INTERMEDIATE ACCOUNTING
Second Canadian Edition

DEDICATED TO

Marilyn	Viola
Lee-Ann	Susan
Cameron	Dianne
Sandra	Daniel

INTERMEDIATE ACCOUNTING
Second Canadian Edition

Donald E. Kieso Ph.D., C.P.A.
Northern Illinois University
DeKalb, Illinois

Jerry J. Weygandt Ph.D., C.P.A.
University of Wisconsin
Madison, Wisconsin

Canadian Edition prepared by

V. Bruce Irvine Ph.D., C.M.A., F.S.M.A.C.
University of Saskatchewan
Saskatoon, Saskatchewan

W. Harold Silvester Ph.D., C.P.A., C.A.
University of Saskatchewan
Saskatoon, Saskatchewan

John Wiley & Sons Canada Limited
Toronto

Canadian Cataloguing in Publication Data

Main entry under title:
Intermediate accounting

Includes bibliographical references and index.
ISBN 0-471-79718-9

1. Accounting.   I. Kieso, Donald E.

HF5635.I57 1986   647'.044   C86-093697-X

Printed and bound in Canada by The Bryant Press Limited.
10 9 8 7 6 5 4 3

PREFACE TO THE SECOND CANADIAN EDITION

The Second Canadian edition of *Intermediate Accounting* discusses in depth the traditional (intermediate) financial accounting topics as well as the recent developments in accounting valuation and reporting practices promulgated by the leading professional accounting organizations and applied by practitioners in public accounting and industry. Explanations and discussions of financial accounting theory are supported and illustrated by examples taken directly from practice and authoritative pronouncements.

In keeping pace with the complexities of the modern business enterprise, we have included a comprehensive set of topics supported by numerous illustrations and judiciously selected appendices. The appendices are concerned primarily with complex subjects, lesser-used methods, or specialized topics. Our intent in using the appendices is to provide the instructor with greater flexibility in choosing topics to cover or omit.

The text is organized into six major parts.

1 Financial Accounting Functions and Basic Theory (Chapters 1 to 6)
2 Assets—Recognition and Measurement (Chapters 7 to 12)
3 Liabilities—Recognition and Measurement (Chapters 13 to 14)

    4 Shareholders' Equity, Dilutive Securities, and Investments (Chapters 15 to 18)
    5 Issues Related to Income Measurement (Chapters 19 to 23)
    6 Preparation and Analysis of Financial Statements (Chapters 24 to 27)

FEATURES

Among the significant features of this edition, Chapter 1 contains a discussion of the nature of financial accounting, the environmental factors influencing its development, and a historical perspective of its evolution in Canada. In Chapter 2, we have integrated coverage of the FASB's Conceptual Framework for Financial Accounting and Reporting with the basic assumptions and principles of accounting as they apply to the Canadian environment. Chapter 3 is a review of the accounting process, including the preparation of the work sheet. Specialized journals and conversion of cash to accrual basis are included in appendices. Chapters 4 and 5 concentrate on issues related to the content and presentation of the income statement, retained earnings statement, balance sheet, and statement of changes in financial position (Chapter 24 is devoted to the preparation of the statement of changes in financial position). Chapter 6 provides the material covering the basics of compound interest, annuities, and present value for those wishing to study or review these topics in preparation for understanding their use in various financial accounting topics covered in subsequent chapters.

Cash, temporary investments, and accounts and notes receivable are examined extensively in Chapter 7. Coverage of inventories in Chapters 8 and 9 emphasize methods most frequently used by businesses in Canada. Such current issues as "capitalization of interest cost" and "special sale agreements" have been included.

Capitalization of interest cost has been included in the coverage of acquisition of plant and equipment in Chapter 10. Chapter 11 includes discussion of accounting for natural resources as well as traditional methods of depreciation, capital cost allowance, and investment credits. Chapter 12 covers issues related to intangible assets. Current and contingent liabilities are examined in Chapter 13. Chapter 14 examines bonds and includes appendices illustrating serial bond amortization and redemption before maturity.

Chapters 15 and 16 on shareholders' equity include a discussion of the related provisions of the Canada Business Corporations Act and such current developments as "redeemable preferred shares". Chapter coverage incorporates only no-par value shares, but an appendix addresses how par shares should be accounted for. Chapter 17 contains a thorough explanation and illustration of the earnings per share requirements of the *CICA Handbook*. Chapter 18 deals with issues associated with accounting for investments in bonds, shares, and funds.

Chapter 19 on revenue recognition has been organized around "product sales transactions" and "service sales transactions". In order to integrate the tax effect of "accounting changes and error analysis", we have placed Chapter 20 on income tax allocation ahead of Chapter 23 on accounting changes. The gross and net change methods of tax computation are presented in Chapter 20. Our coverage of "pension costs" in Chapter 21 includes an explanation of different funding and cost allowance patterns. Chapter 22 on leases provides a complete coverage of Section 3065 of the *Handbook*. Topics in this chapter include "guaranteed and unguaranteed residual values'', ''bargain purchase options'', and ''initial direct cost''.

Chapter 24 on the statement changes in financial position presents the work sheet approach to the preparation of this statement. An appendix to the chapter illustrates the ''T'' account method for those who prefer this approach. A cash flow basis for this statement is emphasized. The coverage of current value/constant dollar accounting includes material from the *CICA Handbook*, Section 4510. The illustrations of different methods of adjusting for specific and general price changes in this chapter use common data and are presented in comparative form. Basic financial statement analysis is covered in Chapter 26. Chapter 27 on ''full disclosure'' contains numerous examples of disclosure from the financial statements of Canadian firms.

QUESTIONS, CASES, EXERCISES, AND PROBLEMS

At the end of each chapter we have provided a comprehensive set of review and homework material consisting of questions, cases, exercises, and problems. The exercises and problems have been carefully selected, and the end-of-chapter material includes up-to-date cases and problems, nearly all of which have been class tested.

The questions are designed for review, self-testing, and classroom discussion purposes as well as homework assignments. The cases generally require essay as opposed to quantitative solutions; they are intended to confront the student with situations calling for conceptual analysis and the exercise of judgement in identifying problems and evaluating alternatives. Typically, an exercise covers a specific topic and requires less time and effort to solve than cases and problems. The problems are designed to develop a professional level of achievement and are more challenging to solve than the exercises.

Probably no more than one-fourth of the total case, exercise, and problem material must be used to cover the subject matter adequately; consequently, problem assignments may be varied from year to year.

SUPPLEMENTARY MATERIALS

Accompanying this textbook is a package of supplements consisting of instructional aids for either students or instructors. These include (1) a comprehensive Solutions Manual for the end-of-chapter material, (2) a separate Instructor's Manual containing lecture outlines, an annotated bibliography, and other enrichment materials, (3) a Checklist of Key Figures, and (4) a Student Study Guide prepared by Ambrose Marsh of Seneca College.

If this book helps teachers instill in their students an appreciation for the challenges and limitations of accounting, if it encourages students to evaluate critically and understand financial accounting theory and practice, and if it prepares students for advanced study, professional examinations, and the successful pursuit of their careers in accounting and business, then we will have attained our objective.

Suggestions and comments from users of this book will be appreciated.

Donald E. Kieso
Northern Illinois University
DeKalb, Illinois

V. Bruce Irvine
University of Saskatchewan
Saskatoon, Saskatchewan

Jerry J. Weygandt
University of Wisconsin
Madison, Wisconsin

W. Harold Silvester
University of Saskatchewan
Saskatoon, Saskatchewan

ACKNOWLEDGEMENTS FOR THE FIFTH U.S. EDITION

We thank the many users of our fourth edition who contributed to this revision through their comments and constructive criticism. Special thanks are extended to the primary reviewers of our fifth edition manuscript:

Floyd D. Beams
  Virginia Polytechnic Institute and
  State University
John C. Borke
  University of Wisconsin–Platteville
Paula Harbecke
  University of Maryland
Wayne Higley
  University of Nebraska

Marilyn Hunt
  Central Florida University
Melvin McClure
  University of Maine
Curtis Norton
  Northern Illinois University
Thomas Nunamaker
  Washington State University
Gene Rozanski
  Illinois State University

Other colleagues in academe who have provided helpful criticisms and made valuable suggestions as adopters of the previous edition or reviewers of selected topics include: Robert J. Brill of St. Bonaventure University; Don Etnier, University of Wisconsin–Eau Claire; Patrick R. Delaney, Ray McClary, Kap Shin, and Thomas Sterling Wetzel of Northern Illinois University; Walker Fesmire, University of Michigan–Flint; M. Zafar Iqbal, California Polytechnic State University; William Larson, Indiana University; Willard J. Lawrence, Austin Community College; Thomas Linsmeier of University of Iowa; Jiwan Merchia and James Tucker of Drexel University; Malcolm McClure of Illinois State University; and Emmanuel Nyadrok, University of Illinois–Chicago.

From the field of professional accountancy we owe thanks to the following practitioners for their technical advice: Michael Crooch and John E. Stewart of Arthur Andersen & Co.; Michael Baker of Price Waterhouse & Co.; Carol Krenek of Wolf & Company; and Scott Szykowny of Peat, Marwick, Mitchell & Co.

We appreciate the exemplary support and professional commitment given us by our office manager, Donna R. Kieso, our word processor operator, Debra J. Kieso, our typist, Enid Weygandt, and by the production and editorial staffs of John Wiley & Sons, including Romayne Ponleithner and Barbara Heaney; and John Beresford, Judy Nolan, and the staff of Allservice Phototypesetting. We especially thank our production manager, David Smith, and our editor, Lucille Sutton, for their counsel on and commitment to this edition.

We appreciate the cooperation of the American Institute of Certified Public Accountants and the Financial Accounting Standards Board in permitting us to quote from their pronouncements. We also acknowledge permission from the American Institute of Certified Public Accountants, the Institute of Management Accounting, and the Institute of Internal Auditors to adapt and use material from the Uniform CPA Examinations, the CMA Examinations, and the CIA Examinations, respectively.

If this book helps teachers instill in their students an appreciation for the challenges and limitations of accounting, if it encourages students to evaluate critcially and understand financial accounting theory and practice, and if it prepares students for advanced study, professional examinations, and the successful pursuit of their careers in accounting or business, then we will have attained our objective.

Suggestions and comments from users of this book will be appreciated.

DeKalb, Illinois   Donald E. Kieso
Madison, Wisconsin   Jerry J. Weygandt
January, 1986

ACKNOWLEDGEMENTS FOR THE SECOND CANADIAN EDITION

We thank the many individuals who contributed to the book through their comments and constructive criticism. Special thanks are extended to the primary reviewers of our manuscript, Ambrose Marsh, Seneca College and Atkinson College, York University; Harvey Babiak, University of Toronto; and Lawrence Pinkney, Instructor for the Society of Management Accountants. We thank Brenda Mallouk, University of Toronto, and Carolyn Watson for their contributions to the final manuscript as accounting proofreaders. Other colleagues in academe who worked on and examined portions of this work and who made valuable suggestions include George Murphy, Jack Vicq, John Brennan, and Maureen Fizzell, University of Saskatchewan. Thanks are also due to all others who contributed to the development of the original material.

From the field of professional accountancy we owe thanks to the following practitioners: Robert G. Bundon, Jim Spinney, and Ivan Thompson of Deloitte, Haskins & Sells; Julie McCartan, Cheryl Brooke, Maxine Maksymetz, Brenda Woodley, James Salamon, and Lorena Eggerman.

We are most grateful to Barbara Consky, Acquisitions Editor, Business Administration, of John Wiley & Sons Canada Limited, and to editor Francine Geraci and proofreader Krista Watson for their work. We also extend our thanks to the production and editorial staff of John Wiley & Sons Canada Limited, including Kaari Turk, Joan Kerr, Kim Koh, and Cathy Johnson.

We appreciate the cooperation of the Canadian Institute of Chartered Accountants in permitting us to quote from their pronouncements. We also acknowledge permission from the Uniform CPA Examinations and the CMA Examinations. We also wish to acknowledge the cooperation of the many Canadian companies from which we have drawn excerpts from financial statements.

Saskatoon, Saskatchewan   V. Bruce Irvine
                                                    W. Harold Silvester

ABOUT THE AUTHORS

Donald E. Kieso, Ph.D., C.P.A., received his doctorate in accounting from the University of Illinois. He has served as chairman of the Department of Accountancy and is currently Professor of Accountancy at Northern Illinois University. He has public accounting experience with Price Waterhouse & Co. (San Francisco and Chicago) and Arthur Andersen & Co. (Chicago) and research experience with the Research Division of the American Institute of Certified Public Accountants (New York). He has done postdoctorate work as a Visiting Scholar at the University of California at Berkeley and is a recipient of NIU's Teaching Excellence Award. Professor Kieso is the author of other accounting and business books and is a member of the American Accounting Association, the American Institute of Certified Public Accountants, the Financial Executives Institute, and the Illinois CPA Society. Most recently he has served as a member of the Board of Directors of the Illinois CPA Society, the Board of Governors of the American Accounting Association's Administrators of Accounting Programs Group, the State of Illinois Comptroller's Commission, as Secretary-Treasurer of the Federation of Schools of Accountancy, and as Secretary-Treasurer of the American Accounting Association. Professor Kieso is currently serving as a member of the American Assembly of Collegiate Schools of Business Accounting Accreditation Visitation Committee, the Board of Directors of Aurora University, and the Ethics Committee of the Illinois CPA Society.

Jerry J. Weygandt, Ph.D., C.P.A., is professor of Accounting at the University of Wisconsin–Madison. He holds a Ph.D. in accounting from the University of Illinois. Articles by Professor Weygandt have appeared in the *Accounting Review, Journal of Accounting Research,* the *Journal of Accountancy,* and other professional journals. These articles have examined such financial reporting issues as accounting for price-level adjustments, pensions, convertible securities, stock option contracts, and interim reports. He is a member of the American Accounting Association, the American Institute of Certified Public Accountants, and the Wisconsin Society of Certified Public Accountants. He has served on numerous committees of the American Accounting Association and as a member of the editorial board of the *Accounting Review.* In addition, he is actively involved with the American Institute of Certified Public Accountants and has been a member of the Accounting Standards Executive Committee (AsSEC) of that organization. He has served as a consultant to a number of businesses and state agencies on financial reporting issues and currently is serving on an FASB task force that is examining the problems of "accounting for income taxes." Professor Weygandt recently received the Chancellor's Award for Excellence in Teaching; he is currently serving as Secretary-Treasurer of the American Accounting Association.

CANADIAN EDITION

V. Bruce Irvine, Ph.D., C.M.A., F.S.M.A.C., is a professor of Accounting at the University of Saskatchewan. He received his Ph.D. in accounting from the University of Minnesota. Among his publications are articles and reviews in such journals as *Cost and Management, Managerial Planning, Canadian Chartered Accountants,* and *The Accounting Review.* Designated "Professor of the Year" five times, Dr. Irvine has extensive teaching experience in financial and managerial accounting and has been instrumental in establishing innovative pedagogical techniques and instructional materials at the University of Saskatchewan. His close relationship with practising accountants has been enhanced by his provincial and national involvement with the Society of Management Accountants. He has served on many working committees of the Society, including the Ad Hoc Committee on Examinations, and has acted as chairman of the SMAC's Curriculum Committee of

Canada and of the Society's National Education Services Committee. He has also been involved with the Canadian Institute of Chartered Accountants and has been a member of the Saskatchewan Institute of Chartered Accountants' Education Committee and Exam Board. Recently, he has served as a Canadian representative to the Board of the International Accounting Standards Committee.

W. Harold Silvester, Ph.D., C.P.A., C.A., received his doctorate from the University of Missouri, Columbia, and is Professor of Accounting at the University of Saskatchewan. In his teaching capacity, he has played a key role in introducing pedagogical improvements at the University of Saskatchewan and in developing instructional materials for the Accounting program there. He has been named "Professor of the Year" in recognition of his important contributions to the College of Commerce. An important recent contribution has been the development of materials to integrate computers with accounting instruction. Articles by Professor Silvester have appeared in *CA Magazine* and other academic and professional journals. He maintains an active involvement with the educational programs of the professional organizations and does consultative work in financial accounting for practitioners.

CONTENTS

PART 3
LIABILITIES—RECOGNITION AND MEASUREMENT

PART 4
SHAREHOLDERS' EQUITY, DILUTIVE SECURITIES, AND INVESTMENTS

PART 5
ISSUES RELATED TO INCOME MEASUREMENT

21 Accounting for Pension Costs   979–1008

The Nature of Pension Plans 980; Employer versus Plan (Fund) Accounting 980; Cash Basis versus Accrual Basis 982; Past Service Cost and Current Service Pension Cost 982; Amendments to Pension Plans and Prior Service Cost 985; Actuarial Cost Methods 985; Accumulated Plan Benefits and Vesting 986; Interest Equivalents 987 **Accounting for Pension Costs 987** Two Views of Pension Cost 993; Experience (Actuarial) Gains or Losses 993; Plan Cancellation or Termination 994; Disclosure of Pensions in Financial Statements 994; Past and Prior Service—Financial Statement Presentation 995 **Key Points 995**

22 Accounting for Leases   1009–1062

Advantages of Leasing 1010; Lease Provisions 1011 **Conceptual Nature of a Lease 1011** To Capitalize or Not to Capitalize 1012; If Capitalization, What Amount? 1013 **Accounting for Leases—A Brief Background 1013 Accounting by Lessees 1013 Examination of Capitalization Criteria 1014** Transfer of Ownership Test 1014; Economic Life Test (75% Test) 1015; Recovery of Investment Test (90% Test) 1015; Asset and Liability Accounted for Differently 1017; Capitalized Lease Method Illustrated (Lessee) 1018; Operating Method (Lessee) 1020; Comparison of Capital Lease with Operating Lease 1021 **Accounting by Lessors 1022** Economics of Leasing 1022; Classification of Leases by the Lessor 1023; Classification of Lease Obligation/Net Investment 1028; Operating Method (Lessor) 1029 **Special Accounting Problems 1030** Residual Values 1030; Sales-Type Lease (Lessor) 1036; Bargain Purchase Option (Lessee) 1037; Initial Direct Costs (Lessor) 1038; Sale-Leaseback 1039; Sale-Leaseback Illustration 1040 **Lease Accounting—The Unsolved Problem 1040 Reporting Lease Data in Financial Statements 1043** Disclosures Required of the Lessee 1043; Disclosures Required of the Lessor 1043; Illustrated Disclosures 1043; Illustration of Different Lease Arrangements 1046 **Key Points 1049**

Appendix 22A   Real Estate Leases   1051

Land 1051; Land and Buildings 1051; Real Estate and Equipment 1052

23 Accounting Changes and Error Analysis   1063–1106

Accounting Changes 1064 Types of Accounting Changes 1064; Correction of an Error in Previously Issued Financial Statements 1064; Changes in Accounting Policy 1065; Three Types of Accounting Changes 1066; Change in Accounting Estimate 1070; Reporting a Change in Entity 1072; Correction of an Error 1072; Summary of Accounting Changes and Corrections of Errors 1074 **Error Analysis 1076** Type of Error Involved 1076; Balance Sheet Errors 1076; Income

PART
1

FINANCIAL ACCOUNTING FUNCTIONS AND BASIC THEORY

1

THE ENVIRONMENT OF FINANCIAL ACCOUNTING AND THE DEVELOPMENT OF ACCOUNTING STANDARDS

Is accounting a service activity, a descriptive/analytical discipline, or an information system? It is all three. **As a service activity,** accounting provides interested parties with quantitative financial information that helps them make decisions about the deployment and use of resources in business and nonbusiness entities and the economy. **As a descriptive/analytical discipline,** it identifies the great mass of events and transactions that characterize the economic activity of an entity and, through measurement, classification, and summarization, reduces those data to relatively small, highly significant, and interrelated items. When properly assembled and reported, these describe the entity's financial condition and results of operations. **As an information system,** it collects economic information about a business enterprise or other entity and communicates this information to a wide variety of interested persons.

Each of these descriptions of accounting—different though they may seem—contains the three essential characteristics of accounting: (1) **identification, measurement, and communication of financial information about** (2) **economic entities to** (3) **interested persons.** These characteristics have been peculiar to accounting for hundreds of years. Yet, in the last sixty years, economic entities have increased so greatly in number and diversity that the responsibility placed on the accounting profession is greater today than ever before.

NATURE AND ENVIRONMENT OF FINANCIAL ACCOUNTING

Financial Accounting

For purposes of study and practice, the discipline of accounting is commonly divided into the following areas or subsets: financial accounting, managerial (cost) accounting, tax accounting, and not-for-profit or fund accounting. This text concentrates on financial accounting. Financial accounting has been characterized as "the branch of accounting that focuses on the general-purpose reports on financial position and results of operations known as financial statements."[1] These statements provide "a continual history quantified in money terms of economic resources and obligations of a business enterprise and of economic activities that change these resources and obligations."[2] **Financial accounting** is the process that culminates in the preparation of financial reports relative to the enterprise as a whole for use by internal and external parties. In contrast, **managerial accounting** pertains to the process of identification, measurement, accumulation, analysis, preparation, interpretation, and communication of financial information used by management to plan, evaluate, and control within an organization, and to assure appropriate use of, and accountability for, its resources.[3]

Financial Statements and Financial Reporting

Financial statements are the principal means through which financial information is communicated to those outside an enterprise. The **financial statements** most frequently provided are (1) the balance sheet, (2) the income statement, (3) the statement of changes in financial position, and (4) the statement of retained earnings. Appropriate disclosures through notes are an integral part of each of these four basic financial statements.

Some financial information is better provided, or can only be provided, by means of **financial reporting** other than formal financial statements, either because it is required by authoritative pronouncement, regulatory rule, or custom, or because enterprise management wishes to disclose it voluntarily. Financial reporting other than financial statements (and related notes) may take various forms and relate to various matters. Common examples are contained in corporate annual reports (e.g., the president's letter or supplementary schedules), prospectuses, annual reports filed with government agencies, news releases, management's forecasts, plans, or expectations, and descriptions of an enterprise's social or environmental impact.

The primary but not exclusive focus of this text is on the development of financial information that is reported in the basic financial statements and the related disclosures.

---

[1] "Basic Concepts and Accounting Principles Underlying Financial Statements of Business Enterprises," *Statement of Accounting Principles Board No. 4* (New York: AICPA, 1970), par. 9.

[2] *Ibid.*, par. 41.

[3] "Definition of Management Accounting," *Statements on Management Accounting No. 1A* (New York: NAA, 1981), p. 4. These statements adequately reflect the distinction between the two subsets of accounting as understood in Canada.

Environmental Factors That Influence Accounting

Accounting, like other social science disciplines and human activities, is largely a product of its environment. The environment of accounting consists of social, economic, political, and legal conditions, restraints, and influences, which have varied over time. As a result, accounting objectives and practices are not the same today as they were in the past, **because accounting theory has evolved to meet changing demands and influences.** Modern financial accounting is the product of many influences and conditions, three of which deserve special consideration.

First, accounting recognizes that people live in a world of scarce resources. For this reason, people try to conserve their resources, to use them effectively, and to identify and encourage those who can make efficient use of them. Through an efficient use of our resources, the standard of living in our country increases. Accounting plays a useful role in obtaining a higher standard of living because it helps to identify efficient and inefficient users of resources. For example, the measurement, communication, and comparison of various companies' income and assets reveal their relative efficiency or inefficiency. As a result, investors and lenders can assess the relative returns and risks of investment opportunities, and channel resources effectively.

Second, accounting recognizes and accepts society's current legal and ethical concepts of property and other rights when determining equity among the varying interests in the enterprise or entity. Accounting looks to its environment for its standards in regard to which property rights society protects, and what society recognizes as value, or acknowledges as equitable and fair.

Third, accounting recognizes that in highly developed, complex economic systems, some (owners and investors) entrust the custodianship of and control over property to others (managers). One of the results of corporate organization has been the tendency in large enterprises to separate ownership from management. Thus, the function of measuring and reporting information to absentee investors, called the **stewardship function,** has been added to that of recording and presenting financial data for owner-manager use. This development greatly increased the need for accounting standards. The absentee investor, unlike the owner-operator, has no opportunity to combine reported information with first-hand knowledge of the conditions and activities of the enterprise.[4] Accounting has become responsible for providing standards that ensure the fairness, objectivity, and comparability of this reported information. The public accountant (auditor) plays a major role in meeting this responsibility by attesting to the fairness of financial statements and their conformity to generally accepted accounting principles.

The foregoing conditions are impressed on financial accounting by the environment within which it operates and which it is intended to reflect. The following environmental aspects, although not as basic as the three conditions just discussed, also shape financial accounting significantly:

1. The many uses and users that accounting serves.
2. The overall organization of economic activity.
3. The nature of economic activity in individual business enterprises.
4. The means of measuring economic activity.[5]

---

[4]W. A. Paton and A. C. Littleton, *An Introduction to Corporate Accounting Standards* (Sarasota: American Accounting Association, 1940), pp. 1–2.

[5]*APB Statement No. 4*, par. 42.

Many Uses and Users

Some users of financial accounting information have (or contemplate having) a direct interest in economic entities. "Direct interest" users include: present and potential owners, creditors, suppliers; management; taxing authorities; employees; and consumers. Other users have an interest in such entities because their function is to assist or protect persons who have or contemplate having a direct interest in them. Such "indirect interest" users include: financial analysts; stock exchanges; lawyers; regulatory and registration authorities; financial press and reporting agencies; trade associations; and labour unions. In order to provide the most useful and equitable information, the accountant must know the nature of user needs, the decision processes employed by users, and the information that best serves their needs.

Recognizing the various needs of the many potential user groups employing different decision processes (models) can influence choices between accounting alternatives. Indeed, a research study by the Canadian Institute of Chartered Accountants (CICA) proposed that such a user-oriented perspective form the basis for developing Canadian financial accounting standards.[6] This study builds upon the premise that an important objective of financial reporting is the provision of useful information to all potential users in a form and time frame that is relevant to their various needs. It proceeds to identify fifteen user classes (see Table 1-1) and then relates various needs to them (see Table 1-2). From this perspective, a variety of different measurement bases (historical cost, general price-level-adjusted historical cost, current replacement cost, net realizable value) may be relevant to different users, users' needs, and decision processes. Consequently, if financial reports are to provide the most useful information, accountants must be aware of users, their needs, and decision processes.

A user perspective has been a part of the development of accounting reports throughout history. The success of financial reports in meeting such needs has, however, become an increasingly important issue. This is due, in part, to the increased number of user groups, the complexity and diversity of their needs, and the lack of understanding of human decision-making processes. Therefore, while a user orientation is significant in shaping the nature of financial accounting, the full implications of such an orientation have still to be incorporated into financial reporting standards.

Organization of Economic Activity

All societies engage in the fundamental economic activities of production, distribution, exchange, consumption, saving, and investment. In a highly developed economy like that of Canada, these activities become specialized, complex, and intertwined. The continuous nature of these activities means that relationships and accomplishments associated with intervals of time (e.g., a year or portions of a year) can be measured only by making assumptions that result in conventional accounting allocations. Computation of the precise effects of a particular event, transaction, or process is impossible except on an arbitrary basis because the activities are interdependent. This problem is intensified in a dynamic economy because the outcome of economic activity is uncertain at the time decisions are

[6]*Corporate Reporting: Its Future Evolution* (Toronto: CICA, 1980).

Table 1-1
User Classes

User Class	Members of Class
(1) Shareholders	Present and Potential
(2) Creditors—Long-term	Present and Potential
(3) Creditors—Short-term	Present and Potential
(4) Analysts and Advisors serving (1), (2), & (3) (e.g., Brokers, Financial Analysts, Journalists)	Present
(5) Employees	Present, Past, and Potential
(6) Nonexecutive Directors	Present and Potential
(7) Customers	Present, Past, and Potential
(8) Suppliers	Present and Potential
(9) Industry Groups	Present
(10) Labour Unions	Present
(11) Government Departments and Ministers (Federal, Provincial, Municipal—e.g., Tax; Statistics; Consumer and Corporate Affairs; Industry, Trade, and Commerce)	Present
(12) Public—Political Parties Public Affairs Groups Consumer Groups Environment Groups	Present
(13) Regulatory Agencies (e.g., Stock Exchanges and Securities Commissions)	Present
(14) Other Companies (Domestic and Foreign)	Present
(15) Standard Setters, Academic Researchers	Present

Source: *Corporate Reporting: Its Future Evolution* (Toronto: CICA, 1980), p. 44.

made and when action is taken. Fortunately, the continuity of enterprise existence and the framework of law, custom, and traditional patterns of action help to stabilize many aspects of the economic environment. The degree of uncertainty is reduced (and the accounting function greatly assisted) when the society ensures the protection of property rights, the fulfillment of contracts, and the payment of debts.

Economic Activity in Individual Enterprises

Business enterprises are the major units that conduct economic activity; they consist of economic resources (assets), economic obligations (liabilities), and residual interests (owners' equity). These elements are increased or decreased by the economic activities of the enterprise. The resources, obligations, and residual interests (balance sheet items) of an enterprise are the basis for the results of operations—revenues, expenses, and net income (income statement items)—and other changes in financial position with which financial accounting is concerned. Accounting accumulates and reports economic activity as it affects these aspects of each business enterprise.

Table 1-2
Users' Needs

Needs	Classes of Users Having These Needs
(1) Assessment of overall performance	
(a) In absolute terms	(1) to (15)
(b) Compared to goals	(1) to (15)
(c) Compared to other entities	(1) to (15)
(2) Assessment of management quality	
(a) Profit, overall performance, efficiency	(1) to (11) especially
(b) Stewardship	(1) (4) (6) (11) (12) (13)
(3) Estimating future prospects for	
(a) Profits	(1) to (11) especially
(b) Dividends and interest	(1) to (4) especially
(c) Investment and capital needs	(1) to (6), (8) to (14)
(d) Employment	(5) (10) (11) (12) especially
(e) Suppliers	(3) (5) (11) (12) (14) especially
(f) Customers (warranties, etc.)	(7) (9) (11) (12) especially
(g) Past employees	(5) (10) (11) (12) (13)
(4) Assessing financial strength and stability	(1) to (15)
(5) Assessing solvency	(1) to (15)
(6) Assessing liquidity	(1) to (15)
(7) Assessing risk and uncertainty	(1) to (15)
(8) As an aid to resource allocation by	
(a) Shareholders (present and potential)	(1) (4) (11) (12) (13) (14)
(b) Creditors (present and potential; long- and short-term)	(2) (3) (4) (8) (11) (12) (13) (14)
(c) Governments	(11) (12) especially
(d) Other private sector bodies	(4) (9) (12) (13) (14)
(9) In making comparisons	
(a) With past performance	(1) to (15)
(b) With other entities	(1) to (15)
(c) With industry and economy as a whole	(1) to (15)
(10) In valuation of debt and equity holdings in the company	(1) to (4) especially
(11) In assessing adaptive ability	(1) to (15)
(12) Determining compliance with laws or regulations	(11) to (13) especially
(13) Assessing entity's contribution to society, national goals, etc.	(11) (12) especially

Note: The numbers in brackets in Column 2 refer to the user classes in Table 1-1.
Some readers may well feel that one or more of the user classes may have additional needs.

Source: *Corporate Reporting: Its Future Evolution* (Toronto: CICA, 1980) pp. 48–49.

Other types of entities (governments, individuals, not-for-profit organizations) also conduct economic activity. While many of the concepts related to accounting for business enterprises are also appropriate for these other types of entities, some important differences exist because of their nature. This text concentrates on financial accounting and reporting for business entities.

Measuring Economic Activity

Accounting facilitates the comparison and evaluation of diverse economic activities by the **measurement** (or valuation) of an enterprise's resources and obligations and the events that increase or decrease them. As already indicated, the complexity, continuity, and joint nature of economic activity create problems in measuring these activities and associating their economic consequences with relatively short time periods as well as specific segments, processes, and products. Measuring the resources and obligations of an enterprise and measuring the changes in them are two aspects of the same problem; hence, there is an inseparable connection between the accountant's statement of financial position (balance sheet), the statement indicating the results of activities (income statement), and the statement of changes in financial position. Money offers a simple solution to the selection of a common standard for purposes of measurement. **Money permits the measurement of qualitative and quantitative attributes of economic events, resources, and obligations.** Thus, the unit of measurement in accounting is expressed in terms of money or exchange price. Of course, some important activities of enterprises are not measurable in terms of money (e.g., appointing a new president, adopting a trade name or trademark).[7]

Accounting Influences Its Environment

Accounting is critical or important not because it is a product of its environment but rather because it shapes its environment and plays a significant role in the conduct of economic, social, political, legal, and organizational decisions and actions. **Accounting is a system that feeds back to organizations and individuals information which they can use to reshape their environment.** It provides information for the reevaluation of social, political, and economic objectives as well as the relative costs and benefits of the alternative means of achieving them.

More specifically, the effect of publicly reported accounting numbers is to influence the distribution of scarce resources. Resources are channeled where needed at returns commensurate with perceived risk. Accounting information is by nature and design useful in assessing the prospective risks and returns associated with investments.

The **economic effects** of reported accounting numbers can directly and rapidly affect the transfer of resources among entities and individuals. Examples are: the amount of taxes paid based on accounting numbers (historical cost numbers produce a much different answer than numbers adjusted for inflation); the effects on existing contracts when a change in accounting rules impinges upon a restrictive covenant (a change from using the straight-line method to an accelerated method to account for depreciation may reduce income sufficiently to cause a dividend restriction owing to the violation of a bond covenant); and the rates allowed to utilities by regulatory agencies (permitting companies to expense certain capital assets may increase energy costs now rather than later). Other economic effects of accounting information may be indirect but no less critical because they affect people's perceptions of the enterprise's economic status and progress and, hence, their

---

[7]Qualitative attributes, as well as quantitative ones, are measurable (valued) in money terms. For instance, in January, 1985, one ounce of gold measured $396 in money terms while one ounce of silver measured $8. The difference in price per ounce reflected differences in qualitative attributes. A doubling of the quantity would result in doubling the amount of money measurement. As another example of qualitative attributes being reflected by money measurement, one of van Gogh's paintings (*La fin de la journée*, 1890) was sold recently at auction for $800,000, while the author's brother had difficulty selling one of his paintings for $50 at an art fair. Money measures both quality and quantity.

willingness to invest in it, subject it to regulation, work for it, enter into long-term supply contracts with it, purchase its products, and so on.[8]

OBJECTIVES OF FINANCIAL REPORTING

The preceding discussion indicates that financial accounting has evolved to reflect the influences and constraints of the environment as well as to influence decisions and actions taken in the environment. As this evolution will continue, it will always affect any definition regarding the objectives of financial statements. It is important, however, to identify clearly such objectives as they currently exist. In a conscientious, costly, and time-consuming attempt to establish a foundation upon which financial accounting and reporting standards would be based, the following **objectives of financial reporting by business enterprises** were identified. Recognizing the characteristics of the environment, financial reporting should provide information:

(a) that is useful to present and potential investors and creditors and other users in making rational investment, credit, and similar decisions. The information should be comprehensible to those who have a reasonable understanding of business and economic activities and are willing to study the information with reasonable diligence.

(b) to help present and potential investors, creditors, and other users in assessing the amounts, timing, and uncertainty of prospective cash receipts from dividends or interest and proceeds from the sale, redemption, or maturity of securities or loans. Since investors' and creditors' cash flows are related to enterprise cash flows, financial reporting should provide information to help investors, creditors, and others assess the amounts, timing, and uncertainty of prospective net cash inflows to the related enterprise.

(c) about the economic resources of an enterprise, the claims to those resources (obligations of the enterprise to transfer resources to other entities and owners' equity), and the effects of transactions, events, and circumstances that change its resources and claims to those resources.[9]

In summary, the objectives of financial reporting are to provide information that is useful (1) in investment and credit decisions, (2) in assessing cash flow prospects, and (3) in evaluating enterprise resources, claims to those resources, and changes in them.

On first reading these objectives, the emphasis on "assessing cash flow prospects" might lead one to infer that the cash basis is being advocated over the accrual basis. This is not the case. Accountants continue to believe that information about enterprise income based on **accrual accounting** generally provides a better indication of the enterprise's present and continuing ability to generate favourable cash flows than information limited to the financial effects of cash receipts and payments.[10]

---

[8]George J. Benston and Melvin A. Krasney, "The Economic Consequences of Financial Accounting Statements" (a paper prepared for the American Council of Life Insurance for submission to the FASB), presented in *Economic Consequences of Financial Accounting Standards*, Research Report (Stamford, Conn.: FASB, 1978).

[9]"Objectives of Financial Reporting by Business Enterprises," *Statement of Financial Accounting Concepts No. 1* (Stamford, Conn.: FASB, November, 1978), p. viii.

[10]*SFAC No.1*, p. iv. As used here, cash flow means "cash generated and used in operations." The term cash flows is frequently used also to include cash obtained by borrowing and used to repay borrowing, cash used for investments in resources and obtained from the disposal of investments, and cash contributed by or distributed to owners.

The objective of **accrual accounting** (recognizing revenues when earned rather than when cash is received, and recognizing expenses when incurred rather than paid) is the measurement of income. Information about income is useful because it reveals relationships that are likely to be important in predicting future results. For example, under accrual accounting, revenues are recognized when sales are made; thus they can be related to the economic environment of the period in which they occurred. Trends in revenues are therefore more meaningful.

Another noteworthy point regarding these objectives is that they specifically refer to investor and creditor user groups and combine all remaining groups (see Table 1-1) into an "other" category. This reflects a dilemma of contemporary financial accounting and reporting. Traditionally, creditors and investors have been the primary external groups that financial accounting has been designed to serve. The growth in size, significance, power, and concerns of other groups of users has been an important event in our economy. These groups also need financial information when making decisions. At present, the published financial statements of an enterprise represent the only publicly available source of such information. Given the variety of user groups seeking and using them, they are often called **general purpose financial statements**.

As suggested previously, however, the various user groups have different needs (decisions to make) and different perspectives or viewpoints (for example, union leaders representing employees, consumers, shareholders). Consequently, while these statements may be called "general purpose," there is some question as to whether they are adequate for providing the information that specific user groups require. Provision of "specific purpose statements" to a particular user group might help resolve this issue.

The key point is that the basic objective of financial statements is to provide information that is useful for decision making. For most users, financial statement information is only a part (in many cases, a major part) of the total information used to make a decision. The type of information provided in financial statements is designed to report on how resources and obligations of an enterprise have been managed such that user groups may employ it to:

- assess overall financial performance
- assess management performance
- estimate future prospects
- assess financial strength and stability
- assess solvency
- assess liquidity
- assess risk and uncertainty
- make comparisons

when making their decisions.

THE DEVELOPMENT OF ACCOUNTING STANDARDS

Given the objectives of financial accounting and reporting, the question remains as to how they can best be achieved. The accounting profession has responded by the formation of standards for use in accounting practice. The following discussion examines the manner in which accounting standards have been and are being developed. (The terms **principles** and **standards** are used interchangeably in practice and throughout this text.)

The Need to Develop Standards

As previously indicated, the users of financial accounting statements have coinciding and conflicting needs for statements of various types. To meet these needs, and to satisfy the fiduciary reporting responsibility of management, accountants prepare a single set of general purpose financial statements. These statements are expected to present fairly, clearly, and completely the economic facts of the existence and operations of the enterprise. **In preparing financial statements, accountants (like those involved in any communication process) are confronted with the potential dangers of bias, misinterpretation, inexactness, and ambiguity.** In order to minimize these dangers and to render financial statements that can reasonably be compared between enterprises and between accounting periods for the same enterprise, the accounting profession has attempted to develop a body of theory that is generally accepted and universally practised. Without this body of theory, each accountant or enterprise would have to develop its own theoretical structure and set of practices pertaining to financial accounting. If this happened, readers of financial statements would have to familiarize themselves with every company's peculiar accounting and reporting practices. As a result, comparisons would be nearly impossible.

The accounting profession's efforts to establish a body of theory and practice that acts as a general guide have resulted in the adoption of a common set of accounting concepts, standards, and procedures called **generally accepted accounting principles (GAAP).** The term "generally accepted" means either that an authoritative accounting rule-making body has established a principle of reporting in a given area, or that, over time, a given practice has been accepted as appropriate because of its universal application. Although the principles have provoked both debate and criticism, most accountants and members of the financial community recognize them as theories, methods, and practices that, over time, have proved to be most useful.

A historical perspective of the interaction between accounting and its environment fosters an appreciation for and understanding of accounting's heritage and conventions. Such a perspective as it applies to Canada is presented in the remainder of this chapter.

Historical Perspective[11]

Before the twentieth century, the commercial and industrial life of Canada was generally carried on through partnerships and small corporations. From 1900 to 1920 the economy developed rapidly, and this period witnessed the emergence of the large corporations that were eventually to dominate Canadian enterprise. This era marked significant corporate legislation at the provincial and federal levels and initiation of income taxes during the First World War (1914–1918). Like the stock markets in other western nations, the Canadian stock market collapsed in 1929, and the country lapsed into the long depression of the 1930s. Significant corporate legislation in 1934 and 1935 attempted to correct various real or imagined

[11]This material is drawn from G. J. Murphy, "The Evolution of Corporate Reporting Practices in Canada," *The Academy of Accounting Historians Working Papers Series, Volume 1* (Academy of Accounting Historians, 1979), pp. 329–368; and G. J. Murphy, "Financial Statement Disclosures and Corporate Law: The Canadian Experience," *The International Journal of Accounting* (Spring, 1980), pp. 87–99.

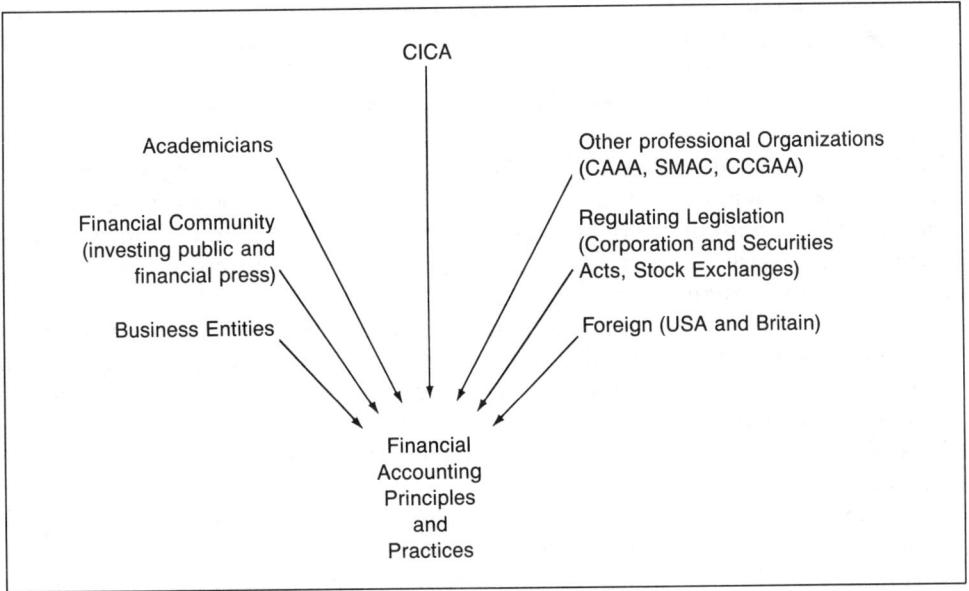

FIGURE 1-1 Influences on the Formulation of Accounting Principles and Practices

abuses. The immediate post-Second World War era witnessed not only the resurgence of commercial and industrial activity but also the increasing awareness by the accounting profession of the role it must play in Canadian life. With considerable help from professional accountants, significant improvement in corporate disclosure legislation was initiated from the mid-1950s to mid-1960s. The importance of the contribution of the Canadian Institute of Chartered Accountants (CICA) in setting accounting standards was reflected in legislation during the 1970s.

Various sources have influenced the evolution of financial accounting practices in Canada. Figure 1-1 depicts some of them; they will be discussed in the following chronology of accounting's evolution in Canada during the twentieth century.

To 1920

The Ontario corporate legislation of 1897 and 1907 and the counterpart Canadian legislation of 1917 likely led that of both England and the U.S.A. with respect to the extent of financial statement disclosure required. The earlier provincial legislation required an "income and expenditure" statement, while the later Act of 1907 additionally required that the balance sheet be audited and that certain assets, liabilities, and equities be distinguished. The federal legislation a decade later virtually copied the Ontario Act. Various influences were at work in these early days. The financial community had been alerted by the abuses in insurance company accounting practices, the rash of bankruptcies at the beginning of World War I, bank failures, and the increasing size and frequency of corporate mergers. The Income Tax Acts of 1916 and 1917 greatly influenced corporate legislation, since their application was based on financial statements that not only disclosed a great deal of information but also were attested to by an independent professional accountant.

At the professional organization level, the Association of Accountants in Montreal in 1880 was the first accounting association chartered in North America.[12] The Institute of Chartered Accountants of Ontario followed in 1883, and the Dominion Association of Chartered Accountants (later named the Canadian Institute of Chartered Accountants) was established in 1902. The strong influence of the Ontario Institute on the early legislation was acknowledged by the assistant provincial secretary at the time. The Dominion Association began publishing its journal, *The Canadian Chartered Accountant* (later changed to *CA Magazine*), in 1911. In those early years, much of its content consisted of reprints from British and American journals.

The provincially and federally legislated disclosure requirements were probably the chief reason for the relatively high quality of the average financial statement of public corporations in Canada during this period. These sources of influence, together with the Income Tax Acts, served to alter the emphasis in financial accounting from the balance sheet toward the income statement and to establish the historical cost principle of valuation.

During the last part of the second decade, England was forced to withdraw much of her financial investment in Canada because of the war—a gap in investment that was later filled by the U.S.A. This change in financial influence also marked a period of transition in which British influence on Canadian accounting began to wane and the American influence increased.

1920–1945

As in most western countries, the economy of Canada, after experiencing a continuing rise in the 1920s and a stock market crash at the end of the decade, endured a severe and prolonged depression during much of the 1930s. The concern over abuses in corporate promotion and capitalization, accompanied by a demand for improved financial statement disclosure (much of it coming from the eminent Queen's University Professor R.G.H. Smails), prompted remedial federal legislation in 1934. The same kind of concerns in the U.S.A. gave rise to the Securities Acts of 1933 and 1934 and the creation of the Securities and Exchange Commission (SEC). In contrast to the American legislation, the Canadian Companies Acts did not attempt to set accounting standards beyond disclosure requirements, nor did they set up institutions or procedures to review annual corporate reports. The revolutionary legislation in the U.S.A. was mirrored in an evolutionary fashion in Canada within the traditional vehicle of the Companies Acts.

The mid-1930s marked a point at which events in the U.S.A. increasingly asserted a strong influence on Canadian accounting (see Appendix 1B for a historical summary of developments in accounting in the U.S.A.).[13] The SEC and the energetic American Institute of Certified Public Accountants (AICPA) began to set forth

---

[12]Harvey Mann, "CA's in Canada . . . The First Hundred Years," *CA Magazine* (December, 1979), pp. 26–30. This article indicates that the Canadian accounting profession has much to be proud of but also that there are some serious problems that require solution.

[13]Financial accounting standards in the U.S.A. tend to be more specific, comprehensive (in terms of the number of issues addressed), regulatory, and limiting than those in Canada. Appendix 1B provides a historical perspective as to some of the reasons for this. As a consequence, a similar item may be accounted for differently in the financial statements of companies in the two countries (even if one company is controlled by the other). While understanding these differences is important, there are many other reasons, identified in the introduction to Appendix 1B, as to why accountants in Canada need to be aware of U.S. standards and the process and history of their development.

numerous recommendations on accounting and auditing matters. Most of these were discussed and many emulated in Canada through the Canadian accounting journals and later through the recommendations of the Canadian Institute of Chartered Accountants. The latter, though not prodded by an SEC, began increasingly to undertake the activities and duties of professional accounting leadership, forwarding briefs to governments, commissioning studies, and establishing research organizations. Though World War II (1939–1945) dampened much of this activity, the CICA was able to put forward, in 1946, its first recommendations on standards of financial statement disclosure (Bulletin #1).

As in the United States, the rise and subsequent fall of prices in the 1920–1940 period lent heavy support to those who argued against the use of any kind of current or appraised value of assets. If value were a function of income, current or appraisal values could be ignored. Emphasis fell therefore on the income statement and on the objectivity of historical cost for valuation purposes. This emphasis clearly reinforced what had emerged in the first two decades of the century.

1945–1965

This era marked a relatively quiet but effective period in which much progress was made at the professional and legislative levels. Though the traditional sources of influence for change continued with steady pressure, there were no important or well-publicized instances of corporate malfeasance or financial reporting inadequacies. In the U.S.A., the AICPA and its ever-present watchdog, the SEC, poured forth a profusion of auditing and accounting recommendations—all of which were carefully scrutinized in Canada. Since the British profession and legislation were far less active, events in the U.S.A. continued to be much more important for Canadian observers.

At the professional level, the Institutes of Chartered Accountants of Quebec in 1946 and of Ontario in 1962 secured the exclusive auditing rights for public corporations for its members. The publication of accounting and auditing recommendations, which began with Bulletin #1 in 1946, continued as a series through 1968. These recommendations became the common standards for financial reporting in Canada.

The financial statement disclosure provisions of the Ontario Corporations Act of 1953 were a virtual copy of this first Institute Bulletin and the briefs of the Institute of Chartered Accountants of Ontario. As in 1907, this provincial legislation became the direct model for federal legislation approximately a decade later in 1964–65. The Ontario Securities Act of 1965 gave to the Ontario Securities Commission continuing surveillance responsibilities of Canada's most important stock exchange, the Toronto Stock Exchange. Though this Commission has powers (relating to financial statement disclosure and practices) not dissimilar to those of the American SEC, it has not promulgated its own set of accounting standards nor has it set up any elaborate process for the review of corporate annual reports.

1965 to Present

Coinciding in time with the legislative approval of the Ontario Securities Act of 1965 and the Canada Corporations Act of 1964–65—but otherwise unrelated—a major scandal broke upon the Canadian financial scene. The fall of the Atlantic

Acceptance Company Limited and, in its wake, several other companies was of grave concern to the investing public, various legislatures, and the accounting profession. This type of concern was of much greater proportions in the U.S. where instances of corporate scandals and legal suits against auditors abounded and had resulted in several Congressional and professional inquiries. These inquiries led to such significant documents as the Metcalf Report, the Moss Report, the Wheat Report, and the Cohen Report. In 1973 the Financial Accounting Standards Board (FASB) was formed as a body independent of the AICPA to establish accounting principles. All of these events in the U.S. were closely observed by the Canadian profession. Other important influences of the United States on the Canadian scene were the existence of numerous U.S. subsidiary corporations in Canada, the close relationship between many American and Canadian public accounting firms, and the fact that many Canadian corporations were listed on U.S. stock exchanges.

Two important differences between the U.S.A. and Canada may help to explain the different responses of the American and Canadian professions during this time period. First, there were many instances of corporate abuse in the United States, while only one (the Atlantic Acceptance debacle) stands out as a unique event in Canada. Second, the prestige of and longstanding respect for the traditions of the accounting profession were much greater in Canada. By comparison, the events in Canada and the responses that they drew were far more subdued.

In 1968 all CICA accounting and auditing recommendations were reorganized into the *CICA Handbook*, which has since been revised continually. In 1969, auditors were required to disclose departure from recommended accounting standards. Of much greater significance, however, was a little-heralded event in 1972 in which National Policy No. 27 of the Canadian Securities Commission, in its concern for uniformity and disclosure inadequacies, required that the *CICA Handbook* be used to determine generally accepted accounting principles. This requirement was quickly incorporated into the Canada Business Corporations Act of 1975 and the Ontario Securities Act of 1978. Legislative deference to the expertise of the CICA was complete. With this legislation, the setting of the laws of the country with regard to financial accounting standards and disclosure became the unique task of the CICA.

The acceptability of the legal authority for Canadian GAAP as represented by recommendations in the *CICA Handbook* (and the process of their development by the accounting profession) came under serious challenge in 1982. The challenger was the federal government (which had granted the power in the first place through the Canada Business Corporations Act). The issue concerned the accounting treatment by Canadian oil companies of grants received under the federal government's Petroleum Incentives Program (PIP grants). This program provided for direct incentive payments for exploration and development. The CICA's position (stated in an accounting guideline issued in February, 1982) was that PIP grants be treated in accordance with Section 3800 of the *Handbook* ("Accounting for Government Assistance," issued in 1975). The required accounting would be that PIP grants be taken into income as the exploration and development efforts they financed resulted in earnings or were written off. The federal government's preference, supported by the oil companies in general, was to have the full amount of the grant reflected immediately in income in the year received. Various reasons existed for taking a stance directly contrary to the *CICA Handbook*, not the least of which was the significantly reduced earnings of oil companies related to other provisions of the National Energy Program. The federal government was seriously considering enacting an Order-in-Council that would have resulted in its legislating a generally accepted accounting principle. This action never took place. These events, however, reflect the most serious challenge in recent history to the acceptability of the Canadian accounting profession acting as a self-regulating and policy-setting group. This heavy responsibility demands an ever-increasing devotion of time and resources, and any perceived failure in this regard may well redound to the crippling discredit of the CICA.

The Standard-Setting Process

Canadian GAAP are formalized through the **recommendations** included in the *CICA Handbook*. These recommendations are set out in italicized type in the *Handbook* so that they may be clearly distinguished from the additional material included as background information.[14]

The development and publication of accounting recommendations and other material is the responsibility of the **Accounting Standards Committee (AcSC)**, established by the Board of Governors of the CICA.[15] Significant amounts of time, effort, and dollars are devoted to the development of accounting recommendations in order to assure that "due process" takes place. A description of this process is presented in Appendix 1A.

While this process is significant and effective, it is recognized that the AcSC cannot develop general recommendations that can be applied to all situations and circumstances. Consequently, accountants must rely heavily on the exercise of **professional judgement** when reaching solutions to particular problems and determining what constitutes fair presentation.[16] In such cases, accountants look to many sources to seek guidance. For example, accounting **Guidelines** are published from time to time under the auspices of the AcSC's Steering Committee, with much of the work being done by the AcSC Section Committees. These guidelines provide interpretation of some *Handbook* recommendations or offer guidance on particular issues (e.g., presentation and disclosure of financial forecasts) faced by the profession. Also, the CICA sponsors and publishes in-depth **Studies** on particular topics. Existing standards and authoritative literature from the U.S. provide other sources to which accountants may refer. To exercise professional judgement, however, means much more than being knowledgeable of GAAP and the multitude of authoritative literature that exists. It reflects a capacity to make appropriate decisions in unfamiliar and changing situations. While knowledge is a necessary requirement of professional judgement, one's own experience and that of others, as well as ethics and the ability to recognize the particular circumstances surrounding a situation, are further important components.

Other Influential Organizations

While the CICA has clearly led, and has the responsibility for, the development and issuance of financial accounting standards in Canada, other organizations

---

[14]*CICA Handbook*, "Introduction to Accounting Recommendations," p. 9.

[15]Prior to 1982, the Accounting Standards Committee was named the Accounting Research Committee. The terms of reference and rules of membership are approved by the Board of Governors. The *Handbook* also includes recommendations and material on auditing (the responsibility of the Auditing Standards Committee); and another group, the Public Sector Accounting and Auditing Committee, is responsible for recommendations applicable to the public sector.

[16]*CICA Handbook*, "Introduction to Accounting Recommendations," p. 9.

play an important role in the Canadian accounting environment. These organizations include the Society of Management Accountants of Canada (SMAC), the Canadian Certified General Accountants' Association (CCGAA), the Canadian Academic Accounting Association (CAAA), and various international accounting bodies. The role of these organizations in developing financial accounting standards has been primarily one of providing both input and reaction to proposals (exposure drafts) developed by the CICA's Accounting Standards Committee (AcSC). The input process usually consists of providing written briefs to be considered by the AcSC when developing standards and, in some cases, membership on committees. Research activities of these organizations have also made an important contribution to accounting in Canada. A brief description of these organizations is presented in the following paragraphs.

The Society of Management Accountants of Canada   As the name implies, the SMAC is the professional organization of management accountants in Canada. Its professional members (Certified Management Accountants or CMAs[17]) are typically employed by business organizations, although they may work for government or in public practice.[18] As preparers of management's financial statements and reports, they must be thoroughly familiar with financial accounting principles. In addition, CMAs are responsible for providing information for management decisions. The SMAC has assumed a leadership role in providing direction regarding management accounting practices through its **Management Accounting Guidelines** as well as in conducting research on management accounting topics, as evidenced by the publication of several **Research Studies.** The Society also publishes a journal, *CMA Magazine* (formerly called *Cost and Management*), which includes contemporary articles on issues and topics of concern to management accounting.

The Canadian Certified General Accountants' Association   Professional members of the CCGAA (Certified General Accountants or CGAs) are employed by governments and industry or may provide accounting services in public practice. Like the SMAC, this organization offers an educational program through which members may acquire the professional designation. Unlike the SMAC, which requires all students to take the same course material, the CCGAA allows its students to choose a sequence of courses, enabling them to specialize in various areas of accounting. The CCGAA publishes a journal (*CGA Magazine*) and has established a research foundation to promote the study of accounting, auditing, and finance issues. It has also financed several **Research Monographs** and published a *GAAP Guide* for use by Canadian professional accountants.

Canadian Academic Accounting Association   This organization is concerned with accounting education and research. Since 1975 it has actively stimulated examination of accounting education problems and encouraged increased funding of accounting and auditing research in Canada. Current membership numbers well over six

---

[17]Prior to July of 1985, the professional designation was Registered Industrial Accountant (RIA). The designation change was made to reflect more appropriately what members do and the variety of organizations in which they are employed.

[18]A common misconception is that CAs (Chartered Accountants) are in public practice (as auditors, tax specialists, etc.), CMAs are accountants in industry, and CGAs are government accountants. While legislation in some provinces and certain stock exchanges may require some audits to be performed by CAs, it is common to find members of all three professional organizations working in industry and government as well as providing services as public accountants.

hundred and includes a good balance of academics and practitioners. This organization publishes a regular newsletter on topics of interest to Canadian accountants, studies of significance to Canadian accounting educators, and a journal titled *Contemporary Accounting Research*.

International Accounting Bodies   International accounting has come of age, and accounting bodies in Canada have been at the forefront of these developments.[19] The first formal organization was the International Accounting Standards Committee (IASC). In 1973 the CICA, the SMAC, and the CCGAA cooperated in making Canada one of the nine founding member nations. The objective of the IASC is ''to formulate . . . standards to be observed in the presentation of audited financial statements. . . .'' The IASC member bodies have agreed to ''use their best endeavours'' to see that the published standards are applied in financial statements. Section 1501 of the *CICA Handbook* formally recognizes and supports the general objective of harmonizing accounting standards.

A number of International Accounting Standards have been published. These standards are generally consistent with recommendations presented in the *CICA Handbook*, although some differences do exist.[20] General support for these standards is growing, as evidenced by their increased use and recognition in the financial statements of Canadian corporations operating in an international environment.

The initial success at developing international standards led to the creation of a world-wide body with broader objectives. The International Federation of Accountants was established in 1977. The CICA, SMAC, and CCGAA are founding members. These Canadian organizations are active in the pursuit of the Federation's activities related to establishing accounting and auditing standards as well as management accounting practices, and to coordinating professional ethical principles and educational processes. All member bodies are committed to work toward ''a coordinated world-wide accounting profession.''

These world-wide bodies are supported by regional organizations. In North America, the relevant body is the Inter-American Accounting Association. Its primary goal is to improve liaison among accountants in the Americas. Conferences and other forms of interaction are organized regularly. Similar activities are promoted by regional bodies in Europe, the Pacific Rim, and South East Asia.

Academe has also adapted to this internationalization. The International Section of the American Accounting Association is the focus of this activity. It attempts to facilitate liaison among the world's accounting academics and to encourage research into international accounting problems.

Conclusion

The purpose of this chapter has been to present a general description of the nature of financial accounting, its objectives, the environmental factors influencing its development, and a historical perspective of its evolution in Canada. From this

[19]W. John Brennan, ed., *The Internationalization of the Accounting Profession* (Toronto: CICA, 1979). This book provides a general description of the institutes, activities, and issues involved in this internationalization process.

[20]*Financial Reporting in an International Environment: A Comparison of International Accounting Standards with Canadian Practice* (Toronto: CICA, 1984). This material is regularly updated and identifies differences that exist.

description, it is evident that accounting serves a utilitarian function—it is a means to an end rather than an end in itself. Since the environment within which accounting exists is constantly changing, one can expect accounting to continue to evolve in response to these changes. Indeed, continuous evolution has been a constant theme throughout the history of accounting. This evolution is understandable, given its utilitarian nature and the fact that accounting principles and practices, usually derived on a piecemeal basis, are subject to various complex, interacting, and sometimes competing influences.

KEY POINTS

1. The three essential characteristics of accounting are (1) identification, measurement, and communication of financial information about (2) economic entities to (3) interested persons.
2. Financial statements most frequently provided are (1) the balance sheet, (2) the income statement, (3) the statement of changes in financial position, and (4) the statement of retained earnings.
3. The objectives of financial reporting are to provide information (1) that is useful to present and potential investors and creditors and other users in making rational investment, credit, and similar decisions; (2) to help present and potential investors and creditors and other users in assessing the amounts, timing, and uncertainty of future cash flows; (3) about the economic resources of the enterprise, the claims to those resources, and the effects of transactions, events, and circumstances that change its resources and claims to those resources.
4. Accountants prepare financial statements in accordance with generally accepted accounting principles (GAAP).
5. Recommendations in the *CICA Handbook* serve as the specific reference point for identifying Canadian GAAP. These recommendations have legal authority conferred by the Canadian Business Corporations Act.
6. Responsibility for *Handbook* recommendations on financial accounting rests with the Accounting Standards Committee of the Canadian Institute of Chartered Accountants.
7. Determining specific accounting principles to apply in particular situations requires accountants to rely heavily on the exercise of professional judgement.
8. Standards and authoritative literature in the U.S.A. are an important reference source for guidance when Canadian accountants exercise professional judgement.
9. In addition to the Canadian Institute of Chartered Accountants, the Society of Management Accountants of Canada, the Canadian Certified General Accountants Association, and the Canadian Academic Accounting Association are major organizations in the Canadian accounting environment.
10. International accounting bodies, primarily the International Accounting Standards Committee and the International Federation of Accountants, provide organizational means through which harmonization of accounting standards in different countries evolves. Canada has strongly supported these endeavours, and the standards developed by these groups closely parallel those used in Canada.

APPENDIX

1A

THE CANADIAN STANDARD-SETTING PROCESS

The recommendations in the *CICA Handbook* represent formally written Canadian GAAP. The *Handbook*'s content regarding financial accounting is developed by the Accounting Standards Committee (AcSC). The structure of this committee and its operating procedures permit the exercise of due process when formulating recommendations. They constitute the formal process that generates Canadian GAAP.

The AcSC consists of twenty-two appointed voting members. While at least one-half of the members will actively engage in public practice, accountants from a variety of other occupations (industry, finance, academe, etc.) also serve on the committee. Up to six members may be appointed from organizations other than the Canadian Institute of Chartered Accountants (e.g., financial analysts, financial executives, and members of the Society of Management Accountants). Such nonaccountants as lawyers, economists, and government employees may be considered for appointment. The AcSC as a whole has three **Section Committees** —Western, Central, and Eastern Canada—each with its own chairman. The work of the AcSC is supported by the professional personnel in the Research Department of the CICA. The **Steering Committee** of the AcSC consists of the AcSC chairperson, the three section chairpersons, and the Institute's General Director of Research and Accounting Standards Director.

Given this structure, the various stages in the process for formulation of *CICA Handbook* recommendations as illustrated in Figure 1A-1 may be examined.

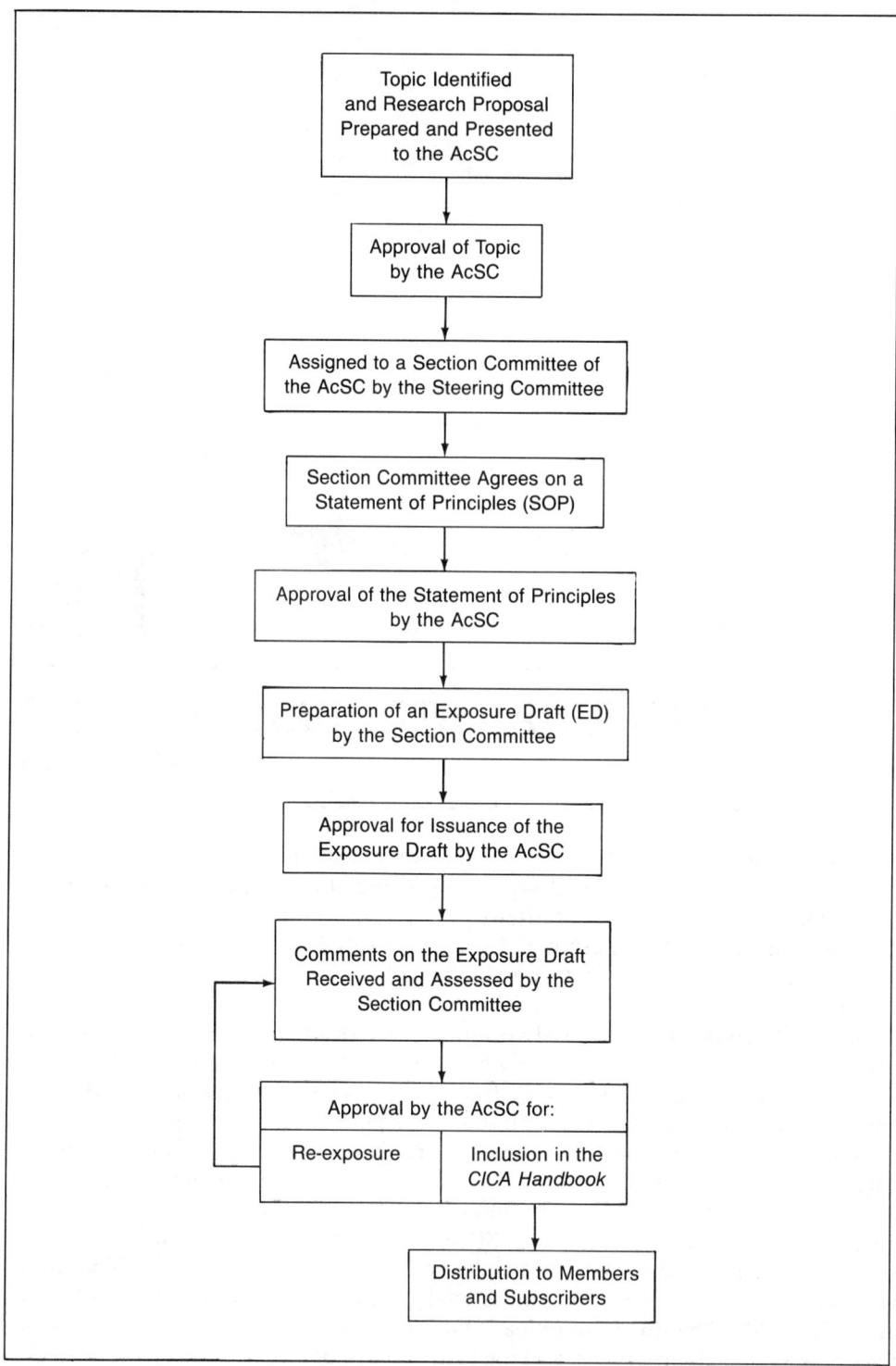

FIGURE 1A-1 Formulation of *CICA Handbook* Recommendations

To initiate this process, a formal research proposal must be approved by the AcSC. While suggested projects are primarily identified by the Committee or its support staff, any interested party may submit proposals.

Once proposals are approved by the AcSC, the Steering Committee assigns them to one of the three Section Committees. The Section Committee discusses and debates the issues and then agrees on a Statement of Principles which must be presented to and approved by the AcSC. The Statement of Principles identifies the Section Committee's consideration of the issues, analysis, and direction that the recommendations are likely to take. Should approval to continue be given by the AcSC, the Section Committee will then be responsible for preparation of an Exposure Draft. This document presents the proposed contents of a new section or an amendment to an existing section of the *Handbook*.

Approval by the AcSC for release of an Exposure Draft would result in its becoming a public document available to all interested persons or organizations. The purpose of issuing an Exposure Draft is to solicit public input on the proposed accounting recommendations. Such input is considered by the Section Committee when formulating its submission to the AcSC for adding recommendations to the *Handbook*. If the Section Committee's recommendations are approved for inclusion in the *Handbook*, they are distributed to all members of the Institute, other *Handbook* subscribers, and other persons expressing interest. Once the recommendations are part of the *Handbook*, they are considered Canadian GAAP. Unless otherwise stated, these recommendations become effective for inclusion in financial statements of companies with fiscal year ends on or after the first of the month in which the recommendation was published in the *Handbook* and this date appears at the bottom of each page in the *Handbook*. The AcSC may determine that the final proposed recommendations are sufficiently different from those in the Exposure Draft and, accordingly, may decide that a Re-exposure Draft is necessary to obtain additional public feedback. Any submissions on the Re-exposure Draft are given to the Section Committee as shown in Figure 1A-1.

This representation of the financial accounting standard-setting process in Canada is very basic and has omitted some of the complexities, such as the voting requirements for approval to progress at the various stages, the role of associates (volunteers selected by members to provide assistance) in deliberations, and the use of Task Forces. Even given this oversimplification of the process, it should be evident that a conscientious, thorough, and time-consuming effort is put into the development of recommendations. A major strength is the great deal of attention paid to a concern for ''due process.''

APPENDIX

1B

THE DEVELOPMENT OF ACCOUNTING STANDARDS IN THE U.S.A.

The development of financial accounting standards in the U.S.A. has been carefully observed by Canadian practitioners. In many instances, accounting standards and practices developed in the U.S.A. have later become a part of Canadian pronouncements. Also, when no Canadian standard or practice is documented, practitioners will often rely on U.S. pronouncements for guidance (as has been done in some cases in preparing the Canadian edition of this text). The facts that many U.S. subsidiary companies operate in Canada, that there is a close relationship between many American and Canadian public accounting firms, and that there are a number of Canadian companies listed on various U.S. stock exchanges are additional reasons for Canadians to be familiar with developments in the United States. For these reasons, this appendix is appropriate for a Canadian text. Also, a comparison of the histories of the U.S.A. and Canada with respect to development of financial standards reveals somewhat different approaches. As indicated in the following pages, many different agencies and boards have influenced the development of standards in the U.S.A., whereas in Canada the CICA remains the primary organization for setting standards and procedures to guide financial accounting practice.

Prior to 1900, the economy of the United States required a relatively unsophisticated type of accounting function, and an accounting profession *per se* was virtually nonexistent. Before the beginning of this century, single ownership was the predominant form of business organization. Accounting reports emphasized solvency and liquidity and were limited to internal use and scrutiny by banks and other lending institutions. From 1900 to 1929, the growth of large corporations, with their absentee ownership, and the increasing investment and speculation in corporate shares, resulted in the demand for greater disclosure and a change from the concern with solvency to a concern with income-producing ability. The constitutional amendment in 1913 authorizing the federal government to impose an income tax on businesses and individuals intensified the emphasis on income measurement. As a result of the stock market crash of 1929, the Great Depression, and widespread dissatisfaction with accounting reports, the federal government, the stock exchanges, and the accounting profession all made efforts to improve accounting. Since that time, environmental influences on the development of accounting principles have been primarily institutional (or organizational).

PARTIES INVOLVED IN STANDARD SETTING

Although the needs of interested parties have been the focus in the development of accounting principles, certain professional organizations, government agencies, and legislative acts have also exerted a significant influence. The major organizations discussed in the remainder of this Appendix, which have been and are currently instrumental in the development of financial accounting standards (GAAP) in the United States, are:

1. American Institute of Certified Public Accountants (AICPA)
2. Financial Accounting Standards Board (FASB)
3. Government Accounting Standards Board (GASB)
4. Securities and Exchange Commission (SEC)
5. American Accounting Association (AAA)
6. Such other bodies as the Financial Executives Institute (FEI) and the National Association of Accountants (NAA).

The AICPA

The efforts of the **American Institute of Certified Public Accountants (AICPA),** the national professional organization of practising Certified Public Accountants (CPAs), have been vital to the development of generally accepted accounting principles in the United States. In 1905 the Institute began monthly publication of *The Journal of Accountancy*, which has been the most popular forum for the practising CPA since then. In 1917 an Institute committee, at the request of the Federal Trade Commission, prepared a pamphlet on "Uniform Accounting," which suggested procedures for standardizing the preparation of financial statements. In 1930 the Institute appointed a special committee to cooperate with the New York Stock Exchange on matters of common interest to accountants, investors, and the exchanges. An outgrowth of this special committee was the Committee on Accounting Procedure which, during the years 1939 to 1959, issued 51 *Accounting Research Bulletins (ARBs)* dealing with a variety of timely accounting problems. These bulletins, however, were not directives to the members of the Institute. Their authority rested only on their general acceptance by the profession. Although these bulletins narrowed the range of alternative practices to some extent, this problem-by-problem approach of the Committee on Accounting Procedure failed to provide the well-defined and well-structured body of accounting principles that was so badly needed and desired.

In 1959 the AICPA created the **Accounting Principles Board (APB)** as part of a program to advance the written expression of accounting principles, to determine appropriate practices, and to narrow the areas of difference and inconsistency in practice.[21] The objectives of this reorganization were fourfold: (1) to establish basic postulates,[22] (2) to formulate a set of broad principles, (3) to set up rules to guide the application of principles in specific situations, and (4) to base the entire program on research. Accordingly, a permanent accounting research staff was employed to carry on the research and to publish research studies.

Accounting Research Studies

Research projects were conducted by independently employed consultants or by members of the research staff under the guidance of the Director of Accounting Research and a project advisory committee. Research usually was undertaken on a subject to be considered and acted on by the APB. (The APB was designated as the AICPA's sole authority for public pronouncements on accounting principles.) Upon completion of a research project, the results of the study and the conclusions and recommendations were published and circulated for comment and discussion. The published *Accounting Research Studies* were not official pronouncements of the AICPA; they were the responsibility of their authors and were published under the authority of the Director of Accounting Research. Fifteen research studies were published between 1960 and 1973.

APB Opinions

The APB had more authority and responsibility than did its predecessor, the Committee on Accounting Procedure. The Board's 18 to 21 members were selected primarily from public accounting but also included representatives from industry and the academic community. The Board's official pronouncements, called *APB Opinions*, were intended to be based mainly on research studies and to be supported by reasoning. Between its inception in 1959 and its dissolution in 1973, the APB issued 31 opinions.

APB Opinions were enforced primarily through the prestige of the AICPA and its APB, which was recognized as the body that regulated the accounting profession and determined and enforced accounting principles. Probably the most critical and the most important enforcement pressure resulted from the Securities and Exchange Commission's willingness to recognize the AICPA and to support *APB Opinions*.

In 1964 the Council (the governing body) of the AICPA circumscribed the long-used but officially undefined term **generally accepted accounting principles.** In a document published as a Special Bulletin and later as an appendix to *APB Opinion No. 6*, the Council adopted the following resolution:

---

[21]*Organization and Operation of the Accounting Research Program and Related Activities* (New York: AICPA, 1959), p. 9.

[22]Postulates are basic assumptions of self-evident propositions that are generally accepted as valid. Few in number and broad in nature, they provide the basis from which principles or standards may be deduced.

1. "Generally accepted accounting principles" are those principles which have substantial authoritative support.
2. Opinions of the Accounting Principles Board constitute "substantial authoritative support."
3. "Substantial authoritative support" can exist for accounting principles that differ from Opinions of the Accounting Principles Board.
4. No distinction should be made between the bulletins issued by the former Committee on Accounting Procedure on matters of accounting principles and Opinions of the Accounting Principles Board.

Also important was the fact that the Council and the APB declared that all material departures by companies from *APB Opinions* and effective Research Bulletins must be disclosed and explained in the companies' published financial statements. Although the AICPA recognizes other sources as constituting substantial authoritative support, the decision and burden of proof in these cases rest with the reporting members.[23] It is because of this burden of proof and related risk of liability from lawsuits that the pronouncements issued to that date and since have been followed. Thus, the policy of strong **persuasion** gave way to a more effective one of professional (not legislative) **compulsion**.

Financial Accounting Standards Board

The APB was beleaguered throughout its 13-year existence. It came under fire early, charged with lack of productivity and failure to act promptly to correct alleged accounting abuses. Later the APB tackled numerous thorny accounting issues, only to meet a buzz-saw of industry opposition and occasional government interference. In 1971 the accounting profession's leaders, anxious to avoid governmental rule making, responded by appointing a Study Group on Establishment of Accounting Principles (commonly known as the Wheat Committee) "to examine the organization and operation of the Accounting Principles Board and determine what changes are necessary to attain better results faster." The Study Group's recommendations were submitted to the AICPA Council in the late spring of 1972, adopted in total, and implemented by early 1973.

The Wheat Committee's recommendations caused the demise of the APB and the creation of a new standard-setting structure comprising three organizations—the Financial Accounting Foundation (FAF), the Financial Accounting Standards Board (FASB), and the Financial Accounting Standards Advisory Council (FASAC). The **Financial Accounting Foundation** is responsible for selecting the members of the FASB and its Advisory Council, funding their activities, and overseeing the FASB. Its Board of Trustees is made up of nominees from six sponsoring organizations[24] whose members have special knowledge of, and interest in, financial reporting.

The major operating part of this three-part structure is the **Financial Accounting Standards Board.** Its mission is to establish and improve the standards of financial accounting and reporting for the guidance and education of the public, including

---

[23]A member of the AICPA is prohibited from expressing an opinion that financial statements conform with generally accepted accounting principles if those statements contain a material departure from an accounting principle promulgated by the FASB, unless the member can demonstrate that because of unusual circumstances the financial statements otherwise would have been misleading.

[24]The Financial Accounting Foundation members are appointed by representatives of the American Accounting Association, the American Institute of CPAs, the Financial Executives Institute, the National Association of Accountants, the Financial Analysts Federation, and the Securities Industry Association.

issuers, auditors, and users of the financial information. The expectation of success and support for the new FASB was based on several significant differences between it and its predecessor, APB:

1. **Smaller membership.** The FASB is composed of seven members, replacing the relatively large 18-member APB.
2. **Full-time, remunerated membership.** FASB members are well-paid, full-time members appointed for renewable five-year terms, whereas the APB members were unpaid and part-time.
3. **Greater autonomy.** The APB was a senior committee of the AICPA, whereas the FASB is not an organ of any single professional organization. It is appointed by and answerable only to the Financial Accounting Foundation.
4. **Increased independence.** APB members had retained their private positions with firms, companies, or institutions; FASB members sever all such ties.
5. **Broader representation.** All APB members were required to be CPAs and members of the AICPA; currently, it is not necessary to be a CPA to be a member of the FASB.

In recognition of the misconceptions caused by the term ''principles,'' the FASB uses the term **financial accounting standards** in its pronouncements.

Two of the basic premises of the FASB are that in establishing financial accounting standards (1) it should be responsive to the needs and viewpoints of the entire economic community, not just the public accounting profession, and (2) it should operate in full view of the public through due process, giving interested persons ample opportunity to make their views known. To ensure the achievement of these goals, the following steps are taken in the evolution of a typical FASB Statement:

1. A topic or project is identified and placed on the Board's agenda.
2. A task force of experts from various sectors is assembled to define problems, issues, and alternatives related to the topic.
3. Research and analysis are conducted by the FASB technical staff.
4. A **discussion memorandum** is drafted and released.[25]
5. A public hearing is often held, usually 60 days after release of the memorandum.
6. The Board analyzes and evaluates the public response.
7. The Board deliberates on the issues and prepares an **exposure draft** (prepublication copy) for release.
8. After a 30-day (minimum) exposure period for public comment, the Board evaluates all of the responses received.
9. A committee studies the exposure draft in relation to the public responses, reevaluates its position, and revises the draft if necessary.
10. The full Board gives the revised draft final consideration and votes on issuance of a **Standards Statement**.

The passage of a new accounting standard in the form of an *FASB Statement* requires the support of four of the seven Board members. *FASB Statements* are considered GAAP and therefore binding in practice. All *ARBs* and *APB Opinions* that were in effect when the FASB became effective continue to be effective until amended or superseded by FASB pronouncements.

In addition to issuing financial accounting standards, the FASB also issues

[25]Sometimes, in place of or before issuing a discussion memorandum, the FASB will issue an *Invitation to Comment. Invitations to Comment* are written either by an FASB or AICPA task force in an effort to stimulate research, gather information, and invite reactions to an existing but nonauthoritative pronouncement. An *Invitation to Comment* is not deliberated upon by the FASB and has no authoritative status.

documents called *Interpretations, Statements of Financial Accounting Concepts,* and *Technical Bulletins.*

Interpretations   These represent modifications or extensions of existing standards. The FASB interpretations have the same authority as standards and require the same majority votes for passage. In the formulation of an interpretation, however, it is not considered necessary to operate in full view of the public through due process, as required for the FASB Standards. It should be noted that during the time the APB was in operation, it also issued interpretations of *APB Opinions.* Both types of interpretations are now considered authoritative support for purposes of determining generally accepted accounting principles.

Financial Accounting Concepts   As part of a long-range effort to move away from the ''problem-by-problem approach,'' the FASB in November 1978 issued the first in a series of *Statements of Financial Accounting Concepts.* The purpose of the series is to set forth fundamental objectives and concepts that the Board will use in developing future standards of financial accounting and reporting. Individual concept statements are issued serially; they are intended to form a cohesive set of interrelated concepts, a body of theory or a conceptual framework, that will serve as tools for solving existing and emerging problems in a consistent, sound manner. Unlike a Statement of Financial Accounting Standards, a Statement of Financial Accounting Concepts does not establish GAAP. Concepts statements, however, pass by due process through the same system (discussion memo, public hearing, exposure draft, etc.) as do standards statements. Chapter 2 identifies and discusses the contents of particular concepts statements.

Technical Bulletins   The FASB receives many requests from various sources for guidelines on implementing or applying *FASB Standards* or *Interpretations, APB Opinions,* and *Accounting Research Bulletins.* In addition, there is a strong need for timely guidance on financial accounting and reporting problems that GAAP does not cover. For example, when the Tax Reform Act of 1984 was enacted, certain income taxes that companies had accrued as liabilities were forgiven. The question was how should the forgiven taxes be reported—as a reduction of income tax expense, a prior-period adjustment, or as an extraordinary item? A technical bulletin was quickly issued requiring that the tax reduction be reported as a reduction of income tax expense in the current period. It should be emphasized that a technical bulletin is issued only when (1) it is not expected to cause a major change in accounting practice for a number of enterprises, (2) its cost of implementation is low, and (3) the guidance provided does not conflict with a broad fundamental accounting principle.

Since it has become operational, the FASB has undeniably been hard at work and quite productive. However, it is debatable whether the Board is any more effective or productive than the APB. Like the APB, the FASB in its first twelve years adopted the ''problem-by-problem approach'' in establishing standards and has been under constant pressure to perform more expeditiously and be more responsive and productive. Recognizing that it must use the resources and talents of others, the FASB has consulted with numerous individuals and engaged them to develop materials and to research and draft discussion memoranda, and follow-up studies.[26] Critics and supporters alike agree that the FASB will have the best chance of survival if it deals with problems promptly, sets proper priorities, takes whatever action it thinks is right and in the public interest, and handles pressures responsibly without overreacting to them.

Changing Role of AICPA

When the APB was dissolved and replaced with the FASB, the AICPA established the Accounting Standards Division to act as its official voice on accounting and reporting issues. The **Accounting Standards Executive Committee (AcSEC)** was established within the Division and was designated as the senior technical committee authorized to speak for the AICPA in the area of financial accounting and reporting.

During the first five years of its operation, AcSEC (1) responded to pronouncements of both the FASB and the SEC and (2) devoted attention to emerging problems not addressed by the FASB or the SEC through the issuance of *Statements of Position (SOPs)*. Unlike FASB pronouncements, the *SOPs* do not represent enforceable standards required by AICPA members; they are issued with the objective of influencing the development of accounting and reporting standards and of providing guidance where none exists.

Late in 1978, the FASB publicly expressed concern that the AICPA was evolving into a competing standard-setting body because of the number of *SOPs* being issued. The FASB proposed first to consolidate that work into a single, standard-setting body—its own—by rewriting the *SOPs* into FASB style and format. After exposure to public comment, they would be issued as final *Statements of Financial Accounting Standards*. Second, the FASB proposed to establish a new series of FASB *Technical Bulletins* that would offer timely guidance on preferred accounting and reporting practice (as discussed earlier).

The AICPA agreed in general with the FASB proposal, urging that the FASB adopt existing *SOPs* as authoritative, as it did with *Accounting Research Bulletins* and *APB Opinions*. In 1979 "the FASB agreed to exercise responsibility for the specialized accounting and reporting principles and practices in AICPA *Statements of Position* and *Guides* on accounting and auditing matters by extracting those specialized principles and practices from those documents and issuing them as FASB *Statements*, after appropriate due process."[27]

A major role of AcSEC, therefore, has become the preparation of issue papers to inform the FASB of financial reporting problems that are developing in practice. **Issue papers** identify current problems, present alternative treatments of the issue, and recommend preferred solutions. This procedure provides the FASB with an

[26]Examples of special research projects are: A. Rashad Abdel-khalik et al., *The Economic Effects of Lessees of FASB Statement No. 13*, Research Report (Stamford, Conn.: FASB, 1981); Yuji Ijiri, *Recognition of Contractual Rights and Obligations*, Research Report (Stamford, Conn.: FASB, 1980); Henry R. Jaenicke, *Survey of Present Practices in Recognizing Revenues, Expenses, Gains, and Losses*, Research Report (Stamford, Conn.: FASB, 1981); Paul A. Griffin, *Usefulness to Investors and Creditors of Information Provided by Financial Reporting*, Research Report (Stamford, Conn.: FASB, 1982); L. Todd Johnson and Reed K. Storey, *Recognition in Financial Statements: Underlying Concepts and Practical Conventions*, Research Report (Stamford, Conn.: FASB, 1982).

[27]"Specialized Accounting and Reporting Principles and Practices in AICPA Statements of Position and Guides on Accounting and Auditing Matters," *Statement of Financial Accounting Standards No. 32* (Stamford, Conn.: FASB, 1979). Until "due process" was accomplished, *FASB No. 32* designated a large number of *SOPs* and *Guides* on accounting and auditing as containing preferable accounting principles.

early warning device to insure the timely issuance of FASB *Standards, Interpretations,* and *Technical Bulletins.*

The AICPA is still the leader in developing auditing standards through its **Auditing Standards Board**, in regulating accounting practice, in developing and enforcing professional ethics, and in providing continuing professional education programs. The AICPA also develops and grades the CPA examination, which is administered in all fifty states.

Governmental Accounting Standards Board

Many accountants have criticized financial statements prepared by state and local governments because these statements are not comparable with those prepared by private business organizations. For example, many state and local governments use a simple cash basis and do not include such items as depreciation in their income statements. This lack of comparability was particularly highlighted in the 1970s when a number of larger cities such as New York and Cleveland faced potential bankruptcy. As a result, a new Governmental Accounting Standards Board (GASB), under the supervison of the Financial Accounting Foundation, was created in 1984 to address reporting issues in the areas of state and local government.

Except for a few minor details, the operational structure of the GASB is similar to that of the FASB. That is, it has an advisory council and is assisted by its own technical staff and task forces.

The creation of GASB is controversial. Many believe that there should be only one standard-setting body—the FASB. Hopefully, the partitioning of standard setting, where the GASB deals with only state and local government reporting and the FASB with reporting for all other entities, will not lead to conflict.

The Securities and Exchange Commission

The Great Depression of the 1930s, which resulted in the widespread collapse of businesses and the securities market, was the impetus for government intervention in and regulation of business. Concern regarding financial statements and accounting principles resulted in the creation of the **Securities and Exchange Commission (SEC)** as an independent regulatory agency of the United States government to administer the Securities Act of 1933, the Securities Exchange Act of 1934, and several other acts. Companies that issue securities to the public or are listed on stock exchanges are required to file annual audited financial statements with the SEC. The SEC, in turn, was given broad powers to prescribe, in whatever detail it desires, the accounting practices and principles to be employed by companies that fall within its jurisdiction. The SEC filing requirements[28] and accounting opinions are published in (1) its *Financial Reporting Releases (FRRs),*[29] (2) *Regulation S-X,*

---

[28]The Securities and Exchange Acts of 1933 and 1934 require that companies issuing securities file registration statements and periodic reports with the SEC. Most commercial and industrial companies file a Form S-1 registration statement upon the initial issuance of securities. (Forms S-2 through S-18 are filed by companies in certain specialized industries.) Form 10-K is the annual report form required to be filed, and Form 10-Q the report that must be filed for the first three quarters of each fiscal year. Form 8-K must be filed after the occurrence of a material event.

[29]In the past (prior to 1982), these pronouncements were referred to as Accounting Series Releases (ASRs). The SEC has changed the title of new releases to reflect better their nature and to differentiate FRRs (nonenforcement, nondisciplinary type releases) from the new AAERs (Accounting and Auditing Enforcement Releases—disciplinary in nature).

which contains instructions and forms for filing financial statements, and (3) decisions on cases coming before the SEC. Yet, the SEC until recently acted with remarkable restraint in the area of developing accounting principles. For the most part, until 1960 it relied on the AICPA to regulate the accounting profession and develop and enforce accounting principles.

During the APB era, however, the SEC took a more active interest in the development of accounting standards, pressing for quicker action, specific pronouncements, and eventually for the demise of the APB. Over the past decade the SEC has interacted with the FASB as both a supporter and a prodder. The SEC frequently identifies emerging problems for the FASB to address because it confronts the financial accounting and reporting practices of U.S. businesses on a daily basis. The Commission communicates these problems to the FASB, responds to FASB drafts and exposures, and provides the FASB with counsel and advice upon request.

The SEC has reaffirmed its support for the FASB (in *ASR No. 150*), indicating "that financial statements conforming to standards set by the FASB will be presumed to have authoritative support." In addition, the SEC has indicated in its reports to Congress "that it continues to believe that the initiative for establishing and improving accounting standards should remain in the private sector, subject to Commission oversight."[30]

The American Accounting Association

The **American Accounting Association (AAA),** an organization of college professors and practising accountants, seeks, as part of its stated objective, to influence the development of accounting theory by encouraging and sponsoring accounting research. Functioning through a series of committees, the Association has published numerous monographs and committee reports and a series of statements on accounting principles, standards, and theory.

The AAA in its role as critic appraises accounting practice and recommends improvements through its quarterly publication, *The Accounting Review*, and the work of its committees. Its concern is more for "what should be, as opposed to what was, or what is." Unconcerned about immediate adoption of its proposals, the AAA takes a long-range point of view and attempts to lead practice rather than follow it.

Other Influential Organizations

Several other organizations have influenced the development of accounting theory. The **National Association of Accountants (NAA),** formerly the National Association of Cost Accountants, has been interested in research primarily in cost accounting and in managerial accounting since its origin in 1919. *Management*

---

[30]One writer has described the relationship of the FASB and SEC and the development of financial reporting standards using the analogy of a pearl. The pearl (financial reporting standard) "is formed by the reaction of certain oysters (FASB) to an irritant (the SEC)—usually a grain of sand—that becomes embedded inside the shell. The oyster coats this grain with layers of nacre, and ultimately a pearl is formed. The pearl is a joint result of the irritant (SEC) and oyster (FASB); without both, it cannot be created." (John C. Burton, "Government Regulation of Accounting and Information," the proceedings of the 1979 round-table discussion at the University of Florida, Gainesville, edited by A. Rashad Abdel-khalik, 1980, Board of Regents of the State of Florida.)

Accounting is the monthly publication of the NAA. In 1968 the NAA broadened its research program to ''encompass the entire range of socio-economic information needed by those who manage a business and by those who provide its capital.''[31]

The **Financial Executives Institute** **(FEI)** and its subsidiary, the Financial Executives Research Foundation, have published several interesting accounting and reporting studies. The FEI's monthly publication is *The Financial Executive.* The FEI has influenced the development of accounting standards through its Panel on Accounting Principles. This panel reviews the Discussion Memoranda and the prepublication drafts of proposed pronouncements of the FASB and submits its views and recommendations. More recently, the FEI established committees to parallel task forces of the FASB that are responsible for developing various standards.

The **state societies of CPAs** also provide sounding boards and forums for the airing of support and criticism of FASB exposure drafts on accounting standards. Comments and proposals are formally obtained by each state CPA society and submitted to the FASB, thus providing the Board with the grassroots reaction to its proposed opinions.

The **Internal Revenue Service (IRS),** which derives its authority from the Internal Revenue Code and its amendments and legal interpretations, constitutes one of the strongest influences on accounting practice. In an effort to lessen the impact of taxes, and to avoid keeping two sets of books, business managers frequently adopt ''acceptable'' accounting procedures that minimize taxable income. Note, however, that ''good tax accounting'' is not necessarily ''good financial accounting'' because the objectives of the tax law differ from the objectives of financial accounting. As noted throughout this text, tax laws and ''tax effects'' are a pervasive influence in business decision making and on the selection of accounting methods. Differences between tax accounting and financial accounting are generally permissible; therefore, in the preparation of financial statements, tax considerations must give ground to the requirements of sound accounting.

The **Cost Accounting Standards Board (CASB)** also has influenced the development of accounting thought. The CASB was established in 1970 as an agency of the U.S. Congress to promote uniformity and consistency in the cost accounting practices for defence contracts by establishing **Cost Accounting Standards.** The CASB's interest in any cost that may be charged to a government contract necessarily overlaps topics relevant to financial accounting and reporting. Although Congress dissolved the CASB in 1980, the 17 standards that it issued remain in force.

STANDARD SETTING IN THE POLITICAL ENVIRONMENT OF THE U.S.A.

The earlier discussion of the environment of accounting disclosed some of the factors that shape and influence the nature and development of accounting standards and practices in the U.S.A. Possibly the most influential environmental force flows from various user groups (Figure 1B-1). User groups consist of the parties who are the most interested in or affected by accounting standards, rules, and procedures. User groups play a significant role because the setting of accounting standards is a social decision; that is, **accounting standards are as much a product of political action as of careful logic or empirical findings.**[32]

---

[31]''Report and Recommendations of the Long-Range Objectives Committee of the NAA,'' *Management Accounting* (1968), Section 3.

[32]Charles T. Horngren, ''The Marketing of Accounting Standards,'' *Journal of Accountancy* (October, 1973), p. 61.

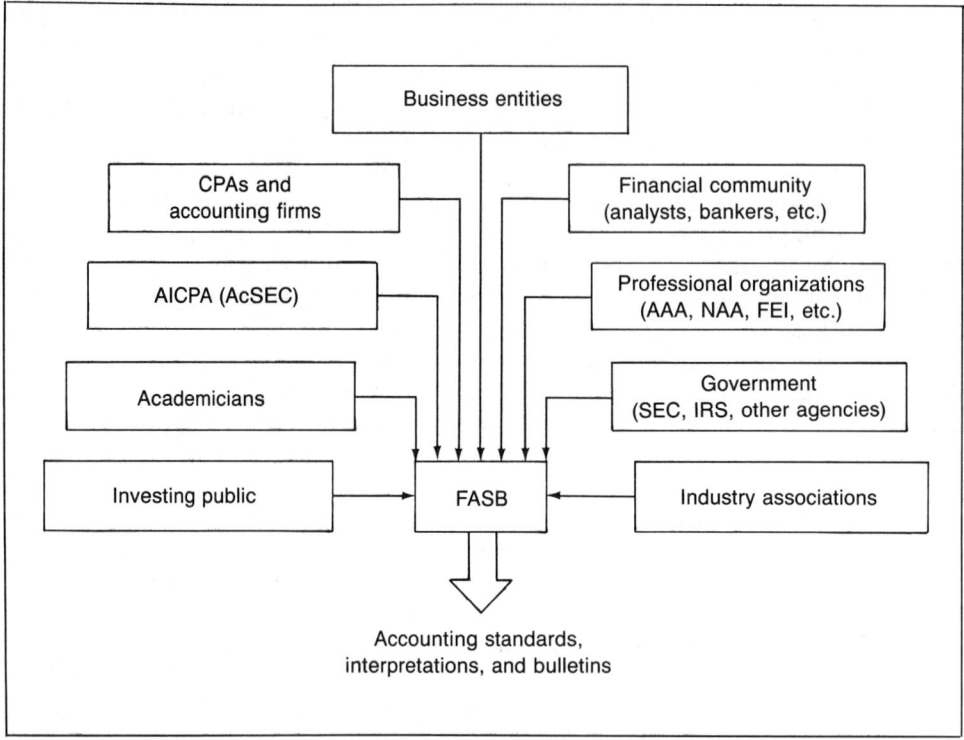

FIGURE 1B-1 User Groups That Influence the Formation of U.S. Accounting Standards

User groups may want particular economic events accounted for or reported in a particular way, and they fight hard to get what they want. They know that the most effective way to influence the standards that dictate accounting practice is to participate in the formulation of these standards and the development of new ones.[33] Pressures such as increased complexity and interrelatedness of economic activity, and the ever-increasing dependence on financial accounting, have been multiplying because of the accelerated rate of change in the economy. Some influential groups demand that the accounting profession act more quickly and decisively to solve its problems and remedy its deficiencies; other groups resist such action, preferring to implement change more slowly, if at all.

The sources of influence are innumerable, but the most intense and continuous pressure comes from government agencies, financial analysts, bankers, industry associations, clients of CPAs, individual companies, academicians, other accounting organizations, and public opinion. Several of these groups significantly influence accounting standards.

Should there be politics in setting financial accounting and reporting standards? We have politics at home; at school; at the fraternity, sorority, and dormitory; at the office; at church; politics is everywhere! The FASB does not exist in a vacuum. Standard setting is part of the real world and, as such, it cannot escape politics and political pressures. That is not to say that politics per se in standard setting is evil.

[33]Former FASB chairman Marshall S. Armstrong acknowledged that several of the Board's projects, including ''Accounting for Contingencies,'' ''Accounting for Changes in General Purchasing Power,'' and ''Accounting for Certain Marketable Equity Securities,'' were targets of political pressure.

Considering the **economic consequences**[34] of many accounting standards, it is not surprising that special interest groups become vocal and critical (some supporting, some opposing) when these standards are being formulated. The Board must be attentive to the politics and economic consequences of its actions. What the Board should not do is issue pronouncements whose primary motivation is political. The politics of the day (contemporary wisdom) cannot be the guiding light in setting standards. While paying attention to its constituencies, the Board should base its standards on sound research and a conceptual framework founded in economic reality. Even so, the FASB can continue to expect politics and special interest pressures since, as T. S. Eliot said, "Humankind cannot bear very much reality."

A current illustration of an economic consequence is the depressed situation in the savings and loan industry (S&Ls). To acquire more liquidity, many S&Ls would like to sell part of their investment portfolio. If they did so, however, large losses would be reported, because the market value of these investments is considerably below their book value. As a consequence, these losses would reduce shareholders' equity to such an extent that many S&Ls would violate regulatory requirements. The S&Ls argue that they should be permitted to defer these losses and amortize them over an appropriate future period. The accounting profession, on the other hand, argues that under generally accepted accounting principles a full loss should be reported in the period during which the sale transaction is completed. We agree with the latter position. Such a situation demonstrates why certain industries will argue strongly for a position that does not accord with generally accepted accounting principles. (The Canadian experience regarding PIP grants discussed earlier in this Chapter is another example.)

Continued Interest in Standard Setting

Since many interests may be affected by the implementation of an accounting standard, it is not surprising that there is much discussion about who should develop these standards and to whom they should apply. Some of the major issues are discussed below.

Public Versus Private Sector

All professions have come under increasing scrutiny by the government in the last ten years: lawyers, doctors, and engineers all have received attention as the government has assumed an increasingly active role in protecting the public interest. The accounting profession has not been ignored. Owing to some well-publicized instances of corporate fraud, domestic and foreign bribery, and sudden bankruptcies, critics of the accounting profession started to question its dedication and performance. Add to this society's general desire for greater accountability from all institutions, and it is not surprising that Congress began to inquire into the structure and practices of the accounting profession, the accounting and auditing standard-setting process, and the role of accountancy in the business world.

[34]"Economic consequences" in this context means the impact of accounting reports on the wealth positions of issuers and users of financial information and the decision-making behaviour resulting from that impact. The resulting behaviour of these individuals and groups could have detrimental financial effects on the providers (enterprises) of the financial information. For a more detailed discussion of this phenomenon, see Stephen A. Zeff, "The Rise of Economic Consequences," *Journal of Accountancy* (December, 1978), pp. 56–63.

In 1976, for example, a House of Representatives committee chaired by Representative John E. Moss **(Moss Committee)** issued a report that criticized the FASB for not moving quickly enough to eliminate some of the alternative reporting practices in accounting. It recommended that the SEC take a more active role in establishing accounting principles and that a framework for uniform accounting principles be developed. In 1977 a Senate committee chaired by Senator Lee Metcalf **(Metcalf Committee)** also examined the accounting profession and arrived at a number of conclusions that were critical and also inaccurate.

Recently, Representative John D.Dingell **(Dingell Committee)** held hearings to determine whether the FASB and the SEC are issuing effective and timely standards. The hearings were precipitated by some massive bankruptcies and frauds that occurred in the early 1980s such as Penn Square Bank and Drysdale Government Securities, Inc. Some in Congress complain that these bankruptcies could have been averted if more timely information had been provided.

The profession's response to these criticisms has been direct and immediate. For example, the AICPA established an Accounting Firms Division (in addition to the existing division for individual AICPA members) with two sections: one for firms auditing SEC clients (called the **SEC Practice Section**) and the other for firms auditing privately owned, non-SEC clients (called the **Private Companies Section**).[35] To help assure the public that the SEC Practice Section is meeting its responsibilities, the AICPA established as part of this structure an independent **Public Oversight Board.** The Board, composed of distinguished nonaccountants, has its own staff and is free to conduct its own inquiries and to report publicly as it wishes. The Private Companies Section also has its own quality control standards and peer review requirements.

Competing Standard-Setting Bodies

The right of the FASB to establish accounting principles has been challenged continually. As previously stated, the AICPA started issuing SOPs because it believed that immediate guidance was needed for specific reporting problems and that the FASB was unable to respond promptly. More recently, after much debate, the Financial Accounting Foundation consented to establish a separate Governmental Accounting Standards Board for state and local governments.

These developments demonstrate the tenuous nature of the FASB's ultimate authority to establish accounting standards. Other groups may also decide to pursue such an approach. For example, trade associations and special industry organizations have begun to issue pronouncements on accounting matters. As a result, it is possible that someday there may be attempts to develop separate accounting standards boards for specific industries. Each of these competing standard setters would represent a challenge to the FASB's authority.

Summary

A delicate balance still exists between the private sector and the public sector. Some people in government, some in the financial community, and some in the

---

[35]CPA firms that audit SEC registered firms must join the SEC Practice Section and thereby must comply with more comprehensive practice requirements (such as compulsory peer practice review) than are required by the Private Companies Section.

profession itself are continually challenging the accounting profession to assume more responsibility and to be more responsive to the needs of its constituencies. At present, the accounting profession is reacting responsibly and effectively to remedy identified shortcomings. The private sector, because of its substantive resources and expertise, should be able to develop and maintain high standards, but it is a difficult process requiring time, logic, and diplomacy. By a judicious mix of these three ingredients, and a measure of luck, the profession may be able to continue to develop its own standards and regulate itself with minimal intervention.

Note: All asterisked Questions, Cases, Exercises, or Problems relate to material in an Appendix.

QUESTIONS

1. What is "accounting"?
2. What is it in today's environment that places a greater responsibility on accounting than ever before?
3. Into what areas can the discipline of accounting be divided?
4. Differentiate broadly between financial accounting and managerial accounting.
5. Differentiate between "financial statements" and "financial reporting."
6. Accounting is an unchanging discipline independent of its environment and other influences. Comment.
7. Name several environmental conditions that shape financial accounting to a significant extent.
8. It is an acknowledged fact that we live in a world of scarce resources. In what ways does accounting recognize this fact?
9. How are current legal and ethical standards related to the basic nature of accounting?
10. In what way does accounting shape its environment and play a role in the conduct of economic, social, political, and legal actions?
11. What are the objectives of financial reporting?
12. How valuable is a common body of theory to financial accounting and reporting?
13. What is the likely limitation of "general-purpose financial statements"?
14. What are some of the developments or events that occurred in Canada between 1900 and 1945 that helped bring about changes in accounting theory or practice?
15. If you had to explain or define "generally accepted accounting principles or standards" to a nonaccountant, what essential characteristics would you include in your explanation?
16. What are the sources of pressure that change and influence the development of accounting principles and standards?
17. What is the legal source in Canada for GAAP? Why does it have legal authority?
18. What is a Recommendation in the *CICA Handbook*? What is the significance of these Recommendations to financial accounting?
19. Who has the responsibility for developing *CICA Handbook* Recommendations for financial accounting?
20. Why is professional judgement necessary in financial accounting?
21. If you were given complete authority in the matter, how would you propose that accounting principles or standards be developed and enforced?
22. *The Canada Business Corporations Act* (1975) requires that the *CICA Handbook* be used to determine generally accepted accounting principles for financial statement reporting of companies incorporated federally. Explain the significance of this requirement in terms of the apparent role the federal government has delegated to the CICA. How well has the CICA performed this role? Do you think there is a possibility of

government agencies taking over the role of setting accounting standards in Canada? Would such a situation be favourable or unfavourable to the accounting profession?

23. Identify CICA, SMAC, CCGAA. What are the differences between these organizations in terms of their role in developing financial accounting standards, and in terms of what their professional members do?

*24. What is an Exposure Draft and what role does it play in developing *CICA Handbook* Recommendations?

*25. Under what circumstances may a Reexposure Draft be issued?

CASES

C1-1 At the completion of the Wetzel Industries, Inc. audit, the president, Thomas Wetzel, Sr., questions the meaning of the phrase "in conformity with generally accepted accounting principles" that appears in your audit report on the management's financial statements. He observes that the phrase must mean more than what he ordinarily thinks of as "principles."

Instructions

(a) Explain the meaning of the term "accounting principles" as used in the audit report. (Do **not** discuss in this part the significance of "generally accepted.")

(b) Thomas Wetzel, Sr. wants to know how you determine whether or not an accounting principle is generally accepted. Discuss the sources of evidence for determining whether an accounting principle has substantial authoritative support. Do not merely list the titles of publications.

(c) Thomas Wetzel, Sr. believes that diversity in accounting practice will always exist among independent entities despite continual improvements in comparability. Discuss the arguments that **support** his belief.

C1-2 Some accountants have said that politicization in the development and acceptance of generally accepted accounting principles (i.e., standard-setting) is taking place. Some use the term "politicization" in a narrow sense to mean the influence by government agencies on the development of generally accepted accounting principles. Others use it more broadly to mean the compromise that takes place in bodies responsible for developing generally accepted accounting principles because of the influence and pressure of interested groups (Canadian Academic Accounting Association, provincial securities commissions, businesses through their various organizations, Society of Management Accountants, Certified General Accountants Association, financial analysts, bankers, lawyers, etc.).

Instructions

(a) What are the arguments to support the "politicization" of accounting standard-setting?

(b) What are the arguments against the "politicization" of accounting standard-setting?

(CMA adapted)

C1-3 From time to time, it has been suggested that the various professional accounting bodies in Canada should merge into a single organization. Discuss the potential advantages and disadvantages of such a merger.

C1-4 Presented below are three models for setting accounting standards.

1. The purely political approach, where national legislative action decrees accounting standards.

2. The private, professional approach, where financial accounting standards are set and enforced by private professional actions only.

3. The public/private mixed approach, where standards are basically set by private sector bodies that behave as though they were public agencies and whose standards to a great extent are enforced through government agencies.

Instructions

    (a)   Which of these three models best describes standard-setting in Canada? Explain your answer.

    (b)   Why do companies, financial analysts, labour unions, industry trade associations, and others take such an active interest in standard-setting?

    (c)   In 1982, during the PIP grants controversy, the federal government came close to legislating an accounting practice. Why would such an action have tremendous consequences regarding Canadian accounting if it had been carried out? Speculate as to why the federal government wished to set its own standard, which was contradictory to that of the *Handbook*.

C1-5   Peter Buck recently entered the wholesale business by forming a limited company. He rented warehouse space, bought inventory, and made sales and deliveries over a period of several months. His inventory management was of significant importance to the likely success of his business, and he maintained a record of the purchases made. Because these had been made at varying quantities and unit prices, he was becoming quite confused as to how the inventory should be valued for such purposes as pricing decisions, insurance coverage, renewing a bank loan, preparing financial statements, and determining income tax obligations.

    Having taken a basic bookkeeping course, he understood that the *CICA Handbook* was the source for generally accepted accounting principles in Canada. He obtained the *Handbook* to look for clear-cut answers as to how his inventory should be valued in order to satisfy his purposes. He was rather disappointed in what he read. Several methods for inventory valuation were identified as generally acceptable, but none was recommended as that which would uniquely satisfy his needs.

    That evening he met his friend Barbara, a professional accountant, at a reception. During their conversation, he mentioned his dilemma and his frustration with the *Handbook*. She understood his problem and explained the need for accountants to exercise professional judgement in finding solutions to particular accounting problems. Their discussion continued for the rest of the evening.

Instructions

    (a)   What, in your opinion, is meant by the phrase "professional judgement"?

    (b)   Given that GAAP, as expressed in the *CICA Handbook*, establish acceptable financial accounting principles and practices, why is professional judgement important?

    (c)   What important factors would you take into consideration if you were to recommend to Peter Buck how his inventory should be valued?

2

CONCEPTUAL FRAMEWORK UNDERLYING FINANCIAL ACCOUNTING

Accounting may appear to be primarily procedural in nature. The visible portion of accounting—record keeping and preparation of financial statements—too often suggests the application of a low-level skill in an occupation devoted to mundane objectives and devoid of challenge and imagination. However, a large body of theory in accounting does exist, comprising philosophical objectives, normative theories, interrelated concepts, precise definitions, and rationalized rules. This conceptual framework may be unknown to many people in the business community.[1] Thus, **accountants philosophize, theorize, judge, create, and deliberate as a significant part of their professional practice.** The subjective aspects that are so critical to current accounting practice, such as searching for truth and fact, judging

---

[1] Perhaps the most significant documents in this area are: Maurice Moonitz, *Accounting Research Study No. 1: The Basic Postulates of Accounting* (New York: AICPA, 1961); Robert T. Sprouse and Maurice Moonitz, *Accounting Research Study No. 3: A Tentative Set of Broad Accounting Principles for Business Enterprises* (New York: AICPA, 1962); *APB Statement No. 4: Basic Concepts and Accounting Principles Underlying Financial Statements of Business Enterprises* (New York: AICPA, 1970); "Objectives of Financial Reporting by Business Enterprises," *Statement of Financial Accounting Concepts No. 1* (Stamford, Conn.: FASB, 1978); "Conceptual Framework for Financial Accounting and Reporting: Elements of Financial Statements and Their Measurement," *FASB Discussion Memorandum* (Stamford, Conn.: FASB, 1976); and subsequent documents related to the U.S. conceptual framework project of the FASB. *Corporate Reporting: Its Future Evolution* (Toronto: CICA, 1980) is the major Canadian statement regarding a conceptual framework.

what is fair presentation, and considering the behaviour induced by presentations, are overshadowed by the appearance of exactitude, precision, and objectivity that are inherent in the use of numbers to express the financial results of the enterprise.

The principles of accounting are unlike the principles of the natural sciences and mathematics, because they cannot be derived from or proved by the laws of nature, and they are not viewed as fundamental truths or axioms. **Accounting principles cannot be discovered; they are created, developed, or decreed. Accounting principles are supported and justified by intuition, authority, and acceptability**. Arguments concerning accounting principles can degenerate into quasi-religious dogmatism because it is difficult to substantiate them objectively or by experimentation. As a result, the sanction for and credibility of accounting principles rest upon their general recognition and acceptance, which depend upon such criteria as usefulness, fairness, relevance, reliability, and cost-benefit considerations.

NATURE OF A CONCEPTUAL FRAMEWORK

A conceptual framework is like a **constitution**; it is "a coherent system of interrelated objectives and fundamentals that can lead to consistent standards and that prescribes the nature, function, and limits of financial accounting and financial statements."[2]

Why is a conceptual framework necessary? First, to be useful, standard setting should build on and relate to an established body of concepts and objectives. A soundly developed conceptual framework should thus enable the development and issuance of **a coherent set of standards and practices** built upon the same foundation. Second, new and emerging **practical problems should be more quickly solvable by reference to an existing framework** of basic theory. As an illustration of an emerging problem, unique types of debt instruments have been issued by companies as a response to high interest and inflation rates. Examples are "shared appreciation mortgages" (debt in which the lender receives equity participation), "deep discount bonds" (debt with no stated interest rate), and "commodity-backed bonds" (debt that may be repaid in a commodity). Examining the commodity-backed bonds a little further, we find that companies are issuing debt that will be repaid either in cash or in some commodity, such as silver, oil, coal, and so on (also referred to as asset-linked bonds). For example, in 1980, Sunshine Mining (a silver-mining company) sold two issues of bonds that it would redeem either with $1,000 in cash or with 50 ounces of silver (or the cash equivalent), whichever was greater at maturity. Both bond issues are due in 1995 and both have a low stated interest rate—8.5%. At what amounts should the bonds be recorded by Sunshine or the buyers of the bonds? What is the amount of the premium or discount on the bonds and how should it be amortized, if the bond redemption payments are to be made in silver (the future value of which is currently unknown)?

It is difficult, if not impossible, for the CICA to prescribe the proper accounting treatment quickly for situations like this. Practising accountants, however, must resolve such problems on a day-to-day basis. Through the exercise of professional judgement and with the help of an accepted conceptual framework, it is hoped that practitioners will be able to dismiss certain alternatives quickly because they fall outside the conceptual framework, and then to focus upon a logical and acceptable treatment.

[2]"Conceptual Framework for Financial Accounting and Reporting: Elements of Financial Statements and Their Measurement," *FASB Discussion Memorandum* (Stamford, Conn.: FASB, 1976), page 1 of the section, "Scope and Implications of the Conceptual Framework Project."

Third, a conceptual framework should **increase financial statement users' understanding of and confidence in financial reporting** and, fourth, such a framework should **enhance comparability among companies' financial statements.** Similar events and phenomena should be similarly accounted for and reported; dissimilar events properly should not be.

DEVELOPMENT OF A CONCEPTUAL FRAMEWORK

The development of a conceptual framework for financial accounting and reporting has been the focus of much time, talent, and expense.

In Canada, the CICA research study, *Corporate Reporting: Its Future Evolution (1980)*, represents the major document encompassing such a conceptual framework. Its contribution to the evolutionary process of deriving a framework for accounting practice resided primarily in its discussion of objectives and suggestions for criteria in developing standards for financial reporting. While it is a unique Canadian study, the essence of its contents closely paralleled the conclusions derived in documents issued by the Financial Accounting Standards Board (FASB) in the U.S.A. Given the similarity in the two countries, this consistency is not surprising. The fact of the matter is that the FASB has committed far more human and financial resources to the development of a conceptual framework. Thus, the FASB's results provide a far more comprehensive source for studying the nature of a conceptual framework for financial accounting, even as it applies in Canada. Therefore, it is worthwhile to examine this material in order to gain an appreciation for the underlying theory that shapes contemporary accounting.

The development of a conceptual framework in the U.S.A. has had a fairly long history which has not been free of criticism. While significant efforts took place prior to the establishment of the FASB, it is the work of this Board that has been particularly important to the contemporary understanding of a conceptual framework. Recognizing the need for a generally accepted framework, the FASB in 1976 issued a massive three-part Discussion Memorandum entitled *Conceptual Framework for Financial Accounting and Reporting: Elements of Financial Statements and Their Measurement*, which detailed the major issues considered necessary to establish a basic framework for resolving financial reporting controversies. This project was to facilitate pronouncements on the following matters:

1. **Establishment of the objectives of financial statements.** It is necessary to determine (a) for what purposes financial statements are intended; (b) to whom should they be directed; (c) what information should be included; and (d) the limitations of financial statements.
2. **Determination of the essential qualitative characteristics of financial statement information.** What qualities (e.g., relevance, reliability, and comparability) make accounting information useful to financial statement readers, and what are the appropriate trade-offs when conflicts between these characteristics (e.g., relevance and reliability) occur?
3. **Definition of the basic elements of accounting.** What is an asset, liability, revenue, or expense? Are some of these elements more important than others in determining net income? For example, should net income be defined in terms of changes in an enterprise's net assets (excluding capital transactions) over a period of time, or should assets and liabilities be determined only after revenues, expenses, and net income are defined?
4. **Determination of the basis of measurement.** Even after the basic elements are developed, how should assets be measured? For example, should we use historical cost, replacement

cost, current selling price, expected cash flow, present value of expected cash flow, or some other valuation system?

5. **Change in the measuring unit.** Should the basic measuring unit of accounting be adjusted for changes in purchasing power of the dollar, should these changes be ignored, or should supplementary information be presented?

Since publication of the Discussion Memorandum, the FASB has issued four *Statements of Financial Accounting Concepts* that relate to financial reporting for business enterprises:[3]

1. *SFAC No. 1.* "Objectives of Financial Reporting by Business Enterprises," presents the goals and purposes of accounting (November, 1978).
2. *SFAC No. 2.* "Qualitative Characteristics of Accounting Information," examines the characteristics that make accounting information useful (May, 1980).
3. *SFAC No. 3.* "Elements of Financial Statements of Business Enterprises," provides definitions of items that financial statements comprise, such as assets, liabilities, revenues, and expenses (December, 1980).
4. *SFAC No. 5.* "Recognition and Measurement in Financial Statements of Business Enterprises," sets forth fundamental recognition criteria and guidance on what information should be formally incorporated into financial statements, how the information is to be quantified, and when it should be reported (January, 1985).

We will draw on the CICA study and these FASB concept statements, as well as other sources, to present a capsule examination of a conceptual framework for financial accounting.

This framework should provide the reader with an understanding of the underlying perspective from which accounting standards are, and are likely to continue to be, established. Furthermore, from the point of view of a preparer of financial information, awareness of this framework should furnish guidance in choosing what to present in reports, making decisions between alternative ways of representing economic events, and selecting appropriate means of communicating such information. Finally, this framework may be useful to those who use information in financial reports through increasing their understanding of both the usefulness and limitations of such information.

Figure 2-1 provides an overview of the conceptual framework in accounting.[4] At the first level, the objectives identify the goals and purposes of accounting and are the building blocks for the conceptual framework. At the second level are the **qualitative characteristics** of accounting information and definitions of the **elements** of financial statements. The former are the characteristics that make accounting information useful, and the latter are definitions of financial statement components (assets, liabilities, and so on). Together these two categories provide the foundation for developing recognition and measurement guidelines to be used in practice. At the final or third level are the **measurement and recognition guidelines** that the accountant uses in establishing and applying accounting practices. The measurement and recognition guidelines encompass the use of **assumptions, principles, and constraints** to describe the present reporting environment.

---

[3]A "Statement of Financial Accounting Concepts," like a CICA research study, does not constitute a change in existing generally accepted accounting principles. Rather, the contents of such publications serve as a basis for examining standards and developing future pronouncements. The FASB has also issued "Objectives of Financial Reporting by Nonbusiness Organizations," *Statement of Financial Accounting Concepts No. 4* (Stamford, Conn.: FASB, December, 1980).

[4]Adapted from William C. Norby, *The Financial Analyst's Journal* (March–April, 1982), p. 22.

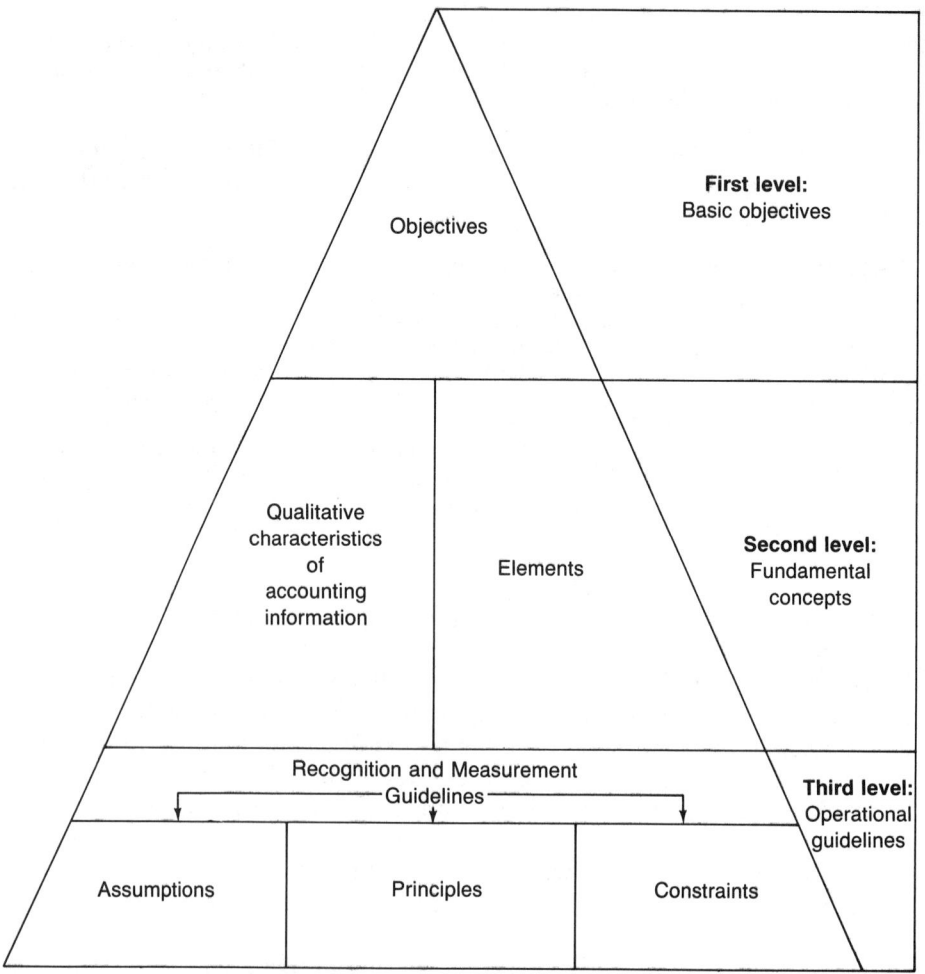

FIGURE 2-1 A Conceptual Framework for Accounting

FIRST LEVEL: BASIC OBJECTIVES

Chapter 1 considered the objectives of financial statements and reporting. In general, when providing information to users of financial statements, the accounting profession has relied on general-purpose financial statements. The intent of these is to provide the most useful information possible to various user groups at minimal cost. Underlying these objectives is the notion that users have a reasonably sophisticated understanding of matters related to business and financial accounting. This point is important because it means that, in the preparation of financial statements, accountants may assume a level of reasonable competence; this has an impact on the way and the extent to which information is reported.

As stated earlier, the objectives of financial reporting include providing information that (1) is useful for making investment, credit, and other decisions by those who have a reasonable understanding of business and economic activities; (2) is helpful to present and potential investors, creditors, and other users in assessing the amount, timing, and uncertainty of future cash flow; and (3) is financially descriptive of economic resources, the claims to those resources, and the changes in them.

While these objectives presuppose a variety of user groups, tradition has emphasized investors and creditors. The broad concern for general information useful for such decision makers is frequently narrowed to their interest in the prospect of receiving cash from their investments in, or loans to, business enterprises. Recent economic events (i.e., bankruptcies or serious cash flow problems of many Canadian corporations) have served to emphasize the usefulness of financial statements to enable reasonable assessment of prospective cash flows of a business enterprise. Nevertheless, while economic events at the time may be related to a particular orientation regarding the usefulness of financial statements, the broad perspective of providing useful information to various groups remains paramount.

A statement of objectives, general though they may appear, is a necessary starting point for developing the framework. Objectives may vary, and their nature may exert tremendous impact upon the practice of accounting. For example, if the only objective of financial statements were to determine the minimum taxable income each year, we would proceed from a substantially different framework than presently exists.

SECOND LEVEL: FUNDAMENTAL CONCEPTS

The objectives (first level) deal with the goals and purposes of accounting. Later, we will discuss the ways in which these goals and purposes are implemented (third level). Between these two levels, it is necessary to provide certain conceptual building blocks that explain the qualitative characteristics of accounting information and define the elements that financial statements comprise. These conceptual building blocks form a bridge between the **why** (objectives) and the **how** (operational guidelines) of accounting.

QUALITATIVE CHARACTERISTICS OF ACCOUNTING INFORMATION

How does one decide whether financial reports should provide information on an historical cost basis or on a current value basis? Or how does one decide whether the three main companies that constitute the Molson Companies Limited—Molson Breweries of Canada Limited, Beaver Lumber Company Limited, and Diversey Corporation—should be combined and shown as one company or disaggregated as three separate companies for financial reporting purposes? To answer such diverse yet basic questions, one looks to some criterion as a guide in choosing among alternatives.

Choosing an acceptable accounting method, the amount and types of information to be disclosed, and the format in which information should be presented involves determining which alternative provides the best (i.e., most useful) information for decision-making purposes. The FASB (in *SFAC No. 2*) identified the qualitative characteristics of accounting information that distinguish better (more useful) from inferior (less useful) information for decision-making purposes.[5] In addition, the FASB has identified certain constraints (cost-benefit and materiality) as part of

---

[5]"Qualitative Characteristics of Accounting Information," *Statement of Financial Accounting Concepts No. 2* (Stamford, Conn.: FASB, May, 1980).

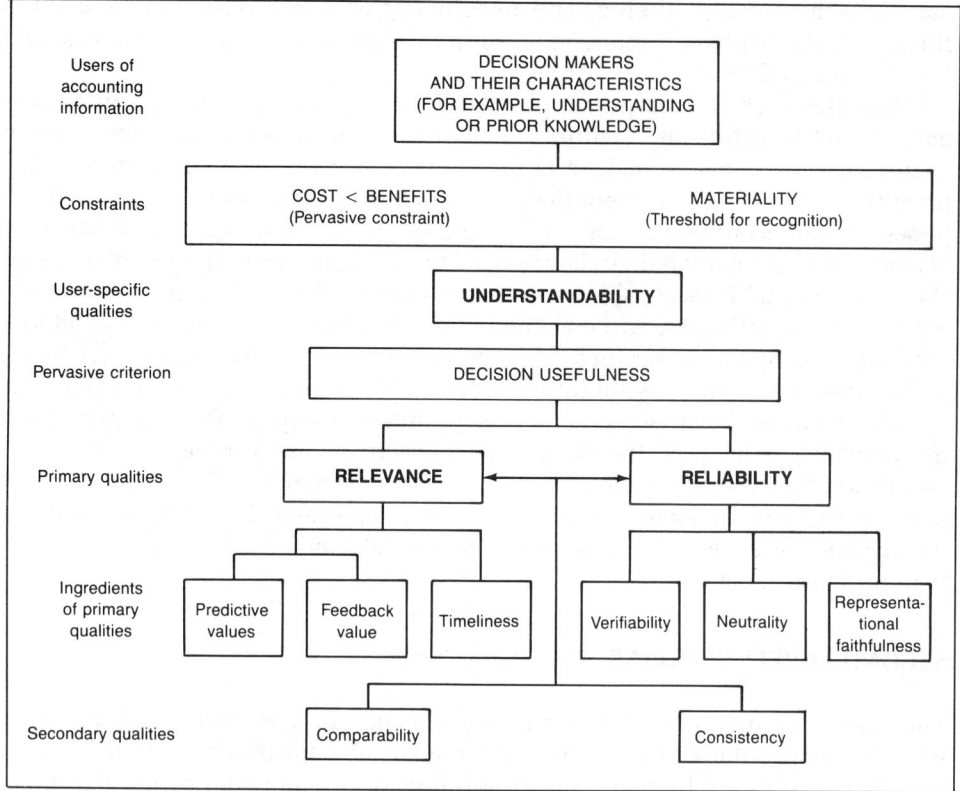

FIGURE 2-2 A Hierarchy of Qualitative Characteristics for Financial Accounting Information

the conceptual framework. These are discussed later in the chapter. The characteristics may be viewed as a hierarchy, as illustrated in Figure 2-2.

Pervasive Criterion of Decision Usefulness

Financial reporting is concerned with decision making. As a consequence, **the overriding criterion by which accounting choices can be judged is that of decision usefulness**; that is, providing information that is the most useful for decision making. Without usefulness, there would be no justification for accounting activity, nor a basis against which to assess the costs of providing reports. Usefulness depends on the appropriate linking of users and their qualities with the qualities (primary and secondary) of the information, recognizing constraints.

Decision Makers (Users) and Understandability

Decision makers vary widely in the types of decisions they make, the methods of decision making they employ, the information they already possess or can obtain from other sources, and their ability to process the information. Consequently, accountants should consider decision makers and their characteristics when formulating financial reports. (See Chapter 1 for an elaboration of this point.) When considering the usefulness of accounting information to decision makers, a critical notion is their ability to understand what it is and is not. **Understandability** means that a reasonably informed user is able to perceive the significance of the information. To illustrate the importance of understandability to usefulness, assume that DuPont Canada Inc. issues a three-months' earnings report (interim report) that provides relevant and reliable information for decision-making purposes. Unfortunately, certain users do not understand the content and significance of the interim report. Thus, although the information presented is highly relevant and reliable, it is useless to users who do not understand it.

The primary consequence of the concept of understandability to preparers of financial reports is that one must think about the users and whether the disclosures made will be intelligible to the intended audience. The basic assumption generally made about the users of general-purpose financial statements is that they have a reasonable understanding of business and economic activity and are willing to study the information with reasonable diligence.

Primary Qualities

It is generally believed that **relevance and reliability are the two primary qualities that make accounting information useful for decision making.** As stated in *Concepts Statement No. 2*, "the qualities that distinguish 'better' (more useful) information from 'inferior' (less useful) information are primarily the qualities of relevance and reliability, with some other characteristics that those qualities imply."[6]

Relevance   To be relevant, accounting information must be capable of making a difference in a decision.[7] Relevant information helps users make predictions about the outcome of past, present, and future events (**predictive value**), or confirm or correct prior expectations (**feedback value**). For example, when DuPont Canada Inc. issues an interim report, this information is considered relevant because it provides a basis for forecasting annual earnings and furnishes feedback on past performance. It follows that for information to be relevant, it must also be available to decision makers before it loses its capacity to influence their decisions (**timeliness**). For example, if DuPont did not report its interim results until six months after the end of the period, the information would be much less useful for decision-making purposes. Thus, **for information to be relevant, it should have the ingredients of predictive value, feedback value, and timeliness.**

Reliability   Accounting information is reliable to the extent that users can depend on it to represent the economic conditions or events that it purports to represent. **Reliability is the quality of information that gives assurance that it is reasonably free of error and bias and is a faithful representation.** To be reliable, accounting information must possess three key ingredients: verifiability, representational faithfulness, and neutrality.

Verifiability   Verifiability is an ingredient that is demonstrated when a high degree of consensus can be secured among independent persons using the same measurement methods. When measurements are based on such objective evidence as invoices, they are likely to be highly verifiable. Alternatively, when measure-

---

[6]*Ibid.*, par. 15.
[7]*Ibid.*, par. 47.

ments require the making of estimates without the benefit of objective evidence (e.g., asset lives or uncollectible accounts), less verifiability can be expected and the results are, to a large extent, based on the accountant's judgement, observation, and experience.

Representational faithfulness   Representational faithfulness (called isomorphism in the CICA study *Corporate Reporting: Its Future Evolution*) means correspondence or agreement between the accounting numbers and descriptions and the resources or events that these numbers and descriptions purport to represent. For example, if DuPont's interim report presents cash sales of $1 billion when in fact it had cash sales of only $800 million, it would not represent what it purports to represent; that is, it would not be a faithful representation.

Neutrality   Neutrality is also an ingredient of reliability. Neutrality means that, when making a choice between accounting alternatives, the choice is free from bias toward a predetermined result. In other words, the primary concern when formulating or implementing accounting practices should be the relevance and reliability of the information that results and not just the economic consequence. For example, the applicability of a standard that requires a drug company to disclose in its notes that numerous lawsuits have been filed against it because of an inferior product should not be decided on the basis of the harm that such disclosure might inflict on the drug company. Similarly, neutrality precludes the choice of accounting policies for the explicit purpose of smoothing out fluctuations in reported income, thereby leading users to conclude there is less risk in a company's operations than there really is.

Reliability of information is a necessity for individuals who have neither the time nor the expertise to evaluate the factual content of the information. It is especially important to the independent audit process. Auditors would have a difficult time justifying their opinions about financial information if the information were not reasonably reliable.

Secondary Qualities

The potential use of different acceptable accounting methods by one enterprise in different years or by different companies in a given year would make comparison of financial results difficult. Consequently, in order to enhance the usefulness of accounting reports, the qualities of comparability and consistency are components of the conceptual framework. They are considered to be secondary to the qualities of relevance and reliability in the sense that, if information is to be useful, it must first be relevant and reliable. Achieving these primary qualities may require forgoing the secondary qualities, although in the most desirable state of affairs, financial accounting information would satisfy both qualitative levels.

Comparability   This is a qualitative characteristic that can improve both relevance and reliability. Comparability of financial information of a company over time periods or against some other enterprise contributes significantly to its usefulness. This occurs because the significance of information in a financial report depends to a great extent on a user's ability to relate it to some benchmark.

Consistency   This characteristic is achieved by an enterprise when it uses the same selected accounting methods over a period of years; that is, these methods are consistently applied. Consistency results in making financial statements of an enterprise comparable.

The standard opinion in an auditor's report also refers to consistency. The relevant portion of this report is: "In our opinion, the accompanying financial statements present fairly the financial position, results of operations, and changes in financial position for the period under review in accordance with generally accepted accounting principles applied on a basis consistent with that of the preceding year."

While consistency in applying the same methods across different enterprises **(uniformity)** may improve comparability, it has not become an aspect of practice. The difficulty associated with uniformity is that sometimes dissimilar circumstances must be similarly reported. Moreover, consistency does not mean that a company can never change an accounting method once selected. Indeed, **flexibility** is encouraged if it can be justified as resulting in more useful reports. When changes are made in a company's methods, however, they must be **fully disclosed** in the financial statements. (More will be said later concerning the meaning of full disclosure.)

Qualitative Characteristics, a Concluding Comment

The purpose of establishing qualitative characteristics of accounting information is to provide a framework for accountants when making choices regarding measurements and disclosures in financial reports. Using such a framework does not provide obvious solutions to accounting problems; rather, it simply identifies and defines aspects that should be considered in reaching a solution. Indeed, many accounting choices require trade-offs between the qualitative characteristics.[8] For example, some believe that financial reports based on current costs could provide more relevant information than reports based on historical costs which are more reliable. There is not, however, any clear-cut consensus on the relative weighting (importance) of relevance and reliability (or other characteristics) that would assist in deciding on such issues. Consequently, while awareness of the qualitative characteristics may help in choosing between alternatives, the actual decisions, in most cases, require the exercise of professional judgement.

BASIC ELEMENTS

An important aspect of any theoretical structure is the establishment of a body of elements or definitions. At present, accounting uses many terms that have peculiar and specific meanings in the language of business. One such term is **asset.** Is it something we own? If the answer is yes, can we assume that any asset leased would never be shown on the balance sheet? Is it something we have the right to use, or is it anything of value used by the enterprise to generate earnings? If the answer is yes, then why should the management of the enterprise not be reported

---

[8]As discussed previously, the CICA research study, *Corporate Reporting: Its Future Evolution* specified a set of criteria that could be used to develop standards in Canada. The criteria identified in this study are very similar to the qualitative characteristics in *SFAC No. 2*, but the latter has been used as the primary reference source herein because it provides more explicit definitions. The CICA study, however, provides many examples (particularly of trade-off situations) of the use of criteria.

as an asset? It seems necessary, therefore, to develop a basic definitional framework for the elements of accounting. Such definitions provide some guidance for identifying what to include and exclude from the financial statements. *Concepts Statement No. 3* defines ten interrelated elements that are most directly related to measuring the performance and financial status of an enterprise as follows:[9]

Elements of Financial Statements

Assets. Probable future economic benefits obtained or controlled by a particular entity as a result of past transactions or events.

Liabilities. Probable future sacrifices of economic benefits arising from present obligations of a particular entity to transfer assets or provide services to other entities in the future as a result of past transactions or events.

Equity. Residual interest in the assets of an entity that remains after deducting its liabilities. In a business enterprise, the equity is the ownership interest.

Investments by owners. Increases in net assets of a particular enterprise resulting from transfers to it from other entities of something of value to obtain or increase ownership interests (or equity) in it. Assets are most commonly received as investments by owners, but that which is received may also include services or satisfaction or conversion of liabilities of the enterprise.

Distributions to owners. Decreases in net assets of a particular enterprise resulting from transferring assets, rendering services, or incurring liabilities by the enterprise to owners. Distributions to owners decrease ownership interests (or equity) in an enterprise.

Comprehensive income. Change in equity (net assets) of an entity during a period from transactions and other events and circumstances from nonowner sources. It includes all changes in equity during a period except those resulting from investments by owners and distributions to owners.

Revenues. Inflows or other enhancements of assets of an entity or settlement of its liabilities (or a combination of both) during a period from delivering or producing goods, rendering services, or other activities that constitute the entity's ongoing major or central operations.

Expenses. Outflows or other using up of assets or incurrences of liabilities (or a combination of both) during a period from delivering or producing goods, rendering services, or carrying out other activities that constitute the entity's ongoing major or central operations.

Gains. Increases in equity (net assets) from peripheral or incidental transactions of an entity and from all other transactions and other events and circumstances affecting the entity during a period except those that result from revenues or investments by owners.

Losses. Decreases in equity (net assets) from peripheral or incidental transactions of an entity and from all other transactions and other events and circumstances affecting the entity during a period except those that result from expenses or distributions to owners.

Each of these elements will be explained and examined in detail in subsequent chapters.

Two important points should be noted regarding these definitions. First, the term **comprehensive income** represents a unique concept. Comprehensive income is more inclusive than our traditional notion of **net income**; if the FASB's definition is taken literally, it includes net income and all other changes in equity exclusive of owners' investments and distributions. Net income, therefore, is an intermediate amount that comprises part, but not all, of comprehensive income. For example, prior-period adjustments and correction of a prior period's errors, which are

---

[9]"Elements of Financial Statements of Business Enterprises," *Statement of Financial Accounting Concepts No. 3* (Stamford, Conn.: FASB, December, 1980). These definitions provide a reasonable perspective of the general nature of these items and reflect the way in which they are generally interpreted in the Canadian accounting environment.

currently excluded from net income (they are reported in the statement of retained earnings), may be included under comprehensive income. The concept of comprehensive income is, therefore, not applied in Canadian practice. Consequently, the more limited notion of net income is used throughout this book. Net income is defined as revenues minus expenses plus gains minus losses as they pertain to a particular time period.

Second, it is useful to think of the elements as two distinct groups. The first group of three elements—assets, liabilities, and equity—describes amounts of resources and claims to resources at a **moment in time.** The other seven elements (income and its components—revenues, expenses, gains, and losses—as well as investments by owners and distributions to owners) describe transactions, events, and circumstances that affect an enterprise during a **period of time.** The first group is changed by elements of the second group and at any time is the cumulative result of all changes. This interaction is referred to as **articulation**, and results in financial statements that are fundamentally interrelated. Thus, a statement (e.g., the balance sheet) that reports elements of the first group depends on a statement (e.g., the income statement) that reports elements of the second group, and vice versa.

THIRD LEVEL: OPERATIONAL GUIDELINES

SFAC No. 5, ''Recognition and Measurement in Financial Statements,''[10] provides guidelines for determining what information should be included in financial statements, how that information should be quantified, and when the information should be reported. The Statement specifies that four fundamental criteria should be met if an item or event is to be recognized. These are: (1) **definitions**—the item or event should satisfy the definition of an element of financial statements; (2) **measurability**—it has a relevant attribute measurable with sufficient reliability; (3) **relevance**—the information about it is capable of making a difference in user decisions; and (4) **reliability**—the information is verifiable, representationally faithful, and neutral. The recognition and measurement concepts do not call for any major changes from present accounting. Specifically, the concepts statement indicates that most aspects of current practice are consistent with the proposed recognition and measurement guidelines. Of necessity, therefore, the accounting profession continues to use operational guidelines which we have identified as assumptions, principles, and constraints. These serve as aids in developing rational responses to controversial financial reporting issues.

BASIC ASSUMPTIONS

What are the basic assumptions of accounting? In most cases, they are so obvious that we might ask why they have to be stated at all. Nevertheless, they merit special attention because they are critical to the development of proper and consistent accounting. If we do not understand the basic assumptions made by accountants, we cannot understand why the data are presented in a given manner.

Four basic assumptions underlying the financial accounting structure are (1) **an**

---

[10]''Recognition and Measurement in Financial Statements,'' *Statement of Financial Accounting Concepts No. 5* (Stamford, Conn.: FASB, January, 1985).

economic entity assumption, (2) **a going concern assumption,** (3) **a monetary unit assumption,** and (4) **a periodicity assumption.**

Economic Entity Assumption

A major assumption in accounting is that economic activity can be identified with a particular unit of accountability. In other words, the activity of a business enterprise can be kept separate and distinct from its owners and any other business unit.[11] If there were no meaningful way to separate all of the economic events that occur, no basis for accounting would exist. Imagine the results, for example, if the activities of General Motors could not be distinguished from those of Ford, Chrysler, or American Motors.

The economic entity assumption does not apply solely to the segregation of activities among given business enterprises. Although we usually think of entities as business enterprises, an individual, a department or division, or an entire industry could be considered a separate entity if we chose to define the unit in such a manner. Thus **the economic entity assumption is not necessarily a legal-entity concept;** a parent and its subsidiaries are separate legal entities, but merging their activities for accounting and reporting purposes when providing consolidated financial statements is not a violation of the economic entity assumption.

Going Concern Assumption

Most accounting methods are based on **the assumption that the business enterprise will have a long life.** Experience indicates that, in spite of numerous business failures, companies have a fairly high continuance rate, and it has proved useful to adopt a going concern or continuity assumption for accounting purposes. Although accountants do not believe that business firms will last indefinitely, they do expect them to last long enough to fulfill their objectives and commitments.

The implications of adopting this assumption are critical: it provides credibility to the historical cost principle, which would be of limited use if liquidation were assumed. Under a liquidation approach, for example, asset values are better stated at net realizable value (sales price less costs of disposal) than at acquisition cost. **Only if we assume some permanence to the enterprise are depreciation and amortization policies justifiable and appropriate.** If a liquidation approach were adopted, the current-noncurrent classification of assets and liabilities would lose much of its significance. Labelling anything a fixed or long-term asset would be difficult to justify. The listing of the liabilities on the basis of priority in liquidation, for example, would be more reasonable.

The going concern assumption is generally applicable in most business situations. **Only where liquidation appears imminent is the assumption inapplicable,** and in these cases a total revaluation of the assets and liabilities can provide information that closely approximates net realizable value of the entity. (Discussion of the accounting problems related to an enterprise in liquidation is presented in advanced accounting texts.)

---

[11]Surprisingly, such a distinction is not always made in practice. A *Wall Street Journal* article, for example, noted that audit committees of six publicly held companies wanted their chief executive to reimburse the companies an additional $1 million in personal expenses for such items as company yachts, speedboats, refurbishing, and rent money on personal apartments. (''Posners Asked to Repay Firms $1.1 Million More,'' *Wall Street Journal*, November 27, 1978, p. 6.)

Monetary Unit Assumption

Accounting is based on the assumption that money is the common denominator by which economic activity is conducted, and thus provides an appropriate basis for accounting measurement and analysis. This assumption implies that the monetary unit is the most effective means of expressing to interested parties changes in capital and exchanges of goods and services. Support for this assumption lies in the fact that **the monetary unit is relevant, simple, universally available, understandable, and useful.** Application of this assumption is dependent on the even more basic assumption that quantitative data are useful in communicating economic information and in making rational economic decisions.

In Canada, financial accounting practice (until recently, as discussed in Chapter 25) had chosen generally to ignore the phenomenon of price-level changes (inflation and deflation) by adopting the monetary unit assumption that **the unit of measure —the dollar—remains reasonably stable.** This second assumption about the monetary unit allows the accountant to add 1970 dollars to 1986 dollars without any adjustment. Arguments submitted in support of this stable dollar assumption are that the effects of price-level changes are not significant, and that presentation of price-level adjusted data is not easily understood.

Periodicity Assumption

The most accurate way to measure the results of enterprise activity would be to measure them at the time of the enterprise's eventual liquidation. Business, government, investors, and various other user groups, however, cannot wait indefinitely for such information. If accountants did not provide financial information periodically, someone else would.

The periodicity or time period assumption simply implies that **the economic activities of an enterprise can be divided into artificial time periods.** These time periods vary, but the most common are monthly, quarterly, and yearly. It is because accountants have to divide continuous operations into arbitrary time periods that they must determine the relevance of each business transaction or event to one specific accounting period. The shorter the time period, the more difficult it becomes to determine the proper net income for it. Problems of allocation[12] mean that a month's results are usually less reliable than a quarter's results. This phenomenon provides an interesting example of the trade-off between reliability and timeliness in preparing financial data. Investors desire and demand that information be quickly processed and disseminated; yet the quicker the information is released, the more it is subject to error.

BASIC PRINCIPLES OF ACCOUNTING

In view of the qualitative characteristics of accounting information and the basic assumptions of accounting, what are the principles that the accountant follows in

---

[12]Arthur L. Thomas, ''The Allocation Problem in Financial Accounting Theory,'' *Studies in Accounting Research No. 3* (Evanston, Ill.: American Accounting Association, 1969), and ''The Allocation Problem: Part Two,'' *Studies in Accounting Research No. 9* (Sarasota, Fla.: American Accounting Association, 1974). These studies provide an excellent examination of the difficulties and problems associated with arbitrary allocations in accounting as well as a thought-provoking discussion of the basis and usefulness of allocation in financial reporting.

deciding when and how to measure, record, and report assets, liabilities, revenues, and expenses? We will now discuss four such principles: (1) **the historical cost principle,** (2) **the revenue realization principle,** (3) **the matching principle,** and (4) **the full disclosure principle.**

Historical Cost Principle

The determination of the amounts to be recorded and reported for various assets and liabilities creates one of the most difficult problems in accounting. A wide range of values may exist for a single item: replacement cost, current selling price, present value of future cash flows, and original cost (less depreciation, where appropriate). Which should the accountant use?

Traditionally, preparers and users of financial statements have found that the historical acquisition cost is generally the most useful basis for accounting measurement and reporting. As a result, existing GAAP requires that most assets and liabilities be accounted for and reported on the basis of acquisition price. This is often referred to as the **historical cost principle. Historical cost has an important advantage over other valuations: it is reliable.** To illustrate the importance of this advantage, let us consider the problems that would arise if we adopted some other basis for keeping records. If we were to select current selling price, for instance, we might have a difficult time in attempting to establish a sales value for a given item without selling it. Every member of the accounting department might have his or her own opinion of the proper valuation of the asset, and management might desire still another figure. And how often would we find it necessary to establish sales value? All companies close their accounts at least annually, and some compute their net income every month. These companies would find it necessary to place a sales value on every asset each time they wished to determine income—a laborious task and one that would result in a figure of net income materially affected by opinion on sales value of the many assets involved. Similar objections have been levelled against current cost (replacement cost, present value of future cash flows) and other bases of valuation except historical cost.

Historical cost is usually definite and verifiable. Once established, it is fixed as long as the asset remains the property of the company. These characteristics are of real importance to those who use accounting data. To rely on the information supplied, both internal and external parties must know that the information is accurate and based on fact. **By using historical cost as their basis for record keeping, accountants can provide objective and verifiable data in their reports.**

The question of "what is cost?" is, however, not always easy to answer; a variety of problems arise. If fixed assets are to be carried in the accounts at cost, are cash discounts to be deducted in determining cost? Does cost include freight and insurance? Does it include cost of installation as well as the price of a machine itself? And what of the cost of reinstallation if the machine is later moved? When land is purchased for a building site and is already occupied by old structures, is the cost of razing these structures part of the cost of the land? These and similar questions must be considered and answered in arriving at cost figures for assets purchased.

Furthermore, purchase is not the only method of acquiring assets. How do we determine the cost of items received as a gift? It is not unusual for a developing community to offer plant sites free as an inducement to companies to establish themselves in that locality. At what price should such assets be carried? Also, certain assets may be acquired by the issuance of the share capital of the acquiring company, or perhaps through the issuance of bonds or notes payable. If no money price is stated in the transaction, how is cost to be established? These questions are answered in later chapters; they are raised here only to point out some of the difficulties regularly encountered in accounting for costs.

The basic financial statements include liabilities and assets. It may seem strange that liabilities are accounted for on a basis of cost, but this is because we ordinarily think of cost as relating only to assets. **If we convert the term "cost" to "exchange price," we will find that it applies to liabilities as well.** Such liabilities as bonds, notes, and accounts payable are incurred by a business enterprise in exchange for assets, or perhaps services, upon which an agreed price has usually been placed. This price, established by the exchange transaction, is a "cost" of the liability and provides, under the historical cost principle, the figure at which it should be recorded in the accounts and in financial statements.

Although there is general agreement that assets and liabilities should be accounted for on the basis of acquisition cost, there is also considerable criticism of this practice. Criticism is especially strong during a period when general and specific price levels are changing substantially. At such times cost is said to go "out of date" almost as soon as it is determined. In a period of rising or falling prices, the cost figures of the preceding year are viewed as not comparable with current cost figures. For example, assuming a rate of inflation of 1% per month, a McDonald's "quarter-pounder with cheese," which costs $1.45 today, will cost approximately $153.00 in 39 years if its cost directly followed the inflation rate. In a similar manner, financial statements that present the cost of fixed assets acquired 10 or 20 years ago may be misleading, because readers of such statements may tend to think in terms of current price levels, not in terms of the price levels at the time the fixed assets were purchased. A further complication follows from the fact that depreciation figures are based on recorded costs. As depreciation expense enters into income calculations, even the net income figure is suspect because of price-level changes.

Revenue Realization Principle (or Revenue Recognition Principle)[13]

The revenue realization principle provides guidance in answering the question of when revenue should be recognized. Revenue is recognized in the accounts when (1) **the earning process is virtually complete** and (2) **there is objective, verifiable evidence of the amount.**

Generally, these two requirements are met when a sale to independent parties occurs. Thus, recognition of revenue (recording it in the accounts) would take place at that time. Any basis for revenue recognition short of actual sales opens the door to wide variations in practice. Conservative business individuals might wait until sale of their securities; more optimistic individuals could watch market quotations and take up gains as market prices increased; yet others might recognize increases that are merely rumoured; and unscrupulous persons could "write up" their investments as they pleased to suit their own purposes. To give accounting

---

[13]Technically, realization means the process of converting noncash resources and rights into money and is used in accounting to refer to the sale of assets for cash or claims to cash. Recognition is formally recording an item in the financial statements (*SFAC No. 3, par. 83*). It is for this reason that the revenue realization principle is also referred to as the revenue recognition principle. (Revenue realization is discussed in depth in Chapter 19.)

reports uniform meaning, a rule for revenue recognition comparable to the cost rule for asset valuation is essential. **Realization through sale provides a uniform and reasonable test for recognition in most cases.**

There are, however, exceptions to recognition of revenue at the point of sale, as identified below.

Percentage-of-Completion Approach   Recognition of revenue is allowed in certain long-term construction contracts before the contract is completed. The advantage of this method is that income is recognized periodically on the basis of percentage of job completion, rather than at completion of the entire job. Although technically an exchange transaction has not occurred (transfer of ownership), the earning process is substantially completed as construction progresses. Naturally, if it is not possible to obtain dependable estimates of price, cost, and progress, then the accountant should wait and record the revenue at the completion date.

End of Production   At times, revenue might be recognized before sale, but after the production cycle has ended. This is the case where the price is certain as well as the quantity. An example would be the mining of certain minerals for which, once the mineral is mined, a ready market at a standard price exists. The same holds true for some guaranteed price supports set by the government in establishing agricultural prices.

Receipt of Cash   Receipt of cash is another basis for revenue recognition. The cash basis approach should be used only when it is impossible to establish the revenue figure at the time of the sale because of the uncertainty of collection. This approach is commonly referred to as the **instalment sales method** where payment is required in periodic instalments over a long period of time. Its most common use is in the retail field where various types of farm and home equipment and furnishings are sold on an instalment basis. The instalment method is frequently justified on the basis that the risk of not collecting an account receivable may be so great that the sale is not sufficient evidence that the two criteria for revenue recognition have been met. In some instances, this reasoning may be valid, but not in a majority of such transactions. If a sale has been completed, it should be recognized; and if bad debts are expected, they should be recorded as separate estimates of uncollectibles.

In summary, revenue is deemed to be realized and, therefore, recorded in the period when there is objective, verifiable evidence of the amount, and the earning process is virtually completed. Normally, this is the date of sale, but circumstances may dictate application of the percentage-of-completion approach, the end-of-production approach, or the receipt-of-cash approach.

Conceptually, the proper accounting treatment for revenue recognition should be apparent and should fit nicely into one of the conditions mentioned above, but often it does not. For example, consider two developments on the business scene —**franchises** and **motion picture sales to television.**

During the 1960s and 1970s franchising appeared to be the "updated version of the Canadian dream." Franchising operations were established for a wide variety of businesses from restaurants to pet-care centres. One need not have travelled too widely to appreciate the significant increases in such fast-food chains as McDonald's or Kentucky Fried Chicken. One of the problems that faced accountants of the franchisor (seller of the franchise) was when to recognize revenue from the sale of a franchise. In nearly all cases, as soon as the franchisor found an individual franchisee (buyer of the franchise) and received a down payment (no matter how small), the entire franchise price was treated as revenue. Consequently, to avoid any income slump that could impair their growth reputation, many franchisors signed up franchisees at an accelerating rate each year to perpetuate growth in earnings. This was necessary because the initial franchise fees were treated immediately as revenue—even though in many situations those fees were payable over a period of years, were refundable or uncollectible in the case of franchises that never got started, or were earned only as certain services were performed by the franchisor. In effect the franchisors were counting their fried chickens before they were hatched. Accountants had to change the basis for revenue recognition from the date the franchise contract was signed to a basis that more clearly reflected the requirements of the revenue realization principle, because of the abuses that developed in the area of franchise accounting.[14]

How should such motion picture companies as the National Film Board of Canada, Metro-Goldwyn-Mayer Inc., Warner Brothers, and United Artists account for the sale of rights to show motion picture films on such television networks as cable networks, CBC, CTV, ABC, CBS, or NBC? Should the revenue from the sale of the rights be reported when the contract is signed, when the motion picture film is delivered to the network, when the cash payment is received by the motion picture company, or when the film is shown on television? The problem of revenue recognition is complicated because the TV networks are often restricted to the number of times the film may be shown in total as well as to specified periods.

For example, Metro-Goldwyn-Mayer Inc. (MGM) sold CBS the rights to show *Gone With The Wind* for $35 million. For this $35 million, CBS is permitted to show this classic movie twenty times over a twenty-year period. MGM contends that revenue reporting should coincide with the right to telecast on first and subsequent showings as included in the licence agreement. They argued that the right to show *Gone With The Wind* twenty times over a twenty-year period is a significant contract restriction and, therefore, revenue recognition should coincide with the showings. The accounting profession, on the other hand, argued that when (1) the sales price and cost of each film is known, (2) collectibility is assured, and (3) the film is available and accepted by the network, revenue recognition should occur. The restriction that *Gone With The Wind* be shown only once a year for twenty years is not considered significant enough or appropriate justification for deferring revenue recognition. When MGM, in the first quarter of 1979, reported essentially the entire $35 million in revenue in one period, the following headline appeared in the *Wall Street Journal*: ''MGM's Net Tripled in the First Quarter That Ended Nov. 30.''

Matching Principle

In recognizing expenses, accountants attempt to follow the approach of ''let the expenses follow the revenues.'' Expenses are recognized not when wages are paid, or when the work is performed, or when a product is produced, but when the work (service) or the product actually makes its contribution to revenue. Thus, expense recognition is tied to revenue recognition. In some cases it is difficult to determine the period in which an expense contributes to the generation of revenues, but

[14]''Franchise Fee Recognition,'' *Accounting Guideline* (Toronto: CICA, 1984).

many expenses can be associated with particular revenues. This practice is referred to as the **matching principle** because it dictates that efforts (expenses) be matched with accomplishment (revenues) whenever it is reasonable and practicable to do so.

For those costs for which it is difficult to adopt some type of rational association between the expense and revenue, some other approach must be developed. Often, the accountant must develop a "rational and systematic" allocation policy that will approximate the matching principle. This type of expense recognition pattern always involves assumptions about the benefits that are being received as well as the cost associated with those benefits. The cost of a long-lived asset, for example, must be allocated over all of the accounting periods during which the asset is used because the asset contributes to the generation of revenue throughout its useful life.

Some costs are charged to the current period as expenses (or losses) simply because no future benefit is anticipated or no apparent connection with revenue is available. Examples of these types of costs are officers' salaries and advertising and promotion expenses.

Summarizing, we might say that costs are analyzed to determine whether a relationship exists with revenue. Where this association holds, the costs are expensed and matched against the revenue in the period when the revenue is recognized. If no direct connection appears between costs and revenues, an allocation of cost on some systematic and rational basis may be appropriate. Where such an allocation approach does not seem appropriate or reasonable, the costs may be expensed immediately.

Costs are generally classified into two groups: **product costs and period costs.** Such product costs as material, labour, and overhead attach to the product and are carried into future periods if the revenue from the product is realized in subsequent periods. Such period costs as officers' salaries and selling expenses are charged immediately to income because no direct relationship between cost and revenue can be determined.

The problem of expense recognition is as complex as that of revenue recognition. For example, at one time a large oil company spent a considerable amount of money in an introductory advertising campaign. The company obviously hoped that this advertising campaign would attract new customers and develop brand loyalty. Over how many years should this outlay be expensed? For another example, CP Air may depreciate its planes over 10 years, while Air Canada may write off its DC9 jets over a period as long as 16 years. Would the revenue flow from these two fleets justify that much of a difference in the expense recognition?

The conceptual validity of the matching principle has been a subject of debate. A major concern is that matching permits certain costs to be deferred and treated as assets on the balance sheet when in fact these costs may not have future benefits. If abused, this principle permits the balance sheet to become a "dumping ground" for unmatched costs. In addition, there appears to be no objective definition of "systematic and rational." Therefore, while the matching principle is an important guideline for determining when expenses are to be recognized, its application requires substantial judgement in many situations.

Full Disclosure Principle

In deciding what information to report, accountants follow the general practice of providing information that is sufficiently important to influence the judgement and decisions of an informed user. Often referred to as the **full disclosure principle**, this principle recognizes that the nature and amount of information included in financial reports reflects a series of judgemental trade-offs. These trade-offs strive for (1) sufficient detail to disclose matters that **make a difference** to users, and (2) sufficient combination and condensation to make the **information understandable**, keeping in mind costs of preparing and using it.[15] The accountant can place information about financial position, income, and cash flows in one of three places: (1) within the main body of financial statements, (2) in the notes to those statements, or (3) as supplementary information. The following paragraphs provide some broad guidelines for deciding where to place certain kinds of financial information.

The **financial statements** are a formalized, structured means of communicating. To be recognized in the main body of financial statements, an item should meet the definition of an element as well as other recognition conditions. The item must have been measured, recorded in the books, and passed through the double-entry system of accounting.

The **notes** to financial statements generally amplify or explain the items presented in the main body of the statements. If the information in the main body of the financial statements gives an incomplete picture of the performance and position of the enterprise, additional information that is needed to complete the picture should be included in the notes. Information in the notes does not have to be quantifiable, nor does it need to qualify as an element. Notes can be partially or totally narrative. Examples of notes are: descriptions of the accounting policies and methods used in measuring the elements reported in the statements; explanations of uncertainties and contingencies; and statistics and details too voluminous for inclusion in the statements. Information provided in the notes is not only helpful but also essential to an understanding of the performance and position of the enterprise.

Supplementary information may include information that presents a different perspective from that adopted in the financial statements. This may be quantifiable information that is high in relevance but low in reliability, or information that is helpful but not essential. The primary example of supplementary information is the data and schedules provided by certain companies on the effects of changing prices (constant dollar and current cost information). Supplementary information may also include management's explanation of the financial information and a discussion of its significance.

The full disclosure principle is not always easy to put into operation because the business environment is complicated and ever-changing. For example, during the past decade many business combinations have produced innumerable conglomerate-type business organizations and financing arrangements that demand new and different accounting and reporting practices and principles. Leases, investment credits, pension funds, franchising, stock options, and mergers have had to be studied, and appropriate reporting practices have had to be developed. In each of these situations, the accountant is faced with the problem of ensuring that enough information is presented so that the mythical, **reasonably prudent investor** will not be misled.

A classic illustration of the problems of determining adequate disclosure guidelines is the past turmoil related to bribes and political gifts to foreign countries. How much disclosure, if any, is necessary in the financial statements for these

[15]"Reporting Income, Cash Flows, and Financial Position of Business Enterprises," *Proposed Statement of Financial Accounting Concepts* (Stamford, Conn.: FASB, 1982), p. viii.

types of expenditures? On the one hand, it is contended that payoffs are unavoidable and should be looked upon as a cost of doing business. In addition, many of the transactions are generally small in comparison with the corporation's revenues and are not considered material in relation to its financial statements. Conversely, others argue that these types of payoffs raise questions about the quality of both management and earnings. They contend that shareholders have the right to know if the continuation of a company's operations in a foreign country depends on making payoffs, and what effect stopping the payoffs might have on the financial statements. The emergence of such a problem demonstrates the complexity and subjectivity of devising disclosure rules that meet the needs of society.[16]

CONSTRAINTS

In providing information with the qualitative characteristics that make it useful, two overriding constraints must be considered: (1) the **cost-benefit relationship** and (2) **materiality.** Two other less dominant yet important constraints that are part of the reporting environment are **industry practices** and **conservatism**.

Cost-Benefit Relationship   Too often, users assume that information is a cost-free commodity, but preparers and providers of accounting information know that it is not. The costs of providing the information must be weighed against the benefits that can be derived from using it. Obviously the benefits should exceed the costs. Practising accountants have traditionally applied this constraint through the notions of **expediency** or **practicality**. In order to justify requiring a particular measurement or disclosure, the benefits perceived to be derived from it must exceed the costs perceived to be associated with it.

The difficulty in cost-benefit analysis is that the costs and especially the benefits are not always evident or measurable. The costs are of several kinds, including costs of collecting and processing, disseminating, auditing, potential litigation, disclosure to competitors, and analysis and interpretation. Benefits accrue to preparers (that is, in terms of greater efficiency, control, and financing) as well as users (in terms of allocation of resources, tax assessment, and rate regulation), but they are generally more difficult to quantify than are costs. An increasing number of individuals and organizations are urging that cost-benefit analysis be required as part of the accounting standards development process, because the costs are usually more immediate and measurable while the benefits are not.

Among both the providers and the users of accounting information, there are those who believe that the costs associated with implementing certain standards are too high when compared with the benefits received. For example, some believe that Canadian GAAP, as represented in the *CICA Handbook*, are too cumbersome

---

[16]In the United States, the Foreign Corrupt Practices Act of 1977, which resulted from these developments, has been called by many the most significant piece of legislation affecting business enterprise in the last twenty years. This legislation requires business enterprises to keep books and records accurately to reflect accounting transactions and to maintain a system of internal accounting controls sufficient to provide reasonable assurance that transactions are handled properly. It establishes criminal penalties for making payments to foreign officials, political parties, or candidates in order to obtain or retain business. Such legislation provides guidance to accountants who, prior to this legislation, often were forced to make their own moral judgements on these questions. Since U.S. developments influence Canadian practice, it is likely that this legislation will have some impact on Canadian accounting practices. Codes of ethics of professional accounting organizations are also useful reference sources for reaching conclusions in such situations.

and expensive for smaller businesses to adhere to, relative to the benefits perceived as resulting from them. Consequently, they have argued that the financial
statements of smaller businesses should be governed by less demanding standards. The issues are related to what is called the ''big GAAP, little GAAP''
controversy which concerns the advantages and disadvantages of having all
enterprises adhere to the same standards, compared to having somewhat different
standards deemed acceptable for smaller versus larger enterprises.

Materiality   An item is material if its inclusion or omission would influence or
change the judgement of a reasonable person. It is immaterial and, therefore,
irrelevant if its inclusion or omission would have no impact on a decision maker.
In short, **it must make a difference** or it need not be disclosed. The point here is
one of **relative size and importance**. If the amount involved is significant when
compared with the other revenues and expenses, assets and liabilities, or net
income of the entity, sound and acceptable standards should be followed. If the
amount is so small that it is unimportant when compared with other items, application of a particular standard may be considered less important. It is difficult to
provide firm guidelines to determine when a given item is or is not material,
because materiality varies both with relative amount (the size of the item relative
to the size of other items) and with relative importance (the nature of the item
itself). The two sets of numbers presented below illustrate relative size.

	Company A	Company B
Sales	$10,000,000	$100,000
Costs and expenses	9,000,000	90,000
Income from operations	$ 1,000,000	$ 10,000
Unusual gain	$ 20,000	$ 5,000

During the period in question, the revenues and expenses and, therefore, the net
incomes from operations of Company A and Company B have been proportional.
Each has had an unusual gain which is not extraordinary. In looking at the
abbreviated income figures for Company A, it does not appear significant whether
the amount of the unusual gain is set out separately or merged with the costs and
expenses of regular operating income. It is only 2% of the operating income and, if
merged, would not seriously distort the net operating income figure. Company B
has had an unusual gain of only $5,000 but, as this item amounts to 50% of its
income from operations, it is relatively much more significant than the larger gain
realized by A. Obviously, the inclusion of such an item in ordinary operating
income would affect the amount of that income materially. Thus we see the importance of the **relative size** of an item in determining its materiality.

The **nature of the item** may also be important. For example, if a company violates a
statute, the amounts involved likely should be separately disclosed. Or, a misclas-
sification of assets that would not be material in amount if it affected two categories of
plant and equipment might be material if it changed the classification between a
noncurrent and a current category.

Materiality is a difficult concept, as these practical examples indicate:

1. General Dynamics disclosed that at one time its Resources Group had improved its
   earnings by $5.8 million at the same time that its Stromberg Datagraphix subsidiary
   had taken write-offs of $6.7 million. Although both numbers were far larger than
   the $2.5 million that General Dynamics as a whole earned for the year, neither was

disclosed as a separate item in the annual report; apparently the effect on net income was not considered material.

2. In the first quarter, GAC's earnings rose from 76 cents to 77 cents a share. Nowhere did the annual report disclose that a favourable tax carry-forward of 4 cents a share prevented GAC's earnings from sliding to 73 cents a share. The company took the position that this carry-forward should not be shown as an extraordinary item because it was not material (6%). As one executive noted, "You know that accountants have a rule of thumb that says that anything under 10% is not material."

These examples should illustrate one point: in practice, the answer to what is material is not clear-cut, and difficult decisions must be made each period. Only by the exercise of good judgement and professional expertise can the accountant arrive at answers that are reasonable and appropriate.

Materiality is a factor in a great many accounting decisions, only some of which are concerned with reporting items in the financial statements. For example, the amount of classification required in a subsidiary expense ledger, the degree of accuracy required in prorating expenses among the departments of a business, and the extent to which adjustments should be made for accrued and deferred items, are examples of judgements that should finally be determined on a basis of reasonableness and practicability, which is the materiality constraint sensibly applied.

Industry Practices   Another practical consideration that sometimes requires departure from basic theory is **the peculiar nature of some industries and business concerns.** For example, banks often report certain investment securities at market value because these securities are traded frequently, and many believe a cash equivalent price provides more useful information. In the public utility industry, noncurrent assets may be reported first on the balance sheet to highlight the capital-intensive nature of the industry. In the agricultural industry, crops are often reported at market value because it is costly to develop accurate cost figures on individual crops. Such variations from basic theory are few; yet they do exist, and so, whenever we find what appears to be a violation of basic accounting theory, it is important to determine whether it is explained by some peculiar feature of the type of business involved before being critical of the procedures followed.

Conservatism   Few conventions in accounting are as misunderstood as the constraint of conservatism. The practising accountant must make many decisions, some of them very difficult. For example, in a particular case the accountant may be in doubt about whether a given expenditure should be charged to an expense account or to an asset account. In reaching a decision he or she uses accounting theory as modified by cost-benefit considerations, materiality, industry practices, and the influence that this item will have on the financial statements. If this approach does not give the accountant a clear decision, he or she then tends to rely on the convention of conservatism that says, in effect: **when in doubt, choose the solution that will be least likely to overstate assets and income.** There is nothing in the conservatism convention urging the accountant to understate assets or income, although unfortunately it has been interpreted by some accountants to mean just that. All that conservatism does, properly applied, is to give the accountant a guide in difficult situations, and then the guide is a very reasonable one: refrain from overstatement of net income and net assets. Examples of conservatism in accounting are the use of the lower of cost and market approach in valuing inventories, and the rule that accrued net losses should be recognized on firm purchase commitments for goods for inventory. If the issue is in doubt, it is better to understate than overstate. Of course, if there are no doubts, there is no need to apply this constraint.

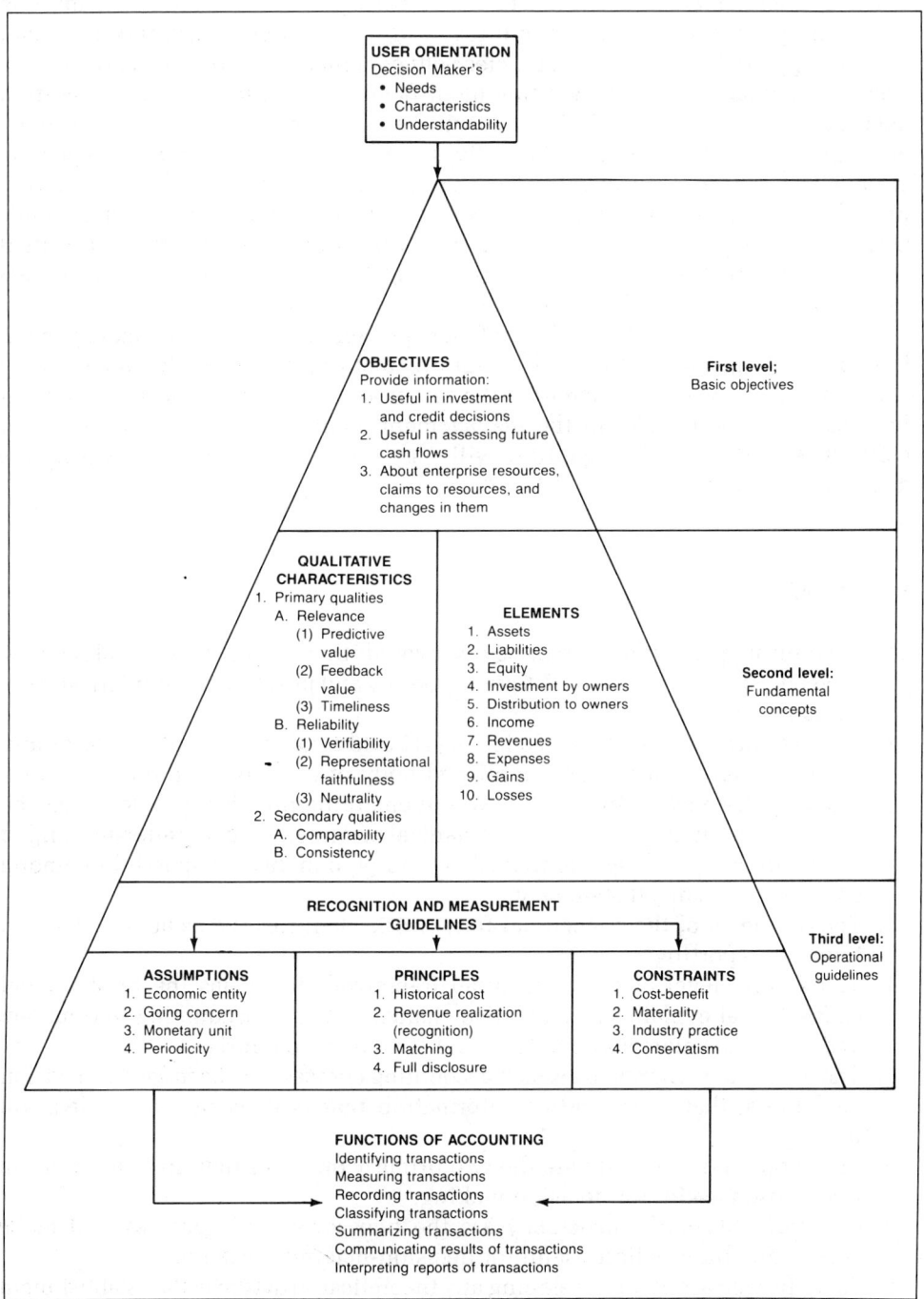

FIGURE 2-3 Conceptual Framework For Financial Accounting

SUMMARY OF THE CONCEPTUAL FRAMEWORK

Figure 2-3 summarizes the essential components of the conceptual framework of financial accounting developed in Chapters 1 and 2. We cannot overemphasize the usefulness of this theoretical framework in understanding many of the problem areas that are examined in subsequent chapters.

Throughout the remainder of this book, the basic perspective is one of examining the techniques, mechanics, procedures, and issues of contemporary financial accounting practice. In many cases, clear-cut conclusions as to what a preparer of financial reports should do regarding identification, measurement, and reporting decisions are not possible. Indeed, it will become obvious that there are many generally accepted accounting alternatives available for measuring and reporting various transactions and events. They are acceptable because of the flexibility provided by the framework and the trade-offs that, by necessity, must be made between its components. The consequence of this is that professional judgement is a critical aspect of financial reporting; that is, preparers of financial reports must relate the framework to the circumstances involved.

The financial statements are those of management; thus it is really management that selects the generally accepted accounting methods to be used in preparing the financial statements. It is, therefore, the senior accountant who, because of his or her position as a member of the management team, and because of his or her conceptual and practical expertise, will play a crucial role in determining the accounting policies.

KEY POINTS

1. Accounting principles cannot be discovered; they are created, developed, or decreed. Accounting principles are supported and justified by intuition, authority, and acceptability.
2. A conceptual framework is needed to (1) build a coherent set of standards and practices that relates to an established body of concepts and objectives, (2) provide a framework in which new and emerging practical problems may be solved more quickly, (3) increase financial statement users' understanding of and confidence in financial reporting, and (4) enhance comparability among companies' financial statements.
3. The first level of the conceptual framework identifies the basic objectives of financial reporting.
4. The second level of the conceptual framework identifies the fundamental concepts that explain the qualitative characteristics of accounting information and define the elements that financial statements comprise.
5. The overriding criterion by which accounting choices may be judged is decision usefulness, that is, providing information that is most useful for decision making.
6. Relevance and reliability are the two primary qualities that make accounting information useful for decision making.
7. Comparability and consistency are the two secondary qualities that make accounting information useful for decision-making purposes.
8. An important aspect of developing any theoretical structure is the establishment of a body of elements or definitions. Ten interrelated elements that are most

directly related to measuring the performance and financial status of an enterprise were identified and defined.

9. The third level of the conceptual framework relates to operational guidelines that are used to develop responses to controversial financial reporting issues. These operational guidelines are segregated into assumptions, principles, and constraints.

10. As the environment changes, so to some degree will the components of this theoretical structure.

APPENDIX

2A

APPROACHES TO ACCOUNTING THEORY FORMULATION

As indicated in Chapter 2, accountants have attempted to develop a general theory or conceptual framework to resolve the many financial accounting issues facing their profession. Complete agreement on all aspects of a single conceptual framework is highly unlikely, because accounting both affects and is influenced by its environment. The theory necessary to resolve accounting controversies will continue to be updated, modified, and at times completely changed.

The purpose of this appendix is to show that the proper approach to accounting theory formulation is very much a matter of debate, and that different individuals have different perceptions about what approaches the profession should take to resolve financial accounting issues. The different views of accounting theory can be classified in the following manner:[17]

1. True income approach
2. Decision model approach
3. Individual user approach — behavioural
4. Aggregate user approach — efficient markets
5. Information economics approach

[17]The general approach to this section was heavily influenced by the AAA Committee on Concepts and Standards for External Financial Reports, *Statement on Accounting Theory and Theory Acceptance* (Sarasota, Fla.: American Accounting Association, 1977).

True Income Approach

Some accountants argue that, if we search long enough, we will ultimately find the one proper method to account for various business transactions. This approach has been referred to as the **true income approach** because it implies that there is a single accounting method that will correctly identify the economic substance of a business transaction.

Many of the writings in the early and mid-1900s, for example, seemed to adopt this position.[18] No consideration was given to the fact that information requirements might be different for different users of financial statements. These writers generally agreed that current values were superior to historical cost, although they differed as to how current values should be implemented. In short, the true income approach adopts the position that there is one correct reporting method and that research should be directed to finding this method.

Decision Model Approach

In the **decision model** or **decision usefulness approach** to accounting theory formulation, an appropriate decision model based on the hypothesized needs of financial statement users is developed. For example, one theorist might argue that the greatest concern of users is that a company maintain its physical capacity. Using physical capacity as the economic attribute of interest to financial statement users, the theorist might then argue that replacement cost is the appropriate method for the valuation of business transactions. Conversely, another theorist might argue that command over consumer goods is the most important economic attribute of interest to financial statement users, and would suggest that selling prices or exit values is the appropriate basis for the valuation of business transactions. In other words, the decision model theorist establishes a set of normative assumptions about the goals, decisions, and information needs of users and, given these assumptions, derives the accounting methods best suited for meeting these needs.

The decision model approach has been used to justify accounting methods based on (1) replacement cost, (2) selling price, and (3) present value of future cash flows.[19] The proponents of each accounting method argue forcefully that their method is correct, given their underlying assumptions as to what users of financial statements desire. Unlike the proponents of the true income approach, the decision model theorists acknowledge that different information may be needed for different users of the financial statements or for different kinds of decisions.

Individual User Approach—Behavioural

Some accountants have suggested that accounting theory should be developed not by postulating a set of normative assumptions about how accounting information is used (decision model approach), but rather by examining actual user decision

---

[18]See, for example, John B. Canning, *The Economics of Accountancy* (New York: Ronald Press, 1929); Henry W. Sweeney, *Stabilized Accounting* (New York: Harper, 1936); Kenneth MacNeal, *Truth in Accounting* (New York: Ronald Press, 1939).

[19]See, for example, Lawrence Revsine, *Replacement Cost Accounting* (Englewood Cliffs, N.J.: Prentice-Hall, 1973); Robert R. Sterling, *Theory of the Measurement of Enterprise Income* (Lawrence: University Press of Kansas, 1970); George J. Staubus, *A Theory of Accounting to Investors* (Berkeley: University of California Press, 1961).

behaviour. This approach has sometimes been referred to as the **individual user** or **behavioural approach** to accounting theory formulation.

To illustrate this approach, consider the controversy over whether some form of price-level adjusted information should be reported in the financial statements. The behavioural/accounting theorist might solicit opinions from various financial statement users, primarily financial analysts and bankers, about the usefulness of price-level adjusted information. If the majority of users indicated that price-level adjusted information would be useful, it would then be argued that this information should be provided. Another technique used by behavioural theorists is to ask a group of financial statement users to make a series of investment or loan decisions based on some accounting information set (e.g., conventional financial statements). Another group of users is then asked to make the same decisions on the basis of a different information set (e.g., price-level adjusted financial statements). The decisions are then compared, and the behavioural theorist attempts to infer which information set (conventional or price-level adjusted) is more useful.

Aggregate User Approach—Efficient Markets

The **aggregate user** or **efficient market approach**[20] holds that all publicly available information about a company is quickly incorporated into its share price because of the sophistication of the many financial analysts and individual investors who comprise the stock market. This approach does not say that the price of the share is necessarily ''correct'' but rather that it reflects all publicly available information.

To illustrate the implications of the efficient market approach, suppose that we were concerned about whether price-level adjustments should be used to report financial information. Advocates of the efficient market approach would argue that, if reporting price-level adjusted information is a costless venture, both conventional and price-level adjusted information should be disclosed. Because the market is efficient, the marketplace will decide on what information to use. In other words, why be concerned about a specific reporting approach? Disclose the alternatives, and the marketplace (aggregate users) will decide what information is useful.

Implicitly, this approach suggests that if the information is publicly disclosed, the market as a whole cannot be fooled, although individual investors may be deceived. For example, assume that two companies are alike in all respects except that one company uses straight-line depreciation and the other accelerated depreciation. In such a case, one company will have higher reported profits than the other, but efficient market theorists would argue that the share price would be the same as long as the alternative reporting methods are disclosed or can be determined from available financial information. The market is not fooled by this difference in accounting methods.

Information Economics Approach

The **information economics approach** to accounting theory maintains that all accounting reporting decisions should be evaluated within a cost-benefit framework. Essentially this approach looks upon accounting information as a product, just as

[20]See, for example, William H. Beaver, ''What Should Be the FASB Objectives?'' *The Journal of Accountancy* (August, 1973) for a simplified explanation of this approach.

bread and butter are products, and asks the relative costs of producing this product compared with the benefits.[21] For example, comments are often made that a given reporting alternative is too costly in view of the benefits obtained, but few attempts have been made to measure the costs and benefits. Conversely, to say simply that a reporting method reflects the economic substance of a transaction and, therefore, should be used is equally inappropriate. What must be considered are all the ramifications of the alternative ways of reporting.

For example, the *CICA Handbook* mandates that ordinarily all research and development costs should be expensed as incurred. Assuming that this treatment reflects the economic substance of the situation, does it necessarily follow that we should adopt this practice? One might argue that to report research and development expenditures in such a manner might incur social costs that far outweigh the benefits. For example, forcing companies to expense research and development costs as incurred might result in curtailment of their research and development projects, which might produce long-run social consequences that are undesirable.

In the FASB's research carried out to assess the economic consequences of a standard (*Statement No. 8*) on foreign currency translation, two studies were commissioned. The first tried to determine whether share price behaviour is significantly affected by the manner in which foreign exchange gains and losses are reported. This stock market study concluded that the method of reporting translation gains and losses had no significant effect on the share price of the company involved. A second study attempted to determine whether companies would forgo profitable investments overseas or employ foreign exchange practices that might be considered uneconomical because of the way foreign translation gains and losses were reported. The conclusion was that *FASB Statement No. 8* was causing business enterprises to make bad economic decisions.

Concluding Remarks

We have attempted to provide a brief overview of the alternative approaches to theory formulation currently being discussed in the accounting literature. Although the descriptions are necessarily brief, it is hoped that they provide sufficient insight into the essence of each approach. Exposure to these ideas and thoughts develops a broader and better framework for judging the advancement of the accounting profession.

It has been suggested frequently that present-day generally accepted accounting principles should be made more consistent internally and should provide more useful information. Accounting is a social discipline. This is why the best way to report a given item or event is often difficult to determine, because different users have different perspectives and different sets of objectives. It is, therefore, important to establish some framework on which to base the standard-setting process. Some believe that the search for a framework is hopeless, and that an issue-by-issue approach is the only practical method in resolving accounting controversies. Only one thing appears certain at this point—accounting principles and procedures will grow and change as internal attempts at improvement continue and external pressures for change persist.

---

[21]See, for example, Joel Demski, "Choice Among Financial Reporting Alternatives," *Accounting Review* (April, 1974).

Note: All asterisked Questions, Cases, Exercises, or Problems relate to material contained in an Appendix.

QUESTIONS

1. What is a conceptual framework? Why is a conceptual framework useful in financial accounting?
2. What are the primary objectives of financial reporting?
3. What is meant by the term "qualitative characteristics of accounting information"?
4. Briefly describe the two primary qualities of useful accounting information.
5. What is the distinction between comparability and consistency?
6. Discuss whether the changes described in each of the cases below require recognition in the independent auditor's report as to consistency. (Assume that the amounts are material.)
    (a) After three years of computing depreciation under the declining balance method for income tax purposes and under the straight-line method for reporting purposes, the company adopted the declining balance method for reporting purposes.
    (b) The company disposed of one of the two subsidiaries that had been included in its consolidated statements for prior years.
    (c) The estimated remaining useful life of plant property was reduced because of obsolescence.
    (d) The company is using an inventory valuation method that is different from those used by other companies in their industry.
7. Why is it necessary to develop a definitional framework for the basic elements of accounting?
8. Expenses, losses, and distributions to owners are all decreases in net assets. What are the distinctions among them?
9. Revenues, gains, and investments by owners are all increases in net assets. What are the distinctions among them?
10. What are the four basic assumptions that underlie the financial accounting structure?
11. If the going concern assumption is not made in accounting, what difference does it make in the amounts shown in the financial statements for the following items?
    (a) Land.
    (b) Unamortized bond premium.
    (c) Depreciation expense on equipment.
    (d) Long-term investments in common shares of other companies.
    (e) Merchandise inventory.
    (f) Prepaid insurance.
12. The life of a business is divided into specific time periods, usually a year, to measure results of operations for each such time period and to portray financial conditions at the end of each period.
    (a) This practice is based on the accounting assumption that the life of the business consists of a series of time periods and that it is possible to measure accurately the results of operations for each period. Comment on the validity and necessity of this assumption.
    (b) What has been the effect of this practice on accounting? What is its relation to the accrual system? What influence does it have on accounting entries and methodology?
13. What is the basic accounting problem related to the monetary unit assumption when there is significant inflation?
14. The chairman of the board of directors of the company for which you are chief accountant has told you that he is entirely out of sympathy with accounting figures based on cost. He believes that replacement values are far more significant to the board of directors than "out-of-date costs." Present some arguments to convince him that accounting data should still be based on cost.

15. Develop an argument supporting the adjustment of cost figures in financial statements for general price-level changes or, at least, the preparation of supplementary statements adjusted for changes in the general price level.

16. What are the accounting requirements regarding revenue recognition? Why has the date of sale been chosen as the point at which to recognize the revenue resulting from the entire producing and selling process in most cases?

17. What is the justification for the following deviations from recognizing revenue at the time of sale?
    (a) Instalment sales method of recognizing revenue.
    (b) Recognition of revenue during production for certain agricultural products.
    (c) The percentage-of-completion basis in long-term construction contracts.

18. Bradley Company paid $81,000 for a machine in 1984. The Accumulated Depreciation account has a balance of $27,000 at the present time. The company could sell the machine today for $94,000. The company president believes that the company has a "right to this gain." What does the president mean by this statement? Do you agree?

19. Three expense recognition points (associating cause and effect, systematic and rational allocation, and immediate recognition) were discussed in the text under the matching principle. Indicate the basic nature of each of these types of expenses and give two examples of each.

20. Explain how you would decide whether to record each of the following expenditures as an asset or an expense.
    (a) Legal fees paid in connection with the purchase of land are $650.
    (b) Daley, Inc. paves the driveway leading to the office building at a cost of $9,000.
    (c) A meat market purchases a meat-grinding machine at a cost of $180.
    (d) On June 30, Smith and Johnson, medical doctors, pay six months' office rent to cover the month of June and the next five months.
    (e) The Logan Hardware Company pays $3,000 in wages to labourers for the construction of a building to be used in the business.
    (f) Sally's Florists pays wages of $1,400 for November to an employee who serves as driver of their delivery truck.

21. Briefly describe the types of information concerning financial position, income, and cash flows that might be provided (a) within the main body of the financial statements, (b) in the notes to the financial statements, or (c) as supplementary information.

22. In January, 1986, Dain, Inc. doubled the amount of its outstanding shares by selling on the market an additional 10,000 shares to finance an expansion of the business. You propose that this information be shown by a note on the balance sheet as of December 31, 1985. The president objects, claiming that this sale took place after December 31, 1985, and therefore should not be shown. Explain your position.

23. Describe the two major constraints inherent in the presentation of accounting information.

24. What are some of the costs of providing accounting information? What are some of the benefits of accounting information? Describe the cost/benefit factors that should be considered when new accounting standards are being proposed.

25. How are materiality (and immateriality) related to the proper presentation of financial statements? What factors and measures should an accountant consider in assessing the materiality of a misstatement in the presentation of a financial statement?

26. The president of Egger Enterprises has heard that conservatism is a doctrine that is followed in accounting and, therefore, proposes that several policies be followed that are conservative in nature. State your opinion with respect to each of the policies below.
    (a) The inventory should be valued at "cost or market, whichever is lower" because the losses from price declines should be recognized in the accounts in the period in which the price decline takes place.

(b) The company gives a two-year warranty to its customers on all products sold. The estimated warranty costs incurred from this year's sales should be entered as an expense this year instead of an expense in the period in the future when the warranty is made good.

(c) When sales are made on account, there is always uncertainty about whether the accounts are collectible. Therefore, the president recommends recording the sale when the cash is received from the customers.

(d) A lawsuit is pending against the company. The president believes there is an even chance that the company will lose the suit and have to pay damages of $90,000 to $150,000. The president recommends that a loss be recorded and a liability created in the amount of $150,000.

*27. What is the difference between the true income approach and the decision model approach to resolving accounting controversies?

CASES

C2-1 After having read the first two chapters of this text, two students were discussing the various aspects of existing statements of financial accounting objectives. One student said that he felt such statements provide little, if any, guidance to the practising professional in resolving accounting controversies. He felt that the objectives stated were so broad and general that they were impossible to apply to solve present-day reporting problems. The other student conceded that the objectives were general but said that she felt they were needed to provide a starting point for accountants to help them improve financial reporting.

Instructions

(a) Describe the basic objectives of financial accounting.

(b) What do you think is the meaning of the second student's statement that the accounting profession needs objectives as a starting point to resolve accounting controversies?

C2-2 Accounting statements provide useful information about business transactions and events. Those who provide financial reports must often evaluate and select from a set of accounting alternatives. The qualitative characteristics that relate to making accounting information useful for decision making were identified and discussed in Chapter 2. It was also pointed out that trade-offs or sacrifices of one quality for another are often necessary when carrying out the identification, measurement, and communication functions of accounting.

Instructions

(a) Describe briefly what is meant by the following qualities of useful accounting information:

1. Understandability.
2. Relevance.
3. Reliability.
4. Comparability.
5. Consistency.

(b) Why is the distinction between primary qualities (relevance and reliability) and secondary qualities (comparability and consistency) made?

(c) For each of the following pairs of information qualities, give an example of a situation in which one may be sacrificed in return for a gain in the other:

1. Relevance and reliability.
2. Relevance and consistency.
3. Comparability and consistency.
4. Relevance and understandability.

(d) What criterion should be used to evaluate trade-offs between information qualities?

C2-3   Figure 2-2 provided an identification of qualitative characteristics for financial accounting information. Within this framework of qualitative characteristics are primary qualities of information (and their basic ingredients) and secondary qualities of information. Presented below are a number of questions. If an answer reflects an absence of one of the primary qualities of information, specify what it is and the ingredient that is most likely to be missing.

1. Winnipeg Co. Ltd. switches from FIFO to weighted average to FIFO over a two-year period. Which quality of information is missing?

2. Assume that the profession permits the savings and loan industry to defer losses on investments it sells because immediate recognition of the loss may have adverse economic consequences on the industry. Which quality of information is missing?

3. What are the two primary qualities that make accounting information useful for decision making?

4. Cross, Inc. does not issue its second quarter report until after the third quarter's results are reported. Which information quality is missing?

5. Predictive value is an ingredient of which of the two primary qualities that make accounting information useful for decision-making purposes?

6. Leggett, Inc. is the only company in its industry to depreciate its plant assets on a straight-line basis. Which quality of accounting information may be absent?

7. Laclede Company has attempted to determine the replacement cost of its inventory. Three different appraisers arrive at substantially different amounts for this value. The president, nevertheless, decides to report the middle value for external reporting purposes. Which quality of information is lacking in this data?

8. What is the ingredient of information that enables users to confirm or correct prior expectations?

9. Identify the two overall or pervasive constraints.

10. It was once noted that "if it becomes accepted or expected that accounting principles are determined or modified in order to secure purposes other than economic measurement—we assume a grave risk that confidence in the credibility of our financial information system will be undermined." Which quality of accounting information should ensure that such a situation will not occur?

C2-4   The president of the Wark Manufacturing Company received an income statement from his controller. The statement covered the calendar year 1986. "Gail," he said to the controller, "this statement indicates that a net income of two million dollars was earned last year. You know the value of the company is not that much more than it was a year earlier."

"You're probably right," replied the controller. "You see, there are factors in accounting that sometimes keep reported operating results from reflecting the change in the value of the company."

Instructions

Prepare a detailed explanation of the accounting factors to which the controller referred. Justify, to the extent possible, generally accepted accounting methods.

C2-5   Presented below is a statement that appeared about Weyerhaeuser Company in a financial magazine.

The land and timber holdings are now carried on the company's books at a mere $422 million. The value of the timber alone is variously estimated at $3 billion to $7 billion and is rising all the time. "The understatement of the company is pretty severe," conceded Charles W. Bingham, a senior vice-president. Adds Robert L. Schuyler, another senior vice-president, "We have a whole stream of profit nobody sees and there is no way to show it on our books."

Instructions

(a) What does Schuyler mean when he says that "we have a whole stream of profit nobody sees and there is no way to show it on our books?"

(b) If the understatement of the company's assets is severe, why does accounting not report this information?

C2-6   On June 8, 1986, Larson Corporation signed a contract with Flad Associates under which Flad agreed (1) to construct an office building on land owned by Larson, (2) to accept responsibility for procuring financing for the project and finding tenants, and (3) to manage the property for 35 years. The annual net income from the project, after debt service, was to be divided equally between Larson Corporation and Flad Associates. Flad was to accept its share of future net income as full payment for its services in construction, obtaining finances and tenants, and managing the project.

By May 31, 1987, the project was nearly completed and tenants had signed leases to occupy 90% of the available space at annual rentals totalling $3,000,000. It was estimated that, after operating expenses and debt service, the annual net income would amount to $1,100,000. The management of Flad Associates believed that the economic benefit derived from the contract with Larson should be reflected on its financial statements for the fiscal year ended May 31, 1987, and directed that revenue be accrued in an amount equal to the commercial value of the services Flad had rendered during the year, that this amount be carried in contracts receivable, and that all related expenditures be charged against the revenue.

Instructions

   (a)   Discuss the factors to be considered in determining when revenue has been realized for the purpose of accounting measurement of periodic income.

   (b)   Is the belief of Flad's management in accord with generally accepted accounting principles for the measurement of revenues and expenses for the year ended May 31, 1987? Support your opinion by discussing the application to this case of the factors to be considered for asset measurement and revenue and expense recognition.

                                                                    (AICPA adapted)

C2-7   After your presentation of the financial statements to the board of directors of the Strother Publishing Company, one new director expresses surprise that the income statement assumes that an equal proportion of the revenue is earned with the publication of each issue of the company's magazine. He feels that the "crucial event" in the process of earning revenue in the magazine business is the cash sale of the subscription. He says that he does not understand why most of the revenue cannot be "recognized" in the period of the sale.

Instructions

   (a)   List the various accepted methods for recognizing revenue in the accounts and explain when the methods are appropriate.

   (b)   Discuss the propriety of timing the recognition of revenue in the Strother Publishing Company's account with

      1.   The cash sale of the magazine subscription.
      2.   The publication of the magazine every month.
      3.   Both events, by realizing a portion of the revenue with cash sale of the magazine subscription and a portion of the revenue with the publication of the magazine every month.

                                                                    (AICPA adapted)

C2-8   A common objective of accountants is to prepare income statements that are as accurate as possible. A basic requirement in preparing accurate income statements is to match costs with revenues properly. Proper matching of costs with revenues requires that costs resulting from typical business operations be recognized in the period in which they expire.

Instructions

   (a)   List three approaches (rational conditions) that can be used to determine whether such typical costs should appear as charges in the income statement for the current period.

   (b)   As generally presented in financial statements, the following items or procedures have been criticized as improperly matching costs with revenues. Briefly discuss each item from the viewpoint of matching costs with revenues and suggest corrective or alternative means of presenting the financial information.

1. Cash discounts on purchases being treated as "other revenue."
2. Valuation of inventories at the lower of cost and market.
3. Receiving and handling costs of inventory being expensed in the period incurred.

C2-9   An accountant must be familiar with the concepts involved in determining the earnings of a business entity. The amount of earnings reported for a business entity depends upon the proper recognition, in general, of revenues and expenses for a given time period. In some situations, costs are recognized as expenses in the time period of the product sale; in other situations, guidelines have been developed for recognizing costs as expenses or losses by other criteria.

Instructions

(a) Explain the rationale for recognizing costs as expenses at the time of product sale.

(b) What is the rationale underlying the appropriateness of treating costs as expenses of a period instead of assigning the costs to an asset? Explain.

(c) In what general circumstances would it be appropriate to treat a cost as an asset instead of as an expense? Explain.

(d) Some expenses are assigned to specific accounting periods on the basis of systematic and rational allocation of asset costs. Explain the underlying rationale for recognizing expenses on the basis of systematic and rational allocation of asset costs.

(e) Identify the conditions in which it would be appropriate to treat a cost as a loss.

(AICPA adapted)

C2-10   Pick Homes sells and erects shell houses: that is, frame structures that are completely finished on the outside but are unfinished on the inside except for flooring, partition studding, and ceiling joists. Shell houses are sold chiefly to customers who are handy with tools and who have time to do the interior wiring, plumbing, wall completion and finishing, and other work necessary to make the shell houses into livable dwellings.

Pick buys shell houses from a manufacturer in unassembled packages consisting of all lumber, roofing, doors, windows, and similar materials necessary to complete a shell house. Upon commencing operations in a new area, Pick buys or leases land as a site for its local warehouse, field office, and display houses. Sample display houses are erected at a total cost of from $3,600 to $7,700 including the cost of the unassembled packages. The chief element of cost of the display houses is the unassembled packages, inasmuch as erection is a short low-cost operation. Old sample models are torn down or altered into new models every three to seven years. Sample display houses have little salvage value because dismantling and moving costs amount to nearly as much as the cost of an unassembled package.

Instructions

(a) A choice must be made between (1) expensing the costs of sample display houses in the periods in which the expenditure is made and (2) spreading the costs over more than one period. Discuss the advantages of each method.

(b) Would it be preferable to amortize the cost of display houses on the basis of (1) the passage of time or (2) the number of shell houses sold? Explain.

(AICPA adapted)

C2-11   You are engaged in the audit of Data Base, Inc., which opened its first branch office in 1985. During the audit Sharon Thomas, president, raises the question of the accounting treatment of the operating loss of the branch office for its first year, which is material in amount.

The president proposes to capitalize the operating loss as a "start-up" expense to be amortized over a five-year period. She states that branch offices of other firms engaged in the same field generally suffer a first-year operating loss that is invariably capitalized, and you are aware of this practice. She argues, therefore, that the loss should be capitalized so that the accounting will be "conservative"; further, she argues that the accounting must be "consistent" with established industry practice.

Instructions

Discuss the president's use of the words "conservative" and "consistent" from the standpoint of accounting terminology. Discuss the accounting treatment that you would recommend.

(AICPA adapted)

C2-12 The general ledger of MBS, Inc., a corporation engaged in the development and production of television programs for commercial sponsorship, contains the following asset accounts before amortization at the end of the current year:

Account	Balance
Monk & Cindy	$60,000
Supertown	41,000
The Badman	21,500
Spacetrack	9,000
Studio Rearrangement	4,000

An examination of contracts and records reveals the following information:

1. The first two accounts listed above represent the total cost of completed programs that were televised during the accounting period just ended. Under the terms of an existing contract, Monk & Cindy will be rerun during the next accounting period, at a fee equal to 50% of the fee for the first televising of the program. The contract for the first run produced $600,000 of revenue. The contract with the sponsor of Supertown provides that he may, at his option, rerun the program during the next season at a fee of 75% of the fee on the first televising of the program.
2. The balance in The Badman account is the cost of a new program that has just been completed and is being considered by several companies for commercial sponsorship.
3. The balance in the Spacetrack account represents the cost of a partially completed program for a projected series that has been abandoned.
4. The balance of the Studio Rearrangement account consists of payments made to a firm of engineers that prepared a report relative to the more efficient use of existing studio space and equipment.

Instructions

(a) State the general principle (or principles) of accounting that are applicable to the first four accounts.

(b) How would you report each of the first four accounts in the financial statements of MBS, Inc.? Explain.

(c) In what way, if at all, does the Studio Rearrangement account differ from the first four? Explain.

(AICPA adapted)

*C2-13 Two students in intermediate accounting are arguing about the merits of various theory approaches to resolving financial reporting controversies. The first student indicates that we should develop some type of normative criterion, such as prediction of cash flows, and then decide which accounting procedure or which reporting approach best meets this criterion. The second student believes that an analysis of the costs and the benefits of a proposed accounting alternative should be determined, and then, after assessing the costs and benefits, it can be determined whether or not this alternative should be selected.

Instructions

(a) What general type of theory approach involves the establishment of some normative criterion, such as prediction of cash flows, to resolve accounting controversies? Discuss.

(b) What general approach is employed when the costs and benefits of a proposed accounting standard are examined? Discuss.

PROBLEMS

P2-1   Each of the following statements represents a decision made by the controller of Sampson Enterprises on which your advice is asked.

1.   A flood during the year destroyed or damaged a considerable amount of uninsured inventory. No entry was made for this loss because the controller reasons that the ending inventory will, of course, be reduced by the amount of the destroyed or damaged merchandise. Therefore, its cost will be included in cost of goods sold, and the net income figure will be correct.

2.   The company provides housing for certain employees and adjusts their salaries accordingly. The controller contends that the cost to the company of maintaining this housing should be charged to "Wages and Salaries."

3.   Material included in the inventory that cost $90,000 has become obsolete. The controller contends that no loss can be realized until the goods are sold, and so the material is included in the inventory at $90,000.

4.   Inasmuch as profits for the year appear to be extremely small, no depreciation of fixed assets is to be recorded as an expense this year.

5.   The company occupies the building in which it operates under a long-term lease requiring annual rental payments. It sublets certain office space not required for its own purposes. The controller credits rents received against rents paid to get net rent expense.

6.   The entire cost of a new delivery truck is to be charged to an expense account.

7.   The company has paid a large sum for an advertising campaign to promote a new product that will not be placed on the market until the following year. The controller has charged this amount to a prepaid expense account.

8.   A customer leaving the building slipped on an icy spot on the stairway and wrenched his back. He immediately entered suit against the company for permanent physical injuries and claims damages in the amount of $110,000. The suit has not yet come to trial. The controller has made an entry charging a special loss account and crediting a liability account.

9.   A building purchased by the company five years ago at $75,000, including the land on which it stands, can now be sold for $115,000. The controller instructs that the new value of $115,000 be entered in the accounts.

10.   The company operates a cafeteria for the convenience of its employees. Sales made by the cafeteria are credited to the regular sales account for product sales; food purchased and salaries paid for the cafeteria operations are recorded in the regular purchase and payroll accounts.

Instructions

You are to state (a) whether you agree with his decision and (b) the reasons supporting your position. Consider each decision independently of all others.

P2-2   Presented below are a number of facts related to Rotterman Co. Assume that no mention of these facts was made in the financial statements and the related notes.

1.   The company is a defendant in a patent-infringement suit involving a material amount; you have received assurance from the company's counsel that the possibility of loss is remote.

2.   During the year, an assistant controller for the company embezzled $5,000. Rotterman's net income for the year was $1,400,000. The assistant controller and the money have not been found.

3.   Because of the recent gasoline shortage, it is possible that Rotterman may suffer a costly shutdown in the near future similar to those suffered by other companies both within and outside the industry.

4.   Rotterman has reported its ending inventory at $1,300,000 in the financial statements. No other information related to inventories is presented in the financial statements and related notes.

5.   The company changed its method of depreciating equipment from the double-

declining balance to the straight-line method. No mention of this change was made in the financial statements.

6. The company decided that, for the sake of conciseness, only net income should be reported on the income statement. Details as to revenues, cost of goods sold, and expenses were omitted.

7. Equipment purchases of $70,000 were partly financed during the year through the issuance of $60,000 in notes payable. The company offset the notes payable against the equipment and reported plant assets at $10,000.

Instructions

Assume that you are the auditor of Rotterman Co., and that you have been asked to explain the appropriate accounting and related disclosure necessary for each of these items. Provide your answers.

P2-3 Presented below is information related to Sanchez, Inc.

1. Materials were purchased on January 1, 1986, for $60,000, and this amount was entered in the Materials account. On December 31, 1986, the materials would have cost $72,000, so the following entry is made.

Inventory	12,000	
Gain on Inventories		12,000

2. An order for $16,000 has been received from a customer for products on hand. This order was shipped on January 3, 1987. The company made the following entry in 1986.

Accounts Receivable	16,000	
Sales		16,000

3. During the year, the company purchased equipment through the issuance of common shares. The shares had a fair market value of $300,000. The fair market value of the equipment was not easily determinable. The company recorded this transaction as follows:

Equipment	300,000	
Common Shares		300,000

4. Depreciation expense on the building for the year was $23,000. Because the building was increasing in value during the year, the controller decided to charge the depreciation expense to retained earnings instead of to net income. The following entry is recorded.

Retained Earnings	23,000	
Accumulated Depreciation—Buildings		23,000

5. During the year, the company sold certain equipment for $110,000, recognizing a gain of $7,000. Because the controller believed that new equipment would be needed in the near future, the controller decided to defer the gain and amortize it over the life of any new equipment purchased.

Instructions

Comment on the appropriateness of the accounting procedures followed by Sanchez, Inc.

P2-4 Each of the items below involves the question of materiality to Carlson, Inc.

1. The amount of $600 is paid during 1986 for an assessment of additional income taxes for the year 1984. The amount originally paid in 1984 was $18,000, and the amount of this year's income taxes will be $26,000.

2. Land that had originally been purchased for expansion is sold in 1986 at a gain of $7,000. Net income for the year is $53,000, including the gain of $7,000. The company has experienced similar types of gains in the past.

3. The company purchases several items of equipment each year that cost less than $90 each. Most of them are used for several years, but some of them last for less than a year. The total cost of these purchases is about the same each year.

Instructions

State your recommendation as to how each item should be treated in the accounts and in the statements, giving proper consideration to the aspects of materiality and practicability.

P2-5 A number of accounting procedures and practices are described below.

1. Ken Janson, manager of University Bookstore, Inc., bought a radio for his own use. He paid for the set by writing a cheque on the Bookstore chequing account and charged the "Office Equipment" account.

2. Goldman, Inc. recently completed a new 120-storey office building which houses their home offices and many other tenants. All the office equipment purchased for the building that had a per-item or per-unit cost of $900 or less was expensed even though the office equipment has an average life of 10 years. The total cost of such office equipment was approximately $25 million.

3. A large lawsuit has been filed against Losso Corp. by Rand Co. Losso has recorded a loss and related estimated liability equal to the maximum possible amount it feels it might lose. They are confident, however, that either they will not lose the suit or they will owe a much smaller amount.

4. Canada Discount Centres buys its merchandise by the truck and train-car load. Canada does not defer any transportation costs in computing the cost of its ending inventory. Such costs, although varying from period to period, are always material in amount.

5. Rollet, Inc., a fast-food company, sells franchises for $60,000, accepting a $500 down payment and a 50-year note for the remainder. Rollet promises within 3 years to assist in site selection, building, and management training. Rollet records the $60,000 franchise fee as revenue in the period in which the contract is signed.

6. Toronto Chemical Company "faces possible expropriation (i.e., take-over) of foreign facilities and possible losses on sums owed by various customers on the verge of bankruptcy." The company president has decided that these possibilities should not be noted on the financial statements because Toronto still hopes that these events will not take place.

7. The treasurer of Winnipeg Co. wishes to prepare financial statements only during downturns in their wine production, which occur periodically when the rhubarb crop fails. He states that it is at such times that the statements could most easily be prepared. In no event would more than 30 months pass without statements being prepared.

8. The LPS Power & Light Company has purchased a large amount of property, plant, and equipment over a number of years. They have decided that because the general price level has changed materially over the years, they will issue only price-level adjusted financial statements.

9. Wright Manufacturing Co. decided to manufacture its own widgets because it would be cheaper to do so than to buy them from an outside supplier. In an attempt to make Wright's statements more comparable with those of its competitors, management charged the inventory account for what they felt the widgets would have cost had they been purchased from an outside supplier.

Instructions

For each of the foregoing, list the major accounting assumption, principle, or constraint that would be violated. Do not use components of the qualitative characteristics.

P2-6 Presented below are a number of operational guidelines and practices that have developed over time.

1. All payments out of petty cash are charged to Miscellaneous Expense.

2. The use of consolidated statements is justified.

3. Reporting must be done at defined time intervals.
4. An allowance for doubtful accounts is established.
5. Anticipate no profits and recognize all possible losses.
6. Goodwill is recorded only when it is purchased (i.e., not when it is built up).
7. Brokerage firms use market value for purposes of valuation of all marketable securities.
8. Each enterprise is kept as a unit distinct from its owner or owners.
9. All significant postbalance sheet events are reported.
10. Revenue is recorded at point of sale.
11. Price-level changes are not recognized in the accounting records.
12. Lower of cost and market is used to value inventories.
13. Financial information is presented so that reasonably prudent investors will not be misled.
14. Intangibles are capitalized and amortized over periods benefited.
15. Repair tools are expensed when purchased.
16. All important aspects of bond indentures are presented in financial statements.

Instructions

Select the assumption, principle, or constraint that most appropriately justifies these procedures and practices. Do not use components of the qualitative characteristics.

P2-7 Presented below are a number of business transactions that occurred during the current year for Tuttle, Inc.

1. Because of a fire sale, equipment obviously worth $140,000 was acquired at a cost of $110,000. The following entry was made:

Equipment	140,000	
Cash		110,000
Revenue		30,000

2. Merchandise inventory that cost $380,000 is reported on the balance sheet at $460,000, the expected selling price less estimated selling costs. The following entry was made to record this increase in value:

Merchandise Inventory	80,000	
Revenue		80,000

3. Tuttle, Inc. has been concerned about whether intangible assets could generate cash in case of liquidation. As a consequence, goodwill arising from a purchase transaction during the current year and recorded at $600,000 was written off as follows:

Retained Earnings	600,000	
Goodwill		600,000

4. Because the general level of prices increased during the current year, Tuttle, Inc. determined that there was an $8,000 understatement of depreciation expense on its equipment and decided to record it in its accounts. The following entry was made:

Depreciation Expense	8,000	
Accumulated Depreciation—Equipment		8,000

5. The company is being sued for $90,000 by a customer who claims damages for personal injury apparently caused by a defective product. Company attorneys feel extremely confident that the company will have no liability for damages resulting from the situation. Nevertheless, the company decides to make the following entry:

Loss from Lawsuit	90,000	
Liability for Lawsuit		90,000

6. The president of Tuttle, Inc. used his expense account to purchase a new boat solely for personal use. The following entry was made:

Miscellaneous Expense	8,000	
Cash		8,000

Instructions

In each of the situations above, discuss the appropriateness of the journal entries in light of the components of the conceptual framework.

P2-8 You are engaged to review the accounting records of Dennis Corporation prior to the closing of the revenue and expense accounts as of December 31, the end of the current fiscal year. The following information comes to your attention.

1. For a number of years the company had used the average cost method for inventory valuation purposes. During the current year, the president noted that all the other companies in their industry had switched to the LIFO method. The company decided not to switch to LIFO because net income would decrease $280,000.

2. During the current year, Dennis Corporation changed its policy in regard to expensing purchases of small tools. In the past, these purchases had always been expensed because they amounted to less than .01% of net income, but the president has decided that capitalization and subsequent depreciation should now be followed. It is expected that purchases of small tools will not fluctuate greatly from year to year.

3. Dennis Corporation constructed a warehouse at a cost of $350,000. The company had been depreciating the asset on a straight-line basis over ten years. In the current year, the controller doubled depreciation expense because the replacement cost of the warehouse had increased significantly.

4. The company decided in October of the current fiscal year to start a massive advertising campaign to enhance the marketability of its product. In November, the company paid $400,000 for advertising time on a major television network to advertise its product during the subsequent twelve months. The controller expensed the $400,000 in the current year on the basis that "once the money is spent, it can never be recovered from the television network."

5. In preparing the balance sheet, detailed information as to the amount of cash on deposit in each of several banks was omitted. Only the total amount of cash under a caption "Cash in Banks" was presented.

6. On June 6 of the current year, Dennis Corporation purchased an undeveloped tract of land at a cost of $285,000. The company spent $60,000 in subdividing the land and getting it ready for sale. An appraisal of the property at the end of the year indicated that the land was now worth $400,000. Although none of the lots were sold, the company recognized revenue of $115,000, less related expenses of $60,000, for a net income on the project of $55,000.

Instructions

State whether or not you agree with the decisions made by Dennis Corporation. Support your answers with reference, whenever possible, to the appropriate aspects of the conceptual framework developed in this chapter and any assumptions about the circumstances of the Corporation that you think would be helpful.

3

A REVIEW OF THE ACCOUNTING PROCESS

Accounting systems vary widely from one business to another, depending on the **nature of the business** and the **transactions** in which it engages, its **size** and the **volume of data** to be handled, and the **informational demands** that management and others place on the system.

The broadest definition of an accounting system includes all of the activities required to provide management with the quantified information needed for planning, controlling, and reporting the financial condition and operations of the enterprise. Managers and investors, confronted with questions such as those listed below, depend on the accounting system to provide or help to provide the answers.

What is the composition of our asset structure?
What is the composition of our capital structure?
Did we make a profit last period?
What did it cost us to produce one unit of product?
Were our sales higher this period than last?
Are any of our product lines or divisions operating at a loss?
Can we safely increase our dividends to shareholders?
Is our rate of return on net assets increasing?

Many similar questions can be answered when there is an efficient accounting system to provide the data. A well-devised accounting system is a necessity for every business enterprise. A company that does not keep an accurate record of its business transactions is likely to lose revenue and operate inefficiently. Although most companies have satisfactory accounting systems, some companies are likely to be inefficient partly because of poor accounting procedures. Consider, for example, the case of the Canadian Commercial Bank failure in the fall of 1985. Testimony during the judicial inquiry into the failure indicated serious weaknesses in the policies used to account for loans—"bad loans" were classified as "good loans"; and, while the financial credibility of some organizations receiving loans was definitely suspect, this type of information was apparently not a significant criterion in their obtaining the loans. In another example, the Long Island Railroad,[1] the busiest commuter line in the United States, lost money at one time because its cash position was unknown; large amounts of money owed the railroad had not been billed; some payables were erroneously recorded twice; and redemptions of bonds were not recorded. Similarly, one of the largest gold and silver retailers, the International Gold Bullion Exchange (IGBE) was forced to declare bankruptcy; the records were in such shambles that it was difficult to determine how much money it lost. It was noted that the company failed to keep track of its revenues and wrote cheques on uncollected funds. IGBE even allowed its employee health insurance to lapse but continued to collect premiums from workers. Although rare in large enterprises, these examples illustrate the point that accounts and detailed records must be kept by every business enterprise.

PROCEDURES EMPLOYED IN ACCOUNTING

Financial accounting rests on a framework for identifying, recording, classifying, and interpreting transaction data relating to enterprises as discussed in Chapter 2. It is important that the accountant understand the **basic terminology employed in collecting accounting data.** The terms most commonly used are defined below.

Basic Terminology

Event. A happening of consequence to an entity. An event generally is the source or cause of changes in assets, liabilities, and equity. Events may be categorized as external and internal, as discussed later.

Transactions. An **external event** involving the transfer or exchange of something of value between two (or more) entities.

Account. A systematic arrangement that shows the effect of transactions on a specific asset or equity. A separate account is kept for each asset, liability, revenue, expense, and for capital (owners' equity).

Real and nominal accounts. Real (also called permanent) accounts are asset, liability, and owners' equity accounts that appear on the balance sheet. Nominal (also called temporary) accounts are revenue and expense accounts, and they appear on the income statement. Nominal accounts are periodically closed; real accounts are not.

Ledger. The book (or computer print-outs) containing the accounts is called a ledger. It usually has a separate page for each account. A **general ledger** is a collection of all the asset, liability, owners' equity, revenue, and expense accounts. A **subsidiary ledger** contains a group of accounts related to a specific general ledger account.

Journal. The book of original entry that initially records the essential facts and figures in connection with all transactions and selected other events. From the book of original entry the various amounts are transferred to the ledger.

Posting. The mechanical process of transferring the essential facts and figures from the book of original entry to the accounts in the ledger.

---

[1]"Long Island Railroad Is Said to Be Losing Revenue Due to 'Weak' Accounting System," *The Wall Street Journal*, February 19, 1971, p. 4.

Trial balance. A list of all open accounts in the ledger and their balances. A trial balance may be prepared at any time. A trial balance taken immediately after all adjustments have been posted is called an **adjusted trial balance.** A trial balance taken immediately after closing entries have been posted is designated an **after-closing** or **post-closing trial balance.**

Adjusting entries. Entries made at the end of an accounting period to bring all accounts up to date on an accrual accounting basis so that correct financial statements can be prepared.

Financial statements. Statements that reflect the collection, tabulation, and final summarization of the accounting data. Basically, four statements are involved: (1) the **balance sheet,** which shows the financial condition of the enterprise at the end of a period, (2) the **income statement,** which measures the results of operations during the period, (3) the **statement of changes in financial position,** which measures the resources provided during the period and uses to which they are put, and (4) the **statement of retained earnings,** which reconciles the balance of the retained earnings account from the beginning to the end of the period.

Closing entries. The formal process by which all nominal accounts are reduced to zero and the net income or net loss is determined and transferred to the owners' equity account is known as "closing the ledger," "closing the books," or merely "closing."

DOUBLE-ENTRY ACCOUNTING RECORDING PROCESS

There are established rules for recording transactions as they occur. These rules, often referred to as double-entry accounting, are the ones you probably learned in your basic principles course. Debit and credit in accounting simply mean left and right or, depending on the account, positive or negative. The left side of any account is the debit side; the right side, the credit side. In arithmetic, plus and minus signs indicate addition or subtraction; in accounting, addition or subtraction is indicated by the side of the account on which the amount is shown. All asset and expense accounts are increased on the left or debit side and decreased on the right or credit side. Conversely, all liability, revenue, and capital accounts are increased on the right or credit side and decreased on the left or debit side. The basic rules for a double-entry accounting system are presented below.

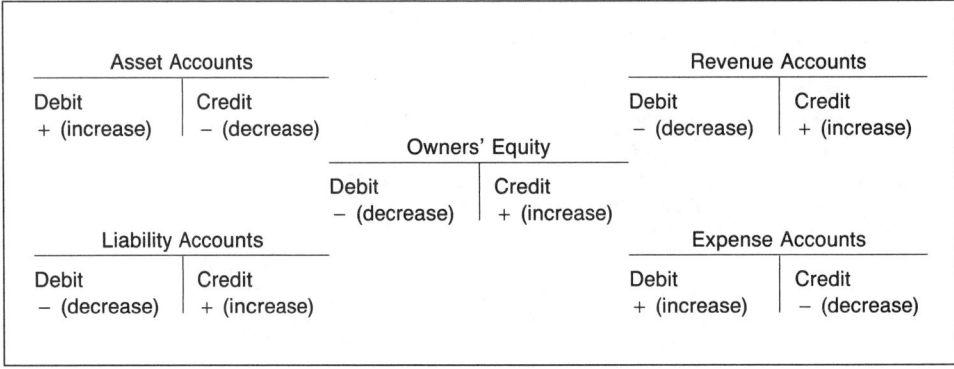

Assume a transaction in which service is rendered for cash. Two accounts are affected; both an asset account (Cash) and a revenue account (Sales) are increased. Cash is debited and Sales is credited. Therein are revealed the essentials of a **double-entry system**—for every debit there must be a credit and vice versa. This leads us, then, to the following basic equation in accounting:

$$\text{Assets} = \text{Liabilities} + \text{Owners' Equity}$$

or simply

$$\text{Assets} = \text{Equities}$$

Every time a transaction occurs, the elements of the equation change, but the basic equality remains. To illustrate, here are seven different transactions.

1. Investment by the owner of $30,000 for use in the business:

    assets = liabilities + owners' equity
    +30,000   +30,000

2. Disburse $600 cash for secretarial wages:

    assets = liabilities + owners' equity
    −600   −600 (expense)

3. Purchase office equipment priced at $5,200 giving a 10% promissory note in exchange:

    assets = liabilities + owners' equity
    +5,200   +5,200

4. Pay off a short-term liability of $7,000:

    assets = liabilities + owners' equity
    −7,000   −7,000

5. Declare a cash dividend of $5,000:

    assets = liabilities + owners' equity
    +5,000   −5,000

6. Convert a long-term liability of $9,000 into common shares:

    assets = liabilities + owners' equity
    −9,000   +9,000

7. Pay cash of $8,000 for delivery van:

    assets = liabilities + owners' equity
    −8,000
    +8,000

Revenue and expense accounts are elements of owners' equity—revenues being increases or credits to owners' equity and expenses being decreases or debits. The difference between revenues and expenses for a period of time becomes a net increase (income) or net decrease (loss) in owners' equity.

The type of ownership structure employed by a business enterprise will dictate the types of accounts found in the owners' equity section. In a proprietorship or partnership, in addition to revenue and expenses, a Drawing account is sometimes used to indicate withdrawals by owners. In a corporation, the owners' equity (Shareholders' Equity) is divided into at least two categories: Share Capital and Retained Earnings. The retained earnings section sometimes includes a Dividends account to indicate the amount of dividends declared during the year. This account is closed to retained earnings at the end of the accounting period.

Transactions Affecting Owners' Equity	Impact on Owners' Equity	Ownership Structure			
		Proprietorships and Partnerships		Corporations	
		Nominal (Temporary) Accounts	Real (Permanent) Accounts	Nominal (Temporary) Accounts	Real (Permanent) Accounts
Investment by owner(s)	Increase		Capital		Share Capital and related accounts
Revenues earned	Increase	Revenue	Capital	Revenue	Retained Earnings
Expenses incurred	Decrease	Expense		Expense	
Withdrawal by owner(s)	Decrease	Drawing		Dividends	

FIGURE 3-1 Transactions Affecting Owners' Equity

Figure 3-1 summarizes and relates the transactions affecting owners' equity to the nominal and real accounts involved according to the types of business ownership.

THE ACCOUNTING CYCLE

Using the definitions of the basic terminology and the rules of debit and credit, accountants have established procedures that result in the periodic reporting of the effects of transactions and selected other events on an entity in the form of financial statements. The basic procedures normally used to ensure that the data are recorded correctly and transmitted to the user are often called the steps in the accounting cycle. The accounting cycle (which is completed at least once every period) presented in Figure 3-2 illustrates the necessary procedures followed from one accounting period to another. Each step is discussed and illustrated in the remaining parts of this chapter.

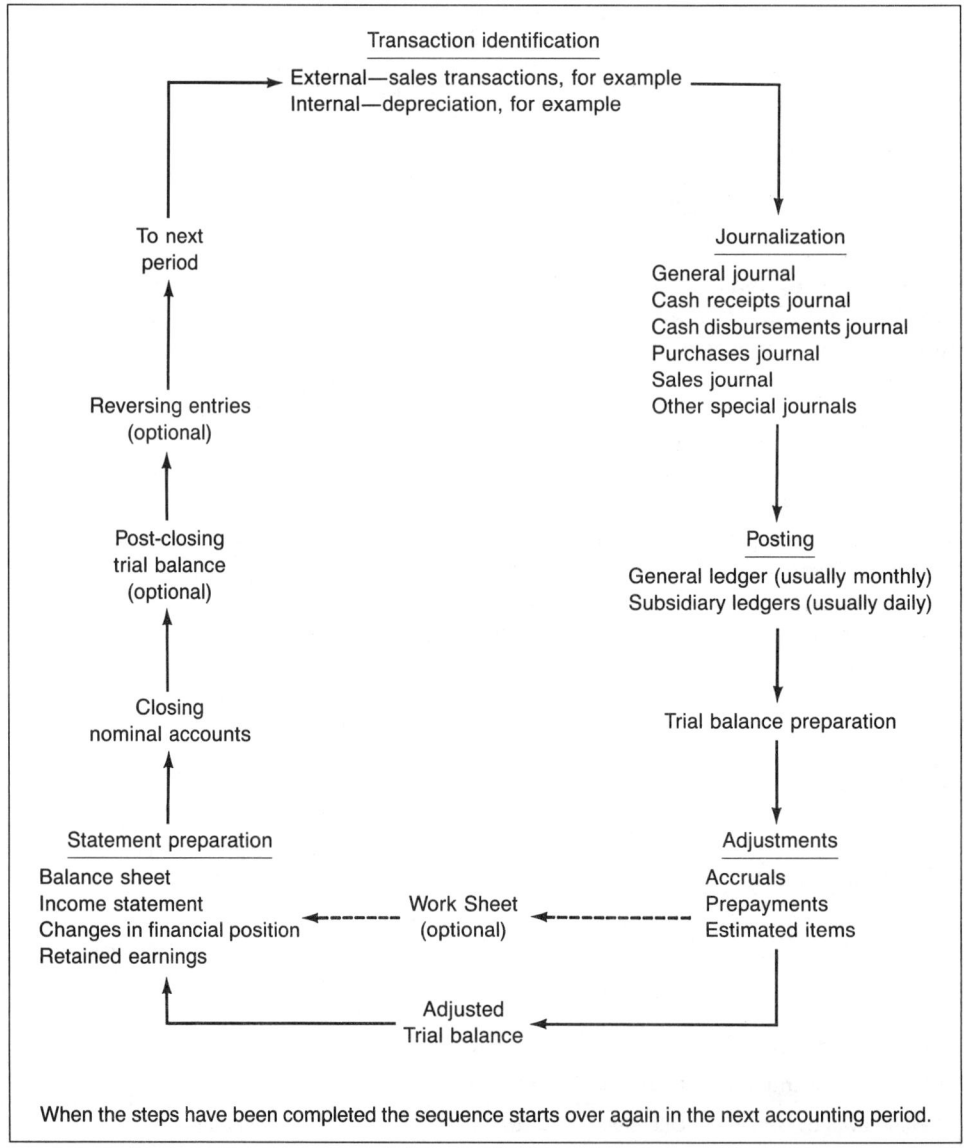

FIGURE 3–2 The Accounting Cycle

IDENTIFICATION AND RECORDING OF TRANSACTIONS AND OTHER EVENTS

The first step in the accounting cycle is analysis of transactions and other selected events. The problem is to determine what to record; that is, to **identify recordable events.** No simple rules exist for stating whether an event should be recorded. For example, most accountants agree that changes in personnel, changes in managerial policies, and the value of human resources are important; but none of these items is recorded in the accounts. On the other hand, when the company makes a cash sale, we have no reservations about recording this transaction.

What makes the difference? Generally, two criteria are applied in determining whether an event or item should be recorded: Can the event or item **be measured objectively (with reliability)** in financial terms? And does this event or item **affect the financial position** of the company? If the answer is no to either question, the event should not be recorded. Events that can be measured and that directly affect the financial statements should be recorded. To illustrate, consider the problem of human resources. Should human resources be recognized on financial statements? R. G. Barry & Co., for example, at one time reported as supplemental data total assets of $14,055,926, including $986,094 for "net investments in human resources." Other companies, including some in Canada, have experimented with human resource accounting and, in a broader sense, social responsibility accounting. Should accountants value employees for balance sheet purposes and also for income statement purposes? Certainly skilled employees are an important asset, but the problems of determining their value and measuring it objectively have not yet been solved. Consequently, human resources are not recorded; perhaps when measurement techniques become more sophisticated and accepted, such information will be presented, if only in supplemental form.

The phrase "transactions and other events and circumstances affecting an entity" is used to describe the sources or causes of changes in an entity's assets, liabilities, and equity.[2] **Events** are of two types: (1) **External events** involve interaction between an entity and its environment, such as a transaction with another entity, a change in the price of a good or service that an entity buys or sells, a flood or earthquake, or an improvement in technology by a competitor; (2) **Internal events** occur within an entity, such as using buildings and machinery in its operation or transferring or consuming raw materials in production processes.

Many events include both external and internal aspects. For example, acquiring the services of employees or others involves exchange transactions, which are external events; using those services (labour), often simultaneously with their acquisition, is part of production, which is a series of internal events. Events may be initiated and controlled by an entity, such as the purchase of merchandise or the use of a machine, or they may be partly or wholly beyond the control of an entity and its management, such as an interest rate change, an act of theft or vandalism, or the imposition of taxes.

Transactions, as particular kinds of external events, may be an exchange in which each entity both receives and sacrifices value, such as purchases and sales of goods or services. Or transactions may be nonreciprocal transfers (transfers in one direction) in which an entity incurs a liability or transfers an asset to another entity without directly receiving (or giving) value in exchange, such as investments by owners, impositions of taxes, gifts, charitable contributions, and thefts.

---

[2]"Elements of Financial Statements of Business Enterprises," *Statement of Financial Accounting Concepts No. 3* (Stamford, Conn.: FASB, 1980), pars. 75-78.

In short, accountants record as many events as possible that affect the financial position of the enterprise, but events or items are often omitted because the problems of measuring them are too complex. The accounting profession, through the efforts of individuals and numerous organizations, as indicated in Chapter 1, is continually working to refine its measurement techniques.

JOURNALIZATION

Accounts are the means by which differing effects on the basic business elements (assets, liabilities, and equities) are categorized and collected. The **general ledger** is a collection of all the asset, liability, owners' equity, revenue, and expense accounts. A **T account** (as illustrated on page 90) is a convenient method of illustrating the effect of transactions on particular asset, liability, owners' equity, revenue, and expense items.

In practice, transactions are not recorded originally in the ledger because a transaction affects two or more different accounts, each of which is on a different page in the ledger. To circumvent this problem and to have a complete record of each transaction in one place, a **journal (book of original entry)** is employed. The simplest form of a journal is a chronological listing of transactions and other selected events expressed in terms of debits and credits to particular accounts. This type of journal is called a **general journal** and is illustrated below for the following transactions.

Nov. 1 Buy a new delivery truck on account from Chevy Motor Co., $14,700.
      3 Receive an invoice from the *Evening Journal* for advertising, $80.
      4 Return merchandise to Crane Supply for credit, $175.
     16 Receive a $45 debit memo from Stafford & Co., indicating that freight on a purchase from Stafford & Co. was prepaid, terms, f.o.b. shipping point (i.e., we have an obligation to pay it).

GENERAL JOURNAL			Page 12	
Date		Acct.	Amount	
1986		No.	Dr.	Cr.
Nov. 1	Delivery Equipment	8	14,700	
	Accounts Payable	34		14,700
	(Purchased delivery truck on account from Chevy Motor Co.)			
3	Advertising Expense	65	80	
	Accounts Payable	34		80
	(Received invoice for advertising from *Evening Journal*)			
4	Accounts Payable	34	175	
	Purchase Returns	53		175
	(Returned merchandise for credit to Crane Supply)			
16	Transportation-In	55	45	
	Accounts Payable	34		45
	(Received debit memo for freight on merchandise purchased f.o.b. shipping point from Stafford & Co.)			

Transactions and other events entered in the general journal record much the same data as are recorded in the T accounts. Each general journal entry consists of four parts: (1) the accounts and amounts to be debited (Dr.), (2) the accounts and amounts to be credited (Cr.), (3) a date, and (4) an explanation. The debit account titles and amounts are entered first, followed by the credit account titles and amounts, which are slightly indented to differentiate them from debits. The explanation is begun on the line below the last account to be credited and may take one or more lines. The Acct. No. column is completed at the time the accounts are posted.

Specialized Journals

Most businesses use special journals in addition to the general journal. Special journals permit greater division of labour, reduce the time necessary to accomplish the various bookkeeping tasks, and summarize transactions possessing a common characteristic. Specialized journals are discussed in Appendix 3A at the end of this chapter.

POSTING TO THE LEDGER

The items entered in a general journal must be transferred to the general ledger. This procedure, **posting,** is considered part of the summarizing and classifying activity of the accounting process. Because the debit and credit analysis of the transaction or event takes place as the entry is recorded in the general journal, posting consists of transferring to the proper ledger accounts the amounts entered in the general journal.

For example, the November 1 entry in the general journal expressed a debit to Delivery Equipment of $14,700 and a credit to Accounts Payable of $14,700. This entry indicates that the amount in the debit column is posted from the journal to the debit side of the ledger account, and that the amount in the credit column is posted from the journal to the credit side of the ledger account.

The numbers in the Acct. No. column refer to the number of the accounts in the ledger to which the respective items are posted. For example, the "8" to the right of the words "Delivery Equipment" means that Delivery Equipment is account No. 8 in the ledger, to which the $14,700 was posted. Similarly, the "34" placed in the column to the right of "Accounts Payable" indicates that this $14,700 item was posted to account No. 34 in the ledger. The posting of the general journal is completed when all of the account numbers have been recorded opposite the account titles in the journal. Thus the number in the Acct. No. column serves two purposes: (1) to indicate the ledger account number of the account involved, and (2) to indicate that the posting has been completed for the particular item. Each business enterprise selects its own numbering system for its ledger accounts. One practice is to begin numbering with asset accounts and to follow with liabilities, owners' equities, revenue, and expense accounts in that order.

The various ledger accounts affected by the journal entries in the preceding illustration appear as on page 90 after the posting process is completed. The source of the data transferred to the ledger account is indicated by the reference GJ12 (General Journal, page 12).

Delivery Equipment					No. 8
Nov. 1	GJ12	14,700			

Accounts Payable					No. 34
Nov. 4	GJ12	175	Nov. 1	GJ12	14,700
			3	GJ12	80
			16	GJ12	45

Purchase Returns			No. 53
	Nov. 4	GJ12	175

Transportation-In					No. 55
Nov. 16	GJ12	45			

Advertising Expense					No. 65
Nov. 3	GJ12	80			

UNADJUSTED TRIAL BALANCE

At the end of a given period, after the entries have been recorded in the journal and posted to the ledger, it is customary and desirable to prepare a trial balance. A **trial balance** is a list of all open accounts in the general ledger and their balances. The trial balance accomplishes two principal purposes:

1. It proves that debits and credits of an equal amount are in the ledger.
2. It supplies a listing of open accounts and their balances which is the basis for any adjustments and is used in preparing the financial statements and in supplying financial data about the concern.

The unadjusted trial balance for Ruddy Bros. Wholesale is illustrated below.

Ruddy Bros. Wholesale
TRIAL BALANCE
December 31, 1986

	Debit	Credit
Cash	$ 13,000	
Accounts Receivable	14,650	
Notes Receivable	8,000	
Inventory, January 1, 1986	89,500	
Office Equipment	16,000	
Furniture and Fixtures	12,300	

Accounts Payable		$ 14,100
Notes Payable		24,000
Ruddy Bros. Capital		91,240
Sales		896,000
Sales Returns	3,760	
Sales Allowances	960	
Purchases	713,450	
Purchase Returns		4,140
Transportation-In	6,570	
Sales Salaries Expense	65,700	
Travelling Expenses	4,900	
Advertising Expense	21,200	
General Office Salaries	39,800	
Rent Expense	18,000	
Insurance Expense	2,780	
Utilities Expense	4,310	
Telephone Expense	1,260	
Auditing and Legal Expense	2,780	
Miscellaneous Administrative Expense	2,200	
Purchase Discounts		13,500
Sales Discounts	1,860	
	$1,042,980	$1,042,980

ADJUSTMENTS

The employment of an accrual system means that numerous adjustments are necessary before financial statements are prepared because certain accounts are not accurately stated. For example, if we handle transactions on a cash basis, only cash transactions during the year are recorded. Consequently, if a company's employees are paid every two weeks and the end of an accounting period occurs in the middle of these two weeks, neither liability nor expense is shown for the last week.[3] In order to bring the accounts up to date for the preparation of financial statements, both the wage expense and the wage liability accounts need to be increased. This change is accomplished by means of an adjusting entry.

A necessary step in the accounting process, then, is the adjustment of all accounts to an accrual basis. **Adjusting entries** are therefore necessary to achieve an appropriate matching of revenues and expenses in the determination of net income for the current period and to provide a more complete statement of the assets and equities existing at the end of the period. Each adjusting entry affects both a real (asset or equity) account and a nominal (revenue or expense) account.

Normally the adjustments are classified in the following manner:

   Prepaid (deferred) items:
     Prepaid expenses (e.g., prepaid insurance)
     Unearned revenues (e.g., rent received in advance)
   Accrued items:
     Accrued liabilities or expenses (e.g., unpaid salaries)
     Accrued assets or revenues (e.g., interest earned but not collected)
   Estimated items (e.g., depreciation)

---

[3]See Appendix 3B for a brief discussion of the accrual and cash based accounting systems and procedures that may be used to convert from the cash basis to the accrual basis.

Prepaid Expenses

A prepaid expense is an item paid and recorded in advance of its use or consumption in the business, part of which properly represents expense of the current period and part of which represents an asset on hand at the end of the period. If a three-year insurance premium is paid in advance at the beginning of the current year, one-third of the amount paid represents expense of the current year and two-thirds represent an asset at the end of the year, an amount properly to be deferred to, and expensed in, future years.

Illustration   If a three-year insurance policy is purchased for $1,200 on January 2, 1986, and the books are closed annually on December 31, the asset account appears as follows on December 31, 1986, before the adjusting entry is made:

Unexpired Insurance			
1986			
Jan. 2	Cash Paid	1,200	

Because one-third of the three-year period has now passed, one-third of the amount is shown as an expense for 1986, and the asset account is reduced by the same amount. The adjusting entry required on December 31, 1986 is:

	Dec. 31		
Insurance Expense		400	
Unexpired Insurance			400
(To charge one-third of insurance premium to expense)			

The ledger now shows an expense for insurance of $400 and an asset, Unexpired Insurance, of $800.

Unexpired Insurance						
1986			1986			
Jan. 2	Cash Paid	1,200	Dec. 31	To Insurance Expense		400

Insurance Expense			
1986			
Dec. 31	Insurance Expired	400	

Unearned Revenue

Unearned revenue is revenue received and recorded as a liability or as a revenue before the revenue has been earned by providing goods or services to customers. As dictated by the "revenue realization principle" in accounting, revenue is reported in the period in which it is earned; therefore, when it is received in advance of being earned, the amount applicable to future periods is deferred to future periods. The amount unearned is considered a liability because it represents an obligation to perform a service or supply goods in the future.

Some common unearned revenue items are rent received in advance, interest received in advance on notes receivable, subscriptions and advertising fees received in advance by publishers, and deposits from customers received before delivery of merchandise.

Illustration   Assume that a business rents part of a building for a three-year period from January 1, 1986 for $6,000, and the tenant has paid the full three years' rent in advance. The business makes the following entry.

Jan. 1

Cash	6,000	
Unearned Rent Revenue		6,000
(To record rent for three years received in advance)		

At the end of 1986, one-third of this amount has been earned and, therefore, an adjusting entry is made.

Dec. 31

Unearned Rent Revenue	2,000	
Rent Revenue		2,000
(To take up as revenue one-third of $6,000)		

The entry reduces the liability and records $2,000 in the Rent Revenue account, which represents the amount of revenue earned during the year. These two accounts now show the following balances after adjustment.

Unearned Rent Revenue					
1986			1986		
Dec. 31	Adjusting entry	2,000	Jan. 1	Cash Received	6,000

Rent Revenue					
			1986		
			Dec. 31	Adjusting entry	2,000

For prepaid expense or unearned revenue items, it makes no difference if an original transaction entry is recorded in a real account (asset or liability) or in a nominal account (expense or revenue). After appropriate adjusting entries, the balances of the respective accounts are the same, regardless of the original entry.

Accrued Liabilities or Expenses

Accrued liabilities or accrued expenses are items of expense that have been incurred during the period, but have not yet been recorded or paid. As such, they represent liabilities at the end of the period. The related debits for such items are included in the income statement as expenses.

Some common accrued liabilities are interest payable, wages and salaries payable, and property taxes payable.

Illustration   When employees are paid on a monthly basis on the last day of the month, there are no accrued wages and salaries at the end of the month or year because all employees will have been paid all amounts due them for the month or the year. However, when they are paid on a weekly or biweekly basis, it is usually necessary to make an adjusting entry for wages and salaries earned but not paid at the end of the fiscal period.

Assume that a business pays its sales staff every Friday for a five-day week, that the total weekly payroll is $8,000, and that December 31 falls on Thursday. On

December 31, the end of the fiscal period, the employees have worked four-fifths of a week for which they have not been paid and for which no entry has been made. The adjusting entry on December 31 is:

Sales Salaries Expense	6,400	
Salaries Payable		6,400
(To record accrued salaries as of Dec. 31: 4/5 × $8,000)		

As a result of this entry, the income statement for the year includes the salaries earned by the sales staff during the last four days in December, and the balance sheet shows salaries payable of $6,400 as a liability.

Sales Salaries Expense					
1986					
Paid in 1986		409,600			
Dec. 31	Adjusting entry	6,400			
Total 1986		416,000			

Salaries Payable				
	1986			
	Dec. 31	Adjusting entry	6,400

Accrued Assets or Revenues

Items of revenue that have been earned during the period but that have not yet been collected are called accrued assets, accrued revenues, or revenues receivable. Adjusting entries must be made for these items to record the revenue that has been earned but not yet received and to record as an asset the amount receivable.

Some examples of accrued assets are rent receivable and interest receivable.

Illustration   Assume that office space is rented to a tenant at $1,000 per month, that the tenant has paid the rent for the first 11 months of the year, and that the tenant has paid no rent for December. The adjusting entry on December 31 is:

	Dec. 31		
Rent Receivable		1,000	
Rent Revenue			1,000
(To record December rent)			

As a result of this entry, an asset of $1,000, Rent Receivable, appears on the balance sheet, disclosing the amount due from the tenant as of December 31. The income statement discloses rent revenue of $12,000, the $11,000 received for the first 11 months, and the $1,000 for December entered by means of the adjusting entry. After adjustment the accounts appear as follows.

Rent Revenue					
		1986			
		Received in 1986		11,000	
		Dec. 31	Adjusting entry	1,000	
		Total 1986		12,000	

Rent Receivable				
1986				
Dec. 31	Adjusting entry	1,000		

Estimated Items

Uncollectible accounts and depreciation of fixed assets are ordinarily called estimated items because the amounts are not exactly determinable. In other words, an **estimated item** is a function of unknown future events and developments, which means that current period charges can be evaluated on a subjective basis only. It is known, for example, that some accounts receivable arising from credit sales will prove to be uncollectible. To prevent an understatement of expenses and losses of the period, it is necessary to estimate and record the bad debts that are expected to result.

Also, when a long-lived fixed asset is purchased, it is assumed that ultimately it will be scrapped or sold at a price much below the purchase price. This difference between an asset's cost and its scrap (salvage) value represents an expense to the business that should be apportioned over the asset's useful life. We must estimate the probable life of the fixed asset and its scrap value to determine the expense that is charged in each period.

Adjusting Entries for Bad Debts   Proper matching of revenues and expenses dictates recording bad debts as an expense of the period in which the sale is made instead of the period in which the accounts or notes are written off. This method requires an adjusting entry.

At the end of each period, an estimate is made of the bad debts expense to be recorded. The estimate is based on factors such as the amount of bad debts experienced in one or more past years, general economic conditions, and the age of the receivables. The amount of the adjusting entry may be determined as a specified percentage of sales on account for the period (Percentage of Sales Method) or as the amount required to bring the Allowance for Doubtful Accounts account balance to a level reflecting the estimated uncollectible portion of the trade accounts and notes receivable at the end of the period (Aging Method).

Assume, for example, that experience reveals that bad debts usually approximate one-half of one percent of the net sales on account, and that net sales on account for the year are $300,000. The adjusting entry for bad debts is:

Dec. 31

Bad Debts Expense	1,500	
Allowance for Doubtful Accounts		1,500
(To record estimated bad debts for the year: $300,000 × .005)		

Whenever a particular customer's account is determined to be uncollectible, the Allowance for Doubtful Accounts is debited and Accounts Receivable is credited for the amount of the write-off. Methods of determining the amount of the adjusting entry, and how to account for a write-off and a write-off reversal, are examined in Chapter 7.

Adjusting Entries for Depreciation   Entries for depreciation are similar to those made for reducing the prepaid expenses in which the original amount was debited to an asset account. The principal difference is that for depreciation the credit is made to a separate account, Accumulated Depreciation, instead of to the asset account.

In estimating depreciation, the original cost of the asset, its length of useful life, and its estimated salvage or trade-in value are used. Assume that a truck costing $9,000 has an estimated life of five years and an estimated trade-in value of $1,000 at the end of that period. Because the truck is expected to be worth $8,000 less at the time of its disposal than it was at the time of its purchase, the amount of $8,000 represents an expense that is apportioned over the five years of its anticipated use in operations. It is neither logical nor good accounting practice to consider the $8,000 as an expense entirely of the period in which it was acquired or the period in which it was sold, inasmuch as the business receives the benefit of the use of the truck during the entire five-year period.

If the straight-line method of depreciation is used, each year shows as an expense one-fifth of $8,000, or $1,600. Each full year the truck is used the following adjusting entry is made.

Dec. 31

Depreciation Expense—Delivery Equipment	1,600	
Accumulated Depreciation—Delivery Equipment		1,600
(To record depreciation on truck for the year)		

Summary of Adjustments

We have summarized the basic adjustments and defined them individually:

Prepaid expense. An expense paid in cash and recorded in advance of its use or consumption.

Unearned revenue. A revenue received and recorded in a liability or revenue account before it is earned.

Accrued liabilities (expenses). Expense incurred but not yet paid.

Accrued assets (revenues). Revenue earned but not yet received.

Estimated items. An expense recorded on the basis of subjective estimates because the expense is a function of unknown future events or developments.

As soon as these adjusting entries have been recorded and posted, another trial balance is prepared before closing. The second or **adjusted trial balance** is used to prepare the financial statements. The basic set of financial statements is discussed in the next two chapters.

YEAR-END PROCEDURE FOR INVENTORY AND RELATED ACCOUNTS

When the inventory records are maintained on a **perpetual inventory system,** purchases and issues are recorded directly in the Inventory account as they occur. Therefore, the balance in the Inventory account should represent the ending inventory amount, and no adjusting entries are needed. No Purchases account is used because the purchases are debited directly to the Inventory account. However, a Cost of Goods Sold account is used to accumulate the issuances from inventory.

When the inventory records are maintained on a **periodic inventory system,** a Purchases account is used and the Inventory account is unchanged during the period. The Inventory account represents the beginning inventory amount throughout the period. At the end of the accounting period, the Inventory account must be adjusted by closing out the **beginning inventory** amount and recording the **ending inventory** amount. The ending inventory is determined by physically counting the items on hand and valuing them at cost or at the lower of cost and market. Under the periodic inventory system, cost of goods sold is, therefore, determined by adding the beginning inventory together with the net purchases and deducting the ending inventory.

Computation of cost of goods sold using the periodic inventory system has the characteristics of both an adjusting entry and a closing entry; thus, there is more than one way to prepare the entries that update inventory, record cost of goods sold, and close the other related nominal accounts. To illustrate, Collegiate Apparel Shop has a beginning inventory of $30,000; Purchases $200,000; Transportation-In $6,000; Purchase Returns $1,200; Purchase Allowances $800; Purchase Discounts $2,000; and the ending inventory is $26,000.

One approach for closing out the beginning inventory, setting up the ending inventory, and closing the various merchandise purchase accounts into the Cost of Goods Sold account is to use three entries, as indicated below:

(1)	Cost of Goods Sold	30,000	
	Inventory (beginning)		30,000
	(To transfer beginning inventory balance to Cost of Goods Sold)		
(2)	Inventory (ending)	26,000	
	Cost of Goods Sold		26,000
	(To set up the ending inventory balance and adjust Cost of Goods Sold accordingly)		
(3)	Purchase Discounts	2,000	
	Purchase Allowances	800	
	Purchase Returns	1,200	
	Cost of Goods Sold	202,000	
	Purchases		200,000
	Transportation-In		6,000
	(To transfer net purchases to Cost of Goods Sold)		

While making three entries may facilitate one's understanding of the way in which the balance for ending inventory or Cost of Goods Sold is derived, the same conclusions in terms of account balances result when the above entries are combined into one as follows:

Inventory (ending)	26,000	
Purchase Discounts	2,000	
Purchase Allowances	800	
Purchase Returns	1,200	
Cost of Goods Sold	206,000	
Inventory (beginning)		30,000
Purchases		200,000
Transportation-In		6,000
(To transfer beginning inventory and net purchases to Cost of Goods Sold and to record ending inventory)		

The following diagram illustrates, in T-account form, the process of determining the cost of goods sold through adjusting the inventory balance and closing the accounts related to net purchases on an item-by-item basis. Using the one entry approach as shown would simply result in fewer amounts being posted to the Cost of Goods Sold account.

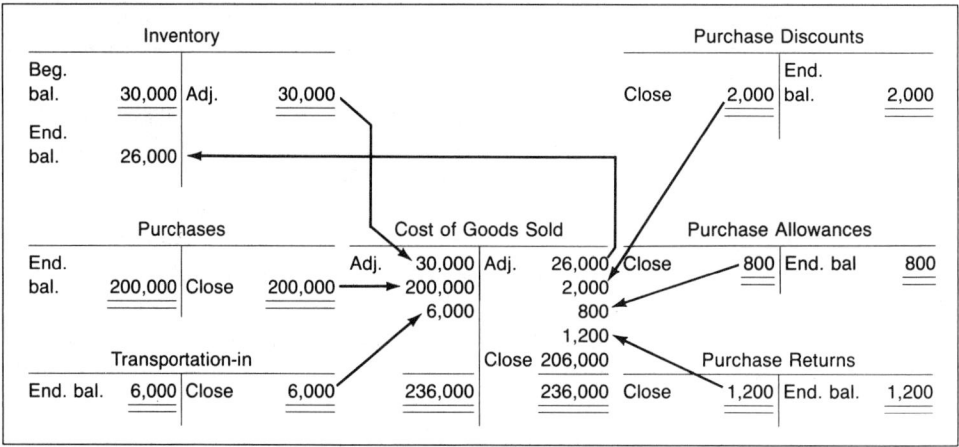

CLOSING

The procedure generally followed to reduce the balance of nominal (temporary) accounts to zero in order to prepare the accounts for the next period's transactions is known as the **closing process.** In the closing process, all of the revenue and expense account balances (income statement items) are transferred to a clearing or suspense account called Income Summary, which is used only at the end of each accounting period. Revenues and expenses are matched in the Income Summary account and the net result of this matching, which represents the net income or net loss for the period, is then transferred to an owners' equity account (retained earnings for a corporation, and capital accounts normally for proprietorships and partnerships). Note that all closing entries are posted to the appropriate general ledger accounts.

For example, assume that revenue accounts of Collegiate Apparel Shop have the following balances, after adjustments, at the end of the year:

Revenue from Sales	$280,000
Rental Revenue	27,000
Interest Revenue	5,000

These **revenue accounts** would be closed and the balances transferred to the Income Summary account through the following closing journal entry:

Revenue from Sales	280,000	
Rental Revenue	27,000	
Interest Revenue	5,000	
Income Summary		312,000
(To close revenue accounts to Income Summary)		

Assume that the expense accounts, including Cost of Goods Sold, have the following balances, after adjustments, at the end of the year:

Cost of Goods Sold	$206,000
Selling Expenses	25,000
General and Administrative Expenses	40,600
Interest Expense	4,400
Income Tax Expense	13,000

These **expense accounts** would be closed and the balances transferred to the Income Summary account through the following closing journal entry:

Income Summary	289,000	
Cost of Goods Sold		206,000
Selling Expenses		25,000
General and Administrative Expenses		40,600
Interest Expense		4,400
Income Tax Expense		13,000
(To close expense accounts to Income Summary)		

The Income Summary account now has a credit balance of $23,000 which is the amount of the net income. The **net income is transferred to owners' equity** by closing the Income Summary account to Retained Earnings as follows:

Income Summary	23,000	
Retained Earnings		23,000
(To close Income Summary to owners' equity)		

Assuming that dividends of $7,000 were declared and distributed during the year, the Dividends account is closed directly to Retained Earnings as follows:

Retained Earnings	7,000	
Dividends		7,000
(To close Dividends to Retained Earnings)		

After the closing process is completed, each income statement (nominal) account is balanced out to zero and is ready for use in the next accounting period.

The following diagram illustrates in T-account form the closing process.

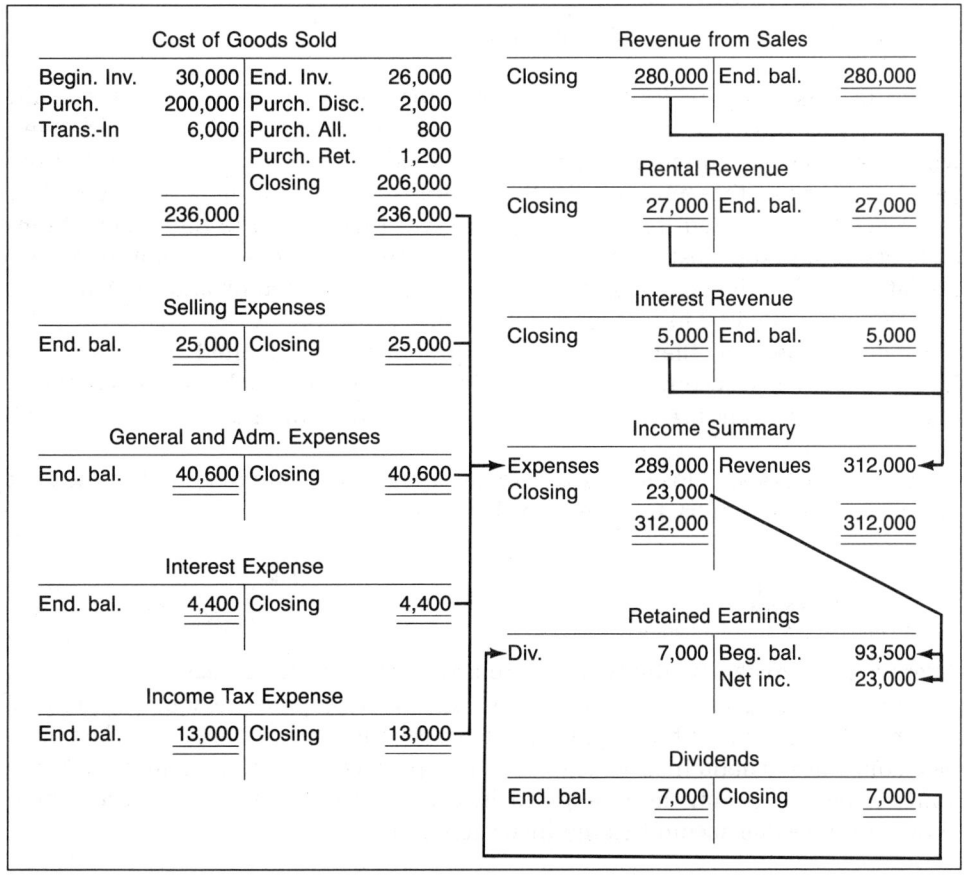

POST-CLOSING TRIAL BALANCE

We already mentioned that a trial balance is taken after the regular transactions of the period have been entered, and that a second trial balance (adjusted trial balance) is taken after the adjusting entries have been posted. A third trial balance may be taken after posting closing entries; often called the **post-closing trial balance,** it shows that equal debits and credits have been posted to the Income Summary. The post-closing trial balance consists only of asset, liability, and owners' equity accounts.

REVERSING ENTRIES

After the financial statements have been prepared and the books closed, it is sometimes useful to reverse some of the adjusting entries before entering the regular transactions of the next period. Such entries are called reversing entries.

A **reversing entry** is the exact reverse, both in amount and in account titles, of an adjusting entry. **Any adjusting entries that create an asset or a liability account could be reversed.** Reversing entries are generally recorded at the beginning of the next accounting period. Such entries are optional. They are made only to simplify the recording of a subsequent transaction related to an adjusting entry. When an adjusting entry is reversed, the related subsequent transaction can be recorded as if the adjusting entry had never been recorded.

Reversing Entries for Prepaid Expenses

Earlier in this chapter, the adjusting entry for unexpired insurance (a prepaid expense) was illustrated. An asset account, Unexpired Insurance, was debited when the three-year premium of $1,200 was paid in advance. At the end of the year, one-third of that amount, $400, was transferred from the asset account to Insurance Expense, and Insurance Expense was then closed to the Income Summary account in the closing process. This adjusting entry does not require reversing; at the end of the next year, the asset account is reduced by another $400 and that amount is debited to Insurance Expense.

Suppose, however, that the insurance premium was debited initially to the Insurance Expense account. In the adjusting entry, Insurance Expense is credited and Unexpired Insurance is debited for $800, the unexpired portion of the insurance coverage.

After the books are closed and before any transactions are recorded in the next period, a reversing entry may be recorded.

Jan. 1

Insurance Expense	800	
Unexpired Insurance		800
(To reverse the adjusting entry of Dec. 31)		

After we post this entry, the two accounts appear as shown in page 101.

Here a reversing entry was made to return to the expense account the cost of unexpired insurance at the beginning of the second year of the policy. The business continues to debit Insurance Expense for purchases of other insurance during 1987; to be consistent, the unexpired insurance at the beginning of the year is shown in the same account as the insurance purchased.

Insurance Expense					
1986			1986		
Jan. 2	Cash paid	1,200	Dec. 31	Adjusting entry	800
			Dec. 31	To Income	
				Summary	400
		1,200			1,200
1987					
Jan. 1	Reversing entry	800			

Unexpired Insurance					
1986			1987		
Dec. 31	Adjusting entry	800	Jan. 1	Reversing entry	800

Reversing entries are also made for prepaid revenue transactions if the initial entry is made to a revenue account.

With respect to prepaid items, why are all such items not entered originally into real accounts (assets and liabilities), thus making reversing entries unnecessary? This practice is often followed. It is particularly advantageous for items that need to be apportioned over several periods. Despite this, a company may prefer to treat payments for such items initially as an expense, then adjust and reverse them, because such a practice is perceived to facilitate accounting in the coming period, or it is believed to be desirable to reverse all adjusting entries, given that accrued amounts are being reversed. In essence, the accounting treatment is a matter of preference.

Reversing Entries for Accrued Items

Each accrued item resulting from adjusting entries involves either a later receipt of cash for revenue earned or a later disbursement of cash for an expense incurred. An entry reversing these adjustments facilitates the accounting when the cash is received or paid, as the full amount may be credited to the revenue account or debited to the expense account. The net balance from the reversing entries and the cash transaction represents the revenue earned or expense incurred for that period. To illustrate, we continue with the Sales Salaries account after the adjustment that was shown previously (page 94). The Sales Salaries Expense account, being an expense account, is closed to the Income Summary on December 31. On January 1 this reversing entry is made.

	Jan. 1		
Salaries Payable		6,400	
Sales Salaries Expense			6,400
(To reverse the adjusting entry of Dec. 31)			

This entry closes the Salaries Payable account and puts a credit balance of $6,400 in the Sales Salaries Expense account. On January 1, after we post the reversing entry, the accounts appear as follows.

Sales Salaries Expense						
1986			1986			
Paid in 1986		409,600	Dec. 31	To Income		
Dec. 31	Adjusting entry	6,400		Summary	416,000	
		416,000			416,000	
			1987			
			Jan. 1	Reversing entry	6,400	

Salaries Payable						
			1986			
			Dec. 31	Adjusting entry	6,400	
1987						
Jan. 1	Reversing entry	6,400				

On Friday, January 1, the weekly payroll of $8,000 is paid, and the usual debit to Sales Salaries Expense and credit to Cash are recorded. The Sales Salaries Expense account now contains a debit of $8,000 and a credit of $6,400. The balance of $1,600 represents the expense incurred during the first day of January. This is illustrated below.

Sales Salaries Expense					
1987			1987		
Jan. 1	Cash paid	8,000	Jan. 1	Reversing entry	6, 400

This item was reversed so that the entry for payment of salaries on the first Friday of 1987 is the same as that for any other payroll. If the entry had not been reversed, it would have been necessary to debit Sales Salaries Payable for $6,400, and Sales Salaries Expense for $1,600. Analysis of this sort can be time-consuming and impractical.

In general, all adjusting entries for prepaid items for which the original amount was entered in a revenue or expense account and for all accrued items could be reversed. It follows, of course, that all other adjusting entries are not reversed; in other words, adjusting entries for prepaid items, for which the original amount was entered in a real account, and for estimated items, are not reversed.

Some accountants avoid reversing entries entirely, but frequently it is desirable to use them under the conditions described to ensure consistent treatment of the accounts and to establish standardized procedures for transactions that occur regularly.

THE ACCOUNTING CYCLE SUMMARIZED

A summary of the steps in the accounting cycle shows a logical sequence of the accounting procedures used during a fiscal period. The process begins with the identification and analysis of transactions and other selected events for which business documents provide evidence of the accounts and amounts. From this the following steps take place:

1. Enter the transactions of the period in appropriate journals.
2. Post from the journals to the ledger(s).
3. Take a trial balance (unadjusted trial balance).
4. Prepare adjusting journal entries and post to the ledger(s).
5. Take a trial balance after adjusting (adjusted trial balance).
6. Prepare the financial statements from the second trial balance.
7. Prepare closing journal entries and post to the ledger(s).
8. Take a trial balance after closing (postclosing trial balance).
9. Prepare reversing entries and post to the ledger (optional step).

This list of procedures constitutes a complete accounting cycle that is normally performed in every fiscal period.

USING A WORK SHEET TO PREPARE FINANCIAL STATEMENTS

To facilitate the end-of-period accounting and reporting process, accountants frequently use a work sheet. A **work sheet** is a columnar sheet of paper that may be used to help in adjusting the account balances and preparing the financial statements. The **ten-column work sheet** illustrated in this chapter provides columns for the first trial balance, adjustments, adjusted trial balance, income statement, and balance sheet. The work sheet does not in any way replace the journalizing, posting, or financial statements as previously discussed; instead, it is the accountant's informal device for accumulating and sorting the information that is needed for the preparation of financial statements. The satisfactory completion of the work sheet provides considerable assurance that all of the details related to the end-of-period accounting and statement preparation have been properly brought together.

An illustration of a completed work sheet and the steps related to its derivation appears on page 105.

Adjustments Entered on the Work Sheet

The information that serves as the basis for the adjusting entries made in the work sheet illustration on page 105 follows.

(a) Furniture and equipment is depreciated at the rate of 10% per year based on original cost.
(b) Estimated bad debts expense, one-quarter of 1% of sales.
(c) Insurance expired during the year, $360.
(d) Interest accrued on notes receivable as of December 31, $800.
(e) The Interest Expense account contains $500 interest paid in advance, which is applicable to next year.
(f) Property taxes accrued December 31, $2,000.

The adjusting entries, reflected in the Adjustments columns of the work sheet are:

(a)

Depreciation Expense—Furniture and Equipment	6,700	
Accumulated Depreciation of Furniture and Equipment		6,700

(b)

Bad Debts Expense	1,000	
Allowance for Doubtful Accounts		1,000

(c)

Insurance Expense	360	
Unexpired Insurance		360

	(d)		
Interest Receivable		800	
Interest Revenue			800

	(e)		
Prepaid Interest Expense		500	
Interest Expense			500

	(f)		
Property Tax Expense		2,000	
Property Tax Payable			2,000

These adjustments are entered into the Adjustments columns of the work sheet, and each may be designated by letter. The accounts that are set up as a result of the adjusting entries and that are not already in the trial balance are listed below the totals of the trial balance, as illustrated in the work sheet. The Adjustments columns are then totalled and balanced.

The illustration does not include in the Adjustments columns the adjustments for cost of goods sold. Although these adjustments are sometimes included in these columns on a ten-column work sheet, this illustration assumes that these entries will be made during the closing procedures.

Adjusted Trial Balance Columns

The amounts shown in the Trial Balance columns are combined with the amounts in the Adjustments columns and are extended to the Adjusted Trial Balance columns. For example, the amount of $2,000, shown opposite the Allowance for Doubtful Accounts in the Trial Balance Cr. column, is added to the $1,000 in the Adjustments Cr. column, and the total of $3,000 is extended to the Adjusted Trial Balance Cr. column. Similarly, the $900 debit opposite Unexpired Insurance is reduced by the $360 credit in the Adjustments column, and the $540 is shown in the Adjusted Trial Balance Dr. column. The Adjusted Trial Balance columns are then totalled and determined to be in balance.

Income Statement and Balance Sheet Columns

All the debit items in the Adjusted Trial Balance are extended into one of the two debit columns to the right, depending on the financial statement in which the items will appear. Similarly, all the credit items in the Adjusted Trial Balance are extended into one of the two credit columns to the right. It should be observed that the January 1 inventory, which was the inventory at the beginning of the year, is extended to the Income Statement Dr. column, because this item will appear as an addition in the cost of goods sold section of the income statement.

Ending Inventory

The December 31 inventory, which is the inventory at the end of the year, is not in either of the trial balances but is listed as a separate item below the accounts already shown. In the illustration the amount of the ending inventory is assumed to be $40,000, and this amount is shown on the work sheet as both debit and credit. It is listed in the Balance Sheet Dr. column because it is an asset at the end of the year, and in the Income Statement Cr. column because it will be used as a deduction in the cost of goods sold section of the income statement.

The Spencer Company
TEN-COLUMN WORK SHEET

December 31, 1986

Accounts	Trial Balance Dr.	Trial Balance Cr.	Adjustments Dr.	Adjustments Cr.	Adjusted Trial Balance Dr.	Adjusted Trial Balance Cr.	Income Statement Dr.	Income Statement Cr.	Balance Sheet Dr.	Balance Sheet Cr.
Cash	1,200				1,200				1,200	
Notes receivable	16,000				16,000				16,000	
Accounts receivable	41,000				41,000				41,000	
Allowance for doubtful accounts		2,000		(b) 1,000		3,000				3,000
Inventory, Jan. 1, 1986	36,000				36,000		36,000			
Unexpired insurance	900			(c) 360	540				540	
Furniture and equipment	67,000				67,000				67,000	
Accumulated depreciation of furniture and equipment		12,000		(a) 6,700		18,700				18,700
Notes payable		20,000				20,000				20,000
Accounts payable		13,500				13,500				13,500
Bonds payable		30,000				30,000				30,000
Common shares		50,000				50,000				50,000
Retained earnings, Jan. 1, 1986		14,200				14,200				14,200
Sales		400,000				400,000		400,000		
Purchases	320,000				320,000		320,000			
Sales salaries expense	20,000				20,000		20,000			
Advertising expense	2,200				2,200		2,200			
Travelling expense	8,000				8,000		8,000			
Salaries, office and general	19,000				19,000		19,000			
Telephone and telegraph expense	600				600		600			
Rent expense	4,800				4,800		4,800			
Property tax expense	3,300		(f) 2,000		5,300		5,300			
Interest expense	1,700			(e) 500	1,200		1,200			
Totals	541,700	541,700								
Depreciation expense— furniture and equipment			(a) 6,700		6,700		6,700			
Bad debts expense			(b) 1,000		1,000		1,000			
Insurance expense			(c) 360		360		360			
Interest receivable			(d) 800		800				800	
Interest revenue				(d) 800		800		800		
Prepaid interest expense			(e) 500		500				500	
Property tax payable				(f) 2,000		2,000				2,000
Totals			11,360	11,360	552,200	552,200				
Inventory, Dec. 31, 1986								40,000	40,000	
Totals							425,160	440,800		
Income before income taxes							15,640			
Totals							440,800	440,800		
Income before income taxes								15,640		
Income tax expense			(g) 3,440				3,440			
Income tax payable				(g) 3,440						3,440
Net Income							12,200			12,200
							15,640	15,640	167,040	167,040

Income Taxes and Net Income

The next step is to total the Income Statement columns; the figure necessary to balance the debit and credit columns is the income or loss for the period before income taxes. In this illustration the income before income taxes of $15,640 is shown in the Income Statement Dr. column because the revenues exceeded the expenses by that amount.

The income tax expense and related tax liability are then computed (in this case an effective rate of 22% was applied). This adjustment is entered in the Income Statement Dr. column as Income Tax Expense $3,440 and in the Balance Sheet Cr. column as Income Tax Payable $3,440, because the Adjustments columns have been balanced. Next, the Income Statement columns are balanced with the income taxes included. The $12,200 difference between the debit and credit columns in this illustration represents net income. The net income of $12,200 is entered in the Income Statement Dr. column to achieve equality and in the Balance Sheet Cr. column as the increase in retained earnings. The following adjusting journal entry, as well as those previously entered in the work sheet, is recorded and posted to the general ledger.

	(g)		
Income Tax Expense		3,440	
Income Tax Payable			3,440

Eight-Column and Twelve-Column Work Sheets

An eight-column instead of a ten-column work sheet may be used to accumulate the same information. The only difference between the two is that the eight-column work sheet omits the Adjusted Trial Balance columns. The amounts shown in the Trial Balance columns (the first two columns) are combined with the amounts in the Adjustments columns and are extended directly into the Income Statement and Balance Sheet columns.

A twelve-column work sheet may be prepared to accommodate increases and decreases in retained earnings merely by adding Retained Earnings Dr. and Cr. columns. Dividends and net income would appear as adjustments to the beginning Retained Earnings.

Preparation of Financial Statements from Work Sheet

The work sheet provides the information needed for preparation of the financial statements without reference to the ledger or other records. In addition, the data have been sorted into appropriate columns, which facilitate the preparation of the statements.

The financial statements prepared from the ten-column work sheet illustrated are:

Statement of Income for the Year Ended December 31, 1986.
Statement of Retained Earnings for the Year Ended December 31, 1986.
Balance Sheet as of December 31, 1986.

Statement of Income

The income statement presented here is that of a trading or merchandising concern; if a manufacturing concern were illustrated, three inventory accounts would be involved: raw materials, work in process, and finished goods. When these accounts are used, a supplementary statement entitled Cost of Goods Manufactured must be prepared.

The Spencer Company
INCOME STATEMENT
For the Year Ended December 31, 1986

Net sales			$400,000
Cost of goods sold			
Inventory, Jan. 1, 1986		$ 36,000	
Purchases		320,000	
Cost of goods available for sale		$356,000	
Deduct inventory, Dec. 31, 1986		40,000	
Cost of goods sold			316,000
Gross profit on sales			$ 84,000
Selling expenses			
Sales salaries expense		$ 20,000	
Advertising expense		2,200	
Travelling expense		8,000	
Total selling expenses		$ 30,200	
Administrative expenses			
Salaries, office and general	$19,000		
Telephone and telegraph expense	600		
Rent expense	4,800		
Property tax expense	5,300		
Depreciation expense—furniture			
and equipment	6,700		
Bad debts expense	1,000		
Insurance expense	360		
Total administrative expenses		37,760	
Total selling and administrative expenses			67,960
Income from operations			$ 16,040
Other revenue			
Interest revenue			800
			$ 16,840
Other expense			
Interest expense			1,200
Income before income taxes			$ 15,640
Income taxes			3,440
Net income			$ 12,200

Statement of Retained Earnings

The net income earned by a corporation may be retained in the business or it may be distributed to shareholders by payment of dividends. In the illustration, the net income earned during the year was added to the balance of retained earnings on January 1, thereby increasing the balance of retained earnings to $26,400 on December 31. No dividends were declared or paid during the year.

```
                          The Spencer Company
                      STATEMENT OF RETAINED EARNINGS
                      For the Year Ended December 31, 1986

Retained earnings, Jan. 1, 1986                                  $14,200
Add: Net income for 1986                                          12,200
Retained earnings, Dec. 31, 1986                                 $26,400
```

Balance Sheet

The balance sheet prepared from the ten-column work sheet contains more new items resulting from year-end adjusting entries. Interest receivable, unexpired insurance, and prepaid interest expense are included as current assets, because these assets will be converted into cash or consumed in the ordinary routine of the business within a relatively short period of time. The amount of Allowance for Doubtful Accounts is deducted from the total accounts and notes receivable because it is estimated that only $54,000 of the total of $57,000 will be collected in cash.

In the property, plant, and equipment section, the accumulated depreciation is deducted from the cost of the furniture and equipment; the difference represents the book or carrying value of the furniture and equipment.

Property tax payable is shown as a current liability because it is an obligation that is payable within a year. Other short-term accrued liabilities would also be shown as current liabilities.

The bonds payable, due in 1994, are long-term or fixed liabilities and are shown in a separate section. (Interest on the bonds was paid on December 31.)

The Spencer Company is a corporation, and the capital section of the balance sheet, called the shareholders' equity section in the illustration, is somewhat different from the capital section of the proprietorship. The total capital or shareholders' equity consists of the common shares, which is the original investment by shareholders, and the earnings retained in the business.

```
                          The Spencer Company
                            BALANCE SHEET
                        As of December 31, 1986

                                Assets
Current assets
  Cash                                                          $   1,200
  Notes receivable                           $16,000
  Accounts receivable                         41,000   $57,000
  Less: Allowance for doubtful accounts                  3,000     54,000
  Interest receivable                                                800
  Merchandise inventory on hand                                   40,000
  Unexpired insurance                                                540
  Prepaid interest expense                                           500
    Total current assets                                        $ 97,040
Property, plant, and equipment
  Furniture and equipment                    $67,000
  Less: Accumulated depreciation              18,700
    Total property, plant, and equipment                          48,300
Total assets                                                    $145,340
```

Liabilities and Shareholders' Equity		
Current liabilities		
Notes payable		$ 20,000
Accounts payable		13,500
Property tax payable		2,000
Income taxes payable		3,440
Total current liabilities		$38,940
Long-term liabilities		
Bonds payable, due June 30, 1994		30,000
Total liabilities		$68,940
Shareholders' equity		
Common shares issued		
and outstanding, 50,000 shares	$50,000	
Retained earnings	26,400	
Total shareholders' equity		76,400
Total liabilities and shareholders' equity		$145,340

Closing and Reversing Entries

The entries for the closing process are as follows:

GENERAL JOURNAL

Inventory (December 31)	40,000	
Cost of Goods Sold	316,000	
Inventory (January 1)		36,000
Purchases		320,000
(To record ending inventory balance and to determine cost of goods sold)		
Interest Revenue	800	
Sales	400,000	
Cost of Goods Sold		316,000
Sales Salaries Expense		20,000
Advertising Expense		2,200
Travelling Expense		8,000
Salaries, Office and General		19,000
Telephone and Telegraph Expense		600
Rent Expense		4,800
Property Tax Expense		5,300
Depreciation of Furniture and Equipment		6,700
Bad Debt Expense		1,000
Insurance Expense		360
Interest Expense		1,200
Income Tax Expense		3,440
Income Summary		12,200
(To close revenues and expenses to Income Summary)		
Income Summary	12,200	
Retained Earnings		12,200
(To close Income Summary to Retained Earnings)		

After the financial statements have been prepared, the enterprise may use reversing entries to facilitate the accounting next period. The following reversing entries would be made if a reversing system were used.

(a)

Interest Revenue	800	
Interest Receivable		800

(b)

Interest Expense	500	
Prepaid Interest Expense		500

(c)

Property Tax Payable	2,000	
Property Tax Expense		2,000

Reversing entries would not appear on the ten-column work sheet because they are recorded in the next year (1987). The main object of the work sheet is to obtain the correct balances at the end of the year for financial statement presentation for the current year (1986).

Monthly Statements, Yearly Closing

The use of a work sheet at the end of each month or quarter permits the preparation of interim financial statements even though the books are closed only at the end of each year. For example, assume that a business closes its books on December 31 but that monthly financial statements are desired. At the end of January, a work sheet similar to the one illustrated in this chapter can be prepared to supply the information needed for statements for January. At the end of February, a work sheet can be used again but, because the accounts were not closed at the end of January, the income statement taken from the work sheet on February 28 will present the net income for two months. An income statement for the month of February can be obtained by subtracting the items in the January income statement from the corresponding items in the income statement for the two months of January and February.

A statement of retained earnings for February only may be obtained also by subtracting the January items. The balance sheet prepared from the February work sheet, however, shows the assets and equities as of February 28, the specific date for which a balance sheet is used.

The March work sheet would show the revenues and expenses for three months, and the subtraction of the revenues and expenses for the first two months could be made to supply the amounts needed for an income statement for the month of March.

COMPUTERS AND ACCOUNTING SOFTWARE

The principles of recording, classifying, and summarizing accounting data described in this chapter are generally applicable to most enterprises. While the activities related to data processing may be done manually, the mass of data in many enterprises is so great that such an approach would be very time consuming and costly. Consequently, most businesses use relatively low-cost equipment to carry out the data processing in a quick and efficient manner. The nature and type of the equipment being used varies according to the nature and size of the business, what it does, and its cost.

In the past, various accounting and bookkeeping machines were widely used. These were essentially posting machines that could be operated by a clerk. They made it possible to post a transaction simultaneously to several different records. For example, a purchase invoice would be recorded in the purchases journal and posted to the subsidiary accounts payable ledger at the same time. Summary totals were then posted manually either daily or monthly to the purchases account and the accounts payable control account in the general ledger. The major benefits of an accounting or bookkeeping machine are that (1) the posting process is expedited, (2) the records are neater and easier to read, and (3) the equality of debits and credits is maintained. While equipment of this type is still in use, computers are rapidly making such items obsolete.

A computer is a machine that can perform with amazing speed many internal operations from a specific set of instructions. The computer has revolutionized data processing not only because of its speed and accuracy in processing data, but also because it can be programmed to process the data in almost any manner desired by management.

Nearly every medium- or large-sized business owns or rents a computer, but until recently a computer was too expensive for a small business to own or rent. Small businesses generally avoided investing large sums of money but gained the use of computers through **EDP service centres** or through **time-sharing arrangements.** However, with the recent emergence of **mini-computers** and **micro-computers,** even small businesses can own a computer and obtain the operating and record-keeping efficiencies provided.

The growth in computers is nothing short of phenomenal. From the beginning of time through 1980, there were approximately 1 million computer systems. By 1987, the number of personal computers alone is estimated to be 80 million. This is not surprising, given the level of technological change in this area. As one executive noted, "The amount of raw computing power available at a given price has been improving 25% a year. That which cost $1,000,000 in 1970 will cost $10,000 in 1990." As a result, in 1984 it was estimated that one out of every three white-collar workers had a personal computer. By 1990, the ratio is expected to be one to one.

While the availability of relatively low-cost and technologically advanced hardware has been one of the most significant events in the recent history of the business environment, the related development of low-cost accounting software packages is of equal importance to the accounting profession.[4] Such packages (programs) are capable of carrying out most of the mechanical steps in the accounting cycle. That is, once transactions and events have been identified and analyzed as to the accounts affected and amounts involved, these software packages can take this input and process it through all the steps, resulting in the financial statements.

These technological advances have been a great boon to accountants. As a result, accountants are no longer required to devote hours to the routine tasks of recording, posting, and summarizing data. Therefore, more attention to the activities of analyzing and interpreting financial information is possible. To an extent, the use of computers and accounting software has provided the opportunity to take much of the bookkeeping drudgery out of accounting.

These developments, however, do not mean that the accountant no longer has to be an expert in knowing and understanding the accounting process. The nature of this process as represented by the procedures in the accounting cycle provides a basic model by which an accountant can analyze the effect of various transactions and events on the financial reports. This is particularly important when choosing a

---

[4]In a 1984 study conducted by Dun & Bradstreet of 2,000 buyers and users of software in all sectors of the North American economy, it was reported that 81% of the smaller firms used micro-computers for accounting purposes. Large companies used micros to a lesser extent (64%) for accounting purposes (probably because their accounting systems were more likely to be on larger computers). The study also reported substantial use of micros in such areas as financial analysis, inventory control, purchasing, credit analysis of customers, word processing and data-base management.

method from various generally accepted accounting alternatives. If one is simply entering a transaction or event into a computer without knowing why or what happens afterwards, significant problems are likely to result (i.e., errors made, not being able to find information in the system, accepting the results without understanding what they mean or how they are determined). With understanding of the steps in the cycle, such problems are less likely to occur. Also, the accountant is responsible for the design of the information system of an enterprise. Such a design would require a complete understanding of the process by which financial statements are derived. While the procedures outlined in this chapter are basic to most accounting systems, it must also be accepted that the accounting system for each enterprise is likely to have some unique characteristics. Determining, understanding, and implementing these require the accountant to have a thorough knowledge of the accounting process.

In conclusion, while the use of computers can greatly assist in carrying out the mechanical activities in the accounting cycle, the accountant must know what the process is if the information input and output relationships are to be appropriate and understood.

KEY POINTS

1. Accounting systems vary widely from one business to another, depending on the nature of the business and the transactions in which it engages, the size of the firm, the volume of data to be handled, and the informational demands that management and others place on the system.

2. There are established rules for recording transactions and other events as they occur. These rules are the basis of double-entry accounting.

3. The basic steps in the accounting cycle are (1) identification and measurement of transactions and other events, (2) journalization, (3) posting, (4) trial balance preparation, (5) adjustments, (6) adjusted trial balance, (7) statement preparation, and (8) closing. Optional procedures are the use of a worksheet, post-closing trial balance, and reversing entries.

4. Events are of two types: (1) external events and (2) internal events. Accountants record many events that affect the financial position and results of operations of the enterprise, but some events are omitted because the problems of measuring them are too complex.

5. Journalization is the process where essential facts and figures in connection with transactions and selected events are recorded initially in a book of original entry.

6. Posting is the mechanical process of transferring the essential facts and figures from the book of original entry to the accounts in the ledger.

7. A trial balance is a listing of all open accounts in the ledger and their balances. A trial balance taken immediately after all adjustments have been posted is called an adjusted trial balance. A trial balance taken immediately after closing entries have been posted is designated an after-closing or post-closing trial balance.

8. Adjustments are used to achieve an appropriate matching of revenues and expenses in the determination of net income for the current period and to provide a more complete statement of the assets and equities existing at the end of the period.

9. The closing process reduces the balances of nominal (temporary) accounts to zero in order to prepare the accounts for the next period's transactions.

10. Reversing entries are used to simplify accounting. Accrued items and prepaid items debited or credited to a nominal account are often reversed. Reversing entries, however, are not necessary to record transactions correctly.

11. A work sheet is often prepared to facilitate the preparation of financial statements. The work sheet does not in any way replace the financial statements; instead, it is the accountant's informal device for accumulating and sorting the information that is needed for the financial statements.

12. Computers and accounting software packages are frequently used to assist in carrying out most of the mechanical steps in the accounting cycle. While such technology is tremendously useful, the accountant must still have a thorough understanding of the accounting cycle. Such an understanding is necessary in order to make sure the process is working for a particular enterprise, to know where information is located, and to be able to properly analyze, assess, and comprehend the information input and output relationships.

3A

SPECIALIZED JOURNALS AND METHODS OF PROCESSING ACCOUNTING DATA

Most businesses use special journals in addition to the general journal. Special journals permit greater division of labour, which facilitates improved internal control, reduces the time necessary to accomplish the various bookkeeping tasks, and summarizes transactions possessing a common characteristic. Therefore, the special journals used by any given business depend largely on the specific transactions common to that business. Most trading concerns have many transactions grouped into these categories:

Receipts of cash
Sales on account
Purchases on account
Payments of cash

A business that engages in many of each of these transactions is likely to use the following five journals.

1. **Cash receipts journal.** Records entries for all cash received by the business.
2. **Sales journal.** Records entries for all sales of merchandise on account.
3. **Purchases journal.** Records entries for all purchases of merchandise on account.
4. **Cash payments journal** (cheque register).Records entries for all cash paid.
5. **General journal.** Records entries for all transactions that cannot be recorded in any of the special journals.

Cash Receipts Journal

Every transaction entered in the cash receipts journal represents a debit to cash and a credit to each of the accounts in the "account credited" column. In other words, the cash receipts journal is the book of original entry in which **all** receipts of cash are recorded before being posted to the ledger. Special columns are used in the cash receipts journal to save time in posting. Although all transactions entered in this journal are based on receipts of cash, not all cash receipts are necessarily from customers. Thus a one-column journal is not sufficient to accommodate all cash receipts transactions; columns must be provided for cash and the common sources of cash as illustrated below. It should be noted that the format (e.g., location of the Account Title column, number, and nature of columns used) of specialized journals may vary between companies. The formats used in this Appendix for such journals should, therefore, be considered only as examples of what is possible.

CASH RECEIPTS JOURNAL							Page 8
Date 1986	Acct. No.	Account Title	Explanation	Cash Dr.	Sales Discount Dr.	Accounts Receivable Cr.	Sales Cr.	Sundry Cr.
April 7	208	M. L. King	In full	182.28	3.72	186.00		
8	✓	Sales	Per cash register	25.00			25.00	
9	16	Notes Payable	60-day, 12%, First Nat'l	300.00				300.00
16	206	J. Lahey	On account	200.00		200.00		
18	204	A. Pushkin	On account	735.00	15.00	750.00		
19	✓	Sales	Per cash register	185.00			185.00	
				1,627.28	18.72	1,136.00	210.00	300.00
				(1)	(74)	(3)	(20)	✓

The columns in the cash receipts journal indicate that the business receives cash from customers (credit to Accounts Receivable), sells goods for cash (credit Sales), and has miscellaneous sources of cash (credits entered in the Sundry column). Additional specific credit columns are used if business needs demand them. For example, if cash were borrowed from the bank frequently, a separate Notes Payable Credit column could be used.

Posting from Cash Receipts Journal

The posting procedures from a cash receipts journal are relatively simple. The total of the columns for Cash, Sales Discount, Accounts Receivable, and Sales are posted to those general ledger accounts at the end of the month. Amounts entered in the Sundry Credit column must be posted to the general ledger as individual amounts to the accounts named in the Account Title column, because the ledger does not contain a Sundry account and because the purpose of this column in the journal is to provide a place to identify miscellaneous sources of cash receipts. The use of a Sundry column avoids having a column for every different credit account entered in the journal.

In addition to these ledger postings, all amounts in the Accounts Receivable

Credit column are posted to the credit side of the subsidiary ledger account named in the Account Title column. A **subsidiary ledger** is a group of accounts with a common characteristic (e.g., all are accounts receivable) assembled together principally to facilitate the accounting process by freeing the general ledger from details concerning individual balances. Business concerns of medium and large sizes frequently have accounts receivable from thousands of customers and accounts payable with hundreds of creditors. A continuous record of the transactions affecting each customer and each creditor is necessary, and individual accounts with each customer and each creditor are better kept in ledgers separate from the ledger containing other asset, liability, equity, and nominal accounts. Thus the average trading concern has one or more subsidiary ledgers containing nothing but accounts with customers, one or more subsidiary ledgers containing nothing but accounts with creditors, and one general ledger containing the other accounts of the business. The enterprise still maintains a **controlling account** (or control account) in the general ledger that summarizes the results that the customers' ledgers contain in detail. A general ledger is self-balancing (debit balances equal credit balances); subsidiary ledgers are not self-balancing.

The **advantages of subsidiary ledgers** are that they:

1. Permit the transactions affecting a single customer or single creditor to be shown in a single account.
2. Free the general ledger of details relating to accounts receivable and accounts payable.
3. Assist in locating errors in individual accounts by reducing the number of accounts combined in one ledger and by using controlling accounts.
4. Permit the division of labour by separating groups of accounts.

A business may establish and use controlling accounts and subsidiary ledgers for other than accounts receivable and accounts payable (e.g., for inventory; property, plant, and equipment; investments; general expenses; and selling expenses).

In the illustrated Cash Receipts Journal the numbers in the Acct. No. column opposite the names of individual customers refer to the account or page numbers in the customers' subsidiary ledger. Care must be taken to post the amount appearing in the Accounts Receivable Cr. column. These postings are generally made on a daily basis, if possible, so that information on the status of any customer's account is up to date. Because each amount in the Accounts Receivable Cr. column is posted as a part of the column total to the Accounts Receivable (control account) in the general ledger and also to the individual customer account in the subsidiary ledger, each amount may be said to be **double posted.**

Check marks are used in the Acct. No. column opposite the two items titled "Sales." These check marks indicate that these items should not be posted individually to the Sales account because they are posted in total as a credit to the Sales account. Thus, individual postings would merely duplicate the amounts posted to Sales. Also, a check mark below the Sundry Cr. total indicates that the total is not to be posted. Here the individual amounts that make up this total have been posted to the specific general ledger accounts identified in the entry.

The totals of the columns of the Cash Receipts Journal are then posted to the account involved. Cash is posted to account 1 in the general ledger; Sales Discount to account 74; Accounts Receivable to account 3; Sales to account 20; and the Sundry total is not posted, because it was posted on a transaction-by-transaction basis. The total debited to various general ledger accounts equals the total credited.

The Sales Journal

Entries in the sales journal are based on sales invoices or charge sales issued. Remember that the sales journal is used only for sales of merchandise on account. Sales of merchandise for cash are entered in the cash receipts journal.

The sales journal may take a variety of forms, depending on the specific needs of a business. In its simplest form, it has an amount column on the right side of the page, with space for the date, posting reference (Acct. No.), account title, and explanation to the left. If a business concern wishes to accumulate the sales according to the major types of merchandise sold, several amount columns are used, each denoting sales of one type of merchandise.

		SALES JOURNAL			Page 6
Date 1986	Acct. No.	Account Debited	Explanation	Sales Invoice No.	Amount
April 1	208	M. L. King	2/10,n/30	62	186.00
2	202	Randy Ryan	Net	63	910.00
4	206	J. Lahey	2/10,n/30	64	816.00
6	204	A.Pushkin	2/10,n/30	65	750.00
					2,662.00
					3/20

GENERAL LEDGER

Cash No. 1

1986					
March 31	Balance	600.00			
April 30	CR8	1,627.28			

Accounts Receivable No. 3

1986					
March 31	Balance	672.00	April 30	CR8	1,136.00
April 30	S6	2,662.00			

Notes Payable No. 16

			1986		
			April 9	CR8	300.00

Sales No. 20

			1986		
			March 31	Balance	7,826.00
			April 30	S6	2,662.00
			April 30	CR8	210.00

Sales Discount No. 74

1986					
April 30	CR8	18.72			

Accounts Receivable
SUBSIDIARY LEDGER

Randy Ryan					202
1986					
March 31	Balance	520.00			
April 2	S6	910.00			

A. Pushkin					204
1986					
March 31	Balance	30.00	April 18	CR8	750.00
April 6	S6	750.00			

J. Lahey					206
1986					
March 31	Balance	122.00	April 16	CR8	200.00
April 4	S6	816.00			

M. L. King					208
1986					
April 1	S6	186.00	April 7	CR8	186.00

The illustration on page 117 shows the headings employed in a simple sales journal for a business concern that maintains only one Sales account.

Notice that the sales journal follows basically the same procedure for posting as the cash receipt journal. The T accounts following the Sales Journal illustrate how these postings are recorded in the general ledger and the subsidiary ledger.

Purchases Journal and Voucher Register

The purpose of a purchases journal is to record entries for all purchases of merchandise on account. Each invoice received for purchases of merchandise is the basis for an entry in the purchases journal. Transactions for purchases on account are entered in a separate journal in a manner similar to that described for the sales journal. The columns in a purchases journal are similar to those in a sales journal. If the business concern requires an analysis of purchases by product or department, the purchases journal is expanded to contain a separate money column for each product or department. The headings for a purchases journal are shown below.

PURCHASES JOURNAL				
Date 1986	Acct. No.	Name of Creditor	Explanation	Amount
Nov. 1	105	Hendricks Produce	Oct. 30,n/30	765.00

Each entry in this journal is recorded on one line to show each purchase invoice received. The total of the items entered in the purchases journal represents the total purchases on account for the month or other accounting period. At the end of each accounting period, the purchases journal is totalled and posted to the purchases and accounts payable accounts in the general ledger. At frequent intervals during the accounting period, the accounts payable are posted to the individual accounts in the subsidiary ledger.

A **voucher register** is a book of original entry that often replaces the purchases journal. Entries in the voucher register are not limited to purchases of merchandise on account but include purchases of services, supplies, and fixed assets. In other words, credit purchases of all descriptions are properly entered in the voucher register. In addition, when the voucher system operates in its most complete form, a voucher is prepared for every payment, so that cash purchases also are entered in the voucher register. To voucher such a payment, it is necessary only to make out a voucher form giving the facts about the amount to be paid. The types of columns generally employed in a voucher register are illustrated below.

VOUCHER REGISTER

Date 1986	Voucher No.	Creditor	Payment Made Cheque No.	Payment Made Date	Vouchers Payable Cr.	Purchases Dr.	Advertising Dr.	Sundry Items Dr. Account Title	Amount
Jan. 2	200	W. C. Crane	205	Jan. 5	343.00	343.00			
Jan. 3	201	R. M. Higgins	206	Jan. 6	150.00		150.00		
Jan. 4	202	R. Haugen	208	Jan. 9	200.00		200.00		
Jan. 5	203	C. Kroncke	209	Jan. 10	285.00	285.00			

Each voucher is numbered consecutively for control purposes, and the entries are made in numerical order. Also, two columns are provided for Payment Made —one for the number of the cheque used to pay the voucher; and one for the date of payment. Because all entries made in the voucher register are for vouchers to be paid, the single credit money column needed is for Vouchers Payable. Also, because the vouchers are prepared for several different items, we find several money debit columns, as shown in the illustration.

The use of the voucher system assumes that with few exceptions all current obligations are set up as liabilities in the form of vouchers payable, and that cash payments reduce liabilities thus set up. In other words, expressed in general journal form, the voucher system requires the following entries for every payment:

In the Voucher Register		
Expense (or asset)	XXX	
Vouchers Payable		XXX
In the Cash Payments Journal (Cheque Register)		
Vouchers Payable	XXX	
Cash		XXX

Cash Payments Journal

Every transaction entered in the cash payments journal represents a credit to Cash and a debit to each of the accounts named in the Account Debited column. Any transaction that does not stand this test of debits and credits cannot be entered in the cash payments journal. Here is the basic format of a cash payments journal (without a voucher system):

CASH PAYMENTS JOURNAL

Date 1986	Acct. No.	Account Title	Explanation	Cheque No.	Cash Cr.	Purchase Discounts Cr.	Accounts Payable Dr.	Sundry Dr.
April 1	302	Bennett Co.	In full	50	514.50	10.50	525.00	
April 3	65	Advertising	*Star Times*	51	173.00			173.00

The cash payments journal operates in principle much like the cash receipts journal. The totals of the Cash Cr., Purchase Discounts Cr., and Accounts Payable Dr. columns are posted at the end of the month. The items in the Sundry Dr. column are posted as individual items from time to time during the month. The amounts entered in the Accounts Payable Dr. column are posted daily, if possible, as debits to the individual accounts in the accounts payable subsidiary ledger.

Whenever a voucher system is employed, the enterprise replaces accounts payable with vouchers payable and adds another column to its cash payments journal (often called a cheque register in a voucher system) entitled Voucher No. to indicate which voucher is being paid. The column headings are illustrated in the following example:

CASH PAYMENTS JOURNAL
(or cheque register)
Entries for Vouchers Paid

Date 1986	Cheque No.	Payee	Voucher No.	Cash Cr.	Purchase Discounts Cr.	Vouchers Payable Dr.
Jan. 5	205	W. C. Crane	200	336.14	6.86	343.00
Jan. 6	206	R. M. Higgins	201	150.00		150.00
Jan. 8	207	Pappas Supply	195	190.00		190.00
Jan. 9	208	R. Haugen	202	196.00	4.00	200.00
Jan. 10	209	C. Kroncke	203	280.00	5.00	285.00

The totals of the Cash, Purchase Discounts, and Vouchers Payable columns are posted at the end of the month. The amounts entered in the Vouchers Payable column are posted daily, if possible, as debits to the individual accounts in the accounts payable (vouchers payable) subsidiary ledger.

Flexibility in Selection of Journals

In addition to the journals described in this Appendix, other specialized journals are used by various businesses. For example, if a business finds that it has a large volume of returned sales or returned purchases, it could use a sales returns journal or a purchases returns journal. A notes receivable journal could be used by a business that regularly receives notes.

Each business decides on the appropriate journals to use after a study of the transactions in which it regularly engages. Most businesses have a general journal and the cash journals, whereas many trading companies also find a sales and a purchases journal necessary. A cash-and-carry grocery, on the other hand, has no need for a sales journal, because few sales are made on account. Thus, there is no established rule for a business to follow in choosing its books of original entry. It selects the books that result in the greatest convenience and saving of time in processing the many transactions in which it engages. The design of the journals and ledgers is part of the work involved in the design of an accounting system.

Journals Not Always "Books"

Journals are usually called books of original entry, but some "books" of original entry are in reality not books at all; they are merely **files of business papers** preserved in an orderly manner in a filing or binding device.

For example, some concerns use carbon copies of sales invoices as a sales journal. These invoices give the essential facts about the sale, and a copy of each sales invoice for the period provides the data necessary to debit Accounts Receivable and credit Sales for the period. Thus the principle of the sales journal is applied in handling the sales transactions even though a journal is not used.

In a similar manner loose-leaf purchase invoice records, sales returns records, and purchase allowance records, for example, may take this form. Regardless of the arrangement used for the initial recording of transactions, all transactions are ultimately posted to the ledger accounts in accordance with the principles developed in this Appendix for the several journals. These principles are fundamental; they do not change when a different means of recording and processing the data is used, whether it be by loose-leaf records, adding machine tapes, bookkeeping machines, magnetic tapes, diskettes, or other mechanical or electrical devices.

3B

CONVERSION OF CASH BASIS TO ACCRUAL BASIS

As part of Chapter 2's discussion of the principles of revenue realization (recognition) and matching, we briefly contrasted the accrual basis of accounting with the cash basis of accounting. Given the material in Chapter 3, we are now in a better position to elaborate on the differences and understand how one may convert from the cash basis to an accrual basis.

Most companies use the **accrual basis of accounting,** recording revenue when it is realized (earned) and recognizing expenses in the period incurred, without regard to the time of receipt or payment of cash. Some enterprises and the average individual taxpayer, however, use a strict or modified cash basis approach. Under the **strict cash basis,** revenue is recorded only when the cash is received, and expenses are recorded only when the cash is paid. The determination of income on the cash basis rests upon the collection of revenue and the payment of expenses, and the matching principle of accrual accounting is ignored. Consequently, cash basis financial statements do not conform with generally accepted accounting principles.

The **modified cash basis,** a mixture of cash basis and accrual basis, may be used by practising professionals. Expenditures having an economic life of more than one year are capitalized as assets and depreciated or amortized over future years. Prepaid expenses and accrued expenses are not treated in a consistent manner.

Prepayments of expenses are deferred and deducted in the year to which they apply, while expenses paid after the year of incurrence (accrued expenses) are deducted only in the year paid. Revenue is reported in the year of receipt.

Not infrequently an accountant is required to convert a cash basis set of financial statements to the accrual basis for presentation and interpretation to a banker or for audit by an independent public accountant. The following simplified diagram illustrates how cash basis financial data are converted to the accrual basis through various types of adjusting items.

Cash Basis ——————————————————————→ Accrual Basis		
Receipts	− Beginning accounts receivable + Ending accounts receivable	= Net sales
Rent receipts	+ Beginning unearned rent revenue − Ending unearned rent revenue − Beginning rent revenue receivable + Ending rent revenue receivable	= Rent revenue
Payment for goods	+ Beginning inventory − Ending inventory − Beginning accounts payable + Ending accounts payable	= Cost of goods sold
Payments for expenses	+ Beginning prepaid expenses − Ending prepaid expenses − Beginning accrued expenses + Ending accrued expenses	= Operating expenses (except depreciation and similar write-offs)
Payments for property, plant, and equipment	− Cash payments for property, plant, and equipment + Periodic write-off of the asset cost through some formula(s)	= Depreciation or amortization expense

FIGURE 3B-1   Conversion of Cash Basis to Accrual Basis

As indicated in Figure 3B-1, cash receipts are converted to **net sales** by subtracting beginning accounts receivable and adding ending accounts receivable. By expanding the formula to include all the accounts related to sales, cash receipts can be converted to **gross sales:**

Cash receipts from customers		XXX
Plus: Cash discounts	XX	
Sales returns and allowances	XX	
Accounts written off	XX	
Ending accounts receivable	XX	XX
		XXX
Less: Beginning accounts receivable		XX
Gross sales		XXX

Cash receipts from customers can be converted to net sales also merely by adding or subtracting the change in the balance of accounts receivable from the beginning to the end of the year:

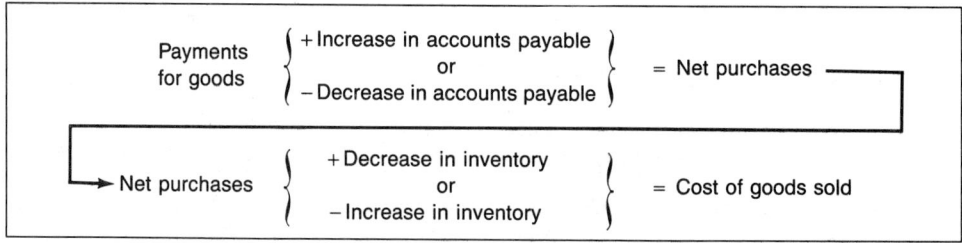

The example in Figure 3B-1 regarding rent illustrates the procedure that can be used to convert other revenue sources (interest is another example) from a cash to accrual basis.

Similarly, cash payments for goods can be converted to cost of goods sold by adding or deducting the change from the beginning to the end of the year in the accounts payable balance and in the inventory balance as follows:

Figure 3B-1 also presents the procedure for the conversion of cash payments for all expenses to the accrual basis operating expenses in the aggregate and, therefore, involves both prepaid and accrued expenses in the conversion. Generally, each expense item is affected by a related accrual or a related prepayment, but not both. For example, the conversion of wages expense and the conversion of insurance expense are illustrated separately below.

Illustration Conversion of cash basis income statement data to the accrual basis will be illustrated for Olivia Newton, D.D.S., a dentist who keeps her accounting records on a cash basis. During 1986, Dr. Newton collected $80,000 from her patients and paid $30,000 for operating expenses, resulting in a cash basis net income of $50,000. At January 1 and December 31, 1986, she has fees receivable, unearned fees, accrued expenses, and prepaid expenses as follows:

	January 1, 1986	December 31, 1986
Fees receivable	$12,000	$5,000
Unearned fees	-0-	1,000
Accrued expenses	3,800	6,800
Prepaid expenses	2,000	3,000

Restatement of Olivia Newton's income statement data is presented in work sheet form below:

Olivia Newton, D.D.S
Conversion of Income Statement from Cash Basis to Accrual Basis
For the Year 1986

	Cash Basis	Adjustments Add	Adjustments Deduct	Accrual Basis
Revenue from fees:	$80,000			
– Fees receivable, Jan. 1			$12,000	
+ Fees receivable, Dec. 31		$5,000		
– Unearned fees, Dec. 31			1,000	
Restated				$72,000
Operating expenses:	30,000			
– Accrued expenses, Jan. 1			3,800	
+ Accrued expenses, Dec. 31		6,800		
+ Prepaid expenses, Jan. 1		2,000		
– Prepaid expenses, Dec. 31			3,000	
Restated				32,000
Net income—cash basis	$50,000			
Net income—accrual basis				$40,000

The computation of income on the cash basis can result in a material misstatement when there is a lag in time between the exchange transactions and the related cash receipt or disbursement transactions.

Note: All asterisked Questions, Cases, Exercises, or Problems relate to material in an Appendix.

QUESTIONS

1. Why are revenue and expense accounts called temporary or nominal accounts?
2. Do the following events represent business transactions? Explain your answer in each case.
   (a) Merchandise is ordered for delivery next month.
   (b) A truck is purchased on account.
   (c) A customer returns merchandise and is given credit on account.
   (d) A prospective employee is interviewed.
   (e) The owner of the business withdraws cash from the business for personal use.
3. Give an example of a transaction that results in:
   (a) A decrease in one asset and an increase in another asset.
   (b) A decrease in an asset and a decrease in a liability.
   (c) A decrease in one liability and an increase in another liability.
4. Name the accounts debited and credited for each of the following transactions:
   (a) Purchase of office supplies on account.
   (b) Purchase of 40 L of gasoline for the delivery truck.
   (c) Billing a customer for work done.
   (d) Receipt of cash from customer on account.
5. Is it necessary that a trial balance be taken periodically? What purpose does it serve?

6. Indicate whether each of the items below is a real or nominal account and whether it appears in the balance sheet or the income statement.
   (a) Furniture.
   (b) Revenue from Services.
   (c) Office Salaries.
   (d) Supplies on Hand.
   (e) Prepaid Insurance Expense.
   (f) Wages Payable.
   (g) Merchandise Inventory (ending balance).
   (h) Accumulated Depreciation.

7. Employees are paid every Saturday. If a balance sheet is prepared on Wednesday, December 31, what does the amount of wages earned during the first 3 days of the week (December 29, 30, 31) represent? Explain.

8. Why is the Purchases account debited both when merchandise is purchased for cash and when it is purchased on account? Why is the inventory amount as determined at the end of the fiscal period under a periodic inventory system deducted from the cost of goods available for sale?

9. What is the purpose of the Cost of Goods Sold account? (Assume a periodic inventory system.)

10. Under a periodic system, is the amount shown for Inventory the same in a trial balance taken before closing as it is in a trial balance taken after closing? Why?

11. If the cost of a new typewriter ($900) purchased for office use were recorded as a debit to Purchases, what would be the effect of the error on the balance sheet and income statement in the period in which the error was made?

12. What differences are there between the trial balance before closing and the trial balance after closing with respect to the following?
    (a) Revenue accounts.
    (b) Retained earnings account.
    (c) Cash.
    (d) Expense accounts.
    (e) Accounts payable.

13. What are "adjusting entries" and why are they necessary?

14. What are "closing entries" and why are they necessary?

15. What are "reversing entries" and why are they necessary?

*16. Why would a company use several journals instead of only a general journal? How would the company determine which special journals it should use?

*17. When the special journals illustrated in Appendix 3A are used, how many postings are made to the Cash account? Why?

*18. For each of the following transactions name the book of original entry and the accounts to be debited and credited, assuming that the 5 journals discussed in Appendix 3A are used:
     (a) Sale of merchandise for cash.
     (b) Purchase of office equipment on account.
     (c) Payment of cash to a creditor, no discount.
     (d) Receipt of cash from a customer on account.
     (e) Loan from bank on a promissory note; interest payable at maturity date.
     (f) Purchase of merchandise on account (periodic inventory system).
     (g) Return of damaged merchandise to a supplier.

*19. What is a controlling account? What is its relationship to a subsidiary ledger?

*20. How does the use of controlling accounts and subsidiary ledgers affect (a) the taking of a trial balance, (b) the appearance of the trial balance, and (c) the equality of debits and credits in the trial balance?

*21. Differentiate between a purchase order, a purchase invoice, a voucher, and a cheque. What journal entry, if any, generally results from each of these documents? (Assume a periodic inventory system.)

*22. List two types of transactions that would receive different accounting treatment using (a) a strict cash basis accounting, and (b) a modified cash basis.

*23. Why are beginning accrued wages subtracted from, and ending accrued wages added to, wages paid during the year when wages expense for the year is computed?

EXERCISES

E3-1 The trial balance of the Wirlwind Company does not balance.

Wirlwind Co.
TRIAL BALANCE
April 30

Cash	$ 5,902	
Accounts Receivable	6,300	
Supplies on Hand	1,600	
Furniture and Equipment	5,200	
Accounts Payable		$ 4,500
Wirlwind Capital		10,000
Revenue from Fees		4,700
Office Expenses	1,980	
	$20,982	$19,200

An examination of the ledger shows these errors.

1. Cash received from a customer on account was recorded (both debit and credit) as $1,400 instead of $1,120.
2. The purchase on account of a typewriter costing $780 was recorded as a debit to Office Expenses and a credit to Accounts Payable.
3. Services were performed on account for a client; $1,780 was debited to Accounts Receivable, and Revenue from Fees was credited for $178.
4. A payment of $80 for telephone charges was entered as a debit to Office Expenses and a debit to Cash.
5. The Revenue from Fees account was totalled at $4,700 instead of $4,720.

Instructions

From this information prepare a corrected trial balance.

E3-2 Information concerning the first month of operations of Linda Lahey Boutique is presented below:

Transportation–in	$ 900
Total purchases on account	18,000
Purchase returns on account	720
Transportation–out	540
Total recorded as cash purchases	8,280
Purchase allowances on account	1,260
Inventory at the end of the month	3,600
Sales discounts	585
Refunds for defective items purchased for cash	378
Error made by bookkeeper debiting Supplies Expense, when in reality the item was a cash purchase of merchandise	576

Instructions

(a) Prepare a cost of goods sold T account.
(b) Prepare the cost of goods sold section of the income statement.
(c) Indicate in which section of the income statement items in this exercise that were not used in the cost of goods sold section should appear.

E3-3 When the accounts of S. Pritchett Donut Shoppe are examined, the adjusting data listed below are uncovered on December 31, the end of an annual fiscal period.

1. The unexpired insurance account shows a debit of $1,800, representing the cost of a 3-year fire insurance policy dated September 1 of the current year.

2. On November 1, Rental Revenue was credited for $1,200, representing revenue from a subrental for a 3-month period beginning on that date.

3. Purchase of advertising materials for $800 during the year was recorded in the advertising expense account. On December 31, advertising materials of $120 are on hand.

4. Interest of $180 has accrued on notes payable.

Instructions

Prepare in general journal form: (a) the adjusting entry for each item; (b) the reversing entry for each item where appropriate.

*E3-4 Presented below are various transactions of the Spanish Company.

Sept. 1 Purchases office equipment for cash, $706.

3 Sells merchandise on account to S. Adams, $1,063. f.o.b. shipping point.

3 Pays freight on sale to S. Adams, $56. By agreement, Adams will reimburse us.

4 Receives a refund of $52 on office equipment because of a difference in the specifications of equipment ordered and received.

7 Purchases merchandise on account from R. Barnes, $1,500, 2/10, n/30, f.o.b. destination (record at gross amount).

9 R. Barnes has paid freight on shipment, $44.

13 Receives a cheque in full payment of account from S. Adams.

18 Because of increased business, Spanish Company purchases additional office equipment at a price of $600, giving in exchange its own no-par shares having a total market price of $310, with the balance payable in 30 days.

21 Cash sales of $6,250 are made.

25 An invoice for heat, light, and water of $50 is received.

27 Pays R. Barnes the full amount due.

29 Office salaries of $438 and the utilities bill received on September 25 are paid.

Instructions

Prepare general journal entries for each transaction and indicate in which journal they normally are recorded. (Spanish Company uses a periodic inventory system.)

*E3-5 The general ledger of the Watts Company contains the following Accounts Payable control account. Also shown is the related subsidiary ledger.

Accounts Payable

Feb. 28	General journal	13,500	Feb.	1	Balance	37,538
28		33,450		5	General journal	180
				11	General journal	53
				28	Cash receipts	300
				28	General journal	990
				28	Purchases	21,750

Creditor's Ledger

French	Greek	Elliott
Balance 4,783	Balance 8,417	Balance ?

Instructions

For the data above:

(a) Indicate the missing posting reference in the control account and the missing ending balance in the subsidiary ledger.

(b) Indicate the amounts in the control account that were double posted.

(c) What is meant by "double posting"? (Explain in full.)

*E3-6 Here are selected records and documents for the voucher system of the John Penkowski Company.

VOUCHER REGISTER

Date 1986	Vou. No.	Creditor	Cheque No.	Date	Vouchers Payable Cr.	Purchases Dr.	Account Title	Amount
			Payment Made				Sundry Items Dr.	
2/5	300	Russell Supply	113	2/7	900		Supplies	900
2/9	301	Dick & Jane	114	2/26	2,340	2,340		
2/15	302	Betts & Bore	115	2/26	5,220	5,220		
2/17	303	Capps Co.	117	2/28	3,150		Furniture	3,150
2/20	304	*Daily Courier*			450		Advertising	450
2/24	305	K. Comfort			63		Miscellaneous expenses	63
2/25	306	Dick & Jane			1,980	1,980		
2/28	307	Otey Realty	116	2/28	2,430		Rent	2,430

UNPAID VOUCHERS

Voucher No. 304	Voucher No. 305
Date: 2/20 To: *Daily Courier*	Date: 2/24 To: K. Comfort
Amount $450	Amount $63
Acct. Dr. Advertising	Acct. Dr. Miscellaneous Expenses
Voucher No. 301	Voucher No. 299
Date: 2/9 To: Dick & Jane	Date: 2/3 To: Jeri Delaney
Amount $2,340	Amount $423
Acct. Dr. Purchases	Acct. Dr. Repair Expenses

GENERAL LEDGER
Vouchers Payable

Feb. 28	CP	13,680	Feb. 28	VR	16,533

Instructions

(a) Determine the balance in the control account.

(b) Try to prove the vouchers payable account by reconciling the voucher file with the detail in the register.

(c) Determine the causes of any lack of agreement between the control account and subsidiary records. (Label all amounts.)

(d) What is the correct vouchers payable balance?

*E3-7 Cricket Company maintains its books on the accrual basis. The company reported insurance expense of $17,450 in its 1986 income statement. Prepaid insurance at December 31, 1986, amounted to $3,220; cash paid for insurance during the year 1986 totalled $19,800. There was no accrued insurance expense either at the beginning or at the end of 1986.

Instructions

What was the amount, if any, of prepaid insurance at January 1, 1986? Show computations.

*E3-8 Needles Corporation, which uses the accrual basis of accounting, reported interest expense of $90,280 in its 1986 income statement. Accrued interest at December 31, 1986, amounted to $14,710; cash paid for interest during 1986 totalled $84,400. There was no prepaid interest either at the beginning or at the end of 1986.

Instructions

What was the amount, if any, of accrued interest at January 1, 1986? Show computations.

*E3-9 Chip Dip Corp. maintains its financial records on the cash basis of accounting. Interested in securing a long-term loan from its regular bank, Chip Dip Corp. requests you to convert its cash basis income statement data to the accrual basis. You are provided with the following summarized data covering 1984, 1985, and 1986.

	1984	1985	1986
Cash receipts from sales:			
On 1984 sales	$240,000	$ 45,000	$15,000
On 1985 sales	-0-	270,000	90,000
Cash payments for expenses:			
On 1984 expenses	150,000	21,000	9,000
On 1985 expenses	180,000[1]	150,000	42,000
On 1986 expenses		15,000[2]	

[1]Prepayments of 1985 expense.
[2]Prepayments of 1986 expense.

Instructions

(a) Using the data above, prepare abbreviated income statements for the years 1984 and 1985 on the cash basis.

(b) Using the data above, prepare abbreviated income statements for the years 1984 and 1985 on the accrual basis.

PROBLEMS

P3-1 The accounts listed appeared in the December 31 trial balance of the Broadway Theater.

Equipment	$180,000	
Accumulated Depreciation of Equipment		$ 54,000
Notes Payable		72,000
Revenue from Admissions		378,000
Revenue from Concessions		36,000
Advertising Expense	13,680	
Salaries Expense	57,600	
Interest Expense	1,080	

Instructions

(a) From the account balances listed and the information given below, prepare the adjusting entries necessary on December 31.

1. The equipment has an estimated life of 20 years and a trade-in value of $36,000 at the end of that time. (Use straight-line method.)
2. The note payable is a 90-date note given to the bank October 22 and bearing interest at 12%. (Use a 360-day-year to calculate interest.)
3. In December 2,000 coupon admission books were sold at $18 each; they can be used for admission any time after January 1.

4. The concession stand is operated by a concessionaire who pays 10% of gross receipts for the privilege of selling popcorn, candy, and soft drinks in the lobby. Sales for December were $21,600, and the 10% due for December has not yet been received or entered.
5. Advertising expense paid in advance, $900.
6. Salaries accrued but unpaid, $3,100.

(b) What amounts should be shown for each of the following on the income statement for the year.

1. Interest expense.
2. Revenue from admissions.
3. Revenue from concessions.
4. Advertising expense.
5. Salaries expense.

P3-2 Presented below are the trial balance and the other information related to I. M. Amazing, a consulting engineer.

I. M. Amazing, Consulting Engineer
TRIAL BALANCE
December 31, 1986

Cash	$ 37,800	
Accounts Receivable	13,100	
Allowance for Doubtful Accounts		$ 972
Engineering Supplies Inventory	1,980	
Unexpired Insurance	666	
Furniture and Equipment	24,660	
Accumulated Depreciation of Furniture and Equipment		3,960
Notes Payable		5,400
I. M. Amazing, Capital		18,914
Revenue from Consulting Fees		90,000
Rent Expense	9,360	
Office Salaries	29,880	
Heat, Light, and Water	1,080	
Miscellaneous Office Expense	720	
	$119,246	$119,246

1. Fees received in advance from clients, $5,400.
2. Services performed for clients that were not recorded by December 31, $3,600.
3. The Allowance for Doubtful Accounts account should be adjusted to 7% of the accounts receivable balance (adjusted).
4. Insurance expired during the year, $234.
5. Furniture and equipment is being depreciated at 10% of cost per year.
6. I. M. Amazing gave the bank a 90-day, 12% note for $5,400 on December 1, 1986.
7. Rent of the building is $720 per month. The rent for 1986 has been paid, as has that for January 1987.
8. Office salaries earned but unpaid December 31, 1986, $1,080.

Instructions

(a) From the trial balance and other information given, prepare adjusting entries as of December 31, 1986.
(b) Prepare an income statement for 1986, a balance sheet, and a statement of capital. I. M. Amazing withdrew $18,000 cash for personal use during the year.

P3-3 Following is the December 31 trial balance of Infocus TV Store.

Infocus TV Store
TRIAL BALANCE
December 31

Cash	$ 10,000	
Accounts Receivable	56,000	
Allowance for Doubtful Accounts		$ 4,000
Inventory, January 1	70,000	
Furniture and Equipment	60,000	
Accumulated Depreciation of Furniture and Equipment		24,000
Prepaid Insurance	3,600	
Notes Payable		20,000
Infocus, Capital		60,000
Sales		600,000
Purchases	400,000	
Sales Salaries	40,000	
Advertising	2,400	
Administrative Salaries	60,000	
Office Expenses	6,000	
	$708,000	$708,000

Instructions

(a)   Construct T accounts and enter the balances shown.

(b)   Prepare adjusting journal entries for the following and post to the T accounts. (The books are closed yearly on December 31.)

1.   Adjust the Allowance for Doubtful Accounts to 10% of the accounts receivable.
2.   Furniture and equipment is depreciated at 10% of cost per year.
3.   Insurance expired during the year, $1,600.
4.   Interest accrued on notes payable, $800.
5.   Sales salaries earned but not paid, $1,200.
6.   Advertising paid in advance, $600.
7.   Office supplies on hand, $1,000, charged to Office Expenses when purchased.

(c)   Prepare closing entries and post to the accounts. The inventory on December 31 was $90,000.

P3-4   Listed below are the transactions of E. Z. Pull, D.D.S., for the month of September.

Sept. 1   E. Z. Pull begins practice as a dentist and invests $12,000 cash.
       2   Purchases furniture and dental equipment on account from Meyer Co. for $17,280.
       4   Pays rent for office space, $540 for the month.
       4   Employs a receptionist.
       5   Purchases dental supplies for cash, $856.
       8   Receives cash of $306 from patients.
      10   Pays miscellaneous office expenses, $126.
      14   Bills patients $1,620 for services performed.
      18   Pays Meyer Co. on account, $3,600.
      19   Withdraws $2,000 cash from the business for personal use.
      20   Receives $720 from patients on account.
      25   Bills patients $1,530 for services performed.
      30   Pays the following expenses in cash: office salaries, $900; miscellaneous office expenses, $72.
      30   Dental supplies used during September, $150.

Instructions

(a) Enter the transactions shown above in appropriate ledger accounts. Allow 10 lines for the Cash account and 5 lines for each of the other accounts needed. Record depreciation using an 8-year life on the furniture and equipment, the straight-line method, and no salvage value.

(b) Take a trial balance.

(c) Prepare an income statement, a balance sheet, and a statement of capital.

(d) Close the ledger.

(e) Take a post-closing trial balance.

P3-5 The balance sheet of Remmers Company as of December 31, 1985, is presented below.

Remmers Company
BALANCE SHEET
as of December 31, 1985

Assets		Liabilities and Owner's Equity	
Cash	$ 3,900	Accounts payable	$ 2,325
Accounts receivable	4,395	Notes payable	3,000
Inventory	3,000	Total liabilities	$ 5,325
Office equipment	3,800		
Accumulated depreciation—office equip.	(975)		
Furniture and fixtures	6,300		
Accumulated depreciation—furniture and fixtures	(1,500)	Remmers, capital	13,595
Total assets	$18,920	Total liabilities and capital	$18,920

The following transactions occurred during the month of January, 1986.

Jan. 2 Receives payment of $1,050 on accounts receivable.

3 Purchases merchandise on account from R. Walsh for $1,875, 2/30, n/60, f.o.b. shipping point. (Record at gross amount.)

4 Receives an invoice from *Tops*, a trade magazine, for advertising, $24.

4 Sells merchandise on account to Marvin Roy for $825, 2/10, n/30, f.o.b. shipping point.

4 Makes a cash sale to Phil Inc. for $1,613.

6 Sends a letter to R. Walsh regarding a slight defect in 1 item of merchandise received.

9 Purchases merchandise on account from Heather's Novelty Company, $563.

11 Pays freight on merchandise received from R. Walsh, $53.

11 Receives a credit memo from R. Walsh granting an allowance of $18 on defective merchandise. (See January 6.)

15 Receives $500 on account from Marvin Roy.

19 Sells merchandise on account to R. Urban, $713, 2/10, n/30.

21 Pays display clerk's salary of $488.

25 Sells merchandise for cash, $1,402.

27 Purchases office equipment on account, $750. (Begin depreciating in February.)

29 Pays R. Walsh the full amount due.

30 Receives a note from R. Urban in full amount of his account.

31 A count of the inventory on hand reveals $2,510 of salable merchandise.

Instructions

(a) Open ledger accounts at January 1, 1986 (T account format).

(b) Enter the transactions into ledger accounts.

(c) Take a trial balance and adjust for depreciation; use 10-year life, straight-line method, and no salvage for all long-term assets.

(d) Prepare a balance sheet and income statement.

(e) Close the ledger.

(f) Take a post-closing trial balance.

P3-6 On January 1, 1986, after reversing entries were made, the trial balance of Scott Grometer Co. contained the following account balances, all of which relate to prepaid or unearned items.

Interest Expense	$ 100	
Prepaid Insurance		
($480 was paid Oct. 1, 1985		
for one year's premium)	360	
Subscription Revenue		$2,200
Newsprint on Hand		
(Balance was $8,500 before adjusting)	4,400	
Stationery and Postage Expense	1,220	
Unearned Advertising Revenue		
(Balance was $36,000 before		
adjusting)		6,000

Instructions

(a) Give the December 31, 1985, adjusting entry that involved each of the accounts shown.

(b) Which of the adjusting entries shown in (a) were probably reversed on January 1, 1986?

P3-7 Presented below is information related to Noel Batten, realtor, at the close of the fiscal year ending December 31.

1. He had paid the local newspaper $108 for an advertisement to be run in January of the next year, charging it to Advertising Expense.

2. On October 31 he had his 3-month note for $3,000 discounted at the bank at 12% and received cash for the proceeds. (Interest Expense was debited for 3 months' interest on October 31.)

3. Salaries and wages due and unpaid December 31: sales, $950; office clerks, $750.

4. Interest accrued to date on a note receivable held by the company, $150.

5. Estimated loss on bad debts, $1,120 for the period.

6. Stamps and stationery on hand, $180, charged to Stationery and Postage Expense account when purchased.

7. He has not yet paid the December rent on the building his business occupies, $800.

8. Insurance paid November 1 for 1 year, $648, charged to Unexpired Insurance when paid.

9. Property taxes accrued, $1,400.

10. On December 1 he gave Carol & Company his 60-day, 12% note for $5,000 on account.

11. On October 31 he received $2,040 from Eric Grinter in payment of 6 months' rent for office space occupied by him in the building and credited Unearned Rent Revenue.

12. On September 1 he paid 6 months' rent in advance on a warehouse, $9,000, and debited Prepaid Rent Expense.

13. The bill from the City Light & Power Company for December has been received but not yet entered or paid, $470.

14. Estimated depreciation on furniture and equipment, $1,150.

Instructions

    (a)   Prepare adjusting entries as of December 31.

    (b)   List the numbers of the entries that could be reversed.

P3-8 The following list of accounts and their balances represent the unadjusted trial balance of Omeomy Company at December 31, 1986.

	Dr.	Cr.
Cash	$ 83,124	
Accounts Receivable	106,200	
Allowance for Doubtful Accounts		$ 3,060
Merchandise Inventory	59,400	
Prepaid Insurance	2,232	
Investment in India Inc. Bonds	22,000	
Land	27,000	
Building	121,500	
Accumulated Depreciation—Building		13,500
Equipment	32,400	
Accumulated Depreciation—Equipment		5,400
Goodwill	30,600	
Accounts Payable		117,000
Bonds Payable (20-year, 6%)		180,000
Discount on Bonds Payable	14,400	
Common Stock		162,000
Retained Earnings		36,211
Sales		180,000
Rental Revenue		4,860
Advertising Expense	27,000	
Supplies Expense	10,800	
Purchases	97,200	
Purchase Discounts		1,800
Office Salary Expense	18,900	
Sales Salary Expense	42,300	
Interest Expense	8,775	
	$703,831	$703,831

Additional information:

1.   Actual advertising costs amounted to $1,800 per month. The company has already paid for advertisements in *People Magazine* for the first quarter of 1987.

2.   The building was purchased and occupied January 1, 1984, with an estimated life of 18 years. (The company uses straight-line depreciation.)

3.   Prepaid insurance contains the premium costs of 2 policies: Policy A, cost of $756, 1-year term taken out on Sept. 1, 1985; Policy B, cost of $1,728, 3-year term taken out on April 1, 1986.

4.   A portion of their building has been converted into a snack bar that has been rented to the Yummy Tummy Food Corp. since July 1, 1985, at a rate of $3,240 per year payable each July 1.

5.   One of the company's customers declared bankruptcy December 30, 1986, and it has been definitely established that the $2,700 due from him will never be collected. This fact has not been recorded. Omeomy estimates that 4% of the Accounts Receivable balance on December 31, 1986, will become uncollectible.

6.   Nine hundred dollars, which was advanced to a salesperson on December 31, 1986, was charged to Sales Salary Expense. Sales salaries are paid on the 1st and 16th of each month for the following half month.

7.   When the company purchased a competing firm on July 1, 1984, it acquired goodwill in the amount of $36,000, which is being amortized.

8. On October 1, 1982, Omeomy issued 180 $1,000 bonds at 90% of par value. Interest payments are made semiannually on March 31 and September 30. (Use straight-line method for amortization of the bond discount and presume that amortization is recorded at interest dates and year end.)

9. On August 1, 1986, Omeomy purchased 22 $1,000, 10% bonds maturing on August 31, 1990, at par value. Interest payment dates are July 31 and January 31.

10. Inventory on hand at December 31, 1986, was $82,800 per a physical inventory. Record the adjustment for inventory by using a Cost of Goods Sold account.

Instructions

(a) Prepare adjusting and correcting entries in general journal form using the information above.

(b) Indicate which of the adjusting entries will probably be reversed.

P3-9 The following list of accounts and their balances represents the unadjusted trial balance of Rita Co. at December 31, 1986:

	Dr.	Cr.
Cash	$ 4,000	
Accounts Receivable	46,000	
Allowance for Doubtful Accounts		$ 720
Inventory	55,000	
Prepaid Insurance	2,760	
Prepaid Rent	14,400	
Investment in Zorp. Corp. Bonds	10,000	
Property, Plant, and Equipment	104,000	
Accumulated Depreciation		15,600
Accounts Payable		10,930
Bonds Payable		50,000
Premium on Bonds Payable		950
Capital Stock		100,000
Retained Earnings		51,600
Sales		216,000
Rent Revenue		7,200
Purchases	170,000	
Purchase Discounts		3,400
Transportation–out	10,000	
Transportation–in	4,400	
Salaries and Wages	32,000	
Interest Expense	2,950	
Miscellaneous Expense	890	
	$456,400	$456,400

Additional data:

1. On November 1, 1986, Rita received $7,200 rent from its lessee for an 18-month lease beginning on that date, crediting Rent Revenue.

2. Rita estimates that 4% of the Accounts Receivable balances on December 31, 1986, will become uncollectible. On December 28, 1986, the bookkeeper incorrectly credited Sales for a receipt on account in the amount of $1,000. This error had not yet been corrected on December 31.

3. Per a physical inventory, inventory on hand at December 31, 1986, was $54,000. Record the adjusting entry for inventory by using a Cost of Goods Sold account.

4. Prepaid insurance contains the premium costs of 2 policies: Policy A, cost of $840, 1-year term, taken out on September 1, 1986; Policy B, cost of $1,920, 3-year term, taken out on April 1, 1986.

5. The regular rate of depreciation is 10% of cost per year. Acquisitions and retirements during a year are depreciated at half this rate. There were no retirements during the year. On December 31, 1985, the balance of Property, Plant, and Equipment was $96,000.

6. On April 1, 1986, Rita issued 50 $1,000, 12% bonds, maturing on April 1, 1996, at 102% of par value. Interest payment dates are April 1 and October 1.

7. On August 1, 1986, Rita purchased 10 $1,000, 10% Zorp. Corp. bonds, maturing on July 31, 1988, at par value. Interest payment dates are July 31 and January 31.

8. On May 30, 1986, Rita rented warehouse space for $600 per month, paying $14,400 in advance, debiting Prepaid Rent.

Instructions

(a) Prepare adjusting and correcting entries in general journal form using the information above.

(b) Indicate the adjusting entries that could be reversed.

P3-10 Following is the trial balance of the Exclusive Country Club as of December 31. The books are closed annually on December 31.

Exclusive Country Club
TRIAL BALANCE
December 31

Cash	$ 16,000	
Dues Receivable	13,200	
Allowance for Doubtful Accounts		$ 1,200
Land	400,000	
Buildings	120,000	
Accumulated Depreciation of Buildings		40,000
Equipment	160,000	
Accumulated Depreciation of Equipment		70,000
Unexpired Insurance	6,000	
Capital		562,800
Dues Revenue		180,000
Revenue from Green Fees		6,000
Rent Revenue		13,200
Utilities Expense	54,000	
Salaries Expense	80,000	
Maintenance	24,000	
	$873,200	$873,200

Instructions

(a) Enter the balances in ledger accounts. Allow 5 lines for each account.

(b) From the trial balance and the information given below, prepare adjusting entries and post to the ledger accounts.

1. The buildings have an estimated life of 40 years with no salvage value (straight-line method).
2. The equipment is depreciated at 10% of cost per year.
3. Insurance expired during the year, $2,500.
4. The rent revenue represents the amount received for 11 months for dining facilities. The December rent has not yet been received.
5. It is estimated that 20% of the dues receivable will be uncollectible.
6. Salaries earned but not paid by December 31, $2,400.
7. Dues paid in advance by members, $7,500.

(c) Prepare an adjusted trial balance.

(d) Prepare closing entries and post.

(e)   Prepare reversing entries and post.

(f)   Prepare a trial balance after the reversing entries.

P3-11   Presented below is the trial balance for Tom Brown, proprietor.

<table>
<tr><td colspan="3" align="center">Tom Brown
TRIAL BALANCE
December 31, 1986</td></tr>
<tr><td>Cash</td><td>$ 11,100</td><td></td></tr>
<tr><td>Accounts Receivable</td><td>64,800</td><td></td></tr>
<tr><td>Allowance for Doubtful Accounts</td><td></td><td>$ 2,000</td></tr>
<tr><td>Inventory, January 1</td><td>76,000</td><td></td></tr>
<tr><td>Land</td><td>27,000</td><td></td></tr>
<tr><td>Building</td><td>90,000</td><td></td></tr>
<tr><td>Accumulated Depreciation of Building</td><td></td><td>14,400</td></tr>
<tr><td>Furniture and Fixtures</td><td>17,300</td><td></td></tr>
<tr><td>Accumulated Depreciation of Furniture
   and Fixtures</td><td></td><td>5,700</td></tr>
<tr><td>Unexpired Insurance</td><td>7,800</td><td></td></tr>
<tr><td>Accounts Payable</td><td></td><td>32,400</td></tr>
<tr><td>Notes Payable</td><td></td><td>27,000</td></tr>
<tr><td>Mortgage Payable</td><td></td><td>36,000</td></tr>
<tr><td>Tom Brown, Capital</td><td></td><td>79,380</td></tr>
<tr><td>Sales</td><td></td><td>720,000</td></tr>
<tr><td>Sales Returns and Allowances</td><td>3,600</td><td></td></tr>
<tr><td>Purchases</td><td>558,000</td><td></td></tr>
<tr><td>Purchase Returns and Allowances</td><td></td><td>5,900</td></tr>
<tr><td>Transportation–in</td><td>14,800</td><td></td></tr>
<tr><td>Sales Salaries</td><td>21,600</td><td></td></tr>
<tr><td>Advertising</td><td>4,700</td><td></td></tr>
<tr><td>Salaries, Office and General</td><td>16,200</td><td></td></tr>
<tr><td>Heat, Light, and Water</td><td>4,300</td><td></td></tr>
<tr><td>Telephone and Telegraph</td><td>1,600</td><td></td></tr>
<tr><td>Miscellaneous Office Expenses</td><td>2,000</td><td></td></tr>
<tr><td>Purchase Discounts</td><td></td><td>9,600</td></tr>
<tr><td>Sales Discount</td><td>9,500</td><td></td></tr>
<tr><td>Interest Expense</td><td>2,080</td><td></td></tr>
<tr><td></td><td>$932,380</td><td>$932,380</td></tr>
</table>

Instructions

(a)   Copy the trial balance above in the first two columns of a 10-column work sheet.

(b)   Prepare adjusting entries in journal form from the following information. (The fiscal year ends December 31.)

1.   Estimated bad debts, one-quarter of 1% of sales less returns and allowances.
2.   Depreciation on building, 2% of cost per year; on furniture and fixtures, 10% of cost per year.
3.   Insurance expired during the year, $3,500.
4.   Interest at 12% is payable on the mortgage on January 1 of each year.
5.   Sales salaries accrued, December 31, $2,000.
6.   Advertising expenses paid in advance, $700.
7.   Office supplies on hand December 31, $2,000. (Charged to Miscellaneous Office Expenses when purchased.)
8.   Interest accrued on notes payable December 31, $1,500.

(c)   Transfer the adjusting entries to the work sheet and complete it. Merchandise inventory on hand December 31, $60,000.

(d) Prepare an income statement, a balance sheet, and a statement of proprietor's capital.

(e) Prepare closing journal entries.

(f) Indicate the adjusting entries that could be reversed.

P3-12 The Saddle Up Company Ltd. closes its books only once a year on December 31 but prepares monthly financial statements by estimating month-end inventories and by using work sheets.

The company's unadjusted trial balance on January 31, 1986, is presented below. Selling Expenses and Administrative Expenses are controlling accounts.

Saddle Up Company Ltd.		
TRIAL BALANCE		
January 31, 1986		
Cash	$ 1,150	
Accounts Receivable	10,000	
Notes Receivable	2,600	
Allowance for Doubtful Accounts		$ 1,250
Inventory, Jan. I, 1986	15,000	
Furniture and Fixtures	25,000	
Accumulated Depreciation of Furniture and Fixtures		5,000
Unexpired Insurance	600	
Supplies on Hand	1,050	
Accounts Payable		6,000
Notes Payable		5,000
Common Shares		20,000
Retained Earnings		10,125
Sales		101,600
Sales Returns and Allowances	1,600	
Purchases	70,000	
Transportation–in	2,000	
Selling Expenses	11,000	
Administrative Expenses	9,000	
Interest Revenue		75
Interest Expense	50	
	$149,050	$149,050

Instructions

(a) Copy the trial balance in the first 2 columns of an 8-column work sheet.

(b) Prepare adjusting entries in journal form (administrative expenses includes bad debts, depreciation, insurance, supplies, and office salaries).

   1. Estimated bad debts, one-quarter of 1% of net sales.
   2. Depreciation of furniture and fixtures, 12% of cost per year.
   3. Insurance expired in January, $60.
   4. Supplies used in January, $250.
   5. Office salaries accrued, $400.
   6. Interest accrued on notes payable, $110.
   7. Interest unearned on notes receivable, $65.

(c) Transfer the adjusting entries to the work sheet.

(d) Estimate the January 31 inventory and enter it on the work sheet. The average gross profit earned by the company is 35% of net sales.

(e) Complete the work sheet.

(f) Prepare a balance sheet, an income statement, and a statement of retained earnings. Dividends of $2,000 were paid on the common shares during the month.

P3-13 Phillips Wholesale Distributors, Inc. operates on a fiscal year ending on January 31. The agreement with the Bank of Montreal for its loan to Phillips requires that Phillips submit quarterly financial statements to the bank.

You have just been hired by Phillips Wholesale Distributors, Inc. as their accountant, and your first responsibility is to prepare financial statements for the quarter ended April 30, 1986, for submission to the bank. The following is the trial balance at April 30, 1986 prepared by the bookkeeper.

Phillips Wholesale Distributors, Inc.
TRIAL BALANCE
April 30, 1986

Cash	$ 37,540	
Accounts Receivable	124,700	
Allowance for Doubtful Accounts	700	
Notes Receivable	25,000	
Interest Receivable	700	
Inventory, February 1, 1986	47,600	
Unexpired Insurance	1,600	
Supplies on Hand	3,700	
Land	40,000	
Building	135,000	
Accumulated Depreciation—Building		$ 19,600
Equipment	90,000	
Accumulated Depreciation—Equipment		45,400
Delivery Truck	24,000	
Accumulated Depreciation—Delivery Truck		5,000
Accounts Payable		64,500
Salaries and Wages Payable		-0-
Interest Payable		-0-
Payroll Taxes Payable (including withholding)		-0-
Income Taxes Payable		-0-
Notes Payable, 16%, due March 31, 1987		70,000
Mortgage Payable, 12%, due January 1, 2004		126,300
Common Shares, no-par value, 1,000 shares issued and outstanding		114,700
Retained Earnings		54,020
Dividends Declared	5,000	
Sales		324,600
Sales Discounts	4,600	
Purchases	216,300	
Purchase Discounts		470
Purchase Returns and Allowances		1,300
Transportation–in	6,300	
Executive Salary Expense	10,000	
Wages Expense	42,000	
Payroll Tax Expense	1,700	
Utilities Expense	2,400	
Supplies Expense	-0-	
Truck Expense	3,100	
Depreciation Expense	-0-	
Bad Debt Expense	-0-	
Miscellaneous Expense	390	
Interest Expense	3,560	
Interest Revenue		-0-
Gain or Loss on Sale of Assets		-0-
Income Tax Expense	-0-	
	$825,890	$825,890

You determine the following information about the ledger accounts which may need adjustment or correction. Phillips does *not* use reversing entries.

1. The accounts receivable consist of $104,200 of current accounts and $20,500 of past due accounts. In estimating bad debts, the balance in the allowance account is determined by using 1% of current accounts and 10% of past due accounts.

2. The notes receivable consist of the following:

   (a) Able Sales Co., $10,000 face dated June 30, 1985, interest at 12%, interest and principal due June 30, 1986.

   (b) Caraco Retailers, $15,000 face dated February 15, 1986, interest at 16%, interest and principal due June 15, 1986.

   (c) Phillips computes interest using 30-day months, 360-day years.

3. The land has a fair market value of $60,000 and the building has a fair market value of $150,000.

4. The building, when purchased, had an estimated useful life of 25 years and an estimated salvage value of $5,000. Phillips uses the straight-line method of depreciation for the building.

5. The equipment consists of 3 forklifts. In your discussions with the bookkeeper, you learn that on February 1, 1986, forklift Number 2 was sold for $7,000 and the selling price was credited to accumulated depreciation, and a new forklift purchased.

	Date Acquired	Cost	Salvage Value
Forklift No. 1	February 1, 1984	$20,000	$1,000
Forklift No. 2	February 1, 1984	20,000	1,000
Forklift No. 3	February 1, 1984	20,000	1,000
Forklift No. 5	February 1, 1986	30,000	2,000

The forklifts are depreciated on the double-declining balance method of depreciation over 5 years. A full year's depreciation is taken on the forklifts owned at the end of the year.

6. The delivery truck was purchased on February 1, 1984, for $24,000. The truck has a useful life of 4 years, estimated life in kilometres of 200,000, and a salvage value of $4,000. On January 31, 1986, the truck had been driven 50,000 km. You ascertain the truck has been driven 6,000 km since January 31, 1986, and that Phillips depreciates the truck on the basis of kilometres driven.

7. The unexpired insurance consists of a combination policy that covers the building, the equipment, and the trucks. The 3-year policy was purchased February 1, 1984, for $4,800 (Debit Miscellaneous Expense).

8. The estimate of supplies on hand at April 30, 1986, is $2,900.

9. The company pays its employees once a month on the fifth day of the month for the prior month. The payroll of April, 1986, consists of the following:

	Gross Pay	Taxes to be Withheld	Net Pay
Executives	$ 5,000	$1,000	$ 4,000
Other employees	23,000	3,700	19,300
	$28,000	$4,700	$23,300

Phillips also will pay for April payroll taxes totalling $900.

10. The three notes payable at 16%, due March 31, 1987, were taken out on January 31, 1984, to finance the purchase of the forklifts and delivery truck. The interest is payable every January 31, and the principal is due at maturity.

11. The mortgage payable of $130,000 was for the purchase of the land and building. The mortgage is payable over 20 years with $1,375 monthly payments, including principal and interest at 12% due at month end. All payments have been made and recorded.

12. You discover that the company estimates inventory for quarterly financial statements. The company has had a gross profit equal to 40% of net sales since it started in business on February 1, 1984.

13. The company's average tax rate is 30%. Compute to the nearest dollar.

Instructions

(a) Prepare a 12-column work sheet for preparation of the quarterly financial statements.

(b) Prepare a combined statement of income and retained earnings for the 3 months ended April 30, 1986, and the balance sheet at April 30, 1986.

*P3-14 Presented below is information related to the Colonial Company.

Journals

Sales journal	Page 17
Purchases journal	Page 8
Cash receipts journal	Page 43
Cash payments journal	Page 44
General journal	Page 12

Ledger Accounts

Title	Balance July 1	Acct. No.
Cash	$6,000	2
Accounts Receivable	8,000	5
Delivery Equipment	7,000	8
Sales Equipment	1,000	21
Accounts Payable	5,000	35
Advertising Expense	-0-	65
Purchases	-0-	52
Purchase Returns	-0-	53
Sales	-0-	69
Transportation–in	-0-	70

The following transactions occurred during the month of July.

July 1 Sells merchandise for cash, $9,000.
3 Buys a new delivery truck on account from L. Canary Motors, $9000.
3 Receives an invoice from the *Daily Advertiser* for an advertisement, $150, which appeared in the paper on July 2.
5 Receives a purchase requisition for display equipment from the sales manager; the equipment sells for $1,130.
6 Returns merchandise for credit of $130 on a cash purchase.
7 Sells merchandise on account to Peggy Graham, $10,000.
8 Purchases merchandise on account from Kelly Smith, $9,000, f.o.b. shipping point.
10 Receives cash of $130 for merchandise returned July 6.
11 Receives a debit memo for $70 from Kelly Smith, indicating that the merchandise purchased July 8 was shipped with freight prepaid.
13 Purchases display equipment for $1,130; the invoice is paid immediately. (See July 5 information.)
17 Sells merchandise on account to Lisa Jacobson, $1,000.
20 Pays Kelly Smith the full amount due.
24 Purchases merchandise on account from Sherrie Strain, $3,400.
28 Pays the *Daily Advertiser.*
31 Receives full payment from Peggy Graham.

Instructions

Complete the following:

(a) Open ledger accounts and enter the July 1 balances.

(b) Record the July transactions in appropriate journals.

(c) Post from the journals to the ledger with posting references in good form. (Omit subsidiary ledger postings.)

*P3-15 The E. T. Elsner Company maintains a voucher register with debit columns for Purchases, Office Salaries, Sales Salaries, Advertising Expense, Office Supplies Expense, and Sundry, and a credit column for Vouchers Payable. The cheque register contains a debit column for Vouchers Payable and credit columns for Cash and Purchase Discounts.

May 3   Purchases merchandise from Montreal Supply Company for $10,800, terms 1/10, n/30. (Purchases are recorded at gross amount).

     6   Purchases merchandise from F. Kort for $6,300, 2/10, n/30.

     9   Pays office payroll of $2,160 and sales payroll of $4,500.

    11   Purchases office equipment for $3,600 from Alcan Equipment Company, terms 1/15, n/45.

    12   Returns damaged merchandise of $800 to the Montreal Supply Company and pays the balance due.

    15   Receives an invoice from the Power and Light Company for utilities of $41.

    17   Pays Alcan Equipment Company the full amount due.

    20   Purchases office supplies of $1,000 from Office Equipment Company, making immediate payment by cheque.

    21   Receives an invoice for advertising from CKON Radio Station, $270.

    23   Pays F. Kort in full.

    27   Pays the telephone bill of $47 received from the telephone company.

    28   Pays the invoices for utilities and advertising.

    31   Supplies on hand are valued at $558.

Instructions

Record the transactions in the books of original entry of the E. T. Elsner Company beginning with voucher number 1 and cheque number 101.

*P3-16 On January 2, 1986, Wetzel-Pretty, Inc. was organized with two shareholders, Thomas Wetzel and Mary Ann Pretty. Thomas Wetzel purchased 500 common shares for $50,000 cash; Mary Ann Pretty received 500 common shares in exchange for the assets and liabilities of a men's clothing shop that she had operated as a sole proprietorship. The trial balance immediately after incorporation appears on the work sheet provided.

No formal books have been kept during 1986. The following information has been gathered from the cheque books, deposit slips, and other sources:

1. Most balance sheet account balances at December 31, 1986, have been determined and recorded on the work sheet.

2. Cash receipts for the year are summarized as follows:

Advances from customers	$ 800
Cash sales and collections on accounts receivable (after sales discounts of $1,520 and sales returns and allowances of $1,940)	126,540
Sale of equipment costing $5,000 on which $1,000 of depreciation had accumulated	4,500
	$131,840

3. During 1986, the depreciation expense on the building was $800; depreciation expense on the equipment was $1,750.

4. Cash disbursements for the year are summarized as follows:

Insurance Premiums	$ 900
Purchase of equipment	18,000
Addition to building	4,600
Cash purchases and payments on accounts payable (after purchase discounts of $1,150 and purchase returns and allowances of $1,800)	82,050
Salaries paid to employees	39,820
Utilities	1,850
Total cash disbursements	$147,220

5.   Bad debts are estimated to be 1.2% of total sales for the year. The ending accounts receivable balance of $18,700 has been reduced by $650 for specific accounts that were written off as uncollectible.

Instructions

Complete the work sheet for the preparation of accrual basis financial statements. Formal financial statements and journal entries are not required.

(AICPA adapted)

Wetzel-Pretty, Inc.
WORK SHEET FOR PREPARATION OF ACCRUAL BASIS
FINANCIAL STATEMENTS
For the Year Ended December 31, 1986

	Balance Sheet January 2, 1986		Adjustments		Income Statement 1986		Balance Sheet December 31, 1986	
	Debit	Credit	Debit	Credit	Debit	Credit	Debit	Credit
Cash	$ 60,000							
Accounts receivable	12,400						18,700	
Merchandise inventory	23,000						24,500	
Unexpired insurance	350						200	
Land	15,000						15,000	
Buildings	20,000							
Accumulated depreciation— buildings		$ 7,000						
Equipment	8,000							
Accumulated depreciation— equipment		2,400						
Accounts payable		17,850						9,229
Advances from customers		900						550
Salaries payable		600						1,595
Common shares		110,000						110,000
	$138,750	$138,750						

(Prepare your own work sheet, because you will need additional accounts)

4

STATEMENT OF INCOME AND RETAINED EARNINGS

The statement of income, or statement of earnings as it is frequently called,[1] is the report that measures the success of enterprise operations for a given period of time. The business and investment community uses this report to measure investment value, credit worthiness, and income success, for instance. Whether this confidence is well founded is a matter of conjecture, because the derived income is at best a rough estimate, and great caution should be exercised not to give it more significance than it deserves.

As indicated in Chapter 2, the measurement of income in accounting is a reflection of the many assumptions and principles (standards) established over the years by accountants, such as the periodicity assumption, the revenue realization principle, and the matching principle. If for any reason the assumptions and principles are ill founded, weaknesses will appear in the income statement.

Importance of the Statement of Income

As indicated above, the business and investment community pay close attention to a company's statement of income. The *Globe and Mail*, for example, continually

[1]*Financial Reporting in Canada—1983* (Toronto: CICA, 1983), p.170, indicates that for the 325 companies surveyed in 1982 the term "earnings" is employed in the title of 155 income statements. The term "income" is second in acceptance with 142, while the term "operations" is used by only 14 companies.

reports the income and the earnings per share consequences for Canadian companies like this: Rogers Cable Systems Inc. reported a 6 months' loss of $9.7 million with a per share loss of 49 cents; Canada Tungsten Mining Corp. Ltd. had a loss for a year of $5.63 million with a corresponding per share loss of $1.10.

Why is the income statement of such importance? A major reason is that it provides investors and creditors with information that **aids in predicting the amount, timing, and uncertainty of future cash flows.** Predictions of future cash flows enable investors to assess better the economic value of the enterprise and creditors to determine the probability of repayment of their claims against the enterprise.

The income statement helps users of the financial statements to predict future cash flows in a number of different ways. First, investors and creditors may use the information on the income statement **to evaluate the past performance of the enterprise.** Although success in the past does not necessarily mean success in the future, some important trends can be determined. It follows that if a reasonable correlation exists between past and future performance, predictions of future cash flows are more reliable.

Second, the income statement helps users of the financial statements **to determine the risk (level of uncertainty) of achieving future cash flows.** By providing information on the components of income, revenues, expenses, gains, and losses, the relationships among these various components are highlighted; for example, the extent to which a change in demand for a company's product affects revenue and expense (and therefore income). Similarly, segregating operating performance from other aspects of enterprise performance provides useful insights. In other words, operations are usually the major means by which revenues and ultimately cash are generated. Results from continuing operations therefore usually have greater significance than results from nonrecurring activities and events. To illustrate the importance of the income statement, consider the case of National Patent Development, a company that specializes in the soft contact lens market. Recently, it reported $18.6 million in income from continuing operations before taxes. A closer examination of this income, however, revealed that (1) $7.5 million in income came from the sale of investments by a subsidiary; (2) $2.4 million represented a gain on the exchange of a licence to sell its product for shares in the company it licensed; (3) $3.6 million came from the sale of shares in its portfolio; and (4) $3.2 million came from settlement of lawsuits related to patent infringements. In addition, its largest revenue source, $9.9 million from royalties on its soft contact lenses, may not continue because a note indicated that its patent on this process was to expire the following year. Our point here is that income, "the bottom line," does not tell the whole story. The income statement, however, is useful in providing information on the nature of the revenue sources and expense items, the likelihood of income continuing in the future, and other important considerations.

The income statement is used by parties other than investors and creditors. For example, customers may use the income statement to determine the company's ability to provide needed goods or services; unions may examine earnings closely as a basis for contract negotiations; and the government uses earnings of companies as a basis for formulating tax and economic policies.

Limitations of the Statement of Income

The statement of income based on generally accepted accounting principles is not without limitations. For example, economists have often criticized accountants for their definition of income, because accountants **do not include many items** that contribute to the general growth and well-being of an enterprise. For example, the noted economist, J. R. Hicks, has defined income as the maximum value a person can consume during a period and still be as well off at the end as at the beginning.[2] This definition provides the essential elements of measuring an individual's income. Any effort to measure how well off an individual is at any point in time, however, will prove fruitless unless certain restrictive assumptions are developed and applied.

For example, what was your net income for last year? Let us suppose that you worked during the summer and earned $5,600. Because you paid taxes and incurred tuition and living expenses for school, your income statement may show a loss for the year, if measured in terms of straight dollar value. But have you sustained a loss? How do you value the education obtained during the one year? According to one interpretation of Hicks' definition, you would measure not only monetary income but also psychic income. Psychic income is defined as a measure of increase in net wealth arising from qualitative features, in this case the value of your educational experience. Accountants undoubtedly recognize that the measurement of such experiences may be useful, but the problem of measurement has not been solved. Items that cannot be quantified with any degree of reliability have been discarded as part of accounting for income because of the impracticality of their measurement.

Furthermore, the **income numbers are often affected by the accounting methods employed**. For example, one company may choose to depreciate its plant assets on an accelerated basis; another on a straight-line basis. Assuming all other factors equal, the income of the first company will be lower than that of the latter during the earlier years of the life of the plant assets, even though the company is essentially the same. Thus the **quality of earnings** of a given enterprise is important. Companies that tend to use liberal accounting policies report higher income numbers in the short run. In those cases, we say that the quality of its earnings is low. Furthermore, some companies generate income in the short run because of some unusual event that is not sustainable over a period of time. For example, Coleco Industries' share price skyrocketed in the early 1980s because of the talk of "Adam," a revolutionary computer that was going to transform the home computer market and greatly increase Coleco's earnings. In fact, in the third quarter of 1983 income was up over 17% from the same quarter the previous year; but a closer look revealed that the increase in income was suspect, having been the result of lower tax rates and high profits on sales, neither of which would likely be sustained in future periods.

Capital Maintenance Approach vs. Transaction Approach

One interpretation of Hicks' definition of income assumes that net income is measured by subtracting beginning net assets (assets minus liabilities) from ending net assets and adjusting for any additional investments or dividends during the period. When income is calculated in this manner, accountants state that a capital maintenance approach to income measurement is employed. The **capital maintenance approach** (sometimes referred to as the change-in-equity approach) takes the net assets or capital values based on some valuation (e.g., historical cost, discounted cash flows, current cost, or fair market value) and measures income by the difference in capital values at two points in time. Here is an illustration, assuming the use of historical costs.

[2]J. R. Hicks, *Value and Capital* (Oxford: Clarendon Press, 1946), p.172.

Suppose that a corporation had beginning net assets of $10,000 and end-of-the-year net assets of $18,000, and that during this same period additional owners' investments of $5,000 were made. Calculation of the net income for the period, employing the capital maintenance approach, is shown below.

Net assets, December 31, 1986	$18,000
Less: Net assets, January 1, 1986	− 10,000
	$ 8,000
Less:	
Owners' investments during the year	5,000
Net income for 1986	$ 3,000

With the capital maintenance approach we compute the net income for the period, but there is one important drawback. Detailed information concerning the composition of the income is not evident: all of the revenue and expense amounts are not presented to the financial statement reader.

An alternative procedure measures the basic income-related transactions that occur during a period and summarizes them in an income statement. This method is normally called the **transaction approach.** This approach focuses on the activities that have occurred during a given period: instead of presenting only a net change, the components that constitute the change are disclosed. Income may be classified by customer, product line, or function. In addition, classification into such groupings as ordinary and extraordinary is developed to aid user groups. The transaction approach to income measurement is the method that you learned in your basic accounting course.

Elements of the Income Statement

The transaction approach to income measurement is believed to be superior to the capital maintenance approach because it provides information on the elements of income. As indicated in Chapter 2, the major elements of the income statement are as follows:

ELEMENTS OF THE INCOME STATEMENT

Revenues. Inflows or other enhancements of assets of an entity or settlements of its liabilities (or a combination of both) during a period from delivering or producing goods, rendering services, or carrying out other activities that constitute the entity's ongoing major or central operation.

Expenses. Outflows or other using up of assets or incurrences of liabilities (or a combination of both) during a period from delivering or producing goods, rendering services, or carrying out other activities that constitute the entity's ongoing major or central operations.

Gains. Increases in equity (net assets) from peripheral or incidental transactions of an entity and from all other transactions and other events and circumstances affecting the entity during a period except those that result from revenues or investments by owners.

Losses. Decreases in equity (net assets) from peripheral or incidental transactions of an entity and from all other transactions and other events and circumstances affecting the entity during a period except those that result from expenses or distributions to owners.[3]

---

[3]"Elements of Financial Statements of Business Enterprises," *Statement of Financial Accounting Concepts No.3* (Stamford, Conn.: FASB, 1980), p.xii.

Revenues take many forms: sales, fees, interest, dividends, and rents. Expenses also take many forms: cost of goods sold, depreciation, interest, rent, salaries and wages, and taxes. Gains and losses also are of many types, such as gains or losses resulting from the sale of investments, sale of plant assets, settlement of liabilities, write-offs of assets due to obsolescence or casualty, and theft.

The distinction between revenues and gains and the distinction between expenses and losses depend to a great extent on the typical activities of the enterprise. For example, the sales price of investments sold by an insurance company may be classified as revenues, whereas the sales price less book value on the sale of an investment by a manufacturing enterprise would be classified as a gain or loss. The different treatment results because the sale of investments by an insurance company is part of its regular operations, whereas in a manufacturing enterprise it is not.

The importance of reporting these elements should not be underestimated. For most decision makers, the parts of a financial statement will often be more useful than the whole. As indicated earlier, investors and creditors are interested in predicting the amounts, timing, and uncertainty of future income and cash flows. Revenues, expenses, gains, and losses occur as a result of numerous events and activities that vary in their stability, risk, and predictability. By reporting these income statement elements in some detail and in comparative form with prior years' data, companies will ensure that decision makers are better able to assess future income and cash flows.

Single-Step Income Statements

When using a transaction approach and reporting revenues, gains, expenses, and losses, one resulting concern is the format for the income statement. Many accountants prefer a format known as the **single-step** income statement.

For example, here is the income statement of Kaiser, Ltd.

Kaiser, Ltd. INCOME STATEMENT For the Year Ended December 31, 1986	
Net sales	$343,000
Other revenue	6,000
Total revenue	$349,000
Expenses	
Cost of goods sold	$258,000
Selling and administrative expenses	49,000
Interest on long-term debt	3,961
Other expenses	1,104
Total expenses	$312,065
Income before taxes	$ 36,935
Income taxes	16,000
Net income	$ 20,935
Earnings per share	$1.36

A single-step income statement features two major groupings or classifications: revenues on the one hand, and expenses on the other. The expenses are deducted from the revenues to arrive at the net income or loss; the expression "single-step" derives from the single subtraction necessary to arrive at net income. Frequently, however, income taxes are shown as a separate last item.

The use of the single-step form of income statement predominates in business reporting today; in recent years, however, the multiple-step form has regained some of its former popularity.

The primary advantage of the single-step format lies in the simplicity of presentation and the absence of any implied priority of one type of revenue or expense item over another. This approach thus eliminates potential classification problems.

Multiple-Step Income Statements

Some accountants contend that revenue and expense data contain additional important relationships, and that when the income statement shows these relationships it becomes more informative and more useful. Further classification and association of data within the statement make the report even more informative. Among the features are the following:

1. A separation of results achieved through regular operations and those obtained through the subordinate or nonoperating activities of the company. This separation is helpful because it provides a sound basis for evaluating the results of the nonoperating, as well as regular, activities. For example, enterprises often present a figure for income from operations, and then a section entitled Other Revenue or Expense that includes dividend and interest revenue and interest expense, and gains (losses) on miscellaneous items.
2. A classification of expenses by such functions as merchandising or manufacturing (cost of goods sold), selling, and administration. This presentation of the total expense of each activity permits immediate comparison with costs of previous years and with the cost of different segments during the same year (if reported).

Accountants who show these additional relationships in the operating data favour what is called the **multiple-step** income statement, rather than the single-step statement. In a multiple-step statement the basic distinction lies between operating and nonoperating activities, with both revenues and expenses separated into these two groups. This statement format is recommended because it recognizes a separation of operating transactions from nonoperating transactions, and matches expenses with related revenues to provide more information to the financial statement reader. For illustration, see Caine Company Ltd's multiple-step statement of income, presented on page 151.

For a manufacturing company, the section concerned with the cost of goods manufactured and sold is usually too extensive to include in the income statement. Normally, a separate schedule is used for the presentation of this data, if it is presented at all.

Components of the Income Statement

The components (often referred to as sections and subsections) within the income statement are described as follows:

1. **Operating section.** A report of the revenues and expenses of the company's principal operations. (This section may or may not be presented on a departmental and/or seg-

Caine Company Ltd.
INCOME STATEMENT
For the Year Ended December 31, 1986

Sales

Sales			$3,053,081
Less: Sales discounts		$ 44,241	
Sales returns and allowances		36,427	80,668
Net sales			$2,972,413

Cost of Goods Sold

Merchandise inventory, Jan.1, 1986		$ 461,219	
Purchases	$1,989,693		
Less: Purchase discounts	19,270		
Net purchases	$1,970,423		
Freight and transportation-in	40,612	2,011,035	
Total merchandise available for sale		$2,472,254	
Less: Merchandise inventory, Dec.31, 1986		489,713	
Cost of goods sold			1,982,541
Gross profit on sales			$ 989,872

Operating Expenses

Selling expenses			
Sales salaries and commissions	$ 202,644		
Sales office salaries	59,200		
Travel and entertainment	48,940		
Advertising expense	38,315		
Freight and transportation-out	41,209		
Shipping supplies and expense	24,712		
Postage and stationery	16,788		
Depreciation of sales equipment	9,005		
Telephone and telegraph	12,215	$ 453,028	
Administrative expenses			
Officers' salaries	$ 186,000		
Office salaries	61,200		
Legal and professional services	23,721		
Utilities expense	23,275		
Insurance expense	7,029		
Depreciation of building	8,059		
Depreciation of office equipment	6,000		
Stationery, supplies, and postage	2,875		
Miscellaneous office expenses	2,612	320,771	773,799
Income from operations			$ 216,073

Other Revenue

Dividend Revenue		$ 8,500	
Rental Revenue		2,910	11,410
			$ 227,483

Other Expense

Interest on bonds and notes			26,060
Income before taxes			$ 201,423
Income taxes			102,000
Net income for the year			$ 99,423
Earnings per share			$3.06

mented basis.) Section 1700 of the *CICA Handbook* requires that certain large firms report revenues and expenses on a segmented basis. These requirements are discussed in detail in Chapter 27.

   a. **Sales and revenue section.** A subsection within the operating section to present the pertinent facts about sales, discounts, allowances, returns, and other related information, arriving at the net amount of sales revenue.

   b. **Cost of goods sold section.** A subsection within the operating section that shows the cost of goods that were sold to obtain the sales revenue, and that displays in adequate detail the components of this cost figure.

   c. **Selling expenses.** A subsection within the operating section that states expenses resulting from the company's efforts to make sales.

   d. **Administrative or general expenses.** A subsection within the operating section reporting expenses of general administration of the company's operations.

   e. **Special gains or losses** that are material in amount and unusual or infrequent, but not both, and are deemed to be of an operating nature are generally shown in this section.

2. **Nonoperating section.** A report of the revenues and expenses resulting from secondary or auxiliary activities of the company. In addition, special gains and losses that are infrequent or unusual, but not both, and are deemed to be of a nonoperating nature are normally reported in this section. Generally, these items break down into two main subsections.

   a. **Other revenues and gains.** A list of revenues earned or gains incurred (generally net of related expenses) from nonoperating transactions.

   b. **Other expenses and losses.** A list of expenses or losses incurred (generally net of any related revenues) from nonoperating transactions.

3. **Income taxes.** A short section to report as a separate item the amount of federal and provincial taxes levied on income.

4. **Extraordinary items.** Unusual and infrequent gains and losses of material amounts, shown net of income taxes.

5. **Earnings per share.**[4]

Although the content of the operating section is always the same, the organization of the material need not be as just described. The breakdown above uses a **natural expense classification** and is commonly used for manufacturing concerns and for merchandising companies in the wholesale trade. Another classification of operating expenses recommended for a retail store's use is a **functional expense classification** of administrative, occupancy, publicity, buying, and selling expenses. Thus any reasonable classification that serves to inform those who use the statement is satisfactory. The present tendency in statements prepared for management is to present considerable detailed expense data grouped along lines of responsibility. This permits evaluation of the effectiveness of the work of individuals and departments according to work done and amount expended.

Whether a single-step or a multiple-step income statement is used, extraordinary gains and losses, net of income taxes, should be reported separately following the line item ''Income Before Extraordinary Items,'' as explained later in this chapter.

Refer to the income statement of Indal Limited, Appendix 5A, page 223, for a practical illustration of an income statement.

Condensed Income Statements

In some cases it is impossible to present in a single report of convenient size all of the desired detail related to expenses in the statement of income. This problem is solved by including only the totals of expense groups in the statement of income

---

[4]*CICA Handbook*, Section 3500, requires that earnings per share or net loss per share be included on the face of the income statement or in a note cross-referenced to the income statement.

and preparing supplementary schedules of expenses to support the totals in the statement. When this is done, the income statement proper may be reduced to only a few lines on a single sheet. For this reason, readers who study all the reported data on operations must give their attention to the supporting schedules of expenses as well. The following income statement for Caine Company Ltd. is a condensed version of the more detailed statement presented earlier, and is more representative of the type found in practice. If used, it should be accompanied by supporting schedules to present as much detail as is desirable.

Caine Company Ltd. INCOME STATEMENT For the Year Ended December 31, 1986		
Net sales		$2,972,413
Cost of goods sold		1,982,541
Gross profit		$ 989,872
Selling expense	$453,028	
Administrative expense	320,771	773,799
Income from operations		$ 216,073
Other revenue		11,410
		$ 227,483
Other expense		26,060
Income before taxes		$ 201,423
Income taxes		102,000
Net income for the year		$ 99,423
Earnings per share		$3.06

There is always a problem concerning the amount of detail to include in the financial statements. On the one hand, we want to present a simple, summarized statement so that a reader can readily discover the important facts. On the other hand, there is the necessity for full disclosure of the results of all activities and a desire to provide more than just a skeleton report. Supplementary schedules in the notes that provide the detailed information that cannot fit conveniently into the principal statement satisfy both requirements. They make it possible to present brief, summarized statements and to report as much additional detail as desired separately from, but in conjunction with, the basic statements.

Professional Pronouncements and the Income Statement

The profession has not taken a position on whether the single-step or the multiple-step income statement should be employed. Flexibility in the presentation of the components of the income statement data has been permitted. There are areas, however, where some guidelines have been developed. These relate to what should be included in the income statement as opposed to the statement of retained earnings.

What should be included in net income had been a controversy for many years. For example, should unusual and/or infrequent gains and losses and corrections of revenues and expenses of prior years be closed directly to Retained Earnings and therefore not reported in the income statement? Or should they first be presented in the income statement and then carried to Retained Earnings along with the net income or loss for the period? Or should unusual and/or infrequent gains and losses be treated differently than prior period adjustments? When all the items are first presented in the income statement, the Retained Earnings account normally includes for any given year only the net income (or loss) for the year and any dividends declared.

To illustrate, assume that Brooke Corp. has a retained earnings balance on January 1, 1986, of $80,000. For 1986 the corporation has earned revenue of $100,000 and incurred expenses of $30,000, exclusive of an extraordinary gain on the expropriation of properties of $10,000, net of tax. The following indicates how this information would be reported under two concepts, one called the all-inclusive income statement approach, and the other the current operating income statement approach.

	All-Inclusive	Current Operating
Revenues	$100,000	$100,000
Expenses	30,000	30,000
Income before extraordinary item	$ 70,000	$ 70,000
Extraordinary item:		
Gain on expropriation of properties		
(net of tax)	10,000	
Net income	$ 80,000	$ 70,000
Beginning retained earnings	$ 80,000	$ 80,000
Add:		
Net income	80,000	70,000
Extraordinary gain on expropriation		
of properties (net of tax)		10,000
Ending retained earnings	$160,000	$160,000

Advocates of the **current operating performance income statement** argue that the net income figure should show the regular, recurring earnings of the business based on its normal operations. Extraordinary gains and losses are neither representative nor reflective of an enterprise's future earning power. Therefore, they should not be included in computing net income but should be carried directly to Retained Earnings as special items. In addition, they note that many readers are not trained to differentiate between regular and irregular items and, therefore, would be confused if such items were included in computing net income.

Advocates of the **all-inclusive income statement** insist that such items be included in net income because they reflect the long-range income-producing ability of the enterprise. They state that any gain or loss experienced by the concern, whether directly or indirectly related to operations, contributes to its long-run profitability and should be included in its computation. They point out that extraordinary gains and losses can be separated from the results of ordinary operations to arrive at a figure of income from operations, but that in determining the net income for the year, all transactions should be included. They believe that when judgement is allowed to determine the location of extraordinary items, differences may develop in the treatment of such items, resulting in a danger of manipulating income data. For example, at one time American Standard wrote off $17.9 million in losses from discontinued operations directly to Retained Earnings. This enabled the company to report earnings per share of $1.01; if the write-off had been charged against income, American Standard would have reported a loss of 78 cents per share. If permitted, it could be to the advantage of the corporation to run losses through retained earnings, but gains through income. Supporters of the all-inclusive concept argue that this flexibility should not be allowed because it leads to poor financial reporting practices. In other words, Gresham's Law applies: poor accounting practices drive out good ones.

Prior to 1969, there was no agreement in Canadian practice regarding the use of either the all-inclusive or the current operating approach. Both were used, even when comparable situations existed. Since then, however, the most convincing arguments regarding the reporting of extraordinary items must have been given by those who favour the all-inclusive concept. **The *CICA Handbook* (Sections 1520 and 3480) adopts a modified all-inclusive concept for reporting extraordinary items and requires application of this approach in practice with few exceptions.** While extraordinary items are to be included in the income statement, they are to be specifically shown as such in a separate section of the statement.

The adoption of this modified all-inclusive approach for Canadian practice is based on the conclusion that the net income figure is intended to disclose the results of all activities for a period and should, therefore, reflect all gains and losses during the period except for prior period adjustments.[5] Accordingly, the *Handbook* provides guidance on what various items are and where and how they should be reported. For purposes of discussion, we will consider some specific items in the following general categories:

1. Extraordinary items related to the current period.
2. Certain gains and losses that do not constitute extraordinary items, even though they are unusual or infrequent in nature and material in amount.
3. Prior period adjustments.
4. Correction of errors made in prior periods.
5. Changes in estimates.
6. Changes in accounting principles.
7. Discontinued operations.

Extraordinary Items Related to the Current Period   These are defined as **material** "gains, losses, and provisions for losses which result from occurrences, the underlying nature of which is not typical of the normal business activities of the enterprise, are not expected to occur regularly over a period of years, and are not considered as recurring factors in any evaluation of the ordinary operations of the enterprise."[6]

Thus, the category of "extraordinary items" on the income statement is reserved for those items that are both:

(a) **unusual in nature**—items that do not arise in the course of normal business activities

(b) **occur infrequently**, or are expected to occur only infrequently, over a period of years.

---

[5]*CICA Handbook*, Section 3480, pars. 2 and 6.
[6]*Ibid.*, par. 4.

Examples given in the *Handbook* that could meet these two criteria are:

1. the discontinuance of, or substantial change in, a business program or policy (e.g., sale or abandonment of a plant or other significant segment of the enterprise, sale of investments not acquired for resale);
2. intervention by government or other regulatory bodies, such as property expropriation or revaluation of foreign currency;
3. such acts of God as earthquakes or floods.

For further clarification, the *CICA Handbook* specifies that the following gains and losses, although unusual, do not constitute extraordinary items:

(a) losses and provisions for losses (regardless of size) with respect to bad debts or inventories;
(b) gains and losses from fluctuations of foreign exchange rates;
(c) adjustments with respect to contract prices.[7]

The items listed above do not constitute extraordinary items in a going concern because they "result from occurrences, the underlying nature of which is typical of the customary business activities of the enterprise, even though caused by unusual circumstances."[8] Given these examples, it is clear that judgement must be exercised when determining whether or not an event or transaction results in an extraordinary item according to the criteria specified in Section 3480.[9]

In determining whether an item is an extraordinary item, **the environment in which the entity operates is of primary importance.** The environment of an entity includes such factors as the characteristics of the industry or industries in which it operates, the geographical location of its operations, and the nature and extent of governmental regulations. Thus, extraordinary item treatment may be accorded the loss arising from hail damages to a tobacco grower's crops because severe damage from hailstorms in the locality is rare. On the other hand, frost damage to orchards in parts of the Okanagan Valley might not qualify as extraordinary because frost damage is normally experienced every three or four years. In this environment, the criterion of infrequency is not met. Similarly, when a company sells the only security investment it has ever owned, the gain or loss probably meets the criteria of an extraordinary item. Another company, however, that has a portfolio of securities which it has acquired for investment purposes, might not have an extraordinary item upon the sale of such securities. Because the company owns several securities for investment purposes, sale of such securities is considered part of its ordinary and typical activities in the environment in which it operates.

It should be noted that there are **exceptions** to the general criteria of extraordinary items being both unusual and infrequent. For instance, the **tax benefits of loss carry-forwards** recognized in periods subsequent to the loss must be reported as an extraordinary item in those periods regardless of their frequency (discussed in Chapter 20).[10]

Unfortunately, it is often difficult to determine what is extraordinary because accountants have never clearly defined materiality. As indicated in Chapter 2, firm guidelines to follow in judging when an item is or is not material have not been established. For example, companies have shown as extraordinary gains and losses

---

[7]*Ibid.*, par. 11.

[8]*Ibid.*

[9]*Financial Reporting in Canada—1983* indicates that one-third of the 325 firms surveyed reports at least one extraordinary item.

[10]*CICA Handbook*, Section 3470, par. 56.

items that accounted for less than 1% of income before extraordinary items. Our point is that as long as the definition of materiality is not sharply outlined, it will be difficult in some cases to differentiate an ordinary from an extraordinary item. In determining whether an extraordinary event or transaction is material in relation to income before extraordinary items, to the trend of earnings, or by other appropriate criteria, items should be considered individually and not in the aggregate.

As previously stated, considerable judgement must be exercised in determining whether an item should be reported as extraordinary. For example, some paper companies have had their forest lands expropriated by the government for parks and forests. Is such an event extraordinary or is it part of normal operations? Such determination is not easy; much depends on the frequency of previous expropriations, the expectation of future expropriations, materiality, and so on.

Extraordinary items are to be shown net of taxes in a separate section in the income statement, just before net income. After listing the usual revenues, costs and expenses, and income taxes, the remainder of the statement shows:

Income before extraordinary items
Extraordinary items (less applicable income taxes of $_____)
Net income

For example, the AHL Group Limited (formerly Automotive Hardware Limited) reported extraordinary items in its 1984 financial statements as follows:

The AHL Group Limited

	(thousands of dollars, except per share amounts)	
	1984	1983
Earnings (loss) before extraordinary income	2,027	(2,345)
Extraordinary income (Note 9)	381	3,591
Net earnings	2,408	1,246
Earnings (loss) per share:		
Before extraordinary item	$ .59	$ (.68)
After extraordinary item	$ .70	$ .36

Notes:
9. **Extraordinary income**

	(thousands of dollars)	
	1984	1983
Special operator development program	$(1,315)	$ —
Write-down of land held for sale to net realizable value	(330)	—
Income taxes recovered through the application of losses carried forward	2,109	—
Share of extraordinary income of nonconsolidated subsidiaries	1,644	3,570
Loss on disposal of nonconsolidated subsidiaries	(1,824)	—
Other, net of income taxes	97	21
	$ 381	$ 3,591

The share of extraordinary income of nonconsolidated subsidiaries principally related to the gain on disposal of property, plant, and equipment and income taxes recovered through the application of losses carried forward.

Material gains and losses not constituting extraordinary items   Because of Section 3480's narrow criteria for extraordinary items, financial statement users must examine carefully the financial statements for items that are **unusual or infrequent but not both.** As indicated earlier, Section 3480 provides examples of such items as write-downs of inventories and gains and losses from fluctuations of foreign exchange rates that should be reflected in the determination of income before extraordinary items. Thus, these items are shown with the normal, recurring revenues, costs, and expenses. If they are not material in amount, they are combined with other items in the statement. If they are material, they should be disclosed separately, but are shown above "income (loss) before extraordinary items."

The following excerpt from the 1984 financial statements of Shell Canada Limited shows how an unusual item may be disclosed. This example also illustrates a presentation that clearly distinguishes unusual from extraordinary items.

Shell Canada Limited

	($millions, except per share amounts)		
	1984	1983	1982
Earnings before unusual item	**158**	102	148
Unusual item, after income tax (Note 3)	**—**	—	17
Earnings before extraordinary item	**158**	102	131
Extraordinary item, after income tax (Note 2)	**35**	—	—
Earnings for the year	**123**	102	131
Earnings per Class "A" Common Share (dollars)			
Before extraordinary item	**1.27**	0.83	1.07
After extraordinary item	**0.96**	0.83	1.07

Notes:
2. Extraordinary item   The extraordinary item represents the costs of $70 million less income taxes of $35 million associated with restructuring the Corporation's organization, relocating corporate headquarters to Calgary, and reducing staff, including severance pay, relocation costs, the present value of additional pensions to those otherwise entitled to early retirement, and gain on the disposal of the Head Office building in Toronto. Additional pension benefits, having a present value of $55 million less related income taxes of $24 million, payable under the enhanced voluntary retirement program to those entitled to retire early, will be provided out of earnings and funded over a period not exceeding 15 years.

3. Unusual item   In 1982, the Corporation announced the closing of the refineries at Oakville, Ontario, and St. Boniface, Manitoba. Closing of the Oakville refinery had no adverse effect on earnings or financial position and no provision was recorded in the accounts in this regard. Closing of the St. Boniface refinery resulted in a one-time charge to earnings in 1982 of $32 million before reduction for deferred income taxes of $15 million. This charge included the write-down of assets to net realizable value, and provisions for employee relocation, termination costs, and other associated shutdown costs.

In dealing with events that are either unusual or infrequent but not both, the CICA attempted to prevent a practice that many accountants believed was misleading. Companies often reported these transactions on a net-of-tax basis and prominently displayed the earnings per share effect of these items. Although not captioned extraordinary items, they were presented in the same manner, and indeed some had referred to these as "first cousins" to extraordinary items. As a consequence, the *CICA Handbook* stipulates that these items are to be reported in the income statement before "income before extraordinary items.[11]

Prior Period Adjustments   The accounting treatment for prior period adjustments is relatively straightforward. *CICA Handbook*, Section 3600, requires that items having all four of the following characteristics shall be accounted for and reported as prior period adjustments and excluded from the determination of net income for the current period:

   (a)   specifically identified with and directly related to the business activities of particular prior periods;
   (b)   not attributed to economic events occurring subsequent to the date of the financial statements for such prior periods;
   (c)   depend primarily on decisions or determinations by persons other than management or owners;
   (d)   could not reasonably be estimated prior to such decisions or determinations.[12]

Examples of prior period adjustments are rare. The most common are nonrecurring adjustments or settlements of income taxes and settlements of litigation.

   Prior period adjustments should be charged or credited (net of tax) to the opening balance of retained earnings and, thus, excluded from the determination of net income for the current period. The following serves as an example of how this can be accomplished:[13]

STATEMENT OF RETAINED EARNINGS
For the Year Ended December 31, 1984
(In thousands of dollars)

	1984	1983
Retained earnings, beginning of year		
As previously reported	$60,100	$54,100
Adjustments of prior years' income taxes (Note X)	7,500	5,100
As restated	$52,600	$49,000
Net income for the year	5,300	5,600
	$57,900	$54,600
Dividends	2,000	2,000
Retained earnings, end of year	$55,900	$52,600

Note X. As a result of income tax reassessments applicable to the years 1980 to 1983, the balance of retained earnings at January 1, 1984 has been adjusted by the cumulative amount by which income taxes as at that date had been increased; $2,400,000 of the adjustment is applicable to 1983 and has been charged to income for that year. The remainder is applicable to years prior to January 1, 1983, and the balance of retained earnings at that date has been adjusted accordingly.

Correction of Errors Made in Prior Period   While it may be a rare event, accountants do make mistakes when preparing financial statements. A mistake or error may occur because of incorrect computation, oversight in considering available information, or misinterpretation of information. For example, depreciation may be incorrectly calculated. When such errors are discovered in a subsequent period

[11]*Ibid.*, Section 3480, par. 12.
[12]*Ibid.*, Section 3600, par. 3.
[13]*Ibid.*, Section 3600A. Example 2.

and are material, **retroactive adjustment** of the financial statements presented in the year of discovery is required.[14] This means that the correction is to be accounted for by restating the financial statements for the periods affected by the error if they are presented for comparative purposes with the current period's statements. If the error affected periods prior to the comparative statements presented, the opening balance of retained earnings for the earliest period presented is adjusted. All such adjustments should reflect any related tax effects.

Changes in Accounting Estimates   Making estimates is a necessary consequence of preparing periodic financial statements. When estimates are made, they are based on available information and experience. However, as experience increases, new events unfold, and additional information is acquired, the initial estimates may need to be revised. Examples of such revisions are a change in the estimated life of an asset or estimated liability for warranty costs or realizability of receivables or inventories.

A change in an estimate is not the same as a correction of an error. The latter results from not having correctly calculated or used information that was available at the time. A change in estimate becomes necessary because new information has arisen or new events become important. Consequently, a change in estimate is accounted for differently. Because the change is the result of events and information emerging in the current period, it is accounted for on a **prospective basis**; that is, its consequences are reflected in the current and future period's statements and no retroactive adjustment takes place. Furthermore, because changes in estimates are normal and recurring, they are not treated as extraordinary items. Only if it is rare or unusual would specific disclosure be made in the financial statements.[15]

Changes in Accounting Policies   Accounting policies include the specific accounting principles and the methods of applying them in preparation of a firm's financial statements. A change in accounting policy occurs when an accounting principle is adopted that is different from the one previously used. Examples of changes in accounting principles would include: a change in the method of inventory valuation from FIFO to average cost, or a change in depreciation from the declining-balance to straight-line method.[16]

These types of changes are recognized through **retroactive adjustment.** This involves the determination of the effect on the income of the prior periods affected. The financial statements for all prior periods that are presented for comparative purposes should be restated to reflect the new accounting policy except when the effect is not reasonably determinable for specific prior periods. If this exception is applicable, an adjustment would be made to the beginning retained earnings of the current or an appropriate earlier period to show the cumulative effect from all previous periods. Appropriate disclosure related to a change in an accounting policy should occur.

To illustrate, McCartan, Inc. decided at the beginning of 1986 to change from an accelerated depreciation method (double declining balance) of computing depreciation on its plant assets to the straight-line method. The declining balance rate of

[14]*Ibid.*, Section 1506, par. 28.

[15]*Ibid.*, Section 1506, par. 24.

[16]*Ibid.*, Section 1506. Chapter 23 examines in greater detail the problems related to accounting changes; our purpose now is to provide general guidance for the major types of transactions affecting the income and retained earnings statements.

40% is the same as the capital cost allowance rate that has been and will continue to be used to determine taxable income. The assets originally cost $100,000 and have a service life of five years. Here are the data assumed for this illustration and the manner of reporting the change.

Year	Accelerated Depreciation	Straight-Line Depreciation	Excess of Accelerated Depreciation over Straight-Line
1984	$40,000	$20,000	$20,000
1985	24,000	20,000	4,000
Total			$24,000

The adjustment for this accounting policy change as shown in the 1986 financial statements could be shown as follows. (No comparative statements are shown and the tax rate is 48%.)

Retained earnings, January 1, 1986, as previously reported	$250,000
Cumulative effect on prior periods of retroactive application of new depreciation method (net of $11,520 tax)	12,480
Adjusted balance of retained earnings at January 1, 1986	$262,480

Discontinued Operations   A company may discontinue a part of its operations (e.g., a subsidiary, product line, or division) by closing it down, selling it, or making a "substantial" change in it. In such cases, two aspects must be dealt with in the financial statements: the reporting of the gain or loss related to the discontinuance and the reporting of the results of its operations up to the discontinuance.

The gain or loss from discontinuance would be reported as an extraordinary item if it meets the criteria for such items.[17] Otherwise, it would likely be shown as a separate item in the determination of income before extraordinary items.

Various practices exist regarding the reporting of the results of operations of the discontinued unit. In past years' financial statements, the revenues and expenses related to the now discontinued unit would have been included in the total revenues and expenses reported for the whole company or consolidated enterprises. Consequently, some companies continue to report the results of operations of a discontinued unit in the same way during the year of discontinuance. This approach has the disadvantage of mixing results of operations from continued and discontinued operations in deriving a total net income from operations. To the extent that net income from operations is used to predict future results, the mixing of the two types of operations may distort trends. Therefore, another practice is to separate the results of discontinued from continued operations in the income statement.

---

[17]*Financial Reporting in Canada—1983* showed that of the 13 companies having a gain or loss from discontinued operations in 1982, 11 reported it as an extraordinary item. The other 2 companies disclosed the gain and loss in conjunction with the results of the discontinued operations, but not as an extraordinary item.

This separation would apply to figures presented for previous years when comparative statements are provided. While the *CICA Handbook* makes no formal recommendation on the issue, it does make the following statement regarding a disposal of a subsidiary company:

> . . . In the period of a disposal, it is desirable to report the results of continuing operations separately from the results of discontinued operations: this segregation would be made for both the current period and any prior periods which are presented for comparative purposes.[18]

It should be noted that the results of discontinued operations, while they may be reported separately in the income statement, are not an extraordinary item. These results were a part of normal operations of previous periods. The separate identification of these results in the determination of Income before Extraordinary Items is to help the user predict results from continuing operations, given that a discontinuance has taken place. The following examples from Canadian incorporated companies indicate how they have reported the results of discontinued operations and the gain or loss on discontinuance. Both EMCO Limited and AMCA International Limited separate the results of discontinued operations from the results of continuing operations. EMCO Limited indentifies the loss on discontinuance as an extraordinary item while AMCA International Limited includes their loss with the results of discontinued operations in a special section of the income statement labelled Discontinued Operations. AMCA's disclosure follows U.S. requirements which call for a separate section on discontinued operations and prohibit the loss or gain on discontinuance from being shown as an extraordinary item.[19]

EMCO Limited	(thousands of dollars, except per share amounts)	
	1984	1983
Earnings from continuing operations before extraordinary item	**6,219**	4,119
Loss from discontinued operations (Note 8)*	**(1,024)**	(450)
Earnings before extraordinary item	**5,195**	3,669
Extraordinary item: Provision for loss on disposal of discontinued operations, net of applicable income taxes (Note 8)*	**(1,300)**	—
Net earnings	**$ 3,895**	3,669
Earnings (loss) per share:		
From continuing operations	**$ 1.20**	.80
From discontinued operations	**$(.20)**	(.09)
Before extraordinary item	**$ 1.00**	.71
Net earnings	**$ .75**	.71

[18]*CICA Handbook*, Section 1600, par. 72.

[19]"Reporting the Results of Operations," *Opinions of the Accounting Principles Board No. 30* (New York: AICPA, 1973).

AMCA International Limited

	1984	1983	1982
	(thousands of U.S. dollars, except per share amounts)		
Income (Loss) from Continuing Operations before Income Taxes	**(11,447)**	(43,210)	43,397
Income Tax Benefit (Note 4)*	**(16,514)**	(39,605)	(4,396)
Income (Loss) from Continuing Operations	5,067	(3,605)	47,793
Discontinued Operations (Note 2)*			
Income (loss) from operations (less income tax benefit of $2,627 in 1984 and $12,126 in 1983 and income tax provision of $46 in 1982)	**(3,162)**	(13,089)	49
Loss on disposal (less income tax benefit of $3,157 in 1984 and $20,400 in 1983)	**(3,560)**	(22,600)	—
	(6,722)	(35,689)	49
Net Income (Loss)	**$ (1,655)**	$(39,294)	$47,842
Earnings (Loss) Per Common Share (Note 1)*			
Continuing operations	**$(.07)**	$ (.11)	$1.68
Discontinued operations	**(.20)**	(1.08)	—
Net Income (Loss)	**$(.27)**	$(1.19)	$1.68

*Notes not included in this illustration.

Summary

The public accounting profession now tends to accept a modified all-inclusive income concept instead of the current operating performance concept. The only items ordinarily charged or credited directly to Retained Earnings, other than dividends and income, are **prior period adjustments**, **error corrections**, and **consequences of changes in accounting principles** that require restatement of prior period financial statements. Unusual gains and losses or nonrecurring items are closed to Income Summary and are included in the income statement. Gains and losses that are **both unusual and infrequent** are shown in a separate section for "extraordinary items" in the income statement just before net income. Other items of a material amount that are of an **unusual or nonrecurring** nature and are **not considered extraordinary** are separately disclosed before the "extraordinary items" section.

Because of the numerous intermediate income figures that are created by the reporting of these items, careful evaluations of information reported by the financial press are needed. For example, when RCA recently released its first-quarter results, the *Wall Street Journal* reported that "RCA earnings climbed by 47% in the first quarter" as compared to the first quarter of last year. Conversely, the *New York Times* reported the following regarding RCA's first-quarter results: "RCA Slides 46%." Which article was right? Both were factually correct. The difference arose because the *Times* article, in making its comparison to the quarter of the previous year, included extraordinary gains in the income of the earlier quarter; the *Wall Street Journal* did not. Such an illustration demonstrates the importance of understanding the intermediate components of net income.

SUMMARY OF CICA HANDBOOK RECOMMENDATIONS§

Type of Situation	Criteria	Examples	Placement on Financial Statements
Extraordinary items	Material, and both unusual and nonrecurring (infrequent).	Gains or losses resulting from casualties, an expropriation, or a prohibition under a new law.	Separate section in the income statement entitled extraordinary items. (Shown net of tax)
Material gains or losses, not considered extraordinary	Material; character typical of the customary business activities; unusual or infrequent but not both.	Write-downs of receivables, inventories; adjustments of contract prices; gains or losses from fluctuations of foreign exchange.	Separate section in income statement above income before extraordinary items. (Not shown net of tax)
Prior period adjustments	Meet all four characteristics in *CICA Handbook*, Section 3600, par. 03.	Income tax reassessments for previous years; settlements of litigation.	Adjust the beginning balance of retained earnings. (Shown net of tax)
Correction of an error made in a prior period	Is the result of a mistake in computation, oversight of available information or misinterpretation of information that is material.	Incorrectly calculated depreciation or allowance for doubtful accounts.	Retroactive adjustment by restating the financial statements of the prior periods presented for comparative purposes. If error was in periods prior to the comparative statements presented, adjust opening balance of the earliest period presented. Adjustments reflect related tax effects.
Changes in estimates	Result from occurrence of new events, more experience, and new or additional information.	Changes in the realizability of receivables and inventories; changes in estimated lives of equipment, intangible assets; changes in estimated liability for warranty costs, income taxes, and salary payments.	Prospective adjustment by incorporating the change in current and future periods' statements as affected. No retroactive adjustment is made.
Changes in accounting policies	Change from one generally accepted principle to another.	Changing the basis of inventory pricing from FIFO to average cost; change in the method of depreciation from accelerated to straight-line.	Retroactive adjustment to all financial statements presented and adjustment of beginning retained earnings of earliest period presented. Adjustments are net of tax.
Discontinued operations	Disposal by selling or closing down a segment of a business or making a substantial change in a product line.	Sale by diversified company of major division which represents only activities in electronics industry. Food distributor that sells wholesale to supermarket chains and through fast-food restaurants decides to discontinue the division that sells to one of two classes of customers.	Show gain or loss on discontinued operations as an extraordinary item if the criteria (unusual and nonrecurring) are met, otherwise as an unusual item. Results of operations of discontinued activity may be separately shown in determination of income before extraordinary items.

§This summary provides only the general rules to be followed in accounting for the various situations described above. Exceptions do exist in some of these situations.

The chart on page 164 summarizes the basic concepts previously examined. Although the chart is simplified, it provides a useful framework for determining the proper treatment of special items affecting the income statement.

INTRAPERIOD TAX ALLOCATION

Allocation within a Period

Whenever an extraordinary item, prior period adjustment, change in accounting principle, or correction of an error made in a prior period occurs, most accountants believe that the resulting income tax effect should be directly associated with that event or item. In other words, the tax for the year should be related, where possible, to specific items on the income statement to provide a more informative disclosure to statement users. This procedure is called **intraperiod tax allocation.** Its main purpose is to relate the income taxes to the following items which affect the amount of the tax provisions: (1) income before extraordinary items, (2) extraordinary items, (3) prior period adjustments, (4) correction of errors in prior periods, and (5) changes in accounting principles. The general rule is "let the tax follow the item."

The income tax expense attributable to "income before extraordinary items" is simply computed by ascertaining the income tax expense related to revenue and expense transactions entering into the determination of this income. In this computation, no effect is given to the tax consequences of the items excluded from the determination of "income before extraordinary items." The income tax expense attributable to other items is determined by the tax consequences of transactions involving these items. Because all these items are ordinarily material in amount, the applicable tax effect is also material and is disclosed separately and in close association with the related items.

Extraordinary Losses For example, assume that a company has income before extraordinary items of $250,000 and an extraordinary loss from a major casualty of $100,000. Because the casualty is not expected to occur frequently, has a material effect, and is not considered usual to the ordinary operating processes of the business, it is reported as an extraordinary item. The loss is deductible for tax purposes, however. Therefore, if the income tax rate is assumed to be 48%, the income tax payable for the year will be computed as follows:

Income before loss deduction	$250,000
Less: Extraordinary item—loss from casualty	100,000
Taxable income	$150,000
Income tax payable at 48%	$ 72,000

The income tax expense applicable to the $250,000 income before extraordinary items is $120,000, and the tax reduction applicable to the loss of $100,000 from the major casualty is $48,000. If the tax reduction of $48,000 is **not** associated with the extraordinary loss, the income statement would appear incorrectly as follows:

Income before tax and extraordinary item	$250,000
Income tax	72,000
Income before extraordinary item	$178,000
Less: Extraordinary item—loss from casualty	(100,000)
Net income	$ 78,000

The report above does not disclose an appropriate relationship between the income tax expense, the "income before extraordinary item," and the "loss." Without the tax benefit of the loss, the $250,000 of operating income would have been taxed at the 48% rate for an income tax of $120,000. The income before the extraordinary item would have appeared as $130,000 instead of $178,000. Thus we have the paradoxical situation of a loss of $100,000 making the income before extraordinary item appear larger by $48,000 instead of smaller.

To avoid such a misleading presentation, we may report the tax effect in the income statement along with the loss in the following way.

Income before tax and extraordinary item		$250,000
Income tax		120,000
Income before extraordinary item		$130,000
Extraordinary item—loss from casualty	$100,000	
Less: Applicable income tax reduction	48,000	(52,000)
Net income		$ 78,000

Or, it may be reported "net of tax" with note disclosure as illustrated below.

Income before tax and extraordinary item	$250,000
Income tax	120,000
Income before extraordinary item	$130,000
Extraordinary item, less applicable income tax (Note 1)	(52,000)
Net income	$ 78,000

Note 1. During the year the Company suffered a major casualty loss of $52,000 after applicable income tax reduction of $48,000.

Extraordinary Gains   If a company realizes an extraordinary gain, the tax expense is allocated between the gain and the income before gain. If we assume a $100,000 extraordinary gain, the income statement disclosure is as follows.

Income before tax and extraordinary item		$250,000
Income tax (48%)		120,000
Income before extraordinary item		$130,000
Extraordinary gain	$100,000	
Less: Applicable income tax	48,000	52,000
Net income		$182,000

Prior Period Adjustments The possibility of misleading reports resulting from carrying prior period adjustments directly to retained earnings also results unless the tax effect is reported with the adjustment. Again, "let the tax follow the item" expresses the basic idea. A prior period adjustment having a current tax effect is disclosed in this statement of retained earnings as follows.

Retained earnings at beginning of year:		
As previously reported		$2,000,000
Prior period adjustment	$200,000	
Less: Applicable income tax reduction	96,000	(104,000)
Adjusted balance of retained earnings at beginning of year		$1,896,000
Net income		160,000
Retained earnings at end of year		$2,056,000

Under this arrangement the net income for the year shows the income tax expense related to the revenue and expense transactions that determine such income.

Reporting correction of errors made in prior periods and the consequences of a change in accounting policy are somewhat more complicated, as they involve retroactive adjustment of statements provided for comparative purposes with the current year and, possibly, adjustment of the beginning retained earnings of the earliest period presented. Also, because timing differences occur when amounts are recognized in financial statements and in tax returns, the tax effects of changes in accounting policies are likely to affect deferred tax amounts (a topic discussed in Chapter 20). Consequently, discussion of the complexities related to reporting these two types of items is deferred to Chapter 23.

Earnings per Share

The results of a company's operations are customarily summed up in one important figure: net income. As if this condensation were not enough of a simplification of a complex operation, the financial world has widely accepted an even more distilled and compact figure as its most significant business indicator—"earnings per share."

The computation of earnings per share amounts can become quite complex (as discussed in Chapter 17). For the time being, however, we will concentrate on a straightforward computation of basic earnings per share. This is determined by **dividing net income available to common shareholders (i.e., net income minus preferred dividends) by the weighted-average number of common shares outstanding during the year.** To illustrate, assume that Lancer, Inc. reports net income of $350,000 and declares and pays preferred dividends of $50,000 for the year; the weighted-average number of shares outstanding during the year is 100,000 shares. The earnings per share is $3.00 as computed below:

$$\frac{\text{Net Income} - \text{Preferred Dividends}}{\text{Weighted-Average Number of Shares Outstanding}} = \text{Earnings per Share}$$

$$\frac{\$350,000 - \$50,000}{100,000} = \$3.00$$

"Net income per share" or "earnings per share" is a ratio commonly used in prospectuses, proxy material, and annual reports to shareholders, and in the compilation of business earnings data for the press and other statistical services. Because of the inherent dangers of focusing attention on earnings per share by itself, the profession concluded that **earnings per share must be disclosed either on the face of the income statement or in a note to the financial statements.** In addition to net income per share, per share amounts should be shown for "income before extraordinary items."[20]

To illustrate comprehensively both the income statement order of presentation and the earnings per share data, assume that Juarez Industries, Ltd. had the condensed income statement shown below and that 100,000 common shares have been outstanding for the entire year.

Juarez Industries, Ltd.		
INCOME STATEMENT		
For the Year Ended December 31, 1986		
(In thousands of dollars)		
Sales		$1,480,000
Cost of goods sold		600,000
Gross profit		$ 880,000
Selling and administrative expenses		320,000
Income from operations		$ 560,000
Other revenues and expenses, gains and losses		
Income from discontinued operations—Hartley Div.	$ 90,000	
Interest revenue	10,000	
Loss on disposal of equipment	(5,000)	
Loss on sale of investments	(45,000)	50,000
Income before income taxes and extraordinary items		$ 610,000
Income taxes		244,000
Income before extraordinary items		$ 366,000
Extraordinary items		
Loss on disposal of Hartley Division,		
less applicable income taxes of $60,000	$(90,000)	
Loss from earthquake, less applicable		
income taxes of $30,000	(45,000)	(135,000)
Net income		$ 231,000
Basic earnings per common share		
Income before extraordinary items		$ 3.66
Extraordinary loss, net of tax		(1.35)
Net Income		$ 2.31

The earnings per share data also may be disclosed parenthetically by a corporation, as illustrated below. (This form is especially applicable when only one per share amount is involved.)

Net income (per share $4.02)	$804,000

[20]*CICA Handbook*, Section 3500, pars. 9 and 11.

As indicated earlier, amounts for extraordinary items need not be stated on a per share basis. These per share amounts can be determined simply by subtraction if not reported as separate per share amounts. For example, Huskey Oil reported basic earnings per share before an extraordinary item of $1.10 and basic earnings per share of $3.67. This means it had an extraordinary gain of $2.57 per share, net of income tax. Many corporations have simple capital structures that include only common shares. For these companies, a presentation such as ''earnings per common share'' is appropriate on the income statement. In an increasing number of instances, however, companies' earnings per share are subject to dilution (reduction) in the future because existing contingencies permit the further issuance of common shares.[21] Examples of such instances are (1) outstanding preferred shares or debt that is convertible into common shares, (2) outstanding stock options or warrants, and (3) agreements for the issuance of common shares for little or no consideration in the satisfaction of certain conditions (e.g., the attainment of specified levels of earnings following a business combination). The presentation of earnings per share information in such complex situations as these is frequently done through a note to the financial statements that is cross-referenced to the income statement. The computational problems involved in accounting for these dilutive securities in earnings per share computations are discussed in Chapter 17.

In summary, the simplicity and availability of figures for per share earnings lead inevitably to their widespread use. Because of the importance (justified or not) that the public, even when well informed, attaches to earnings per share, accountants have an obligation to make the earnings per share figures as meaningful as possible.

STATEMENT OF RETAINED EARNINGS

A statement of retained earnings is generally included, together with an income statement and a balance sheet, in the financial statements of an enterprise. Actually, rather than being a statement that merely reports related data, **it is a reconciliation of the balance of the retained earnings account from the beginning to the end of the year.**

Every effort should be made to prepare as useful and informative a statement of retained earnings as possible. Given that the retained earnings account may receive direct charges and credits for certain prior period adjustments or other items, the income statement will not reveal such information. The statement of retained earnings must, therefore, be studied in conjunction with the income statement; otherwise, important changes in owners' equity may be overlooked. Therefore, the statement of retained earnings makes full use of descriptive terminology so that readers can relate the appropriate items to the income statement.

Items Disclosed

The following are some significant relationships and data recorded in the account for retained earnings that should be clearly disclosed in the statement:

1. **Prior period adjustments, adjustments for change in accounting policies, and error corrections.** Such items indicate that one or more income statements for prior years were incorrect, and that the amounts shown as adjustments do not appear in any prior period income statement. Such items should be described clearly. They may require

---

[21]*Ibid.*, par. 30.

the restatement of prior period financial statements that are presented for comparative purposes.

2. **The relationship of dividend distributions to net income for the period.** An association of these two items indicates whether management is distributing all earnings, is "plowing" part of the earnings back into the business, or is distributing not only current income but also the accumulated earnings of previous years.

3. **Transfers to and from retained earnings.** Transfers to and from retained earnings may be made in accordance with contract requirements, a continuing policy, or the apparent necessity of the moment. In any case, the amounts of retained earnings appropriated for stated reasons and the amounts returned should be clearly presented for evaluation by the user of the statement. Additionally, changes in retained earnings due to various share capital transactions may occur (e.g., stock dividends, purchase and cancellation of shares).

An example of a statement of retained earnings follows:

Fairfield Limited
STATEMENT OF RETAINED EARNINGS
For the Year Ended December 31, 1986
(In thousands of dollars)

Retained earnings January 1, 1986		$ 21,159
Add: Net income for the year		99,423
		$120,582
Deduct dividends declared on:		
Preferred shares, at $5 per share	$15,000	
Common shares, at $7 per share	28,000	43,000
Retained earnings December 31, 1986		$ 77,582

Combined Statement of Income and Retained Earnings

Some accountants believe that the statements of income and retained earnings are so closely related that they present both statements in one combined report. The principal advantage of a combined statement is that all items affecting income and retained earnings appear in one statement. Therefore, the user can assess such items as net income before extraordinary items, prior period adjustments, correction of prior period errors, and changes in accounting principles by examining this single statement. On the other hand, the figure of net income for the year is "buried" in the body of the statement, a feature that some find objectionable. A former trend toward this method of presentation has recently abated. When a combined statement is prepared, the income statement is presented as if it were an independent report but, instead of closing that statement with the amount of net income, it is extended to include retained earnings as shown below.

Magnavox Limited
COMBINED STATEMENT OF INCOME
AND RETAINED EARNINGS
(lower portion only)

Net income for the year	$ 42,290,385
Retained earnings at beginning of the year	106,734,310
	$149,024,695
Cash dividends paid	15,764,250
Retained earnings at end of year	$133,260,445

If the company has other capital accounts such as Contributed Surplus, a good practice is to present a statement of these accounts reconciling the beginning and ending balances. *CICA Handbook*, Section 3250.13, requires that changes in both retained earnings and contributed surplus during the period be disclosed. Disclosure of such changes takes the form of separate statements or is made either in the basic financial statements or in the notes.

Examples of income statements, retained earnings sections, and contributed surplus sections are presented in Appendix 5A of Chapter 5 and in Chapter 16.

KEY POINTS

1. The statement of income, or statement of earnings as it is frequently called, is the report that measures the success of enterprise operations for a given period in time.

2. The transaction approach is the method used to report income-related information. This approach focuses on the activities that have occurred during a given period; instead of presenting only a net change, the components that constitute the change are disclosed.

3. The distinction between revenues and gains and the distinction between expenses and losses depend to a great extent on the typical activities of the enterprise.

4. A single-step income statement features two major categories or groupings: revenues on the one hand, and expenses on the other. The expenses are deducted from the revenues to arrive at the net income or loss; the expression "single-step" derives from the single subtraction necessary to arrive at net income.

5. A multiple-step income statement provides a basic division between operating and nonoperating activities, and both revenues and expenses are separated into these two groups.

6. Advocates of the current operating performance income statement argue that the net income figure should show only the regular, recurring earnings of the business based on its normal operations. Conversely, advocates of the all-inclusive income statement believe that both regular and irregular earnings of the business should be reported.

7. The modified all-inclusive method, with a few exceptions, is the approach used in practice.

8. Special procedures are followed for reporting the following items: extraordinary items, unusual or infrequent gains and losses, prior period adjustments, correction of errors made in prior periods, changes in accounting principles, and discontinued operations.

9. Intraperiod tax allocation is the procedure where the tax expense for the year should be related, where possible, to specific items on the income statement and retained earnings to provide a more informative disclosure to statement users.

10. Earnings per share must be disclosed either on the face of the income statement or in a note to the statements. In addition to net income per share, per share amounts should be shown for "income before extraordinary items."

11. The statement of retained earnings should disclose prior period adjustments,

retroactive effects of error corrections and any change in accounting policies, net income (loss), dividends, and transfers to and from retained earnings (appropriations).

QUESTIONS

1. Why should caution be exercised in using the net income figure derived in an income statement? What are the objectives in applying generally accepted accounting principles to the income statement?

2. What is the difference between the capital maintenance approach to income measurement and the transaction approach? Is the final income figure the same under both approaches?

3. What are the advantages and disadvantages of the single-step income statement?

4. What usually are the main sections of a multiple-step income statement?

5. What are the advantages and disadvantages of a combined statement of income and retained earnings? What is the basis for distinguishing between operating and non-operating items?

6. Distinguish between the "all-inclusive" income statement and the "current operating performance" income statement. According to present generally accepted accounting principles, which is recommended? Explain.

7. What is the significance of a nonrecurring item's materiality in deciding its proper placement in the statement of retained earnings or in the income statement? Explain.

8. How should adjustments to prior years' income be reported in the financial statements? Give an example of such adjustments.

9. Discuss the appropriate treatment in the financial statements of each of the following:
   (a) Rent received from subletting a portion of the office space.
   (b) A patent infringement suit, brought 2 years ago against the company by another company, was settled this year by a cash payment of $132,000.
   (c) A reduction in the Allowance for Doubtful Accounts balance, because the account appears to be considerably in excess of the probable loss from uncollectible receivables.
   (d) An amount of $71,000 realized in excess of the cash surrender value of an insurance policy on the life of one of the founders of the company who died during the year.
   (e) A profit-sharing bonus to employees computed as a percentage of net income.
   (f) Additional depreciation on factory machinery because of an error in computing depreciation for the previous year.

10. Give the section of a multiple-step income statement in which each of the following is shown.
    (a) Loss on sale of machinery.
    (b) Interest expense.
    (c) Depreciation expense.
    (d) Material write-offs of notes receivable.
    (e) Bad debt expense.
    (f) Loss on disposal of a segment of the business.
    (g) Loss on inventory write-down.
    (h) Loss from a strike.

11. Indicate where the following items would ordinarily appear on the financial statements of Fry Limited for the year 1986.
    (a) Fry Limited changes its depreciation method for machinery from straight-line to double-declining balance in 1986. The cumulative effect of the change is $300,000 (net of tax).
    (b) In 1981, a supply warehouse with an expected useful life of 7 years was erroneously expensed.
    (c) An income tax refund related to the 1984 tax year was received.

(d) In 1986 the company wrote off $1,000,000 of inventory that was considered obsolete.

(e) In 1986 an earthquake destroyed a warehouse that had a book value of $200,000. Earthquakes are rare in this locality.

(f) The service life of certain equipment was changed from 7 to 5 years. If a 5-year life had been used previously, additional depreciation of $35,000 would have been charged.

12. What is meant by "tax allocation within a period"? What is the justification for such practice?

13. When does tax allocation within a period become necessary? How should this allocation be handled?

14. During the year the Jones Company earned income of $400,000 before income taxes and realized a gain of $250,000 on a government-forced expropriation sale of a division plant facility. The income is subject to income taxation at the rate of 46%; the gain on the sale of the plant is taxed at 25%. Proper accounting suggests that the gain be reported as an extraordinary item. Illustrate an appropriate presentation of these items in the income statement.

15. Recently Scott Paper Company decided to close 2 small pulp mills in Coquitlam, B. C. How would these closings be reported?

16. On January 30, 1981, a suit was filed against Olin Corporation. On August 6, 1986, Olin Corporation agreed to settle the action and pay $180,000 in damages to certain current and former employees. How should this settlement be reported in the 1986 financial statements? Discuss.

17. What major types of items are reported in the retained earnings statement?

18. The controller for Harlight, Inc. is discussing the possibility of presenting a combined statement of income and retained earnings for the current year. Indicate a possible advantage and disadvantage of this presentation format.

19. Generally accepted accounting principles usually require the use of accrual accounting for a "fair presentation" of income. If the cash receipts and disbursements method of accounting could "clearly reflect" taxable income, why does this method not usually also "fairly present" income?

20. State some of the more serious problems encountered in seeking to achieve the ideal measurement of periodic net income. Explain what accountants do as a practical alternative.

CASES

C4-1   Information concerning the operations of a corporation can be presented in an income statement or in a combined statement of income and retained earnings. Income statements could be prepared on the basis of current operating performance or on an "all-inclusive" basis. Proponents of the two types of income statements do not agree upon the proper treatment of material nonrecurring and unusual charges and credits.

Instructions

(a) Define "current operating performance" and "all-inclusive" as the terms are used above.

(b) Explain the differences in content and organization of a "current operating performance" income statement and an "all-inclusive" income statement. Include a discussion of the proper treatment of material nonrecurring and unusual charges and credits.

(c) Give the principal arguments for the use of each: all-inclusive income statement, current operating performance income statement, combined statement of income and retained earnings.

(AICPA adapted)

C4-2 Ace Limited was incorporated and began business on January 1, 1986. It has been successful and now requires a bank loan for additional working capital to finance expansion. The bank has requested an audited income statement for the year 1986. The bookkeeper for Ace Limited provides you with the following income statement which Ace plans to submit to the bank:

INCOME STATEMENT

Sales		$932,100
Dividends		12,300
Gain on recovery of insurance proceeds from flood loss (extraordinary)		28,400
		$972,800
Less:		
Selling expenses	$101,100	
Cost of goods sold	532,200	
Advertising expense	13,700	
Loss on obsolescence of inventories	34,000	
Loss on discontinued operations	48,600	
Administrative expense	73,400	803,000
Income before income taxes		$169,800
Income taxes		84,300
Net income		$ 85,500

Instructions

Indicate the deficiencies in the income statement presented above. Assume that the company desires a single-step income statement.

C4-3 Holmes, Inc. is a real estate firm that derives approximately 30% of its income from the Executive Management Division, which manages apartment complexes. As auditor for Holmes, Inc., you have recently overheard the following discussion between the controller and financial vice-president.

Vice-president: If we sold the Executive Management Division, it seems ridiculous to segregate the results of the sale in the income statement. Separate categories tend to be absurd and confusing to the shareholders. I believe that we should simply report gain on the sale as other income or expense.

Controller: Professional pronouncements would indicate that we disclose this information separately in the income statement. If a sale of this type is considered unusual and infrequent, it must be reported as an extraordinary item.

Vice-president: What about the walkout we had last month when our employees were upset about their commission income? Would this situation not also be an extraordinary item?

Controller: I am not sure whether this item would be reported as extraordinary or not.

Vice-president: Oh well, it doesn't make any difference, because the net effect of all these items is immaterial, so no disclosure is necessary.

Instructions

Based on the foregoing discussion, answer the following questions:
(a) Who is correct about handling the sale? What would be in the income statement presentation for the sale of the Executive Management Division?
(b) How should the walkout by the employees be reported?
(c) What do you think about the vice-president's observation on materiality?

C4-4 Lars Ewell, vice-president of finance for Axleson, Inc., has recently been asked to discuss with the company's division controllers the proper accounting for extraordinary items. Lars Ewell prepares the factual situations presented below as a basis for discussion.

1. A company experiences a material loss in the repurchase of a large bond issue that has been outstanding for 3 years. The company regularly repurchases bonds of this nature.

2. A railroad experiences an unusual flood loss to part of its track system. Flood losses normally occur every 3 or 4 years.

3. A machine tool company sells the only land it owns. The land was acquired 10 years ago for future expansion, but shortly thereafter the company abandoned all plans for expansion and decided to hold the land for speculation.

4. An earthquake destroys one of the oil refineries owned by a large multinational oil company. Earthquakes are rare in this geographical location.

5. A publicly held company has incurred a substantial loss in the unsuccessful registration of a bond issue.

6. A large portion of a cigarette manufacturer's tobacco crops are destroyed by a hailstorm. Severe damage from hailstorms is rare in this locality.

7. A large diversified company sells a block of shares from its portfolio of securities acquired for investment purposes.

8. A company sells a block of common shares of a publicly traded company. The block of shares, which represents less than 10% of the publicly held company, is the only security investment the company has ever owned.

9. A company that operates a chain of warehouses sells the excess land surrounding one of its warehouses. When the company buys property to establish a new warehouse, it usually buys more land than it expects to use for the warehouse with the expectation that the land will appreciate in value. Twice during the past 5 years the company had sold excess land.

10. A textile manufacturer with only one plant moves to another location and sustains relocation costs of $400,000.

Instructions

Determine whether the foregoing items should be classified as extraordinary items. Present a rationale for your position.

C4-5 The following financial statement was prepared by employees of the Cason Corporation:

Cason Corporation
STATEMENT OF INCOME AND RETAINED EARNINGS
Year Ended December 31, 1986

Revenues:	
Gross sales, including sales taxes	$877,900
Less: Returns, allowances, and cash discounts	19,800
Net sales	$858,100
Dividends, interest, and purchase discounts	30,250
Recoveries of accounts written off in prior years	13,850
Total revenues	$902,200
Costs and expenses:	
Cost of goods sold, including sales taxes	$415,900
Salaries and related payroll expenses	60,500
Rent	19,100
Freight-in and freight-out	3,400
Bad debt expense	24,000
Addition to reserve for possible inventory losses	3,800
Total costs and expenses	$526,700
Income before extraordinary items	$375,500

Extraordinary items:	
Loss on discontinued styles (note 1)	$ 27,000
Loss on sale of marketable securities (note 2)	49,050
Loss on sale of warehouse (note 3)	86,350
Retroactive settlement of federal income taxes for 1984 and 1985 (note 4)	34,600
Total extraordinary items	$197,000
Net income	$178,500
Retained earnings at beginning of year	310,700
Total	$489,200
Less: Federal income taxes	$120,000
Cash dividends on common stock	21,900
Total	$141,900
Retained earnings at end of year	$347,300
Net income per share of common stock	$1.81

Notes to the Statement of Income and Retained Earnings:
1. New styles and rapidly changing consumer preferences resulted in a $27,000 loss on the disposal of discontinued styles and related accessories.
2. The corporation sold an investment in marketable securities at a loss of $49,050. The corporation normally sells securities of this nature.
3. The corporation sold one of its warehouses at a loss of $86,350.
4. The corporation was charged $34,600 retroactively for additional income taxes resulting from a settlement in 1986. Of this amount, $17,000 was applicable to 1985 and the balance was applicable to 1984. Litigation of this nature is recurring for this company.

Instructions

Identify and discuss the weaknesses in classification and disclosure in this single-step statement of income and retained earnings. You should explain why these treatments are weaknesses and what the proper presentation of the items is in accordance with recent professional pronouncements.

C4-6 As the audit partner for Foot and Crossfoot, you are in charge of reviewing the classification of the following unusual items that have occurred during the current year:

1. An automobile dealer sells for $96,000 an extremely rare 1926 Type 37 Bugatti which was purchased for $15,000 ten years ago. The Bugatti is the only such display item the dealer owns.
2. A drilling company during the current year extended the estimated useful life of certain drilling equipment from 9 to 15 years. As a result, depreciation for the current year was materially lowered.
3. A merchandising company incorrectly overstated its ending inventory two years ago by a material amount. Inventory for all other periods is correctly computed.
4. A retail outlet changed its computation for bad debt expense from 1% to 0.5% of sales because of changes in its clientele.
5. A mining concern sells a foreign subsidiary engaged in uranium mining, although the seller continues to engage in uranium mining in other countries. (Consider only the resulting gain or loss on the sale, not the results of its operations up to the time of the sale.)
6. A steel company changes from straight-line depreciation to accelerated depreciation in accounting for its plant assets.
7. A construction company, at great expense, prepares a major proposal for a government loan. The loan is not approved.
8. A water pump manufacturer has had large losses resulting from a strike by its employees early in the year.

9. Depreciation for a prior period was incorrectly understated by $58,000. The error was discovered in the current year.

10. A large sheep rancher suffered a major loss because the government required that all sheep in the province be killed to halt the spread of a rare disease. Such a situation has not occurred in the province for 20 years.

Instructions

From the foregoing information, indicate in what section of the income statement or retained earnings statement these items should be classified. Provide a brief rationale for your position.

C4-7 R. D. Nair, controller for W & M, Inc., has recently prepared an income statement for 1986. Mr. Nair admits that he has not examined any recent professional pronouncements, but believes that the following presentation presents fairly the financial progress of this company during the current period.

W & M, Inc.
INCOME STATEMENT
For the Year Ended December 31, 1986

Sales			$347,852
Less: Sales returns and allowances			6,320
Net sales			$341,532
Cost of goods sold:			
Inventory, January 1, 1986		$ 50,235	
Purchases	$182,143		
Less: Purchase discounts	3,142	179,001	
Cost of goods available for sale		$229,236	
Inventory, December 31, 1986		37,124	
Cost of goods sold			192,112
Gross profit			$149,420
Selling expenses		$ 41,850	
Administrative expenses		32,142	73,992
Income from operations			$ 75,428
Other revenue			
Dividends received			31,000
			$106,428
Income taxes			41,342
Net income			$ 65,086

W & M, Inc.
STATEMENT OF RETAINED EARNINGS
For the Year Ended December 31, 1986

Retained earnings, January 1, 1986			$176,000
Add:			
Net income for 1986	$65,086		
Gain from casualty (net of tax)	10,000		
Gain on sale of plant assets	21,400	$ 96,486	
Deduct:			
Loss on expropriation (net of tax)	$ 8,000		
Cash dividends on common shares	30,000		
Correction of mathematical error in depreciating plant assets in 1984 (net of tax)	7,186	(45,186)	51,300
Retained earnings, December 31, 1986			$227,300

Instructions

    (a) Determine whether these statements are prepared under the current operating or all-inclusive concept of income. Cite specific details.

    (b) Which method do you favour and why?

    (c) Which method should be used, and how should the information be presented? Common shares outstanding for the year are 100,000 shares.

        For questionable items, use the classification that ordinarily would be appropriate.

C4-8 MarjoFood Company is a major manufacturer of foodstuffs whose products are sold in grocery and convenience stores throughout Canada. The company's name is well known and respected because its products have been marketed nationally for over 50 years.

    In April, 1986, the company was forced to recall one of its major products. A total of 35 persons were treated for severe intestinal pain, and eventually 3 people died from complications. All of the people had consumed MarjoFood's product.

    The product causing the problem was traced to one specific lot. MarjoFood keeps samples from all lots of foodstuffs. After thorough testing, MarjoFood and the legal authorities confirmed that the product had been tampered with after it left the company's plant and was no longer under the company's control.

    All of the product was recalled from the market—the only time a MarjoFood product has been recalled nationally and the only time for tampering. Persons who still had the product in their homes, even though it was not from the affected lot, were encouraged to return the product for credit and refund. A media campaign was designed and implemented by the company to explain what had happened and what the company was doing to minimize any chance of recurrence. MarjoFood decided to continue the product with the same trade name and same wholesale price. However, the packaging was redesigned completely to be tamper-resistant and safety sealed. This required the purchase and installation of new equipment.

    The corporate accounting staff recommended that the costs associated with the tampered product be treated as an extraordinary charge on the 1986 financial statements. Corporate accounting was asked to identify the various costs that could be associated with the tampered product and related recall. These costs are as follows ($000 omitted):

1. Credits and refunds to stores and consumers	$20,000
2. Insurance to cover lost sales and costs for possible future recalls	4,000
3. Transportation costs and off-site warehousing of returned product	4,000
4. Future security measures for other MarjoFood products	6,000
5. Testing of returned product and inventory	800
6. Destroying returned product and inventory	2,400
7. Public relations program to re-establish brand credibility	1,800
8. Communication program to inform customers, answer inquiries, prepare press releases, etc.	1,600
9. Higher cost arising from new packaging	700
10. Investigation of possible involvement of employees, former employees, competitors, etc.	500
11. Packaging redesign and testing	2,000
12. Purchase and installation of new packaging equipment	5,000
13. Legal costs for defence against liability suits	600
14. Lost sales revenue due to recall	22,000

    MarjoFood's estimated earnings before income taxes and before consideration of any of the above items for the year ending December 31, 1986, are $200 million.

Instructions

(a) MarjoFood Company plans to recognize the costs associated with the product tampering and recall as an extraordinary charge.
  1. Explain why MarjoFood could classify this occurrence as an extraordinary charge.
  2. Describe the placement and terminology used to present the extraordinary charge in the 1986 income statement.

(b) Refer to the 14 costs identified by the corporate accounting staff of MarjoFood Company.
  1. Identify the cost items by number that should be included in the extraordinary charge for 1986.
  2. For any item that is not included in the extraordinary charge, explain why it would not be included in the extraordinary charge and how it would be reported in the 1986 financial statements.

(CMA adapted)

EXERCISES

E4-1 Presented below is certain information pertaining to the Outer Space Attire Company for the current year:

Cash balance, January 1	$ 8,000
Accounts receivable, January 1	20,000
Collections from customers during year	180,000
Capital account balance, January 1	40,000
Total assets, January 1	60,000
Cash investment added, July 1	4,000
Total assets, December 31	68,000
Cash balance, December 31	10,000
Accounts receivable, December 31	27,000
Merchandise taken for personal use during year	10,000
Total liabilities, December 31	26,000

Instructions

Compute the net income for the year.

E4-2 Presented below are changes in the account balances of Antler Manufacturing Co. during the current year, except for retained earnings.

	Increase (Decrease)		Increase (Decrease)
Cash	$ 80,000	Accounts payable	$ (26,000)
Accounts receivable (net)	14,000	Bonds payable	80,000
Inventory	126,000	Common shares	120,000
Investments	(42,000)	Contributed surplus	11,000

Instructions

Compute the net income for the current year, assuming that there were no entries in the retained earnings account except for a dividend payment of $26,000.

E4-3 Presented below are certain account balances of Cricket, Inc.

Ending inventory	$ 55,000	Sales returns	$ 7,200
Rental revenue	8,400	Sales discounts	18,100
Interest expense	10,300	Selling expenses	98,800
Purchase allowances	8,200	Sales	372,400
Beginning retained earnings	105,300	Income taxes	33,000
Ending retained earnings	124,100	Beginning inventory	44,400
Freight-in	10,100	Purchases	184,200
Dividends earned	75,000	Purchase discounts	17,300
		Administrative expenses	82,000

Instructions

From the foregoing, compute the following: (a) net revenue, (b) cost of goods sold, (c) net income, (d) dividends declared during the current year.

E4-4   The financial records of Harbor, Inc. were destroyed by fire at the end of the current year. Fortunately the controller had kept certain statistical data related to the income statement as presented below.

1. The income tax rate is 45%.
2. Cost of goods sold amounts to $460,000.
3. Administrative expenses are 20% of cost of goods sold but only 8% of gross sales.
4. Four-fifths of the operating expenses relate to sales activities.
5. The beginning merchandise inventory was $88,000 and decreased 25% during the current year.
6. Sales discounts amount to $17,800.
7. 20,000 common shares were outstanding for the entire year.
8. Interest expense was $28,000.

Instructions

From the foregoing information prepare an income statement for the current year in single-step form.

E4-5   Two accountants for the firm of Check and Doublecheck are arguing about the merits of presenting an income statement on the basis of a multiple-step versus a single-step format. The discussion involves the following information related to Davis Company.

Administrative expenses	
Officers' salaries	$ 6,000
Depreciation of office furniture and equipment	4,250
Purchase returns	6,150
Purchases	51,250
Rental revenue	16,650
Selling expenses	
Transportation-out	4,450
Sales commissions	7,320
Depreciation of sales equipment	5,850
Merchandise inventory, beginning inventory	12,550
Merchandise inventory, ending inventory	14,150
Sales	77,450
Transportation-in	2,280
Income taxes	13,360
Interest expense on bonds payable	1,860

Instructions

(a) Prepare an income statement for the year using the multiple-step form. There were 50,000 common shares outstanding during the year.

(b) Prepare an income statement for the year using the single-step form.

(c) Which one do you prefer? Discuss.

E4-6   The bookkeeper of Kin-So Enterprises has compiled the following information from the company's records as a basis for an income statement for the year ended December 31, 1986.

Merchandise inventory, January 1, 1986	$ 85,000
Merchandise inventory, December 31, 1986	71,000
Purchase returns and allowances	9,000
Net sales	952,000
Sales taxes payable	40,000
Depreciation on plant assets	
(75% selling, 25% administrative)	52,000

Dividends declared	22,000
Rental revenues	17,000
Interest on notes payable	10,000
Market appreciation on temporary investments	18,000
Merchandise purchases	389,000
Transportation-in—merchandise	45,000
Wages and salaries—sales	104,000
Materials and supplies—sales	29,500
Income taxes	53,300
Wages and salaries—administrative	142,000
Other administrative expense	45,000

There were 10,000 common shares outstanding throughout the year.

Instructions

(a) Prepare a multiple-step income statement.

(b) Prepare a single-step income statement.

(c) Which format do you prefer? Discuss.

E4-7 Presented below is information related to Sampler Square, Inc. for the year 1986. There were 10,000 common shares outstanding during 1986. Assume that the loss due to damage from fire is an extraordinary item.

Purchases	$26,000
Interest revenue	6,000
Selling expense	20,000
Sales	80,000
Transportation-in	4,000
Administrative expenses	11,000
Income tax expense	12,000
Inventory, January 1, 1986	4,000
Inventory, December 31, 1986	6,000
Cash dividend paid ($5,000 declared)	4,000
Loss due to uninsured fire loss (net of tax)	10,000
Accrued rent payable	2,000
Appropriation for contingencies	12,000

Instructions

(a) Prepare a multiple-step income statement.

(b) Prepare a single-step income statement.

(c) Which format do you prefer? Discuss.

E4-8 Presented below is income statement information related to Fallon Corporation for the year.

Earthquake damage (pretax extraordinary item, tax rate 25%)	$ 50,000
Purchases	575,000
Sales	850,000
Transportation-in	10,000
Purchase discounts	7,000
Inventory (beginning)	135,000
Sales returns and allowances	17,000
Selling expenses:	
Sales salaries	55,000
Depreciation expense—store equipment	12,000
Store supplies expense	9,000
Administrative expenses:	
Officers' salaries	45,000
Depreciation expense—building	11,900
Office supplies expense	7,000
Income tax applicable to uninsured earthquake	12,500
Inventory (ending)	140,000

In addition, the corporation has other income from dividends received of $30,000 and other expense of interest on notes payable of $9,000. There are 10,000 common shares outstanding for the year. The tax rate on income is 40%.

Instructions

(a) Prepare a multiple-step income statement for the year.

(b) Prepare a single-step income statement for the year.

(c) Discuss the relative merits of the 2 income statements.

E4-9   Presented below is information related to O'Reilly, Inc. for the year 1986.

Net sales	$1,500,000
Cost of goods sold	900,000
Selling expenses	110,000
Administrative expenses	60,000
Dividend revenue	15,000
Interest revenue	6,000
Write-off of inventory due to obsolescence	60,000
Depreciation expenses omitted by accident in 1985	15,000
Casualty loss (extraordinary item)	20,000
Dividends declared	30,000
Retained earnings at December 31, 1985	2,500,000
Federal tax rate of 40% on all items	

Instructions

(a) Prepare a multiple-step income statement for 1986. Assume that 100,000 common shares are outstanding.

(b) Prepare a separate statement of retained earnings at December 31, 1986.

E4-10   The following balances were taken from the books of the Modern Health Studios Corporation on December 31, 1986.

Interest revenue	$ 70,000
Sales	1,200,000
Sales returns and allowances	200,000
Sales discounts	30,000
Inventory January 1, 1986	225,000
Inventory Dec. 31, 1986	320,000
Purchases	700,000
Purchase returns and allowances	125,000
Purchase discounts	55,000
Selling expenses	150,000
Administrative and general expenses	100,000
Interest expense	30,000
Loss from flood damage (extraordinary item)	120,000

Income tax rates are:
(1) 50% on ordinary income.
(2) 25% on extraordinary gains and losses.

Instructions

Prepare a multiple-step income statement. Assume that 100,000 common shares were outstanding during the year.

E4-11 During 1986 Entertainment Enterprises had pretax earnings of $500,000 exclusive of a realized and tax deductible loss of $200,000 from the expropriation of properties (extraordinary item). In addition, the company discovered that depreciation expense was overstated by $90,000 in 1980. Retained earnings at January 1, 1986, amounted to $1,000,000; dividends of $150,000 were declared on common shares during 1986. One hundred thousand common shares were outstanding during 1986.
Assume that the income tax rate on income is 45% for both 1980 and 1986.

Instructions

Prepare a combined statement of income and retained earnings beginning with income before taxes and extraordinary item.

E4-12 The shareholders' equity section of Danna Corporation appears below as of December 31, 1986:

Cumulative preferred shares, $2.50 dividend,		
100,000 shares authorized, outstanding 90,000 shares		$ 4,500,000
Common shares, authorized and issued 10 million		10,000,000
Contributed surplus		20,000,000
Retained earnings Dec. 31, 1985	$200,000,000	
Net income	24,000,000	224,000,000
		$258,500,000

Net income for 1986 reflects a tax rate of 40%. Included in the net income figure is a loss of $10,000,000 (before tax) as a result of a major casualty loss (extraordinary item).

Instructions

Compute earnings per share data as it should appear on the financial statements of the Danna Corporation.

E4-13 The following information was taken from the records of Logan, Inc. for the year 1986: income tax applicable to income from operations, $250,000; income tax applicable to extraordinary loss on disposal of Airtex Division, $30,000; income tax applicable to extraordinary gain, $40,000; income tax applicable to extraordinary loss from a flood, $20,000.

Retained earnings January 1, 1986	$ 500,000
Cost of goods sold	800,000
Selling expenses	200,000
Sales	1,600,000
Extraordinary gain	90,000
Extraordinary loss on disposal of	
Airtex Division	110,000
Administrative expenses	110,000
Rent revenue	35,000
Extraordinary loss, flood	50,000
Cash dividends declared	40,000

Shares outstanding during 1986 were 10,000 shares.

Instructions

(a) Prepare a single-step income statement for 1986. Include per share data.
(b) Prepare a combined single-step income and retained earnings statement.
(c) Which one do you prefer? Discuss.

PROBLEMS

P4-1 Selected accounts and related amounts appearing in the income statement and balance sheet columns of Roth Corporation for December 31 are listed in alphabetical order below.

Administrative expenses		Merchandise inventory	
(total)	$105,000	January 1	$ 87,500
Share capital	300,000	December 31	92,500
Dividends declared and		Purchases	587,500
paid	40,000	Purchase discounts	13,000
Freight-in	10,500	Rent revenue	15,000
Gain on sale of land	10,000	Sales discounts	7,500
Retained earnings (January 1)	230,000	Sales returns	3,500
Salaries payable	11,000	Selling expenses (total)	186,000
Sales	960,000		

The gain on sale of land is not an extraordinary item. All income is taxed at a uniform rate of 45% except for the gain on sale of land, which is taxed at a 30% rate.

Instructions

Prepare a combined statement of income and retained earnings using the single-step form. Assume that the only change in the unappropriated retained earnings balance during the current year was for dividends. Ten thousand common shares were outstanding during the entire year.

P4-2 The president of Sue Kinney Corporation provides you with the following account balances as of December 31, 1986.

	Dr.	Cr.
Sales		$2,500,000
Sales office salaries	$ 180,000	
Officers' salaries	195,000	
Building depreciation (50% of building is directly related to sales)	90,000	
Freight-out	50,000	
Cost of goods sold	1,050,000	
Dividends paid	75,000	
Dividends received		45,000
Interest expense—7% bonds	60,000	
Retained earnings—January 1, 1986		250,000
Expropriation of foreign holdings (extraordinary item)	500,000	
Damages payable from litigation		75,000
Federal income taxes paid	172,500	

The president informs you that the damages payable from litigation in 1986 arose out of a lawsuit initiated in 1977, and the bookkeeper debited retained earnings for $75,000. Assume that the company is continually involved in litigation of this nature. The bookkeeper had also credited cash for $172,500 in payment of the federal income taxes for 1986. The president requests your help in constructing an income statement. She advises you that the corporation had 100,000 common shares outstanding, and was taxed at a straight rate of 40% on all income-related items.

Instructions

(a) Prepare a combined statement of income and retained earnings in multiple-step form.

(b) Prepare a combined statement of income and retained earnings in single-step form.

P4-3 The following account balances were included in the trial balance of the Brown Toaster Corporation at June 30, 1986.

Sales	$1,495,625
Sales discounts	28,352
Purchases	895,450
Freight-in	20,500
Purchase returns	5,150
Purchase discounts	18,670
Sales salaries	31,750
Sales commissions	88,700
Travel expense—salespersons	23,650
Freight-out	19,500
Entertainment expense	15,150
Telephone and telegraph—sales	8,700
Depreciation of sales equipment	4,980
Building expense—prorated to sales	6,200
Miscellaneous selling expenses	2,980
Office supplies	3,450
Telephone and telegraph—administration	2,820
Depreciation of office furniture and equipment	5,340
Real estate and other local taxes	6,525
Bad debt expense—selling	4,315
Building expense—prorated to administration	8,210
Miscellaneous office expenses	6,000
Sales returns	22,450
Dividends received	25,000
Bond interest expense	14,000
Income taxes	162,190
Depreciation understatement due to error—1982 (net of tax)	6,680
Dividends declared on preferred shares	9,000
Dividends declared on common shares	32,000
Merchandise inventory—July 1, 1985	225,000

The merchandise inventory at June 30, 1986, amounted to $260,000. The Unappropriated Retained Earnings account had a balance of $195,000 at June 30, 1986, before closing; the only entry in that account during the year was a debit of $35,000 to establish an Appropriation for Bond Indebtedness account. There are 70,000 common shares outstanding.

Instructions

(a) Using the multiple-step form, prepare a combined statement of income and unappropriated retained earnings for the year ended June 30, 1986.

(b) Using the single-step form, prepare a combined statement of income and unappropriated retained earnings for the year ended June 30, 1986.

P4-4 Below is the Retained Earnings account for the year 1986 for Haley, Inc.

Retained earnings, January 1, 1986		$274,155
Add:		
Gain on sale of investments (net of tax)	$33,400	
Net income	61,800	
Refund on litigation with government, related to the year 1982 (net of tax)	12,750	
Recognition of income earned in 1985, but omitted from income statement in that year (net of tax)	9,100	117,050
		$391,205
Deduct:		
Loss on discontinued operations (net of tax)	$20,000	
Write-off of goodwill	48,000	
Cumulative effect on income in changing from straight-line depreciation to accelerated depreciation in 1986 (net of tax)	15,470	
Cash dividends	9,000	92,470
Retained earnings, December 31, 1986		$298,735

Instructions

(a) Prepare a statement of retained earnings. Haley, Inc. normally sells investments of the type mentioned above.

(b) State where the items that do not appear in the retained earnings statement should be shown.

P4-5 Presented below is information related to the Hope Company for 1986.

Retained earnings balance January 1, 1986	$ 980,000
Sales for the year	25,000,000
Cost of goods sold	17,000,000
Interest revenue	50,000
Selling and administrative expenses	5,000,000
Write-off of goodwill (not tax deductible)	500,000
Federal income taxes for 1986, excluding extraordinary items	1,100,000
Assessment for additional 1982 income taxes (normally recurring)	250,000
Gain on the sale of investments	90,000
Loss from disposal of foreign subsidiary (net of tax)	450,000
Dividends declared on common shares	250,000
Dividends declared on preferred shares	75,000

Instructions

Prepare a combined statement of income and retained earnings using the single-step form. Hope Company ordinarily sells investments of the type mentioned above. The foreign subsidiary constituted a significant segment of the firm. There were 500,000 common shares outstanding during 1986.

P4-6 Mandell Corporation has 100,000 common shares outstanding. In 1986, the company reports income from continuing operations before taxes of $1,570,000. Additional transactions not considered in the $1,570,000 are as follows:

1. In 1986, Mandell Corporation sold equipment for $86,000. The machine had originally cost $68,000 and had accumulated depreciation of $26,000. The gain or loss (considered ordinary) is taxed at the rate of 40%.

2. The company discontinued operations of one of its subsidiaries during 1986 at a loss of $180,000 before taxes. The loss on operations of the discontinued subsidiary was $80,000 before taxes; the loss from disposal of the subsidiary was $100,000 before taxes.

3. The sum of $84,000, applicable to a breached 1981 contract, was received as a result of a lawsuit. Prior to the award, legal counsel was uncertain about the outcome of the suit and had not established a receivable.

4. In 1986, the company reviewed its accounts receivable and wrote off as an expense of that year $18,400 of accounts receivable that had been carried for years and appeared unlikely to be collected. Assume this is an acceptable charge.

5. An internal audit discovered that amortization of intangible assets was understated by $32,000 (net of tax) in a prior period because of a calculation error. The amount was charged against retained earnings.

6. The company sold its only investment in common shares during the year at a gain of $120,000. The gain is taxed at a rate of 25%. Assume that the transaction meets the requirements of an extraordinary item.

Instructions

Prepare an income statement for the year 1986 starting with income from operations before taxes. Compute earnings per share as it should be shown on the face of the income statement. (Assume a tax rate of 40% on all items, unless indicated otherwise.)

P4-7 The Gabriel Corporation reported income from operations before taxes during 1986 of $720,000. Additional transactions occurring in 1986 but not considered in the $720,000 are as follows:

1. Sale of a part of its portfolio of securities resulted in a loss of $80,000 (pretax).

2. When its president died, the corporation realized $90,000 in an insurance policy. The cash surrender value of this policy had been carried on the books as an investment in the amount of $51,000. (The gain is nontaxable.)

3. The corporation disposed of its recreational division at a loss of $80,000 before taxes. Assume that this transaction meets the criteria for extraordinary items.

4. The corporation decided to change its method of inventory pricing from average cost to the FIFO method. The effect of this change on prior years is to increase 1984 income by $60,000 and decrease 1985 income by $20,000 before taxes. The FIFO method has been used for 1986. The tax rate on these items is 40%.

5. The corporation experienced an uninsured flood loss (extraordinary) in the amount of $50,000 during the year. The tax rate on this item is 45%.

6. At the beginning of 1984 the corporation purchased a machine for $60,000 (salvage value of $6,000) that had a useful life of 6 years. The bookkeeper uses straight-line depreciation, but failed to deduct the salvage value in computing the depreciation base.

Instructions

Prepare an income statement for the year 1986 starting with income from operations before taxes. Compute earnings per share as it should be shown on the face of the income statement. Common shares outstanding for the year are 10,000 shares. (Assume a tax rate of 45% on all items, unless indicated otherwise.)

P4-8 The Merill Corporation commenced business on January 1, 1983. Recently the corporation has had several unusual accounting problems related to the presentation of their income statement for financial reporting purposes.

You have been the CA for Merill Corporation for several years and have been asked to examine the following data.

Merill Corporation
STATEMENT OF INCOME
For the Year Ended December 31, 1986

Sales	$9,500,000
Cost of goods sold	6,000,000
Gross profit	$3,500,000
Selling and administrative expense	1,250,000
Income before income taxes	$2,250,000
Income tax (40%)	900,000
Net income	$1,350,000

In addition, this information was provided:

1. Retained earnings as of January 1, 1986, was $3,600,000. Cash dividends of $500,000 were declared and paid in 1986.

2. In January, 1986, Merill Corporation changed its method of accounting for plant assets from the straight-line method to the accelerated method (double-declining balance). The controller has prepared a schedule indicating what depreciation expense would have been in previous periods if the double-declining balance method had been used. (The effective tax rate for 1983, 1984, 1985 was 30%.)

	Depreciation Expense under Straight-Line	Depreciation Expense under Double-Declining Balance	Difference
1983	$ 90,000	$140,000	$50,000
1984	90,000	121,000	31,000
1985	90,000	105,000	15,000
	$270,000	$366,000	$96,000

3. In 1986, Merill discovered that two errors were made in previous years. First, when it took a physical inventory at the end of 1983, one of the count sheets was apparently lost. The ending inventory for 1983 was therefore understated by $80,000. The inventory was correctly taken in 1984, 1985, and 1986. Also, the corporation found that, in 1985, it had failed to record a $16,000 expense for sales commissions. The effective tax rate for 1983, 1984, and 1985 was 30%. The sales commissions for 1985 are included in 1986 expenses.

4. The controller mentioned that the corporation has had difficulty in collecting on several of their receivables. For this reason, the bad debt write-off was increased to 1 1/2% of sales from 1%. The controller estimates that if this rate had been used in past periods, an additional $25,000 worth of expense would have been charged. The bad debt expense for the current period was calculated and is part of selling and administrative expense.

5. Common shares outstanding at the end of 1986 totalled 1,000,000. No additional shares were purchased or sold during 1986.

6. Merill noted also that:
   (a) inventory in the amount of $48,000 was obsolete;
   (b) the major casualty loss suffered by the corporation was partially uninsured and cost $60,000, net of tax (extraordinary item).

Instructions

Prepare (a) the income statement and (b) the statement of retained earnings for Merill Corporation in accordance with professional pronouncements. Do not prepare notes.

P4-9 A condensed statement of income and retained earnings of the MacDowell Company for the year ended December 31, 1986, is presented below.

The MacDowell Company
CONDENSED STATEMENTS OF INCOME
AND RETAINED EARNINGS
For the Year Ended, December 31, 1986

Sales	$5,000,000
Cost of goods sold	2,800,000
Gross margin	$2,200,000
Selling, general, and administrative expenses	1,500,000
Income before extraordinary item	$ 700,000
Extraordinary item	(500,000)
Net income	$ 200,000
Retained earnings, January 1	800,000
Retained earnings, December 31	$1,000,000

Presented below are three unrelated situations involving accounting changes and classification of certain items as ordinary or extraordinary. Each situation is based upon the condensed statements of income and retained earnings of the MacDowell Company and requires revisions of these statements.

1. At the end of 1986, MacDowell's management decided that the estimated loss rate on uncollectible accounts receivable was too low. The loss rate used for the years 1985 and 1986 was 1% of total sales, and owing to an increase in the write-off of uncollectible accounts, the rate has been raised to 3% of total sales. The amount recorded in bad debt expense under the heading of selling, general, and administrative expenses for 1986 was $50,000 and for 1985 was $30,000. The extraordinary item in the condensed statement of income and retained earnings of 1986 relates to a loss incurred in the abandonment of outmoded equipment formerly used in the business.

2. On January 1, 1984, MacDowell acquired machinery at a cost of $200,000. The company adopted the double-declining balance method of depreciation for this

machinery, and had been recording depreciation over an estimated life of 10 years, with no residual value. At the beginning of 1986, a decision was made to adopt the straight-line method of depreciation for this machinery. Owing to an oversight, however, the double-declining balance method was used for 1986. For financial reporting purposes, depreciation is included in selling, general, and administrative expenses. The extraordinary item in the condensed statement of income and retained earnings relates to shutdown expenses incurred by the company during a major strike by its operating employees during 1986.

3. During the latter part of 1986, the company discontinued its retail and apparel fabric divisions. The loss on sale of these two discontinued divisions amounted to $500,000. This amount was considered part of selling, general, and administrative expenses. The transaction meets the criteria for extraordinary items. The extraordinary item in the condensed statement of income and retained earnings for 1986 relates to a loss sustained as a result of damage to the company's merchandise caused by a tornado that struck its main warehouse in Beaumont City. This natural disaster was considered an unusual and infrequent occurrence for that section of the country.

Instructions

For each of the three unrelated situations, prepare a revised condensed statement of income and retained earnings of the MacDowell Company. Ignore income tax considerations and earnings per share computations.

(AICPA adapted)

P4-10 Presented below is a combined single-step statement of income and retained earnings for Pearson Company for 1986.

	(000 omitted)
Net sales	$600,000
Cost and expenses:	
Cost of goods sold	480,000
Selling, general, and administrative expenses	66,000
Other, net	17,000
	563,000
Income before income taxes	37,000
Income taxes	16,800
Net income	20,200
Retained earnings at beginning period, as previously reported	141,000
Adjustment required for correction of error	(7,000)
Retained earnings at beginning of period, as restated	134,000
Dividends on common shares	(12,200)
Retained earnings at end of period	$142,000

Additional facts are as follows:

1. "Selling, general, and administrative expenses" for 1986 included a usual but infrequently occurring charge of $9,000,000.

2. "Other, net" for 1986 included an extraordinary item (charge) of $10,000,000. If the extraordinary item (charge) had not occurred, income taxes for 1986 would have been $21,800,000 instead of $16,800,000.

3. "Adjustment required for correction of error" was a result of a change in estimate (useful life of certain assets reduced to 7 years and a catch-up adjustment made).

4. Pearson Company disclosed earnings per common share for net income in the Notes to the Financial Statements.

Instructions

Determine from these additional facts whether the presentation in the above Pearson Company's statement of income and retained earnings is appropriate. If the presentation is not appropriate, describe the appropriate presentation and discuss its theoretical rationale.

5

BALANCE SHEET AND STATEMENT OF CHANGES IN FINANCIAL POSITION

Investors have often focused their attention primarily on the income statement and earnings per share to the virtual exclusion of the balance sheet and statement of changes in financial position. However, high inflation rates, coupled with the related credit "crunches" of the 1970s and 1980s, have taught investors an important lesson—many surprises in earnings per share could have been anticipated if these financial statements had not been overlooked. Liquidity and financial flexibility are necessary conditions for any profitable enterprise, and only through careful analysis of balance sheets and statements of changes in financial position can information about these conditions be obtained.

BALANCE SHEET

Usefulness of the Balance Sheet[1]

The balance sheet provides information about the nature and amounts of investments in enterprise resources, obligations to enterprise creditors, and the owners'

---

[1]*Financial Reporting in Canada—1983* (Toronto: CICA, 1983) indicated that, in 1982, 90% of the companies surveyed used the term "balance sheet." The term "statement of financial position" is used infrequently, although it is conceptually appealing.

equity in net enterprise resources. That information not only complements information about the components of income, but also contributes to financial reporting by providing a basis for (1) computing rates of return, (2) evaluating the capital structure of the enterprise, and (3) assessing the liquidity and financial flexibility of the enterprise. In order to make certain judgements about enterprise risk[2] and assessments of future cash flows, one must analyze the balance sheet and determine enterprise liquidity and financial flexibility.

Liquidity describes "the amount of time that is expected to elapse until an asset is realized or otherwise converted into cash or until a liability has to be paid."[3] Both short-term and long-term credit grantors are interested in the relationship of current assets to current liabilities as one means to help assess the enterprise's ability to meet current and maturing obligations. Similarly, present and prospective equity holders study the liquidity of an enterprise to assess the likelihood of continuing or increasing cash dividends or the possibility of expanding operations. Generally, the greater the liquidity, the lower the risk of enterprise failure.

Financial flexibility is the "ability of an enterprise to take effective actions to alter the amounts and timing of cash flows so it can respond to unexpected needs and opportunities."[4] For example, a company may become so loaded with debt that its sources of monies to finance expansion or to pay off maturing debt are limited or nonexistent; thus, it lacks financial flexibility. An enterprise with a high degree of financial flexibility is better able to survive bad times, to recover from unexpected setbacks, and to take advantage of profitable and unexpected investment opportunities. Generally, the greater the financial flexibility, the lower the risk of enterprise failure.

The serious effects of a lack of liquidity and inadequate financial flexibility are illustrated by the experience of the airline industry in the United States during the early 1980s. Pan Am, American, Eastern, United, and TWA all reported quarterly operating losses that stemmed primarily from high interest rates, deregulation and increased competition, increased fuel costs, and price cutting. Because of operating losses and lowered liquidity, some airlines asked their employees to sign labour contracts that provided no wage increases. Other airlines, already heavily in debt and lacking financial flexibility and liquidity, had to cancel orders for new, more efficient aircraft of the 757 and 767 variety. They were not even able to generate cash through the sale of their old airplanes because of lowered air traffic (controllers' strike and layoff) and the lower fuel efficiency of the older aircraft. Pan Am was forced to sell its Manhattan skyscraper for $400 million to maintain its liquidity. The problem became so acute that one of the major airlines (Braniff) declared bankruptcy. An examination of the airlines' balance sheets revealed their financial inflexibility and low liquidity prior to the occurrence of these consequences.

Limitations of the Balance Sheet

As indicated in earlier Chapters, the balance sheet **does not reflect current values** because accountants have adopted a historical cost basis in valuing and reporting the assets and liabilities. For example, when a balance sheet is prepared in accor-

---

[2]Risk is an expression of the unpredictability of future events, transactions, circumstances, and results of the enterprise.

[3]"Reporting Income, Cash Flows, and Financial Position of Business Enterprises," *Proposed Statement of Financial Accounting Concepts* (Stamford, Conn.: FASB, 1981), par. 29.

[4]*Ibid.*, par. 25.

dance with generally accepted accounting principles, most assets are stated at cost; exceptions would include receivables and some marketable securities, inventories and long-term investments. Many accountants believe that all the assets should be restated in terms of current values; there are, however, widely differing opinions about the exact type of valuation basis to be employed. Some contend that statements based on historical cost should be adjusted to constant dollars (general price-level changes) when inflation is significant; others believe that a current cost concept (specific price-level changes) is more useful; still others believe that a fair market value concept should be adopted. Regardless of the method favoured, all are significantly different from the historical cost approach. Each approach has the advantage over the historical cost basis of presenting a more appropriate assessment of the current value of the enterprise, although the question of whether reliable values can be obtained is still unresolved. These issues are discussed further in Chapter 25.

Another basic limitation of historical cost statements is that they **depend on estimated values.** Determining these amounts requires the exercise of judgement. Even if significant changes in price levels do not occur, the determination of the collectibility of receivables, the salability of inventory, and the useful life of long-term tangible and intangible assets is difficult. Although the depreciation of long-term assets is a generally accepted practice, the recognition of accretion and enhancement in value is generally ignored by accountants for such fixed assets.

In addition, the balance sheet necessarily **omits many items that are of financial value to the business** but cannot be measured objectively. As indicated earlier, the value of a company's human resources is certainly significant, but it is omitted because such assets are difficult to quantify as a result of the uncertainty surrounding their ultimate value. Such omissions are understandable and excusable, but many items that could appear on the balance sheet (most are liabilities or commitments) are sometimes reported in an ''off-balance sheet'' manner, if reported at all.[5] Several of these items (e.g., sales of receivables with recourse, leases, throughput arrangements, and take-or-pay contracts) are discussed in later chapters.

Classification in the Balance Sheet

In the balance sheet, accounts are classified so that similar items are grouped together to arrive at significant subtotals; furthermore, the material is arranged to show important relationships and focus attention on the most important items.

The three general classes of items included in the balance sheet are assets, liabilities, and owners' equity. Here is how we defined them in Chapter 2:

1. **Assets** are probable future economic benefits obtained or controlled by a particular entity as a result of past transactions or events.
2. **Liabilities** are probable future sacrifices of economic benefits arising from present obligations of a particular entity to transfer assets or provide services to other entities in the future as a result of past transactions or events.
3. **Equity** is the residual interest in the assets of an entity that remains after deducting its liabilities. In a business enterprise, the equity is the ownership interest.

[5]For a discussion of various methods that businesses have devised to remove debt from the balance sheet, see Richard Dieter and Arthur R. Wyatt, ''Get It Off the Balance Sheet, '' *Financial Executive* (Vol. 48, June, 1980), pp. 42, 44–48.

These items are then divided into several subclassifications that provide the reader with additional information. The following table indicates the general format of balance sheet presentation for a corporation.

BALANCE SHEET

Assets	Liabilities and Shareholders' Equity
Current assets	Current liabilities
Noncurrent assets	Noncurrent liabilities
Investments	Shareholders' equity
Property, plant, and equipment	Share capital
Intangible assets	Contributed surplus
Other assets	Retained earnings

The balance sheet may be classified in some other manner, but these are the major subdivisions of this statement, and there is little departure from them in practice. In the case of a proprietorship or partnership, the classifications within the owners' equity section are presented differently.

Current Assets

Current assets are cash and other assets that are expected to be converted into cash, sold, or consumed either in one year or in the operating cycle, whichever is longer. Within this definition, the operating cycle of any given enterprise is considered to be the average time between the acquisition of materials and supplies and the realization of cash through sales of the product for which the materials and supplies were acquired. Thus the time it takes to process the material, to sell the product, and to collect from customers is included in the operating cycle. The cycle operates **from cash**, through inventory and receivables, and back **to cash**. This definition ignores the arbitrary one-year period except when there are several operating cycles within one year; then the one-year period is used. If the operating cycle is more than one year, the longer period is used.

Current assets are presented in the balance sheet in the order of their liquidity. The five major items found in the current assets section are cash, temporary investments in marketable securities, receivables, inventories, and prepayments. **Cash** is included at its value; **temporary investments in marketable securities** are valued at cost or the lower of cost and market; **accounts receivable** are stated at the estimated amount collectible; **inventories** generally are included at cost or the lower of cost and market; and **prepaid items** are valued at unexpired cost.

These items are not considered current assets if they are not expected to be realized in one year or in the operating cycle, whichever is longer. For example, cash restricted for purposes other than payment of current obligations or for use in current operations is excluded from the current asset section. **Generally, the rule is that if an asset is to be turned into cash or is to be used to pay a current liability within a year or the operating cycle, whichever is longer, it is classified as current.** This requirement is subject to exceptions. Marketable securities, for example, pose a problem. Depending on the intent of management, an investment in common shares is classified as either a current asset or a noncurrent asset. The problem is especially difficult when a company has small holdings of common shares or bonds of another company. Should these assets be classified as current? The differentiation can be made only on the basis of intent: What does management plan to do with these securities?

Note also that although a current asset is well defined, certain theoretical problems develop. One problem is justifying the inclusion of prepaid expenses in the current asset section. The normal justification is that if these items had not been paid in advance, they would require the use of current assets during the operating cycle. If we follow this logic to its ultimate conclusion, however, any asset purchased previously saves the use of current assets during the operating cycle. Prepaid expenses are not material in amount, however, and their placement on the balance sheet has been of little concern.

Another problem occurs in the definition of current assets when fixed assets are consumed during the operating cycle. A literal interpretation of the accounting profession's position on this matter would indicate that an amount equal to the following period's depreciation and amortization charges on the noncurrent assets should be placed in the current asset section reported at the current year end, because it will be consumed in the next operating cycle. This conceptual problem is generally ignored, which illustrates that the formal distinction made between current and noncurrent assets is, nonetheless, "flexible."[6]

Cash   Any restrictions on the general availability of cash or any commitments on its probable disposition must be disclosed. This may be done through notes or in the body of the balance sheet as exemplified below:

Current assets		
Cash		
Restricted in accordance with terms of the purchase contract	$48,500.00	
Unrestricted—available for current use	14,928.92	$63,428.92

In this example, it was assumed that an amount of cash ($48,500) was restricted to meet an obligation due currently and, therefore, the restricted cash was included under current assets. If cash is restricted for purposes other than current obligations, it is excluded from the current assets, as shown below:

Current assets		
Cash	$78,327.45	
Less: Cash restricted for bond redemption	45,000.00	$33,327.45
Other Assets		
Cash restricted for bond redemption in accordance with the bond indenture		$45,000.00

[6]For an interesting discussion of the shortcomings of the current and noncurrent classification framework, see Loyd Heath, "Financial Reporting and the Evaluation of Solvency," *Accounting Research Monograph No. 3* (New York: AICPA, 1978), pp. 43–69. The principal recommendation is that the current and noncurrent classification be abolished, and that assets and liabilities simply be listed without classification in their present order. This approach is justified on the basis that any classification scheme is arbitrary and that users of the financial statements can assemble the data in the manner they believe most appropriate.

Temporary Investments   The basis of valuation and any differences between cost and current market value should be included in the balance sheet presentation of temporary investments. The generally accepted method of accounting for such investments, often referred to as marketable securities, is cost and market, whichever is lower.[7]

Current assets

   Marketable securities—at cost that
     approximates market $26,342.00

Receivables   The amount and nature of any nontrade receivables, and any amounts pledged or discounted should be clearly stated. Additionally, the anticipated loss due to uncollectibles may be separately disclosed rather than simply reporting a net figure for receivables less the related allowance. The following serves to illustrate one of the many possible ways of presenting receivables.

Current assets

  Notes and accounts receivable
    Customers—
      Notes $ 35,000.00
      Accounts (of which $40,000 is pledged
        as security for a note payable)   146,528.75
    Subsidiary company   18,247.12
    Officers and employees   17,912.11
                                    $217,687.98
    Less: Allowance for doubtful accounts   11,200.00 $206,487.98

Inventories   For a proper presentation of inventories, the basis of valuation, the method of pricing (costing), and, for a manufacturing concern, the stages of completion of the inventories are disclosed.

Current assets

  Inventories—at the lower of cost (determined
    by the first-in, first-out method) and market
    Finished goods $ 47,258.91
    Work in process   12,246.88
    Raw materials   188,764.21 $248,270.00

Some accountants contend that, in a company that assembles a final product from both purchased and manufactured parts and also sells some of these parts, a distinction among finished goods, work in progress, and raw materials is arbitrary and misleading. They prefer a classification that indicates the source or nature of the inventory amount as shown on page 196.

---

[7]Special rules that apply for both short-term and long-term marketable securities are discussed in Chapters 7 and 18.

Current assets

Inventories—at the lower of cost (determined
    by the first-in, first-out method) and market

Materials	$195,696.25	
Direct labour	37,300.25	
Manufacturing overhead	15,273.50	$248,270.00

Long-Term Investments

Long-term investments, often referred to simply as investments, normally consist of one of three types:

1. Investments in such securities as bonds, common shares, or long-term notes.
2. Investments in tangible fixed assets not currently used in operations, such as land held for speculation.
3. Investments set aside in special funds (e.g., a sinking fund, pension fund, or plant expansion fund). The cash surrender value of life insurance is included here.

Long-term investments are to be held for many years, and are not acquired with the intention of disposing of them in the near future. Long-term investments are usually presented on the balance sheet just below Current Assets in a separate section called Investments. Many securities that are properly shown among the long-term investments are readily marketable; however, they should not be included as current assets if they are not held with the intention of converting them to cash in a year or in the operating cycle, whichever is longer.[8]

Investments

Investments in companies—at equity			
Leelco, Inc.			
1,000 shares (45% of common shares)	$86,425		
Cash advance	10,000	$96,425	
Career Co., Inc.			
2,000 shares (40% of common shares)		42,000	$138,425
Miscellaneous other investments— at cost, which is approximately $13,500 below current market value			84,600	$223,025

Property, Plant, and Equipment and Intangible Assets

Property, plant, and equipment are assets of a durable nature used in the regular operations of the business. These assets consist of such physical items as land, buildings, machinery, furniture, tools, and wasting or natural resources (timberland, minerals). In some cases, natural resources may be classified under their own heading in the balance sheet. With the exception of land, most assets within this classification are either depreciable (e.g., buildings) or consumable (e.g., timberland).

[8]A discussion of issues related to accounting for long-term investments is presented in Chapter 18.

Property, plant, and equipment			
Land		$ 80,000	
Buildings (subject to a first mortgage lien of $100,000)	$420,000		
Less: Accumulated depreciation	176,000	244,000	
Equipment	$350,000		
Less: Accumulated depreciation	120,000	230,000	$554,000
Intangible assets			
Franchise— at cost less amortization of $4,712		$ 8,244	
Licences, trademarks, and patents— at cost less amortization of $12,444		16,556	
Goodwill—at cost less amortization of $10,000		70,000	$ 94,800

Intangible assets lack physical substance. They include, for example, patents, copyrights, franchises, goodwill, trademarks, trade names, and secret processes. Generally, all of these intangibles are written off (amortized) against income. Intangibles can represent significant economic resources, yet financial analysts often ignore them, and accountants write them down or off arbitrarily because valuation is difficult. Intangibles are not generally capitalized and amortized unless acquired in arm's length transactions.

The basis of valuing the property, plant and equipment and intangible assets, any liens against the properties, and accumulated depreciation should be shown. It is seldom advisable to show a detailed classification of the property, plant and equipment in the balance sheet; a supplementary schedule or analysis in the notes to the financial statements generally provides a better means of presenting such information.

Other Assets

The items included here vary widely in practice (e.g., deferred charges—long-term prepaid expenses—noncurrent receivables, assets in special funds, and advances to subsidiaries). Such classification is, unfortunately, too general; it should properly be restricted to unusual items significantly different from assets included in the categories above. Some deferred costs (e.g., organization costs incurred during the early life of the business) are commonly classified here. Even these costs, however, may be more properly placed in the intangible assets section.

Current Liabilities

Current liabilities are the obligations that are reasonably expected to be liquidated either through the use of current assets or the creation of other current liabilities. This classification includes:

1. Payables resulting from the acquisition of goods and services: accounts payable, wages payable, taxes payable, and so on.
2. Collections received in advance for the delivery of goods or performance of services: for example, rent revenue received in advance or subscription revenue received in advance.

3. Other liabilities whose liquidation will take place within the operating cycle. This includes such liabilities as bonds to be paid in the current period, or obligations arising from the purchase of equipment.

At times, even though a liability will be paid next year, it is not included in the current liability section. This occurs either when the debt is expected to be refinanced through another long-term issue,[9] or when the retirement of the debt occurs out of noncurrent assets. This approach is used because liquidation does not require the use of current assets or the creation of other current liabilities. Current liabilities frequently are reported on the balance sheet in the order in which they will be paid.

Here is an example of a current liability section.

Current liabilities			
Notes payable to bank (secured by pledge of raw materials inventory)		$ 45,000.00	
Accounts payable			
Trade	$185,917.18		
Customers' deposits and advances	32,412.81		
Employees' payroll deductions	18,912.88	237,242.87	
Bank overdraft		7,245.12	
Current maturities of instalment note payable, secured by lien against land and buildings		50,000.00	
Dividend payable		18,000.00	
Income taxes		23,000.00	
Miscellaneous accrued liabilities		17,245.86	$397,733.85

Current liabilities include such items as trade payables, nontrade notes and accounts payable, advances received from customers, and current maturities of long-term debt. Income taxes and other accrued items are classified separately, if material. Any secured liability (e.g., investment in shares held as collateral on notes payable) is fully described so that the assets providing the security can be determined.

The difference between current assets and current liabilities is called working capital. **Working capital** is frequently analyzed as a means to assess the short-term debt-paying ability of a company. In order to highlight working capital, some companies show current liabilities deducted from current assets in their balance sheet. This format, however, is not the common practice.

Long-Term Liabilities

Long-term liabilities are obligations that are not reasonably expected to be liquidated within the normal operating cycle of the business but, instead, are payable at some date beyond that time. Bonds payable, notes payable, deferred income taxes, lease obligations, and pension obligations are the most common long-term liabilities. Generally, a great deal of supplementary disclosure is needed for this section because most long-term debt is subject to various covenants and restrictions for the protection of the lenders. Long-term liabilities that mature within the current operating cycle are classified as current liabilities if their liquidation requires the use of assets included in the current asset group.

[9]A detailed discussion of accounting for debt expected to be refinanced is found in Chapter 10.

Generally, long-term liabilities are of three types:

1. Obligations arising from specific financing arrangements where additional assets are acquired (e.g., the issuance of bonds, long-term lease obligations, and long-term notes payable).
2. Obligations arising from the ordinary operations of the enterprise (e.g., pension obligations and deferred income taxes).
3. Obligations extending beyond the coming year that are dependent upon the occurrence or nonoccurrence of one or more future events to confirm the amount payable, or the payee, or the date payable (e.g., service or product warranties).

For issued bonds payable it is desirable to report any premium or discount separately as an addition to or subtraction from the principal (par value) amount. The terms of all long-term liability agreements including maturity date or dates, rates of interest, nature of obligation, and any security pledged to support the debt should be described as illustrated below.

Long-term liabilities			
First mortgage 9% notes payable in semiannual instalments of $25,000	$500,000		
Less: Current maturities	50,000	$450,000	
Bond payable 9 1/2% (due in 1996)	$850,000		
Less: Discount	35,000	815,000	$1,265,000

Notes in the amount of $50,000, which mature currently and have been deducted above, are shown as current liabilities.

Shareholders' Equity

The complexity of share capital agreements and the various restrictions on residual equity imposed by federal and provincial corporation laws, debt contracts, and voluntary actions of boards of directors make the shareholders' equity section one of the most difficult to prepare and understand. The legal basis for examples and problems presented in this book is **The Canada Business Corporations Act** (CBCA) which came into force on January 1, 1976. Companies may incorporate under the provincial corporation acts which may vary to some extent from the federal act, although differences are becoming less significant as provinces revise their acts. For example, prior to the CBCA, federally incorporated companies could have par value stock. Under the CBCA the concept of par value was abolished, which meant that the entire proceeds from the sale of shares were to be credited to the appropriate share account. An amendment to the **Ontario Business Corporations Act** in 1983 included a similar provision (as do many provincial Incorporation Acts). The notion of par value, however, has not disappeared from the Canadian accounting scene.[10] Because of this, a very limited number of examples as well as cases, exer-

---

[10]*Financial Reporting in Canada—1983 op. cit.*, indicated that in 1982 a few of the Canadian companies surveyed still carried a "Premium on shares" amount in their Contributed Surplus. Also, of the 325 companies surveyed, 94 made reference to a par value or stated value in general or as existing for at least one class of their shares. Also, the CBCA permits a restricted use of the notion of par value for reasons having to do with some particular tax issues. Par value shares are allowed under incorporation statutes of British Columbia, Newfoundland, Nova Scotia, Prince Edward Island, Quebec, and the Northwest Territories.

cises, and problems in this book will reflect the existence of par value shares.[11] Another point is that the CBCA states that corporations are to issue shares by "classes" and "series of classes." The terms "preferred" and "common" may continue to be used and, thus, will be used herein.

The major requirements for reporting share capital accounts are that the amounts authorized, issued, and outstanding be disclosed. The contributed surplus is usually presented in one amount, although breakdowns are informative if the sources of additional capital obtained are varied and material. The retained earnings section may be divided between the unappropriated (the amount that is available for dividend declaration) and any amounts that are legally or voluntarily restricted (called appropriated retained earnings).

The ownership or shareholders' equity accounts in a corporation are considerably different from those in a partnership or proprietorship. Partners' permanent capital accounts and the balance in their temporary accounts (Drawing accounts) are shown separately. Proprietorships may use a single capital account that handles all of the owner's equity transactions.

Presented below are illustrations of various shareholders' equity sections.

Shareholders' investment		
Share capital		
Authorized and issued, 100,000 shares of no-par value	$540,000.00	
Earnings reinvested in the business (of which $16,500 is not available for dividends under terms of the bank loan payable)	27,200.00	$567,200.00

Investment of shareholders, represented by			
Share capital:			
Class A, cumulative, $2 dividend, preferred shares, no-par value Authorized and issued, 10,000 shares		$250,000.00	
Class B, common shares, no-par value Authorized 500,000 shares; issued and outstanding, 450,000 shares		450,000.00	
Contributed surplus		33,000.00	
Earnings retained in the business:			
Appropriated for future inventory losses	$20,000.00		
Unappropriated	15,000.00	35,000.00	$768,000.00

---

[11]Most of these examples, cases, exercises, and problems occur in later chapters, particularly Chapters 15 and 16, where the issue is discussed in depth. Some instructors may choose to deal only with no par value shares. If so, one approach would be simply to assume that all proceeds from the sale of shares are to be credited to the appropriate stock account, even when a par value is given (i.e., there would be no Premium accounts in Contributed Surplus).

Shareholders' equity			
Share capital:			
6% cumulative preferred—			
Authorized, 2,500 shares of $50			
par value; issued, 2,000 shares		$100,000.00	
(redeemable at $52.50 per share)			
Common—			
Authorized, 60,000 shares without			
par value; issued and			
outstanding; 50,000 shares		160,000.00	
Total share capital		$260,000.00	
Retained earnings:			
Appropriated for			
plant expansion	$100,000.00		
Unappropriated	250,000.00	$350,000.00	
Total shareholders' equity			$610,000.00

Additional Information Reported

The balance sheet is not complete simply because a listing of the assets, liabilities, and owners' equity accounts has been presented. Great importance is given to supplemental information that is completely new or is an elaboration or qualification of items in the balance sheet. There are normally four types of information that are supplemental to account titles and amounts presented in the balance sheet.

1. **Contingencies.** An existing condition or situation involving uncertainty as to possible gain or loss to an enterprise that will be resolved ultimately when one or more future events occur or fail to occur.
2. **Valuation and accounting policies.** Explanations of the valuation methods used or the basic assumptions made concerning, for example, inventory valuations, depreciation methods, and investments in subsidiaries.
3. **Contractual situations.** Explanations of certain restrictions or covenants attached either to specific assets or, more likely, to liabilities.
4. **Post-balance sheet disclosures.** Disclosures of certain events that have occurred after the balance sheet date but before the financial statements have been issued.

Each of these topics is considered briefly in the following paragraphs, and in greater detail in later chapters.

Gain Contingencies   The term **gain contingencies** designates claims or rights to receive assets (or have a liability reduced) whose existence is uncertain but which may become valid property rights eventually.

The typical gain contingencies are:

1. Possible receipts of monies from gifts, donations, bonuses, and so on.
2. Possible refunds from the government in tax disputes.
3. Pending court cases where the probable outcome is favourable.

Accountants have adopted a conservative policy in this area. Gain contingencies are not recorded but are disclosed in notes to the financial statements only when the probabilities are high that a gain contingency will become a reality.

Loss Contingencies   The *CICA Handbook* requires that an estimated loss from loss contingencies be accrued by a charge to income and the recording of a liability if both of the following conditions are met:

1. It is **likely** that future events will confirm that an asset had been impaired or a liability incurred at the date of the financial statements.
2. The amount of loss can be **reasonable estimated**.[12]

The establishment of a liability for service or product warranties would ordinarily meet these two conditions.

In most loss contingency cases, however, one or both of the conditions will not be present. For example, assume that a company is involved in a lawsuit with one of its competitors. The company's lawyer indicates a reasonable possibility that they may lose. In such a case, there is only a **reasonable possibility** of loss rather than a **likely possibility** (i.e., having a high chance of occurrence) and, therefore, a liability would not be recorded. However, disclosure of the nature of the contingency and, where possible, the amount involved should be made in notes to the financial statements. If a reasonable estimate of the amount of the contingency is not possible, disclosure is made in general terms, describing the loss contingency and explaining that no estimated amount is determinable. Because these types of contingencies are only possibilities, they should not enter into the determination of net income.

The diverse practices in accounting for contingencies stem from varied interpretations of the words "likely" and "reasonably possible." This area of practice requires the accountant to use professional judgement, as the determination of what constitutes full and proper accounting and disclosure entails a high degree of subjectivity.[13]

Some of the more common sources of **loss contingencies that ordinarily will not be accrued as liabilities are:**

1. Guarantees of indebtedness of others.
2. Obligations of commercial banks under "standby letters of credit" (commitments to finance projects under certain circumstances).
3. Guarantees to repurchase receivables (or any related property) that have been sold or assigned.
4. Disputes over additional income taxes for prior years.
5. Pending lawsuits whose outcome is uncertain.

It should be noted that reporting for loss contingencies is complex and presented here only in general terms. In Chapter 10 the subject is discussed at greater length. **General risk contingencies** that are inherent in the business operations, such as the possibility of war, strike, losses from catastrophes not ordinarily insured against, or a business recession, are not reflected in financial statements either by incorporation in the accounts or by other disclosures.

Valuations and Accounting Policies   As subsequent chapters of this text indicate, accountants use many different methods and bases in valuing assets and allocating costs. For instance, inventories can be computed under several cost-flow assump-

---

[12]*CICA Handbook*, Section 3290.

[13]G. Richard Chaley and Heather A. Wier, "The Challenge Of Contingencies; Adding Precision to Probability," *CA Magazine*, (April, 1985) pp. 38–41. The diversity of interpretation of the words "likely," "unlikely," "not reasonably estimable," and "possible" among accountants and lawyers is well identified in this article. A solution to improved understanding—assigning a range of probabilities—is suggested.

tions (e.g., LIFO, average cost, and FIFO), plant and equipment can be depreciated under several accepted methods of cost allocation (e.g., double-declining balance and straight-line), and investments can be carried at different valuations (e.g., cost, equity, and market). Many users of financial statements know of these possibilities and examine the statements closely to determine the methods used.

Generally, requirements have been established to ensure that these valuation methods are disclosed either in the statement itself or in the notes to the statements. The *CICA Handbook* requires disclosure in the financial statements of all significant accounting principles and methods chosen from among alternatives and/or those that are peculiar to a given industry.[14] The *CICA Handbook* states that the disclosure is particularly useful if given in a separate **Summary of Significant Accounting Policies** cross-referenced to the financial statements or as the initial note. See the specimen financial statements in Appendix 5A following this chapter for an example of such a summary (page 222) and further discussion of this topic in Chapter 27.

Contracts and Negotiations   In addition to the contingencies and different methods of valuation disclosed as supplementary data to the financial statements, any contracts and negotiations of significance are disclosed in the notes to the statements.

It is mandatory, for example, that the essential provisions of lease contracts, pension obligations, and stock option plans be clearly stated in the notes to the financial statements. The analyst who examines a set of financial statements wants to know not only the amount of the liabilities, but also how the different contractual provisions of these debt obligations affect the company at present and in the future.

In addition to the exacting disclosure requirements for certain obligations, the accountant must pay heed to many other items that have a significant effect on the enterprise. It is here that he or she must exercise professional judgement: would omission of such information be misleading to the financial statement user? The axiom, "When in doubt, disclose," suggests that it is better to disclose a little too much information than not enough.

Post-Balance Sheet Events   Notes to the financial statements should include adequate explanations of any significant financial events taking place after the formal date of the balance sheet, but before the date of its completion.[15] A period of several weeks, and sometimes months, may elapse after the end of the year before the financial statements are completed. Determining the quantity and valuation of inventory, reconciling subsidiary ledgers with controlling accounts, preparing necessary adjusting entries, assuring that all transactions for the period have been entered, obtaining an audit of the financial statements by independent accountants, and printing the annual report all take time. During the period between the balance sheet date and its distribution to shareholders and creditors, important transactions or other events may have occurred that materially affect the company's financial position or operating situation.

Those who read a balance sheet may think of the balance sheet condition as remaining constant, and project it into the future. Numerous events or transactions

---

[14]*CICA Handbook*, Section 1500.

[15]*Ibid.*, Section 3820. The date of completion is a matter of judgement and depends on the particular circumstances and reporting requirements.

may make this projection inappropriate, however. If the company has sold one of its plants, acquired a subsidiary, suffered extraordinary losses, settled significant litigation, or experienced any other important event in the post-balance sheet period, such an event should be brought to the attention of financial statement readers. Without an explanation of such an occurrence in a note, the reader (not knowing of its existence) might easily be misled, reaching conclusions that would differ from those made if all the facts had been disclosed.

Two types of events or transactions occurring after the balance sheet date (commonly referred to as **subsequent events**) may have a material effect on the financial statements or may need to be considered to interpret these statements accurately.

The first type consists of events or transactions that (1) provide additional evidence about conditions that existed at the balance sheet date, (2) affect the estimates that are used in preparing financial statements, and (3) result in adjustments of the financial statements. The accountant is obligated to use all of the information that is available prior to the issuance of the financial statements in evaluating estimates previously made. To ignore these subsequent events is to pass an opportunity to improve the accuracy of the financial statements. This first type of event encompasses information that would have been recorded in the accounts had it been available at the balance sheet date: for example, subsequent events that affect the realization of such assets as receivables and inventories or the settlement of estimated liabilities. Such events typically represent the culmination of conditions that have existed for some time.

The second type consists of events that provide evidence about conditions that (1) did not exist at the balance sheet date but arise subsequent to that date and (2) do not require adjustment of the financial statements. Some of these events may have to be disclosed to keep the financial statements from misleading users. These disclosures take the form of notes, supplemental schedules or, possibly, even *pro forma* financial data presented as though the event had occurred on or prior to the date of the balance sheet. Below are examples given in the *CICA Handbook*, Section 3820, of subsequent events that require disclosure (but do not result in adjustment):

1. an event such as a fire or flood which results in a loss;
2. a decline in the market value of investments;
3. purchase of a business;
4. commencement of litigation where the cause of action arose subsequent to the date of the financial statements;
5. changes in foreign currency exchange rates;
6. the issue of share capital or long-term debt.

Identifying events that require adjustment of, or disclosure in, the financial statements under the criteria stated above calls for knowledge of the facts and circumstances and the exercise of judgement. For example, if a loss on an uncollectible trade account receivable results from a customer's deteriorating financial condition, leading to bankruptcy subsequent to the balance sheet date, the financial statements are adjusted before their issuance because the event (bankruptcy) indicates conditions existing at the balance sheet date. However, a similar loss resulting from a customer's major casualty, such as a fire or flood, after the balance sheet date does not indicate conditions existing at that date, and adjustment of the financial statements is not necessary; disclosure is appropriate depending on the materiality of the loss. The same criterion applies to settlements of litigation. If the events that gave rise to the litigation, such as personal injury or patent infringement, took place prior to the balance sheet date, adjustment of the financial statements is necessary. If the event giving rise to the claim took place subsequent to the balance sheet date, no adjustment is necessary, but disclosure is. Such subsequent events as changes in the quoted market prices of securities ordinarily do not result in adjustment of the financial statements, because such changes typically reflect a concurrent evaluation of new conditions.

Further, **many subsequent events or developments are not likely to require either adjustment of, or disclosure in, the financial statements.** These are non-accounting events or conditions that managements normally communicate by other means, and include legislation, product changes, management changes, strikes, unionization, marketing agreements, and loss of important customers.

Techniques of Disclosure

The effect of various contingencies on financial condition, the methods of valuing assets, and the company's contracts and agreements should be disclosed as completely as possible in the financial statements. These methods of disclosing pertinent information are available:

> Parenthetical explanations
> Notes to the financial statements
> Cross reference and contra items
> Supporting schedules

Appendix 5A contains specimen financial statements that illustrate some of these methods.

Parenthetical Explanations   Additional information or description is often given by means of parenthetical explanations following the item. For example, investments in common shares may be shown on the balance sheet under Investments as below.

Investments in Common Shares at cost (market value, $330,586)—$280,783

This device permits disclosure of additional pertinent information that adds clarity and completeness to the balance sheet. Its advantage over a note is that it brings the additional information into the body of the statement, where it is less likely to be overlooked. Of course, inasmuch as lengthy parenthetical explanations might distract the reader from, or even appear to contradict, the balance sheet information, they must be used with care.

Notes   If additional explanations or descriptions do not lend themselves conveniently as parenthetical explanations, notes are used. For example, Develcon Electronics disclosed its inventories in the following way:

Develcon Electronics Ltd

	(thousands of dollars)	
Under Current Assets:	1983	1982
Inventory (Note 3)	4,221	1,640

Notes:

3. Inventory

Costs of the company's inventories include materials, labour, and manufacturing overhead. Inventories are valued on a first-in, first-out basis at the lower of cost or net realizable value and consist of:

	1983	1982
	(thousands of dollars)	
Raw materials	$2,409	$ 638
Work in progress	340	229
Finished goods	1,472	773
	$4,221	$1,640

Notes commonly present such other information as the existence and amount of any dividends in arrears for preferred shares; the terms of, or obligations imposed by, purchase commitments; special financial arrangements; depreciation policies; any changes in the application of accounting principles; and the existence of contingencies. The following examples illustrate the use of notes to disclose such information.

Dupont Canada Ltd.
(1984 Financial Statements)

SUMMARY OF SIGNIFICANT ACCOUNTING POLICIES

Basis of Consolidation

Dupont Canada Inc. is incorporated under the laws of Canada and the consolidated financial statements are prepared in accordance with accounting principles generally accepted in Canada and conform in all material respects with International Accounting Standards.

Inventories

Inventories are carried at the lower of average cost and net realizable value. Finished goods inventories are based on material and product-related conversion costs.

Plants and Properties and Related Depreciation

Plants and properties are carried at cost. Preproduction expenses related to manufacturing and interest on borrowed money incurred in connection with new facilities are charged to expense as incurred.

Depreciation is provided based on the average useful life of assets. For manufacturing facilities, the diminishing balance method is used and rates of 12% or 10% are applied to the net investment at each plant site, provided that amounts set aside in the accounts are not less than 5% of the original cost. Thus the provision for depreciation is higher in the early life of the assets when the risk is greater. Generally, depreciation is not charged on new assets until they become operative. When assets are retired, sold, or otherwise disposed of, the gross book value and dismantling costs are charged to accumulated depreciation; any recovery is credited to accumulated depreciation.

Goodwill, Patents, and Processes

Goodwill was acquired prior to 1974 and is not amortized. Purchased patents and processes are amortized over their economic life.

Dome Petroleum Limited
(1984 Financial Statements)

20. Contingencies and Commitments

In addition to the commitments described under Debt Rescheduling Agreement in Long-Term Debt, the Company has the following contingent liabilities:

(a) The Company is contingently liable for $225 million advanced to Dome Canada by the Arctic Petroleum Corporation of Japan.

(b) In 1983, Revenue Canada–Taxation issued reassessments to the Company disallowing the frontier exploration allowance claimed in 1980. Management believes that these amounts were validly claimed and intends to contest the issue. If the Company is not successful, a prior period adjustment will be made relating to 1980 which will increase the deficit and deferred income taxes by $443 million.

There are no pending legal proceedings to which the Company or any of its subsidiaries is a party, or of which any of their properties is the subject, that in management's view would have a material effect on the Company's consolidated financial position or results of operations.

22. Subsequent Events

(a) On February 5, 1985, the Company and certain of its lenders closed the Debt Rescheduling Agreement effective December 31, 1984.

(b) On February 5, 1985, in connection with the closing of the Debt Rescheduling Agreement, the Company issued 12, 223, 757 common shares at $2.22 per common share having an aggregate value of $27. 1 million from which no cash proceeds were received.

(c) On March 11, 1985, the Company sold all of its shares in Davie for nominal consideration.

In the preparation of notes, we must be sure that they present all essential facts as completely and succinctly as possible. Careless wording may result in misleading instead of aiding readers. Notes should add to the total information in the financial statements, not raise unanswered questions or contradict other portions of the statements.

Cross-Reference and Contra Items   Cross-referencing calls the reader's attention to the direct relationship between an asset and a liability. For example, on December 31, 1986, this item might appear among the current assets:

| Cash on deposit with sinking fund trustee for redemption of bonds payable—see current liabilities | $800,000 |

Included among the current liabilities is the amount of bonds payable to be redeemed currently:

| Bonds payable to be redeemed in 1987—see current assets | $2,300,000 |

This cross reference points out that $2,300,000 of bonds payable are to be redeemed currently, for which only $800,000 in cash has been set aside; therefore the additional amount of cash needed must come from the general cash, from sales of investments, or from some other source. The same information can appear parenthetically, if that approach is preferred.

Another common procedure is to establish contra or adjunct accounts. A **contra account** is one that reduces either an asset or a liability on a balance sheet. As examples, Accumulated Depreciation is considered a contra account, as is Discount on Bonds Payable. Contra accounts provide the accountant with some flexibility in presenting the financial information. With the use of the Accumulated Depreciation account, for example, a reader of the statement can see the original cost of the asset as well as the depreciation to date.

An **adjunct account,** on the other hand, increases either an asset or a liability. An example is Premium on Bonds Payable which, when added to the Bonds Payable account, provides a picture of the total liability of the enterprise.

Supporting Schedules   Often a separate schedule is needed to present more detailed information about certain assets or liabilities. Here is a single item in the balance sheet for long-term tangible assets that might be appropriate:

Property, plant and equipment
  Land, building, equipment, and other fixed assets
    (see Schedule 3) $643,300

A separate schedule then might be presented as follows:

Schedule 3
LAND, BUILDINGS, EQUIPMENT, AND OTHER FIXED ASSETS

	Total	Land	Buildings	Equip.	Other Fixed Assets
Balance January 1, 1986	$740,000	$46,000	$358,000	$260,000	$76,000
Additions in 1986	161,200		120,000	38,000	3,200
	$901,200	$46,000	$478,000	$298,000	$79,200
Assets retired or sold in 1986	31,700			27,000	4,700
Balance December 31, 1986	$869,500	$46,000	$478,000	$271,000	$74,500
Depreciation taken to January 1, 1986	$196,000		$102,000	$78,000	$16,000
Depreciation taken in 1986	56,000		28,000	24,000	4,000
	$252,000		$130,000	$102,000	$20,000
Depreciation on assets retired in 1986	25,800			22,000	3,800
Depreciation accumulated December 31, 1986	$226,200		$130,000	$ 80,000	$16,200
Book value of assets	$643,300	$46,000	$348,000	$191,000	$58,300

Balance Sheet Form

One common arrangement of the balance sheet is called the **account form.** It details the assets on the left side and the liabilities and shareholders' equity on the right side. To avoid the use of facing pages, another arrangement lists the liabilities and shareholders' equity directly below the assets on the same page in what is

Ecological Management, Inc.
BALANCE SHEET
December 31, 1986
Assets

Current assets

Cash		$ 42,485
Marketable securities—cost that approximates market value		28,250
Accounts receivable	$165,824	
Less: Allowance for doubtful accounts	1,850	163,974
Notes receivable		23,000
Inventories—at average cost		489,713
Supplies on hand		9,780
Prepaid expenses		16,252

Total current assets		$ 773,454

Long-term investments

Securities at cost (market value $94,000)		87,500

Property, plant, and equipment

Land—at cost		$125,000
Buildings—at cost	$975,800	
Less: Accumulated depreciation	341,200	634,600
Property, plant, and equipment		759,600

Intangible assets

Goodwill		100,000
Total assets		$1,720,554

Liabilities and Shareholders' Equity

Current liabilities

Notes payable to banks		$ 50,000
Accounts payable		197,532
Accrued interest on notes payable		500
Accrued federal income taxes		62,520
Accrued salaries, wages, and other expenses		9,500
Deposits received from customers		420
Total current liabilities		$ 320,472

Long-term debt

Twenty-year 8% debentures, due January 1, 1996		500,000
Total liabilities		$ 820,472

Shareholders' equity

Share capital
Preferred, $7 cumulative
Authorized and outstanding,

30,000 shares	$300,000	

Common
Authorized, 500,000 shares,
without par value,
issued and outstanding,

400,000 shares	400,000	$700,000
Contributed surplus		37,500

Earnings retained in the business

Appropriated	$ 85,000	
Unappropriated	77,582	162,582
Total shareholders' equity		900,082
Total liabilities and shareholders' equity		$1,720,554

often called the **report form**.[16] (This arrangement is illustrated on page 209 for Ecological Management, Inc.) Other presentations appear infrequently: for example, current liabilities are sometimes deducted from current assets to highlight the amount of working capital, or total liabilities are deducted from total assets to emphasize the "net assets" (equal to shareholders' equity). Refer to the financial statements of Indal Limited, Appendix 5A, pages 224-225 for a practical illustration of a balance sheet presentation in account form.

Questions on Terminology

The account titles in the general ledger do not necessarily represent the best terminology for balance sheet purposes; they are often brief, and include technical terms that are understood only by those keeping the records and by other accountants. Since balance sheets are examined by many persons who are not acquainted with the technical vocabulary of accounting, they should contain descriptions that will be generally understood and not be subject to misinterpretation. Accountants are becoming aware of the need for better terminology in financial statements. This awareness is evident in the helpful descriptions used in recent published financial statements and in the attention given this subject by professional groups, periodicals, and textbooks.

For example, the CICA recommended that the word "reserve" be used only to describe an appropriation of retained earnings. Formerly, this term had been used in several ways: to describe amounts deducted from assets (contra accounts, e.g. Accumulated Depreciation and Allowance for Doubtful Accounts), as part of the title of Estimated Liabilities, and to describe certain charges in the income statement. Because of the different meanings attached to this term, its significance in the balance sheet was questionable, and subject to misinterpretation. Limiting the use of the term "reserve" to describe appropriated earnings has resulted in a better understanding of its significance. Perhaps use of the word should be discontinued entirely, because to the nonaccountant a "reserve" is something quite different from what is signified by the term on a balance sheet. The term "appropriated" appears more logical, and its use should be encouraged.

It has also been recommended that the word "surplus" be discontinued in balance sheet presentations of shareholders' equity. Outside the field of accounting, this term connotes something quite different from its meaning in the balance sheet. The use of the terms Capital Surplus, Paid-in Surplus, and Earned Surplus may confuse the nonaccountant and encourage misinterpretation. Although inappropriate, these terms appear all too frequently in current financial statements and literature. We have discussed them only to enable you to understand these terms when you encounter them in practice.

Most of the profession's recommendations on changes in terminology have related to the balance sheet presentation of shareholders' equity in order to ensure that the words or phrases used for these unique accounts truly describe the amounts shown.

Aggregation

How does one determine the various items to be reported in a balance sheet, their classifications and subclassifications? The answer depends upon one's judgement

---

[16]*Financial Reporting in Canada—1983 op. cit.*, indicates that, in 1982, 94% of the companies surveyed use the "report or account form" (197 the account form, 107 the report form).

as to what provides the most useful information. For users, the various sections and subsections of financial statements can be more informative than the whole. Therefore, as one would expect, the reporting of summary accounts (total assets, net assets, total liabilities, and so on) alone is discouraged. Individual items should be separately reported and classified in sufficient detail to permit users to assess the amounts, timing, and uncertainty related to financial position, results of operations, and future cash flows. In the preparation of a balance sheet, emphasis should be placed on providing information that permits the evaluation of liquidity and financial flexibility. In the words of the FASB, "the main basis for deciding the number of classes and the content of each is that the result should help users to assess the nature, amounts, and liquidity of available resources, including management's intentions regarding their function in use, and the amounts and timing of obligations that require liquid resources for settlement."[17] The following guides provide a basis for decisions on the optimal number of asset and liability items to be reported.[18]

1. Assets that differ in their **type or expected function** in the central operations or other activities of the enterprise should be reported as separate items; for example, merchandise inventories should be reported separately from property, plant, and equipment.
2. Assets and liabilities with **different implications for the financial flexibility** of the enterprise should be reported as separate items; for example, assets used in operations, assets held for investment, and assets subject to restrictions (e.g., leased equipment).
3. Assets and liabilities with **different general liquidity characteristics** should be reported as separate items; for example, cash should be separately reported from inventories.
4. Assets and liabilities with **different measurement bases** should be reported in separate categories; for example, inventories measured at historical cost and those measured at net realizable value.

Given these emphases, it appears that the form, content, and classification of the balance sheet will not change significantly. We already prepare balance sheets that provide information about the functions of assets, the types of claims on assets, the bases of measuring assets and liabilities, and the liquidity and financial flexibility.

STATEMENT OF CHANGES IN FINANCIAL POSITION

If you were asked to determine the additions to or dispositions of property, plant, and equipment for the past year or the amount of money borrowed or share capital issued by a company during the year, you would best proceed by analyzing its **statement of changes in financial position.** This statement of changes in financial position helps answer these questions because it provides information concerning the **operating, financing,** and **investing** activities of the company.[19] As such, this statement is useful for evaluating a company's solvency and liquidity, and ability to repay debt, purchase assets, and pay dividends.

Although the income statement, balance sheet, and statement of retained earnings contain information on financing and investing activities, they present this information only in a partial, fragmented manner. Only the statement of changes in financial position indicates where the resources (funds) came from during the period and how they were used. *CICA Handbook* in Section 1500, paragraph 3,

---

[17]"Reporting Income, Cash Flows, and Financial Position of Business Enterprises," *op. cit.*, par. 50.

[18]*Ibid.*, par. 51.

[19]*CICA Handbook*, Section 1540. Procedures for preparing this statement are discussed in more detail in Chapter 24. The major purpose of this discussion is to focus on the content and use of the statement.

states that the statement of changes in financial position normally accompanies the balance sheet and statement of income and retained earnings and, thus, can be considered as **a basic financial statement.**

Prior to fall of 1985, the *CICA Handbook* permitted the statement of changes in financial position to present a company's operating, financing, and investing activities in terms of the consequences with regard to changes in cash **or** changes in working capital. Thus, the statement's format generally showed the sources and uses of either cash or working capital.[20] In June, 1985, the AcSC approved a revision to the *CICA Handbook*, Section 1540, with the recommendation that this statement should be based on the changes in "cash and cash equivalents" (cash and temporary investments less short-term borrowings) during a period.[21] Furthermore, it was recommended that, rather than use the traditional format of reporting sources and uses under separate headings, the statement would summarize changes under the classifications of operating activities, financing activities, and investing activities.[22] Under each classification, activities resulting in increases and decreases of cash and cash equivalents are reported. Also, **all** financing and investing activities are to be incorporated into the statement, even though cash may not have directly been affected: this is often referred to as the **all-financial resources concept**. Examples of such transactions are the acquisition of property for other property, issuance of shares for property, and conversion of debt into share capital.

Lambert Co. Ltd.
STATEMENT OF CHANGES IN FINANCIAL POSITION
For the Year Ended December 31, 1986

Operating Activities		
Cash from operations:		
Income before extraordinary items		$1,200,000
Add (deduct): Items not affecting cash		
Depreciation expense	$ 150,000	
Bond discount amortization	6,000	
Deferred income taxes	(50,000)	
Equity in earnings of a 25% owned company	(20,000)	
Net adjustment for changes in receivables,		
payables, and inventories related to operations	(75,000)	11,000
Total		$1,211,000
Investing Activities		
Purchase of equipment	$(250,000)	
Extraordinary item — proceeds from expropriation		
of land	80,000	
Proceeds from sale of building	150,000	
Total		(20,000)
Financing Activities		
Sale of Class B shares	$ 100,00	
Redemption of bonds	(800,000)	
Dividends paid	(90,000)	
Total		(790,000)
Increase in cash during year		$ 401,000
Cash at beginning of year		50,000
Cash at year end		$ 451,000

[20]*Financial Reporting in Canada—1983 op. cit.*, showed that 86% of the companies surveyed used a working capital basis while 7% used a strict cash basis. The remaining companies would likely be using a cash and cash equivalent basis.

[21]*CICA Handbook*, Section 1540, par. 4.

[22]*Ibid.*, Section 1540, par. 18.

The Statement of Changes in Financial Position for Lambert Co. Ltd., as shown on page 212, illustrates a form and content that reflects the *Handbook*'s recommendations.

The 1985 *CICA Handbook* recommendations regarding the basis and format of the statement of changes in financial position had just been introduced at the time of writing this text. Therefore, the way in which they would be interpreted by practitioners was not evident. The Lambert Co. Ltd. example reflects a prediction of what these statements may look like. Determining the classification under which dividends and extraordinary cash flows fall, as well as selecting an approach by which to present cash flow from operations, are examples of issues for which alternative solutions are possible and permissible.

While Canadian GAAP now use the change in cash and cash equivalents as the prescribed basis for preparing the statement of changes in financial position, an alternative basis (change in working capital) was acceptable in Canada prior to 1985 and is presently permitted and used in most other countries. The following example, derived from the data previously presented for the Lambert Co. Ltd., illustrates the application of the working capital basis for presenting a statement of changes. While the all-financial resources concept is used, the major classifications are sources (operations and other) and applications of working capital rather than operating, investing, and financing activities.

Lambert Co. Ltd.
STATEMENT OF CHANGES IN FINANCIAL POSITION
For the Year Ended December 31, 1986
(Working Capital Basis)

Sources of Working Capital		
Operations:		
Income before extraordinary items		$1,200,000
Add (deduct): Items not affecting working capital		
Depreciation expense	$150,000	
Bond discount amortization	6,000	
Deferred income taxes	(50,000)	
Equity in earnings of a 25% owned company	(20,000)	86,000
Working capital from operations		$1,286,000
Other Sources:		
Extraordinary item—proceeds from expro-		
priation of land	$ 80,000	
Proceeds from sale of building	150,000	
Sale of Class B shares	100,000	300,000
Total Sources		$1,616,000
Applications of Working Capital		
Purchase of equipment	$250,000	
Redemption of bonds	800,000	
Dividends paid	90,000	
Total Applications		1,140,000
Increase in Working Capital		$ 476,000

Comparison of the statements prepared on the two bases shows that working capital increased $75,000 more than did cash and cash equivalents during the year. Otherwise, the two statements contain generally the same information, albeit classified under different headings. The recommendations in the *CICA Handbook* to provide a cash and cash equivalents based statement with classification by operating, investing, and financing activities are based on the perception that such information is more relevant to financial statement users. Many support this view.

Appendix 5A, page 226, provides another illustration of a statement of changes in financial position. Chapter 24 presents a comprehensive discussion of this subject and illustrates the techniques of preparing and presenting the statement of changes in financial position.

The statement of changes in financial position provides information about the flow of funds (cash and cash equivalents) into and out of the business enterprise during a period. This type of information is useful for assessing the amount, timing, and uncertainty of future fund flows. For example, by identifying different sources and applications of funds and classifying them as due to operating, investing, or financing activity, the user has a better understanding of the **liquidity** and **financial flexibility** of the enterprise. Similarly, these statements are useful in **providing feedback** about the flow of enterprise resources. This information should help users make more accurate predictions of future flows. In addition, some individuals have expressed concern about the "quality of the earnings" because the measurement of income depends on a number of accruals and estimates that may be somewhat subjective. As a result, the higher the ratio of funds provided by operations to income, the more comfort some users have in the quality of the earnings.[23]

KEY POINTS

1. The balance sheet provides information about the nature and amounts of investments in enterprise resources, obligations to enterprise creditors, and owners' equity in net enterprise resources. This information provides a basis for computing rates of return, evaluating the capital structure of the enterprise, and assessing its liquidity and financial flexibility.

2. Limitations of the balance sheet are (1) it does not reflect current values, (2) estimates requiring judgement must be used in allocating costs, and (3) it omits many items that are of financial value to the business but cannot be recorded objectively.

3. The three general elements of the balance sheet are assets, liabilities, and owners' equity.

4. The major classifications within the balance sheet on the asset side are current assets; long-term investments; property, plant, and equipment; intangible assets; and other assets.

5. The major classifications of liabilities are current liabilities and long-term liabilities.

6. In a corporation, shareholders' equity is generally classified as share capital, contributed surplus, and retained earnings.

---

[23]Numerous empirical studies have been made regarding the usefulness of the statement of changes in financial position. Morton Backer and Martin L. Gosman, "Financial Reporting and Business Liquidity" (New York: National Association of Accountants, 1978), show that the ratio of resources provided by operations to total debt is useful in assessing credit-worthiness for intermediate- and long-term debt. Similarly, William H. Beaver, "Alternative Accounting Measures as Predictors of Failure," *The Accounting Review* (January, 1968), found the same types of information useful in assessing bankruptcy. David F. Hawkins and Walter J. Campbell, "Equity Valuation: Models, Analysis and Implications," *Financial Executive* (New York: Financial Executives Research Institute, 1978), found that institutional investors and research firms used resource flow information to determine a company's ability to fund capital expenditures and dividends internally, and that a comparison of cash flows to earnings was used as a basis for evaluating the quality of earnings.

7. There are normally four types of information that are supplemental to assets, liabilities, and owners' equity accounts presented in the balance sheet. These are (1) contingencies, (2) valuation and accounting policies, (3) contractual situations, and (4) post-balance sheet disclosures.

8. The methods of disclosing pertinent information are (1) parenthetical explanations, (2) notes, (3) cross-reference and contra items, and (4) supporting schedules.

9. Balance sheets may follow either the account form or report form. The account form is the more common.

10. The statement of changes in financial position is considered a basic financial statement and summarizes information concerning the operating, financing, and investing activities of the company.

11. The *CICA Handbook* recommends that the statement of changes in financial position be prepared on the basis of changes in cash and cash equivalents. Such changes are to be classified as being due to operating, investing, or financing activities. All significant financing and investing activities must be incorporated in the statement even though cash is not directly affected; this is referred to as the all-financial resources concept.

APPENDIX

5A

SPECIMEN FINANCIAL STATEMENTS

The following pages consist of material drawn from the 1984 Annual Report of Indal Limited, a company incorporated under Canadian laws. This material is presented in order to provide the student with a comprehensive example of the contents of such a report, in the expectation that it will be useful in studying and understanding the nature of such information. The specific portions of the report reproduced in this Appendix include

1. Financial Review
2. Financial Statements—including (a) the management's report to the shareholders, (b) the auditor's report to shareholders, (c) significant accounting policies (shown on a separate page and not as the first note in the statements), (d) the consolidated statement of earnings (income) and retained earnings, (e) the consolidated balance sheet, (f) the consolidated statement of changes in financial position, (g) the notes to the financial statements, and (h) segmented information, which was an appendix to the financials
3. Quarterly Financial Information
4. Ten-Year Financial Summary
5. Glossary (to clarify the business terms used by the company)
6. Shareholder Information.

Indal Limited was founded and incorporated in 1964. Its subsidiaries and divisions extrude aluminum, cold rollform and stamp aluminum and steel, die-cast zinc, tempered and laminate glass, and fabricate a broad range of metal, wood, and glass products. The company's products are principally sold in three markets: residential construction, nonresidential construction, and industrial, which includes automotive and design engineering. Indal Limited has 23 operating subsidiaries and divisions in Canada and 16 in the United States. More than 7,000 people are employed by the company in over 60 locations in North America. Its corporate office is in Weston, Ontario.

While the student will likely be familiar with many of the items and disclosures made in this material, several items may be new. Consequently, one should not expect to comprehend everything fully during the first reading of this information. It is hoped, however, that by the time this text is completed the student's level of understanding and interpretative ability will have increased significantly.

Appendix 5A might be scanned in order to familiarize the reader with the contents. The following chapters will direct the student to specific parts of Indal Limited's financial statements as an example of the topic being discussed. Upon completion of this book, the student might reexamine Indal's financials in their entirety.

This Appendix contains only 19 of the 40 pages of the published Annual Report. The selection of the material was based on the criteria of including that which pertained primarily to financial portions of the report and information that was particularly useful to understanding such portions.

Shareholder information

The Company

The Company was incorporated under the laws of Canada on October 9, 1964

Capital stock

At December 31, 1984 the issued capital stock of the Company comprised 24,334,122 fully paid common shares

Listing of stock

The common shares of the Company were listed on the Toronto and Montreal stock exchanges on March 24, 1969. The shares are listed on these exchanges under the stock symbol "ICL"

Transfer agents and registrars

The transfer agents and registrars for the common shares of the Company are The Royal Trust Company at its offices in Toronto, Montreal, Winnipeg, Calgary, Regina and Vancouver.

Principal issues of common shares

The principal issues of common shares since listing in 1969 have been:

		Shares
1972	Rights issue: 1 for 2 at $9.75	479,059
1973	Rights issue: 1 for 3 at $10.50	539,287
1975	Rights issue: 1 for 3 at $9.25	752,098
1977	Stock split: 2 for 1	3,045,760
1978	Public issue at $12.75	3,000,000
1983	Private placement at $16.50	950,000
1983	Stock split: 2 for 1	10,631,911
1984	Private placement at $10.65	3,000,000

Stock prices and volumes traded

The following table sets out the high and low closing prices of the Company s common shares on The Toronto Stock Exchange and the volumes of shares traded on the Toronto and Montreal stock exchanges over the past five years:

	High	Low	Volume
1980	$ 9.13	$ 5.75	3,289,000
1981	10.00	5.50	2,800,000
1982	7.75	4.75	1,820,000
1983	13.63	7.75	3,125,000
1984	13.75	10.00	2,174,000

Note: figures in the above table have been adjusted to reflect subsequent stock splits.

Investment data

The following table sets out the averages of the high and low closing prices of the Company's common shares on The Toronto Stock Exchange, the dividends paid per share and the average dividend yields based on these average share prices:

	Average share price	Dividends paid	Dividend yield %
1969	$ 4.01	$ 0.05	1.2
1970	2.16	0.05	2.3
1971	2.19	0.05	2.3
1972	3.26	0.07½	2.3
1973	3.12	0.15	4.8
1974	2.69	0.19½	7.3
1975	2.73	0.22½	8.2
1976	3.30	0.23	7.0
1977	4.22	0.24¾	5.9
1978	6.31	0.28	4.4
1979	6.78	0.35	5.2
1980	7.44	0.40	5.4
1981	7.75	0.40	5.2
1982	6.25	0.22½	3.6
1983	10.69	0.25	2.3
1984	11.87	0.55	4.6

Note: figures in the above table have been adjusted to reflect subsequent stock splits.

Financial calendar

Financial year-end:	December 31
Quarterly results:	late April, July and October
Quarterly reports:	late April, July and October
Annual figures:	mid-February
Annual report:	early April
Annual meeting:	early May
Dividend payments:	March 15, June 15, September 15 and December 15

1984 Annual Report

Additional copies of the 1984 Annual Report may be obtained from the Secretary, Indal Limited, 4000 Weston Road, Weston, Ontario M9L 2W8

1985 Annual Meeting

The 1985 annual meeting of the common shareholders of the Company will be held on May 8, 1985 at 4:00 p.m. in The Territories Room of The Royal York Hotel, 100 Front Street West, Toronto, Ontario.

Financial review

The year 1984 proved to be a most successful one for Indal as significant improvements in earnings were achieved and its financial position was greatly strengthened.

As noted in detail in the "Operations Review" section of this Report, the basis of segmentation of the Company's business was amended in 1984. The information presented in the financial statements and other sections of this Report reflects the revised segment structure.

Earnings

First quarter earnings were better than anticipated, following the improving trend evident at the end of 1983, and set the tone for the rest of the year. The extremely rapid first half growth in the U.S. economy assisted this trend, especially in the residential construction and automotive sectors. A comparison of earnings by quarter with 1983's performance illustrates this:

in millions of dollars	1984	1983
Net earnings		
First quarter	$ 3.1	$ 0.8
Second quarter	9.0	6.2
Third quarter	11.9	8.3
Fourth quarter	9.5	8.2
	$33.5	$23.5

in dollars		
Earnings per share		
First quarter	$0.13	$0.01
Second quarter	0.40	0.28
Third quarter	0.50	0.38
Fourth quarter	0.38	0.36
	$1.41	$1.03

Although the rate of growth in the United States slowed appreciably in the second half of the year, normal seasonal increases in activity in the Company's markets in the final six months of 1984 ensured a substantial improvement in earnings compared with the previous year.

The Company's consolidated results show a marginal increase in gross profit as a percentage of sales compared to 1983. The favourable impact of higher volumes and declining costs for some raw materials

were offset by the high cost of prime aluminum supplies in the United States and the resistance to selling price increases in many markets.

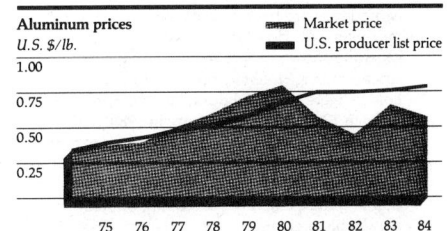

Aluminum prices
U.S. $/lb.

▬▬▬ Market price
▬▬▬ U.S. producer list price

75 76 77 78 79 80 81 82 83 84

Operating expenses as a percentage of sales were appreciably lower than in 1983 due principally to lower interest expenses and the favourable impact of increased volume on administration costs. Moderating interest rates and improved cash generation, including the impact of the share issue in August, were the major influences in the reduction of interest expenses.

Selling and distribution expenses as a percentage of sales increased compared with 1983. This situation reflects an increased contribution to sales from U.S.-based operations, which generally cover larger geographic market areas and have correspondingly higher distribution and selling expenses.

Financial position

Net cash inflow showed a significant increase in 1984 as the following abbreviated statement illustrates:

in millions of dollars	1984	1983
Cash inflow from operations	$79.2	$60.0
Cash outflow		
Investment in fixed assets	30.5	15.9
Investment in working capital	(8.0)	35.8
Taxation payments	7.9	0.8
Dividends to shareholders	14.8	7.4
Other	1.8	(6.2)
	47.0	53.7
Net cash inflow before capital stock transactions	32.2	6.3
Issue of capital stock	32.2	16.0
Redemption of preferred shares	(25.0)	—
Net cash inflow	$39.4	$22.3

Key items in the improved cash generation in 1984 were higher earnings and much lower investment in working capital, despite the significant increase in sales. The consumption of excess prime aluminum inventories carried forward from 1983 contributed towards this improvement. However, working capital utilization generally showed improvement and will continue to be strictly managed. Dividends paid to common shareholders were increased during the year from $0.25 per share in 1983 to $0.55 per share in 1984. This represents a distribution of 39% of the Company's earnings attributable to common shareholders. The issue of 3.0 million new common shares in August 1984 raised $31.9 million enabling the Company's $25.0 million floating rate retractable preferred shares, Indal's most costly financing, to be redeemed.

The currency translation account, an element of shareholders' equity, showed a substantial increase in 1984. This account represents the cumulative increase in value in Canadian dollar terms of the Company's foreign net assets arising from exchange rate movements. During the year, the U.S. dollar, in Canadian dollar terms, increased in value from $1.24 to $1.32 giving rise to the bulk of the 1984 increase.

In 1984 the term of the Company's U.S. $39.3 million loan was renegotiated until 1991, and a more favourable interest rate obtained. Towards the end of the year the interest rate on U.S. $20.0 million of this loan was fixed at approximately 12½% until 1990 by way of interest-rate swaps.

The combination of the foregoing factors resulted in the strongest balance sheet in the Company's history as the following statistics show:

	1984	1983
Current ratio	2.7:1	2.6:1
Liquidity ratio	1.5:1	1.2:1
Working capital/sales %	20.2	25.7
Debt/equity ratio	0.37:1	0.65:1

At the end of the year, the Company had available for its use approximately $150 million of unutilized, unsecured borrowing facilities which, combined with the strength of the Company's balance sheet at the end of 1984, will enable full advantage to be taken of any investment opportunities which may arise.

Reporting the effects of changing prices

In the 1983 Annual Report, the reasons for not reporting the effects of changing prices on the Company's results were explained and deserve repetition because they remained equally valid in 1984, as inflation moderated. In 1983 it was stated:

"The issues that have to be addressed in the area of inflation accounting are often hypothetical, open to very subjective judgement, or both, and the conclusions reached are consequently of questionable value. It seems that we do not yet have practical solutions to the many aspects of the inflation reporting problem and it may be, in fact, that there are no practical accounting solutions. In any event, it seems likely that further revisions of the current pronouncements will have to be made."

Indal's management remains firmly of the opinion that, for these reasons, there is little value in disclosure of financial data adjusted to reflect changing prices.

Earnings per common share
dollars

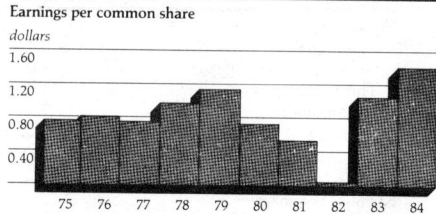

Dividends per common share
dollars

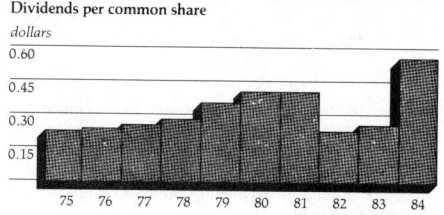

Book value per common share
dollars

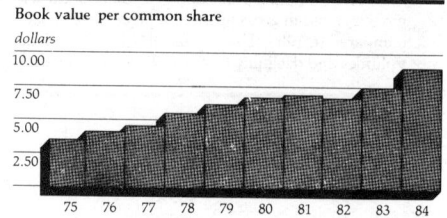

Management's report to the shareholders

Indal Limited

The accompanying financial statements and all information in the Annual Report have been prepared by management and approved by the Board of Directors of the Company. The financial statements were prepared in accordance with accounting principles generally accepted in Canada. The significant accounting policies followed by the Company are set out on page 22. Management is responsible for the accuracy, integrity and objectivity of the consolidated financial statements within reasonable limits of materiality and for the consistency of financial data included in the text of the Report.

To assist management in the discharge of these responsibilities, the Company maintains a system of internal control designed to provide reasonable assurance that its assets are safeguarded; that only valid and authorized transactions are executed; and that accurate, timely and comprehensive financial information is prepared. Management believes that the system is appropriate in terms of cost and risk to meet the objectives outlined. The Company's internal audit department, working under the direction of management, monitors the system of internal control to ensure that adequate standards are maintained.

The consolidated financial statements have been independently examined by Coopers & Lybrand on behalf of the shareholders, in accordance with generally accepted auditing standards. Their report outlines the nature of their examination and expresses their opinion on the consolidated financial statements of the Company.

The Company's Audit Committee is appointed by the Board of Directors annually and is comprised of non-management Directors. The Committee meets with management as well as with the internal and external auditors to satisfy itself that each group is properly discharging its responsibilities and to review the financial statements and the independent auditors' report. The Audit Committee reports its findings to the Board of Directors for consideration in approving the financial statements for presentation to the shareholders.

P. G. Selley
Senior Vice-President, Finance
February 20, 1985

Auditors' report to the shareholders

We have examined the consolidated balance sheet of Indal Limited as at December 31, 1984 and the consolidated statements of earnings and retained earnings and changes in financial position for the year then ended. Our examination was made in accordance with generally accepted auditing standards, and accordingly included such tests and other procedures as we considered necessary in the circumstances.

In our opinion, these consolidated financial statements present fairly the financial position of the Company as at December 31, 1984 and the results of its

operations and the changes in its financial position for the year then ended in accordance with generally accepted accounting principles applied on a basis consistent with that of the preceding year.

Coopers & Lybrand
Toronto, Ontario
February 11, 1985

Significant accounting policies

Accounting standards

The consolidated financial statements are prepared in accordance with accounting principles generally accepted in Canada.

Basis of consolidation

The consolidated financial statements include the financial statements of the Company and all subsidiaries. The operating results and gains or losses on the disposal or discontinuance of an operation are included in "other income/(expenses)" in the consolidated statement of earnings and identified in a note to the consolidated financial statements. All material inter-company items and transactions are eliminated on consolidation. Acquisitions are consolidated from the date of acquisition.

Foreign currency translation

Assets and liabilities in foreign currencies are translated to Canadian dollars at the rate of exchange in effect at the year-end. Income and expenses in foreign currencies are translated to Canadian dollars at rates approximating the average rates of exchange during the year. Exchange differences arising on translation of the financial statements of foreign subsidiaries are taken to a currency translation account in the shareholders' equity section of the consolidated balance sheet.

Inventories

Inventories are valued at the lower of cost and net realizable value. Cost is generally determined on a first-in, first-out basis.

Fixed assets

Fixed assets, including expenditures which improve or prolong the useful lives of the assets, are stated at cost. Fixed assets obtained through acquisitions are stated at the values assigned, based on appraisals, at date of acquisition.

Depreciation is computed on a straight-line basis at rates based on the estimated useful lives of the assets. Estimated useful lives range from twenty to forty years for buildings, eight to ten years for machinery and equipment, seven to ten years for office furniture and equipment, three to four years for motor vehicles and two to ten years for tools and dies. Leasehold improvements are amortized over the terms of the leases.

Maintenance and repair costs of a routine nature are expensed as incurred.

Capital leases

Leases that transfer substantially all the benefits and risks of ownership are capitalized. Other leases are accounted for as operating leases.

Goodwill

Goodwill resulting from acquisitions or agreements entered into prior to January 1, 1974 is not amortized. Goodwill resulting from acquisitions subsequent to January 1, 1974 is amortized on a straight-line basis, over its estimated life or forty years, whichever is less. Any goodwill remaining on the sale or discontinuance of an operation is written off in the year of sale or discontinuance.

Inter-segment sales

Inter-segment sales are accounted for at prices comparable to open market prices.

Long-term contracts

Sales and earnings relating to long-term construction and design engineering contracts are recognized on a percentage of completion basis. Full provision is made for estimated losses on contracts as soon as these are identified.

Deferred charges

Deferred charges are written off over periods not exceeding five years.

Income taxes

The deferral method is used in accounting for income taxes. Timing differences giving rise to deferred income taxes relate primarily to:

–depreciation and amortization—where the cumulative amounts claimed for income tax purposes differ from the amounts written off for accounting purposes.

–accounts receivable holdbacks—where amounts are not taxed until released.

–inventories—where values determined on the last-in, first-out method have been restated on consolidation on the first-in, first-out method.

The flow-through method is used to account for investment tax credits.

Earnings per common share

Earnings per common share are calculated after deducting dividends on preferred shares and using the weighted average number of shares outstanding during the year.

Fully diluted earnings per common share are computed as though outstanding stock options had been exercised at the beginning of the year.

Consolidated statements of earnings and retained earnings   Indal Limited
for the year ended December 31, 1984

in thousands of dollars		1984	%	1983	%
Earnings	Sales	$834,782	100.0	$694,946	100.0
	Cost of sales	623,036	74.6	521,379	75.0
	Gross profit	211,746	25.4	173,567	25.0
	Expenses				
	Selling and distribution	81,023	9.7	66,302	9.5
	Administration	57,572	6.9	52,931	7.6
	Financial	10,969	1.3	14,373	2.1
		149,564	17.9	133,606	19.2
		62,182	7.5	39,961	5.8
	Other income/(expenses) (note 2)	(8,800)	(1.1)	159	—
	Earnings before income taxes (note 3)	53,382	6.4	40,120	5.8
	Income taxes (note 4)	18,832	2.3	15,525	2.2
	Earnings before minority shareholders' interests	34,550	4.1	24,595	3.6
	Minority shareholders' interests	1,080	0.1	1,078	0.2
	Net earnings	$ 33,470	4.0	$ 23,517	3.4
	Earnings per common share				
	Basic	$1.41		$1.03	
	Fully diluted	1.39		1.03	
Retained earnings	Balance—beginning of year	$ 74,480		$ 58,366	
	Net earnings	33,470		23,517	
		107,950		81,883	
	Dividends paid				
	Preferred shares	1,822		1,911	
	Common shares	12,644		5,321	
	Share issue expenses, net of tax	—		171	
		14,466		7,403	
	Balance—end of year	$ 93,484		$ 74,480	

Consolidated balance sheet
as at December 31, 1984

in thousands of dollars	1984	1983
Assets		
Current assets		
Cash	$ 17,872	$ 4,109
Accounts receivable	117,800	105,708
Inventories (note 5)	117,821	134,918
Other accounts receivable and prepaid expenses	9,293	9,805
Net assets of discontinued operation (note 2)	1,825	3,746
	264,611	258,286
Fixed assets (note 6)		
Land	10,648	10,310
Buildings	64,314	58,248
Machinery and equipment	114,279	96,686
Leasehold improvements	6,779	5,940
Office furniture and equipment	9,216	7,531
Motor vehicles	8,402	7,495
	213,638	186,210
Accumulated depreciation	(81,136)	(68,270)
	132,502	117,940
Tools and dies—at cost, less amortization	5,785	4,838
	138,287	122,778
Intangible assets		
Goodwill (note 7)	36,779	35,111
Deferred charges, less amortization (note 8)	–	1,016
	36,779	36,127
	$439,677	$417,191

Signed on behalf of the Board:

W.E. Stracey, Director
P.G. Selley, Director

Indal Limited

	1984	1983

Liabilities

Current liabilities

Bank advances	$ –	$ 5,237
Accounts payable	40,854	43,063
Other accounts payable and accrued charges	34,055	29,649
Income taxes payable	13,670	845
Other taxes payable	3,478	3,199
Deferred income taxes relating to current items	2,395	9,849
Current portion of long-term liabilities (note 9)	2,434	7,086
	96,886	98,928
Long-term liabilities less current portion (note 9)	98,083	113,849
Deferred income taxes	18,312	10,454
Minority shareholders' interests in subsidiary companies	4,415	5,151
	217,696	228,382

Shareholders' equity

Capital stock (note 10)
Issued and fully paid

1,000,000 floating rate preferred shares	–	25,000
24,334,122 (1983–21,291,022) common shares	114,553	82,386
Currency translation account (note 11)	13,944	6,943
Retained earnings	93,484	74,480
	221,981	188,809
	$439,677	$417,191

Consolidated statement of changes in financial position   Indal Limited

for the year ended December 31, 1984

in thousands of dollars	1984	1983
Source of funds		
Operations:		
Earnings before income taxes	$ 53,382	$ 40,120
Items not affecting funds		
Depreciation and amortization of fixed assets	18,086	16,285
Amortization of goodwill	1,966	2,372
Amortization of deferred charges	1,636	1,245
Loss attributable to discontinued metal trading operation (note 2)	4,164	–
	79,234	60,022
Proceeds from sale of fixed assets	1,901	9,433
Issue of common shares (note 10)	32,167	16,023
Other	797	(1,926)
Total source of funds	114,099	83,552
Application of funds		
Working capital (excluding fund items)		
Accounts receivable and prepaid expenses	11,580	11,944
Inventories	(17,097)	39,597
Accounts payable, accruals and other taxes	(2,476)	(20,999)
Working capital of business sold	–	5,234
	(7,993)	35,776
Purchase of fixed assets	30,548	15,917
Redemption of preferred shares (note 10)	25,000	–
Additions to deferred charges (note 8)	599	740
Net investment in subsidiaries (note 1)	3,777	698
Taxation payments	7,900	755
Dividends		
Preferred shares	1,822	1,911
Common shares	12,644	5,321
Minority shareholders	384	180
Total application of funds	74,681	61,298
Increase in funds	39,418	22,254
Opening funds		
Bank advances (net of cash)	1,128	22,643
Long-term liabilities (including current portion)	120,935	121,674
Net borrowings—beginning of year	122,063	144,317
Closing funds		
Bank advances (net of cash)	(17,872)	1,128
Long-term liabilities (including current portion)	100,517	120,935
Net borrowings—end of year	$ 82,645	$122,063

Note: funds are defined as cash, bank advances and long-term liabilities. For the change in long-term liabilities see note 9.

Notes to consolidated financial statements
for the year ended December 31, 1984

Indal Limited

1. Investment in subsidiaries

During the year, the Company acquired additional equity in Peachtree Doors, Inc. (5.0%); Tempglass Southern, Inc. (5.0%) and disposed of its interest in Deltaglass S.A. (51.0%)

The net consideration paid in respect of these changes in holdings during the year amounted to $3,777,000.

2. Other income/(expenses)

An analysis of other income/(expenses) is:

in thousands of dollars	1984	1983
Income/(loss) before income taxes attributable to operations sold or discontinued.....	$ (2,154)	$ 581
Income/(loss) before income taxes attributable to discontinued metal trading operation	(4,164)	1,659
	(6,318)	2,240
Amortization of goodwill	(1,966)	(2,130)
Other	(516)	49
	$ (8,800)	$ 159

Income/(loss) attributable to operations sold or discontinued:

During the year, the investment in Deltaglass S.A. was disposed of and the business of Commercial Aluminum (Western) Division was discontinued. Comparative figures reflect the sale of the assets of Tennessee Building Products, Inc.

The operating results and losses on disposal or discontinuance of these operations were:

in thousands of dollars	1984	1983
Sales.......	$ 2,240	$ 18,755
Operating income/(loss)	(588)	692
Gain/(loss) on disposal or discontinuance............	(1,566)	(111)
Income/(loss) from operations disposed of or discontinued............	$ (2,154)	$ 581

Income/(loss) attributable to discontinued metal trading operation:

The current year losses attributable to the discontinued metal trading operation reflect full provision for an amount receivable from a customer who is being sued for non-payment of the debt.

The net assets of the discontinued metal trading operation, amounting to $1,825,000 as at December 31, 1984, mainly represent pension refunds due and deferred tax debits.

3. Earnings before income taxes

Earnings before income taxes are stated after charging:

in thousands of dollars	1984	1983
Depreciation and amortization of fixed assets............	$ 18,086	$ 16,285
Amortization of goodwill............	1,966	2,130
Write-off of goodwill relating to operations sold	–	242
Amortization of deferred charges............	1,636	1,245
Interest on bank advances............	1,210	3,095
Interest on long-term liabilities............	11,848	12,219

4. Income taxes

Income taxes based on earnings are:

in thousands of dollars	1984	1983
Canadian		
Income tax payable	$ 15,226	$ 6,313
Deferred income tax	(3,944)	1,210
	11,282	7,523
Foreign		
Income tax payable	12,859	6,013
Deferred income tax	(5,309)	1,989
	7,550	8,002
Total		
Income tax payable	28,085	12,326
Deferred income tax	(9,253)	3,199
	$ 18,832	$ 15,525

Of the total amount of deferred income tax, $592,000 (1983–$829,000) relates to non-current items.

The Company's effective income tax rate is:

percentages	1984	1983
Canadian corporate tax rate	45.1	45.2
Effect of higher foreign tax rates	1.7	3.3
Effect of financing and inventory allowances	(7.5)	(10.1)
Effect of non-deductible goodwill amortization and appraisal-surplus depreciation	1.9	3.6
Investment tax credits	(4.0)	(3.2)
Effect of recognition for tax purposes of foreign losses and investment tax credits	(2.3)	0.1
Adjustment of amounts previously provided	0.3	(1.1)
Other	0.1	0.9
	35.3	38.7

Deferred income tax arises from timing differences. The sources and tax effects of these timing differences and other movements through the deferred income tax account are:

in thousands of dollars	1984	1983
Tax depreciation and amortization in excess of accounting depreciation and amortization	$ 592	$ 425
Accounts receivable holdbacks	(1,835)	946
Provision for bad debts and pension contributions not currently deductible for income tax purposes	(2,951)	–
Deferred recognition for income tax purposes of profit on long-term contracts	(3,142)	1,040
Inventories restated on the first-in, first-out method	(232)	379
Adjustment of amounts previously provided and other items	(1,685)	409
Deferred income tax provision for the year	(9,253)	3,199
Transfer to income tax payable in respect of income tax losses and investment tax credits recognized, and other adjustments	9,657	5,714
	$ 404	$ 8,913

5. Inventories
in thousands of dollars

	1984	1983
Raw materials	$ 67,041	$ 84,479
Work in process	29,248	28,713
Finished goods	21,532	21,726
	$117,821	$134,918

6. Leases
Assets financed by capital leases, accounted for and depreciated as company-owned facilities and included in fixed assets are:
in thousands of dollars

	1984	1983
Land and buildings	$ 8,052	$ 7,564
Machinery and equipment	6,007	6,408
	14,059	13,972
Accumulated depreciation	(4,932)	(4,740)
	$ 9,127	$ 9,232

Aggregate future minimum lease payments at December 31, 1984 are:
in thousands of dollars

	Capital leases	Operating leases
1985	$ 1,322	$ 8,700
1986	1,267	6,789
1987	1,242	5,585
1988	1,196	4,285
1989	994	3,036
Thereafter	12,342	12,297
Total minimum lease payments	18,363	40,692
Less: amount representing interest	7,317	—
	$ 11,046	$ 40,692

7. Goodwill
in thousands of dollars

Resulting from acquisitions or agreements entered into	Prior to January 1, 1974	After January 1, 1974	1984	1983
Balance—beginning of year	$ 13,669	$ 21,442	$ 35,111	$ 36,673
Additions	—	2,335	2,335	642
Amortization—continuing operations	(1,290)	(676)	(1,966)	(2,130)
Write-off—operations sold	—	—	—	(242)
Exchange rate adjustments	—	1,299	1,299	168
Balance—end of year	$ 12,379	$ 24,400	$ 36,779	$ 35,111

8. Deferred charges, less amortization
in thousands of dollars

	1984	1983
Balance—beginning of year	$ 1,016	$ 1,602
Additions	599	740
Amortization	(1,636)	(1,245)
Exchange rate adjustments	21	(81)
Balance—end of year	$ —	$ 1,016

9. Long-term liabilities

in thousands of dollars

	1984	1983
Long-term debt:		
U.S. $39,324,000 unsecured bank term loan, repayable in increasing annual instalments between 1989 and 1991, with interest at LIBOR plus from $1/2$% to 1% over the term of the loan. The Company has entered into separate interest rate swap agreements which effectively convert the interest cost on U.S. $20,000,000 of this loan to a fixed rate of approximately $12^1/_2$% for five years.	$ 51,908	$ 48,762
U.S. $35,000,000 unsecured bank revolving credit facility of a U.S. subsidiary with interest at U.S. prime or at from $3/4$% to $7/8$% over LIBOR or CD rate at the option of the subsidiary. The loan is also convertible to a five year term loan at the borrower's option	3,960	26,040
$8^1/_2$% Sinking Fund Debentures, Series A, due March 15, 1993 secured by a charge on certain assets of the Company and the pledge of the shares of a Canadian subsidiary, with annual sinking fund repayments of $259,000 in 1986, $400,000 in 1987 and 1988 and $550,000 from 1989 to 1992 with the balance of $1,900,000 repayable on maturity	5,159	5,989
Mortgages maturing:		
Within 5 years, at from 8% to $14^3/_4$%	11,099	6,431
Within 5-10 years, at from $8^1/_2$% to $13^1/_2$%	1,184	3,485
After 10 years, at from 4% to 10%	3,322	4,065
10% Industrial Revenue Development Bonds repayable between 1991 and 1993	7,920	7,440
Other	4,919	7,923
	89,471	110,135
Capital leases:		
Manufacturing plant leases payable in varying monthly or annual instalments at interest rates of between 2% and 16%. At the end of each lease term the Company has the option to purchase the property on payment of a nominal sum	11,046	10,800
	100,517	120,935
Portion due within one year	2,434	7,086
	$ 98,083	$113,849

The change during the year in long-term liabilities, including the current portion, was:

in thousands of dollars

	1984	1983
Balance—beginning of year	$120,935	$121,674
New borrowings	19,639	14,792
Repayments	(43,541)	(13,391)
Reduction related to sale of Tennessee Building Products, Inc.	—	(2,583)
Exchange rate adjustments	3,484	443
Balance—end of year	$100,517	$120,935

Maximum repayments over the next five years are: 1985–$2,434,000; 1986–$8,278,000; 1987–$2,604,000; 1988–$2,683,000; and 1989–$15,029,000.

10. Capital stock

Authorized share capital:

The authorized share capital of the Company consists of an unlimited number of preferred shares of no par value, issuable in series, and an unlimited number of common shares of no par value.

Changes during the year in issued capital stock:

Preferred shares:

The 1,000,000 cumulative floating rate preferred shares Series A were redeemed by the Company at their stated value of $25 per share on December 3, 1984.

Common shares:

in thousands of units/dollars	Shares	1984	1983
Balance—beginning of year	21,291	$ 82,386	$ 66,363
Treasury issue	3,000	31,934	15,675
Exercise of stock options..	43	233	348
Balance—end of year..	24,334	$114,553	$ 82,386

The weighted average number of shares outstanding in 1984 was 22,524,000 (1983–20,908,000).

Stock options:
At December 31, 1984 stock options were outstanding in respect of 277,300 common shares of the Company. These options are exercisable by members of senior management of the Company and its subsidiaries (some of whom are also Directors or Officers of the Company) at between $4.56 and $11.62½ per share and expire on various dates between 1985 and 1991.

11. Currency translation account
The movement in the currency translation account is principally the result of the movement in the exchange rate between the U.S. and Canadian dollars during the year.

12. Commitments and contingencies
Minority shareholders in four subsidiaries have the option to require the Company to purchase their shareholdings at prices based on the earnings of these companies. In respect of two subsidiaries, these options were not yet exercisable at December 31, 1984 and hence the total potential cost cannot be determined. For those subsidiaries in respect of which options were already exercisable, the cost based on earnings to December 31, 1984 would be approximately $484,000.

A Canadian subsidiary of the Company has received federal and provincial income tax assessments totalling $4,000,000 including interest and penalties in respect of the years 1971-1976. Certain of these assessments allege that additional income was earned in those years and the remainder allege that the subsidiary failed to withhold tax on amounts paid or credited to a non-resident corporation. These assessments are being resisted and no provision therefore has been made in the financial statements.

At December 31, 1984, capital commitments in respect of fixed asset additions amounted to $7,000,000.

There were no material transactions during the year between the Company and related parties.

13. Pension plans
Various pension plans exist within the Company. Pension plan contributions charged to income during the year amounted to $6,002,000 (1983–$4,600,000). In addition to the normal annual cost, the 1984 figure reflects full provision for a deficit of $6,579,000 in one plan, arising from a change in the actuarial method of calculating benefits, and full credit for a surplus of $4,700,000 in a second plan, arising principally from an actuarial revaluation.
The Company's pension plans are actuarially revalued at least every three years. The cost of normal pension fund contributions is provided and funded on a current basis. Provisions for this cost are adjusted to reflect the amounts of actuarial revaluation surpluses and deficiencies in the year in which they arise, and amounts funded are adjusted to reflect these surpluses and deficiencies over periods of up to ten years.

14. Segmented information (appendix 1)
Based on the products and operations of the Company, the classes of business as determined by the Directors are:

Residential construction products: For use in residential construction, including new housing and home improvement.

Non-residential construction products: For use in industrial, commercial, institutional and agricultural construction.

Industrial products: Principally for incorporation as a part or sub-assembly in industrial products.

Segmented information (appendix 1)

Indal Limited

in thousands of dollars/ % of sales

Industry segments	Sales		Operating profit				
	1984	1983	1984	%	1983	%	
Residential construction	$369,139	$309,191	$32,917	8.9	$28,060	9.1	
Non-residential construction	155,309	141,111	11,175	7.2	9,290	6.6	
Industrial	336,374	268,243	36,620	10.9	30,286	11.3	
Consolidation eliminations	(26,040)	(23,599)	(3,826)	–	(2,206)	–	
	$834,782	$694,946	76,886	9.2	65,430	9.4	
Corporate expense			(10,446)	(1.2)	(9,996)	(1.4)	
Interest expense			(13,058)	(1.6)	(15,314)	(2.2)	
Earnings before income taxes			53,382	6.4	40,120	5.8	
Income taxes			18,832	2.3	15,525	2.2	
Earnings before minority shareholders' interests			$34,550	4.1	$24,595	3.6	

	Capital expenditures		Depreciation and amortization		Identifiable assets	
	1984	1983	1984	1983	1984	1983
Residential construction	$ 8,187	$ 5,779	$ 5,766	$ 5,192	$184,255	$170,233
Non-residential construction	4,034	3,631	4,221	3,995	105,732	92,338
Industrial	17,592	5,918	7,073	6,107	190,333	169,504
Consolidation eliminations					(66,702)	(26,619)
					413,618	405,456
Net assets—discontinued operation					1,825	3,746
Corporate assets					24,234	7,989
					$439,677	$417,191

Geographic segments	Sales		Operating profit		Identifiable assets	
	1984	1983	1984	1983	1984	1983
Canada	$340,519	$313,960	$ 36,965	$ 36,998	$191,084	$176,825
United States	520,303	404,585	43,747	30,638	289,236	255,250
Consolidation eliminations	(26,040)	(23,599)	(3,826)	(2,206)	(66,702)	(26,619)
	$834,782	$694,946	$ 76,886	$ 65,430	$413,618	$405,456

External and inter-segment sales	External		Inter-segment		Total	
	1984	1983	1984	1983	1984	1983
Industry segments:						
Residential construction	$368,897	$308,757	$ 242	$ 434	$369,139	$309,191
Non-residential construction	148,028	133,971	7,281	7,140	155,309	141,111
Industrial	317,857	252,218	18,517	16,025	336,374	268,243
	834,782	694,946	26,040	23,599	860,822	718,545
Geographic segments:						
Canada	321,264	295,403	19,255	18,557	340,519	313,960
United States	513,518	399,543	6,785	5,042	520,303	404,585
	$834,782	$694,946	$26,040	$23,599	$860,822	$718,545

Canadian sales include exports of $129,156,000 in 1984 (1983—$102,181,000) primarily to the United States.

Quarterly financial information (unaudited)
for the year ended December 31, 1984

Indal Limited

in thousands of dollars

1984	Three months ended				Year ended
	March 31	June 30	September 30	December 31	December 31
Sales[1]	$175,671	$214,730	$224,894	$219,487	$834,782
Gross profit[1]	39,752	52,484	58,357	61,153	211,746
Gross profit percentage[1]	22.6	24.4	25.9	27.9	25.4
Net earnings	3,105	8,965	11,916	9,484	33,470
Earnings per common share					
Basic	$0.13	$0.40	$0.50	$0.38	$1.41
Fully diluted	0.13	0.39	0.50	0.37	1.39
Market price of common shares[2]					
High	$13¾	$12¼	$11⅞	$11¾	$13¾
Low	11	10⅞	10	10¼	10
Number of shares traded[3]					
(in thousands)	744	380	460	590	2,174

in thousands of dollars

1983	Three months ended				Year ended
	March 31	June 30	September 30	December 31	December 31
Sales[1]	$136,877	$181,820	$191,233	$185,016	$694,946
Gross profit[1]	30,864	43,223	51,475	48,005	173,567
Gross profit percentage[1]	22.5	23.8	26.9	25.9	25.0
Net earnings	774	6,234	8,339	8,170	23,517
Earnings per common share[4]					
Basic	$0.01	$0.28	$0.38	$0.36	$1.03
Fully diluted	0.01	0.28	0.38	0.36	1.03
Market price of common shares[2][4]					
High	$9¼	$11½	$13	$13⅝	$13⅝
Low	7¾	9	9¾	9¾	7¾
Number of shares traded[3][4]					
(in thousands)	245	1,794	495	591	3,125

(1) Sales, gross profits and gross profit percentages for the first three quarters of the year have been restated to exclude figures for operations discontinued during the year.
(2) High/low market prices reflect prices quoted on The Toronto Stock Exchange.
(3) The number of shares traded reflects the combined volume of shares traded on the Toronto and Montreal stock exchanges.
(4) Figures have been restated to reflect the 2 for 1 stock split in May 1983.

33

Ten year financial summary

in millions of dollars	1984	1983
Earnings		
Sales	$835	$695
Gross profit	212	174
Earnings before income taxes[1]	53.4	40.1
Net earnings	33.5	23.5
Preferred dividends	1.8	1.9
Common dividends	12.6	5.3
Performance statistics		
Gross profit percentage	25.4%	25.0%
Net earnings as a percentage of sales	4.0%	3.4%
Sales/assets ratio	1.9	1.7
Return on total assets (based on net earnings)	7.6%	5.6%
Return on common shareholders' equity (based on net earnings after preferred dividends and on average opening and closing equity)	16.4%	14.7%
Common share data[2]		
Earnings per common share	$1.41	$1.03
Dividends per common share	55¢	25¢
Book value per common share	9.12	7.69
Average number of common shares outstanding (in millions)	22.5	20.9
Assets		
Working capital	168	159
Current ratio	2.7:1	2.6:1
Fixed assets	138	123
Total assets	440	417
Shareholders' equity		
Preferred shareholders' equity	—	25
Common shareholders' equity	222	164
Number of common shares outstanding at year-end (in millions)	24.3	21.3
Cash flow		
Funds from operations	79	60
Purchase of fixed assets	31	16
Depreciation of fixed assets	18	16

(1) Figures prior to 1984 have been restated to reflect the operating results and gains or losses on the disposal or discontinuance of operations sold or discontinued.

(2) Figures prior to 1983 have been restated to reflect the 2 for 1 stock split in May 1983. Figures prior to 1977 have also been restated to reflect the 2 for 1 stock split in that year.

(3) Percentages and ratios have been calculated using figures in thousands of dollars.

Indal Limited

1982	1981	1980	1979	1978	1977	1976	1975
$565	$584	$443	$450	$363	$212	$159	$109
129	145	110	116	93	55	43	32
4.7	16.9	28.5	45.0	28.0	19.3	19.2	15.1
3.2	12.5	15.8	23.6	13.8	9.3	9.5	7.5
2.6	2.5	2.2	1.8	1.1	0.1	0.1	0.1
4.3	7.7	7.7	6.7	3.6	3.1	2.8	2.2
22.9%	24.8%	24.8%	25.8%	25.5%	25.9%	27.1%	29.1%
0.6%	2.2%	3.6%	5.2%	3.8%	4.4%	6.0%	6.8%
1.5	1.6	1.5	1.6	1.4	1.4	1.3	1.2
0.8%	3.5%	5.2%	8.1%	5.3%	6.3%	7.7%	7.9%
0.4%	7.6%	10.6%	18.1%	14.8%	17.1%	20.5%	20.6%
$0.03	$0.52	$0.71	$1.14	$0.96	$0.74	$0.78	$0.77
22.5¢	40¢	40¢	35¢	27.9¢	24.8¢	22.9¢	22.5¢
6.78	6.89	6.78	6.25	5.47	4.46	4.05	3.52
19.2	19.2	19.2	19.2	13.4	12.4	12.2	9.6
107	116	103	92	98	33	32	24
2.0:1	2.4:1	3.0:1	2.5:1	3.1:1	1.6:1	2.1:1	1.9:1
127	119	105	95	77	46	39	31
376	362	304	290	259	148	122	94
25	25	25	25	25	1	1	1
131	133	130	128	113	59	49	42
9.7	9.6	9.6	9.6	9.6	6.5	3.0	3.0
25	45	41	51	38	24	21	18
23	22	22	33	20	11	9	10
16	15	12	11	8	6	4	3

Glossary

Manufacturing and production terms

Aluminum billet casting: *pouring molten aluminum into long, vertical, cylindrical moulds which form the metal into log-shaped sections which are then cut into shorter lengths, called billets, for use in aluminum extruding.*

Aluminum extruding: *forcing preheated and softened aluminum billet horizontally through a steel die under pressure from a hydraulic ram. The aluminum takes on the shape of the die as it emerges from the press and is cut into lengths for use in fabrication processes.*

Aluminum recycling: *billet casting from sorted and remelted aluminum scrap.*

CAD/CAM: *Computer-aided design and computer-aided manufacturing systems which provide greater speed and precision for repetitive design, drafting and manufacturing tasks.*

Die: *a press tool, usually made of steel, which matches within very close tolerances either two or three dimensions of a metal product and which imparts its shape to the metal passing through the press process. An extrusion die has the form of the two-dimensional extruded section; a pressure-casting die has the complete form of a three-dimensional product.*

Glass laminating: *a method of making safety glass by sandwiching and bonding an interlayer of clear, flexible material with two outer layers of plain or tempered glass. Can also be used to make multi-layer product for use as vandal-proof or bullet-resistant glass.*

Glass tempering: *passing sheets of glass through a high-temperature furnace and then air-cooling them rapidly. This strengthens the glass and changes its molecular structure so that if broken, it will shatter into a myriad of tiny, crystal-like and relatively harmless fragments.*

Steel or aluminum cold rollforming: *passing coiled sheets of steel or aluminum through a series of roller dies that form the metal into sections of various shapes, sizes and thicknesses for use in construction products and general manufacturing.*

Steel stamping: *placing and punching metal blanks in punch presses containing dies, so that the processed blanks, called stampings, have the shape of the die.*

Zinc diecasting: *molten zinc is forced under pressure into the cavities of moulds or dies that shape the metal to their pattern. Door handles, window locks and other hardware are made in this manner.*

Product and market terms

Architectural products or systems: *refers generally to the fabrication of large windows and entrance systems for commercial and industrial buildings.*

Cladding: *steel and aluminum sheet produced in a variety of profiles by cold rollforming for use as roofing and siding on agricultural, commercial and industrial buildings.*

Curtainwall: *windows, panels and frames assembled and affixed to the outer walls of multi-storey buildings.*

Design engineering: *products designed and engineered for custom applications.*

Double-hung windows: *windows consisting of two sashes which slide vertically past each other, held in any open position by balancing devices.*

Glazing: *glass installed in window and door frames.*

Helicopter hauldown systems: *systems engineered by DAF Indal Ltd. to link a hovering helicopter securely to the deck of a naval vessel shortly before touchdown, and, in the U.S. Navy application, to manoeuvre it along a track into the vessel's hangar. These systems are invaluable operating aids in rough weather.*

Insulated steel entry doors: *residential entry doors manufactured from stamped steel panels on a wood frame with a centre core of insulating material.*

Insulating glass units: *energy-efficient products comprising two or three sheets of glass separated by metal spacers and thoroughly sealed, for use in windows and doors.*

Prime aluminum: *aluminum made from alumina as opposed to secondary aluminum made from recycled scrap.*

Prime windows: *windows installed in new buildings or extensions to existing buildings.*

Replacement windows: *windows for installation in existing buildings to upgrade insulating characteristics and lower maintenance requirements.*

Shipboard helicopter hangars: *hangars to house helicopters on the decks of ships not normally of an aircraft-carrying type.*

Spandrel glass: *opaque glass produced by coating glass with paint, then passing it through a high temperature furnace to bake on the coating.*

Thresholds: *adjustable strips at the base of entry door frames, used to exclude air filtration.*

Weatherstripping: *plastic or metal strip used to reduce air filtration around door and window frames.*

Wind turbines: *wind-driven rotary blade systems producing the motive power for electrical generators.*

QUESTIONS

1. How does information from the balance sheet help users of the financial statements?
2. A recent article in a financial magazine indicated that a drug company had good financial flexibility. What is meant by financial flexibility and why is it important?
3. What are the major limitations of the balance sheet as a source of information?
4. Indicate the measurement basis upon which each of the amounts for the following assets would be stated in the balance sheet under generally accepted accounting practice.
   (a) Inventories.
   (b) Prepaid expenses.
   (c) Trade accounts receivable.
   (d) Machinery and equipment.
   (e) Marketable securities consisting of common shares (current asset account).
5. In what section of the balance sheet should the following items appear, and what balance sheet terminology would you use?
   (a) Chequing account at bank.
   (b) Land (held as an investment).
   (c) Reserve for sinking fund.
   (d) Unamortized premium on bonds payable.
   (e) Investment in copyrights.
   (f) Employees' pension fund (consisting of cash and securities).
   (g) Long-term investments (pledged against bank loans payable).
6. Where should the following items be shown on the balance sheet, if shown at all?
   (a) Allowance for doubtful accounts receivable.
   (b) Merchandise held on consignment by the company.
   (c) Advances received on sales contracts.
   (d) Cash surrender value of life insurance.
   (e) Merchandise out on consignment.
   (f) Pension fund on deposit with a trustee (under a trust revocable at depositor's option).
   (g) Intangible assets.
   (h) Accumulated depreciation of plant and equipment.
   (i) Materials in transit—f.o.b. shipping point.
7. What is the relationship between a current asset and a current liability?
8. The creditors of a company agree to accept promissory notes for the amount of its indebtedness with a proviso that three-fourths of the annual profits must be applied to their liquidation. How should these notes be shown on the balance sheet of the issuing company? Give a reason for your answer.
9. What are some of the techniques of disclosure for the balance sheet?
10. If cash is restricted for purposes other than to pay current obligations, should it be classified as a current asset?
11. What are the major types of subsequent events? Indicate how each of the following "subsequent events" would be reported.
    (a) Collection of a note written off in a prior period.
    (b) Issuance of a large preferred stock offering.
    (c) Acquisition of a company in a different industry.
    (d) Destruction of a major plant in an earthquake.
    (e) Death of company president.
    (f) Settlement of a four-week strike at additional wage costs.
    (g) Settlement of a federal income tax case at considerably more tax than anticipated at year end.
    (h) Change in the product mix from consumer goods to industrial goods.

12.   What is a gain contingency? A loss contingency? Give two examples of each.

13.   What is the difference between the report form and the account form for the purpose of balance sheet presentation?

14.   What is a "summary of significant accounting policies"?

15.   What types of contractual obligations must be disclosed in great detail in the notes to the balance sheet? Why do you think these detailed provisions should be disclosed?

16.   What is the purpose of the statement of changes in financial position? How does it differ from a balance sheet or income statement?

17.   The net income for the year for Alsask Enterprises is $810,000, but the statement of changes in financial position indicates that the cash provided by operations is $880,000. What might account for the difference?

18.   Each of the following items must be considered in preparing a statement of changes in financial position. State where each item is to be reported in the statement, if at all.

   (a)   During the year, 1,000 common shares were issued at $40 per share.

   (b)   The company had a net income for the year of $90,000. Depreciation expense amounted to $14,000 and bond premium amortization to $6,000.

   (c)   Uncollectible accounts receivable in the amount of $12,000 were written off against the allowance for doubtful accounts.

19.   The president of your company has recently read an article that disturbs him greatly. The author of this article stated that "although the balance sheet and income statement balance to the penny, they are full of estimates and subject to material error." Indicate items found in these statements that are based on estimates and explain why you must resort to exercising judgement to determine their amount.

20.   What guides might accountants use to provide a basis for decisions on the optimal number of asset and liability items to be reported?

CASES

C5-1   At December 31, 1986, Buckley, Inc. has assets of $9,000,000, liabilities of $6,000,000, common stock of $2,000,000 (representing 2,000,000 shares) , and retained earnings of $1,000,000. Net sales for the year 1986 were $18,000,000 and net income was $800,000. As auditor, you are making a review of subsequent events of this company on February 13, 1987, and find the following:

   1.   On February 3, 1987, one of Buckley's customers declared bankruptcy. At December 31,1986, this company owed Buckley $200,000, of which $20,000 was paid in January, 1987.

   2.   On January 18, 1987, one of the three major plants of the client was destroyed in a fire.

   3.   On January 23, 1987, a strike was called at one of Buckley's largest plants which halted 30% of its production. As of today (February 13) the strike has not been settled.

   4.   A major electronics enterprise has introduced a line of products that would compete directly with Buckley's primary line, now being produced in a specially designed new plant. Because of manufacturing innovations, the competitor has been able to achieve quality similar to that of Buckley's products, but at a price 50% lower. Buckley officials say they will meet the lower prices, which are high enough to cover variable manufacturing and selling costs but which permit recovery of only a portion of fixed costs.

   5.   Merchandise traded in the open market is recorded in the company's records at $1.40 per unit on December 31, 1986. This price had prevailed for two weeks, after release of an official market report that predicted vastly enlarged supplies; however, no purchases were made at $1.40. The price throughout the preceding year had been about $2.00, which was the level experienced over several years. On January 18, 1987, the

price returned to $2.00, after public disclosure of an error in the market report which destroyed the expectations of excessive supplies. Inventory at December 31, 1986, was on a lower of cost and market basis.

6. On February 1, 1987, the board of directors adopted a resolution accepting the offer of an investment banker to guarantee the marketing of $1,000,000 of preferred shares.

Instructions

For each case, state what adjustments or disclosures you would make regarding the December 31, 1986, financial statements.

C5-2 The following items were brought to your attention during the course of the year-end audit:

1. The client expects to recover a substantial amount in connection with a pending refund claim for a prior year's taxes. Although the claim is being contested, counsel for the company has confirmed this expectation.

2. Your client is a defendant in a patent infringement suit involving a material amount; you have received from the client's counsel a statement that the loss can be reasonably estimated and that it is likely that it will occur.

3. Cash includes a substantial sum specifically set aside for immediate reconstruction of a plant and replacement of machinery.

4. Because of a general increase in the number of labour disputes and strikes, both within and outside the industry, it is possible that the client will suffer a costly strike in the near future.

5. Trade accounts receivable include a large number of customers' notes, many of which had been renewed several times and may have to be renewed continually for some time in the future. The interest is settled on each maturity date, and the makers are in good financial condition.

6. At the beginning of the year the client entered into a 10-year nonrenewable lease agreement. Provisions in the lease require the client to make substantial reconditioning and restoration expenditures at the termination of the lease.

7. Inventory includes retired equipment, some at regularly depreciated book value, and some at scrap or sale value.

Instructions

For each of the situations above describe the accounting treatment you recommend for the current year. Justify your recommended treatment for each situation.

C5-3 In an examination of the Davis Corporation as of December 31, 1986, you have learned that the following situations exist. No entries have been made in the accounting records for these items.

1. On December 15, 1986, the Davis Corporation declared a common stock dividend of 1,000 shares on 100,000 of its common shares outstanding, payable February 1, 1987, to the common shareholders of record December 31, 1986.

2. Davis Corporation, which is on a calendar-year basis, changed its inventory method as of January 1, 1986. The inventory for December 31, 1985, was costed by the FIFO method, and the inventory for December 31, 1986, was costed by the weighted-average method.

3. Davis Corporation has guaranteed the payment of interest on the 20-year first mortgage bonds of the Poper Company, an affiliate. Outstanding bonds of the Poper Company amount to $150,000 with interest payable at 12% per annum, due June 1 and December 1 of each year. The bonds were issued by the Poper company on December 1, 1982, and all interest payments have been met by the company with the exception of the payment due December 1, 1986. The Davis Corporation states that it will pay the defaulted interest to the bondholders on January 15, 1987.

4. During the year 1986, the Davis Corporation was named as a defendant in a suit for damages by the Long Company for breach of contract. The case was decided in favour of Long Company, and it was awarded $60,000 damages. At the time of the audit, the case was under appeal to a higher court.

5. The corporation erected its present factory building in 1971. Depreciation was calculated by the straight-line method, using an estimated life of 35 years. Early in 1986, the board of directors conducted a careful survey and estimated that the factory building had a remaining useful life of 25 years as of January 1, 1986.

6. An additional assessment of 1986 income taxes was levied and paid in 1986.

7. When calculating the accrual for officers' salaries at December 31, 1986, it was discovered that the accrual for officers' salaries for December 31, 1985, had been overstated.

Instructions

Describe fully how each of the items above should be reflected in the financial statements of Davis Corporation for the year 1986.

C5-4   The assets of Loghorn, Inc. are presented below:

Loghorn, Inc.
BALANCE SHEET
December 31, 1986

Assets

Current Assets		
Cash		$ 80,000
Unclaimed dividend cheques		7,500
Marketable securities (cost $20,000) at market		24,500
Accounts receivable (less bad debt reserve)		75,000
Inventories—at lower of cost (determined by the next-in, first-out method) and market		250,000
Total current assets		$ 437,000
Tangible Assets		
Land (less accumulated depreciation)		$ 70,000
Buildings and equipment	$800,000	
Less: Accumulated depreciation	300,000	500,000
Net tangible assets		$ 570,000
Long-term Investments		
Shares and bonds		$ 100,000
Sinking fund		40,000
Total long-term investments		$ 140,000
Other Assets		
Discount on bonds payable		$ 14,200
Claim against Canadian government (pending)		975,200
Total other assets		$ 989,200
Total Assets		$2,136,200

Instructions

Indicate the deficiencies, if any, in the foregoing assets of Loghorn, Inc.

C5-5   Presented below is the balance sheet of Widener Corporation.

Widener Corporation
BALANCE SHEET
December 31, 1986

Assets

Current Assets		
Cash	$ 9,000	
Marketable securities	9,000	
Accounts receivable	25,000	
Merchandise inventory	20,000	
Supplies inventory	4,000	
Stock investment in subsidiary company	20,000	$ 87,000
Investments		
Bond sinking fund		26,000
Property, Plant, and Equipment		
Buildings and land	$71,000	
Less: Reserve for depreciation	20,000	51,000
Deferred Charges		
Unamortized discount on bonds payable		1,000
Other Assets		
Cash surrender value of life insurance		18,000
		$183,000

Liabilities and Capital

Current Liabilities		
Accounts payable	$15,000	
Reserve for income taxes	14,000	
Customers' accounts with credit balances	1	$ 29,001
Long-term Liabilities		
Bonds payable		46,000
Total liabilties		$ 75,001
Share Capital		
Common shares	$75,000	
Earned surplus	24,999	
Cash dividends declared	8,000	107,999
		$183,000

Instructions

Indicate your criticism of the balance sheet presented above. State briefly the proper treatment of the item criticized.

C5-6 The financial statement below was prepared by employees of your client, Godfrey Manufacturing Company. The statement is unaccompanied by notes.

Godfrey Manufacturing Company
BALANCE SHEET
As of November 30, 1986

Current Assets

Cash		$ 179,200	
Accounts receivable (less allowance of			
$15,000 for doubtful accounts)		240,700	
Inventories		2,554,000	$2,973,900

Less: Current Liabilities

Accounts payable		$ 206,400	
Accrued payroll		8,260	
Accrued interest on mortgage note		12,000	
Estimated taxes payable		66,000	292,660
Net working capital			$2,681,240

Property, Plant, and Equipment (at cost)

	Cost	Depreciation	Value	
Land and buildings	$ 983,300	$ 310,000	$ 673,300	
Machinery and equipment	1,135,700	568,699	567,001	
	$2,119,000	$ 878,699		$1,240,301

Deferred Charges

Prepaid taxes and other expenses		$ 11,700	
Unamortized discount on mortgage note		10,800	22,500
Total net working capital and noncurrent assets			$3,944,041

Less: Deferred Liabilities

Mortgage note payable		$ 300,000	
Unearned revenue		1,898,000	2,198,000
Total net assets			$1,746,041

Shareholders' Equity

$6 preferred shares	$ 400,000
Common shares	697,000
Paid-in surplus	210,000
Retained earnings	439,041
Total shareholders' equity	$1,746,041

Instructions

Indicate the deficiencies, if any, in the balance sheet above.

C5-7 The following balance sheet, which was submitted to you for review, has been prepared for inclusion in the published annual report of the Cruise Corporation for the year ended December 31, 1986.

Cruise Corporation
BALANCE SHEET
As of December 31, 1986

Assets

Current Asset

Cash		$ 1,800,000
Accounts receivable	$3,900,000	
Less: Reserve for bad debts	50,000	3,850,000
Inventories—at the lower of cost (determined by the first-in, first-out method) and market		3,600,000
Total current assets		$ 9,250,000

Plant Assets

Land (at cost)	$ 400,000	
Building, machinery and equipment, and furniture (at cost)	4,000,000	
Less: Reserve for depreciation	(1,490,000)	2,910,000

Deferred Charges and Other Assets

Cash surrender value of life insurance	$ 20,000	
Unamortized discount on first mortgage note	42,000	
Prepaid expenses	40,000	102,000
		$12,262,000

Liabilities

Current Liabilities

Notes payable to bank—unsecured		$ 750,000
Current maturities of first mortgage note		600,000
Accounts payable—trade		1,900,000
Reserve for income taxes for the year ended December 31, 1986		700,000
Accrued expenses		550,000
		$ 4,500,000

Long-term Debt

8% first mortgage note payable in quarterly instalments of $150,000	$4,200,000	
Less: Current maturities	600,000	3,600,000

Reserves

Reserve for contingencies	$ 500,000	
Reserve for additional income tax	100,000	
Reserve for damages	50,000	
Reserve for possible future inventory losses	300,000	950,000

Capital

Share capital—authorized, issued, and outstanding, 100,000 shares	$1,000,000	
Capital surplus—donated land	300,000	
Earned surplus	1,912,000	3,212,000
		$12,262,000

Additional data:

1. Reserve for contingencies was set up by charges against earned surplus over a period of several years by the board of directors to provide for a possible future recession.

2. Reserve for income taxes was set up in prior years and relates to additional taxes that Revenue Canada contends the company owes. The company believes that Revenue Canada will settle for the amount of $100,000 set up on the balance sheet.

3. Reserve for damages was set up by a charge against the current fiscal year's net income to cover damages possibly payable by the company as a defendant in a lawsuit in progress at the balance sheet date. The suit was subsequently settled for $50,000 prior to the completion of the statement.

4. Reserve for possible future inventory losses was set up in prior years by action of the board of directors by charges against earned surplus. No charges occurred in the account during the current year.

Instructions

State what changes in classification or terminology you would advocate in the presentation of this balance sheet to make it conform with generally accepted accounting principles and with present-day terminology. State reasons for your suggested changes.

C5-8 The following year-end financial statements were prepared by the Windsor Corporation's bookkeeper. The Windsor Corporation operates a chain of retail stores.

Windsor Corporation
BALANCE SHEET
June 30, 1986

Assets

Current Assets		
Cash		$ 100,000
Notes receivable		100,000
Accounts receivable, less reserve for doubtful accounts		75,000
Inventories		395,500
Investment securities (at cost)		100,000
Total current assets		$ 770,500
Property, Plant, and Equipment		
Land (at cost) (Note 1)	$180,000	
Buildings, at cost less accumulated depreciation of $350,000	500,000	
Equipment, at cost less accumulated depreciation of $180,000	400,000	1,080,000
Intangibles		450,000
Other Assets		
Prepaid expenses		6,405
Total assets		$2,306,905

Liabilities and Shareholders' Equity

Current Liabilities

Accounts payable		$ 25,500
Estimated income taxes payable		160,000
Contingent liability on discounted notes receivable		75,000
Total current liabilities		$ 260,500

Long-term Liabilities

9% serial bonds, $50,000 due annually on December 31		
Maturity value	$865,000	
Less: Unamortized discount	35,000	830,000
Total liabilities		$1,090,500

Shareholders' Equity

Common shares			
(authorized and issued, 75,000 shares)		$750,000	
Retained earnings			
Appropriated (Note 2)	$110,000		
Free	356,405	466,405	1,216,405
Total liabilities and shareholders' equity			$2,306,905

Windsor Corporation
INCOME STATEMENT
As at June 30, 1986

Sales			$2,500,000
Interest revenue			6,000
Total revenue			$2,506,000
Cost of goods sold			1,780,000
Gross profit			$ 726,000
Operating expenses			
Selling expenses			
Salaries	$ 95,000		
Advertising	85,000		
Sales returns and allowances	50,000	$230,000	
General and administrative expenses			
Salaries	$ 84,000		
Property taxes	38,000		
Depreciation and amortization	86,000		
Rent (Note 3)	75,000		
Interest on serial bonds	48,000	331,000	561,000
Income before taxes			$ 165,000
Income taxes			80,000
Net income			$ 85,000

Notes to financial statements:

Note 1. Includes a future store site acquired during the year at a cost of $80,000.

Note 2. Retained earnings in the amount of $110,000 have been set aside to finance expansion.

Note 3. During the year the corporation acquired certain equipment under a long-term lease.

Instructions

Identify and discuss the defects in the financial statements of Windsor Corporation with respect to terminology, disclosure, and classification. Your discussion should explain why you consider them to be defects. Do not prepare revised statements.

(AICPA adapted)

C5-9 Below are a number of debit and credit items as they might appear on the balance sheet of the Pappas Corporation as of October 31, 1986.

Debits	Credits
Cash in bank	Accrued payroll
Land	Amounts payable to lawyer for
Inventory of operating parts and	renegotiation of government contracts
supplies	Notes payable
Inventory of raw materials	Accrued interest on bonds
Patents	Accumulated depreciation
Cash and Canadian government bonds	Accounts payable
set aside for property additions	Contributed surplus
Investment in subsidiary	Accrued interest on notes payable
Accounts receivable	8% first mortgage bonds to be
Government contracts	redeemed in 1986 out of current
Regular	assets
Instalments—due in 1986	Share capital—preferred
Instalments—due in 1987-88	9 1/2% first mortgage bonds due in
Goodwill	1992
Inventory of finished goods	Preferred shares dividend, payable
Inventory of work in process	Nov. 1, 1986
Deficit	Allowance for doubtful accounts
Interest accrued on Canadian	receivable
government securities	Provision for income taxes
Notes receivable	Customers advances (on contracts to
Petty cash fund	be completed in 1987)
Canadian government securities	Appropriation for possible decline
Unamortized bond discount	in value of raw materials inventory
	Premium on bonds redeemable in 1986
	Officers' 1986 bonus accrued

Instructions

Select the current asset and current liability items from among these debits and credits. If there are certain borderline cases that you are unable to classify without further information, mention them and explain your difficulty, or give your reasons for making questionable classifications, if any.

(AICPA adapted)

EXERCISES

E5-1 Presented below are the captions of a balance sheet:
1. Current assets
2. Investments
3. Property, plant, and equipment
4. Intangible assets
5. Other assets
6. Current liabilities
7. Noncurrent liabilities
8. Share capital
9. Contributed surplus
10. Retained earnings

Instructions

Indicate by number where each of the following items would be classified:

(a)	Goodwill	(k)	Cash surrender value of life insurance
(b)	Preferred shares	(l)	Notes payable (due next year)
(c)	Wages payable	(m)	Taxes payable
(d)	Trade accounts payable	(n)	Land
(e)	Buildings	(o)	Bond sinking fund
(f)	Marketable securities	(p)	Merchandise inventory
(g)	Current portion of long-term debt	(q)	Office supplies
(h)	Premium on bonds payable	(r)	Prepaid insurance
(i)	Allowance for doubtful accounts	(s)	Bonds payable
(j)	Appropriation for contingencies	(t)	Common shares

E5-2   Presented below are a number of balance sheet accounts:

1.	Investment in Common Shares	8.	Marketable Securities (short-term)
2.	Bonds Payable	9.	Income Taxes Payable
3.	Common Shares	10.	Accrued Interest on Notes Payable
4.	Accumulated Depreciation— Buildings	11.	Unearned Subscription Revenue
5.	Warehouse in Process of Construction	12.	Work in Process Inventory
6.	Petty Cash	13.	Accrued Vacation Pay
7.	Deficit	14.	Cash Dividends Payable

Instructions

For each of the accounts above, indicate the proper balance sheet classification. In the case of borderline items, indicate the additional information that would be required to determine the proper classification.

E5-3   Assume that Rothchild, Inc. has the following accounts at the end of the current year.

1.	Common Shares	15.	Notes Receivable Discounted
2.	Discount on Bonds Payable	16.	Cash Restricted for Plant Expansion
3.	Goodwill	17.	Land Held for Future Plant Site
4.	Raw Materials	18.	Allowance for Doubtful Accounts—
5.	Preferred Shares Investments (long-term)		Accounts Receivable
6.	Unearned Rent Revenue	19.	Retained Earnings—Unappropriated
7.	Appropriation for Plant Expansion	20.	Contributed Capital—Donated land
8.	Work in Process	21.	Unearned Subscription Revenue
9.	Copyrights	22.	Receivables—Officers (due in 1 year)
10.	Buildings	23.	Finished Goods
11.	Notes Receivable (short-term)	24.	Accounts Receivable
12.	Cash	25.	Bonds Payable (due in 4 years)
13.	Accrued Salaries Payable		
14.	Accumulated Depreciation—Buildings		

Instructions

Prepare a balance sheet in good form. (No monetary amounts are necessary.)

E5-4   Assume that Harlow Enterprises uses the following headings on its balance sheet:

1.	Current assets	6.	Current liabilities
2.	Investments	7.	Long-term liabilities
3.	Property, plant, and equipment	8.	Share capital
4.	Intangible assets	9.	Contributed surplus
5.	Other assets	10.	Retained earnings

Instructions

Indicate by number where each of the following usually should be classified. If an item should appear in a note to the financial statements, use the letter "N" to indicate this fact. If an item need not be reported at all on the balance sheet, use the letter "X."

(a) Advances to suppliers.
(b) Unearned rental revenue.
(c) Common shares issued.
(d) Unexpired insurance
(e) Shares owned in affiliated companies.
(f) Unearned subscriptions revenue.
(g) Preferred shares.
(h) Copyrights.
(i) Bond sinking fund.
(j) Sale of large issue of common shares days after balance sheet date.
(k) Accrued interest on notes receivable.
(l) Twenty-year issue of bonds payable which will mature within the next year. (No sinking fund exists and refunding is not planned.)

(m) Machinery retired from use and held for sale.
(n) Fully depreciated machine still in use.
(o) Organization costs.
(p) Salaries which company budget shows will be paid to employees within the next year.
(q) Company is a defendant in a lawsuit for $1 million. (Possibility of loss is remote.)
(r) Discount on bonds payable. Assume related to bonds payable in (l).
(s) Accrued interest on bonds payable.
(t) Accumulated depreciation.

E5-5 Focus Company has decided to expand their operations. The bookkeeper recently completed the balance sheet presented below in order to obtain additional funds for expansion.

Focus Company
BALANCE SHEET
For the Year Ended 1986

Current Assets	
Cash (net of bank overdraft of $40,000)	$180,000
Accounts receivable (net)	325,000
Inventories at lower of average cost and market	420,000
Marketable securities—at market (cost $110,000)	125,000
Property, Plant, and Equipment	
Building (net)	460,000
Office equipment (net)	185,000
Land held for future use	150,000
Intangible Assets	
Goodwill	75,000
Cash surrender value of life insurance	64,000
Prepaid expenses	2,200
Current Liabilities	
Accounts payable	95,000
Notes payable (due next year)	100,000
Pension obligation	71,000
Rent payable	85,000
Premium on bonds payable	68,000
Long-term Liabilities	
Bond payable	500,000
Reserve for plant expansion	75,000
Shareholders' Equity	
Common shares, authorized 400,000 shares, issued 280,000	280,000
Contributed surplus—donations	70,000
Retained earnings	?

Instructions

Prepare a revised balance sheet given the available information. Assume that the accumulated depreciation balance for the buildings is $95,000 and for the office equipment, $55,000. The allowance for doubtful accounts has a balance of $25,000. The pension obligation is considered a long-term liability.

E5-6   The bookkeeper for Pet Food Company has prepared the following balance sheet as of July 31, 1986.

Pet Food Company
BALANCE SHEET
As of July 31, 1986

Cash	$ 64,000	Notes and accounts payable	$ 41,000
Accounts receivable (net)	38,000	Long-term liabilities	64,000
Inventories	50,000	Shareholders' equity	141,000
Equipment (net)	73,000		
Patents	21,000		
	$246,000		$246,000

The following additional information is provided.

1.   Cash includes $800 in a petty cash fund and $10,000 in a bond sinking fund.
2.   The net accounts receivable balance comprises the following three items: (a) accounts receivable—debit balances; $45,000; (b) accounts receivable—credit balances; $5,000; (c) allowance for doubtful accounts; $2,000.
3.   Merchandise inventory costing $2,400 was shipped out on consignment on July 31, 1986. The ending inventory balance does not include the consigned goods. Receivables in the amount of $3,200 were recognized on these consigned goods.
4.   Equipment had a cost of $95,000 and an accumulated depreciation balance of $22,000.
5.   Taxes payable of $4,000 were accrued on July 31. The Pet Food Company, however, had set up a cash fund to meet this obligation. This cash fund was not included in the cash balance, but was offset against the taxes payable amount.

Instructions

Prepare a corrected balance sheet as of July 31, 1986, from the available information.

E5-7   The current asset and liability sections of the balance sheet of Cheryl, Inc. appear as follows:

Cheryl, Inc.
PARTIAL BALANCE SHEET
December 31, 1986

Cash		$ 30,000	Accounts payable	$ 48,000
Accounts receivable	$80,000		Notes payable	70,000
Less: Allowance for doubtful accounts	6,000	74,000		
Inventories		170,000		
Prepaid expenses		10,000		
		$284,000		$118,000

The following errors in the corporation's accounting have been discovered:

1. Sales for the first four days in January, 1987, in the amount of $26,000 were entered in the sales book as of December 31, 1986. Of these, $23,000 were sales on account and the remainder were cash sales.

2. Cash, not including cash sales, collected in January, 1987, and entered as of December 31, 1986, totalled $30,384. Of this amount, $20,384 was received on account after cash discounts of 2% had been deducted; the remainder represented the proceeds of a bank loan.

3. January, 1987, cash disbursements entered as of December, 1986, included payments of accounts payable in the amount of $37,000, on which a cash discount of 2% was taken.

4. The inventory included $24,000 of merchandise that had been received at December 31, but for which no purchase invoices had been received or entered. Of this amount, $10,000 had been received on consignment; the remainder was purchased f.o.b. destination, terms 2/10, n/30.

Instructions

(a) Restate the current asset and liability sections of the balance sheet in accordance with good accounting practice. (Assume that both accounts receivable and accounts payable are recorded gross.)

(b) State the net effect of your adjustments on Cheryl, Inc.'s retained earnings balance.

E5-8 Condensed financial data of the Maxine Company Ltd. for the years ended December 31, 1985, and December 31, 1986, are presented below:

Maxine Company Ltd.
COMPARATIVE BALANCE SHEET DATA
as of December 31, 1985 and 1986

	1985	1986
Cash	$ 18,400	$134,800
Receivables, net	49,000	83,200
Inventories	61,900	92,500
Investments	100,000	90,000
Plant assets	220,000	240,000
	$449,300	$640,500
Accounts payable	$ 67,300	$100,000
Mortgage payable	73,500	50,000
Accumulated depreciation	50,000	30,000
Common shares	125,000	175,000
Retained earnings	133,500	285,500
	$449,300	$640,500

Maxine Company Ltd.
INCOME STATEMENT
For the Year Ended December 31, 1986

Sales	$300,000	
Interest and other revenue	10,000	$310,000
Less:		
Cost of goods sold	$100,000	
Selling and administrative expenses	10,000	
Depreciation	22,000	
Income taxes	5,000	
Interest charges	3,000	
Loss on sale of plant assets	8,000	148,000
Net income		$162,000
Dividends		10,000
Income retained in business		$152,000

Additional information:

New plant assets costing $80,000 were purchased during the year. Investments were sold at book value.

Instructions

From the foregoing information, prepare a statement of changes in financial position based on *CICA Handbook*, Section 1540, recommendations. (Hint: The adjustment for changes in current receivables, payables, and inventory is a deduction of $32,100.)

E5-9   Presented below is a condensed version of the balance sheet for Pana Corporation for the last two years:

	December 31	
	1986	1985
Current assets	$320,000	$245,000
Investments	60,000	71,000
Equipment	305,000	260,000
Less: Accumulated depreciation	(110,000)	(98,000)
Current liabilities	140,000	142,000
Share capital	130,000	130,000
Retained earnings	305,000	206,000

Additional information:

Investments were sold at a loss (not extraordinary) of $3,000; no equipment was sold; cash dividends were $31,000; and net income was $130,000.

Instructions

Prepare a statement of changes in financial position for 1986 for Pana Corporation using (a) the working capital basis, (b) cash and cash equivalent basis following the *CICA Handbook*, Section 1540. (Assume cash is the only current asset.)

PROBLEMS

P5-1   Presented below is a list of accounts in alphabetical order.

Accounts Payable	Franchise
Accounts Receivable	Gain on Sale of Equipment
Accrued Wages	Interest Receivable
Accumulated Depreciation—Buildings	Inventory—Beginning Inventory
Accumulated Depreciation—Equipment	Inventory—Ending Inventory
Advances to employees	Land for Future Plant Site
Advertising	Patent
Allowance for Doubtful Accounts	Pension Fund
Appropriation for Plant Expansion	Pension Obligations
Appropriation for Possible Inventory	Petty Cash
Price Declines	Preferred Shares
Bond Sinking Fund	Premium on Bonds Payable
Bonds Payable	Prepaid Expenses
Buildings	Purchase Returns and Allowances
Cash in Bank	Purchases
Cash on Hand	Retained Earnings—Unappropriated
Cash Surrender Value of Life Insurance	Sales
Commission Expense	Sales discounts
Common Shares	Sales Salaries
Dividends Payable	Temporary Investments
Employee Income Taxes Withheld	Transportation-in
Equipment	Unearned Subscription Revenue

Instructions

Prepare a balance sheet in good form. (No monetary amounts are to be shown.)

P5-2   Presented below are a number of balance sheet items for Anderson, Inc. for the current year:

Notes receivable	$ 627,905	Inventories	$ 225,468
Notes payable to banks	241,652	Rent payable (short-term)	33,600
Accounts payable	701,244	Taxes payable	70,541
Equipment	1,766,874	Long-term rental obligations	460,296
Marketable securities		Common shares	156,162
(short-term)	96,000	Preferred shares	160,000
Accumulated depreciation—		Prepaid expenses	109,662
building	80,800	Goodwill	124,263
Building	1,802,823	Payroll taxes payable	168,000
Retained earnings	?	Bonds payable	240,000
Refundable income taxes	92,632	Discount on bonds payable	12,000
Unsecured notes payable		Cash	240,000
(long-term)	1,633,154	Land	280,000
Accumulated depreciation—			
equipment	272,084		

Instructions

Prepare a balance sheet in good form. Assume that notes receivable and notes payable are short-term unless stated otherwise. There were 30,000 authorized preferred shares of which 16,000 were issued, and 35,000,000 common shares authorized of which 1,561,620 were issued.

P5-3   Presented on page 253 is the balance sheet of Krammer Corporation as of December 31, 1986:

Krammer Corporation
BALANCE SHEET
December 31, 1986

Assets

Building (Note 1)	$1,425,000
Land	823,500
Cash on hand	187,500
Assets allocated to trustee for plant expansion	
Cash in bank	60,000
Treasury notes, at cost	165,000
Accounts receivable	130,500
Inventories	151,500
Goodwill (Note 2)	108,000
	$3,051,000

Equities

Common shares	$1,558,500
Notes payable (Note 3)	480,000
Income taxes payable	46,500
Reserve for repairs of machinery (Note 4)	39,000
Reserve for contingencies	67,500
Reserve for depreciation of building	315,000
Appreciation capital (Note 1)	288,000
Retained earnings	256,500
	$3,051,000

Note 1. Buildings are stated at cost, except for one building that was recorded at appraised value. The excess of appraisal value over cost was $288,000.

Note 2. Goodwill in the amount of $108,000 was recognized because the company believed that their book value was not an accurate representation of the fair market value of the company.

Note 3. Notes payable are long-term except for the current instalment due of $15,000.

Note 4. A reserve for repairs was set up by a charge to income. Upon consultation with the company's auditors, it was determined that this contingency did not meet the criteria of a loss contingency. The company still wishes to show this amount in shareholders' equity.

Instructions

Prepare a corrected balance sheet in good form.

P5-4   Presented below is the balance sheet of Charlatan Corporation for the current year, 1986.

Charlatan Corporation
BALANCE SHEET
December 31, 1986

Current assets	$ 435,000	Current liabilities	$ 380,000
Investments	640,000	Long-term liabilities	1,040,000
Property, plant, and		Shareholders' equity	1,680,000
equipment	1,720,000		
Intangible assets	305,000		
	$3,100,000		$3,100,000

The following information is presented:

1. The current asset section includes: cash, $100,000; accounts receivable, $170,000 less $10,000 for allowance for doubtful accounts; inventories $180,000; and a deduction for revenue received in advance of $5,000. The cash balance is $116,000, less a bank overdraft of $16,000. Inventories are stated on the lower of FIFO cost and market basis.

2. The investments section includes the cash surrender value of a life insurance contract, $40,000; investments in common shares, short-term $80,000 and long-term $140,000; bond sinking fund, $200,000; and organization costs, $180,000.

3. Property, plant, and equipment includes buildings, $1,040,000 less accumulated depreciation, $360,000; equipment, $420,000 less accumulated depreciation, $180,000; land, $500,000; and land held for future use, $300,000.

4. Intangible assets include a franchise, $165,000; goodwill, $100,000; and discount on bonds payable, $40,000.

5. Current liabilities include accounts payable, $90,000; notes payable, short-term $120,000 and long-term $80,000; taxes payable, $40,000; and appropriation for short-term contingencies, $50,000.

6. Long-term liabilities comprise only 10% bonds payable due 1996.

7. Shareholders' equity has preferred stock, no-par value, authorized 300,000 shares, issued 150,000 shares for $450,000, and common stock, authorized 400,000 shares, issued 100,000 shares at an average price of $10. In addition, the corporation has unappropriated retained earnings of $230,000.

Instructions

Prepare a balance sheet in good form.

P5-5 The adjusted trial balance of Wollman Bros. and other related information for the year 1986 is as follows:

Wollman Bros.
ADJUSTED TRIAL BALANCE
December 31, 1986

Cash	$ 18,000	
Accounts receivable	144,000	
Allowance for doubtful accounts		$ 5,940
Prepaid expenses	1,620	
Inventory	270,000	
Long-term investments	324,000	
Land	72,000	
Construction work in progress	108,000	
Patents	18,000	
Equipment	360,000	
Accumulated depreciation of equipment		108,000
Unamortized discount on bonds payable	7,200	
Accounts payable		162,000
Accrued expenses		3,600
Notes payable		72,000
Bonds payable		360,000
Share capital		563,400
Retained earnings		37,080
Appropriation for contingencies		10,800
	$1,322,820	$1,322,820

Additional information:

1. The inventory has a replacement market value of $320,400. The lower of cost (FIFO) and market method of inventory valuation is used.
2. The market value of the long-term investments that consist of stocks and bonds is $330,000.
3. The amount of the Construction Work in Progress account represents the costs expended to date on a building in the process of construction. (The company rents factory space at the present time.) The land on which the building is being constructed cost $72,000, as shown in the trial balance.
4. The patents were purchased by the company at a cost of $28,800 and are being amortized on a straight-line basis.
5. Of the unamortized discount on bonds payable, $600 will be amortized in each year to maturity.
6. The notes payable represent bank loans that are secured by long-term investments carried at $144,000. These bank loans are due in 1987.
7. The bonds payable bear interest at 11% and are due January 1, 1998.
8. 600,000 common shares were authorized, of which 540,000 shares were issued and are outstanding.
9. The Appropriation for Contingencies was created by action of the board of directors.

Instructions

Prepare a balance sheet as of December 31, 1986, so that all important information is fully disclosed.

P5-6 You have been engaged to examine the financial statements of Warren Corporation for the year 1986. The bookkeeper who maintains the financial records has prepared all the unaudited financial statements for the corporation since its organization on January 2, 1980. The client has provided you with the December 31, 1986, balance sheet (page 256) and the supplementary information below.

1. A major competitor has introduced a line of products that will compete directly with Warren's primary line, now being produced in a specially designed new plant. Because of manufacturing innovations, the competitor's line will be of comparable quality but priced 50% below the client's line. The competitor announced its new line on January 14, 1987. The client indicates that the company will meet the lower prices that are high enough to cover variable manufacturing and selling expenses, but permit recovery of only a portion of fixed costs.
2. You learned on January 28, 1987, prior to completion of the audit, of heavy damage because of a recent fire to one of the client's two plants; the loss will not be reimbursed by insurance. The newspapers described the event in detail.
3. On May 1, 1986, the corporation issued $750,000 of bonds to finance plant expansion. The long-term bond agreement provided for the annual payment of principal and interest over five years. The existing plant was pledged as security for the loan.
4. The bookkeeper made the following mistakes:
   (a) In 1984, the ending inventory was overstated by $183,000. The ending inventories for 1985 and 1986 were correctly computed.
   (b) In 1986, accrued wages in the amount of $330,000 were omitted from the balance sheet and these expenses were not charged on the income statement.
   (c) In 1986, a gain of $150,000 (net of tax) on the sale of certain plant assets was credited directly to retained earnings.

Instructions

Prepare the balance sheet for Warren Corporation in accordance with proper accounting principles. Describe the nature of any notes that might need to be prepared.

Warren Corporation
BALANCE SHEET
As of December 31, 1986

Assets		Liabilities	
Current assets	$1,823,130	Current liabilities	$ 813,513
Other assets	6,480,000	Long-term liabilities	1,500,000
		Capital	5,989,617
	$8,303,130		$8,303,130

An analysis of current assets discloses the following:

Cash (restricted in the amount of $480,000 for plant expansion)	$1,113,195
Investments in land	106,500
Accounts receivable less allowance of $48,000	118,710
Inventories	484,725
	$1,823,130

Other assets include:

Prepaid expenses	$ 47,073
Plant and equipment less accumulated depreciation of $1,506,000	5,123,490
Cash surrender value of life insurance policy	90,198
Unamortized bond discount	47,130
Claim for income tax refund	182,148
Goodwill, at cost less amortization of $4,500	347,100
Land	642,861
	$6,480,000

Current liabilities include:

Accounts payable	$ 480,000
Notes payable (due, 1988)	183,513
Estimated income taxes payable	150,000
	$ 813,513

Long-term liabilities include:

Unearned revenue	$ 527,730
Dividends payable (cash)	222,270
12% serial bonds payable ($150,000 maturing each year for 1987–1991)	750,000
	$1,500,000

Capital includes:

Retained earnings (unappropriated)	$2,130,000
Capital stock, authorized 200,000 shares, 150,000 shares issued	1,638,252
Reserve for contingencies	2,221,365
	$5,989,617

P5-7 Anchor, Inc. had the following condensed balance sheet at the end of 1985:

<table>
<tr><td colspan="4" align="center">Anchor, Inc.
BALANCE SHEET
December 31, 1985</td></tr>
<tr><td>Current assets (all cash)</td><td>$ 37,500</td><td>Current liabilities</td><td>$ 15,000</td></tr>
<tr><td>Investments</td><td>20,000</td><td>Long-term notes payable</td><td>16,500</td></tr>
<tr><td>Plant assets (net)</td><td>67,500</td><td>Bonds payable</td><td>25,000</td></tr>
<tr><td>Land</td><td>31,000</td><td>Share capital</td><td>75,000</td></tr>
<tr><td></td><td></td><td>Retained earnings</td><td>24,500</td></tr>
<tr><td></td><td>$156,000</td><td></td><td>$156,000</td></tr>
</table>

During 1986 the following occurred:

1. Anchor, Inc. sold part of its investment portfolio for $10,300. This transaction resulted in a gain of $300. The company often sells and buys securities of this nature.
2. A tract of land was purchased for $6,000.
3. Bonds payable in the amount of $5,000 were retired at par.
4. Additional common shares were sold for $10,000.
5. Dividends totalling $7,500 were declared and paid to shareholders.
6. Net income for 1986 was $21,000 after allowing for depreciation of $9,000.
7. Land was purchased through the issuance of $18,000 in bonds.

Instructions

(a) Prepare a statement of changes in financial position for 1986 (cash basis as recommended in CICA Handbook, Section 1540). Assume that current liabilities remained at $15,000.
(b) Prepare the condensed balance sheet for Anchor, Inc. as it would appear at December 31, 1986. Assume that current liabilities remained at $15,000.
(c) How might the statement of changes in financial position help the user of the financial statements?

6

ACCOUNTING AND THE TIME VALUE OF MONEY

Would you like to be a millionaire? If you are 20 years old now, can save $100 every month, and can invest those savings to earn an after-tax rate of return of 1% per month (over 12% per year), you could be a millionaire before you are 59 years old. Or if you could invest just $10,000 today at that same interest rate, you would have over a million dollars by age 59. Such is the power of **interest,** especially when it is energized with a generous dosage of **time.** With interest rates in double digits, interest becomes one of the most significant factors affecting business decisions.

Business enterprises both invest and borrow large sums of money. **Investments** are made in the expectation of realizing future benefits through receiving cash returns in future periods. **Borrowing** is performed in contemplation of full repayment: that is, a sum of money is received in return for a promise to repay certain sums of money in the future. The common characteristic in these two transactions is the **time value of the money** (i.e., the **interest factor**). The timing of the returns on the investment has an important effect on the worth of the investment (asset), and the timing of debt repayments has an effect on the value of the commitment (liability). Business people have become acutely aware of this timing factor, and invest and borrow only after carefully analyzing the relative values of the cash outflows and inflows. The accountant is expected to make value measurements and to understand their implications. To do so, the accountant must understand and be able to measure the present value of future cash inflows and outflows. This measurement requires an understanding of compound interest, annuities, and present value concepts.

APPLICATIONS OF TIME VALUE CONCEPTS

Compound interest, annuities, and present value concepts are fundamental to understanding much of the information in succeeding chapters of this text. Some typical applications of these concepts in accounting are:

1. **Notes.** Valuing receivables and payables that carry no stated interest rate or a lower than market interest rate (Chapter 7).
2. **Leases.** Valuing assets to be capitalized under long-term leases and measuring the amount of the lease payments and annual leasehold amortization (Chapter 22).
3. **Amortization of premiums and discounts.** Measuring amortization of premium or discount on both investments and bonds payable (Chapter 14).
4. **Pensions.** Measuring amortization, accruals, and interest equivalents relative to unfunded past or prior service cost (Chapter 21).
5. **Capital assets.** Evaluating alternative long-term investments by discounting future cash flows (Chapter 18). Determining the value of assets acquired under deferred payment contracts (Chapter 10).
6. **Sinking funds.** Determining the contributions necessary to accumulate a fund for debt retirements (Chapter 14).
7. **Business combinations.** Determining the value of receivables, payables, liabilities, accruals, and commitments acquired or assumed in a "purchase" (Chapter 18).
8. **Depreciation.** Measuring depreciation charges under the sinking fund and the annuity methods (Chapter 11).
9. **Instalment contracts.** Measuring periodic payments on long-term purchase contracts (Chapter 14).

In addition to accounting and business applications, time value concepts are relevant to such personal finance and investment decisions as purchasing a home, planning for retirement, and evaluating alternative investments. This chapter discusses the essentials of compound interest, annuities, and present value in a variety of situations to provide you with the background for applying these techniques in later chapters.

NATURE OF INTEREST

Interest is the payment for the use of money. It is the excess cash received or repaid over and above the amount lent or borrowed (often referred to as the **principal**). For example, if the Corner Bank lends you $1,000 with the understanding that you will repay $1,150, the excess over $1,000, or $150, represents interest expense to you. Or, if you lend your roommate $100 and then collect $110 in full payment, the $10 excess represents interest revenue to you.

The amount of interest to be paid is generally stated as a rate over a specific period of time. For example, if you used the $1,000 for one year before repaying $1,150, the rate of interest is 15% per year ($150 ÷ $1,000). That is, the interest is 15% of the principal each year. The custom of expressing interest as a rate is an established business practice.[1] In fact, business managers make investing and borrowing decisions on the basis of the rate of interest involved rather than on the actual dollar amount of interest to be received or paid.

---

[1]Various federal and provincial legislation requires the disclosure of the effective interest rate on an **annual basis** in contracts. That is, instead of stating the rate as "1% per month," it must be stated as "12% per year" if it is simple interest or "12. 68% per year" if it is compounded monthly.

The rate of interest is commonly applied to the time interval of one year. Interest of 12% represents a rate of 12% per year unless stipulated otherwise. The statement that a corporation will pay bond interest of 12%, payable semiannually, means a rate of 6% every six months, not 12% every six months.

How is the interest rate determined? The interest rate is the result of several factors, but one of the most important is the level of credit risk (risk of nonpayment). Other factors being equal, the higher the credit risk, the higher the interest rate. Every borrower's risk is evaluated by the lender. A low-risk borrower like Seagram may obtain a loan at or slightly below the going market rate of interest. You or the neighbourhood delicatessen, however, may obtain a loan at several percentage points above the market rate. Another important factor is inflation (change in the general purchasing power of the dollar). Lenders desire to protect the purchasing power of the future cash flows they will receive (interest payments and return of the principal). If inflation is expected to be significant in the future, lenders will require more dollars (i.e., a higher interest rate) in order to offset the anticipated reduction of the purchasing power of these dollars. In addition to receiving compensation to offset the risk of default and inflation, lenders also desire a pure return from the service provided of letting someone else use their money. These factors and others help to determine the interest rate.

The following three variables must be known when determining the amount of interest related to any financing transaction:

1. **Principal**—the amount borrowed or invested.
2. **Interest rate**—a percentage of the outstanding principal.
3. **Time**—the number of years or fractional portion of a year that the principal is outstanding.

Simple Interest

Simple interest is the term used to describe interest that is computed on the amount of the principal only. It is the return on (or growth of) the principal for one time period or for each period in a succession of periods at a given rate per period applied to the principal at the beginning of the series.

Simple interest[2] is commonly expressed as:

$$\text{Interest} = p \times i \times n$$

where

p = principal
i = rate of interest for a single period
n = number of periods

To illustrate, if you were to borrow $1,000 for a three-year period, with a simple interest rate of 15% per year, the total interest you would pay would be $450, computed as follows:

$$\begin{aligned}\text{Interest} &= (p)\,(i)\,(n) \\ &= (\$1,000)\,(.15)\,(3) \\ &= \$450\end{aligned}$$

Compound Interest

Compound interest is the term used to describe interest that is computed on principal and on any interest earned that has not been paid. It is the return on (or growth

---

[2]Simple interest is traditionally expressed in textbooks in business mathematics or business finance as i(interest) = P(principal) × R(rate) × T(time).

of) the principal for two or more time periods, assuming that the growth (the interest) in each time period is added to the principal at the end of the period and earns a return in all subsequent periods. Compounding means that interest is computed not only on the principal but also on the interest earned to date on that principal, assuming the interest is left on deposit.[3] To illustrate the difference between simple interest and compound interest, assume that you deposit $1,000 in the Last Canadian Bank, where it will earn simple interest of 6% per year, and you deposit another $1,000 in the First Canadian Bank where it will earn compound interest of 6% per year compounded annually. Also assume that in both cases you will not withdraw any principal or interest until three years from the date of deposit. The calculation of interest to be received would be as indicated below.

		Simple Interest Last Canadian	Compound Interest First Canadian
First year	($1,000 × 6%)	$ 60.00	$ 60.00
Second year	($1,000 × 6%)	60.00	60.00
	($60 × 6%)	-0-	3.60
Third year	($1,000 × 6%)	60.00	60.00
	($123.60 × 6%)	-0-	7.42
Total interest, three year period		$180.00	$191.02

Obviously if you had a choice between investing your money at simple interest or at compound interest, you would choose compound interest, all other things —especially risk—being equal. The amounts of interest received from the two banks differ by $11.02 because of the calculation of the compound interest —effectively, interest on interest. For practical purposes in computing compound interest, it may be assumed that unpaid interest earned becomes a part of the principal and is entitled to interest. That is, with compound interest the accumulated amount at the end of each year becomes the new principal sum on which interest is earned during the next year. Applying this notion to the previous illustration, the computation of compound interest in the second year would be 6% times $1,060 ($1,000 plus $60), and in the third year would be 6% times $1,123.60 ($1,000 plus $60 plus $63.60).

Compound interest is the typical computation applied in business situations, particularly in our economy where large amounts of long-lived capital are used productively and financed over long periods of time. Financial managers view and evaluate their investment opportunities in terms of a series of periodic returns, each of which can be reinvested. Simple interest usually applies only on short-term investments and debts that involve a time span of one year or less.

---

[3]Here is an illustration of the power of time and compounding interest on money. In 1626, Peter Minuit bought Manhattan Island from the Manhattoe Indians for $24 worth of trinkets and beads. If the Indians had taken a boat to Holland, invested the $24 in Dutch securities returning just 6% per year, and kept the money and interest invested at 6%, by 1971 they would have had $13 billion, enough to buy back all the land on the island and still have a couple of billion dollars left for doodads (Forbes, Vol. 107, #11, June 1, 1971).By 1981, 355 years after the trade, the $24 would have grown to $23 billion. An annual increase in the interest rate of only 2% from 6% to 8% would have caused the $24 to have grown to over $17 trillion by 1981.

Compound Interest Tables

Five different types of compound interest tables are presented at the end of this chapter for use in solving problems involving interest throughout this book. The titles of these five tables and their contents are:

1. **Future Amount of 1.** Contains the amounts to which $1.00 will accumulate if deposited now at a specified rate and left for a specified number of periods. (Table 6-1)
2. **Present Value of 1.** Contains the amounts that must be deposited now at a specified rate of interest to amount to $1.00 at the end of a specified number of periods. (Table 6-2)
3. **Future Amount of an Ordinary Annuity of 1.** Contains the amounts to which periodic rents of $1.00 will accumulate if the rents are invested at the **end** of each period at a specified rate of interest and are continued for a specified number of periods. This table may also be used as a basis for converting to the amount of an annuity due of 1. (Table 6-3)
4. **Present Value of an Ordinary Annuity of 1.** Contains the amounts that must be deposited now at a specified rate of interest to permit withdrawals of $1.00 at the **end** of regular periodic intervals for the specified number of periods. This table may also be used as a basis for converting to the present value of an annuity due of 1. (Table 6-4)
5. **Present Value of an Annuity Due of 1.** Contains the amounts that must be deposited now at a specified rate of interest to permit withdrawals of $1.00 at the **beginning** of regular periodic intervals for the specified number of periods. (Table 6-5)

The excerpt below from Table 6-1, "Future Amount of 1," illustrates the general format and content of these tables. In this case, the figures indicate the amount of principal plus interest to which a dollar accumulates at the end of each of five periods at three different rates of compound interest.

FUTURE AMOUNT OF 1 AT COMPOUND INTEREST
(Excerpt from Table 6-1)

Period	9%	10%	11%
1	1.09000	1.10000	1.11000
2	1.18810	1.21000	1.23210
3	1.29503	1.33100	1.36763
4	1.41158	1.46410	1.51807
5	1.53862	1.61051	1.68506

As the table shows, if $1.00 is invested for three periods at a compound interest rate of 9% per period, the $1.00 will amount to $1.30 (1.29503 × $1.00), the **compound amount**; if the investment were for five periods, it would amount to $1.54. If $1.00 were invested at 11%, at the end of four periods it would amount to $1.52. If the investment were $1,000 instead of $1.00, the respective amounts would be as shown below:

> If invested for 3 periods at 9% ($1,000 × 1.29503) = $1,295.03
> If invested for 5 periods at 9% ($1,000 × 1.53862) = $1,538.62
> If invested for 4 periods at 11% ($1,000 × 1.51807) = $1,518.07

Throughout the foregoing discussion of compound interest tables (and most of the discussion that follows), the use of the term **periods** instead of **years** is intentional. Interest is generally expressed in terms of an annual rate, but in many business circumstances the compounding period is less than one year. In such circumstances the annual interest rate must be converted to correspond to the length of the period. The process is to convert the "annual interest rate" into the "compounding period interest rate" by **dividing the annual rate by the number of**

compounding periods per year. In addition, the number of periods is determined by **multiplying the number of years involved by the number of compounding periods per year.** To illustrate, assume that $1.00 is invested for six years at 8% annual interest compounded quarterly. Using Table 6-1, we can determine the amount to which this $1.00 will accumulate by reading the factor that appears in the 2% column on the 24th row, namely $1.60844, or approximately $1.61. Thus, the term periods, not years, is used in all compound interest tables to express the quantity of n. The following schedule shows how to determine (1) the interest rate per period and (2) the number of compounding periods in four situations of differing compounding frequency.

12% Annual Interest Rate Compounded	Interest Rate per Compounding Period	Number of Compounding Periods
Annually for 5 years	.12 ÷ 1 = .12	5 years × 1 compounding per year = 5 periods
Semiannually for 5 years	.12 ÷ 2 = .06	5 years × 2 compoundings per year = 10 periods
Quarterly for 5 years	.12 ÷ 4 = .03	5 years × 4 compoundings per year = 20 periods
Monthly for 5 years	.12 ÷ 12 = .01	5 years × 12 compoundings per year = 60 periods

As another point on the frequency of compounding, because interest is theoretically earned (accruing) every second of every day, it is possible to calculate interest that is **compounded continuously**. Computations involving continuous compounding are facilitated through the use of the natural, or Napierian, system of logarithms. In spite of the soundness of continuous compounding, most business situations involving interest are resolved through the discrete compounding techniques illustrated in this chapter.

How interest is compounded can make a substantial difference in the level of return achieved. For example, 9% interest compounded daily provides a 9.42% annual yield, or a difference of .42% compared to annual compounding. The 9.42% is referred to as the **effective yield** or **rate**[4] whereas the annual interest rate is called the **stated, nominal,** or **face rate**. When the compounding frequency is greater than once a year, the effective interest rate is greater than the stated rate. Shown below are some effective interest rates at four different periods of compounding:

Annually	Quarterly	Monthly	Daily
8%	8.24%	8.30%	8.33%
9%	9.31%	9.38%	9.42%
10%	10.38%	10.47%	10.52%
11%	11.46%	11.57%	11.63%

[4]The formula for calculating the effective rate in situations where the compounding frequency (f) is greater than once a year is as follows:

$$\text{Effective rate} = (1 + i)^f - 1$$

where

i = the interest rate per compounding period

Fundamental Variables

The following four variables are fundamental to all compound interest problems:

1. **Rate of interest.** This rate, unless otherwise stated, is an annual rate. It must be converted to the interest rate per compounding period if the compounding period is less than a year.
2. **Number of time periods.** This is the number of compounding periods for which interest is to be computed.
3. **Future amount.** The value at a future date of a given sum or sums invested at compound interest.
4. **Present value.** The value now (present time) of a future sum or sums discounted at compound interest.

The relationship of these four variables is depicted in the following **time-diagram**:

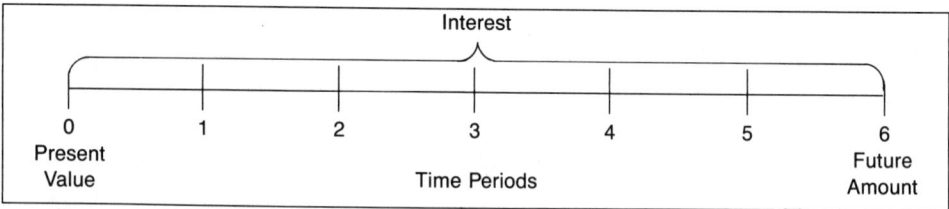

In some cases all four of these variables are known, but in many business situations at least one variable is unknown. Frequently, it is the accountant who is expected to solve the problem of the unknown. As an aid to understanding the problems and finding solutions, we encourage you to sketch compound interest problems in the form of a time-diagram.

The remainder of this chapter covers the following six major concepts of the time value of money, using both formula and interest table approaches to solve problems:

1. Future amount of a single sum.
2. Present value of a single sum.
3. Future amount of an ordinary annuity.
4. Future amount of an annuity due.
5. Present value of an ordinary annuity.
6. Present value of an annuity due.

SINGLE SUM PROBLEMS

Many business and investment decisions involve a single amount of money that either exists now or will exist in the future. Single sum problems can generally be classified into one of the following two categories:

1. Problems that require the computation of the unknown **future amount** of a known single sum of money that is invested for a certain number of periods at a certain interest rate.
2. Problems that require the computation of the unknown **present value** of a known single sum of money that is discounted for a certain number of periods at a certain interest rate.

Future Amount of a Single Sum

In the context of compound interest, the term "amount" refers only to a future value. The amount of a sum of money is therefore the future value of that sum when left to accumulate for a certain number of periods at a specified rate of interest per period.

The amount to which 1 (one) will accumulate may be expressed as a formula:

$$a_{\overline{n}|i} = (1 + i)^n$$

where

$a_{\overline{n}|i}$ = compound amount of 1
i = rate of interest for a single period
n = number of periods

The symbol $a_{\overline{n}|i}$ is expressed as "lower case a angle n at i." It is the amount to which $1.00 will accumulate at i rate of interest per period for n periods.

To illustrate, assume that $1.00 is invested at 9% interest for three periods. The amounts to which the $1.00 will accumulate at the end of each period are:

$a_{\overline{n}|i} = (1 + .09)^1$ for the end of the first period
$a_{\overline{n}|i} = (1 + .09)^2$ for the end of the second period
$a_{\overline{n}|i} = (1 + .09)^3$ for the end of the third period

These compound amounts accumulate as follows:

Period	Beginning-of-Period Amount	×	Multiplier (1 + i)	=	End-of-Period Amount*
1	1.00000		1.09		1.09000
2	1.09000		1.09		1.18810
3	1.18810		1.09		1.29503

* The amounts appear in Table 6-1 in the 9% column.

The formula $a_{\overline{n}|i}$ can be expanded to compute the future amount of **any single sum** as follows:

$$a = p(a_{\overline{n}|i})$$

where

a = future amount
p = beginning principal or sum (present value)
$a_{\overline{n}|i} = (1 + i)^n$ = future amount of 1

To illustrate, what is the future amount of $50,000 invested for five years at a compound interest rate of 11%? In time-diagram form, this investment situation would appear as follows:

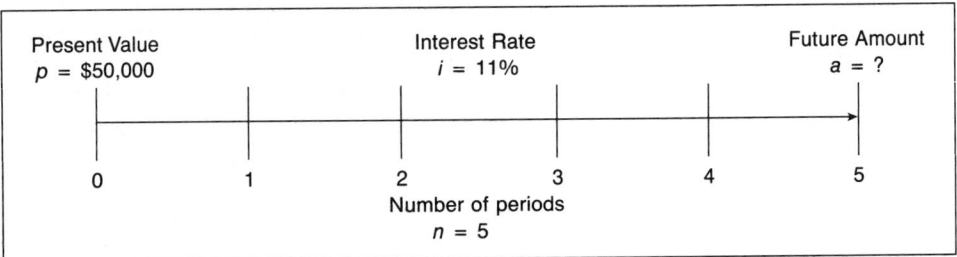

Using the formula, this investment problem is solved as follows:

$a = p(a_{\overline{n}|i})$
  $= $50,000 \, (a_{\overline{5}|11\%})$
  $= $50,000 \, (1 + .11)^5$
  $= $50,000 \, (1.68506)$
  $= $84,253$

Determination of the future amount factor of 1.68506 in the above formula is facilitated by the use of a calculator or by reading the appropriate table, in this case Table 6-1 in the 11% column and the 5-period row.

This time-diagram and formula approach can be applied in a more complex business situation. To illustrate, assume that at the beginning of 1986 Ontario Hydro Corp. deposited $250 million in an escrow account with Canada Trust Company as a commitment toward a small nuclear power plant to be completed December 31, 1989. How much will be on deposit at the end of four years if interest is compounded semiannually at 10%?

With a known present value of $250 million, a total of 8 compounding periods (4 × 2), and an interest rate of 5% (.10 ÷ 2), this problem can be time-diagramed and the future amount determined as follows:

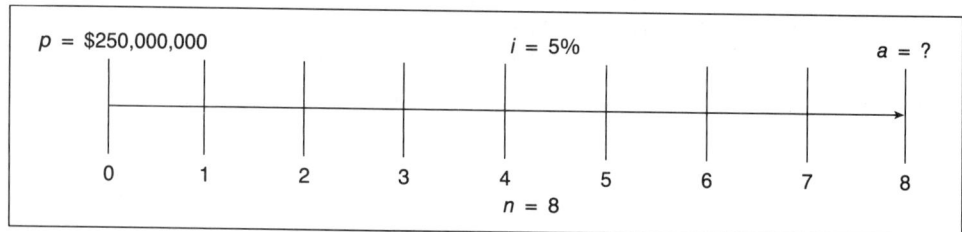

$$a = \$250,000,000\ (a_{\overline{8}|5\%})$$
$$= \$250,000,000\ (1.47746)$$
$$= \$369,365,000$$

The deposit of $250 million will accumulate to $369,365,000 by December 31, 1989.

Present Value of a Single Sum

A preceding example showed that $50,000 invested at a compound interest rate of 11% will be worth $84,253 at the end of five years. It follows then that $84,253 to be received five years from now is presently worth $50,000 given the 11% interest rate; that is, $50,000 is the present value of this $84,253. The **present value** is the amount that must be invested now to produce the known future value. In the compound amount illustrations, it was the future value of a known present value that was determined; in present-value problems, it is the present value of a known future amount that must be determined. **The present value is always a smaller amount than the known future amount because interest will be earned and accumulated on the present value to the future date.** In determining the future amount we move forward in time using a process of **accumulation**, while in determining present value we move backward in time using the process of **discounting**.

The present value of 1 (one) may be expressed as a formula:

$$p_{\overline{n}|i} = 1/a_{\overline{n}|i} = \frac{1}{(1+i)^n}$$

where

$p_{\overline{n}|i}$ = present value of 1
$a_{\overline{n}|i} = (1+i)^n$ = compound amount of 1

The symbol $p_{\overline{n}|i}$ is expressed as "lower case p angle n at i." It is the present value of $1.00 discounted at i rate of interest per period for n periods. To illustrate, assume that $1.00 is discounted for three periods at 9%. The present value of the $1.00 is discounted each period as follows:

$p_{\overline{1}|9\%} = 1/(1\ +\ .09)^1$ for the first period
$p_{\overline{2}|9\%} = 1/(1\ +\ .09)^2$ for the second period
$p_{\overline{3}|9\%} = 1/(1\ +\ .09)^3$ for the third period

Therefore, the $1.00 is discounted as follows:

Discount Periods	Future Amount	÷	Divisor $(1 + i)$	=	Beginning-of-Period Present Value*
1	1.00000		1.09		.91743
2	.91743		1.09		.84168
3	.84168		1.09		.77218

*These amounts appear in Table 6-2 in the 9% column.

Quick computation of present values is frequently needed. As a result, from the formula, tables have been developed showing how much must be invested at various compound interest rates for various periods of time to equal 1 at a future date. A "Present Value of 1" table appears at the end of this chapter. The excerpt below illustrates the nature of such a table by indicating the present value of 1 for five different periods at three different rates of interest.

PRESENT VALUE OF 1 AT COMPOUND INTEREST (Excerpt from Table 6-2)			
Period	9%	10%	11%
1	0.91743	0.90909	0.90090
2	0.84168	0.82645	0.81162
3	0.77218	0.75132	0.73119
4	0.70843	0.68301	0.65873
5	0.64993	0.62092	0.59345

The present value of 1 formula $p_{\overline{n}|i}$ can be expanded for use in computing the present value of **any single sum** as follows:

$$p = a(p_{\overline{n}|i})$$

where

p = present value of a single sum
a = future amount
$p_{\overline{n}|i} = \dfrac{1}{(1\ +\ i)^n}$ = present value of 1

To illustrate, what is the present value of $84,253 to be received or paid in five years discounted at 11% compounded annually? In time-diagram form, this problem is drawn as follows:

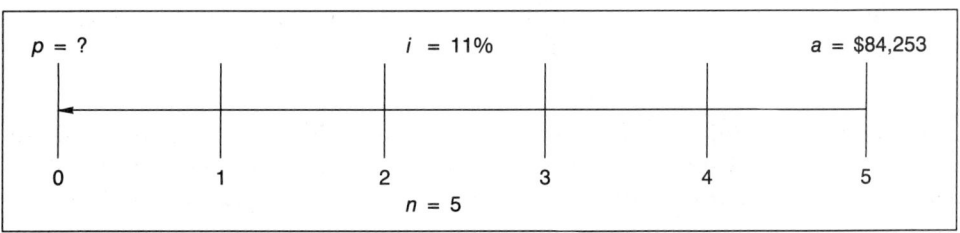

Using the formula, this problem is solved as follows:

$$p = a(p_{\overline{n}|i})$$
$$= \$84{,}253\ (p_{\overline{5}|\ 11\%})$$
$$= \$84{,}253\ (1/(1 + .11)^5)$$
$$= \$84{,}253\ (.59345)$$
$$= \$50{,}000$$

Determination of the present value factor of .59345 is facilitated by the use of a calculator or by reading Table 6-2 (11% column, 5-period row).

The time-diagram and formula approach can be applied in more complex situations. For example, assume that your rich uncle proposes to give you $2,000 for a trip to Europe when you graduate three years from now. He proposes to finance the trip by investing a sum of money now at 12% compound interest that will provide you with $2,000 upon your graduation. The only conditions are that you graduate and that you tell him how much to invest now.

To impress your uncle you might set up the following time-diagram and solve this problem as follows:

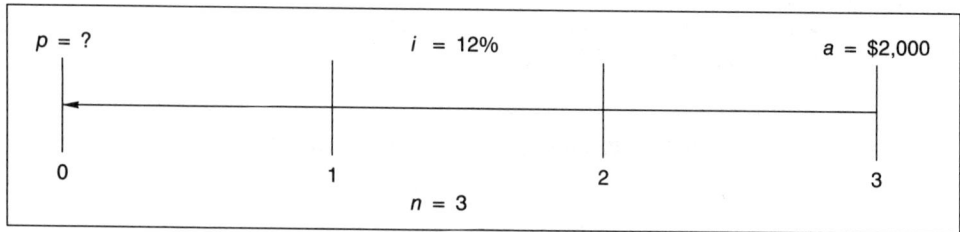

$$p = \$2{,}000\ (p_{\overline{3}|\ 12\%})$$
$$= \$2{,}000\ (.71178)$$
$$= \$1{,}423.56$$

Advise your uncle to invest $1,423.56 now to provide you with $2,000 upon graduation. (To satisfy your uncle's other condition, you must simply pass this course—and many more.)

Solving for Other Unknowns—Single Sum Problems

In computing either the future amount or the present value in the previous single sum illustrations, both the number of periods and the interest rate were known. In many business situations, both the future amount and the present value are known and either the number of periods or the interest rate is unknown. The following two illustrations are single sum problems (future amount and present value) with either an unknown number of periods (n) or an unknown interest rate (i). These illustrations and the accompanying solutions demonstrate that if any three of the four values (future amount, a; present value, p; number of periods, n; interest rate, i) are known, the one unknown can be derived.

Illustration—Computation of the Number of Periods   The city of Regina wants to accumulate $70,000 for the construction of a veterans' monument in one of its parks. If, at the beginning of the current year, the city deposited $47,811 in a memorial fund that earns 10% interest compounded annually, how many years will it take to accumulate $70,000 in the memorial fund?

In this illustration, both the present value ($47,811) and the future amount ($70,000) are known, along with the interest rate of 10%. A time-diagram of this investment is as follows:

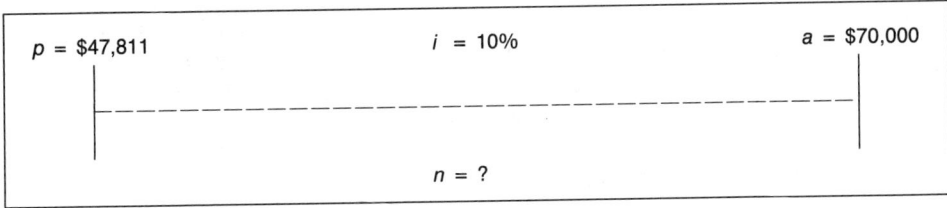

Because both the present value and the future amount are known, we can solve for the unknown number of periods by using either the future amount or the present value formula as shown below:

Future Amount
Approach

$$a = p(a_{\overline{n}|\,10\%})$$
$$\$70{,}000 = \$47{,}811\,(a_{\overline{n}|\,10\%})$$
$$a_{\overline{n}|\,10\%} = \frac{\$70{,}000}{\$47{,}811} = 1.46410$$

Present Value
Approach

$$p = a(p_{\overline{n}|\,10\%})$$
$$\$47{,}811 = \$70{,}000\,(p_{\overline{n}|\,10\%})$$
$$p_{\overline{n}|\,10\%} = \frac{\$47{,}811}{\$70{,}000} = .68301$$

Using the future amount factor of 1.46410 we refer to Table 6-1, and reading down the 10% column we find that factor in the 4-period row. Thus, it will take 4 years for the $47,811 to accumulate to $70,000 invested at 10% compound interest.

Using the present value factor of .68301 we refer to Table 6-2, and reading down the 10% column we again find that factor in the 4-period row.

Illustration—Computation of the Interest Rate   The Canadian Academic Accounting Association wants to have $141,000 available 5 years from now in order to provide scholarships to individuals who undertake a Ph.D. program of studies. At present, the CAAA membership, through its executive, has determined that $80,000 may be invested for this purpose. What rate of interest must be earned on the investments in order to accumulate the $141,000?

A time-diagram of this investment problem is as follows:

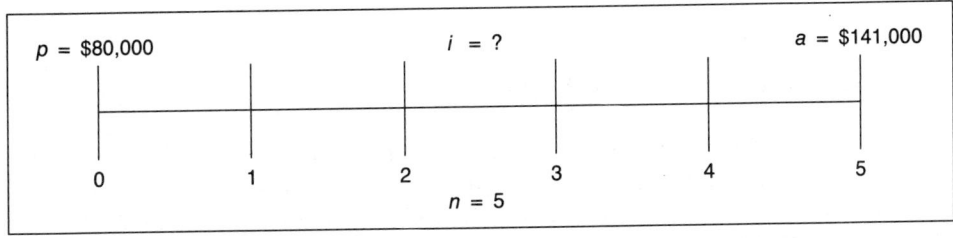

Given that the present value, future amount, and number of periods are known, the unknown interest rate can be determined by using either the future amount or present value formula as shown on the next page:

Future Amount Approach	Present Value Approach
$a = p(a_{\overline{5}|i})$	$p = a(p_{\overline{5}|i})$
$\$141{,}000 = \$80{,}000\,(a_{\overline{5}|i})$	$\$80{,}000 = \$141{,}000\,(p_{\overline{5}|i})$
$a_{\overline{5}|i} = \$141{,}000 \div \$80{,}000$	$p_{\overline{5}|i} = \$80{,}000 \div \$141{,}000$
$= 1.7625$	$= 0.5674$

Using the future amount factor of 1.7625 and referring to Table 6-1, we can read across the 5-period row to find a close match of this future amount factor in the 12% column. Therefore, the $80,000 would have to be invested at 12% interest rate in order to have $141,000 at the end of 5 years.

Similarly, using the present value factor of 0.5674, and Table 6-2, reading across the 5-period row shows this factor in the 12% column.

ANNUITIES

The preceding discussion has involved only the accumulation or discounting of a single principal sum. Individuals frequently encounter situations in which a series of dollar amounts are to be paid or received periodically (e.g., loans or sales to be repaid in instalments, invested funds that will be recovered partially at regular intervals, and cost savings that are realized repeatedly). A life insurance contract is probably the most common and most familiar type of transaction involving a series of equal payments made at equal intervals. Such a process of periodic saving represents the accumulation of a sum of money through an annuity. An **annuity** by definition requires that (1) the periodic payments or receipts (called **rents**) always be the **same amount**, (2) the **interval** between such rents always be the same, and (3) the **interest be compounded** once each interval. In other words, the interval of time between each rent and the interval of time between each compounding of interest must be identical.

The **future amount of an annuity** is the sum (future value) of all the rents (payments or receipts) plus the accumulated compound interest on them. It should be noted that the rents may occur at either the beginning or the end of the periods (not necessarily January 1 or December 31). To distinguish annuities under these two alternatives, an annuity is classified as an **ordinary annuity** if the rents occur at the end of the period, and as an **annuity due** if the rents occur at the beginning of the period.

Future Amount of an Ordinary Annuity

One approach to the problem of determining the future amount to which an annuity will accumulate is to compute the amount to which each of the rents in the series will accumulate and then aggregate their individual future amounts. For example, assume that $1 is deposited at the end of each of five years (an ordinary annuity) and earns 12% interest compounded annually. The future amount can be computed as follows, using the "Future Amount of 1" table (Table 6-1) for each of the five $1 rents:

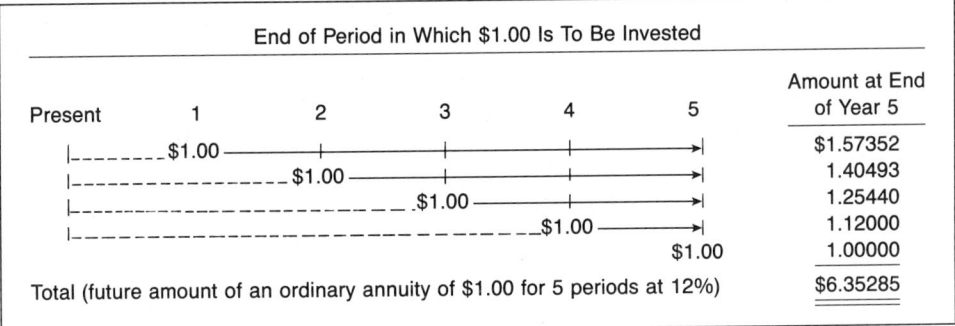

End of Period in Which $1.00 Is To Be Invested						Amount at End of Year 5
Present	1	2	3	4	5	
$1.00 ────────────────────────────────→						$1.57352
$1.00 ─────────────────────────→						1.40493
$1.00 ──────────────→						1.25440
$1.00 ──────→						1.12000
					$1.00	1.00000
Total (future amount of an ordinary annuity of $1.00 for 5 periods at 12%)						$6.35285

Rents that compose an ordinary annuity can earn no interest during the period in which they are originally deposited because they are deposited at the end of the period. For example, the third rent earns interest for only two periods. Obviously, the third rent can earn no interest for the first two periods since it is not deposited until the third period; but, additionally, it can earn no interest for the third period since it is deposited at the end of the third period. Any time the future amount of an ordinary annuity is computed, the number of compounding periods will always be one less than the number of investment periods.

Although the above procedure for computing the future amount of an ordinary annuity will always produce the correct answer, it can become cumbersome if the number of investment periods is large. A more efficient way of expressing the future amount of an ordinary annuity of 1 is in a formula that is a summation of the individual rents plus the compound interest:

$$A_{\overline{n}|i} = \frac{(1 + i)^n - 1}{i}$$

where

$A_{\overline{n}|i}$ = future amount of an ordinary annuity
of 1 for n periods at i rate of interest

i = rate of interest

n = number of periods

The symbol $A_{\overline{n}|i}$ is expressed "capital A angle n at i;" for example, $A_{\overline{5}|12\%}$ is expressed "capital A angle 5 at 12%" and refers to the amount to which an ordinary annuity of 1 will accumulate in five periods at 12% interest.

Using this formula, Table 6-3 has been developed to show the "Future Amount of an Ordinary Annuity of 1" for various interest rates and investment periods. The following is an excerpt from this table:

FUTURE AMOUNT OF AN ORDINARY ANNUITY OF 1 (Excerpt from Table 6-3)			
Period	10%	11%	12%
1	1.00000	1.00000	1.00000
2	2.10000	2.11000	2.12000
3	3.31000	3.34210	3.37440
4	4.64100	4.70973	4.77933
5	6.10510	6.22780	6.35285*

*Note that this annuity table factor is the same as the sum of the future amounts of 1 factors shown in the previous schedule.

As the table shows, if $1.00 is invested at the end of each year for four years at 11% interest compounded annually, the amount of the annuity at the end of the fourth year will be $4.71 (4.70973 × $1.00). The amount of an ordinary annuity of 1 is the accumulated sum of the rents plus the compound interest to the date of the last rent payment. In this example, the $4.71 is made up of $4 of rent payments ($1 at the end of each of the 4 years) and compound interest of $0.71.

The $A_{\overline{n}|i}$ formula can be expanded for use in computing the future amount of an ordinary annuity of any constant rent as follows:

$$A = R(A_{\overline{n}|i})$$

where

A = future amount of an ordinary annuity
R = periodic rents
$$A_{\overline{n}|i} = \frac{(1 + i)^n - 1}{i}$$

To illustrate, what is the future amount of five $5,000 deposits made at the end of each of the next five years, earning interest at 12%?

In time-diagram form, this problem is drawn as follows:

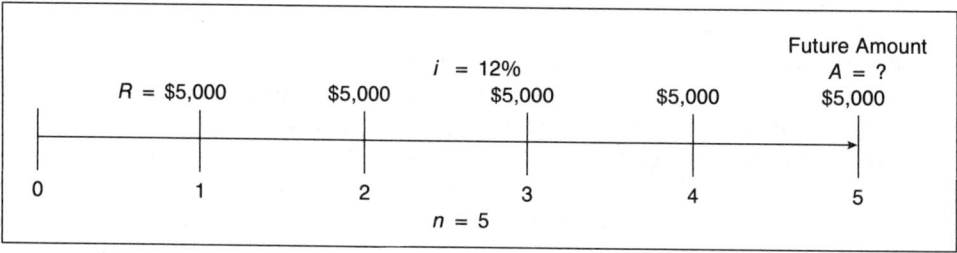

Using the formula, this investment problem is solved as follows:

$$
\begin{aligned}
A &= R(A_{\overline{n}|i}) \\
&= \$5,000\ (A_{\overline{5}|\,12\%}) \\
&= \$5,000 \times \frac{(1 + .12)^5 - 1}{.12} \\
&= \$5,000\ (6.35285) \\
&= \$31,764.25
\end{aligned}
$$

The future amount of an ordinary annuity factor of 6.35285 in the above formula is facilitated by the use of a calculator or by reading the appropriate table, Table 6-3, in the 12% column and the 5-period row.

To illustrate these computations in a business situation, assume that Lightning Electronics Limited's management decides to deposit $75,000 at the end of each six-month period for the next three years for the purpose of accumulating enough money to meet debts that mature in three years. What is the future amount that will be on deposit at the end of three years if the annual interest rate is 10%?

The time-diagram and formula solution are as follows:

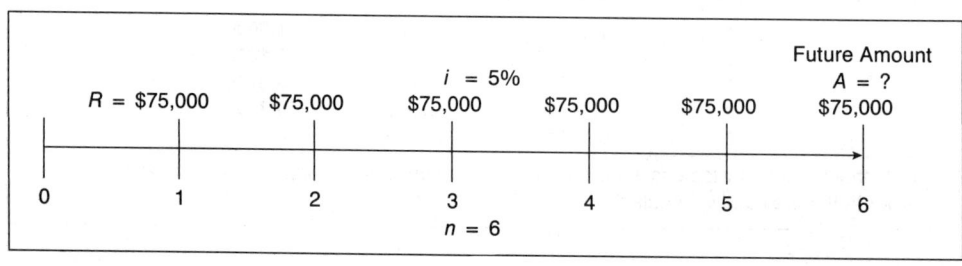

$$A = R(A_{\overline{n}|i})$$
$$= \$75,000\ (A_{\overline{6}|5\%})$$
$$= \$75,000\ (6.80191)$$
$$= \$510,143.25$$

Thus, six deposits of $75,000 made at the end of every six months and earning 5% per period will grow to $510,143.25 at the end of the last deposit.

Future Amount of an Annuity Due

The preceding analysis of an **ordinary annuity** was based on the fact that the **periodic rents** occur at the **end** of each period. An **annuity due** is based on the fact that the **periodic rents** occur at the **beginning** of each period. This means that each rent will accumulate interest during the period in which it is paid or received, whereas for an ordinary annuity each rent will not accumulate interest during the period in which it is paid because the payment is not made until the end of the period. Consequently, assuming all other things to be equal, the future amount of an annuity due will always be greater than the future amount of an ordinary annuity. The following illustration shows the distinctions between the two types of annuities. Both annuities consist of five rents of $1 each year and earn interest of 12% (accumulated amounts are rounded to the nearest cent).

Future Amount of an Ordinary Annuity of $1.00 at 12%					
	Present				Future
	1/1/86 1/1/87	1/1/88	1/1/89	1/1/90	1/1/91
5 Rents (occur at 12/31)	$1	$1	$1	$1	$1
	Period 1 Period 2	Period 3	Period 4	Period 5	
4 Interest periods	(No interest) (Interest)	(Interest)	(Interest	(Interest)	
Accumulated Amount (per Table 6-3)	0 $1.00	$2.12	$3.37	$4.78	$6.35

Future Amount of an Annuity Due of $1.00 at 12%					
	1/1/86 1/1/87	1/1/88	1/1/89	1/1/90	1/1/91
5 Rents (occur at 1/1)	$1 $1	$1	$1	$1	
	Period 1 Period 2	Period 3	Period 4	Period 5	
5 Interest periods	(Interest) (Interest)	(Interest)	(Interest)	(Interest)	
Accumulated Amount	$1.00 $1.12	$2.37	$3.78	$5.35	$7.11

The generalization that "the periodic interest earnings under an ordinary annuity will always be lower by one period's interest than the interest earned by an annuity due" suggests the basis for converting an ordinary annuity table to an annuity due table. **If the last rent in an ordinary annuity is deducted from the end-of-period accumulation, the remainder will represent the amount of an annuity due for one less period.** For example, if one rent is deducted from the ordinary annuity of five periods at 12%, in the illustration above, the result will be the amount of an annuity due for four periods at 12%.

1. Future amount of ordinary annuity of $1 a period for five periods at 12%	$ 6.35
2. Deduct last payment	− 1.00
3. Future amount of annuity due of $1 per period for four periods at 12%	$ 5.35

In the case of an ordinary annuity, there is one rent (the last) on which no interest is involved. That is the reason for subtracting the last payment as shown on page 273. The annuity due has one more interest period than the ordinary annuity.

To illustrate the use of the ordinary annuity tables in converting to an annuity due, assume that Hank Lotadough plans to deposit $800 a year on each birthday of his son Howard, starting today, his tenth birthday, at 12% interest compounded annually. Hank wants to know the amount he will have accumulated for college expenses by his son's eighteenth birthday.

If the first deposit is made on his son's tenth birthday, Hank will make a total of 8 deposits over the life of the annuity (assume no deposit on the eighteenth birthday). All the deposits will be made at the beginning of the periods, therefore representing an annuity due. This annuity due problem is time-diagrammed as follows:

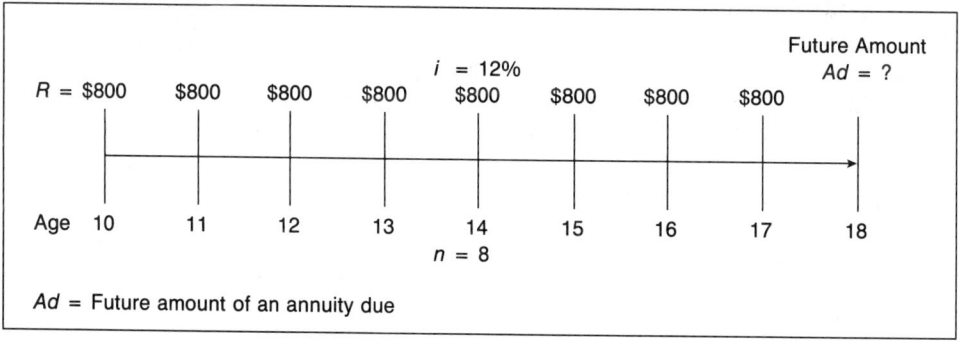

Refer to the "Future Amount of an Ordinary Annuity of 1" table for 9 periods at 12% and deduct 1 [(factor for $n + 1$ rents) $- 1$] to arrive at the annuity due for 8 periods.

1. Future amount of an ordinary annuity of 1 for 9 periods at 12% (Table 6-3)	$ 14.77566
2. Deduct one	$-$ 1.00000
3. Future amount of an annuity due of 1 for 8 periods at 12%	$ 13.77566
4. Periodic deposit (rent)	$\times$ $800
5. Accumulated amount on son's eighteenth birthday	$11,020.53

The same solution can be arrived at in the following manner.

1. Future amount of an ordinary annuity of $800 per period at 12% for 9 periods (14.77566 × $800)	$11,820.53
2. Deduct last payment (rent)	$-$ 800.00
3. Future amount of an annuity due of $800 a period at 12% for 8 periods	$11,020.53

Illustrations of Future Amount of Annuity Problems

In the previous annuity example three values were known (amount of each rent, interest rate, and number of periods) and were used to determine the unknown fourth value (future amount). Indeed, if any three of the four values are known, the fourth can be derived as illustrated in the following examples. The first two future amount problems illustrate the computations of (1) the amount of the rents and (2) the number of rents in ordinary annuity situations. The third problem illustrates the computation of the future amount of an annuity due.

Illustration—Computation of the Amount of Each Rent   Assume that you wish to accumulate $14,000 for a down payment on a condominium apartment five years from now; for the next five years you can earn an annual return of 8% compounded semiannually. How much should you deposit at the end of each six-month period?

The $14,000 is the future amount of 10 (5 × 2) payments of an unknown amount, at an interest rate of 4% (8% ÷ 2). This problem appears in the form of a time-diagram as follows:

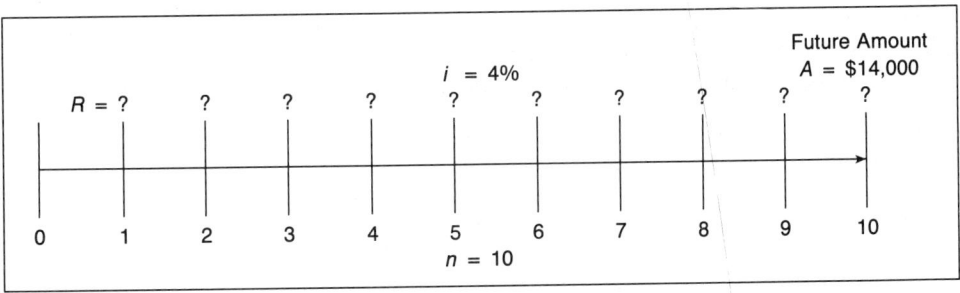

Using the formula for the future amount of an ordinary annuity, the amount of each rent is determined as follows:

$$A = R(A_{\overline{n}|i})$$
$$\$14,000 = R(A_{\overline{10}|4\%})$$
$$\$14,000 = R(12.00611)$$
$$R = \$1,166.07$$

Thus, you must make 10 semiannual deposits of $1,166.07 each in order to accumulate $14,000 for your down payment.

Illustration—Computation of the Number of Periodic Rents   As an accountant you may be called upon to determine the number of payments necessary to accumulate a certain sum of money. For example, your company wishes to accumulate $117,332 by making periodic deposits of $20,000 at the end of each year that will earn 8%. How many deposits must be made?

The $117,332 represents the future amount of n(?) $20,000 deposits, at an 8% rate of interest. This problem appears in the form of a time-diagram as follows:

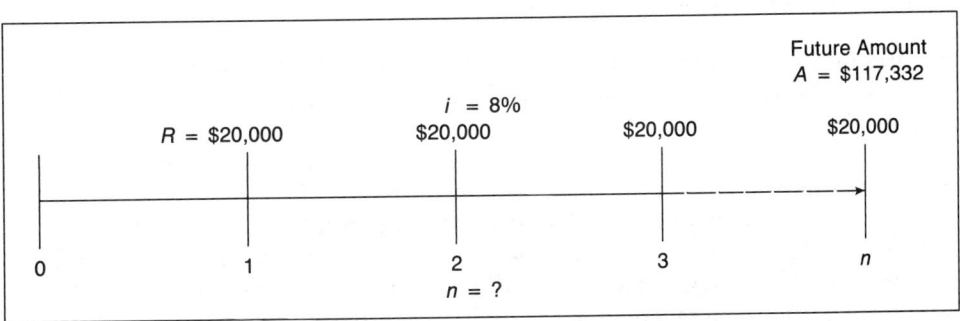

Using the future amount of an ordinary annuity formula, we obtain the following factor:

$$A = R(A_{\overline{n}|i})$$
$$\$117,332 = \$20,000\ (A_{\overline{n}|8\%})$$
$$A_{\overline{n}|8\%} = \frac{\$117,332}{\$20,000} = 5.86660$$

Using Table 6-3 and reading down the 8% column, we find 5.86660 in the 5-period row. Thus, five deposits of $20,000 each must be made at the end of each year.

Illustration—Computation of the Future Amount of an Annuity Due   Walter Goodwrench, a mechanic, has taken on weekend work in the hope of creating his own retirement fund. Mr. Goodwrench deposits $2,500 today in a savings account that earns 9% interest. He plans to deposit $2,500 at the beginning of every year for 30 years, including the present payment. How much cash will have accumulated in Mr. Goodwrench's retirement savings account when he retires at the end of the 30 years? This future amount of an annuity due problem is time-diagramed as follows:

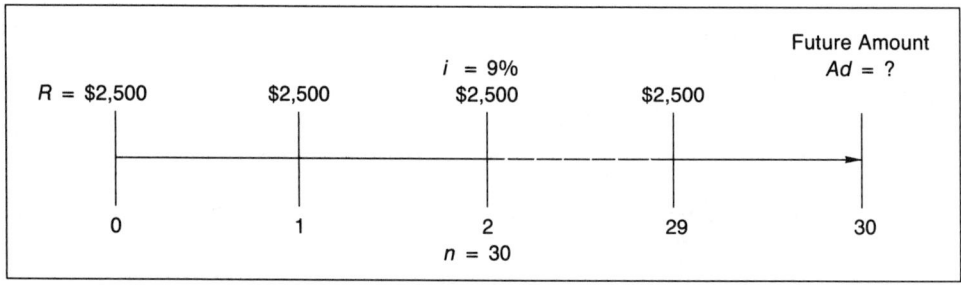

Using the "Future Amount of an Ordinary Annuity of 1" table, the solution is computed as follows:

1. Future amount of an ordinary annuity of 1 for 31 periods at 9%		$149.57522
2. Deduct one	−	1.00000
3. Future amount of an annuity due of 1 for 30 periods at 9%		$148.57522
4. Periodic deposit	×	$2,500
5. Accumulated amount at end of 30 years		$371,438

Present Value of an Ordinary Annuity

The present value of an annuity may be viewed as **the single sum** that, if invested at compound interest now, would provide for an annuity (a series of withdrawals) of a certain amount per period for a certain number of future periods. In other words, the present value of an ordinary annuity is the present value of a series of rents to be made at equal intervals in the future.

One approach to the problem of valuing at the present an annuity consisting of a series of future rents is to determine the present value of each of the rents in the series and then aggregate their individual present values. For example, an annuity of $1.00 to be received at the end of each period for five periods may be viewed as separate amounts, and the present value of each computed from the table of present values (Table 6-2). Assuming an interest rate of 12%, the present value can be computed:

End of Period in Which $1.00 Is To Be Received

Present Value at Beginning of Year 1	1	2	3	4	5
$0.89286 ◄———————	$1.00				
0.79719 ◄———————————————		$1.00			
0.71178 ◄——————————————————————————			$1.00		
0.63552 ◄—————————————————————————————————————				$1.00	
0.56743 ◄———					$1.00
$3.60478 Total (present value of an ordinary annuity of $1.00 for five periods at 12%)					

This computation tells us that if we invest the single sum of $3.60 today at 12% interest for five periods, we will be able to withdraw $1.00 at the end of each period for five periods.

This cumbersome procedure can be made more efficient through the following formula:

$$P_{\overline{n}|i} = \frac{1 - \dfrac{1}{(1 + i)^n}}{i}$$

The symbol $P_{\overline{n}|i}$ is expressed "capital P angle n at i;" for example, $P_{\overline{5}|12\%}$ is expressed "capital P angle 5 at 12%" and refers to the present value of an ordinary annuity of 1 for five periods at 12% interest. From this formula, "present value of an ordinary annuity" tables are prepared; an excerpt from such a table (Table 6-4) is shown below:

PRESENT VALUE OF AN ORDINARY ANNUITY OF 1
(Excerpt from Table 6–4)

Period	10%	11%	12%
1	0.90909	0.90090	0.89286
2	1.73554	1.71252	1.69005
3	2.48685	2.44371	2.40183
4	3.16988	3.10245	3.03735
5	3.79079	3.69590	3.60478*

*Note that this annuity table factor is equal to the sum of the present value of 1 factors shown in the previous schedule.

The formula for the present value of any ordinary annuity of any rent value is as follows:

$$P = R(P_{\overline{n}|i})$$

where

P = present value of an ordinary annuity
R = periodic rent (ordinary annuity)

$$P_{\overline{n}|i} = \frac{1 - \dfrac{1}{(1 + i)^n}}{i}$$

To illustrate, what is the present value of rental receipts of $6,000 each to be received at the end of each of the next five years when discounted at 12%? This problem may be time-diagrammed and solved as follows:

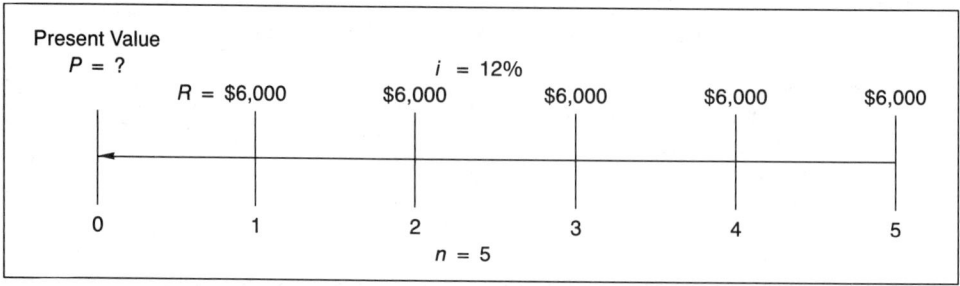

$$P = R(P_{\overline{n}|i})$$
$$= \$6,000 \ (P_{\overline{5}|\,12\%})$$
$$= \$6,000 \ (3.60478)$$
$$= \$21,628.68$$

The present value of the five ordinary annuity rental receipts of $6,000 each is thus $21,628.68.

Present Value of an Annuity Due

As stated previously, the rents of an ordinary annuity occur at the end of each period, whereas the rents for an annuity due occur at the beginning of each period. Consequently, when computing the present value of an ordinary annuity, the first rent can be discounted for one period, the second rent for two periods, and so on. For an annuity due, however, there is no discounting of the first rent because it occurs at the present date (on the first day the annuity is begun). That is, the present value of the first rent is equal to the amount of the rent. Therefore, in determining the present value of an annuity due, there is one less discount period than in determining the present value of an ordinary annuity. Assuming all other things equal, the present value of an annuity due will always be greater than that of an ordinary annuity because of the timing difference of the rents. The distinction between the two is shown in the following illustration. Both annuities consist of five rents of $1 each being discounted at a rate of 12% per period (present values are rounded to the nearest cent).

Present Value of an Ordinary Annuity of $1.00 at 12%					
Present 1/1/86	1/1/87	1/1/88	1/1/89	1/1/90	Future 1/1/91
5 Rents (occur at 12/31)	$1	$1	$1	$1	$1
5 Discount Periods	Period 1 (Discount)	Period 2 (Discount)	Period 3 (Discount)	Period 4 (Discount)	Period 5 (Discount)
Present value at 1/1 (per Table 6-4)	$3.60	$3.04	$2.40	$1.69	$.89

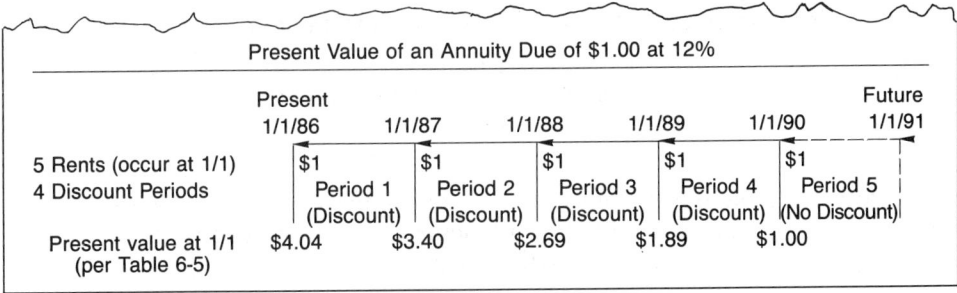

Present Value of an Annuity Due of $1.00 at 12%					
	Present				Future
	1/1/86	1/1/87	1/1/88	1/1/89	1/1/90	1/1/91
5 Rents (occur at 1/1)	$1	$1	$1	$1	$1	
4 Discount Periods	Period 1 (Discount)	Period 2 (Discount)	Period 3 (Discount)	Period 4 (Discount)	Period 5 (No Discount)	
Present value at 1/1 (per Table 6-5)	$4.04	$3.40	$2.69	$1.89	$1.00	

We could compute the present value of an annuity due simply by adding together the present value of each of the periodic rents, but we can use the present value tables for ordinary annuities to simplify the computation. The diagrams in this section illustrate that **in an ordinary annuity the number of discount periods and the number of rents are the same, whereas in an annuity due, the number of discount periods is always one less than the number of rents.** The basis then for converting a table of present value of an ordinary annuity of 1 factor to a factor for the present value of an annuity due of 1 involves taking the factor for an ordinary annuity **of one less period** and adding 1. The present value discounting factor may, therefore, be expressed as: $(P_{\overline{n-1}|i} + 1)$. Referring to Table 6-4 of "Present Value of an Ordinary Annuity of 1," this procedure is illustrated as follows:

1. Present value of an ordinary annuity of 1 for four periods at 12% (Table 6-4)	$3.03735
2. Add 1	+ 1.00000
3. Present value of an annuity due of 1 for five periods at 12%	$4.03735

Due to the fact that payment and receipt of rent at the beginning of periods (e.g., leases, insurance, and subscriptions) are as common as those at the end of the periods (referred to as "in arrears"), we have provided present value of annuity due factors in Table 6-5.

To illustrate a present value of an annuity due problem, assume Space Odyssey Inc. rents a communications satellite for four years with annual rental payments of $4.8 million to be made at the beginning of each year. Assuming the relevant interest rate is 11%, what is the present value of the rental obligations?

This problem is time-diagrammed as follows:

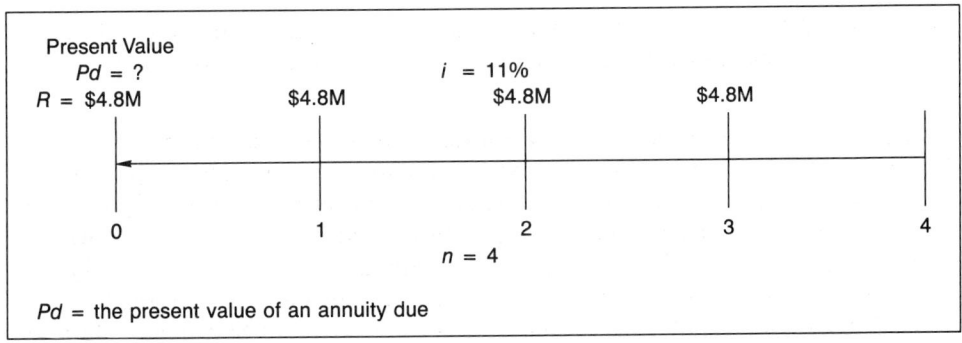

Pd = the present value of an annuity due

This problem can be solved using the following formula:

$$Pd = R(P_{\overline{n-1}|i} + 1) = R(Pd_{\overline{n}|i})$$
$$= \$4.8M\,(P_{\overline{3}|11\%} + 1) = \$4.8M\,(Pd_{\overline{4}|11\%})$$
$$= \$4.8M\,(3.44371)$$
$$= \$16,529,808$$

Since we have Table 6-5 for present value of an annuity due problems, we can simply use $Pd_{\overline{4}|11\%}$ to locate the desired factor 3.44371 and compute the present value of the lease payments to be $16,529,808.

Illustrations of Present Value of Annuity Problems

The following three illustrations use financial and investment situations to demonstrate the computation of (1) the present value, (2) the interest rate, and (3) the amount of each rent for annuity problems.

Illustration—Computation of the Present Value of an Ordinary Annuity   You have just won Lotto B.C. totalling $4,000,000 and learned that the province will pay you the money by sending a cheque in the amount of $200,000 at the end of each of the next twenty years. What is the amount you have really won? That is, if the interest rate is 10%, what is the present value of the $200,000 cheques you will receive over the next twenty years? A time-diagram of this enviable situation is as follows:

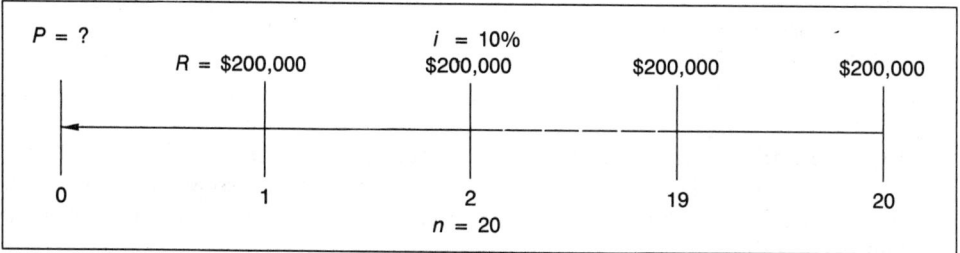

The present value is determined as follows:

$$P = R(P_{\overline{n}|i})$$
$$= \$200,000\,(P_{\overline{20}|10\%})$$
$$= \$200,000\,(8.51356)$$
$$= \$1,702,712$$

As a result, if the province deposits $1,702,712 now and earns 10% interest, it can draw $200,000 a year for twenty years to pay you the $4,000,000.

Illustration—Computation of the Interest Rate   It is not uncommon to make purchases using a credit card. When you receive the invoice for payment, you may pay the total amount due or you may pay the balance in a certain number of payments. For example, if you receive an invoice with a balance due of $528.77 and are invited to pay it off in twelve equal monthly payments of $50.00 each with the first payment due one month from now, what rate of interest are you paying?

The $528.77 represents the present value of the twelve $50 payments at an unknown rate of interest. This situation in the form of a time-diagram appears as follows:

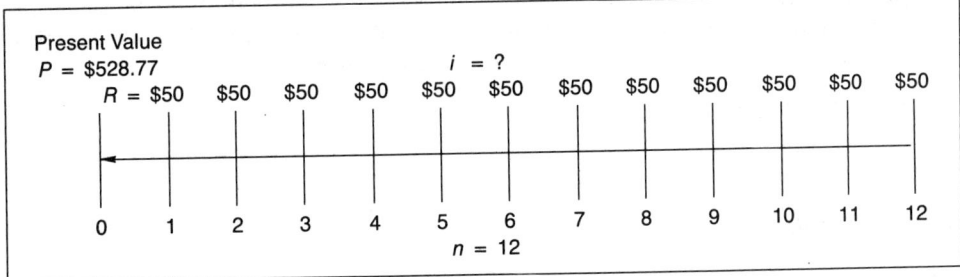

The rate is determined as follows:

$$P = R(P_{\overline{n}|i})$$
$$\$528.77 = \$50\ (P_{\overline{12}|i})$$
$$P_{\overline{12}|i} = \frac{\$528.77}{\$50} = 10.57534$$

Referring to Table 6-4 and reading across the 12-period row, we find 10.57534 in the 2% column. Since 2% is a monthly rate, the nominal annual rate of interest is 24% (12 × 2%), and the effective annual rate is 26.82413%.

Illustration—Computation of Each Periodic Rent   Norm and Jackie have saved $18,000 to finance their daughter Dawn's university education. The money has been deposited in the Permanent Savings and Loan Association and is earning 10% interest compounded semiannually. What equal amounts can their daughter withdraw at the end of every six months during the next four years while she attends university and exhausts the fund with the last withdrawal? This problem appears as follows in the form of a time-diagram:

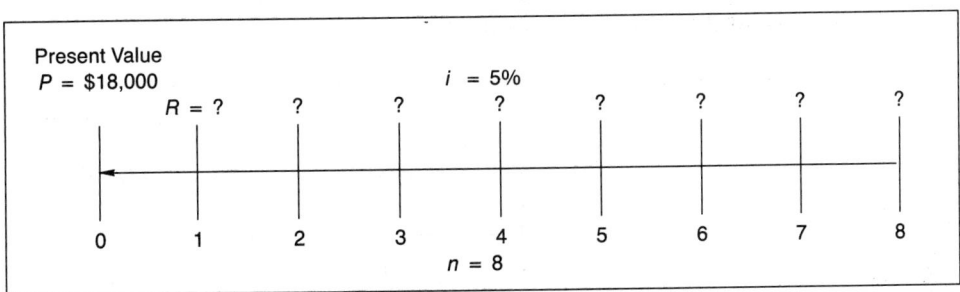

The answer is not determined by simply dividing $18,000 by 8 withdrawals because that ignores the interest earned on the money remaining on deposit. Taking into consideration that interest is compounded semiannually at 5% (10% ÷ 2) for eight periods (4 years × 2), and using the present value of an ordinary annuity formula, we determine the amount of each withdrawal as follows:

$$P = R(P_{\overline{n}|i})$$
$$\$18,000 = R(P_{\overline{8}|5\%})$$
$$\$18,000 = R(6.46321)$$
$$R = \$2,784.99$$

COMPLEX SITUATIONS

Often it is necessary to use more than one table to solve time-value problems. For example, a business problem may require that both present value of a single sum and present value of an ordinary annuity computations be made. To illustrate the more commonplace situations, two problems are presented:

1. Deferred annuities.
2. Bond problems.

Deferred Annuities

A **deferred annuity** is one in which the rents begin a specified number of periods after the arrangement or contract is made. In other words, a deferred annuity does not begin to produce rents until two or more periods have expired. For example, "an **ordinary annuity** of six annual rents deferred four years" means that no rents will occur during the first four years, and that the first of the six rents will occur at the end of the fifth year. "An **annuity due** of six annual rents deferred four years" means that no rents will occur during the first four years, and that the first of six rents will occur at the beginning of the fifth year.

Future Amount of a Deferred Annuity In the case of the future amount of a deferred annuity the computations are relatively straightforward. There is no accumulation or investment on which interest may accrue during the deferred periods; therefore the future amount of a deferred annuity is the same as the future amount of an annuity with the same number of payments not deferred.

To illustrate, assume that Sutton Corporation plans to purchase a land site in six years for the construction of its new corporate headquarters. Cash flow problems mean that Sutton is able to budget deposits of $80,000 only at the end of the fourth, fifth, and sixth years, which are expected to earn 12% annually. What future amount will Sutton have accumulated at the end of the sixth year?

A time-diagram of this situation is as follows:

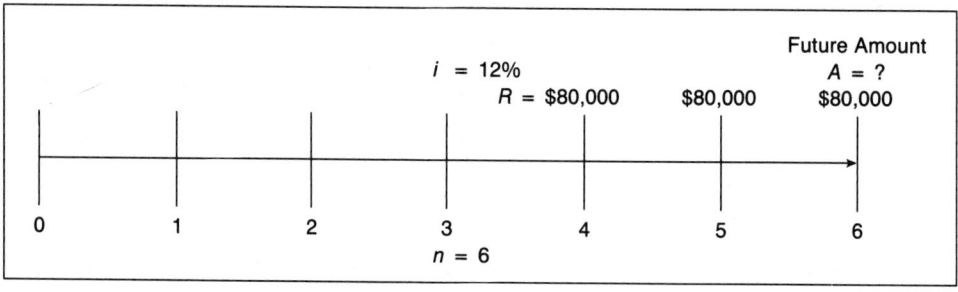

The amount accumulated is determined by using the standard formula for the future amount of an ordinary annuity:

$$
\begin{aligned}
A &= R(A_{\overline{n}|}\,i) \\
&= \$80,000\ (A_{\overline{3}|\,12\%}) \\
&= \$80,000\ (3.37440) \\
&= \$269,952
\end{aligned}
$$

Present Value of a Deferred Annuity   In computing the present value of a deferred annuity, recognition must be given to the facts that no rents occur during the deferral period and that the future actual rents must be discounted for the entire period.

To illustrate, Tom Hacker has developed and copyrighted a software computer program that is a tutorial for students in intermediate accounting. He agrees to sell the copyright to Campus Micro Systems for six annual payments of $5,000 each, the payments to begin five years from today. The annual interest rate is 8%. What is the present value of the six payments?

This situation may be viewed as an ordinary annuity of six payments deferred four periods. The following time-diagram helps to visualize this sales agreement:

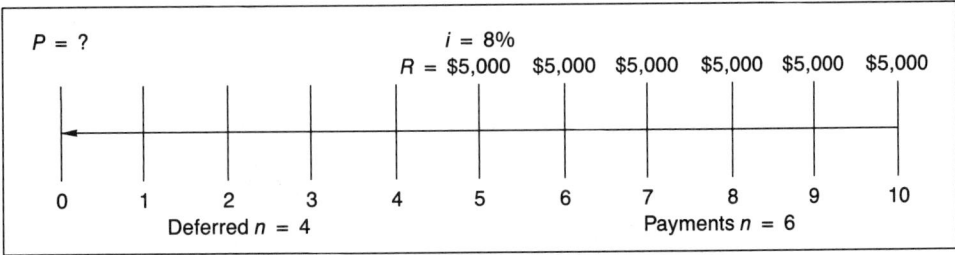

Two approaches are available to solve this problem. The first is to compute the present value of an ordinary annuity as if the rents had occurred for all periods, and then subtract the present value of those rents not received during the deferral periods. We are then left with the present value of the rents actually received subsequent to the deferral. This approach requires the use of only Table 6-4 as follows:

1. Each periodic rent	$5,000
2. Present value of an ordinary annuity of 1 for total periods (10) involved [number of rents (6) plus number of deferred periods (4)] at 8%	6.71008
3. Less: Present value of an ordinary annuity of 1 for the number of deferred periods (4) at 8%	− 3.31213
4. Difference (times amount of periodic rents)	× 3.39795
5. Present value of six rents of $5,000	$16,989.75

The subtraction of the present value of an annuity of 1 for the deferred periods eliminates the nonexistent rents during the deferral period and converts the present value of an ordinary annuity of $1.00 for 10 periods to the present value of 6 rents of $1.00, deferred 4 periods.

The second approach is a two-step one that requires the use of both Tables 6-2 and 6-4. The first step is to determine the present value of an ordinary annuity for the number of rent payments involved, using Table 6-4. This step provides the present value of the ordinary annuity as at the beginning of first payment period. (This is the same as the present value at the end of the last deferral period). The second step is to discount the amount determined in step one for the number of deferral periods, using Table 6-2. This approach applies to the illustration as follows:

Step 1: $P = R(P_{\overline{n}|i})$
= $5,000 $(P_{\overline{6}|8\%})$
= $5,000 (4.62288), Table 6-4 (present value of an
ordinary annuity)
= $23,114.40

Step 2: $p = a(p_{\overline{n}|i})$ (a is the amount P determined in Step 1)
= $23,114.40 $(p_{\overline{4}|8\%})$
= $23,114.40 (.73503), Table 6-2 (present value of a
single sum)
= $16,989.78

A time-diagram reflecting the completion of this two-step approach is as follows:

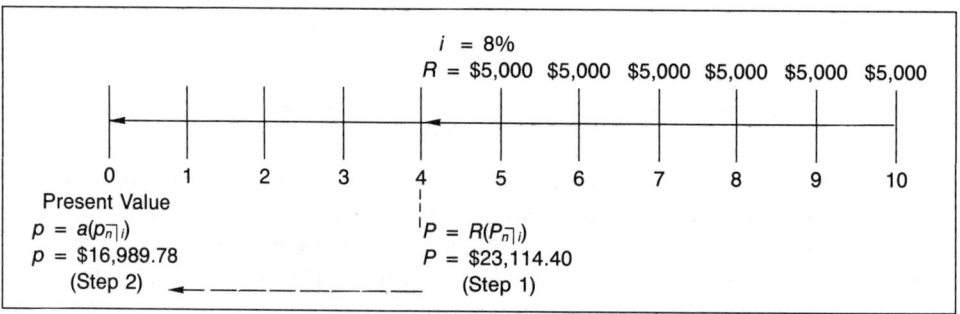

Applying the P formula discounts the annuity six periods, but because the annuity is deferred four periods, the present value of the annuity must be treated as a future amount to be discounted another four periods.[5]

Valuation of Long-Term Bonds

A long-term bond contains two cash flows: (1) periodic interest payments during the life of the bond, and (2) the principal (face value) paid at maturity. At the date of issue the buyers of the bonds determine the present value of these two cash flows using the applicable current market rate of interest.

The periodic interest payments represent an annuity problem, while the principal represents a single sum problem. The current market value of the bonds is the combined present values of the interest annuity and the principal amount.

To illustrate, Servicemaster Corp. issues $100,000 of 9% bonds due in five years with interest payable annually at year end. The current market rate of interest for bonds of similar risk is 11%. What will the buyers pay for this bond issue?

The time-diagram depicting both cash flows is shown on page 285:

---

[5]Deferred annuity contracts are common in professional sports. Rich Gossage's contract with the San Diego Padres, for example, in addition to salary and bonuses over the first five or six years, will pay him compensation at the rate of $240,000 a year from 1990 to 2006 and $125,000 from 2007 to 2016. The payouts from 1990 through 2016 total $5.33 million, but the present value of this deferred annuity is estimated at $1.5 million.

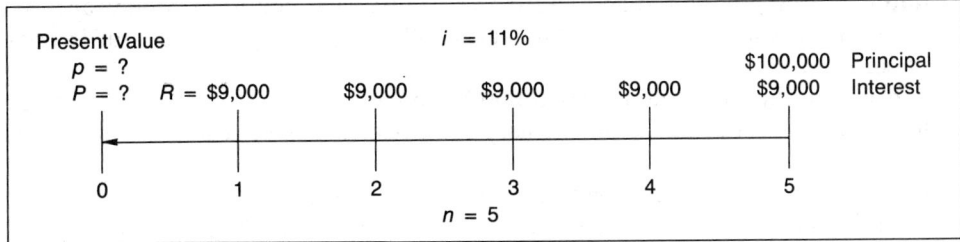

The present value of the two cash flows is computed as follows:

Present value of the principal:
$p = a\,(p_{\overline{5}|\,11\%}) = \$100{,}000\,(.59345) =$ \$59,345.00

Present value of interest payments:
$P = R(P_{\overline{5}|\,11\%}) = \$9{,}000\,(3.69590) =$ 33,263.10

Combined present value (market price)   \$92,608.10

By paying \$92,608.10 at date of issue, the buyers of the bonds will realize an effective yield of 11% over the 5-year term of the bonds. This is true because the cash flows were discounted at 11%.

INTERPOLATION OF TABLES TO DERIVE INTEREST RATES

Throughout the previous discussion, our illustrations were designed to produce interest rates and factors that could be found in the tables. Frequently it is necessary to **interpolate** to derive the exact or required interest rate. Interpolation is useful in finding a particular unknown value that lies between two given table values. The following examples illustrate the method of interpolation, using Tables 6-1 and 6-4.

Example 1 If \$2,000 accumulates to \$5,900 after being invested for 20 years, what is the annual interest rate that the investment paid?

By dividing the future amount of \$5,900 by the investment of \$2,000, we obtain the amount to which \$1.00 would have grown if invested for 20 years: that is, \$2.95. Referring to Table 6-1 and reading across the 20-period line, we find that the value under 5% is 2.65330 and the value under 6% is 3.20714. The factor 2.95 is between 5% and 6%, which means that the interest rate is also between 5% and 6%. By interpolation, the rate is determined more precisely as follows (i = unknown rate and d = difference between 5% and i):

$$.01 \left\{ \begin{array}{l} d \left\{ \begin{array}{l} .05 = 2.65330 \\ i = 2.95000 \end{array} \right\} .29670 \\ .06 = 3.20714 \end{array} \right\} .55384$$

$$\therefore \frac{d}{.01} = \frac{.29670}{.55384} \qquad d = \frac{.29670}{.55384}(.01) = .00536$$

$$\therefore i = .05 + .00536 = .05536$$

The approximate interest rate is 5.536%, or 5.5% rounded.

Example 2   You are offered an annuity of $1,000 a year beginning one year from now for 25 years for investing $15,000 cash. What rate of interest is your investment earning?

By dividing the investment of $15,000 by the annuity of $1,000 we obtain 15, which is the "present value of an ordinary annuity of 1" for 25 years at an unknown interest rate.

Referring to Table 6-4 and reading across the 25-period line, we find that the value under 4% is 15.62208 and the value under 5% is 14.09394. The factor 15 is between 4% and 5%, which means that the unknown interest rate is also between 4% and 5%. By interpolation, the rate is determined more precisely as follows (i = unknown rate and d = difference between 4% and i):

$$\begin{array}{c}
.04 = 15.62208 \\
.01 \left[\; d \left[\begin{array}{c} \\ i = 15.00000 \end{array} \right. \right] .62208 \quad \right] \; 1.52814 \\
.05 = 14.09394
\end{array}$$

$$\therefore \; \frac{d}{.01} = \frac{.62208}{1.52814} \qquad d = \frac{.62208}{1.52814} (.01) = .00407$$

$$\therefore \; i = .04 + d = .04 + .00407 = .04407$$

The approximate interest rate is 4.407%, or 4.4% rounded.

Interpolation assumes that the change between any two values in the table is linear. Although such an assumption is not correct, if the table value ranges are not too wide, the margin of error is generally insignificant.

CHOOSING AN APPROPRIATE INTEREST RATE

Up to this point, we have assumed a known or given interest rate, and therefore illustrated only the mechanics of computing accumulated values and present values. However, one of the more perplexing problems facing the accountant is the selection of an appropriate interest rate. Consider the following debates that have taken place in practice.

1. In pension accounting, the amount payable to pension claimants in the future **does not** anticipate inflation. The interest rate used to determine present value of the amount payable in the future, however, is a market rate of interest that **does** reflect inflation. Some argue, therefore, that the present value of estimated benefits payable is understated, because the smaller the estimate of benefits payable in the future, and the larger the interest rate used as a discount factor, the smaller the computed present value of the pension obligation will be.

2. In oil and gas accounting, it was at one time recommended that the fair value of oil and gas reserves in the ground be computed at the present value of the future revenues discounted at a flat 10% rate. It was argued that the use of one rate leads to comparability, and that a rate of this magnitude provides a reasonable representation of the present value of future oil and gas reserves. Others disagreed, noting that a 10% rate was unrealistic for two reasons. First, in many cases the rate should have been much higher than 10%, considering the existing prime rate. Second, not all companies and situations deserved the same rate because of differences in risk.

3. In trying to resolve the problem of capitalizing interest cost incurred during construction, the profession encountered support for two different bases to the measurement of interest cost. Some accountants favoured capitalizing the interest cost of the specific borrowing. Others disagreed, arguing that a weighted-average interest rate is prefer-

able because the borrowing on any specific project affects the borrowing costs of the entire company on other projects.

These are just a few examples of the practical problems encountered in selecting an appropriate discount (interest) rate. How then should we select an interest rate for purposes of present value computations? In the past, interest rates have often been selected on the basis of expediency (availability), regulatory stipulations, and ease of auditability. No consistent approach has been adopted. This is not surprising, given the wide variety of rates from which to choose; for example, the general borrowing rate (prime rate), a specific borrowing rate for a given company, opportunity cost rate, investment rate of return, cost-of-capital rate on a weighted-average basis, and so on.

The appropriate interest rate is not always obvious. This is so because an interest rate generally has three components:

1. **Pure rate of interest** (2% to 4%). This would be the amount a lender would charge if there were no possibilities of default and no expectation of inflation.
2. **Credit risk rate of interest** (0 to 5%). The government has little or no credit risk (i.e., risk of nonpayment) when it issues bonds; a business enterprise, however, depending upon factors such as its financial stability or profitability can have a low or a high credit risk.
3. **Expected inflation rate of interest** (0 to ?). Lenders recognize that, in an inflationary economy, they are being paid back with less valuable dollars. As a result, they increase their interest rate to compensate for this loss in purchasing power. When inflationary expectations are high, interest rates are high.

Identifying and mixing these three components in the appropriate ratio for any given company or investor at any given moment is not easy but, because inflation has been substantial in the last twenty years, the relevance and reliability of accounting information increasingly depends on selecting appropriate interest rates.

FUNDAMENTAL TERMS AND CONCEPTS

The following list of terms and their definitions is provided as a summary and review of the essential items presented in this chapter.

1. **Simple interest.** Interest on principal only, regardless of interest that may have accrued in the past.
2. **Compound interest.** Interest accrues on the unpaid interest of past periods as well as on the principal.
3. **Rate of interest.** Interest is usually expressed as an annual rate, but when the interest period is shorter than one year, the interest rate for the shorter period must be determined.
4. **Annuity.** A series of payments or receipts (called rents) that occur at equal intervals of time.
5. **Amount.** Value at a later date of a given sum that is invested at compound interest.
   (a) **Amount of 1** (or amount of a given sum). The future value of $1.00 (or a single given sum), a, at the end of n periods at i compound interest rate (Table 6-1).
   (b) **Amount of an annuity.** The amount of a series of rents invested at compound interest; in other words, the accumulated total that results from a series of equal deposits at regular intervals invested at compound interest. Both deposits and interest increase the accumulation.

(i) **Amount of an ordinary annuity.** The future value on the date of the last rent; therefore, there is one less interest period than rents. (This is taken into account in the development of Table 6-3.)

(ii) **Amount of an annuity due.** The future value one period after the date of the last rent; therefore, there are the same number of interest periods as rents. When an annuity due table is not available, use Table 6-3 with the following formula:

Amount of annuity due of 1 for n rents = Amount of ordinary annuity for (n + 1 rents) − 1.

6. **Present value.** The value at an earlier date (usually now) of a given sum in the future discounted at compound interest.

(a) **Present value of 1** (or present value of a single sum).The present value (worth) of $1.00 (or a given sum) due n periods hence, discounted at i compound interest (Table 6-2).

(b) **Present value of an annuity.** The present value (worth) of a series of rents discounted at compound interest; in other words, it is the sum when invested at compound interest that will permit a series of equal withdrawals at regular intervals.

(i) **Present value of an ordinary annuity.** The value now of $1.00 to be received or paid at the end of each period for n periods, discounted at i compound interest (Table 6-4).

(ii) **Present value of an annuity due.** The value now of $1.00 to be received or paid at the beginning of each period for n periods, discounted at i compound interest; thus, there is one less discount period than rents (Table 6-5). To use Table 6-4 for an annuity due, apply this formula:

Present value of annuity due of 1 for n rents = Present value of ordinary annuity of (n − 1 rents) + 1.

QUESTIONS

1. What is the time value of money? Why should accountants have an understanding of compound interest, annuities, and present value concepts?

2. What is the nature of interest? Distinguish between simple interest and compound interest.

3. Presented below are a number of values taken from compound interest tables involving the same number of periods and the same rate of interest. Indicate what each of these four values represents.
   (a) .10367   (c) 9.64629
   (b) 7.46944   (d) 72.05244

4. Thomas Linsmeier deposited $15,000 in a money market certificate that provides interest of 12% compounded quarterly if the amount is maintained for three years. How much will Linsmeier have at the end of three years?

5. Thomas Buttars will receive $25,000 on December 31, 1991 (five years from now) from a trust fund established by his father. Assuming the interest rate for discounting is 12% (compounded semiannually), what is the present value of this amount today?

6. What are the primary characteristics of an annuity? Differentiate between an ordinary annuity and an annuity due.

7. Hillside, Inc. owes $25,000 to Lowery Company. How much would Hillside have to pay each year if the debt is retired through four equal payments (made at the end of the year) given an interest rate on the debt of 15%?

8. The Hogans are planning for a retirement home. They estimate they will need $100,000 four years from now to purchase this home. Assuming an interest rate of 10%, what amount must be deposited at the end of the four years to fund the home price?

9. Assume the same situation as in Question 8, except that the four equal amounts are deposited at the beginning of the period rather than at the end. In this case, what amount must be deposited at the beginning of each period?

10. Explain how the amount of an ordinary annuity interest table is converted to the amount of an annuity due table.

11. Explain how the present value of an ordinary annuity interest table is converted to the present value of an annuity due interest table.

12. Albrecht Enterprises leases property to Erin, Inc. Because Erin, Inc. is experiencing financial difficulty, Albrecht agrees to receive five rents of $8,000 at the end of each year, with the rents deferred three years and interest accruing at the rate of 12%. What is the present value of the five rents?

13. Warner, Inc. invests $20,000 initially, which accumulates to $38,000 at the end of five years. What is the annual interest rate earned on the investment? (Hint: Interpolation will be needed.)

14. What are the components of an interest rate? Why is it important for accountants to understand these components?

15. (a) On May 1, 1986, Sanchez Company sold some machinery to Hargrove Company on an instalment contract basis. The contract required five equal annual payments, with the first payment due on May 1, 1986. What present value concept is appropriate for this situation?

    (b) On June 1, 1986, Sunset, Inc. purchased a new machine that it does not have to pay for until May 1, 1988. The total payment on May 1, 1988, will include both principal and interest. Assuming interest at a 15% rate, the cost of the machine would be the total payment multiplied by what time value of money concept?

    (c) Fortune, Inc. wishes to know how much monies it will have available in five years if five equal amounts of $20,000 are invested, with the first amount invested immediately. What interest table is appropriate for this situation?

    (d) El Cerro invests in a "jumbo" $100,000 three-year certificate of deposit at a bank. What table would be used to determine the amount accumulated at the end of three years?

EXERCISES

(Interest rates are per annum unless otherwise stated.)

E6-1 Joanie Schmidt invests $2,000 at 8% annual interest, leaving the money invested without withdrawing any of the interest for ten years. At the end of the ten years, Joanie withdraws the accumulated amount of money.

Instructions

(a) Compute the amount Joanie would withdraw, assuming the investment earns **simple interest**.

(b) Compute the amount Joanie would withdraw, assuming the investment earns **interest compounded annually**.

(c) Compute the amount Joanie would withdraw, assuming the investment earns **interest compounded semiannually**.

E6-2 For each of the following cases, indicate (a) to what interest rate columns and (b) to what number of periods you would refer in looking up the interest factor.

1. In a Future Amount of 1 table (Table 6-1):

	Annual Rate	Number of Years Invested	Compounded
a.	6%	15	Annually
b.	10%	6	Quarterly
c.	8%	15	Semiannually

2. In a Present Value of an Ordinary Annuity of 1 table (Table 6-4):

	Annual Rate	Number of Years Involved	Number of Rents Involved	Frequency of Rents
a.	12%	20	20	Annually
b.	10%	5	10	Semiannually
c.	8%	4	16	Quarterly

Note: Exercises and Problems continue on page 300.

TABLE 6–1   FUTURE AMOUNT OF 1

$$a_{\overline{n}|i} = (1 + i)^n$$

(n) Periods	2%	2½%	3%	4%	5%	6%
1	1.02000	1.02500	1.03000	1.04000	1.05000	1.06000
2	1.04040	1.05063	1.06090	1.08160	1.10250	1.12360
3	1.06121	1.07689	1.09273	1.12486	1.15763	1.19102
4	1.08243	1.10381	1.12551	1.16986	1.21551	1.26248
5	1.10408	1.13141	1.15927	1.21665	1.27628	1.33823
6	1.12616	1.15969	1.19405	1.26532	1.34010	1.41852
7	1.14869	1.18869	1.22987	1.31593	1.40710	1.50363
8	1.17166	1.21840	1.26677	1.36857	1.47746	1.59385
9	1.19509	1.24886	1.30477	1.42331	1.55133	1.68948
10	1.21899	1.28008	1.34392	1.48024	1.62889	1.79085
11	1.24337	1.31209	1.38423	1.53945	1.71034	1.89830
12	1.26824	1.34489	1.42576	1.60103	1.79586	2.01220
13	1.29361	1.37851	1.46853	1.66507	1.88565	2.13293
14	1.31948	1.41297	1.51259	1.73168	1.97993	2.26090
15	1.34587	1.44830	1.55797	1.80094	2.07893	2.39656
16	1.37279	1.48451	1.60471	1.87298	2.18287	2.54035
17	1.40024	1.52162	1.65285	1.94790	2.29202	2.69277
18	1.42825	1.55966	1.70243	2.02582	2.40662	2.85434
19	1.45681	1.59865	1.75351	2.10685	2.52695	3.02560
20	1.48595	1.63862	1.80611	2.19112	2.65330	3.20714
21	1.51567	1.67958	1.86029	2.27877	2.78596	3.39956
22	1.54598	1.72157	1.91610	2.36992	2.92526	3.60354
23	1.57690	1.76461	1.97359	2.46472	3.07152	3.81975
24	1.60844	1.80873	2.03279	2.56330	3.22510	4.04893
25	1.64061	1.85394	2.09378	2.66584	3.38635	4.29187
26	1.67342	1.90029	2.15659	2.77247	3.55567	4.54938
27	1.70689	1.94780	2.22129	2.88337	3.73346	4.82235
28	1.74102	1.99650	2.28793	2.99870	3.92013	5.11169
29	1.77584	2.04641	2.35657	3.11865	4.11614	5.41839
30	1.81136	2.09757	2.42726	3.24340	4.32194	5.74349
31	1.84759	2.15001	2.50008	3.37313	4.53804	6.08810
32	1.88454	2.20376	2.57508	3.50806	5.76494	6.45339
33	1.92223	2.25885	2.65234	3.64838	5.00319	6.84059
34	1.96068	2.31532	2.73191	3.79432	5.25335	7.25103
35	1.99989	2.37321	.281386	3.94609	5.51602	7.68609
36	2.03989	2.43254	2.89828	4.10393	5.79182	8.14725
37	2.08069	2.49335	2.98523	4.26809	6.08141	8.63609
38	2.12230	2.55568	3.07478	4.43881	6.38548	9.15425
39	2.16474	2.61957	3.16703	4.61637	6.70475	9.70351
40	2.20804	2.68506	3.26204	4.80102	7.03999	10.28572

FUTURE AMOUNT OF 1   **TABLE 6–1**

8%	9%	10%	11%	12%	15%	(n) Periods
1.08000	1.09000	1.10000	1.11000	1.12000	1.15000	1
1.16640	1.18810	1.21000	1.23210	1.25440	1.32250	2
1.25971	1.29503	1.33100	1.36763	1.40493	1.52088	3
1.36049	1.41158	1.46410	1.51807	1.57352	1.74901	4
1.46933	1.53862	1.61051	1.68506	1.76234	2.01136	5
1.58687	1.67710	1.77156	1.87041	1.97382	2.31306	6
1.71382	1.82804	1.94872	2.07616	2.21068	2.66002	7
1.85093	1.99256	2.14359	2.30454	2.47596	3.05902	8
1.99900	2.17189	2.35795	2.55803	2.77308	3.51788	9
2.15892	2.36736	2.59374	2.83942	3.10585	4.04556	10
2.33164	2.58043	2.85312	3.15176	3.47855	4.65239	11
2.51817	2.81267	3.13843	3.49845	3.89598	5.35025	12
2.71962	3.06581	3.45227	3.88328	4.36349	6.15279	13
2.93719	3.34173	3.79750	4.31044	4.88711	7.07571	14
3.17217	3.64248	4.17725	4.78459	5.47357	8.13706	15
3.42594	3.97031	4.59497	5.31089	6.13039	9.35762	16
3.70002	4.32763	5.05447	5.89509	6.86604	10.76126	17
3.99602	4.71712	5.55992	6.54355	7.68997	12.37545	18
4.31570	5.14166	6.11591	7.26334	8.61276	14.23177	19
4.66096	5.60441	6.72750	8.06231	9.64629	16.36654	20
5.03383	6.10881	7.40025	8.94917	10.80385	18.82152	21
5.43654	6.65860	8.14028	9.93357	12.10031	21.64475	22
5.87146	7.25787	8.95430	11.02627	13.55235	24.89146	23
6.34118	7.91108	9.84973	12.23916	15.17863	28.62518	24
6.84847	8.62308	10.83471	13.58546	17.00000	32.91895	25
7.39635	9.39916	11.91818	15.07986	19.04007	37.85680	26
7.98806	10.24508	13.10999	16.73865	21.32488	43.53532	27
8.62711	11.16714	14.42099	18.57990	23.88387	50.06561	28
9.31727	12.17218	15.86309	20.62369	26.74993	57.57545	29
10.06266	13.26768	17.44940	22.89230	29.95992	66.21177	30
10.86767	14.46177	19.19434	25.41045	33.55511	76.14354	31
11.73708	15.76333	21.11378	28.20560	37.58173	87.56507	32
12.67605	17.18203	23.22515	31.30821	42.09153	100.69983	33
13.69013	18.72841	25.54767	34.75212	47.14252	115.80480	34
14.78534	20.41397	28.10244	38.57485	52.79962	133.17552	35
15.96817	22.25123	30.91268	42.81808	59.13557	153.15185	36
17.24563	24.25384	34.00395	47.52807	66.23184	176.12463	37
18.62528	26.43668	37.40434	52.75616	74.17966	202.54332	38
20.11530	28.81598	41.14479	58.55934	83.08122	232.92482	39
21.72452	31.40942	45.25926	65.00087	93.05097	267.86355	40

TABLE 6–2   PRESENT VALUE OF 1

$$p_{\overline{n}|i} = \frac{1}{(1+i)^n} = (1+i)^{-n}$$

(n) Periods	2%	2½%	3%	4%	5%	6%
1	.98039	.97561	.97087	.96154	.95238	.94340
2	.96117	.95181	.94260	.92456	.90703	.89000
3	.94232	.92860	.91514	.88900	.86384	.83962
4	.92385	.90595	.88849	.85480	.82270	.79209
5	.90573	.88385	.86261	.82193	.78353	.74726
6	.88797	.86230	.83748	.79031	.74622	.70496
7	.87056	.84127	.81309	.75992	.71068	.66506
8	.85349	.82075	.78941	.73069	.67684	.62741
9	.83676	.80073	.76642	.70259	.64461	.59190
10	.82035	.78120	.74409	.67556	.61391	.55839
11	.80426	.76214	.72242	.64958	.58468	.52679
12	.78849	.74356	.70138	.62460	.55684	.49697
13	.77303	.72542	.68095	.60057	.53032	.46884
14	.75788	.70773	.66112	.57748	.50507	.44230
15	.74301	.69047	.64186	.55526	.48102	.41727
16	.72845	.67362	.62317	.53391	.45811	.39365
17	.71416	.54720	.60502	.51337	.43630	.37136
18	.70016	.64117	.58739	.49363	.41552	.35034
19	.68643	.62553	.57029	.47464	.39573	.33051
20	.67297	.61027	.55368	.45639	.37689	.31180
21	.65978	.59539	.53755	.43883	.35894	.29416
22	.64684	.58086	.52189	.42196	.34185	.27751
23	.63416	.56670	.50669	.40573	.32557	.26180
24	.62172	.55288	.49193	.39012	.31007	.24698
25	.60953	.53939	.47761	.37512	.29530	.23300
26	.59758	.52623	.46369	.36069	.28124	.21981
27	.58586	.51340	.45019	.34682	.26785	.20737
28	.57437	.50088	.43708	.33348	.25509	.19563
29	.56311	.48866	.42435	.32065	.24925	.18456
30	.55207	.47674	.41199	.30832	.23138	.17411
31	.54125	.46511	.39999	.29646	.22036	.16425
32	.53063	.45377	.38834	.28506	.20987	.15496
33	.52023	.44270	.37703	.27409	.19987	.14619
34	.51003	.43191	.36604	.26355	.19035	.13791
35	.50003	.42137	.35538	.25342	.18129	.13011
36	.49022	.41109	.34503	.24367	.17266	.12274
37	.48061	.40107	.33498	.23430	.16444	.11579
38	.47119	.39128	.32523	.22529	.15661	.10924
39	.46195	.38174	.31575	.21662	.14915	.10306
40	.45289	.37243	.30656	.20829	.14205	.09722

PRESENT VALUE OF 1   **TABLE 6–2**

8%	9%	10%	11%	12%	15%	(n) Periods
.92593	.91743	.90909	.90090	.89286	.86957	1
.85734	.84168	.82645	.81162	.79719	.75614	2
.79383	.77218	.75132	.73119	.71178	.65752	3
.73503	.70843	.68301	.65873	.63552	.57175	4
.68058	.64993	.62092	.59345	.56743	.49718	5
.63017	.59627	.56447	.53464	.50663	.43233	6
.58349	.54703	.51316	.48166	.45235	.37594	7
.54027	.50187	.46651	.43393	.40388	.32690	8
.50025	.46043	.42410	.39092	.36061	.28426	9
.46319	.42241	.38554	.35218	.32197	.24719	10
.42888	.38753	.35049	.31728	.28748	.21494	11
.39711	.35554	.31863	.28584	.25668	.18691	12
.36770	.32618	.28966	.25751	.22917	.16253	13
.34046	.29925	.26333	.23199	.20462	.14133	14
.31524	.27454	.23939	.20900	.18270	.12289	15
.29189	.25187	.21763	.18829	.16312	.10687	16
.27027	.23107	.19785	.16963	.14564	.09293	17
.25025	.21199	.17986	.15282	.13004	.08081	18
.23171	.19449	.16351	.13768	.11611	.07027	19
.21455	.17843	.14864	.12403	.10367	.06110	20
.19866	.16370	.13513	.11174	.09256	.05313	21
.18394	.15018	.12285	.10067	.08264	.04620	22
.17032	.13778	.11168	.09069	.07379	.04017	23
.15770	.12641	.10153	.08170	.06588	.03493	24
.14602	.11597	.09230	.07361	.05882	.03038	25
.13520	.10639	.08391	.06631	.05252	.02642	26
.12519	.09761	.07628	.05974	.04689	.02297	27
.11591	.08955	.06934	.05382	.04187	.01997	28
.10733	.08216	.06304	.04849	.03738	.01737	29
.09938	.07537	.05731	.04368	.03338	.01510	30
.09202	.06915	.05210	.03935	.02980	.01313	31
.08520	.06344	.04736	.03545	.02661	.01142	32
.07889	.05820	.04306	.03194	.02376	.00993	33
.07305	.05340	.03914	.02898	.02121	.00864	34
.06763	.04899	.03558	.02592	.01894	.00751	35
.06262	.04494	.03235	.02335	.01691	.00653	36
.05799	.04123	.02941	.02104	.01510	.00568	37
.05369	.03783	.02674	.01896	.01348	.00494	38
.04971	.03470	.02430	.01708	.01204	.00429	39
.04603	.03184	.02210	.01538	.01075	.00373	40

TABLE 6–3 FUTURE AMOUNT OF AN ORDINARY ANNUITY OF 1

$$A_{\overline{n}|i} = \frac{(1 + i)^n - 1}{i}$$

(n) Periods	2%	2½%	3%	4%	5%	6%
1	1.00000	1.00000	1.00000	1.00000	1.00000	1.00000
2	2.02000	2.02500	2.03000	2.04000	2.05000	2.06000
3	3.06040	3.07563	3.09090	3.12160	3.15250	3.18360
4	4.12161	4.15252	4.18363	4.24646	4.31013	4.37462
5	5.20404	5.25633	5.30914	5.41632	5.52563	5.63709
6	6.30812	6.38774	6.46841	6.63289	6.80191	6.97532
7	7.43428	7.54743	7.66246	7.89829	8.14201	8.39384
8	8.58297	8.73612	8.89234	9.21423	9.54911	9.89747
9	9.75463	9.95452	10.15911	10.58280	11.02656	11.49132
10	10.94972	11.20338	11.46338	12.00611	12.57789	13.18079
11	12.16872	12.48347	12.80780	13.48635	14.20679	14.97164
12	13.41209	13.79555	14.19203	15.02581	15.91713	16.86994
13	14.68033	15.14044	15.61779	16.62684	17.71298	18.88214
14	15.97394	16.51895	17.08632	18.29191	19.59863	21.01507
15	17.29342	17.93193	18.59891	20.02359	21.57856	23.27597
16	18.63929	19.38022	20.15688	21.82453	23.65749	25.67253
17	20.01207	20.86473	21.76159	23.69751	25.84037	28.21288
18	21.41231	22.38635	23.41444	25.64541	28.13238	30.90565
19	22.84056	23.94601	25.11687	27.67123	30.53900	33.75999
20	24.29737	25.54466	26.87037	29.77808	33.06595	36.78559
21	25.78332	27.18327	28.67649	31.96920	35.71925	39.99273
22	27.29898	28.86286	30.53678	34.24797	38.50521	43.39229
23	28.84496	30.58443	32.45288	36.61789	41.43048	46.99583
24	30.42186	32.34904	34.42647	39.08260	44.50200	50.81558
25	32.03030	34.15776	36.45926	41.64591	47.72710	54.86451
26	33.67091	36.01171	38.55304	44.31174	51.11345	59.15638
27	35.34432	37.91200	40.70963	47.08421	54.66913	63.70577
28	37.05121	39.85980	42.93092	49.96758	58.40258	68.52811
29	38.79223	41.85630	45.21885	52.96629	62.32271	73.63980
30	40.56808	53.90270	47.57542	56.08494	66.43885	79.05819
31	42.37944	46.00027	50.00268	59.32834	70.76079	84.80168
32	44.22703	48.15028	52.50276	62.70147	75.29883	90.88978
33	46.11157	50.35403	55.07784	66.20953	80.06377	97.34316
34	48.03380	52.61289	57.73018	69.95791	85.06696	104.18376
35	49.99448	54.92821	60.46208	73.65222	90.32021	111.43478
36	51.99437	57.30141	63.27594	77.59831	95.83632	119.12087
37	54.03425	59.73395	66.17422	81.70225	101.62814	127.26812
38	56.11494	62.22730	69.15945	85.97034	107.70955	135.90421
39	58.23724	64.79298	72.23423	90.40915	114.09502	145.05846
40	60.40189	67.40255	75.40126	95.02552	120.79977	154.76917

FUTURE AMOUNT OF AN ORDINARY ANNUITY OF 1   **TABLE 6-3**

8%	9½%	10%	11%	12%	15%	(*n*) Periods
1.00000	1.00000	1.00000	1.00000	1.00000	1.00000	1
2.08000	2.09000	2.10000	2.11000	2.12000	2.15000	2
3.24640	3.27810	3.31000	3.34210	3.37440	3.47250	3
4.50611	4.57313	4.64100	4.70973	4.77933	4.99338	4
5.86660	5.98471	6.10510	6.22780	6.35285	6.74238	5
7.33592	7.52334	7.71561	7.91286	8.11519	8.75374	6
8.92280	9.20044	9.48717	9.78437	10.08901	11.06680	7
10.63663	11.02847	11.43589	11.85943	12.29969	13.72682	8
12.48756	13.02104	13.57948	14.16397	14.77566	16.78584	9
14.48656	15.19293	15.93743	16.72201	17.54874	20.30372	10
16.64549	17.56029	18.53117	19.56143	20.65458	24.34928	11
18.97713	20.14072	21.38428	22.71319	24.13313	29.00167	12
21.49530	22.95339	24.52271	26.21164	28.02911	34.35192	13
24.21492	26.01919	27.97498	30.09492	32.39260	40.50471	14
27.15211	29.36092	31.77248	34.40536	37.27972	47.58041	15
30.32428	33.00340	35.94973	39.18995	42.75328	55.71747	16
33.75023	36.97371	40.54470	44.50084	48.88367	65.07509	17
37.45024	41.30134	45.59917	50.39593	55.74972	75.83636	18
41.44626	46.01846	51.15909	56.93949	63.43968	88.21181	19
45.76196	51.16012	57.27500	64.20283	72.05244	102.44358	20
50.42292	56.76453	64.00250	72.26514	81.69874	118.81012	21
55.45676	62.87334	71.40275	81.21431	92.50258	137.63163	22
60.89330	69.53194	79.54302	91.14788	104.60289	159.27638	23
66.76476	76.78981	88.49733	102.17415	118.15524	184.16784	24
73.10594	84.70090	98.34706	114.41331	133.33387	212.79302	25
79.95442	93.32398	109.18177	127.99877	150.33393	245.71197	26
87.35077	102.72314	121.09994	143.07864	169.37401	283.56877	27
95.33883	112.96822	134.20994	159.81729	190.69889	327.10408	28
103.96594	124.13536	148.63093	178.39719	214.58275	377.16969	29
113.28321	136.30754	164.49402	199.02088	241.33268	434.74515	30
123.34587	149.57522	181.94343	221.91317	271.29261	500.95692	31
134.21354	164.03699	201.13777	247.32362	304.84772	577.10046	32
145.95062	179.80032	222.25154	275.52922	342.42945	644.66553	33
158.62667	196.98234	245.47670	306.83744	384.52098	765.36535	34
172.31680	215.71076	271.02437	341.59855	431.66350	881.17016	35
187.10215	236.12472	299.12681	380.16441	484.46312	1014.34568	36
203.07032	258.37595	330.03949	143.07864	543.59869	1167.49753	37
220.31595	282.62978	364.04343	470.51056	609.83053	1343.62216	38
238.94122	309.06646	401.44778	523.26673	684.01020	1546.16549	39
259.05652	337.88245	442.59256	581.82607	767.09142	1779.09031	40

TABLE 6–4   PRESENT VALUE OF AN ORDINARY ANNUITY OF 1 (payment at end of period)

$$P_{\overline{n}|i} = \frac{1 - \dfrac{1}{(1 + i)^n}}{i} = \frac{1 - P_{\overline{n}|i}}{i}$$

(n) Periods	2%	2½%	3%	4%	5%	6%
1	.98039	.97561	.97087	.96154	.95238	.94340
2	1.94156	1.92742	1.91347	1.88609	1.85941	1.83339
3	2.88388	3.85602	2.82861	2.77509	2.72325	2.67301
4	3.80773	3.76197	3.71710	3.62990	3.54595	3.46511
5	4.71346	4.64583	4.57971	4.45182	4.32948	4.21236
6	5.60143	5.50813	5.41719	5.24214	5.07569	4.91732
7	6.47199	6.34939	6.23028	6.00205	5.78637	5.58238
8	7.32548	7.17014	7.01969	6.73274	6.46321	6.20979
9	8.16224	7.97087	7.78611	7.43533	7.10782	6.80169
10	8.98259	8.75206	8.53020	8.11090	7.72173	7.36009
11	9.78685	9.51421	9.25262	8.76048	8.30641	7.88787
12	10.57534	10.25776	9.95400	9.38507	8.86325	8.38384
13	11.34837	10.98319	10.63496	9.98565	9.39357	8.85268
14	12.10625	11.69091	11.29607	10.56312	9.89864	9.29498
15	12.84926	12.38138	11.93794	11.11839	10.37966	9.71225
16	13.57771	13.05500	12.56110	11.65230	10.83777	10.10590
17	14.29187	13.71220	13.16612	12.16567	11.27407	10.47726
18	14.99203	14.35336	13.75351	12.65930	11.69859	10.82760
19	15.67846	14.97889	14.32380	13.13394	12.08532	11.15812
20	16.35143	15.58916	14.87747	13.59033	12.46221	11.46992
21	17.01121	16.18455	15.41502	14.02916	12.82115	11.76408
22	17.65805	16.76541	15.93692	14.45112	13.16300	12.04158
23	18.29220	17.33211	16.44361	14.85684	13.48857	12.30338
24	18.91393	17.88499	16.93554	15.24696	13.79864	12.55036
25	19.52346	18.42438	17.41315	15.62208	14.09394	12.78336
26	20.12104	18.95061	17.87684	15.98277	14.37519	13.00317
27	20.70690	19.46401	18.32703	16.32959	14.64303	13.21053
28	21.28127	19.96489	18.76411	16.66306	14.89813	13.40616
29	21.84438	20.45355	19.18845	16.98371	15.14107	13.59072
30	22.39646	20.93029	19.60044	17.29203	15.37245	13.76483
31	22.93770	21.39541	20.00043	17.58849	15.59281	13.92909
32	23.46833	21.84918	20.38877	17.87355	15.80268	14.08404
33	23.98856	22.29188	20.76579	18.14765	16.00255	14.23023
34	24.49859	22.72379	21.13184	18.41120	16.19290	14.36814
35	24.99862	23.14516	21.48722	18.66461	16.37419	14.49825
36	25.48884	23.55625	21.83225	18.90828	16.54685	14.52099
37	25.96945	23.95732	22.16724	19.14258	16.71129	14.73678
38	26.44064	24.34860	22.49246	19.36786	16.86789	14.84602
39	26.90259	24.73034	22.80822	19.58448	17.01704	14.94907
40	27.35548	25.10278	23.11477	19.79277	17.15909	15.04630

PRESENT VALUE OF AN ORDINARY ANNUITY OF 1 (payment at end of period)   **TABLE 6–4**

8%	9%	10%	11%	12%	15%	(n) Periods
.92593	9.1743	.90909	.90090	.89286	.86957	1
1.78326	1.75911	1.73554	1.71252	1.69005	1.62571	2
2.57710	2.53130	2.48685	2.44371	2.40183	2.28323	3
3.31213	3.23972	3.16986	3.10245	3.03735	2.85498	4
3.99271	3.88965	3.79079	3.69590	3.60478	3.35216	5
4.62288	4.48592	4.35526	4.23065	4.11141	3.78449	6
5.20637	5.03295	4.86842	4.71220	4.56376	4.16042	7
5.74664	5.53482	5.33493	5.14612	4.96764	4.48732	8
6.24689	5.99525	5.75902	5.53705	5.32825	4.77158	9
6.71008	6.41766	6.14457	5.88923	5.65022	5.01877	10
7.13896	6.80519	6.49506	6.20652	5.93770	5.23371	11
7.53608	7.16073	6.81369	6.49236	6.19437	5.42062	12
7.90378	7.48690	7.10336	6.74987	6.42355	5.58315	13
8.24424	7.78615	7.36669	6.98187	6.62817	5.72448	14
8.55948	8.06069	7.60608	7.19087	6.81086	5.84737	15
8.85137	8.31256	7.82371	7.37916	6.97399	5.95424	16
9.12164	8.54363	8.02155	7.54879	7.11963	6.04716	17
9.37189	8.75563	8.20141	7.70162	7.24967	6.12797	18
9.60360	8.95012	8.36492	7.83929	7.36578	6.19823	19
9.81815	9.12855	8.51356	7.96333	7.46944	6.25933	20
10.01680	9.29224	8.64869	8.07507	7.56200	6.31246	21
10.20074	9.44243	8.77154	8.17574	7.64465	7.36866	22
10.37106	9.58021	7.77322	8.26643	7.71843	6.39884	23
10.52876	9.70661	8.98474	8.34814	7.78432	6.43377	24
10.67478	9.82258	9.07704	8.42174	7.84314	6.46415	25
10.80998	9.92897	9.16094	8.48806	7.89566	6.49056	26
10.93516	10.02658	9.23722	8.54780	7.94255	6.51353	27
11.05108	10.11613	9.30657	8.60162	7.98442	6.53351	28
11.15841	10.19828	9.36961	8.65011	8.02181	6.55088	29
11.25778	10.27365	9.42691	8.69379	8.05518	6.56598	30
11.34980	10.34280	9.47901	8.73315	8.08499	6.57911	31
11.43500	10.40624	9.52638	8.76860	8.11159	6.59053	32
11.51389	10.46444	9.56943	8.80054	8.13535	6.60046	33
11.58693	10.51784	9.60858	8.82932	8.15656	6.60910	34
11.65457	10.56682	9.64416	8.85524	8.17550	6.61661	35
11.71719	10.61176	9.67651	8.87859	8.19241	6.62314	36
11.77518	10.56299	9.70592	8.89963	8.20751	6.62882	37
11.82887	10.69082	9.73265	8.91859	8.22099	6.63375	38
11.87858	10.72552	9.75697	8.93567	8.23303	6.63805	39
11.92461	10.75736	9.77905	8.95105	8.24378	6.64178	40

TABLE 6–5   PRESENT VALUE OF AN ANNUITY DUE OF 1 (payment at beginning of period)

$$PD_{\overline{n}|i} = 1 + \frac{1 - \dfrac{1}{(1+i)^{n-1}}}{i} = (1+i)\left(\frac{1 - p_{\overline{n}|i}}{i}\right) = (1+i)P_{\overline{n}|i}$$

(n) Periods	2%	2½%	3%	4%	5%	6%
1	1.00000	1.00000	1.00000	1.00000	1.00000	1.00000
2	1.98039	1.97561	1.97087	1.96154	1.95238	1.94340
3	2.94156	2.92742	2.91347	2.88609	2.85941	2.83339
4	3.88388	3.85602	3.82861	3.77509	3.72325	3.67301
5	4.80773	4.76197	4.71710	4.62990	4.54595	4.46411
6	5.71346	5.64583	5.57971	5.45182	5.32948	5.21246
7	6.60143	6.50813	6.41719	6.24214	6.07569	6.91732
8	7.47199	7.34939	7.23028	7.00205	6.78637	7.20979
9	8.32548	7.17014	7.01969	7.73274	7.46321	7.20979
10	9.16224	8.97087	8.78611	8.43533	8.10782	7.80169
11	9.98259	9.75206	9.53020	9.11090	8.72173	8.36009
12	10.78685	10.51421	10.25262	9.76048	9.30641	8.88687
13	11.57534	11.25776	10.95400	10.38507	9.86325	9.38384
14	12.34837	11.98319	11.63496	10.98565	10.39357	9.85268
15	13.10625	12.69091	12.29607	11.56312	10.89863	10.29498
16	13.84926	13.38138	12.93794	12.11839	11.37966	10.71225
17	14.57771	14.05500	13.56110	12.65230	11.83777	11.10590
18	15.29187	14.71220	14.16612	13.16567	12.27407	11.47726
19	15.99203	15.35336	14.75351	13.65930	12.68959	11.82760
20	16.67846	15.97899	15.32380	14.13394	13.08532	12.15812
21	17.35142	16.58916	15.87747	14.59033	13.46221	12.46992
22	18.01121	17.18455	16.41502	15.02916	13.82115	12.76408
23	18.65805	17.76541	16.93692	15.45112	14.16300	13.04158
24	19.29220	18.33211	17.44361	15.85684	14.48857	13.30338
25	19.91393	18.88499	17.93554	16.24696	14.79864	13.55036
26	20.52346	19.42438	18.41315	16.62208	15.09394	13.78336
27	21.12104	19.95061	18.87684	16.98277	15.37519	14.00317
28	21.70690	20.46401	19.32703	17.32959	15.64303	14.21053
29	22.28127	20.96489	19.76411	17.66306	15.89813	14.40616
30	22.84438	21.45355	20.18845	17.98371	16.14107	14.59072
31	23.39646	21.93029	20.60044	18.29203	16.37245	14.86483
32	23.93770	22.39541	21.00043	18.58849	16.59281	14.92909
33	24.46833	22.84918	21.38877	18.87355	16.80268	15.08404
34	24.98856	23.29188	21.76579	19.14765	17.00255	15.23023
35	25.49859	23.72379	22.13184	19.41120	17.19290	15.36814
36	25.99862	24.14516	22.48722	19.66461	17.37419	15.49825
37	26.48884	24.55625	22.83225	19.90828	17.54685	15.62099
38	26.96945	24.95732	23.16724	20.14258	17.71129	15.73678
39	27.44064	25.34860	23.49246	20.36786	17.86789	15.84602
40	27.90259	25.73034	23.80822	20.58448	18.01704	15.94907

Handwritten annotations: in the 6% column, row 5 value "4.46411" is struck through with "4.46511" written beside it; row 7 has "5" written before "6.91732"; row 8 value "7.20979" is struck through with "6.58238" written beside it.

PRESENT VALUE OF AN ANNUITY DUE OF 1 (payment at beginning of period) **TABLE 6–5**

8%	9%	10%	11%	12%	15%	(n) Periods
1.00000	1.00000	1.00000	1.00000	1.00000	1.00000	1
1.92593	1.91743	1.90909	1.90090	1.89286	1.86957	2
2.78326	2.75911	2.73554	2.71252	2.69005	2.62571	3
3.57710	3.53130	3.48685	3.44371	3.40183	3.28323	4
4.31213	4.23972	4.16986	4.10245	4.03735	3.85498	5
4.99271	4.88965	4.79079	4.69590	4.60478	4.35216	6
5.62288	5.48592	5.35526	5.23054	5.11141	4.78448	7
6.20637	6.03295	5.86842	5.71220	5.56376	5.16042	8
6.74664	6.53482	6.33493	6.14612	5.96764	5.48732	9
7.24689	6.99525	6.75902	6.53705	6.32825	6.77158	10
7.71008	7.41766	7.14457	6.88923	6.65022	6.01877	11
8.13896	7.80519	7.49506	7.20652	6.93770	7.23371	12
8.53608	8.16073	7.81369	7.49236	7.19437	6.42062	13
8.90378	8.48690	8.10336	7.74987	7.42355	6.58315	14
9.24424	8.78615	8.36669	7.98187	7.62817	6.72448	15
9.55948	9.06069	8.60608	8.19087	7.81086	6.84737	16
9.85137	9.31256	8.82371	8.37916	7.97399	6.95424	17
10.12164	9.54363	9.02155	8.54879	8.11963	7.04716	18
10.37189	9.75563	9.20141	8.70162	8.24967	7.12797	19
10.60360	9.95012	9.36492	8.83929	8.36578	7.19823	20
10.81815	10.12855	9.51356	8.96333	8.46944	7.25933	21
11.01680	10.29224	9.64869	9.07507	8.56200	7.31246	22
11.20074	10.44243	9.77154	9.17574	8.64465	7.35866	23
11.37106	10.58021	9.88322	9.26643	8.71843	7.39884	24
11.52876	10.70661	9.98474	9.34814	8.78432	7.43377	25
11.67478	10.82258	10.07704	9.42174	8.84314	7.46415	26
11.80998	10.92897	10.16094	9.48806	8.89566	7.49056	27
11.93518	11.02658	10.23722	9.54780	8.94255	7.51353	28
12.05108	11.11613	10.30657	9.60162	8.98442	7.53351	29
12.15841	11.19828	10.36961	9.65011	9.02181	7.55088	30
12.25778	11.27365	10.42691	9.69379	9.05518	7.56598	31
12.34980	11.34280	10.47901	9.73315	9.08499	7.57911	32
12.43500	11.40624	10.52638	9.76860	9.11159	7.59053	33
12.51389	11.46444	10.56943	9.80054	9.13535	7.60046	34
12.58693	11.51784	10.60858	9.82932	9.15656	7.60910	35
12.65457	11.56682	10.64416	9.87859	9.17550	7.61661	36
12.71719	11.61176	10.67651	9.87859	9.19241	7.62314	37
12.77518	11.61176	10.67651	9.89963	9.20751	7.62882	38
12.82887	11.69082	10.73265	9.91859	9.22099	7.63375	39
12.87858	11.72552	10.75697	9.93567	9.23303	7.63805	40

E6-3   Merriment Company recently signed a lease for a new office building, for a lease period of 25 years. Under the lease agreement, a security deposit of $10,000 is made, with the deposit to be returned at the expiration of the lease, with interest compounded at 10% per year.

Instructions

What amount will the company receive at the time the lease expires?

E6-4   Under the terms of his salary agreement, President Joe Leo has an option of receiving either an immediate bonus of $20,000, or a deferred bonus of $40,000, payable in 20 years. Ignoring tax considerations, and assuming a relevant interest rate of 6%, which form of settlement should President Leo accept?

E6-5   Determine the amount that must be deposited now at compound annual interest to provide the desired sum at the end of the following designated periods at the interest rate specified.

(a)   Dollars to be invested and held for 5 years at 8% per year to amount to $1,500.

(b)   Dollars to be invested and held for 8 years at 6% per year, then invested at 8% per year and held for another 5 years to amount to $10,000.

(c)   Dollars to be invested now at 12% per year and held for 30 years to have $100,000 at retirement.

E6-6   Using the appropriate interest table, compute the amounts to be invested now at compound annual interest in order to provide the following sums at the end of the designated periods.

(a)   Amount invested for 5 periods at 6% to amount to $15,000.

(b)   Amount invested for 15 periods at 10% to amount to $15,000.

(c)   Amount invested for 5 years at 6%, then at 8% for another 5 years to amount to $15,000.

E6-7   Using the appropriate interest table, compute the amounts to which the following periodic investments would accumulate at compound annual interest by the end of the last period in which an investment is made (end-of-period payments).

(a) $12,000 each period for 10 periods at 8%.

(b) $12,000 each period for 30 periods at 6%.

(c) $12,000 each period for 10 periods at 8% and then $12,000 each period for the eleventh through the twentieth periods at 10%.

E6-8   Musical Corporation, having recently issued a $10 million, ten-year bond issue, is committed to make annual sinking fund deposits of $600,000. The deposits are made on the last day of each year, and yield a return of 10%. Will the fund at the end of ten years be sufficient to retire the bonds? If not, what will the deficiency be?

E6-9   Determine the amount that Zaf Iqbal would have at the end of 1995 if investments were made under the following conditions:

(a) $1,000 is to be invested at the end of each year, 1986 through 1995, at 9% interest, compounded annually.

(b) $1,000 is to be invested at the beginning of each year, 1986 through 1995, at 9% interest, compounded annually.

E6-10   Using the appropriate interest table, answer each of the following questions. (Each case is independent of the others.)

(a)   What is the future amount of $2,500 at the end of ten periods at 8% compounded interest?

(b) What is the present value of $2,500 due eight periods hence, discounted at 10%?

(c) What is the future amount of 15 periodic payments of $2,500 each, made at the end of each period and compounded at 6%?

(d) What is the present value of $2,500 to be received at the end of each of 30 periods, discounted at 5% compound interest?

E6-11 Using the appropriate interest table, answer the following questions. (Each case is independent of the others.)

(a) What is the future amount of 15 periodic payments of $1,200 each made at the beginning of each period and compounded at 10%?

(b) What is the present value of $1,000 to be received at the beginning of each of 30 periods, discounted at 9% compound interest?

(c) What is the future amount of 10 deposits of $500 each made at the beginning of each period and compounded at 8%? (Future amount as of the end of the tenth period.)

(d) What is the present value of 8 receipts of $900 each received at the beginning of each period, discounted at 10% compound interest?

E6-12 What would you pay for a $10,000 bond that matures in 30 years and pays $1,000 a year in interest if you wanted to earn a yield of:

(a) 8%?

(b) 10%?

(c) 12%?

E6-13 Mr. Greg Garious, a super salesman contemplating retirement on his fifty-fifth birthday, decides to create a fund on a 10% basis that will enable him to withdraw $5,000 per year on June 30, beginning in 1992, and continuing through 1995. To develop this fund, Greg intends to make equal contributions on June 30 of each of the years 1988–1991.

Instructions

(a) How much must the balance of the fund equal on June 30, 1991, in order for Greg Garious to satisfy his objective?

(b) What is each of Greg's contributions to the fund?

E6-14 Using the appropriate interest table, compute the present values of the following periodic amounts due at the end of the designated periods.

(a) $18,500 receivable at the end of each period for ten periods compounded at 8%.

(b) $18,500 payments to be made at the end of each period for 16 periods at 10%.

(c) $18,500 payable at the end of the seventh, eighth, ninth, and tenth periods at 8%.

E6-15 Leslie Topple wishes to invest $10,000 on July 1, 1986, and have it accumulate to $22,000 by July 1, 1996.

Instructions

At what exact annual rate of interest must Leslie invest the $10,000? (Interpolation is required.)

E6-16 On July 17, 1986, Eric Stottrup borrowed $40,000 from his grandfather to open a clothing store. Starting July 17, 1987, Eric has to make five equal annual payments of $10,500 each to repay the loan.

Instructions

What interest rate is Eric Stottrup paying? (Interpolation is required.)

E6-17 As the purchaser of a new house, Sara Silverman has signed a mortgage note to pay the Honorable Canadian Bank and Trust Co. $5,000 every six months for 15 years, at the end of which time she will own the house. At the date the mortgage is signed the cash value of the house is $60,000. The first payment will be made six months after the date the mortgage is signed.

Instructions

Compute the exact rate of interest earned on the mortgage by the bank. (Interpolate if necessary.)

E6-18 Laura Vessely intends to invest $16,000 in a trust on January 10 of every year, 1986 to 2000, inclusive. She anticipates that interest rates will change during that period of time as follows:

January 10, 1986–January 10, 1989	5%
January 10, 1989–January 10, 1996	6%
January 10, 1996–January 10, 2000	8%

How much will Laura have in trust on January 10, 2000?

PROBLEMS

(Interest rates are per annum unless otherwise stated.)

P6-1 Using the appropriate interest table, provide the solution to each of the following four questions by computing the unknowns.
- (a) Scott Marks has $15,000 to invest today at 8% to pay a debt of $25,707.30. How many years will it take him to accumulate enough to liquidate the debt?
- (b) Geneen Deutsch has an $8,500 debt which she wishes to repay five years from today; she has $5,524.43 which she intends to invest for the five years. What rate of interest will she need to earn annually in order to accumulate enough to pay the debt?
- (c) What is the amount of the payments that Steve Robinson must make at the end of each of eight years to accumulate a fund of $30,000 by the end of the eighth year, if the fund earns 8% interest, compounded annually?
- (d) Maria Resch wishes to accumulate $200,000 by her fifty-fifth birthday so she can retire to her summer place on Lake Holiday. She wishes to accumulate this amount by equal deposits on each of her next twenty-five birthdays, her thirtieth through her fifty-fourth. What annual deposit must Maria make if the fund will earn 12% interest compounded annually?

P6-2 Answer each of these unrelated questions.

- (a) Electric Corporation bought a new machine and agreed to pay for it in equal annual instalments of $5,000 at the end of each of the next five years. Assuming that a prevailing interest rate of 15% applies to this contract, how much should Electric record as the cost of the machine?
- (b) Electric Corporation purchased a special tractor on December 31, 1986. The purchase agreement stipulated that Electric should pay $10,000 at the time of purchase and $10,000 at the end of each of the next five years. The tractor should be valued on December 31, 1986, at what amount, assuming an appropriate interest rate of 12%?
- (c) Electric Corporation wants to withdraw $30,000 (including principal) from an investment fund at the end of each year for five years. What should be the required initial investment at the beginning of the first year if the fund earns 10%?

(d) On January 1, 1986, Electric Corporation sold a building that cost $190,000 and that had accumulated depreciation of $80,000 on the date of sale. The company received as consideration a $200,000 noninterest-bearing note due on January 1, 1989. There was no established exchange price for the building, and the note had no ready market. The prevailing rate of interest for a note of this type on January 1, 1986, was 10%. At what amount should the proceeds from the sale of the building be reported?

(e) On January 1, 1986, Electric Corporation purchased 100 of the $1,000 face value, 8% ten-year bonds of Ruth, Inc. The bonds mature on January 1, 1997, and pay interest annually on January 1. Electric Corporation purchased the bonds to yield 12%. How much did Electric pay for the bonds? (Hint: Payment for bonds must consider both principal and interest.)

P6-3 Mack Aroni, a bank robber, is worried about his retirement. He decides to start a savings account. Mack deposits annually his net share of the "loot," which consists of $50,000 per year, for three years beginning January 1, 1986. Mack is arrested on January 4, 1988 (after making the third deposit) and spends the rest of 1988 and most of 1989 in jail. He escapes in September of 1989. He resumes his savings plan with semiannual deposits of $15,000 each beginning January 1, 1990. Assume that the bank's interest rate was 5% compounded annually from January 1, 1986, through January 1, 1989, and 6% annual rate compounded semiannually thereafter.

Instructions

When Mack retires on January 1, 1993 (six months after his last deposit), what is the balance in his savings account?

P6-4 John Sanford borrowed $40,000 on March 1, 1986. This amount plus accrued interest at 8% compounded semiannually is to be repaid March 1, 1996. To retire this debt, John plans to contribute to a debt retirement fund in five equal amounts starting on March 1, 1991 and for the next four years. The fund is expected to earn 10% per annum.

Instructions

How much must be contributed each year by John Sanford to provide a fund sufficient to retire the debt on March 1, 1996?

P6-5 Your client, Lowrental Leasing Company, is preparing a contract to lease a machine to Neverown Corporation for a period of 20 years. Lowrental has an investment cost of $249,245 in the machine, which has a useful life of 20 years and no salvage value at the end of that time. Your client is interested in earning a 12% return on its investment and has agreed to accept 20 equal rental payments at the end of each of the next 20 years.

Instructions

You are requested to provide Lowrental with the amount of each of the 20 rental payments that will render a 12% return on investment.

P6-6 Your client, Universal, Inc., has acquired Brockabrella Manufacturing Company in a business combination that is to be accounted for as a purchase transaction (at fair market value). Along with the assets and business of Brockabrella, Universal assumed an outstanding debenture bond issue having a principal amount of $5,000,000 with interest payable semiannually at a stated rate of 7%. Brockabrella received $4,800,000 in proceeds from the issuance five years ago. The bonds are currently 15 years from maturity. Equivalent securities command a 10% current market rate of interest.

Instructions

Your client requests your advice regarding the amount to record for the acquired bond issue.

P6-7   Hardhat, Inc. has decided to surface and maintain for ten years a vacant lot next to one of its discount retail outlets to serve as a parking lot for customers. Management is considering the following bids involving two different qualities of surfacing for a parking area of 10,000 m².
Bid A. A surface that costs $8.00/m² to install. This surface has a probable useful life of ten years and will require annual maintenance in each year except the last, at an estimated cost of 3 cents/m².
Bid B. A surface that costs $4.50/m² to install. This surface will have to be replaced at the end of five years. The annual maintenance cost on this surface is estimated at 12 cents/m² for each year of its service but the last. The replacement surface will be similar to the initial surface.

Instructions

Prepare computations showing which bid should be accepted by Hardhat, Inc. You may assume that the cost of capital is 10%, that the annual maintenance expenditures are incurred at the end of each year, and that prices are not expected to change during the next ten years.

P6-8   Terry & Melissa Corporation has a contractual debt outstanding. The corporation has available two means of settlement: either it can make immediate payment of $750,000, or it can make annual payments of $115,000 for ten years, each payment due on the last day of the year. Which method of payment do you recommend, assuming an expected effective interest rate of 10% during the future period?

P6-9   Assuming the same facts as those in Problem 6-8 except that the payments must begin now and be made on the first day of each of the ten years, what payment method would you recommend?

P6-10   Solve for the unknowns in each of the following three situations using the interest tables.

(a)   On June 1, 1986, Rich Cushing purchases 20 ha of farm land from his neighbour, Nita Doty, and agrees to pay the purchase price in five payments of $12,000 each, the first payment to be payable June 1, 1990, with interest compounded annually at the rate of 15%. What is the purchase price of the 20 ha?

(b)   Ruth Washington wishes to invest $45,201 today to insure $8,000 payments to her son at the end of each year for the next ten years. At what interest rate must the $45,201 be invested?

(c)   Mr. and Mrs. Greg Taylor have decided to provide for their handicapped son by investing $230,000 today in an annuity at 10% interest, compounded annually. They feel their son should receive approximately $25,400 per year beginning one year from today. The investment of the $230,000 will provide approximately $25,400 per year for how many years before being depleted?

P6-11   Paul Bearer died, leaving to his wife Mona an insurance policy contract that provides that the beneficiary (Mona) can choose any one of the following four options:

(a) $40,000 immediate cash.

(b) $1,600 every three months payable at the end of each quarter for ten years.

(c) $20,000 immediate cash and $800 every three months for eight years, payable at the beginning of each three-month period.

(d) $2,800 every three months for three years and $800 each quarter for the following 25 quarters, all payments payable at the end of each quarter.

Instructions

If money is worth 2% per quarter, compounded quarterly, which option would you recommend that Mona exercise?

P6-12   Provide a solution to each of the following situations by computing the unknowns. (Use the interest tables.)

(a) Jean Isham owes a debt of $15,000 from the purchase of her new sports car. The debt bears interest of 12% payable annually. Jean wishes to pay the debt and interest in four annual instalments, beginning one year hence. What equal annual instalments will pay the debt and interest?

(b) On January 1, 1986, Willie Hayseed offers to buy Barney Olfield's used combine for $18,000, payable in five equal instalments, which are to include 10% interest on the unpaid balance and a portion of the principal with the first payment to be made on January 1, 1986. How much will each payment be?

(c) Evelyn Reed invests in a $50,000 annuity insurance policy at 5% compounded annually on February 8, 1986. The first of 20 receipts from the annuity is payable to Evelyn ten years after the annuity is purchased (on February 8, 1996). What will be the amount of each of the 20 equal annual receipts?

P6-13 During the past year Edward Chablis planted a new vineyard on 100 ha of land which he leases for $15,000 a year. He has asked you, as his accountant, to assist him in determining the value of his vineyard operation.

The vineyard will bear no grapes for the first five years (1–5). In the next five years (6–10), Edward estimates that the vines will bear grapes that can be sold for $40,000 each year. For the next 20 years (11–30) he expects the harvest will provide annual revenues of $60,000. But during the last ten years (31–40) of the vineyard's life he estimates that revenues will decline to $50,000 per year.

During the first five years the annual cost of pruning, fertilizing, and caring for the vineyard is estimated at $4,000; during the years of production, 6–40, these costs will rise to $6,000 per year. The relevant market rate of interest for the entire period is 8%. Assume that all receipts and payments are made at the end of each year.

Instructions

Dolores Hass has offered to buy Edward's vineyard business by assuming the 40-year lease. On the basis of the current value of the business, what is the minimum price Edward should accept?

P6-14 Mary Ann Wetzel plans to establish an annuity arrangement whereby her three children would each receive $5,000 on December 25 of the years 1986 to 2000, inclusive. Variations in the interest rates during that period of time are estimated as follows:

December 26, 1985–December 25, 1990 12%
December 26, 1990–December 25, 1996 10%
December 26, 1996–December 25, 2000 8%

Instructions

Compute the amount that Mrs. Wetzel must invest on December 26, 1985, to assure these annual payments to her children.

P6-15 Answer the following questions related to Hadley, Inc.

(a) Hadley, Inc. loans money to Fairchild Corporation in the amount of $100,000. Hadley accepts a note due in five years at 10% compounded semiannually. After two years (and receipt of interest for two years), Hadley needs money and therefore sells the note to First Canadian Bank, which demands interest on the note of 16% compounded semiannually. What is the amount Hadley will receive on the sale of the note?

(b) Hadley, Inc. wishes to accumulate $500,000 by December 31, 1996, to retire bonds outstanding. The company deposits $100,000 on December 31, 1986, which will earn interest at 8% compounded quarterly, to help in the retirement of this debt. In addition, the company wants to know how much should be deposited at the end of each quarter for ten years to insure that $500,000 is available at the end of 1996. (The quarterly deposits will also earn a rate of 8%, compounded quarterly.) Round to even dollars.

(c) Hadley, Inc. has $80,000 to invest. The company is trying to decide between two alternative uses of the funds. One alternative provides $15,000 at the end of each year for ten years, and the other is to receive a single lump sum payment of $200,000 at the end of ten years. Which alternative should Hadley select? Assume the interest rate is constant over the entire investment.

(d) Hadley, Inc. has completed the purchase of a new computer. The fair market value of the equipment is $452,500. The purchase agreement specifies an immediate downpayment of $100,000 and semiannual payments of $71,685 beginning at the end of six months for three years. What is the interest rate, to the nearest percent, used in discounting this purchase transaction?

PART
2

ASSETS — RECOGNITION AND MEASUREMENT

PART 2

ASSETS – RECOGNITION AND MEASUREMENT

7

CASH AND RECEIVABLES

Assets are the heart of the enterprise. Assets generate revenues that turn into cash inflows that pay off creditors, compensate employees, reward owners, provide for asset replacement, and produce growth.

One characteristic of assets is their **liquidity**; that is, the amount of time that is expected to elapse until an asset is realized or otherwise converted into cash. An asset that is available for conversion into cash quickly is a liquid asset. Liquidity is one indication of an enterprise's ability to meet its obligations as they come due. An enterprise with greater liquidity is likely to have a lower risk of failure than one which does not and, generally, it has greater financial flexibility to accept unexpected new investment opportunities. Non liquidity is a cause of bankruptcy; consider the Canadian Commercial Bank, Braniff Airlines, White Farm, and numerous other industry leaders that have gone under owing to lack of liquidity. Thus accountants must provide information that allows management, creditors, and investors to assess the enterprise's current liquidity and prospective cash flows.

The primary liquid assets of most enterprises are cash, temporary investments, and receivables. This first of six asset chapters covers cash and cash equivalents, accounts receivable, and notes receivable. Temporary investments (marketable securities) are discussed in Chapter 18 along with long-term investments.

CASH

Nature and Composition of Cash

Cash, the most liquid of assets, is the standard medium of exchange, providing the basis for measuring and accounting for all other items. It is generally classified as a current asset. To be reported as **"cash,"** it must be readily available for the payment of current obligations, and free from any contractual restriction that limits its use in satisfying debts.

Cash consists of coin, currency, and available funds on deposit at the bank. Such negotiable instruments as money orders, certified cheques, cashiers' cheques, personal cheques, and bank drafts are also viewed as cash.

Savings accounts are usually classified as cash, although the bank has a legal right to demand notice before withdrawal; but, since the privilege of prior notice is rarely exercised by banks, savings accounts are considered cash.

Certificates of deposit, deposit receipts, treasury bills, commercial and finance company paper, similar types of deposits and "short-term paper"[1] that provide small investors with an opportunity to earn high rates of interest are more appropriately classified as temporary investments than as cash. The logic for this classification is that these situations usually contain restrictions or penalties on their conversion to cash.

A classification title that has recently become popular is **"cash and cash equivalents."** Cash and cash equivalents generally include cash items plus certificates of deposit, and similar types of deposits (even though a possibility exists that redemption prior to maturity will result in some type of penalty).

Items that present classification problems are postdated cheques, IOUs, travel advances, postage stamps, and special cash funds. **Postdated cheques and IOUs** are treated as receivables. **Travel advances** are properly treated as receivables if the advances are to be collected from the employees or deducted from their salaries. Otherwise, classification of the travel advance as a prepaid expense is more appropriate. **Postage stamps on hand** are classified as part of office supplies inventory or as a prepaid expense. **Petty cash funds and change funds** are included in current assets as cash because these funds are used to meet current operating expenses and to liquidate current liabilities.

Cash that is restricted or in escrow is segregated from the general cash account. The **restricted cash** is classified either in the current asset or in the long-term asset section, depending on the date of availability for disbursement. If the cash is to be used (within a year or the operating cycle, whichever is longer) for payment of existing or maturing obligations, classification in the current section is appropriate. On the other hand, if the cash is to be held for a longer period of time, the restricted cash is shown in the long-term section of the balance sheet. Generally, cash to be held for long periods is invested and not held in the form of cash.

---

[1]A variety of "short-term paper" is available for investment. **Certificates of deposit** (CDs) represent formal evidence of indebtedness, issued by a bank, subject to withdrawal under the specific terms of the instrument. Issued in $10,000 and $100,000 denominations, they mature in 30 to 360 days and generally pay interest at the short-term interest rate in effect at date of issuance. **Savings certificates** are issued by banks and trust companies in various denominations. The interest rate is tied to current savings rates. **Treasury bills** are government obligations generally having 91- and 182-day maturities; they are sold on a discount basis in $10,000 denominations at weekly government auctions. **Commercial paper** is a short-term note (30 to 270 days) issued by corporations with good credit ratings: Issued in $5,000 and $10,000 denominations, these notes generally yield a higher rate than treasury bills.

However, in those infrequent circumstances when cash is set aside for noncurrent purposes, it should be classified in the long-term section of the balance sheet.

In summary, cash includes the medium of exchange and most negotiable instruments. If the item cannot be converted immediately to coin or currency, it is separately classified as an investment, as a receivable, or as a prepaid expense. Cash that is not available for payment of currently maturing liabilities is segregated and classified in the long-term asset section.

Compensating Balances

Occasionally, banks and other lending institutions may require customers to whom they lend money or extend credit to maintain minimum cash balances on deposit. These minimum balances are called **compensating balances**. By requiring a compensating balance, the bank achieves an effective interest rate on a loan that is higher than the stated rate because of the restricted amount that must remain on deposit.

In order to provide financial statement users with adequate information, accountants should report **restricted deposits** held as compensating balances against short-term borrowing arrangements separately among the "cash and cash items" in current assets. Restricted deposits held as compensating balances against **long-term** borrowing arrangements should be separately classified as noncurrent assets in either the "investments" or "other assets" sections, using such a caption as "Cash on deposit maintained as compensating balance."

In cases where compensating balance arrangements exist without agreements that restrict the use of cash amounts shown on the balance sheet, the arrangements and the amounts involved should be described in notes to the financial statements. Compensating balances that are maintained under an agreement to assure future credit availability must also be disclosed separately in the notes together with the amount and duration of such an agreement.

Management and Control of Cash

Cash presents special management and control problems not only because it enters into a great many transactions but also for these reasons:

1. **Cash is the single asset readily convertible into any other type of asset.** It is easily concealed and transported, and it is almost universally desired. Correct accounting for cash transactions therefore requires that controls be established to insure that cash belonging to the enterprise is not improperly converted to personal use by someone in or connected with the enterprise.

2. **The amount of cash owned by an enterprise should be regulated carefully so that neither too much nor too little is available at any time.** An adequate supply must always be maintained without tying up too much of the firm's resources. As the medium of exchange, cash is required to pay for all assets and services purchased by the company and to meet all its obligations as they mature. The disbursement of cash is thus a daily occurrence, and a sufficient fund of cash must be kept on hand to meet these needs. On the other hand, cash as such is not a productive asset; it earns no return. Hence it is undesirable to keep on hand a supply of cash any larger than necessary to meet day-by-day needs, with a reasonable margin for emergencies. Cash in excess of what is needed should be invested either in income-producing securities or in other productive assets.

Two problems of accounting for cash transactions face the accounting department: (1) proper controls must be established to insure that no unauthorized transactions are entered into by officers or employees; (2) information necessary to the proper management of cash on hand and cash transactions must be provided. Most companies fix the responsibility for obtaining proper record control over cash transactions in the accounting department. Record control, of course, is not possible without adequate physical control; therefore the accounting department must take an interest in preventing intentional or unintentional mistakes in cash transactions. Even with sophisticated control devices errors can and do happen. The *Wall Street Journal* ran a story entitled "A $7.8 Million Error Has a Happy Ending for a Horrified Bank," which described how Manufacturers Hanover Trust Co., one of the largest banks in the United States, mailed about $7.8 million too much in cash dividends to its shareholders. Happily most of the monies were subsequently returned.

Regulating the amount of cash on hand is primarily a management problem, but accountants must be able to provide the information required by management for regulating cash on hand through the special transactions of borrowing or investing.

Using Bank Accounts   A company can vary the number and location of banks and the types of bank accounts to obtain desired control objectives. For large companies operating in multiple locations, the location of bank accounts can be important. Establishing collection accounts in strategic locations can accelerate the flow of cash into the company by shortening the time between a customer's mailing of a payment and the company's receipt and use of the cash. Multiple collection centres are generally used to reduce the size of a company's **collection float,** which is the difference between the amount on deposit according to the company's records and the amount of collected cash according to the bank's record.

The **general chequing account** is the principal bank account in most companies and frequently the only bank account in small businesses. Cash is deposited in and disbursed from this account as all transactions are cycled through it. Deposits from and disbursements to all other bank accounts are made through the general chequing account.

Imprest bank accounts are used to make a specific amount of cash available for a limited purpose. The account acts as a clearing account for a large volume of cheques or for a specific type of cheque. The specific and intended amount to be cleared through the imprest account is deposited therein by transferring that amount from the general chequing account or other source. Imprest bank accounts are often used for disbursing payroll cheques, dividends, commissions, bonuses, confidential expenses (e.g., officers' salaries), and travel expenses.

Lockbox accounts are frequently used by large, multilocation companies to make collections in cities within areas of heaviest customer billing. The company rents a local post office box and authorizes a local bank to pick up the remittances mailed to that box number. The bank empties the box at least once a day and immediately credits the company's account for collections. The greatest advantage of a lockbox is that it accelerates the availability of collected cash. Generally, in a lockbox arrangement the bank microfilms the cheques for record purposes and provides the company with a deposit slip, a list of collections, and any other correspondence mailed by the customer. If the control over cash is improved and if the income generated from accelerating the receipt of funds exceeds the cost of the lockbox system, it is considered worth undertaking.

Electronic Funds Transfer (EFT)   Business and individuals in North America use about 35 billion cheques annually to pay their bills. This process is not without its cost. Preparing, issuing, receiving, and clearing a cheque through the banking system is estimated to cost between 55 cents and $1.00, and the cost is rising rapidly with inflation.[2] It is not surprising, therefore, that in this electronic age new methods are being developed to transfer funds among parties without the use and movement of paper. We are entering the age of **electronic funds transfer (EFT)**, a process that uses wire, telephone, telegraph, computer (maybe even satellite), or other electronic device rather than paper to make instantaneous transfers of funds.

Canada's major banks are now in the process of developing national automated teller machine (ATM) networks. The pace of development has been so hectic that greater strides were made in 1984 than in the whole decade of the 1970s. National electronic banking networks have consolidated most retail banking services in much the same way that Visa and MasterCard unified consumer credit services; but the new ATM electronic networks will be far more powerful than the credit card networks of Visa and MasterCard because they will operate with the **debit card**, which can give access to all of a customer's accounts within a bank. Using an ATM, customers are able to withdraw cash and make deposits to both their chequing and savings accounts, as well as to transfer funds between accounts and make balance inquiries. By linking ATMs nationally, the networks are building the first electronic funds transfer system capable of processing large-volume retail fund transfers between computers at different banks. Already the use of cheques has disappeared for certain fund transfers. For example, none of the authors of this book receives a formal payroll cheque from his employer university; the university sends his bank a magnetic tape that transfers money from the university's account to his account. Within a short time the services provided by these ATM networks will accommodate electronic transfers from home and retail point-of-sale terminals. When this occurs, the banks will have the power to replace many of the estimated 35 billion cheques with electronic transactions.

Safeguards and controls must be built into these electronic systems to reduce the exposure to massive frauds that come with heavy reliance on computer technology, which makes possible funds transfer without personal intervention.

The Imprest Petty Cash System   Almost every company finds it necessary to pay small amounts for a great many things such as employees' lunches and taxi fare, purchase of minor office supply items, and small expense payments. It is frequently impractical to require that such disbursements be made by cheque, and yet some control over them is important. A common method of obtaining reasonable control, simplicity of operation, and general adherence to the rule of disbursement by cheque is the **imprest system** for petty cash disbursements.

This is how the system works:

1. An individual is designated as the petty cash custodian and given a small amount of cash as a fund from which small payments are made. The entry in the general journal would be:

Petty Cash Fund   300
   Cash   300
    (To establish a petty cash fund)

[2]Alfred Hunt, *Corporate Cash Management Including Electronic Funds Transfer* (New York: AMACOM, 1978), p. 142.

2. As disbursements are made, the petty cash custodian obtains signed receipts from each individual to whom cash is paid. If possible, evidence of the disbursements should be attached to the petty cash receipt. (Petty cash transactions are not recorded until the fund is reimbursed, and then such entries are recorded by someone in accounting, not the petty cash custodian.)

3. When the supply of cash runs low, the custodian presents to the general cashier a request for reimbursement supported by the petty cash receipts and other evidence that has been obtained for all disbursements, and receives a company cheque drawn to "Cash" to replenish the fund. The journal entry would be:

Office Supplies Expense	42	
Postage Expense	53	
Entertainment Expense	76	
Cash Over and Short	2	
Cash		173
(To replenish petty cash fund)		

4. If it is decided that the amount of cash in the petty cash fund is excessive, an adjustment may be made as follows (lowering the fund balance from $300 to $250):

Cash	50	
Petty Cash		50
(To reduce petty cash fund)		

Entries are made to the Petty Cash account only to increase or decrease the size of the fund or to adjust the petty cash account balance and related expenses if the fund is not replenished at year end. The reimbursement entry does not affect the Petty Cash account, but it does affect the amount of petty cash on hand.

A **Cash Over and Short** account is used when the fund fails to prove out. If cash proves out short (that is, the sum of the vouchers and cash in the fund is less than the imprest amount), the shortage is debited to the Cash Over and Short account. If it proves out over, the overage is credited to Cash Over and Short. This account is left open until the end of the year, when it is closed and generally shown on the income statement as a miscellaneous expense or income.

There are usually expense items in the fund except immediately after reimbursement; therefore, if accurate financial statements are desired, the funds must be reimbursed at the end of each accounting period and also when nearly depleted.

Under the imprest system the petty cash custodian is responsible at all times for the amount of the fund on hand either as cash or in the form of signed vouchers. These vouchers provide the evidence required by the disbursing officer to issue a reimbursement cheque. Two additional procedures are followed to obtain more complete control over the petty cash fund:

1. Surprise counts of the funds are made from time to time by a superior of the petty cash custodian to determine that the fund is being accounted for satisfactorily.

2. Petty cash vouchers are cancelled or mutilated after they have been submitted for reimbursement, so that they cannot be used to secure a second and improper reimbursement.

Physical Protection of Cash Balances   Cash receipts and cash disbursements must be safeguarded through internal control measures, just as cash on hand or in banks must be protected. Adequate control of receipts and disbursements is a part of the protection of cash balances, because receipts become cash on hand and cash disbursements are made from cash in banks. Certain other procedures, however, should be given some consideration.

Physical protection of cash is so elementary a necessity that it requires little discussion. Every effort should be made to hold the cash on hand in the office to a minimum. A petty cash fund, perhaps change funds, and the current day's receipts should be all that is on hand at any one time, and these funds should be kept, insofar as possible, in a vault, safe, or locked cash drawer. Each day's receipts should be transmitted intact to the bank as soon as practicable.

Related to the problem of protecting cash balances is the problem of accurately stating the amount of available cash both in internal reports for management and in financial statements for external use.

Every company has, in its cash books and cash account, a record of all cash received and disbursed and the balance. Due to the many cash transactions, however, errors or omissions may be made in keeping this record. Therefore, it is necessary to prove periodically the balance shown in the general ledger. Cash actually present in the office—petty cash, change funds, and undeposited receipts —can be counted and the amount determined in that way, for comparison with the company records. Cash on deposit with a bank is not available for count and is proved through the **preparation of a bank reconciliation;** that is, a reconciliation of the company's record of cash in the bank and the bank's record of the company's cash that is on deposit.

Reconciliation of Bank Balances   Generally, once a month the bank supplies each customer with a **bank statement** (a copy of the bank's account with the customer) together with the customer's cheques that have been paid by the bank during the month. If no errors were made by the bank or the customer, if all deposits made and all cheques drawn by the customer reached the bank within the same month, and if no other transactions occurred that affected either the company's or the bank's record of cash, the balance of cash reported by the bank to the customer should be the same as that shown in the customer's own records as of the same date. Thus, comparison of the balance shown on the bank statement with the balance shown in the customer's own records should verify the latter.

This condition seldom occurs for one or more of the following reasons:

1. **Deposits in transit.** End-of-month deposits of cash recorded on the depositor's books in one month are received and recorded by the bank in the following month.
2. **Outstanding cheques.** Cheques written by the depositor are recorded when written, but because they have not cleared the bank, the bank has not yet recorded them.
3. **Bank charges.** Charges recorded by the bank against the depositor's balance for such items as bank services, printing cheques, not-sufficient-funds (NSF) cheques, and safety-deposit box rentals. The depositor may not be aware of these charges until receipt of the bank statement.
4. **Bank credits.** Collections or deposits by the bank for the benefit of the depositor that may be unknown to the depositor until receipt of the bank statement (e.g., collection of a note for the depositor and interest earned on certificates of deposit).
5. **Bank or depositor errors.** Errors on the part of the bank or the depositor cause the bank balance to disagree with the depositor's book balance.

Hence, there regularly are differences between the depositor's record of cash and the bank's record, and the two must be reconciled to determine the nature of the differences between the two amounts.

A **bank reconciliation,** then, is a schedule indicating and explaining any differences between the bank's and the company's records of cash. If the difference results only from transactions with customers not yet recorded by the bank, the company's record of cash is considered correct; but, if some part of the difference arises from other items, either the bank's records or the customer's records or both must be adjusted.

Two forms of bank reconciliation may be prepared. One form reconciles from the bank statement balance to the book balance, or *vice versa*. The other, more widely used, form reconciles from both the bank balance and the book balance to a correct cash balance; this form of reconciliation and the common reconciling items are shown below.

BANK RECONCILIATION AND CONTENT

Balance per bank statement (end of period)		$$$
Add: Deposits in transit	$$	
Bank errors that understate the bank statement balance	$$	$$
		$$$
Deduct: Outstanding cheques	$$	
Bank errors that overstate the bank		
statement balance	$$	$$
Corrected cash balance		$$$
Balance per depositor's books		$$$
Add: Bank credits and collections not yet		
recorded in the books	$$	
Book errors that understate the book balance	$$	$$
		$$$
Deduct: Bank charges not yet recorded in the books	$$	
Book errors that overstate the book balance	$$	$$
Corrected cash balance		$$$

This form of reconciliation consists of two sections, (1) ''balance per bank statement'' and (2) ''balance per depositor's books,'' with both sections ending with the same ''corrected cash balance.'' The corrected cash balance is the amount to which the books must be adjusted and is the amount reported on the balance sheet. The adjusting journal entries are prepared from the addition and deduction items appearing in the ''balance per depositor's books.'' Any errors attributable to the bank should be called to the bank's attention immediately upon discovery.

To illustrate, Nugget Mining Company's books show a cash balance of $20,502 at the Bank of Montreal on November 30, 1986. The bank statement covering the month of November showed an ending balance of $22,190. An examination of Nugget's accounting records and November bank statement identified the following reconciling items:

1. A deposit of $3,680 was mailed November 30 but does not appear on the bank statement.

2. Cheques written in November but not charged to the November bank statement are:

Cheque #7327	$ 150
#7348	4,820
#7349	31

3. Interest of $600 on Quebec Hydro bonds held by the bank for Nugget was collected by the bank on Nov. 20 for Nugget, but has not been recorded by Nugget.

4. Bank service charges of $18 are not yet recorded on Nugget's books.

5. One of Nugget's customers' cheques for $220 was returned with the bank statement and marked ''NSF.'' The bank treated this bad cheque as a disbursement.

6. Nugget discovered that cheque #7322, written in November for $131 in payment of an account payable, was recorded in the books incorrectly as $311.
7. A cheque issued by Nugent Oil Co. in the amount of $175 accompanied the bank statement and was incorrectly charged to Nugget Mining.

The reconciliation of bank and book balances to the corrected cash balance of $21,044 would appear as follows when completed:

Nugget Mining Company
BANK RECONCILIATION
Bank of Montreal, November 30, 1986

Balance per bank statement (end of period)		$22,190
Add: Deposit in transit	$3,680	
Bank error—incorrect cheque charged to account by bank	175	3,855
		26,045
Deduct: Outstanding cheques		
#7327	$ 150	
#7348	4,820	
#7349	31	5,001
Corrected cash balance		$21,044
Balance per books		$20,502
Add: Interest collected by the bank	$ 600	
Error in recording cheque #7322	180	780
		$21,282
Deduct: Bank service charges	18	
NSF cheque returned	220	238
Corrected cash balance		$21,044

The journal entries required to adjust and correct Nugget Mining's books at November 30, 1986, are taken from the items in the "Balance per books" section and are as follows:

November 30

Cash	600	
Interest Revenue		600

(To record interest on Quebec Hydro bonds, collected by bank)

November 30

Cash	180	
Accounts Payable		180

(To correct error in recording amount of cheque #7322)

November 30

Office Expense—Bank Charges	18	
Cash		18

(To record bank service charges for November)

November 30

Accounts receivable	220	
Cash		220

(To record customer's cheque returned NSF)

When the entries are posted, Nugget's cash account will have a balance of $21,044. Nugget should return the Nugent Oil Co. cheque to the Bank of Montreal, informing the bank of the error.

Another widely used form of bank reconciliation is the **four-column reconciliation** ("proof of cash"), which is discussed and illustrated in Appendix 7A.

RECEIVABLES

Receivables are claims held against customers and others for money, goods, or services. For financial statement purposes, receivables are classified as either **current** (short-term) or noncurrent (long-term). Those receivables expected to be collected within a year or the current operating cycle, whichever is longer, are classified as **current receivables;** all other receivables are classified as **noncurrent.** Receivables are further classified in the balance sheet as either trade receivables or nontrade receivables.

Trade receivables are amounts owed by customers for goods sold and services rendered as part of the normal operations of the business. Trade receivables, usually the most significant receivable an enterprise possesses, may be subclassified into accounts receivable and notes receivable. **Accounts receivable** are nonwritten (oral) promises to pay for goods and services sold, are normally collectible within 30 to 60 days, and are represented by "open accounts" resulting from short-term extensions of credit. **Notes receivable** are written promises to pay a certain sum of money on a specified future date and may arise from sales, financing, or other transactions. Notes may be short-term or long-term.

Nontrade receivables arise from a variety of transactions and are oral or written promises to pay or deliver. Some examples of nontrade receivables are:

1. Advances to officers and employees.
2. Advances to subsidiaries.
3. Deposits to cover potential damages or losses.
4. Deposits as a guarantee of performance or payment.
5. Dividends and interest receivable.
6. Share subscriptions receivable.
7. Claims against
   (a) Insurance companies for casualties sustained.
   (b) Defendants under suit.
   (c) Government bodies for tax refunds.
   (d) Common carriers for damaged or lost goods.
   (e) Creditors for returned, damaged, or lost goods.
   (f) Customers for returnable items (crates, containers, etc.).

The remainder of this chapter is divided into two parts—accounts receivable and notes receivable. In our coverage of accounts receivable, emphasis is given to trade accounts receivable because of their importance. Our coverage of notes receivable includes both short-term and long-term notes.

Accounts Receivable

The three primary accounting problems associated with accounts receivable are:

1. Recording receivables.

2. Valuation of receivables.
3. Disposition of receivables.

Recording Receivables   Once the receivable transaction is identified, the appropriate amount to record must be determined. Receivables are recorded at their face value; that is, the amount due from the debtor (a customer or a borrower). **The face value or the amount due is the exchange price established in the transaction** which is generally evidenced by some types of business document, often an invoice. Determination of the exchange price requires the proper treatment of such items as trade discounts, cash discounts, and interest.

Trade Discount. Customers are often quoted prices on the basis of list or catalogue prices that may be subject to a trade or quantity discount. Trade discounts are used to avoid frequent changes in catalogues, or to quote different prices for different quantities purchased, or to hide the true invoice price from competitors. They are commonly quoted in percentages. For example, if your textbook has a list price of $40.00 and the publisher sells it to college book stores for list less a 30% discount, the receivable recorded by the publisher is $28.00 per textbook. The normal pricing practice is simply to deduct the discount from the list price and bill the customer the net amount.

For another example, the producers of Nabob recently sold a 285 g jar of its instant coffee that had a list price of $4.65 to various supermarkets for $3.90, a trade discount of approximately 16%. The supermarkets in turn sold the instant coffee for $3.99 per jar. Nabob would record the receivable and related sales revenue at $3.90 per jar, not $4.65.

Cash Discounts (Sales Discounts)   Cash discounts (sales discounts) are offered as an inducement for prompt payment and communicated in terms that read 2/10, n/30 (2% if paid within 10 days, gross amount due in 30 days), or 2/10, E.O.M. (2% if paid within 10 days of the end of the month). Companies that fail to take sales discounts are usually not employing their money advantageously. An enterprise that receives a 1% reduction in the sales price for payment within 10 days, total payment due within 30 days, is effectively earning 18.25% (.01 ÷ 20/365), or at least avoiding that rate of interest cost. For this reason, it is usual for companies to take the discount unless their cash is severely limited.

The easiest and most commonly used method of recording sales and related sales discount transactions is to enter the receivable and sale at the gross amount. Under this method, sales discounts are recognized in the accounts only when payment is received within the discount period. Sales discounts would then be shown in the income statement as a deduction from sales to arrive at net sales.

Some accountants contend that sales discounts are not actually discounts but penalties added to an established price to encourage prompt payment. That is, the seller offers sales on account at a slightly higher price than if selling for cash, and the increase is offset by the cash discount offered. Thus, customers who pay within the discount period purchase at the cash price; those who pay after expiration of the discount period are penalized because they must pay an amount in excess of the cash price. If this approach is adopted, sales and receivables are recorded net, and any discounts not taken are subsequently debited to Accounts Receivable and credited to Sales Discounts Forfeited. To illustrate the difference between the gross and net methods, assume the following transactions.

Entries under Gross and Net Methods

Gross Method			Net Method		
Sale of $10,000, terms 2/10, n/30:					
Accounts Receivable	10,000		Accounts Receivable	9,800	
Sales		10,000	Sales		9,800
Payment of $4,000 received within discount period:					
Cash	3,920		Cash	3,920	
Sales Discount	80		Accounts receivable		3,920
Accounts Receivable		4,000			
Payment of $6,000 received after discount period:					
Cash	6,000		Accounts Receivable	120	
Accounts Receivable		6,000	Sales Discounts Forfeited		120
			Cash	6,000	
			Accounts Receivable		6,000

As noted earlier, if the gross method is employed, sales discounts should be reported as a deduction from sales in the income statement. If the net method is used, Sales Discounts Forfeited should be considered as an "other revenue" item. Theoretically, the recognition of Sales Discounts Forfeited is correct, because the receivable is stated closer to its realizable value and the net sale figure measures the revenue earned from the sale. As a practical matter, the net method is seldom used because it requires additional analysis and bookkeeping. For example, adjusting entries are required under the net method to record sales discounts forfeited on accounts receivable that have passed the discount period.

Nonrecognition of Interest Element   When expected cash receipts require a waiting period, the receivable face amount is not worth the amount that is ultimately received. To illustrate, assume that a company makes a sale on account for $1,000 with payment due in four months. Also assume that the applicable rate of interest in this case is 12% and that payment is made at the end of the four months. The present value of that receivable is not $1,000 but $961.54 ($1,000 × .96154, Table 6-2, n = 1, i = 4). In other words, $1,000 to be received four months from now is not the same as $1,000 received today.

Any revenue after the period of sale is interest revenue (actual and implicit). Accountants have chosen to ignore this idea for the most part in connection with accounts receivable because the amount of the discount is not usually material in relation to the net income for the period. Unearned discounts, finance charges, and interest included in the face amount of a receivable are shown as deductions from the related receivables, whenever they are material.[3] In general practice, trade receivables are excluded from present value considerations.[4]

[3]"Status of Accounting Research Bulletins," *Opinions of the Accounting Principles Board No. 6* (New York: AICPA, 1965), par. 14.

[4]In the United States, *APB Opinion No. 21*, "Interest on Receivables and Payables," provides that all receivables are subject to present value measurement techniques and interest imputation, if necessary, except for the following specifically excluded types:
1. Normal accounts receivable due within one year.
2. Security deposits, retainages, advances, or progress payments.
3. Transactions between parent and subsidiary.
4. Receivables due at some determinable future date.

Valuation of Receivables

Having recorded the receivables at their face value (the amount due), the accountant then faces the problem of reporting them in the financial statements. Reporting of receivables involves (1) their classification and (2) their valuation on the balance sheet. Classification, as already discussed, involves a determination of the length of time the receivable will be outstanding. Receivables expected to be collected within a year or the operating cycle, whichever is longer, are classified as current; all other receivables are classified as long-term.

The valuation of receivables is considerably more complex. Short-term receivables are valued and reported at **net realizable value,** which is the net amount expected to be received in cash (not necessarily the amount legally receivable). Determining net realizable value requires an estimation of uncollectible receivables, along with returns and allowances to be granted. The methods of estimating these reductions or offsets to the amount due are discussed below.

Uncollectible Accounts Receivable

As one accountant so aptly noted: "The credit manager's idea of heaven probably would envisage a situation in which everybody (eventually) paid his debts."[5] Sales on any basis other than for cash make subsequent failure to collect the account a real possibility. An uncollectible account receivable is a loss of revenue that requires, through proper entry in the accounts, a decrease in the asset accounts receivable and a related decrease in income and shareholders' equity.

The chief problem in recording uncollectible accounts receivable is establishing the time at which to record the loss. Two general procedures are in use:

1. No entry is made until a specific account has definitely been established as uncollectible. Then the loss is recorded by crediting Accounts Receivable and debiting Bad Debt Expense. This is normally referred to as the "direct write-off" method for receivables.
2. An estimate is made of the expected uncollectible accounts from all sales made on account or from the total of outstanding receivables. This estimate is entered as an expense and a reduction in accounts receivable (via an increase in the allowance account) in the period in which the sale is recorded. This is usually called the "allowance" method.

The direct write-off method records the bad debt in the year it is determined that a specific receivable cannot be collected; the allowance method enters the expense on an estimated basis in the accounting period in which the sales on account are made. Either method is acceptable for tax purposes, as long as it is consistently applied.

Supporters of the **direct write-off method** contend that facts, not estimates, are recorded. It assumes that a good account receivable resulted from each sale, and that later events proved certain accounts to be uncollectible and worthless. From a practical standpoint this method is simple and convenient to apply, although we must recognize that receivables do not generally become worthless at an identifiable moment of time. The direct write-off is theoretically deficient because it usually does not match costs with revenues of the period, nor does it result in receivables being stated at estimated realizable value on the balance sheet. As a result, its use

[5]"Accounting for Contingencies," *Statement of Financial Accounting Standards No. 5* (Stamford, Conn.: FASB, 1975), par. 8.

is not considered appropriate, except when the uncollectible amount is immaterial.

Advocates of the **allowance method** believe that bad debt expense should be recorded in the same period as the sale to obtain a proper matching of expenses and revenues and to achieve a proper carrying value for accounts receivable at the end of the period. They support the position that although estimates are involved, the percentage of receivables that will not be collected can be predicted from past experiences, present market conditions, and an analysis of the outstanding balances.

Because the collectibility is considered a loss contingency, the allowance method is appropriate only in situations where it is probable that an asset has been impaired and that the amount of the loss can be reasonably estimated. Accountants, for the most part, have accepted the challenge of estimating the proportion of uncollectible accounts. A receivable is a prospective cash inflow, and the probability of its collection must be considered in valuing this inflow. These estimates normally are made either (1) on the basis of percentage of sales, or (2) on the basis of outstanding receivables.

Percentage of Sales (Income Statement Approach)   When the percentage-of-sales approach is employed, a company's past experience with uncollectible accounts is analyzed. If there is a fairly stable relationship between previous years' charge sales and bad debts, that relationship can be turned into a percentage and used to determine this year's bad debt expense.

The percentage-of-sales method matches costs with revenues because it relates the charge to the period in which the sale is recorded. To illustrate, assume that E. T. Elsner's, Inc. estimates from past experience that about 2% of charge sales become uncollectible. If E. T. Elsner's, Inc. had charge sales of $400,000 in 1986, the entry to record bad debt expense using the percentage-of-sales method is as follows:

Bad Debt Expense	8,000	
Allowance for Doubtful Accounts		8,000

The Allowance for Doubtful Accounts is a valuation account (i.e., contra asset) and is subtracted from the trade receivables on the balance sheet. The amount of bad debt expense and the related credit to the allowance account is unaffected by any balance currently existing in the allowance account. This method is frequently referred to as the income statement approach, because the bad debt expense is related to a nominal account (Sales) and any balance in the allowance is ignored. A proper matching of cost and revenues is therefore achieved.

Percentage of Outstanding Receivables (Balance Sheet Approach)   Using past experience, a company can estimate the percentage of its outstanding receivables that will become uncollectible, without identifying specific accounts. This procedure provides a reasonably accurate estimate of the realizable value of the receivables at any time, but does not fit the concept of matching cost and revenues. Rather, its objective is to report receivables in the balance sheet at net realizable values, and it accomplishes that objective reasonably well; hence it is referred to as the balance sheet approach.

The percentage of receivables may be applied using one **composite rate** that reflects an estimate of the uncollectible receivables. Another approach that is more sensitive to the actual status of the accounts receivable is achieved by setting up an **aging schedule** and applying a different percentage to the various age categories established. The percentages used are developed from past experience. An aging schedule is a method frequently used in practice. This schedule indicates which accounts require special attention by providing the age of such accounts receivable. The following schedule of Wilson & Co. is an example.

Wilson & Co. AGING SCHEDULE					
Name of Customer	Balance Dec. 31	Under 60 days	61–90 days	91–120 days	Over 120 days
Western Stainless Steel Corp.	$ 98,000	$ 80,000	$18,000	$	$
Brockway Steel Co.	320,000	320,000			
Freeport Sheet & Tube Co.	55,000				55,000
Allegheny Iron Works	74,000	60,000		14,000	
	$547,000	$460,000	$18,000	$14,000	$55,000

Summary			
Age	Amount	Percentage Estimated to be Uncollectible	Required Balance in Allowance
Under 60 days old	$460,000	1%	$ 4,600
61-90 days old	18,000	5%	900
91-120 days old	14,000	10%	1,400
Over 120 days	55,000	20%	11,000
Year-end balance of allowance for doubtful accounts			$17,900

The amount $17,900 would be the bad debt expense to be reported for this year, assuming that no balance existed in the allowance account. To change the illustration slightly, assume that the allowance account had a credit balance of $800 before adjustment. In this case, the amount to be added to the allowance account is $17,100 ($17,900 - $800), and the following entry is made:

Bad Debt Expense	17,100	
Allowance for Doubtful Accounts		17,100

The balance in the allowance account is therefore correctly stated at $17,900. If the allowance account balance before adjustment had a debit balance of $200, then the amount to be recorded for bad debt expense would be $18,100 ($17,900 desired balance + $200 debit balance). In the percentage of outstanding receivables method, the balance in the allowance account cannot be ignored because the percentage is related to a real account (accounts receivable).

An aging schedule is usually prepared not only to determine the bad debt expense but also as a control device to determine the composition of receivables and to identify delinquent accounts. The estimated loss percentage developed for each category is based on previous loss experience and the advice of credit department personnel. Regardless of whether a composite rate or an aging schedule is employed, the primary objective of the percentage of outstanding receivables method for financial statement purposes is to report receivables in the balance sheet at net realizable value. However, it is deficient in that it may not match the bad debt expense to the period in which the sale takes place.

In summary, the percentage-of-sales method results in a direct entry to an expense account and the allowance account because the amount calculated is related to the year's sales and not to the balance remaining in accounts receivable. Generally, the percentage-of-sales approach provides the best results from a matching viewpoint, but the percentage of receivables method results in a more accurate valuation of receivables on the balance sheet. The following diagram relates these methods to the basic theory:

Comparison of Bases of Estimating Uncollectibles	
Percentage of Sales	Percentage of Receivables
Matching	Net Realizable Value
Sales ◄— —► Bad Debts Expense	Accounts Receivable ◄— —► Allowance for Bad Debts

If no consistent pattern of uncollectible accounts to sales is established, other approaches might be desirable. The account description employed for the allowance account is usually "Allowance for Doubtful Accounts," "Allowance for Bad Debts," or simply "Allowance."[6]

Writing Off an Uncollectible Account   When it has been determined that it is very unlikely that a particular account will be collected, that account should be written off. This requires crediting Accounts Receivable and debiting the Allowance for Doubtful Accounts for the amount of the delinquent customer's account. For example, assume that a customer who has owed Hi Value Hardware Ltd. $1,200 since last year has just declared bankruptcy. The journal entry to record the write-off of this account would be:

Allowance for Doubtful Accounts   1,200
   Accounts Receivable   1,200

It is important to note that writing off an account recognizes the fact that the ultimate collection appears unlikely and not that efforts to collect will cease.

Collection of Accounts Receivable Written Off   If a collection is made on a receivable that was previously written off, the procedure to be followed is first to reestablish the receivable by debiting Accounts Receivable and crediting Allowance for Doubtful Accounts. An entry is then made to debit Cash and credit the customer's account in the amount of the remittance received.

If the direct write-off approach is employed, the amount collected is debited to Cash and credited to a revenue account entitled Uncollectible Amounts Recovered, with proper notation in the customer's account.

Special Allowance Accounts

To match expenses to sales revenues properly, it is sometimes necessary to establish allowance accounts. These allowance accounts are reported as contra accounts to accounts receivable and establish the receivables at **net realizable value.** The most common allowances are:

1. Allowance for sales returns and allowances.
2. Allowance for collection expenses.

[6]*Accounting Trends and Techniques* (Toronto: CICA, 1984), for example, indicates that approximately 90% of the companies surveyed used "allowance" in their description. Approximately 10%, in addition to deducting an allowance for doubtful accounts from receivables, also deducted amounts for unearned discounts, finance charges, or sales returns.

Sales Returns and Allowances   Many accountants question the soundness of recording returns and allowances in the current period when they are derived from sales made in the preceding period. Normally, however, the amount of mismatched returns and allowances is not material, if such items are handled consistently from year to year. Yet, if a company completes a few special orders involving large amounts near the end of the accounting period, returns and allowances should be anticipated in the period of the sale to avoid distorting the income statement of the current period.

As an example, Astro Turf Limited recognizes that approximately 5% of its $1,000,000 trade sales outstanding are returned or some adjustment is made to the sales price. Omission of a $50,000 charge could have a material effect on net income for the period.

The entry to reflect this anticipated sales return and allowance is:

Sales Returns and Allowances	50,000	
Allowance for Sales Returns and Allowances		50,000

Sales returns and allowances are reported as an offset to sales revenue in the income statement. Returns and allowances are accumulated separately instead of debited directly to the sales account simply to let the business manager and the statement reader know the magnitude of the returns and allowances. The allowance is an asset valuation account (contra asset) and is deducted from total accounts receivable; the receivables are thus stated at net realizable value.

In most cases, the inclusion in the income statement of all returns and allowances made during the period, whether or not they resulted from the current period's sales, is an acceptable accounting procedure justified on the basis of practicality and immateriality.[7]

Collection Expense   A similar concept holds true for collection expense. If significant costs are incurred to collect the open accounts receivable at the end of the year, an allowance for collection expenses should be recorded. For example, Sears, Roebuck and Company reports its receivables as follows:

Sears, Roebuck and Company	
Receivables	
Customer instalment accounts receivable	
Easy payment accounts	$2,221,017,167
Revolving charge accounts	1,372,874,725
	3,593,891,892
Other customer accounts	101,904,882
Miscellaneous accounts and notes receivable	96,446,334
	3,792,243,108
Less: Allowance for collection expenses and losses on customer accounts	236,826,866
	$3,555,416,242

[7]An interesting sidelight to the entire problem of returns and allowances has developed in recent years. Determination of when a sale is a sale has become difficult, because in certain circumstances the seller is exposed to such a high risk of ownership through possible return of the property that the entire transaction is nullified and the sale not recognized. Such situations have developed particularly in sales to related parties. This subject is discussed in more detail in Chapters 8 and 19.

OMIT

Disposition of Accounts Receivable

Accounts receivable are liquidated and removed from the books in the normal course of events as a result of payment. As generally expected, the amounts due are collected in the form of cash and the operating cycle is completed, but as credit sales and receivables have grown in size and significance, the "normal course of events" has changed. The following paragraphs recount a short history of the changing liquidation of receivables.

The significance and character of accounts receivable parallels the development of credit as a tool to facilitate all types of business transactions. From the centuries-old use of factoring (selling of receivables) by the textile industry through the post-World War II growth in consumer instalment debt, and the modern development of commercial finance companies, accounts receivable have grown to become one of the largest and highest-quality assets for a majority of industrial companies. As such, receivables are used extensively as a basis to obtain additional funds. For example, in order to advance the timing of the cash receipt from receivables, the owner may transfer the receivables to another company or other third party for cash, thereby shortening the cash-to-cash operating cycle.

In many industries, providing sales financing for customers is virtually mandatory for competitive reasons. In the sale of such durable goods as automobiles, trucks, industrial and farm equipment, computers, and appliances, a large majority of the sales are on the instalment contract basis. Many of the major companies in these industries have created wholly owned subsidiaries to serve as vehicles for accounts receivable financing. For example, General Motors of Canada Ltd. has its General Motors Acceptance Corp. of Canada (GMAC), Sears has its Sears Acceptance Corp., and Chrysler Corporation of Canada has its Chrysler Finance Corporation.

A more recent development has been the use of such outside, third-party entities as banks or other financial organizations, in large-scale transfer-of-receivables transactions. Included in these are the arrangements that every size and type of business makes with third-party credit card companies—MasterCard, VISA, American Express, Diners Club, and others. In times of tight and expensive money, firms turn to the transfer of receivables as a means to obtain essential funds because access to normal credit markets is not available, or if available, the cost of the funds is prohibitive.

The transfer of accounts receivable to a third party for cash is generally accomplished in one of two ways:[8]

1. Assignment of accounts receivable (pledging a security interest in accounts receivable).
2. Sale (factoring) of accounts receivable.

Assignment of Accounts Receivable

In an assignment of accounts receivable, the owner of the receivables (the assignor) borrows cash from a lender (the assignee) by writing a promissory note that contains a provision designating the accounts receivable as collateral. If the note is not paid when due, the assignee has the right to convert the collateral to cash; that is, to collect the receivables. The term **pledging** is sometimes used instead of assignment to describe this transaction.

---

[8]*Accounting Trends and Techniques* (1983) reports that, of the 600 companies surveyed, 26 assigned receivables and 96 sold their receivables.

General Assignment   If the assignment is general, all the receivables serve as collateral for the note. New receivables can be substituted for the ones collected. To illustrate, Machlin Motor Company assigns its accounts receivable to First City Finance Company as collateral for a loan of $946,000. The entry to record this transaction is as follows:

Cash	946,000	
Notes Payable		946,000

No special entries are made to the receivable accounts to record the assignment. Information concerning the assigned receivables is disclosed in a note or in a parenthetical explanation. To illustrate, United Air Industries, Inc. reports its general assignment in the following manner:

United Air Industries, Inc.

Current Assets

Trade accounts, notes, and other receivables, less
  allowance of $95,000 for doubtful accounts (Note B) $8,695,372

Note B. **Other Notes Payable.** Under the terms of the amended revolving credit agreement with a commercial finance company, the corporation may borrow up to 90% of eligible trade accounts receivable and 60% of certain inventories. The maximum that may be borrowed under this agreement is $7,000,000. The corporation's trade accounts, notes, and other receivables and inventories are pledged as collateral.

Specific Assignment In a specific assignment, the borrower and lender enter into an agreement as to (1) who is to receive the collections—the borrower or the lender, (2) the finance charges (which are in addition to the interest on the note), (3) the specific accounts that serve as security, and (4) notification or nonnotification of account debtors. In this case the total of the specifically assigned accounts should be transferred to a special general ledger control account, and the individual accounts in the subsidiary ledger should be segregated or clearly marked as assigned. Collections on the assigned accounts are generally made by the assignor. To illustrate, on March 1, 1986, Howat Mills Ltd. assigns a group of its accounts receivable totalling $700,000 to the Royal Bank as collateral for a $500,000 note. Howat Mills will continue to make collections of the accounts receivable; the account debtors are not notified of the assignment. The Royal Bank assesses a finance charge of 1% of the accounts receivable assigned and interest on the note of 12%.Settlement is made monthly for all cash collected on the assigned receivables.

Entries for Assignment of Specific Accounts Receivable

Howat Mills, Inc.   Royal Bank

Assignment of accounts receivable and issuance of note on March 1, 1986:

Cash	493,000	Notes Receivable	500,000	
Finance Charge	7,000*	Finance Revenue		7,000*
Accounts Receivable		Cash		493,000
Assigned	700,000			
Notes Payable	500,000			
Accounts Receivable	700,000			

*(1% × $700,000)

Collection in March of $440,000 of assigned accounts less cash discounts of $6,000. In addition sales returns of $14,000 were received:

Cash	434,000		
Sales Discounts	6,000		
Sales Returns	14,000	(no entry)	
Accounts Receivable			
Assigned		454,000	
($440,000 + $14,000 = $454,000)			

Remitted March collection plus accrued interest to the bank on April 1:

Interest Expense	5,000*	Cash	439,000
Notes Payable	434,000	Interest Revenue	5,000
Cash	439,000	Notes Receivable	434,000
*($500,000 × .12 × 1/12)			

Collection in April of the balance of assigned accounts less $2,000 written off as uncollectible:

Cash	244,000		
Allowance for			
Doubtful Accounts	2,000	(no entry)	
Accounts Receivable			
Assigned	246,000*		
*($700,000 − $454,000)			

Remitted the balance due of $66,000 ($500,000 − $434,000) on the note plus interest on May 1:

Interest Expense	660*	Cash	66,660
Notes Payable	66,000	Interest Revenue	660*
Cash	66,660	Notes Receivable	66,000
*($66,000 × .12 × 1/12)			

If the account debtors had been notified to make remittance directly to the Royal Bank, the bank would have communicated monthly on the amount of collections and sales discount on the assigned accounts and the amount of interest due. A liability account ("Payable to Howat Mills, Inc.") would be used by the bank to record cash collections during the period. The bank would not record the assigned accounts receivable as an asset of the bank. Upon full payment of principal and interest on the note, the bank would remit to Howat Mills any cash collections in excess of the note along with any uncollected accounts.

Specifically assigned accounts receivable should be reported in the financial statements as a separate asset account if material. The assignor's equity in the assigned accounts should be disclosed. For instance, Howat Mills, Inc. has equity of $200,000 in its assigned receivables at March 1 ($700,000 − $500,000).

Sale (Factoring) of Accounts Receivable

Factoring is the sale of accounts receivable. Factors are finance companies or banks that buy receivables from businesses for a fee and then collect the remittances directly from the customers. Factoring, traditionally associated with the textiles, apparel, footwear, furniture, and home furnishing industries, has now spread to many other types of businesses and represents billions of dollars in North America. As an illustration, Sears, Roebuck & Co. recently arranged to sell $550 million of customer accounts receivable at 99.015% of face value. Credit cards like MasterCard and VISA are a type of factoring arrangement.

The **holder** of receivables frequently resorts to a sale because it is the only reasonable source of funds. Also, a firm may have to sell its receivables as opposed to borrowing and assigning them in order to avoid violating existing lending agreements. The **purchaser** of receivables may be prompted to enter into the purchase in order to obtain the legal protection afforded a purchaser of assets (e.g., rights of ownership) as opposed to the lesser rights afforded a secured creditor. In addition, banks and other lending institutions may be forced to purchase receivables because of legal lending limit restrictions; that is, they cannot make any additional loans but they can buy receivables and charge a fee for this service.

Factoring arrangements vary widely, but typically the purchaser charges a commission of from 3/4 to 1 1/2% of the net amount of receivables purchased (except for the credit card factoring which costs the seller 4 to 5%). The following diagram illustrates in sequential process the basic procedures in factoring.

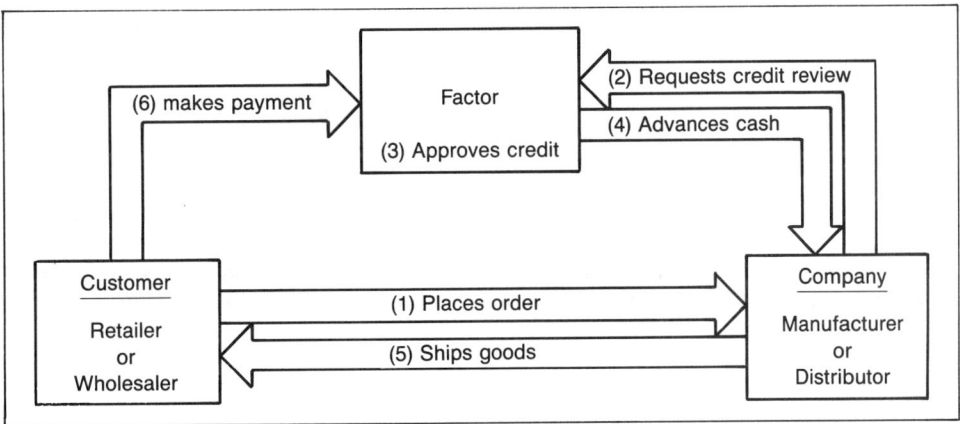

In many factoring transactions the company sells the receivables without recourse, but in even more transactions, receivables are sold with recourse.[9]

Transfer without Recourse   When a seller sells receivables **without recourse,** the purchaser assumes the risk of collectibility and absorbs any credit losses. The transfer of accounts receivable in a nonrecourse transaction is both in form (transfer of title) and substance (transfer of the risk and reward) an outright sale of receivables.

In nonrecourse transactions, as in any sale of assets, Cash is debited for the proceeds, Accounts Receivable is credited for the carrying value of the receivables, and the difference, reduced by any provision for probable adjustments (discounts, returns, allowances, and so on), is recognized as a Loss on the Sale of Receivables. A "Due from Factor" account is used by the seller to account for the amount of proceeds retained by the factor to cover the probable adjustments in the form of sales discounts, sales returns, and sales allowances.

To illustrate, Crest Textiles Ltd. factors $500,000 of accounts receivable with Commercial Factors Ltd. on a **without-recourse** basis. On May 1 the receivable

[9]**Recourse** is the right of a transferee of receivables to receive payment from the transferor of those receivables for (a) failure of the debtors to pay when due, (b) the effects of prepayments, or (c) adjustments resulting from defects in the eligibility of the transferred receivables. See "Reporting by Transferors for Transfers of Receivables with Recourse," *Statement of Financial Accounting Standards No. 77* (Stamford, Conn.: FASB, 1983), p. 7.

records are transferred to Commercial Factors Ltd., which will receive the collections. Commercial Factors assesses a finance charge of 3% of the amount of accounts receivable and retains an amount equal to 5% of the accounts receivable. Crest Textiles handles returned goods, claims for defective goods (allowances), and disputes concerning shipments. The factor handles the sales discounts and absorbs the credit losses. Based on analysis, Commercial Factors allows $4,100 for uncollectible accounts.

Entries for Factored Receivables without Recourse

Crest Textiles Ltd.			Commercial Factors Ltd.		
Sales of accounts receivable without recourse on May 1:					
Cash	460,000		Accounts Receivable	500,000	
Due from Factor	25,000*		Due to Crest Textiles		25,000
Loss on Sale of			Financing Revenue		15,000
Receivables	15,000**		Cash		460,000
Accounts Receivable		500,000			
			Bad Debt Expense	4,100	
			Allowance for		
			Doubtful Accounts		4,100
*(5% × $500,000)					
**(3% × $500,000)					

Transactions in May and June—collections of $483,800 by factor; sales returns and allowances of $9,500; sales discounts taken of $2,600; and uncollectibles of $4,100 are written off by the factor.

Crest Textiles Ltd.			Commercial Factors Ltd.		
Sales Returns			Cash	483,800	
and Allowance	9,500		Due to Crest Textiles	12,100	
Sales Discounts	2,600		Accounts Receivable		495,900
Due from Factor		12,100	Allowance for Doubtful		
			Accounts	4,100	
			Accounts Receivable		4,100

Final settlement between Crest Textiles and Commercial Factors:

Crest Textiles Ltd.			Commercial Factors Ltd.		
Cash	12,900		Due to Crest Textiles	12,900	
Due from Factor		12,900	Cash		12,900
($25,000 − $9,500 − $2,600)					

As shown in the above entries, the factor's income is the difference between the financing revenue of $15,000 and the bad debt expense of $4,100. As indicated earlier, in a without-recourse transfer of receivables, the factor absorbs the loss from uncollectibles. Crest Textiles absorbs the cost of sales discounts and sales returns and allowances.

Transfer with Recourse If the seller sells receivables with recourse, the seller guarantees payment to the purchaser in the event the debtor does not pay. The question is: Is this a **sale transaction,** in which a gain or loss should be recognized immediately? Or, is the sale of receivables on a with-recourse basis a **borrowing transaction,** in which the difference between the proceeds and the receivables is a financing cost (interest) that should be amortized over the term of the receivables?

In the United States the FASB requires that a transfer of receivables with recourse be accounted for and reported as a sale, and a gain or loss recognized, if all three of the following conditions are met:[10]

1. The transferor surrenders control of the future economic benefits of the receivables.
2. The transferor's obligation under the recourse provisions can be reasonably estimated.
3. The transferee cannot require the transferor to repurchase the receivables.[11]

If the transfer with recourse does not meet these three conditions, the amount of the proceeds from the transfer of the receivable is recorded and reported as a liability. That is, instead of crediting the receivables account for the transfer, Cash is debited and a current liability is credited in a like amount; the liability might be titled "Liability on Transferred Accounts Receivable."

To illustrate the differences in accounting for a transfer of receivables with recourse that is in one case a sale and in another case a borrowing, we will use the same data for both cases as that which appeared in the previous Crest Textiles/ Commercial Factors illustration. (We have chosen to use the same data for purposes of comparability, even though the situations in real life would dictate different rates, risks, and so on between with-recourse and without-recourse transactions.) Crest estimates that $4,100 of the accounts transferred to Commercial Factors will not be paid by the debtors.

First, note that in the with-recourse borrowing situation (page 332), Crest Textiles credited a liability on May 1 instead of crediting accounts receivable. **Second,** in both with-recourse cases Crest Textiles reimburses the factor for the $4,100 of uncollectible accounts and records the bad debt expense on its books, whereas in the without-recourse illustration (page 330), Commercial Factors absorbed the loss due to uncollectibility. However, because accounts receivable are removed from the books when the transfer is treated as a sale, it is meaningless to credit an allowance account when recognizing the bad debt expense. Hence, Crest immediately credited Due from Factor for the $4,100, thereby reimbursing the factor for the bad debts anticipated. **Third,** Crest recognized interest expense of $15,000 over the two months the receivables were outstanding instead of recording the loss on sale of $15,000 at May 1.

Notes Receivable

A note receivable is supported by a formal **promissory note** which is a written promise to pay a certain sum of money at a specific future date. Such a note is a negotiable instrument that is signed by a **maker** in favour of a designated **payee,** who may legally and readily sell or otherwise transfer the note to others. Although all notes bear an interest element owing to the time value of money, notes are classified as interest-bearing or noninterest-bearing. **Interest-bearing notes** contain a stated rate, while **noninterest-bearing notes** include the interest as part of its face amount instead of stating it explicitly.

---

[10]"Reporting by Transferors for Transfers of Receivables with Recourse," *ibid.*, par. 5

[11]The transferor's ability to initiate repurchase, however, does not violate a sale accounting. For example, because Motorola, Inc. wishes to maintain long-term service relationships with its customers, it reserves the unlimited right to repurchase receivables contracts that it has sold to its factor, Associates Capital Services Corporation. This arrangement allows Motorola to restructure existing receivables contracts, to accept customers' prepayments, and to trade in or redesign customers' products, and still account for the receivables transfer as a sale.

Crest Textiles Ltd. Entries for Factored Receivables **with** Recourse

Treated as a Sale by Crest			Treated as a Borrowing by Crest		

Transfer of accounts receivable on May 1:

Cash	460,000		Cash	460,000	
Due from Factor	25,000*		Due from Factor	25,000*	
Loss on Sale of			Discount on Transferred		
Receivables	15,000**		Accounts Receivable	15,000**	
Accounts Receivable		500,000	Liability on Transferred		
			Accounts Receivable		500,000

*(5% × $500,000)
**(3% × $500,000)

Recognition of doubtful accounts on May 1:

Bad Debt Expense	4,100		Bad Debt Expense	4,100	
Due from Factor		4,100	Allowance for Doubtful		
			Accounts		4,100

Transactions in May and June—collections of $483,800 by the factor; sales returns and allowances of $9,500; sales discounts taken of $2,600; and uncollectibles of $4,100 materialize:

Sales Returns and			Sales Returns and		
Allowance	9,500		Allowance	9,500	
Sales Discounts	2,600		Sales Discounts	2,600	
Due from Factor		12,100	Due from Factor		12,100
			Allowance for Doubtful		
			Accounts	4,100	
			Due from Factor		4,100
			Liability on Transferred		
			Accounts Receivable	500,000	
			Accounts Receivable		500,000
			($483,800 + $9,500 + $2,600 + $4,100)		
			Interest Expense	15,000	
			Discount on Transferred		
			Accounts Receivable		15,000

Final settlement between Crest Textiles and the Factor:

Cash	8,800		Cash	8,800	
Due from Factor		8,800*	Due from Factor		8,800*

*($25,000 − $9,500 − $2,600 − $4,100)

Notes receivable are frequently accepted from customers who need to extend the payment period on an outstanding receivable. Signed notes are sometimes required of high-risk or new customers; and in some industries (e.g., the pleasure- and sport-boat industry) all credit sales are supported by signed notes. The majority of notes, however, originate from lending transactions. As with accounts receivable, the basic issues in accounting for notes receivable are:

1. Recording of notes receivable.
2. Valuation of notes receivable.
3. Disposition of notes receivable.

Recording Interest-Bearing Notes   Notes receivable should be valued and reported at the **present value** of the cash expected to be collected. When the effective interest on an interest-bearing note is equal to its stated rate, the note sells at its face value. When the stated rate is different from the effective interest, the cash exchanged (present value) will be different from the face value of the note. The difference between the face value and the cash exchanged is a discount or a premium that should be recorded and amortized over the life of a note to approximate the effective interest rate.

To illustrate these differences, assume that Bigelow Corp. lends Scandinavian Imports $10,000 in exchange for a $10,000, three-year note bearing interest at 10% annually. The market rate of interest for a note of similar risk is also 10%. The present value or selling price of the note is computed as follows:

Face value of the note	$10,000
Present value of the principal:	
$10,000 \times p_{\overline{3}|\,10\%} = $10,000 \times .75132$ $7,513	
Present value of the interest:	
$1,000 \times P_{\overline{3}|\,10\%} = $1,000 \times 2.48685$ 2,487	
Present value of the note	10,000
Difference	$ -0-

In this case, because the effective rate of interest and the stated rate are the same, the present value of the note and the face value are the same; that is, $10,000. The receipt of the note is recorded by Bigelow Corp. as follows:

Notes Receivable	10,000	
Cash		10,000

Bigelow Corp. would recognize the interest earned each year as follows:

Cash	1,000	
Interest Revenue		1,000

If the market rate of interest for Scandinavian Imports' $10,000, 10% note had been 12%, the present value would have been computed as follows:

Face value of the note		$10,000
Present value of the principal:		
$10,000 \times p_{\overline{3}|\,12\%} = $10,000 \times .71178$	$7,118	
Present value of the interest:		
$1,000 \times P_{\overline{3}|\,12\%} = $1,000 \times 2.40182$	2,402	
Present value of the note		9,520
Difference (Discount)		$ 480

In this case, because the effective rate of interest (12%) is greater than the stated rate, the present value of the note is less than the face value; that is, the note was exchanged at a discount. The receipt of the note at a discount is recorded by Bigelow as follows:

Notes Receivable	10,000	
Discount on Notes Receivable		480
Cash		9,520

The discount on notes receivable is a valuation account and is reported on the balance sheet as a contra-asset account to notes receivable. The discount is amortized, and interest revenue is recognized annually by the effective interest method. The three-year discount amortization and interest revenue schedule is shown below:

	Cash Interest 10%	Effective Interest 12%	Discount Amortized	Unamortized Discount Balance	Present Value of Note
	Schedule of Note Discount Amortization Effective Interest Method 10% Note Discounted at 12%				
Date of issue				$480	$9,520
End of year 1	$1,000[a]	$1,142[b]	$142[c]	338[d]	9,662[e]
End of year 2	1,000	1,159	159	179	9,821
End of year 3	1,000	1,179	179	-0-	10,000
	$3,000	$3,480	$480		

[a]$10,000 × 10% = $1,000   [d]$480 − $142 = $338
[b]$9,520 × 12% = $1,142   [e]$9,520 + $142 = $9,662
[c]$1,142 − $1,000 = $142

Receipt of the annual interest and amortization of the discount (unearned interest) for the first year is recorded by Bigelow as follows (amounts per amortization schedule):

Cash	1,000	
Discount on Notes Receivable	142	
Interest Revenue		1,142

If the note were issued at a premium (where the present value exceeds the face value), the premium would be recorded as a debit and amortized by the effective interest method over the life of the note as annual reductions in the amount of interest revenue recognized.

Recording Noninterest- or Unreasonable Interest-Bearing Notes   Interest is an inherent and natural ingredient in notes receivable, most especially when the note is long-term. It is unrealistic and improbable for any business to lend money interest free. Yet during the 1960s and 1970s numerous business transactions that were material in amount were consummated either with no apparent interest or with a very low stated interest rate.

The accounting profession in the United States responded to this practice by issuing a standard that insures proper accounting for transactions where the form does not reflect the economic substance of the arrangement because of failure to provide for a realistic interest rate on monies receivable or payable in the future.[12] Whenever the face amount of the note does not reasonably represent the present value of the consideration given or received in the exchange, the accountant must evaluate the entire arrangement to determine the amounts involved for properly recording the exchange and subsequent related interest. This circumstance is most apparent when the note is noninterest-bearing or has a stated interest rate that is different from the rate of interest appropriate for the transaction at the date of issuance. Unless such notes are recorded at present value, the sales price and profit

[12]"Interest on Receivables and Payables," *Opinions of the Accounting Principles Board No. 21* (New York: AICPA, 1971), par. 12.

to the seller (accepting the note) and the purchase price and cost to the buyer (issuing the note) in the year of the transaction are misstated. In addition, the interest revenue and interest expense in subsequent periods are also misstated.

In discussing the appropriate accounting for notes receivable having an unrealistic stated interest rate, the following categories are important:

1. Notes received solely for cash.
2. Notes received for cash, but with some right or privilege also being exchanged. For example, a corporation may lend a supplier cash that is receivable five years hence with no stated interest, in exchange for which the supplier agrees to make products available to the lender at lower than prevailing market prices.
3. Notes received in a noncash exchange for property, goods, or services.

Notes Received Solely for Cash   If a noninterest-bearing note is received solely for cash, it is presumed to have a present value measured by the cash paid to the issuer of the note. The difference between the face amount and the present value (cash paid) is recorded as a discount or premium and amortized to interest revenue over the life of the note. **When a note is issued solely for cash, the interest factor is assumed to be the stated or coupon rate plus or minus the amortization of the discount or premium.** Interest other than that provided by the coupon or stated rate plus or minus amortization of the discount or premium should not be considered unreasonable because the note issued for cash has a present value equal to cash.

Notes Received for Cash and Other Rights   The lender may also accept a **note in exchange for cash and other rights and privileges**. For example, Ideal Equipment Co. accepts a five-year $100,000 noninterest-bearing note from Outland Steel Corp. plus the right to purchase 10,000 tonnes of steel at 93% of regular selling price in exchange for $100,000 in cash. If the current rate of interest applicable to this kind of transaction is 10%, the acceptance of the note is recorded and the present value of the note is computed as follows:

Notes Receivable	100,000	
Prepaid Purchases	37,908	
Discount on Notes Receivable		37,908*
Cash		100,000

*Present value = $100,000 \times p_{\overline{5}|\,10\%} = \$100{,}000 \times .62092 = \$62{,}092$;
Discount = $100,000 - $62,092 = $37,908.

The difference between the $62,092 present value of the note and its maturity value of $100,000 represents interest of $37,908 which is amortized to interest revenue over the five-year life of the note under the effective interest method. The excess of the $100,000 cash paid over the $62,092 present value of the note represents an asset, prepaid purchases, that is allocated to purchases or inventory in proportion to the number of tonnes of steel purchased each year as compared to the next 10,000 tonnes to be purchased. For example, if 3,000 tonnes of steel were purchased during the first year of the five-year discount period, the following entry would be recorded by Ideal Equipment:

Purchases (Inventory)	11,372	
Prepaid Purchases		11,372
(3,000/10,000 $\times$ $37,908)		

Although the amounts recorded as prepaid purchases and as discount on notes receivable are the same at $37,908, they are written off dissimilarly—prepaid purchases in the ratio of the tonnes purchased during the year to the total 10,000 tonnes and the discount by the effective interest method. The value of the right or privilege, in this case the price discount, may aid in determining the interest implicit in the transaction.

Notes Received for Property, Goods, or Services   When a **note is received in exchange for property, goods, or services** in a bargained transaction entered into at arm's length, the stated interest rate is presumed to be fair unless

1. no interest rate is stated
2. the stated interest rate is unreasonable
3. the stated face amount of the note is materially different from the current cash sales price for the same or similar items or from the current market value of the debt instrument.

In these circumstances the present value of the note is measured by the fair value of the property, goods, or services or by an amount that reasonably approximates the market value of the note. To illustrate, Oasis Development Co. sold a corner lot to Rusty Pelican as a restaurant site and accepted in exchange a five-year note having a maturity value of $35,247. The land originally cost Oasis $14,000 and had an appraised fair value of $20,000. An imputed interest rate of 12% is determined by using the fair market value of the land as the present value of the note. The entry to record the sale is as follows:

Notes Receivable	35,247	
Discount on Notes Receivable ($35,247 − $20,000)		15,247
Land		14,000
Gain on Sale of Land ($20,000 − $14,000)		6,000

The discount is amortized to interest revenue over the five-year life of the note under the effective interest method.

Imputing an Interest Rate   In each of the previously illustrated situations, the effective or real interest rate was evident or determinable by such other factors in the exchange as the fair market value of what was either given or received; but if the fair value of the property, goods, services, or other rights is not determinable; and, if the note has no ready market, the problem of determining the present value of the note is more difficult. To estimate the present value of a note under such circumstances, an applicable interest rate is approximated that may differ from the stated interest rate. This process of interest rate approximation is called **imputation**, and the resulting interest rate is called an **imputed interest rate.** The imputed interest rate is used to establish the present value of the note by discounting, at that rate, all future receipts (interest and principal) on the note.

APB Opinion No. 21 provides the following general guidelines for imputing the appropriate interest rate:

> The prevailing rate for similar instruments of issuers with similar credit ratings will normally help determine the appropriate interest rate for determining the present value of a specific note at its date of issuance. In any event, the rate used for valuation purposes will normally be at least equal to the rate at which the debtor can obtain financing of a similar nature from other sources at the date of the transaction. The objective is to approximate the rate which would have resulted if an independent borrower and an independent lender had negotiated a similar transaction under comparable terms and conditions with the option to pay the cash price upon purchase or to give a note for the amount of the purchase which bears the prevailing rate of interest to maturity.[13]

[13]*Ibid.*, par. 13.

The choice of a rate may be affected specifically by the credit standing of the issuer, restrictive covenants, the collateral, payment, and other terms pertaining to the debt, and the existing prime interest rate. The interest rate is imputed upon receipt of the note; any subsequent changes in prevailing interest rates are ignored.

Accounting for Imputed Interest   On December 31, 1986, Brown Interiors Limited rendered architectural services and accepted in exchange a long-term promissory note with a face value of $550,000, a due date of December 31, 1991, and a stated interest rate of 2%, interest receivable at the end of each year. The fair value of the services is not readily determinable and the note is not readily marketable. When the credit rating of the maker of the note, the absence of collateral, the prime interest rate at that date, and the prevailing interest on the maker's outstanding debt are considered, an 8% interest rate is imputed as appropriate in this circumstance. The present value of the note and the imputed fair value of the architechtural services are determined as follows:

Face value of the note		$550,000
Present value of $550,000 due in 5 years		
at 8%—$550,000 × $p_{\overline{5}\rvert 8\%}$ = $550,000 × .068058	$374,319	
Present value of $11,000 ($550,000 × .02) payable		
annually for 5 years at 8% =		
$11,000 × $P_{\overline{5}\rvert 8\%}$ = $11,000 × 3.99271	43,920	
Present value of the note		418,239
Discount		$131,761

The receipt of the note in exchange for the services is recorded as follows:

December 31, 1986

Notes Receivable	550,000	
Discount on Notes Receivable		131,761
Revenue from Services		418,239

The five-year amortization schedule appears below.

Schedule of Note Discount Amortization
Effective Interest Method
2% Note Discounted at 8% (Imputed)

Date	Cash Interest (2%)	Effective Interest (8%)	Discount Amortized	Unamortized Discount Balance	Present Value of Note
12/31/86				$131,761	$418,239
12/31/87	$11,000[a]	$ 33,459[b]	$ 22,459[c]	109,302[d]	440,698[e]
12/31/88	11,000	35,256	24,256	85,046	464,954
12/31/89	11,000	37,196	26,196	58,850	491,150
12/31/90	11,000	39,292	28,292	30,558	519,442
12/31/91	11,000	41,558[f]	30,558	-0-	550,000
	$55,000	$186,761	$131,761		

[a]$550,000 × 2% = $11,000
[b]$418,239 × 8% = $33,459
[c]$33,459 − $11,000 = $22,459

[d]$131,750 − $22,459 = $109,291
[e]$418,239 + $22,459 = $440,689
[f]$3 adjustment to compensate for rounding.

Receipt of the annual interest and amortization of the discount is recorded as follows:

December 31, 1987

Cash	11,000	
Discount on Notes Receivable	22,459	
Interest Revenue		33,459

In the case of a **noninterest-bearing note** where a reasonable rate must be imputed, the periodic cash receipt for interest would be zero; therefore, the entry would be simply for the imputed interest—debit Discount on Notes Receivable and credit Interest Revenue.

Valuation of Notes Receivable

As with accounts receivable, notes receivable are valued and reported at net realizable value. That is, the notes reported at their face amount are offset by any necessary allowances. The primary allowance account for notes receivable is Allowance for Doubtful Accounts. The computations and estimations involved in valuing notes receivable at net realizable value and in recording the proper amount of bad debt expense and the related allowance are exactly the same as for accounts receivable. That is, a percentage of sales revenue or an analysis of the receivables is used to estimate the amount of uncollectibles.

Notes receivable can pose additional estimation problems because these receivables are often longer in term. As a result, the difficulty of estimating collection is increased. As an example, we need only look at the problems of many financial institutions, most notably our largest banks, in collecting their receivables from energy loans, agricultural loans, and loans to less developed countries.

Our purpose here is to indicate that the same procedures used earlier to compute the allowance for doubtful accounts apply here, but that estimation may be more difficult. Allowance accounts for such items as sales returns and allowances (where appropriate) and collection expenses also can be established if deemed material.

OMIT

Disposition of Notes Receivable

Notes are usually held to maturity date at which time the face value plus any accrued interest is collected and the note is removed from the accounts. Not infrequently, however, the holder of the note speeds up the conversion to cash by discounting the note before maturity date.

Discounting Notes Receivable   Notes receivable, because of their greater negotiability, are readily converted to cash through discounting at a bank. The bank accepts the note and pays the holder cash in an amount equal to the note's maturity value less a discount that represents the bank's financing (interest) charge. At maturity the bank collects the face value of the note plus interest from the maker.

Notes may be discounted with or without recourse. In those rare instances when a note is discounted **without recourse** (a qualified endorsement), the notes receivable account is credited as in an outright sale. The transferor conveys all the risks and benefits of ownership to the transferee in discounting a note without recourse. Having transferred all the risks and benefits of ownership, the transferor no longer has an asset. In a nonrecourse transfer the difference between the book carrying value of the note and the cash proceeds is recorded as a gain or loss on sale.

The more common transaction is the discounting of a note at a bank **with recourse.** If the maker fails to pay at maturity, the bank presents the note to the transferor (endorser), who is then liable for payment. In most discounting transactions, the bank will insist on having recourse. Is the discounting of a note a sale with a gain or loss to be recognized and a contingent liability to be disclosed? Or is it a borrowing transaction that is accounted for by retaining the notes receivable in the accounts, reporting the endorser's obligation among the current liabilities, and recognizing interest expense or interest revenue?

As discussed in connection with accounts receivable factored with recourse, good accounting practice requires that the transfer (discounting) of notes receivable with recourse be accounted for and reported as a sale, and a gain and loss recognized, if all three of the conditions listed on page 331 are met. Likewise, if the transfer with recourse does not meet those same three conditions, the transaction is accounted for as a borrowing with a liability recorded and reported along with interest expense.

Whether the transfer is a sale or a borrowing, accounting for a discounted note receivable is a six-step process:

1. Compute the maturity value of the note (face value plus interest to maturity).
2. Compute the discount (the bank's discount rate times the maturity value times the time to maturity).
3. Compute the proceeds (maturity value minus the bank's discount).
4. Compute the book carrying value of the note (face value plus interest accrued to date of discounting).
5. Compute the gain or loss, if a sale, or the interest revenue expense, if a borrowing (proceeds minus the book carrying value).
6. Record the journal entry.

To illustrate, on July 30, the Reliable Appliance Ltd. discounts at the bank a customer's 3-month $10,000 note receivable dated June 30 and bearing interest at 12%; the bank accepts the note **with recourse** and discounts it at 15%. The maturity value, discount, proceeds, book carrying value, and interest element are computed as follows:

Discounting with Recourse		
	Face value of note	$10,000.00
	Plus: Interest ($10,000 × .12 × 3/12)	300.00
Step 1.	Maturity value	10,300.00
Step 2.	Less: Discount ($10,300 × .15 × 2/12)	257.50
Step 3.	Proceeds	10,042.50
Step 4.	Book carrying value [$10,000 + ($10,000 × .12 × 1/12)]	10,100.00
Step 5.	Interest expense or loss on sale	$ 57.50

Entries for Sale or Borrowing			
Discounting a Sale		**Discounting a Borrowing**	
Receipt of a 3-month note from an overdue customer, June 30:			
Notes Receivable 10,000.00		Notes Receivable 10,000.00	
Accounts Receivable	10,000.00	Accounts Receivable	10,000.00

Interest accrued (June 30-July 30) at date of discounting, July 30:

Interest Receivable	100.00		Interest Receivable	100.00
Interest Revenue		100.00	Interest Revenue	100.00

Discounting of notes receivable with recourse, July 30:

Cash	10,042.50		Cash	10,042.50
Loss on Sale of Note	57.50		Interest Expense	57.50
Notes Receivable		10,000.00	Liability on Discounted	
Interest Receivable		100.00	Notes Receivable	10,000.00
			Interest Receivable	100.00

If payment of note by the maker at maturity date, September 30:

	Liability on Discounted	
(No entry)	Notes Receivable 10,000.00	
	Notes Receivable	10,000.00

If maker defaults and endorser pays note the following day with interest of $300 plus the bank protest fee of $25, October 1:

Notes Receivable			Notes Receivable	
Past Due*	10,325.00		Past Due*	10,325.00
Cash		10,325.00	Cash	10,325.00
			Liability on Discounted	
			Notes Receivable 10,000.00	
			Notes Receivable	10,000.00

*Accounts Receivable is frequently used as the account to reinstate the default.

In the above discounting transaction that is a sale, the endorser would disclose its contingent liability on the discounted notes with recourse by reporting the contingency in a note to the financial statements. Alternatively, the endorser could credit Notes Receivable Discounted, instead of Notes Receivable, for $10,000 and report it as a contra asset deducted from Notes Receivable in the current asset section of the balance sheet. This would serve to disclose the endorser's contingent liability for default by the maker of the note.

Dishonoured Notes   Notes receivable that are not paid at maturity (whether discounted or not) remain notes receivable and are considered notes receivable past due. Defaulted notes should be separately classified on the balance sheet. If all efforts to collect fail, the note is written off as a loss. Whether the loss is charged to the allowance for doubtful accounts or directly to a loss account depends on (1) whether the company has an allowance for doubtful accounts and (2) whether the periodic provisions cover losses only on accounts receivable or on both accounts and notes receivable.

Conceptual Issues Related to the Transfer of Receivables

As indicated, the transfer of receivables to a third party for cash takes one of three forms.[14]

1. One form is to borrow from a third party and **assign or pledge the receivables** as collateral. Both the form of this transaction and its substance suggest that it be accounted for and reported as a borrowing.

[14]Understanding these transactions is made more difficult by the inconsistent use of terms to describe these transactions in practice. When you encounter such transactions, we recommend that you attempt to classify them in accordance with their basic nature as one of these three types.

2. A second form is to **transfer the receivables** to a third party in exchange for cash and in a manner whereby the third party is **without recourse** to the transferor in connection with the receivables. Both the form of this transaction and its substance suggest that it be accounted for and reported as a **sale.**

3. A third form is to **transfer the receivables** to a third party in exchange for cash but in a manner whereby the third party has full or partial recourse (**with recourse**) to the transferor in connection with the receivables. In this case the form of the transaction may either be a sale or a borrowing, depending on the facts.

The essence of a transfer of receivables in a **borrowing transaction** is that the transferor retains the same risks of collectibility on the receivables after the transaction that it had before the transaction. This is the situation in the first and in some cases the third form presented above. In the second form, where the receivables are transferred without recourse, the transferor has substantially eliminated its risks on the receivables transferred. The transferee assumes the risk of uncollectibles. As is required in other sale transactions, the substantial (or complete) risk transfer test has been met.

In the absence of official pronouncements in Canada, the authors recommend that the proceeds from the transfer of receivables with recourse should be reported initially as a liability, and that the transfer not be treated as a sale of the receivables unless the transferor transfers both the future economic benefits embodied in the receivables and the related inherent risks of uncollectibility. The transferor's retention of credit risk through the recourse provisions leaves the transferor in an economic position in substance undistinguishable from that of a borrower.

Accounts and Notes Receivable: Balance Sheet Presentation

The general rules in classifying the typical transactions in the receivable section are: (1) segregate the different receivables that an enterprise possesses, if material; (2) insure that the valuation accounts are appropriately offset against the proper receivable accounts; (3) determine that receivables classified in the current asset section will be converted into cash within the year or the operating cycle, whichever is longer; (4) disclose any loss contingencies that exist on the receivables; and (5) disclose any receivables assigned or pledged as collateral.

Any discount or premium resulting from the determination of present value in notes receivable transactions is not an asset or a liability separable from the note that gives rise to it. Therefore, the discount or premium is reported in the balance sheet as a direct deduction from or addition to the face amount of the note. It is not classified as a deferred charge or deferred credit. The face amount of the note is disclosed in the balance sheet or in the footnotes, and the description of the note should include the effective interest rate. If several notes are involved, the principal amount of such notes and the balance of total unamortized discount are presented in the balance sheet with the details disclosed individually in footnotes or a separate schedule to the balance sheet.

For transfers of receivables with recourse accounted for as a sale, the transferor could disclose (1) the proceeds received during each period for which an income statement is presented and (2) if the information is available, the balance of the transferred receivables that remain uncollected at the date of each balance sheet presented.

The following asset sections of Colton Corporation's balance sheet illustrate many of the disclosures required for receivables:

Colton Corporation
PARTIAL BALANCE SHEET
As of December 31, 1985

Current assets

Cash and cash equivalent		$1,870,250
Accounts receivable (Note 2)	$8,977,673	
Less: Allowance for doubtful accounts	500,226	
	8,477,447	
Advances to subsidiaries due 9/30/86	2,090,000	
Notes receivable-trade (Note 2)	1,532,000	
Dividends and interest receivable	75,500	
Federal income taxes refundable	146,704	
Other receivables and claims (including debit balances in accounts payable)	174,620	12,496,271
Total current assets		14,366,521

Noncurrent receivables

Notes receivable from officers and key employees for purchase of company's shares	376,090
Claims receivable (litigation settlement to be collected over four years)	585,000

Note 2—Accounts and notes receivable.

In November 1985, the Company arranged with a finance company to refinance a part of its indebtedness. The loan is evidenced by a 12% note payable. The note is payable on demand and is secured by substantially all the accounts receivable.

In May 1985, the Company entered into an agreement with a financial institution whereby the Company had the right to sell designated receivables, with recourse, not to exceed $3,000,000 at any time. During the period May 1 through September 20, 1985, proceeds totalling $2,480,000 were received from such sales. Losses totalling $202,640 were recognized on these sales during 1985. As of December 31, 1985, $171,500 of transferred receivables remains uncollected.

In several countries outside the United States, notes receivable are discounted with banks. The contingent liability under such arrangements amounted to $751,000 at December 31, 1985.

KEY POINTS

1. **Cash** includes the medium of exchange and most negotiable instruments.
2. To be reported as cash, a medium must be readily available for the payment of current obligations, and it must be free from any contractual restrictions.
3. **Restricted cash** is classified separately either in the current asset or in the long-term asset section, depending on the expected date of availability or disbursement.
4. A **compensating balance** is that portion of any demand or time deposit maintained by a depositor as support for existing borrowing arrangements or future credit availability with a lending institution.
5. **Compensating balances** that are legally restricted deposits must be stated separately among cash and cash equivalent items in current assets while noncontractual compensating balance arrangements should be described only in the notes to the financial statements.
6. Cash presents special management and control problems because it enters into a great many transactions; it is the asset most readily convertible into any

other type of asset (i.e., most subject to embezzlement); and its amount must be managed carefully so that neither too much nor too little is available at any time.

7. An **imprest petty cash system** is frequently used to pay small amounts of money for things like postage, minor office supplies, taxi fare, and other small expense payments.

8. Cash on deposit with a bank is not available for count and must therefore be proved through the preparation of a **bank reconciliation:** that is, a schedule indicating and explaining the differences between the depositor's record of cash in the bank and the bank's record **(bank statement)** of the cash on deposit.

9. A four-column bank reconciliation called a **proof of cash** may be prepared in lieu of the simpler single-column reconciliation when stronger control and evidence is needed to match the bank's and the company's records of cash transactions and balances.

10. Short-term receivables are claims against others for money, goods, or services collectible within one year or the operating cycle, whichever is longer.

11. Short-term receivables are valued at net realizable value, which is the net amount expected to be received in cash.

12. Although the net method of recording credit sales is theoretically correct, the gross method is used almost universally because of bookkeeping convenience and lack of materiality.

13. In accounting for uncollectible receivables, the **allowance method,** which conforms to the matching principle, should be used over the direct write-off method, which violates the matching principle.

14. The **percentage-of-sales approach** (income statement approach) emphasizes the matching principle by relating the bad debt expense to the amount of the credit sales, ignoring any balance in the allowance account.

15. The **percentage-of-receivables approach** (balance sheet approach) emphasizes reporting accounts receivable at net realizable value by adjusting the balance in the allowance account.

16. The allowance method may also be applied to other items that affect the cash realization of accounts receivable; for example, sales returns and allowances, freight, and collection expenses.

17. To advance the timing of the cash receipts from accounts receivable, many companies assign (pledge as security for a loan) or factor (sell) their accounts receivable.

18. Receivables may be factored or discounted without recourse or with recourse. Transference without recourse is accounted for as a sale while transference with recourse may be a sale or a borrowing, depending on the circumstances.

19. The sale of receivables results in the recognition of a loss on sale and removal of the receivables from the transferor's books. Borrowing against receivables results in the recognition of a liability and interest expense.

20. Interest is inherent in all borrowing transactions, even though some commercial notes have no stated interest rate. In the absence of an explicit interest rate, or if an unreasonably low rate is stated, a reasonable interest must be imputed and accounted for.

7A

FOUR-COLUMN BANK RECONCILIATION

In addition to the form presented in this chapter, another form of reconciliation frequently used by auditors and typically illustrated in auditing textbooks, is the so-called **proof of cash** of "four-column bank reconciliation." It is an expanded version of the bank reconciliation previously illustrated on page 317.

The proof-of-cash form of reconciliation is actually four reconciliations in one:

1. Reconciliation of the **beginning of the period cash balances** per the bank statement and the books (first column).
2. Reconciliation of the current period cash receipts (deposits) per the bank statement to receipts recorded in the books (second column).
3. Reconciliation of the **current period cash disbursements** per the bank statement to disbursements recorded in the books (third column).
4. Reconciliation of the **end of the period cash balances** per the bank statement and the books (fourth column).

The top line across the four-column reconciliation ("per bank statement") is a summary of the transactions for the period covered, as taken from the bank statement or statements. The beginning and ending bank balances are shown on the bank statement, as are the bank receipts (as shown in the "deposits" column), and the bank disbursements (as shown in the "charges" or "cheques cashed" column).

The "Per books" line is a summary of the cash transactions as recorded in the books. These totals should be taken directly from the books, preferably from the Cash account itself, which should, of course, show receipts and disbursements as debit and credit entries and the beginning and ending cash balances.

The left-hand and right-hand columns are simply **end-of-the-prior-period** and **end-of-the-current-period** reconciliations, the preparation of which is illustrated below. The two centre columns, receipts and disbursements, tie the left-hand column and right-hand column reconciliations together. With few exceptions, the amounts needed to complete these centre columns may be found in the figures included in either the top or bottom lines, or in the left-hand columns; no new data need be added. The exceptions consist of such items as bank error corrected by the bank within the month in which it was made, so that transactions but not balances are affected. A customer's cheque deposited, returned N.S.F., and redeposited without entry in the same period would have the same effect.

The four-column proof of cash is preferred by auditors as a means of identifying all differences between the books and the bank statement during the period covered by the reconciliation. It is generally prepared by auditors when a company has weak internal control over cash.

Nugget Mining Company
Proof of Cash for November 1986
Bank of Montreal—Chequing Account

	Balance October 31	November Receipts	November Disbursements	Balance November 30
Per bank statement	$17,520	$96,450	$91,780	$22,190
Deposits in transit				
at October 31	4,200	(4,200)		
at November 30		3,680		3,680
Outstanding cheques				
at October 31	(3,700)		(3,700)	
at November 30			5,001	(5,001)
Bank error—incorrect cheque				
charged by bank			(175)	175
Correct amounts	$18,020	$95,930	$92,906	$21,044
Per books	$18,044	$95,330	$92,872	$20,502
Interest collected by bank		600		600
Error in recording cheque				
#7322			(180)	180
Unrecorded service charges				
at October 31	(24)		(24)	
at November 30			18	(18)
NSF cheque returned			220	(220)
Correct amounts	$18,020	$95,930	$92,906	$21,044

To illustrate the four-column reconciliation, the data provided for the Nugget Mining Company at November 30 on page 316 will be used in conjunction with the following information:

1. The cash balance as of October 31, 1986 per the bank statements (the beginning of November balance) was $17,520.
2. The cash balance as of October 31, 1986 per Nugget's books was $18,044.

3. The total cash receipts (deposits) per the November bank statement are $96,450. These receipts include the deposit in transit of $4,200 at October 31.
4. The total cash receipts per Nugget's books during November are $95,330.
5. The total cash disbursements per the bank statement for November are $91,780. These disbursements include $3,700 of cheques outstanding at October 31.
6. The total cash disbursements per the books during November are $92,872.
7. The October bank service charge was $24.

The completed reconciliation would appear as shown on page 345.

An alternative procedure for preparing a bank reconciliation involves reconciling from the bank balance to the book balance as opposed to reconciling both amounts to a correct cash balance. This same alternative can also be applied to the four-column, proof of cash reconciliation, as illustrated below:

	(Bank to Book Form) Nugget Mining Company Proof of Cash for November 1986 Bank of Montreal—Chequing Account			
	Balance October 31	Balance Receipts	Disbursements	November 30
Per bank statement	$17,520	$96,450	$91,780	$22,190
Deposits in transit				
at October 31	4,200	(4,200)		
at November 30		3,680		3,680
Outstanding cheques				
at October 31	(3,700)		(3,700)	
at November 30			5,001	(5,001)
Bank error—incorrect cheque			(175)	175
Interest collected by bank		(600)		(600)
Error per books—cheque #7322			180	(180)
Unrecorded service charges				
at October 31	24		24	
at November 30			(18)	18
NSF cheque returned by bank			(220)	220
Per books	$18,044	$95,330	$92,872	$20,502

The above "bank to book" reconciliation form is generally illustrated in auditing textbooks. The auditors frequently use this form because their main objective is to identify all of the items that make up the difference between the bank's records and the depositor's records. Preparation of the adjusting entries is secondary to them. This form is usually more difficult for students because each of the reconciling items must be analysed carefully to determine whether an addition or subtraction from the top of the column "Per bank" amount is the logical reconciliation treatment.

QUESTIONS

1. What may be included under the heading of "cash"?

2. Distinguish among the following: (1) certificates of deposit, (2) money market savings certificates, (3) money market funds, (4) treasury bills, and (5) commercial paper.

3. Define a "compensating balance." How should a compensating balance be reported?

4. Distinguish among the following: (1) a general chequing account, (2) an imprest bank account, and (3) a lockbox account.

5. What is electronic funds transfer, and what effect is its widespread use likely to have on record-keeping and accounting?

6. In what accounts should the following items be classified?
   (a) Travel advances.
   (b) Cash (to be used for retirement of long-term bonds).
   (c) Savings and chequing accounts.
   (d) Petty cash.
   (e) Cash in a bank that is in receivership.
   (f) Deposits in transit.
   (g) Coins and currency.
   (h) Certificate of deposit.
   (i) Postdated cheques.
   (j) NSF cheque (returned with bank statement).
   (k) Deposit in foreign bank (exchangeability limited).
   (l) Stamps.

7. What is the difference between trade receivables and nontrade receivables? Give two examples of each type.

8. What are the basic problems that occur in the valuation of accounts receivable?

9. What are the reasons that a company gives trade discounts? Why are trade discounts not recorded in the accounts like cash discounts?

10. What are two methods of recording accounts receivable transactions when a cash discount situation is involved? Which is theoretically the more correct? Which is used in practice most of the time? Why?

11. Why is the account "Allowance for Sales Returns and Allowances" sometimes used? What other types of allowance accounts (similar to Allowance for Sales Returns and Allowances) are employed? What is their purpose?

12. What is the normal procedure for handling the collection of accounts receivable previously written off using the direct write-off method? The allowance method?

13. Because of calamitous earthquake losses, Pelican Company, one of your client's oldest and largest customers, suddenly and unexpectedly became bankrupt. Approximately 25% of your client's total sales had been made to Pelican Company during each of the past several years. The amount due from Pelican Company—none of which is collectible—equals 20% of total accounts receivable, an amount that is considerably in excess of what was determined to be an adequate provision for doubtful accounts at the close of the preceding year. How would your client record the write-off of the Pelican Company receivable if it is using the allowance method of accounting for bad debts? Justify your suggested treatment.

14. What is the theoretical justification of the allowance method as contrasted with the direct write-off method of accounting for bad debts?

15. Indicate how well the percentage-of-sales method and the aging method accomplish the objectives of the allowance method of accounting for bad debts.

16. Of what merit is the contention that the allowance method lacks the objectivity of the direct write-off method? Discuss in terms of accounting's measurement function.

17. Mesmerism Shop shows a balance in Accounts Receivable on December 31, 1986, of $150,000. Of this amount $80,000 is assigned to the Canadian Finance Co. as security for a loan of $60,000. Illustrate three satisfactory methods for showing this information on the balance sheet for December 31, 1986.

18. The Pinnacle Company includes in its trial balance for December 31 an item for "Accounts Receivable, $477,000." This balance consists of the following items:

Due from regular customers	$301,000
Refund receivable on prior year's income taxes (an established claim)	10,000
Loans to officers	22,000
Loan to wholly owned subsidiary	45,500
Advances to creditors for goods ordered	61,000
Accounts receivable assigned as security for loans payable	31,500
Notes receivable past due plus interest on these notes	6,000
Total	$477,000

    Illustrate how these items should be shown in the balance sheet as of December 31.

19. Differentiate between assigning and factoring accounts receivable.

20. Identify three forms by which receivables can be transferred to a third party for cash. Conceptually, what is the nature or substance of each form?

21. Identify the different methods of disclosing the loss contingency for notes receivable discounted with recourse.

22. What is "imputed interest"? In what situations is it necessary to impute an interest rate for notes receivable? What are the considerations involved when imputing an appropriate interest rate?

23. On January 1, 1986, Pipedream, Inc. sells property for which it had paid $500 to Seltzer Company, receiving in return Seltzer's noninterest-bearing note for $1,000 payable in five years. What entry would Pipedream make to record the sale, assuming that Pipedream frequently sells similar items of property for a cash sales price of $600?

CASES

C7-1 Jose Supply Limited conducts a wholesale merchandising business that sells approximately 5,000 items per month with a total monthly average sales value of $150,000. Its annual bad debt ratio has been approximately 1 1/2% of sales. In recent discussions with his bookkeeper, Mr. Jose has become confused by all the alternatives apparently available in handling the Allowance for Doubtful Accounts balance. The following information has been shown.

1. An allowance can be set up (a) on the basis of a percentage of sales or (b) on the basis of a valuation of all past due or otherwise questionable accounts receivable—those considered uncollectible being charged to such allowance at the close of the accounting period; or specific items are charged off directly against (c) gross sales, or to (d) bad debt expense in the year in which they are determined to be uncollectible.

2. Collection agency and legal fees, and so on, incurred in connection with the attempted recovery of bad debts can be charged to (a) bad debt expense, (b) allowance for doubtful accounts, (c) legal expense, or (d) general expense.

3. Debts previously written off in whole or in part but currently recovered can be credited to (a) other revenue, (b) bad debt expenses, or (c) allowance for doubtful accounts.

Instructions

    Which of the foregoing methods would you recommend to Mr. Jose in regard to (a) allowances and charge-offs, (b) collection expenses, and (c) recoveries? State briefly and clearly the reasons supporting your recommendations.

C7-2 **Part 1** On July 1, 1987, Carme Corp., a calendar-year company, sold special order merchandise on credit and received in return an interest-bearing note receivable from the customer. Carme Corp. will receive interest at the prevailing rate for a note of this type. Both the principal and interest are due in one lump sum on June 30, 1988.

Instructions

(a) When should Carme Corp. report interest income from the note receivable? Discuss the rationale for your answer.

(b) Assume that the note receivable was discounted without recourse at a bank on December 31, 1987. How would Carme Corp. determine the amount of the discount, and what is the appropriate accounting for the discounting transaction?

Part 2 On December 31, 1987, Carme Corp. had significant amounts of accounts receivable as a result of credit sales to its customers. Carme Corp. uses the allowance method based on credit sales to estimate bad debts. Based on past experience, 1% of credit sales normally will not be collected. This pattern is expected to continue.

Instructions

(a) Discuss the rationale for using the allowance method based on credit sales to estimate bad debts. Contrast this method with the allowance method based on the balance in the trade receivables accounts.

(b) How should Carme Corp. report the allowance for bad debts account on its balance sheet at December 31, 1987? Also, describe the alternatives, if any, for presentation of bad debt expense in Carme Corp.'s 1987 income statement.

(AICPA adapted)

C7-3 Henderson Limited operates a full-line department store that is dominant in its market area, is easily accessible to public and private transportation, has adequate parking facilities, and is near a large permanent military base. The president of the company, Susan Bannerman, seeks your advice on a recently received proposal.

A local credit union in which your client has an account recently affiliated with a popular national credit card plan and has extended an invitation to your client to participate in the plan. Under the plan affiliated banks and credit unions mail credit card applications to persons in the community who have good credit ratings regardless of whether they are customers of the credit union. If the recipients wish to receive a credit card, they complete, sign, and return the application and instalment credit agreement. Holders of cards thus activated may charge merchandise or services at any participating establishment throughout the nation.

The credit union guarantees payment to all participating merchants on all presented invoices that have been properly completed, signed, and validated with the impression of credit cards that have not expired or been reported stolen or otherwise cancelled. Local merchants including your client may turn in all card-validated sales tickets or invoices to their affiliated local credit union at any time and receive immediate credits to their chequing accounts of 96.5% of the face value of the invoices. If card users pay the credit union or bank in full within 30 days for amounts billed, the credit union levies no added charges against the customer. If they elect to make their payments under a deferred payment plan, the credit union adds a service charge that amounts to an effective interest rate of 18% per annum on unpaid balances. Only the local affiliated credit unions, banks, and the franchisor of the credit card plan share in these revenues.

The 18% service charge approximates what your client has been billing customers who pay their accounts over an extended period on a schedule similar to that offered under the credit card plan. Participation in the plan does not prevent your client from continuing to carry on its credit business as in the past.

Instructions

(a) What are (1) the positive and (2) the negative financial and accounting-related factors that Henderson Ltd. should consider in deciding whether to participate in the described credit card plan? Explain.

(b) If Henderson Ltd. does participate in the plan, which income statement and balance sheet accounts may change materially as the plan becomes fully operative? (Such factors as market position, sales mix, prices, markup, etc. are expected to remain about the same as in the past.) Explain.

C7-4   Abbott Company sells office equipment and supplies to many organizations in the city and surrounding area on contract terms of 2/10, n/30. In the past, over 75% of credit customers have taken advantage of the discount by paying within ten days of the invoice date.

The number of customers taking full 30 days to pay has increased within the last year. Current indications are that less than 60% of the customers are now taking the discount. Bad debts as a percentage of gross credit sales have risen from 1.5% provided in the past years to about 4% in the current year.

The Controller has responded to a request for more information on the deterioration in collections of accounts receivable with the report reproduced below.

Abbott Company
FINANCE COMMITTEE REPORT
ACCOUNTS RECEIVABLE COLLECTIONS
May 31, 1987

The fact that some credit accounts will prove uncollectible is normal. Annual bad debt write-offs have been 1.5% of gross credit sales over the past five years. During the last fiscal year, this percentage increased to slightly less than 4%. The current Accounts Receivable balance is $1,200,000. The condition of this balance in terms of probability of collection is as follows:

Proportion of Total	Age Categories	Probability of Collection
68%	not yet due	99%
15%	less than 30 days past due	96 1/2%
8%	31 to 60 days past due	95%
5%	61 to 120 days past due	91%
2 1/2%	121 to 180 days past due	75%
1 1/2%	over 181 days past due	20%

The Allowance for Doubtful Accounts had a credit balance of $30,250 on June 1, 1986. Abbott has provided for a monthly bad debt expense accrual during the fiscal year based on the assumption that 4% of gross credit sales will be uncollectible. Total gross credit sales for the 1986–87 fiscal year amounted to $3,000,000. Write-offs of bad accounts during the year totalled $108,750.

Instructions

(a)   Prepare an accounts receivable aging schedule for the Abbott Company using the age categories identified in the Controller's report to the Finance Committee showing:
1.   The amount of accounts receivable outstanding for each age category and in total.
2.   The estimated amount that is uncollectible for each category and in total.

(b)   Compute the amount of the year-end adjustment necessary to bring Allowance for Doubtful Accounts to the balance indicated by the age analysis. Then prepare the necessary journal entry to adjust the accounting records.

(c)   In a recessionary environment with tight credit and high interest rates:
1.   Identify steps Abbott Company might consider to improve the accounts receivable situation, and
2.   Then evaluate each step identified in terms of the risks and costs involved.
(CMA adapted)

C7-5   On July 1, 1987, Marie Company sold special-order merchandise on credit and received in return an interest-bearing note receivable from the customer. Marie will receive interest at the prevailing rate for a note of this type. Both the principal and interest are due in one lump sum on June 30, 1988.

On September 1, 1987, Marie sold special-order merchandise on credit and received a noninterest-bearing note receivable from the customer. The prevailing rate of interest for a note of this type is determinable. The note receivable is due in one lump sum on August 31, 1989.

Marie also has significant amounts of trade accounts receivable as a result of credit sales to its customers. On October 1, 1987, some trade accounts receivable were assigned to Daniel Finance Company on a with recourse, nonnotification basis for an advance of 75% of their amount at an interest charge of 20% on the balance outstanding.

On November 1, 1987, other trade accounts receivable were factored on a without recourse basis. The factor withheld 5% of the trade accounts receivable factored as protection against sales returns and allowances and charged a finance charge of 3%.

Instructions

(a) How should Marie determine the interest income for 1987 on the:
   1. Interest-bearing note receivable? Why?
   2. Noninterest-bearing note receivable? Why?

(b) How should Marie report the interest-bearing note receivable and the noninterest-bearing note receivable on its balance sheet at December 31, 1987?

(c) How should Marie account for subsequent collections on the trade accounts receivable assigned on October 1, 1987, and the payments to Daniel Finance? Why?

(d) How should Marie account for the trade accounts receivable factored on November 1, 1987? Why?

(AICPA adapted)

C7-6 Soon after beginning the year-end audit work on March 10 at Resurrection Company, the auditor has the following conversation with the controller.

Controller: The year ended March 31 should be our most profitable in history and, as a consequence, the Board of Directors has just awarded the officers generous bonuses.

Auditor: I thought profits were down this year in the industry, according to your latest interim report.

Controller: Well, they were down but ten days ago we closed a deal that will give us a substantial increase for the year.

Auditor: Oh, what was it?

Controller: Well, you remember a few years ago our former president bought shares in Carson Enterprises because he had those grandiose ideas about becoming a conglomerate. For six years we have not been able to sell this stock, which cost us $1,500,000 and has not paid a nickel in dividends. Thursday we sold this stock to Casino Ltd. for $2,000,000. So, we will have a gain of $350,000 ($500,000 pretax) which will increase our net income for the year to $2,000,000 compared with last year's $1,900,000. As far as I know, we'll be the only company in the industry to register an increase in net income this year. That should help the market value of the company's shares!

Auditor: Do you expect to receive the $2,000,000 in cash by March 31, your fiscal year-end?

Controller: No. Although Casino Ltd. is an excellent company, they are a little tight for cash because of their rapid growth. Consequently, they are going to give us a $2,000,000 noninterest-bearing note due $200,000 per year for the next ten years. The first payment is due on March 31 of next year.

Auditor: Why is the note noninterest-bearing?

Controller: Because that's what everybody agreed to. Since we don't have any interest-bearing debt, the funds invested in the note do not cost us anything and besides, we were not getting any dividends on the Carson Enterprises shares.

Instructions

Do you agree with the way the controller has accounted for the transaction? If not, how should the transaction be accounted for?

EXERCISES

E7-1 The following information was available from Dontar Corporation's books:

Month	Purchases	Sales
Jan.	$42,000	$72,000
Feb.	48,000	66,000
Mar.	36,000	60,000
Apr.	54,000	78,000

Collections from customers are normally 70% in the month of sale, 20% in the month following the sale, and 9% in the second month following the sale. The balance is expected to be uncollectible. Dontar takes full advantage of the 2% discount allowed on purchases paid for by the tenth of the following month. Purchases for May are budgeted at $60,000, while sales for May are forecasted at $66,000. Cash disbursements for expenses are expected to be $14,400 for the month of May. Dontar's cash balance at May 1 was $22,000.

Instructions

Prepare the following schedules:
(a) Expected cash collections during May.
(b) Expected cash disbursements during May.
(c) Expected cash balance at May 31.

(AICPA adapted)

E7-2 The petty cash fund of Tim's Auto Repair Service, a sole proprietorship, contains the following:

1.	Coins and currency		$ 15.46
2.	Fourteen 20-cent stamps		2.80
3.	An IOU from Mary Mechanic, an employee, for cash advance		50.00
4.	Cheque payable to Tim's Auto Repair from John Brakeshoe, an employee, marked NSF		30.00
5.	Vouchers for the following:		
	Stamps	$20.00	
	Two Grey Cup tickets for Tim	70.00	
	Typewriter repairs	9.85	99.85
			$198.11

The general ledger account Petty Cash has a balance of $200.00.

Instructions

Prepare the journal entry to record the reimbursement of the petty cash fund.

E7-3 Golfpro Company has just received the August 31, 1986, bank statement, which is summarized below:

Toronto Dominion Bank	Disbursements	Receipts	Balance
Balance, August 1			$ 8,600
Deposits during August		$28,000	36,600
Note collected for depositor, including $24 interest		924	37,524
Cheques cleared during August	$32,200		5,324
Bank service charges	15		5,309
Balance, August 31			5,309

The general ledger Cash account contained the following entries for the month of August:

Cash			
Balance, August 1	8,200	Disbursements in August	32,500
Receipts during August	31,000		

Deposits in transit at August 31 are $3,000, and cheques outstanding at August 31 are determined to total $900. Cash on hand at August 31 is $190. The bookkeeper improperly entered one cheque in the books at $155.39 which was written for $165.39 for supplies; it cleared the bank during the month of August.

Instructions
(a) Prepare a bank reconciliation dated August 31, 1986, proceeding to a corrected balance.
(b) Prepare any entries necessary to make the books correct and complete.
(c) What amount of cash should be reported in the August 31 balance sheet?

E7-4 Falcon Ltd. deposits all receipts and makes all payments by cheque. The following information is available from the cash records.

June 30 BANK RECONCILIATION

Balance per bank	$4,610
Add: Deposits in transit	1,200
Deduct: Outstanding cheques	(1,500)
Balance per books	$4,310

Month of July Results

	Per Bank	Per Books
Balance, July 31	$7,000	$6,600
July deposits	4,100	4,590
July cheques	2,500	2,300
July notes collected (not included in July deposits)	1,000	-0-
July bank service charge	10	-0-
July NSF cheque of a customer returned by the bank (recorded by bank as a charge)	200	-0-

Instructions
(a) Prepare a bank reconciliation going from balance per bank and balance per book to corrected cash balance.
(b) Prepare the general journal entry to correct the cash account.

E7-5 Scott's Hospitality Inc. shows a balance of $134,250 in the accounts receivable account on December 31, 1986. The balance consists of the following:

Due from regular customers, of which $30,000 represents accounts pledged as security for a bank loan	$75,000
Advances to employees	700
Advance to subsidiary company (made in 1982)	24,000
Instalment accounts due in 1987	15,000
Instalment accounts due after 1987	18,000
Overpayments to creditors	1,550

Instructions
Illustrate how the information above should be shown on the balance sheet of the Scott's Hospitality Inc. on December 31, 1986.

E7-6 Your accounts receivable clerk, Mr. Rod Robertson, to whom you pay a salary of $950 per month, has just purchased a new Cadillac. You decided to test the accuracy of the accounts receivable balance of $60,200 as shown in the ledger. The following information is available for your **first year** in business:

Collections from customers	$225,000
Merchandise purchased	300,000
Ending merchandise inventory	80,000
Goods are marked to sell at 40% above cost	

Instructions

Compute an estimate of the ending balance of accounts receivable from customers that should appear in the ledger, and any apparent shortages. Assume that all sales are made on account.

E7-7 On June 3, Rotunda Company sold to Jan Scharf merchandise having a sale price of $2,000 with terms of 2/10, n/60, f.o.b. shipping point. An invoice totalling $90, terms n/30, was received by Jan Scharf on June 8 from the Madsen Transport Service for the freight cost. On receipt of the goods, June 5, Jan Scharf notified the Rotunda Company that merchandise costing $200 contained flaws that rendered it worthless; the same day Rotunda Company issued a credit memo covering the worthless merchandise and asked that it be returned at company expense. The freight on the returned merchandise was $20, paid by Rotunda Company on June 7. On June 12, the company received a cheque for the balance due from Jan Scharf.

Instructions

(a) Prepare journal entries on the Rotunda Company books to record all the events noted above under each of the following bases:
1. Sales and receivables are entered at gross selling price.
2. Sales and receivables are entered at net of cash discounts.

(b) Prepare the journal entry under basis 2, assuming that Jan Scharf did not remit payment until July 29.

E7-8 At January 1, 1986, the credit balance in the allowance for doubtful accounts of the Ackerman Company was $400,000. For 1986, the provision for doubtful accounts is based on a percentage of net sales. Net sales for 1986 were $60,000,000. On the basis of the latest available facts, the 1986 provision for doubtful accounts is estimated to be 0.7% of net sales. During 1986, uncollectible receivables amounting to $450,000 were written off against the allowance for doubtful accounts.

Instructions

Prepare a schedule computing the balance in Ackerman's allowance for doubtful accounts at December 31, 1986.

E7-9 The trial balance before adjustment of Ken Shulzke Auto Parts shows the following balances:

	Dr.	Cr.
Accounts Receivable	60,000	
Allowance for Doubtful Accounts	750	
Sales (all on credit)		581,200
Sales Returns and Allowances	15,000	

Instructions

Give the entry for estimated bad debts assuming that the allowance is to provide for doubtful accounts on the basis (a) 4% of gross accounts receivable and (b) 3% of net sales.

E7-10 The Reding Company includes the following account among its trade receivables.

Galtaco Inc.

1/1	Balance forward	500	1/28	Cash (#1710)	1,300
1/20	Invoice #1710	1,300	4/2	Cash (#2116)	890
3/14	Invoice #2116	890	4/10	Cash	125
4/12	Invoice #2412	1,420	4/30	Cash (#2412)	1,000
9/5	Invoice #3614	490	9/20	Cash (#3614 and	
10/17	Invoice #4912	860		part of #2412)	790
11/18	Invoice #5681	2,300	10/31	Cash (#4912)	860
12/20	Invoice #6347	630	12/1	Cash (#5681)	1,700
			12/29	Cash (#6347)	630

Instructions

Age the balance and specify any items that apparently require particular attention.

E7-11 The chief accountant for the Robinson Corporation provides you with the following list of accounts receivable written off in the current year.

Date	Customer	Amount
Mar. 31	GLC Designs	$7,600
June 30	Harley Associates	5,700
Sept. 30	Susan's Dress Shop	6,120
Dec. 31	Drew Corporation	4,800

Robinson Corporation follows the policy of debiting Bad Debt Expense as accounts are written off. The chief accountant maintains that this procedure is appropriate for financial statement purposes because Revenue Canada will not accept other methods for recognizing bad debts.

All of Robinson Corporation's sales are on a 30-day credit basis. Sales for the current year total $1,500,000, and research has determined that bad debt losses approximate 2% of sales.

Instructions

(a) Do you agree or disagree with the Robinson Corporation policy concerning recognition of bad debt expense? Why or why not?

(b) By what amount would net income differ if bad debt expense was computed using the percentage-of-sales approach?

E7-12 Presented below is information related to Bambi Corp.

June 1   Bambi Corp. sold to Moat Co. merchandise having a sales price of $6,000 with terms 2/10, n/60. Bambi records its sales and receivables net.

June 3   Moat Co. returned defective merchandise having a sales price of $600.

OMIT June 5   Accounts receivable of $8,000 are factored with Mohr Credit Corp. without recourse at a financing charge of 10%. Cash is received for the proceeds; collections are handled by the finance company. (These accounts were all past the discount period.)

June 9   Specific accounts receivable of $9,000 are assigned to Chase Credit Corp. as security for a loan of $6,000 at a finance charge of 6% of the amount of the loan. The finance company will make the collections. (All the accounts receivable are past the discount period.)

December 30   Moat Co. notifies Bambi that it is bankrupt and will pay only 10% of its account. Give the entry to write off the uncollectible balance using the allowance method. (Note: First record the increase in the receivable on June 11 when the discount period passed.)

Instructions

Prepare all necessary entries in general journal form for Bambi Corp.

E7-13 Presented below is information related to Andy's Wines Ltd., Inc.

1. Customers' accounts in the amount of $36,000 are assigned to the Macks Finance Company as security for a loan of $20,000. The finance charge is 3% of the amount borrowed.

2. Cash collections on assigned accounts amount to $12,600.

3. Collections on assigned accounts to date, plus a $300 cheque for interest on the loan, are forwarded to Macks Finance Company.

4. Additional collections on assigned accounts amount to $14,200.

5. The loan is paid in full plus additional interest of $100.

6. Uncollected balances of the assigned accounts are returned to the regular customers' ledger.

Instructions

Prepare entries in journal form for Andy's Wines Ltd.

E7-14   The trial balance before adjustment for the Leather Goods Company shows the following balances:

	Dr.	Cr.
Accounts Receivable	$64,800	
Allowance for Doubtful Accounts	1,080	
Sales		$373,000
Sales Returns and Allowances	1,800	

Instructions

Using the data above, give the journal entries required to record each of the following cases. (Each situation is independent.)

(a)   The company wants to maintain the Allowance for Doubtful Accounts at 4% of gross accounts receivable.

(b)   The company wishes to increase the allowance by 1 1/2% of net sales.

(c)   To obtain additional cash, Leather factors, without recourse, $18,000 of Accounts Receivable with Tri-County Finance. The finance charge is 10% of the amount factored.

(d)   To obtain a one-year loan of $45,000, Leather assigns $54,000 of specific receivable accounts to Blair Financial. The finance charge is 9% of the loan; the cash is received and the accounts turned over to Blair.

E7-15   Steg, Inc. factors receivables with a carrying amount of $173,120 to Lisa Company for $140,000 on a with recourse basis.

Instructions

(a)   Assuming that this transaction should be reported as a sale, prepare the appropriate journal entry.

(b)   Assuming that this transaction should be reported as a borrowing, prepare the appropriate journal entry.

E7-16   The Guide Company requires additional cash for its business. Guide has decided to use its accounts receivable to raise the additional cash as follows:

1.   On July 1, 1986, Guide assigned $200,000 of accounts receivable to the Cell Finance Company. Guide received an advance from Cell of 85% of the assigned accounts receivable less a commission on the advance of 3%. Prior to December 31, 1986, Guide collected $150,000 on the assigned accounts receivable, and remitted $160,000 to Cell, $10,000 of which represented interest on the advance from Cell.

2.   On December 1, 1986, Guide sold $300,000 of net accounts receivable to the Factoring Company for $260,000. The receivables were sold outright on a nonrecourse basis.

3.   On December 31, 1986, an advance of $100,000 was received from the Domestic Bank by pledging $120,000 of Guide's accounts receivable. Guide's first payment to Domestic is due on January 30, 1987.

Instructions

Prepare a schedule showing the income statement effect for the year ended December 31, 1986, as a result of the above facts. Show supporting computations in good form.

(AICPA adapted)

E7-17   Presented below is information related to Nofftz Co. and Niagara, Inc.

May   1   Nofftz Co. gave Niagara, Inc. a $5,400, 60-day, 10% note in payment of its account of the same amount.

May 16   Niagara, Inc. discounted the note at the bank at an 11% discount rate.

June 30   On the maturity date of the note, Nofftz Co. paid the amount due.

Instructions

    (a) Record the transactions above on both the books of Nofftz Co. and the books of Niagara, Inc. (Assume it is a borrowing transaction.)

    (b) Assume that Nofftz Co. dishonoured its note and the bank notified Niagara, Inc., that it had charged the maturity value plus a protest fee of $25 to the Niagara, Inc. bank account. What entry (entries) should Niagara, Inc. make upon receiving this notification?

E7-18 On July 1, 1986, Greek Company made two sales:

    1. It sold land having a fair market value of $500,000 in exchange for a four-year noninterest-bearing promissory note in the face amount of $786,760. The land is carried on Greek Company's books at a cost of $425,000.

    2. It rendered services in exchange for a 3%, eight-year promissory note having a face value of $200,000 (interest payable annually).

        Greek Company recently had to pay 8% interest for monies that it borrowed from Continental Bank. The customers in these two transactions have credit ratings that require them to borrow money at 12% interest.

Instructions

    Record the two journal entries that should be recorded by Greek Company for the sales.transactions above that took place on July 1, 1986.

E7-19 On December 31, 1986, Tulip Company sold some of its product to Three M Company, accepting a $210,000 noninterest-bearing note, receivable in full on December 31, 1989. Tulip Company enjoys a high credit rating and, therefore, borrows funds from its several lines of credit at 10%. Three M Company, however, pays 15% for its borrowed funds. The product sold is carried on the books of Tulip Company at a manufactured cost of $110,000. Assume that the effective interest method is used for amortization payments.

Instructions

    (a) Prepare the journal entry to record the sale on December 31, 1986, by the Tulip Company. Assume that a perpetual inventory system is used.

    (b) Prepare the journal entries on the books of Tulip Company for the year 1987 that are necessitated by the sales transaction of December 31, 1986.

    (c) Prepare the journal entries on the books of Tulip Company for the year 1988 that are necessitated by the sale on December 31, 1986.

PROBLEMS

P7-1 Northgate Foundry closes its books regularly on December 31, but at the end of 1986 it held its cash book open so that a more favourable balance sheet could be prepared for credit purposes. Cash receipts and disbursements for the first ten days of January were recorded as December transactions. The following information is given.

    1. January cash receipts recorded in the December cash book totalled $32,730, of which $18,000 represents cash sales and $14,730 represents collections on account for which cash discounts of $270 were given.

    2. January cash disbursements recorded in the December cheque register liquidated accounts payable of $21,750 on which discounts of $512 were taken.

    3. The ledger has not been closed for 1986.

    4. The amount shown as inventory was determined by physical count on December 31, 1986.

Instructions

    (a) Prepare any entries you consider necessary to correct Northgate Foundry Company's accounts at December 31.

(b) To what extent was Northgate Foundry Company able to show a more favourable balance sheet at December 31 by holding its cash book open? Assume that the balance sheet that was prepared by the company showed the following amounts:

	Dr.	Cr.
Cash	$45,000	
Receivables	30,000	
Inventories	75,000	
Accounts payable		$45,000
Other current liabilities		15,000

P7-2 Presented below is information related to Shiffman Products Company.
Balance per books at October 31, $32,965.58; receipts, $164,834.34; disbursements, $159,225.68. Balance per bank statement November 30, $45,328.44.
The following cheques were outstanding at November 30:

No. 1224	$1,600.34
No. 1230	3,335.78
No. 1232	2,285.60
No. 1233	391.18

Included with the November bank statement and not recorded by the company were a bank debit ticket for $33.60 covering bank charges for the month, a debit ticket for $375.60 for a customer's cheque returned and marked NSF, and a credit ticket for $1,200.00 representing bond interest collected by the bank in the name of Shiffman Products Company. Cash on hand at November 30 recorded and awaiting deposit amounted to $1,649.50.

Instructions

(a) Prepare a bank reconciliation (bank balance to book balance) at November 30, 1986, for Shiffman Products Company from the information above.
(b) Prepare any journal entries required to adjust the cash account at November 30.
(c) State the amount of cash available for disbursement at November 30.

P7-3 The cash account of Badger Co. showed a ledger balance of $4,112.78 on June 30, 1986. The bank statement as of that date showed a balance of $3,278.85. Upon comparing the statement with the cash records, the following facts were determined:

1. The bank had charged the Badger Co.'s account for a customer's uncollectible cheque amounting to $505.20 on June 29.
2. A 60-day, 6%, $1,000 customer's note dated April 25, and discounted by Badger on June 12, remained unpaid by the customer on the due date. On June 28 the bank charged Badger Co. for $1,012.90, which included a protest fee of $2.90. (Badger discloses discounted notes receivable by use of a footnote.)
3. A customer's cheque for $90 had been entered as $70 in the cash receipts journal by Badger on June 15.
4. Cheque no. 742 in the amount of $392 had been entered in the cashbook as $329, and cheque no. 747 in the amount of $47.10 had been entered as $471. Both cheques had been issued to pay for purchases of equipment.
5. There were bank service charges for June of $25.00.
6. A bank memo stated that W. W. Briscoe's note for $600 and interest of $24 had been collected on June 29, and the bank had made a charge of $5.50 on the collection. (No entry had been made on Badger's books when Briscoe's note was sent to the bank for collection.)
7. Receipts for June 30 of $1,735 were not deposited until July 2.
8. Cheques outstanding on June 30 totalled $1,444.77.

Instructions

(a) Prepare a bank reconciliation dated June 30, 1986, proceeding to a corrected cash balance.

(b) Prepare any entries necessary to make the books correct and complete.

P7-4 Presented below is information related to Hawkeye Company.

Hawkeye Company
BANK RECONCILIATION
May 31, 1986

Balance per bank statement		$30,928.46
Less outstanding cheques		
No. 6124	$2,125.00	
No. 6138	932.65	
No. 6139	960.57	
No. 6140	1,420.00	5,438.22
		25,490.24
Add deposit in transit		4,710.56
Balance per books		$30,200.80

CHEQUE REGISTER—JUNE

Date	Payee	No.	V. Pay	Discount	Cash
June 1	Lund Mfg.	6141	$ 237.50		$ 237.50
1	Geo. Bates Mfg.	6142	915.00	$ 9.15	905.85
8	Office Supply Co., Inc.	6143	122.90	2.45	120.45
9	Lund Mfg.	6144	306.40		306.40
10	Petty Cash	6145	89.93		89.93
17	Allservice Photo	6146	706.00	14.12	691.88
22	Linda Elbert Publishing	6147	447.50		447.50
23	Payroll Account	6148	4,130.00		4,130.00
25	Warren Tools, Inc.	6149	390.75	3.91	386.84
28	Mutual Insurance Agency	6150	1,050.00		1,050.00
28	Riley Construction	6151	2,250.00		2,250.00
29	S. Hargrove, Inc.	6152	750.00		750.00
30	Wixon Bros.	6153	295.25	5.90	289.35
			$11,691.23	$35.53	$11,655.70

STATEMENT
Canadian Imperial Bank of Commerce
General Chequing Account of Hawkeye Co.—June 1986

Debits			Date	Credits	Balance
					$30,928.46
$2,125.00	$ 237.50	$ 905.85	June 1	$4,710.56	32,370.67
932.65	120.45		12	1,507.06	32,824.63
1,420.00	447.50	306.40	23	1,458.55	32,109.28
4,130.00		11.05 (BC)			27,968.23
89.93	2,250.00	1,050.00	28	4,157.48	28,735.78

Cash received June 29 and 30 and deposited in the mail for the general chequing account June 30 amounted to $4,407.96. Because the cash account balance at June 30 is not given, it must be calculated from other information in the problem.

Instructions

From the information above, prepare a bank reconciliation (bank balance to book balance) as of June 30, 1986, for the Hawkeye Company.

P7-5 The balance sheet of Rooster, Inc. at December 31, 1985 includes the following:

Notes receivable	$ 43,000	
Less: Notes receivable discounted	15,000	$ 28,000
Accounts receivable	$166,400	
Less: Allowance for doubtful accounts	12,400	154,000

Transactions in 1986 include the following:

1. Notes receivable discounted at December 31, 1985, matured and were paid with the exception of a $3,000 note for which the company had to pay $3,050, which included $50 interest and protest fees. Recovery is expected in 1986. (Use Notes Receivable Past Due account.)
2. Cash collected on accounts receivable totalled $135,000 including accounts of $25,000 on which 2% sales discounts were allowed.
3. $4,200 was received in payment of an account which was written off the books as worthless in 1983. (Hint: Reestablish the receivable account.)
4. Customer accounts of $14,400 were written off during the year.
5. At year-end the allowance for doubtful accounts was estimated to need a balance of $18,000. This estimate is based on an analysis of aged accounts receivable.
6. Rooster, Inc. discounted a $12,000, 90-day note dated November 1, 1986, on December 1, 1986. The note bears a 12% interest rate and was discounted at 10%. (Treat as a sale.)

Instructions

Prepare all journal entries necessary to reflect the transactions above.

P7-6 Presented below is information related to the accounts receivable accounts of Designor Creations, Inc. during the current year 1986.

1. The accounts receivable control account has a debit balance of $366,500 on December 31, 1986.
2. Two entries were made in the Bad Debt Expense account during the year: (1) a debit on December 31 for the amount credited to Allowance for Doubtful Accounts, and (2) a credit for $1,810 on November 3, 1986, because of a bankruptcy.
3. The Allowance for Doubtful Accounts is as follows for 1986.

Allowance for Doubtful Accounts

Nov. 3 Uncollectible accounts written off	1,810	Jan. 1 Beginning balance	6,660
		Dec. 31 5% of $366,500	18,325

4. An aging schedule of the accounts receivable as of December 31, 1986, is as follows:

Age	Net debit balance	% to be applied after correction made
Under 60 days	$164,664	1%
61–90 days	139,140	3%
91–120 days	39,924*	6%
Over 120 days	22,772	$3,600 definitely uncollectible; estimated remainder collectible 75%
	$366,500	

*The $1,810 write-off of receivables is related to the 91–120 day category.

5. A credit balance exists in the Accounts Receivable (61–90 days) of $3,960, which represents an advance on a sales contract.

Instructions

Assuming that the books have not been closed for 1986, make the necessary correcting entries.

P7-7 From inception of operations 1982, Summit carried no allowance for doubtful accounts. Uncollectible receivables were expensed as written off and recoveries were credited to income as collected. On March 1, 1986 (after the 1985 financial statements were issued), management recognized that Summit's accounting policy with respect to doubtful accounts was not correct, and determined that an allowance for doubtful accounts was necessary. A policy was established to maintain an allowance for doubtful accounts based on Summit's historical bad debt loss percentage applied to year-end accounts receivable. The historical bad debt loss percentage is to be recomputed each year based on all available past years up to a maximum of five years.

Information from Summit's records for five years is as follows:

Year	Credit Sales	Accounts Written Off	Recoveries
1982	$1,500,000	$15,000	$0
1983	2,250,000	38,000	2,700
1984	2,950,000	52,000	2,500
1985	3,300,000	65,000	4,800
1986	4,000,000	83,000	5,000

Accounts receivable balances were $1,250,000 and $1,460,000 at December 31, 1985, and December 31, 1986, respectively.

Instructions

(a) Prepare the journal entry, with appropriate explanation, to set up the allowance for doubtful accounts as of January 1, 1986. Show supporting computations in good form.

(b) Prepare a schedule analyzing the changes in the Allowance for Doubtful Accounts account for the year ended December 31, 1986. Show supporting computations in good form.

(AICPA adapted)

P7-8 Grafton Corporation operates in an industry that has a high rate of bad debts. On December 31, 1986, before any year-end adjustments, the balance in Grafton's accounts receivable account was $505,000 and the allowance for doubtful accounts had a balance of $25,000. The year-end balance reported in the statement of financial position for the allowance for doubtful accounts will be based on the aging schedule shown below.

Days Account Outstanding	Amount	Probability of Collection
Less than 15 days	$300,000	.98
Between 16 and 30 days	100,000	.90
Between 31 and 45 days	50,000	.80
Between 46 and 60 days	30,000	.70
Between 61 and 75 days	10,000	.60
Over 75 days	15,000	.00

Instructions

(a) What is the appropriate balance for the allowance for doubtful accounts on December 31, 1986?

(b) Show how accounts receivable would be presented on the balance sheet prepared on December 31,1986.

(c) What is the dollar effect of the year-end bad debt adjustment on the before-tax income for 1986?

P7-9 Honeywell Company finances some of its current operations by assigning accounts receivable to a finance company. On July 1, 1986, it assigned, under guarantee, specific accounts amounting to $50,000, the finance company advancing to Honeywell 80% of the accounts assigned (20% of the total to be withheld until the finance company has made its full recovery), less a finance charge of 1/2% of the total accounts assigned.

On July 31, Honeywell Company received a statement that the finance company had collected $24,000 of these accounts, and had made an additional charge of 1/2% of the total accounts outstanding as of July 31, this charge to be deducted at the time of the first remittance due Honeywell Company from the finance company. (Hint: Make entries at this time.) On August 31, 1986, Honeywell Company received a second statement from the finance company, together with a cheque for the amount due. The statement indicated that the finance company had collected an additional $19,000 and had made a further charge of 1/2% of the balance outstanding as of August 31.

Instructions

(a) Make all entries on the books of Honeywell Company that are involved in the transactions above.

(b) Explain how these accounts should be presented in the financial statements of Honeywell Company at July 31 and at August 31.

(AICPA adapted)

P7-10 Douglas Sports Company produces soccer, football, and track shoes. The treasurer has recently completed negotiations in which Douglas Sports agrees to loan Ehrlich Company, a leather supplier, $500,000. Ehrlich Company will issue a noninterest-bearing note due in five years (a 15% interest rate is appropriate), and has agreed to furnish Douglas Sports with leather at prices that are 10% lower than those usually charged.

Instructions

(a) Prepare the accounting entry to record this transaction on Douglas Sports Company's books.

(b) Determine the balances at the end of each year the note is outstanding for the following accounts for Douglas Sports Company:
Notes receivable
Unamortized discount
Interest revenue

P7-11 On December 31, 1986, Rexroad Company rendered services to Alberta Corporation at an agreed price of $80,000, accepting $20,000 down and agreeing to accept the balance in four equal instalments of $15,000 receivable each December 31. An assumed interest rate of 12% is implicit in the agreed price.

Instructions

Prepare the journal entries that would be recorded by the Rexroad Company for the sale and for the receipts and interest on the following dates. (Assume that the effective interest method is used for amortization purposes.)

(a) December 31, 1986.
(b) December 31, 1987.
(c) December 31, 1988.
(d) December 31, 1989.
(e) December 31, 1990.

P7-12 You are engaged in your fifth annual examination of the financial statements of NIU Corporation. Your examination is for the year ended December 31, 1986. The client prepared the following schedules of Trade Notes Receivable for you at December 31, 1986. You have verified the opening balances with your prior year's audit workpapers.

NIU Corporation
TRADE NOTES RECEIVABLE AND RELATED INTEREST RECEIVABLE
Trade Notes Receivable

Maker	Issue Date	Terms	Interest Rate	Bal. Dec. 31, 1985	1986		Bal. Dec. 31, 1986
					Debits	Credits	
Morley Co.	Apr. 1, 1985	One year	12%	$60,000		$ 60,000	
Exberg Co.	May 1, 1986	90 days after date	—		$ 20,000	19,625	$ 375
Clark Ind.	July 1, 1986	60 days after date	12%		4,000		4,000
J. Schmidt	Aug. 3, 1986	Demand	12%		10,000		10,000
Morreale Corp.	Oct. 2, 1986	60 days after date	12%		40,000 40,000	40,000	40,000
Slezak, Inc.	Nov. 1, 1986	90 days after date	8%		42,000	35,000	7,000
Petro Co.	Nov. 1, 1986	90 days after date	14%		24,000		24,000
			Totals	$60,000	$180,000	$154,625	$85,375

Interest Receivable

Due From	Bal. Dec. 31, 1985	1986		Bal. Dec. 31, 1986
		Debits	Credits	
Morley Co.	$5,400	$1,800	$7,200	
Clark Ind.		80		$ 80
J. Schmidt		400		400
Morreale Corp.		800	460	340
Slezak, Inc.		560		560
Petro Co.		560		560
Totals	$5,400	$4,200	$7,660	$1,940

Your examination reveals this information:

1. Interest is computed on a 360-day basis. In computing interest, it is the corporation's practice to exclude the first day of the note's term and to include the due date.

2. The Exberg Company's 90-day noninterest-bearing note was discounted on May 16 at 9%, and the proceeds were credited to the Trade Notes Receivable account. The note was paid at maturity.

3. Clark Industries became bankrupt on August 31, and the corporation will recover 75 cents on the dollar. The corporation uses the direct write-off method for recording bad debt expense. All of NIU Corporation's notes receivable provide for interest at a rate of 12% on the maturity value of a dishonoured note.

4. Jeannie Schmidt, president of NIU Corporation, confirmed that she owed NIU Corporation $10,000 and that she expected to pay the note within six months. You are satisfied that the note is collectible.

5. Morreale Corporation's 60-day note was discounted on November 1 at 10%, and the proceeds were credited to the Trade Notes Receivable and Interest Receivable accounts. On December 2, NIU Corporation received notice from the bank that Morreale Corporation's note was not paid at maturity and that it had been charged against NIU's chequing account by the bank. Upon receiving the notice from the bank, the bookkeeper recorded the note and the accrued interest in the Trade Notes Receivable and Interest Receivable accounts. Morreale Corporation paid NIU Corporation the full amount due in January, 1987.

6. Slezak, Inc.'s 90-day note was pledged as collateral for a $35,000, 60-day, 10% loan from the Royal Bank on December 1.

7. On November 1, the corporation received four, $6,000, 90-day notes from Petro Co. On December 1, the corporation received payment from Petro Co. for one of the $6,000 notes with accrued interest. Prepayment of the notes is allowed without penalty. The bookkeeper credited the Petro Company Accounts Receivable account for the cash received.

Instructions

Prepare the adjusting journal entries that you would suggest at December 31, 1986, for the transactions above. Reclassify all past due notes and related carrying costs to accounts receivable.

(AICPA adapted)

P7-13 Manitoba Woolens, Inc. factors $1,000,000 of accounts receivable with Dundee Credit Corp. on a without-recourse basis. On June 1, the receivable records are transferred to Dundee Credit which will make the collections. Dundee Credit assesses a finance charge of 4% of the total accounts receivable factored and retains an amount equal to 5% of the total receivables to cover sales discounts, returns, and allowances. Manitoba Woolens handles any returned goods, claims and allowances for defective goods, and disputes concerning shipments. Dundee handles the sales discounts and absorbs the credit losses.

During the month of June, the factor collects $680,000; merchandise totalling $13,500 is returned; sales discounts of $9,500 are taken; and allowances of $4,300 are granted.

During the month of July, the factor collects $279,000; merchandise totalling $1,700 is returned; no sales discounts are allowed; and allowances of $2,100 for defective goods are granted.

On August 1, Manitoba Woolens and Dundee Credit agree that any further returns, discounts, and allowances will be absorbed by Manitoba Woolens; Dundee therefore returns the balance of the retainer held for such events. Uncollectibles are estimated to be $4,800.

Instructions

(a) Prepare the entries on Manitoba Woolens' books at June 1, for the June transactions, for the July transactions, and at August 1.

(b) Prepare the entries on Dundee Credit's books at June 1, for the June transactions, for the July transactions, and at August 1.

P7-14 Allservice Photosetting Co. holds Wiley Company's $20,000, 6-month note receivable, dated July 31, 1985, payable on January 31, 1986 and bearing interest at 15%. On October 31, Allservice discounts with recourse Wiley's note at 10% at the Canadian National Bank.

Instructions

(a) Prepare journal entries on Allservice's books on the following dates, treating the discounting as a sale transaction:

1. July 31, 1985—receipt of the note.
2. October 31, 1985—discounted note with recourse.
3. January 31, 1986—Wiley pays principal and interest to Phoenix National Bank.
4. Assume that, instead of paying off the note on February 1, 1986, Wiley defaults and Allservice pays the note, interest, and a bank protest fee of $85.

(b) Prepare journal entries on Allservice's books on each of the four dates listed in (a), treating the discounting as a borrowing transaction.

8

VALUATION OF INVENTORIES: A COST BASIS APPROACH

Inventories are among the most significant assets of many enterprises; therefore, their description and measurement demand careful attention. For manufacturing and retail business enterprises, the sale of inventory at a price greater than total cost is the primary source of income; matching inventory cost appropriately against revenue is necessary for the determination of net income. Consequently, inventories are particularly significant because they may materially affect both the income statement and the balance sheet.

Inventories are asset items held for sale in the ordinary course of business or goods that will be used or consumed in the production of goods to be sold. Assets specifically excluded from inventory because they are not normally sold in the course of business include such items as plant and equipment awaiting final disposition and securities being held for sale. The accounting problems associated with inventory valuation are complex; Chapters 8 and 9 discuss the basic issues involved in recording, valuing, and reporting inventoriable items.

MAJOR CLASSIFICATIONS OF INVENTORY

Inventories are commonly considered in the context of merchandising concerns. A **merchandising (trading) concern** ordinarily purchases its merchandise in a form ready for sale to customers and reports the cost assigned to unsold units left on hand at the end of the period as merchandise inventory. Only one inventory account, Merchandise Inventory, appears in the financial statements of a trading concern. Many large businesses, however, are manufacturing concerns whose function is to produce goods to be sold to the merchandising firms (either wholesale or retail). A **manufacturing firm** normally has three inventory accounts—raw materials, work in process, and finished goods. The cost assigned to goods and materials on hand but not yet placed into production is reported as **raw materials inventory.** Raw materials include such items as the wood to make a baseball bat or the steel to make a car. These materials ultimately can be traced directly to the end product. At any point in a production process, some units generally are not completely processed. The cost of the raw material on which production has been started, but not completed, plus the cost of direct labour applied specifically to this material, and a ratable share of manufacturing overhead costs constitute the **work in process inventory.** The costs identified with the completed but unsold units on hand at the end of the fiscal period are reported as **finished goods inventory.** The relationship between these inventory accounts and the flow of costs through a manufacturing company is shown in the following illustration and contrasted to that of a merchandising firm.

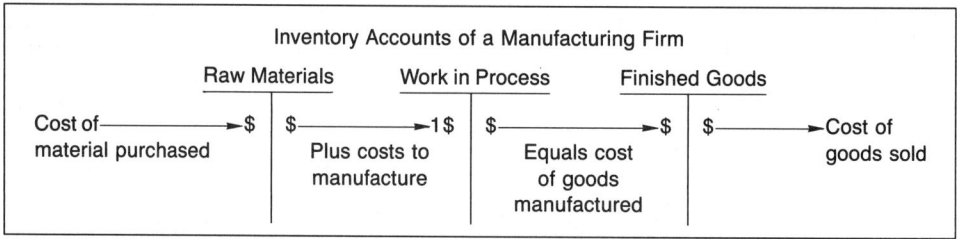

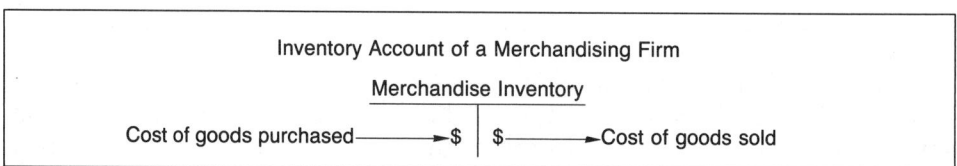

The *CICA Handbook* indicates that it is desirable to disclose the amounts of the major categories that make up total inventory.[1] It is, therefore, common to see three inventory accounts on the balance sheet of a manufacturer: (1) raw materials, (2) work in process, and (3) finished goods.[2] A **manufacturing** or **factory supplies inventory** account might also be included. This account includes such items as machine oils, nails, and cleaning materials that are used in production but are not the primary materials being processed. An annual report of Scott Paper Company illustrates the reporting of these accounts.

[1] *CICA Handbook* (Toronto: The Canadian Institute of Chartered Accountants), Section 3030, par. 10.

[2] *Financial Reporting in Canada—1983* (Toronto: CICA, 1983) indicated that all components of inventory were set out by approximately 43% of the 325 companies surveyed. Lack of such segregation by the remaining companies would, in part, be because they had only one category; for example, they were merchandising companies.

Scott Paper Company	
Current assets	(Thousands of dollars)
Inventories	
Finished products	$401,966
Work in process	15,231
Pulp, logs, and pulpwood	22,412
Other materials and supplies	29,836

MANAGEMENT INTEREST IN ACCOUNTING FOR INVENTORIES

From the standpoint of management, inventories constitute an extremely important asset. The investment in inventories is frequently the largest current asset in manufacturing and retail establishments, and also may be a material portion of the company's total assets. If unsaleable items have accumulated in the inventory, a potential loss exists. If products ordered by customers are not available in the desired style, quality, and quantity, sales and customers may be lost. Excessive or unsaleable inventories may result from an inefficient purchasing procedure, faulty manufacturing techniques, or inadequate sales efforts. In an economic environment that places significant importance on cash flow management and where interest costs are relatively high, businesses must monitor inventory levels carefully in order to avoid excessive investment in inventory and to control the related financing costs.

In many respects, inventories are more sensitive to general business fluctuations than are other assets. In periods of prosperity when sales are high, merchandise can be disposed of readily, and quantities on hand may not appear excessive; but, with even a slight downward trend in the business cycle, many lines of merchandise begin to move slowly, stocks pile up, and obsolescence becomes a possibility.[3]

For these and other reasons, management (and therefore the accounting department) is vitally interested in inventory planning and control. One essential of inventory control is an accounting system with accurate, up-to-date records, containing the information needed by management to implement its manufacturing, merchandising, and financial policies. This degree of control often requires a perpetual inventory system.

DETERMINING INVENTORY QUANTITIES

As indicated in Chapter 3, inventory records may be maintained on a perpetual or periodic inventory system basis. In a **perpetual inventory system,** purchases and issues of goods are recorded directly in the inventory account as they occur. No Purchases account is used because the purchases are debited directly to the inventory account. A Cost of Goods Sold account is used to accumulate the issuances from inventory. The balance in the inventory account at the end of the year should represent the ending inventory amounts.

---

[3]North American manufacturers are particularly sensitive to the level of inventory that they maintain in light of competition with the Japanese. For example, auto makers now carry $700 to $1,000 worth of inventory per automobile, and it is estimated that inventory levels can be cut by 20% to 30%. However, this will still not match the Japanese, who maintain an inventory of approximately only $200, per car. The Japanese have certain advantages, such as no strikes and proximity of suppliers to manufacturers.

When the inventory records are maintained on a **periodic inventory system,** a Purchases account is used and the beginning balance in the Inventory account is unchanged during the period. At the end of the accounting period the Inventory account must be adjusted by closing out the beginning inventory amount and recording the ending inventory amount. Cost of goods sold is therefore determined by adding the beginning inventory together with the net purchases and deducting the ending inventory.

To illustrate the difference between a perpetual and a periodic system, assume that Katt, Ltd. has the following transactions during the current year:

Sales	600 units at $12 = $7,200
Beginning inventory	100 units at $ 6 = $ 600
Purchases	900 units at $ 6 = $5,400
Ending inventory	400 units at $ 6 = $2,400

The entries to record these transactions during the current year are as follows:

Entries under Perpetual and Periodic Inventory Systems

Perpetual Inventory System			Periodic Inventory System		
Purchase merchandise for resale:					
Inventory (900 at $6)	5,400		Purchases (900 at $6)	5,400	
Accounts Payable		5,400	Accounts Payable		5,400
Record sale:					
Accounts Receivable	7,200		Accounts Receivable	7,200	
Sales (600 at $12)		7,200	Sales (600 at $12)		7,200
Cost of Goods Sold			(No entry necessary)		
(600 at $6)	3,600				
Inventory		3,600			
Adjusting/Closing entries:					
(No entry necessary)			Cost of Goods Sold	600	
			Inventory (beginning)		600
			Inventory (ending)	2,400	
			Cost of Goods Sold		2,400
			Cost of Goods Sold	5,400	
			Purchases		5,400

In the past, few companies maintained inventory records in both quantities and dollars. However, with the advent of computers, particularly the mini- and micro-computers, small as well as large businesses today maintain perpetual inventories that report both quantities and dollars and much more. The additional data might consist of such items as catalogue or reference number, supplier, location, and reorder points. Perpetual inventory systems are used extensively for such high-cost items as automobiles and appliances. Conversely, enterprises that sell a large variety of low-cost items (e.g., hardware and drug stores) rely heavily on the periodic inventory system.

How is the ending inventory determined in a periodic system? One method is to take a physical inventory count once a year. However, most companies need more current information on the quantities of their inventory items to protect against stockouts or overpurchasing, and to aid in the preparation of monthly or quarterly financial data. As a consequence, many companies use a **modified perpetual inven-**

tory system in which increases and decreases in quantities are kept in a detailed inventory record. As the detailed inventory record does not include dollar amounts, it is therefore merely an informational memorandum device outside the double-entry system that helps in determining the level of inventory at any point in time.

Whether a company maintains a perpetual inventory in quantities and dollars, quantities only, or has no perpetual inventory record at all, it probably takes a physical inventory count once a year. No matter what type of inventory records are used or how well organized the procedures for recording purchases and requisitions, the danger of error is always present. Waste, breakage, theft, improper entry, failure to prepare or record requisitions, and any number of similar possibilities may cause the inventory records to differ from the actual inventory on hand. The inventory records must therefore be verified periodically by actual count, weight, or measurement of the inventory items. These counts are compared with the detailed inventory records. When a difference exists between the perpetual inventory account amount, a separate entry is needed to adjust the perpetual inventory account. To illustrate, assume that at the end of the reporting period the perpetual inventory account contained an inventory balance of $4,000, but a physical count indicated $3,800. The entry to record this writedown is as follows:

Inventory Over & Short	200	
Inventory		200

Perpetual inventory overages and shortages generally represent a misstatement of cost of goods sold, especially if the difference is a result of normal and expected shrinkage, breakage, shoplifting, etc. Inventory Over and Short would therefore be an adjustment of cost of goods sold. In practice, the account Inventory Over and Short is sometimes reported in the other revenues and gains or other expenses and losses section, depending on its balance. Note that in a periodic inventory system the account Inventory Over and Short does not arise because there are no accounting records available against which to compare the physical count. Thus, inventory overages and shortages are buried in cost of goods sold.

As indicated above, most companies take a **physical inventory count** only once a year.[4] More frequent counts are desirable in businesses that deal in extremely costly merchandise, but in general an annual physical inventory is sufficient to assure reasonable accuracy of the records. Insofar as possible, the physical inventory should be taken close to the end of the company's fiscal year so that correct inventory quantities are available for use in preparing annual accounting reports and statements. However, this is not always possible; therefore, physical inventories taken within two or three months of the year's end are quite satisfactory, if the detailed inventory records are maintained with a fair degree of accuracy.

BASIC ISSUES IN INVENTORY VALUATION

Because goods sold or used during an accounting period seldom correspond exactly to the goods bought or produced during that period, the physical inventory either increases or decreases from the beginning to the end of the period. Accounting for these increases or decreases requires that the cost of all the goods available for sale or use be allocated between the goods that were sold or used and those that are still

---

[4]In recent years, some companies have developed inventory controls or methods of determining inventories, including statistical sampling, that are highly effective in determining inventory quantities and sufficiently reliable to make unnecessary an annual physical count of each item of inventory.

on hand. The **cost of goods available for sale or use** is the sum of (1) the cost of the goods on hand at the beginning of the period and (2) the cost of the goods acquired or produced during the period. The **cost of goods sold** is the difference between the cost of goods available for sale during the period and the cost of goods on hand at the end of the period as shown below:

Beginning inventory, Jan. 1	$100,000
Cost of goods acquired or produced during the year	800,000
Total cost of goods available for sale	$900,000
Ending inventory, Dec. 31	200,000
Cost of goods sold during the year	$700,000

Inventory accounting involves the determination of each of the items listed above, but the focus is generally on the valuation of the ending inventory.

The valuation of inventories can be a complex process that requires determination of:

1. the physical goods or items to be included in inventory
2. the cost to be included in inventory
3. the cost flow assumption to be adopted.

GOODS OR ITEMS TO BE INCLUDED IN INVENTORY

Goods in Transit

Technically, purchases should be recorded when legal title to the goods passes to the buyer. General day-to-day practice, however, is to record acquisitions when the goods are received, because it is difficult for the buyer to determine the exact time of legal passage of title for every purchase, and because no material error is likely to result from such a practice if it is consistently applied.

Even though the legal rule is not followed in day-to-day transactions, purchased merchandise in transit at the end of a fiscal period, to which legal title has passed, should be recorded as purchases of the fiscal period. This means that ordinarily all goods shipped f.o.b. (free on board) shipping point that are in transit at the end of the period belong to the buyer and should be shown in the buyer's records, because legal title to these goods passed to the buyer when the goods were shipped. To disregard such purchases would result in an understatement of inventories and accounts payable in the balance sheet and an understatement of purchases and ending inventories in the income statement.

The accountant normally prepares a purchase cut-off schedule or worksheet at the end of the period and analyzes the transactions near the end of the year to ensure that the purchases and inventories are recorded in the proper period. Preparation of a purchase cut-off requires application of the "passage of title" rule in the following manner: if the goods are shipped **f.o.b. shipping point,** title passes to the buyer when the seller delivers the goods to the common carrier (transporter) who acts as an agent for the buyer; if the goods are shipped **f.o.b. destination,** title does not pass until the buyer receives the goods from the common carrier. "Shipping point" and "destination" are designated by a particular location; for example, f.o.b. Montreal. When the purchase-sales contract makes no reference to the freight charges it is assumed that (1) the buyer pays the freight when the terms are f.o.b. shipping point and (2) the seller pays the freight when the terms are f.o.b. destination. This assumption, however, does not always hold. In buying a new car from General Motors or Ford, title does not pass until the buyer accepts delivery of the car from the local automobile dealer (f.o.b. destination), but the customer may be required to pay the freight from the manufacturing site (freight collect). The term **freight collect** means that the freight charges are paid by the purchaser; **freight prepaid** means that the freight is paid by the seller. For example, "f.o.b. shipping point, freight prepaid" means that title passes to the buyer when the seller places the goods in the hands of the freight company. In addition, the seller is required to pay the freight charges. To illustrate further, "f.o.b. shipping point, freight collect" means that title passes to the buyer when the seller places the goods in the hands of the freight company, but the buyer is required to pay the freight charges.

In cases where there is some question as to whether title has passed, the accountant should exercise judgement, taking into consideration the practices common to the industry, the intent of the sales agreement, the policies of the parties involved, and any other available evidence of intent.

Consigned Goods

A specialized method of marketing certain types of products makes use of a device known as a consignment shipment. Under this arrangement, one party, the consignor, ships merchandise to another, the consignee, who is to act as an agent for the consignor in selling the goods. The consignee agrees to accept the goods without any liability, except to exercise due care and reasonable protection from loss or damage, until the goods are sold to a third party. When the goods are sold by the consignee, the sale price, less a selling commission and expenses incurred in accomplishing the sale, is remitted to the consignor.

Goods out on consignment remain the property of the consignor and must be included in the consignor's inventory at purchase price or production cost plus the cost of handling and shipping involved in the transfer to the consignee. Occasionally, the inventory out on consignment is shown as a separate item, but unless the amount is large there is little need for this. No entry to adjust the inventory account is made by the consignee for goods received because they are the property of the consignor. The consignee should be extremely careful not to include any of the goods consigned as a part of inventory. Accounting for consignments is discussed in Chapter 19.

Special Sale Agreements

As indicated earlier, transfer of legal title is the general guideline that accountants follow in determining whether an item should be included in inventory. Unfortunately, transfer of legal title and the underlying economics of the situation may not match, and therefore considerable professional judgement must be exercised. For example, it is possible that legal title has passed to the purchaser but that the economic substance of the transaction is such that the seller of the goods retains the risks of ownership. Conversely, transfer of legal title may not occur, but the economic substance of the transaction is that the seller no longer holds the risks of ownership. Three special situations are illustrated here to indicate the types of problems encountered in practice. These are as follows:

1. Sales with buybacks.
2. Sales with high rates of return.
3. Sales on instalments.

Sales with Buybacks (often referred to as **product financing arrangements**)   A variety of approaches are used in practice whereby an enterprise finances its inventory without reporting on its balance sheet the liability or the inventory. Such an approach usually involves the "sale" of a good with either an implicit or explicit "buyback" arrangement. To illustrate, Hill Enterprises transfers ("sells") inventory to Chase, Inc., and as part of the same transaction agrees to repurchase this merchandise at a specified price over a specified period in the future. Chase, Inc. then uses the inventory as collateral and borrows against the value of the product from a bank and remits the proceeds to Hill Enterprises as "payment" for the inventory. Hill Enterprises then repurchases the inventory in the future and Chase, Inc. employs the proceeds from repayment to meet its loan obligation.

The essence of this transaction is that Hill Enterprises is financing its inventory even though technical title to the merchandise was transferred to Chase, Inc. The advantages to Hill Enterprises for structuring a transaction in this manner are the possible avoidance of personal property taxes (in some Canadian municipalities), the removal of the current liability from its balance sheet, and the ability to manipulate income. The advantages to Chase, Inc. are that the purchase of the goods may solve a LIFO liquidation problem (discussed later) and that it may be interested in a reciprocal agreement at a later date.

Legal title has transferred in this situation, but the economic substance of the transaction is that the risks of ownership are retained by Hill Enterprises (the seller). These transactions are often described as **parking transactions** in practice, because the seller simply parks the inventory on another enterprise's balance sheet for a short period of time. In the United States, the profession has taken steps to curtail this practice by requiring that when a repurchase agreement exists at a set price and this price covers all costs of the inventory plus related holding costs, the inventory and related liability remain on the seller's books.[5] While this U.S. standard may be a useful Canadian reference source, since there is no comparable Canadian standard, Canadian practitioners must continue to exercise their judgement regarding substance over form in such situations.

Sales with High Rates of Return   Formal or informal agreements often exist in such industries as publishing, records and tapes, and toys and sporting goods that permit merchandise to be returned for a full refund or that allow for an adjustment to be made to the amount owed. To illustrate, MEM Publishing Company sells textbooks to University Bookstores with an agreement that any books not sold may be returned for full credit. In the past, approximately 25% of the textbooks sold to University Bookstores were returned. How should MEM Publishing report its sales transactions? One alternative is to record the sale at the full amount and establish an Estimated Sales Returns and Allowances account. A second possibility is not to record any sales until circumstances indicate that the buyer will not return the inventory. The key question is: Under what circumstances should the inventory be

---

[5] "Accounting for Product Financing Arrangements," *Statement of Financial Accounting Standards No. 49* (Stamford, Conn.: FASB, 1981).

considered sold and removed from MEM's inventory? An acceptable accounting position for such cases is that, if a reasonable prediction of the returns can be established, then the goods should be considered sold. Conversely, if returns are unpredictable, then removal of these goods from the inventory does not appear warranted.[6]

Sales on Instalment   "Goods sold on instalment" describes any type of sale in which payment is required in periodic instalments over an extended period of time. Because the risk of loss from uncollectibles is higher in instalment sale situations than in other sale transactions, the seller often asks for protection in the form of a conditional sales contract that withholds legal title to the merchandise until all the payments have been made. The question is whether the inventory should be considered sold, even though legal title has not passed. The economic substance of the transaction is that the goods should be excluded from the seller's inventory if the percentage of bad debts can be reasonably estimated. Chapter 19 covers in detail the accounting for instalment sales. Instalment sales are discussed here to show that in some cases legal title may not have passed, but the goods should be removed from the inventory.

Effect of Inventory Errors

If items are incorrectly included in or excluded from inventory, there will be errors in the financial statements. To illustrate, suppose that certain goods in transit that we owned were not recorded as a purchase and were not counted in ending inventory. To disregard such purchases would result in an understatement of inventories and accounts payable in the balance sheet and an understatement of purchases and ending inventories in the income statement. The net income for the period would not be affected by the omission of such purchases, since purchases and ending inventory would both be understated by the same amount, the error thereby offsetting itself in cost of goods sold. Total working capital would not change, but the **current ratio** would be higher because of the omission of equal amounts from the inventory and accounts payable.

To illustrate the effect on working capital items, Barker Ltd. reports the following at the end of a fiscal period:

Current assets	$120,000
Current liabilities	40,000
Current ratio $\left(\dfrac{\$120,000}{\$\ 40,000}\right)$	3 to 1

If Barker Ltd. would have included goods in transit of $40,000 in ending inventory, then the following would be presented:

Current assets	$160,000
Current liabilities	80,000
Current ratio $\left(\dfrac{\$160,000}{\$\ 80,000}\right)$	2 to 1

[6]"Revenue Recognition When Right of Return Exists," *Statement of Financial Accounting Standards No. 48* (Stamford, Conn.: FASB, 1981).

The correct current ratio is 2 to 1 instead of 3 to 1, because the goods in transit should be reported in both the inventory and accounts payable.

What would happen if the beginning inventory and the goods purchased are recorded correctly, but some items on hand are not included in ending inventory? In this situation the ending inventory, net income, current ratio, and working capital are all understated. Net income is understated because cost of goods sold is larger than it should be; the current ratio and working capital are understated because a portion of ending inventory is omitted.

To illustrate the effect on net income, assume that the ending inventory of Antonio Ltd. is understated by $10,000 and that all other items are correctly stated. The effect of this error will be to show a lower net income in the current year and a higher net income in the following year relative to the correct net income figures. The error will affect the following year because the beginning inventory will be understated, thereby causing net income to be overstated. Both net income figures are misstated, but the total for the two years is correct, as the two errors will be counterbalanced (offset) as illustrated below:

Antonio Ltd.
Effect of Inventory Error on Two Periods
(all figures assumed)

	1986		1987	
	Correct	Incorrect	Incorrect	Correct
Revenues	$100,000	$100,000	$100,000	$100,000
Cost of goods sold				
Beginning inventory	25,000	25,000	20,000	30,000
Purchased or produced	45,000	45,000	60,000	60,000
Goods available for sale	70,000	70,000	80,000	90,000
Less: Ending inventory	30,000	20,000	40,000	40,000
Cost of goods sold	40,000	50,000	40,000	50,000
Gross profit	60,000	50,000	60,000	50,000
Administrative and				
selling expenses	40,000	40,000	40,000	40,000
Net income	$ 20,000	$ 10,000	$ 20,000	$ 10,000

total income for two
years correct ($30,000)

If a purchase is not recorded, but the goods are included in ending inventory, the reverse effect occurs. Net income, the current ratio, and working capital are all overstated in the year of the error. The effect of the error on the net income will be counterbalanced in the subsequent year (assuming purchases are recorded in the next year), but both years' income statements will be misstated.

We cannot overemphasize the importance that proper inventory computation plays in presenting financial statements. One has only to read the financial press to learn how the misstatement of inventory can generate high income numbers. For example, Anixter Bros. Inc. recently had to restate its income by $1.7 million because an accountant in the antenna manufacturing division overstated the ending inventory, thereby reducing its cost of sales. The practice of some Canadian farm equipment manufacturers of treating deliveries to dealers as sales of the company (with concurrent reductions in inventory) can also significantly inflate reported income when sales to the ultimate consumer are not keeping pace with such deliveries. These illustrations indicate that an accurate computation of purchases and inventory is needed to ensure that appropriate income and asset figures are presented.

COSTS TO BE INCLUDED IN INVENTORY

One of the most important problems in dealing with inventories concerns the amount at which the inventory should be carried in the accounts and stated in the accounting reports. Inventories, like other assets, are generally accounted for on a basis of cost (other bases are discussed in Chapter 9).

Product Costs

In defining cost as it applies to inventories, it becomes necessary to define inventoriable costs **(product costs)**; that is, those costs that are said to attach to the inventory and are considered to be a part of the total inventory valuation. Charges directly connected with the bringing of goods to the place of business of the buyer and converting such goods to a saleable condition are accepted as proper inventoriable costs. Such charges would include freight and hauling charges on goods purchased, other direct costs of acquisition, and labour and other production costs incurred in processing the goods up to the time of sale.

It would seem proper also to allocate to inventories a share of any buying costs or expenses of a purchasing department, storage costs, and other costs incurred in storing or handling the goods before they are sold. Because of the practical difficulties involved in allocating such costs and expenses, however, these items are not ordinarily included in valuing inventories.

Period Costs

Selling expenses and, under ordinary circumstances, **general and administration expenses** are not considered to be directly related to the acquisition or production of goods and, therefore, are not considered to be a part of the cost of inventories. Such costs are **period costs** rather than product costs. Conceptually, these expenses are as much a cost of the product as the initial purchase price and related freight charges attached to the product. Why then are these costs not considered inventoriable?

In some industries these charges are not material, and no real purpose is served by making an allocation of these costs to inventory. In other cases, especially where selling expenses are significant, the cost is more directly related to the cost of goods sold than to the unsold inventory. In most cases the costs, especially administrative expenses, are so unrelated or indirectly related to the immediate production process that any allocation is purely arbitrary. One guideline that may be followed is to charge to inventory those costs that bear a fairly direct relationship to the quantity produced. If, for example, an increase in administrative expenses occurs, without subsequent increase in inventories, justification exists for treating the cost as a period charge on the basis that the inventory quantities were not affected.

Interest costs associated with getting inventories ready for sale usually are expensed as incurred. A major argument for this approach is that interest costs are a cost of financing and should not be considered a cost of the asset. Others have argued, however, that interest costs incurred to finance activities associated with bringing inventories to a condition ready for sale are as much a cost of the asset as materials, labour, and overhead and, therefore, should be capitalized.[7] In the United States, the FASB indicated that interest cost related to assets constructed for its own use or assets produced as discrete projects (such as ships or real estate projects) for sale or lease should be capitalized.[8] It is emphasized that these discrete projects should take considerable time, entail substantial expenditures, and be likely to involve significant amounts of interest cost. Interest costs should not be capitalized for inventories that are routinely manufactured or otherwise produced in large quantities on a repetitive basis because the informational benefit does not justify the cost of doing so.

Treatment of Purchase Discounts

In accordance with practice, **purchase discounts** have been treated in the accounts either as a financial revenue or as a reduction of purchases. From a theoretical standpoint, the arguments for treatment as a reduction of purchases are stronger than those usually presented in support of financial revenue. If discounts received for prompt payment of purchase invoices are shown as revenue, this would result in recognizing revenue as realized before the goods have been sold, at least to the extent that such purchases are still in the inventory at the end of the accounting period. It is generally held that a business does not realize revenue by buying goods and paying bills; it realizes revenue by selling goods, the sale transaction being an essential step in the revenue realization process.

The treatment of purchase discounts as financial revenue has been supported by the argument that it is similar to interest earned in that it represents a reduction allowed by the seller so that cash may be obtained promptly. This argument has little merit; it may be countered by the statement that the buyer is not in any sense lending money to the seller; the buyer is merely paying a bill for purchases, and the amount paid is the cost of such purchases.

The use of a Purchase Discounts account indicates that the company is reporting its purchases and accounts payable at the gross amount. An alternative approach is to record the purchases and accounts payable at an amount net of the cash discounts. This treatment is often considered more appropriate because the net amount (1) provides a correct reporting of the cost of the asset and related liability and (2) presents the opportunity to measure the inefficiency of financial management if the discount is not taken. In the net approach, the failure to take a purchase discount within the discount period is recorded in a Purchase Discounts Lost

[7]The reporting rules related to interest cost capitalization have their greatest impact in accounting for long-term assets and, therefore, are discussed in detail in Chapter 11. This brief overview provides the basic issues when inventories are involved.

[8]"Capitalization of Interest Cost," *Statement of Financial Accounting Standards No. 34* (Stamford, Conn.: FASB, 1979). While the CICA has initiated a move to study similar issues in Canada, no formal document on the subject has yet been published.

account. The following example serves to illustrate the difference between the gross and net methods.

Entries under Gross and Net Methods			
Gross Method		**Net Method**	
Purchase cost $10,000, terms 2/10, net 30:			
Purchases	10,000	Purchases	9,800
Accounts Payable	10,000	Accounts Payable	9,800
Invoices of $4,000 are paid within discount period:			
Accounts Payable	4,000	Accounts Payable	3,920
Purchase Discounts	80	Cash	3,920
Cash	3,920		
Invoices of $6,000 are paid after discount period:			
Accounts Payable	6,000	Accounts Payable	5,880
Cash	6,000	Purchase Discounts Lost	120
		Cash	6,000

As indicated earlier, if the **gross method** is employed, purchase discounts should be reported as a deduction from purchases on the income statement. If the **net method** is used, purchase discounts lost should be considered a financial expense and reported in the Other Expense section of the income statement. In addition, when purchases are recorded net, beginning and ending inventories are reported on the same basis. Many believe that the difficulty involved in using the somewhat more complicated net method is not justified by the resulting benefits, which may account for the widespread use of the less logical but simpler gross method. In addition, some contend that management is reluctant to report the amount of purchase discounts lost in the financial statements.

Manufacturing Costs

As previously indicated, a business that manufactures goods uses three inventory accounts—raw materials, work in process, and finished goods. Work in process and finished goods include raw materials, direct labour, and manufacturing overhead costs. Manufacturing overhead costs include all manufacturing costs except direct materials and direct labour. Items included in manufacturing overhead are indirect material, depreciation, taxes, insurance, heat, electricity, and other costs that are incurred to manufacture the finished products. To illustrate how these different costs affect the inventory accounts, a **cost of goods manufactured statement** for Leonard Ltd. is presented on page 378.

The Cost of Raw Materials Consumed section is presented in a format similar to that used for reporting cost of goods sold in the income statement. Cost of goods manufactured statements are prepared primarily for internal use; such details are rarely disclosed in published financial statements. The Cost of Goods Sold section in the income statement for a manufacturing firm is similar to that of a merchandising concern. The principal difference is the substitution of cost of goods manufactured during the year for the details related to purchases of merchandise.

Leonard Ltd.
STATEMENT OF COST OF GOODS MANUFACTURED
Year Ended December 31, 1986

Raw materials consumed			
Raw materials inventory, Jan. 1, 1986			$ 14,000
Add net purchases:			
Purchases		$126,000	
Less: Purchase returns and allowances	$1,800		
Purchase discounts	1,200	3,000	123,000
Raw materials available for use			$137,000
Less: Raw materials inventory, Dec. 31, 1986			17,000
			$120,000
Direct labour			200,000
Manufacturing overhead			
Supervisors' salaries		$52,000	
Indirect labour		20,000	
Factory supplies used		18,000	
Taxes		15,000	
Heat, light, power, and water		13,000	
Depreciation on building and equipment		12,000	
Factory rent		11,000	
Tools expense		2,000	
Patent expense		1,000	
Miscellaneous factory expenses		6,000	150,000
Total manufacturing costs for the period			$470,000
Work in process inventory, Jan. 1, 1986			33,000
Total manufacturing costs			$503,000
Less: Work in process inventory, Dec. 31, 1986			28,000
Cost of goods manufactured during the year			$475,000

If the inventory of finished goods was $16,000 at the beginning of the year and $10,000 at the end of the year, the Cost of Goods Sold section of the income statement would appear as follows:

Cost of Goods Sold	
Finished goods inventory, Jan. 1, 1986	$ 16,000
Cost of goods manufactured during 1986	475,000
Cost of goods available for sale	$491,000
Finished goods inventory, Dec. 31, 1986	10,000
Cost of goods sold	$481,000

The principles that are applied in classifying inventory amounts on the income statement and on the balance sheet are the same for a manufacturing firm as for a merchandising concern.

Variable Costing versus Absorption Costing

Fixed manufacturing overhead costs present a special problem in costing inventories, because two concepts exist relative to the costs of the product as it flows through the manufacturing process. These two concepts are (1) **variable costing,** frequently called **direct costing,** and (2) **absorption costing,** also called **full costing.**

In a variable cost system all costs must be classified as variable or fixed. **Variable costs** are those that fluctuate in direct proportion to changes in input or output, and **fixed costs** are those that remain constant in spite of changes in output. Under variable costing only costs that vary directly with the volume of production are charged to products as manufacturing takes place. Only direct material, direct labour, and the variable costs in manufacturing overhead are charged to work in process and finished goods inventories and appear as cost of goods sold. Such fixed overhead costs as property taxes, insurance, depreciation on plant building, and salaries of supervisors are considered to be **period costs.** All fixed costs are charged as expenses to the current period under variable costing. Because the fixed costs are not viewed as costs of the products being manufactured, they are not associated with inventories.

Under **absorption costing,** all manufacturing costs, variable and fixed, direct and indirect, incurred in the factory or production process attach to the product and are included in the cost of inventory. Direct material, direct labour, and all manufacturing overhead—fixed as well as variable—are charged to output and allocated to cost of goods sold and inventories.

Proponents of the variable costing system believe that it provides data that are more useful to management in formulating pricing policies and in controlling cost than are data prepared under the conventional absorption costing method. Information for marginal income analysis, for fixed and variable expense analysis, and for cost-volume-profit analysis is readily available. Also, because fixed costs are included in inventory under the absorption costing system, it may be argued that such a system would result in distorting net income from period to period when production volume fluctuates each period. If such is the case, variable costing may be a more appropriate basis for reporting income. Absorption costing, however, is the more frequently used basis for external financial reporting. Its supporters believe that it provides a more reasonable representation of a firm's investment in inventories.

In the *CICA Handbook,* the position on inventory costing is as follows:

> In the case of inventories of work in process and finished goods, cost should include the laid-down cost of materials plus the cost of direct labour applied to the product and the applicable share of overhead expense properly chargeable to production.[9]

This statement leaves to one's judgement the issue of how fixed overhead costs are to be treated in terms of whether or not they are "properly chargeable to production." In Section 3030, paragraph 3, the *CICA Handbook* states that "in some cases, a portion of fixed overhead is excluded where its inclusion would distort the net income for the period by reason of fluctuating volume of production." Therefore, this guideline appears to suggest that variable costing would be considered more the exception than the rule for external financial reporting. Clearly, however, judgement is called for when making a decision in particular circumstances.

METHODS OF INVENTORY VALUATION

After having determined the number of units of ending inventory and what costs are to be included in the inventory account, another decision must be made before

[9]*CICA Handbook,* Section 3030, par. 6.

the inventory valuation can be carried out. The decision requires making a choice of which of several methods or approaches for inventory costing is to be used. The methods available include the following:

Cost Flow Methods:
    Specific Identification
    First-in, First-out (FIFO)
    Average Cost (weighted average or moving average)
    Last-in, First-out (LIFO)
    Base Stock
    Standard Cost
Cost Modified for Market Value Changes Methods:
    Lower of Cost and Market
    Current Replacement Cost
Cost Approximation (Estimation) Methods:
    Gross Profit
    Retail Inventory
Long-term Construction Contract Methods:
    Completed Contract Approach
    Percentage of Completion Approach

The method chosen will depend on several factors. The remainder of this chapter will consider the various aspects of the cost flow methods identified above. The lower of cost and market, gross profit, and retail inventory methods are examined in Chapter 9. Because the choice of approach to account for long-term construction contracts is related to a revenue recognition (timing) decision, these methods will be examined in Chapter 19. The current replacement cost method will be discussed in Chapter 25.

WHICH COST FLOW ASSUMPTION SHOULD BE ADOPTED?

During any given fiscal period it is likely that merchandise will be purchased at several different prices. If inventories are to be priced at cost and numerous purchases have been made at different unit costs, the question arises as to which of the various cost prices should be used. That is, which unit costs are to be assigned to inventory on the balance sheet, and which costs are to be charged to Cost of Goods Sold on the income statement? Conceptually, a specific identification of the given items sold and unsold seems optimal, but this measure is often not only difficult but impossible to achieve. Consequently, for practical reasons and in the interests of reliable financial reporting, the accountant must turn to the consistent application of one of several cost methods that are based on differing but systematic inventory cost flow assumptions. Therefore, the actual physical flow of goods and the cost flow assumption are often quite different. There is no requirement that the cost flow assumption adopted be consistent with the physical movement of goods.

Date	Purchases	Sold or Issued	Balance
Mar. 2	2,000 @ $4.00		2,000 units
Mar. 15	6,000 @ 4.40		8,000 units
Mar. 19		4,000 units	4,000 units
Mar. 30	2,000 @ 4.50		6,000 units

The ending inventory consisted of 6,000 units. Also, the 4,000 units were sold for $10.00 each for a total sales revenue of $40,000.

Issues regarding the various cost flow methods will be illustrated and discussed in the remainder of this chapter using the data on page 380, which summarize inventory-related activities of a company during its first month of operations. The company experienced increasing unit prices for its purchases throughout the month.

The problem is to determine which price or prices to use in order to assign a valuation to the 6,000 units of ending inventory and to the 4,000 units sold. The solution will depend on what one wishes to accomplish. There are, as previously indicated, several acceptable alternative cost flow methods which may be chosen. These methods are based on different assumptions and accomplish different objectives. A suggested approach to selecting a method is as follows:

1. Identify possible objectives to be accomplished.
2. Know the different acceptable methods, their assumptions and how they work.
3. Evaluate the advantages and disadvantages of the different methods for achieving the objectives.
4. Choose the method appropriate to the situation and the primary objective(s) to be accomplished.

OBJECTIVES OF INVENTORY VALUATION

The following general objectives are often associated with making a decision as to which inventory cost flow method to choose:

1. To match expenses (cost of goods sold) realistically against revenue.
2. To report inventory on the balance sheet at a realistic amount.
3. To minimize income taxes.

While the first two are legitimate objectives of financial statements, the third should not be relevant to financial statement accounting; however, it sometimes enters into financial accounting systems for expediency.

The financial statement objectives of inventory valuation are inherently logical and useful when assessing the merits and limitations of the various cost flow methods of inventory valuation within the framework of generally accepted accounting principles. They do, however, beg the question of "what is realistic?" The answer will depend on the purpose of preparing the financial statements. More will be said of this later in this chapter under the heading "Which Method to Select?"

COST FLOW METHODS OF INVENTORY VALUATION: THEIR ASSUMPTIONS AND HOW THEY WORK

Specific Identification

Specific identification calls for identifying each item sold and each item in inventory. The costs of the specific items sold are included in the cost of goods sold, while the costs of specific items on hand are included in the inventory. This method may be used only in instances where it is practical to separate physically the different purchases made. Any goods on hand may then be identified as quantities remaining from specific purchases, and the invoice cost of each lot or item may be separately determined. Obviously this method has a very limited application because of the impossibility or impracticability of segregating separate purchases in most instances. It can be successfully applied, however, in situations where a relatively small number of costly, easily distinguishable items are handled. In the retail trade this includes some types of jewellery, fur coats, automobiles, and some furniture and appliances. In manufacturing it includes special orders and many products manufactured under a job cost system.

Given the previous example data, suppose it was determined that the 6,000 units of inventory consisted of 1,000 from the March 2 purchase, 3,000 from the March 15 purchase, and 2,000 from the March 30 purchase. Ending inventory and cost of goods sold would be determined as follows:

Specific Identification Method			
Ending Inventory: Date Purchased	Units	Unit Cost	Total
Mar. 2	1,000	$4.00	$4,000
Mar. 15	3,000	4.40	13,200
Mar. 30	2,000	4.50	9,000
	6,000		$26,200
Cost of Goods Sold:			
Goods available for sale (total of beginning inventory and purchases)			$43,400
Deduct: Ending inventory			26,200
Cost of goods sold			$17,200

Conceptually, this method appears to be ideal because actual cost is matched against actual revenue, and ending inventory at its actual cost. On closer observation, however, deficiencies can be found in using this method as a basis for inventory valuation and income measurement. One argument against specific identification is that it facilitates manipulation of net income. For example, assume that a wholesaler purchases plywood early in the year at three different prices. When the plywood is sold, the wholesaler can, if desired, select either the lowest or the highest price to charge against income simply by selecting the plywood from a specific lot for delivery to the customer. A business manager is, therefore, afforded the opportunity to manipulate net income simply by delivering to the customer the higher or lower priced item, depending on whether lower or higher reported earnings are desired for the period.

Another problem relates to the arbitrary allocation of costs that sometimes occurs with specific inventory items.[10] In certain circumstances, it is difficult to relate adequately, for example, shipping charges and discounts directly to a given inventory item. The alternative, then, is to allocate these costs somewhat arbitrarily, leading to a "breakdown" in the precision of the specific identification method.

First-In, First-Out (FIFO)

Under the **FIFO method,** costs are allocated between inventory on hand and goods sold on the assumption that goods are sold in the order in which they are purchased;

[10]A good illustration of the cost allocation problem arises in the motion picture industry. Often actors and actresses receive a percentage of net income for a given movie or television program. Actors like James Garner and Fess Parker, who have such arrangements, have alleged that their programs have been extremely profitable to the motion picture studios, but they have received little in the way of profit sharing. Actors contend that the studios allocate additional costs to successful projects to ensure that there will be no profits to share.

in other words, the first goods purchased are the first used (in a manufacturing concern) or sold (in a merchandising concern). The cost of the inventory remaining would therefore come from the most recent purchases. Therefore, the determination of ending inventory valuation is based on the assumption of "last-in, still here" (LISH).

Inventory-Related Activities

Date	Purchased	Sold or Issued	Balance
Mar. 2	2,000 @ $4.00		2,000 units
Mar. 15	6,000 @ 4.40		8,000 units
Mar. 19		4,000 units	4,000 units
Mar. 30	2,000 @ 4.50		6,000 units

Ending Inventory: Periodic System—FIFO Method

Date of Invoice	No. Units	Unit Cost	Total Cost
Mar. 30	2,000	$4.50	$9,000
Mar. 15	4,000	4.40	17,600
	6,000		$26,600

Cost of Goods Sold: Periodic System—FIFO Method

Cost of goods available for sale	$43,400
Deduct: Ending inventory	26,600
Cost of goods sold	$16,800

Using the data previously stated on inventory-related activities, and assuming that the company is using the FIFO method and the periodic system, calculation of ending inventory and cost of goods sold would be as shown above. The cost of the inventory on hand on March 31 is computed by starting with the most recent purchase and working back until all units in the inventory are accounted for.

If a perpetual inventory system in quantities and dollars is used, a cost figure is attached to each withdrawal. Then the cost of the 4,000 units removed on March 19 would be made up of the items purchased on March 2 and March 15. The perpetual inventory record on a FIFO basis as shown below discloses the ending inventory cost ($26,600) and the cost of goods sold of $16,800 (2,000 @ $4.00 + 2,000 @ $4.40).

Perpetual Inventory—FIFO Method

Date	Purchased	Sold or Issued	Balance
Mar. 2	(2,000 @ $4.00) $ 8,000		2,000 @ $4.00 $8,000
Mar. 15	(6,000 @ 4.40) 26,400		2,000 @ 4.00 } 6,000 @ 4.40 } 34,400
Mar. 19		2,000 @ $4.00 } 2,000 @ 4.40 } ($16,800)	4,000 @ 4.40 17,600
Mar. 30	(2,000 @ 4.50) 9,000		4,000 @ 4.40 } 2,000 @ 4.50 } 26,600

When FIFO is used, the ending inventory and cost of goods sold for a period would be the same amount regardless of whether a periodic or perpetual system is used. This is true because the same costs are first in, and therefore first out, whether cost of goods sold is computed as goods are sold throughout the accounting period (the perpetual system) or as a residual at the end of the period (the periodic system).

One objective of FIFO is to follow an approximation of the physical flow of goods. When the physical flow of goods is actually first-in, first-out, the FIFO method very nearly represents specific identification. At the same time, it does not permit manipulation of income because the enterprise is not free to pick a certain cost item to be charged as an expense.

A major advantage of the FIFO method is that the ending inventory is stated in terms of an approximate current cost figure. Because the first goods in are the first goods out, the ending inventory amount will be composed of the most recent purchases. This is particularly true where the inventory turnover is rapid. This approach provides an approximation of replacement cost of inventory on the balance sheet, although this is true only where price changes have not occurred since the most recent purchases.

The basic disadvantage of this method is that current costs are not matched against current revenues on the income statement. The oldest costs are charged against the more current revenue, which can lead to distortions in the results of operations.

Average Cost

As the name implies, the **average cost method** prices items in the inventory on the basis of the average cost of all similar goods available during the period. If perpetual inventory records are not kept, the cost of the inventory is computed only at the end of the period. The periodic average cost method is often referred to as the **weighted-average method.** The application of the weighted-average cost method for a periodic inventory system is as follows:

	Periodic Inventory—Weighted-Average Method			
	Date	No. Units	Unit Cost	Total Cost
Inventory	Mar. 1	—	—	—
Purchases	Mar. 2	2,000	$4.00	$ 8,000
Purchases	Mar. 15	6,000	4.40	26,400
Purchases	Mar. 30	2,000	4.50	9,000
Total goods available		10,000		$43,400
Weighted-average cost per unit		$\dfrac{\$43,400}{10,000} = \$4.34$		
Inventory Mar. 31		6,000 units		
Cost of inventory Mar. 31		6,000 × $4.34 = $26,040		
Cost of goods sold		4,000 × $4.34 = $17,360		

As implied in this example, any beginning inventory is included both in the total units available and in the total cost of goods available in computing the average cost per unit.

Another average cost method is the **moving-average method,** which is used with perpetual inventory records. The application of the moving-average cost method for perpetual records is shown on page 385.

Perpetual Inventory—Moving-Average Method			
Date	Purchased	Sold or Issued	Balance
Mar. 2	(2,000 @ $4.00) $ 8,000		(2,000 @ $4.00) $ 8,000
Mar. 15	(6,000 @ 4.40) 26,400		(8,000 @ 4.30) 34,400
Mar. 19		(4,000 @ $4.30)	
		$17,200	(4,000 @ 4.30) 17,200
Mar. 30	(2,000 @ 4.50) 9,000		(6,000 @ 4.367) 26,200

As indicated above, a new average unit cost is computed each time a purchase is made. On March 15, after 6,000 units are purchased for $26,400, 8,000 units costing $34,400 ($8,000 plus $26,400) are on hand. The average unit cost is $34,400 divided by 8,000, or $4.30. This unit cost is used in costing withdrawals until another purchase is made, when a new average unit cost is computed. Accordingly, the cost of the 4,000 units withdrawn on March 19 is shown at $4.30, or a total of $17,200, and on March 30 a new unit cost of $4.367 is determined.

The use of the average cost methods is usually justified on the basis of practical rather than conceptual reasons. They are simple to apply, objective, and not as subject to income manipulation as some of the other inventory pricing methods. In addition, proponents of the average cost methods argue that it is often impossible to measure a specific physical flow of inventory and therefore it is better to cost items on an average price basis. This argument is particularly persuasive when the inventory involved is relatively homogeneous in nature. A moving average probably more accurately represents the costs to be associated with the product, although a weighted average can give approximately the same results.

In terms of financial statement objectives, an average cost method represents a compromise between the results obtained by using either the FIFO or LIFO method. As a compromise, it has, to an extent, the advantages of neither and the disadvantages of both—the inventory valuation on the balance sheet is not as current as under the FIFO method, and the cost of goods sold on the income statement is not as current as when using LIFO. On the other hand, an average cost method would give a more current cost of goods sold than FIFO and a more current cost of ending inventory represented on the balance sheet than that given by LIFO. Also, as discussed later, in Canada an average cost method can provide some income tax advantages during periods of rising prices.

Last-In, First-Out (LIFO)

The **LIFO method** allocates costs on the assumption that the cost of the most recent purchases are matched against revenue. Therefore, the determination of ending inventory valuation is based on the assumption of "first-in, still-here" (FISH).

If the periodic inventory system is used, then it would be assumed that the total quantity sold or issued would have come from the most recent purchases, even though such purchases may have taken place after the actual date of sale. Conversely, the ending inventory costs would consist first of costs from the beginning inventory and then of costs from purchases early in the period as appropriate. Using the data on inventory-related activities presented previously, the assumption would be made that the 4,000 units withdrawn absorbed the 2,000 units purchased on March 30 and 2,000 of the 6,000 units purchased on March 15. Therefore, the cost of the ending inventory of 6,000 units would be assumed to come from the cost of any beginning inventory (none, in this example) and then the earliest purchases in the period (2,000 units on March 2 and 4,000 units on March 15). The inventory and cost of goods sold would then be computed at the end of the period as shown below.

Inventory-Related Activities

Date	Purchased	Sold or Issued	Balance
Mar. 2	(2,000 @ $4.00)		2,000 units
Mar. 15	(6,000 @ 4.40)		8,000 units
Mar. 19		4,000 units	4,000 units
Mar. 30	(2,000 @ 4.50)		6,000 units
Total	10,000 units	4,000 units	

Ending Inventory: Periodic System—LIFO Method

Date of Invoice	No. Units	Unit Cost	Total Cost
Mar. 2	2,000	$4.00	$8,000
Mar. 15	4,000	4.40	17,600
	6,000		$25,600

Cost of Goods Sold: Periodic System—LIFO Method

Cost of goods available for sale	$43,400
Deduct: Ending inventory	25,600
Cost of goods sold	$17,800

If a perpetual inventory record is kept in quantities and dollars, and costs are computed at the time of each withdrawal, application of the last-in, first-out method will result in different amounts for ending inventory ($25,800) and cost of goods sold ($17,600) as shown below.

Perpetual Inventory—LIFO Method

Date	Purchased	Sold or Issued	Balance	
Mar. 2	(2,000 @ $4.00) $ 8,000		2,000 @ $4.00	$8,000
Mar. 15	(6,000 @ 4.40) 26,400		2,000 @ 4.00 6,000 @ 4.40	34,400
Mar. 19		(4,000 @ $4.40) $17,600	2,000 @ 4.00 2,000 @ 4.40	16,800
Mar. 30	(2,000 @ 4.50) 9,000		2,000 @ 4.00 2,000 @ 4.40 2,000 @ 4.50	25,800

The month-end periodic computation (inventory, $25,600, and cost of goods sold, $17,800) shows a different amount from the perpetual inventory computation (inventory, $25,800, and cost of goods sold, $17,600), because the former matches the total withdrawals for the month with the total purchases for the month in applying the last-in, first-out method; the latter, by contrast, matches each withdrawal with the immediately preceding purchases. In effect, the first computation assumed that goods that were not purchased until March 30 were included in the sale or issue of March 19. While this is not physically possible, it must be remembered that it is not necessary to match physical item flows with cost flows when measuring income. That is, the perspective to be taken regarding income determination is that of determining which costs will be matched against the revenues.

OMIT FROM HERE ↓

A variation of the LIFO approach and the weighted-average method is the **unit LIFO method**, which eliminates the need for identifying specific unit costs. When a large number of purchase and issue transactions are coupled with a large number of inventory items, this inventory costing method greatly reduces record keeping and the number of computations. Under this method, the weighted-average unit cost of the items purchased during the period is used to cost any additions to the inventory for the period. Using the purchase information previously presented, the unit LIFO inventory at the end of March would be computed as follows:

Unit LIFO Method		
Number of units purchased in March		10,000
Cost of March purchases		$43,400
Weighted-average unit price ($43,400 ÷ 10,000)		$4.34
LIFO cost of ending inventory:		
Beginning inventory, Mar. 1	0 units	$ 0
Increase in March	6,000 units @ $4.34	26,040
Total	6,000	$26,040

Increases in inventory quantities from period to period form successive **inventory layers.** When the inventory is decreased, the most recently added inventory layer is the first layer eliminated, given the LIFO assumption. If the ending inventory is never lower than the quantity on hand at the beginning of the period, the original unit cost prices remain intact in inventory. For example, in the illustration above, if a beginning inventory cost had existed on March 1, the $26,040 increase would have constituted a layer added to the beginning inventory and would be the layer first reduced if a decrease in the number of units on hand took place in the next period. Where there is a net liquidation of inventory, as between the beginning and end of the year, the original cost is lost. That is, if a layer has been eliminated, it cannot be rebuilt in future periods.

Last-In, First Out—Pooled Approach

Up to this point, we have emphasized a single goods approach to costing inventories on a LIFO basis. Such an approach may be unrealistic for many enterprises because they have numerous goods in inventory and costing (pricing) them all on a single goods basis (i.e., individually) could be extremely expensive and time-consuming.

As a consequence, goods are often combined into natural groups, or pools. Each pool is then assumed to be one unit for purposes of costing. For example, all units contained in each pool of the opening inventory are considered as having been acquired at the same time for the same price so that the unit cost is obtained by dividing the beginning amount by the total number of units in the pool. Any increment in inventory is usually priced at the average cost of goods purchased during the year, as illustrated in the discussion of the unit LIFO method, although other variations are possible.

To illustrate, assume that Mary Lane Cosmetics in its first year of operations has four raw materials, musk, wax, lavender, and gum, that constitute the basic ingredients for its cosmetics manufacturing process. Mary Lane's beginning inventory is as follows:

Raw Materials	Beginning Inventory		
	Quantity	Price	Total
Musk	24,000 kg	$4.00	$ 96,000
Wax	36,000	6.10	219,600
Lavender	22,000	9.00	198,000
Gum	8,000	3.30	26,400
	90,000 kg		$540,000
		Average cost/kg $6.00	

Assuming that the raw materials are one pool, the average cost for this pool is $6.00/kg ($540,000 divided by 90,000 kg). The following transactions for Mary Lane Cosmetics occurred in the next period:

Raw Materials	Beginning Inventory Quantity	Transactions				Ending Inventory Quantity
		Purchases			Requisitions	
		Quantity	Price	Total	(Quantities Used)	
Musk	24,000 kg	30,000 kg	$ 4.50	$135,000	30,000 kg	24,000 kg
Wax	36,000	40,000	6.40	256,000	42,000	34,000
Lavender	22,000	35,000	10.00	350,000	30,000	27,000
Gum	8,000	15,000	5.00	75,000	15,000	8,000
	90,000 kg	120,000 kg		$816,000	117,000 kg	93,000 kg
			Average cost/kg $6.80			

The average cost computation of purchases made during the current month is $6.80/kg ($816,000 divided by 120,000 kg). The average cost figure of $6.80 per kilogram would be used to value any inventory increase that occurred in the current month. Because the total ending inventory was higher than the total beginning inventory by 3,000 kilograms (93,000 − 90,000), the ending inventory is computed as follows:

Pooled LIFO Cost of Ending Inventory			
	Quantity	Cost	Total
Beginning inventory	90,000 kg	$6.00	$540,000
Increase during the year	3,000	6.80	20,400
	93,000 kg		$560,400

The result is that the inventory would now consist of two layers. When inventory is decreased, the most recently added inventory layer is the first to be eliminated in accordance with the LIFO concept. For example, if a decrease in the number of units (kg) on hand takes place by the end of the next period, the 3,000 kg ($6.80) layer, as the most recent increment, would be the first reduced.

The pooled approach reduces record-keeping and clerical costs. In addition, it is more difficult to erode the layer because the reduction in one item in the pool may be offset by an increase in another. For example, Mary Lane had a decrease in the quantity of wax from the beginning to the end of the period, but in the aggregate the pool increased; thus, no adjustment in the quantity of the initial layer was necessary.

Dollar-Value LIFO

As indicated above, the pooled approach eliminates some of the disadvantages of the single-good approach to accounting for LIFO inventories. The pooled approach's use of quantities as its measurement basis, however, creates other problems. First, most companies are continually changing the mix of their products, materials, and production methods. A business once engaged in manufacturing train locomotives may now be involved in the automobile or aircraft business. A business that had used cotton fabric in its clothing now uses synthetic fabric (dacron, nylon, etc.). If a pooled approach using quantities is employed, it means that the pools must be continually redefined; this can be time-consuming and costly. Second, even when such an approach is practical, an erosion of the base layers often results, thereby losing much of the LIFO costing benefits.

An erosion of the layers results because a specific good or material in the pool may be replaced by another good or material, either temporarily or permanently. This replacement may occur for competitive reasons or simply because a shortage of a certain material exists. Whatever the reason, the new item may not be similar enough to be treated as part of the old pool, and therefore any inflationary profit (excess of current cost over old cost) deferred in the old goods may have to be recognized as they are replaced.

To overcome these problems, the dollar-value LIFO method was developed. The important feature of the dollar-value LIFO method is that increases and decreases in a pool are determined and measured in terms of total dollar value, not the physical quantity of the goods in the inventory pool. Such an approach has two important advantages over the regular LIFO pool approach. First, a broader range of goods may be included in a dollar-value LIFO pool than in a regular LIFO pool. Second, in a dollar-value LIFO pool, replacement is permitted if it is similar as to type of material, or similar in use, or interchangeable. (In a regular LIFO pool, the replacement of any item requires the substitute to be substantially identical.) As a result, changes in quantities and product mix are often ignored. Thus, it is more difficult to erode the LIFO layers using the dollar-value LIFO techniques than with a regular LIFO pool concept. It follows that the dollar-value LIFO method has all the advantages of the regular LIFO pool approach and more. Only in situations where few goods are employed and little change in product mix is predicted would the more traditional LIFO approaches be utilized.

Under the dollar-value LIFO method, it is possible to have the entire inventory in only one pool, although several pools are usually employed. In general, the more goods included in a pool, the more likely that decreases in the quantities of some goods will be offset by increases in others in the same pool; thus liquidation of the LIFO layers is avoided.

Basic Dollar-Value LIFO Illustration   To illustrate how the dollar-value LIFO method works, assume that dollar-value LIFO was first adopted on December 31, 1985 (base period), that the inventory at current prices on that date was $20,000, and that the inventory on December 31, 1986, at current prices is $26,400. We should not conclude that the quantity has increased 32% during the year ($26,400 ÷ $20,000 = 132%). First, we need to ask: What is the value of the ending inventory in terms of beginning-of-the-year prices? Assuming that prices have increased 20% during the year, the ending inventory at beginning-of-the-year prices amounts to $22,000 ($26,400 ÷ 120%). Therefore, the inventory quantity has increased 10%, or from $20,000 to $22,000, in terms of beginning-of-the-year prices.

The next step is to price this real dollar quantity increase. This real dollar quantity increase of $2,000 valued at year-end prices is $2,400 (120% × $2,000). This increment (layer) of $2,400, when added to the beginning inventory of $20,000, gives a total of $22,400 for the December 31, 1986, inventory, as shown below:

First layer—(beginning inventory) in terms of 100	$20,000
Second layer—(1986 increase) in terms of 120	2,400
Dollar-value LIFO inventory, December 31, 1986	$22,400

It should be emphasized that a layer is formed only when the ending inventory at base-year prices exceeds the beginning inventory at base-year prices.

While this example identifies the basic aspects of the dollar-value LIFO method, many complex calculations are often required when using this approach. Because the method is not often used by Canadian companies, these complexities will not be examined. Those interested in pursuing the mechanics of this method will find more detailed coverage in the U.S. edition of this text.

OMIT TO HERE

Evaluation of LIFO

In certain situations the LIFO cost flow may approximate the physical flow of the goods in and out of inventory. For instance, in the case of a coal pile, it can be shown that the last goods in are the first goods out because the coal remover is not going to take the coal from the bottom of the pile. The goods that are going to be taken first are the goods that were placed on the pile last.

Because the coal pile situation is one of only a few situations where the actual physical flow corresponds to LIFO, most adherents of LIFO use other arguments for its employment, as follows:

Major Advantages of LIFO

Matching   In LIFO, the more recent costs are matched against current revenues to provide what may be viewed as a more realistic measure of current earnings. With the present inflationary trend, which is expected to continue, many accountants have challenged the quality of non-LIFO earnings, noting that by failing to match current costs against current revenues, transitory or "paper" profits ("inventory profits") are created. Inventory profits occur when the inventory costs matched against sales are less than the replacement cost of the inventory. The cost of goods sold therefore is understated, and profit is considered overstated. By using LIFO (rather than some such method as FIFO), more recent costs are matched against revenues and inventory profits are thereby reduced.

Future Earnings Hedge   With LIFO, a company's future reported earnings will not be affected substantially by future price declines. LIFO eliminates or substantially minimizes write-downs to market as a result of price decreases, because the inventory value ordinarily will be much lower than net realizable value. This contrasts sharply with the FIFO method, which ordinarily has a higher inventory value than LIFO. Inventory costed under FIFO is more vulnerable to price declines, which can reduce net income substantially.

Major Disadvantages of LIFO

Reduced Earnings   Many corporate managers view the lower profits reported under the LIFO method as a distinct disadvantage. This view assumes that prices are increasing; in some industries where prices are declining, the opposite effect may occur. Some fear that an accounting change to LIFO may be misunderstood and that, as a result of the lower profits, the price of the company's shares will fall. It should be noted that there is some evidence to refute this contention. Some studies have indicated that the users of financial data exhibit a much higher sophistication than might be expected and, as a consequence, share prices are the same and, in some cases, even higher under LIFO in spite of lower reported earnings.[11]

Inventory Understated   The inventory valuation on the balance sheet is normally outdated because the oldest costs remain in inventory. This understatement presents several problems, but manifests itself most directly in evaluating the working capital position of the company. The magnitude and direction of this variation in the carrying amount of inventory and its current price depend on the degree and direction of the changes in price and the amount of inventory turnover.

Physical Flow   LIFO does not approximate the physical flow of the items except in peculiar situations. However, matching more recent costs against revenues may be viewed as a higher priority criterion than reflecting the physical flow of goods when choosing an inventory valuation method.

Current Cost Income Not Measured   LIFO falls short of measuring current cost (replacement cost) income. In order to measure current cost income, the cost of goods sold should consist not of the most recently incurred costs but rather of the cost that will be incurred to replace the goods that have been sold. Using replacement cost is referred to as the next-in, first-out method, a method not currently acceptable for purposes of inventory costing.

[11]See, for example, Shyam Sunder, "Relationship between Accounting Changes and Stock Prices: Problems of Measurement and Some Empirical Evidence," *Empirical Research in Accounting: Selected Studies, 1973* (Chicago: University of Chicago), pp. 1–40; but see Robert Moren Brown, "Short-Range Market Reaction to Changes to LIFO Accounting Using Preliminary Earnings Announcement Dates," *Journal of Accounting Research* (Spring, 1980), which found that companies that do change to LIFO suffer a short-term decline in the price of their shares.

Involuntary Liquidation LIFO also raises the problem of involuntary inventory liquidation. If the base or layers of old costs are eliminated, strange results can occur because old, irrelevant costs can be matched against current revenues. A distortion in reported income for a given period may result.

Poor Buying Habits LIFO may cause poor buying habits because of this liquidation problem. A company may simply purchase more goods and match these costs against revenue. Furthermore, the possibility always exists with LIFO that a company will attempt to manipulate its net income at the end of the year simply by altering its pattern of purchases.

Not Allowable for Tax Purposes Except in a few special circumstances, LIFO inventory valuation is not allowed by Revenue Canada for purposes of determining taxable income.

Summary Analysis of FIFO, Weighted-Average, and LIFO Methods

A summary of the differing effects of the three major cost flow methods on the financial statements is shown on page 393. The numbers used were derived in the previous discussion of each method when illustrating the use of the single goods, periodic system for the month of March. The sales revenue was derived assuming that the 4,000 units were sold for $10 each. Since there was no beginning inventory, the cost of goods available for sale is the same for all methods. The continuation of this example for the month of April is presented in Appendix 8A at the end of this chapter. The difference in gross profit and, therefore, net income (other expenses would be the same) is due to the differing assumptions of inventory valuation associated with each method. Since the example incorporated a period of rising prices, the gross profit (and, therefore, net income) is highest under FIFO and lowest under LIFO.

At the bottom of the summary is a listing of the three objectives previously identified as being most commonly associated with choosing an inventory method. As developed in the prior discussion, the strongest argument favouring LIFO for financial statement reporting purposes is that it matches more current costs against current revenue. FIFO results in a more current cost for inventory on the balance sheet.

In terms of income tax minimization or deferral of tax payments, the method resulting in the lowest taxable income for the period would be preferred. While LIFO results in the lowest income in periods of rising prices, assuming there is little or no liquidation of old layers, it is not permitted for calculating taxable income in Canada for most businesses. Consequently, the weighted-average method, which is permitted by Revenue Canada, would more effectively accomplish this objective in a period of rising prices.

The fact that LIFO is not allowed for determining taxable income in Canada for most businesses is in direct contrast to the situation in the U.S., where it is accepted for tax purposes. Furthermore, the Internal Revenue Service in the U.S. has required that companies employing LIFO for tax purposes use LIFO for financial reporting purposes as well (this was known as the LIFO conformity rule). Recently, however, the IRS has relaxed its requirements such that it is now permitted to provide non-LIFO income numbers as supplementary information. Such information, however, may not be placed on the face of the income statement. While one may argue the merits of LIFO for financial reporting purposes on a more conceptual level, the

Summary Analysis of FIFO, Weighted-Average, and LIFO Inventory Methods—Periodic System

	METHOD		
	FIFO	Weighted-Average	LIFO
Partial Income Statement:			
Sales revenue	$40,000	$40,000	$40,000
Cost of goods sold:			
Beginning inventory	$-0-	$-0-	$-0-
Purchases	43,400	43,400	43,400
Goods available	$43,400	$43,400	$43,400
Deduct:			
Ending inventory	26,600	26,040	25,600
Cost of goods sold	16,800	17,360	17,800
Gross profit	$23,200	$22,640	$22,200
Balance Sheet:			
Inventory	$26,600	$26,040	$25,600
Objectives:			
1. Matching	Old costs against current revenue	Average cost against current revenue	"Current" costs against current revenue*
2. Balance Sheet Valuation	"Current" costs*	Average cost	Old costs
3. Income Tax Minimization	Results in higher taxable income in periods of rising prices.	Best in Canada in periods of rising prices as results in highest cost of goods sold next to LIFO*	Not allowed in Canada in most situations. If it were, it would be best in periods of rising prices.

*Results in a realistic accomplishment of objective relative to other methods.

IRS rulings are likely primarily responsible for the more common use of the LIFO method in financial statements in the U.S. as compared to Canada.[12]

Which Method to Select?

Section 3030 of the *CICA Handbook* indicates that Specific Identification, FIFO, Average Cost, and LIFO are all generally acceptable for financial reporting purposes. The *Handbook* also states:

> The method selected for determining cost should be one which results in the fairest matching of costs against revenues regardless of whether or not the method corresponds to the physical flow of goods.[13]

[12]*Financial Reporting in Canada—1983* reported that, of 286 inventory cost method disclosures, 138 (48%) used FIFO, 11 (4%) used LIFO, 91 (32%) used the average cost, 9 (3%) used specific identification, 9 (3%) used standard cost, 11 (4%) used the retail method, and 17 (6%) used other methods. For comparison, a similar U.S. study, *Accounting Trends and Techniques—1984*, reported that, of 1,061 method disclosures, 408 (38%) used LIFO, 366 (35%) used FIFO, 235 (22%) used average cost, and 52 (5%) used other methods. The data from the U.S. indicates a significant shift from FIFO to LIFO during the 1970s and early 1980s. The high rate of inflation and tax advantages of LIFO in such circumstances are, no doubt, at least partially responsible for the shift. Although inflation was also significant in Canada, a shift to LIFO was not evidenced.

[13]*CICA Handbook*, Section 3030, par. 9.

Which method will provide the fairest matching? The answer can be derived only by exercising professional judgement, given knowledge of the particular circumstances and the desired objectives of the financial statements. As indicated in Chapter 1, a primary objective of financial reporting is to provide useful information to assist users in making their decisions. Therefore, the inventory valuation method that leads to the accomplishment of this objective would certainly be the fairest and most relevant one to choose. The appropriate choice, however, depends on a number of things (e.g., who the users are, the decisions they must make, and what information fits their decision models). If one method were the fairest and most relevant for all situations, then the accounting profession would certainly not have acceptable alternative methods. Consequently, in our present state of understanding, professional judgement is the basis for determining the method to use.

An important point is that it is possible for a company to use one method (FIFO, for example) for financial statement reporting and another method (Average Cost) for tax purposes. This is legal and reasonable as the objectives of financial reporting are different from those of income tax determination. Having "two sets of books" may, however, be inefficient—a judgement requiring the accountant to be fully cognizant of the circumstances.

While the cost-based methods discussed so far are the ones most frequently considered for adoption, two other methods—base stock and standard cost—can also be adopted.

Base Stock

OMIT FROM HERE

The **base stock method** is based on the assumption that a minimum normal stock of goods is required at all times to carry on normal business activity, and that such normal stock be carried at a long-run "normal" price, which may be, and often is, the lowest cost experienced or likely to be experienced. The lowest cost is used to avoid showing an "unrealized" inventory profit. Proponents of this method contend that the minimum inventory quantity is similar to a fixed asset and should not be affected by fluctuations in purchase prices; the costs of maintaining and replenishing this normal stock are charged to operations. The cost of any excess on hand above the base quantity is considered as a temporary increment and is priced at the appropriate costs by the application of the LIFO, FIFO, average cost, or any other suitable method selected. Any shortage in the base stock compared with units on hand is also considered temporary and is charged against revenue at current replacement cost.

If the base stock inventory is assumed to be 5,000 units at $3.80 per unit, then the inventory on hand of 6,000 units on March 31 might be computed as follows (using the data from the prior section and assuming that the excess over the normal stock is to be priced on a first-in, first-out basis):

Base stock (5,000 units @ $3.80)	$19,000
Excess above base quantity (1,000 units @ $4.50)	4,500
Inventory, Mar. 31	$23,500

If the base stock is assumed to be 7,000 units at $3.80 per unit, then the inventory on hand of 6,000 units on March 31 would be computed as follows:

Base stock (7,000 units @ $3.80)	$26,600
Temporary deficiency (1,000 units @ $4.50, current replacement cost)	4,500
Inventory, Mar. 31	$22,100

The application of the base stock method represents a departure from the cost principle as applied to assets, because the base stock quantity is carried at an amount that has no necessary relationship to the cost of units now in inventory. Like the LIFO method, the base stock method matches current costs with current revenues. It is also subject to some of the same objections as the LIFO method; in addition, the "normal" quantity is subject to manipulation. Consequently, it is not a method of inventory pricing that is much used in practice.

Standard Cost

A manufacturing concern that uses a **standard cost system** predetermines the unit costs for material, labour, and manufacturing overhead. Usually the standard costs used are determined on the basis of the costs that should be incurred per unit of finished goods when the plant is operating at normal capacity. The approximate ideal or expected costs are useful to management in its objective of controlling actual costs. Deviations from actual costs are reflected in variance accounts that may be analyzed to determine the reasons for such deviations so that management may take appropriate action to achieve greater control over manufacturing costs.

For financial reporting purposes the pricing of inventories at standard costs is considered acceptable if there is no significant difference between actual and standard. If there is a significant difference, the inventory amounts should be adjusted to estimated actual cost.[14] Otherwise the net income will be misstated in the income statement, and both the assets and the retained earnings will be misstated in the balance sheet. A detailed examination of standard costing is available in most managerial and cost accounting texts but is beyond the scope of this book.

CONCLUDING COMMENT

All of the inventory valuation methods described in the preceding sections of this chapter are used to some extent. Indeed, a company may use different valuation approaches for different types of inventory.

The existence of a variety of inventory pricing methods, each of which has a somewhat different effect on net income when prices are increasing or decreasing, points out that the freedom to shift from one pricing method to another at will would permit a wide range of possible net income figures for a given company for any given period. This in turn would make financial statements less meaningful. This variety of methods has evolved to assist appropriate computation of net income rather than to permit manipulation. Hence, it is necessary that the pricing method most suitable to a company be selected and, once selected, be applied consistently thereafter. If conditions indicate that the inventory pricing method in use is unsuitable, serious consideration should be given to all other possibilities before selecting another method. If a change is then made, it should be clearly explained and its effect disclosed in the financial statements.

[14]*Ibid.*, par. 4.

KEY POINTS

1. Inventories are basically items held for sale in the ordinary course of business or goods that will be used or consumed in the production of goods to be sold. Inventories are among the most significant assets of most manufacturing and merchandising enterprises in terms of size and importance to management.

2. Raw materials, work in process, and finished goods are the major categories of inventory for manufacturing companies. Since merchandising companies ordinarily purchase goods in a form ready for sale, only one inventory account —Merchandise Inventory—appears in their financial statements. Factory or office supplies accounts may also be inventory items.

3. The valuation (assigning a dollar amount) of inventory has impact on balance sheet and income statement (through cost of goods sold) amounts and relationships.

4. Valuation of inventory requires determination of the quantities of inventory and the price to assign to these quantities. Inventory errors may occur for many reasons throughout the valuation process and, when they occur, can have important consequences regarding interpretation of the financial statements.

5. Two inventory systems are common—perpetual and periodic. The perpetual system results in an up-to-date accounting record of units and cost of inventory items. In it, additions and reductions of inventory are recorded as they occur. No such record is kept under the periodic system. Instead, under the periodic system, year-end inventory must be determined by a physical count upon which the amount of ending inventory and cost of goods sold is based. Even under the perpetual system, an annual count is desirable to test the accuracy of the records.

6. Determining quantities requires knowledge of goods in transit, consignments, and special sale agreements. Awareness of the terms of contract for such items is important when determining whether items should be included or excluded.

7. Determining the price to assign to quantities of inventory requires specification of which costs should be included. Basically, the costs should be the laid-down costs (those incurred to get the inventory to its current condition and location). Application of this definition is fairly straightforward for some costs (purchase price, freight, discounts) but difficult for others (interest charges, storage costs, fixed manufacturing costs). Consequently, for practical reasons, allocating the latter type of costs to inventory may not be done.

8. If the unit cost is different for various purchases, the question is which costs will be assigned to ending inventory and, as a consequence, to cost of goods sold. Various cost-flow methods exist for making such an assignment: Specific Identification, FIFO, Average Cost, and LIFO.

9. Determining which cost-flow method to use requires (a) identifying the objectives to be accomplished in the financial reports, (b) knowing the various methods that can be used, their assumptions, and how they work, (c) evaluating the methods relative to the objectives, and (d) choosing the method that most satisfies the objectives. Inevitably, trade-offs exist between methods and objectives such that no one method most appropriately satisfies all objectives.

10. The only guidance provided by the *CICA Handbook* is that the method chosen should result in "the fairest matching of costs against revenues regardless of whether or not the method corresponds to the physical flow of goods." Consequently, choice of a costing method requires an exercise of judgement.

8A

INVENTORY VALUATION METHODS—
AN EXTENSION OF THE EXAMPLE

The basic data used in the chapter to illustrate the mechanics of the FIFO, Average Cost, and LIFO inventory methods assumed a situation of no beginning inventory and a period of rising prices. The material in this Appendix carries the example one more month. As such, the ending inventory on March 31 as calculated in the chapter illustrations becomes the beginning inventory for the month of April. The material in this Appendix assumes the use of the periodic system and continuing rising prices. If the perpetual system were being used, the purchases and sales of April would be recorded in the perpetual inventory record on a basis consistent with the procedures illustrated in the chapter.

The following schedules should be studied carefully for a clear understanding of how each financial statement figure is calculated and why the results differ among inventory methods. Because the weighted-average method will result in the lowest taxable income and, therefore, taxes paid (given that LIFO is not acceptable for tax purposes in Canada), it has been used to determine the amount of cash paid for income taxes when determining cash balances at the end of April, as shown on the last schedule of this Appendix. (A simplifying assumption for this determination is that taxes are paid at the end of each month.) It should be noted, however, that the calculation of income tax expense when determining net income for each inventory method was based on multiplying the respective income before taxes by

40% (the assumed tax rate). Consequently, this results in a difference between the tax expense and the tax paid for the FIFO and LIFO methods. The difference is due to the fact that the financial statements are being prepared using an inventory method different from that used for preparing tax returns. The amount of the difference between the tax expense and tax paid would result in an entry to adjust a Deferred Income Taxes account. The complexities of interperiod tax allocation and the use of a Deferred Income Taxes Account will be examined in Chapter 20.

Selected Data for April			
Beginning cash balance			$ 7,000
Beginning retained earnings			10,000
Beginning inventory (from March 31), 6,000 units:			
FIFO cost			26,600
Weighted-average cost			26,040
LIFO cost			25,600

Inventory related activities in April:			
Date	Purchases	Sales	Balance in Units
Beginning			6,000
April 5		4,000 @ $11.00	2,000
April 10	3,000 @ $5.00		5,000
April 20	4,000 @ $5.20		9,000
April 25		3,000 @ $11.50	6,000
April 30	1,000 @ $5.25		7,000
Operating expenses for April			$10,000
40% tax rate			

The comparative results of using FIFO, Weighted-Average Cost, and LIFO on net income are computed as follows:

Comparative Results of FIFO, Weighted-Average Cost, LIFO			
	FIFO	Weighted-Average	LIFO
Sales	$78,500	$78,500	$78,500
Cost of goods sold	31,600	33,545	36,050
Gross profit	$46,900	$44,955	$42,450
Operating expenses	10,000	10,000	10,000
Income before taxes	$36,900	$34,955	$32,450
Income tax expense	14,760	13,982	12,980
Net income	$22,140	$20,973	$19,470
Cost of Goods Sold:			
Beginning inventory	$26,600	$26,040	$25,600
Purchases	41,050	41,050	41,050
Goods available	$67,650	$67,090	$66,650
Deduct: Ending inventory	36,050	33,545	30,600
Cost of goods sold	$31,600	$33,545	$36,050

The following schedule shows the final balances of selected items at the end of April:

		Balance of Selected Items, April 30				
Method:	Inventory	Gross Profit	Tax Expense	Net Income	Retained Earnings	Cash*
FIFO	$36,050 (1,000 @ $5.25) (4,000 @ $5.20) (2,000 @ $5.00)	$46,900	$14,760 (0.40 × $36,900)	$22,140	$32,140 ($10,000 + $22,140)	$20,468
Weighted-Average	$33,545 ($\frac{\$67,090}{14,000} \times 7,000$)	$44,955	$13,982 (0.40 × $34,955)	$20,973	$30,973 ($10,000 + $20,973)	$20,468
LIFO	$30,600 (6,000 of Beginning Inventory for $25,600 plus 1,000 @ $5.00)	$42,450	$12,980 (0.40 × $32,450)	$19,470	$29,470 ($10,000 + $19,470)	$20,468

*Cash at month end	= Beginning Balance	+ Sales	– Purchases	– Operating Expenses	– Taxes Paid**
FIFO: $20,468	= $7,000	+ $78,500	– $41,050	– $10,000	– $13,982
Weighted-Average: $20,468	= $7,000	+ $78,500	– $41,050	– $10,000	– $13,982
LIFO: $20,468	= $7,000	+ $78,500	– $41,050	– $10,000	– $13,982

** Taxes paid in all cases are based on weighted-average method calculations which result in the lowest amount under Canadian tax reporting in this situation. Any difference between tax expense and tax paid would result in adjusting Deferred Income Taxes as discussed in Chapter 20.

QUESTIONS

1. In what ways are the inventory accounts of a merchandising business different from those of a manufacturing enterprise?
2. What is the difference between a perpetual inventory system and a periodic inventory system? If a company maintains a perpetual inventory, should its physical inventory at any date be equal to the amount indicated by the perpetual inventory records? Why?
3. Why should inventories be included (a) in the balance sheet and (b) in the computation of net income?
4. Define ''cost'' as applied to the valuation of inventories.
5. Where, if at all, should the following items be classified on a balance sheet?
   (a) Raw materials.
   (b) Goods received on consignment.
   (c) Manufacturing supplies.
   (d) Goods out on approval to customers.
   (e) Goods in transit that were recently purchased f.o.b. shipping point.
   (f) Land held by a realty firm for sale.
6. At the balance sheet date the Wiglet Company held title to goods in transit amounting to $48,110. This amount was omitted from the purchases figure for the year and also from the ending inventory. What is the effect of this omission on the

net income for the year as calculated when the books are closed? On the company's financial position as shown in its balance sheet? Is materiality a factor in determining whether an adjustment for this item should be made?

7. Briefly indicate the arguments pro and con for variable costing. Indicate how each of the following conditions would affect the amounts of net profit reported under conventional absorption and variable costing.

   (a) Sales and production are in balance at a standard volume.

   (b) Sales exceed production.

   (c) Production exceeds sales.

8. What is the difference between variable costing and conventional absorption costing? Is variable costing acceptable for external financial reporting? Explain.

9. X purchases 150 units of an item at an invoice cost of $2,700. What is the cost per unit? If the goods are shipped f.o.b. shipping point and the freight bill was $300, what is the cost per unit if X pays the freight charges? If these items were bought on 2/15, n/30 terms and the invoice and the freight bill were paid within the discount period, what would be the cost per unit?

10. Specific identification is sometimes said to be the ideal method of assigning cost to inventory and to cost of goods sold. Briefly indicate the arguments for and against this method of inventory valuation.

11. First-in, first-out; weighted-average; and last-in, first-out methods are often used instead of specific identification for inventory valuation purposes. Compare these methods with the specific identification method, discussing the theoretical propriety of each method regarding the determination of income and asset valuation.

12. In what respects is the LIFO method of costing inventories similar to the base stock method? In what respects is it dissimilar?

13. As compared with the FIFO method of costing inventories, does the LIFO method result in a larger or smaller net income in a period of rising prices? What is the comparative effect on net income in a period of falling prices?

14. What is the advantage of combining inventory goods into natural groups or pools when using LIFO? What is the distinction between a LIFO pool and a dollar-value LIFO pool? What are the advantages of a dollar-value LIFO pool?

15. On December 31, 1986, the inventory of the Duffy Company amounts to $800,000. During 1987, the company decides to use the dollar-value LIFO method of costing inventories. On December 31, 1987, the inventory is $884,000 at December 31, 1987, prices. Using the December 31, 1986, price level of 100 and the December 31, 1987, price level of 104, compute the inventory value at December 31, 1987, under the dollar-value LIFO method.

16. Define standard costs. What are the advantages of a standard cost system? Present arguments in support of each of the following three methods of treating standard cost variances (actual costs—standard costs) for purposes of financial reporting:

   (a) They may be carried as deferred charges or credits on the balance sheet.

   (b) They may appear as charges or credits on the income statement.

   (c) They may be allocated between inventories and cost of goods sold.

17. What is meant by the term "sales with buybacks" (a product financing arrangement)? How should such an arrangement be reported in the financial statements of the "seller"?

18. In an article that appeared in the *Wall Street Journal*, the phrases "phantom (paper) profits" and "high LIFO profits through involuntary liquidation of inventory" were used. Explain what was likely meant by these phrases.

CASES

C8-1 Salmon Company has been growing rapidly, but during this period the accounting records have not been properly maintained. You were recently employed to correct the accounting records and to assist in the preparation of the financial statements for the fiscal year ended February 28, 1986. One of the accounts you have been analyzing is entitled "Merchandise." That account follows in summary form. Numbers in parentheses following each entry correspond to related numbered explanations and additional information that you have accumulated during your analysis.

Merchandise

Balance, March 1, 1985	(1)	Merchandise sold	(5)
Purchases	(2)	Consigned merchandise	(6)
Freight-in	(3)		
Insurance	(4)		
Freight-out on consigned merchandise	(7)		
Freight-out on merchandise sold	(8)		

Explanations and additional information:

1. You have satisfied yourself that the March 1, 1985, inventory balance represents the approximate cost of the few units in inventory at the beginning of the year. Salmon employs the FIFO method of accounting for inventories.

2. The merchandise purchased was recorded in the account at the sellers' catalogue list price, which is the price appearing on the face of each vendor's invoice. All purchased merchandise is subject to a trade (chain) discount of 20%–10%. These discounts have been accounted for as revenue when the merchandise was paid for.
   All merchandise purchased was also subject to cash terms of 2/15, n/30. During the fiscal year Salmon recorded $3,500 in purchase discounts as revenue when the merchandise was paid for. Some purchase discounts were lost because payment was made after the discount period ended. All purchases of merchandise were paid for in the fiscal year they were recorded as purchased.

3. All merchandise is purchased f.o.b. sellers' business locations. The freight-in amount is the cost of transporting the merchandise from the sellers' business locations to Salmon.

4. The insurance charge is for an all-perils policy to cover merchandise in transit to Salmon from sellers.

5. The credit to this account for merchandise sold represents the sellers' catalogue list price of merchandise sold plus the cost of the beginning inventory; the debit side of the entry was made to the cost of goods sold account.

6. Consigned merchandise represents goods that were shipped to Mark Company during January, 1986, priced at the sellers' catalogue list price. The offsetting debit was made to accounts receivable when the merchandise was shipped to Mark.

7. The freight-out on consigned goods is the cost of trucking the consigned goods to Mark from Salmon.

8. Freight-out on merchandise sold is the amount paid trucking companies to deliver merchandise sold to Salmon's customers.

Instructions

Consider each of the eight numbered items independently and explain specifically how and why each item should (if correctly accounted for) have affected:

(a) The amount of cost of goods sold to be included in Salmon's earnings statement, and

(b) The amount of any other account to be included in Salmon's February 28, 1986, financial statements.

Organize your answer in the following format:

Item Number	How and Why the Amount of Cost of Goods Sold Should Have Been Affected	How and Why the Amount of Any Other Account Should Have Been Affected

C8-2 The controller for Sutton Enterprises has recently hired you as assistant controller. She wishes to determine your expertise in the area of inventory accounting and therefore requests that you answer the following unrelated situations:

1. A company is involved in the wholesaling and retailing of automobile tires for foreign cars. Most of the inventory is imported, and it is valued on the company's records at the actual inventory cost plus freight-in. At year-end, the warehousing costs are allocated to the cost of goods sold and the ending inventory. Are warehousing costs considered to be a product cost or a period cost?

2. A certain portion of a company's "inventory" is composed of obsolete items. Should obsolete items that are not currently consumed in the production of "goods or services to be available for sale" be classified as part of inventory?

3. A company purchases airplanes for sale to others. However, until they are sold, the company charters and services the planes. What is the proper way to report these airplanes in the company's financial statements?

4. A competitor uses standard costs for valuing inventory. Is this permissible?

5. A company wants to buy coal deposits but does not want the financing for the purchase to be reported on its financial statements. The company therefore establishes a trust to acquire the coal deposits. The company agrees to buy the coal over a certain period of time at specified prices. The trust is able to finance the coal purchase and pay off the loan as it is paid by the company for the minerals. How should this transaction be reported?

6. A company has decided that part of its inventory is similar to a long-term asset in that a portion must always be available for potential stockout problems. The company therefore decides to use the base stock method of inventory valuation. Is this permissible? Discuss.

C8-3 You are asked to travel to Calgary to observe and verify the inventory of the Calgary branch of one of your clients. You arrive on Thursday, December 30, and find that the inventory procedures have just been started. You note that there is a railway car spotted on the sidetrack at the unloading door and ask the warehouse superintendent how she plans to inventory the contents of the car. She responds: "We are not going to include the contents in the inventory."

Later in the day, you ask the bookkeeper for the invoice on the carload and the related freight bill. The invoice lists the various items, prices, and extensions of the goods in the car. You note that the carload was shipped December 24 from Montreal, f.o.b. Montreal, and that the total invoice price of the goods in the car was $30,300. The freight bill called for a payment of $1,150. Terms were net 30 days. The bookkeeper affirms the fact that his invoice is to be held for recording in January.

Instructions

(a) Does your client have a liability that should be recorded at December 31? Discuss.

(b) Prepare a journal entry (entries) to reflect any adjustment required.

(c) For what possible reason(s) might your client wish to postpone recording the transaction?

C8-4 You have a client engaged in a manufacturing business with relatively heavy fixed costs and large inventories of finished goods. These inventories constitute a very material item on the balance sheet. The company has a cost accounting system that assigns all manufacturing costs to the product each period.

The controller of the company has informed you that the management is giving serious consideration to adopting direct costing as a method of accounting for plant operations and inventory valuation. The management wishes to have your opinion of the effect, if any, that such a change would have on: (1) the year-end financial position and (2) the net income for the year.

Instructions

State your reply to the request and the reasons for your conclusions.

C8-5 Ronald Fisher, president of Delightful Products, Inc., a Canadian company merchandising trophies, recently read an article in a U.S. trade magazine that claimed that many American businesses similar to his were either adopting or considering adopting the LIFO method for costing inventories. The article stated that these companies were switching to LIFO to (1) neutralize the effect of inflation in their financial statements, (2) eliminate inventory profits, and (3) reduce income taxes. Mr. Fisher wonders if the switch would benefit his company.

Delightful Products, Inc. currently uses the FIFO method of inventory valuation in its periodic inventory system. The company has a high inventory turnover rate and inventories represent a significant proportion of the assets.

Mr. Fisher wishes to use the inventory method that is best for the company in the long run rather than select a method because it is a current fad.

Instructions

(a) Explain to Mr. Fisher what "inventory profits" are and how the LIFO method of inventory valuation could reduce them.

(b) Explain to Mr. Fisher how the choice of an inventory method may affect the income taxes paid with particular reference to what he read in the article regarding LIFO.

(c) Would Mr. Fisher have to use the same inventory method for financial reporting as is used for income tax determination? Explain why.

C8-6 "Accounting Change Aids White Farm" was the headline for a February 8, 1985, report in the *Saskatoon Star Phoenix*. This report contained the following comments from White Farm Manufacturing Canada Ltd.'s vice-president of marketing with regard to the company's attempts to recover under new ownership after being placed in receivership in June, 1983:

> In the past, most manufacturers, including the old White, treated a sale as a sale when a piece of equipment was put on a dealer's lot. Once we had a wholesale order for a combine or tractor, most companies booked it as a sale. Whatever the invoice read as revenue was revenue, and whatever costs were incurred up to that point were expenses. And then they'd book a profit. Until that piece of equipment was actually sold to a farmer, the company in most cases finances that equipment on the dealer's lot.

The report went on to state that the practice of booking a profit before it is realized led to a series of problems. Consequently, the company changed its accounting policy so that it did not book profits until a unit was sold at the retail level. At that point, all the firm's costs were behind it and it was recording real profits.

Instructions

(a) Within the framework of GAAP, discuss the appropriateness or lack thereof of the original accounting policy of White Farm and other farm equipment manufacturers in terms of recognizing revenue and cost of goods sold (i.e., inventory reductions).

(b) What type of problems could such an accounting policy have led to?

(c) Given this practice, how would one account for the equipment that remained on a dealer's lot at a fiscal year end?

(d) How could the new policy aid the company?

C8-7 Max Hillery, an inventory control specialist, is interested in better understanding the accounting for inventories. Although Max understands the more sophisticated computer inventory control systems, he has little knowledge of how inventory cost is determined. In studying the records of Harmon Enterprises which sells normal brand-name goods from its own store and on consignment through Darien, Inc., he asks you to answer the following questions.

Instructions

(a) Should Harmon Enterprises include in its inventory normal brand-name goods purchased from its suppliers but not yet received if the terms of purchase are f.o.b. shipping point (manufacturer's plant)? Why?

(b) Should Harmon Enterprises include freight-in expenditures as an inventory cost? Why?

(c) Harmon Enterprises purchased cooking utensils for sale in the ordinary course of business three times during the current year, each time at a higher price than the previous purchase. What would have been the effect on ending inventory and cost of goods sold had Harmon used the weighted-average cost method instead of the FIFO method?

(d) What are products on consignment? How should they be treated in the financial records?

(AICPA adapted)

EXERCISES

E8-1 Three or more items are omitted in each of the following tabulations of income statement data. Fill in the amounts that are missing.

	1986	1987	1988
Sales	$245,000	$320,000	$ _____
Sales Returns	_____	7,500	12,500
Net Sales	_____	_____	340,000
Beginning Inventory	_____	15,000	_____
Ending Inventory	_____	_____	22,500
Purchases	119,000	_____	175,000
Purchase Returns and Allowances	4,000	5,000	7,500
Transportation-in	5,000	7,000	5,000
Cost of Goods Sold	125,000	150,000	_____
Gross Profit on Sales	110,000	_____	160,000

E8-2 How would you recommend that the following items be reported on the balance sheet?

1. An appropriation of retained earnings for possible inventory declines.   _____

2. Materials received from a customer for processing.   _____

3. Merchandise produced by special order and set aside to be picked up by customer.   _____

4. Janitorial supplies.   _____

5. Unsold goods in the hands of consignees.   _____

6. Raw materials pledged by means of warehouse receipts on notes payable to bank.   _____

7. Raw materials in transit from suppliers, f.o.b. shipping point.   _____

8. An allowance to reduce the inventory cost to market.   _____

E8-3 The net income per books was determined without knowledge of the errors indicated.

Year	Net Income per Books	Error in Ending Inventory	
1982	$41,000	Overstated	$ 3,000
1983	44,000	Overstated	6,000
1984	42,000	Understated	10,000
1985	44,600	No error	
1986	43,800	Understated	2,000
1987	45,000	Overstated	9,000

Instructions

Prepare a work sheet to show the adjusted net income figure for each of the six years after taking into account the inventory errors.

E8-4 Harbour Company has a calendar-year accounting period. The following errors have been discovered in 1986.

1. The December 31, 1984, merchandise inventory had been understated by $15,000.

2. Merchandise purchased on account during 1985 was recorded on the books for the first time in February, 1986, when the original invoice for the correct amount of $2,750 arrived. The merchandise had arrived December 28, 1985, and was included in the December 31, 1985, merchandise inventory. The invoice arrived late because of a mix-up on the wholesaler's part.

3. Accrued interest of $315 at December 31, 1985, on notes receivable had not been recorded until the cash for the interest was received in March, 1986.

Instructions

(a) Compute the effect each error had on the 1985 net income.

(b) Compute the effect, if any, each error had on the December 31, 1985, balance sheet items.

E8-5 The following purchase transactions occurred during the last few days of the Frank Company's business year, which ends October 31, or in the first few days after that date. A periodic inventory system is used.

1. An invoice for $2,200, terms f.o.b. shipping point, was received and entered November 1. The invoice shows that the material was shipped October 29, but the receiving report indicates receipt of goods on November 3.

2. An invoice for $1,800, terms f.o.b. destination, was received and entered November 2. The receiving report indicates that the goods were received October 29.

3. An invoice for $2,840, terms f.o.b. shipping point, was received October 15 but never entered. Attached to it is a receiving report indicating that the goods were received October 18. Across the face of the receiving report is the following notation: "Merchandise not of same quality as ordered—returned for credit October 19."

4. An invoice for $3,600, terms f.o.b. shipping point, was received and entered October 27. The receiving report attached to the invoice indicates that the shipment was received October 27 in satisfactory condition.

5. An invoice for $1,500, terms f.o.b. destination, was received and entered October 28. The receiving report indicates that the merchandise was received November 2.

Before preparing financial statements for the year, you are instructed to review these transactions to determine whether any correcting entries are required and whether the inventory of $65,700 determined by physical count should be changed.

Instructions

Complete the following schedule, and state the correct inventory at October 31. Assume that the books have not been closed.

Transaction	Purchase and Related Payable Should Be Recognized in (Month)	Purchase and Related Payable Were Recognized in (Month)	Correcting Journal Entries Needed	Should Inventory Be Included in October Ending Inventory?	Was Inventory Included in October Ending Inventory?	Dollar Adjustments Needed to October Ending Inventory?

E8-6 Presented below are the transactions related to Tronto, Inc.

May 10 Purchased goods billed at $12,450 subject to cash discount terms of 2/10, n/60.

11 Purchased goods billed at $9,500 subject to terms of 1/15, n/30.

19 Paid invoice of May 10.

22 Purchased goods billed at $9,000 subject to cash discount terms of 2/10, n/30.

Instructions

(a) Prepare general journal entries for the transactions above under the assumption that purchases are to be recorded at net amounts after cash discounts and that discounts lost are to be treated as financial expense.

(b) Assuming no purchase or payment transactions other than those given above, prepare the adjusting entry required on May 31 if financial statements are to be prepared as of that date.

E8-7 The Bock Manufacturing Company maintains a general ledger account for each class of inventory, debiting such accounts for increases during the period, and crediting them for decreases. The transactions below relate to the Raw Materials Inventory account, which is debited for materials purchased and which is credited for materials requisitioned for use.

1. An invoice for $6,000, terms f.o.b. shipping point, was received and entered December 30, 1986. The receiving report shows that the materials were received January 1987, and the bill of lading shows that they were shipped January 2, 1987.

2. Materials costing $15,000 were received December 30, 1986, but no entry was made for them because "they were ordered with a specified delivery of no earlier than January 10, 1987."

3. An invoice for $8,600, terms f.o.b. destination, was received and entered January 2, 1987. The receiving report shows that they were received December 28, 1986.

4. Materials costing $22,000, shipped f.o.b. destination, were not entered by December 31, 1986, "because they were in a railroad car on the company's siding on that date and had not been unloaded."

5. Materials costing $3,600 were returned on December 29, 1986, to the creditor, and were shipped f.o.b. shipping point. They were entered on that date, even though they were not expected to reach the creditor's place of business until January 6, 1987.

Instructions

Prepare correcting general journal entries required December 31, 1986, assuming that the books have not been closed.

E8-8 In an annual audit at December 31, 1986, you find the following transactions near the closing date.

1. A packing case containing a product costing $408 was standing in the shipping room when the physical inventory was taken. It was not included in the inventory

because it was marked "Hold for shipping instructions." Your investigation revealed that the customer's order was dated December 18, 1986, but that the case was shipped and the customer billed on January 10, 1987. The product was a stock item of your client.

2. Merchandise received on January 6, 1987, costing $360 was entered in the purchase journal on January 7, 1987. The invoice showed shipment was made f.o.b. supplier's warehouse on December 31, 1986. Because it was not on hand at December 31, it was not included in inventory.

3. A special machine, fabricated to order for a customer, was finished and specifically segregated in the back part of the shipping room on December 31, 1986. The customer was billed on that date and the machine excluded from inventory although it was shipped on January 1987.

4. Merchandise costing $911 was received on January 3, 1987, and the related purchase invoice recorded January 5. The invoice showed the shipment was made on December 29, 1986, f.o.b. destination.

5. Merchandise costing $310 was received on December 28, 1986, and the invoice was not recorded. You located it in the hands of the purchasing agent; it was marked on consignment.

Instructions

Assuming that each of the amounts is material, state whether the merchandise should be included in the client's inventory and give your reason for your decision on each item.

E8-9   The board of directors of Remarkable Computer Corporation is considering whether or not it should instruct the accounting department to shift from a first-in, first-out (FIFO) basis of pricing inventories to a last-in, first-out (LIFO) basis. The following information is available.

Sales	20,000 units @ $50
Inventory Jan. 1	4,000 units @ 30
Purchases	2,000 units @ 30
	12,000 units @ 33
	8,000 units @ 35
Inventory Dec. 31	6,000 units @ ?
Operating expenses	$100,000

Instructions

Prepare a condensed income statement for the year on both bases for comparative purposes.

E8-10   The following accounts, among others, appear on the trial balance of the El Paso Corporation at the end of the year 1986:

Raw Materials Inventory, January 1, 1986	$ 30,000
Goods in Process Inventory, January 1, 1986	40,000
Finished Goods Inventory, January 1, 1986	50,000
Raw Materials Purchased	66,000
Direct Labour	76,000
Manufacturing Overhead	55,000
Sales	200,000
General and Administrative Expense	50,000

Instructions

Assuming that no other nominal accounts existed, give the adjusting and closing entries that would be made at the end of the year. Inventories on December 31, 1986, are: raw materials, $26,000; goods in process, $36,000; finished goods, $40,000. Ignore income tax effects.

E8-11   The following is a record of transactions for transistor radios for the month of January:

Jan. 1 Balance 400 units @ $ 9.00	Jan. 10 Sale 300 units @ $14
12 Purchase 200 units @ $10.00	30 Sale 200 units @ $16
28 Purchase 200 units @ $11.00	

1. Assuming that perpetual inventories are **not** maintained and that a physical count at the end of the month shows 300 units to be on hand, what is the cost of the ending inventory using (1) FIFO? (2) LIFO? (3) weighted average?
2. Assuming that perpetual records are maintained and they tie into the general ledger, calculate the ending inventory using (1) FIFO; (2) LIFO; (3) moving average.

E8-12   Inventory information for Part 311 discloses the following for the month of June:

June I	Balance	300 units @ $10
11	Purchased	500 units @ $ 8
20	Purchased	400 units @ $ 7
June 10	Sold	200 units @ $12
23	Sold	400 units @ $11
27	Sold	200 units @ $11

Instructions

(a) Assuming that the periodic inventory method is used, compute the cost of goods sold and ending inventory under (1) LIFO; (2) FIFO; (3) weighted average.

(b) Assuming that the perpetual inventory record is kept in dollars, and costs are computed at the time of each withdrawal, what is the cost of the ending inventory at (1) LIFO? (2) FIFO? (3) moving average?

(c) Why is it that LIFO usually produces a lower gross profit than FIFO?

E8-13   The Stoughton Sports Shop began operations on January 1, 1986. The following stock record card for footballs was taken from the records at the end of the year.

Date	Voucher	Terms	Units Received	Unit Invoice Cost	Gross Invoice Amount
Jan. 15	10624	Net 30	60	$15.00	$ 900.00
Mar. 15	11437	1/5, net 30	24	14.00	336.00
June 6	21332	1/10, net 30	120	13.00	1,560.00
Sept. 12	27644	1/10, net 30	84	12.00	1,008.00
Nov. 24	31269	1/10, net 30	96	12.00	1,152.00
	Totals		384		$4,956.00

A physical inventory on December 31, 1986, reveals that 150 footballs were in stock. The bookkeeper informs you that all the discounts were taken. Assume that Stoughton uses the invoice price less discount for recording purchases. Use the periodic system.

Instructions

(a) Compute the December 31, 1986, inventory using the FIFO method.

(b) Compute the 1986 cost of goods sold using the LIFO method.

(c) Compute the December 31, 1986, inventory using the weighted-average method.

E8-14   The Pauley Company's record of transactions for the month of May was as follows:

Purchases

May I	(balance on hand)	700 @ $5.00
4		300 @ 5.20
8		300 @ 5.20
13		1,000 @ 5.10
21		400 @ 5.50
29		300 @ 5.60
		3,000

Sales

May 3	400 @ $9.00
9	500 @ 8.50
11	300 @ 9.20
23	600 @ 8.60
27	800 @ 8.70
	2,600

Instructions

(a) Assuming that the periodic system is used, compute the inventory at May 31 using (1) LIFO; (2) average cost.

(b) Assuming that perpetual inventory records are kept in dollars and costs are computed at the time of each withdrawal, determine the inventory using (1) FIFO; (2) LIFO.

(c) Compute cost of goods sold assuming periodic inventory procedures and inventory priced at FIFO.

(d) In an inflationary period, which of the inventory methods (FIFO, LIFO, average cost) will show the highest net income?

E8-15   Rorry Halverson, the vice-president of finance of Swimsuit Corporation, a retail company, made two different schedules of gross margin for the first quarter ended March 31, 1986. These schedules appear below:

	Sales ($5 per unit)	Cost of Goods Sold	Gross Margin
Schedule 1	$140,000	$115,700	$24,300
Schedule 2	140,000	116,900	23,100

The computation of cost of goods sold in each schedule is based on the following data:

	Units	Cost per Unit	Total Cost
Beginning inventory, January 1	10,000	$4.10	$41,000
Purchase, January 10	8,000	4.20	33,600
Purchase, January 30	5,000	4.16	20,800
Purchase, February 11	7,000	4.30	30,100
Purchase, March 17	12,000	4.00	48,000

Doreen Chase, the president of the corporation, cannot understand how two different gross margins can be computed from the same set of data. As the vice-president of finance, you have explained to Ms. Chase that the two schedules are based on different assumptions concerning the flow of inventory costs (i.e., first-in, first-out; and last-in, first-out). Schedules 1 and 2 were not necessarily prepared in this sequence of cost-flow assumptions.

Instructions

Prepare two separate schedules computing cost of goods sold plus supporting schedules showing the composition of the ending inventory under both cost-flow assumptions.

E8-16   The Frate Company was formed on December 1, 1985. The following information is available from Frate's inventory records for Product Ply:

	Units	Unit Cost
January 1, 1986 (beginning inventory)	800	$ 9.00
Purchases:		
January 5, 1986	1,500	$10.00
January 25, 1986	1,200	$10.50
February 16, 1986	600	$11.00
March 26, 1986	900	$11.50

A physical inventory on March 31, 1986, shows 1,600 units on hand.

Instructions

Prepare schedules to compute the ending inventory at March 31, 1986, under each of the following inventory methods:

(a)   FIFO

(b)   LIFO

(c)   Weighted-average

(AICPA adapted)

PROBLEMS

P8-1   Plug Company is a wholesale distributor of automotive replacement parts. Initial amounts taken from Plug's accounting records are as follows:

Inventory at December 31, 1986 (based on physical count of goods in Plug's warehouse on December 31, 1986)	$1,250,000

Accounts payable at December 31, 1986.

Vendor	Terms	Amount
L. Poe Company	2% 10 days, net 30	$ 280,000
Joy Corporation	Net 30	210,000
Chestnut Company	Net 30	300,000
Vanessa Enterprises	Net 30	225,000
Firefox Products	Net 30	—
R. Casey Company	Net 30	—
		$1,015,000
Sales in 1986		$9,000,000

Additional information is as follows:

1.   Parts received on consignment from Joy Corporation by Plug, the consignee, amounting to $160,000, were included in the physical count of goods in Plug's warehouse on December 31, 1986, and in accounts payable at December 31, 1986.

2. $20,000 of parts that were purchased from Firefox and paid for in December, 1986 were sold in the last week of 1986, and appropriately recorded as sales of $28,000. The parts were included in the physical count of goods in Plug's warehouse on

December 31, 1986, because the parts were on the loading dock waiting to be picked up by customers.

3.   Parts in transit on December 31, 1986, to customers, shipped f.o.b. shipping point on December 28, 1986, amounted to $34,000. The customers received the parts on January 6, 1987. Sales of $44,000 to the customers for the parts were recorded by Plug on January 2, 1987.

4.   Retailers were holding $215,000 at cost ($260,000 at retail) of goods on consignment from Plug, the consignor, at their stores on December 31, 1986.

5.   Goods were in transit from Casey to Plug on December 31, 1986. The cost of the goods was $30,000, and they were shipped f.o.b. shipping point on December 29, 1986.

6.   A quarterly freight bill in the amount of $2,500 specifically relating to merchandise purchases in December, 1986, all of which was still in the inventory at December 31, 1986, was received on January 3, 1987. The freight bill was not included in the inventory or in accounts payable at December 31, 1986.

7.   All of the purchases from Poe occurred during the last seven days of the year. These items have been recorded in accounts payable and accounted for in the physical inventory at cost before discount. Plug's policy is to pay invoices in time to take advantage of all cash discounts, adjust inventory accordingly, and record accounts payable, net of cash discounts.

Instructions

Prepare a schedule of adjustments to the initial amounts, using the format shown below. Show the effect, if any, of each of the transactions separately. If any of the transactions would not affect the amount shown, state **none**.

	Inventory	Accounts Payable	Sales
Initial amounts	$1,250,000	$1,015,000	$9,000,000
Adjustments—increase (decrease)			
1			
2			
3			
4			
5			
6			
7			
Total adjustments			
Adjusted amounts	$	$	$

(AICPA adapted)

P8-2   Lee-Ann Corporation, a manufacturer of small tools, provided the following information from its accounting records for the year ended December 31, 1986:

Inventory at December 31, 1986 (based on physical count of goods in Lee-Ann's plant at cost on December 31, 1986)	$1,750,000
Accounts payable at December 31, 1986	1,200,000
Net sales (sales less sales returns)	8,500,000

Additional information follows:

1.   Included in the physical count were tools billed to a customer f.o.b. shipping point on December 31, 1986. These tools had a cost of $28,000 and were billed at $35,000. The shipment was on Lee-Ann's loading dock waiting to be picked up by the common carrier.

2. Goods were in transit from a vendor to Lee-Ann on December 31, 1986. The invoice cost was $50,000, and the goods were shipped f.o.b. shipping point on December 29, 1986.

3. Work in process inventory costing $20,000 was sent to an outside processor for plating on December 30, 1986.

4. Tools returned by customers and held pending inspection in the returned goods area on December 31, 1986, were not included in the physical count. On January 8, 1987, the tools costing $26,000 were inspected and returned to inventory. Credit memos totalling $40,000 were issued to the customers on the same date.

5. Tools shipped to a customer f.o.b. destination on December 26, 1986, were in transit at December 31, 1986, and had a cost of $25,000. Upon notification of receipt by the customer on January 2, 1987, Lee-Ann issued a sales invoice for $42,000.

6. Goods, with an invoice cost of $30,000, received from a vendor at 5:00 p.m. on December 31, 1986, were recorded on a receiving report dated January 2, 1987. The goods were not included in the physical count, but the invoice was included in accounts payable at December 31, 1986.

7. Goods received from a vendor on December 26, 1986, were included in the physical count. However, the related $60,000 vendor invoice was not included in accounts payable at December 31, 1986, because the accounts payable copy of the receiving report was lost.

8. On January 3, 1987, a monthly freight bill in the amount of $4,000 was received. The bill specifically related to merchandise purchased in December 1986, one-half of which was still in the inventory at December 31, 1986. The freight charges were not included in either the inventory or in accounts payable at December 31, 1986.

Instructions

Using the format shown below, prepare a schedule of adjustments as of December 31, 1986, to the initial amounts per Lee-Ann's accounting records. Show separately the effect, if any, of each of the eight transactions on the December 31, 1986, amounts. If the transactions would have no effect on the initial amount shown, state **none**.

	Inventory	Accounts Payable	Net Sales
Initial amounts	$1,750,000	$1,200,000	$8,500,000
Adjustments—increase (decrease)			
1			
2			
3			
4			
5			
6			
7			
8			
Total adjustments			
Adjusted amounts	$	$	$

(AICPA adapted)

P8-3   As manager of a summer resort hotel, you noticed after a few months' operations that the receipts of the cigar counter were less than those in corresponding periods of previous seasons. The receipts from other hotel activities have not decreased, and you determine the following:

1. No inventories are carried over at the counter from the previous season.
2. Cigars and cigarettes are added to the counter from the general storeroom in full boxes and cartons as needed.
3. No inventory records are kept at the counter.
4. The cashier's record shows $6,120.00 received up to date of examination.
5. Four office employees are allowed to serve customers at the counter.
6. All sales are at the established unit selling prices.
7. All cash in excess of a $20 change fund is to be deposited with the cashier at the close of each day. An inventory was taken under your supervision and the following statement was prepared:

Boxes of 50 Cigars
Cartons of 10 Packages Cigarettes

Unit Selling Prices	Received from Stockroom	Boxes and Cartons	Single Cigars and Packages	Cost per Box or Carton
Cigars				
50¢	10 boxes	3	25	$18.00
2/50¢	20 boxes	4	10	9.00
20¢	30 boxes	6	40	7.50
Cigarettes				
$2.60	25 cartons	4	6	$17.50
$2.50	300 cartons	77	5	17.00

Instructions

Prepare a summary of cigar counter transactions, showing sales, cost of sales and profit on each of cigars and cigarettes as well as the amount of any shortage.

P8-4 Some of the transactions of Thorn Bird Company during August are listed below.

August 10 Purchased merchandise on account, $8,000, terms 2/10, n/30.
13 Returned part of the purchase of August 10, $500, and received credit on account.
15 Purchased merchandise on account, $12,000, terms 1/10, n/60.
25 Purchased merchandise on account, $6,000, terms 2/10, n/30.
28 Paid invoice of August 15 in full.

Instructions

(a) Assuming that purchases are recorded at gross amounts and that discounts are to be recorded when taken:
1. Prepare general journal entries to record the transactions.
2. Describe how the various items would be shown in the financial statements.
(b) Assuming that purchases are recorded at net amounts and that discounts lost are treated as financial expenses:
1. Prepare general journal entries to enter the transactions.
2. Prepare the adjusting entry necessary on August 31 if financial statements are to be prepared at that time.
3. Describe how the various items would be shown in the financial statements.
(c) Which of the two methods do you prefer and why?

P8-5 The books of Dana Bethard Corporation on December 31, 1986, are in agreement with the following balance sheet:

Dana Bethard Corporation
BALANCE SHEET
As of December 31, 1986

Assets

Cash	$ 30,000
Accounts and notes receivable	40,000
Inventory	80,000
	$150,000

Liabilities and Capital

Accounts and notes payable	$ 24,000
Common shares	100,000
Retained earnings	26,000
	$150,000

The following errors were made by the corporation on December 31, 1985, and were not corrected: the inventory was overstated by $8,000; prepaid expense of $1,500 was omitted; and accrued income of $1,000 was omitted. On December 31, 1986, the inventory was understated by $12,000; prepaid expense of $1,200 was omitted, accrued expense of $800 was omitted; and unearned income of $1,400 was omitted.

The net income shown by the books for 1986 was $15,000.

Instructions

(a) Compute the corrected net income for 1986.

(b) Prepare a corrected balance sheet for December 31, 1986.

P8-6 Summarized below are certain quarterly data relative to the Beresford Company. Assume that there was no inventory on hand at the beginning of the first quarter.

	Purchases	Sales
First quarter	10,000 @ $3.00	8,000 @ $3.75
	5,000 @ 3.10	3,000 @ 3.80
Second quarter	8,000 @ 3.10	6,000 @ 3.90
	4,000 @ 3.25	4,000 @ 4.00
Third quarter	9,000 @ 3.30	10,000 @ 4.00
	3,000 @ 3.40	2,000 @ 4.10
Fourth quarter	5,000 @ 3.40	4,000 @ 4.20
	8,000 @ 3.50	5,000 @ 4.25

Instructions

(a) Compute the gross profit for the Beresford Company by quarters under each of the following methods of inventory pricing, assuming that inventory costs are determined only at the end of each quarter.
  1. First-in, first-out (FIFO).
  2. Last-in, first-out (LIFO).
  3. Weighted-average cost (carry unit costs to the nearest cent).

(b) Evaluate the effect of each of these three methods on gross profit in a period of rising prices as presented above.

P8-7 Teddy Bear Manufacturing Company manufactures two products: Andy Panda and Cuddly Cub. At December 31, 1985, Teddy used the first-in, first-out (FIFO) inventory method. Effective January 1, 1986, Teddy changed to the last-in, first-out (LIFO) inventory method. The cumulative effect of this change is not determinable and, as a result, the ending inventory of 1985, for which the FIFO method was used, is also the beginning inventory for 1986 for the LIFO method.

Any layers added during 1986 should be costed by reference to the first acquisitions of 1986, and any layers liquidated during 1986 should be considered a permanent liquidation.

The following information was available from Teddy's inventory records for the two most recent years:

	Andy Panda		Cuddly Cub	
	Units	Unit Cost	Units	Unit Cost
1985 purchases				
January 7	5,000	$4.00	22,000	$2.00
April 16	12,000	4.50		
November 8	17,000	5.50	18,500	3.00
December 13	10,000	6.00		
1986 purchases				
February 11	3,000	7.00	23,000	3.50
May 20	8,000	7.50		
October 15	20,000	8.00		
December 23			15,500	4.00
Units on hand				
December 31, 1985	15,000		14,500	
December 31, 1986	17,000		13,000	

Instructions

Compute the effect on income before income taxes for the year ended December 31, 1986, resulting from the change from the FIFO to the LIFO inventory method.

(AICPA adapted)

P8-8 Hoyt Corporation's record of transactions concerning Part 453 for the month of April was as follows:

Purchases

Apr. I (balance on hand)	100 @ $4.00
Apr. 4	300 @ 4.10
Apr. 11	400 @ 4.00
Apr. 18	200 @ 3.75
Apr. 26	600 @ 3.50
Apr. 30	300 @ 3.30

Sales

Apr. 5	300
Apr. 12	200
Apr. 27	700
Apr. 28	100

Instructions

(a) Compute the inventory at April 30 on each of the following bases. Assume that the periodic system is used for inventory valuation. Carry unit costs to the nearest cent.
1. First-in, first-out (FIFO).
2. Last-in, first-out (LIFO).
3. Weighted-average cost.

(b) Assuming that the perpetual inventory system is used, what amount would be shown as ending inventory under the FIFO, LIFO, and moving-average methods? Carry unit costs to the nearest cent.

P8-9 Here is some of the information found on a detail inventory card for Kurt Reding, Inc. for the first month of operations.

Date	Received No. of Units	Received Unit Cost	Issued, No. of Units	Balance, No. of Units
Jan. 2	1,200	$3.00		1,200
7			700	500
10	500	3.20		1,000
13			600	400
18	1,500	3.20	300	1,600
20			1,000	600
23	1,000	3.40		1,600
26			900	700
28	1,500	3.50		2,200
31			1,200	1,000

Instructions

(a) From this information, compute the ending inventory on each of the following bases. (Assume that perpetual inventory records are kept in units only; carry unit costs to the nearest cent.)
   1. First-in, first-out (FIFO).
   2. Last-in, first-out (LIFO).
   3. Weighted-average cost.
   4. Base stock. (Assume 500 units at $3.00 to be the base stock with receipts and issues over that figure to be priced on a first-in, first-out basis.)

(b) If the perpetual inventory record is kept in dollars, and costs are computed at the time of each withdrawal, would the amounts shown as ending inventory in 1, 2, and 3 above be the same? Explain.

P8-10 The management of Logan Products Company has asked its accounting department to describe the effect upon the company's financial position and its income statement of accounting for inventories on the LIFO rather than the FIFO basis during 1985 and 1986. The accounting department is to assume that the change to LIFO would have been effective on January 1, 1985, and that the initial LIFO base would have been the inventory value on December 31, 1984. Presented below are the company's financial statements and other data for the years 1985 and 1986 when the FIFO method was in fact employed.

Financial Position as of	December 31, 1984	December 31, 1985	December 31, 1986
Cash	$ 67,700	$121,300	$176,050
Accounts receivable	40,000	54,000	61,750
Inventory	69,000	75,000	84,000
Other assets	114,000	114,000	114,000
Total assets	$290,700	$364,300	$435,800
Accounts payable	$ 23,000	$ 30,000	$ 36,400
Other liabilities	40,000	40,000	40,000
Common shares	140,000	140,000	140,000
Retained earnings	87,700	154,300	219,400
Total equities	$290,700	$364,300	$435,800

Income for Years Ended	December 31, 1985	December 31, 1986
Sales	$540,000	$617,500
Less: Cost of goods sold	$294,000	$355,000
Other expenses	135,000	154,000
	$429,000	$509,000
Net income before income taxes	$111,000	$108,500
Income tax expense (40%)	44,400	43,400
Net income	$ 66,600	$ 65,100

Other data:

1. Inventory on hand at December 31, 1984, consisted of 30,000 units valued at $2.30 each.
2. Sales (all units sold at the same price in a given year):
   1985—120,000 units @ $4.50 each
   1986—130,000 units @ $4.75 each
3. Purchases (all units purchased at the same price in given year):
   1985—120,000 units @ $2.50 each
   1986—130,000 units @ $2.80 each
4. Income tax expense is at the effective rate of 40%.

Instructions

Name the account(s) presented in the financial statement that would have different amounts for 1986 if LIFO rather than FIFO had been used and state the new amount for each account that is named. The income tax expense is based on the net income before taxes amount. For purposes of determining taxes paid, assume that the FIFO method is continued to be used for determining taxable income. The difference between tax expense and taxes paid is charged to a Deferred Income Taxes account, and this account would incorporate the effect of the different methods in the financial statements for only the two-year period.

(CMA adapted)

P8-11 As the controller of Nessinger Farms, Inc., a retail company, you made three different schedules of gross profit for the third quarter ended September 30. These schedules appear below.

	Sales ($10 per Unit)	Cost of Goods Sold	Gross Profit
Schedule A	$560,000	$234,700	$325,300
Schedule B	560,000	233,386	326,614
Schedule C	560,000	231,030	328,970

The computation of cost of goods sold in each schedule is based on the following data:

	Units	Cost per Unit	Total Cost
Beginning inventory, July 1	10,000	$4.00	$ 40,000
Purchase, July 25	15,000	4.20	63,000
Purchase, August 15	33,000	4.13	136,290
Purchase, September 5	6,000	4.30	25,800
Purchase, September 25	20,000	4.25	85,000

Tom Nessinger, president of the corporation, cannot understand how three different gross profits can be computed from the same set of data. As controller, you have explained that the three schedules are based on three different assumptions concerning the flow of inventory costs (i.e., first-in, first-out; last-in, first-out; and weighted-average). Schedules A, B, and C were not necessarily prepared in this sequence of cost-flow assumptions.

Instructions

Prepare three separate schedules computing cost of goods sold and supporting schedules showing the composition of the ending inventory under each of the three cost-flow assumptions.

P8-12 Sawtell Company cans two food commodities that it stores at various warehouses. The company employs a perpetual inventory accounting system under which the finished goods inventory is charged with production and credited for sales at standard cost. The detail of the finished goods inventory is maintained by the computing department in units and dollars for the various warehouses.

Company procedures call for the accounting department to receive copies of daily production reports and sales invoices. Units are then extended at standard cost and a summary of the day's activity is posted to the Finished Goods Inventory general ledger control account. Next the sales invoices and production reports are sent to the computing department for processing. Every month the control account and detailed records are reconciled and adjustments recorded. The last reconciliation and adjustments were made at November 30, 1986.

Your audit firm observed the taking of the physical inventory at all locations on December 31, 1986. The inventory count began at 3:00 p.m. and was completed at 8:00 p.m. The company's figure for the physical inventory is $331,400. The general ledger control account balance at December 31 was $373,900, and the final computer run of the inventory showed a total of $392,300.

Unit cost data for the company's two products are as follows:

Product	Standard Cost
A	$2.00
B	3.00

A review of December transactions disclosed the following:

1. Sales invoice #1603, dated December 2, 1986, was priced at standard cost for $11,700 but was listed on the accounting department's daily summary at $11,200.

2. A production report for $23,900, dated December 15, 1986, was processed twice in error by the computing department.

3. Sales invoice #1481, dated December 9, 1986, for 1,200 units of product A, was priced at a standard cost of $1.50 per unit by the accounting department. The computing department noticed and corrected the error but did not notify the accounting department.

4. A shipment of 3,400 units of product A was invoiced by the billing department as 3,000 units on sales invoice #1703, dated December 27, 1986. The error was discovered in your review of transactions.

5. On December 27 the Toronto warehouse notified the computing department to remove 2,200 unsalable units of product A from the finished goods inventory, which it did without receiving a special invoice from the accounting department. The accounting department received a copy of the Toronto warehouse notification on December 29 and made up a special invoice that was processed in the normal manner. The units were not included in the physical inventory.

6. A production report for the production on January 3 of 2,500 units of product B was processed for the Oshawa plant as of December 31.

7. A shipment of 300 units of product B was made from the St. John warehouse to Ken's Markets, Inc. at 8:30 p.m. on December 31 as an emergency service. The sales invoice was processed as of December 31. The client prefers to treat the transaction as a sale in 1986.

8. The working papers of the auditor observing the physical count at the Winnipeg warehouse revealed that 700 units of product B were omitted from the client's physical count. The client concurred that the units were omitted in error.

9. A sales invoice for 600 units of product A shipped from the Halifax warehouse was mislaid and was not processed until January 5. The units involved were shipped on December 30.

10. The physical inventory of the Victoria warehouse excluded 350 units of product A that were marked "reserved." Upon investigation it was ascertained that this merchandise was being stored as a convenience for Steve's Markets, Inc., a customer. This merchandise, which has not been recorded as a sale, is billed as it is shipped.

11. A shipment of 10,000 units of product B was made on December 27 from the Halifax warehouse to the Winnipeg warehouse. The shipment arrived on January 6 but had been excluded from the physical inventories.

Instructions

Prepare a work sheet to reconcile the balances for the physical inventory, Finished Goods Inventory general ledger control account, and computing department's detail of finished goods inventory. The following format is suggested for the work sheet.

	Physical Inventory	General Ledger Control Account	Computing Department's Detail of Inventory
Balance per client	$331,400	$373,900	$392,300

(AICPA adapted)

P8-13 You are engaged in an audit of the Underwood Manufacturing Company for the year ended December 31, 1986. To reduce the workload at year end the company took its annual physical inventory under your observation on November 30, 1986. The company's inventory account, which includes both raw material and work in process, is kept on a perpetual basis, using the first-in, first-out method of pricing. There is no finished goods inventory. The company's physical inventory revealed that the book inventory of $55,570 was understated by $4,000. To avoid distorting the interim financial statements the company decided not to adjust the book inventory until year end except for obsolete inventory items.

Your audit revealed the following information regarding the November 30 inventory:

1. Pricing tests showed that the physical inventory was overpriced by $2,200.
2. Footing and extension errors resulted in a $150 understatement of the physical inventory.
3. Direct labour included in the physical inventory amounted to $10,000. Overhead was included at the rate of 200% of direct labour. You determined that the amount of direct labour was correct and the overhead rate was proper.
4. The physical inventory included obsolete materials recorded at $400. During December these obsolete materials were removed from the inventory account by a charge to Cost of Sales. Your audit also disclosed the following information about the December 31 inventory:

    (a) Total debits to certain accounts during December are listed below.

	December
Purchases	$26,700
Direct labour	12,100
Manufacturing expense	25,200
Cost of goods sold	68,600

    (b) The cost of goods sold of $68,600 included direct labour of $13,800.
    (c) Normal scrap loss on established product lines is negligible. A special order started and completed during December had excessive scrap loss of $800, however, which was charged to Manufacturing Expense.

Instructions

(a) Compute the correct dollar amount of the physical inventory at November 30, 1986.
(b) Without prejudice to your solution to (a), assume that the correct amount of the physical inventory at November 30, 1986, was $59,700. Compute the amount of the inventory at December 31, 1986.

(AICPA adapted)

P8-14 On January 1, 1982, Grover Company changed its inventory cost flow method to the LIFO cost method from the FIFO cost method for its raw materials inventory. Grover uses the multiple-pools approach, under which substantially identical raw materials are grouped into LIFO inventory pools; weighted-average costs are used in valuing annual incremental layers. The composition of the December 31, 1984, inventory for the Class F inventory pool is as follows:

	Units	Weighted-Average Unit Cost	Total Cost
Base year inventory—1982	9,000	$10.00	$ 90,000
Incremental layer—1983	3,000	11.00	33,000
Incremental layer—1984	2,000	12.50	25,000
Inventory, December 31, 1984	14,000		$148,000

Inventory transactions for the Class F inventory pool during 1985 were as follows:

1. On March 1, there were 4,800 units purchased at a unit cost of $13.50 for $64,800.
2. On September 1, there were 7,200 units purchased at a unit cost of $14.00 for $100,800.
3. A total of 15,000 units were used for production during 1985.

The following transactions for the Class F inventory pool took place during 1986:

1. On January 10, there were 7,500 units purchased at a unit cost of $14.50 for $108,750.
2. On May 15, there were 5,500 units purchased at a unit cost of $15.50 for $85,250.
3. On December 29, there were 7,000 units purchased at a unit cost of $16.00 for $112,000.
4. A total of 16,000 units were used for production during 1986.

Instructions

(a) Prepare a schedule to compute the inventory (units and dollar amounts) of the Class F inventory pool at December 31, 1985. Show supporting computations in good form.

(b) Prepare a schedule to compute the cost of Class F raw materials used in production for the year ended December 31, 1985.

(c) Prepare a schedule to compute the inventory (units and dollar amounts) of the Class F inventory pool at December 31, 1986. Show supporting computations in good form.

9

INVENTORIES: ADDITIONAL VALUATION PROBLEMS

In Chapter 8, different methods for computing the unit cost for inventories were explained by examining the various cost flow assumptions used in accounting. Other possibilities will be explored now. For example, what happens if the value of the inventory increases or decreases after the initial purchase date? Does the accountant recognize these increases and decreases in value before the point of sale? What happens if there is a fire and a physical count cannot be made? How does the accountant determine the ending inventory for insurance purposes? Or, what happens in large department stores where monthly inventory figures are needed, but monthly counts are not feasible?

These questions involve the development and use of estimation techniques to value the ending inventory without a physical count. Estimation methods that are widely used are discussed in this chapter.

LOWER OF COST AND MARKET

A major departure from adherence to the historical cost principle is made in the area of inventory valuation. Applying the constraint of conservatism in accounting means recognizing known losses in the period of occurrence. In contrast, known gains are not recognized until realized. If the inventory declines in value below its original cost for whatever reason (e.g., obsolescence, price level changes, or damaged goods), the inventory should be written down to reflect this loss. **The general rule is that the historical cost principle is abandoned when the future utility (revenue-producing ability) of the asset is no longer as great as its original cost.** A departure from cost is justified on the basis that a loss of utility should be reflected as a charge against the revenues in the period in which the loss occurs. Inventories are valued, therefore, on the basis of the lower of cost and market instead of on an original cost basis. The term **"market"** in the phrase "the lower of cost and market" (cost or market, whichever is lower) requires a more specific definition, as the *CICA Handbook* notes:

> In view of the lack of precision in meaning, it is desirable that the term "market" not be used in describing the basis of valuation. A term more descriptive of the method of determining market, such as "replacement cost," "net realizable value," or "net realizable value less normal profit margin" would be preferable.[1]

Replacement cost generally means the cost to replace the item, by purchase or production, as it would be incurred in the normal course of business operations (e.g., buying or manufacturing from usual sources in normal quantities). **Net realizable value** is the estimated selling price of the items in the ordinary course of business less reasonably predictable future costs to complete and dispose of the items. **Net realizable value less normal profit margin** is determined by deducting a normal profit margin from the previously defined net realizable value amount. For example, a retailer may have in inventory calculator wrist-watches that had cost $15.00 each. If their purchase cost is presently $14.00, that would be their replacement cost. If their selling price today is $25.00, and there were no additional costs to sell them, then this amount would be their net realizable value. If a normal profit margin is 35% of selling price, the net realizable value less normal profit margin would be $16.25. Consequently, in this example, this inventory would be valued at $15.00 per unit (its historical cost) under the lower of cost and market rule if market were either net realizable value or net realizable value less normal profit margin, but would be valued at $14.00 per unit if market were the replacement cost.

Given that there are different interpretations as to what market can be, the question of which to use when applying the lower of cost and market rule requires consideration. The *CICA Handbook* recognizes several possibilities (as indicated by the previous quotation) but is silent on which one is appropriate in particular circumstances. This is understandable, given the various practical problems in considering the implications of any definition of market in particular situations for various types of inventories. (Some of these considerations are identified later under the heading "Evaluation of the Lower of Cost and Market Rule".) Clearly, however, net realizable value is the most frequently used method of determining "market" in Canada.[2] This is most likely due to the conclusions reached by a CICA research study which stated that

> . . . selling prices do not necessarily fluctuate with costs and that, as a result, a decline in the cost of replacement or reproduction, in itself, is not conclusive evidence that a

[1]*CICA Handbook* (Toronto: CICA), Section 3030, par. 11.

[2]*Financial Reporting in Canada—1983* (Toronto: CICA, 1983) reports that, of the interpretations of market disclosed in 1982 financial statements of the surveyed companies, net realizable value was used 237 times, replacement cost 64 times, net realizable value less normal profit margin 13 times, and other methods 44 times.

loss will be incurred. It is only if selling prices vary directly with changes in costs that replacement cost provides an accurate measure of the anticipated loss of gross profits and, under such conditions, exactly the same result can be accomplished by using net realizable value less normal profits. Due to its obvious limitations and because consistent use may produce unreasonable results, the lower of cost and replacement cost can hardly be classified as a practical interpretation of the lower of cost and market basis of valuing inventories.

The only reasonable choice of interpretation seems to be between net realizable value and net realizable value less normal profit. Both of these interpretations have the desired quality of being capable of consistent application. The choice between the two reduces itself to the question of which interpretation provides the more accurate measurement of the loss which will actually be experienced. Under the net realization theory, the loss charged against the income of the current period is limited to irrecoverable cost which is, in effect, the true loss (cost incurred without return or benefit) that is expected to be suffered. Under the net realizable value less normal profit theory, all or part of the charge against income does not represent a true loss.

Since any departure from cost disrupts the normal process of matching costs with related revenues and is an arbitrary shifting of income from one period to another, it would seem most logical to insist on that interpretation of market which causes the lesser disruption of or shift away from the normal matching process. Net realizable value wins over net realizable value less a normal profit because the latter interpretation results in a larger inventory adjustment and, therefore, unnecessarily accentuates the shift in income.

. . . If the lower of cost and market basis of inventory valuation in the ordinary course of business operations is to be used, market should be limited to net realizable value since this is the most reasonable interpretation from the point of view of both income measurement and balance sheet presentation.[3]

In the United States the AICPA has adopted a different approach for determining "market" in the application of the lower of cost and market rule. Generally, it means the cost to replace the item (by purchase or reproduction). "Market," however, is limited to an amount that should not exceed the net realizable value (the ceiling) and "should not be less than net realizable value reduced by an allowance for an approximately normal profit margin (the floor)."[4]

Basically, under the U.S. procedures, the accountant determines the replacement cost of the inventory, and when it is lower than cost, uses that valuation for pricing the inventory unless it either exceeds net realizable value or is less than net realizable value less a normal margin. Therefore, the value used for "market" is the middle value of these three possibilities.

The U.S. approach is based on the premise that declines in replacement cost reflect or predict a decline in selling price. The ceiling and floor limits are introduced to protect against situations where this premise is in serious error. Consequently, while the underlying rationale of attempting to reflect a decline in utility (selling price) of inventory is common to both Canada and the U.S.A.,

[3]Gertrude Mulcahy, *Use and Meaning of "Market" in Inventory Valuation* (Toronto: CICA, 1963), p. 19.

[4]"Restatement and Revision of Accounting Research Bulletins," *Accounting Research Bulletin No. 43*, (New York: AICPA, 1953), Ch. 4, par. 8. It also should be noted that a literal interpretation of the rules of the lower of cost and market is frequently not applied in practice. For example, the lower limit, net realizable value less a normal markup, is rarely computed and applied because it results in an extremely conservative approach to inventory valuation. In addition, inventory is often not reduced to market unless its disposition is expected to result in a loss. Furthermore, if the net realizable value of finished goods exceeds cost, it is usually assumed that both work in process and raw materials do as well. In practice, therefore, *ARB No. 43* is considered a guide, and professional judgement is often exercised in lieu of following this pronouncement literally. Indeed, *Accounting Research Study No. 13*, "The Accounting Basis of Inventories" (New York: AICPA, 1973) recommends that net realizable value be adopted.

each has reached a different conclusion as to how this is to be accomplished in practice.

How Lower of Cost and Market Works

The lower of cost and market rule requires that the inventory be valued at cost unless "market" is lower than cost, in which case the inventory is valued at "market." To apply this rule, the market value must be determined and then compared to the cost as determined on an acceptable historical cost basis. The cost or market figure, whichever is lower, would then be used for inventory valuation on the financial statements.

To illustrate, consider the following information:

		Market		
Case	Cost	Net Realizable Value	Replacement Cost	Net Realizable Value Less Normal Profit Margin
1	$1.00	$1.50	$1.10	$1.20
2	1.00	1.00	.90	.70
3	1.00	.80	.95	.56
4	1.00	.80	.40	.56
5	1.00	.95	1.05	.80

The Lower of Cost and Market Approach

If net realizable value were the designated "market" value, as is commonly the case for Canadian companies, the application of a "lower of cost and net realizable value" approach would mean that inventory would be shown at cost in cases 1 and 2 and net realizable value in cases 3, 4, and 5. If, however, net realizable value less normal profit margin were the designated "market" value, inventory would be shown at cost in case 1 and net realizable value less normal profit margin in cases 2, 3, 4, and 5. Use of replacement cost as market would result in using cost in cases 1 and 5 and replacement cost in cases 2, 3, and 4.

If market were determined using the AICPA approach, then ending inventory under the lower of cost and market rule would be valued as follows:

Case 1. Cost selected because it is lower than any of the possible market values.

Case 2. Replacement cost selected because it is lower than cost and the middle value of the three market possibilities.

Case 3. Net realizable value (ceiling) selected because replacement cost, while lower than cost, is higher than net realizable value and net realizable value is less than cost.

Case 4. Net realizable value less a normal margin (floor) is selected because replacement cost is below this figure, which is the lower limit for market and is less than cost.

Case 5. Net realizable value (ceiling) is selected because replacement cost is above this upper constraint. Cost is not selected because it is higher than net realizable value.

Recording "Market" Instead of Cost

In those cases in which "market" rather than cost is used as the inventory price, some accountants consider it undesirable accounting procedure merely to substitute the market figure for cost when pricing the new inventory. **Recording the**

ending inventory at market increases the cost of goods sold by the amount of the loss recognized and thus fails to reflect this loss separately. This objection may be overcome by first **recording the inventory at cost** in the adjusting or closing process **and then making a separate entry to reduce the inventory to market**. The following illustration of entries under both approaches assumes an inventory cost of $82,000 and a determined market value of $70,000:

Ending Inventory Recorded at Market		Ending Inventory Recorded at Cost and Reduced to Market		
To record inventory at year end:				
Inventory	70,000	Inventory	82,000	
Cost of Goods Sold	70,000	Cost of Goods Sold		82,000
To write down inventory to market:				
No entry		Loss Due to Market		
		Decline of Inventory	12,000	
		Inventory		12,000

The advantage of reporting the loss is that it may then be shown as a separate item in the income statement, but not as an extraordinary item, and the cost of the sales for the year is not distorted by its inclusion. Consequently, the rate of gross profit for the year is not affected by the loss due to market decline.

The advantage of recording a market decline in this manner is indicated in the following comparison:

Inventory Priced at Market

Sales		$200,000
Cost of goods sold		
Inventory, beginning	$ 65,000	
Purchases	125,000	
Goods available	$190,000	
Inventory, ending	70,000	
Cost of goods sold		120,000
Gross profit on sales		$ 80,000

Inventory Priced at Cost and Reduced to Market by Separate Journal Entry

Sales		$200,000
Cost of goods sold		
Inventory, beginning	$ 65,000	
Purchases	125,000	
Goods available	$190,000	
Inventory, ending	82,000	
Cost of goods sold		108,000
Gross profit on sales		$ 92,000
Loss due to market decline of inventory		12,000
		$80,000

The second presentation is preferable, because it clearly discloses the loss resulting from the market decline of inventory prices, which is ''buried'' in the cost of goods sold figure in the first presentation. Although this presentation is preferred to direct pricing of the inventory at market because the loss due to market decline is shown separately, it does include an inconsistency: the inventory is shown at $82,000 in the income statement but it is included in the balance sheet at only $70,000. In overcoming this inconsistency, some accountants have advocated the use of a special account to receive the credit for such an inventory write-down. Instead of the inventory account being credited directly, the entries to record ending inventory at cost and to write down the inventory from cost to the lower of cost and market are as follows:

Inventory	82,000	
Cost of Goods Sold		82,000
(To record inventory at year end)		
Loss Due to Market Decline of Inventory	12,000	
Allowance to Reduce Inventory to Market		12,000
(To write down inventory to market)		

The Allowance to Reduce Inventory to Market (contra asset) would be shown on the balance sheet as a deduction from the inventory of $82,000, thereby reducing it to the lower of cost and market. This deduction permits both the income statement and the balance sheet to show the amount of $82,000, although the inventory extension in the balance sheet is a net amount of $70,000. It also keeps subsidiary inventory ledgers and records in correspondence with the control account without changing unit prices.

Although this practice permits disclosure on the balance sheet of the amount of inventory both at cost and at the lower of cost and market, it raises the additional problem of how to dispose of the balance of the new account in the following period. If the merchandise in question is still on hand, the account may be retained but, if it is assumed that the goods that suffered the decline have been sold, this account should be removed from the books. Because the inventory account is currently stated at cost, the beginning inventory and thus the cost of goods sold in the next period are overstated if the allowance balance is not closed. **Closing the allowance account against beginning inventory** (or to Cost of Goods Sold if beginning inventory has already been removed from the accounts) **corrects the misstatement**. A "new" allowance account is then established for the decline in inventory value that has taken place in the current period. Another possibility is to close the allowance account to the Income Summary account.

Some accountants leave this account on the books and merely adjust the balance at the next year end to agree with the discrepancy between cost and the lower of cost and market at that balance sheet date. Thus, if prices are falling, a loss is recorded; if prices are increasing, a loss recorded in prior years is recovered, and a gain is recorded, as illustrated in the following example.

Date	Inventory at Cost	Inventory at Market	Amount Required in Valuation Account	Adjustment of Valuation Account Balance	Effect on Net Income
Dec. 31/83	$188,000	$176,000	$12,000	$12,000 inc.	Loss
Dec. 31/84	194,000	187,000	7,000	5,000 dec.	Gain
Dec. 31/85	173,000	174,000	-0-	7,000 dec.	Gain
Dec. 31/86	182,000	180,000	2,000	2,000 inc.	Loss

This "gain" can be thought of as the excess of the credit effect of closing the beginning allowance balance over the debit effect of setting up the current year-end allowance account. Recognition of such a gain or loss has the same effect on net income as closing the allowance balance to beginning inventory or to cost of goods sold.

This discussion indicates some of the basic problems of presentation surrounding the lower of cost and market approach. It also illustrates the complications that arise when deviations are made from basic accounting theory. To the alert student of business, one conclusion seems inevitable: as long as a number of treatments and practices are followed, real understanding of accounting reports requires some knowledge of all possibilities and their effect on the reported data.

Methods of Applying the Lower of Cost and Market Rule

The lower of cost and market rule may be applied to each item of the inventory, to the total of the components of each major category of inventory, or to the total of the entire inventory. The method chosen should be the one that is judged to reflect periodic income most clearly. Ordinarily the application of the rule to the total of the entire inventory, or to the total of the components of each major category, results in an amount that more nearly approaches cost than would be the case if the rule were applied to each item. Under the total or category methods, increases in market prices of some items offset, to some extent, the decreases in market prices of other items, as illustrated below. Assume that the major categories of inventory for this business are radios and TVs.

Methods of Applying Lower of Cost and Market

	Cost	Market	Lower of Cost and Market: Individual Items	Lower of Cost and Market: Major Categories	Lower of Cost and Market: Total Inventory
Radios					
Type A	$ 800	$ 750	$ 750		
B	1,500	1,600	1,500		
C	900	800	800		
Total Radios	$ 3,200	$ 3,150		$ 3,150	
TV Sets					
Type X	$ 3,000	$ 3,400	3,000		
Y	4,500	4,300	4,300		
Z	2,000	1,900	1,900		
Total TVs	$ 9,500	$ 9,600		9,500	
Total Inventory	$12,700	$12,750	$12,250	$12,650	$12,700

If the lower of cost and market rule is applied by individual items, the amount of inventory is $12,250. If applied by major categories, it is $12,650 and, if applied to the total inventory, it is $12,700.

In Canada the most common practice is to price the inventory on a total basis. Companies favour the application of the rule to the total of the inventory because Canadian income tax rules require this treatment. The tax rules in the United

States require the application of the lower of cost and market to individual items and, consequently, that method is more common in the United States.

Whichever method is selected for financial reporting, it should be applied consistently from one period to the next. **As soon as the inventory is written down to market, this new basis is considered to be the cost basis for future periods.** Generally, a rise in the market prices of the inventory after it has been written down should not be recognized.

Evaluation of Lower of Cost and Market Rule

Conceptually, the lower of cost and market rule has some deficiencies. First, if the inventory is written down because of a loss in utility, does it not seem appropriate to write up the value of the inventory when the utility of the asset increases? Decreases in the value of the asset and the charge to income are recognized in the period in which the loss in utility occurs—not in the period of sale. On the other hand, increases in the value of the asset are recognized only at the point of sale. This situation is inconsistent and can lead to distortions in the presentation of income data.

Even if we accept this inconsistency, another problem arises in defining market. **Basically, three different types of valuations could be used in Canada: replacement cost, net realizable value, and net realizable value less a normal profit margin.**[5] Replacement cost could be chosen because changes in replacement cost are easily identified and may reflect a corresponding decline in sales value. Frequently, however, a reduction in the replacement cost of an item does not indicate a corresponding reduction in the utility of the item. To illustrate, assume that a retailer has several T-shirts that were bought for $3.00 each. The replacement cost of these shirts falls to $2.50, but the selling price remains the same. The problem that must be addressed in this case is whether or not the retailer has suffered a loss. To recognize a loss in this period misstates this year's income and also that of future periods because, upon sale of the shirts in future periods, the full price is received.

The second valuation approach—net realizable value—is the most logical method for valuing inventory. The net realizable value reflects the future service potential of the asset and, for that reason, is conceptually sound. Unfortunately, net realizable value may sometimes be difficult to measure with a sufficient degree of certainty and, therefore, replacement cost may be the only available option. Also, replacement cost may be the most reasonable and practical for raw materials and work in process inventories, given that they do not have a selling price *per se*.

Another alternative is net realizable value less a normal profit margin. This method requires dealing with the difficult problems of determining both the net realizable value and a normal profit margin. In addition, under this approach, a loss recognized in one period is partially offset by the recognition of profit in a future period. To illustrate, assume that an item costing $10 has a net realizable value of $8, and that the normal profit margin is 30% of the cost. Firms using net realizable value would recognize a loss of only $2 ($10 − $8); firms using net realizable value less a normal profit margin would show a loss of $5 ($10 − $2 − $3)

[5]As previously mentioned, market is usually defined as net realizable value in Canadian practice. The other methods of determining market are recognized in the *CICA Handbook* (Section 3030, par. 11) and are used to some extent (see footnote 2 of this chapter).

and then, in a later period when the item is sold, record a profit of $3. The purpose of the latter approach is to show a normal profit margin in the period of sale.

From the standpoint of accounting theory there is little to justify the lower of cost and market rule. Despite this, lower of cost and market is, by far, the most common basis for valuation of inventories in Canada.[6] Its acceptance is based on the practical constraint of conservatism and tradition in financial statement reporting. The rule does result in conservatism from a balance sheet point of view and lower net income in the period in which write-downs occur. Consequently, the loss is matched to the period in which it is deemed to occur, and the amount carried forward as inventory is matched against the revenue of the periods in which it is sold. Therefore, despite the conservatism in the current period, the result is to show higher income in future periods than would be the case if costs had been carried forward. Since the total income over several periods will be the same whether or not the lower of cost and market rule is applied, the real concern regarding its acceptability lies in determining in which period the loss should be matched against revenue.

THE GROSS PROFIT METHOD OF DETERMINING INVENTORY

The basic purpose of taking a physical inventory is to verify the accuracy of the inventory records or, if no records exist, to arrive at an inventory amount. Sometimes estimation methods are used to accomplish the same purpose. One such method of verifying or determining the inventory amount is called the gross profit method. This method is widely used in situations requiring only an estimate of the amount of the company's inventory (e.g., for determining monthly or quarterly inventory amounts), or where both inventory and inventory records have been destroyed by fire or other catastrophe.

The **gross profit method** is based on the assumption that (1) the beginning inventory plus purchases equals total goods to be accounted for; (2) goods not sold must be on hand; and (3) if the sales, reduced to cost, are deducted from the sum of the opening inventory plus purchases, the result is the goods on hand or, in other words, the inventory.

To illustrate, assume that a department has a beginning inventory of $60,000 and purchases of $200,000 both at cost. Sales at selling price amount to $280,000. The average rate of gross profit (margin) on selling price for the department is 30%. The calculation of inventory on hand would be as follows:

Beginning inventory (at cost)		$ 60,000
Purchases (at cost)		200,000
Goods available (at cost)		$260,000
Sales (at selling price)	$280,000	
Less: Gross profit (30% of $280,000)	84,000	
Sales (at cost)		196,000
Approximate inventory (at cost)		$ 64,000

---

[6]*Financial Reporting in Canada—1983* reported that lower of cost and market was used by 288 companies, cost by 46 companies, market by 13 companies, and other approaches by 15 companies. Only 15 companies indicated that market was not used in valuations.

All the information to compute the inventory at cost, except for the gross profit percentage, is available in the current period's accounting records. The gross profit percentage is determined by reviewing prior period records. In some cases, this percentage must be adjusted if prior periods are not considered representative of the current period's operations.

Calculation of Gross Profit Percentage

In most situations, the gross profit percentage is given as a percentage of selling price. The previous illustration indicated that a 30% gross profit on sales was used. Gross profit on selling price is the common method for quoting the profit because (1) most goods are stated on a retail basis, not a cost basis; (2) a percentage based on selling price is lower than one based on cost, and the lower rate gives a favourable impression to the consumer; and (3) the gross profit based on selling price can never exceed 100%.[7]

To see how gross profit is computed, assume that an article costs $15 and sells for $20, a gross profit of $5.00. This markup is one-quarter or 25% of retail and one-third or 33 1/3% of cost.

$$\frac{markup}{retail} = \frac{\$\ 5.00}{\$20.00} = 25\% \text{ of retail} \qquad \frac{markup}{cost} = \frac{\$5.00}{\$15.00} = 33\ 1/3\% \text{ of cost}$$

Although it is normal to compute the gross profit on the basis of selling price, the accountant should understand the basic relationship between markup on cost and markup on selling price.

For example, assume that you were told that the markup on cost for a given item is 25%. What is the **gross profit on selling price?** To find the answer, assume that the sales price of the item is $1.00. In this case, the following holds.

$$\text{Cost + Gross Profit = Selling Price}$$
$$C + .25C = SP$$
$$1.25C = 1.00$$
$$C = \$0.80$$

The gross profit equals $0.20 ($1.00 − $0.80), and the rate of gross profit on sales is therefore 20% ($0.20 ÷ $1.00).

Conversely, assume that you were told that the gross profit on selling price is 20%. What is the **markup on cost?** To find the answer, again assume that the sales price is $1.00. Again the following formula holds:

$$\text{Cost + Gross Profit = Selling Price}$$
$$C + .20SP = SP$$
$$C = .80SP$$
$$C = \$0.80$$

As above, the markup equals $0.20 ($1.00 − $0.80), and the markup on cost is 25% ($0.20 ÷ $0.80).

Selling price is greater than cost; it therefore follows that the markup (gross

---

[7]The terms gross profit percentage, gross margin, rate of gross profit, and percentage markup are synonymous terms, although it sounds more acceptable to use markup in reference to cost and gross profit in reference to sales.

profit) on cost will be greater than the gross profit on selling price. This is because the gross profit amount will be the same for both but the denominator in the equation will be smaller for the cost based calculation compared to the selling price based calculation.

Retailers use the following formulas to express these relationships:

1. Percentage markup on selling price $= \dfrac{\text{percentage markup on cost}}{100\% + \text{percentage markup on cost}}$

2. Percentage markup on cost $= \dfrac{\text{percentage markup on selling price}}{100\% - \text{percentage markup on selling price}}$

To illustrate how these formulas are employed, the following different relationships are provided:

Percentage Markup on Selling Price	Percentage Markup on Cost
Given: 20% $\longrightarrow$	$\dfrac{.20}{1.00 - .20} = 25\%$
Given: 25% $\longrightarrow$	$\dfrac{.25}{1.00 - .25} = 33\ 1/3\%$
$\dfrac{.25}{1.00 + .25} = 20\%$ $\longleftarrow$	Given: 25%
$\dfrac{.50}{1.00 + .50} = 33\ 1/3\%$ $\longleftarrow$	Given: 50%

Appraisal of Gross Profit Method

The gross profit method is not normally acceptable for annual financial reporting purposes because it is only an estimate, and a physical inventory is needed as additional verification that the inventory indicated in the records is on hand. Nevertheless, as indicated earlier, the gross profit method is quite useful whenever an estimate of the ending inventory is needed (e.g., for interim reporting). Note that the gross profit method should follow closely the inventory method used (FIFO, LIFO, average cost) because it is based on historical records, reflecting the use of one of these inventory flow assumptions.

One major disadvantage of the gross profit method is that **it is an estimate**; as a result, a physical inventory must be taken once a year to verify that the inventory is actually on hand.

A second disadvantage is that the gross profit method **uses past percentages** for determination of the markup, and although the past can often provide answers to the future, a current rate is more appropriate.

Third, when the inventory is approximated by this method, **care must be taken in applying a blanket rate of gross profit.** A blanket rate is an average of the gross profit rates for several different items. Frequently a store or department handles merchandise with widely varying rates of gross profit. In these situations, the gross profit method may have to be applied by subsections, lines of merchandise, or a similar basis that classifies merchandise according to rates of gross profit. If a blanket rate is used in these situations, a change in the quantity of one line relative to another, or a change in the markup of one line could lead to an inappropriate final inventory value.

RETAIL INVENTORY METHOD

Retailers with certain types of inventory may use the specific identification method for valuation of their inventories. For example, when individual inventory units are significant (e.g., automobiles, pianos, or fur coats), such an approach makes sense. However, imagine attempting to use such an approach with Canadian Tire or Eaton's retailers, that have many different types of merchandise at low unit costs and also have a large volume of transactions. In such situations, it would be extremely difficult to determine the cost of each sale, enter cost codes on the tickets, change the codes to reflect declines in value of the merchandise, allocate such costs as transportation, and so on. As a result, any type of unit cost method would be unsatisfactory in most department stores selling enormous numbers of items in a huge volume of transactions. An alternative is to compile the inventories at retail prices. In most retail concerns, an observable pattern between cost and sales price lends itself to the computation of inventory on hand through the use of retail prices. These retail prices can then be converted to cost through an adjustment process.

This method, called **the retail inventory method, requires that a record be kept of (1) the total cost and retail value of goods purchased, (2) the total cost and retail value of the goods available for sale, and (3) the sales for the period.** The sales for the period are deducted from the retail value of the goods available for sale to produce an estimated inventory at retail. The ratio of cost to retail for all goods passing through a department or company is then determined by dividing the total goods available for sale at cost by the total goods available at retail. The inventory valued at retail is reduced to approximate cost by applying the cost to retail ratio. The retail inventory method is illustrated for Marshy Field, Ltd. below:

	Cost	Retail
Marshy Field, Ltd.		
Retail Inventory Method		
(current period)		
Beginning inventory	$14,000	$ 20,000
Purchases	63,000	90,000
Goods available	$77,000	$110,000
Deduct: Sales		85,000
Ending inventory, at retail		$ 25,000
Ratio of cost to retail ($77,000 ÷ $110,000)		70%
Ending inventory at cost (70% of $25,000)		$ 17,500

This calculation is based on the relationship that the total goods available for sale (at retail) less the goods sold (at retail) equals the goods on hand (at retail). The goods on hand at retail are then converted to goods on hand at cost by application of the cost to retail ratio. To avoid a potential misstatement of the inventory, periodic inventory counts are made, especially in retail operations where loss due to shoplifting and breakage is common.

The retail method is sanctioned by various retail associations, the accounting profession, and (except for methods approximating a LIFO valuation) by Revenue Canada. One advantage of the retail inventory method is that the inventory balance **can be approximated without a physical count.** This method is particularly useful for any type of interim report, because a fairly quick and reliable measure of the inventory value can be determined. Insurance adjusters often use this approach when estimates of the inventory are needed because of a fire, flood, or other type of casualty. This method also acts as a **control device,** because any deviations from a physical count at the end of the year will have to be explained. In addition, the retail method also **expedites the physical inventory count** at the end of the year. The inventory crew need take only the retail prices of each item. There is no need to look up each item's invoice cost, thus saving time and expense.

Retail Method Terminology

The amounts shown in the Retail column of the preceding illustration represent the original retail prices (cost plus an original markup or markon), assuming no other price increases or decreases. Sales prices are frequently changed; that is, they are additionally marked up or marked down from the original price. For retailers, **markup** is considered as an additional markup on original selling price; normally, we think of markup on the basis of cost. **Markup cancellations** are decreases in prices of merchandise that had been marked up above the original retail price.

Markdowns below the original sale prices may be necessary because of a decrease in the general level of prices, special sales, soiled and damaged goods, overstocking, or competition. Markdowns are a fairly common phenomenon. **Markdown cancellations** occur when the markdowns are partially offset at a later date by increases in the prices of goods that had been marked down below the original sales price. Neither a markup cancellation nor a markdown cancellation can exceed the initial markup or markdown.

To illustrate these different concepts, let us assume that the Hub Clothing Store recently purchased 100 high-fashion knit shirts from Marroway, Ltd. The cost for these shirts was $1,500 or $15.00 a shirt. Hub Clothing established the selling price at $25.00 a shirt. The manager noted that the shirts were selling quickly, so he added a markup of $1.50 per shirt. This markup made the price of $26.50 too high and sales lagged; the manager then reduced the price to $26.00. At this point we would say that Hub Clothing has had a markup of $1.50 and a markup cancellation of $0.50. As soon as the major marketing season passed, the manager marked the remaining shirts down to a sales price of $20.00. At this point, an additional markup cancellation of $1.00 has taken place, and a $5.00 markdown has occurred. If the shirts are later written up to $21.00, a markdown cancellation of $1.00 will have occurred.

Retail Inventory Method with Markups and Markdowns

Retailers use these concepts in developing the inventory valuation at the end of the accounting period. To obtain the appropriate inventory figures, proper treatment must be given to markups, markup cancellations, markdowns, and markdown cancellations. To illustrate the different possibilities, assume the following conditions for Donovan Stores, Ltd.

	Cost	Retail
Beginning inventory	$ 500	$ 1,000
Purchases (net)	20,000	35,000
Markups		3,000
Markup cancellations		1,000
Markdowns		2,500
Markdown cancellations		2,000
Sales (net)		25,000

Donovan Stores, Ltd.
Retail Inventory Method

	Cost		Retail
Beginning inventory	$ 500		$ 1,000
Purchases (net)	20,000		35,000
Merchandise available for sale	$20,500		$36,000
Cost ratio $\dfrac{\$20,500}{\$36,000} = 56.9\%$ .... (A)			
Add:			
Markups		$ 3,000	
Less: Markup cancellations		(1,000)	
Net markup			2,000
	$20,500		$38,000
Cost ratio $\dfrac{\$20,500}{\$38,000} = 53.9\%$ .... (B)			
Deduct:			
Markdowns		$ 2,500	
Less: Markdown cancellations		(2,000)	
Net markdowns			500
	$20,500		$37,500
Cost ratio $\dfrac{\$20,500}{\$37,500} = 54.7\%$ .... (C)			
Deduct: Sales (net)			25,000
Ending inventory at retail			$12,500

Computation of ending inventory at cost under different assumptions:

A	$12,500 × 56.9% = $7,112.50
B	12,500 × 53.9% = 6,737.50
C	12,500 × 54.7% = 6,837.50

The first percentage (A) considers only the sum of the beginning inventory and net purchases, and represents a cost percentage before markups or markdowns. The second percentage (B) reflects a cost percentage after the additional markups and markup cancellations but before the markdowns. Finally, the third percentage (C) is computed after both the markups and markdowns and related cancellations.

Which percentage should be employed to compute the ending inventory valuation?

The conventional retail inventory method is designed to approximate the lower of average cost and market. In this approach the accountant computes the cost to retail percentage after the net markups (markups less markup cancellations) but before the net markdowns (markdowns less markdown cancellations). To understand why the markups but not the markdowns are considered in the cost to retail ratio, we must understand how a retail outlet operates. When a company has an additional markup, it normally indicates that the market value of that item has increased. On the other hand, if the company has a net markdown, it means that a decline in the utility of that item has occurred. Therefore, if we attempt to approximate the lower of average cost and market, markdowns would be considered a current loss; in order to reflect this in the inventory valuation, they are not calculated into the cost to retail ratio. For example, assume two items were purchased for $5 apiece, and the original sales price was established at $10 each. One item was subsequently written down to $2.00. Assuming no sales for the period, if markdowns are considered in the cost to retail ratio, we compute the ending inventory in the following manner.

Cost Method
Markdowns Considered in Cost Ratio

	Cost	Retail
Purchases	$10.00	$20.00
Deduct: Markdowns		8.00
Ending inventory, at retail		$12.00

Cost to retail ratio $\dfrac{\$10.00}{\$12.00}$ = 83.3%

Ending inventory at cost ($12.00 × .833) = $10.00

This approach incorporates the average actual cost of the two items of the commodity into the inventory valuation without considering the loss on the one item. If a lower of average cost and market approach is adopted, the calculation is made in the following manner.

Conventional Method
Lower of Average Cost and Market

	Cost	Retail
Purchases	$10.00	$20.00
Cost to retail ratio $\dfrac{\$10.00}{\$20.00}$ = 50%		
Deduct: Markdowns		8.00
Ending inventory at retail		$12.00

Ending inventory, at lower of average cost and market ($12 × .50) = $6.00

Under the conventional retail inventory method, when markdowns are **not** considered in computing the cost to retail ratio, the ratio would be 50% ($10/$20) and ending inventory would be $6 ($12 × .50).

The inventory valuation of $6 reflects two inventory items, one inventoried at $5, the other at $1.00. Basically, the sale price was reduced from $10 to $2 and the cost reduced from $5.00 to $1.00.[8] To approximate the lower of average cost and market, therefore, the **cost to retail ratio** must be established by dividing the cost of goods available by the sum of the original retail price of these goods plus the net markups; the markdowns and markdown cancellations are excluded from the ratio. The basic format for the retail inventory method using the lower of average cost and market approach is illustrated below, using the Donovan Stores information.

Donovan Stores, Ltd.
Retail Inventory Method—Lower of Average Cost and Market Approach

	Cost		Retail
Beginning inventory	$ 500.00		$ 1,000.00
Purchases (net)	20,000.00		35,000.00
Totals	$20,500.00		$36,000.00
Add net markups:			
Markups		$3,000.00	
Markup cancellations		(1,000.00)	2,000.00
Totals	$20,500.00		38,000.00
Deduct net markdowns:			
Markdowns		$2,500.00	
Markdown cancellations		(2,000.00)	500.00
Sales price of goods available			$37,500.00
Deduct: Sales			25,000.00
Ending inventory, at retail			$12,500.00

$$\text{Cost to retail ratio} = \frac{\text{cost of goods available}}{\text{original retail price of goods available, plus net markups}}$$

$$= \frac{\$20,500}{\$38,000} = 53.9\%$$

Ending inventory at lower of average cost and market (53.9% × $12,500.00)	$ 6,737.50

An exact lower of average cost and market inventory valuation is not ordinarily obtained because an averaging effect occurs, but an adequate approximation can be achieved. Also, as indicated previously, net realizable value less normal profit is the interpretation of market that results. By computing the cost ratio from the totals after adding net markups **and** deducting net markdowns, it is possible to arrive at **approximate average cost** instead of approximating the lower of average cost and market.

Thus there are many possible cost to retail ratios that may be calculated, depending upon whether or not the beginning inventory, net markups, and net markdowns are included. The conventional method includes beginning inventory and net markups in the cost to retail ratio. The result is an ending inventory that approximates the lower of average cost and market rule. The following schedule summarizes the methods of inventory valuation approximated by the inclusion or

---

[8]This figure reflects market as net realizable value less the normal profit that is allowed. In other words, the sale price of the goods written down is $2.00 but, when a normal profit of 50% of selling price (or 100% of cost) is subtracted, the figure becomes $1.00.

exclusion of various items in the cost to retail ratio. (Net purchases are always included in the ratio.)

Retail Inventory Method—Identification of Inventory Valuation Method Approximated by Including Various Items in the Cost to Retail Ratio			
Beginning Inventory	Net Markups	Net Markdowns	Inventory Valuation Method Approximated
Include	Include	Include	Average Cost
Include	Include	Exclude	Lower of Average Cost and Market (Conventional Method)
Exclude	Include	Include	FIFO Cost
Exclude	Include	Exclude	Lower of FIFO Cost and Market

It is also possible to use the retail approach to approximate the LIFO cost or dollar-value LIFO valuation methods, but these complex calculations will not be examined in this book as they are seldom used in Canada.[9]

Special Items Relating to the Retail Inventory Method

The retail inventory method becomes more complicated when such items as freight-in, purchase returns and allowances, and purchase discounts are involved. **Freight costs** are treated as a part of the cost of the purchases; **purchase returns and allowances** are ordinarily considered as a reduction of the cost price and the retail price; **purchase discounts** usually are considered as a reduction of purchases unless these discounts are recorded as financial income. When the purchase allowance is not reflected by a reduction in the selling price, no adjustment is made to the retail column. In short, the treatment for the items affecting the cost column of the retail inventory approach follows the computation for cost of goods available for sale. Note also that **sales returns and allowances** are considered as proper adjustments to gross sales; **sales discounts,** however, are not recognized when sales are recorded gross. To adjust for the sales discount account in such a situation would provide an ending inventory figure at retail that would be overvalued.

In addition, there are a number of special items that require careful analysis. **Transfers-in** from another department, for example, should be reported in the same way as purchases. Instead of purchasing from an outside enterprise, a department is purchasing from another department in the same entity. **Normal shortage** (breakage, damage, theft), should reduce the retail column because these goods are no longer available for sale. A certain amount of shortage is considered normal in a retail enterprise; therefore these costs are reflected in the selling price. As a result, this amount is not considered in computing the cost to retail percentage but is shown as a deduction similar to sales to arrive at ending inventory at retail. **Abnormal shortage** should be deducted from both the cost and retail columns and reported as

---

[9]The U.S. edition of this text would be a useful reference for those interested in LIFO retail concepts and calculations.

a special inventory amount or as a loss. To do otherwise distorts the cost to retail ratio and overstates ending inventory. Finally, companies often provide their employees with special discounts to encourage loyalty, better performance, and so on. **Employee discounts** should be deducted from the retail column, in the same way as sales. These discounts should not be considered in the cost to retail percentage because they do not reflect an overall change in the selling price.

To illustrate some of these treatments in more detail, assume that Big and Tall Executive Apparel determines its inventory using the conventional retail inventory method as follows:

Big and Tall Executive Apparel
Conventional Retail Inventory Method—Lower of Average Cost and Market

	Cost	Retail
Beginning inventory	$ 1,000	$ 1,800
Purchases	30,000	60,000
Freight-in	600	—
Purchase returns	(1,500)	(3,000)
Totals	$30,100	$58,800
Net markups		9,000
Abnormal shrinkage	(1,200)	(2,000)
Totals	$28,900	$65,800
Net markdowns		1,400
Sales	$36,000	
Sales returns	(900)	35,100
Employee discounts		800
Normal shrinkage		1,300
Ending inventory at retail		$27,200

Cost to retail ratio $= \dfrac{\$28,900}{\$65,800} = 43.9\%$

Ending inventory at lower of average cost and market (43.9% × $27,200) = $11,940.80

Appraisal of Retail Inventory Method

The retail inventory method of estimating is used widely (1) to permit the computation of net income without the necessity of a physical count of the inventory, (2) as a control measure in determining inventory shortages, (3) in controlling quantities of merchandise on hand, and (4) as a basis of information needed for insurance and tax purposes.

One characteristic of the retail inventory method is that it **has an averaging effect on varying rates of gross profit.** When applied to the operations of an entire business where rates of gross profit vary among departments, no allowance is made for possible distortion of results because of the differences in rates of gross profit. Some concerns use a refinement of the retail method under such conditions, by computing the inventory separately by departments or by classes of merchandise with similar rates of gross profit. In addition, the reliability of this method rests on the assumption that the distribution of items in the inventory is roughly the same as the "mix" in the total collection of goods available for sale.

ADDITIONAL ISSUES RELATED TO INVENTORY VALUATION

MIT
ROM
HERE
↓

While this and the previous chapter have addressed many important issues, three additional concerns require identification and discussion in order to complete our consideration of inventory determination and valuation for financial reporting purposes. These are valuation of inventory using the relative sales value method, valuation of inventory at selling price, and accounting for purchase contracts.

Valuation Using the Relative Sales Value Method

A special problem of pricing inventory items arises when a group of varying units is purchased at a single lump sum price. For example, assume that Stark Developers purchases land for $1 million that can be subdivided into 400 lots. These lots are of different sizes and shapes but can be roughly sorted into three groups graded A, B, and C. As lots are sold, it becomes necessary to apportion the purchase cost of $1 million among the lots sold and the lots remaining on hand.

It is unfair to divide 400 lots into the total cost of $1 million to get a cost of $2,500 for each lot, because they vary in size, shape, and attractiveness. When such a situation is encountered—and it is not at all unusual—the common and most logical practice is to allocate the total cost among the various units on the basis of their relative sales value (e.g., the percentage of their particular sales prices to the total of all sales prices). For the example given, the allocation works out as follows:

				Allocation of Cost				
Lots	Number of Lots	Sales Price per Lot	Total Sales Price	Relative Sales Price	Total Cost	Cost Allocated to Lots	Cost per Lot
A	100	$10,000	$1,000,000	100/250	$1,000,000	$ 400,000	$4,000
B	100	6,000	600,000	60/250	1,000,000	240,000	2,400
C	200	4,500	900,000	90/250	1,000,000	360,000	1,800
			$2,500,000			$1,000,000	

The cost of lots sold can be computed by using the amounts given in the column for "Cost per Lot," and the gross profit determined as follows:

		Determination of Gross Profit			
Lots	Number of Lots Sold	Cost per Lot	Cost of Lots Sold	Sales	Gross Profit
A	77	$4,000	$308,000	$ 770,000	$ 462,000
B	80	2,400	192,000	480,000	288,000
C	100	1,800	180,000	450,000	270,000
			$680,000	$1,700,000	$1,020,000

This information may be applied in a slightly different way. The ratio of the cost to the selling price of all the lots is $1 million divided by $2,500,000, or 40%. Accordingly, if the total sales price of lots sold is, say, $1,700,000, then the cost of these lots sold is 40% of $1,700,000, or $680,000. The inventory of lots on hand is $1 million less $680,000, or $320,000.

Valuation of Inventory at Selling Prices

Certain circumstances may warrant **recording inventory at selling price less estimated costs to complete and sell** (net realizable value) regardless of its cost. For example, an exception to the normal realization rule is permitted where (1) there is a controlled market with a fixed price applicable to all quantities and (2) no significant costs of disposal are involved. Inventories of certain minerals, for example, may be reflected at selling price when there is a government-controlled market without significant costs of disposal. A similar treatment may be given to agricultural products that are immediately marketable at fixed prices.

Another reason for allowing this method of valuation is that often the cost figures are too difficult to obtain. For example, it is difficult to allocate the cost of an animal "on the hoof" into the costs of ribs, chuck, shoulders, and so on. It seems much more useful to determine the market price of the end product less costs of disposal than to make an arbitrary allocation of costs. Recognition of inventories at selling price less cost of disposal means that income is recognized before the goods are transferred to an outside party. If this approach is adopted, the use of such basis should be fully disclosed in the financial statements.

Accounting for Purchase Contracts

In many lines of business the survival and continued profitability of an enterprise depends upon having a sufficient stock of merchandise to meet all customer demands. Consequently, it is quite common for a corporation to contract for the purchase of merchandise or materials weeks, months, or even years in advance. Such commitments may be made on the basis either of estimated sales demands or firm commitments by the company's customers. Generally, title to the merchandise or materials described in these purchase commitments has not passed (indeed, the goods may exist only as natural resources or, in the case of commodities, as unplanted seed).

Usually it is neither necessary nor proper for the buyer to make any entries to reflect commitments for purchases of goods that have not been shipped by the seller. Ordinary orders, for which the prices are determined at the time of shipment and **that are subject to cancellation** by the buyer or seller, do not represent either an asset or a liability to the buyer and need not be reflected in the books or in the financial statements.

Formal purchase contracts for which a firm price has been established, however, if of material amount, should be disclosed in the balance sheet of the buyer by means of a note[10] such as the following:

Note 4. Contracts for the purchase of raw materials in 1987 have been executed in the amount of $600,000. The market price of such raw materials on December 31, 1986, is $640,000.

---

[10]*CICA Handbook*, Section 3280, par. 1.

In the foregoing illustration we assumed that the contracted price was less than the market price at the date of the balance sheet. If the contracted price exceeds the purchase price and losses are expected to occur at the time of purchase, losses should be recognized in the accounts in the period during which such declines in prices take place. For example, if purchase contracts for delivery in 1987 have been executed at a firm price of $800,000 and the market price of the materials on December 31, 1986, is $750,000, the following entry is made:

Loss on Purchase Contracts	50,000	
Accrued Loss on Purchase Contracts		50,000

This loss would be closed out to the Income Summary and shown on the income statement; the Accrued Loss on Purchase Contracts is shown in the liability section of the balance sheet. When the goods are delivered in 1987, the entry will be:

Purchases	750,000	
Accrued Loss on Purchase Contracts	50,000	
Accounts Payable		800,000

If the price is partially or fully recovered before the inventory is received, the Accrued Loss on Purchase Commitments could be reduced. A resulting gain would then be reported in the period of the price increase for the amount of the partial or full recovery.

Accounting for purchase commitments (and, for that matter, all commitments) is controversial. Some argue that these contracts should be reported as assets or liabilities at the time the contract is signed; others believe that recognition at the delivery date is most appropriate.[11] Clearly, the treatment of such contracts in practice is far from uniform. What is done for certain contracts in particular situations rests on the exercise of judgement within the context of generally accepted accounting principles and experience.

FINANCIAL STATEMENT PRESENTATION OF INVENTORIES

Inventories are among the most significant assets of manufacturing and merchandising business enterprises; therefore, the accounting profession has adopted standards for reporting inventory on financial statements. Section 3030 of the *CICA*

The Oshawa Group Limited
For the year ended January 26, 1985

Balance Sheet - in current assets	1985	1984
Inventories (in thousands of dollars)	176,744	172,339

From the summary of significant accounting policies:

Inventories
Warehouse inventories are valued at the lower of cost and net realizable value with cost being determined on a first-in, first-out basis. Retail inventories are valued at the lower of cost and net realizable value less normal profit margins as determined by the retail method of inventory valuation.

---

[11]See, for example, Yuji Ijiri, *Recognition of Contractual Rights and Obligations, Research Report* (Stamford, Conn.,: FASB, 1980), who argues that firm purchase commitments might be capitalized. "Firm" means it is unlikely that performance under the contract can be avoided without severe penalty.

Handbook covers the requirements for financial statement presentation in Canada. Essentially, the requirements are to state the basis of valuation and to disclose any changes in the basis and the effect of such changes on the net income for the period. It is also desirable that the amounts of the major categories making up the total inventory (e.g., finished goods, work in process, and raw materials) be disclosed.

Examples illustrating presentations of inventory in financial statements are shown at the bottom of page 441 and below.

Imasco Limited
For the year ended March 31, 1985

Balance Sheet - in current assets	1985	1984
Inventories (in thousands of dollars)	909,704	534,261

From the summary of significant accounting policies:

Inventories
Inventories are valued at the lower of cost and net realizable value. Cost is determined substantially as follows:

    Tobacco: average cost
    Drug Stores—Peoples Drug Stores: first-in, first-out
             —Shoppers Drug Mart: retail inventory method
    Restaurant: first-in, first-out
    Other—retail stores: retail inventory method

Genstar Corporation

From the summary of significant accounting policies:

Inventories
Inventories are valued at the lower of cost or net realizable value. Cost of manufactured goods is determined principally at average on the first-in, first-out basis and includes all overhead elements except depreciation. Cost of land and housing inventories is determined on a specific item basis and includes service such as roads, sewage, and water systems on land under development. Land inventories are those parcels which are expected to be sold within the five-year operating cycle of the land development business. Other parcels are classified as development land.

From notes to the financial statements:

2. Inventories

	(thousands of dollars)	
Finished goods	149,083	140,941
Work in process	37,781	84,645
Raw materials, supplies, and repair parts	66,918	78,645
Land	402,383	335,675
Revenue property held for sale	—	55,298
	$656,165	$695,204

These examples show disclosure of the basis for inventory valuation (lower of cost and market), the cost method used, and the definition of market used for the major categories making up the total inventory. It is quite acceptable, as shown in these illustrations, for a company to use different pricing approaches for different components of its inventory. The use of notes is the basic means for disclosing such information.

Section 3030, paragraph 12, of the *CICA Handbook* states that "reserves for future decline in inventory values, or any similar reserves, should not be deducted in arriving at inventory valuation." This requirement does not preclude an enterprise from appropriating a portion of retained earnings for the anticipated decline.

Also, Section 4510 of the *CICA Handbook*, which became effective for large, publicly owned Canadian companies whose fiscal periods commenced on or after January 1, 1983, holds important implications for inventory valuation. This section deals with reporting the effects of changing prices. Basically, it has the effect of maintaining the use of the historical cost basis within financial statements, but recommends that supplementary information (not part of the statements) be provided to disclose the effects of changing prices. The current cost amounts for inventory and cost of goods sold are a part of this supplementary information.

This current cost reporting is highly controversial, because many companies contend that the high cost of preparing this information is not warranted by the benefits received. Others disagree, noting that historical cost income numbers are misleading in a period of rising prices. Many accountants believe historical cost based profits to be illusory because the company must replace that inventory at a higher price. Thus, it is argued, disclosure of changing price information is useful for a better assessment of the quality of enterprise income. The detailed computations for reporting changes in price are discussed in Chapter 25.

KEY POINTS

1. In addition to having different methods for determining the unit cost for inventories as explained in Chapter 8, there are other means for assigning a valuation for inventories. Primary among these are lower of cost and market, gross profit, and retail inventory valuation approaches.

2. The lower of cost and market method reflects the application of the constraint of conservatism in accounting. Under this method, the cost (FIFO, average, LIFO, etc.) and market (replacement cost, net realizable value, or net realizable value less normal profit margin) of inventory are separately determined. The inventory valuation is then the lower of the two amounts.

3. The lower of cost and market amount may be determined on an item-by-item basis, major category basis, or total inventory basis.

4. Lower of cost and market applied on a total inventory basis is the most commonly used inventory valuation method in Canada. Net realizable value is, by far, the most frequently used definition of market employed by Canadian companies, although the other interpretations are recognized as acceptable in the *CICA Handbook* and are used to some extent.

5. The lower of cost and market approach is justified on the basis that a decline in market value below cost reflects a loss in utility (worth) of the inventory. Application of the constraint of conservatism means that such a loss should be recognized in the period of occurrence. Future periods would, therefore, not be penalized by such losses. Many argue that a lower of cost and market approach has little theoretical justification. They point out that its application to losses but not gains is somewhat inconsistent in the total realm of accounting. Also, it is conservative only in the current period, as it shows higher income in future periods.

6. The gross profit method of inventory valuation is based on reducing net sales to their cost and deducting that determined amount from cost of goods available for sale to get ending inventory at cost.

7. To reduce net sales to cost under the gross profit method, a gross profit on sales percentage is determined. The difference between the amount of sales and gross profit is the cost of sales. Gross profit on sales may be determined from examining accounting records or policy regarding a company's markup on retail price or cost.

8. The gross profit method results in an estimated value for ending inventory that is determined from accounting information rather than a physical count. Consequently, it is useful for preparing financial statements when there is no count taken or when no count can be taken (e.g., fire or other catastrophic losses).

9. The retail inventory method is a technique for determining ending inventory that is based on multiplying a cost to retail percentage derived from accounting information by the retail price of ending inventory determined by a count or from accounting records.

10. The retail inventory method is particularly appropriate for retail businesses that have a large number of items and a high volume of transactions. It enables taking a physical inventory at retail prices rather than having to make a count and then assign a cost to each item. Also, inventory at cost may be determined directly from accounting information when a count is not taken or cannot be taken.

11. To apply the retail method, records must be kept of the cost and retail prices for beginning inventory, net purchases, and abnormal spoilage, and the retail amount of net markups, net markdowns, and net sales. Determination of the items going into the numerator and denominator amounts of the cost to retail ratio depends on the type of inventory valuation estimate desired. The most common composition of the components of the cost to retail ratio is in what is called the conventional retail method, which results in an approximation of inventory valuation at the lower of average cost and market, market being defined as net realizable value less a normal profit.

12. Other issues related to inventory valuation include using the relative sales value method, valuation of inventory at selling prices, and accounting for purchase contracts.

13. Disclosure of the basis of inventory valuation, and any change in the basis are required by the *CICA Handbook*. Also, it is desirable to disclose major categories of inventory, the method used to determine cost, and the definition of market applied under the lower of cost and market method. It is also recommended that large, publicly held Canadian companies disclose, as supplementary information, the current cost of inventory and cost of goods sold.

QUESTIONS

1. Where there is evidence that the "market value" of inventory is less than cost, what is the appropriate accounting treatment?

2. Why are inventories valued at the lower of cost and market? What are the arguments against the use of the lower of cost and market method of valuing inventories?

3. (a) Determine the ending inventory for the Hat Department of the Michaels Depart-

ment Store from the following data using the conventional retail approach (approximation of lower of average cost and market).

	Cost	Retail
Inventory, Jan. 1	$ 94,500	$ 141,750
Purchases	720,000	1,080,000
Freight-in	35,000	
Markups, net		46,000
Markdowns, net		24,000
Sales		1,122,000

(b) If the results of a physical inventory indicated an inventory at retail of $120,000, what inferences would you draw?

4. In some instances accounting principles require a departure from valuing inventories at cost alone. Determine the proper unit inventory price in the following cases, assuming (a) use of the most frequently used interpretation of market in Canadian practice and (b) U.S. rules are applied.

	Cases				
	1	2	3	4	5
Cost	$4.00	$4.00	$4.00	$4.00	$4.00
Net realizable value	2.60	4.10	3.60	4.80	3.80
Net realizable value less normal profit	2.20	3.70	3.20	4.40	3.40
Replacement cost	2.40	4.20	3.70	4.30	3.20

5. What method(s) might be used in the accounts to record a loss when the "market" value of inventory is less than cost? Discuss.

6. What methods may the accountant employ in applying the lower of cost and market procedure when there are several items and major categories in the total inventory? What is the method normally used and why?

7. (a) Distinguish between gross profit as a percentage of cost and gross profit as a percentage of sales price.
   (b) Convert the following gross profit percentages based on cost to gross profit percentages based on sales price: 20% and 33.3%.
   (c) Convert the following gross profit percentages based on sales price to gross profit percentages based on cost: 33.3% and 60%.

8. List the major uses of the gross profit method.

9. A retailer with annual net sales of $3 million maintains a markup of 25% based on cost. Her expenses average 15% of net sales. What is her gross profit and net profit in dollars?

10. What conditions must exist for the retail inventory method to provide valid results?

11. The conventional retail inventory method yields results that are essentially the same as those yielded by the lower of average cost and market method. Explain. Prepare an illustration of how the conventional retail method reduces inventory to market. What is the definition of market that results from using this method?

12. At December 31, 1986, the Toby Company has outstanding contracts for the purchase of 350,000 L, at $0.55/L, of a raw material to be used in their manufacturing process. The company prices its raw material inventory at cost or market, whichever is lower. Assuming that the market price as of December 31, 1986, is $0.51/L, how would you treat this situation in the accounts under each of the following situations?
   (a) The contracts are significant in relation to current financial position and future operations, are not subject to cancellation, and the price is firm.
   (b) The contracts can be cancelled by Toby Company on payment of a cancellation fee of $10,000.
   (c) The contracts may be cancelled by either party without penalty.
   How would the contracts be accounted for in the above situations if the market price on December 31, 1986, was $0.56/L?

13. What factors might justify valuing inventory at sales prices?

14. The Madden Corporation provides the following information with respect to its inventories:

Inventories $4,800,000

What additional disclosure is necessary to present the inventory in accordance with generally accepted accounting practices?

CASES

C9-1 You have just been hired as a new accountant for the accounting firm of Jennings and Jones. The manager of the office is interested in how you can apply your formal education and provides you with the following situations that have taken place in their practice.

1. One of our clients' major business activities is the purchase and resale of used heavy mining and construction equipment, including trucks, cranes, shovels, conveyors, crushers, etc. The company was organized in 1975. In its earlier years, it purchased individual items of heavy equipment and resold them to customers throughout Canada. In the early 1980s, the company began negotiating the "package" purchase of all the existing equipment at mine sites, concurrent with the closing down of several of the large iron mines in Ontario and exhausted coal mines in Saskatchewan. The mine operators preferred to liquidate their mine assets on that basis rather than hold auctions or leave the mine site open until all of the equipment could be liquidated. As there were numerous pieces of equipment in these package purchases, the client found it difficult to assign costs to each individual item. As a result, the company followed the policy of valuing these "package" purchases by the cost recovery method. Under this method, the company recognized no income until the entire cost had been recovered through sales revenues. This produced the effect of deferring income to later periods and represented, for financial reporting purposes, a "conservative" valuation of inventories in what was essentially a new field for the company where its level of experience had not been demonstrated.

Instructions

Comment on the propriety of this approach.

2. In December, 1985, one of our clients had a major management change and a new president was hired. After reviewing the various policies of the company, the president's opinion was that prior systems employed by the company did not allow for adequate testing of obsolescence (including discontinued products) and overstocks in inventories. Accordingly, the president changed the mechanics of the procedures for reviewing obsolete and excess stock and determining the amount. These reviews resulted in a significant increase between years in the amount of inventory that was written off. You are satisfied that these procedures are accurate and provide reliable results. The amounts charged against operations for excess and obsolete stock for the last three years were: 1985—$440,000; 1984—$114,000; and 1983—$113,000. Net income for 1985 before adjustment for these additional obsolescence charges was $540,000.

Instructions

How should these charges be reported in the financial statements, if at all?

3. Another of our clients, Mogel Foods, was upset because we forced them to write down their inventory on an item-by-item basis. For example, our computation resulted in a writedown of approximately $300,000 as follows:

	Frozen	Cans
Cut beans	—	$ 25,000
Peas	—	45,000
Mixed vegetables	$ 5,000	15,000
Spinach	183,000	8,000
Carrots	12,000	7,000
	$200,000	$100,000

The company argued that the products are sold on a line basis (frozen or canned) with customers taking all varieties, and only rarely are sales made on an individual product basis. As a result, they argued that the application of the lower of cost and market rule to the total product line would result in the proper determination of income (loss). A pricing of the inventory on this basis would result in a $60,000 write-off.

Instructions

Why do you think our accounting firm argued for the item-by-item approach? Which method should be used, given the information in this case?

C9-2   Woodley Products Company manufactures and sells four products, the inventories of which are priced at cost or market, whichever is lower. A normal profit margin rate of 30% is usually maintained on each of the four products.

The following information was compiled as of December 31, 1986.

Product	Original Cost	Cost to Replace	Estimated Cost to Dispose	Expected Selling Price[a]	Units on Hand
A	$17.50	$15.00	$15.00	$ 30.00	5,000
B	45.00	46.00	26.00	100.00	1,000
C	35.00	42.00	15.00	80.00	3,000
D	47.50	45.00	20.50	95.00	2,000

[a]Normal margin is 30% of selling price.

Instructions

(a)   Why are expected selling prices important in the application of the lower of cost and market rule?

(b)   Prepare a schedule for determining the lower of cost and market on a total inventory basis. The schedule should contain for each product the unit value for the purpose of inventory valuation resulting from the application of the lower of cost and market rule which is the most frequently applied in Canada.

C9-3   You are in charge of the audit of Manor Nylons, Incorporated. The following items were in Manor Nylons' inventory at November 30, 1986 (fiscal year end).

Product Number	075936	078310	079104	081111
Selling price per unit November 30, 1986	$15.00	$23.00	$28.00	$13.00
Standard cost, per unit, as included in inventory at November 30, 1986	$ 7.90	$11.25	$14.26	$ 7.40

In discussion with Manor's marketing and sales personnel you were told that there will be a general 9% (rounded to the next highest 5 cents) increase in selling prices, effective December 1, 1986. This increase will affect all garments except those that have 081 as the first three digits of the product code. The 081 codes are assigned to new apparel introductions, and for product code 081111, the selling price will be $9.00 effective December 1, 1986.

In addition, you were told by the controller that Manor plans to earn a 50% gross profit on the selling price of all their nylons.

From the cost department you obtained the following standards, which will be used for fiscal year 1987:

Product number	1987 Standard
075936	$ 8.25
078310	$10.75
079104	$14.71
081111	$ 7.51

Sales commissions and estimates of other costs of disposal approximate 25% of standard manufacturing costs. Assume that standard costs provide an accurate assessment of the replacement cost of the product.

Instructions

(a) Determine the net realizable value of each item expected for 1987.

(b) Assuming the net realizable values for (a) are to be used to determine the lower of cost and market valuation for the November 30, 1986, inventory, and that there were 5,000 units of each item on hand, how and at what amount would the inventory be shown on the balance sheet using an item-by-item approach? A total inventory approach?

(c) When market is lower than cost, why should inventories be reported at market? Why are inventories reported at cost when market is greater than cost?

C9-4 Dri-Fast Company, your client, manufactures paint. The company's president, Ms. Fast, has decided to open a retail store to sell Dri-Fast paint as well as wallpaper and other supplies that would be purchased from other suppliers. She has asked you for information about the conventional retail method of pricing inventories at the retail store.

Instructions

Prepare a report to the president explaining the conventional retail method of pricing inventories. Your report should include these points:

(a) Description and accounting features of the method.

(b) The conditions that may distort the results under the method.

(c) A comparison of the advantages of using the retail method with those of using cost methods of inventory pricing.

(d) The accounting theory underlying the treatment of net markdowns and net markups under the method.

C9-5 Presented below are a number of items that may be encountered in computing the cost to retail percentage when using the conventional retail method or the average cost retail method.

1. Markdowns
2. Markdown cancellations
3. Cost of items transferred in from other departments
4. Retail value of items transferred in from other departments
5. Sales discounts
6. Purchase discounts (purchases recorded gross)
7. Estimated retail value of goods broken or stolen
8. Cost of beginning inventory
9. Retail value of beginning inventory
10. Cost of purchases
11. Retail value of purchases
12. Markups
13. Markup cancellations
14. Employee discounts (sales recorded net)

Instructions

For each of the items listed, indicate whether this item would be considered in the cost to retail percentage under (a) conventional retail and (b) average cost retail.

EXERCISES

E9-1 The inventory of Hamsmith Company on December 31, 1986, consists of these items:

Part No.	Quantity	Cost per Unit	Net Realizable Value per Unit
110	200	$100	$110
111	500	60	52
112	1,500	80	76
113	100	160	180
120	300	205	208
121a	2,000	16	0.20
122	100	240	244

aPart No. 121 is obsolete and each unit has a realizable value of $0.20.

Instructions

Determine the inventory as of December 31, 1986, applying the method of cost or market, whichever is lower, (a) directly to each item and (b) to the total of the inventory.

E9-2 Iqbal Company follows the practice of pricing its inventory at the lower of cost and market, on an individual-item basis.

Item No.	Quantity	Cost per Unit	Cost to Replace	Estimated Selling Price	Cost of Completion and Disposal	Normal Profit
1320	1,000	$3.00	$3.05	$4.50	$.35	$1.25
1333	1,100	2.50	2.40	3.50	.50	.50
1426	600	4.00	3.90	5.00	.40	1.00
1437	1,000	3.60	3.10	3.00	.25	.90
1510	900	2.25	2.00	3.25	.70	.60
1522	400	3.00	2.50	3.50	.40	.50
1573	3,200	1.60	1.50	2.50	.75	.50
1626	1,000	4.50	5.25	6.00	.50	1.00

Instructions

From the information above, determine the amount of Iqbal Company inventory assuming:

(a) Use of the most commonly used definition of "market" in Canadian practice.

(b) Application of U.S. rules to determine market.

E9-3 Presented below is information related to Appalachian Enterprises.

	Jan. 31	Feb. 28	Mar. 31	Apr. 30
Inventory	$16,000	$15,500	$17,000	$13,000
Inventory at the lower of cost and market	15,000	13,500	15,500	12,500
Purchases for the month		20,000	24,000	22,000
Sales for the month		28,000	35,000	30,000

Instructions

(a) From the information prepare (as far as the data permit) monthly income statements in columnar form for February, March, and April. The inventory is to be shown in the statement at cost, the profit or loss due to market fluctuations is to be shown separately, and a valuation account is to be set up for the difference between cost and the lower of cost and market as it exists at year end.

(b) Prepare the journal entry required to establish the valuation account at January 31 and entries to adjust it monthly thereafter.

E9-4 Oshkosh Boat Company has been having difficulty obtaining key raw materials for its manufacturing process. The company decides to sign a long-term noncancellable purchase commitment with its largest supplier of this raw material on November 30, 1986, at an agreed price of $380,000. At December 31, 1986, the raw material drops in price to $350,000, and it is further anticipated that the price would drop another $15,000, so that at the date of delivery the value of the inventory would be $335,000.

Instructions

What entries would you make on December 31, 1986, to recognize these facts?

E9-5 At December 31, 1986, the Alta Crunch Company has outstanding purchase commitments for 225 m³, of raw material at $660/m³, to be used in its manufacturing process. The company prices its raw material inventory at cost or market, whichever is lower.

Instructions

(a) Assuming that the market price as of December 31, 1986, is $680/m^3, how would this matter be treated in the accounts and statements? Explain.

(b) Assuming that the market price as of December 31, 1986, is $640/m^3, how would you treat this situation in the accounts and statements?

(c) Give the entry in January, 1987, when the 225 m^3 shipment is received, assuming that the situation given in (b) above existed at December 31, 1986. Give an explanation of your treatment.

E9-6 The Glass Bottle Corporation began business on January 1, 1985. Information about its inventories under different valuation methods is presented below.

		Inventory		
	LIFO Cost	FIFO Cost	Replacement Cost	Lower of Cost and Market
December 31, 1985	$20,400	$20,000	$19,200	$17,800
December 31, 1986	18,200	18,000	17,600	17,000

Instructions

(a) Indicate the inventory basis that will show the highest net income in (1) 1985 and (2) 1986.

(b) Indicate whether the FIFO cost basis would provide a higher or lower profit than the lower of cost or market basis in 1986, and by how much.

E9-7 Hallam Furniture Company purchases, during 1986, a carload of wicker chairs at a cost of $43,200. The manufacturer sells the chairs to Hallam for a lump sum of $43,200, because it is discontinuing manufacturing operations and wishes to dispose of its entire stock. Three types of chairs are included in the carload. The three types and the estimated selling price for each are listed below.

Type	No. of Chairs	Estimated Selling Price Each
Lounge chairs	500	$90
Armchairs	300	60
Straight chairs	200	45

During 1986 Hallam sells 150 lounge chairs, 80 armchairs, and 110 straight chairs.

Instructions

What is the amount of gross profit realized during 1986? What is the amount of inventory of unsold wicker chairs on December 31, 1986?

E9-8 Century Twenty Realty Corporation purchased a tract of unimproved land for $38,140. This land was improved and subdivided into building lots at an additional cost of $15,200. These building lots were all of the same size but owing to differences in location were offered for sale at different prices as follows:

Group	No. of Lots	Price per Lot
1	12	$2,500
2	18	2,000
3	6	1,700

Operating expenses for the year allocated to this project totalled $13,500. Lots unsold at the year end were as follows:

Group 1	4 lots
Group 2	6 lots
Group 3	1 lot

Instructions

Determine the year-end inventory and net income from these operations.

E9-9   A fire destroys all of the merchandise of the P.E.I. Company on February 10, 1986. Presented below is information compiled up to the date of the fire.

Inventory, January 1, 1986	$ 250,000
Sales to February 10, 1986	1,500,000
Purchases to February 10, 1986	1,250,000
Freight-in to February 10, 1986	50,000
Rate of gross profit on selling price	40%

Instructions

From the information above, compute the approximate inventory on February 10, 1986.

E9-10   Presented below is information related to Lakehead Corporation for the current year:

Beginning inventory	$ 300,000
Purchases	1,200,000
Total goods available for sale	1,500,000
Sales	2,000,000

Instructions

Compute the ending inventory, assuming that (a) gross profit is 30% of sales; (b) gross profit is 33 1/3% of cost; (c) gross profit is 50% of cost; and (d) gross profit is 25% of sales.

E9-11   Humphry Bougart requires an estimate of the cost of goods lost by fire on March 9. Merchandise on hand on January 1 was $32,000. Purchases since January 1 were $22,500; freight-in, $2,500; purchase returns and allowances, $1,500. Sales are made at 25% above cost and totalled $28,000 to March 9. Goods costing $6,125 were left undamaged by the fire; remaining goods were destroyed.

Instructions

(a)   Compute the cost of goods destroyed.

(b)   Compute the cost of goods destroyed, assuming that the gross profit is 25% of sales.

E9-12   Northern Lumber Company handles three principal lines of merchandise with these varying rates of gross profit on cost:

Lumber	40%
Millwork	25%
Hardware and fittings	30%

On August 18 a fire destroyed the office, lumber shed, and a considerable portion of the lumber stacked in the yard. To file a report of loss for insurance purposes, the company must know what the inventories were immediately preceding the fire. No detailed or perpetual inventory records of any kind were maintained. The only pertinent information you are able to obtain are the following facts from the general ledger, which was kept in a fireproof vault and thus escaped destruction.

	Lumber	Millwork	Hardware
Inventory, Jan. 1	$ 187,500	$ 67,500	$ 27,750
Purchases to Aug. 18	1,470,000	375,000	117,750
Sales to Aug. 18	1,875,000	510,000	180,000

Instructions

Submit your estimate of the inventory amounts immediately preceding the fire.

E9-13 You are called by Gary Fish of Cycle Co. on July 16 and asked to prepare a claim for insurance as a result of a theft that took place the night before. You suggest that an inventory be taken immediately. The following data are available:

Inventory, July 1	$32,000
Purchases—goods placed in stock July 1–15	18,600
Sales—goods delivered to customers (gross)	34,000
Sales returns—goods returned to stock	2,500

Your client reports that the goods on hand on July 16 cost $30,000, but you determine that this figure includes goods of $9,000 received on a consignment basis. Your past records show that sales are made at approximately 50% over cost.

Instructions

Compute the claim against the insurance company.

E9-14 Presented below is information related to Simon's Sporting Goods, Ltd.

	Cost	Retail
Beginning inventory	$ 150,000	$ 200,000
Purchases	1,350,000	1,800,000
Markups		75,000
Markup cancellations		15,000
Markdowns		37,500
Markdown cancellations		7,500
Sales		1,950,000

Instructions

Compute the inventory using the conventional retail inventory method.

E9-15 The records of The Clothes Horse Corp. show the following data for the month of September.

Sales	$50,000
Sales returns	1,000
Additional markups	10,000
Markup cancellations	1,500
Markdowns	7,500
Markdown cancellations	2,500
Freight on purchases	1,000
Purchases (at cost)	20,000
Purchases (at sales price)	30,000
Purchase returns (at cost)	1,000
Purchase returns (at sales price)	1,500
Beginning inventory (at cost)	40,000
Beginning inventory (at sales price)	60,000

Instructions

Compute the ending inventory using the conventional retail inventory method.

E9-16 M & M Company began operations on January 1, 1985, adopting the conventional retail inventory system. None of its merchandise was marked down in 1985 and, because there was no beginning inventory, its ending inventory for 1985 of $21,740 would have been the same under either the conventional system or the average cost system. All pertinent data regarding purchases, sales, markups, and markdowns for 1986 are shown below.

	Cost	Retail
Inventory, Jan. 1, 1986	$ 21,740	$ 32,000
Markdowns (net)		12,000
Markups (net)	20,000	
Purchases (net)	129,540	196,000
Sales (net)		152,000

Instructions

Determine the cost of the 1986 ending inventory under (a) the conventional retail method and (b) the average cost retail method.

PROBLEMS

P9-1 Biagioni Company manufactures desks. Most of the company's desks are standard models and are sold on the basis of catalogue prices. At December 31, 1986, the following finished desks appear in the company's inventory:

Finished Desks	A	B	C	D
1986 catalogue selling price	$440	$470	$ 870	$1,040
FIFO cost per inventory list Dec. 31, 1986	450	440	840	980
Estimated current cost to manufacture				
(at December 31, 1986, and early 1987)	460	430	710	1,000
Sales commissions and estimated				
other costs of disposal	40	70	120	260
1987 catalogue selling price	480	520	1,000	1,200

The 1986 catalogue was in effect through November, 1986, and the 1987 catalogue is effective as of December 1, 1986. All catalogue prices are net of the usual discounts. Generally, the company attempts to obtain a 25% gross profit on selling price and has usually been successful in doing so.

Instructions

At what amount should each of the four desks appear in the company's December 31, 1986, inventory, assuming that the company has adopted a lower of FIFO cost and market approach for valuation of inventories on an individual item basis? Use net realizable value as the definition of market.

P9-2 Guchi Leather Co. follows the practice of valuing its inventory at the lower of cost and market. The following information is available from the company's inventory records as of December 31, the company's year end.

Item	On Hand Quantity	Unit Cost	Replacement Cost/Unit	Estimated Unit Selling Price	Completion and Disposal Costs/Unit	Normal Unit Profit
A	1,500	$4.50	$5.50	$ 7.50	$1.50	$1.40
B	1,200	7.20	8.00	8.00	.90	.90
C	800	4.20	4.00	6.00	1.10	.60
D	200	8.20	9.00	8.00	.60	2.00
E	800	4.80	7.40	10.00	3.20	3.70

Instructions

(a) Indicate the inventory price that should be used for each item under the lower of cost and market rule assuming (1) the most commonly used Canadian practice and (2) U.S. rules.

(b) Guchi Company applies the lower of cost and market rule directly to each item in the inventory but maintains its inventory account at cost to account for the items above. Give the adjusting entry, if one is necessary, to write down the ending inventory from cost to market, assuming (1) the common Canadian interpretation of market and (2) U.S. rules.

(c) Guchi Company applies the lower of cost and market rule to the total of the inventory. What is the dollar amount for inventory as of December 31, assuming (1) the most common Canadian interpretation of market and (2) U.S. rules?

P9-3 Kenny Company is a food wholesaler that supplies independent grocery stores in the immediate region. The first-in, first-out (FIFO) method of inventory valuation is used to determine the cost of the inventory at the end of each month. Transactions and other related information regarding two of the items (instant coffee and sugar) carried by Kenny are given below for October, the last month of Kenny's fiscal year.

	Instant Coffee	Sugar
Standard unit of packaging	Case containing 24 1 kg jars	Baler containing 12 5 kg bags
Inventory, Oct. 1	1,200 cases @$53.22 per case	600 balers @$6.50 per baler
Purchases	1. Oct. 10—1,600 cases @$56.40 per case plus freight of $480 2. Oct. 20—1,600 cases @$57.00 per case plus freight of $480	1. Oct. 5—640 balers @$5.76 per baler plus freight of $320 2. Oct. 16—640 balers @$5.40 per baler plus freight of $320 3. Oct. 24—640 balers @ $5.04 per baler plus freight of $320
Purchase terms	2/10, net/30, f.o.b. shipping point	Net 30 days, f.o.b. shipping point
October sales	3,400 cases @$76.00 per case	2,200 balers @$7.80 per baler
Returns and allowances	A customer returned 50 cases that had been shipped by error. The customer's account was credited for $3,800.	As the October 16 purchase was unloaded, 20 balers were discovered to be damaged. A representative of the trucking firm confirmed the damage, and the balers were discarded. Credit of $108 for the merchandise and $10 for the freight was received by Kenny.
Inventory values including freight and net of purchase discounts—Oct. 31		
• Most recently quoted price	$56.65 per case	$5.30 per baler
• Net realizable value	$60.80 per case	$5.20 per baler
• Net realizable value less a normal markup of 12 1/2%	$53.20 per case	$4.55 per baler

Kenny's sales terms are 1/10, net /30, f.o.b. shipping point. Kenny records all purchases net of purchase discounts and takes all purchase discounts.

Instructions

(a) Calculate the number of units in inventory and the FIFO unit cost for instant coffee and sugar as of October 31.

(b) Kenny Company applies the lower of cost and market (net realizable value) rule in valuing its year-end inventory. Calculate the total dollar amount of the inventory for instant coffee and sugar, applying the lower of cost and market rule on an individual product basis.

(c) Could Kenny Company apply the lower of cost and market rule to groups of products or the inventory as a whole rather than on an individual product basis? Explain your answer.

(CMA adapted)

P9-4 Luoma, Inc. lost most of its inventory in a fire in December just before the year-end physical inventory was taken. The corporation's books disclosed the following:

Beginning inventory	$120,000	Sales	$440,000
Purchases for the year	360,000	Sales returns	10,000
Purchase returns	34,000	Rate of gross profit on sales	20%

Merchandise with a selling price of $12,000 remained undamaged after the fire. Damaged merchandise with an original selling price of $8,000 had a net realizable value of $2,000.

Instructions

Compute the amount of the loss as a result of the fire, assuming that the corporation had no insurance coverage.

P9-5 Brooke Products Corporation, which began operations in 1983, always values its inventories at the current replacement cost. Its annual inventory figure is arrived at by taking a physical inventory and then pricing each item in the physical inventory at current prices determined from recent vendors' invoices or catalogues. Here is the condensed income statement for this company for the last four years.

	1983	1984	1985	1986
Sales	$800,000	$840,000	$920,000	$900,000
Cost of goods sold	580,000	610,000	650,000	660,000
Gross profit	220,000	230,000	270,000	240,000
Operating expenses	150,000	164,000	180,000	178,000
Income before income taxes	$ 70,000	$ 66,000	$ 90,000	$ 62,000

Instructions

(a) Do you see any objections to their procedure for valuing inventories? Explain.

(b) Assuming that the inventory at cost, and as determined by the corporation at the end of each of the four years is as follows, restate the condensed income statements, using cost for inventories.

Ending Inventory	At Cost	As Determined by Company
1983	$120,000	$102,000
1984	130,000	104,000
1985	125,000	98,000
1986	135,000	115,000

P9-6 University Supplies, Inc. lost most of its inventory in a fire in December just before the year-end physical inventory was taken. Corporate records disclose the following:

Inventory (beginning)	$ 85,000	Sales	$350,000
Purchases	240,000	Sales returns	8,000
Purchase returns	15,000	Gross profit % based on selling price	25%

Merchandise with a selling price of $20,000 remained undamaged after the fire, and damaged merchandise has a salvage value of $3,750. The company does not carry fire insurance on its inventory. It is estimated that the year-end inventory would have been subject to a normal 10% writedown for obsolescence.

Instructions

Prepare a formal, well-labelled schedule computing the fire loss incurred by University Supplies, Inc. (Do not use the retail inventory method.)

P9-7 On June 30, 1986, a flash flood damaged the warehouse and factory of Risky Corporation, completely destroying the work in process inventory. There was no damage to either the raw materials or finished goods inventories. A physical inventory taken after the flood revealed the following valuations:

Raw materials	$ 50,000
Work in process	-0-
Finished goods	125,000

The inventory on January 1, 1986, consisted of the following:

Raw materials	$ 30,000
Work in process	120,000
Finished goods	140,000
	$290,000

A review of the books and records disclosed that the gross profit historically approximated 25% of sales. The sales for the first six months of 1986 were $360,000. Raw material purchases were $115,000. Direct labour costs for this period were $80,000 and manufacturing overhead has historically been applied at 50% of direct labour.

Instructions

Compute the value of the work in process inventory lost at June 30, 1986.

P9-8 The records for the Shoe Department of the Kresge Department Store are summarized below for the month of January.

Inventory, January 1, at retail, $12,000; at cost, $8,400
Purchases in January, at retail, $90,000; at cost, $60,000
Freight-in, $5,000
Purchase returns, at retail, $3,000; at cost, $2,000
Purchase allowances, $1,500
Transfers-in from Department B, at retail, $3,000; at cost, $2,100
Net markups, $8,000
Net markdowns, $3,000
Inventory losses due to normal breakage, etc., at retail, $600
Sales at retail, $60,000
Sales returns, $1,600

Instructions

Compute the inventory for this department as of January 31, at (a) sales price and (b) lower of average cost and market.

P9-9 Presented below is information related to McComb's, Inc. for 1986:

	Cost	Retail
Inventory, Dec. 31, 1985	$195,000	$ 300,000
Purchases	900,000	1,350,000
Purchase returns	60,000	90,000
Purchase discounts	15,000	—
Gross sales (after employee discounts)	—	1,325,000
Sales returns	—	97,500
Markups	—	90,000
Markup cancellations	—	50,000
Markdowns	—	30,000
Markdown cancellations	—	15,000
Freight-in	80,000	—
Employee discounts granted	—	6,000
Loss from breakage (normal)	—	1,500

Instructions

Assuming that McComb's, Inc. uses the conventional retail inventory method, compute the amount of their ending inventory at December 31, 1986.

P9-10 Bloomington Department Store, Inc. uses the retail inventory method to estimate ending inventory for its monthly financial statements. The following data pertain to a single department for the month of October:

Inventory, October 1	
At cost	$ 40,000
At retail	60,000
Purchases (exclusive of freight and returns)	
At cost	245,000
At retail	350,000
Freight-in	13,660
Purchase returns	
At cost	4,900
At retail	7,000
Additional markups	6,500
Markup cancellations	1,500
Markdowns (net)	1,600
Normal spoilage and breakage	9,000
Sales	282,500

Instructions

(a) Using the conventional retail method, prepare a schedule computing the estimated lower of average cost and market inventory for October 31.

(b) A department store using the conventional retail inventory method estimates the cost of its ending inventory at $58,000. An accurate physical count reveals only $44,000 or inventory at lower of cost and market. List the factors that may have caused the difference between the computed inventory and the physical count.

P9-11 As of January 1, 1986, the Downhill Ski Store adopted the retail method of accounting for its merchandise inventory.

To prepare the store's financial statements at June 30, 1986, you obtain these data:

	Cost	Selling Price
Inventory, January 1	$26,900	$ 42,000
Markdowns		10,500
Markups		19,500
Markdown cancellations		7,500
Markup cancellations		4,500
Purchases	86,200	109,800
Sales		122,000
Purchase returns and allowances	1,500	1,800
Sales returns and allowances		6,000

Instructions

Prepare a schedule to compute the Downhill Ski Store's inventory at June 30, 1986, using the retail method which approximates:

(a) lower of average cost and market (the conventional method).

(b) average cost.

(c) FIFO cost.

(d) lower of FIFO cost and market.

P9-12 The Video Corporation is an importer and wholesaler. Its merchandise is purchased from several suppliers and is warehoused by Video Corporation until sold to consumers.

In conducting his audit for the year ended June 30, 1986, the corporation's auditor determined that the system of internal control was good. Accordingly, he observed the physical inventory at an interim date, May 31, 1986, instead of at year end.

The following information was obtained from the general ledger.

Inventory, July 1, 1985	$ 97,500
Physical inventory, May 31, 1986	95,000
Sales for 11 months ended May 31, 1986	900,000
Sales for year ended June 30, 1986	980,000
Purchases for 11 months ended May 31, 1986 (before audit adjustments)	668,000
Purchases for year ended June 30, 1986 (before audit adjustments)	800,000

The audit disclosed the following information.

Shipments received in May and included in the physical inventory but recorded as June purchases.	7,500
Shipments received in unsalable condition and excluded from physical inventory; credit memos had not been received nor had chargebacks to vendors been recorded.	
Total at May 31, 1986.	1,000
Total at June 30, 1986 (including the May unrecorded chargebacks).	1,500
Deposit made with vendor and charged to purchases in April, 1986. Product was shipped in July, 1986.	2,000
Deposit made with vendor and charged to purchases in May, 1986. Product was shipped, f.o.b. destination, on May 29, 1986, and was included in May 31, 1986, physical inventory as goods in transit.	5,500
Through the carelessness of the receiving department, a June shipment was damaged by rain. This shipment was later sold in June at its cost of $10,000.	

Instructions

In audit engagements in which interim physical inventories are observed, a frequently used auditing procedure is to test the reasonableness of the year-end inventory by the application of gross profit ratios.

Prepare in good form the following schedules:

(a)   Computation of the gross profit ratio for the 11 months ended May 31, 1986.

(b)   Computation by the gross profit method, of the cost of goods sold during June, 1986.

(c)   Computation by the gross profit method, of the June 30, 1986, inventory.

(AICPA adapted)

P9-13   On April 15, 1986, fire damaged the office and warehouse of Kenosha Tool Corporation. The only accounting record saved was the general ledger, from which the trial balance below was prepared.

Kenosha Tool Corporation
TRIAL BALANCE
March 31, 1986

Cash	$ 9,000	
Accounts receivable	30,000	
Inventory, December 31, 1985	60,000	
Land	20,000	
Building and equipment	120,000	
Accumulated depreciation		$ 37,200
Other assets	3,600	
Accounts payable		23,700
Other expense accruals		10,200
Common shares		100,000
Retained earnings		47,700
Sales		90,400
Purchases	40,000	
Other expenses	26,600	
	$309,200	$309,200

The following data and information have been gathered:

1. The fiscal year of the corporation ends on December 31.

2. An examination of the April bank statement and cancelled cheques revealed that cheques written during the period April 1–15 totalled $11,600: $5,700 paid to accounts payable as of March 31; $2,000 for April merchandise shipments; and $3,900 paid for other expenses. Deposits during the same period amounted to $10,700, which consisted of receipts on account from customers with the exception of a $500 refund from a vendor for merchandise returned in April.

3. Correspondence with suppliers revealed unrecorded obligations at April 15 of $9,000 for April merchandise shipments, including $1,500 for shipments in transit on that date.

4. Customers acknowledged indebtedness of $28,000 at April 15, 1986. It was also estimated that customers owed another $5,000 that would never be acknowledged or recovered. Of the acknowledged indebtedness, $600 would probably be uncollectible.

5. The companies insuring the inventory agreed that the corporation's fire-loss claim should be based on the assumption that the overall gross profit ratio for the past two years was in effect during the current year. The corporation's audited financial statements disclosed this information:

	Year Ended December 31	
	1985	1984
Net sales	$440,000	$360,000
Net purchases	264,000	226,000
Beginning inventory	45,000	50,000
Ending inventory	60,000	45,000

6. Inventory with a cost of $6,500 was salvaged and sold for $3,000. The balance of the inventory was a total loss.

Instructions

Prepare a schedule computing the amount of inventory fire loss. The supporting schedule of the computation of the gross profit ratio should be in good form.

(AICPA adapted)

10

ACQUISITION AND DISPOSITION OF PROPERTY, PLANT, AND EQUIPMENT

Almost every business enterprise of any size or activity uses assets of a durable nature in its operations. Such assets, commonly referred to as **property, plant, and equipment; plant assets;** or **fixed assets,** include land, building structures (offices, factories, warehouses), and equipment (machinery, furniture, tools). These terms are used interchangeably throughout this text. The major characteristics of property, plant, and equipment are:

1. **They are acquired for use in operations and not for sale.** Only assets used in the normal operations of the business should be classified as property, plant, and equipment. An idle building is more appropriately classified separately as an investment; land held by land developers is classified as inventory.

2. **They are long-term in nature and usually subject to depreciation.** Property, plant, and equipment yield services over a number of years. The investment in these assets is assigned to future periods through periodic depreciation charges. The exception is land, which is not depreciated, except where a material erosion in value occurs, such as a loss in fertility of agricultural land because of poor crop rotation, drought, or soil erosion.

3. **They possess physical substance.** Property, plant, and equipment are characterized by physical existence or substance and thus differentiated from such intangible assets as patents or goodwill. Unlike raw material, however, property, plant, and equipment do not physically become part of the product held for resale.

This chapter discusses the basic accounting problems associated with (1) the incurrence of costs related to property, plant, and equipment and (2) retaining these costs. The methods of allocating costs of property, plant, and equipment to accounting periods are presented in Chapter 11.

ACQUISITION OF PROPERTY, PLANT, AND EQUIPMENT

Historical cost is the usual basis for valuing property, plant, and equipment. **Historical cost is measured by the cash or cash equivalent price of obtaining the asset and getting it ready for its intended use.** The purchase price, freight costs, and installation costs of a productive asset are considered part of the cost of the asset. Any costs related to the asset that are incurred after its acquisition, such as additions, improvements, or replacements, are added to the carrying value of the asset if they provide future service potential; otherwise they are expensed in the period of incurrence.

Accountants agree that cost should be the basis used at the date of acquisition because the cash or cash equivalent price best measures the value of the asset at that time. Disagreement does exist concerning accounting recognition of substantial differences arising subsequent to acquisition between historical cost and such other valuation methods as current replacement cost or fair market value. Current standards as stated in Section 3060 of the *CICA Handbook* are that "the writing up of fixed asset values should not occur in ordinary circumstances." Although minor exceptions are noted, current standards indicate that departures from historical cost should be rare.

Currently, the profession for the most part has taken the position that property, plant, and equipment should be reported at historical cost. The main reasons for the profession's position are: (1) at the date of acquisition, cost reflects fair value; (2) historical cost involves actual, not hypothetical, transactions, and as a result is objective; and (3) gains and losses should not be anticipated but should be recognized when the asset is sold. As indicated earlier, there are several other concepts of valuation that might be used to value property, plant, and equipment, such as (1) constant dollar accounting (adjustments for general price-level changes), (2) current cost accounting (adjustments for specific price-level changes), (3) net realizable value, or (4) a combination of constant dollar accounting and current cost or net realizable value. These alternative valuation concepts are discussed in Chapter 25.

Cost of Land

All expenditures made to acquire land and to ready it for use should be considered part of the land cost. Land costs typically include (1) the purchase price; (2) costs incurred in "closing" (e.g., registering title to the land, attorney's fees); (3) costs incurred in getting the land in condition for its intended use (e.g., grading, filling, draining, and clearing); (4) assumption of any liens or mortgages or encumbrances on the property; and (5) any additional land improvements that have an indefinite life.

When land has been purchased for the purpose of constructing a building, all costs incurred up to the excavation for the new building are considered land costs. Removal of old buildings, clearing, grading, and filling are considered costs of the land because these costs are necessary to get the land in condition for its intended purpose. Any proceeds obtained in such processes as salvage receipts on the demolition of an old building or the sale of timber that has been cleared are treated as reductions in the price of the land.

In some cases, the purchaser of land has to assume such obligations on it as back taxes or possible liens on the property. In these situations, the cost of the land is the cash paid for it, plus the encumbrances. If land is purchased for $50,000 cash, but the buyer assumes property taxes of $5,000, the land is recorded at $55,000.

Such **special assessments** for local improvements as pavements, street lights, sewers, and drainage systems are usually charged to the Land account because they are relatively permanent in nature and are maintained and replaced by the local government body. In addition, if the improvement made by the owner is rather permanent in nature, such as landscaping, then the item is properly chargeable to the Land account. Such **improvements with limited lives** as private driveways, walks, fences, and parking lots, are best recorded separately as Land Improvements so that they may be depreciated over their estimated lives.

Generally, land is considered part of property, plant, and equipment. If the major purpose of acquiring and holding land is speculative, however, it is more appropriately classified as an investment. If the land is held by a real estate concern for resale, it should be classified as part of inventory. In cases where land is held as an investment, a question develops regarding the accounting treatment that should be given taxes, insurance, and other direct costs incurred while holding the land. Many accounting theorists believe these costs should be capitalized because the revenue from the investment still has not been received. This approach is reasonable and seems justified except in cases where the asset is currently producing income (e.g., rental property).

Cost of Buildings

The cost of buildings should include all expenditures related directly to their acquisition or construction. These costs include (1) materials, labour, and overhead costs incurred during construction and (2) such fees as attorney's and architect's, and building permits. Generally, companies contract to have their buildings constructed. All costs incurred starting with excavation to completion of the building are considered part of the building costs.

One accounting problem in determining the costs of buildings is deciding what to do about an old building that is on the site of a newly proposed building. Is the cost of removal of the old building a cost of the land or a cost of the building? Accountants take the position that if land is purchased with an old building on it, the cost of demolition of the old building less its salvage value is a cost of getting the land ready for the intended use and relates to the land rather than to the construction of the new building. As indicated earlier, the general rule is that all costs of getting an asset ready for its intended use are costs of that asset.

Cost of Equipment

The term **equipment** includes delivery equipment, office equipment, furniture and fixtures, factory machinery, and similar fixed assets. The cost of such assets includes the purchase price, freight and handling charges incurred, insurance on the equipment while in transit, cost of special foundations if required, assembling and installation costs, and costs of conducting trial runs. Costs thus include all expenditures in acquiring the equipment and preparing it for use.

Self-Constructed Assets

not too heavy

Determining the cost of machinery and equipment is a problem when companies (e.g., in the railroad and utilities industries) construct their own assets. Without a purchase price or contract price, the company must allocate costs to arrive at the construction cost to be entered in the property records. Materials and direct labour used in construction pose no problem because these costs can be traced directly to work and material orders related to the fixed assets constructed.

The assignment of indirect costs of manufacturing creates special problems, however. These indirect costs, called **overhead** or burden, consist of such items as power, heat, light, insurance, property taxes on factory buildings and equipment, factory supervisory labour, depreciation of fixed assets, and supplies.

These costs may be handled in one of three ways.

1. **Assign no fixed overhead to the cost of the constructed asset.** The major reason for this treatment is that indirect overhead is generally fixed in nature and does not increase as a result of constructing one's own plant and equipment. This approach assumes that the company will have the same costs regardless of whether the company constructs the asset or not; thus, to charge a portion of the overhead costs to the equipment will normally reduce current expenses and consequently overstate income of the current period. However, variable overhead costs that increase as a result of the construction should be assigned to the cost of the asset.

GAAP

2. **Assign a portion of all overhead to the construction process.** This approach, a full costing concept, is appropriate if one believes that costs attach to all products and assets manufactured or constructed. The procedure assigns overhead costs to construction as it would to normal production. This method is employed extensively because most accountants believe a better matching of costs with revenues is obtained. Advocates of this approach indicate that failure to allocate overhead costs understates the initial cost of the equipment and results in an inaccurate allocation in the future.

3. **Allocate on basis of lost production.** A third alternative is to allocate to the construction project the cost of any curtailed production that occurs because the asset is built instead of purchased. This method is conceptually appealing, but is based on ''what might have occurred,'' which is essentially an opportunity cost concept. The practicality of this approach is questionable because valuation problems would be extremely difficult.

In practice, a *pro rata* portion of the fixed overhead should be assigned to the asset to obtain its cost. If the allocated overhead results in recording the construction costs in excess of the costs that would be charged by an outside independent producer, the excess overhead should be recorded as a period loss rather than capitalized in order to avoid capitalizing the asset at more than its probable market value.

the amt of int. capitalized should be disclosed.

Interest Costs During Construction

The proper accounting for interest costs has been a long-standing controversy in accounting. Three approaches have been suggested to account for the interest incurred in financing the construction or acquisition of property, plant, and equipment:

1. **Capitalize no interest charges during construction.** Under this approach interest is considered a cost of financing and not a cost of construction. It is contended that, if

the company had used equity financing rather than debt financing, this cost would not have been incurred. The major arguments against this approach are that an implicit interest cost is associated with the use of cash regardless of its source; if equity financing is employed, a real cost exists to the shareholders although a contractual claim does not develop.

in Canada only. ✳ 2. **Capitalize only the actual interest costs incurred during construction.** This approach relies on the historical cost concept that only actual transactions are recorded. It is argued that interest incurred is as much a cost of acquiring the asset as the cost of the materials, labour, and other resources used. As a result, a company that uses debt financing will value a similar asset at a higher cost than an enterprise that uses equity financing. The results achieved by this approach are held to be unsatisfactory by some because the cost of an asset should be the same whether cash, debt financing, or equity financing is employed.

3. **Capitalize construction with all costs of funds employed, whether identifiable or not.** This method is an economic cost approach that maintains that one part of the cost of construction is the cost of financing, whether by debt, cash, or equity financing. An asset should be charged with all costs necessary to get it ready for its intended use. Interest, whether actual or imputed, is a cost of building, just as labour, materials, and overhead are costs. A major criticism of this approach is that imputation of a cost of equity capital is subjective and falls outside the framework of a historical cost system.

The CICA has not established standards for capitalizing interest cost as part of the historical cost of acquiring assets. Consequently, practitioners must use their judgement when allocating interest costs. In the United States, the FASB has issued a *Statement of Financial Accounting Standard* that prescribes proper accounting procedures for certain interest costs.[1] Under this standard, assets require a period of time in which they are prepared for their intended use in order to qualify for interest cost capitalization. Interest capitalization on these assets is, however, required only if the effect of capitalization is material compared to the effect of expensing the interest.[2]

Interest costs are capitalized, starting with the first expenditure related to the asset, and capitalization continues until the asset is substantially completed and ready for its intended use. The amount of interest to be capitalized is the **actual interest incurred** on an enterprise's debt obligations and does not include a **cost of capital charge** for shareholders' equity. Assets that qualify for interest cost capitalization include assets under construction for an enterprise's own use (e.g., buildings, plants, and large machinery) and assets intended for sale or lease that are constructed or otherwise produced as discrete projects (e.g., ships or real estate developments). Examples of assets that do not qualify for interest capitalization are (1) assets that are in use or ready for their intended use in the earnings of the enterprise, and (2) assets that are not being used in the earnings activities of the enterprise and that are not undergoing the activities necessary to get them ready for use (such as land that is not being developed and assets not being used because of obsolescence, excess capacity, or need for repair).

In *Statement No. 34*, the amount of interest that may be capitalized for qualifying assets is that portion of total interest cost incurred during the period that theoretically could have been avoided if expenditures for the assets had not been made. To apply this concept, the potential amount of interest that may be capitalized during an accounting period is determined by multiplying an interest rate(s) by the weighted-average amount of accumulated expenditures (**average accumulated expenditures**) for qualifying assets during the period. For our purposes we will refer to this amount as **avoidable interest.** The interest rates to be used are:

[1]"Capitalization of Interest Costs," *Statement of Financial Accounting Standards No. 34* (Stamford, Conn.: FASB, 1979).

[2]*Ibid.*, summary paragraph.

1. For the portion of average accumulated expenditures that is less than or equal to any amounts borrowed specifically to finance construction of the assets, use the interest rate incurred on the specific borrowings.
2. For the portion of average accumulated expenditures that is greater than any debt incurred specifically to finance construction of the assets, use a weighted average of interest rates incurred on all outstanding debt during the period.

The capitalization period (that is, period of time during which interest must be capitalized) begins when three conditions are present:

1. Expenditures for the asset have been made.
2. Activities that are necessary to get the asset ready for its intended use are in progress.
3. Interest cost is being incurred.

Interest capitalization continues as long as those three conditions are met. The capitalization period ends when the asset is substantially complete and ready for its intended use.

The amount of interest cost to be capitalized is the "avoidable interest," explained above, or the total actual interest cost incurred, whichever is less. Interest cost that is capitalized should be written off over the useful lives of the assets involved and not over the term of the debt. Disclosure should be made of the total interest cost incurred during the period, indicating the portion charged to expense and the portion capitalized.

To illustrate, assume that on November 1, 1985, Gardner Company contracted with Wesleyan Construction Co. to have a building constructed for $1,500,000 on land Gardner purchased years earlier. Gardner made the following payments to the construction company during 1986:

March 1	May 1	December 31	Total
$510,000	$540,000	$450,000	$1,500,000

Construction was completed, and the building was ready for occupancy on December 31, 1986. Gardner Company had the following debt outstanding at December 31, 1986:

1. 15% three-year note to finance construction of the building, dated March 31, 1986, with interest payable annually on March 31. $750,000
2. 10% five-year note payable, dated December 31, 1982, with interest payable annually on December 31. $550,000
3. 12% ten-year bonds issued December 31, 1981, with interest payable annually on December 31. $600,000

Computation of Average Accumulated Expenditures

Date	Expenditures	×	Capitalization Period*	=	Average Accumulated Expenditures
March 1	$ 510,000		10/12		$425,000
May 1	540,000		8/12		360,000
Dec. 31	450,000		—		–0–
	$1,500,000				$785,000

*Months elapsing between the date expenditures were made and the date interest capitalization stops (Dec. 31, 1986).

Average accumulated expenditures: $785,000

(handwritten margin note: omit as too heavy)

Computation of Avoidable Interest

	Expenditures	×	Interest Rate	=	Avoidable Interest
Average Accumulated Expenditures	$785,000				
Financing provided by:					
Construction note, dated 3/31					
$750,000 × 9/12	562,500	×	.15	=	$ 84,375
Balance (all other debt)	$222,500	×	.1104*	=	24,564
Total Avoidable Interest					$108,939

*Weighted-average interest rate computation:

	Principal	Interest
10% five-year note	$ 550,000	$ 55,000
12% ten-year bonds	600,000	72,000
	$1,150,000	$127,000

$$\frac{\text{Total interest}}{\text{Total principal}} = \frac{\$ 127,000}{\$1,150,000} = 11.04\%$$

The average accumulated expenditures during 1986 and the avoidable interest that is potentially capitalizable during 1986 are computed on page 465 and above.

The actual interest cost that represents the maximum amount of interest that may be capitalized during 1986 is computed as follows:

Construction note	$750,000 × .15 × 9/12	=	$ 84,375
Five-year note	$550,000 × .10	=	55,000
Ten-year bonds	$600,000 × .12	=	72,000
			$211,375

Actual interest: $211,375

The interest cost to be capitalized is the lesser of $108,939 (avoidable interest) and $211,375 (actual interest), which is $108,939.

The journal entries to be made by Gardner Company during 1986 would be as follows:

March 1

Building Under Construction	510,000	
Cash		510,000

March 31

Cash	750,000	
Notes Payable		750,000

May 1

Building Under Construction	540,000	
Cash		540,000

December 31

Building Under Construction	450,000	
Cash		450,000

Building	108,939	
Interest Expense ($211,375 − $108,939)	102,436	
Interest Payable ($750,000 × .15 × 9/12)		84,375
Cash ($55,000 + $72,000)		127,000

At December 31, 1986, Gardner should disclose the amount of interest capitalized either as a reduction of interest expense in the income statement or in the notes accompanying the financial statements. Both forms of disclosure are illustrated below:

Capitalized Interest Reported in the Income Statement		
Income from operations		XXX
Other expenses:		
Interest expense	$211,375	
Less: Capitalized interest	108,939	102,436
Income before income taxes		XXXXX
Income tax expense		XXX
Net income		XXXX

Capitalized Interest Disclosed in a Note	
Interest expense (Note 1)	$102,436

Note 1—Accounting Policies
<u>Capitalized interest</u>. During 1986 total interest cost was $211,375 of which $108,939 was capitalized as part of the cost of buildings.

Two additional points should be noted regarding interest capitalization. First, when interest cost is incurred in connection with the purchase of land that will be used in the near future as a building site, the interest to be capitalized should be debited to the building account and not to the land account. Second, companies frequently borrow money to finance construction of assets and temporarily invest the excess borrowed funds in interest-bearing securities until the funds are needed to pay for construction. During the early stages of construction, interest revenue earned may exceed the interest cost incurred on the borrowed funds. Some accountants have wondered whether it is appropriate to offset interest revenue against interest cost when determining the amount of interest to be capitalized as a part of the construction cost of assets. Those who oppose this argue that temporary or short-term investment decisions are not related to interest incurred as part of the acquisition cost of assets. On the other hand, others believe that firms should not be permitted to defer interest cost while recognizing interest revenue in the current period. The FASB supports the former view and, in *Technical Bulletin No. 81-5*, has stated that **interest revenue should not be netted or offset against interest cost**.

Many Canadian companies have adopted a policy of interest capitalization as mandated by the FASB in *Statement No. 34* although the CICA has not yet established an accounting standard. The possibility of interest capitalization is currently being studied by the CICA in Canada, and a great deal of controversy is expected. From a conceptual viewpoint, many believe that either no interest cost should be capitalized or all interest costs, actual or imputed, should be capitalized for the reasons mentioned earlier in this section. In addition, some difficult practi-

cal problems exist. For example, capitalization is supposed to take place only when the benefits of the information provided exceed the costs of providing the information.

ACQUISITION AND VALUATION

An asset should be recorded at the fair market value of what is given up to acquire it or at its own fair market value, whichever is more clearly evident. Fair market value, however, is sometimes obscured by the process through which the asset is acquired. As an example, assume that land and buildings are bought together for one price. How are separate values for the land and buildings computed? A number of accounting problems of this nature are examined in the following sections.

Cash Discounts

When plant assets are purchased subject to cash discounts for prompt payment, the question of how the discount should be handled occurs. If the discount is taken, it should be considered a reduction in the purchase price of the asset. What is not clear, however, is whether a reduction in the asset cost should occur if the discount is not taken. Two points of view exist on this matter. Under one approach, the discount, whether taken or not, is considered a reduction in the cost of the asset. The rationale for this approach is that the real cost of the asset is the cash or cash equivalent price of the asset. In addition, some argue that the terms of cash discounts are so attractive that failure to take a discount is a loss because management is inefficient. On the other hand, some argue that the discount should not be considered a loss because the terms may be unfavourable or because it would not be prudent for the company to take the discount. At present, both methods are employed in practice. The former method is generally preferred because it records the asset at the current cash equivalent price to acquire the asset at the date of acquisition.

Deferred Payment Contracts

Plant assets are purchased frequently on long-term credit contracts through the use of notes, mortgages, bonds, or equipment obligations. **Assets purchased on long-term credit contracts should be accounted for at the present value of the consideration exchanged between the contracting parties at the date of the transaction.** An asset purchased today, therefore, in exchange for a $10,000 noninterest-bearing note, payable four years from now, should not be recorded originally at $10,000. The present value of the $10,000 note is the purchase price of the asset. If the appropriate interest rate at which to discount this single payment of $10,000 due four years from now is 12%, this asset should be recorded at $6,355.20 ($10,000 × .63552; see Table 6-2).

If no interest rate is stated or if the specified rate is unreasonable, an appropriate interest rate must be imputed. The objective is to approximate the interest rate that the buyer and seller would negotiate at arm's length in a similar borrowing transaction. Some factors to be considered in imputing an interest rate are the borrower's credit rating, the amount and maturity date of the note, and prevailing interest rates. In determining the interest rate, the cash exchange price of the asset acquired (if determinable) may be used as the basis for recording the asset and for measuring the interest element.

To illustrate, Sutter Company purchases a specially built robot spray painter for its production line. The company issues a $100,000, 5-year, noninterest-bearing note to Wrigley Robotics, Ltd. for the new equipment when the prevailing market rate of interest for obligations of this nature is 10%. Sutter is to pay off the note in five $20,000 instalments at the end of each year. The fair market value of this particular specially built robot cannot be determined readily in the market place and is thus approximated by establishing the market value (present value) of the note. The computation of the present value of the note and entries at the date of purchase and the dates of payment are as follows:

At date of purchase

Equipment	75,816*	
Discount on Notes Payable	24,184	
Notes Payable		100,000

*Present value of note $= \$20,000 \ (p_{\overline{5}|10\%})$
$= \$20,000 \ (3.79079) \ \text{(Table 6-4)}$
$= \$75,816$

At end of first year

Interest Expense	7,582*	
Notes Payable	20,000	
Cash		20,000
Discount on Notes Payable		7,582

*[($100,000 − $24,184) × 10%]

At end of second year

Interest Expense	6,340*	
Notes Payable	20,000	
Cash		20,000
Discount on Notes Payable		6,340

*[($100,000 − $24,184) − ($20,000 − $7,582)] × 10%

If an interest rate is not imputed in such deferred payment contracts, the asset will be recorded at an amount greater than its fair value, or actual historical cost. In addition, interest expense would be understated in the income statement in all periods involved. The use of the effective interest method relates the interest cost to the unpaid balance during each period.

Lump Sum Purchase

A special problem of pricing fixed assets arises when a group of plant assets is purchased at a single lump sum price. When such a situation occurs, and it is not at all unusual, the practice is to allocate the total cost among the various assets on the basis of their relative fair market values. The assumption is that costs will vary in direct proportion to sales value.

Although the accountant may not be an expert in this area, responsibility for determining that the valuations associated with the different assets are reasonable and that they can be verified to some degree must be accepted. Generally, an appraisal that was employed for insurance purposes, the assessed valuation for property taxes, or simply an independent appraisal by an engineer or other appraiser might be used. Normally, the seller's book value should not be employed as a basis for allocation.

To illustrate, Norduct Heating Ltd. decides to purchase several assets of a small heating concern, Harker Heating, for $80,000. Harker Heating is in the process of liquidation, and its assets sold are:

	Book Value	Fair Market Value
Inventory	$30,000	$ 25,000
Land	20,000	25,000
Building	35,000	50,000
	$85,000	$100,000

The $80,000 purchase price would be allocated on the basis of the relative fair market values in the following manner:

Inventory $\dfrac{\$\,25,000}{\$100,000} \times \$80,000 = \$20,000$

Land $\dfrac{\$\,25,000}{\$100,000} \times \$80,000 = \$20,000$

Building $\dfrac{\$\,50,000}{\$100,000} \times \$80,000 = \$40,000$

Issuance of Shares

When property is acquired by issuance of securities, such as common shares, the cost of the property is not properly measured by the par or stated value of such shares. If the shares are being actively traded, **the market value of the shares issued is a fair indication of the cost of the property acquired because the shares are a good measure of the current cash equivalent price.**

For example, Coyle-Lukkin decides to purchase some adjacent land for expansion of its carpeting and cabinet operation. In lieu of paying cash for the land, the company issues to Starret Company 5,000 no-par value common shares that have a fair market value of $12 per share. Coyle-Lukkin would make the following entry:

Land (5,000 × $12)   60,000
  Common Shares   60,000

If the market value of common shares exchanged is not determinable, the market value of the property should be established and used as a basis for recording the asset and issuance of the common shares.

When the fair market value of the shares is used as the basis of valuation, careful consideration must be given to the effect that the issuance of additional shares will have on the existing market price. Where the effect on market price appears significant, an independent appraisal of the asset received should be made. This valuation should be employed as the basis for valuation of the asset as well as for the shares issued. In the unusual case where the fair market value of the shares or the fair market value of the asset cannot be determined objectively, the board of directors of the corporation may set the value.

Exchanges of Property, Plant, and Equipment (Nonmonetary Assets)

Accounting for exchanges of nonmonetary assets (e.g., inventories and property, plant, and equipment) has not yet been included in the *CICA Handbook*. Consequently, the following discussion is based on U.S. accounting standards which, under the circumstances, would be acceptable in Canadian practice. Proper accounting for exchanges of nonmonetary assets is controversial.[3] Some accountants argue that the accounting for these types of exchanges should be based on the fair value of the asset given up with a gain or loss recognized; others believe that the accounting should be based on the recorded amount (book value) of the asset given up with no gain or loss recognized; and still others favour an approach that would recognize losses in all cases, but defer gains in special situations.

Ordinarily accounting for exchange of nonmonetary assets should be based on **the fair value of the asset given up or the fair value of the asset received, whichever is clearly more evident.**[4] If the fair value of either asset is not reasonably determinable, the book value of the asset given up is usually used as the basis for recording the nonmonetary exchange. Thus, any gains or losses on the exchange should be recognized immediately. The rationale for this approach is that **the earnings process related to these assets is completed** and, therefore, a gain or loss should be recognized. This approach is always employed when the assets are **dissimilar** in nature, such as the exchange of land for a building, or the exchange of equipment for inventory.

The general rule is modified when exchanges of **similar nonmonetary** assets occur. For example, when a company exchanges inventory items with inventory of another company because of colour or size to facilitate sale to an outside customer, the earnings process is not considered completed, and a **gain** should not be recognized. Likewise, if a company trades **similar productive assets** (assets held for or used in the production of goods or services) such as land for land or equipment for equipment, the enterprise is not considered to have completed the earnings process and, therefore, a **gain should not be recognized.** However, if the exchange transaction involving **similar assets** would result in a loss, **the loss is recognized immediately**.

In certain situations, gains on exchange of similar nonmonetary assets may be involved where **monetary consideration (boot)** is received. When such monetary consideration as cash is received in addition to the nonmonetary asset, it is assumed that a portion of the earnings process is completed and, therefore, a partial gain is recognized.

In summary, losses on nonmonetary transactions are always recognized whether the exchange involves dissimilar or similar assets. Gains on nonmonetary transactions are recognized if the exchange involves dissimilar assets; gains are deferred if the exchange involves similar assets, unless cash or some other form of monetary consideration is received, in which case a partial gain is recognized. Any gain or loss on disposal of nonmonetary assets is computed by comparing the book value of the asset given up with the fair value of the asset given up.

---

[3]Nonmonetary assets are items whose price in terms of the monetary unit may change over time, whereas monetary assets are fixed in terms of units of currency by contract or otherwise; for example, cash and short- or long-term accounts and notes receivable.

[4]"Accounting for Nonmonetary Transactions," *Opinions of the Accounting Principles Board No. 29* (Stamford, Conn.: FASB, 1973), par. 18.

To illustrate the accounting for these different types of transactions, the discussion is divided into three sections as follows:

1. Accounting for dissimilar assets.
2. Accounting for similar assets—loss situation.
3. Accounting for similar assets—gain situation.

Dissimilar Assets   The cost of a nonmonetary asset acquired in exchange for a dissimilar nonmonetary asset is usually recorded at the **fair value of the asset given up,** and a gain or loss is recognized. The **fair value of the asset received** should be used only if it is more clearly evident than the fair value of the asset given up. If the fair value of either asset is not reasonably determinable, the **book value of the asset given up** is used as a basis for recording the nonmonetary exchange.

To illustrate, Newbold Transportation Company exchanged a number of used trucks plus cash for vacant land that might be used for a future plant site. The trucks have a combined book value of $42,000 (cost $64,000 less $22,000 accumulated depreciation). Newbold's purchasing agent, who has had previous dealings in the second-hand market, indicates that the trucks have a fair market value of $49,000. In addition to the trucks, Newbold must pay $17,000 cash for the land. The cost of the land is $66,000 computed as follows:

	Computation of Land Cost
Fair value of trucks exchanged	$49,000
Cash paid	17,000
Cost of land	$66,000

The journal entry to record the exchange transaction is:

Land	66,000	
Accumulated Depreciation—Trucks	22,000	
Trucks		64,000
Gain on Disposal of Trucks		7,000
Cash		17,000

The gain is the difference between the fair value of the trucks ($49,000) and their book value ($42,000). It is verified as follows:

		Computation of Gain
Fair value of trucks		$49,000
Cost of trucks	$64,000	
Less: Accumulated depreciation	22,000	
Book value of trucks		42,000
Gain on disposal of used trucks		$ 7,000

If the fair value of the trucks were $39,000 instead of $49,000, a loss on the exchange of $3,000 ($42,000 − $39,000) would be reported. In either case, as a result of the exchange of dissimilar assets, the earnings process on the used trucks had been completed and a gain **or** loss should be recognized.

Similar Assets—Loss Situation   Similar nonmonetary assets are those of the same general type, that perform the same function, or are employed in the same line of business. When similar nonmonetary assets are exchanged and a loss results, the loss should be recognized immediately. For example, Information Processing, Ltd. trades its used accounting machine for a new model. The accounting machine given up has a book value of $8,000 (original cost $12,000 less $4,000 accumulated depreciation) and a fair value of $6,000. It is traded for a new model that has a list price of $16,000. In negotiations with the seller, a trade-in allowance of $9,000 is finally agreed on for the used machine. The cash payment that must be made for the new asset and the cost of the new machine is computed as follows:

	Cost of New Machine
List price of new machine	$16,000
Less: Trade-in allowance for used machine	9,000
Cash payment due	7,000
Fair value of used machine	6,000
Cost of new machine	$13,000

The journal entry to record this transaction is:

Equipment	13,000	
Accumulated Depreciation—Equipment	4,000	
Loss on Disposal of Equipment	2,000	
Equipment		12,000
Cash		7,000

The loss on the disposal of the used machine is the difference between its book value ($8,000) and its fair value ($6,000).

Why was the trade-in allowance or the book value of the old asset not used as a basis for the new equipment? The trade-in allowance is not employed because it included a price concession (similar to a price discount) to the purchaser. For example, few individuals pay list price for a new car. Trade-in allowances on the used car are often so inflated that actual selling prices are below list prices. In short, the list price of a new car is usually inflated, and to record the car at list price would state it at an amount in excess of its cash equivalent price. Use of book value in this situation would overstate the value of the new accounting machine by $2,000. Because assets should not be valued at more than their cash equivalent price, the loss should be recognized immediately rather than added to the cost of the newly acquired asset.

Similar Assets—Gain Situation (no cash received)   The accounting treatment for exchanges of **similar** nonmonetary assets when a gain develops is more complex. If the exchange does not complete the earnings process, then any **gain should be deferred**. The real estate industry provides a good example of why the profession decided not to recognize gains on exchanges of similar nonmonetary assets. In the early 1970s when the real estate business was booming, it was common practice for companies to "swap" estate holdings. To illustrate, Landmark Company and Hillfarm, Inc. each had undeveloped land on which they intended to build shopping centres. Appraisals indicated that the land of both companies had increased significantly in value. The companies decided to exchange their undeveloped land, record a gain, and report their new parcels of land at current fair value. But should income be recognized at this point? The profession's position was that the earnings process is not completed because the companies remain in the same economic position after the swap as before; therefore, the asset acquired should be recorded at the book value of the assets disposed of with no gain recognized. If, however, the book value exceeds fair value, a loss should be recognized.

To illustrate, Davis Rent-a-Car has a rental fleet of automobiles that are primarily Ford Motor Company products. Davis's management is interested in increasing the variety of automobiles in its rental fleet by adding numerous models of General Motors products. During a long delay in delivery from the manufacturer, Davis arranges with Nertz Rent-a-Car to exchange a group of Ford Fairmonts and Futuras with a fair value of $160,000 and a book value of $135,000 (cost $150,000 less accumulated depreciation $15,000) for a number of Chevy Citations and Pontiac Phoenixes. The fair value of the automobiles received from Nertz is $170,000; Davis, therefore, pays $10,000 in cash in addition to the Ford automobiles exchanged. The total gain to Davis Rent-a-Car is computed as follows:

	Computation of Gain
Fair value of Ford automobiles exchanged	$160,000
Book value of Ford automobiles exchanged	135,000
Total gain (unrecognized)	$ 25,000

The entry by Davis to record this transaction is as follows:

Automobiles (GM)	145,000	
Accumulated Depreciation—Automobiles	15,000	
Automobiles (Ford)		150,000
Cash		10,000

The 145,000 cost debited to Automobiles is computed by adding the amount of cash paid to the book value of the cars traded in ($10,000 + $135,000). Alternatively, the $145,000 could be calculated by deducting the amount of gain deferred ($25,000) from the fair value of the GM automobiles ($170,000). The total gain is deferred because the earnings process is not considered to be completed.

The deferred gain that reduced the basis of the new automobiles will be recognized when those automobiles are sold to an outside party. If these automobiles are held for an extended period of time, depreciation charges will be lower and net income higher in subsequent periods because of the reduced basis.

Similar Assets—Gain Situation (some cash received)   The accounting issue of gain recognition becomes difficult if such monetary consideration (boot) as cash is **received** in an exchange of similar nonmonetary assets. When cash is received, part of the nonmonetary asset is considered sold and part exchanged; therefore, only a portion of the gain is deferred.[5] The general formula for gain recognition when some cash is received is as follows:

---

[5]The part-sold, part-exchanged treatment is applicable to exchanges of similar nonmonetary assets irrespective of the amount of monetary consideration involved in the transaction. See James B. Hubbs and D. R. Bainbridge, ''Nonmonetary Exchange Transactions: Clarification of APB Opinion No. 29,'' *The Accounting Review* (January, 1982), pp. 171–175.

$$\frac{\text{Cash Received (Boot)}}{\text{Cash Received (Boot)} + \text{Fair Value of Asset Received}} \times \text{Total Gain} = \text{Recognized Gain}$$

For example, consider recording the foregoing exchange of automobiles on the books of Nertz Rent-a-Car. If the book value of Nertz's Chevy and Pontiac automobiles exchanged is $136,000 (cost $200,000 less accumulated depreciation $64,000), the total gain on the exchange to Nertz would be computed as follows:

	Computation of Total Gain to Nertz
Fair value of GM automobiles exchanged	$170,000
Book value of GM automobiles exchanged	136,000
Total gain	$ 34,000

But, because Nertz received $10,000 in cash, the recognized gain on this transaction is computed as follows using the formula above:

$$\frac{\$10,000}{\$10,000 + \$160,000} \times \$34,000 = \$2,000$$

The ratio of monetary assets ($10,000) to the total consideration received ($10,000 + $160,000) is the portion of the total gain ($34,000) to be recognized; that is, $2,000. Because only a gain of $2,000 is recognized on this transaction, the remaining $32,000 ($34,000 − $2,000) is deferred and reduces the basis of the new automobiles:

Basis of New Automobiles to Nertz

Fair value of Ford automobiles	$160,000	Book value of GM automobiles	$136,000
Less: Gain deferred	(32,000) OR	Portion of book value	
Basis of Ford automobiles	$128,000	presumed sold*	(8,000)
		Basis of Ford automobiles	$128,000

$$\frac{*\$10,000}{\$170,000} \times \$136,000 = \$8,000$$

The entry by Nertz to record this transaction is as follows:

Cash	10,000	
Automobiles (Ford)	128,000	
Accumulated Depreciation—Automobiles (GM)	64,000	
Automobiles (GM)		200,000
Gain on Disposal of GM Automobiles		2,000

The profession's rationale for this treatment is that, before the exchange, Nertz Rent-a-Car had an unrecognized gain of $34,000, as evidenced by the difference between the book value ($136,000) and the fair value ($170,000) of its GM automobiles. When the exchange occurred, a portion ($10,000/$170,000 or 1/17) of the fair value was converted to a more liquid asset. The ratio of this liquid asset ($10,000) to the total consideration received ($160,000 + $10,000) is the portion of the gain ($34,000) realized. Thus, a gain of $2,000 (1/17 × $34,000) is realized and recorded.

Presented below in summary form are the accounting requirements for recognizing gains and losses on exchanges of nonmonetary assets.[6]

1. Compute the total gain or loss on the transaction, which is equal to the difference between the fair value of the asset given up and the book value of the asset given up.
2. If a loss is computed in 1, always recognize the entire loss.
3. If a gain is computed in 1,
   (a) and the earnings process is considered completed, the entire gain is recognized (dissimilar assets).
   (b) and the earnings process is not considered completed (similar assets),
       (1) and no cash is involved, no gain is recognized.
       (2) and some cash is given, no gain is recognized.
       (3) and some cash is received, the following portion of the gain is recognized:

$$\frac{\text{Cash Received (Boot)}}{\text{Cash Received (Boot)} + \text{Fair Value of Assets Received}} \times \text{Total Gain}$$

An enterprise that engages in one or more nonmonetary exchanges during a period should disclose in financial statements for the period the nature of the transactions, the basis of accounting for the assets transferred, and gains or losses recognized on transfers.[7]

Acquisition and Disposition by Donation or Gift

An enterprise may be both the recipient of donations or the maker of donations. Such exchanges are referred to as **nonreciprocal transfers** because they are transfers of assets in one direction. When assets are acquired in this manner, a strict cost concept dictates that the valuation of the asset should be zero. A departure from the cost principle seems justified, however, because the only costs incurred, legal fees and other relatively minor expenditures, do not constitute a reasonable basis of accounting for the assets acquired. To record nothing, we believe, is to ignore the economic realities of an increase in wealth and asset utility. Therefore, **the appraisal or fair market value of the asset should be used to establish a proper basis of asset valuation for purposes of enterprise accountability.**

The classification of the offsetting credit to the asset received, however, is controversial. Some believe that the credit should be to Donated Capital (a contributed surplus account) because these donations increase the amount of assets and, therefore, shareholders' equity available to the enterprise. Others argue that capital is contributed only by the owners of the business and that donations are benefits to the enterprise which should be reported as income. An issue related to the income approach is whether the income should be reported immediately or over the period that the asset is employed. If the asset is donated by a government organization, the purpose of the donation will determine how the credit should be recorded. For example, to attract new industry, a city may offer land; but the receiving enterprise may incur additional costs in the future (transportation, higher

---

[6]Adapted from an article by Robert Capettini and Thomas E. King, "Exchanges of Nonmonetary Assets: Some Changes," *The Accounting Review* (January, 1976).

[7]"Accounting for Nonmonetary Transactions," *op. cit.*, par. 28.

taxes, etc.) because the location is not the most desirable. As a consequence, the income should be deferred and recognized as these costs are incurred. If known additional costs are to be incurred, an Unrealized Government Grant account could be established in the liability section and written off over the term during which the additional costs are incurred.

Regardless of whether assets or funds to acquire assets are received from federal, provincial, or local governments, *CICA Handbook*, Section 3800, requires that recipients follow certain prescribed accounting methods. These methods are based on an ''income approach'' which requires that the amount received should be deferred and recognized over the period in which the related assets are employed. This is accomplished by either (1) reducing the cost of the asset by the amount of government assistance received, or (2) recording the amount of assistance received from the various government sources as a deferred credit and amortizing it to income over the life of the related asset. To illustrate, Max Wayer Meat Packing, Inc. has recently received a grant of $225,000 from the federal government to upgrade its sewage treatment facility. The entry to record receipt of the grant, if Max Wayer wishes to use the cost reduction method, would be as follows:

Cash	225,000	
Equipment		225,000

This results in the equipment being carried on the books at cost minus the related government assistance. As a result the annual depreciation charge for the equipment would be reduced over its useful life and net income would be increased.

Alternatively, an unrealized income account could be credited with the amount of the grant. This unrealized income account would then be amortized periodically to income over a term equal to the useful life of the equipment. The entries to record the grant and amortization for the first year (assuming a 10-year term) would be as follows:

Cash	225,000	
Deferred Revenue—Government Grants		225,000
Deferred Revenue—Government Grants	22,500	
Revenue—Government Grants		22,500

Whether the capital approach or the unrealized income approach is used, if the donation is contingent upon some performance (such as building a plant), this contingency should be reported in the notes to the financial statements.

In practice, enterprises permit cash donations in the form of government assistance related to current expenses and revenues to flow through the income statement while cash and noncash donations from shareholders and other nongovernment entities or individuals are generally credited to contributed surplus.

When a nonmonetary asset is donated, that is, given away, the amount of the donation should be recorded at the fair market value of the donated asset. If a difference exists between the fair market value of the asset and its book value, a gain or loss should be recognized.[8] To illustrate, Kline Industries donates land that cost $80,000 and has a fair market value of $110,000 to the City of Halifax for a park. The entry to record this donation would be:

Donation	110,000	
Land		80,000
Gain on Disposition of Land		30,000

[8]''Accounting for Nonmonetary Transactions,'' *op. cit.* , par. 18.

The donation cost would ordinarily be classified in the Other Expense section of the income statement.

COSTS SUBSEQUENT TO ACQUISITION

After plant assets are installed and ready for use, additional costs are incurred that range from ordinary repair costs to significant additions. The major problem in this area is allocating these costs to individual periods. Accountants for the most part have adopted the position that costs incurred to achieve greater future benefits should be capitalized (debited to an asset account), whereas expenditures that simply maintain a given level of services should be expensed. In order for costs to be capitalized (capital expenditures), one of three future benefit conditions must be present: (1) **the useful life of the asset must be increased;** (2) **the quantity of units produced from the asset must be increased;** or (3) **the quality of the units produced must be enhanced.**

Expenditures (revenue expenditures) that do not increase the service benefits of the assets are expensed. Ordinary repairs, for example, are expenditures that maintain the existing condition of the asset or restore it to normal operating efficiency and should be expensed immediately. In addition, most expenditures below an established arbitrary minimum amount are expensed rather than capitalized. For example, many enterprises have adopted the rule that expenditures below, say, $500 should always be expensed. Although conceptually this treatment may not be correct, expediency demands that this approach be followed; otherwise, accountants would have to set up depreciation schedules for such things as waste baskets and ash trays.

The distinction between a **capital (asset)** and **revenue (expense)** expenditure is not always clear-cut. For example, determination of the **property unit** with which costs should be associated is critical. If a fully equipped steamship is considered a property unit, then replacement of the engine might be considered an expense, whereas if the ship's engine is considered a property unit, then its replacement would be capitalized. It follows that the disposition and treatment of many items require considerable analysis and judgement before the proper distinction can be made. In many cases, consistent application of a capital/expense policy is justified as more important than attempting to provide general theoretical guidelines.

Generally, four major types of expenditures are incurred relative to existing assets.

1. **Additions.** Increase or extension of existing assets.
2. **Improvements and replacements.** Substitution of an improved asset for an existing one.
3. **Reinstallation and rearrangement.** Movement of assets from one location to another.
4. **Repairs.** Expenditures that maintain assets in condition for operation.

Additions

Additions should present no major accounting problems. By definition, any addition to plant assets is capitalized because a new asset has been created. The addition of a wing to a hospital or the addition of an air conditioning system to an office, for example, increases the service potential of that facility and should be capitalized and matched against the revenues that will result in future periods.

The most difficult problem that develops in this area is accounting for any changes related to the existing structure as a result of the addition. Is the cost that is incurred to tear down a wall of the old structure to make room for the addition a cost of the addition or an expense or loss of the period? The answer is that it depends on the original intent. If the company had anticipated that an addition was going to be added later, then this cost of removal is a proper cost of the addition. But if the company had not anticipated this development, it should properly be reported as a loss in the current period on the basis that the company was inefficient in its planning. Normally, the carrying amount of the old wall remains in the accounts, although theoretically it should be removed.

Improvements and Replacements

Improvements (often referred to as betterments) and replacements are substitutions of one asset for another. The distinguishing feature between an improvement and a replacement is that an improvement is the substitution of a better asset for the one currently used (say, a concrete floor for a wooden floor). A replacement, on the other hand, is the substitution of a similar asset (a wooden floor for a wooden floor).

Many times improvements and replacements occur as a result of a general policy to modernize or rehabilitate an older building or piece of equipment. The problem lies in differentiating these types of expenditures from normal repairs. The accountant should ask: Does the expenditure increase the **future** service potential of the asset, or does it merely maintain the existing level of service? Many times the answer is not clear-cut, and good judgement must be used in order to classify these expenditures properly.

If it is determined that the expenditure increases the future service potential of the asset and, therefore, should be capitalized, this capitalization is handled in one of three ways, depending on the circumstances.

1. **Substitution Approach.** Conceptually, the substitution approach is the correct procedure if the carrying amount of the old asset is available. If the carrying amount of the old asset can be determined, it is a simple matter to remove the cost (book value) of the old asset and replace it with the cost of the new asset.

   To illustrate, Instinct Enterprises decides to replace the pipes in its plumbing system. A plumber suggests that in place of the cast iron pipes and copper tubing, a newly developed plastic tubing be used. The old pipe and tubing have a book value of $15,000 (cost of $150,000 less accumulated depreciation of $135,000), and a fair market value of $1,000. The plastic tubing system has a market value of $125,000. Assuming that Instinct has to pay $124,000 for the new tubing after exchanging the old tubing, the entry is:

Plumbing System	125,000	
Accumulated Depreciation	135,000	
Loss on Disposal of Plant Assets	14,000	
Plumbing System		150,000
Cash		124,000

   The problem with this approach is determining the book value of the old asset. Generally, the components of a given asset depreciate at different rates, but no separate accounting is made of each component. As an example, the tires, motor, and body of a truck depreciate at different rates, but most concerns use only one depreciation rate for the truck. Separate depreciation rates could be set for each component, but practicality precludes the use of this approach. If the carrying amount of the old asset cannot be determined, one of two other approaches is adopted.

2. **Capitalizing the New Cost.** The justification for capitalizing the cost of the improvement or replacement is that even though the carrying amount of the old asset is not removed from the accounts, sufficient depreciation was taken on the item to reduce the carrying amount almost to zero. Whether this assumption is true in all cases is unlikely, but in many situations the differences would not be significant. Improvements especially are handled in this manner.

3. **Charging to Accumulated Depreciation.** There are times when there has not been an improvement in the quantity or quality of the asset itself, but the useful life of the asset has been extended. Replacements, particularly, may extend the useful life of the asset, yet they may not improve the quality or quantity of service or product in a given period. In these circumstances, the expenditure may be debited to Accumulated Depreciation rather than to the asset; it thereby recaptures some or all of the past depreciation. The main justification for this approach is that it is a recovery of past depreciation charges. The carrying amount of the asset is the same whether the asset is charged or the accumulated depreciation is charged—it is only in the manner of presentation that a difference arises.

Rearrangement and Reinstallation

Rearrangement and reinstallation costs are expenditures that are intended to benefit future periods but are not additions, replacements, or improvements. An example is the rearrangement or reinstallation of a group of machines to facilitate future production. If the original installation cost can be estimated along with the accumulated depreciation to date, the rearrangement and reinstallation cost might properly be handled as a replacement. If not, which is generally the case, the new costs should be carried forward as an asset to be amortized over future periods expected to benefit.[9] If these costs are not material, or if they cannot be separated from other operating expenses, or if their future benefit is questionable, they should be expensed in the period in which they were incurred.

Repairs

Ordinary repairs are expenditures made to maintain plant assets in operating condition; they are charged to an expense account in the period in which they are incurred on the basis that it is the only period benefited. Replacement of minor parts, lubricating and adjusting of equipment, repainting, and cleaning are examples of the type of maintenance charges that occur regularly and are treated as ordinary operating expenses. It is often difficult to distinguish a repair from an improvement or replacement. The major consideration is whether the expenditure increases the future service potential. If a **major repair,** such as an overhaul, occurs, several periods will benefit and the cost should be handled as an addition, improvement, or replacement, depending on the type of repair made.

If operating and income statements are prepared for short periods of time, say, monthly or quarterly, the same principles must be applied to accounting for repair

---

[9]Another cost of this nature is relocation costs. For example, when Shell Oil moved its world headquarters from New York to Houston, it amortized the dollar amount of relocating over four years. Conversely, relocation costs necessitated by the company's move to Calgary were charged to revenue. The point is that no definitive guidelines have been established in this area, and generally costs are deferred over some arbitrary period in the future. Some writers have argued that these costs should generally be expensed as incurred. See, for example, Charles W. Lamden, Dale L. Gerboth, and Thomas W. McRae, ''Accounting for Depreciable Assets,'' *Accounting Research Monograph No. 1* (New York: AICPA, 1975), pp. 54–61.

costs. Ordinary repairs and other regular maintenance charges for an annual period may benefit several quarters, and allocation of the cost among periods concerned might be required. For example, a concern will often find it advantageous to concentrate its repair program at a certain time of the year, perhaps during the period of least activity or when the plant is shut down for vacation. Short-term comparative statements might be misleading if such expenditures are shown as expenses of the quarter in which they were incurred. To give comparability to monthly or quarterly income statements, an account such as Allowance for Repairs might be used so that repair costs are better assigned to periods that benefited.

To illustrate, Cricket Tractor Company estimated that its total repair expense for the year would be $720,000. It decided to charge each quarter for a portion of the repair cost even though the total cost for the year would occur only in two quarters.

End of first quarter (zero repair costs incurred):

Repair Expense	180,000	
Allowance for Repairs (1/4 × $720,000)		180,000

End of second quarter ($344,000 repair costs incurred):

Allowance for Repairs	344,000	
Cash, Wages Payable, Inventory, etc.		344,000
Repair Expense	180,000	
Allowance for Repairs (1/4 × $720,000)		180,000

End of third quarter (zero repair costs incurred):

Repair Expense	180,000	
Allowance for Repairs (1/4 × $720,000)		180,000

End of fourth quarter ($380,800 repair costs incurred):

Allowance for Repairs	380,800	
Cash, Wages Payable, Inventory, etc.		380,800
Repair Expense	184,800	
Allowance for Repairs		184,800
($344,000 + $380,800 − $180,000 − $180,000 − $180,000)		

Ordinarily, no balance should be carried over to the following year in the Allowance for Repairs account, and the fourth quarter would normally absorb the variation from estimates. If balance sheets are prepared during the year, the allowance account could be reported as an accrued liability or added to or subtracted from the property, plant, and equipment section to obtain a proper valuation during the year.

Some accountants advocate the accrual of estimated repair costs beyond one year. This approach is based on the assumption that the allocation of asset cost via depreciation charges does not take into consideration the incurrence of repair costs. For example, in aircraft overhaul and steel furnace rebuilding, an allowance for repairs is sometimes established because the amount of repairs can be established with a high degree of certainty. Although conceptually this approach may be appealing, there are many drawbacks. First, it is difficult to justify the Allowance for Repairs account as a liability because one might ask: To whom is the company liable? Placement in the shareholders' equity section is also illogical because no addition to the shareholders' investment has taken place. One possibility might be to treat allowance for repairs as an addition to or subtraction from the asset on the basis that the value has increased or decreased, depending on when the repairs were made. The fact is that expenses should not be anticipated before they arise unless estimates of the future are predictable within a reasonable range.

Summary

The schedule summarizing the accounting treatment discussed in this section for costs incurred subsequent to the acquisition of capitalized assets is presented below:

SUMMARY OF COSTS SUBSEQUENT TO ACQUISITION OF PROPERTY, PLANT, AND EQUIPMENT		
Type of Expenditure	Characteristics	Normal Accounting Treatment
Additions	Extend, expand, or enlarge existing asset.	Capitalize cost to asset account.
Improvements and Replacements	(a) Carrying value of old asset known.	Remove cost of and accumulated depreciation on old asset. Recognize gain or loss on old asset. Capitalize cost of improvement/ replacement.
	(b) Carrying value of old asset unknown.	(1) If the asset's useful life is extended, debit accumulated depreciation for the cost.
		(2) If the quantity or quality of the asset's productivity is increased and carrying value near fully depreciated, capitalize cost to asset account.
Rearrangement and Reinstallation	(a) Original installation cost known.	Treat as a replacement.
	(b) Original cost unknown, new costs are material in amount and benefit future periods.	Capitalize as an asset.
	(c) Cost not material or future benefit questionable.	Expense the cost when incurred.
Repairs	(a) Ordinary maintenance.	Expense the cost when incurred.
	(b) Major—material in amount, increases the use value or extends the useful life.	Treat as an addition, improvement, or replacement depending on the type of repair.

DISPOSITIONS OF PLANT ASSETS

Plant assets may be retired voluntarily or disposed of by sale, exchange, involuntary conversion, or abandonment. **Regardless of the time of disposal, depreciation should be taken up to the date of disposition, and all accounts related to the retired asset should be removed from the accounts.** Ideally, the book value of the specific plant asset would be equal to its disposal value. This is generally not the case, however, and a resulting gain or loss occurs.

This gain or loss develops because depreciation is a process of cost allocation and not a process of valuation. The gain or loss in most situations is in reality a correction of net income for the years during which the fixed asset was used. If it had been possible at the time of acquisition to forecast the exact date of disposal and the amount to be realized at disposition, then a more accurate estimate of depreciation could have been recorded and no gain or loss would have developed.

In accordance with Section 3480 of the *CICA Handbook*, gains and losses on the retirement of plant assets should normally be shown in the income statement along with other items that arise from customary business activities. If, however, the disposal involves ''sale or abandonment of a plant or significant segment of the enterprise,'' the gain or loss should be reported as an extraordinary item. These reporting requirements were discussed in Chapter 4.

Sale of Plant Assets

The problems related to the outright sale of a plant asset are relatively simple. Depreciation should be recorded for the period of time between the date of the last depreciation entry and the date of retirement. To illustrate, assume that depreciation on a machine costing $18,000 has been recorded for nine years at the rate of $1,200 per year. If the machine is sold in the middle of the tenth year for $7,000, the entry to record depreciation to the date of sale is:

Depreciation Expense	600	
Accumulated Depreciation of Machinery		600

The entry for the sale of the asset is:

Cash	7,000	
Accumulated Depreciation of Machinery	11,400	
($1,200 × 9 plus $600)		
Machinery		18,000
Gain on Disposal of Plant Assets		400

The book value of the machinery at the time of the sale is $6,600 ($18,000 − $11,400); because it is sold for $7,000, the amount of the gain on the sale is $400.

Involuntary Conversion

Sometimes, an asset's service is terminated through some type of involuntary conversion such as fire, theft, expropriation, and so on. The accounting problems in this area are not difficult, inasmuch as the gains and losses are no different from those in any other type of disposition.

To illustrate, Camel Transport Corp. was forced to sell a plant located on company property that stood directly in the path of a proposed highway. For a number of years the province had sought to purchase the land on which the plant stood but the company resisted. The province ultimately exercised its right of eminent domain and was upheld by the courts. In settlement, Camel received $500,000, which was substantially in excess of the $200,000 book value of the plant (cost of $300,000 less accumulated depreciation of $200,000) and land (cost of $100,000). The following entry was made:

Cash	500,000	
Accumulated Depreciation of Plant Assets	200,000	
Plant Assets		300,000
Land		100,000
Gain on Disposal of Plant Assets		300,000

The gain or loss that develops on these types of unusual, nonrecurring transactions should normally be shown as an extraordinary item in the income statement. Similar treatment would be given to other types of involuntary conversions such as those resulting from a major casualty (e.g., an earthquake) or an expropriation, assuming that it meets the conditions for extraordinary item treatment. The difference between the amount recovered (condemnation award or insurance recovery), if any, and the book value of the asset would be reflected as a gain or loss. The determination of the insurance proceeds to be received in a casualty situation is sometimes quite complex; it is discussed in the appendix to this chapter.

Miscellaneous Problems

If an asset is scrapped or abandoned without any cash recovery, a loss should be recognized in the amount of the asset's book value. If scrap value exists, the gain or loss that occurs is the difference between the asset's scrap value and its book value. If an asset still can be used even though it is fully depreciated, either the asset may be kept on the books at historical cost less its related depreciation, or the asset may be carried at scrap value. If the asset is written up or down to scrap value, the gain or loss could be recognized, although many accountants believe that recognition of the gain or loss violates the principle of realization. Note disclosure of fully depreciated assets in service should be made in the financial statements.

OTHER ASSET VALUATION METHODS

We have generally assumed that accountants have used cost as the basis for valuing assets at acquisition. The major exception has been the acquisition of plant assets through donation. Another approach that is sometimes allowed and not considered a violation of historical cost is a concept often referred to as **prudent cost.** This concept states that if for some reason you were ignorant about a certain price and paid too much for the asset originally, it is theoretically preferable to charge a loss immediately. As an example, assume that a company constructs an asset at a cost substantially in excess of its present economic usefulness. In this case, an appropriate procedure would be to charge these excess costs as a loss to the current period, rather than capitalize them as part of the cost of the asset. This problem seldom develops because at the outset individuals either use good reasoning in paying a given price or fail to recognize any such errors. On the other hand, a purchase that is obtained at a bargain, or a piece of equipment internally constructed at what amounts to a cost savings, should not result in immediate recognition of income under any circumstances. Although immediate recognition of income is conceptually appealing, the implications of such a treatment would be to change completely the entire basis of accounting.

There are several concepts of valuation other than historical cost that might be used to value property, plant, and equipment, such as (1) constant dollar accounting (adjustments for general price-level changes), (2) current cost accounting (adjustments for specific price-level changes), (3) fair market value, or (4) a combination of constant dollar accounting and one of these other methods. These valuation methods are discussed in Chapter 25.

The general accounting rule of lower of cost and market does not apply to property, plant, and equipment. Even when property, plant, and equipment have suffered partial obsolescence, accountants are reluctant to write it down to net realizable value. This reluctance stems from the fact that it is difficult to arrive at a net realizable value that is not subjective and arbitrary for property, plant, and equipment, unlike inventories, for which values can be obtained more easily. In addition, many argue that depreciation is a method of cost allocation and, therefore, should not be concerned with valuation. Finally, there is some concern that permitting write-offs of this type may lead companies to make unreasonable write-offs in bad years to ensure that future periods will be relieved of these costs (the "big bath" phenomenon). We are not sympathetic with these arguments and believe that whenever a **permanent impairment** in the revenue-producing ability of property, plant, and equipment occurs, a loss should be recognized.

KEY POINTS

1. **Historical cost**, as measured by the cash or cash equivalent price of obtaining an asset and bringing it to the location and condition necessary for its intended use, is the usual basis for valuing property, plant, and equipment.

2. Recording an asset at the fair market value of what is given up to acquire it or at its own fair value is complicated by such things as cash discounts, deferred payment plans, lump sum purchases, issuance of securities, interest capitalization, acquisition by gift, internal construction, and nonmonetary exchanges.

3. **Interest** may be capitalized as part of certain assets under construction, starting with the first expenditure related to the asset and continuing until the asset is substantially complete and ready for use.

4. The general rule in accounting for **exchanges of nonmonetary assets** is to record the fair value inherent in the exchange. Exceptions to this general policy occur if fair value is not determinable or if the exchange is not the completion of the earning process.

5. The exchange of **dissimilar nonmonetary assets** is viewed as a completion of the earning process requiring measurement and recognition of either a gain or a loss. In exchanges of **similar nonmonetary assets**, the earnings process is not considered complete and gains are not recognized (unless some cash is received), but losses are recognized immediately.

6. **Nonreciprocal transfers** of assets are one-sided transactions, either receipts of gifts or donations of assets. The appraisal or fair market value of the asset should be used to establish a reasonable basis of valuation.

7. **Costs subsequent to acquisition** are either capitalized or expensed, depending on whether they are incurred to achieve greater future benefits (capitalize) or to maintain a given level of services (expense). In order for such costs to be capitalized, one of three conditions must be present: (1) the useful life of the asset must be increased; (2) the quantity of units produced must be increased; or (3) the quality of the units produced must be enhanced.

8. At the time of **disposal of plant assets**, depreciation should be taken up to the date of disposition, all accounts related to the retired assets should be removed from the accounts, and any gain or loss should be recognized.

9. **Disposals of plant assets** may result from sale, involuntary conversion, abandonment, or exchange and may result in gains or losses includable in income determination.

10A

CASUALTY INSURANCE

Business enterprises constantly face the risk of loss of assets by fire, storm, theft, accident, or other casualties. Generally companies shift the burden of such losses by entering into a casualty insurance contract whereby an insurance company in consideration for a premium payment assumes the risk of all or a portion of these losses. The premium, a charge per $100 of insurance carried, is paid in advance. Many companies pay insurance premiums in advance because a premium discount is given when the term of the policy exceeds one year, thereby creating the asset (deferred charge) **prepaid insurance.**

When an insured asset is damaged, destroyed, or lost, the relevant accounts must be adjusted and settlement with the insurance company must be completed. The maximum amount recoverable is the **fair market value** of the property at the date of loss and is referred to as the **insurable value.** Although the book value is irrelevant in determining the amount recoverable from the insurance company, it is used for accounting purposes to measure the loss (or gain) resulting from the casualty and any insurance settlement. For example, if $40,000 is recovered under an insurance policy after the complete destruction of an asset having a book value of $34,000, a gain of $6,000 would be recognized. In some instances the amount recoverable is limited by some special feature such as a **deductible clause** in the case of automobile insurance (e.g., $50 or $100 deductible) or a **coinsurance clause** in the case of fire insurance.

Coinsurance

Because most assets are only partially destroyed by any casualty, companies would take out only enough insurance to cover a fraction of the value of the asset and receive full reimbursement of most losses if they were not encouraged through a coinsurance clause to do otherwise. Most casualty insurance policies therefore contain a **coinsurance clause** which provides that if the property is insured for less than a certain percentage (frequently 80%) of its fair market value (insurable value) at the time of the loss, the insurance company will be liable for only a portion of any loss; that is, the owner becomes a **coinsurer** with the insurance company.

Coinsurance means that the amount recoverable is in the same proportion to the loss as the face value of the policy (amount of insurance carried) is to the coinsurance requirement (amount of insurance that should be carried). As a formula, coinsurance may be stated as follows:

$$\frac{\text{Face value of policy}}{\text{Coinsurance requirement}} \times \text{Loss} = \text{Amount Recoverable}$$

The following example illustrates the use of the formula in determining the amount recoverable using an 80% coinsurance clause.

Amount Recoverable Under Coinsurance	Case 1	Case 2	Case 3	Case 4
Fair market value	$10,000	$10,000	$10,000	$10,000
Face value of policy	7,000	5,000	9,000	8,000
Coinsurance requirement	8,000	8,000	8,000	8,000
Amount of loss	6,000	6,000	6,000	9,000
Amount recoverable	5,250[a]	3,750[b]	6,000[c]	8,000[d]

[a]$\dfrac{\$7,000}{\$8,000} \times \$6,000 = \$5,250$

[c]$\dfrac{\$9,000}{\$8,000} \times \$6,000 = \$6,750*$

[b]$\dfrac{\$5,000}{\$8,000} \times \$6,000 = \$3,750$

[d]$\dfrac{\$8,000}{\$8,000} \times \$9,000 = \$9,000**$

*Amount recoverable limited to amount of loss.
**Amount recoverable limited to face value of policy.

As illustrated above, **the amount recoverable from the insurance company is the lowest of (1) the amount of the loss, (2) the face value of the policy, or (3) the coinsurance formula amount**.

Recovery from Multiple Policies

If an asset is insured under two or more insurance policies, all of which have the same or **no coinsurance** requirement, recovery of a loss is obtained from the different policies in proportion to the face value of each policy. If the policies have **different coinsurance** requirements, the amount recoverable under each of the policies is computed by multiplying the loss by a fraction, the numerator of which is the face value of the individual policy, and the denominator of which is the higher of (1) the total face value of all policies, or (2) the amount required under the coinsurance requirement of the particular policy.

To illustrate, assume that an asset having a fair market value of $100,000 is insured under policies presented below, and that a fire loss of $72,000 is suffered. If the policies contain the same (90%) coinsurance requirement, recovery from each policy would be as follows:

Amount Recoverable under Multiple Policies with Identical Coinsurance					
Policy	Face Value	Coinsurance Requirement	Fraction	Loss	Amount Collectible
A	$30,000	$90,000	30/90	$72,000	$24,000
B	40,000	90,000	40/90	72,000	32,000
C	10,000	90,000	10/90	72,000	8,000
	$80,000				$64,000

If the policies contain different (70%, 85%, and 90%) coinsurance requirements, recovery from each policy would be as follows:

Amount Recoverable under Multiple Policies with Different Coinsurance					
Policy	Face Value	Coinsurance Requirement	Fraction	Loss	Amount Collectible
A	$30,000	$70,000	30/80	$72,000	$27,000
B	40,000	85,000	40/85	72,000	33,882
C	10,000	90,000	10/90	72,000	8,000
	$80,000				$68,882

Accounting for Casualty Losses

In the event of a casualty loss, the accounting records as maintained or as reconstructed (if destroyed in the casualty) must be adjusted as of the date of the casualty. The loss may be summarized in a casualty loss account, charging such account for the book value of the assets destroyed or damaged and crediting it for amounts recoverable from salvage and from insurance companies. The total amount recoverable (receivable) from the insurance companies would be classified as a current asset if current settlement is anticipated. If the casualty loss is material and the consequence of an unusual and infrequent event or circumstance, it would be classified as an extraordinary item.

Because the amount recovered under insurance policies is based upon fair market and appraised values, the insurance proceeds may exceed the book value of the assets destroyed or damaged. The excess of insurance proceeds over the book value should be presented as a book gain.

Note: All **asterisked** Questions, Cases, Exercises, or Problems relate to material contained in an Appendix.

QUESTIONS

1. What are the major characteristics of plant assets?
2. Indicate where the following items would be shown on a balance sheet.
    (a) A parking lot servicing employees in the building.
    (b) The cost of demolishing an old building that was on the land when purchased.
    (c) A lien that was attached to the land when purchased.
    (d) Landscaping costs.
    (e) Attorney's fees and recording fees related to purchasing land.
    (f) Variable overhead related to construction of machinery.
    (g) Cost of temporary building for workers during construction of building.
    (h) Interest expense on bonds payable incurred during construction of a building.
    (i) Sidewalks that are maintained by the city.
3. Once equipment has been installed and placed in operation, subsequent expenditures relating to this equipment are frequently thought of as being in the nature of repairs or general maintenance and, hence, chargeable to operations in the period in which the expenditure is made. Actually, determination of whether such an expenditure should be charged to operations or capitalized involves a much more careful analysis of the character of the expenditure. What are the factors that should be considered in making such a decision? Discuss fully.
4. What accounting treatment is normally given to the following items in accounting for plant assets?
    (a) Additions.
    (b) Major repairs.
    (c) Improvements and replacements.
5. Name the items, in addition to the amount paid to the former owner or contractor, that may be properly included as part of the acquisition cost of the following plant assets:
    (a) Land.
    (b) Machinery and equipment.
    (c) Buildings.
6. Three positions have normally been taken with respect to the recording of fixed manufacturing overhead as an element of the cost of plant assets constructed by a company for its own use:
    (a) It should be excluded completely.
    (b) It should be included at the same rate as is charged to normal operations.
    (c) It should be allocated on the basis of the lost production that occurs from normal operations.
    What are the circumstances or rationale that support or deny the application of these methods?
7. What interest rates should be used in determining the amount of interest to be capitalized? How should the amount of interest to be capitalized be determined?
8. How should the amount of interest capitalized be disclosed in the notes to the financial statements? How should interest revenue from temporarily invested excess funds borrowed to finance the construction of assets be accounted for?
9. Expenditures may be divided into two general categories: (1) capital expenditures and (2) revenue expenditures.
    (a) Distinguish between these two categories of expenditures and between their treatments in the accounts.
    (b) Discuss the impact on both present and future balance sheets and income statements of improperly distinguishing between capital and revenue expenditures.
    (c) What criteria do accountants generally use in establishing a policy for classifying expenditures under these two general categories?

10. The Hunt Trucking Company purchased a heavy-duty truck on July 1, 1982, for $30,000. It was estimated that it would have a useful life of ten years and then would have a trade-in value of $6,000. It was traded on October 1, 1986, for a similar truck costing $38,000; $14,000 was allowed as trade-in value (also fair value) on the old truck, and $24,000 was paid in cash. What is the entry to record the trade-in? The company uses the straight-line method.

11. The Buildings account of a corporation includes the following items that were used in determining the basis for depreciating the cost of a building:
    (a) Organization and promotion expenses.
    (b) Architect's fees.
    (c) Interest and taxes during construction.
    (d) Commission paid on the sale of capital stock.
    (e) Bond discount and expenses.
    Do you agree with these charges? If not, how would you deal with each of the items above in the corporation's books and in its annual financial statements?

12. New machinery, which replaced a number of employees, was installed and put in operation in the last month of the fiscal year. The employees had been dismissed after payment of an extra month's wages, and this amount was added to the cost of the machinery. Discuss the propriety of the charge and, if it was improper, describe the proper treatment.

13. To what extent do you consider the following items to be proper costs of the fixed asset? Give reasons for your opinions.
    (a) Freight on equipment returned before installation, for replacement by other equipment of greater capacity.
    (b) Cost of moving machinery to a new location.
    (c) Cost of plywood partitions erected as part of the remodeling of the office.
    (d) Replastering of a section of the building.
    (e) Cost of a new motor for one of the trucks.
    (f) Overhead of a business that builds its own equipment.
    (g) Cost of constructing new models of machinery.
    (h) Cash discounts on purchases of equipment.
    (i) Interest paid during construction of a building.
    (j) Cost of a safety device installed on a machine.

14. Discuss the basic accounting problem that arises in handling each of the following situations.
    (a) Assets purchased by issuance of share capital.
    (b) Acquisition of plant assets by gift or donation.
    (c) Purchase of a plant asset subject to a cash discount.
    (d) Assets purchased on a long-term credit basis.
    (e) A group of assets acquired for a lump sum.
    (f) An asset traded in or exchanged for another asset.

15. Recently, Atlantic Manufacturing Co. presented the account "Allowance for Repairs" in the long-term liability section. Evaluate this procedure.

16. Electrohome Enterprises has a number of fully depreciated assets that are still being used in the main operations of the business. Because the assets are fully depreciated, the president of the company decides not to show them on the balance sheet or disclose this information in the notes. Evaluate this procedure.

17. Recently, Gremlin, Inc. decided to discontinue production of one of its product lines because demand for it had fallen substantially. Although it is highly unlikely that the plant may be used for this type of production in the future, the controller is reluctant to write the plant down to its net realizable value. Why might the controller be reluctant to write the asset down?

*18. What is the objective of a coinsurance clause in a casualty insurance policy?

CASES

C10-1 Wetzel Medical, Inc. began operations five years ago producing stetrics, a new type of instrument it hoped to sell to doctors, dentists, and hospitals. The demand for stetrics far exceeded initial expectations, and the company was unable to produce enough stetrics to meet demand.

The company was manufacturing its product on equipment that it built at the start of its operations. To meet demand, more efficient equipment was needed. The company decided to design and build the equipment, since the equipment currently available on the market was unsuitable for producing stetrics.

In 1986, a section of the plant was devoted to development of the new equipment, and a special staff of personnel was hired. Within six months a machine was developed at a cost of $420,000 which successfully increased production and reduced labour costs substantially. Sparked by the success of the new machine, the company built three more machines of the same type ot a cost of $260,000 each.

Instructions

    (a)   In general, what costs should be capitalized for self-constructed equipment?

    (b)   Discuss the propriety of including in the capitalized cost of self-constructed assets:

        1.   The increase in overhead caused by the self-construction of fixed assets.

        2.   A proportionate share of overhead on the same basis as that applied to goods manufactured for sale.

    (c)   Discuss the proper accounting treatment of the $160,000 ($420,000 − $260,000) by which the cost of the first machine exceeded the cost of the subsequent machines. This additional cost should not be considered research and development costs.

C10-2   Your client, Steetly Industries Ltd., found three suitable sites, each having certain unique advantages, for a new plant facility. In order to investigate thoroughly the advantages and disadvantages of each site, one-year options were purchased for an amount equal to 6% of the contract price of each site. The costs of the options could not be applied against the contracts. Before the options expired, one of the sites was purchased at the contract price of $180,000. The option on this site had cost $10,800. The two options not exercised had cost $7,000 each.

Instructions

Present arguments in support of recording the cost of the land at each of the following amounts.

    (a) $180,000.

    (b) $190,800.

    (c) $204,800.

                             (AICPA adapted)

C10-3   You have recently been hired as a junior accountant in the firm of Toe and Crossfoot. Mr. Crossfoot is an alumnus of the same school from which you graduated and, therefore, is quite interested in your accounting training. He therefore presents the following situations and asks for your response.

    1.   Recently a construction company agreed to construct a new hospital for its client at the construction company's cost; that is, the contractor was to realize no profit. The construction company was interested in performing this service because it had substantial interests in the community and wanted to make the community more attractive. The building was completed in 1986, and the costs of the hospital were $17,000,000. An appraisal firm indicated, however, that the fair market value of the properties was $18,500,000, the difference due to the $1,500,000 that the company did not charge the hospital.

Instructions

At what amount should the hospital value the asset? A related question is whether the donated profit on the hospital should be reported as revenue or as a capital contribution. What is your answer to this question?

2.   Recently, one of our clients asked whether it would be appropriate to capitalize a portion of the salaries of the corporate officers for time spent on construction activities. During construction, one of the officers devotes full time to the supervision of construction projects. His activities are similar to those of a construction superintendent for a general contractor. During periods of heavy construction activity, this officer also employs several assistants to help with administrative matters related to construction. All other officers are general corporate officers.

The compensation and other costs related to the construction officer do not depend upon the level of construction activity in a particular period (except to the extent that additional assistants are employed on a short-term basis). These expenses would continue to be incurred even if there were no construction activity unless the company decided to discontinue permanently, or in the foreseeable future, all construction activities. In that case, it could well reach the decision to terminate the service of the construction officer. The company has, however, aggressive expansion plans that anticipate continuing construction of shopping centre properties.

Instructions

What salary costs, if any, should be capitalized to the cost of properties?

3.   Every few years one of our clients publishes a new catalogue for distribution to its sales outlets and customers. The latest catalogue was published in 1982. Periodically, current price lists and new product brochures are issued. The company is now contemplating the issue of a new catalogue during the latter part of 1986. The cost of the new catalogue has been accounted for as follows:

(a)   Estimated total cost of the catalogue is accounted for over a period beginning with the initial planning (1983) and is expected to end at time of publication.

(b)   Estimated costs are accumulated in an accrued liability account through monthly charges to selling expenses.

(c)   Monthly charges were based upon the estimated total cost of the guide and the estimated number of months remaining before publication; periodic revisions were made to the estimates as current information became available.

(d)   Actual costs were recorded as charges to the accrued liability account as they were accrued.

In summary, the company accrues the entire estimated cost (including anticipated costs to be incurred) of a contemplated catalogue through charges to operations prior to the expected publication date.

Instructions

Comment on the propriety of this treatment.

C10-4   You have been engaged to examine the financial statements of Pipeline Corporation for the year ending December 31, 1986. Pipeline Corporation was organized in January, 1986, by Messrs. Norton and Sanders, original owners of options to acquire oil leases on 5,000 ha of land for $700,000. They expected that first the oil leases would be acquired by the corporation and subsequently 180,000 shares of the corporation's common stock would be sold to the public at $12 per share. In February 1986, they exchanged their options, $300,000 cash, and $100,000 of other assets for 75,000 shares of common stock of the corporation. The corporation's board of directors appraised the leases at $1,200,000, based on the price of other parcels recently leased in the same area. The options were therefore recorded at $500,000 ($1,200,000—$700,000 option price).

The options were exercised by the corporation in March, 1986, prior to the sale of common stock to the public in April, 1986. Leases on approximately 500 ha of land were abandoned as worthless during the year.

Instructions

(a)   Why is the valuation of assets acquired by a corporation in exchange for its own common shares sometimes difficult?

(b)   1.   What reasoning might Pipeline Corporation use to support valuing the leases at $1,200,000, the amount of the appraisal by the board of directors?

2. Assuming that the board's appraisal was sincere, what steps might Pipeline Corporation have taken to strengthen its position to use the $1,200,000 value and to provide additional information if questions were raised about possible overvaluation of the leases?

(c) Discuss the propriety of charging one-tenth of the recorded value of the leases to expense at December 31, 1986, because leases on 500 ha of land were abandoned during the year.

(AICPA adapted)

C10-5 The invoice price of a machine is $30,000. Various other costs relating to the acquisition and installation of the machine including transportation, electrical wiring, special base, and so on amount to $5,000. The machine has an estimated life of 10 years, with no residual value at the end of that period.

The owner of the business suggests that the incidental costs of $5,000 be charged to expense immediately for the following reasons:

1. If the machine should be sold, these costs cannot be recovered in the sales price;

2. The inclusion of the $5,000 in the machinery account on the books will not necessarily result in a closer approximation of the market price of this asset over the years, because of the possibility of changing demand and supply levels; and

3. Charging the $5,000 to expense immediately will reduce income taxes.

Instructions

Discuss **each** of the points raised by the owner of the business.

(AICPA adapted)

C10-6 Flypaper Airline is converting from piston-type planes to jets. Delivery time for the jets is three years, during which period substantial progress payments must be made. The multimillion-dollar cost of the planes cannot be financed from working capital; Flypaper must borrow funds for the payments.

Because of high interest rates and the large sum to be borrowed, management estimates that interest costs in the second year of the period will be equal to one-third of income before interest and taxes, and one-half of such income in the third year.

After conversion, Flypaper's passenger-carrying capacity will be doubled with no increase in the number of planes, although the investment in planes would be substantially increased. The jet planes have a seven-year service life.

Instructions

Give your recommendation concerning the proper accounting for interest during the conversion period. Support your recommendation with reasons **and** suggested accounting treatment. (Disregard income tax implications.)

(AICPA adapted)

C10-7 Curt See Company purchased land for use as its corporate headquarters. A small factory that was on the land when it was purchased was torn down before construction of the office building began. Furthermore, a substantial amount of rock blasting and removal had to be done to the site before construction of the building foundation began. Because the office building was set on the land far from the public road, Curt See Company had the contractor construct a paved road that led from the public road to the parking lot of the office building.

Three years after the office building was occupied, Curt See Company added four storeys to the office building. The four storeys had an estimated useful life of five years more than the remaining useful life of the original office building.

Ten years later, the land and building were sold at an amount more than their book value, and Curt See Company had a new office building constructed in another province for its new corporate headquarters.

Instructions

(a) Which of the above expenditures should be capitalized? How should each be depreciated or amortized? Discuss the rationale for your answer.

(b)   How would the sale of the land and building be accounted for? Include in your answer how to determine the net book value at the date of sale. Discuss the rationale for your answer.

EXERCISES

E10-1   Read Limited, a newly formed corporation, incurred the following expenditures related to Land, to Buildings, and to Machinery and Equipment.

Architect's fees		$ 2,200
Cash paid for land and dilapidated building thereon		66,000
Removal of old building	$9,000	
Less: Salvage	1,200	7,800
Realtor's fee for title search		270
Surveying before construction		450
Interest on short-term loans during construction		6,500
Excavation before construction for basement		13,700
Machinery purchased (subject to 3% cash discount, which was not taken); record net		44,000
Freight on machinery purchased		750
Storage charges on machinery, necessitated by noncompletion of building when machinery was delivered		1,070
New building constructed (building construction took six months from date of purchase of land and old building)		400,000
B Assessment by city for drainage project		900
M Hauling charges for delivery of machinery from storage to new building		300
L Trees, shrubs, and other landscaping after completion of building (permanent in nature)		4,500
M Installation of machinery		1,400

Instructions

Determine the amounts that should be debited to Land, to Buildings, and to Machinery and Equipment accounts. Assume the benefits of capitalizing interest during construction exceed the cost of implementation.

E10-2   Moore Co. purchased land as a factory site for $300,000. The process of tearing down two old buildings on the site and constructing the factory required six months.

   The company paid $12,000 to raze the old buildings and sold salvaged lumber and brick for $2,100. Legal fees of $1,560 were paid for title registration and drawing the purchase contract. Payment to an engineering firm was made for a land survey, $1,800, and for drawing the factory plans, $60,000. The land survey had to be made before definitive plans could be drawn. Title insurance on the property cost $1,500, and a liability insurance premium paid during construction was $600. The contractor's charge for construction was $2,250,000. The company paid the contractor in two instalments: $1,200,000 at the end of three months and $1,050,000 upon completion. Interest costs of $45,000 were incurred to finance the construction.

Instructions

Determine the cost of the land and the cost of the building as they should be recorded on the books of the Moore Co. Assume that the land survey was for the building.

E10-3   Triple Value Construction Company started construction of a combination office and warehouse building for their own use at an estimated cost of $3,500,000 on October 1, 1986. Triple Value expects to complete the building by June 30, 1987. Triple Value has the following debt obligations during the construction period.

	Balance October 1, 1986
Construction loan—15%, interest payable monthly, principal due one month after completion of the new building.	$1,200,000
Short-term loan—20%, interest and principal payable at maturity on September 30, 1987.	500,000
Long-term loan—10%, interest payable on January 1st of each year. Principal payable on January 1, 1992.	900,000

Instructions

(a) If Triple Value Construction completed the office and warehouse building on June 30, 1987, as planned at a total cost of $3,600,000 and the average accumulated expenditures were $1,900,000, compute the avoidable interest on this project. (Round all decimals to four places.)

(b) Assuming the actual interest incurred exceeded the avoidable interest, compute the depreciation expense for the year ended December 31, 1987. Triple Value elected to depreciate the building on a straight-line method and determined that the asset has a useful life of ten years and a salvage value of $23,000.

E10-4 On July 31, 1986, the Downing Company engaged the Collins Machine Tooling Company to construct a special-purpose piece of factory machinery. Construction was begun immediately and was completed on November 1, 1986. To help finance construction, on July 31 Downing discounted a $160,000, 3-year noninterest-bearing note, payable at the Bank of Montreal. Interest on the note should be imputed at 12%, and the discount is to be amortized using the straight-line method. (Hint: Calculate the present value of the note to find the proceeds received by Downing.) Seventy-five thousand dollars of the proceeds of the note was paid to Collins on July 31. The remainder of the proceeds was temporarily invested in short-term marketable securities at 10% until November 1. On November 1, Downing made a final $75,000 payment to Collins. Other than the note to the Bank of Montreal, the only outstanding liability at December 31, 1986 is a $20,000, 8%, 6-year note payable, dated January 1, 1984, on which interest is payable each December 31.

Instructions

(a) Calculate the interest revenue, average accumulated expenditures, avoidable interest, and total interest cost to be capitalized during 1986. Round all computations to the nearest dollar.

(b) Prepare the journal entries needed on the books of Downing Company on each of the following dates:
1. July 31, 1986
2. November 1, 1986 (Capitalize interest at year end.)
3. December 31, 1986 (Ignore depreciation entry.)

E10-5 Woodley's Machine Shop builds machines for its regular manufacturing department. During 1986, the company built a machine that had the following costs associated with it:

	Machinery Cost
Material and purchased parts	$10,000
Freight on material and parts	700
Insurance in transit	90
Implicit interest on tied-up working capital	210
Labour to build	12,000
Labour to test	2,500
Overhead	7,000
	$32,500

The machine immediately after construction has a fair market value of $35,000.

Instructions

What dollar amount should appear in Woodley's balance sheet for this machinery?

E10-6   Prozit, Inc. has decided to purchase equipment from Tillie Industries on January 1, 1986, to expand its production capacity to meet customers' demand for its product. Prozit issues a $600,000, 5-year, noninterest-bearing note to Tillie for the new equipment when the prevailing market rate of interest for obligations of this nature is 12%. The company will pay off the note in five equal instalments of $120,000 due at the end of each year over the life of the note.

Instructions

(a)   Prepare the journal entry (entries) at the date of purchase. (Round to nearest dollar in all computations.)

(b)   Prepare the journal entry (entries) at the end of the first year to record the payment and interest, assuming that the company employs the effective interest method.

(c)   Prepare the journal entry (entries) at the end of the second year to record the payment and interest.

(d)   Assuming that the equipment had a ten-year life and no salvage value, prepare the journal entry necessary to record depreciation in the first year. (Straight-line depreciation is employed.)

E10-7   Wasco Ltd. purchased a computer on December 31, 1985, for $90,000, paying $15,000 down and agreeing to pay the balance in five equal instalments of $15,000 payable each December 31 beginning in 1986. An assumed interest of 12% is implicit in the purchase price.

Instructions

(a)   Prepare the journal entry (entries) at the date of purchase. (Round to two decimal places.)

(b)   Prepare the journal entry (entries) at December 31, 1986, to record the payment and interest (effective interest method employed).

(c)   Prepare the journal entry (entries) at December 31, 1987, to record the payment and interest (effective interest method employed).

E10-8   The Spats Corporation, which manufactures shoes, hired a recent college graduate to work in their accounting department. On the first day of work, the accountant was assigned to total a batch of invoices with the use of an adding machine. Before long, the accountant, who had never before seen such a machine, managed to break it. Spats Corporation gave the machine plus $680 to Brent Business Machines Ltd. in exchange for a new one. Assume the following information about the machines:

	Spats Corp. (Old Machine)	Brent Business Machines Ltd. (New Machine)
Machine cost	$600	$540
Accumulated depreciation	310	-0-
Fair value	170	850

Instructions

For each company, prepare the necessary journal entry to record the exchange.

E10-9   Doreen Company exchanged equipment used in its manufacturing operations plus $3,000 in cash for similar equipment used in the operations of Atle Sutland Company. The following information pertains to the exchange:

	Doreen Co.	Atle Sutland Co.
Equipment (cost)	$25,000	$23,000
Accumulated depreciation	21,000	6,000
Fair value of equipment	12,000	15,000
Cash given up	3,000	

Instructions

Prepare the journal entries to record the exchange on the books of both companies.

E10-10 Jackie Kiss Ltd. has negotiated the purchase of a new piece of automatic equipment at a price of $48,000, f.o.b. factory. Jackie Kiss Ltd. paid $8,000 cash, gave an instalment note calling for monthly payments of $4,000 for ten months plus interest at 12% on the unpaid balance, and traded in used equipment. The used equipment had originally cost $30,000; it had a book value of $12,000 and a second-hand market value of $7,300, as indicated by recent transactions involving similar equipment. Freight and installation charges for the new equipment amounted to $1,600.

Instructions

(a) Prepare the general journal entry to record this transaction, assuming that the assets Jackie Kiss Ltd. exchanged are similar in nature.

(b) Assuming the same facts as in (a) except that the asset traded in has a fair market value of $15,000, prepare the general journal entry to record this transaction.

E10-11 Wicks Company purchased an electric wax melter on June 30, 1986, by trading in their old gas model and paying the balance in cash. The following data relate to the purchase:

List price of new melter	$16,000
Cash paid	9,700
Cost of old melter (eight-year life, $400 residual value)	11,200
Accumulated depreciation—old melter (straight-line)	5,400
Second-hand market value of old melter	5,320

Instructions

Prepare the journal entry (entries) necessary to record this exchange, assuming that the melters exchanged are (a) similar in nature and (b) dissimilar in nature. Wick's fiscal year ends on December 31, and depreciation has been recorded through December 31, 1985.

E10-12 On October 1, Jock's, a local entertainment establishment, acquired a new piano that had a list price of $2,700. Jock's received a trade-in allowance of $1,200 on its old piano, which had a book value of $900 (original cost $1,400). The fair market value of the old piano was $800. The balance owed by Jock's was paid in cash.

Instructions

(a) Prepare the journal entry to record this transaction.

(b) What significance does the list price have for this computation?

E10-13 Presented below is information related to Readyrite Company.

1. On July 6 Readyrite Company acquired the plant assets of Tom Hack Company, which had discontinued operations. The appraised value of the property is:

Land	$ 200,000
Building	1,200,000
Machinery and Equipment	400,000
Total	$1,800,000

Readyrite Company gave 12,000 shares of its no-par common stock in exchange. The stock had a market value of $120 per share on the date of the purchase of the property.

2. Readyrite Company expended the following amounts in cash between July 6 and December 15, the date when it first occupied the building.

Repairs to building	$ 75,000
Construction of bases for machinery to be installed later	120,000
Driveways and parking lots	110,000
Remodelling of office space in building, including new partitions and walls	160,000
Special assessment by city	12,000

3. On December 20, the company paid $200,000 cash for machinery, subject to a 2% cash discount, and freight of $7,000.

Instructions

Prepare entries on the books of Readyrite Company for these transactions.

E10-14 Below are transactions related to McDonald Manufacturing Company.

1. On March 10, 1986, McDonald Manufacturing Company purchases land with an appraised value of $12,000 and buildings with an appraised value of $30,000 for $37,800.

2. Between March 10, 1986, and September 1, 1986, the date of occupancy, the company expends the following amounts in cash.

Additional wing constructed	$22,000
Replastering	3,600
Additional windows and doors	2,500
Repairs to roof	2,640
Brick pointing and masonry repairs	4,540
Painting and decorating	4,920

Instructions

(a) Prepare entries on the books of the McDonald Manufacturing Company to reflect the information given above.

(b) Prepare entries to record depreciation on a straight-line basis at December 31, 1986, assuming a 20-year life.

E10-15 Below are transactions related to Lindbergh Company.

1. The City of Saskatoon gives the company five ha of land as a plant site. The market value of this land is determined to be $45,000.

2. Ten thousand common shares were issued in exchange for land and buildings. The property has been appraised at a fair market value of $560,000, of which $200,000 has been allocated to land and $360,000 to buildings. The shares of the Lindbergh Company are not listed on any exchange, but a block of 100 shares was sold by a shareholder 12 months ago at $60 per share, and a block of 200 shares was sold by another shareholder 18 months ago at $55 per share.

3. No entry has been made to remove from the accounts for Materials, Factory Supplies, Direct Labour, and Overhead the amounts properly chargeable to plant asset accounts for machinery constructed during the year. The following information is given relative to costs of the machinery constructed.

Materials used	$ 9,000
Factory supplies used	800
Direct labour incurred	10,000
Additional overhead (over regular) caused by adaptation of equipment to construct special machine	1,800
Fixed overhead rate applied to regular manufacturing operations	50% of direct labour cost
Cost of similar machinery if it had been purchased from outside suppliers	31,000

Instructions

Prepare journal entries on the books of the Lindbergh Company to record these transactions.

E10-16   The following transactions occurred during 1986. Assume that depreciation of 12 1/2% per year is charged on all machinery and 5% per year on buildings, on a straight-line basis, with no estimated salvage value. Depreciation is charged for a full year on all fixed assets acquired during the year, and no depreciation is charged on fixed assets disposed of during the year.

Jan. 30   A building that cost $45,000 in 1968 is torn down to make room for a new building. The wrecking contractor was paid $3,000 and was permitted to keep all materials salvaged.

Mar. 10   Machinery that was purchased in 1979 for $12,000 is sold for $1,350 cash, f.o.b. purchaser's plant. Freight of $300 is paid on this machinery.

Mar. 20   A gear breaks on a machine that cost $9,000 in 1980, and the gear is replaced at a cost of $400.

May 18   A special base installed for a machine in 1981 when the machine was purchased has to be replaced at a cost of $4,500 because of defective workmanship on the original base. The cost of the machinery was $10,500 in 1981; the cost of the base was $3,300, and this amount was charged to the Machinery account in 1981.

June 23   One of the buildings is repainted at a cost of $4,500. It has not been painted since its construction in 1982.

Instructions

Prepare general journal entries for the transactions. (Round to nearest dollar.)

E10-17   Cain Corporation purchased conveyor equipment with a list price of $6,000. The vendor's credit terms were 2/10, n/30. Presented below are three independent cases related to the equipment. Assume that the purchases of equipment are recorded gross.

1.   Cain paid cash for the equipment 8 days after the purchase.

2.   Cain traded in equipment with a book value of $300, and paid $5,700 in cash one month after the purchase. The old equipment could have been sold for $300 at the date of trade.

3.   Cain gave the vendor a $6,050 noninterest-bearing note for the equipment on the date of purchase. The note was due in one year and was paid on time. Assume that the effective interest rate in the market was 10%. (Round to the nearest dollar.)

Instructions

Prepare the general journal entries required to record the acquisition and payment in each of the independent cases above.

E10-18   Presented below is information related to CanWest Company.

1.   In January, 1982, CanWest Company built a loading dock to accommodate heavy tractor- and trailer-type trucks at a cost of $19,000 as follows:

Labour	$8,000
Materials	7,000
Estimated overhead	4,000

It was estimated that this structure would have a useful life of 20 years.

2.   During 1984 several planks in the loading platform split and were weakened to such an extent that they had to be replaced at a cost of $150.

3.   In July, 1985, the entire dock was repainted at a cost of $325.

4.   An inexperienced driver backed into the end of the dock and damaged it in February, 1986. The company for which he worked was insured against such accidents, and a settlement of $1,800 was obtained. Cost to CanWest Company of repairing the damage was: labour, $700; materials, $500; and overhead, $350.

5.   In June, 1986, a hailstorm damaged the roof. A settlement of $1,500 was obtained from the insurance company. It was decided, however, that a new roof would soon be needed and repairs were not worthwhile. Therefore nothing was done

until October, when a roofing contractor was engaged to reroof the loading dock at a price of $4,000.

Instructions

State how each of the items above should be recorded in the accounts and support your conclusions.

*E10-19 Presented below are data for three independent cases involving coinsurance coverage.

	Case 1	Case 2	Case 3
Fair market value at date of loss	$66,000	$54,000	$60,000
Face value of policy	39,600	47,520	36,000
Coinsurance requirement (80%)	52,800	43,200	48,000
Amount of loss	33,000	32,400	60,000

Instructions

For each of the cases above, compute the amount recoverable.

PROBLEMS

P10-1 Selected accounts included in the property, plant, and equipment section of the Kingston Corporation's balance sheet at December 31, 1985, had the following balances:

Land	$175,000
Land improvements	90,000
Buildings	900,000
Machinery and equipment	850,000

During 1986 the following transactions occurred:

1. A tract of land was acquired for $125,000 as a potential future building site.

2. A plant facility consisting of land and building was acquired from the Nostrand Company in exchange for 10,000 shares of Kingston's common stock. On the acquisition date, Kingston's stock had a closing market price of $45 per share on the national stock exchange. The plant facility was carried on Nostrand's books at $89,000 for land and $130,000 for the building at the exchange date. Current appraised values for the land and building are $120,000 and $240,000, respectively.

3. Items of machinery and equipment were purchased at a total cost of $300,000. Additional costs were incurred as follows:

Freight and unloading	$ 5,000
Sales taxes	12,000
Installation	25,000

4. Expenditures totalling $75,000 were made for new parking lots and sidewalks at the corporation's various plant locations. These expenditures had an estimated useful life of 15 years.

5. A machine costing $50,000 on January 1, 1978, was scrapped on June 30, 1986. Double-declining-balance depreciation has been recorded on the basis of a ten-year life.

6. A machine was sold for $20,000 on July 1, 1986. Original cost of the machine was $36,000 on January 1, 1983, and it was depreciated on a straight-line basis over an estimated useful life of seven years and a salvage value of $1,000.

Instructions

(a) Prepare a detailed analysis of the changes in each of the following balance sheet accounts for 1986:

Land
Land improvements
Buildings
Machinery and equipment

(Hint: Disregard the related accumulated depreciation accounts.)

(b) List the items in the problem that were not used to determine the answer to (a), showing the pertinent amounts and supporting computations in good form for each item. In addition, indicate where, or if, these items should be included in Kingston's financial statements.

(AICPA adapted)

P10-2 At December 31, 1985, certain accounts included in the property, plant, and equipment section of the McCartney Company's balance sheet had the following balances:

Land	$100,000
Buildings	850,000
Leasehold improvements	500,000
Machinery and equipment	725,000

During 1986 the following transactions occurred:

Land site number 621 was acquired for $1,125,000. In addition, to acquire the land McCartney paid $60,000 in commission to a real estate agent. Costs of $20,000 were incurred to clear the land. During the course of clearing the land, timber and gravel were recovered and sold for $7,000.

A second tract of land (site number 622) with a building was acquired for $350,000. The closing statement indicated that the land value was $250,000 and the building value was $100,000. Shortly after acquisition, the building was demolished at a cost of $30,000. A new building was constructed for $150,000 plus the following costs.

Excavation fees	$11,000
Architectural design fees	9,000
Building permit fee	1,000
Imputed interest on funds used	
during construction (stock financing)	6,000

The building was completed and occupied on September 30, 1986.

A third tract of land (site number 623) was acquired for $700,000 and was put on the market for resale.

During December 1986 costs of $70,000 were incurred to improve leased office space. The related lease will terminate on December 31, 1988, and it is not expected to be renewed. (Hint: Leasehold improvements should be handled in the same manner as land improvements.)

A group of new machines was purchased under a royalty agreement that provides for payment of royalties based on units of production for the machines. The invoice price of the machines was $75,000, freight costs were $2,500, unloading charges were $1,500, and royalty payments for 1986 were $14,000.

Instructions

(a) Prepare a detailed analysis of the changes in each of the following balance sheet accounts for 1986:

Land
Buildings
Leasehold improvements
Machinery and equipment

Disregard the related accumulated depreciation accounts.

(b) List the items in the problem that were not used to determine the answer to (a) above, and indicate where, or if, these items should be included in McCartney's financial statements.

(AICPA adapted)

P10-3 Presented below is a schedule of property dispositions for James Camper Ltd.

SCHEDULE OF PROPERTY DISPOSITIONS

	Cost	Accumulated Depreciation	Cash Proceeds	Fair Market Value	Nature of Disposition
Land	$22,000	—	$19,000	$19,000	Expropriation
Building	6,800	—	1,800	—	Demolition
Warehouse	60,000	$7,978	61,000	61,000	Destruction by fire
Machine	4,000	1,700	500	3,300	Trade-in
Furniture	8,200	6,560	—	2,000	Contribution
Automobile	6,000	2,250	3,100	3,100	Sale

The following additional information is available:

Land. On February 15, land held primarily as an investment was expropriated by the city and, on March 31, another parcel of unimproved land to be held as an investment was purchased at a cost of $21,500.

Building. On April 2, land and building were purchased at a total cost of $34,000 at which 20% was allocated to the building on the corporate books. The real estate was acquired with the intention of demolishing the building, and this was accomplished during the month of November. Cash proceeds received in November represent the net proceeds from demolition of the building.

Warehouse. On June 30, the warehouse was destroyed by fire. The warehouse was purchased January 2, 1973, and had depreciated by $7,978. On December 27, part of the insurance proceeds was used to purchase a replacement warehouse at a cost of $57,000.

Machine. On December 26, the machine was exchanged for another machine having a fair market value of $2,800, and cash of $500 was received. (Round to nearest dollar.)

Furniture. On August 15, furniture was contributed to a recognized charitable organization. No other contributions were made or pledged during the year.

Automobile. On November 3, the automobile was sold to Jeff Light, a shareholder.

Instructions

Indicate how these items would be reported on the income statement of James Camper Ltd.

(AICPA adapted)

P10-4 During 1986, Argo Company of Canada manufactured a machine for its own use. At December 31, 1986, the account related to that machine is as follows:

Machinery

Machine cost	$ 4,800	Old Machine—cost	$4,800
Cost of dismantling old machine	900	Cash proceeds from sale of old machine	500
Raw materials used in construction of new machine	18,000	Depreciation for 1986, 10% of $44,400	4,440
Labour in construction of new machine	12,600		
Cost of installation	2,040		
Materials used in trial runs	960		
Profit on construction	10,400		

An analysis of the details in the account discloses the following:

1. The old machine, which was removed during installation of the new one, has been fully depreciated.

2. Cash discounts received on the payments for materials used in construction totalled $500 and were reported in the "purchases discount" account.

3. The factory overhead account shows a balance of $300,000, which includes variable overhead and total fixed overhead, for the year ended December 31, 1986. Of the variable overhead, $3,600 is attributable to the production of the machine. Fixed overhead is normally priced to operations at $2 per man-hour of labour. Nine hundred and eighty man-hours of labour were consumed in the production of the machine.

4. A profit was recognized on construction for the difference between costs incurred and the price at which the machine could have been purchased. The profit was credited to "self-construction gains."

5. Machinery has an estimated life of ten years with no salvage value. The new machine was used for production beginning July 1, 1986.

Instructions

Prepare the entries necessary to correct the Machinery account as of December 31, 1986, and to record depreciation expense for the year 1986.

P10-5 The Brinkley Furniture Company was incorporated on January 2, 1986, but was unable to begin manufacturing activities until July 1, 1986, because new factory facilities were not completed until that date.

The Land and Building account at December 31, 1986, was as follows:

January 31, 1986	Land and building	$ 98,000
February 28, 1986	Cost of removal of building	1,700
May 1, 1986	Partial payment of new construction	35,000
May 1, 1986	Legal fees paid	2,000
June 1, 1986	Second payment on new construction	30,000
June 1, 1986	Insurance premium	1,800
June 1, 1986	Special tax assessment	1,900
June 30, 1986	General expenses	12,000
July 1, 1986	Final payment on new construction	35,000
December 31, 1986	Asset write-up	12,600
		$230,000
December 31, 1986	Depreciation—1986 at 1%	2,300
	Account balance	$227,700

The following additional information is to be considered.

1. To acquire land and building the company paid $48,000 cash and 500 of its $5 cumulative preferred shares. Fair market value of the shares was $105 per share. The shares were recorded at an arbitrary value of $100 per share.

2. Cost of removal of old buildings amounted to $1,700, and the demolition company retained all materials of the building.

3. Legal fees covered the following:

Cost of organization	$ 400
Examination of title covering purchase of land	900
Legal work in connection with construction contract	700
	$2,000

4. Insurance premium covered the building for a two-year term beginning May 1, 1986.

5. General expenses covered the following for the period from January 12, 1986, to June 30, 1986.

President's salary	$ 7,000
Plant superintendent's salary	3,800
Office salaries	1,200
	$12,000

6. The special tax assessment covered street improvements that are permanent in nature.

7. Because of a general increase in construction costs after entering into the building contract, the board of directors increased the value of the building $12,600, believing that such an increase was justified to reflect the current market at the time the building was completed. Retained earnings was credited for this amount.

8. Estimated life of building—50 years. Write-off for 1986—1% of asset value (1% of $230,000, or $2,300).

Instructions

(a) Prepare entries to reflect correct land, building, and accumulated depreciation allowance accounts at December 31, 1986.

(b) Show the proper presentation of land, building, and accumulated depreciation accounts on the balance sheet at December 31, 1986.

(AICPA adapted)

P10-6   Kemp Corporation wishes to exchange a machine used in its operations. Kemp has received the following offers from other companies in the industry:

1. The Fisk Company offered to exchange a similar machine plus $15,000.
2. The Baines Company offered to exchange a similar machine.
3. The Edmonton Company offered to exchange a similar machine, but wanted $20,000 in addition to Kemp's machine.

In addition, Kemp contacted the Park Corporation, a dealer in machines. To obtain a new machine, Kemp must pay $150,000 in addition to trading in its old machine.

	Kemp	Fisk	Baines	Edmonton	Park
Machine cost	$175,000	$115,000	$275,000	$180,000	$185,000
Accumulated depreciation	85,000	40,000	225,000	108,000	-0-
Fair value	75,000	60,000	75,000	95,000	225,000

Instructions

For each of the four independent situations, prepare the journal entries to record the exchange on the books of each company. (Round to nearest dollar.)

P10-7   On August 1, 1986, Harrison, Inc. exchanged productive assets with Clapton, Inc. Harrison's asset is referred to below as "Asset A" and Clapton's is referred to as "Asset B." The following facts pertain to these assets:

	Asset A	Asset B
Original cost	$96,000	$110,000
Accumulated depreciation (to date of exchange)	40,000	52,000
Fair market value at date of exchange	60,000	75,000
Cash paid by Harrison, Inc.	15,000	
Cash received by Clapton, Inc.		15,000

Instructions

(a) Assume that Assets A and B are similar, and record the exchange for both Harrison, Inc. and Clapton, Inc. in accordance with generally accepted accounting principles.

    (b)   Assume that Assets A and B are dissimilar, and record the exchange for both Harrison, Inc. and Clapton, Inc. in accordance with generally accepted accounting principles.

P10-8   Presented below are unrelated transactions related to the acquisition of plant assets for Chaffless Grain Ltd. for the current year.

    1. Chaffless Grain Ltd. acquired a machine with a list price of $130,000 on May 1 of the current year. To acquire this machine, Chaffless Grain Ltd. exchanged 5,000 shares of its no-par common stock, and paid cash of $40,000. The shares of Chaffless Grain Ltd. were selling for $15 each on May 1.

    2. A used truck costing $13,000 with a book value of $4,000 is exchanged for a new truck with a fair market value of $8,000, and $5,000 cash is given. Assume that the assets exchanged are similar productive assets.

    3. Used machinery having a fair market value of $12,000 and $4,000 in cash is received in exchange for a newer piece of machinery having a book value of $10,000 (original cost $10,500 less accumulated depreciation of $500). Assume that the assets exchanged are similar productive assets.

    4. Chaffless Grain Ltd. purchased plant assets which included land and building for cash of $90,000. Chaffless Grain Ltd. borrowed $40,000 in cash at 11% interest (principal and interest are due in one year) to finance part of the purchase. The property was appraised for tax purposes as follows: land, $20,000 and building, $60,000. It is decided to use the tax appraisals to allocate cost between the land and the building because the relative tax values appear reasonable.

    5. An old computer has a book value of $41,000 (original cost $100,000 less $59,000 accumulated depreciation) and a fair market value of $56,000. A new computer having a fair market value of $140,000 is obtained by paying $84,000 cash and trading in the old computer. Assume that the assets exchanged are considered similar in nature.

Instructions

    (a)   Prepare the general journal entries necessary to record these transactions during the current year.

    (b)   Assume that the assets exchanged in the foregoing transactions were dissimilar in nature, and prepare the general journal entries necessary to record these transactions during the current year.

P10-9   During the current year, Condo Construction trades an old crane that has a book value of $96,000 (original cost $120,000 less accumulated depreciation $24,000) for a new crane from Bombay Manufacturing Co. The new crane cost Bombay $140,000 to manufacture. The following information is also available:

	Condo Const.	Bombay Mfg. Co.
Fair market value of old crane	$84,000	
Fair market value of new crane		$180,000
Cash paid	96,000	
Cash received		96,000

Instructions

    (a)   Assume that this exchange is considered to involve dissimilar assets (culmination of the earnings process), and prepare the journal entries on the books of (1) Condo Construction, and (2) Bombay Manufacturing Co.

    (b)   Assume that this exchange is considered to involve similar assets (no culmination of the earnings process), and prepare the journal entries on the books of (1) Condo Construction, and (2) Bombay Manufacturing Co.

    (c)   Assuming the same facts as those in (a), except that the fair market value of the old crane is $102,000 and the cash paid $78,000, prepare the journal entries on the books of (1) Condo Construction, and (2) Bombay Manufacturing Co.

(d)   Assuming the same facts as those in (b), except that the fair market value of the old crane is $108,000 and the cash paid $72,000, prepare the journal entries on the books of (1) Condo Construction, and (2) Bombay Manufacturing Co.

P10-10   On March 1, 1986, Southland Corporation acquired a tract of land as a plant site. Southland paid $20,000 cash and gave a $50,000, 3-year, 12% note payable, on which interest is payable annually. Construction was started immediately on the plant, and it was completed on October 31, 1986. Expenditures for construction were $300,000 monthly for eight months beginning on March 1. In order to help finance construction, Southland borrowed $2,000,000 on March 1 on a 2-year 10%, note payable. Interest on this note is payable at maturity. Excess funds that are not needed to pay construction costs were invested in temporary securities at 14%. Other than these two notes, Southland had no outstanding debt during 1986.

Instructions

(a)   Calculate interest revenue, average accumulated expenditures, avoidable interest, total interest cost incurred, and interest cost to be capitalized during 1986. In computing avoidable interest, start with the specific borrowing on the land. Round all computations to the nearest dollar.

(b)   Prepare the journal entry needed on the books of Southam at December 31, 1986, to record interest cost incurred and interest cost capitalized.

P10-11   Ontario Winery Co. received a $535,000 low bid from a reputable manufacturer for the construction of special production equipment needed by Ontario Winery in an expansion program. Because the company's own plant was not operating at capacity, Ontario Winery decided to construct the equipment there and recorded the following production costs related to the construction.

Services of consulting engineer	$ 20,000
Work subcontracted	30,000
Materials	265,000
Plant labour normally assigned to production	80,000
Plant labour normally assigned to maintenance	130,000
Total	$525,000

Management prefers to record the cost of the equipment under the incremental cost method. Approximately 40% of the corporation's production is devoted to government supply contracts which are all based in some way on cost. The contracts require that any self-constructed equipment be allocated its full share of all costs related to the construction.

The following information is also available:

1.   The production labour was for partial fabrication of the equipment in the plant. Skilled personnel were required and were assigned from other projects. The maintenance labour would have been the idle time of nonproduction plant employees who would have been retained on the payroll whether or not their services were used.

2.   Payroll taxes and employee fringe benefits are approximately 30% of labour cost and are included in manufacturing overhead cost. Total manufacturing overhead for the year was $6,969,000, including the $130,000 maintenance labour used to construct the equipment.

3.   Manufacturing overhead is approximately 50% variable and is applied on the basis of production labour cost. Production labour cost for the year for the corporation's normal products totalled $8,420,000.

4.   General and administrative expenses include $30,000 of allocated executive salary cost and $12,500 of postage, telephone, supplies, and miscellaneous expenses identifiable with this equipment construction.

Instructions

(a) Prepare a schedule computing the amount that should be reported as the full cost of the constructed equipment to meet the requirements of the government contracts. Any supporting computations should be in good form.

(b) Prepare a schedule computing the incremental cost of the constructed equipment.

(c) What is the greatest amount that should be capitalized as the cost of the equipment? Why?

(AICPA adapted)

*P10-12 Jimmy Cricket, Inc. has two fire insurance policies. Policy A covers the office building at a face value of $720,000 and the furniture and fixtures at a face value of $182,400. Policy B covers only the office building at an additional face value of $345,600. Each policy is with a different insurance company. A fire caused losses to the office building and the furniture and fixtures. The relevant data are summarized below:

	Furniture and Fixtures	Office Building	
Insurance policy	A	A	B
Fair market value of the property before fire	$240,000	$1,440,000	$1,440,000
Fair market value of the property after fire	$ 20,000	$ 880,000	$ 880,000
Face of insurance policy	$182,400	$ 720,000	$ 345,600
Coinsurance requirement	80%	80%	80%

Instructions

Compute the amount due from each insurance company for the loss on each asset category. Show computations in good form.

11

DEPRECIATION AND DEPLETION

Accountants, engineers, lawyers, and economists all define depreciation differently, because each group uses depreciation in a different context. All agree, however, that most assets are on an inevitable "march to the rubbish heap," and some type of write-down or write-off of costs is needed to indicate that the usefulness of an asset has declined. **Depreciation** is the term most often employed to indicate that tangible assets (other than natural resources) have declined in service potential. Where such natural resources as timber, oil, and coal are involved, the term **depletion** is employed. The expiration of intangible assets, such as patents or goodwill, is called **amortization.** For accounting purposes, **these terms are used to describe the allocation of the cost of various assets, less any salvage value, over their useful economic lives in a systematic and rational manner.**

DEPRECIATION—A METHOD OF COST ALLOCATION

Most people at one time or another are party to the trade-in and purchase of an automobile. In discussions with the automobile dealer, depreciation is a consideration on two points. First, how much has the old car "depreciated"? That is, how much is the trade-in value? Second, how fast will the new car depreciate? That is, what will its trade-in value be? In both cases the concept of depreciation is viewed as a valuation approach; depreciation is thought of as a loss in value.

To accountants, **depreciation is not a matter of valuation but a means of cost allocation.** Assets are not depreciated on the basis of a decline in their fair market value, but on the basis of systematic charges of cost to expense. Therefore, depreciation is the result of an accounting process of allocating the cost of tangible assets as expense in a systematic and rational manner to those periods expected to benefit from the use of the assets.

It is undeniably true that between the time the asset is purchased and the time it is sold or scrapped, fluctuations in the value of the asset may take place. Attempts to measure these interim value changes have, however, not been well received by accountants, because values are difficult to measure objectively. Therefore, accountants charge the cost of the asset to depreciation expense over its estimated life, making no attempts at valuation of the asset between acquisition and disposition. The cost allocation approach is justified because a matching of costs with revenues occurs, and because fluctuations in market value are tenuous and difficult to measure.

FACTORS IN THE DEPRECIATION PROCESS

Before a pattern of charges to revenue can be established, three basic questions must be answered:

1. What depreciation base is to be used for the asset?
2. What is the asset's useful life?
3. What method of cost apportionment is best for the asset?

The answers to these questions determine the particular calculation of a periodic depreciation charge and the mathematics of the method selected. Answering these questions requires the prediction of future events. This requires a distillation of several estimates into the resulting depreciation charge. Consequently, since perfect knowledge of the future is never attainable, a perfect measure of depreciation for each period cannot be expected to occur. Nevertheless, the accountant and management must exercise their collective judgement when deriving answers to these questions in order to achieve an appropriate matching of expenses against revenues in the income statement. A key point, however, is to recognize that the depreciation charge is not intended to measure change of value; **it is an allocation of the cost of the asset to the periods from which benefits are derived.**

Depreciation Base for the Asset

The base established for depreciation is a function of two factors: the original cost of the asset and its salvage or disposal value. In the previous chapter, the procedures used in establishing a cost basis for assets were illustrated; little attention was given to salvage value. Salvage value is the estimated amount that will be received at the time the asset is sold or removed from service. The salvage value is the amount to which the asset is to be written down or depreciated during its useful life. To illustrate, if an asset has a cost of $10,000 and a salvage value of $1,000, the depreciation base is $9,000.

Original cost	$10,000
Less: Salvage value	1,000
Depreciation base	$9,000

Companies differ as to their estimate of salvage value. For example, many companies depreciate their computer equipment on a straight-line basis, but estimated salvage values vary considerably. Consequently, although companies have similar assets and depreciate them using the same method, differences in estimated salvage value would result in different amounts being charged to depreciation expense each year.

From a practical standpoint, salvage value is often ignored when depreciating an asset because the valuation is immaterial. Some long-lived assets, however, have substantial residual values and, when this is the case, these amounts should be considered. Examples presented in this chapter include salvage value to illustrate how it affects the calculation of depreciation expense under the various methods.

Estimation of Service Life

There is a basic difference between the service life of an asset and its physical life. A piece of machinery may be physically capable of producing a given product for many years beyond its service life, but the equipment is not used for all of those years because the cost of producing the product in later years may be too high. For example, many tractors in the Western Development Museum at Saskatoon are preserved in remarkable physical condition as a historic reminder of the development of Canadian farming, although their service lives were terminated many years ago.

Assets are retired for two reasons: **physical factors** (e.g., casualty or expiration of physical life) and **economic factors** (obsolescence).

Physical factors relate to such things as decay, or wear and tear that result from use and the passage of time. These physical factors set the outside limit for the service life of an asset.

Economic or functional factors are other constraints that shorten the service life of an asset. The reasons why an asset is scrapped before its physical life expires are varied. New processes or techniques or improved machines, for example, may provide the same service at lower costs and with higher quality. Changes in the product may shorten the service life of the asset, or public requirements may demand that the asset be retired. Ecological factors, for instance, often influence a decision to retire a given asset.

The economic or functional factors can be classified into three categories: inadequacy, supersession, and obsolescence. **Inadequacy** results when an asset ceases to be useful to a given enterprise because the demands of the firm have changed; for example, the need for a larger building to handle increased production. Although the old building may still be sound, it may have become inadequate for that enterprise's purposes. **Supersession** is the replacement of one asset with another more efficient and economical asset; for example, the replacement of a second-generation computer (transistor type) with a third-generation computer (integrated circuit type) or the replacement of the Boeing 727 with the Boeing 767. **Obsolescence** is the catch-all term for situations not involving inadequacy and supersession. Because the distinction between these categories is artificial, it is probably best to consider economic factors in total instead of trying to make distinctions that are not clear-cut.

To illustrate these concepts, consider a new nuclear power plant. What do you think would be the most important factors in determining its useful life: physical factors or economic factors? An answer may not be possible on the basis of the limited data provided, but some observations seem valid. The limiting factors seem to be: (1) ecological considerations, (2) competition from other power sources (non-nuclear) and (3) safety concerns.

In this situation, the physical life does not appear to be the primary factor affecting useful life. Although the plant's physical life may be far from over, the plant may become obsolete in ten years. For a house, physical factors undoubtedly supersede economic or functional factors relative to useful life. Whenever the physical nature of the asset is the primary determinant of useful life, maintenance plays a vital role. The better the maintenance, the longer the life of the asset.[1]

The problem of estimating service life is difficult; experience and judgement are the primary means of determining service lives. In some cases, arbitrary lives are selected; in others, fairly sophisticated statistical methods are employed to establish a useful life for accounting purposes. In many cases, the primary basis for estimating the useful life of an asset is the enterprise's past experience with the same and similar assets. In a highly industrial economy such as that of Canada, where research and innovation are so prominent, economic and technological factors have as much, if not more, effect on the service lives of tangible assets as do physical factors.

METHODS OF COST APPORTIONMENT (DEPRECIATION)

Given that the depreciation base and useful life of an asset is determined, the depreciation charge depends on the method selected to calculate the depreciation. The accounting profession recognizes that the depreciation method employed should be "systematic and rational." The arbitrary assignment of cost to accounting periods without regard to the probable pattern of losses in an asset's services is not acceptable.

Depreciation methods may be classified as follows:[2]

1. Straight-line method
2. Activity method (units of use or production)
3. Decreasing charge methods
    (a) Declining balance
    (b) Sum-of-the years'-digits

---

[1] The airline industry also illustrates the problems of estimation. In the past, aircraft were assumed not to wear out—they just became obsolete. However, some jets have been in service as long as twenty years, and maintenance of these aircraft has become increasingly expensive. As a result, some airlines are finding it necessary to replace aircraft not because of obsolescence but because of their physical deterioration. The oil tanker industry provides another example of this problem.

[2] *Financial Reporting in Canada—1983* (Toronto: CICA, 1983) reports that, of the companies surveyed, 276 disclosed use of the straight-line method, 104 used a diminishing balance method, 85 used the units of production (activity) method, and 9 used the sinking fund method (all in real estate development operations). In the U.S.A., *Accounting Trends and Techniques—1984* reported 564 cases of straight-line method, 148 cases of a diminishing balance method, and 65 cases of the units of production method.

4. Tax method of capital cost allowance
5. Special depreciation methods
    (a) Inventory method
    (b) Retirement and replacement methods
    (c) Group and composite-life methods
    (d) Compound interest methods

To illustrate, Barek Co. Ltd. recently purchased a crane for construction purposes. Pertinent data concerning the purchase of the crane are:

Cost of crane	$500,000
Estimated useful life in years	5 years
Estimated salvage value	$ 50,000
Productive life in hours	30,000 hours

Straight-Line Method

Under the straight-line method, depreciation is considered a function of the passage of time. This method is widely used because of its simplicity. The straight-line procedure is often justified on a more theoretical basis as well. When creeping obsolescence is the primary reason for a limited service life, a decline in usefulness may be constant from period to period. In this situation, the straight-line approach is appropriate. The depreciation charge per year for the crane is computed as follows:

$$\frac{\text{Cost less salvage}}{\text{Estimated service life}} = \text{Depreciation charge}$$

$$\frac{\$500,000 - \$50,000}{5} = \$90,000$$

The major objection to the use of the straight-line approach is that it rests on tenuous assumptions that the asset's economic usefulness is the same each year and that the repair and maintenance expense is essentially the same each period (given constant revenue flows). If such is not the case, a rational matching of costs with revenues would not result from application of this method.

One additional problem that occurs in using the straight-line method is that distortions in the rate of return analysis (income/assets) develop. For example, Table 11-1 indicates how the rate of return increases, given constant revenue flows.

TABLE 11-1   Depreciation and Rate of Return Analysis—Crane Example

Year	Depreciation Expense	Undepreciated Asset Balance (book value)	Income Flow (after depreciation expense)	Rate of Return (income ÷ book value)
0		$500,000		
1	$90,000	410,000	$100,000	24.4%
2	90,000	320,000	100,000	31.2%
3	90,000	230,000	100,000	43.5%
4	90,000	140,000	100,000	71.4%
5	90,000	50,000	100,000	200.0%

This illustration indicates that analysis of rate of return can be misleading when the straight-line method is employed because the income flow remains the same, whereas the book value of the asset decreases. With the exception of the compound interest methods, the rate of return analysis is similarly distorted by other depreciation methods that systematically allocate cost. A student of accounting soon realizes that any cost allocation procedure has several assumptions, and that simplicity and ease of understanding are valid considerations in making the final selection of a depreciation method.

Activity Method

The activity method (often called the variable charge approach) assumes that depreciation is a function of use or productivity instead of the passage of time. The life of the asset is considered in terms of either the output it provides (units it produces), or the number of hours it works. Conceptually, the proper cost association is established in terms of an **output measure** instead of hours used, but often the output is not homogeneous and is difficult to measure. In such cases, an **input measure** such as machine hours is an appropriate basis for determining the amount of depreciation charge for a given accounting period.

The crane poses no particular problem because the usage (hours) is relatively easy to measure. If we assume that the crane is used 4,000 hours the first year, the depreciation charge for that year is calculated as:

$$\frac{\text{(Cost less salvage)} \times \text{Hours this year}}{\text{Total estimated hours}} = \text{Depreciation charge}$$

$$\frac{(\$500,000 - \$50,000) \times 4,000}{30,000} = \$60,000$$

The major limitation of this method is that it is not appropriate in situations in which depreciation is a function of time instead of activity. For example, a building is subject to a great deal of steady deterioration from the elements (a function of time) regardless of its use. In addition, where an asset is subject to economic or functional factors, independent of its use, the activity method loses much of its significance. For example, if a company is expanding rapidly, a particular building may soon become obsolete for its intended purposes, without activity playing any role in its loss of utility.

Another problem in using an activity method is that the total units of output or service hours that will be received are often difficult to estimate. While still resulting in a subjective estimate, data may be more frequently available concerning estimated lives of given assets in relation to time rather than the number of units of output that will be achieved.

Where loss of services (use value) is a function of activity or productivity, a units of production method may best match costs and revenues. Those companies that want low depreciation during periods of low productivity and higher depreciation during high productivity either adopt or switch to an activity method. Inland Steel in 1982, for example, switched to units of production depreciation and reduced its losses by $43 million or $1.20 per share.[3]

---

[3]"Double Standard," *Forbes* (November 22, 1982), p. 178.

Decreasing Charge Methods

The decreasing charge methods (often called accelerated depreciation methods) provide for a higher depreciation expense charge in the earlier years and lower charges in later periods compared to the straight-line method. The main justification for this approach is that, inasmuch as the asset is more efficient or suffers the greatest decline of services in the earlier years, more depreciation should be charged in those years. Another argument is that repair and maintenance costs are often higher in the later periods, and the accelerated methods thus provide a constant total cost (for both depreciation and repairs and maintenance) because the depreciation charge is lower in the later periods. Two decreasing charge methods (the declining balance method and the sum-of-the-years' digits method) are considered in the following paragraphs.

Declining Balance Method   The declining balance method uses a depreciation rate (expressed as a percentage) that is some multiple of the rate implied in the straight-line method. For example, the double-declining balance rate for a ten-year life asset would be 20% (double the straight-line rate which is 1/10 or 10%). The declining balance rate remains the same throughout the asset's life (assuming no change in estimates occurs) and is applied to the reduced book value each year. Unlike other methods, in the declining balance method the salvage value is not deducted in computing the depreciation base. The declining balance rate is multiplied by the book value of the asset at the beginning of each period. Since the book value of the asset is reduced each period by the depreciation charge, the constant rate is applied to a successively lower book value and, therefore, there is a lower depreciation charge each year. Conceptually, as is shown in the following example, this process continues until the book value of the asset is reduced to its estimated salvage value, at which time depreciation is discontinued. Using a double-declining balance rate, the depreciation charges for the crane example of Barek Co. Ltd. are presented in Table 11-2.

TABLE 11-2   Double-Declining Depreciation Schedule—Crane Example

Year	Book Value of Asset, Start of Year	Rate on Declining Balance[a]	Debit Depreciation Expense	Balance Accumulated Depreciation	Book Value, End of Year
1	$500,000	40%	$200,000	$200,000	$300,000
2	300,000	40%	120,000	320,000	180,000
3	180,000	40%	72,000	392,000	108,000
4	108,000	40%	43,200	435,200	64,800
5	64,800	40%	14,800[b]	450,000	50,000

[a]Based on twice the straight-line rate of 20% (1 ÷ 5 = 20%; 20% × 2 = 40%).
[b]Limited to $14,800 because book value is not to be less than salvage value.

Enterprises often switch from the double-declining to the straight-line method near the end of the asset's useful life to ensure that the asset is depreciated only to estimated salvage value.[4]

[4]A pure form of the declining balance method (sometimes appropriately called the "fixed percentage of book value method") has also been suggested as a possibility. This approach finds a rate that depreciates the asset exactly to salvage value at the end of its expected useful life. The formula for determination of this rate is as follows:

$$\text{Depreciation rate} = 1 - \sqrt[n]{\frac{\text{Salvage value}}{\text{Acquisition cost}}}$$

The life in years is n. This calculation is not extensively used in practice.

Sum-of-the-Years'-Digits Method   The sum-of-the-years'-digits method results in a decreasing depreciation charge based on a decreasing fraction of depreciable cost (original cost less salvage value). Each fraction uses the sum of the years as a denominator (5 + 4 + 3 + 2 + 1 = 15) and the number of years of estimated life remaining as of the beginning of the year as a numerator. In this method, the numerator decreases year by year, although the denominator remains constant (5/15, 4/15, 3/15, 2/15, and 1/15). At the end of the asset's useful life, the balance remaining should be equal to the salvage value. The example (Table 11-3) involving the crane shows this method of computation.[5] This decreasing charge method has not been used extensively in Canadian practice.

TABLE 11-3   Sum-of-the-Years'-Digits Depreciation Schedule—Crane Example

Year	Depreciation Base	Remaining Life in Years	Depreciation Fraction	Depreciation Expense	Book Value, End of Year
1	$450,000	5	5/15	$150,000	$350,000
2	450,000	4	4/15	120,000	230,000
3	450,000	3	3/15	90,000	140,000
4	450,000	2	2/15	60,000	80,000
5	450,000	1	1/15	30,000	50,000[a]
		15	15/15	$450,000	

[a]Salvage value.

Tax Method of Capital Cost Allowance Determination

This method is used to determine taxable income in Canada regardless of which method is used for financial reporting purposes. Because companies use it for tax purposes, some may also use it for financial reporting rather than keep two sets of records. Such an action, while expedient, may not provide a rational allocation of costs in the financial reports. Therefore, many companies keep a record of capital cost allowance for tax purposes and use another method to determine depreciation for financial statements.

The mechanics of this method are the same as for the declining balance method except that:

- The government, through the Income Tax Act (*Income Tax Regulations, Schedule II*), specifies the rate to be used for an asset class. This rate is called the Capital Cost Allowance (CCA) rate. The Income Tax Act identifies several different classes of assets and the maximum CCA rate for each class. Examination of the definition of each asset class and the examples given in the Income Tax Act is necessary to determine the class into which a particular asset falls.

- CCA is determined for each asset class. Assuming no net additions to a class (purchases less disposals, if any) during a year, the maximum CCA allowed is the CCA rate for the class multiplied by the undepreciated capital cost (UCC) at the year end, before the CCA deduction for the year. When there is a net addition, the maximum CCA on the net addition is one-half of the allowed CCA rate multiplied by the amount of the net

---

[5]What happens if the estimated service life of the asset is, let us say, 51 years? How would you calculate the sum-of-the-years'-digits? Fortunately, mathematicians have developed a formula that permits easy computation.

$$\frac{n(n+1)}{2} = \frac{51(51+1)}{2} = 1,326$$

addition. The CCA for the net addition plus the CCA on the remaining UCC would be the total CCA for the asset class. If there were only one asset in a class, the maximum CCA allowed in the year of its acquisition would be one-half of the CCA rate multiplied by the acquisition cost. Thereafter, the maximum CCA per year would be the allowed rate multiplied by the UCC at year end, before the CCA deduction.

• Regardless of when an asset is bought or sold during a year, a company must own the asset at the year end to be eligible to take any CCA. If the company has been in business for the full year and the asset is owned at year end, the maximum allowed CCA may be taken (even if the asset was bought one week before year end). However, no CCA is allowed on assets sold during a year (even if they were sold just before the year end).

• CCA would be taken even if it resulted in an undepreciated capital cost (book value) less than estimated salvage value.

• It is not required that the maximum rate be taken in any given year, although that would be the normal case as long as a company had taxable income resulting after taking the maximum.

• Instead of calling it depreciation expense, it is called capital cost allowance in tax returns.

Assuming that the crane of Barek Co. Ltd. was a Class 8 asset for which the CCA rate allowed is 20%, Table 11-4 shows the calculations required to determine CCA for tax purposes for the first three years. This example also assumes that no other assets were in the class. If there were other Class 8 assets owned prior to purchase of the crane, or purchased or sold during the three years, Table 11-4 indicates how they would be incorporated. See Appendix 11A at the end of this chapter for a discussion of the tax treatment for additions, retirements, and asset class eliminations.

TABLE 11-4   Capital Cost Allowance Schedule—Crane Example

UCC beginning of year 1	$ -0-
Additions during year	500,000
Deduct the lower of the proceeds from or cost of assets in class disposed of during the year	-0-
UCC before CCA	$500,000
CCA for year 1 (20% × $500,000) × .5	50,000
UCC beginning of year 2	$450,000
Additions	-0-
Deduct disposals	-0-
UCC before CCA	$450,000
CCA for year 2 (20% × $450,000)	90,000
CCA beginning of year 3	$360,000
Additions	-0-
Deduct disposals	-0-
UCC before CCA	$360,000
CCA for year 3 (20% × $360,000)	72,000
UCC beginning of year 4	$288,000
(Continued in Appendix 11A)	

It should be noted that determination of CCA is subject to rules determined by government legislation and, thus, is subject to alteration from time to time. Furthermore, various provincial governments can have different rules with regard to determining CCA for purposes of calculating the income on which provincial taxes are based. This example is based on the 1985 Federal Income Tax Act.

SELECTION OF A DEPRECIATION METHOD

Which method should be selected and why? Conceptually, the selection of a depreciation method (as with the selection of an inventory method) should be determined on the basis of which method best meets the objectives of financial reporting in the particular circumstances. In attempting to achieve these objectives, many believe that **matching** of expenses rationally against benefits (revenues) should occur.

Theoretically, if the method to be chosen is the one that rationally matches depreciation expenses against the benefits to be received from the asset, it is first necessary to identify the pattern of benefits to be received. Possible benefit patterns (net revenues before depreciation) are indicated in the following graph:

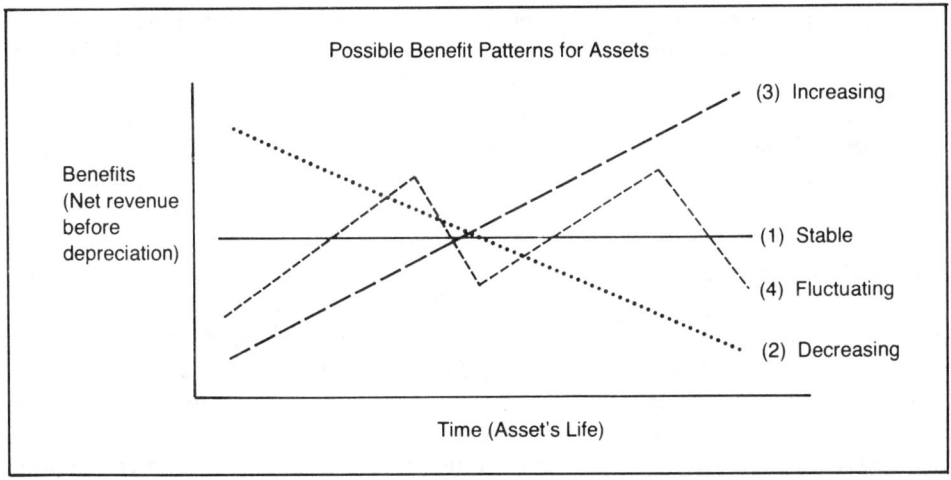

Pattern (1) would represent an asset providing roughly the same level of benefits for each year of its life. A warehouse could be an example. For such assets, the straight-line depreciation method would be rational because it gives a constant depreciation expense each period. An airplane may be an example of an asset with a decreasing benefit pattern (2). When it is new, it is constantly in service on major routes but, as it gets older, it may be repaired more frequently and used for more peripheral routes. Therefore, depreciation expense should decline each year (which is what occurs under decreasing charge methods) if expense is rationally to match benefits. The use of a truck (in terms of kilometres driven) may fluctuate considerably from period to period, yielding a benefit pattern that varies (4). An activity method would rationally match depreciation expense against such a benefit pattern. An increasing benefit pattern (3) may result from ownership of a computer. When bought, it is likely that few and less complicated programs are used and many "bugs" have to be ironed out. As time passes, more complex programs may be added, providing benefits to company operations. Methods of calculating increasing depreciation charges (called compound interest methods) exist, but are beyond the scope of this book. Conceptually, the compound interest methods ("sinking fund method" and "annuity method") have much to offer, but they have found limited acceptance, being used primarily in the public utility industry and the real estate industry. These methods are discussed in more advanced accounting courses.

While the merits of appropriate matching are important to selecting a depreciation method, it may be difficult in many cases to develop projections of future revenues, and therefore **simplicity** may govern. In such cases, it might be argued that the straight-line method of depreciation should be used. However, others might argue that whatever is used for tax purposes should be used for book purposes because it **eliminates some record-keeping costs.** Because Canadian companies must use the capital cost allowance approach for income tax purposes, they may be tempted to use the same for financial reporting purposes. The objectives of financial reporting differ, however, from those of income tax determination. Therefore, for many companies, it is not uncommon to have "two sets of records" when accounting for cost allocations: one for financial reporting and another for income tax determination. While this is legal and acceptable given the differences in objectives, a consequence is that financial statement income before taxes will differ from taxable income in any given year. This is one of the reasons for reporting deferred income taxes in financial statements (a topic examined in Chapter 20).

The **perceived economic consequence** of the resulting financial reporting has also been cited as a factor influencing selection of a depreciation method. For example, in the late 1960s, U.S. Steel changed its method of depreciation from an accelerated to a straight-line method for financial reporting purposes. Many observers noted that the reason for the change was to report higher income so that it would be less susceptible to takeover by another enterprise. In effect, U.S. Steel wanted to report higher income so that the market value of its shares would rise.[6]

As another illustration, the real estate industry in the U.S.A. is frustrated with depreciation accounting because, it is argued, real estate often does not decline in value. In addition, because real estate is highly leveraged, most real estate concerns report losses in earlier years when the sum of depreciation and interest charges exceeds the revenues from the real estate project. The industry argues for some form of increasing charge method of depreciation (lower depreciation at the beginning and higher depreciation at the end), so that higher total assets and net income are reported in the earlier years of the project. Some even use an economic consequences argument that Canadian real estate companies (which may use an increasing charge method) have a competitive edge over U.S. real estate companies. In support of this view, they point to the increasing number of acquisitions by Canadian real estate companies of U.S. real estate companies and real estate properties.

SPECIAL DEPRECIATION SYSTEMS

Sometimes an enterprise does not select one of the more popular depreciation methods because the assets involved have unique characteristics, or the nature of

---

[6]This assumption is highly tenuous. It is based on the belief that stock market analysts will not be able to recognize that the change in depreciation methods is purely cosmetic and therefore will give more value to the shares after the change. In fact, research in this area reports just the opposite. For example, one study showed that companies that switched from accelerated to straight-line (which increased income) experienced declines in share value after the change; see Robert J. Kaplan and Richard Roll, "Investors Evaluation of Accounting Information: Some Empirical Evidence," *The Journal of Business* (April, 1972), pp. 225–257. Similarly, others have noted that switches to move to more liberal accounting policies (generating higher income numbers) have resulted in lower stock market performance. One rationale for such an occurrence is that such changes signal the market that the company is in trouble and also lead to skepticism about management's attitudes and behaviour. See, for example, David F. Hawkins and Walter J. Campbell, "Equity Valuation: Models, Analysis, and Implications," *Research Study and Report* (New York: Financial Executives Research Foundation, 1978); and Tom Harrison, "Different Market Reactions to Discretionary and Nondiscretionary Accounting Changes," *Journal of Accounting Research* (Spring, 1977), pp. 84–107.

the industry dictates that a special depreciation method be adopted. Generally, these systems can be classified into three groups:

1. Inventory systems.
2. Retirement and replacement systems.
3. Group and composite methods.

Inventory Systems

The inventory method (often called the appraisal system) is used to value such small tangible assets as hand tools or utensils. A tool inventory, for example, might be taken at the beginning and the end of the year; the value of the beginning inventory plus the cost of tools acquired for the year less the value of the ending inventory provides the amount of depreciation expense for the year. Separate depreciation schedules for the assets in use are impractical; consequently, this method is appealing.

The major objection to this depreciation method is that it is not "systematic and rational." No set formula exists, and a great deal of subjectivity may be involved in the valuations presented. In many situations, a market or liquidation value is used as the basis for valuation, a practice that is criticized as a violation of the historical cost principle.

Retirement and Replacement Systems

The retirement and replacement methods are used principally by public utilities and railroads that own many similar units of small value, such as poles, ties, conductors, telephones, and so on. The purpose of these approaches is to avoid elaborate depreciation schedules for the individual assets. The distinction between the two methods is that **the retirement system charges the cost of the retired asset (less salvage value) to depreciation expense, and the replacement system charges the cost of units purchased as replacements less salvage value from the units replaced to depreciation expense.** In the replacement method, the original cost of the old assets is maintained in the accounts indefinitely.

To illustrate these two methods, let us assume that the transmission lines of Hi-Test Utility, Ltd. originally cost $1,000,000 in 1980 and that eight years later lines costing $150,000 are replaced with lines having a cost of $200,000.

Entries under Retirement and Replacement System

Retirement System		Replacement System	

Record installation of line — 1980:

Plant assets—Lines	1,000,000	Plant Assets—Lines 1,000,000	
Cash	1,000,000	Cash	1,000,000

Record retirement of old asset as depreciation expense—1988:

Depreciation expense	150,000	(no entry)	
Plant assets—Lines	150,000		

Record cost of new asset as depreciation expense—1988:

(no entry)		Depreciation Expense 200,000	
		Cash	200,000

Record cost of new asset—1988:

Plant assets—Lines	200,000	(no entry)	
Cash	200,000		

Any salvage value from the old transmission lines is considered a reduction of the depreciation expense in the period of retirement or replacement under both methods. Note that neither makes use of an accumulated depreciation account.

Both systems are subject to the criticism that a proper allocation of costs to all periods does not occur, particularly in the early years. To overcome this objection, a special allowance account may be established in the earlier years so that an assumed depreciation charge can be provided. The probability of retirements or replacements being fairly constant is essential to the validity of this concept; otherwise, depreciation is simply a function of when retirement and replacement occur.

Group and Composite Systems

Depreciation methods are usually applied to a single asset. In certain circumstances, however, multiple-asset accounts are depreciated using one rate. For example, an enterprise such as a telephone company might depreciate by equipment groups (e.g., telephone poles, microwave systems, or switchboards). Two methods of depreciating multiple-asset accounts are employed: the group method and the composite method. The term **group refers to a collection of assets that are similar in nature; composite refers to a collection of assets that are dissimilar in nature.** The group method is frequently used where the assets are fairly homogeneous and have approximately the same useful lives. The composite approach is used when the assets are heterogeneous and have different lives. The group method more closely approximates a single-unit cost procedure because the dispersion from the average is not as great. The method of computation for either the group or composite method is essentially the same: find an average and depreciate on that basis.

To illustrate, Smart Motors depreciates its fleet of cars, trucks, and campers on a composite basis. The depreciation rate is established in this manner:

Asset	Original Cost	Residual Value	Depreciable Cost	Estimated Life (years)	Depreciation Per Year (straight-line)
Cars	$145,000	$25,000	$120,000	3	$40,000
Trucks	44,000	4,000	40,000	4	10,000
Campers	35,000	5,000	30,000	5	6,000
	$224,000	$34,000	$190,000		$56,000

$$\text{Depreciation or composite rate} = \frac{\$56,000}{\$224,000} = 25\%$$

Composite life = 3.39 years ($190,000 ÷ $56,000)

If there are no changes in the asset account, the group will be depreciated to the residual or salvage value at the rate of $56,000 ($224,000 × .25) a year for 3.39 years. This system simplifies the procedure for keeping depreciation records when there is a multitude of assets.

The differences between the group or composite method and the single-unit depreciation methods become accentuated in the area of asset retirements. If an asset is retired before the average service life of the group is reached, the resulting gain or loss is buried in the accumulated depreciation account. This practice is justified because some assets will be retired before the average service life and others after the average life. For this reason, the debit to Accumulated Depreciation is the difference between original cost and cash received. No gain or loss on disposition is recorded. To illustrate, suppose that one of the campers with a cost of $5,000 was sold for $2,600 at the end of the third year. The entry is:

Accumulated Depreciation	2,400	
Cash	2,600	
Cars, Trucks, and Campers		5,000

EASY UP TO HERE

If additional assets are purchased (mopeds, for example), a new depreciation rate must be computed and applied in subsequent periods.

SPECIAL DEPRECIATION PROBLEMS

Several special problems related to depreciation remain to be discussed. Although it is difficult to classify these into special categories, the major issues are:

1. How should depreciation be computed for partial periods?
2. Does depreciation provide for the replacement of assets?
3. How are revisions in depreciation rates handled?

Depreciation and Partial Periods

Plant assets are seldom purchased on the first day of a fiscal period and are seldom disposed of on the last day of a fiscal period. A practical question is: How much depreciation should be charged for the partial period involved? Assume, for example, that an automated drill machine with a five-year life is purchased by Algoma Steel for $45,000 (no salvage value) on June 10 and the company's fiscal year ends December 31. Therefore, depreciation would be charged for 6 2/3 months during the year of acquisition. In other words, the total depreciation for a full year (assuming straight-line depreciation) is $9,000 ($45,000/5), and the depreciation for the fraction of the year is:

$$\frac{6\ 2/3}{12} \times \$9,000 = \$5,000$$

In some cases, the previous method is modified to handle acquisitions and disposals of plant assets more simply. For example, depreciation may be computed for the full period on the opening balance in the asset account, and no depreciation is charged on acquisitions during the year. Another variation is to charge a full year's depreciation on assets used for a full year and to charge one-half year's depreciation in the year of acquisition and in the year of disposal.

The schedule at the top of page 522 shows the amounts of depreciation allocated under five different policies using straight-line depreciation on the $45,000 automated drill machine.

A company is at liberty to adopt any one of several fractional-year policies in allocating cost to the first and last years of an asset's life so long as the method is applied consistently. Depreciation, however, is normally computed on the basis of the nearest whole month unless otherwise stipulated.

Fractional-Year Depreciation Policies			
Fractional- Year Policy	Depreciation Year 1	Recognized Each Fiscal Year Year 2–5	Depreciation Year 6
1. Nearest fraction of a year	$5,000[a]	$9,000	$4,000[b]
2. Nearest full month	5,250[c]	9,000	3,750[d]
3. Half-year in period of acquisition and disposal	4,500	9,000	4,500
4. Full year in period of acquisition, none in disposal period	9,000	9,000	-0-
5. None in period of acquisition, full year in disposal	-0-	9,000	9,000

[a]6.667/12 ($9,000)   [c]7/12 ($9,000)
[b]5.333/12 ($9,000)   [d]5/12 ($9,000)

What happens when an accelerated method such as double-declining balance is used when partial periods are involved? As an illustration, assume that an asset was purchased for $10,000 on July 1, 1986, with an estimated useful life of five years: the depreciation figures for 1986, 1987, and 1988 are as below.

	Double-Declining Balance
1st Full Year	(40% × $10,000) = $4,000
2nd Full Year	(40% × 6,000) = 2,400
3rd Full Year	(40% × 3,600) = 1,440

Depreciation from July 1, 1986, to December 31, 1986

0.5 × $4,000 = $2,000

Depreciation for 1987

0.5 × $4,000 = $2,000
0.5 ×   2,400 =   1,200
$3,200

or ($10,000 − $2,000) × 40% = $3,200

Depreciation for 1988

0.5 × $2,400 = $1,200
0.5 ×   1,440 =   720
$1,920

or ($10,000 − $5,200) × 40% = $1,920

In computing depreciation expense for partial periods in this example, the depreciation charge for a full year was first determined and this amount was then prorated on a straight-line basis to depreciation expense between the two accounting periods involved. Alternatively, a simpler approach would be to make the illustrated calculation to determine depreciation expense for the year ended December 31, 1986, and then apply the depreciation rate (40%) to the book value at the beginning of each successive year. This is shown in the illustration as the "or" calculations. The charge for each year is the same under either approach, regardless of the alternative mathematics employed.

Depreciation and Replacement of Fixed Assets

A common misconception about depreciation is that it provides funds (cash) for the replacement of fixed assets. Depreciation is similar to any other expense, in that it reduces net income, and differs from most other expenses, in that it does not involve a current cash outflow.

To illustrate why depreciation does not provide funds for replacement of plant assets, assume that a business starts operating with plant assets of $500,000, which have a useful life of five years. The company's balance sheet at the beginning of the period is:

Plant Assets	$500,000		Owners' Equity	$500,000

Now if we assume that the enterprise earned no revenue over the five years, the income statements are:

	Year 1	Year 2	Year 3	Year 4	Year 5
Revenue	-0-	-0-	-0-	-0-	-0-
Depreciation	(100,000)	(100,000)	(100,000)	(100,000)	(100,000)
Loss	(100,000)	(100,000)	(100,000)	(100,000)	(100,000)

The balance sheet at the end of the five years is:

Plant Assets	-0-		Owners' Equity	-0-

This extreme illustration points out that depreciation in no way provides funds for the replacement of assets. The funds for the replacement of the assets come from the revenues; without the revenues no income materializes, and no cash inflow results. A separate decision must be made by management to set aside cash in order to accumulate asset replacement funds.

Revision of Depreciation Rates

When a plant is purchased, depreciation rates are determined as accurately as possible; the necessary estimates are based on past experience with similar assets and all other pertinent information available. The provisions for depreciation are only estimates, however, and it may be necessary to make revisions in these estimates during the life of the asset. Unexpected physical deterioration or unforeseen obsolescence may indicate that the useful life of the asset is less than originally estimated. Improved maintenance procedures, revision of operating procedures, or similar developments may prolong the life of the asset beyond the expected period.

For example, assume that machinery costing $90,000 and originally estimated to have a life of 20 years with no salvage value at the end of that time has been used for 10 years when it is estimated that it will be used an additional 20 years from that date. Depreciation has been recorded at the rate of 1/20 of $90,000, or $4,500 per year by the straight-line method. On the basis of a 30-year life, depreciation should have been 1/30 of $90,000, or $3,000 per year. In light of the new information, depreciation has been overstated, and net income before taxes has been understated by $1,500 for each of the past 10 years, or a total amount of $15,000. The amount of the difference can be computed as follows:

	Per Year	For 10 Years
Depreciation charged per books (1/20 × $90,000)	$4,500	$45,000
Depreciation based on a 30-year life (1/30 × $90,000)	3,000	30,000
Excess depreciation charged	$1,500	$15,000

The *CICA Handbook*, Section 1506, requires that the effects of changes in estimates be handled in the current and prospective periods; that is, no changes are to be made in previously reported results. Opening balances are not adjusted and no attempt is made to "catch up" for prior periods. The reason for this requirement is that changes in estimates are continual, an inherent part of any estimation process. As new information becomes available it is incorporated into the current and future reports. Therefore, no entry is made at the time the change in estimate occurs, and charges for depreciation in the current and subsequent periods are based on allocating the remaining book value less any salvage value over the remaining estimated life. The book value to be depreciated over the remaining twenty years is determined as follows:

Machinery	$90,000
Less: Accumulated depreciation	45,000
Book value of machinery at end of 10th year	$45,000

The entry to record depreciation for the current and remaining years is:

Depreciation Expense	2,250	
Accumulated Depreciation—Machinery		2,250
($45,000 ÷ 20 years)		

Impairment in Value—A Difficult Accounting Question

As stated in Chapter 10, we believe that whenever a **permanent impairment** in the revenue-producing ability of property, plant, and equipment exists, it would be appropriate to recognize that a loss has occurred. Such a treatment is judged acceptable by the accounting profession in the case of long-term investments (*CICA Handbook*, Section 3050, par. 31) but has not generally been carried out for property, plant, and equipment. Recent economic events and technological advancements will cause the profession to examine this situation carefully. At present, however, it is useful to address the issue regarding how the accounting for such permanent impairment could be handled.

An impairment in value could be partial or total. In some cases the asset will continue in use at a greatly reduced carrying value, while in other cases the asset becomes valueless for its original intent and is worth only its salvage value. In any case the impairment in value must be permanent in nature and material in amount.[7]

A permanent impairment in the value of property, plant, and equipment may be recorded by recognizing a loss and reducing the book value of the asset through a credit to accumulated depreciation. If the asset is to continue in use, estimates of the remaining useful life and the salvage value may be revised as well.

To illustrate, in 1983, Hi-Tech Industries purchased equipment for producing high-speed chain-drive contact printers. The equipment cost $1,000,000, had an expected life of 8 years, and an estimated salvage value of $200,000. With the emergence of the laser printer as a faster, higher quality printer than the chain-drive contact type, it became apparent to Hi-Tech's management in 1985 that its production equipment had suddenly suffered a permanent impairment in value. In early 1985 when the book value of the equipment was $800,000, management determined that (1) it should be only $300,000, (2) the life should be reduced from 6 to 2 remaining years, and (3) the salvage value should be reduced to $50,000.

The entry to record the permanent impairment in value would be as follows:[8]

Loss Due to Equipment Obsolescence	500,000	
Accumulated Depreciation—Equipment		500,000
($800,000 − $300,000)		

The loss of $500,000 is probably not extraordinary, but because it occurs infrequently and is material in amount it should be reported separately in the income statement among other expenses and losses. Future depreciation would be based on the new carrying value of $300,000, a remaining life of two years, and a salvage value of $50,000.

If no future use of the equipment is expected, an entry similar to the one above could be made for an amount that reduces the book value to salvage value. In addition, the equipment would be reclassified to nonoperating assets on the balance sheet.

DISCLOSURE OF PROPERTY, PLANT, AND EQUIPMENT, AND DEPRECIATION

The basis of valuation for property, plant, and equipment should be stated: it is usually historical cost less accumulated depreciation. Pledges, liens, and other commitments related to these assets should be disclosed also. Any liability secured by property, plant, and equipment should not be offset against these assets, but should be reported in the liability section. Property, plant, and equipment not currently employed as producing assets in the business (e.g., idle facilities and land held as an investment) should be segregated from assets being used in operations. When assets are depreciated, a valuation account normally called Accumulated Depreciation or Allowance for Depreciation, is credited. The employment of an Accumulated Depreciation account permits the reader of the financial statements to determine

[7]Examples of two partial write-downs in late 1984 are Philip Morris' $280 million write-down of a newly completed Miller brewery that was not opened because there was no market for its output, and Texaco's $765 million write-down of tankers, refineries, and interests in exploration leases because of excess capacity. The questionable aspect of these two write-downs is the lack of permanency in the impairment in value, since these assets are either continued in use or intended for future use when "beer consumption grows" and "oil prices turn around," respectively.

[8]Some accountants who support partial write-downs due to impairment in value advocate the use of a special contra asset account such as "Allowance for Reduction in Carrying Value of Assets."

the original cost of the asset, and provides the reader with information concerning the amount of depreciation that has been charged to income in past years.

With regard to depreciation, the *CICA Handbook* states that:

> The accumulated allowance for depreciation and depletion should be disclosed and deducted from the fixed assets. Disclosure of fixed assets and accumulated allowances by major category (e.g., land, buildings, machinery and leasehold improvements) is desirable.
> . . . The income statement should disclose the amount charged for depreciation, depletion, and amortization of leasehold improvements. Disclosure should be made of the methods and rates used in such computations. Where they are significant, disclosure of separate amounts would be desirable.[9]

The financial report of Andres Wines Ltd. illustrates an acceptable disclosure (also see Indal Limited's financial statements in Appendix 5A of Chapter 5).

Andres Wines Ltd.

Balance Sheet	1982	1981
FIXED ASSETS (Note 2)	$9,843,039	$10,025,795

Notes to financial statements:
1. Accounting policies (in part)
Fixed Assets
Depreciation on fixed assets is calculated on the straight-line basis over the estimated useful lives of the assets as follows:

Buildings ....2.5% per year
Manufacturing machinery and equipment ....7.5% per year
Other equipment ....10% to 33.3% per year
2. FIXED ASSETS

	1982			1981
	Cost	Accumulated Depreciation	Net	Net
	$	$	$	$
Land	878,145	—	878,145	763,582
Buildings	6,019,128	1,273,443	4,745,685	4,861,771
Machinery and equipment	11,035,762	6,816,553	4,219,209	4,400,442
	17,933,035	8,089,996	9,843,039	10,025,795

Many individuals argue that the disclosure requirements are still not sufficient. For example, some accountants believe that the average useful life of the assets or the range of years for asset life is significant information that should be disclosed.[10]

The effects of changing prices on property, plant, and equipment are substantial. To help deal with this problem, the *CICA Handbook*, Section 4510, recommends that relatively large, publicly held companies disclose supplementary information on such things as the current cost amounts of the carrying value for property, plant, and equipment, the changes during the reporting period in such amounts, and current cost amounts for depreciation, depletion, and amortization. The detailed

---

[9]*CICA Handbook*, Section 3060.

[10]Charles W. Lamden, Dale L. Gerboth, and Thomas W. McRae, ''Accounting for Depreciable Assets,'' *Accounting Research Monograph No. 1* (New York: AICPA, 1975), p. 111. Also, one writer found that variances in useful life had a greater impact on the variation among companies than the depreciation methods selected. See Robert R. Sterling, ''A Test of the Uniformity Hypothesis,'' *Abacus* (September, 1969), pp. 39–47.

computational aspects related to the provision of such information are discussed in Chapter 25.

OMIT
FROM
HERE

INVESTMENT TAX CREDIT

In recent years, the federal government and certain provincial governments have attempted to stimulate the economy by permitting special tax advantages to enterprises that invest in capital assets. One such advantage that has occurred is the investment tax credit. For example, assume that the investment credit allows a taxpayer to reduce taxes payable by an amount up to 10% of the cost of qualified depreciable property purchased. Suppose that an enterprise purchases an asset for $100,000 in 1986 that qualifies for the investment credit. If the company has a tax liability of $30,000 before the credit, the company's final tax liability is:

Taxes payable for 1986 prior to investment credit	$30,000
Less: Investment credit ($100,000 × 10%)	10,000
Final tax liability	$20,000

A vigorous controversy has existed within the accounting profession about how the investment credit should be handled for financial reporting purposes. Many believe that the investment credit is a government reduction in the cost of qualified property similar to a purchase discount, and should be accounted for over the same period as that of the related asset (cost reduction or deferral approach). Others believe that the investment credit is a selective reduction in the tax expense for the year of the purchase, and should be handled as such for financial reporting purposes (tax reduction or flow-through approach). The arguments for the two approaches are presented below.

Cost Reduction or Deferral Method   Advocates for this position argue that earnings (or reduction in tax expense) do not arise from the purchase of qualified property. Instead, the use of the asset creates the benefits to be received from the investment credit. Additional support is given to this argument if part of the investment credit must be refunded; for example, if the property is not kept for a given number of years.

Another position taken is that the true cost of the asset is not the invoice cost but the invoice cost, less the investment credit. Many believe that a company would not buy the property unless the credit were available, and the invoice cost of the asset should be reduced accordingly.

When this method for financial statement purposes is used, the tax credit is either deducted from the cost of the asset with depreciation calculated on the net amount, or deferred and amortized to income on the same basis on which the cost of the related asset is depreciated.

Tax Reduction or Flow-Through Method   In the tax-reduction method the investment credit is considered to be a selective tax reduction in the period of the purchase and, therefore, tax expense for that period is reduced by the full amount of the credit. Advocates of this approach indicate that realization of the credit does not depend on future use of the property, and the benefits of the credit should therefore not be deferred. The investment credit is earned by the act of investment. The credit is not affected by the use or nonuse, retention or nonretention, of the asset.

The following illustration indicates how the investment credit is handled under the two approaches.

Illustration   Kane, Inc. purchases machinery on January 1, 1986, for $100,000 that qualifies for a 10% investment tax credit. The machinery has a useful life of 10 years and no salvage value. Assume that the company intends to use straight-line depreciation ($10,000 per year) for both book and tax purposes,[11] and net income before depreciation and income taxes is $35,000. The tax rate is 50%. In this illustration, it has been assumed that a Deferred Investment Credit amount is created and amortized to income over the 10 years rather than deducting the tax credit from the cost of the machinery with depreciation then calculated on the net amount.

Entries under Cost Reduction and Tax Reduction Bases

Cost Reduction (Deferral)			Tax Reduction (Flow-through)		
At time of purchase, 1/1/86:					
Machinery	100,000		Machinery	100,000	
Cash		100,000	Cash		100,000
Recognition and payment of taxes in 1986:					
Income Tax Expense	12,500		Income Tax Expense	2,500	
Cash		2,500	Cash		2,500
Deferred Investment			(The $10,000 investment tax credit		
Credit		10,000	is deducted from the $12,500 tax		
			expense before the credit to get		
			the $2,500 tax expense for 1986)		
Deferred Investment					
Credit	1,000				
Income Tax Expense		1,000			
Recognition of depreciation in 1986:					
Depreciation Expense	10,000		Depreciation Expense	10,000	
Accumulated Depreciation		10,000	Accumulated Depreciation		10,000
Annual entries in subsequent periods, assuming income before depreciation and income taxes of $35,000:					
Income Tax Expense	11,500		Income Tax Expense	12,500	
Deferred Investment			Cash		12,500
Credit	1,000				
Cash		12,500			
Depreciation Expense	10,000		Depreciation Expense	10,000	
Accumulated Depreciation		10,000	Accumulated Depreciation		10,000

The effects on the income statement and the balance sheet for 1986, 1987, and the 10 years combined are illustrated on page 529.

[11]While the CCA method would usually be used for tax purposes, this assumption has been made to avoid the complexities of having to deal with deferred income taxes in financial statements that result from different methods being used for financial reporting and tax determination (to be examined in Chapter 20). This simplifies the illustration, allowing concentration on the differences between the two approaches regarding investment tax credits. The principles illustrated would apply even if the straight-line method were used for financial statements and CCA for tax purposes. It should also be noted that the capital cost allowance for tax purpose would differ from the depreciation expense for financial statements because the Tax Act deems the capital cost to be $90,000 in this example, even if straight-line amounts were taken for tax purposes.

Income Statement and Balance Sheet
under Cost Reduction and Tax Reduction Methods
of Recording Investment Credit

Income Statement

	1986		1987		Ten Years Combined	
	Cost Reduction	Tax Reduction	Cost Reduction	Tax Reduction	Cost Reduction	Tax Reduction
Income before depreciation and income taxes	$35,000	$35,000	$35,000	$35,000	$350,000	$350,000
Depreciation expense	10,000	10,000	10,000	10,000	100,000	100,000
Income before income taxes	$25,000	$25,000	$25,000	$25,000	$250,000	$250,000
Income tax expense	11,500	2,500	11,500	12,500	115,000	115,000
Net income	$13,500	$22,500	$13,500	$12,500	$135,000	$135,000

Balance Sheet

	1986		1987		At End of Ten Years	
	Cost Reduction	Tax Reduction	Cost Reduction	Tax Reduction	Cost Reduction	Tax Reduction
Machinery	$100,000	$100,000	$100,000	$100,000	$100,000	$100,000
Accumulated depreciation	(10,000)	(10,000)	(20,000)	(20,000)	(100,000)	(100,000)
	$90,000	$90,000	$80,000	$80,000	-0-	-0-
Deferred investment credit (liability)	$9,000	-0-	$8,000	-0-	-0-	-0-

The key issue related to the selection of one method over the other is how one views the economic substance of investment tax credits: is the government providing part of the cost of acquiring the asset, or is the government reducing its demand for current taxes of companies that invest in new assets?[12] Investment tax credits appear to possess the characteristics of both perspectives. After having gone through due process, the Accounting Standards Committee issued Section 3805 of the *CICA Handbook* dealing with investment tax credits in July, 1984, with its recommendations becoming effective for fiscal periods beginning on or after January 1, 1985. Recognizing the arguments for each approach, the Committee concluded that those favouring the cost reduction approach were more persuasive. Consequently, the recommendations state that "investment tax credits should be accounted for using the cost reduction approach."[13] Such credits would be either deducted from the asset's cost with depreciation or amortization calculated on the net amount, or deferred and amortized to income on the same basis as the related asset. Appropriate disclosure in notes would be useful to the readers of the financial statements.

[12]Jonathan M. Kligman, "Investment Tax Credits: Some Key Issues," *CA Magazine* (October, 1983), pp. 78–80. This article provides a good perspective on the controversy over which approach is appropriate and the type of input the Accounting Standards Committee had to deal with when resolving the issue.

[13]*CICA Handbook*, Section 3805, par. 12.

This *Handbook* recommendation is likely to have significant consequences with regard to the financial reporting of most Canadian companies having investment tax credits, as they had predominantly used the flow-through method given that a choice was available.[14] The use of the flow-through method, in addition to the theoretical reasons for its support, was also viewed favourably for practical reasons, as it could increase reported earnings substantially in the year the tax credit was taken.

OMIT
TO
HERE

DEPLETION

Natural resources, often called wasting assets, include petroleum, minerals, and timber. Natural resources are characterized by two main features: (1) the complete removal (consumption) of the asset, and (2) replacement of the asset only by an act of nature. Unlike plant and equipment, natural resources are consumed physically over the period of use and do not maintain their physical characteristics. For the most part, the accounting problems associated with natural resources are similar to those encountered in the plant asset area. The questions to be answered are:

1. How is the cost basis for write-off (depletion) established?
2. What pattern of allocation should be employed?

Establishment of Depletion Base

How do we determine the proper cost for an oil well? Rather large expenditures are needed to find these natural resources, and for every successful discovery there are many "dry holes." Furthermore, long delays are encountered between the time the costs are initially incurred and the point at which benefits are obtained from the extracted resources. As a result, a conservative policy frequently is adopted in accounting for the expenditures incurred in finding and extracting natural resources.

The **cost of natural resources** can be divided into three categories: (1) acquisition cost of the deposit, (2) exploration costs, and (3) development costs. The **acquisition cost of the deposit** is the price paid to obtain the property right to search and find an undiscovered natural resource or the price paid for an already discovered resource. In some cases, property is leased and special royalty payments paid to the lessor if a productive natural resource is found and is commercially profitable. Generally, the acquisition cost is placed in an account titled Undeveloped Property and assigned to the natural resource if exploration efforts are successful. If they are unsuccessful, the cost is written off as a loss.

As soon as the enterprise has the right to use the property, considerable **exploration costs** are likely to be incurred in finding the resource. The accounting treatment for these costs varies: some firms expense all exploration costs; others capitalize only those costs that are directly related to successful projects **(successful efforts approach)**; others adopt a **full-cost approach** (capitalization of all costs whether related to successful or unsuccessful projects).

Proponents of the full-cost concept believe that unsuccessful ventures are a cost of those that are successful, because the cost of drilling a dry hole is a cost that is needed to find the commercially profitable wells. Those who believe that only the

---

[14]*Financial Reporting in Canada—1983* showed that, of 137 companies affected by an investment tax credit in 1982, 103 used the flow-through method, 23 used one of the two approaches under the deferred (cost reduction) method, with the remainder referring only to the existence of unused credits.

costs of successful projects should be capitalized contend that unsuccessful companies will end up capitalizing many costs that will make them, over a short period of time, show no less income than does a company that is successful. In addition, it is contended that to measure accurately cost and effort for a single property unit, the only measure is in terms of the cost directly related to that unit. The remainder of the costs should be allocated as period charges similar to such period costs as advertising.

Canadian practice is mixed in terms of these two approaches.[15] Larger companies like Gulf Canada Ltd., Imperial Oil Limited, Shell Canada Limited, and Texaco Canada Limited use the successful efforts approach. The smaller to medium-sized companies favour the full-cost approach. Exceptions to this generality regarding size include Dome Petroleum Limited and Petro Canada, which are large companies that use the full-cost method. The differences in net income figures under the two methods can be staggering. For example, until Texaco (world-wide) switched to the successful efforts approach in 1975, it was estimated that full-cost accounting increased Texaco's reported profits by $500 million over the previous ten years.

The final costs that are incurred in finding natural resources are **development costs** which are classified in two ways: (1) tangible equipment, and (2) intangible development costs. Tangible equipment includes all of the transportation and other heavy equipment necessary to extract the resource and get it ready for production and shipment. **Tangible equipment costs are normally not considered in the depletion base;** instead, separate depreciation charges are employed because the asset can be moved from one drilling or mining site to another. Depreciation expense is, therefore, based on a service life relevant to its total usefulness. Tangible assets that cannot be moved should be depreciated over their useful life or the life of the resource, whichever is shorter. **Intangible development costs, on the other hand, are considered part of the depletion base.** These costs are for such items as drilling costs, tunnels, shafts, and wells, which have no tangible characteristics, but are needed for the production of the natural resource.

Write-off of Resource Cost

As soon as the depletion base is established, the next problem is determining how the natural resource cost should be allocated to accounting periods. Normally, depletion expense is computed on the units of production method (activity approach), which means that depletion expense is a function of the number of units withdrawn during the period. When this approach is adopted, the total cost of the natural resource is divided by the number of units estimated to be in the resource deposit to obtain a cost per unit of product. This cost per unit is multiplied by the number of units extracted during a period to compute the period's depletion.

For example, suppose MaClede Oil Co. has acquired the right to use 400 ha of land in northern Alberta to explore for oil. The lease cost is $50,000; the related exploration costs for a discovered oil deposit on the property are $100,000; and

---

[15]*The Oil and Gas Industry in Canada: 1983 Survey of Financial Reporting* (Toronto: Price Waterhouse & Co., Canada, 1983) showed that, of the companies in the survey, 7 used successful efforts and 22 used full cost. This document provides an informative description of issues involved and accounting practices used by those Canadian oil and gas companies surveyed, and would be of considerable use to those interested in the topic.

intangible development costs incurred in erecting and drilling the well are $850,000. Total cost related to the oil deposit before the first barrel is extracted is, therefore, $1,000,000. It is estimated that the well will provide approximately 1,000,000 barrels of oil. The depletion rate established is computed in the following manner:

$$\frac{\text{Total cost}}{\text{Total estimated units available}} = \text{Depletion cost per unit}$$

$$\frac{\$1,000,000}{1,000,000} = \$1.00 \text{ per barrel}$$

If 250,000 barrels are withdrawn in the first year, then the depletion charge for the year is $250,000 (250,000 barrels at $1.00). The entry to record the depletion is:

Depletion Expense	250,000	
Accumulated Depletion		250,000

In some instances an Accumulated Depletion account is not used, and the credit goes directly to the natural resources asset account. The depletion charge would initially become part of the cost of the resource extracted (in addition to labour and other direct costs) and then be charged against revenue as the resource is sold (i.e., the cost flow would be similar to that of depreciation on a factory of a manufacturing company, which is part of the cost of goods manufactured and is charged to the income statement in the period in which the goods are sold). The following presents the cost of the property and the amount of depletion entered to date as it could appear on a balance sheet:

Oil deposit (at cost)	$1,000,000	
Less: Accumulated depletion	250,000	$750,000

The tangible equipment used in extracting the oil may also be depreciated on a units of production basis, especially if the estimated lives of the equipment can be directly assigned to one given resource deposit. If the equipment is utilized in more than one job, such other cost allocation methods as straight-line or accelerated depreciation methods may be more appropriate.

OMIT FROM HERE ↓

Controversy Concerning Oil and Gas Accounting

Accounting for oil and gas resources is currently in a state of evolution. The *CICA Handbook* is silent on most of the accounting issues related to this industry.[16] To a considerable extent, accounting practices of many Canadian companies have been influenced by standards and regulations existing in the United States. A history of developments in the U.S.A. is presented in the U.S. edition of this book and may serve as a useful starting point for those who wish to pursue the issues involved.

What will become the accepted accounting method for the oil and gas industry is difficult to predict. Either the full-cost approach or the successful efforts approach is currently acceptable. It also appears that some form of value-based disclosure of oil and gas reserves eventually will occur, but such disclosure is currently made only on a voluntary basis.

[16]At the time of writing this book, the CICA had established an Accounting Task Force which was to prepare a report to the Accounting Standards Committee proposing accounting policies and procedures for Canadian enterprises that follow the full-cost method. Oil and gas companies are, however, subject to the more generalized standards and guidelines in the *Handbook* (e.g., foreign currency translation, accounting for the effects of changing prices, investment tax credits).

Special Problems in Depletion Accounting

Accounting for natural resources has some interesting problems that are uncommon to most other types of assets. For purposes of discussion we have divided these problems into three categories:

1. Difficulty of estimating recoverable reserves.
2. Problems of discovery value.
3. Accounting for liquidating dividends.

Estimating Recoverable Reserves   Not infrequently the estimate of recoverable reserves has to be changed either because new information becomes available or because production processes become more sophisticated.

Such natural resources as oil and gas deposits and some rare metals have recently provided the greatest challenges. Estimates of these reserves are, in large measure, "knowledgeable guesses," and change frequently in today's environment, where marginal projects are undertaken because of price escalations.

This problem is the same as that faced in accounting for changes in estimates of the useful lives of plant and equipment. The procedure is to revise the depletion rate on a prospective basis by dividing the remaining cost into an estimate of the new recoverable reserves. This approach has much merit in this field because the required estimates are quite tenuous.

Discovery Value   Discovery value accounting and reserve recognition accounting (RRA) are essentially similar. RRA is specifically related to the oil and gas industry, whereas discovery value is a broader term associated with the whole area of natural resources. Essentially, application of these approaches means that, as soon as a company finds a resource, its value would be reported on the balance sheet. In general, practice has not recognized discovery values in the general ledger accounts. If discovery value is recorded, an asset account would be debited, and an Unrealized Appreciation account or income account would be credited. Unrealized Appreciation is part of Shareholders' Equity and, if it is used, amounts would then be transferred to revenue (realized income) as the natural resource is sold.

A similar approach could be applied to such resources as growing timber, aging liquor, and maturing livestock, which increase in value over time. One could record the increase in value as the accretion occurs as a debit to the asset account and as a credit to income or to an unrealized income account. These increases can be substantial. For example, the timber resources of a large lumber company were recently valued at $1.7 billion whereas its book value was approximately $289 million. Accountants have hesitated to record these increases because of the uncertainty regarding the final sales price, and the problem of estimating the costs of readying the resources for sale. As such, the trade-offs that exist between the desired qualitative characteristics of relevancy and reliability of information are particularly evident regarding the reporting of discovery values.

Liquidating Dividend   A company often owns as its only major asset a certain property from which it intends to extract natural resources. If the company does not expect to purchase additional properties, it may distribute gradually to shareholders their capital investment by paying dividends equal to the accumulated amount of net income (after depletion) plus the amount of depletion charged. The major accounting problem is to distinguish between dividends that are a return of capital and those that are not. The company, in issuing a liquidating dividend, should debit the appropriate Contributed Capital Account(s) for that portion related to the original investment instead of Retained Earnings, because the dividend is a return of part of the investor's original contribution. Shareholders must be informed that the total dividend consists of a liquidation of capital as well as a distribution of income.

FINANCIAL REPORTING OF NATURAL RESOURCES AND DEPLETION

As previously indicated, the *CICA Handbook* has no specific recommendations regarding financial statement reporting for natural resource companies. Basically, such reporting would be similar to that required for other fixed assets (proper classification, methods used for establishing cost and depletion charges). Considerable guidance for such reporting has come from the U.S.A. and is frequently followed by Canadian companies. Of particular relevance at the present time is *Statement No. 69* of the FASB, "Disclosures about Oil and Gas Producing Activi-

---

Property, plant, and equipment, at cost: (Note 1)
  Mineral properties and mineral rights:

Producing mineral properties and rights	$3,851,018	
Less: Accumulated depletion	(1,882,125)	$1,968,893

  Operating plant and equipment:

Land and buildings	$ 934,613	
Machinery and equipment	1,865,290	
Furniture, fixtures, and other	1,012,385	
Less: Accumulated depreciation	(1,820,277)	1,992,011

Exploration projects and undeveloped mineral properties		5,143,716

Note 1—Significant Accounting Policies

DEPRECIATION AND DEPLETION—Generally, for producing mining and oil and gas properties, depreciation and depletion are provided on the unit-of-production method so as to write off the cost of property, plant, and equipment over the estimated commercial lives of the properties based upon reserve estimates. The straight-line method is used for other assets; such assets are written off over their estimated useful lives (buildings, 10 to 45 years and machinery, equipment, furniture, and fixtures, 3 to 15 years).

EXPLORATION AND DEVELOPMENT—

Mining: Exploration expenditures are charged to earnings. For some projects, facilities expenditures may be necessary before exploration expenses are incurred. Such costs are capitalized and, if exploration is successful, are depreciated over the estimated life of reserves using the unit-of-production method. If exploration is not successful, remaining capitalized costs are written down to estimated net realizable value. Development costs are those incurred after reserves are shown to exist in commercially marketable quantities but prior to the commencement of production. Such costs are capitalized and when production commences are amortized over the estimated life of the reserves.

Oil and Gas: The Company uses the successful efforts method of accounting for oil and gas expenditures. Leasehold acquisition costs are capitalized. Such costs are reflected in producing properties if commercial reserves are discovered or they are charged to expense if it is determined that a property is nonproductive. All geological and geophysical costs and delay rentals are expensed as incurred. Exploratory drilling costs are initially capitalized and costs of unsuccessful wells are charged to expense when they are determined to be dry holes. Costs of development wells are capitalized.

ties.''[17] It states that both publicly traded and privately held companies engaged in significant oil and gas producing activities are required to disclose in their financial statements (1) the basic method of accounting for costs incurred in those activities (e.g., full-cost or successful efforts), and (2) the manner of disposing of costs relating to those activities (e.g., expensing immediately, or capitalizing followed by depreciation and depletion). Public companies, in addition to these two disclosures, must report as supplementary information numerous schedules disclosing reserve quantities; capitalized costs; acquisition, exploration, and development activities; and operating results by geographic area.

The illustration on page 534 indicates the type of classifications, descriptions, and disclosures commonly practised. (Read Note 1 to determine the accounting policies applied by this natural resources company.) In many instances, the financial statement disclosures of natural resource (particularly oil and gas) companies are much more complex than is indicated in this example.

KEY POINTS

1. Depreciation, depletion, and amortization are terms used in accounting to describe the allocation of the cost of various assets (plant and equipment, natural resources, and intangibles respectively), less salvage value, over their useful economic lives in a systematic and rational manner.

2. As depreciation is the result of a cost allocation process to match expenses against revenues systematically and rationally, it is not intended to result in financial statement amounts that reflect value or value changes in the related assets.

3. Determining the amount of depreciation for a period requires determination of the base amount to be depreciated (cost less salvage), the estimated useful life, and the method of cost apportionment to be used.

4. This chapter examined various depreciation methods. The accountant must exercise appropriate judgement when selecting and implementing the method that is most appropriate for the circumstances. Rational matching, tax reporting, simplicity, and perceived economic consequences are factors that have impact on such judgements.

5. Special depreciation problems addressed in the chapter were how to account for depreciation for partial periods, overcoming the misconception that depreciation accounting results in providing funds for asset replacement, and how to account for revisions in estimates that constitute components of the depreciation expense calculation (i.e., reflect the changes in the current and future periods calculations and do not make retroactive adjustments for previous periods).

6. Recognizing a permanent impairment in value for property, plant, and equipment is an issue that can be resolved only by one's judgement in terms of the objectives of financial reporting and awareness of contemporary practice. While sound arguments exist for such recognition in certain circumstances, the tendency in practice has been not to reflect such an impairment in the financial statements.

---

[17]"Disclosure about Oil and Gas Producing Activities," *Statement of the Financial Accounting Standards Board No. 69* (Stamford, Conn.: FASB, 1982).

7. The basis of valuation (usually historical cost) for property, plant, and equipment, major categories of assets, related accumulated depreciation, pledges related to these assets, current period's expense, and the methods and rates used to calculate depreciation should be disclosed in financial statements. The *CICA Handbook* also recommends disclosure of current cost information for fixed assets and such related expenses as supplementary information for relatively large, publicly held companies.

8. Investment tax credits are provided by the government to promote investment in certain assets. Two methods of accounting for these tax credits have been traditionally practised—the cost reduction or deferral method and the tax reduction or flow-through method. While the latter had been used most frequently in Canada prior to 1985, the *CICA Handbook* now requires use of a cost reduction approach.

9. Depletion refers to the allocation of the cost of natural resources. The cost of these resources includes that incurred for acquisition, exploration, and development. The amount of these costs (which are capitalized and then allocated to expense rather than expensed directly) depends on whether the successful efforts or full-cost approach is being used. Capitalized resource costs are usually charged to depletion, using an activity approach (units of production method).

10. Particular issues related to accounting for natural resource industries include the difficulty of estimating recoverable reserves, determining discovery value, and appropriately determining and reporting a liquidating dividend.

11. Disclosure in financial statements of natural resource companies would include proper classification, identifying the method used for establishing cost and depletion charges, and possibly additional supplementary information regarding reserve quantities, operating results by geographic area, acquisition, exploration and development activity, and information on current costs.

11A

TAX METHOD OF CAPITAL COST ALLOWANCE: EXTENSION OF EXAMPLE TO INCLUDE ADDITIONS, RETIREMENTS, AND ASSET CLASS ELIMINATION

Included in this chapter was a basic illustration of the tax method of capital cost allowance determination. Although the mechanics of this method were described, several complexities related to the determination of taxable income remain. The purpose of this appendix is to illustrate some of these complexities—namely, how to account for additions, retirements, and asset class elimination for purposes of determining taxable income. While this material deals exclusively with aspects of determining taxable income, it has implications regarding accounting for deferred income taxes, a financial accounting problem examined in Chapter 20.

Table 11A-1 presents a Capital Cost Allowance Schedule incorporating information to illustrate these complexities. The schedule is a continuation of that shown in Table 11-4 (page 516) dealing with the determination of capital cost allowance for a crane purchased by Barek Co. Ltd. which had a cost of $500,000 and on which capital cost allowance had been taken for three years, resulting in undepreciated capital cost of $288,000 at the beginning of Year 4 for Class 8 assets. The continuation of this schedule is based on the assumption of the following transactions:

1. In Year 4, the company bought another crane (or any other Class 8 asset) for $700,000.
2. In Year 5, the company sold the first crane (No. 1) for $300,000.
3. In Year 6, the company sold the second crane (No. 2) for $500,000. This resulted in no assets remaining in Class 8.

Additions to Asset Class The purchase of another crane (No. 2) in Year 4 resulted in a net addition of $700,000 to the undepreciated capital cost at the end of Year 4. Consequently, the balance of undepreciated capital cost at the end of Year 4 is made up of this $700,000 plus the $288,000 undepreciated capital cost of crane No. 1. The capital cost allowance for Year 4 is, therefore, 20% of $288,000 ($57,600) plus one-half of 20% of the net addition of $700,000 ($70,000) for a total of $127,600.

TABLE 11A-1   Capital Cost Allowance Schedule—Continuation of Table 11-4

UCC beginning of Year 4	$288,000
Additions during Year 4—crane No. 2	700,000
UCC before CCA	$988,000
CCA for Year 4 [(20% × $288,000) + (.5 × 20% × $700,000)]	127,600
UCC beginning of Year 5	$860,400
Deduct the lower of the proceeds from ($300,000) or cost	
of ($500,000) crane No. 1 disposed of during the year	300,000
UCC before CCA	$560,400
CCA for Year 5 (20% × $560,400)	112,080
UCC beginning of Year 6	$448,320
Deduct the lower of the proceeds from ($500,000) or cost	
of ($700,000) crane No. 2 disposed of during the year	500,000
Note: This disposal eliminates all Class 8 assets of the company.	
Recaptured capital cost	$ 51,680

Retirements from an Asset Class, Continuation of Class   When there is more than one asset in a class from which the disposal of an asset takes place, and when the proceeds from or cost of the asset disposed of, whichever is lower, is less than the undepreciated capital cost balance, then the proceeds or cost, whichever is lower, is simply deducted from the undepreciated capital cost balance for the class. This is what happened in Year 5 when the company sold crane No. 1 for $300,000. Since the proceeds were less than the $500,000 original cost, the $300,000 amount was deducted from the $860,400 undepreciated capital cost balance before determining the capital cost allowance for Year 5.

Retirements from an Asset Class, Elimination of Class When the disposal of an asset results in the elimination of an asset class (either because there are no more assets remaining in the class or because the disposal results in the elimination of the undepreciated capital cost balance of the class), the following may result:

1. A recapture of capital cost allowance.
2. A recapture of capital cost allowance and a capital gain.
3. A terminal loss (only when the last asset in the class is disposed of and a balance still exists in the UCC of that class after deducting proceeds or cost of the disposed asset, whichever is lower).

The amount of proceeds, original cost of the asset, and balance of the undepreciated capital cost for the class must be examined to determine which of these results occur.

A **recapture of capital cost allowance** occurs when the proceeds from or cost of the asset disposed of, whichever is lower, is greater than the balance of undepreciated capital cost. The difference represents the amount of recaptured capital cost. This recapture would be included in calculating taxable income and, therefore, subject to income tax at the normal rates. The events of Year 6 reflected in Table 11A-1 illustrate this situation. Since the $500,000 proceeds are lower than the cost of crane No. 2, they are deducted from the $448,320 balance of undepreciated capital cost, resulting in the $51,680 recaptured capital cost allowance.

If an asset of a class is sold for more than its cost, a **capital gain** results, regardless of whether or not the asset class is eliminated. For tax purposes, a capital gain (difference between proceeds and cost when proceeds exceed cost) is treated differently from a recapture of capital cost. Essentially, the taxable capital gain (amount subject to tax) is equal to one-half of the capital gain as defined above. The taxable capital gain is subject to a specified tax rate on such capital gains (i.e., 50%). As indicated previously, the full amount of the recaptured capital cost allowance is included in taxable income. Thus, the recaptured amount is subject to the normal tax rate applicable to the taxable income being reported. If crane No. 1 had been sold in Year 5 for $575,000 the capital gain would be $75,000 and the taxable capital gain would be $37,500. The amount of $500,000 would have been deducted from the UCC. If crane No. 2 had been sold for $750,000 in Year 6, a capital gain and a recapture of capital cost allowance would result. The capital gain would be $50,000 and, therefore, a taxable capital gain of $25,000 would occur. The recaptured capital cost allowance would be $251,680 (the $700,000 cost less the $448,320 undepreciated capital cost balance for the asset class being eliminated). While this example illustrated the basic calculations related to the determination of capital gains, taxable capital gains, and recaptured capital cost allowance, it has necessarily been oversimplified in terms of specifying the actual rates of tax applicable to the latter two items. In essence, the tax rate on taxable capital gains is specified by tax law, which may change from time to time and have implications in terms of other considerations (i.e., refundable dividend tax on hand). Similarly, the tax rate applicable to recaptured capital cost allowance is subject to the particular circumstances of the nature of taxable income being reported (of which the recaptured amount is a component). For example, the recapture will be ''active'' income provided the business is ''active'' and, thus, subject to a reduced tax rate on the first $200,000 of active income earned. These technical and definitional aspects are beyond the scope of this text, but have been mentioned here to point out that determining income taxes payable requires considerable specialist knowledge regarding tax laws.

A **terminal loss** occurs when the proceeds from the disposal of the last asset in a class are less than the undepreciated capital cost balance. A terminal loss may be deducted in full when determining taxable income. If crane No. 2 had been sold in Year 6 for $300,000, a terminal loss of $148,320 would result (the $448,320 undepreciated capital cost less the $300,000 proceeds).

Note: All **asterisked** Questions, Cases, Exercises, or Problems relate to material contained in an Appendix.

QUESTIONS

1. Identify the factors that are relevant in determining the annual depreciation charge. Explain whether these factors are determined objectively or whether they are based on judgement.

2. Distinguish between depreciation, depletion, and amortization.

3. What is accounting for depreciation, and what is its objective? Are the decreasing charge methods of depreciation consistent with this objective? Discuss.

4. The plant manager of a manufacturing firm suggested in a conference of the company's executives that accountants should speed up depreciation on the machinery in the finishing department because improvements were rapidly making those machines obsolete, and a depreciation fund big enough to cover their replacement is needed. Discuss the accounting concept of depreciation and the effect on a business concern of the depreciation recorded for plant assets, paying particular attention to the issues raised by the plant manager.

5. What basic questions must be answered before the amount of the depreciation charge can be computed?

6. For what reasons are plant assets retired? Define inadequacy, supersession, and obsolescence.

7. Porter Company purchased machinery for $120,000 on January 1, 1986. It is estimated that the machinery will have a useful life of 20 years, scrap value of $16,000, production of 84,000 units, and working hours of 42,000. During 1986 the company uses the machinery for 14,300 hours, and the machinery produces 20,000 units. Compute depreciation expense for 1986 under the straight-line, units-of-output, working-hours, sum-of-the-years'-digits, and double-declining balance methods.

8. What are the major factors to be considered in determining which depreciation method to use?

9. It has been suggested that plant and equipment could be replaced more quickly if depreciation rates for income tax and accounting purposes were substantially increased. As a result, business operations would receive the benefit of more modern and more efficient plant facilities. Discuss the merits of this proposition.

10. A building that was purchased on December 31, 1961, for $600,000 was originally estimated to have a life of 50 years with no salvage value at the end of that time. Depreciation has been recorded through 1985. During 1986 an examination of the building by an engineering firm discloses that its remaining estimated useful life is 25 years including 1986. What should be the amount of depreciation for 1986?

11. Discuss the accounting justification for recording on the books (a) plant assets received as a gift and (b) their depreciation or depletion.

12. Under what conditions is it appropriate for a concern to use the retirement method of depreciation for plant assets? What are the advantages of this method?

13. If a business that uses the retirement method sells for $12,000 plant assets originally costing $30,000 five years ago, what entry should be made? The assets sold consist of 500 small motors, which usually last about seven years.

14. Under what conditions is it appropriate for a business to use the composite method of depreciation for its plant assets? What are the advantages and disadvantages of this method?

15. If a concern uses the composite method and its composite rate is 7.5% per year, what entry should it make when plant assets that originally cost $40,000 and have been used for ten years are sold for $10,000?

16. List (a) the similarities and (b) the differences in the accounting treatments of depreciation and cost depletion.

17. In the extractive industries, businesses may pay dividends in excess of net income. What is the maximum permissible? How can this practice be justified?

18. Neither depreciation on replacement cost nor depreciation adjusted for changes in the purchasing power of the dollar has been recognized as generally accepted accounting practice for inclusion in the primary financial statements although inclusion as supplementary information is recommended for large, publicly held companies. Briefly present the accounting treatment that might be used to assist in maintaining the ability of a company to replace its productive capacity.

*19. Using the information in Appendix 11A, indicate what is meant by the terms recaptured capital cost, capital gain, and terminal loss.

CASES

C11-1 Presented below are three different and unrelated situations involving depreciation accounting. Answer the question(s) at the end of each situation.

1. Rockwell Company manufactures electrical appliances, most of which are used in homes. Rockwell's engineers have designed a new blender which, with a few attachments, will perform more functions than any blender currently on the market. Demand for the new blender can be projected with reasonable probability. In order to make the blenders, Rockwell needs a specialized machine that is not available from outside sources. It has been decided to make such a machine in Rockwell's own plant.

Instructions

(a) Discuss the effect of projected demand in units for the new blenders (which may be steady, decreasing, or increasing) on the determination of a depreciation method for the machine.

(b) What other matters should be considered in determining the depreciation method? Ignore income tax considerations.

2. Western Paper Company, a subsidiary of Northern Paper Company, operates a 300-tonne-per-day kraft pulp mill and four sawmills in British Columbia. The company is in the process of expanding its pulp mill capacity to 1,000 tonnes per day and plans to replace three of its older, less efficient sawmills with an expanded facility. One of the mills to be replaced has not been operating for most of 1986 (the current year), and there are no plans to reopen it before the new sawmill facility becomes operational.

   In reviewing the depreciation rates and in discussing the residual values of the sawmills that are to be replaced, it is noted that if present depreciation rates are not adjusted, substantial amounts of plant costs on these three mills would not be depreciated by the time the new mill comes on stream.

Instructions

What is the proper accounting for the four sawmills at the end of 1986?

3. Recently, Ottawa Company experienced a strike that affected a number of its operating plants. The controller of this company indicated that it was not appropriate to report depreciation expense during this period because the equipment did not depreciate and an improper matching of costs and revenues would result. He based his position on the following points:

(a) It is inappropriate to charge the period with costs for which there are no related revenues arising from production.

(b) The basic factor of depreciation in this instance is wear and tear, and because equipment was idle no wear and tear occurred.

Instructions

Comment on the appropriateness of the controller's comments.

C11-2   Benjamin Manufacturing Company was set up on January 1, 1986. During 1986, it has used in its reports to management the straight-line method of depreciating its plant assets.

On November 8, 1986, you are having a conference with Benjamin's officers to discuss the depreciation method to be used for shareholder reporting. The president has suggested the use of a new method, which he feels is more suitable than the straight-line method during the coming period of rapid expansion of production and capacity in the company. Following is an example in which the proposed method is applied to a fixed asset with an original cost of $62,000, an estimated useful life of five years, and a scrap value of approximately $2,000.

Year	Years of Life Used	Fraction Rate	Depreciation Expense	Accumulated Depreciation at End of Year	Book Value at End of Year
1	1	1/15	$ 4,000	$ 4,000	$58,000
2	2	2/15	8,000	12,000	50,000
3	3	3/15	12,000	24,000	38,000
4	4	4/15	16,000	40,000	22,000
5	5	5/15	20,000	60,000	2,000

The president favours the new method because he has heard that:

1. It will increase the funds recovered during the years near the end of the assets' useful lives when maintenance and replacement disbursements are high.
2. It will result in increased write-offs in later years when the company is likely to be in a better operating position.

Instructions

(a)   What is the purpose of accounting for depreciation?

(b)   Is the president's proposal within the scope of generally accepted accounting principles? In making your decision discuss the circumstances, if any, under which use of the method would be reasonable and those, if any, under which it would not be reasonable.

(c)   Do depreciation charges recover or create funds? Explain.

C11-3   The independent public accountant is frequently called upon by management for advice regarding methods of computing depreciation. Of comparable importance, although it arises less frequently, is the question of whether the depreciation method should be based on consideration of the assets as units, as a group, or as having a composite life.

Instructions

(a)   Briefly describe the depreciation methods based on treating assets as: (1) Units. (2) A group or as having a composite life.

(b)   Present the arguments for and against the use of each of the two methods.

(c)   Describe how retirements are recorded under each of the two methods.

(AICPA adapted)

C11-4   In 1984, a large corporation decided to construct a large new processing building at one of its mine sites. A smaller building capable of handling one-third of the capacity of the new building had been used for several years. The new building was completed and ready for operation in the spring of 1986. Much of the equipment used in processing in the old building was transferred to the new one.

At the time the new building began operations, the old building had a book value of $500,000. The auditors assessed the circumstances for this major client and indicated that they thought this amount should be written off as a loss in 1986. Management of the corporation protested against this accounting treatment. Their argument against such a write-off was that the old building had not been torn down and was still capable of handling processing activities should the need arise. Indeed, they had left the building standing as a safeguard against the possibility that things might go wrong with the new building or that the new building's capacity may not be sufficient at some time in the future to handle all processing. When the decision to construct the new building was made, management had attempted to forecast product demand and allowed an additional 20% capacity to the new building, but they recognized that in such a business forecasts could be off considerably. Indeed, in 1986, demand for the processed ore had fallen to two-thirds of the amount forecast, leaving the new processing building operating considerably below its capacity. These circumstances led the auditors to conclude that the old building, while capable of being used in operations, was not likely to be used in the foreseeable future.

Instructions

Analyze this situation and make recommendations regarding the accounting for the old building in 1986.

C11-5 Various companies are in the business of developing and marketing computer software packages (word processing, spreadsheets, business graphics, accounting packages). Several important accounting issues exist regarding how to classify, measure, and report the costs related to such operations. Specifically, issues include where the line should be drawn between expensing and capitalizing costs; whether or not the costs expensed should be shown as research and development costs; how capitalized costs should be amortized; and how the various items should be disclosed in the financial statements.

Generally, computer software costs may be categorized into four types as follows. (Categories basically follow the stages of incurrence, although these stages can overlap.)

1. Idea formulation and feasibility: These costs include costs of study and documentation related to market feasibility (potential market, duration of market, expected selling price, etc.), financial feasibility (determining if future revenues will exceed future costs), and management's commitment and ability (its commitment and ability to obtain the necessary resources.)

2. Determining technological feasibility and design of the product: These costs relate to the detailed product design, and coding and testing that are required to determine that the product can be produced to meet design specifications. Completion of this stage occurs when the product is sufficiently defined so that the costs of production can be reliably estimated.

3. Preparation for production: Presuming that the previous stages have been successful in terms of developing a product that has a technological market and financial feasibility as well as a management team with the commitment and ability to produce, the next step would be preparing for mass production and distribution. Cost at this level relates to producing product masters and related coding and testing, as well as completion of documentation and training materials for the customer.

4. Production of software packages: The costs incurred at this stage are for duplicating the software, documentation, and training materials as well as packaging the product for customers.

Instructions

(a) Throughout this process there are various ways to account for the costs incurred: treat as an operating expense of the period; treat as research and development costs; capitalize to a fixed asset account and amortize on a systematic and rational basis; or capitalize to an inventory account and charge to cost of sales when realization takes place. Analyze each of the four categories, considering them as part of a total process related to the continuing operations of a company, and reach conclusions as to how the costs should be accounted for. Also, for any costs you believe should be capitalized, indicate how they should be amortized or otherwise charged to expense.

(b) Because of the rapid technological and product changes related to the software industry, it is proposed by some that an "ongoing recoverability test" be carried out regarding any costs that have been capitalized. What would be the purpose of such tests? What items would they investigate?

*C11-6   A capital gain may occur whenever an asset is disposed of, whereas a terminal loss may occur only when an asset class is eliminated. Explain why this is so. (Refer to the material in Appendix 11A.)

EXERCISES

E11-1   The Bedrock Company purchased equipment for $204,000 on October 1, 1986. It is estimated that the equipment will have a useful life of ten years and a salvage value of $6,000. Estimated production is 40,000 units and estimated working hours 60,000. During 1986 the Bedrock Company uses the equipment for 2,500 hours and the equipment produces 2,000 units.

Instructions

Compute depreciation expense under each of the following methods. Bedrock is on a calendar-year basis ending December 31.

(a) Straight-line method for 1986.
(b) Activity method (units of output) for 1986.
(c) Activity method (working hours) for 1986.
(d) Double-declining balance method for 1987.
(e) What is the capital cost allowance for 1986 and 1987, assuming a CCA rate of 30% and that the equipment was the only item in the asset class?

E11-2   Kitefly Corp. purchased machinery for $112,000 on July 1, 1986. It is estimated that it will have a useful life of ten years, scrap value of $8,000, production of 273,000 units, and working hours of 63,000. During 1987 the Kitefly Corp. uses the machinery for 7,150 hours, and the machinery produces 32,300 units.

Instructions

Compute the depreciation charge for 1987 under each of the following methods. (Round to three decimal places.)

(a) Straight-line.
(b) Units-of-output.
(c) Working-hours.
(d) Sum-of-the-years'-digits.
(e) Declining balance (using 20% as the annual rate).
(f) Capital cost allowance (tax method), assuming a CCA rate of 20%.

E11-3   Keenguy Corporation purchased a new machine for its assembly process on October 1, 1986. The cost of this machine was $111,600. The company estimated that the machine would have a trade-in value of $3,600 at the end of its service life. Its life is estimated at five years and its working hours are estimated at 20,000 hours. Year end is December 31.

Instructions

Compute the depreciation expense under each of the following methods.

(a) Straight-line depreciation for 1986.
(b) Activity method for 1986 (assuming that machine usage was 800 hours).

(c) Sum-of-the-years'-digits for 1987.

(d) Double-declining balance for 1987.

(e) Capital cost allowance for 1986 and 1987, using a CCA rate of 25%.

Each of the foregoing should be considered unrelated.

E11-4 Robotron Company shows the following entries in its Equipment account for 1986; all amounts are based on historical cost.

Equipment

1986			1986		
Jan. 1	Balance	80,000	June 30	Cost of equipment	
Aug. 10	Purchases	20,000		sold (purchased prior	
12	Freight on equipment			to 1986)	8,000
	purchased	320			
25	Installation costs	800			
Nov. 10	Repairs	500			

Instructions

(a) Prepare any correcting entries necessary.

(b) Assuming that depreciation is to be charged for a full year on the ending balance in the asset account, compute the proper depreciation charge for 1986 under each of the methods listed below. Assume an estimated life of ten years, with no salvage value. The machinery included in the January 1, 1986, balance was purchased in 1984.

1. Straight-line.

2. Sum-of-the-years'-digits.

3. Declining balance (assuming twice the straight-line rate).

E11-5 Tall Tree Lumber Company owns a 5,000 hectare tract of timber purchased in 1977 at a cost of $1,000 per hectare. At the time of purchase, the land was estimated to have a value of $150 per hectare without the timber. Tall Tree Lumber Company has not logged this tract since it was purchased. In 1985, Tall Tree had the timber cruised (appraised). The cruise estimated that each hectare contained 10,000 cubic metres of timber. In 1986, Tall Tree built 10 kilometres of roads at a cost of $5,000 per kilometre. After the roads were completed, Tall Tree logged 4,000 trees containing 1,000,000 cubic metres.

Instructions

(a) Determine the depletion expense for 1986.

(b) If Tall Tree depreciates the logging roads on the basis of timber cut, determine the depreciation expense for 1986.

(c) If Tall Tree plants five seedlings at a cost of $3 per seedling for each tree cut, how should Tall Tree treat the reforestation?

E11-6 Elmira Timber Company owns 10,000 hectares of timberland purchased in 1980 at a cost of $1,500 per hectare. At the time of purchase the land without the timber was valued at $500 per hectare. In 1981, Elmira built fire lanes and roads, with a life of 30 years, at a cost of $60,000. Every year Elmira sprays to prevent disease at a cost of $2,000 per year and spends $5,000 to maintain the fire lanes and roads. During 1982 Elmira selectively logged 500,000 cubic metres of timber, of the estimated 2,500,000 cubic metres. In 1983, Elmira planted new seedlings to replace the trees cut at a cost of $100,000.

Instructions

(a) Determine the depreciation expense and depletion expense for 1982.

PART 2 / ASSETS—RECOGNITION AND MEASUREMENT

(b) Elmira has not logged since 1982. If Elmira logged 1,000,000 cubic metres of timber in 1994, when the timber cruise (appraiser) estimated 5,000,000 cubic metres, determine the depletion expense for 1994.

E11-7 On April 10, 1986, Astro Company sells equipment that it purchased for $120,000 on September 25, 1972. It was originally estimated that the equipment would have a life of 15 years and a scrap value of $12,000 at the end of that time, and depreciation had been computed on that basis. The company used the straight-line method of depreciation.

Instructions

(a) Compute the depreciation charge on this equipment for 1972, for 1986, and the total charge for the period from 1972 to 1986, inclusive, under each of the following six assumptions with respect to partial periods:

1. Depreciation is computed for the exact period of time during which the asset is owned. (Use 365 days for a base.)
2. Depreciation is computed for the full year on the January 1 balance in the asset account.
3. Depreciation is computed for the full year on the December 31 balance in the asset account.
4. Depreciation for one-half year is charged on plant assets acquired or disposed of during the year.
5. Depreciation is computed on additions from the beginning of the month following acquisition and on disposals to the beginning of the month following disposal.
6. Depreciation is computed for a full period on all assets in use for over one-half year, and no depreciation is charged on assets in use for less than one-half year. (Use 365 days for a base.)

(b) Briefly evaluate the methods above, considering them from the point of view of basic accounting theory as well as simplicity of application.

E11-8 Lazy Rocker Corporation bought a machine on June 1, 1983, for $12,200, f.o.b. the place of manufacture. Freight to the point where it was set up was $200, and $250 was expended to install it. The machine's useful life was estimated at ten years, with a scrap value of $50. In June, 1984, an essential part of the machine was replaced, at a cost of $1,500, with one designed to reduce the cost of operating the machine. On June 1, 1987, the company buys a new machine of greater capacity for $18,000, delivered, being allowed a trade-in value on the old machine of $2,000. Preparing the old machine for removal from the plant cost $75, and expenditures to install the new one were $225. It is estimated that the new machine has a useful life of ten years, with a scrap value of $200 at the end of that time.

Instructions

Assuming that depreciation is to be computed on the straight-line basis, prepare schedules showing the gain or loss on the machine traded-in on June 1, 1987, and the amount of depreciation on the new machine that should be provided during the year beginning June 1, 1987. (Round to the nearest dollar.)

E11-9 Presented below is information related to the Roxanne Corporation:

Asset	Cost	Estimated Scrap	Estimated Life (in years)
A	$30,000	$3,000	9
B	32,000	4,000	8
C	12,000	2,000	8
D	20,000	3,000	10
E	4,000	500	7

Instructions

(a) Compute the rate of depreciation per year to be applied to the plant assets under the composite method.

(b) Prepare the adjusting entry necessary at the end of the year to record depreciation for the year.

(c) Prepare the entry to record the sale of fixed asset C for cash of $5,000. It was used for six years, and depreciation was entered under the composite method.

E11-10 In 1986, Northern Power Co. replaced 23,000 utility poles at a cost of $100 each. The old poles originally cost $75 apiece.

Instructions

(a) Prepare the entry (entries), assuming that Northern Power Co. uses the retirement method for depreciating their utility poles.

(b) Prepare the entry (entries), assuming that Northern Power Co. uses the replacement method for depreciating their utility poles.

E11-11 The Atlantic Power Company decides to use the retirement method in accounting for house meters that it installs, because they are of small value and are replaced frequently. The life of the meters is from 1 to 15 years, with the average life about 12 years.

Below are the transactions related to the house meters for 1986.

Jan. 10 Purchases 15,000 meters at $400 each.

Apr. 15 Discards 20 of the meters purchased January 10, 1986, as worthless.

June 20 Sells 50 of the meters purchased January 10, 1986, for $500.

Dec. 12 Replaces 750 meters at $420 each.

Instructions

Using the retirement method, prepare entries to record the transactions for 1986.

E11-12 Algonquin Manufacturing Company has approximately 3,000 hand tools, which it uses in its operations. Each is of relatively small value and is frequently replaced. The total cost of such tools is approximately $24,000.

Because of the characteristics of this asset, the company prefers not to keep detailed records of each tool and depreciate it. You are asked to suggest some reasonably simple method of accounting for these tools so that the asset is carried at a fair amount and operating expenses are charged with a fair amount.

Instructions

Indicate what you suggest. Illustrate your suggestion with pro forma entries for the various types of transactions that might occur.

E11-13 Machinery purchased in 1980 for $54,000 was originally estimated to have a life of eight years with a salvage value of $6,000 at the end of that time. Depreciation has been entered for six years on this basis. In 1986, it is determined that the total estimated life (including 1986) should be 12 years with a salvage value of $7,500 at the end of that time. Assume straight-line depreciation.

Instructions

(a) Prepare the entry to correct the prior years' depreciation, if necessary.

(b) Prepare the entry to record depreciation for 1986.

E11-14 In 1955, Apache Company completed the construction of a building at a cost of $1,860,000 and first occupied it in January, 1956. It was estimated that the building would have a useful life of 50 years, and a salvage value of $60,000 at the end of that time.

Early in 1966, an addition to the building was constructed at a cost of $276,000. At that time it was estimated that the remaining life of the building would be, as originally estimated, an additional 40 years, and that the addition would have a life of 40 years, with a salvage value of $6,000.

In 1986, it is determined that the probable life of the building will extend to 2015, or ten years beyond the original estimate.

Instructions

(a) Compute the annual depreciation that would have been charged from 1956 to 1965.

(b) Compute the annual depreciation that would have been charged from 1966 to 1985.

(c) Prepare the entry, if necessary, to adjust the account balances because of the revision of the estimated life in 1986.

(d) Compute the annual depreciation to be charged, beginning with 1986.

E11-15 Comanche Company constructed a building at a cost of $1,500,000 and has occupied it since January, 1966. It was estimated at that time that its life would be 40 years, with no salvage value.

In January, 1986, a new roof was installed at a cost of $180,000, and it was estimated then that the building would have a useful life of 30 years from that date. The cost of the old roof was $90,000.

Instructions

(a) What amount of depreciation should have been charged annually from the years 1966 to 1985? (Assume straight-line depreciation.)

(b) What entry should be made in 1986 to record the replacement of the roof?

(c) Prepare the entry in January, 1986, to record the revision in the estimated life of the building, if necessary.

(d) What amount of depreciation should be charged for the year 1986?

E11-16 Arapaho, Inc. bought a number of machines at a total cost of $90,000 during 1986. All of them qualify for the 10% investment credit. Arapaho, Inc. had income before taxes of $600,000 (at a tax rate of 40%).

Instructions

(a) Prepare the entry (entries) required at December 31, 1986, to account for the investment credit. Assume that the cost reduction (deferral) method is used and that the credit is amortized over a 6-year life.

(b) Prepare the entry (entries) at December 31, 1986, for the investment credit if the tax reduction (flow-through) method is used by Arapaho, Inc.

E11-17 Chippewa, Inc. purchased machinery and equipment during 1986 amounting to $189,000, and all of these acquisitions qualify for the investment credit. Chippewa, Inc. has decided to record the investment credit in a deferred income account and amortize it over the productive life of the acquired property (seven years). The company's income before taxes is $500,000 (the tax rate is 45%). Assume a 10% rate for the investment credit.

Instructions

(a) Prepare the entry (entries) required at December 31, 1986, to account for the income tax expense and investment credit, assuming that a full year's amortization is taken in the first year.

(b) Prepare the entry (entries) required at December 31, 1986, to account for the income tax expense and investment credit, assuming that the tax reduction (flow-through) method was used.

(c) How would the journal entries under these two approaches be different in future periods?

E11-18   You are the assistant controller for Kickapoo & Associates. On January 1, 1986, Kickapoo purchased heavy machinery with an estimated service life of 20 years. The machinery cost $400,000. This machinery qualified for a 10% investment credit. The controller stated that, to follow the *CICA Handbook* recommendations, the cost reduction (deferral) method would be used for handling this transaction. Accordingly, the following entry was made:

Machinery	360,000	
Reserve for Investment Credit	40,000	
Accounts Payable		400,000

Income tax expense for the year prior to any allowable credits was correctly determined to be $112,000. The controller therefore made the following entry on December 31, 1986:

Dec. 31	Income Tax Expense	72,000	
	Deferred Investment Credit	40,000	
	Income Taxes Payable		72,000
	Reserve for Investment Credit		40,000

The controller, however, is unsure of the entries above and asks your opinion. Amortize the investment credit over 20 years.

Instructions

If you believe that the cost reduction method has not been applied correctly, prepare the entry (entries) that will correct the books and bring them into proper adjustment for 1986. (Ignore any depreciation considerations.)

E11-19   Iroquois Drilling Company has leased property on which oil has been discovered. Wells on this property produced 8,000 barrels of oil during the past year that sold at an average sales price of $30.60 per barrel. Total oil resources of this property are estimated to be 100,000 barrels.

The lease provided for an outright payment of $800,000 to the lessor before drilling could be commenced and an annual rental of $10,000. A premium of 6% of the sales price of every barrel of oil removed is to be paid annually to the lessor. In addition, the lessee is to clean up all the waste and debris from drilling and to bear the costs of reconditioning the land for farming when the wells are abandoned. It is estimated that this clean-up and reconditioning will cost no more than $6,000.

Instructions

From the provisions of the lease agreement, you are to compute the cost per barrel, exclusive of operating costs, to the Iroquois Drilling Company. (Round to three decimal places.)

E11-20   Manitoba Mining Company purchased land on February 1, 1986, at a cost of $900,000. It estimated that a total of 66,000 tonnes of mineral was available for mining. After it has removed all the natural resources, the company will be required to restore the property to its previous state because of strict environmental protection laws. It estimates the cost of this restoration at $40,000. It believes it will be able to sell the property afterwards for $50,000. It incurred developmental costs of $100,000 before it was able to do any mining. In 1986, resources removed totalled 15,000 tonnes, of which 10,000 tonnes were sold.

Instructions

Compute the following information for 1986: (a) mineral cost per tonne; (b) total mineral cost in the December 31, 1986, inventory; and (c) total mineral cost in cost of goods sold for 1986.

*E11-21 During 1986, McCartan Co. Ltd. sold its only Class 3 asset. At the time of sale, the balance of the undepreciated capital cost for this class was $40,000. The asset had originally cost $100,000.

Instructions

Indicate what the resulting amounts would be for any recaptured capital cost, capital gain, and terminal loss assuming that the asset was sold for: (a) $110,000; (b) $80,000; and (c) $25,000.

PROBLEMS

P11-1 On January 1, 1984, Pueblo Company, a small machine-tool manufacturer, acquired a piece of new industrial equipment for $1,500,000. The new equipment was eligible for a 5% investment tax credit. Pueblo took full advantage of the credit and accounted for the amount using the cost reduction method. The new equipment had a useful life of five years, and the salvage value was estimated to be $150,000. Pueblo estimates that the new equipment can produce 10,000 machine tools in its first year. It estimates that production will decline by 1,000 units per year over the remaining useful life of the equipment.

The following depreciation methods may be used:

1. Double-declining balance
2. Straight-line
3. Units-of-output

Instructions

Which depreciation method would result in the maximization of net income for financial statement reporting for the three-year period ending December 31, 1986? Prepare a schedule showing the amount of accumulated depreciation at December 31, 1986, under the method selected. Ignore present value, income tax, and deferred income tax considerations in your answer.

(AICPA adapted)

P11-2 The cost of equipment purchased by Potawatomi, Inc. on April 1, 1985, was $58,000. It was estimated that the machine would have a $2,000 salvage value at the end of its service life. Its service life was estimated at eight years; its total working hours were estimated at 32,000 and its total production at 480,000 units. During 1985, the machine was used for 3,000 hours and produced 46,000 units. During 1986, the machine was used for 4,000 hours and produced 62,000 units. (Round per-hour and unit costs to three decimal places.)

Instructions

Compute depreciation expense on the machine for the year ending December 31, 1985, and the year ending December 31, 1986, using the following methods: (a) straight-line; (b) units-of-output; (c) working-hours; (d) sum-of-the-years'-digits; and (e) declining balance (twice the straight-line rate). Also, compute the capital cost allowance for 1985 and 1986 assuming a CCA rate of 30%.

P11-3 Navajo & Mohawk, Inc. purchased Machine #201 on April 1, 1985. The following information relating to Machine #201 was gathered at the end of April.

✓Price	$89,700
Credit terms	2/10,n/30
✓Freight-in costs	$ 2,400
✓Preparation and installation costs	$ 7,800
Labour costs during regular production operations	$ 9,600

It was expected that the machine could be used for ten years, after which the salvage value would be zero. Navajo & Mohawk, Inc. intended to use the machine for only eight years, however, after which it expected to sell it for $9,600. The invoice for Machine #201 was paid April 5, 1985. Navajo & Mohawk used the calendar year as the basis for the preparation of financial statements.

Instructions

(a) Compute the depreciation expense for the years indicated, using the following methods. (Round to the nearest cent.)
  1. Straight-line method for 1985 and 1986.
  2. Double-declining balance method for 1985 and 1986.

(b) Calculate the capital cost allowance for 1985 and 1986, assuming a CCA rate of 25%.

(c) Suppose the president of Navajo & Mohawk, Inc. tells you that because the company is a new organization, she expects it will be several years before production and sales are at optimum levels. She asks you to recommend a depreciation method that will allocate less of the company's depreciation expense to the early years and more to the later years of the assets' lives. Which method would you recommend?

P11-4 The following data relate to the Plant Asset account of Pastrami Company at December 31, 1985:

Plant Asset				
	A	B	C	D
Original cost	$30,000	$30,000	$60,000	$100,000
Year purchased	1980	1981	1982	1984
Useful life	10 years	15,000 hours	10 years	40 years
Salvage value	$ 4,975	$ 3,000	$ 4,000	$ 10,000
Depreciation method	Sum-of-the-years'-digits	Activity	Straight-line	Double-declining balance
Accum. Depr. through 1985[a]	$18,200	$20,000	$16,800	$ 5,000

[a]In the year an asset is purchased, Pastrami Company does not record any depreciation expense on the asset. In the year an asset is retired or traded in, Pastrami Company takes a full year's depreciation on the asset.

The following transactions occurred during 1986:

1. On May 5, Asset A was sold for $22,500 cash. The company's bookkeeper recorded this retirement in the following manner in the cash receipts journal:

Cash	22,500	
Asset A		22,500

2. On December 31, it was determined that Asset B had been used 3,000 hours during 1986.

3. On December 31, before computing depreciation expense on Asset C, the management of Pastrami Company decided the useful life remaining from January 1, 1986 was ten years.

4. On December 31, it was discovered that a plant asset purchased in 1985 had been expensed completely in that year. This asset cost $14,000 and has a useful life of ten years and no salvage value. Management has decided to use the double-declining balance method for this asset, which can be referred to as "Asset E."

Instructions

Prepare the necessary correcting entries for the year 1986. Record the appropriate depreciation expense on the above-mentioned assets.

P11-5 A depreciation schedule for the semitrucks of Sioux Manufacturing Company was requested by your auditor soon after December 31, 1986, showing the additions, retirements, depreciation, and other data affecting the income of the company in the four-year period 1983 to 1986, inclusive. The following data were ascertained:

Balance of semitrucks accounts, Jan. 1, 1983:

Truck No. 1 purchased Jan. 1, 1980, cost	$12,000
Truck No. 2 purchased July 1, 1980, cost	10,800
Truck No. 3 purchased Jan. 1, 1982, cost	7,200
Truck No. 4 purchased July 1, 1982, cost	6,000
Balance, Jan. 1, 1983	$36,000

The Semitrucks—Accumulated Depreciation account previously adjusted to January 1, 1983, and duly entered in the ledger, had a balance on that date of $14,640 (depreciation on the four trucks from the respective dates of purchase, based on a five-year life). No debit charges had been made against the account before January 1, 1983.

Transactions between January 1, 1983, and December 31, 1986, and their record in the ledger were as follows:

July 1, 1983 Truck No. 3 was traded for a larger one (No. 5), the agreed purchase price of which was $9,600. The Sioux Manufacturing Company paid the automobile dealer $4,680 cash on the transaction. The entry was a debit to Semitrucks and a credit to Cash, $4,680.

Jan. 1, 1984 Truck No. 1 was sold for $3,600 cash; entry debited Cash and credited Semitrucks, $3,600.

July 1, 1985 Truck No. 4 was damaged in a wreck to such an extent that it was sold as junk for $300 cash. Sioux Manufacturing Company received $1,800 from the insurance company. The entry made by the bookkeeper was a debit to Cash, $2,100, and credits to Miscellaneous Income, $300, and Semitrucks, $1,800.

July 1, 1985 A new truck (No. 6) was acquired for $7,200 cash and was charged at that amount to the Semitrucks account. (Assume truck No. 2 was not retired.)

Entries for depreciation had been made at the close of each year as follows: 1983, $7,200; 1984, $6,456; 1985, $6,456; 1986, $7,476.

Instructions

(a) For each of the four years, compute separately the increase or decrease in net income arising from the company's errors in determining or entering depreciation or in recording transactions affecting the trucks, ignoring income tax considerations.

(b) Prepare one compound journal entry as of December 31, 1986, for adjustment of the Semitrucks account to reflect the correct balances as revealed by your schedule, assuming that the books have not been closed for 1986.

P11-6 The Pawnee Tool Company records depreciation annually at the end of the year. Its policy is to take a full year's depreciation on all assets used throughout the year and depreciation for one-half a year on all machines acquired or disposed of during the year. The depreciation rate for the machinery is 10% applied on a straight-line basis, with no estimated scrap value.

The balance of the Machinery account at the beginning of 1986 was $135,420; the Accumulated Depreciation on Machinery account had a balance of $51,240. The following transactions affecting the machinery accounts took place during 1986:

Jan. 15   Machine No. 38, which cost $6,540 when acquired June 3, 1978, was retired and sold as scrap metal for $108.

Feb. 27   Machine No. 81 was purchased. The fair market value of this machine was $10,320. It replaces Machines No. 12 and No. 27, which were traded in on the new machine. Machine No. 12 was acquired Feb. 4, 1973, at a cost of $3,600 and is still carried in the accounts although fully depreciated and not in use; Machine No. 27 was acquired June 11, 1978, at a cost of $3,000. In addition to these two used machines, $9,240 was paid in cash. (Assume exchange of similar assets.)

Apr. 7   Machine No. 54 was equipped with electric control equipment at a cost of $420. This machine, originally equipped with simple hand controls, was purchased Dec. 11, 1982, for $1,080. The new electric controls can be attached to any one of several machines in the shop.

Apr. 12   Machine No. 24 was repaired at a cost of $660 after a fire caused by a short circuit in the wiring burned out the motor and damaged certain essential parts.

Jul. 22   Machines No. 25, 26, and 41 are sold for $2,500 cash. The purchase dates and cost of these machines are:

No. 25	$2,800	May 8, 1977
No. 26	2,800	May 8, 1977
No. 41	3,600	June 1, 1981

Nov. 17   Rearrangement and reinstallation of several machines to facilitate material handling and to speed up production are completed at a cost of $16,400.

Instructions

(a) Record each transaction in general journal entry form.

(b) Compute and record depreciation for the year. No machines now included in the balance of the account were acquired before Jan. 1, 1977.

P11-7   Phillips Logging and Lumber Company owns 2,000 hectares of timberland on the north side of Mount St. Helens, which was purchased in 1965 at a cost of $500 per hectare. In 1980, Phillips began selectively logging this timber tract. In May of 1980, Mount St. Helens erupted, burying the timberland of Phillips under a metre of ash. All of the timber on the Phillips tract was downed. In addition, the logging roads, built at a cost of $100,000, were destroyed, as well as the logging equipment, with a net book value of $250,000.

At the time of the eruption, Phillips had logged 20% of the estimated 400,000 cubic metres of timber. Prior to the eruption, Phillips estimated the land to have a value of $200 per hectare after the timber was harvested.

Phillips depreciates logging roads on the basis of timber harvested. It estimates it will take three years to salvage the downed timber at a cost of $800,000. The timber can be sold for pulpwood at an estimated price of $3 per cubic metre. The value of the land is unknown, but until it will grow vegetation again, which scientists say may be as long as 50–100 years, the value is nominal.

Instructions

(a) Determine the depletion expense per cubic metre for the timber harvested prior to the eruption of Mount St. Helens.

(b) Prepare the journal entry to record the depletion expense prior to the eruption.

(c) If this tract represents approximately half of the timber holdings of Phillips, determine the amount of the estimated loss and show how the losses of roads, machinery, and timber and the salvage of the timber should be reported in the financial statements of Phillips for the year ended December 31, 1980.

P11-8 The Mohican Mining Company has purchased a tract of mineral land for $420,000. It is estimated that this tract will yield 100,000 tonnes of ore with sufficient mineral content to make mining and processing profitable. It is further estimated that 5,000 tonnes of ore will be mined the first year and 10,000 tonnes each year thereafter. The land will have no residual value.

The company builds necessary structures and sheds on the site at a cost of $24,000. It is estimated that these structures can serve 15 years but, because they must be dismantled if they are to be moved, they have no scrap value. The company does not intend to use the buildings elsewhere. Mining machinery installed at the mine was purchased second-hand at a cost of $36,000. This machinery cost the former owner $38,000 and was 40% depreciated when purchased. The Mohican Mining Company estimates that about half of this machinery will still be useful when the present mineral resources have been exhausted but that dismantling and removal costs will just about offset its value at that time. The company does not intend to use the machinery elsewhere. The remaining machinery will last until about one-half the present estimated mineral ore has been removed and will then be worthless. Cost is to be allocated equally between these two classes of machinery.

Instructions

(a) As chief accountant of the company, you are to prepare a schedule showing estimated depletion and depreciation costs for each year of the expected life of the mine.

(b) Also draft entries in general journal entry form to record depreciation and depletion for the first year, assuming actual production of 5,300 tonnes. Nothing occurred during the year to cause the company's engineers to change their estimates of either the mineral resources or the life of the structures and equipment.

P11-9 Hamilton Corporation, a manufacturer of steel products, began operations on October 1, 1984. The accounting department of Hamilton has started the fixed-asset and depreciation schedule presented below. You have been asked to assist in completing this schedule. In addition to ascertaining that the data already on the schedule are correct, you have obtained the following information from the company's records and personnel:

1. Depreciation is computed from the first of the month of acquisition to the first of the month of disposition.

2. Land A and Building A were acquired from a predecessor corporation. Hamilton paid $812,500 for the land and building together. At the time of acquisition, the land had an appraised value of $75,000, and the building had an appraised value of $900,000.

3. Land B was acquired on October 2, 1984, in exchange for 3,000 newly issued common shares of Hamilton. At the date of acquisition, the shares had a fair value of $30 each. During October 1984, Hamilton paid $10,400 to demolish an existing building on this land so it could construct a new building.

4. Construction of Building B on the newly acquired land began on October 1, 1985. By September 30, 1986, Hamilton had paid $210,000 of the estimated total construction costs of $300,000. It is estimated that the building will be completed and occupied by July, 1987.

5. Certain equipment was donated to the corporation by a local university. An independent appraisal of the equipment when donated placed the fair value at $20,000 and the salvage value at $2,000.

6. Machine A's total cost of $110,000 includes installation expense of $550 and normal repairs and maintenance of $10,450. Salvage value is estimated at $5,500. Machine A was sold on February 1, 1986.

7. On October 1, 1985, Machine B was acquired with a down payment of $6,000 and the remaining payments to be made in 11 annual instalments of $5,000 each beginning October 1, 1985. The prevailing interest rate was 8%. The following data were abstracted from present-value tables (rounded):

Present value of $1.00 at
8%

10 years	.463
11 years	429
15 years	.315

Present value of an ordinary annuity of $1.00 at
8%

10 years	6.710
11 years	7.139
15 years	8.559

Hamilton Corporation
FIXED ASSET AND DEPRECIATION SCHEDULE
For Fiscal Years Ended September 30, 1985, and September 30, 1986

Assets	Acquisition Date	Cost	Salvage	Depreciation Method	Estimated Life in Years	Depreciation Expense Year Ended September 30 1985	1986
Land A	October 1, 1984	$ (1)	N/A	N/A	N/A	N/A	N/A
Building A	October 1, 1984	(2)	$50,000	Straight-Line	(3)	$17,500	(4)
Land B	October 2, 1984	(5)	N/A	N/A	N/A	N/A	N/A
Building B	Under Construction	210,000 to date	—	Straight-Line	30	—	(6)
Donated Equip.	October 2, 1984	(7)	2,000	15% Declining Balance	10	(8)	(9)
Machine A	October 2, 1984	(10)	5,500	Sum-of-the-Years'-Digits	10	(11)	(12)
Machine B	October 1, 1985	(13)	—	Straight-Line	25	—	(14)

N/A–Not applicable

Instructions

For each numbered item on the foregoing schedule, supply the correct amount. Round each answer to the nearest dollar.

(AICPA adapted)

P11-10 You are engaged in the examination of the financial statements of the Erie Corporation for the year ended December 31, 1986. The schedules on page 556 for the property, plant, and equipment, and related accumulated depreciation accounts, have been prepared by the client. You have verified the opening balances to your pior year's audit workpapers.

Your examination reveals the following information:

1. All equipment is depreciated on the straight-line basis (no salvage value taken into consideration) using the following estimated lives: buildings, 25 years; all other items, 10 years. The company's policy is to take one-half year's depreciation on all asset acquisitions and disposals during the year.

2. On May 1, the company entered into a ten-year lease contract for a die-casting machine with annual rentals of $5,000 payable in advance every May 1. The lease can be cancelled by either party (60 days written notice is required), and there is no option to renew the lease or buy the equipment at the end of the lease. The estimated useful life of the machine is ten years with no salvage value. The company recorded the die-casting machine in the Machinery and Equipment account at $40,400, the present discounted value at the date of the lease; the amount of $2,020, applicable to the machine, has been included in depreciation

expense for the year. (Hint: Leases with these conditions should not be capitalized nor should a liability be recognized.)

3. The company completed the construction of a wing on the plant building on June 30. The useful life of the building was not extended by this addition. The lowest construction bid received was $17,500, the amount recorded in the Buildings account. Company personnel were used to construct the addition at a cost of $16,500 (materials, $7,500; labour, $6,000; and overhead, $3,000).

4. On August 18, $10,000 was paid for paving and fencing a portion of land owned by the company and used as a parking lot for employees. The expenditure was charged to the Land account.

5. The amount shown in the machinery and equipment asset retirement column represents cash received on September 5 upon disposal of a machine purchased in July, 1982, for $50,000. The bookkeeper recorded depreciation expense of $3,700 on this machine in 1986.

6. Quebec City donated land and building appraised at $10,000 and $50,000 respectively, to the Erie Corporation for a plant. On September 1, the company began operating the plant. Because no costs were involved, the bookkeeper made no entry to record the transaction.

Erie Corp.
ANALYSIS OF PROPERTY, PLANT, AND EQUIPMENT, AND
RELATED ACCUMULATED DEPRECIATION ACCOUNTS
Year Ended December 31, 1986

Assets

Description	Final Dec. 31, 1985	Additions	Retirements	Per Books Dec. 31, 1986
Land	$ 32,500	$10,000		$ 42,500
Buildings	120,000	17,500		137,500
Machinery and equipment	385,000	40,400	$26,000	399,400
	$537,500	$67,900	$26,000	$579,400

Accumulated Depreciation

Description	Final Dec. 31, 1985	Additions[a]	Retirements	Per Books Dec. 31, 1986
Buildings	$ 60,000	$ 5,150		$ 65,150
Machinery and equipment	173,250	39,220		212,470
	$233,250	$44,370		$277,620

[a]Depreciation expense for the year.

Instructions

Prepare the formal journal entries that you would suggest at December 31, 1986, to adjust the accounts for the transactions noted above. Disregard income tax implications. The books have not been closed. Computations should be rounded to the nearest dollar.

(AICPA adapted)

*P11-11 Kim Co. Ltd. engaged in the following transactions regarding Class 10 assets (30% CCA rate):

1980—purchased asset No. 1 for $120,000.
1982—purchased asset No. 2 for $90,000.
1983—sold asset No. 1 for $13,860.
1984—purchased asset No. 3 for $200,000.
1986—sold asset No. 2 for $100,000.

Instructions

(a) Prepare a capital cost allowance schedule for Class 10 assets covering the years ended December 31, 1980 through 1986.

(b) Indicate the amounts of any capital gains, recaptured capital cost or terminal loss that would result if, during 1987, asset No. 3 was sold (thereby eliminating Class 10 assets for the Company) for (1) $230,000, (2) $100,000, (3) $20,000.

12

INTANGIBLE ASSETS

Intangible assets are generally characterized by a **lack of physical existence**, and a high degree of uncertainty concerning future benefits. The value of intangible assets is usually derived from legal rights or privileges held by an entity. These criteria are not so clear-cut as they may seem. The following discussion by a well-known accountant typifies some of the major problems encountered in attempting to define intangibles.

Q. I infer, Mr. May, from your experience . . . that you know what in ordinary speech the word tangible means, don't you?

A. Yes.

Q. Well, what do you understand it to mean in ordinary speech?

A. Something that can be touched, I imagine.

Q. Like merchandise?

A. Yes.

Q. You can touch merchandise or horses?

A. Yes.

Q. Can you touch an account receivable?

A. You can touch the debtor.

Q. Is that the basis on which you include the debtor's debt as tangible?

A. It had not occurred to me before, but possibly it is.[1]

This discussion indicates that the lack of physical existence is not by itself a satisfactory criterion for distinguishing a tangible from an intangible asset. Such assets as bank deposits, accounts receivable, and long-term investments lack physical substance, yet accountants classify them as tangible assets.

Some accountants believe that the major characteristic of an intangible asset is the high degree of uncertainty concerning the future benefits that are to be received from its employment. For example, many intangibles (1) have value only to a given enterprise, (2) have indeterminate lives, and (3) are subject to large fluctuations in value because their benefits are based on a competitive advantage. The determination and timing of future benefits are extremely difficult and pose serious valuation problems. Tangible assets possess similar characteristics but they are not so pronounced.

The more common types of intangibles are patents, copyrights, franchises, goodwill, organization costs, and trademarks or trade names. These intangibles may be further subdivided on the basis of the following chartacteristics:

1. **Identifiability.** Separately identifiable or lacking specific identification.
2. **Manner of acquisition.** Acquired singly, in groups, or in business combinations, or developed internally.
3. **Expected period of benefit.** Limited by law or contract, related to human or economic factors, or indefinite or of undetermined duration.
4. **Separability from an entire enterprise.** Rights transferable without title, salable, or inseparable from the enterprise or a substantial part of it.[2]

VALUATION OF PURCHASED INTANGIBLES

Intangibles, like tangible assets, should be **recorded at cost.** Cost includes all costs of acquisition and expenditures necessary to make the intangible asset ready for its intended use. These costs are normally purchase price, legal fees, and other incidental expenses incurred in obtaining the asset.

If intangibles are acquired for shares or in exchange for other assets, **the cost of the intangible is the fair market value of the consideration given or the fair market value of the intangible received, whichever is more clearly evident**. Sometimes both the value of what is given and the value of what is received are difficult to estimate: at this point, exercise of professional judgement is required to establish an appropriate valuation. Essentially the accounting treatment closely parallels that followed for tangible assets. For example, when several intangibles, or a combination of intangibles and tangibles, are bought in a "basket purchase," the cost should be allocated on the basis of fair market values.

The profession has resisted employment of some other basis of valuation, such as current replacement costs or appraisal value for these types of assets. The basic attributes of intangibles, their uncertainty as to future benefits, and their uniqueness, have discouraged valuation in excess of cost.[3]

[1]From testimony given to referee, *In the Matter of the Estate of E. P. Hatch Deceased (1912)*. Reprinted in Bishop Carleton Hunt, ed., *Twenty-Five Years of Accounting Responsibility, 1911-1936* (New York: Price Waterhouse and Company, 1936), I, p. 246. Selected essays and discussions of George O. May.

[2]"Intangible Assets," *Opinions of the Accounting Principles Board No. 17* (New York: AICPA, 1970), par. 10.

[3]For example, Sprouse and Moonitz in *AICPA Accounting Research Study No. 3*, "A Tentative Set of Broad Accounting Principles for a Business Enterprise," advocate abandonment of historical cost in favour of replacement cost for most asset items, but suggest that intangibles should normally be carried at acquisition cost less amortization because valuation problems are so difficult.

AMORTIZATION OF INTANGIBLE ASSETS

Intangible assets should be amortized by systematic charges to revenue over their useful lives. In determining useful life, a number of factors should be considered. These include:

1. Legal, regulatory, or contractual provisions that may limit the maximum useful life.
2. Provisions for renewal or extension may alter a specified limit on useful life.
3. Effects of obsolescence, demand, competition, and other economic factors that may reduce a useful life.
4. A useful life may parallel the service life expectancies of individuals or groups of employees.
5. Expected actions of competitors and others may restrict present competitive advantages.
6. An apparently unlimited useful life may in fact be indefinite, and benefits cannot be reasonably projected.
7. An intangible asset may be a composite of many individual factors with varying effective lives.[4]

One problem relating to the amortization of intangibles is that some intangibles have indeterminable useful lives. This problem, except for goodwill, has not been addressed by the CICA. In the United States, the APB concluded that the value of an intangible asset eventually disappears and that the recorded costs of intangible assets should be amortized by systematic charges to income over the periods estimated to be benefited. An arbitrary limit of a 40-year amortization period is imposed by *APB Opinion No. 17*.[5] The 40-year requirement is based on the premise that only a few, if any, intangibles last for a lifetime. Sometimes, because it is difficult to determine useful life, a 40-year term is practical, although admittedly it is an arbitrary solution. Another reason for this 40-year limitation is simply that it ensures that companies start to write off their intangibles. There was evidence that some companies retained intangibles (notably goodwill) indefinitely on their balance sheet for only one reason—to avoid the charge against income that occurs when goodwill is written off.

Intangible assets acquired from other enterprises (notably goodwill) should not be written off at acquisition. Some accountants contend that certain intangibles should not be carried as assets on the balance sheet under any circumstances but should be written off directly to retained earnings or contributed surplus. The position of the profession is that the immediate write-off to retained earnings and contributed surplus is not acceptable because it denies the existence of an asset that has just been purchased.

Intangible assets are generally amortized on a straight-line basis, although there is no reason why another systematic approach might not be employed if the firm demonstrates that another method is appropriate. In any case the method and period of amortization should be disclosed.

When intangible assets are amortized the charges should be shown as expenses of the years benefited, and the credits should be made either to the appropriate asset accounts or to separate accumulated amortization accounts.

[4]*APB Opinion No. 17*, par. 27.

[5]*Ibid.*, par. 10.

SPECIFICALLY IDENTIFIABLE INTANGIBLE ASSETS

As indicated earlier, a number of bases may be employed to differentiate one group of intangible assets from another. Originally, the accounting profession recognized two types of classification for intangibles: intangibles that have a limited life and intangibles that have an unlimited life.

The classification framework was changed by the CICA through issuance of *CICA Handbook*, Section 1580, to intangibles that are specifically identifiable as contrasted to "goodwill type" intangible assets (unidentifiable values). **Specifically identifiable** means that costs associated with obtaining a given intangible asset can be identified as a part of the cost of that intangible asset. In contrast, **goodwill type** intangibles may create some right or privilege, but it is not specifically identifiable, it has an indeterminable life, and its cost is inherent in a continuing business. The major identifiable assets and goodwill are discussed below.

Patents

Patents are granted by the federal government. A patent gives the holder exclusive right to use, manufacture, and sell a product or process **for a period of 17 years** without interference or infringement by others. If a patent is purchased from an inventor (or other owner), the purchase price represents its cost. Other costs incurred in connection with securing a patent, and attorneys' fees and other unrecovered costs of a successful legal suit to protect the patent, can be capitalized as part of the patent cost. **Research and development costs** related to the **development** of the product, process, or idea that is subsequently patented are usually expensed as incurred, however. See pages 574–579 for a more complete presentation of accounting for research and development costs.

The cost of a patent should be amortized over its legal life or its useful life (that is, over the period in which benefits are expected to be received), whichever is shorter. If a patent is owned from the date it is granted, and it is expected to be useful during its entire legal life, it should be amortized over 17 years. If it appears that the patent will be useful for a shorter period of time, say, for five years, its cost should be amortized against income over five years. Changing demand, new inventions superseding old ones, inadequacy, and other factors often limit the useful life of a patent to less than the legal life.

Legal fees and other costs incurred in successfully defending a patent suit may properly be charged to the Patents account because such a suit establishes the legal rights of the holder of the patent. Such costs should be amortized along with acquisition cost over the remaining useful life of the patent.

Amortization of patents may be computed on a time basis or on a basis of units produced and may be credited directly to the Patents account; it is acceptable also, although less common in practice, to credit an Accumulated Patent Amortization account. Assuming that the cost of a patent is $102,000, that it will be useful for 17 years, and that it is amortized on a straight-line basis, the entry at the end of each year would be:

Patent Amortization Expense	6,000	
Patents (or Accumulated Patent Amortization)		6,000

Amortization on a units of production basis would be computed in a manner similar to that described for depreciation on property, plant, and equipment.

Royalties received from the assignment of patents to other enterprises represent income of the period in which the royalties are earned and should be accrued as income.

Although a patent's useful life should not extend beyond its legal life of 17 years, small modifications or additions may lead to a new patent. The effect may be to extend the life of the old patent, in which case it is permissable to apply the unamortized costs of the old patent to the new patent if the new patent provides essentially the same benefits. Alternatively, if a patent becomes worthless because demand for the product drops, the asset should be written off immediately to operations.

Copyrights

A copyright is a federally granted right that all authors, painters, sculptors, and other artists have in their creations. A copyright is granted for the **life of the creator plus 50 years**, and gives the owner, or heirs, the exclusive right to reproduce and sell artistic or published work. Copyrights, like patents, may be assigned or sold to other individuals. The cost of acquiring and defending a copyright may be capitalized, but the research costs involved must be expensed as incurred.

Generally, the useful life of the copyright is less than the legal life. The costs of the copyright should be allocated to the years in which the benefits are expected to be received. The difficulty of determining the number of years over which benefits will be received normally encourages the company to write these costs off over a fairly short period of time.

Trademarks and Trade Names

A trademark or trade name is a word, phrase, or symbol that distinguishes or identifies a particular enterprise or product. The right to use a trademark or trade name is granted by the federal government. In order to obtain and maintain a protected trademark or trade name, the owner must have made prior and continuing use of it. Trade names like Kleenex, Pepsi-Cola, Oldsmobile, Excedrin, Shreddies, and Sunkist create immediate product identification in our minds, thereby enhancing the marketability of the product.

The capitalizable cost of a trademark or trade name is the purchase price if it is acquired. If a trademark or trade name is developed by the enterprise itself, the capitalizable cost includes attorney fees, registration fees, design costs, successful legal defence costs, and other expenditures directly related to securing it (excluding research costs). When the total cost of a trademark or trade name is insignificant, it can be expensed rather than capitalized.

Although the legal life may be unlimited, for accounting purposes the cost should be amortized over the periods benefited. However, because of the uncertainty involved in estimating their useful life, the cost of trademarks and trade names is frequently amortized over a much shorter period of time.[6]

Leaseholds

A leasehold is a contractual understanding between a lessor and a lessee that grants the lessee the right to use specific property, owned by the lessor, for a

---

[6]To illustrate how various intangibles might arise from a given product, consider what the creators of the highly successful game *Trivial Pursuit* did to protect their creation. First, the creators *copyrighted* the 6,000 questions that are at the heart of the fun. Then they shielded the "Trivial Pursuit" name by applying for a registered *trademark*. As a third mode of protection the creators obtained a *design patent* on the playing board's design, since it represents a unique graphic creation.

specific period of time in return for stipulated, and generally periodic, cash payments. Most lease agreements provide simply for the right of the lessee to use property of the lessor for stipulated periods. In such a case the rent is included as an expense on the books of the lessee. Special problems, however, develop in the following situations.

Lease Prepayments   If the rent for the period of the lease is paid in advance, or if a lump sum payment is made in advance in addition to periodic rental payments, it is necessary to allocate this prepaid rent to the proper periods. The lessee, by payment of the amount agreed upon, has purchased the exclusive right to use the property for an extended period of time. Some accountants advocate presenting this prepayment as an intangible asset; in many published financial statements, prepayments on long-term leases are classified as deferred charges.

Capitalization of Leases   In some cases, the lease agreement transfers substantially all of the benefits and risks incident to ownership of the property so that the economic effect on the parties is similar to that of an instalment purchase. As a result, the asset value recognized when a lease is capitalized is classified as a tangible rather than an intangible asset. Such a lease is referred to as a **capital lease.** And, according to *CICA Handbook,* Section 3065, the lessee must record a capital lease as an asset and an obligation at an amount equal to the present value of the minimum lease payments required during the lease term, excluding that portion of the payments representing such executory costs as insurance, maintenance, and taxes to be paid by the lessor.[7] Further, in such cases, it is appropriate for the lessee to depreciate the capitalized asset in a manner consistent with the lessee's normal depreciation policy for owned assets.

The CICA requires that if the lessee is party to a lease that meets one or more of the following three criteria, the lessee must classify the transaction as a capital lease and record an asset and a liability at an amount equal to the present value of the future lease payments:

1.   There is reasonable assurance that the lessee will obtain ownership of the leased property at the end of the lease term.
2.   The lease term (including any bargain renewal options) is equal to 75% or more of the economic life of the leased property.
3.   The present value of the lease payments (excluding executory costs) equals or exceeds 90% of the fair value of the leased property.[8]

Significant provisions of material leases should be disclosed in the financial statements or in notes to the financial statements, in order that the reader may have knowledge of the financial effect of lease commitments. Chapter 22 is devoted entirely to accounting for leases.

Leasehold Improvements   Long-term leases ordinarily provide that any improvements made to the leased property revert to the lessor at the end of the life of the lease. If the lessee constructs new buildings on leased land or reconstructs and improves existing buildings, the lessee has the right to use such facilities during the life of the lease, but they become the property of the lessor when the lease expires.

The lessee should charge the cost of the facilities to the Leasehold Improvements account and **depreciate the cost as operating expense over the remaining life of**

---

[7]*CICA Handbook*, Section 3065, par. 16.

[8]*Ibid.*, par. 6.

the lease, or the useful life of the improvements, whichever is shorter. If a building with an estimated useful life of 25 years is constructed on land leased for 35 years, the cost of the building should be depreciated over 25 years. On the other hand, if the building has an estimated life of 50 years, it should be depreciated over 35 years, the life of the lease.

If the lease contains an option to renew for a period of additional years and the likelihood of renewal is too uncertain to warrant apportioning the cost over the longer period of time, the leasehold improvements are generally written off over the original term of the lease (assuming that the life of the lease is shorter than the useful life of the improvements). Leasehold improvements are generally shown in the property, plant, and equipment section, although some accountants classify them as intangible assets.

Organization Costs

Costs incurred in the formation of a corporation such as fees to underwriters for handling share or bond issues, legal fees, provincial fees of various sorts, and promotional expenditures involving the organization of a business are classified as **organization costs.**

These items are usually charged to an account called Organization Costs and may be carried as an asset on the balance sheet as expenditures that will benefit the company over its life. Many companies amortize these costs over an arbitrary period, since the life of the corporation is indeterminable. Income tax regulations permit the amortization of 50% of organization costs at the rate of 10% on the declining balance.

It is difficult to draw a line between organization costs, normal operating expenses, and losses. Some accountants contend that **operating losses incurred in the start-up of a business** should be capitalized, since they are unavoidable and are a cost of starting a business. This approach is not sound, since this cost has no future service potential and cannot be considered an asset.

Our position, that operating losses should not be capitalized during the early years, is supported by the FASB in *Statement of Financial Accounting Standards No. 7*, which clarifies the accounting and reporting practices for **development stage enterprises.** The FASB concludes that the accounting practices and reporting standards should be no different for a development stage enterprise trying to establish a new business than they are for other enterprises. Except for some unique notations and disclosures, the same ''generally accepted accounting principles that apply to established operating enterprises shall govern the recognition of revenue by a development stage enterprise and shall determine whether a cost incurred by a development stage enterprise is to be charged to expense when incurred or is to be capitalized or deferred.''[9]

[9]''Accounting and Reporting by Development Stage Enterprises,'' *Statement of Financial Accounting Standards No. 7* (Stamford, Conn.: FASB, 1975), par. 10. A company is considered to be in the developing stages when its efforts are directed toward establishing a new business and either the principal operations have not started or no significant revenue has been earned. The FASB in evaluating the economic impact of applying to development stage enterprises the same accounting principles that apply to established operating enterprises interviewed officers of fifteen venture capital companies. The consensus of those officers was that whether a development stage enterprise defers or expenses preoperating costs has little effect on the amount of or the terms under which venture capital is provided. According to those officers, the venture capital investor relies on an evaluation of potential cash flows resulting from an investigation of the technological, marketing, management, and financial aspects of the enterprise.

Franchises and Licences

When you drive down the street in an automobile purchased from a Chrysler dealer, fill your tank at the corner Texaco station, eat lunch at McDonald's, work at a Coca-Cola bottling plant, live in a home purchased through a Century 21 real estate broker, and vacation at a Holiday Inn resort, you are dealing with franchises. A **franchise** is a contractual arrangement under which the franchisor grants the franchisee the right to sell certain products or services, to use certain trademarks or trade names, or perform certain functions, usually within a designated geographical area.

The franchisor, having developed a unique concept or product, protects it through a patent, copyright, or trademark or trade name. The franchisee acquires the right to exploit the franchisor's idea or product by signing a franchise agreement.

Such franchise arrangements are made between two separate businesses. Another type of franchise is the arrangement commonly entered into by a municipality or other government body and a business enterprise that uses public property. In such cases, a privately owned enterprise is permitted to use public property. Examples are the use of public waterways for a ferry service, the use of public land for telephones or electric lines, the use of phone lines for cable TV, the use of city streets for a bus line, or the use of the airwaves for radio or TV broadcasting. Operating rights obtained through agreements with government units or agencies are frequently referred to as licences or permits.

Franchises or licences may be for a definite period of time, for an indefinite period of time, or perpetual. The enterprise securing the franchise or licence carries an intangible asset account entitled Franchise or Licence on its books only when there are costs such as a lump sum payment in advance, or legal fees and other expenditures that are identifiable with the acquisition of the franchise. **The cost of a franchise (or licence) for a limited period should be amortized as operating expense over the life of the franchise.** A franchise with an indefinite life or a perpetual franchise should be carried at cost and amortized over a reasonable period. If a franchise is deemed to be worthless, it should be written off immediately.

Annual payments made under a franchise agreement should be entered as operating expenses in the period in which they are incurred. They do not represent an asset to the concern since they do not relate to future rights to use public property.

Property Rights

Most of the indentifiable intangibles discussed above represent **rights**—rights to use, produce, sell, or operate something. Other rights that appear to be growing in significance, and therefore in value, are water rights, mineral rights, solar and wind rights (the legal right to free flow of light and air across one's property), and other property rights. Although these rights have a value of their own, they are generally attached to a particular parcel of property. Therefore, the value of such property rights, if inseparable from the property, is accounted for as part of the capitalized land cost. If the right is separable from the property, as in the case of mineral rights, its cost may be capitalized separately. If minerals are later discovered or developed, the cost of the rights should be reclassified and capitalized as part of the cost of the minerals and written off as the mineral deposit is depleted.

GOODWILL

Goodwill is undoubtedly one of the most complex and controversial assets presented in financial statements; it is often referred to as the most "intangible" of the intangibles. Goodwill is unique because unlike receivables, inventories, and patents that can be sold or exchanged individually in the marketplace, goodwill can be identified only with the business as a whole. For example, a substantial list of regular customers and an established reputation are unrecorded assets that give the enterprise a valuation greater than the sum of the fair market value of the individual identifiable assets. Numerous advantageous factors and conditions that might contribute to the value and the earning power of an enterprise can be cited; in the aggregate they represent goodwill:

1. Superior management team
2. Outstanding sales organization
3. Weakness in management of a competitor
4. Effective advertising
5. Secret process or formula
6. Good labour relations
7. Outstanding credit rating
8. Top-flight training program
9. High standing in the community
10. Discovery of talents or resources
11. Favourable tax conditions
12. Favourable government regulation
13. Favourable association with another company
14. Strategic location
15. Unfavourable developments in the operations of a competitor.[10]

Goodwill is recorded only when an entire business is purchased because goodwill is a "going concern" valuation and cannot be separated from the business as a whole.[11] Goodwill generated internally (sometimes referred to as nonpurchased goodwill) should **not** be capitalized in the accounts, because measuring the components of goodwill (as listed above) is simply too complex and associating any costs with future benefits is too difficult. The future benefits of goodwill may have no relationship to the costs incurred in the development of that goodwill. To add to the mystery, goodwill may exist in the absence of specific costs to develop it. In addition, because no objective transaction with outside parties has taken place, a great deal of subjectivity might be involved, possibly even misrepresentation.

Methods of Measuring Goodwill

The following discussion on the valuation of goodwill and of the related methods of estimation is provided not so much as the solution to an accounting problem as it is a basis for developing an acquisition price for a business enterprise. The accountant is frequently called upon to provide this information as part of the purchase negotiations.

---

[10]George R. Catlett and Norman O. Olson, "Accounting for Goodwill," *Accounting Research Study No. 10* (New York: AICPA, 1968), pp. 17–18.

[11]See "Conceptual Framework for Financial Accounting and Reporting: Elements of Financial Statements and Their Measurement," *FASB Discussion Memorandum* (Stamford, Conn.: FASB, 1976), p. 235.

How does one determine the value of goodwill? Conceptually, the answer is to identify the individual attributes that constitute goodwill and attempt to value them individually. This procedure is impossible at present because our measurement techniques are not sophisticated enough to measure accurately the value of, say, a superior management team, or a good reputation. The methods of measuring goodwill are somewhat related to the **two basic views of the nature of goodwill:**

1. Goodwill represents intangible resources and conditions attributable to an enterprise's above-average strength in such areas as technical skill and knowledge, management, and marketing research and promotion that cannot be separately identified and valued.
2. Goodwill represents expected earnings in excess of anticipated normal earnings.[12]

One method, in accordance with the first view of goodwill, simply compares the fair market value of the net tangible and identifiable intangible assets with the negotiated purchase price of the acquired business. The difference is considered goodwill, which is why goodwill is sometimes referred to as a ''plug'' or ''gap filler'' or **''master valuation''** account. Goodwill is the residual or the excess of the cost over the fair value of the identifiable net assets acquired.

Another view of goodwill is reflected in the second method, one that determines the earnings in excess of those that normally could be earned by the tangible and identifiable intangible assets. These excess earnings are discounted to determine the present value of this extra inflow, which is considered the amount of goodwill.

Excess of Cost over the Fair Value of Net Assets Acquired

To illustrate what is meant by the ''excess of cost over fair value of net assets acquired (master valuation account) approach,'' the sequence followed in a possible merger is illustrated. Multi-Diversified, Inc. decides that it needs a parts division to supplement its existing tractor distributorship. The president of Multi-Diversified is interested in a small concern near Toronto (Tractorling Company) that has an established reputation and is seeking a merger candidate. The balance sheet of Tractorling Company follows.

Tractorling Co. BALANCE SHEET as of December 31, 1986			
Assets		**Equities**	
Cash	$ 25,000	Current liabilities	$ 55,000
Receivables	35,000	Share capital	100,000
Inventories	42,000	Retained earnings	100,000
Property, plant, and equipment (net)	153,000		$255,000
Total assets	$255,000		

After considerable negotiation, Tractorling Company decides to accept Multi-Diversified's offer of $400,000. What then is the value of the goodwill, if any?

The answer is not so obvious, because the fair market value of the identifiable assets of Tractorling are not disclosed in the cost-based balance sheet above. Suppose, for example, that as the negotiations progressed, an investigation of the underly-

[12]Accounting for Business Combinations and Purchased Intangibles,'' *FASB Discussion Memorandum* (Stamford, Conn.: FASB, 1976), p. 48.

ing assets of Tractorling was conducted to determine the fair market value of the assets. Such an investigation may be accomplished either through a purchase audit undertaken by Multi-Diversified's auditors in order to estimate the values of the seller's assets, or an independent appraisal from some other source. The following valuations are determined.

Fair Market Values	
Cash	$ 25,000
Receivables	35,000
Inventories	122,000
Property, plant, and equipment	205,000
Patents	18,000
Liabilities	(55,000)
Fair market value of net assets	$350,000

Normally, differences between current fair market value and book value are more common among the long-term assets, although significant differences can also develop in the current asset category. Cash obviously poses no problems, and receivables normally are fairly close to current valuation, although at times certain adjustments need to be made because of inadequate (or excessive) prior provisions for uncollectible accounts. Liabilities usually are stated at their book value, although if interest rates have changed since the liabilities were incurred, a different valuation might be appropriate. Careful analysis must be made in this area to determine that no unrecorded liabilities are present.

It is not surprising to find large variances in most of the other asset areas. The difference in inventories of $80,000 ($122,000 − $42,000) could result from a number of factors, the most likely being that Tractorling Company has followed a LIFO inventory valuation. If prices have been rising for a number of years and the company is expanding, a large difference in valuation could occur. In addition, the company may not have a full cost accounting system and many of the costs of operations may not be embodied in the inventory valuation.

In many cases, the values of such long-term assets as property, plant, and equipment, and intangibles may have increased substantially over the years. This differential may be caused by inaccurate estimates of useful lives, continual expensing of small expenditures (say, less than $300), inaccurate estimates of salvage values, the discovery of some unrecorded assets, or increases in replacement cost.

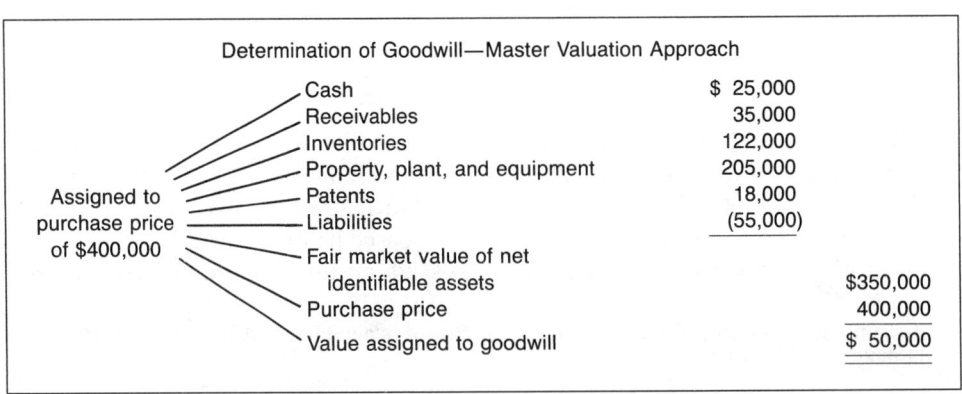

Determination of Goodwill—Master Valuation Approach

Cash	$ 25,000
Receivables	35,000
Inventories	122,000
Property, plant, and equipment	205,000
Patents	18,000
Liabilities	(55,000)
Fair market value of net identifiable assets	$350,000
Purchase price	400,000
Value assigned to goodwill	$ 50,000

Assigned to purchase price of $400,000

Given that the fair market value of the net assets is now determined to be $350,000, how was a purchase price of $400,000 determined? Undoubtedly, the seller pointed to an established reputation, good credit rating, top management team, and so on, as factors that make the value of the business greater than $350,000. On the other hand, Multi-Diversified probably was attempting to assess the future earning power of these attributes as well as the basic asset structure of the enterprise today. At this point in the negotiations, price can be a function of many factors: the most important is probably sheer skill at the bargaining table. Finally, a price of $400,000 is agreed upon. The difference between the purchase price of $400,000 and the fair market value of $350,000 is labelled goodwill. Goodwill is viewed as one or a group of unidentifiable values (intangible assets) the cost of which is measured by the "excess of the cost of the purchase over the acquiring company's interest in identifiable assets acquired and liabilities assumed."[13] This procedure for valuation is referred to as a master valuation approach because goodwill is assumed to cover all the values that cannot be specifically identified with any identifiable tangible or intangible asset.

Excess Earning Power

Conceptually, a more appealing and direct approach to valuing goodwill is to determine the total earning power that a company commands. By determining what a normal rate of return is on the tangible and identifiable intangibles in that industry, the typical earnings are computed. **The difference between what the firm earns and what is normal in the industry is referred to as the excess earning power.** This extra earning power indicates that there are unidentifiable values (intangible assets) that provide this increased earning power. Finding the value of goodwill then is a matter of discounting these excess earnings over their estimated lives.

This approach appears to be a systematic and logical way of attacking the problems for determining goodwill. Each factor necessary to compute a value under this approach is subject to question, however. Generally, the problems relate to getting answers to the following questions:

1. What is a normal rate of return?
2. How does one determine future earnings?
3. What discount rate should be applied to excess earnings?
4. Over what period should excess earnings be discounted?

Normal Rate of Return   Determination of the normal rate of return for tangible and identifiable intangible assets means that companies similar to the enterprise in question must be analyzed. An industry average may be determined by examination of annual reports, financial services, or other related financial data. The problem with this approach is that the rate normally employed is based on the historical value of the other firms' assets, not on their fair value. Suppose, however, that a rate of 15% is decided as normal for such a concern as Tractorling. In this case, the normal earnings are calculated in the following manner:[14]

---

[13]*CICA Handbook*, Section 1580, par. 44(b).

[14]The fair value of Tractorling's assets (rather than historical cost) is used to compute the normal profit, because fair value is more representative of the true value of the company's assets exclusive of goodwill. To use historical cost may result in a misstatement of normal profit and an overstatement of goodwill. This illustration assumes that no significant change in assets has occurred over the past five years; that is, the current fair value of the assets approximates the average fair value for the past five years.

Fair market value of Tractorling's net identifiable assets	$350,000
Normal rate of return	15%
Normal earnings	$ 52,500

Determination of Future Earnings   The starting point for this type of analysis is normally the past earnings of the enterprise. Although estimates of future earnings are needed, the past often provides useful information concerning the future earnings potential of a concern. The past earnings are also useful because estimates of the future are usually overly optimistic, and the hard facts of previous periods bring a sobering sense of reality to the negotiations. Generally a three-to-six-year period is examined to develop past earnings data.

Tractorling's net earnings for the last five years are as follows:

Earnings History—Tractorling

1982	$ 60,000	
1983	55,000	Average Earnings
1984	110,000[a]	$\dfrac{\$375,000}{5 \text{ years}} = \$75,000$
1985	70,000	
1986	80,000	
	$375,000	

[a]Includes extraordinary gain of $25,000.

The average net earnings for the last five years is $75,000. Before we go further, a question that needs answering is whether $75,000 represents the future earnings of this enterprise.

Often past earnings of a company to be acquired need to be adjusted because the acquirer tends to evaluate the average earnings on the basis of its own accounting procedures. Suppose, for example, that in determining earning power, Multi-Diversified measured earnings in relation to a FIFO inventory valuation figure rather than LIFO, which Tractorling employs, and that the use of LIFO reduced Tractorling's net income by $2,000 per year. In addition, Tractorling used accelerated depreciation although Multi-Diversified used a straight-line approach to estimate its earnings; the resulting earnings were therefore lower by the amount of $3,000.

Also, assets discovered on examination that might affect the earnings flow should

Average net earnings per Tractorling computation		$75,000
Add:		
Adjustment for switch from LIFO to FIFO	$2,000	
Adjustment for change from accelerated to straight-line approach	3,000	5,000
		80,000
Deduct:		
Extraordinary gain ($25,000 ÷ 5)	5,000	
Patent amortization on straight-line basis	1,000	6,000
Adjusted average net earnings of Tractorling		$74,000

be considered. For example, the patent costs not previously recorded should be amortized, say, at the rate of $1,000 per period. Finally, because the estimate of future earnings is what we are attempting to determine, some items, like the extraordinary gain of $25,000, probably should not be considered. An analysis can now be made as shown on page 570.

The $74,000 is then evaluated to determine whether it represents a realistic figure for the projected earnings. Assuming that it does, the excess earnings would be determined to be $21,500 ($74,000 − $52,500).

Choosing a Discount Rate to Apply to Excess Earnings   Determination of the discount rate is a fairly subjective estimate. The lower the discount rate, the higher the value of the goodwill. To illustrate, assume that the excess earnings are $21,500 and that these earnings will continue indefinitely. If the excess earnings are capitalized at, say, a rate of 25% in perpetuity[15] the results are:

Capitalization at 25%

$$\frac{\text{Excess earnings}}{\text{Capitalization rate}} \quad \frac{\$21{,}500}{0.25} = \$86{,}000$$

If the excess earnings are capitalized in perpetuity at a somewhat lower rate, say 15%, a much higher goodwill figure results.

Capitalization at 15%

$$\frac{\text{Excess earnings}}{\text{Capitalization rate}} \quad \frac{\$21{,}500}{0.15} = \$143{,}333$$

The higher the discount rate, the lower the value of goodwill. Normally, a rate somewhat higher than the normal rate is employed because the continuance of excess profits is uncertain. Factors that can be considered in this analysis are the stability of past earnings figures along with the speculative nature of the business. Although these factors are often difficult to crystallize into a discount rate, they do provide a basis on which a rate may be established.

Discounting Period for Excess Earnings   Determination of the period over which the excess earnings will exist is perhaps the most difficult problem associated with computing a value for goodwill. If, for example, it is assumed that the excess earnings will last indefinitely, the superior earnings may be capitalized by the discount rate selected. If the discount rate employed is the same as the normal return (15%), then goodwill is $143,333 as computed in the previous section.

Another method of computing goodwill that gives the same answer, using the normal return of 15%, is to discount the total average earnings of the company and subtract the fair market value of the assets as follows:

[15]Why do we divide by the capitalization rate to arrive at the goodwill amount? Recall that the present value of an ordinary annuity is equal to

$$P_{\overline{n}|\,i} = \frac{1 - \dfrac{1}{(1+i)^n}}{i}$$

When a number is capitalized into perpetuity, $(1 + i)^n$ becomes so large that $1/(1 + i)^n$ essentially equals zero, which leaves $1/i$ or, as in the case above, $21{,}500/0.25$.

Average earnings capitalized at 15% in perpetuity	
($74,000 ÷ 15%)	$493,333
Less: Fair market value of assets	350,000
Present value of estimated earnings (goodwill)	$143,333

Frequently, however, the excess earnings are assumed to last a limited number of years, say ten, and then it is necessary to discount these earnings only over that time at a given discount rate.

To illustrate this approach, assume that Multi-Diversified believes that the excess earnings of Tractorling will last ten years, and 15% is considered an appropriate rate of return. The present value of an annuity of $21,500 ($74,000 - $52,500) discounted at 15% for ten years is $107,903.56.[16]

Other Methods of Valuation

Some accountants fail to discount but simply multiply the excess earnings by the number of years they believe the excess earnings will continue. This approach, often referred to as the **number of years method**, is used to provide a rough measure for what the goodwill factor should be. The approach has only the advantage of simplicity; it is sounder to recognize the discount factor.

An even simpler method is one that relies on the prices, as multiples of the most recent annual earnings, that are paid for other companies in the same industry as the company to be purchased. For example, if Skyward Airlines was recently acquired for five times its average yearly earnings of $50 million, or $250 million, then Worldwide Airways, a close competitor, with $80 million in average yearly earnings would be worth $400 million. The method is simple but not very useful in those cases where historical precedents are unenlightening.

In practice, prospective buyers may use all these methods and variations of their own to produce a "valuation curve" or range of prices that vary according to underlying assumptions. The buyer may have accumulated considerable data supporting a specific price range, but the price actually paid may result more from the buyer's or seller's ego and horse-trading acumen.

It seems safe to say that the valuation of goodwill is at best a highly uncertain process. As the illustrations show, the estimated value of goodwill depends on a number of factors, all of which are highly tenuous and subject to bargaining.

Amortization of Goodwill

Once goodwill has been recognized in the accounts, the next question is: What is the proper accounting at this point? Three basic approaches have been suggested.

1. **Charge goodwill immediately to shareholders' equity.** *Accounting Research Study No. 10*, "Accounting for Goodwill," identifies a position that goodwill differs from other types of assets and demands special attention.[17] This argument is based on the proposition that goodwill, unlike other assets, is not separable and distinct from the

---

[16]Generally, the future realization of excess earnings is more uncertain than other earnings. Consequently, it may be appropriate to use a higher discount rate when estimating the present value of future excess earnings.

[17]Catlett and Olson, *op. cit.*, pp. 89-95.

business as a whole and therefore is not an asset in the same sense as cash, receivables, or plant assets. In other words, goodwill cannot be sold without selling the business. Furthermore, *ARS No. 10* notes that the accounting treatment for purchased goodwill and goodwill internally created should be consistent. Goodwill created internally is immediately expensed and does not appear as an asset: the same treatment should be accorded purchased goodwill. It is also contended that amortization of purchased goodwill leads to double counting, because net income is reduced by amortization of the purchased goodwill as well as by the internal expenditure made to maintain or enhance the value of the assets. Perhaps the best rationale for direct write-off is that determination of the periods over which the future benefits are to be received is so difficult that immediate charging to shareholders' equity is justified.

2. **Retain goodwill indefinitely unless reduction in value occurs.** Many accountants believe that goodwill can have an indefinite life and should be maintained as an asset until a decline in value occurs. They contend that inasmuch as internal goodwill is being expensed to maintain or enhance the purchased goodwill, some form of goodwill should always be an asset. In addition, without sufficient evidence that a decline in value has occurred, a write-off of goodwill is both arbitrary and capricious and will lead to distortions in net income.

3. **Amortize goodwill over useful life.** Still other accountants believe that goodwill as service potential eventually disappears, and that the asset should be charged to expense over the periods affected. This procedure provides a better matching of costs and revenues in that amortization over its useful life provides the appropriate charge to expense.

The *CICA Handbook*, Section 1580, takes the position that goodwill should be written off over its useful life, which depends on such myriad factors as regulatory restrictions, demand, competition, and obsolescence. **The profession did note that (1) goodwill should never be written off at the date of acquisition and (2) the period of amortization should not exceed 40 years**.

Immediate write-off was not considered proper, because it would lead to the untenable conclusion that all noncurrent assets should be charged off immediately. It might be noted that the profession merely prohibits the writing off of goodwill in the period of purchase and over a period exceeding 40 years; no other mention is made regarding another period. Some believe that a five-year period for amortization would be appropriate unless, depending on the specific circumstances, such as continued loss of profitability or loss of managerial talent, a shorter period is obviously justified. A single loss year or a combination of loss years does not automatically necessitate a charge-off of the goodwill.

The amortization of the goodwill should be computed using the straight-line method unless another method is deemed more appropriate, and it should be treated as a regular operating expense. Where the amortization is material, a disclosure of the charge is necessary, as well as the method and period of amortization.

Negative Goodwill

Negative goodwill, or bargain purchase, arises when the fair market value of the assets acquired is higher than the purchase price of the assets. Situations do occur where the purchase price is less than the value of the net identifiable assets; thus, a credit develops that is referred to as negative goodwill, or excess of fair value over the cost of assets acquired. This situation is a result of conditions in which the seller would be better off to sell the assets individually than in total. Companies that have negative goodwill occupy an interesting position because the amortization of this negative goodwill to revenue increases earnings.

Negative goodwill is rarely reported in Canadian financial statements, since

CICA Handbook, Section 1580, takes the position that an excess of fair value over purchase price should be allocated to reduce proportionately the values assigned to nonmonetary assets. The *Handbook* does not contemplate the possibility that this allocation might reduce all nonmonetary assets to zero without using the full amount of the excess of fair value acquired over the purchase price. In the rare occasions when this condition does develop, the unallocated excess could be classified as a deferred credit and amortized systematically to income over the period estimated to be benefited.[18]

Negative goodwill most frequently develops in a depressed securities market when the market value of a company's shares is less than their book value. For example, Emhart Corp. offered $23 a share (a premium over market) for U.S.M. Corp. shares which had a per-share book value of $53. Emhart Corp. (in consolidation) was able to write down its newly acquired plant assets by more than $49 million, thereby effecting a reduction in annual depreciation charges of $5.8 million and adding 50 cents annually to its earnings per share, on top of the $2 a share it would gain from consolidating U.S.M.'s reported profits. (This extra $2.50 per share represented a 90% increase over Emhart's prior-year earnings.)

Reporting of Intangibles

The reporting of intangibles differs from the reporting of property, plant, and equipment in that the contra accounts are not normally shown for the intangibles. The amortization of intangibles is generally credited directly to the intangible asset.[19]

The financial statements should disclose the method and period of amortization. Intangible assets of Niagara Structural Steel Company were reported on the company's 1983 financial statements as shown on page 575.

Some companies follow the practice of writing their intangibles down to $1.00 to indicate that they have intangibles of which the values are uncertain. This practice does not accord with good accounting. It would be much better to disclose the nature of the intangible, its original cost, and such other relevant information as competition, danger of obsolescence, and so on.

RESEARCH AND DEVELOPMENT COSTS

Research and development (R&D) costs are not in themselves intangible assets but, because research and development activities frequently result in the development of something that is patented or copyrighted (such as a new product, idea, formula, composition, or literary work), R&D costs are presented in the intangible assets chapter.

Many businesses expend considerable sums of money on research and development for new products or processes, to improve present products, and to discover new knowledge that may be valuable at some future date. The difficulties in accounting for these R&D expenditures are (1) identifying the costs associated with particular activities, projects, or achievements and (2) determining the magnitude

---

[18]*CICA Handbook*, Section 1580, par. 44.

[19]*Financial Reporting in Canada*—1983 (Toronto: CICA, 1983) reports that the most common type of intangible is goodwill, followed by patents, franchises, licences, and trademarks.

Other assets

	1983	1982
Excess of cost of subsidiary over net value of assets at date of acquisition	$1,146,174	$ –0–
Goodwill	25,024	28,600
Deferred costs	210,308	218,661
Patents and trademarks	162,746	–0–
Plant start-up costs	58,955	60,799
	$1,603,207	$308,060

From Note A

Other Assets: The excess of cost of subsidiary over net value of tangible assets at date of acquisition is being amortized on a straight-line basis over ten years resulting in a charge to income this year of $60,325.

Goodwill represents the excess of purchase price of shares of Polyloom Corporation of America over proportionate share of net asset value less amortization. Goodwill is being amortized on a straight-line basis over nine years. The amount of goodwill charged to operations during the year amounted to $3,576 (1982 – $3,575).

Deferred costs consist of organizational and development costs which are being amortized over various periods up to five years. Deferred costs charged to operations during the year amounted to $86,420 (1982 – $5,350). Patents and trademarks are being amortized on a straight-line basis over ten years resulting in a charge to income this year of $13,174.

Plant start-up costs incurred in connection with the Norforge production facility in Sept-Iles, Quebec, are being amortized over an estimated five-year period based upon production. Plant start-up costs charged to operations this year amounted to $27,216 (1982 – $44,679).

Plant start-up costs incurred in connection with newly formed Laykold Corporation in Baltimore, Maryland, are being amortized over one year. Plant start-up costs charged to operations since formation amounted to $25,371.

of the future benefits and the length of time over which such benefits may be realized. Because of these latter uncertainties the accounting profession (through *CICA Handbook*, Section 3450) has greatly standardized and simplified accounting practice in this area by requiring that all research and development costs be charged to expense when incurred except in certain narrowly defined circumstances.

To differentiate research and development costs from each other and from other similar costs, the CICA issued the following definitions:

> **Research** is planned investigation undertaken with the hope of gaining new scientific or technical knowledge and understanding. Such investigation may or may not be directed towards a specific practical aim or application.
>
> **Development** is the translation of research findings or other knowledge into a plan or design for new or substantially improved material, devices, products, processes, systems, or services prior to the commencement of commercial production or use.[20]

Many costs have characteristics similar to those of research and development costs; for instance, costs of relocation and rearrangement of facilities, start-up costs for a new plant or new retail outlet, marketing research costs, promotion costs of a new product or service, and costs of training new personnel. To distinguish between research, development, and these other similar costs, the following

[20]*CICA Handbook*, Section 3450, par. 2.

schedule provides examples of activities that would be excluded from both research and development.[21]

1. **Research Activities**
   (a) Laboratory research aimed at discovery of new knowledge.
   (b) Searching for applications of new research findings or other knowledge.
   (c) Conceptual formulation and design of possible product or process alternatives.

2. **Development Activities**
   (a) Testing in search for or evaluation of product or process alternatives.
   (b) Design, construction, and testing of preproduction prototypes and models.
   (c) Design of tools, jigs, moulds, and dies involving new technology.

3. **Activities Not Considered Either Research or Development**
   (a) Engineering follow-through in an early phase of commercial production.
   (b) Quality control during commercial production, including routine testing of products.
   (c) Trouble-shooting in connection with breakdowns during commercial production.
   (d) Routine or periodic alterations to existing products, production lines, manufacturing processes, and other continuing operations.
   (e) Adaptation of an existing capability to a particular requirement or customer's need as part of a continuing commerical activity.
   (f) Routine design of tools, jigs, moulds, and dies.
   (g) Activity, including design and construction engineering, related to the construction, relocation, rearrangement, or start-up of facilities or equipment other than facilities or equipment whose sole use is for a particular research and development project.

Special Problems

A special problem arises in distinguishing R&D costs from selling and administrative activities. Except for ''routine'' market research costs, research and development costs may include those associated with any product or process regardless of whether related to production, marketing, or administrative activities. For example, the costs of software incurred by an airline in acquiring, developing, or improving its computerized reservation system or for development of a general management information system would be considered development costs.

Costs associated with research and development activities would include direct costs of labour and materials plus a reasonable allocation of overhead. Any indirect costs (general administrative not clearly related to the activity or functional) are to be treated as period costs. The following costs may be properly included as research and development costs:

1. The cost of materials and services consumed in research and development activities.
2. The salaries, wages, and other related costs of personnel directly engaged in research and development activities.
3. The depreciation of equipment and facilities to the extent that they are used for research and development activities.
4. A reasonable allocation of overhead.

[21]*Ibid.*, pars. 4, 5, 6.

5. The amortization of intangibles to the extent that they are related to research and development activities.[22]

The *CICA Handbook* requires that **all** development costs be written off as expenses of the period incurred except when **all** the following criteria for deferral are met:

1. The product or process is clearly defined and the costs attributable thereto can be identified.
2. The technical feasibility of the product or process has been established.
3. The management of the enterprise has indicated its intention to produce and market or use the product or process.
4. The future market for the product or process is clearly defined or, if it is used internally rather than sold, its usefulness to the enterprise has been established.
5. Adequate resources exist, or are expected to be available, to complete the project. Furthermore, the total amount of development costs deferred must be limited to the extent that their recovery can reasonably be regarded as assured.[23]

Next Century Ltd.	
Type of Expenditure	Accounting Treatment
1. Construction of long-range research facility (three-storey, 100,000 m² building) for use in current and future projects.	Capitalize and depreciate as R&D expense.
2. Acquisition of R&D equipment for use on current project only.	Capitalize and depreciate as R&D expense.
3. Purchase of materials to be used on current and future R&D projects.	Inventory and allocate to R&D projects as consumed.
4. Salaries of research staff designing new laser bone scanner.	Expense immediately as research.
5. Research costs incurred under contract for New Horizon Ltd. and invoiced monthly.	Expense as operating expense in period of related revenue recognition.
6. Material, labour, and overhead of prototype laser scanner.	Expense immediately as research.
7. Costs of testing prototype and design modifications.	Expense immediately as research.
8. Legal fees to obtain patent on new laser scanner.	Capitalize as patent and amortize to cost of goods manufactured.
9. Executive salaries. (general and administrative).	Expense as operating expense
10. Cost of marketing research related to promotion of new laser scanner.	Expense as operating expense (selling).
11. Engineering costs incurred to advance the laser scanner to full production stage.	Capitalize as development cost if all criteria [3450.21 (a) – (e)] are met.
12. Costs of successfully defending patent on laser scanner.	Capitalize as patent and amortize to cost of goods manufactured.
13. Commissions to sales staff marketing new laser scanner.	Expense as operating expense (selling).

[22]*Ibid.*, par. 13.

[23]*Ibid.*, par. 13.

Costs of R&D activities conducted for other entities under a **contractual arrangement** are not covered by Section 3450 and, therefore, may be capitalized and deferred rather than expensed when incurred.

To illustrate the identification of R&D activities and the accounting treatment of related costs, assume that Next Century Ltd. conducts research, and produces and markets laser machines for medical, industrial, and defence uses. The types of expenditures related to its laser machine activities are listed on page 577 along with the recommended accounting treatment.

Costs of research and development activities that are unique to companies in the **extractive industries** (for example, prospecting, acquisition of mineral rights, exploration, drilling, mining, and related mineral development) are not covered by Section 3450. However, research and development activities that are comparable in nature to those of firms in other industries must be accounted for in accordance with Section 3450.

Acceptable accounting practice requires that disclosure be made in the financial statements (generally in the notes) of the total R&D costs charged to expense in each period for which an income statement is presented.

An example of an R&D disclosure is the following excerpt from the 1982 annual report of Leigh Instruments Ltd.

Notes to financial statements

1. Accounting Policies
(d) Research and Development Costs:
Development costs relating to specific contracts are included in work-in-progress. Development costs relating to specific product lines, which satisfy certain criteria, are deferred and amortized, beginning in the year that commercial production commences, over the initial series of units expected to be produced, but in any case over a period not to exceed three years. When it is determined that the deferred costs are not likely to be recovered through future revenues, such costs are written off to income. Research and other development costs are charged to earnings in the year in which they are incurred.

5. Other Assets	1982	1981
Deferred development costs (net of amortization of $914,000; 1981 − $225,000)	$1,663,000	$1,105,000

10. Research and Development Costs
Expenditures on research and development, other than costs relating to specific contracts which are billed or included in work-in-progress, were as follows:

	1982	1981
Total expenditures	$3,430,000	$2,165,000
Government assistance	(743,000)	(1,000,000)
	2,687,000	1,165,000
Deferred as other assets	(1,247,000)	(641,000)
	1,440,000	524,000
Amortization of deferred costs	689,000	225,000
	$2,129,000	$ 749,000

Conceptual Questions

The requirement that all research costs incurred internally be expensed immediately is a conservative, practical solution that insures consistency in practice and uniformity among companies. The practice, however, of writing off against revenues of the present period expenditures made in the expectation of benefiting future periods cannot be justified on the grounds that it is good accounting theory.

Defendants of immediate expensing contend that, from the standpoint of the income statement, long-run application of this standard makes little difference. The amount of research costs charged against income each accounting period would be about the same whether there is immediate expensing or capitalization and subsequent amortization because of the continuous nature of most companies' research activities. Aside from the revenue/expense mismatching, which may be minimal, critics of this practice argue that the balance sheet should report an intangible asset related to expenditures that have future benefit. To preclude capitalization of all research expenditures removes from the balance sheet what may be a company's most valuable asset. This standard represents one of the many trade-offs made among relevance, reliability, and cost-benefit considerations.

DEFERRED CHARGES AND LONG-TERM PREPAYMENTS

Deferred charges is a classification often used to describe a number of different items that have debit balances, among them certain types of intangibles. Intangibles sometimes classified as deferred charges include plant rearrangement costs, preoperating and start-up costs, and organization costs. How do these items happen to be classified in this section and not in a separate intangible section? Probably the major reason is that the deferred charge section often serves as a ''dumping ground'' for a number of small items.

Deferred charges also include such items as long-term prepayments for insurance, rent, taxes, and other down payments. The deferred charge classification probably should be abolished because it cannot be clearly differentiated from other amortizable and depreciable assets (which also are deferred charges), and a more informative disclosure could be made of the smaller items often found in this section of the balance sheet. Such a classification has even less relevance today because the conceptual framework project establishes a definition for assets that would apparently exclude deferred charges.

KEY POINTS

1. **Intangible assets** are generally characterized by a lack of physical existence and a high degree of uncertainty concerning future benefits. Intangibles may be categorized according to their separate identity, manner of acquisition, expected periods of benefit, and separability from the enterprise.

2. The **valuation of purchased intangibles** is the acquisition cost (the fair market value of the consideration given or the fair value of the intangible received, whichever is more clearly evident).

3. Intangible assets should be amortized by systematic charges to expense over their estimated useful lives. The straight-line method of amortization is most commonly used.

4. Costs of specifically identifiable intangible assets having determinable lives are capitalized and amortized. Costs related to intangibles not specifically identifiable and developed internally are usually expensed as incurred.

5. Specifically identifiable intangibles that typically have determinable lives include patents, copyrights, trademarks and trade names, leaseholds, franchises, and licences and permits. The capitalized cost of such intangibles are

amortized over their legal, contractual, or useful life, whichever is shorter. Generally, the maximum amortization period would not exceed 40 years.

6. Goodwill is recorded only when an entire business is purchased because goodwill is the "going concern" valuation and cannot be separated from the business as a whole. Costs incurred to generate goodwill internally are not capitalized. Goodwill is recorded at cost and amortized over the estimated useful life, not to exceed 40 years.

7. Goodwill may be measured as the excess of the cost over the fair value of the identifiable net assets acquired in the purchase of a whole business or as the discounted present value of expected earnings in excess of anticipated normal earnings from the tangible and identifiable intangible assets.

8. All research costs are expensed when incurred. Generally, development costs are expensed when incurred. However, when certain criteria are met, development costs may be capitalized and amortized over the period benefiting. The accounting problem is one of differentiating between research, development costs, and other similar costs. Fixed assets used in research and development activities should be capitalized and depreciated.

QUESTIONS

1. What are the major accounting problems related to accounting for intangibles?

2. Many accountants advocate the abandonment of historical cost for plant assets but argue that historical cost should be used in accounting for intangible assets. Are the two viewpoints inconsistent?

3. Intangible assets may be classified on a number of different bases. Indicate three different bases and illustrate how intangibles could be subdivided into these groupings.

4. Accounting authors and practitioners (and this course) have proposed various solutions to the problems of accounting in terms of historical cost for goodwill and similar intangibles. What problems of accounting for goodwill and similar intangibles are comparable to those of accounting for plant assets? What problems are different?

5. What are some examples of internally created intangibles? Why does the accounting profession make a distinction between internally created "goodwill type" intangibles and other intangibles?

6. State the generally accepted accounting procedures for the amortization and write-down or write-off of capitalized intangible assets.

7. It has been argued, on the grounds of conservatism, that all intangible assets should be written off immediately after acquisition. Give the accounting arguments against this treatment.

8. Indicate the period of time over which each of the following should be amortized:
   (a) Franchises.
   (b) Patents.
   (c) Leasehold improvements.
   (d) Copyrights.
   (e) Development costs.
   (f) Trademarks.
   (g) Goodwill.
   (h) A 20-year lease with payments of $44,000 per year on property with an estimated useful life of 50 years. The lessee has the option to renew the lease for 30 additional years at $11,000 per year.

9. What is a lease prepayment? What are property rights capitalized by the lessee? What are leasehold improvements? Should any of these items be classified as an intangible asset?

10. Recently, Heublein Corporation entered into a lease agreement with Mountain Developers, Inc. to lease some land for 20 years in southwest Cambridge. Heublein Corporation as lessee then built on this site a number of apartment buildings having a useful life of 35 years. The lease agreement states that the lessee has the option to renew the lease for another 20 years. Over what period should the apartments be depreciated?

11. Recently, a group of university students decided to incorporate for the purpose of selling a process to recycle the waste product from manufacturing cheese. Some of the initial costs involved were legal fees and office expense incurred in starting the business and incorporation fees. One student wishes to charge these costs against income in the current period; another wishes to defer these costs and amortize them in the future; and another believes these costs should be netted against common shares. Which student is correct?

12. What is goodwill? What is negative goodwill?

13. Under what circumstances is it appropriate to record goodwill in the accounts? How should goodwill, properly recorded on the books, be amortized in order to conform with generally accepted accounting principles?

14. Explain how "average excess earnings" are determined. What is the justification for the use of this method of estimated goodwill?

15. In examining financial statements, financial analysts often write off goodwill immediately. Evaluate this procedure.

16. Discuss two methods for estimating the value of goodwill in determining the amount that should properly be paid for it.

17. What is the nature of research and development costs? What other costs have similar characteristics?

18. Research and development activities may include (a) personnel costs, (b) materials and equipment costs, and (c) indirect costs. What is the recommended accounting treatment for these three types of R&D costs?

19. During the current year, Hydrostatic Railroad spends $600,000 to develop a computer program that will assist in identifying and locating all of its rolling equipment; the railroad also spends $245,000 to develop a unique software package that will be offered on a lease basis to other railroads. How should Hydrostatic account for these two expenditures?

20. Which of the following activities should be expensed currently as R&D costs?
    (a) Engineering follow-through in an early phase of commercial production.
    (b) Legal work in connection with patent applications or litigation, and the sale or licencing of patents.
    (c) Testing in search or evaluation of product or process alternatives.
    (d) Adaptation of an existing capability to a particular requirement or customer's need as a part of continuing commercial activity.

21. In 1984, Southern Corporation developed a new product to be marketed in 1985. In connection with the development of this product, the following costs were incurred in 1984: research and development departmental costs, $200,000; materials and supplies consumed, $50,000; compensation paid to research consultants, $60,000. It is anticipated that these costs will be recovered in 1987. What is the amount of research and development costs that Southern should have recorded in 1984 as a charge to income?

CASES

C12-1 In examining the books of Imagery Manufacturing Company, you find on the December 31, 1985, balance sheet the item "Cost of Patents, $308,440."

Referring to the ledger accounts, you note the following items regarding one patent acquired in 1982:

1982 Legal costs incurred in defending the validity of the patent	$7,200
1984 Legal costs in prosecuting an infringement suit	9,500
1984 Legal costs (additional expenses) in the infringement suit	3,950
1984 Cost of improvements (unpatented) on the patented device	15,700

There are no credits in the account, and no allowance for amortization has been set up on the books for any of the patents. Three other patents issued in 1979, 1981, and 1982 were developed by the staff of the client. The patented articles are currently very marketable, but it is estimated that they will be in demand only for the next few years.

Instructions

Discuss the items included in the Patent account from an accounting standpoint.
(AICPA adapted)

C12-2   On June 30, 1985, your client, Sparatan Corporation, was granted two patents covering plastic cartons that it had been producing and marketing profitably for the past three years. One patent covers the manufacturing process and the other covers the related products.

Sparatan executives tell you that these patents represent the most significant breakthrough in the industry in the past 30 years. The products have been marketed under the registered trademarks Safetainer, Duratainer, and Sealrite. Licences under the patents have already been granted by your client to other manufacturers in Canada and abroad and are producing substantial royalties.

On July 1, Sparatan commences patent infringement actions against several companies whose names you recognize as those of substantial and prominent competitors. Sparatan's management is optimistic that these suits will result in a permanent injunction against the manufacture and sale of the infringing products and collection of damages for loss of profits caused by the alleged infringement.

The financial vice-president has suggested that the patents be recorded at the discounted value of expected net royalty receipts.

Instructions

(a) What is the meaning of "discounted value of expected net receipts"? Explain.
(b) How would such a value be calculated for net royalty receipts?
(c) What basis of valuation for Sparatan's patents would be generally accepted in accounting? Give supporting reasons for this basis.
(d) Assuming no practical problems of implementation and ignoring generally accepted accounting principles, what is the preferable basis of valuation for patents? Explain.
(e) What would be the preferable theoretical basis of amortization? Explain.
(f) What recognition, if any, should be made of the infringement litigation in the financial statements for the year ending September 30, 1985? Discuss.
(AICPA adapted)

C12-3   During the examination of the financial statements of Aurora Company, your assistant calls attention to significant costs incurred in the development of EDP programs (that is, software) for major segments of the sales and inventory scheduling systems.

The EDP program development costs will benefit future periods to the extent that the systems change slowly and the program instructions are compatible with new equipment acquired at three- to six-year intervals. The service value of the EDP programs is affected almost entirely by changes in the technology of systems and EDP equipment and does not decline with the number of times the program is used. Because many system changes are minor, program instructions frequently can be modified with only minor losses in program efficiency. The frequency of such changes tends to increase with the passage of time.

Instructions

(a) Discuss the propriety of classifying the unamortized EDP program development costs as:
1. A prepaid expense.
2. An intangible asset.
3. A tangible fixed asset.

(b) Discuss the propriety of amortizing the EDP program development costs by means of:
1. The straight-line method.
2. A decreasing-charge method (for example, the sum-of-the-years'-digits method).
3. A variable-charge method (for example, the units of production method).

(AICPA adapted)

C12-4 After securing lease commitments from several major stores, Bow Valley Shopping Centre, Inc. built a shopping centre in a growing suburb.

The shopping centre would have opened on schedule on January 1, 1986, if it had not been struck by a severe tornado in December; it opened for business on October 1, 1986. All of the additional construction costs that were incurred as a result of the tornado were covered by insurance.

In July, 1985, in anticipation of the scheduled January opening, a permanent staff had been hired to promote the shopping centre, obtain tenants for the uncommitted space, and manage the property.

A summary of some of the costs incurred in 1985 and the first nine months of 1986 follows.

	1985	January 1, 1986 through September 30, 1986
Interest on mortgage bonds	$75,000	$97,500
Cost of obtaining tenants	33,000	60,000
Promotional advertising	43,500	46,500

The promotional advertising campaign was designed to familiarize shoppers with the centre. Had it been known in time that the centre would not open until October, 1986, the 1985 expenditure for promotional advertising would not have been made. The advertising had to be repeated in 1986.

All of the tenants who had leased space in the shopping centre at the time of the tornado accepted the October occupancy date on condition that the monthly rental charges for the first nine months of 1986 be cancelled.

Instructions

Explain how each of the costs for 1985 and the first nine months of 1986 should be treated in the accounts of Bow Valley. Give the reasons for each treatment.

(AICPA adapted)

C12-5 After extended negotiations, Voltage Corporation bought from Igloo Company most of the latter's assets on June 30, 1986. At the time of the sale, Igloo's accounts (adjusted to June 30, 1986) reflected the following descriptions and amounts for the assets transferred.

	Cost	Contra (Valuation) Account	Book Value
Receivables	$ 85,600	$ 2,500	$ 83,100
Inventory	107,000	5,400	101,600
Land	18,000	—	18,000
Buildings	208,600	73,000	135,600
Fixtures and equipment	203,900	42,000	161,900
Goodwill	50,000	—	50,000
	$673,100	$122,900	$550,200

You ascertain that the contra (valuation) accounts were allowance for doubtful accounts, allowance to reduce inventory to market, and accumulated depreciation.

During the extended negotiations, Igloo held out for a consideration of approximately $625,000 (depending on the level of the receivables and inventory). As of June 30, 1986, however, Igloo agreed to accept Voltage's offer of $475,000 cash plus 1% of the net sales (as defined in the contract) of the next five years with payments at the end of each year. Igloo expected that Voltage's total net sales during this period would exceed $15,000,000.

Instructions

(a) How should Voltage Corporation record this transaction? Explain.

(b) Discuss the propriety of recording goodwill in the accounts of Voltage Corporation for this transaction.

(AICPA adapted)

C12-6 Alberta Corporation, a retail fuel oil distributor, has increased its annual sales volume to a level three times greater than the annual sales of a dealer it purchased in 1985 in order to begin operations.

The board of directors of Alberta Corporation recently received an offer to negotiate the sale of Alberta Corporation to a large competitor. As a result, the majority of the board want to increase the stated value of goodwill on the balance sheet to reflect the larger sales volume developed through intensive promotion and the current market price of sales gallonage. A few of the board members, however, would prefer to eliminate goodwill altogether from the balance sheet in order to prevent "possible misinterpretations." Goodwill was recorded properly in 1985.

Instructions

(a) Discuss the meaning of the term "goodwill."

(b) List the techniques used to calculate the tentative value of goodwill in negotiations to purchase a going concern.

(c) Why are the book and market values of the goodwill of Alberta Corporation different?

(d) Discuss the propriety of:
   1. Increasing the stated value of goodwill prior to the negotiations.
   2. Eliminating goodwill completely from the balance sheet prior to negotiations.

(AICPA adapted)

C12-7 Cormack Company operates several plants at which limestone is processed into quicklime and hydrated lime. The Batavia Plant, where most of the equipment was installed many years ago, continually deposits a dusty white substance over the surrounding countryside. Citing the unsanitary condition of the neighbouring community of Geneva, the pollution of the Fox River, and the high incidence of lung disease among workers at Batavia, the area's Pollution Control Agency has ordered the installation of air pollution control equipment. Also, the Agency has assessed a substantial penalty, which will be used to clean up Geneva. After considering the costs involved (which could not have been reasonably estimated prior to the Agency's action), management decides to comply with the Agency's orders, the alternative being to cease operations at Batavia at the end of the current fiscal year. The officers of Cormack Company agree that the air pollution control equipment should be capitalized and depreciated over its useful life, but they disagree over the period(s) to which the penalty should be charged.

Instructions

Discuss the conceptual merits and reporting requirements of accounting for the penalty as a:

(a) Charge to the current period.

(b) Correction of prior periods.

(c) Capitalizable item to be amortized over future periods.

(AICPA adapted)

C12-8   Honeyall, Inc. is a large, publicly held corporation. Listed below are six selected expenditures made by the company during the current fiscal year ended April 30, 1985. The proper accounting treatment of these transactions must be determined in order that Honeyall's annual financial statements will be prepared in accordance with generally accepted accounting principles.

1.   Honeyall, Inc. spent $2,000,000 on a program designed to improve relations with its dealers. This project was favourably received by the dealers and Honeyall's management believed that significant future benefits should be received from this program. The program was conducted during the fourth quarter of the current fiscal year.

2.   A pilot plant was constructed during 1984–85 at a cost of $4,000,000 to test a new production process. The plant will be operated for approximately five years. At that time, the company will make a decision regarding the economic value of the process. The pilot plant is too small for commercial production, so it will be dismantled when the test is over.

3.   A new product will be introduced next year. The company spent $3,000,000 during the current year for design of tools, jigs, moulds, and dies for this product.

4.   Honeyall, Inc. purchased Merit Company for $5,000,000 in cash in early August, 1984. The fair market value of the identifiable assets of Merit was $4,000,000.

5.   A large advertising campaign was conducted during April, 1985, to introduce a new product to be released during the first quarter of the 1985–86 fiscal year. The advertising campaign cost $2,500,000.

6.   During the first six months of the 1984–85 fiscal year, $500,000 was expended for legal work in connection with a successful patent application. The patent became effective November 1, 1984. The legal life of the patent is 17 years while the economic life of the patent is expected to be approximately 10 years.

Instructions

For each of the six expenditures presented, determine and justify:

(a)   The amount, if any, that should be capitalized and included on Honeyall's Statement of Financial Position prepared as of April 30, 1985.

(b)   The amount that should be included in Honeyall's Statement of Income for the year ended April 30, 1985.

(CMA adapted)

EXERCISES

E12-1   Futuristic Products Company from time to time embarks on a research program when a special project seems to offer possibilities. In 1985 the company expends $300,000 on a research project, but by the end of 1985 it is impossible to determine whether any benefit will be derived from it.

Instructions

(a)   What account should be charged for the $300,000, and how should it be shown in the financial statements?

(b)   The project is completed in 1986, and a successful patent is obtained. The development costs to complete the project are $102,000. The administrative and legal expenses incurred in obtaining patent number 472-1001-86 in 1986 total $12,000. The patent has an expected useful life of five years. Record these costs in journal entry form. Also, record patent amortization (full year) in 1986.

(c)   In 1987 the company successfully defends the patent in extended litigation at a cost of $36,000, thereby extending the patent life to December 31, 1994. What is the proper way to account for this cost? Also, record patent amortization (full year) in 1987.

(d)   Additional engineering and consulting costs incurred in 1987 to improve the quality of the patented product total $40,000. The improvements enhance the salability of the product considerably. Discuss the proper accounting treatment for this cost.

E12-2   Cunningham Products, Inc. has its own research department. In addition, the company purchases patents from time to time. The following statements summarize the transactions involving all patents now owned by the company.

During 1979 and 1980, $109,200 was spent developing a new process that was patented (No. 1) on March 18, 1981, at additional legal and other costs of $13,464. A patent (No. 2) developed by Philip Berger, an inventor, was purchased for $146,850 on November 30, 1982, on which date it had 12 1/2 years yet to run.

During 1981, 1982, and 1983, research and development activities cost amounted to $230,000 ($65,000 and $165,000 respectively). No additional patents resulted from these activities.

A patent infringement suit brought by the company against a competitor because of the manufacture of articles infringing on Patent No. 2 was successfully prosecuted at a cost of $4,970. A decision in the case was rendered in July, 1983.

A competing patent (No. 3) was purchased for $38,400 in August, 1984. This patent had 16 years yet to run. During 1985, $45,500 has been expended on patent development: $22,000 of this amount represents the cost of a device for which a patent application has been filed, but no notification of acceptance or rejection by the Patent Office has been received. The other $23,500 represents costs incurred on uncompleted development projects.

Instructions

(a) Compute the carrying value of these patents as of December 31, 1985, assuming that the legal life and the useful life of each patent is the same and that each patent is to be amortized from the first day of the month following its acquisition.

(b) Prepare a journal entry to record amortization for 1985.

E12-3   Morley Company has provided information on intangible assets as follows:

A patent was purchased from the Doug Company for $1,800,000 on January 1, 1985. Morley estimated the remaining useful life of the patent to be ten years. The patent was carried in Doug's accounting records at a net book value of $1,250,000 when Doug sold it to Morley.

During 1986, a franchise was purchased from the Debbie Company for $600,000. In addition, 5% of revenue from the franchise must be paid to Debbie. Revenue from the franchise for 1986 was $2,400,000. Morley estimates the useful life of the franchise to be ten years and takes a full year's amortization in the year of purchase.

Morley incurred research and development costs in 1986 as follows:

	Research	Development
Materials and equipment	$ 14,000	$130,000
Personnel	140,000	28,000
Indirect costs	24,000	48,000
	$178,000	$206,000

Morley estimates that these costs will be recouped by December 31, 1989.

On January 1, 1986, Morley, because of recent events in the field, estimates that the remaining life of the patent purchased on January 1, 1985, is only five years from January 1, 1986.

Instructions

(a) Prepare a schedule showing the intangibles section of Morley's balance sheet at December 31, 1986. Show supporting computations in good form.

(b) Prepare a schedule showing the income statement effect for the year ended December 31, 1986, as a result of the facts above. Show supporting computations in good form.

(AICPA adapted)

E12-4   As the recently appointed auditor for Allan Thin Corporation, you have been asked to examine selected accounts before the six-month financial statements of

June 30, 1985, are prepared. The controller for Allan Thin Corporation mentions that only one account (shown below) is kept for Intangible Assets.

Intangible Assets

		Debit	Credit	Balance
January 4	Research costs	600,000		600,000
	Development costs	330,000		930,000
January 5	Legal costs to obtain patent	70,000		1,000,000
January 31	Payment of seven months rent			
	on property leased by Rode	77,000		1,077,000
February 1	Share issue costs	53,000		1,130,000
February 11	Premium on common shares		300,000	830,000
March 31	Unamortized bond discount			
	on bonds due March 31,			
	2005	100,000		930,000
April 30	Promotional expenses			
	related to start-up of			
	business	300,000		1,230,000
June 30	Operating losses for first			
	six months	270,000		1,500,000

Instructions

Prepare the entry or entries necessary to correct this account. Assume that the patent has a useful life of ten years, that organization costs are being amortized over a five-year period, and that development costs meet the criteria for capitalizing.

E12-5   Tailwind Airlines leases an old building which it intends to improve and use as a warehouse. To obtain the lease, the company pays a bonus of $25,000. Annual rental for the five-year lease period is $90,000. No option to renew the lease or right to purchase the property is given.

After the lease is obtained, improvements costing $139,000 are made. The building has an estimated remaining useful life of 16 years.

Instructions

(a)   What is the annual cost of this lease to Tailwind Airlines?

(b)   What amount of annual depreciation, if any, on a straight-line basis should Tailwind record?

(c)   How would the annual charges stated above be changed if Tailwind had been granted as part of the lease agreement the right to purchase the building for a nominal sum at the end of the lease period?

E12-6   The net worth of Toronto Company excluding goodwill totals $620,000 and earnings for the last five years total $660,000. Included in the latter figure are extraordinary gains of $60,000, nonrecurring losses of $40,000, and sales commissions of $15,000. A 14% return on net worth is considered normal for the industry, and annual excess earnings are to be capitalized at 20% to arrive at goodwill in developing a sales price for the business.

Instructions

Compute the estimated goodwill.

E12-7   Reisling Corporation's pretax accounting income for the year 1985 was $600,000 and included the following items:

Extraordinary losses	$ 75,000
Extraordinary gains	150,000
Profit-sharing payments to employees	50,000
Amortization of goodwill	33,000
Amortization of identifiable intangibles	35,000
Depreciation on building	90,000

Almaden Industries is seeking to purchase Reisling Corporation. In attempting to measure Reisling's normal earnings for 1985, Almaden Industries determines that the fair market value of the building is triple the book value and that the remaining economic life is double that used by Reisling. Almaden would continue the profit-sharing payments to employees; such payments are based on income before depreciation and amortization.

Instructions

Compute the normal earnings of Reisling Corporation for the year 1985.

E12-8 As the president of British Columbia Records Corp., you are considering purchasing Beatles Corp., whose balance sheet is summarized as follows:

Current assets	$ 200,000	Current liabilities	$ 200,000
Fixed assets (net of depreciation)	800,000	Long-term liabilities	600,000
Other assets	200,000	Common shares	300,000
		Retained earnings	100,000
Total	$1,200,000	Total	$1,200,000

The fair market value of current assets is $400,000 because of the undervaluation of inventory. The normal rate of return on net assets for the industry is 15%. The average expected annual earnings projected for Beatles Corp. is $105,000.

Instructions

Assuming that the excess earnings continue for four years, how much would you be willing to pay for goodwill? (Estimate goodwill by the present-value method.)

E12-9 Assertive Corporation is interested in acquiring Passive Company. It has determined that Passive Company's excess earnings have averaged approximately $90,000 annually over the last six years. Passive Company agrees with the computation of $90,000 as the approximate excess earnings and feels that such amount should be capitalized over an unlimited period at an 18% rate. Assertive Corporation feels that because of increased competition, the excess earnings of Passive Company will continue for eight more years at best, and that a 15% discount rate is appropriate.

Instructions

(a) How far apart are the positions of these two parties?

(b) Is there really any difference in the approaches used by the two parties in evaluating Passive Company's goodwill? Explain.

E12-10 Gymnastics Corporation is contemplating the purchase of Denise L. Rode Industries and evaluating the amount of goodwill to be recognized in the purchase. Rode reported the following net incomes:

1982 — $180,000
1983 — 192,000
1984 — 288,000
1985 — 300,000
1986 — 480,000

Rode has indicated that 1986 net income included the sale of one of its warehouses at a gain of $120,000 (net of tax). Net identifiable assets of Rode have a total fair market value of $900,000.

Instructions

Calculate goodwill in the following cases, assuming that expected income is to be a simple average of **normal income** for the past five years.

(a) Goodwill is determined by capitalizing average net earnings at 20%.

(b) Goodwill is determined by presuming a 15% return on identifiable net assets and capitalizing excess earnings at 25%.

E12-11 Jon Axelson Company bought a business that would yield exactly a 20% annual rate of return on its investment. Of the total amount paid for the business, $54,000 was deemed to be goodwill, and the remaining value was attributable to the identifiable net assets.

Jon Axelson Company projected that the estimated annual future earnings of the new business would be equal to its average annual ordinary earnings over the past four years. The total net income over the past four years was $252,000, which included an extraordinary loss of $18,000 in one year and an extraordinary gain of $54,000 in one of the other three years.

Instructions

Compute the fair market value of the **identifiable** net assets that Jon Axelson Company purchased in this transaction.

E12-12 Rickety Co. has averaged its income for the past three years and finds that its average income equals $110,000. Its net assets have a fair market value of $600,000 exclusive of goodwill. The company is considering a sale of its net assets and wishes to determine an asking price that would include goodwill. Average earnings should be 15% of net assets, and earnings in excess of that amount should be capitalized at 25%.

Instructions

(a) What is the amount of goodwill?

(b) Compute the total value of net assets.

E12-13 Net income figures for Gary Gregor Company are as follows:

> 1981 — $54,000
> 1982 — $30,000
> 1983 — $66,000
> 1984 — $48,000
> 1985 — $36,000

Tangible net assets of this company are appraised at $260,000 on December 31, 1985. This business is to be acquired by Sue Graham Co. early in 1986.

Instructions

What amount should be paid for goodwill if:

(a) 15% is assumed to be a normal rate of return on net tangible assets, and average excess earnings for the last five years are to be capitalized at 24%?

(b) 12% is assumed to be a normal rate of return on net tangible assets, and payment is to be made for excess earnings for the last four years?

E12-14 Mike "the Millionaire" Michaelson is considering acquiring Kroos Company in total as a going concern. He makes the following computations and conclusions:

The fair value of the individual assets of Kroos Company is	$678,000
The liabilities of Kroos Company are	402,000
A fair estimate of annual earnings for the indefinite future is	72,000 per year

Considering the risk and potential of Kroos Company, Mike feels that he must earn a 24% return on his investment.

Instructions

(a) How much should Mike be willing to pay for Kroos Company?

(b) How much (if any) of the above-noted estimates would be goodwill?

PROBLEMS

P12-1 The following information relates to the intangible assets of Metamorphosis Company:

	Organization Costs	Goodwill	Purchased Patent Costs
Original cost at Jan. 1, 1985	$75,000	$400,000	$36,000
Useful life at Jan. 1, 1985 (estimated)	Indefinite[a]	50 years	6 years

[a]The company has decided to write off for accounting and tax purposes the organization costs as quickly as the tax law allows.

Instructions

(a) Assuming straight-line amortization, compute the amount of the amortization of each item for 1985 in accordance with generally accepted accounting principles.

(b) Prepare the journal entries for the amortization of organization costs and goodwill for 1985.

(c) Assume that at January 1, 1986, Metamorphosis Company incurred $3,500 of legal fees in defending the rights to the patents. Prepare the entry for the year 1986 to amortize the patents.

(d) Assume that at the beginning of year 1987, the company decides that the patent costs would be applicable only for the years 1987 and 1988. (A competitor has developed a product that will eventually make that of Metamorphosis obsolete.) Record the amortization of the patent costs at the end of 1987.

P12-2 Environmental Laboratories holds a valuable patent (No. 321-1413-8A) on a precipitator that prevents certain types of air pollution. Environmental does not manufacture or sell the products and processes that it develops; it conducts research, patents the products and processes that it develops, and then assigns the patents to manufacturers on a royalty basis. Occasionally it sells a patent. The history of Environmental's patent No. 321-1413-8A is as follows:

Date	Activity	Cost
1975-1976	Research conducted to develop precipitator	$585,000
Jan. 1977	Design and construction of a prototype	111,420
Mar. 1977	Testing of models	43,000
Jan. 1978	Fees paid to engineers and lawyers to prepare patent application; patent granted July 1, 1978	51,850
Nov. 1979	Engineering activity necessary to advance the design of the precipitator to the manufacturing stage	60,000
Dec. 1980	Legal fees paid to successfully defend precipitator patent	23,100
Apr. 1982	Research aimed at modifying the design of the patented precipitator	50,000
July 1985	Legal fees paid in unsuccessful patent infringement suit against a competitor	30,440

Environmental assumed a useful life of 17 years when it received the initial precipitator patent. On January 1, 1983, it revised its useful life estimate downward to five remaining years. Amortization is computed for a full year if the cost is incurred prior to July 1, and there is no amortization for the year if the cost is incurred after June 30. The company's year ends on December 31.

Instructions

Compute the carrying value of patent No. 321-1413-8A on each of the following dates:

(a) December 31, 1978.

(b) December 31, 1982.

(c) December 31, 1985.

P12-3 During 1983 Creative Company purchased a building site for its proposed research and development laboratory at a cost of $60,000. Construction of the building was started in 1983. The building was completed on December 31, 1984, at a cost of $250,000 and was placed in service on January 2, 1985. The estimated useful life of the building for depreciation purposes was 20 years; the straight-line method of depreciation was to be employed and there was no estimated net salvage value.

Management estimates that about 50% of the projects of the research and development group will result in long-term benefits (i.e., at least ten years) to the company. The remaining projects either benefit the current period or are abandoned before completion. A summary of the number of projects and the direct costs incurred in conjunction with the research and development activities for 1985 follows.

Upon recommendation of the research and development group, Creative Company acquired a patent for manufacturing rights at a cost of $100,000. The patent was acquired on April 1,1984, and has an economic life of ten years.

	Number of Projects	Salaries and Employee Benefits	Other Expenses (Excluding Building Depreciation Charges)
Completed projects with long-term benefits	15	$ 95,000	$45,000
Abandoned projects or projects that benefit the current period	10	20,000	10,000
Projects in process—results indeterminate	5	25,000	10,000
Total	30	$140,000	$65,000

Instructions

If generally accepted accounting principles were followed, how would the items above relating to research and development activities be reported on the company's:

(a) income statement for 1985?

(b) balance sheet as of December 31, 1985?

Be sure to give account titles and amounts, and briefly justify your presentation.

(CMA adapted)

P12-4 Rachael Avery Products Co., organized in 1984, has set up a single account for all intangible assets. The following summary discloses the debit entries that have been recorded during 1984 and 1985.

Intangible Assets

July 1, 1984	5-year franchise; expiration date June 30, 1989	$ 36,000
Oct. 1, 1984	Advance payment on leasehold (4-year lease)	20,000
Dec. 31, 1984	Net loss for 1984 including incorporation fees, $1,000 and related legal fees of organizing, $5,000 (all fees incurred in 1984)	16,000
Jan. 2, 1985	Patent purchased (8-year life)	84,800
Mar. 1, 1985	Cost of developing a secret formula (indefinite life)	100,000
Apr. 1, 1985	Goodwill purchased (indefinite life)	240,000
June 1, 1985	Legal fee for successful defence of patent	14,560
Sept. 1, 1985	Research costs	120,000
Sept. 1, 1985	Development costs	58,000

Instructions

Prepare the necessary entries to clear the Intangible Assets account and to set up separate accounts for distinct types of intangibles. Make the entries as of December 31, 1985, recording any necessary amortization and reflecting all balances accurately as of that date.

P12-5 Okanogan Peaches, Inc. has recently become interested in acquiring a U.S. plant to handle many of its production functions in that market. One possible candidate is Washington, Inc., a closely held corporation, whose owners have decided to sell their business if a proper settlement can be obtained. Washington's balance sheet appears as follows:

Current assets	$150,000	Current liabilities	$ 80,000
Investments	50,000	Long-term debt	100,000
Plant assets (net)	400,000	Common shares	50,000
		Contributed surplus	170,000
		Retained earnings	200,000
Total assets	$600,000	Total equities	$600,000

Okanogan Peaches has hired Canadian Appraisal Corporation to determine the proper price to pay for Washington, Inc. The appraisal firm finds that the investments have a fair market value of $150,000 and that inventory is understated by $75,000. All other assets and equities are properly stated. An examination of the company's income for the last four years indicates that the net income has steadily increased. In 1985 the company had a net operating income of $100,000, and this income should increase 20% each year over the next four years. Okanogan Peaches believes that a normal return in this type of business is 18% on net assets. The asset investment in the Washington plant is expected to stay the same for the next four years.

Instructions

(a) Canadian Appraisal Corporation has indicated that the fair value of the company can be estimated in a number of ways. Prepare an estimate of the value of the firm, assuming that any goodwill will be computed as:
  1. The capitalization of the average excess earnings of Washington, Inc. at 18%.
  2. The purchase of average excess earnings over the next four years.
  3. The capitalization of average excess earnings of Washington, Inc. at 24%.
  4. The present value of the average excess earnings over the next four years discounted at 15%.

(b) Washington, Inc. is willing to sell the business for $1,000,000. How do you think Canadian Appraisal should advise Okanogan Peaches?

(c) If Okanogan Peaches were to pay $750,000 to purchase the assets and assume the liabilities of Washington, Inc., how would this transaction be reflected on Okanogan's books?

P12-6 Presented below are financial forecasts related to Ecumenical Company for the next ten years.

Forecasted average earnings (per year)	$ 25,000
Forecasted market value of net assets, exclusive of goodwill (per year)	144,000

Instructions

You have been asked to compute goodwill under the following methods. The normal rate of return on net assets for the industry is 15%.

(a) Goodwill is equal to five years' excess earnings.

(b) Goodwill is equal to the present value of five years' excess earnings discounted at 12%.

(c) Goodwill is equal to the average excess earnings capitalized at 17%.

(d) Goodwill is equal to average earnings capitalized at the normal rate of return for the industry of 15%.

P12-7 Presented on page 593 is information related to Tornado Cleaner Company for 1986, its first year of operation.

Income Summary

Raw Material Purchased	$123,300	Sales	$474,000
Productive Labour	38,650	Closing Inventories	
Factory Overhead	28,350	Raw Material	32,400
Selling Expenses	37,050	Goods in Process	27,000
Administrative Expenses	27,300	Finished Goods	39,000
Interest Expense	8,650	Appreciation of Land	9,000
Opening Inventories		Profit on Sale of	
Raw Material	29,100	Forfeited Shares	3,000
Goods in Process	24,000		
Finished Goods	30,000		
Extraordinary Loss (net)	6,900		
Income Taxes	81,000		
Net Income	150,100		
	$584,400		$584,400

Instructions

Tornado is negotiating to sell the business after one full year of operation. Compute the amount of goodwill, as 200% of the income before extraordinary items and before taxes, that is in excess of $135,000; $135,000 is considered to be a normal return on investment.

P12-8 Wayne Corp., a high-flying conglomerate, has recently been involved in discussions with Shuster, Inc. As its CA, you have been instructed by Wayne to conduct a purchase audit of Shuster's books to determine a possible purchase price for Shuster's net assets. The following information is found.

Total identifiable assets of Shuster's (fair market value)	$224,000
Liabilities	32,000
Average rate of return on net assets for Shuster's industry	15%
Forecasted earnings per year based on past earnings figures	32,000

Instructions

(a) Wayne asks you to determine the purchase price on the basis of the following assumptions:
 1. Goodwill is equal to three years' excess earnings.
 2. Goodwill is equal to the present value of excess earnings discounted at 15% for three years.
 3. Goodwill is equal to the capitalization of excess earnings at 15%.
 4. Goodwill is equal to the capitalization of excess earnings at 25%.

(b) Wayne asks you which of the methods above is the most theoretically sound. Justify your answer. Any assumptions made should be clearly indicated.

P12-9 Beringer Bros., Inc. has contracted to purchase Chablis Company, including its goodwill. The agreement between purchaser and seller on the price to be paid for goodwill is as follows: "The value of the goodwill to be paid for is to be determined by capitalizing at 18% the average annual earnings from ordinary operations for the last five years in excess of 15% on the net worth, which, for purposes of this computation, is to be considered to be $300,000."

The net income per books for the last five years is:

1982	$40,280
1983	53,840
1984	73,540
1985	53,960
1986	56,360

As assistant to the treasurer of Beringer Bros., you are instructed to review the accounts of Chablis Company and determine the amount to be paid for goodwill in accordance with the terms of the contract. In your review of the accounts, you discover the following:

1. An additional assessment of federal income taxes in the amount of $10,120 for the year 1984 was made and paid in 1986. The amount was charged against Retained Earnings.

2. In 1982 the company reviewed its accounts receivable and wrote off as an expense of that year $15,360 of accounts receivable that had been carried for years and appeared very unlikely to be collected.

3. In 1983 an account for $2,100 included in the 1982 write-off above was collected and credited to "Miscellaneous Income."

4. A fire in 1985 caused a loss, charged to Income, as follows:

Book value of property destroyed	$33,220
Recovery from insurance company	11,000
Net loss	$22,220

5. Expropriation of property in 1985 resulted in a gain of $9,080 credited to income.

6. Amounts paid out under the company's product guarantee plan and charged to expense in each of the five years were as follows:

1982	$ 900
1983	1,200
1984	840
1985	1,300
1986	760

7. In 1986 the president of the company died, and the company realized $75,000 on an insurance policy on his life. The cash surrender value of this policy had been carried on the books as an investment in the amount of $62,240. The excess of proceeds over cash surrender value was credited to income.

Instructions

What is the price to be paid for the goodwill in accordance with the contract agreement? Prepare your computations in good form so that you can answer any questions asked by the treasurer in regard to your conclusions.

P12-10 Tatanka Corporation was incorporated on January 3, 1985. The corporation's financial statements for its first year's operations were not examined by a CA. You have been engaged to examine the financial statements for the year ended December 31, 1986, and your examination is substantially completed. The corporation's trial balance appears below.

Tatanka Corporation
TRIAL BALANCE
December 31, 1986

	Debit	Credit
Cash	$ 10,000	
Accounts Receivable	56,000	
Allowance for Doubtful Accounts		$ 1,120
Inventories	45,600	
Machinery	82,000	
Equipment	34,000	
Accumulated Depreciation		23,200
Patents	113,700	
Leasehold Improvements	36,100	
Prepaid Expenses	14,200	

Organization Expenses	32,000	
Goodwill	28,000	
Licencing Agreement No. 1	60,000	
Licencing Agreement No. 2	57,600	
Accounts Payable		73,000
Unearned Revenue		17,280
Share Capital		300,000
Retained Earnings, January 1, 1986		118,800
Sales		720,000
Cost of Goods Sold	475,000	
Selling and General Expenses	180,000	
Interest Expense	9,200	
Extraordinary Losses	20,000	
Totals	$1,253,400	$1,253,400

The following information relates to accounts that may yet require adjustment.

1. Patents for Tatanka's manufacturing process were acquired on January 2, 1986, at a cost of $88,400. An additional $25,500 was spent in December, 1986, to improve machinery covered by the patents and charged to the Patents account. Depreciation on fixed assets has been properly recorded for 1986 in accordance with Tatanka's practice, which provides a full year's depreciation for property on hand June 30 and no depreciation otherwise. Tatanka uses the straight-line method for all depreciation and amortization and the legal life on its patents.

2. On January 2, 1985, Tatanka purchased licencing agreement No. 1, which was believed to have an unlimited useful life. The balance in the Licencing Agreement No. 1 account includes its purchase price of $57,000 and expenses of $3,000 related to the acquisition. On January 1, 1986, Tatanka purchased licencing agreement No. 2, which has a life expectancy of ten years. The balance in the Licensing Agreement No. 2 account includes its $57,000 purchase price and $3,000 in acquisition expenses, but it has been reduced by a credit of $2,400 for the advance collection of 1987 revenue from the agreement.

   In late December, 1985, an explosion caused a permanent 70% reduction in the expected revenue-producing value of licencing agreement No. 1, and in January, 1987, a flood caused additional damage that rendered the agreement worthless.

3. The balance in the Goodwill account includes (a) $12,000 paid on December 30, 1985, for an advertising program it is estimated will assist in increasing Tatanka's sales over a period of four years following the disbursement, and (b) legal expenses of $16,000 incurred for Tatanka's incorporation on January 3, 1985.

4. The Leasehold Improvements account includes (a) the $15,000 cost of improvements with a total estimated useful life of 12 years, which Tatanka, as tenant, made to leased premises in January, 1985, (b) movable assembly line equipment that cost $18,000 and was installed in the leased premises in December, 1986, and (c) real estate taxes of $3,100 paid by Tatanka in 1986, which under the terms of the lease should have been paid by the landlord. Tatanka paid its rent in full during 1986. A ten-year nonrenewable lease was signed on January 3, 1985, for the leased building that Tatanka used in manufacturing operations.

5. The balance in Organization Expenses account properly includes costs incurred during the organizational period. The corporation has exercised its option to amortize organization costs over a 60-month period for federal income tax purposes and wishes to amortize these for accounting purposes on the same basis.

Instructions

Prepare an eight-column work sheet to adjust accounts that require adjustment. Include columns for an income statement and a balance sheet.

A separate account should be used for the accumulation of each type of amortization and for each prior-period adjustment. Formal adjusting journal entries and financial statements are **not** required. (Hint: Amortize Licencing Agreement No. 1 over 40 years before the explosion damage loss is determined.)

(AICPA adapted)

P12-11 Information concerning Tully Limited's intangible assets is as follows:

1. On January 1, 1987, Tully signs an agreement to operate as a franchisee of Red River Copy Service Inc., for an initial franchise fee of $85,000. Of this amount, $25,000 is paid on signing and the balance is payable in four annual payments of $15,000 each, beginning January 1, 1988. The agreement provides that the down payment is not refundable and no future services are required of the franchisor. The present value at January 1, 1987, of the four annual payments discounted at 14% (the implicit rate for a loan of this type) is $43,700. The agreement also provides that 5% of the revenue from the franchise must be paid to the franchisor annually. Tully's revenue from the franchise for 1987 is $900,000. Tully estimates the useful life of the franchise to be ten years.

2. Tully incurs $78,000 of experimental and development costs in its laboratory to develop a patent which is granted on January 2, 1987. Legal fees and other costs associated with registration of the patent total $16,400. Tully estimates that the useful life of the patent will be eight years.

3. A trademark was purchased from Walton Company for $40,000 on July 2, 1984. Expenditures for successful litigation in defence of the trademark totalling $10,000 are paid on July 1, 1987. Tully estimates that the useful life of the trademark will be 20 years from the date of acquisition.

Instructions

(a) Prepare a schedule showing the intangibles section of Tully's balance sheet at December 31, 1987. Show supporting computations in good form.

(b) Prepare a schedule showing all expenses resulting from the transactions that would appear on Tully's income statement for the year ended December 31, 1987. Show supporting computations in good form.

(AICPA adapted)

P12-12 Loszynski Corporation was founded in 1974 and experienced only moderate growth during its first ten years. However, Loszynski was able to attract several scientists and researchers with technical experience and ability and became a pioneer in the field of robotics.

Loszynski experienced a 30% annual growth rate in revenue for the years 1984–1986 due to the increased demand for its products and consulting services. The company, assured of sufficient financing, planned several expenditures in 1986 that would enable it to meet increased demand and continue its excellent growth rate through the rest of the decade.

Jay Ohara of Loszynski's General Accounting Department is experiencing difficulty in understanding several transactions made during the first quarter of 1987, some of which include expenditures that were planned in 1986. Ohara has asked the controller for assistance in determining how to record the six transactions listed below, and how they will affect the financial statements of Loszynski Corporation in both current and future periods. All amounts are considered material.

1. Loszynski incurred the following costs in securing a trademark:

Design costs	$2,000
Registration fees	300
Attorney's fees	700

Loszynski's attorney informs the company that the trademark registration system provides for an initial registration term of 20 years and an indefinite number of renewals for periods of 20 years each. Loszynski's marketing manager believes the trademark will be of value to the company for 50 years.

2. Loszynski incurred $6,000 of legal fees in defending the rights to a patent. The patent was purchased in the first quarter of 1985 at a cost of $15,000 and is being amortized over a period of 12 years.

3. Loszynski spent $30,000 searching for practical applications of new research findings that are believed to be of use to the company for the next 20 years.

Instructions

As controller of Loszynski Corporation, review the six transactions brought to your attention by Jay Ohara. For each of the six transactions:

(a) Identify whether the item is to be expensed in 1987 or capitalized.

(b) Identify the amount to be capitalized or expensed.

(c) Identify the number of years to be used to write off the items that were capitalized.

(d) Justify your answers by reference to underlying accounting theory or to authoritative accounting pronouncements. You need not cite accounting pronouncements by name, number, or promulgating body.

Income tax implications and calculation of annual depreciation or amortization charges for capitalized items are to be ignored. Use the following format to present your answer.

Item Number	Amount to be Expensed (if any)	Capitalized Items (if any) Amount	Life	Justification of Treatment and/or Life

(CMA adapted)

PART

3

LIABILITIES—RECOGNITION AND MEASUREMENT

13

CURRENT LIABILITIES AND CONTINGENCIES

In recent years the concept of liabilities has undergone a change. One reason for this increased attention is that financial statements have become more complicated because of the increase in special financing and sales agreements, new labour contract formulas and provisions, and more complex tax laws. Also, much accounting thought and analysis has been directed toward the determination of the debit (the valuation of the assets or the charge to expense), with the credit handled as an afterthought and as expediently as possible. Although it is true that all liabilities have credit balances, it is debatable whether all credits appearing above the shareholders' equity section in published balance sheets are liabilities, or even that all liabilities have been recorded.

WHAT IS A LIABILITY?

The question of "What is a liability?" is not easy to answer. It seems clear that liabilities include more than debts arising from borrowings. The acquisition of goods or services on credit terms gives rise to liabilities much like borrowing. Less similar are liabilities resulting from the imposition of taxes, withholdings from employees' wages and salaries, dividend declarations, and product warranties.

Recently, the FASB, as part of its conceptual framework study, defined liabilities as **"probable future sacrifices of economic benefits arising from present obligations of a particular entity to transfer assets or provide services to other entities in the future as a result of past transactions or events."**[1] In other words, a liability has three essential characteristics:

1. It is a present obligation that entails settlement by probable future transfer or use of cash, goods, or services.
2. It must be an unavoidable obligation of a particular enterprise.
3. The transaction or other event obligating the enterprise must have already happened.

Although the FASB definition may be subject to differing interpretations, it is a welcome addition to the professional literature, especially given past definitions developed by professional bodies.[2]

Because liabilities involve future disbursements of assets or services, one of the most important features is the date on which they are payable. Currently maturing obligations represent a demand on the current assets of the enterprise—a demand that must be satisfied promptly and in the ordinary course of business if operations are to be continued. Liabilities with a more distant due date do not, as a rule, represent a claim on the enterprises's current resources and are in a slightly different category. This feature gives rise to the basic division of liabilities into (1) current liabilities and (2) long-term debt.

NATURE OF CURRENT LIABILITIES

For many years payment within the twelve months of the balance sheet date was the characteristic that distinguished a current liability from a long-term debt. This one-year rule, although simple and easy to follow, produced some unreasonable results when the operating cycle of a business exceeded one year. Under currently acceptable practice, both current liabilities and current assets are defined in terms of the operating cycle of the individual enterprise. The **operating cycle** is the period of time elapsing between the acquisition of goods and services involved in the manufacturing process and the final cash realization resulting from sales and subsequent collections. Industries that manufacture products requiring an aging process and certain capital–intensive industries have an operating cycle of considerably more than one year; on the other hand, some processing and most retail establishments have several operating cycles within a year.

Current assets are those assets normally converted into cash or consumed in operations within a single operating cycle or within a year if more than one cycle is completed each year. **Current liabilities are "obligations whose liquidation is reasonably expected to require use of existing resources properly classified as current assets, or the creation of other current liabilities."**[3] This definition has

[1]"Elements of Financial Statements of Business Enterprises," *Statement of Financial Accounting Concepts No. 3* (Stamford, Conn.: FASB, 1980), pars. 28 and 29.

[2]For definitions that are similar to the new FASB definition, see Maurice Moonitz, "The Changing Concept of a Liability," *The Journal of Accountancy* (May, 1960), pp. 41–46; Eldon S. Hendricksen, *Accounting Theory*, 3rd edition (Homewood, Ill.: Richard D. Irwin, Inc., 1977), p. 451; and American Accounting Association, *Accounting and Reporting Standards for Corporate Financial Statements* (Sarasota, Fla.: AAA, 1957), p. 16.

[3]Committee on Accounting Procedure, American Institute of Certified Public Accountants, *Accounting Research and Terminology Bulletin, Final Edition* (New York: AICPA, 1961), p. 21.

gained wide acceptance because it recognizes operating cycles of varying lengths in different industries and takes into consideration the important relationship between current assets and current liabilities. The FASB affirmed this concept of **"maturity within one year or the operating cycle, whichever is longer"** in its definition of short-term obligations in *Statement No. 6*.[4]

VALUATION OF CURRENT LIABILITIES

Theoretically, liabilities should be measured by the present value of the future outlay of cash required to liquidate them but, in practice, current liabilities are usually recorded in accounting records and reported in financial statements at their full maturity amount. Because of the short time periods involved, frequently less than one year, the difference between the present value of a current liability and the maturity value is not usually large. The slight overstatement of liabilities that results from carrying current liabilities at maturity value is justified on the grounds of expediency, conservatism, and immateriality. In the U.S., *APB Opinion No. 21*, "Interest on Receivables and Payables," specifically exempts from present value measurements those payables arising from transactions with suppliers in the normal course of business that do not exceed approximately one year.[5]

DIFFERENCES IN CURRENT LIABILITIES

We have concluded that liabilities are probable future sacrifices arising from obligations resulting from past transactions but, within this sphere of similarity, liabilities possess characteristics that lend themselves to categorization. All liabilities, because they are probable future sacrifices, involve an element of uncertainty. The differences in degrees of uncertainty related to liabilities allow us to discuss current liabilities under the following categories.

1. Determinable current liabilities.
2. Contingent current liabilities.

DETERMINABLE CURRENT LIABILITIES

The types of liabilities discussed in this category are susceptible of precise measurement. The amount of cash that will be needed to discharge the obligation and the date of payment or discharge are reasonably certain. There is nothing uncertain about (1) the fact that the obligation has been incurred and (2) the amount of the obligation. The existence of written or implied contracts or the imposition of legal statutes minimizes the uncertainty in amount, risk, and timing of these liabilities. The primary problem is one of discovery, which arises from the possibility of omitting these liabilities. In contrast to long-term debts, which are normally large in amount and supported by documentary evidence consisting of contracts, authorization, and correspondence, current liabilities may result from unwritten extensions of credit or unrecorded accruals, and may be small. Once these liabilities are discovered, however, the amount is readily determinable.

[4]"Classification of Short-term Obligations Expected to be Refinanced," *Statement of Financial Accounting Standards No. 6* (Stamford, Conn.: FASB, 1975), par. 2.

[5]"Interest on Receivables and Payables," *Opinions of the Accounting Principles Board No. 21* (New York: AICPA, 1971), par. 3.

Accounts Payable

Accounts payable, or **trade accounts payable,** are balances owed to others for goods, supplies, and services purchased on open account. Accounts payable arise because of the time lag between the receipt of services or acquisition of title to assets and the payment for them. This period of extended credit is usually found in the terms of the sale (e.g., 2/10, n/30, or 1/10, E.O.M.) and is commonly 30 to 60 days.

Most accounting systems are designed to record liabilities for purchase of goods when the goods are received or, practically, when the invoices are received. Frequently there is some delay in recording the goods and the related liability on the books. If title has passed to the purchaser before the goods are received, the transaction should be recorded at the time of title passage. As a result, the accountant must pay particular attention to transactions occurring near the end of one accounting period and at the beginning of the next to ascertain that the record of goods received (the inventory) agrees with that of the liability (accounts payable) and that both are recorded in the proper period.

Measuring the amount of an account payable poses no particular difficulty, because the invoice received from the creditor specifies the due date and the exact outlay in money that is necessary to settle the account. The only calculation that may be necessary concerns the amount of cash discount. See Chapter 8 for illustrations of entries related to accounts payable and purchase discounts.

Notes Payable

Obligations in the form of written promissory notes that are classified as current liabilities are usually either (1) trade notes, (2) short-term loan notes, or (3) current maturities of long-term debts.

Trade Notes Trade notes payable represent the unpaid face amount of promissory notes owed to suppliers of goods, services, and equipment. In some industries and for certain classes of customers, promissory notes are required as part of the transaction in lieu of the normal extension of open account or verbal credit. Normally, both the due date and the amount of the outlay necessary to discharge the note are contained on the note. The only calculation that is commonly involved is the calculation of interest if the note is interest bearing.

Short-Term Loan Notes Short-term promissory notes payable to banks or loan companies represent a current liability, and generally arise from cash loans. When these notes are interest bearing, it is necessary to record and report in financial statements any accrued interest payable and to carry the note payable as a liability in the amount of its **face value** (also called **principal amount**).

If a **noninterest-bearing note** is issued, the bank or loan company **discounts** the note and remits the proceeds to the borrower. To illustrate, assume that on October 1 the Hull Company has its $100,000 one-year noninterest-bearing note discounted at 9% at the Corner National Bank. The Hull Company would receive the proceeds of $91,000 and would assume the obligation to pay $100,000 to the bank in 12 months. It should be apparent that the Hull Company has borrowed $91,000 for a period of one year at a cost of $9,000. Although the **stated discount rate** was 9%, the **effective interest rate** was 9.89% ($9,000/$91,000), because the full $100,000 is not available to the Hull Company during the year. A loan under these circumstances is frequently recorded on the date the loan is completed in the following manner:

Cash	91,000	
Discount on Notes Payable	9,000	
Notes Payable		100,000

The balance in the Discount on Notes Payable account would be deducted on the balance sheet from Notes Payable. Interest expense would be recorded in monthly increments of $750 by reducing Discount on Notes Payable through the following entry (assuming straight-line amortization approximates the effective interest method of amortization):

Interest Expense	750	
Discount on Notes Payable		750

Thus, a balance sheet prepared at December 31 would show:

Current Liabilities		
Notes payable	$100,000	
Less: Discount on notes payable	6,750	
		$93,250

The interest expense of $2,250 for the three-month period would be reported in the income statement.

Current Maturities of Long-Term Debts   The portion of bonds, mortgage notes, and other long-term indebtedness that matures within twelve months of the balance sheet date is reported as a current liability. When only a part of a long-term debt is to be paid within the next 12 months, as in the case of serial bonds that are to be retired through a series of annual instalments, **the maturing portion of the long-term debt is reported as a current liability**, and the balance as a long-term debt. Long-term debts maturing currently should not be included as current liabilities if they are (1) to be retired by assets accumulated for this purpose that properly have not been shown as current assets, (2) to be refinanced, or retired from the proceeds of a new debt issue (see next topic below), or (3) to be converted into capital shares. The plan for liquidation of such a debt should be disclosed either parenthetically or by a note to the financial statements. Also included among current liabilities are **long-term obligations that are or will be callable by the creditor** either because (a) the debtor's violation of a provision of the debt agreement at the balance sheet date makes the obligation callable or (b) because the violation, if not cured within a specified grace period, will make the obligation callable. Such callable obligations may continue to be classified as long-term if one of the following conditions is met:[6]

1. The lender either waives or loses the right to demand payment for more than a year from the balance sheet date. For example, a lender might lose the right to demand repayment if a violation existing at the balance sheet date is subsequently cured and the debt is no longer callable at the time the statements are issued.

---

[6]"Classification of Obligations That Are Callable by the Creditor," *Statement of Financial Accounting Standards No. 78* (Stamford, Conn.: FASB, 1983).

2. The obligation will not become callable because it is probable that the violation will be cured within the grace period.

In both of the above cases, the circumstances must be disclosed in notes to the financial statements.

Short-Term Obligations Expected to Be Refinanced

Short-term obligations are those debts that are scheduled to mature within one year after the date of an enterprise's balance sheet or within an enterprise's operating cycle, whichever is longer. Some short-term obligations are expected to be refinanced on a long-term basis and, therefore, are not expected to require the use of working capital during the next year (or operating cycle).[7] Before 1975 the accounting profession generally supported the exclusion of short-term obligations from current liabilities if they were "expected to be refinanced." However, because the profession provided no specific guidelines, determination of whether a short-term obligation was "expected to be refunded" was usually based solely on management's **intent** to refinance on a long-term basis. A company may sell short-term commercial paper to finance new plant and equipment, intending eventually to refinance it on a long-term basis. Or it may obtain a five-year bank loan but, because the bank prefers it, handle the actual financing with 90-day notes, which it must keep turning over (i.e., renewing). Is the obligation a long-term debt or a current liability? To illustrate this problem of classification, the Canadian Commercial Bank (before it went bankrupt) was permitting customers to settle current obligations by signing new notes for unpaid balances including accrued interest. Many of these borrowers, who subsequently defaulted, were able to report the new notes as a noncurrent liability since they were technically long-term although in substance a delinquent current obligation.

In Canadian practice, short-term obligations otherwise classified as current liabilities would be reported as noncurrent liabilities if "contractual arrangements have been made for settlement from other than current assets."[8]

Dividends Payable

A **cash dividend payable** is an amount owed by a corporation to its shareholders as a result of a distribution that the board of directors has formally authorized. At the date of declaration the corporation assumes a liability that places the shareholders in the position of creditors relative to the amount of dividends declared. Cash dividends are classified as current liabilities because they are always paid within one year of declaration (generally within three months).

Accumulated but undeclared dividends on cumulative preferred shares are not a recognized liability because **preferred dividends in arrears** are not an obligation until formal action is taken by the board of directors authorizing the distribution of earnings. Nevertheless, the amount of cumulative dividends unpaid should be

[7]*Refinancing a short-term obligation on a long-term basis* means either replacing it with a long-term obligation or with equity securities, or renewing, extending, or replacing it with short-term obligations for an uninterrupted period extending beyond one year (or operating cycle, if longer) from the date of the enterprise's balance sheet.

[8]*CICA Handbook*, Section 1510, par. 6.

disclosed as a note or it may be shown parenthetically in the share capital section following a description of the shares.

Dividends payable in the form of additional shares of stock are not recognized as a liability because **stock dividends** do not require future outlays of assets or services and they are revocable by the board of directors at any time prior to issuance. Even so, such undistributed stock dividends are generally reported in the shareholders' equity section because they represent retained earnings in the process of transfer to contributed surplus.

Returnable Deposits

Current liabilities of a company may include returnable deposits (monies) received from customers and employees. Deposits may be received from customers to guarantee performance of a contract or service or as guarantees to cover payment of expected future obligations. Deposits may also be received from customers as guarantees for possible damage to property left with the customer. Some companies require their employees to make deposits for the return of keys or other company property or for locker privileges. The classification of these items as current or noncurrent liabilities depends on the time involved between the date of the deposit and the termination of the relationship that required the deposit. Deposits held as security for the return of containers, such as pallets and oil drums, which are often outstanding for several years are especially difficult to classify. Some customers may intend to keep the container and forfeit the deposit but do not indicate their intentions. In other instances, the containers may be reused by the same customer over such an extended period that it becomes a long-term arrangement. In these cases, the deposits should be classified as long-term or written off to income when the return of the container is not likely.

Liability on the Advance Sale of Tickets, Tokens, and Certificates

Transportation companies may issue tickets or tokens that can be exchanged or used to pay for future fares, or restaurants may issue meal tickets that can be exchanged or used to pay for future meals, or retail stores may issue gift certificates that are redeemable in merchandise. In such cases, the businesses have received cash in exchange for promises to perform services or to furnish goods at some indefinite future date.

The balance sheet should reflect the obligation for any outstanding instruments that are redeemable in goods or services; the income statement should reflect the revenues earned as a result of performances during the period. The sale of these tickets, tokens, and certificates is recorded by a debit to Cash and a credit to a current liability account usually described as Deferred or Unearned Revenue. As the claims are redeemed, the liability account is debited and an appropriate revenue account credited but, because these advances are usually small in amount and relatively numerous, some are not presented to the issuing company for redemption. If these claims are rendered void by lapse of time or some other reason as defined by the sales agreement, the amount of forfeited claims may be easily measured; but if, however, the offer is of indefinite duration, it is necessary to reduce the liability balance by an estimate of the claims that will not be redeemed and to credit an appropriate account for the gain that results from forfeitures.

Collections for Third Parties

A common current liability results from a company collecting taxes from customers for a government unit and withholding taxes from employees' payrolls.

Sales Taxes   Sales taxes on transfers of tangible personal property and on certain services must be collected from customers and remitted to the proper government authority. A liability must be set up to provide for the taxes collected from customers but as yet unremitted to the tax authority. If the actual sales total and the sales tax collections are recorded separately at the time of the sale, the sales tax payable account should reflect the liability for sales taxes due the government. The entry below is the proper one for a sale of $3,000 when a 4% sales tax is in effect.

Cash or Accounts Receivable	3,120	
Sales		3,000
Sales Taxes Payable		120

When the sales tax collections credited to the liability account are not equal to the liability computed by the government formula, an adjustment of the liability account may be made by recognizing a gain or a loss on sales tax collections.

In many companies, however, the sales tax and the amount of the sale are not segregated at the time of sale; both are credited in total in the sales account. To reflect correctly the actual amount of sales and the liability for sales taxes, the sales account must be debited for the amount of the sales taxes due the government on these sales and the sales taxes payable account credited for the same amount. As an illustration, assume that the sales account balance is $150,000 and includes sales taxes of 4%. Because the amount recorded in the sales account is equal to sales plus 0.04 of sales, or 1.04 times the sales total, the sales are $150,000 divided by 1.04, or $144,230.77. The sales tax liability is $5,769.23 ($144,230.77 $\times$ 0.04; or $150,000 - $144,230.77), and the following entry would be made to record the amount due the taxing unit:

Sales	$5,769.23	
Sales Taxes Payable		$5,769.23

Income Tax Withholding   Federal income tax laws require employers to withhold from the pay of each employee an amount approximating the applicable income tax due on those wages. The amount of income tax withheld is computed by the employer according to a government-prescribed formula or a government-provided withholding tax table and depends on the length of the pay period and each employee's wages, marital status, and claimed dependants.

Employers are also required to withhold the employees' prescribed share of Canada (Quebec) Pension Plan and Unemployment Insurance contributions. The amount of income tax withheld plus the employee and the employer contributions for the Canada (Quebec) Pension Plan and unemployment insurance must be remitted monthly.

Other Payroll Deductions   In addition to the above payroll deductions, employers frequently deduct insurance premiums, employee savings, and union dues that must be recognized as liabilities to third parties to the extent that the amounts deducted are still among the employer's assets.

Accrued Liabilities

Accrued liabilities (sometimes called accrued expenses) arise through accounting recognition of unpaid costs that come into existence as the result of past contractual commitments, past services received, or by operation of a tax law. The principle of matching requires that incurred but unpaid expenses and the related liabilities be estimated as of the financial statement date, recorded in the accounts, and reported in the financial statements on an accrual basis. In published financial statements these accruals, with the exception of accrued taxes, are often conveniently combined under one heading; but, in recording these liabilities, appropriate account titles should be used, such as Wages Payable, Interest Payable, Property Taxes Payable, Payroll Taxes Payable, Bonuses Payable, and Income Taxes Payable. Payroll taxes payable, liability for compensated absences, and property taxes payable are three accrued expenses, common to every business, that deserve special mention. Income taxes payable and bonuses payable are accrued liabilities accorded special attention in the discussion of conditional payments that follows this section.

Accrued Payroll Taxes   As wages and salaries are earned by employees, the employer's share of Canada (Quebec) Pension Plan (C/QPP) contributions and Unemployment Insurance premiums accrues. The amounts of these payroll taxes are determined from tables supplied by Revenue Canada. In 1985 the rates for C/QPP were 1.8% of pensionable earnings to be deducted from each employee and an equal amount contributed by the employer. The unemployment insurance rate for employees was 2.35% while employers were required to contribute 1.4 times the amount of the employee premiums. The employer is required to remit to the government its share of these payroll taxes along with the amounts of income tax deducted from each employee's gross compensation. All unremitted employer Canada Pension Plan contributions and Unemployment Insurance premiums should be recorded as payroll tax expense and payroll tax payable.

Accounting for employee payroll deductions and employer's payroll taxes is illustrated below. Assume a weekly payroll of $10,000: employee deductions are 1.8% for CPP, 2.35% for Unemployment Insurance, $1,320 for income taxes withheld and $88 withheld for union dues.

The entry to record the wages and salaries expense, the employee payroll deductions, and the payment of cash to employees would be:

Wages and Salaries Expense	10,000	
Employee Income Taxes Withheld		1,320
Canada Pension Plan Payable (1.8% of $10,000)		180
Unemployment Insurance Payable (2.35% of $10,000)		235
Union Dues Payable (to Local No. 257)		88
Cash		8,177

Since employers must match employee CPP contributions and pay unemployment insurance premiums of 1.4 times the employees' premiums (2.35% × 1.4 = 3.29%), the entry to record the employer payroll taxes would be:

Payroll Tax Expense	509	
Canada Pension Plan Payable (1.8% of $10,000)		180
Unemployment Insurance Payable (3.29% of $10,000)		329

The liability for CPP, Unemployment Insurance, and employees' income tax withheld will be eliminated when the employer makes payment to the Receiver General of Canada.

The entries above illustrate the recording of the liabilities associated with withholdings from employees' wages and the employer's share of payroll taxes and fringe benefits. In practice, the cost side of this problem is commonly refined to the extent that all of the payroll costs (wages, payroll taxes, and fringe benefits) are allocated to appropriate cost accounts such as Direct Labour, Indirect Labour, Sales Salaries, Administrative Salaries, and the like.

This abbreviated discussion of payroll accounting does not indicate the volume of records that may be involved in maintaining a sound payroll system.

Compensated Absences Compensated absences are absences from employment, such as vacation, illness, and holidays, for which it is expected that employees will be paid. Employers are required under provincial statutes to give each employee an annual vacation of a stipulated number of days or compensation in lieu of the vacation. As a result, employers have an obligation for vacation pay which accrues to the employees. Usually this obligation is satisfied by paying employees their regular salary for the period that they are absent from work while taking an annual vacation. The employer's obligation for accrued vacation pay is said to be **vested** because employees are entitled to vacation pay even if their employment is terminated; that is, vested rights are not contingent on an employee's future service.

If rights to compensation for work absences may be carried forward to future periods when not used in the period in which they are earned, they are called **accumulated rights**. For example, assume that you have earned four days of vacation pay as of December 31, the end of your employer's fiscal year. In a province where vacation pay is prescribed by statute, your employer will have to pay you for these four days even if you terminate employment. In this case, your vacation pay is vested and accumulates. Now assume that your vacation days are not vested, but that you can carry the four days over into later periods. Although the rights are not vested, they are rights that accumulate and the employer should provide an accrual for these costs in the period during which the benefits have been earned.

Entitlements to **sick pay** vary considerably among employers. In some companies, employees are allowed to accumulate unused sick pay and take compensated time off from work even though they are not ill. In other companies, employees receive sick pay only if they are absent because of illness. In the first case sick pay benefits are vested while in the second case the benefits are not vested and may or may not accumulate. When benefits vest, accrual of the estimated liability is recommended. However, if the sick pay benefits are paid only when employees are absent from work due to illness, then *CICA Handbook*, Section 3290, should be applied. Under this section, accruals are required only if the probability of occurrence is high and the amount can be reasonably estimated.[9] Thus, if the amount of sick pay actually payable in future periods as a consequence of services rendered in the current period can be reasonably estimated, accruals should be recorded. Otherwise, a note to the financial statements would be sufficient.

The expense and related liability for compensated absences should be recognized in the year in which earned by employees. For example, if new employees receive rights to two weeks' paid vacation at the beginning of their second year of employment, the vacation pay is considered to be earned during the first year of employment. After it is determined in what period the employee earned the right

[9]*Ibid.*, Section 3290, par. 12.

to the vacation, an issue arises as to what rate should be used to accrue the compensated absence cost—the current rate or an estimated future rate. It is likely that companies will use the current rate rather than the future rate, which is less certain and raises issues concerning the discounting of the future amount. To illustrate, assume that Helio Topics Inc. began operations on January 1, 1985. The company employs ten people who are paid $280 each per week. Vacation weeks earned by all employees in 1985 were 20 weeks, but none were used during this period. In 1986, the vacation weeks were used when the current rate of pay was $300 per week for each employee. The entry at December 31, 1985, to accrue the accumulated vacation pay is as follows:

Wages Expense	5,600	
Vacation Wages Payable		5,600*
*($280 × 20)		

At December 31, 1985, the company would report on its balance sheet a liability of $5,600. In 1986, the vacation pay related to 1985 would be recorded as follows:

Vacation Wages Payable	5,600	
Wages Expense	400	
Cash		6,000*
*($300 × 20)		

In 1986 the vacation weeks were used; therefore, the liability is extinguished. Note that the difference between the amount of cash paid and the reduction in the liability account is recorded as an adjustment to wages expense in the period when paid. This difference arises because the liability account was accrued at the rates of pay in effect during the period when compensated time was earned. The cash paid, however, is based on the rates in effect during the period in which compensated time is used. If the future rates of pay had been used to compute the accrual in 1985, then the cash paid in 1986 would have been equal to the liability.

Accrued Property Taxes   Local government units generally depend on property taxes as their primary source of revenue. Such taxes are based on the assessed value of real property and become a lien against property at a date determined by law, usually the assessment date. This lien is a liability of the property owner and is a cost of the services of such property. The accounting questions that arise from property taxes are:

1. When should the property owner record the liability?
2. To which income period should the cost be charged?

The date at which the tax becomes a lien against the property is frequently used as the date to recognize and record the liability, but the lien date may not coincide with or occur in the period when the taxpayer pays or benefits from the taxes; that is, the period to which the expense belongs may not be apparent from the lien date.

The accounting profession, in considering the various periods to which property taxes might be charged, contends that "generally, the most acceptable basis of providing for property taxes is monthly accrual on the taxpayer's books during the fiscal period of the taxing authority for which the taxes are levied."[10] Charging the

---

[10]Possible alternatives are: (a) Year in which paid. (b) Year ending on assessment (or lien) date. (c) Year beginning on assessment (or lien) date. (d) Calendar or fiscal year of taxpayer prior to assessment (or lien) date. (e) Calendar or fiscal year of taxpayer including assessment (or lien) date. (f) Calendar or fiscal year of taxpayer prior to payment date. (g) Fiscal year of governing body levying the tax. (h) Year appearing on tax bill. Committee on Accounting Procedure, American Institute of Certified Public Accountants, *op. cit.* Chapter 10, sec. A, par. 10.

taxes to the period subsequent to the levy relates the expense to the period in which the taxes are used by the government unit to provide benefits to the property owner.

Assume that Seaboard Company, which closes its books each year on December 31, receives its property tax bill in May each year. The fiscal year for the city in which Seaboard Company is located begins on May 1 and ends on the following April 30. Property taxes of $36,000 are assessed against Seaboard Company on January 1, 1986, and become a lien on May 1, 1986. However, tax bills are sent out in May and are payable in equal instalments on July 1 and September 1. Even though we agree that in this case the expense should be charged to the period subsequent to the lien date of May 1 (that is, the fiscal year of the city), there are alternative methods of recording the liability.

One alternative is to record the property tax liability on the lien date of May 1, 1986, and amortize the deferred tax expense monthly throughout the fiscal year of the government taxing unit. A **second alternative** is not to recognize the full property tax liability at the lien date of May 1, 1986, but to accrue the liability monthly during the fiscal year of the government taxing unit May 1 to April 30. Entries to record the liability, monthly tax charges, and the tax payments for taxes becoming a lien on May 1, 1986, are shown below under both alternatives.

Entries to Accrue Property Tax Expense

Record Liability on Lien Date			Accrue Liability Monthly		

May 1, 1986 (lien date):

Deferred Property Taxes	36,000		No entry		
Property Taxes Payable		36,000			

May 31 and June 30, 1986 (monthly expense accrual):

Property Tax Expense	3,000		Property Tax Expense	3,000	
Deferred Property Taxes		3,000	Property Taxes Payable		3,000

July 1, 1986 (first tax payment):

Property Taxes Payable	18,000		Property Taxes Payable	6,000	
Cash		18,000	Deferred Property Taxes	12,000	
			Cash		18,000

July 31 and August 31, 1986 (monthly expense accrual):

Property Tax Expense	3,000		Property Tax Expense	3,000	
Deferred Property Taxes		3,000	Deferred Property Taxes		3,000

September 1, 1986 (second tax payment):

Property Taxes Payable	18,000		Deferred Property Taxes	18,000	
Cash		18,000	Cash		18,000

Sept. 30, Oct. 31, Nov. 30 and Dec. 31, 1986, and Jan. 31, Feb. 28, Mar. 31, and Apr. 30, 1987 (monthly expense accrual):

Property Tax Expense	3,000		Property Tax Expense	3,000	
Deferred Property Taxes		3,000	Deferred Property Taxes		3,000

Under both alternatives deferred property taxes of $12,000 will be reported as a current asset on the December 31, 1986, balance sheet, and this amount will be amortized at the rate of $3,000 per month during January, February, March, and April of the following calendar year (1987). Under the first method the deferral is set up when the payable is recorded, whereas under the second method the deferral is set up when the payment is made. Under both alternatives the expense is accrued monthly during the fiscal year of the government taxing unit.

Some accountants advocate accruing property taxes by charges to expense during the fiscal year ending on the lien date, rather than during the fiscal year beginning on the lien date (the fiscal year of the taxing authority). In such instances the property tax for the coming fiscal year must be estimated and charged monthly to Property Tax Expense and must be credited to Property Tax Payable. Under this method the entire amount of the tax accrued by the lien date and the expense is therefore charged to the fiscal period preceding payment of the tax. Justification for this method exists when the assessment date precedes the lien date by a year or more, as is the case in some taxing units. Since, in such instances, the amount is estimated and accrued by the property owner before receipt of the tax bill, it is proper theoretically to categorize property taxes as an estimated current liability rather than as a determinable current liability.

Recognizing that special circumstances may suggest the use of alternative accrual periods, it is important that the period chosen be consistent from year to year. The selection of any of the alternative periods mentioned is a matter for individual judgement.

Conditional Payments

The amount of certain liabilities depends on annual income, which cannot be known for certain until the end of an accounting period. At the end of the year, such items as income taxes, bonuses, and profit-sharing payments can be measured readily. For interim monthly or quarterly financial statements, however, the amounts of these obligations must be viewed as estimates in advance of the final determination of annual income.

Income Taxes Payable Any federal or provincial income tax is a conditional liability because the amount of this tax varies in proportion to the amount of annual income. Some accountants consider the amount of income tax on annual income as an estimate because the computation of income (and the tax thereon) is subject to the review and the approval of Revenue Canada. The meaning and application of numerous tax rules, especially new ones, are debatable and often depend on a court's interpretation. Using the best information and advice available, a business must prepare an income tax return and compute the income tax payable resulting from the operations of the current period. Unpaid taxes payable on the income of a corporation, as computed per the tax return, should be classified as a current liability. Unlike a corporation, a proprietorship or a partnership is not a taxable entity; and because the individual proprietor and the members of a partnership are subject to personal income taxes on their share of the results of the business's operations, income tax liabilities do not appear on the financial statements of proprietorships and partnerships.

Corporations are required to pay monthly instalments based on estimates of their current year's income tax. Three different methods may be used in computing the instalment base. Although the amount of each instalment may differ under each of the alternative instalment bases, the amount of tax paid by instalments should amount to a substantial portion of the tax payable for the year. Any difference between the amount paid in instalments for the year and tax determined upon filing of the tax return for a year will be reported as a current liability.

If in a later year an additional tax is assessed on the income of an earlier year, Income Taxes Payable should be credited. The related debit should be charged to current operations unless the criteria for treating it as a prior period adjustment are met.

Differences between taxable income under the tax laws and accounting income under generally accepted accounting principles have become greater in recent years. Because of these differences and the high income taxes on corporations, the amount of income tax payable to the government in any given year, based on taxable income, may differ substantially from the amount of income tax that relates to the income before taxes, as reported on the published financial statements. The accounting procedure recommended by the *CICA Handbook* to reconcile these differences and to reflect business income correctly is called **interperiod income tax allocation.** Chapter 20 is devoted solely to income tax matters and presents an extensive discussion on this complex and controversial problem.

OM IT FROM HERE

Bonus Agreements   For various reasons, many companies give a bonus to certain or all officers and employees in addition to their regular salary and wage. Frequently the amount of the bonus depends on the company's profits for the year so that, in effect, the employees who are included in the bonus plan participate in the profits of the enterprise.

From the standpoint of the enterprise, **bonus payments to employees** may be considered additional wages and should be included as a deduction in determining the net income for the year.

The problem of computing the amount of bonus to be paid becomes more difficult, however, because the amount of a bonus to employees is an expense of the business. To illustrate, assume a situation in which a company has income of $100,000 determined before considering the bonus as an expense. According to the terms of the bonus agreement, 20% of the income is to be set aside for distribution among the employees. Now if the bonus were not itself an expense to be deducted in determining income, the amount of the bonus could be computed very simply as 20% of the net income of $100,000. The bonus is an expense, however, that must be deducted in arriving at the amount of income on which the bonus is based. Hence, $100,000 reduced by the amount of the bonus is the figure on which the bonus is to be computed. That is, the bonus is equal to 20% of $100,000 less the bonus. Stated algebraically:

$$B = 0.20\,(\$100,000 - B)$$
$$B = \$20,000 - 0.2B$$
$$1.2B = \$20,000$$
$$B = \$16,666.67$$
$$\text{PROOF: } \$16,666.67 = 20\% \text{ of } (\$100,000.00 - \$16,666.67)$$

A similar problem results from the relationship of bonus payments to federal income taxes. Assume the same situation as before, with the income of $100,000 computed without subtracting either the employees' bonus or taxes on income. The bonus is to be based on income after deducting income taxes but before deducting the bonus. The rate of income tax is 40% and the bonus of 20% is a deductible expense for tax purposes. The bonus is, therefore, equal to 20% of

$100,000 minus the tax, and the tax is equal to 40% of $100,000 minus the bonus. Thus we have two simultaneous equations that, using B as the symbol for the bonus and T for the tax, may be stated algebraically as follows:

$$B = 0.20\ (\$100,000 - T)$$
$$T = 0.40\ (\$100,000 - B)$$

These may be solved by substituting the value of T as indicated in the second equation for T in the first equation.

$$B = 0.20[\$100,000 - 0.40(\$100,000 - B)]$$
$$B = 0.20(\$100,000 - \$40,000 + 0.4B)$$
$$B = 0.20(\$60,000 + 0.4B)$$
$$B = \$12,000 + 0.08B$$
$$0.92B = \$12,000$$
$$B = \$13,043.48$$

Substituting this value for B into the second equation allows us to solve for T:

$$T = 0.40(\$100,000 - \$13,043.48)$$
$$T = 0.40(\$86,956.52)$$
$$T = \$34,782.61$$

The relationships may be illustrated and the amounts proven in the following schedule:

Income before bonus and tax	$100,000
Bonus (20% of $100,000 − $34,783)	13,043
Income before tax	86,957
Tax (40% of $86,957)	34,783
Net income	$ 52,174

If the terms of the agreement provide for deducting both the tax and the bonus to arrive at the income figure on which the bonus is computed, the equations would be:

$$B = 0.20(\$100,000 - B - T)$$
$$T = 0.40(\$100,000 - B)$$

Substituting the value of T from the second equation into the first equation enables us to solve for B:

$$B = 0.20[\$100{,}000 - 0.40(\$100{,}000 - B)]$$
$$B = 0.20(\$100{,}000 - B - \$40{,}000 + 0.4B)$$
$$B = 0.20(\$60{,}000 - 0.6B)$$
$$B = \$12{,}000 - 0.12B$$
$$1.12B = \$12{,}000$$
$$B = \$10{,}714.29$$

The value for B may then be substituted in the second equation above, and that equation solved for T:

$$T = 0.40(\$100{,}000 - \$10{,}714.29)$$
$$T = 0.40(\$89{,}285.71)$$
$$T = \$35{,}714.28$$

Inserting these values into a partial income statement, as follows, helps to prove the calculations:

Income before bonus and tax	$100,000
Bonus [20% of $100,000 − ($10,714 + $35,714)]	10,714
Income before tax	89,286
Tax (40% of $89,286)	35,714
Net income	$ 53,572

Drawing up a legal document such as a bonus agreement is a task for a lawyer, not an accountant, although accountants are frequently called on to express an opinion on the feasibility of the provisions of the agreement. In this respect, one should always insist that the agreement states specifically whether income taxes and the bonus itself are expenses deductible in determining the income for purposes of the bonus computation.

It should be apparent from the preceding paragraphs that no entry can be made for a profit-sharing bonus until all other adjusting entries, except the one for accrued taxes on income, have been made and the income before bonus and tax has been calculated. This calculation can be accomplished through the use of a work sheet or by some other method. Once the income before bonus has been calculated, it is possible to make the bonus calculation and to record it by means of an adjusting entry debiting Employee Bonus Expense and crediting Accrued Profit-Sharing Bonus Payable.

The expense account should appear in the income statement as an operating expense. The liability, accrued profit-sharing bonus payable, is usually payable within a short period, and should be included as a current liability in the balance sheet.

Similar to bonus arrangements are contractual agreements covering rents or royalty payments that are conditional on the amount of revenues earned or the quantity of product produced or extracted. Conditional expenses based on revenues or units produced are usually less difficult to compute than the bonus arrangements just illustrated. For example, if a lease calls for a fixed rent payment of $500 per month plus 1% of all sales over $300,000 per year, the annual rent obligation would amount to $6,000 plus $0.01 of each dollar of revenue over $300,000. Or, a royalty agreement may accrue to the patent owner $1.00 for every tonne of product resulting from the patented process, or accrue to the owner of the mineral rights $0.50 on every barrel of oil extracted. As each additional unit of product is produced or extracted, an additional obligation, usually a current liability, is created.

CONTINGENT LIABILITIES

Contingent liabilities are obligations that depend upon the occurrence or nonoccurrence of **one or more future events** to confirm either the **amount payable, or the payee, or the date payable, or its existence**; that is, determination of one or more of these factors is dependent upon a contingency. A contingency is defined in Section 3290 of the *CICA Handbook* as ''an existing condition or situation involving uncertainty as to possible gain or loss to an enterprise that will ultimately be resolved when one or more future events occur or fail to occur.''[11] A liability incurred as a result of a ''loss contingency'' is by definition a **contingent liability.**

When a loss contingency exists, the likelihood that the future event or events will confirm the incurrence of a liability can range from highly probable to only slightly probable. The *CICA Handbook* uses the terms **likely** and **unlikely** to identify two areas within that range and assigns the following meaning:

Likely: The chance of occurrence (or nonoccurrence) of the future event is high.

Unlikely: The chance of the occurrence (or nonoccurrence) of the future event is slight.

Accounting Treatment of Loss Contingencies			
	Usually Accrued	Not Accrued	May Be Accrued*
Loss Related to			
1. Collectibility of receivables	X		
2. Obligations related to product warranties and product defects	X		
3. Premiums offered to customers	X		
4. Risk of loss or damage of enterprise property by fire, explosion, or other hazards		X	
5. General or unspecified business risks		X	
6. Risk of loss from catastrophes assumed by property and casualty insurance companies including reinsurance companies		X	
7. Threat of expropriation of assets			X
8. Pending or threatened litigation			X
9. Actual or possible claims and assessments**			X
10. Guarantees of indebtedness of others			X
11. Obligations of commercial banks under ''standby letters of credit''			X
12. Agreements to repurchase receivables (or the related property) that have been sold			X

*Should be accrued when both criteria are met (likely and reasonably estimable).

**Estimated amounts of losses incurred prior to the balance sheet date but settled subsequently should be accrued as of the balance sheet date.

[11]*CICA Handbook*, Section 3290, par. 2.

An estimated loss from a loss contingency should be accrued by a charge to income and a liability recorded only if both of the following conditions are met:

1. Information available prior to the issuance of the financial statements indicates that it is likely that a future event will confirm that an asset had been impaired or a liability incurred as of the date of the financial statements.
2. The amount of the loss can be reasonably estimated.

Thus contingencies must be evaluated on two scales, the degree of certainty and the degree of measurability, when determining proper accounting treatment. Some items such as warranty costs are likely to occur and are measurable with such reasonable precision that they are not usually thought of as contingencies. The schedule on page 617 illustrates how contingencies vary by degree of certainty and degree of measurability as well as how different items are usually reported in financial statements. Only those loss contingencies that result in the incurrence of a liability are relevant to the discussion in this chapter. Loss contingencies that result in the impairment of an asset (e.g., collectibility of receivables or threat of expropriation of assets) are discussed in other appropriate sections in this text.

The following excerpt from the annual report of The Algoma Steel Corp. Ltd. is an example of disclosure of a loss contingency.

---

2.   Income Taxes

Revenue Canada has issued reassessments relating to earned depletion and 3% inventory allowances which would increase the Corporation's deferred income tax provisions for the years 1975, 1976, and 1977. The basis for the reassessments could have application to subsequent years. Notices of Objection have been filed and representations are being made on these matters. The Corporation and its legal advisors are of the opinion that the Corporation's arguments have merit and that the prospects of successfully opposing the arguments of Revenue Canada are favourable. Accordingly, the potential increase in deferred income taxes for 1975, 1976, and 1977 and subsequent years has not been provided for in the financial statements. In the event of an adverse ruling, the income tax provisions for the years 1975 to 1981 inclusive would be increased approximately $14.2 million and the income tax recovery for 1982 would be decreased by approximately $1.3 million.

The accounting concepts and procedures relating to contingent items are relatively new and unsettled. Practising accountants express concern over the diversity that now exists in the interpretation of "likely" and "unlikely." Current practice relies heavily on the exact language used in responses received from lawyers. (Such language is necessarily biased and protective rather than predictive.) As a result, accruals and disclosures of contingencies vary considerably in practice.

Litigation, Claims, and Assessments

The following factors, among others, must be considered in determining whether a liability should be recorded with respect to **pending or threatened litigation** and actual or possible claims and assessments:

1. The period in which the underlying cause for action occurred.
2. The degree of probability of an unfavourable outcome.
3. The ability to make a reasonable estimate of the amount of loss.

To report a loss and a liability in the financial statements, the cause of litigation must have occurred on or before the date of the financial statements. It does not matter that the company does not become aware of the existence or possibility of the lawsuit or claims until after the date of the financial statements but before they are issued. Among the factors the profession recommended be considered in **evaluating the probability of an unfavourable outcome** are: the nature of the litigation; the progress of the case; the opinion of legal counsel; the experience of the company in similar cases; the experience of other companies; and any decision of management as to how the company intends to respond to the lawsuit.

The outcome of pending litigation, however, can seldom be predicted with any assurance. Even if the evidence available at the balance sheet date does not favour the defendant company, it is hardly reasonable to expect the company to publish in its financial statements a dollar estimate of the probable negative outcome. Such specific disclosures could weaken the company's position in the dispute and encourage the plaintiff to intensify its efforts. A typical example of the wording of such a disclosure is the following note to the financial statements of CBS Inc. relating to its litigation with General Westmoreland:

CBS, Inc.

Note 19.   Litigation

The Company is named as a defendant in numerous defamation actions in the United States, including an action (discussed below) commenced by William C. Westmoreland on September 13, 1982, in the United States District Court for the District of South Carolina. While the Company cannot predict the results of these actions, it believes that it has meritorious defenses and that the liability, if any, resulting from such suits will be substantially covered by insurance and that any uninsured liability from such actions will not have a materially adverse effect on its consolidated operations or consolidated financial position.

In the action referred to above, William C. Westmoreland claims a total of $120 million in compensatory and punitive damages as a result of alleged defamations by a CBS News Special Report entitled "The Uncounted Enemy: A Vietnam Deception," broadcast by CBS on January 23, 1982, and by related broadcasts and publications. CBS has denied the material allegations of the complaint and successfully sought transfer of the action to the United States District Court for the Southern District of New York, where the matter is now pending and in discovery.

With respect to **unfiled suits** and **unasserted claims and assessments,** a company must determine (1) the degree of **probability** that a suit may be filed or a claim or assessment may be asserted and (2) the **probability** of an unfavourable outcome. For example, assume that Nawtee Company is being investigated by the federal government for possible violations of anticombines legislation and enforcement proceedings have been instituted. Such proceedings are often followed by private claims of triple damages for redress. In this case, Nawtee Company must determine the probability of the claims being asserted **and** the probability of triple damages being awarded. If both are probable, the loss reasonably estimable, and the cause for action dated on or before the date of the financial statements, then the liability should be accrued.

Disclosure of Loss Contingencies

If no accrual is made for a loss contingency and a liability is not recorded because one or both of the conditions are not met, or if there has been an accrual of an amount less than the amount of the loss exposure, then the facts must be disclosed by a note to the financial statement.[12]

Presented below is an extensive litigation disclosure note (taken from the financial statements of Raymark Corporation) which shows that although actual losses have been charged to operations and further liability possibly exists, no estimate of this liability is possible:

Raymark Corporation

Note 1.   Litigation

Raymark is a defendant or co-defendant in a substantial number of lawsuits alleging wrongful injury and/or death from exposure to asbestos fibers in the air. The following table summarizes the activity in these lawsuits for fiscal years 1980 to 1982:

	1982	1981	1980
Claims			
Pending at beginning of year	$ 8,719	$5,194	$ 1,965
Received during year	4,494	4,093	3,534
Settled or otherwise disposed of	(1,445)	(568)	(305)
Pending at end of year	11,768	8,719	5,194
Average indemnification cost	$ 3,364	$5,267	$10,724
Average cost per case, including defense costs	$ 6,499	$9,394	$16,080
Trial activity			
Verdicts for the Company	23	7	2
Total trials	36	12	3

The following table presents the cost of defending asbestos litigation, together with related insurance and workers' compensation expenses for each of the three years ending January 2, 1983.

	1982	1981	1980
Included in operating profit	$ 1,872,000	$1,912,000	$1,800,000
Non-operating expense	9,077,000	6,414,000	4,728,000
	$10,949,000	$8,328,000	$6,528,000

The Company is seeking to reasonably determine its liability. However, it is not possible to predict which theory of insurance will apply, the number of lawsuits still to be filed, the cost of settling and defending the existing and unfiled cases, or the ultimate impact of these lawsuits on the Company's consolidated financial statements.

Contingencies involving an unasserted claim or assessment need not be disclosed when there has not been any manifestation by a potential claimant of an awareness of a possible claim or assessment unless (1) it is considered **likely** that a claim will be asserted **and** (2) it is **likely** that the outcome will be unfavourable.

Certain other contingent liabilities that should be disclosed even though the possibility of loss may be remote are as follows:

1. Guarantees of indebtedness of others.
2. Obligations of commercial banks under stand-by letters of credit.
3. Guarantees to repurchase receivables (or any related property) that have been sold or assigned.

Disclosure should include the nature and amount of the guarantee and, if estimable, the amount that could be recovered from outside parties. Cities Service Company disclosed its guarantees of indebtedness of others in the following note:

[12]*Ibid.*, par. 15.

Cities Service Company

Note 10:   Contingent Liabilities
The Company and certain subsidiaries have guaranteed debt obligations of approximately $62 million of companies in which substantial investments are held. Also, under long-term agreements with certain pipeline companies in which stock interests are held, the Company and its subsidiaries have agreed to provide minimum revenue for product shipments. The Company has guaranteed mortgage debt ($80 million) incurred by a 50 percent-owned tanker affiliate for construction of tankers which are under long-term charter contracts to the Company and others. It is not anticipated that any loss will result from any of the above-described agreements.

Guarantee and Warranty Costs

A warranty (product guarantee) is a promise made by a seller to a buyer to make good on a deficiency of quantity, quality, or performance in a product. It is commonly used by manufacturers as a sales promotion technique. For a specified period of time following the date of sale to the consumer, the manufacturer may promise to bear all or part of the cost of replacing defective parts, to perform any necessary repairs or servicing without charge, to refund the purchase price, or even to "double your money back." Warranties and guarantees entail future costs, frequently significant additional costs, which are sometimes called "after costs" or "post-sale costs." Although the future cost is indefinite as to amount, due date, and even customer, a liability is likely in most cases and should be recognized in the accounts if it can be reasonably estimated. The amount of the liability is an estimate of all the costs that will be incurred after sale and delivery and that are incident to the correction of defects or deficiencies required under the warranty provisions.

There are two basic methods of accounting for warranty costs: (1) the cash basis method and (2) the accrual method. Under the **cash basis method,** warranty costs are charged to expense as they are incurred or, in other words, warranty costs are charged to the period in which the seller or manufacturer performs in compliance with the warranty. No liability is recorded for future costs arising from warranties, nor is the period in which the sale is recorded necessarily charged with the costs of making good on outstanding warranties. This method is the only one recognized for income tax purposes and is frequently justified for accounting on the basis of expediency when warranty costs are immaterial or when the warranty period is relatively short. The cash basis method is required in accounting for warranty costs when a warranty liability is not accrued in the year of sale because:

1. It is not likely that a liability has been incurred.
2. The amount of the liability cannot be reasonably estimated.

If, on the basis of available information, it is likely that customers will make claims under warranties relating to goods or services that have been sold and a reasonable estimate of the costs involved can be made, the accrual method must be used. Under the **accrual method,** a provision for warranty costs is made at the time of sale. The accrual method may be divided further into two different accounting treatments: (1) expense warranty treatment (accrual method) and (2) sales warranty treatment (deferral method). The **expense warranty treatment** charges the estimated future warranty costs to operating expense in the year of sale. It is the generally accepted method and should be used whenever the warranty is an integral and inseparable part of the sale and is viewed as a loss contingency. The **sales warranty treatment** defers a certain percentage of the original sales price until some future time when actual costs are incurred or the warranty expires. The following example illustrates the accrual method of accounting for warranty costs and the difference between the accrual and deferral treatments.

The Denson Machinery Company begins production on a new machine in July, 1986, and sells 100 units at $5,000 each by its year end, December 31, 1986. Each machine is under warranty for one year, and the company has estimated, from past experience with a similar machine, that the warranty cost will probably average $200 per unit. Further, as a result of parts replacements and services rendered in compliance with machinery warranties, the company incurs $4,000 in warranty costs in 1986 and $16,000 in 1987.

Entries under Accrual Method of Accounting for Warranties

Expense Warranty Treatment		Sales Warranty Treatment	

Sale of 100 machines at $5,000 each, July through December, 1986:

Cash or Accounts Receivable	500,000		Cash or Accounts Receivable	500,000	
Sales		500,000	Sales		480,000
			Unearned Warranty Revenue		20,000

Recognition of warranty expense, July through December, 1986:

Warranty Expense	20,000		Warranty Expense	4,000	
Estimated Liability			Cash, Inventory, or		
under Warranties		20,000	Accrued Payroll		4,000
($200 × 100 machines)			(Warranty costs incurred)		

Estimated Liability			Unearned Warranty Revenue	4,000	
under Warranties	4,000		Revenue from Warranties		4,000
Cash, Inventory, or			(Warranty revenue earned)		
Accrued Payroll		4,000			
(Warranty costs incurred)					

The December 31, 1986, balance sheet would report Estimated Liability under Warranties at a current liability of $16,000, and the income statement for 1986 would report Warranty Expense of $20,000.

The December 31, 1986, balance sheet would report Unearned Warranty Revenue as a current liability of $16,000. (Note that the $4,000 of Warranty Expense offsets the $4,000 of Warranty Revenue.)

Recognition of warranty costs incurred in 1987 (on 1986 machinery sales):

Estimated Liability			Warranty Expense	16,000	
under Warranties	16,000		Cash, Inventory, or		
Cash, Inventory, or			Accrued Payroll		16,000
Accrued Payroll		16,000	(Warranty costs incurred)		
(Warranty costs incurred)			Unearned Warranty Revenue	16,000	
			Revenue from Warranties		16,000
			(Warranty revenue earned)		

Although the net income in both 1986 and 1987 is the same under both methods, the 1986 income statement would report $16,000 less revenues and $16,000 less operating expenses under the sales warranty method, and the 1987 income statement would report $16,000 more revenues and $16,000 more operating expenses. Notice that the sales warranty treatment above assumes that at the time of sale two items were sold, the product and the warranty. Accordingly, a portion of the total sales price is deferred until the warranty revenue is earned through the replacement of parts and the performance of repairs; that is, as the costs are incurred.

The illustration on page 622 assumed a zero profit from the sale of the warranty. This illustration also assumed that the revenue recognition was a function of costs incurred during the period. Other criteria for revenue recognition for "service sales transactions" similar to this are discussed in Chapter 19.

The sales warranty treatment is applicable to companies that sell warranty contracts separately from the product. For instance, if the Denson Machinery Company had sold each machine for $4,750 with a 90-day warranty and an extended 3-year warranty contract for $250, the sales warranty method clearly would be appropriate. A liability in the form of unearned revenue would be recorded at the time of the sale of the warranty, and the warranty revenues, costs, and any income would be recognized in the periods in which the services, repairs, and replacements under the warranty were performed.

Business managers commonly view warranty costs simply as additional expenses of selling or manufacturing the product rather than as additional sales. It is normally assumed that the selling price of a product covers costs of warranty, not that the warranty is something to be sold separately. Some accountants believe that the deferred warranty revenues must be recognized in the period the sale is made rather than when the cost of repair or replacement is incurred. Neither the expensed warranty nor the sales warranty treatment is allowable for income tax purposes.

If the cash basis method were applied to the facts in the Denson Machinery Company example, $4,000 would be recorded as warranty expense in 1986 and $16,000 as warranty expense in 1987 with all of the sale price being recorded as revenue in 1986. In many instances, application of the cash basis method does not match the warranty costs relating to the products sold during a given period with the revenues derived from such products. Where continuous warranty policies exist year after year, the differences between the cash and the accrual basis would not likely be so great.

Premiums and Coupons Offered to Customers

Many companies offer (either on a limited or on a continuing basis) premiums to customers in return for boxtops, certificates, coupons, labels, or wrappers. The premium may be silverware, dishes, a small appliance, a toy, or other goods. Also, printed coupons that can be redeemed for a cash discount on items purchased are extremely popular. These premium and coupon offers are made to stimulate sales, and their costs should be charged to expense in the period of the sale that benefits from the premium plan. At the end of the accounting period many of these premium offers may be outstanding and, when presented in subsequent periods, must be redeemed. The number of outstanding premium offers that will be presented for redemption must be estimated in order to reflect the existing current liability and to match costs with revenues. The cost of premium offers should be charged to Premium Expense, and the outstanding obligations should be credited to an account titled Estimated Premium Claims Outstanding.

Although the *CICA Handbook* does not include premium offers in its list of loss contingencies, the authors believe that premium offers result in the probable existence of a liability at the date of the financial statements, can be reasonably estimated in amount, are contingent upon the occurrence of a future event (redemption), and therefore are a loss contingency within the guidelines of *CICA Handbook*, Section 3290, paragraph 12.

The following example illustrates the accounting treatment accorded a premium offer. The Fluffy Cakemix Company offered its customers a large unbreakable mixing bowl in exchange for 25 cents and 10 boxtops. The mixing bowl costs the Fluffy Cakemix Company 75 cents, and the company estimates that 60% of the boxtops will be redeemed. The premium offer began in June, 1986, and resulted in the following transactions and entries during 1986.

1. To record purchase of 20,000 mixing bowls

Inventory of Premium Mixing Bowls	15,000	
Cash		15,000

2. To record sales of 300,000 boxes of cake mix at 80 cents

Cash	240,000	
Sales		240,000

3. To record redemption of 60,000 boxtops

Cash [(60,000 ÷ 10) × $0.25]	1,500	
Premium Expense [6,000 bowls × ($0.75 − $0.25)]	3,000	
Inventory of Premium Mixing Bowls (6,000 bowls @ $0.75)		4,500
Computation: [(60,000 ÷ 10) × $0.75 = $4,500]		

4. To record estimated liability for outstanding premium offers

Premium Expense	6,000	
Estimated Premium Claims Outstanding		6,000

Computation (based on 60% redemption):

Total estimated redemptions (60%)	180,000
Boxtops redeemed in 1986	60,000
Estimated future redemptions	120,000

Cost of estimated claims outstanding
(120,000 ÷ 10) × ($0.75 − $0.25) = $6,000

The December 31, 1986, balance sheet of Fluffy Cakemix Company will report an Inventory of 14,000 Premium Mixing Bowls of $10,500 as a current asset and Estimated Premium Claims Outstanding of $6,000 as a current liability. The 1986 income statement will report a $9,000 Premium Expense among the selling expenses.

Risk of Loss Due to Lack of Insurance Coverage

Uninsured risks may arise in a number of ways, including **noninsurance** of certain risks or **co-insurance** or **deductible clauses** in an insurance contract; but the absence of insurance (frequently referred to as self-insurance) does not mean that a liability has been incurred at the date of the financial statements. For example, fires, explosions, and other similar events that may cause damage to a company's own property are random in occurrence and unrelated to the activities of the company prior to their occurrence. The conditions for accrual stated in *CICA Handbook*, Section 3290, are not satisfied prior to the occurrence of the event because until that time there is no diminution in the value of the property. However, if a company lacks adequate insurance coverage against a material risk it may be desirable to disclose this fact.[13]

Exposure to risks of loss resulting from uninsured past injury to others, however, is an existing condition involving uncertainty about the amount and the timing of

[13]*Ibid.*, par. 12.

losses that may develop, in which case a contingency exists. For example, a company with a fleet of vehicles would have to accrue uninsured losses resulting from injury to others or damage to the property of others that took place prior to the date of the financial statements (if the experience of the company or other information enables it to make a reasonable estimate of the liability). Of course, it should not establish a liability for expected future injury to others or damage to the property of others even if the amount of losses is reasonably estimable.

DISCLOSURE OF CURRENT LIABILITIES IN THE FINANCIAL STATEMENTS

The current liability accounts are commonly presented as the top or first classification in the "liabilities and shareholders' equity" section of the balance sheet. In some instances, total current liabilities are deducted from the total current assets to obtain "working capital" or "current assets in excess of current liabilities."

Within the current liability section the accounts may be listed in order of maturity, according to amount (largest to smallest), or in order of liquidation preference. Many companies list "short-term loans and notes payable" first, regardless of relative amount, followed by "accounts payable," and ending the current liability section with "current portion of long-term debt."

Supplemental information concerning current liabilities should be sufficient to meet the requirement of full disclosure. Secured liabilities should be identified, and the related assets pledged as collateral indicated. If the due date of any liability can be extended, the details should be disclosed. Current liabilities should not be offset against assets that are to be applied to their liquidation. Current maturities of long-term debt should be classified as current liabilities. A major exception exists when a currently maturing obligation is to be paid from assets classified as long-term. For example, if payments to retire a bond payable are made from a bond sinking fund classified as a long-term asset, the bonds payable should be reported in the long-term liability section. Presentation of this debt in the current liability section would distort the working capital position of the enterprise.

Existing commitments that will result in obligations in succeeding periods that are material in amount may require disclosure. For example, commitments to purchase goods or services, and for the construction, purchase, or lease of equipment or properties may require disclosure in notes accompanying the balance sheet.

The following is an example of the presentation of current liabilities with appropriate notes.

Weldon Industries, Inc.
In Millions of Dollars—October 31,

	1982	1981
Current Liabilities		
Notes payable—Note G	$ 42.9	$ 39.2
Accounts payable	199.8	150.3
Advances from customers on contracts	83.4	135.3
Accrued compensation	62.9	57.7
Accrued taxes, interest, and other expenses	146.3	141.0
Estimated warranty costs	54.0	38.4
Federal, provincial, and foreign income taxes	50.9	44.8
Current portion of long-term debt	31.0	21.2
Total Current Liabilities	671.2	627.9

NOTE G—SHORT-TERM NOTES PAYABLE
Summary data pertaining to notes payable during 1982 and 1981 is as follows:

	1982		1981	
	Amount (Millions)	Average Interest Rate	Amount (Millions)	Average Interest Rate
Foreign Bank Loans—				
Outstanding at October 31,	$42.9	13.3%[1]	$39.2	23.0%[1]
Average outstanding during the year	39.3		38.8	
Maximum outstanding during the year	42.9		43.5	
Average interest rate during the year		20.8%[1]		23.7%[1]

[1]The relatively high average interest rates on foreign loans reflect the cost of borrowing in certain foreign countries that presently have significantly higher inflation rates than Canada. Such foreign borrowings serve as protection against translation losses related to currencies that decline in value versus the Canadian dollar. Average interest rates during the years are based on weighted-average rates computed quarterly.

At October 31, 1982, the Company had unused lines of credit aggregating $100 million for short-term bank borrowings within Canada. Such lines provide for borrowings at the prevailing prime interest rate. The lines of credit may be terminated at the option of the banks or the Company. None of these lines were used during 1982.

Loan arrangements have been established with banks outside Canada under which the Company's foreign subsidiaries may borrow on an overdraft and short-term note basis. At October 31, 1982, the amount available and unused under these arrangements aggregated $27.4 million.

The Company has understandings with certain of the banks regarding deposit balances as compensation for credit arrangements, but the aggregate amount of such compensating balances was not material at October 31, 1982 and 1981. The Company was not legally restricted from withdrawing all or any portion of the compensating balances at any time during the year.

KEY POINTS

1. Liability recognition entails identifying three essential characteristics: (a) a probable future transfer of assets is involved, (b) an unavoidable obligation of the enterprise exists, and (c) the obligation is a result of past transactions or events.

2. Current liabilities are obligations whose liquidation is reasonably expected to require the use of existing resources properly classified as current assets or the creation of other current liabilities.

3. Short-term obligations can be excluded from current liabilities if the enterprise has made contractual arrangements to refinance the obligation on a long-term basis and it can demonstrate the ability to consummate the refinancing.

4. For some current liabilities (referred to as determinable) there is nothing uncertain about the existence or the amount of the obligation. Examples of determinable current liabilities are accounts and notes payable, current maturities of long-term debts, dividends payable, returnable deposits and advances

from customers, and various taxes payable (sales, payroll, property, and income).

5. Contingent liabilities depend upon the occurrence or nonoccurrence of one or more future events to confirm the amount payable, the payee, the date payable, or the obligation's existence.

6. In order for a loss contingency to be accrued as an expense and recognized as a liability, it must be likely that a liability has been incurred and that the amount of the loss can be reasonably estimated.

7. Contingent liabilities include those that are typically accrued (uncollectible accounts, product warranties, sale premiums), those that are not accrued (risk of fire and other casualties, general and unspecified business risks), and those that may or may not be accrued depending on the circumstances (threat of expropriation, pending or threatened litigation, claims and assessments, guarantees of indebtedness of others).

8. Loss contingencies that are indeterminable either as to the probability of occurrence or amount of loss are not accrued but must be disclosed in the notes to the financial statements.

9. Although the future cost of warranties and guarantees is indefinite as to amount, due date, and even customer, a liability is probable in most cases and should be recognized if it can be reasonably estimated.

10. Premium offers result in a probable liability at the date of the financial statements, can be reasonably estimated in amount, and are contingent upon the occurrence of a future event (redemption). They are therefore loss contingencies requiring expense accrual and liability recognition.

QUESTIONS

1. Assume that your friend, who is an engineering major, asks you to define and discuss the nature of a liability. Assist him or her by preparing a definition of a liability and by explaining what you believe are the elements or factors inherent in the concept of a liability.

2. Distinguish between a current liability and a long-term debt.

3. Why is the liability section of the balance sheet of primary significance to bankers?

4. How are current liabilities related by definition to current assets?

5. How are current liabilities related to a company's operating cycle?

6. How is present value related to the concept of a liability?

7. What is the nature of a "discount" on notes payable?

8. Under what conditions should a short-term obligation be excluded from current liabilities?

9. (a) What evidence is necessary to demonstrate the ability to consummate the refinancing of short-term debt?
   (b) When a financing agreement is relied upon to demonstrate ability to consummate refinancing, what amount of short-term debt may be excluded from current liabilities?

10. Discuss the accounting treatment or disclosure that should be accorded a declared but unpaid cash dividend; an accumulated but undeclared dividend on cumulative preferred shares; and a stock dividend payable.

11. How does deferred or unearned revenue arise? Why can it be classified properly as a current liability? Give several examples of business activities that result in unearned revenues.

12. What are compensated absences?

13. Under what conditions must an employer accrue a liability for the cost of compensated absences?

14. Under what conditions is an employer required to accrue a liability for sick pay? Under what conditions is an employer permitted but not required to accrue a liability for sick pay?

15. Over which two periods of time is the property tax most commonly allocated? Under what circumstances might either of these periods be justified as the period of expense?

16. What is the nature of a conditional payment? How is a conditional payment unlike the other liabilities presented under the classification of determinable current liabilities? List three examples of conditional payment liabilities.

17. Define (a) a contingency and (b) a contingent liability.

18. Under what conditions should a contingent liability be recorded?

19. Distinguish between a determinable current liability and a contingent current liability. Give two examples of each type.

20. How are the terms ''likely'' and ''unlikely'' related to contingent liabilities?

21. Contrast the cash basis method and the accrual method of accounting for warranty costs.

22. How does the expense warranty treatment differ from the sales warranty method?

23. Should a liability be recorded for risk of loss due to lack of insurance coverage? Discuss.

24. What factors must be considered in determining whether or not to record a liability for pending litigation? For threatened litigation?

25. Within the current liability section, how do you believe the accounts should be listed? Defend your position.

26. When should liabilities for each of the following items be recorded on the books of an ordinary business corporation?
    (a) Dividends.
    (b) Purchase commitments.
    (c) Acquisition of goods by purchase on credit.
    (d) Officers' salaries.
    (e) Special bonus to employees.

CASES

C13-1 Kraft Corporation issued $6,000,000 of short-term commercial paper during the year 1985 to finance construction of a plant. At December 31, the corporation's year end, Kraft intends to refinance the commercial paper by issuing long-term debt. However, because the corporation temporarily has excess cash, in January, 1986, it liquidates $2,000,000 of the commercial paper as the paper matures. In February, 1986, Kraft completes a $12,000,000 long-term debt offering. Later during the month of February, it issues its December 31, 1985, financial statements. The proceeds of the long-term debt offering are to be used to replenish $2,000,000 in working capital, to pay $4,000,000 of commercial paper as it matures in March, 1986, and to pay $6,000,000 of construction costs expected to be incurred later that year to complete the plant.

Instructions

(a) How should the $6,000,000 of commercial paper be classified on the December 31, 1985, January 31, 1986, and February 28, 1986, balance sheets? Give support for your answer and also consider the cash element.

(b) What would your answer be if, instead of a completed financing at the date of issuance of the financial statements, a financing agreement existed at that date?

C13-2 The following items are listed as liabilities on the balance sheet of Bow Valley Industrial Co. on December 31, 1986.

Accounts payable	$ 280,000
Notes payable	420,000
Bonds payable	1,460,000

The accounts payable represent obligations to suppliers that are due in January, 1987. The notes payable mature on various dates during 1987. The bonds payable mature on July 1, 1987.

These liabilities must be reported on the balance sheet in accordance with generally accepted accounting principles governing the classification of liabilities as current or noncurrent.

Instructions

(a) What is the general rule for determining whether a liability is classified as current or noncurrent?

(b) Under what conditions may any of Bow Valley Co.'s liabilities be classified as noncurrent? Explain your answer.

(CMA adapted)

C13-3 PRD Corporation reflects in the current liability section of its balance sheet at December 31, 1986 (its year end) short-term obligations of $12,000,000, which includes the current portion of 12% long-term debt in the amount of $8,000,000 (matures in March, 1987). Management has stated its intention to refinance the 12% debt whereby no portion of it will mature during 1987. The date of issuance of the financial statements is March 25, 1987.

Instructions

(a) Is management's intent enough to support long-term classification of the obligation in this situation?

(b) Assume that PRD Corporation issues $10,000,000 of ten-year debentures to the public in January, 1987, and that management intends to use the proceeds to liquidate the $8,000,000 debt maturing in March, 1987. Furthermore, assume that the debt maturing in March, 1987, is paid from these proceeds prior to the issuance of the financial statements. Will this have any impact on the balance sheet classification at December 31, 1986? Explain your answer.

(c) Assume that PRD Corporation issues common shares to the public in January and that management intends to liquidate entirely the $8,000,000 debt maturing in March, 1987, with the proceeds of this equity securities issue. In light of these events, should the $8,000,000 debt maturing in March, 1987, be included in current liabilities at December 31, 1986?

(d) Assume that PRD Corporation, on February 15, 1987, enters into a financing agreement with a commercial bank that permits PRD Corporation to borrow at any time through 1988 up to $12,000,000 at the bank's prime rate of interest. Borrowings under the financing agreement mature three years after the date of the loan. The agreement is not cancellable except for violation of a provision with which compliance is objectively determinable. No violation of any provision exists at the date of issuance of the financial statements. Assume further that $8,000,000 representing the current portion of long-term debt does not mature until August, 1987. In addition, management intends to refinance the $8,000,000 obligation under the terms of the financial agreement with the bank, which is expected to be financially capable of honouring the agreement.

1. Given these facts, should the $8,000,000 be classified as current on the balance sheet at December 31, 1986.

2. Is disclosure of the refinancing method required?

C13-4 1. What is the meaning of the term "contingency" as used in accounting?

2. Distinguish between accounting for a "gain contingency" and accounting for a "loss contingency."

3. How should the following situations be recognized in the calendar year end financial statements of Adams Labs Inc.? Explain.

(a) Pending in a provincial court is a suit against Adams Labs. The suit, which asks for token damages, alleges that Adams has infringed on a 15-year-old patent. Briefs will be heard on March 31.

(b) The C.U.P.E. Union, sole bargaining agent of Adams' production employees, has threatened a strike unless Adams agrees to a proposed profit-sharing plan. Negotiations begin on March 1.

(c) A recently completed (during the calendar year in question) government contract is subject to renegotiation. Although Adams suspects that a refund of approximately $125,000 may be required by the government, the company does not wish, for obvious reasons, to publicize this fact.

(d) Adams has a $170,000, 9% note receivable due next May 1 from Carver Coil Co., its largest customer. Adams discounted the note on December 20, with recourse, at the bank to raise needed cash. Carver Coil Co. has never defaulted on a debt and possesses a high credit rating. (Treated as a sale on December 20.)

C13-5 On February 1, 1986, one of the huge storage tanks of the Scientific Chemical Company exploded. Windows in houses and other buildings within a 1 km radius of the explosion were severely damaged, and a number of people were injured. As of February 15, 1986 (when the December 31, 1985, financial statements were completed and sent to the publisher for printing and public distribution), no suits had been filed or claims asserted against the company as a consequence of the explosion. The company fully anticipates that suits will be filed and claims asserted for injuries and damages. Because the casualty was uninsured and the company was considered at fault, Scientific Chemical will have to cover the damages from its own resources.

Instructions

Discuss fully the accounting treatment and disclosures that should be accorded the casualty and related contingent losses in the financial statements dated December 31, 1985.

C13-6 The following three independent sets of facts relate to (1) the possible accrual or (2) the possible disclosure by other means of a loss contingency.

1. A company offers a one-year warranty for the product that it manufactures. A history of warranty claims has been compiled and the probable amount of claims related to sales for a given period can be determined.

2. Subsequent to the date of a set of financial statements, but prior to the issuance of the financial statements, a company enters into a contract that will probably result in a significant loss to itself. The amount of the loss can be reasonably estimated.

3. A company has adopted a policy of recording self-insurance for any possible losses resulting from injury to others by the company's vehicles. The premium for an insurance policy for the same risk from an independent insurance company would have an annual cost of $2,500. During the period covered by the financial statements, there were no accidents involving the company's vehicles that resulted in injury to others.

Instructions

Discuss the accrual or type of disclosure (if any) necessary, and the reason(s) why such disclosure is appropriate, for each of the three independent sets of facts above. Complete your response to each situation before proceeding to the next.

(AICPA adapted)

C13-7 The two basic requirements for the accrual of a loss contingency are supported by several basic concepts of accounting. Three of these concepts are: periodicity (time periods), measurement, and objectivity.

Instructions

Discuss how the two basic requirements for the accrual of a loss contingency relate to the three concepts listed above.

(AICPA adapted)

EXERCISES

E13-1   On December 31, 1985, Robin Hood Co. had $1,200,000 of short-term debt in the form of notes payable due February 2, 1986. On January 21, 1986, the company issued 100,000 of its common shares for $9 per share, receiving $875,000 in proceeds after brokerage fees and other costs of issuance. On February 1, 1986, the proceeds from the share issue, supplemented by an additional $325,000 cash, were used to liquidate the $1,200,000 debt. The December 31, 1985, balance sheet was issued on February 23, 1986.

Instructions

Show how the $1,200,000 of short-term debt should be presented on the December 31, 1985, balance sheet, including the notes.

E13-2   During the month of June, Jamaican Imports had cash sales of $180,760 and credit sales of $80,000, both of which include the 6% sales tax that must be remitted to the province by July 15.

Instructions

Prepare the adjusting entry that should be recorded to present fairly the June 30 financial statement.

E13-3   Total payroll for the Tropaz Company for September 1986 was $425,000, of which $225,000 represented amounts paid in excess of the maximum pensionable and insurable earnings of certain employees. Income taxes in the amount of $90,000 were withheld, as was $9,000 in union dues. Employee unemployment insurance premium is 2.35% of insurable earnings, and the employer's UI premium is 3.29%. Also, assume that the current CPP(QPP) employee tax is 1.8%, with an equal contribution required of employers.

Instructions

Prepare the necessary journal entries if the wages and salaries paid and the employer payroll taxes are recorded separately.

E13-4   Ontario Jewellery Company's payroll for August, 1986, is summarized below.

Payroll	Wages Due	Amount Subject to Payroll Taxes	
		CPP	Unemployment Insurance
Factory	$120,000	$112,000	$115,000
Sales	44,000	32,000	24,000
Administrative	36,000	12,000	36,000
Total	$200,000	$156,000	$175,000

At this point in the year, some employees have already received wages in excess of those to which payroll taxes apply. Assume that the unemployment insurance rate is 2.35% for employees and 3.29% for employers. The CPP rate is 1.8% for both employee and employer. Income tax withheld amounts to $14,000 for factory, $6,000 for sales, and $7,000 for administrative.

Instructions

(a)   Prepare a schedule showing the employer's total cost of wages for August.

(b)   Prepare the journal entries to record the factory, sales, and administrative payrolls, including the employer's payroll taxes.

E13-5   D. Skorton Company began operations on January 2, 1985. Today it employs seven individuals who work eight-hour days and are paid hourly. Each employee earns ten paid vacation days and six paid sick days annually. Vacation days may be taken after January 15 of the year following the year in which they are earned. Sick days may be taken as soon as they are earned. Additional information follows:

Actual Hourly Wage Rate		Vacation Days Used by Each Employee		Sick Days Used by Each Employee	
1985	1986	1985	1986	1985	1986
$6.00	$6.75	0	9	4	5

D. Skorton Company has chosen to accrue the cost of compensated absences at rates of pay in effect during the period when earned and to accrue sick pay when earned.

Instructions

(a) Prepare journal entries to record transactions related to compensated absences during 1985 and 1986.

(b) Compute the amounts of any liability for compensated absences that should be reported on the balance sheet at December 31, 1986.

E13-6 Assume the facts in the preceding exercise, except that D. Skorton Company has chosen not to accrue paid sick leave until used, and has chosen to accrue vacation time at expected future rates of pay without discounting. The company uses the following projected rates to accrue vacation time:

Year in Which Vacation Time Was Earned	Projected Future Pay Rates Used to Accrue Vacation Pay
1985	$6.70
1986	7.50

Instructions

(a) Prepare journal entries to record transactions related to compensated absences during 1985 and 1986.

(b) Compute the amounts of any liability for compensated absences that should be reported on the balance sheet at December 31, 1985 and 1986.

E13-7 Dave Osborn, president of the Osborn Music Company, has a bonus arrangement with the company under which he receives 20% of the net income (after deducting taxes and bonuses) each year. For the current year, the net income before deducting either the provision for income taxes or the bonus is $162,000. The bonus is deductible for tax purposes, and the effective tax rate may be assumed to be 40%.

Instructions

(a) Compute the amount of Dave Osborn's bonus.

(b) Compute the appropriate provision for federal income taxes for the year.

E13-8 The incomplete income statement of a glue company appears below:

Atlantic Glue Company INCOME STATEMENT For the Year 1986		
Revenue		$5,000,000
Cost of goods sold		3,400,000
Gross profit		1,600,000
Administrative and selling expenses	$500,000	
Profit-sharing bonus to employees	?	?
Income before income taxes		?
Income taxes		?
Net income		$?

The employee profit-sharing plan requires that 20% of all profits remaining after the deduction of the bonus and income taxes be distributed to the employees by the first day of the fourth month following each year end. The corporate income tax rate is 40%, and the bonus is tax deductible.

Instructions

Complete the condensed income statement of the Atlantic Glue Company for the year 1986.

E13-9 Textiles Manufacturing Company sold 200 copymaking machines in 1986 for $4,000 apiece, together with a one-year warranty. Maintenance on each machine during the warranty period averages $300.

Instructions

(a) Prepare entries to record the sale of the machines and the subsequent expenditure of $59,400 to service the machines during the guarantee period, assuming that the expense warranty accrual method is used.

(b) On the basis of the data above, prepare the appropriate entries, assuming that the cash basis (i.e., "tax") method is used and that $28,000 was expended to service the machines in 1986.

E13-10 Crimson Tide Co. includes one coupon in each box of soap powder that it packs, and ten coupons are redeemable for a premium (a kitchen utensil). In 1986, Crimson Tide Co. purchased 5,000 premiums at 80 cents each and sold 80,000 boxes of soap powder at $2.50 per box. Twenty thousand coupons were presented for redemption in 1986. It is estimated that 60% of the coupons will eventually be presented for redemption.

Instructions

Prepare all the entries that would be made relative to sales of soap powder and to the premium plan in 1986.

E13-11 How would each of the following items be reported on the balance sheet?

1. Current maturities of long-term debts to be paid from current assets.
2. Discount on notes payable.
3. Notes receivable discounted.
4. Cash dividends declared but unpaid.
5. Deposit received from customer to guarantee performance of a contract.
6. Dividends in arrears on preferred shares.
7. Loans from officers.
8. Accommodation endorsement.
9. Estimated taxes payable.
10. Employee payroll deductions unremitted.
11. Unpaid bonus to officers.
12. Gift certificates sold to customers but not yet redeemed.
13. Accrued vacation pay.
14. Premium offers outstanding.
15. Personal injury claim pending.
16. Service warranties on appliance sales.

PROBLEMS

P13-1 Described below are certain transactions of Tribec Corporation.

1. On February 2, the corporation purchased goods from Becker Company for $40,000 subject to cash discount terms of 2/10, n/30. Purchases and accounts payable are recorded by the corporation at net amounts after cash discounts. The invoice was paid on February 26.

2. On April 1, the corporation bought a truck for $15,800 from the Elite Company, paying $1,800 in cash and signing a one-year, 12% note for the balance of the purchase price.

3. On May 1, the corporation borrowed $50,000 from the Royal Bank by signing a $57,500 note due one year from May 1.

4. On June 30, the corporation partially refunded $40,000 of its outstanding 10% note payable made one year ago to the Bank of Nova Scotia by paying $40,000 plus interest of $4,000, having obtained the $44,000 by using $18,500 of its own cash and signing a new one-year, $30,000 note discounted at 15% by the bank.

5. On August 1, the Board of Directors declared a $150,000 cash dividend that was payable on September 10 to shareholders of record on August 31.

Instructions

(a) Make all the journal entries necessary to record the transactions above using appropriate dates.

(b) Tribec Corporation's year end is December 31. Assuming that no adjusting entries relative to the transactions above have been recorded at year end, prepare any adjusting journal entries concerning interest that are necessary to present fair financial statements at December 31. Assume straight-line amortization of discounts.

P13-2 Listed below are selected transactions of Drier's Department Store for the current year ending December 31.

1. On December 5, the store received $400 from the Townhouse Players as a deposit to be returned after certain furniture to be used in stage production was returned on January 15.

2. During December, sales totalled $936,000, which included the 4% sales tax that must be remitted to the province by the fifteenth day of the following month.

3. On December 10, the store purchased for cash three delivery trucks for $45,000. The trucks were purchased in a province that applies no sales tax, but the store is located in and must register the trucks in a province that applies an education and health tax of 5% to nonsalable goods bought outside of its tax jurisdiction.

4. The store followed the practice of recording its property tax liability on the lien date and amortizing the tax over the subsequent 12 months. Property taxes of $54,000 became a lien on May 1 and were paid in two equal instalments on July 1 and October 1.

5. During the year, the store estimated that its annual income tax would be $675,000. At year end, income tax expense (for both accounting and tax return purposes) was determined to be $650,000. (Estimated taxes are paid quarterly.)

Instructions

Prepare all the journal entries necessary to record the transactions noted above as they occurred and any adjusting journal entries relative to the transactions that would be required to present fair financial statements at December 31. Date each entry.

P13-3 On December 31, 1986, Doritos Company has $4,000,000 of short-term debt in the form of notes payable to the Royal Bank due periodically in 1987. On January 18, 1987, Doritos enters into a refinancing agreement with the Royal Bank that will permit it to borrow up to 60% of the gross amount of its accounts receivable. Receivables are expected to range between a low of $3,000,000 in May to a high of $4,500,000 in October during 1987. The interest cost of the maturing short-term debt is 15%, and the new agreement calls for a fluctuating interest at 1% above the prime rate on notes due in 1992. Doritos' December 31, 1986, balance sheet is issued on February 15, 1987.

Instructions

Prepare a partial balance sheet for Doritos at December 31, 1986, showing how its $4,000,000 of short-term debt should be presented, including note disclosures.

P13-4 This is a payroll sheet for E-Z Rider Company for the month of September, 1986. The unemployment insurance rate is 2.35% and the maximum monthly amount per employee is $46.84. The employer's liability for unemployment insurance is 1.4 times the amount of employee deductions. Assume a 10% income tax rate for all employees and a 1.8% CPP tax on employee and employer on a maximum of $18,000 annual earnings per employee.

Name	Earnings to Aug. 31	September Earnings	Income Tax Withholding	CPP	Unemployment Insurance
B. Morris	$ 1,200	$ 600			
H. Remmers	2,800	400			
B. Harris	5,400	900			
V. Odom	12,600	1,700			
A. Scaperlanda	38,000	3,200			
E. Wunderlich	30,700	2,700			

Instructions

    (a)   Complete the payroll sheet and make the necessary entry to record the payment of the payroll.

    (b)   Make the entry to record the payroll tax expenses of E-Z Rider Company.

    (c)   Make the entry to pay the payroll liabilities created. Assume that the company pays all payroll liabilities at the end of each month.

P13-5   Knickerbocker Company pays its office employee payroll weekly. Below is a partial list of employees and their payroll data for August. Because August is their vacation period, vacation pay is also listed.

Employee	Earnings to July 31	Weekly Pay	Vacation Pay to Be Received in August
Orlanda Drebit	$2,900	$100	—
Brent Adams	2,465	85	$170
Susan Robinson	6,300	210	420
Les Wall	5,570	130	—
Ken Shiffman	7,000	240	480

    Assume that the federal income tax collected is 10% of wages. Union dues collected are 3% of wages. Vacations are taken the second and third weeks of August by Adams, Robinson, and Shiffman. The unemployment insurance rate is 2.35% for employees and 1.4 times the employee rate for employers, both on a $6,000 monthly maximum. The CPP rate is 1.8% on employee and employer (none of the employees has earned the annual maximum pensionable earnings of $20,000 per employee).

Instructions

    Make the journal entries necessary for each of the four August payrolls. The entries for the payroll and for the company's liability are made separately. Also make the entry to record the monthly payment of accrued payroll liabilities.

P13-6   Elevator Company has a contract with its president, Ann Short, to pay her a bonus during each of the years 1983, 1984, 1985, and 1986. The income tax rate is 40% during the four years. The profit before deductions for bonus and income taxes was $200,000 in 1983, $200,000 in 1984, $400,000 in 1985, and $300,000 in 1986. The president's bonus of 15% is deductible for tax purposes in each year and is to be computed as follows:

    1. In 1983 the bonus is to be based on profit before deductions for bonus and income tax.

    2. In 1984 the bonus is to be based on profit after deduction of bonus but before deduction of income tax.

    3. In 1985 the bonus is to be based on profit before deduction of bonus but after deduction of income tax.

    4. In 1986 the bonus is to be based on profit after deductions for bonus and income tax.

Instructions

    Compute the amounts of the bonus and the income tax for each of the four years.

P13-7 PrairiProv Herbicide Company has a profit-sharing agreement with its employees that provides for deposit, in a pension trust for the benefit of the employees, 20% of the net income after deducting (1) income taxes, (2) the amount of the annual pension contribution, and (3) a return of 8% on the shareholders' equity as of the end of the year 1986.

Instructions

Compute the amount of the pension contribution under the assumption that the shareholders' equity at the end of the year before adding the net income for the year is $1,000,000; that net income for the year before either the pension contribution or tax is $250,000; and that the pension contribution is deductible for tax purposes. Use 45% as the applicable rate of tax.

P13-8 During 1986, Magic Motor Company sells 60,000 high-compression engines under a three-year warranty that requires the company to replace all defective parts during the warranty period at no cost to the purchaser. These engines constitute nearly all of the company's 1986 business.

Instructions

(a) Name two basic methods of accounting for the warranty costs.
(b) What accounts would be used for each of the two methods?
(c) What effect would each method have on net income during the period of the warranties?
(d) In your opinion, which of the two methods is more appropriate for Magic Motor Company?

P13-9 The Potts Products Company sells electric typewriters for $750 each and offers to each customer a three-year warranty contract for $75 that requires the company to perform periodic services and to replace defective parts. During 1986, the company sells 300 typewriters and 250 warranty contracts for cash. It estimates the three-year warranty costs as $20 for parts and $35 for labour, and accounts for warranties on the sales warranty accrual method. Assume that sales occur on December 31, 1986; profit is recognized on the warranties; and that straight-line recognition of revenues occurs.

Instructions

(a) Record any necessary journal entries in 1986.
(b) What amounts relative to these transactions would appear on the December 31, 1986, balance sheet, and how would they be classified? In 1987, the Potts Products Company incurs actual costs relative to 1986 typewriter warranty sales of $1,800 for parts and $3,000 for labour.
(c) Record any necessary journal entries in 1987 relative to 1986 typewriter warranties.
(d) What amounts relative to the 1986 typewriter warranties would appear on the December 31, 1987, balance sheet, and how would they be classified?

P13-10 Weisberg Corporation sells portable computers under a two-year warranty contract that requires the corporation to replace defective parts and to provide the necessary repair labour. During 1986 the corporation sells 250 computers for cash at a unit price of $6,000. On the basis of past experience, the two-year warranty costs are estimated to be $150 for parts and $105 for labour per unit. (For simplicity, assume that all sales occur on December 31, 1986.)

Instructions

(a) Record any necessary journal entries in 1986, applying the cash basis method.
(b) Record any necessary journal entries in 1986, applying the expense warranty accrual method.
(c) What amounts relative to these transactions would appear on the December 31, 1986 balance sheet, and how would they be classified if the cash basis method is applied?

(d) What amounts relative to these transactions would appear on the December 31, 1986 balance sheet, and how would they be classified if the expense warranty accrual method is applied?
In 1987, the actual warranty costs to Weisberg Corporation are $16,700 for parts and $11,650 for labour.

(e) Record any necessary journal entries in 1987, applying the cash basis method.

(f) Record any necessary journal entries in 1987, applying the expensed warranty accrual method.

P13-11 The Elexio Adono Company sells a machine for $4,500 under a 12-month warranty agreement that requires the company to replace all defective parts and to provide the repair labour at no cost to the customers. With sales being made evenly throughout the year, the company sells 1,400 machines in 1985 (warranty expense is incurred one-half in 1985 and one-half in 1986). As a result of product testing, the company estimates that the warranty cost is $150 per machine ($60 parts and $90 labour).

Instructions

Assuming that actual warranty costs are incurred exactly as estimated, what journal entries would be made relative to these facts:

(a) Under application of the expense warranty accrual method for:
1. Sale of machinery in 1985?
2. Warranty expense charged against 1985 revenues?
3. Warranty costs incurred in 1985?
4. Warranty costs incurred in 1986?

(b) Under application of the cash basis method for:
1. Sale of machinery in 1985?
2. Warranty expense charged against 1985 revenues?
3. Warranty costs incurred in 1985?
4. Warranty costs incurred in 1986?

(c) What amount, if any, is disclosed in the balance sheet as a liability for future warranty cost as of December 31, 1985, under each method?

(d) Which method best reflects the income in 1985 and 1986 of the Elexio Adono Company? Why?

P13-12 To stimulate the sales of its Banana-Nuts breakfast cereal, the Better Breakfast Foods Company places one coupon in each box. Five coupons are redeemable for a premium consisting of a children's hand puppet. In 1986, the company purchases 25,000 puppets at 40 cents each and sells 200,000 boxes of Banana-Nuts at 90 cents a box. From its experience with other similar premium offers, the company estimates that 40% of the coupons issued will be mailed back for redemption. During 1986, 40,000 coupons are presented for redemption.

Instructions

Prepare the journal entries that should be recorded in 1986 relative to the premium plan.

P13-13 Sweet Candy Company offers a stereo record as a premium for every five candy bar wrappers presented by customers together with 75 cents. ~~The candy bars are sold by the company to distributors for 30 cents each. The purchase price of each record to the company is 80 cents;~~ in addition, it costs 25 cents to mail each record. The results of the premium plan for the years 1985 and 1986 are as follows (all purchases and sales are for cash):

	UNITS 1985	UNITS 1986
Stereo records purchased	$ 240,000	$ 250,000
Candy bars sold	2,861,420	2,647,500
Wrappers redeemed	924,600	1,350,000
1985 wrappers expected to be redeemed in 1986	360,000	
1986 wrappers expected to be redeemed in 1987		240,000

Instructions

(a) Prepare the journal entries that should be made in 1985 and 1986 to record the transactions related to the premium plan of the Sweet Candy Company.

(b) Indicate the account names, amounts, and classifications of the items related to the premium plan that would appear on the balance sheet and the income statement at the end of 1985 and 1986.

P13-14 Borke Company must make computations and adjusting entries for the following independent situations at December 31, 1986:

1. Its line of amplifiers carries a three-year warranty against defects. On the basis of past experience, the estimated warranty costs related to dollar sales are: first year after sale—1% of sales; second year after sale—2% of sales; and third year after sale—4% of sales. Sales and actual warranty expenditures for the first three years of business are:

	Sales	Warranty Expenditures
1984	$ 800,000	$ 3,800
1985	1,040,000	17,400
1986	1,200,000	48,000

Instructions

Compute the amount that Borke Company should report as a liability in its December 31, 1986, balance sheet. Assume that all sales are made evenly throughout each year, with warranty expenses also evenly spaced relative to the rates above.

2. Borke Company's profit-sharing plan provides that the company will contribute to a fund an amount equal to one-third of its net income after taxes each year. Income before taxes and before deducting the profit-sharing contribution for 1986 is $900,000. The applicable income tax rate is 40%, and the profit-sharing contribution is deductible for tax purposes.

Instructions

Compute the amount to be contributed to the profit-sharing fund for 1986.

3. With some of its products, Borke Company includes coupons that are redeemable in merchandise. The coupons have no expiration date and, in the company's experience, 40% of them are redeemed. The liability for unredeemed coupons at December 31, 1985, was $9,000. During 1986, coupons worth $22,000 were issued, and merchandise worth $8,000 was distributed in exchange for coupons redeemed.

Instructions

Compute the amount of the liability that should appear on the December 31, 1986, balance sheet.

(AICPA adapted)

P13-15 On November 24, 1986, 26 passengers on TransCan Airlines Flight No. 901 were injured upon landing when the plane skidded off the runway. Personal injury suits for damages totalling $3,000,000 were filed on January 11, 1987, against the airline by 18 injured passengers. The airline carried no insurance. Legal counsel studied each suit and advised TransCan that it could reasonably expect to pay 60% of the damages claimed. The financial statements for the year ended December 31, 1986, were issued February 17, 1987.

Instructions

(a) Prepare any disclosures and journal entries required by the airline in the preparation of the December 31, 1986, financial statements.

(b) Ignoring the November 24, 1986, accident, what liability due to the risk of loss from lack of insurance coverage should TransCan Airlines record or disclose? During the past decade the company has experienced at least one accident per year and incurred average damages of $2,500,000. Discuss fully.

P13-16   In preparing its December 31, 1986, financial statements, Universal, Inc. is attempting to determine the proper accounting treatment for each of the following situations:

1. As a result of uninsured accidents during the year, personal injury suits for $300,000 and $50,000 have been filed against the company. It is the judgement of Universal's legal counsel that an unfavourable outcome is unlikely in the $50,000 case but that an unfavourable verdict approximating $180,000 will probably result in the $300,000 case.

2. Universal, Inc. owns a subsidiary in a foreign country that has a book value of $6,780,000 and an estimated fair value of $9,500,000. The foreign government has communicated to Universal its intention to expropriate the assets and business of all foreign investors. On the basis of settlements that other firms have received from this same country, Universal expects to receive 40% of the fair value of its properties as final settlement.

3. Universal's chemical product division, consisting of five plants, is uninsurable because of the special risk of injury to employees and losses due to fire and explosion. The year 1986 is considered one of the safest (or luckiest) in the division's history because no loss due to injury or casualty is suffered. Having suffered an average of three casualties a year during the rest of the past decade (ranging from $45,000 to $800,000), management is certain that next year the company will probably not be so fortunate.

Instructions

(a) Prepare the journal entries that should be recorded as of December 31, 1986, to recognize each of the situations above.

(b) Indicate what should be reported relative to each situation in the financial statements and accompanying notes. Explain why.

P13-17   Zett Inc., a publishing company, is preparing its December 31, 1986, financial statements and must determine the proper accounting treatment for each of the following situations:

1. Zett sells subscriptions to several magazines for a one-year, two-year, or three-year period. Cash receipts from subscribers are credited to magazine subscriptions collected in advance, and this account has a balance of $2,400,000 at December 31, 1986. Outstanding subscriptions at December 31, 1986, expire as follows:

> During 1987—$600,000
> During 1988— 900,000
> During 1989— 400,000

2. On January 2, 1986, Zett discontinues collision, fire, and theft coverage on its delivery vehicles and becomes self-insured for these risks. Actual losses of $45,000 during 1986 are charged to delivery expense. The 1985 premium for the discontinued coverage amounts to $100,000, and the controller wants to set up a reserve for self-insurance by a debit to delivery expense of $55,000 and a credit to the reserve for self-insurance of $55,000.

3. A suit for breach of contract seeking damages of $1,000,000 is filed by an author against Zett on July 1, 1986. The company's legal counsel believes that an unfavourable outcome is probable. A reasonable estimate of the court's award to the plaintiff is in the range between $100,000 and $500,000. No amount within this range is a better estimate of potential damages than any other amount.

4. During December, 1986, a competitor files suit against Zett for industrial espionage, claiming $2,000,000 in damages. In the opinion of management and company counsel, it is reasonably possible that damages will be awarded to the plaintiff. However, the amount of potential damages awarded to the plaintiff cannot be reasonably estimated.

Instructions

For each of the situations above, prepare the journal entry that should be recorded as of December 31, 1986, or explain why an entry should not be recorded. Show supporting computations in good form.

(AICPA adapted)

14

LONG-TERM LIABILITIES

Long-term debt consists of probable future sacrifices of economic resources arising from present obligations that are not payable within the operating cycle of the business, or within a year if there are several operating cycles within one year. Bonds payable, long-term notes payable, mortgages payable, lease obligations, and pension obligations are examples of long-term liabilities. Pension and lease obligations are discussed in Chapters 21 and 22, respectively.

NATURE OF LONG-TERM LIABILITIES

Long-term debt, a more or less permanent means of financing growth, is used to increase the earnings available to shareholders whenever a higher rate of return can be earned on the borrowed funds than is paid out as interest. The excess represents income to the shareholders. **Long-term creditors have no vote in management affairs and receive a stated rate of interest whether the income of the firm is low, high, or nonexistent.** Incurring long-term debt is often accompanied by considerable formality. The bylaws of corporations often require approval by the board of directors and the shareholders before bonds can be issued or other long-term debt arrangements can be contracted.

As we shall see later, the distinction between long-term and equity financing can become hazy. A debt instrument usually has a maturity date when the face value (principal amount) must be repaid to the lender. Additionally, a debt instrument confers no voting rights, but usually bears an interest that must be paid periodically. An equity security, conversely, generally does not have a maturity date; therefore, it need never be redeemed by the issuing corporation. Voting rights may or may not attach to an equity security, and dividends are paid at the direction of the issuing corporation's board of directors.

Generally, long-term debt, in whatever form, is issued subject to various **covenants or restrictions** for the protection of the lenders. The covenants and other terms of the agreement between the borrower and the lender are stated in the **bond indenture or note agreement** and may be printed on (or referred to in) the formal instrument that is evidence of the debt. Items often mentioned in the indenture or agreement include the amounts authorized to be issued, interest rate, due date or dates, property pledged as security, sinking fund requirements, working capital and dividend restrictions, and limitations concerning the assumption of additional debt. Whenever these stipulations are important for a complete understanding of the financial position and the results of operations, they should be described in the body of the financial statements or the notes thereto (*CICA Handbook*, Section 3210). In many cases, the loan instrument or contract is held by a trustee, usually a trust company, who acts as an independent third party to protect the interests of the lender(s) and the borrower.

BONDS PAYABLE

A bond arises from a contract known as an **indenture** and represents a promise to pay: (1) a sum of money at a designated maturity date, plus (2) periodic interest at a fixed or variable rate (dependent upon the level of the prime rate, for example) on the face value. Individual bonds are evidenced by a paper certificate and typically have a maturity amount (face value) of $1,000, although some bond issues are of other denominations. Bond interest payments usually are made semiannually, although the interest rate is generally expressed as an annual rate. Some of the more common types of bonds found in practice are:

Secured and unsecured bonds. Bonds may be **secured** (e.g., mortgage bonds, which have a claim on real estate, and collateral trust bonds, which have securities of other corporations as security) or **unsecured** (e.g., debenture bonds) as to principal.

Term and serial bonds. Bond issues that mature on a single date are called **term bonds**, and issues that mature in instalments are called **serial bonds**. Serially maturing bonds are frequently used by municipalities that borrow money that will be paid back in instalments to be financed through a special levy. The accounting for serial bonds is illustrated in Appendix 14A of this chapter.

Convertible bonds. If bonds are convertible into other securities of the corporation for a specified time after issuance, they are called **convertible bonds**. Accounting for bond conversion is discussed in Chapter 17.

Registered and bearer bonds. Bonds issued in the name of the owner are **registered bonds** and require surrender of the certificate and issuance of a new certificate for the investor to complete a sale. A **bearer** bond, however, is not recorded in the name of the owner and may be transferred from one investor to another by mere delivery. Coupons attached to such bonds are submitted by the holder to receive interest payments.

In addition to the bonds mentioned above, **income bonds** may be issued. Their interest payments depend upon the issuing company's income. If the issuer reserves the right to call and retire the bonds prior to maturity, they are **callable or redeemable bonds.**

While various bonds, such as those mentioned above, have existed for a long time, new types of bonds sometimes appear that have been developed in an attempt to attract capital in a tight money market. The following serve to exemplify some of the more recent developments in this regard.

Retractable bonds provide the holder with the right to sell the bonds back to the company at his or her option. Exercise of this right is typically restricted to specified time periods and prices. AMCA International Limited and British Columbia Telephone Company have retraction rights in some of their long-term debt instruments.

Extendable bonds allow the holder, at his or her option, to extend the date of maturity under specified terms and conditions. Hiram Walker Resources Limited and British Columbia Telephone Company are examples of Canadian companies that have an extension right for some of their bonds.

Commodity-backed bonds (also called ''**asset-linked bonds**'') are redeemable in measures of a commodity, such as barrels of oil, tonnes of coal, or ounces of rare metal. For instance, in 1980 Sunshine Mining, a silver-mining producer, sold two issues of bonds redeemable with either $1,000 in cash or 50 ounces of silver (or the cash equivalent), whichever is greater at maturity. Both issues are due in 1995 and have a stated interest rate of 8 1/2%. The accounting problem for such bonds is one of projecting the maturity value, especially since the price for silver has fluctuated greatly over the past few years.

Deep-discount bonds, also referred to as ''**zero-interest debenture bonds**,'' are sold at a discount. No interest rate is stated and the price paid is simply the market's determination of the present value of the face amount to be received at maturity. Therefore, the buyer's total interest payoff is at maturity (the amount of interest being the difference between the maturity amount and the price for which the bonds were sold). In 1980, J. C. Penney Company sold the first publicly marketed long-term debt securities in the United States that did not bear interest. A unique version of a zero-interest bond (with overtones of a commodity-backed bond) was the 1982 proposal by Caesar's World Inc., a Las Vegas/Lake Tahoe gambling casino operator. Caesar's World proposed to issue 5,000 of $15,000 face amount bonds that would entitle each bondholder to spend two weeks a year at its Lake Tahoe resort in lieu of interest on the bond.[1] The phenomenon of ''deep-discount'' bonds is emerging in Canada under such marketing names as ''Cougars,'' ''Tigers,'' and ''Cats.'' Tax complexities related to such issues have, however, not been totally clarified and, therefore, some degree of risk exists in terms of the tax consequences related to interest. The timing and amount of interest recognition for financial statement reporting also present issues that require considerable judgement to resolve.

The relative risk inherent in any bond issue is often determinable through the quality ratings made public by investment publication companies. Moody's Investors Service and Standard & Poor's Corporation are predominant companies in this regard. The bond quality designations and rating symbols of these two firms are as follows:

---

[1]''Caesar's World May Try Bond Issue Paying in Vacations,'' *The Wall Street Journal* (January 22, 1982), p. 32.

Quality	Symbols	
	Moody's	Standard & Poor's
Prime	Aaa	AAA
Excellent	Aa	AA
Upper medium	A	A
Lower medium	Baa	BBB
Marginally speculative	Ba	BB
Very speculative	B, Caa	B
Default	Ca, C	D

A quality rating is assigned each new public bond issue and may be changed up or down during the issue's outstanding life as the quality is constantly monitored. Dominion Rating Service and Canadian Bond Rating Service are companies that specialize in domestic bond rating.

In short, bonds have many different features and vary in their level of risk. The main purpose of bonds is to borrow from the general public or from institutional investors for the long term when the amount of capital needed is too large for one lender to supply. By issuing bonds in $1,000 or $10,000 denominations, a large amount of long-term indebtedness can be divided into many small investing units, thus enabling more than one lender to participate in the loan.

An entire bond issue may be sold to an investment dealer, who acts as a selling agent in the process of marketing the bonds. The investment dealers often underwrite the entire issue by guaranteeing a certain sum to the corporation, taking the risk of selling the bonds for whatever price they can get, or they may sell the bond issue for a commission to be deducted from the proceeds of the sale. Alternatively, the issuing company may choose to place a bond issue privately by selling the bonds directly to a large institution, financial or otherwise, without the aid of an underwriter.

Figure 14-1 on page 644 shows the events and transactions associated with bonds. As indicated, planning and the making of several important decisions precede the issuance of bonds, the action that initiates accounting activities.

A multitude of complexities arise regarding accounting for bonds. These complexities relate to such things as the proceeds received, the issuance date, the company's year end, interest calculations, and the method of retiring the bonds. While the mechanics involved are fairly complicated, an understanding of them may be enhanced by keeping the following basic purposes of accounting for bonds in mind:

1. To measure the liability appropriately for balance sheet purposes.
2. To match expenses appropriately to the period benefited.

Valuation of Bonds Payable—Discount and Premium

The issuance and marketing of bonds to the public is not an overnight happening—it takes time, often weeks or months, as indicated in Figure 14-1. Approval must be obtained, audits and issuance of a prospectus may be required, certificates must be printed, and underwriters must be arranged. Frequently, therefore, the terms in a bond indenture are established well in advance of the sale of bonds. Between the time the terms are set and the bonds are issued, the market conditions and the

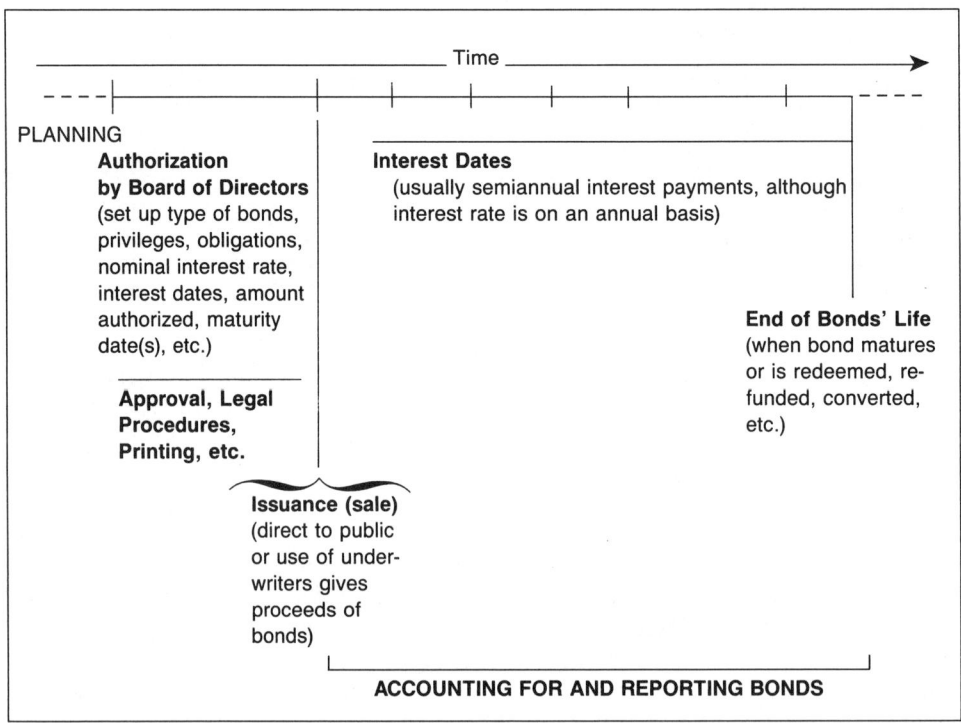

FIGURE 14-1 Events and Transactions Related to Bonds

financial position of the issuing corporation may change significantly. Such changes affect the marketability of the bonds and thus their selling price.

The selling price of a bond issue is set by such familiar economic phenomena as supply and demand of buyers and sellers, relative risk, market conditions, and the state of the economy. The investment community values a bond at the present value of a set of future cash flows consisting of (1) interest and (2) principal. The rate used to compute the present value of these two cash flows is the market interest rate that provides an acceptable return on an investment, given the risk characteristics of the company issuing the bonds and consideration for inflation.

The interest rate written in the terms of the bond indenture and ordinarily appearing on the bond certificate is known as the **stated, coupon, or nominal rate.** This rate, which is set by the issuer of the bonds, is expressed as a percentage of the **face value,** also called the **par value, principal amount, or maturity value,** of the bonds. If the rate employed by the buyers differs from the stated rate, the present value of the bonds computed by the buyers will differ from the face value of the bonds. The difference between the face value and the present value of the bonds is the discount or premium.[2] If the bonds sell for less than face value, they are sold at a **discount.** If the bonds sell for more than face value, they are sold at a **premium.** If

---

[2]Until the 1950s it was common for corporations to issue bonds with low, even-percentage coupons (such as 4%) to demonstrate their financial solidity. Frequently, the result was large discounts. More recently, it has become acceptable to set the stated rate of interest on bonds in precise fractions (such as 10 7/8%). Companies usually attempt to align the stated rate as closely as possible with the market or effective rate. While discounts and premiums continue to occur, their absolute magnitude tends to be much smaller than in the past, to the extent that in several cases the amount of the premium or discount is immaterial.

bonds sell at a discount or premium, the actual interest yield is greater or less than the stated rate. This rate of interest which is actually earned by the bondholders is called the **effective, yield, or market rate.** If bonds sell at a discount, the effective rate is higher than the stated rate. Conversely, if bonds sell at a premium, the effective rate or yield is lower than the stated rate.

To illustrate the computation of the present value of a bond issue, let us assume that the Servicemaster Corp. issues $100,000 in bonds due in five years with 9% interest payable annually at year end when the market rate for such bonds is 11%. The actual principal and interest cash flows are discounted at an 11% rate as follows:

Present value of the principal:
   $a(p_{\overline{5}|11\%})$ = $100,000 (.59345) $59,345.00
Present value of the interest payments:
   $R(P_{\overline{5}|11\%})$ = $9,000 (3.69590)   33,263.10
Combined present value (selling price) $92,608.10

By paying $92,608.10 at the date of issue, the investors will realize an effective yield of 11% over the five-year term of the bonds. These bonds would, therefore, be sold at a discount of $7,391.90, ($100,000 − $92,608.10).[3]

When bonds sell below face value, it means that investors demand a rate of interest higher than the stated rate. The investors are not satisfied with the stated rate because they can earn a greater rate on alternative investments of equal risk. They cannot change the stated rate, and so they refuse to pay the face value for the bonds, opting instead to change the amount invested in order to earn the effective rate of interest. Inasmuch as the company issuing the bonds pays the bondholders cash equal to the stated rate computed on the face value at specified interest dates as well as the face value at maturity, the investors are earning an effective rate that is higher than the stated rate because they paid less than face value for the bonds.

Accounting for Bonds

As indicated in Figure 14-1, accounting for bonds is concerned with recording measured amounts related to the date of issuance, interest dates and year ends, and maturity or extinguishment dates as well as reporting bond-related items appropriately in the financial statements. How this is done is examined in the following paragraphs, which consider the various circumstances that may exist regarding a bond issue.

Bonds Issued at Par on an Interest Date   If bonds are issued on an interest payment date at par (face value), no interest has accrued and no premium or discount exists. The accounting entry is simply made for the cash proceeds and the face value of the bonds. To illustrate, if ten-year bonds of a par value of $800,000, dated January 1, 1986, and bearing interest at an annual rate of 10% payable semiannually on January 1 and July 1, are issued on January 1 at par, the entry on the books of the issuing corporation is:

Cash   800,000
   Bonds Payable   800,000

[3]The price at which the bonds sell is typically stated as a percentage of the face or par value of the bonds. For example, the Servicemaster Corp. bonds above sell for 92.6 (92.6% of par). If Servicemaster has received $102,000, we would say the bonds sell for 102 (102% of par).

The entry to record the first semiannual interest payment of $40,000 ($800,000 × .10 × 1/2) on July 1, would be as follows:

Bond Interest Expense	40,000	
Cash		40,000

If the year end is December 31, then six months' accrued interest would be recorded on that date as follows:

Bond Interest Expense	40,000	
Bond Interest Payable		40,000

On January 1, the interest would be paid and recorded as shown below:

Bond Interest Payable	40,000	
Cash		40,000

Bonds Issued at Discount or Premium on an Interest Date   If the $800,000 of bonds illustrated above were issued on January 1, 1986, at 97, the issuance would be recorded as follows:

Cash ($800,000 × .97)	776,000	
Discount on Bonds Payable	24,000	
Bonds Payable		800,000

The Discount on Bonds Payable does not represent prepaid interest but, because of its relation to interest as previously discussed, **the discount is amortized by a charge to interest expense over the period of time that the bonds are outstanding.** The discount (or premium) may be amortized using the straight-line method or the effective interest method. Under the **straight-line method,** the amount amortized each year is a constant amount. For example, using the above bond issuance at a discount of $24,000, the amount amortized to interest expense each year for ten years is $2,400 ($24,000 ÷ 10 years) and it is recorded annually as follows:

Bond Interest Expense	2,400	
Discount on Bonds Payable		2,400

At the end of the first year, 1986, as a result of the above amortization entry, the unamortized balance in Discount on Bonds Payable account is $21,600 ($24,000 − $2,400). The net charge to Interest Expense for the year would be $82,400 ($40,000 on both July 1 and December 31 as shown previously plus the $2,400 debit to Interest Expense resulting from the discount amortization).

If the bonds were dated and sold on October 1, 1986, with interest dates of October 1 and April 1, and the fiscal year of the corporation ended on December 31, the discount amortized as of December 31, 1986, is only 3/12 of 1/10 of $24,000, or $600. Amortization of this amount and recognition of the accrued interest payable of $20,000 ($800,000 × .10 × 3/12) would result in interest expense of $20,600 for 1986, which would be recorded on December 31 as follows:

Bond Interest Expense	20,600	
Bond Interest Payable		20,000
Discount on Bonds Payable		600

Assuming no reversing entries are made, the entry on April 1, 1987, for the first interest payment would be as follows:

Bond Interest Expense	20,600	
Bond Interest Payable	20,000	
Cash		40,000
Discount on Bonds Payable		600

Premium on Bonds Payable is accounted for in a manner similar to that described for Discount on Bonds Payable. If the ten-year bonds of a par value of $800,000 are sold on January 1, 1986, at 103, then the cash proceeds are $824,000 ($800,000 × 1.03). The entry to record this is:

Cash	824,000	
Bonds Payable		800,000
Premium on Bonds Payable		24,000

Given interest dates of July 1 and January 1, and the company's year end being December 31, the following entries would be made:

July 1, 1986

Bond Interest Expense	38,800	
Premium Bonds Payable	1,200	
Cash		40,000

December 31, 1986

Bonds Interest Expense	38,800	
Premium on Bonds Payable	1,200	
Bond Interest Payable		40,000

January 1, 1987

Bond Interest Payable	40,000	
Cash		40,000

As is evident from these examples, **bond interest expense is increased by amortization of a discount and decreased by amortization of a premium.** Amortization of a discount or premium under the effective interest method will be discussed shortly.

Bonds Issued between Interest Dates   Bond interest payments are usually made semiannually on dates specified in the bond indenture. When bonds are issued on other than the interest payment dates, buyers of the bonds will pay the seller the interest accrued from the last interest payment date to the date of issue. The purchasers of the bonds, in effect, pay the bond issuer in advance for that portion of the full six-month interest payment to which they are not entitled, not having held the bonds during this period. The purchasers will receive the full six-month interest payment on the semiannual interest payment date.

To illustrate, if ten-year bonds of a par value of $800,000, dated January 1, 1986, and bearing interest at an annual rate of 10% payable semiannually on January 1 and July 1, are issued at **par plus accrued interest on March 1, 1986,** the entry on the books of the issuing corporation is (rounding to the nearest dollar):

Cash	813,333	
Bonds Payable		800,000
Bond Interest Expense		13,333
($800,000 × .10 × 2/12)		

The purchaser advances two months' interest, because on July 1, 1986, four months after the date of purchase, six months' interest will be received from the issuing company. The company makes the following entry on July 1, 1986:

Bond Interest Expense	40,000	
Cash		40,000

The expense account now contains a debit balance of $26,667, which represents the proper amount of interest expense, four months at 10% on $800,000. It should be noted that instead of crediting Bond Interest Expense on March 1, a Bond Interest Payable account could have been credited for the $13,333. If this had been the case, the July 1 debit to Bond Interest Expense would have been for $26,667 and the Bond Interest Payable account would have been debited for $13,333.

The above illustration was simplified by having the January 1, 1986, bonds issued on March 1, 1986, **at par.** If, however, these bonds were issued at 102 (a rate that excludes the accrued interest), the entry on March 1 on the books of the issuing corporation would be:

Cash	829,333	
Bonds Payable		800,000
Premium on Bonds Payable		16,000
Bonds Interest Expense (or Interest Payable)		13,333

Since these bonds would mature on January 1, 1996, the period over which the premium would be amortized is 118 months. Therefore, the entry on July 1, 1986, for the interest payment would be:

Bond Interest Expense	39,458	
Premium on Bonds Payable	542	
Cash		40,000

The premium is amortized on a straight-line basis ($16,000 × 4/118 = $542.37, rounded to $542). This amount is deducted from the cash paid to derive the debit amount to interest expense. Considering both the March 1 and July 1 entries, the net amount charged to interest expense for the four months is $26,125 (the July 1 debit for $39,458 less the March 1 credit for $13,333). If Interest Payable had been the account credited on March 1, the July 1 entry would have been:

Bond Interest Expense	26,125	
Bond Interest Payable	13,333	
Premium on Bonds Payable	542	
Cash		40,000

Effective Interest Method

The straight-line method for amortizing a premium or discount results in a constant amount being charged to interest expense for each full year during the life of the bonds. Charging an equal amount to interest expense each year is not conceptually accurate. This is because the relationship of the interest expense to the **carrying value** (face value less discount or plus the premium) of the bonds results in an apparent decrease (in the case of discounts) or increase (for premium situations) in the interest rate for successive years. This phenomenon occurs because, although the interest expense is constant, the carrying value increases each year for discounted bonds and decreases for bonds issued at a premium. The **effective interest method** (also called **present value amortization)** overcomes this problem because it charges to interest expense each year a constant interest rate (the effective rate when the bonds were issued) based on the carrying value of the bonds. Therefore, the interest expense is based on the increasing (for discounts) or decreasing (for premium) carrying value of the bonds. **Under this method the interest cost for each period is the effective interest rate multiplied by the carrying amount (book value) of the bonds at the start of that period. (The carrying amount changes each period by the amount of the amortized discount or premium.)** The amount of amortization of bond discount or premium is the difference between the effective interest expense for the period and the actual interest payments.

Bonds Issued at a Discount   To illustrate amortization of a discount using the effective interest method, assume that Evermaster Corporation issued $100,000 of 8% bonds on January 1, 1986, due on January 1, 1991, with interest payable each July 1 and January 1. Because the investors required effective interest of 10%, they paid $92,278 for the $100,000 of bonds, creating a $7,722 discount. The $7,722 discount is a result of the considerations noted below.

Maturity value of bonds payable		$100,000
Present value of $100,000 due in five years		
at 10%, interest payable semiannually (Table 6-2)	$61,391[4]	
Present value of $4,000 interest payable semiannually		
for five years at 10% annually (Table 6-4)	30,887[4]	
Proceeds from sale of bonds		92,278
Discount on bonds payable		$ 7,722

The five-year amortization schedule appears below.

Schedule of Bond Discount Amortization
Effective Interest Method—Semiannual Interest Payments
5-Year, 8% Bonds Sold to Yield 10%

Date	Credit Cash	Debit Interest Expense	Credit Bond Discount	Carrying Value of Bonds
1/1/86				$ 92,278
7/1/86	$ 4,000[a]	$ 4,614[b]	$ 614[c]	$ 92,892[d]
1/1/87	4,000	4,645	645	93,537
7/1/87	4,000	4,677	677	94,214
1/1/88	4,000	4,711	711	94,925
7/1/88	4,000	4,746	746	95,671
1/1/89	4,000	4,783	783	96,454
7/1/89	4,000	4,823	823	97,277
1/1/90	4,000	4,864	864	98,141
7/1/90	4,000	4,907	907	99,048
1/1/91	4,000	4,952	952	100,000
	$40,000	$47,722	$7,722	

[a]$4,000 = $100,000 × 0.08 × 6/12   [c]$614 = $4,614 − $4,000
[b]$4,614 = $92,278 × 0.10 × 6/12   [d]$92,892 = $92,278 + $614

The entry to record the issuance of Evermaster Corporation's bonds at a discount on January 1, 1986, is:

[4]As determined from present value tables using a 5% rate for ten periods: ($100,000 × 0.61391) and ($4,000 × 7.72173).

Cash	92,278	
Discount on Bonds Payable	7,722	
Bonds Payable		100,000

The journal entry to record the first interest payment and amortization of the discount on July 1, 1986, is:

Bond Interest Expense	4,614	
Discount on Bonds Payable		614
Cash		4,000

Bonds Issued at a Premium If the market had been such that investors were willing to earn an effective interest of 6% on the bond issue described above, they would have paid $108,530 or a premium of $8,530, computed as follows:

Maturity value of bonds payable		$100,000
Present value of $100,000 due in five years at 6%, interest payable semiannually (Table 6-2)	$74,409[5]	
Present value of $4,000 interest payable semi-annually for five years at 6% annually (Table 6-4)	34,121[5]	
Proceeds from sale of bonds		108,530
Premium on bonds payable		$8,530

The five-year amortization schedule appears below.

		Schedule of Bond Premium Amortization		
		Effective Interest Method—Semiannual Interest Payments		
		5-Year, 8% Bonds Sold to Yield 6%		
Date	Credit Cash	Debit Interest Expense	Debit Bond Premium	Carrying Value of Bonds
1/1/86				$108,530
7/1/86	$ 4,000[a]	$ 3,256[b]	$ 744[c]	107,786[d]
1/1/87	4,000	3,234	766	107,020
7/1/87	4,000	3,211	789	106,231
1/1/88	4,000	3,187	813	105,418
7/1/88	4,000	3,162	838	104,580
1/1/89	4,000	3,137	863	103,717
7/1/89	4,000	3,112	888	102,829
1/1/90	4,000	3,085	915	101,914
7/1/90	4,000	3,057	943	100,971
1/1/91	4,000	3,029	971	100,000
	$40,000	$31,470	$8,530	

[a]$4,000 = $100,000 \times 0.08 \times 6/12$
[b]$3,256 = $108,530 \times 0.06 \times 6/12$
[c]$744 = $4,000 - $3,256$
[d]$107,786 = $108,530 - 744

The entry to record the issuance of the Evermaster bonds at a premium on January 1, 1986 is:

Cash	108,530	
Premium on Bonds Payable		8,530
Bonds Payable		100,000

[5]As determined from present value tables using 3% rate for ten periods: ($100,000 × 0.74409) and ($4,000 × 8.53020).

The journal entry to record the first interest payment and amortization of the premium on July 1, 1986, is:

Bond Interest Expense	3,256	
Premium on Bonds Payable	744	
Cash		4,000

Theoretically, a discount or premium should be amortized over the life of the liability in such a way that the interest expense results from applying a **constant rate of interest** to the carrying amount of the debt outstanding at the beginning of the period.[6] Although the effective interest method is the approach to use to accomplish this, the straight-line method may be used in practice on the grounds of expediency and the fact that the results obtained are not materially different from those produced by the effective interest method.

The characteristics of a bond can result in some interesting questions regarding the period over which a premium or discount should be amortized. This is illustrated in the following paragraphs for callable, convertible, and serial bonds.

Some bonds issued are **callable** by the issuer after a certain date at a stated price, so that the issuing corporation may have the opportunity to reduce its bonded indebtedness or take advantage of lower interest rates. Even if bonds are callable, any premium or discount amortization calculations should be based on the life to maturity because early redemption (call of the bonds) is not a certainty.

Also, some bonds may be converted (at the option of the bondholder) into other securities of the corporation during some specified time after issuance. If **convertible bonds** are issued at a discount or premium, it is necessary to amortize the discount or premium on the basis of the maturity date of the issue instead of the conversion date, because it is impossible to predict when, if at all, the conversion privilege will be exercised. Accounting for bond conversions is discussed in Chapter 17.

While an entire bond issue may be due at one maturity date, another approach that may be taken is to have the bonds mature serially; that is, in a series of instalments whereby a specified amount of the bonds issued matures over a specified period of years. Such bonds are called **serial bonds.** Each series of the issue has its own maturity date and stated interest rate.

A serial bond issue may be sold as though each series were a separate bond issue, or it may be sold as a package. Whether sold separately or as a package, one account for the total premium or discount is used in the general ledger for that serial issue. The total premium or discount to be amortized, whether computed for each series separately or for the entire issue, is entered as one amount in the Premium (or Discount) on Bonds Payable account. The accounting for serial bonds is illustrated in Appendix 14A of this chapter.

Balance Sheet Presentation of Unamortized Bond Discount or Premium

Discount on bonds payable is not an asset because it does not provide any future economic benefit. The enterprise has the use of the borrowed funds, but for that use it must pay interest. A bond discount means that the company borrowed less than the face or maturity value of the bond and therefore is faced with an actual (effective) interest rate higher than the stated (nominal) rate. Conceptually, dis-

---

[6]"Interest on Receivables and Payable," *Opinions of the Accounting Principles Board No. 21* (New York: AICPA, 1971), par. 16.

count on bonds payable is a liability valuation account; that is, a reduction of the face or maturity amount of the related liability.

The unamortized portion of premium on bonds payable could be reported in a similar manner. Premium on bonds payable is not itself a liability—it has no existence apart from the related debt. The lower interest costs result because the proceeds of borrowing exceed the face or maturity amount of the debt. Conceptually, premium on bonds payable is a liability valuation account; that is, an addition to the face or maturity amount of the related liability.

In practice, the unamortized portion of a Discount on Bonds Payable has frequently been shown on the balance sheet under Deferred Charges (a separate category under assets or as an item under the heading "Other Assets"). Correspondingly, an unamortized Premium on Bonds Payable has frequently been shown as a deferred credit item under liabilities. This practice tends to obscure the **effective liability** of the bonds by separating the par value from the related discount or premium into different parts of the balance sheet. Consequently, the conceptually correct approach as identified above (showing the unamortized discount or premium as a contra or adjunct account to the maturity value of the bonds) overcomes this criticism. In the United States, *APB Opinion No. 21* requires that bond discount be reported on the balance sheet as a direct deduction from the face amount of the bonds and premiums as a direct addition to the face amount of the bonds.[7] No such decree exists in the *CICA Handbook*, although Section 3070 (on Deferred Charges) states that "major items among the deferred charges should be shown separately (e.g., debt discount and expenses, deferred foreign exchange losses, organization expenses, deferred development costs, and deferred income taxes)." Thus, the *Handbook* recognizes the acceptability of showing bond discounts as deferred charges. One may, however, choose to show discounts and premiums as valuation accounts directly to the face amount of the bonds, the practice preferred by the authors.

When a corporation has numerous bond issues outstanding, each with its own related discount or premium, the total unamortized discount or premium may be shown net at the bottom of a schedule of listed bond issuances. An example of such a disclosure in note form follows:

Note 12—Long-term Debt (First Mortgage Bonds):	
Fixed rate series:	12/31/86
2 7/8% due May 1, 1987	$ 10,000,000
⋮	⋮
8 3/4% due April 15, 2010	37,000,000
Variable rate series:	
Adjustable rate, due December 1, 2001	50,000,000
Floating rate, due June 1, 2010	30,000,000
Total all series	$1,072,165,000
Net unamortized discount	(4,532,000)
	$1,067,633,000
Less: Current portion	(10,365,000)
Long-term bonds outstanding	$1,057,268,000

[7]*Ibid.*

Expenses of Issuing Bonds

The issuance of bonds involves engraving and printing costs, legal and accounting fees, commissions, promotion expenses, and other similar charges. One practice is to merge these items with the discount or premium on bonds, increasing the balance of the discount or decreasing the balance of the premium account, thereby increasing the interest expense over the life of the bonds. This practice relates closely to one of the acceptable treatments put forward by the FASB in *Concepts Statement No. 3,* which takes the position that debt issue cost can be treated as either an expense or a reduction of the related debt liability.[8] Under the latter approach, debt issue cost is not considered an asset for the same reason that debt discount is not; that is, it provides no future economic benefit. The cost of issuing bonds in effect reduces the proceeds from the bonds issued and increases the effective interest rate, and thus may be accounted for in the same way as the unamortized discount.

Alternatively, it is acceptable to debit these debt issue costs to a **deferred charge** account such as Unamortized Bond Issue Costs and amortize them over the life of the debt. Thus this account would appear in the asset section of the balance sheet under the category "Deferred Charges" or "Other Assets." The acceptability of this approach is implied in Section 3070 of the *CICA Handbook,* which indicates that "debt expenses" are an example of Deferred Charges. This procedure is called for in *APB Opinion No. 21* governing U.S. financial reporting.[9] Given this *Opinion's* requirement that discounts be treated as a liability valuation account, it seems clear that it views issue costs as a true deferred charge with characteristics different from those of discounts. It is interesting to note the conflict between the treatment required in *Opinion No. 21* and the concept supported in the FASB's *Concept Statement No. 3.* While the former specifies acceptable GAAP in the U.S.A., the choice of balance sheet presentation in Canada remains, although the tendency is to treat such costs as deferred charges.

To illustrate the accounting for costs of issuing bonds, assume that Microchip Corporation sold $20,000,000 of ten-year debenture bonds for $20,795,000 on January 1, 1986 (also the date of the bonds). Costs of issuing the bonds were $245,000. The entries at January 1, 1986, and December 31, 1986, for issuance of the bonds and amortization of the bond issue costs would be as follows:

	January 1, 1986	
Cash	20,550,000	
Unamortized Bond Issue Costs	245,000	
Premium on Bonds Payable		795,000
Bonds Payable		20,000,000

	December 31, 1986	
Bond Issue Expense	24,500	
Unamortized Bond Issue Costs		24,500
(To amortize one year of bond issue costs—straight-line method)		

While the bond issue costs could be amortized using the effective interest method, the straight-line method is generally used in practice because it is easier and the results are not materially different. The above entries would be made regardless of

[8]"Elements of Financial Statements of Business Enterprises," *Statement of Financial Accounting Concepts No. 3* (Stamford, Conn.: FASB, 1980).

[9]"Interest on Receivables and Payables," *op. cit.,* par. 15.

whether the balance in the Unamortized Bond Issue Costs account was to be shown as a deferred charge or a contra valuation account to the bonds in the balance sheet.

EXTINGUISHMENT OF DEBT

How does the accountant record the payment (often referred to as the extinguishment) of debt? If the bonds (or any other form of debt security) are held to maturity, the answer is relatively straightforward; that is, no gain or loss is computed because the amount of cash required to retire the debt will be equal to its carrying amount. Any premium or discount will have been amortized during the life of the bonds. As a result, the carrying amount will be equal to the maturity or face value of the bonds at that time.

The problems, however, become more complex when the debt is extinguished prior to maturity. Two types of extinguishments are:

1. Reacquisition of debt.
2. In-substance (or economic) defeasance.

Reacquisition of Debt

A reacquisition of debt generally occurs either by payment to the creditor or by reacquisition in the open market. **At the time of reacquisition, the unamortized premium or discount and any costs of issue applicable to the bonds should be amortized up to the reacquisition date.**

The amount paid on extinguishment or redemption before maturity, including any call premium and expense of reacquisition, is called the **reacquisition price.** The **net carrying amount** of the bonds on any specified date is the amount payable at maturity, adjusted for unamortized premium or discount, and the cost of issuance. The difference between the net carrying amount and the reacquisition price is the **gain** or **loss** from extinguishment.

To illustrate, assume that General Bell Corp. issues bonds of a par value of $800,000 due in twenty years, on January 1, 1986, at 97. Bond issue costs totalling $16,000 were incurred. Ten years after the issue date, the entire issue is redeemed at 101 and cancelled. The loss on redemption is computed as follows (straight-line amortization is used for simplicity):

Reacquisition price $\left(\$800,000 \times \dfrac{101}{100}\right)$		$808,000
Net carrying amount of bonds redeemed:		
Face value	$800,000	
Unamortized discount ($24,000 × 10/20)	(12,000)	
Unamortized issue costs ($16,000 × 10/20)		
(both amortized using straight-line basis)	(8,000)	780,000
Loss on redemption		$ 28,000

The entry to record the reacquisition and cancellation of the bonds is:

Bonds Payable	800,000	
Loss on Redemption of Bonds	28,000	
Discount on Bonds Payable		12,000
Unamortized Bond Issue Costs		8,000
Cash		808,000

In some cases, bonds may be reacquired by the issuing corporation or its agent or trustee but not formally cancelled. These are known as **treasury bonds** for the issuing corporation. If the above bonds had been required to be held in treasury, the entry to record the transaction could be the same as shown, except the debit to Bonds Payable may be to an account titled Treasury Bonds. The treasury bonds would then be shown on the balance sheet at their face value as a deduction from the bonds payable issued to arrive at a net figure representing bonds payable outstanding. When they are sold or cancelled, the Treasury Bonds account would be credited.

The issuer of callable bonds is generally required to exercise the call on an interest date. Therefore, the amortization of any discount or premium will be up-to-date, and there will be no accrued interest. However, early extinguishments through purchases of bonds in the open market are more likely to be on other than an interest date. If the purchase is not made on an interest date, the discount or premium must be amortized and the interest payable must be accrued from the last interest date to the date of purchase.

It is often advantageous for the issuing corporation to acquire the entire bond issue outstanding and replace it with a new bond issue bearing a lower rate of interest. The replacement of an existing issuance with a new one is called **refunding.** If refunding takes place prior to the maturity date of a bond issue, a difference between the fair market value of the new bonds issued and the net carrying amount of the refunded issue is likely to result. When this occurs, there are three alternative approaches to accounting for the amount of the difference:

1. Treat it as a loss on bond refunding in the current year's income statement.
2. Amortize it over the remaining life of the bonds that have been refunded.
3. Amortize it over the life of the new bonds issued.

In Canada, the choice of approach is left to judgement, as the *CICA Handbook* contains no recommendations concerning a preference. In the United States only the first alternative is permitted. In accordance with *APB Opinion No. 26*, a gain or loss resulting from early extinguishment of a debt may not be amortized to future periods. This conclusion is based on the opinion that differing reasons for early redemption or differing means by which the bonds are redeemed have no bearing on how to account for the loss or gain.[10]

In-substance Defeasance

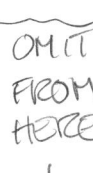
OMIT FROM HERE

Another form of extinguishment emerging particularly in the U.S.A. is referred to as in-substance defeasance. **In-substance defeasance** is an arrangement whereby a company provides for the future repayment of one or more of its long-term debt issues by placing in an irrevocable trust purchased securities, the principal and interest of which are pledged to pay off the interest and principal on its own debt securities as they mature. As such, the company can, in effect, be released economically (although not necessarily legally) from being the primary obligor under the debt which is still outstanding.[11] In some cases, the debt holders are not aware of the transaction and continue to look to the company for repayment.

---

[10]"Early Extinguishment of Debt," *Opinions of the Accounting Principles Board No. 26* (New York: AICPA, 1972), par. 20.

[11]**Legal defeasance** is the release of a debtor from legal liability.

There are several reasons for executing such a transaction. First, the debt obligation may be removed from the balance sheet without actually being purchased. Actual purchase is sometimes a problem because (1) it may be costly as a high call premium is required to be paid, or (2) much of the debt is publicly held and is difficult to buy back in large quantities. Second, because the cost of the purchased securities is usually less than the book value of the company's debt (as interest rates rise, the fair value of the outstanding debt decreases), the company records a gain on its income statement.

To illustrate, in 1982 Exxon placed in trust six of its own bond issues totalling $515 million; the trust purchased $313 million in government securities to service the bond interest and principal. The government securities generated sufficient interest to pay the accrued interest and maturing principal on the bonds. Exxon removed the $515 million bond debt from its balance sheet and reported a sizable gain.

The FASB issued *Statement No. 76* as its prescription for accounting for these in-substance defeasance transactions. To be considered a debt extinguishment (justifying removal of the debt obligation from the balance sheet), the FASB ruled that the debtor must place cash or risk-free securities (those issued or backed by the U.S. government) in an irrevocable trust to be used solely for satisfying the interest and principal of the debt. Also, the possibility that the debtor will be required to make any future payments with respect to the debt must be remote.[12]

This standard is controversial and has been subjected to much criticism. Dissenters from the *Statement* believe that gain or loss recognition should not be extended to situations wherein the debtor is not legally released from being the primary obligor of the debt. They contend that "the setting aside of assets in trust does not, in and of itself, constitute either the disposition of assets with potential gain or loss recognition or the satisfaction of a liability with potential gain or loss recognition."[13] In other words, committing specific assets to a single purpose might ensure that the debt is serviced in timely fashion, but that event alone just matches up cash flows; it does not satisfy, eliminate, or extinguish the obligation. For a debt to be satisfied, the creditor must be satisfied, which is not the case in an in-substance defeasance. Supporters of the *Statement* believe that the effect of an in-substance defeasance is essentially the same as a settlement in cash. Further, they believe that the liability should be removed from the balance sheet, because placing sufficient risk-free assets irrevocably in trust lessens the likelihood of the debtor having to make additional future payments.

Where in-substance defeasance is permitted, the accounting for the extinguishment is the same as for other types of reacquisition. Differing reasons for extinguishment or differing means by which the bonds are redeemed have no bearing on how to account for the loss or gain.[14]

---

[12]Owing to differences in interest rates in different world financing markets, it is possible for a company to borrow at one interest rate and concurrently invest in essentially risk-free assets that yield a higher rate. Immediately placing such assets in an irrevocable trust effects what is referred to as **instantaneous in-substance defeasance.** The U.S. profession does not permit extinguishment of debt through instantaneous defeasance. *FASB Statement No. 76* applies only to the in-substance defeasance of previously outstanding debt, not to newly issued debt. Instantaneous defeasance is accounted for as a borrowing and an investment, not an extinguishment. See "In-Substance Defeasance of Debt," *FASB Technical Bulletin No. 84-4* (Stamford, Conn.: FASB, 1984).

[13]"Extinguishment of Debt," *Statement of Financial Accounting Standards No. 76* (Stamford, Conn.: FASB, 1983), p. 5.

[14]"Early Extinguishment of Debt," *op. cit.*, par. 26.

Reporting Gains and Losses

Once a gain or loss on redemption of bonds has been recorded, the question of where it should be reported in the income statement must be resolved. The *CICA Handbook* states:

> Income before extraordinary items may include gains and losses on the disposal of nonfund assets or the settlement of nonfund liabilities (e.g., gains or losses on sale of fixed assets or the retirement of long-term debt at a discount or premium).[15]

This clearly allows such gains or losses to be shown (perhaps designated as unusual) as a component of income before extraordinary items. Alternatively, reporting such gains and losses as extraordinary items would occur if they satisfy the Canadian criteria for such classification.

Treatment as an extraordinary item, with certain accompanying disclosures, is required in the United States, whether an extinguishment is early, at scheduled maturity date, or later—without regard to the criteria of "unusual nature" and "infrequency of occurrence."[16]

IMPLICIT INTEREST ON LONG-TERM DEBT

Business transactions often involve the exchange of notes or similar instruments for cash or property, goods, or services. If the note is not currently receivable or payable, the transaction is in effect a long-term loan or liability with interest as an inherent and natural ingredient. It is unrealistic and improbable for any business to lend money interest free. Yet, in the past, numerous business transactions that were material in amount were consummated either with no apparent interest or with a very low interest cost.

While there is no reference in the *CICA Handbook* covering such situations, *APB Opinion No. 21* was issued in the United States to identify the accounting for transactions where the form does not reflect the economic substance of the arrangement because of failure to provide for a realistic interest rate on monies payable or receivable in the future. Whenever the face amount of the instrument (notes, bonds, mortgage notes, equipment obligations, and long-term accounts payable) does not reasonably represent the present value of the consideration given or received in the exchange, the accountant must evaluate the entire arrangement to determine the amounts involved for properly recording the exchange and subsequent related interest. This circumstance is most apparent when the note is noninterest bearing, or has a stated interest rate that is different from the rate of interest appropriate for the transaction at the date of occurrence. Unless such notes are recorded at present value, the purchase price and cost of property to the buyer (issuing the note) and the sales price and profit to the seller (accepting the note) in the year of the transaction are misstated. In addition, the interest expense and interest revenue in subsequent periods are also misstated. Examples requiring the accounting recognition of implicit interest are given in the following section on long-term notes payable.

---

[15]*CICA Handbook*, Section 1540, par. 26.

[16]"Reporting Gains and Losses from Extinguishment of Debt," *Statement of Financial Accounting Standards No. 4* (Stamford, Conn.: FASB, 1975), par. 8.

LONG-TERM NOTES PAYABLE

The difference between a current note payable and a long-term note payable is the maturity date. As discussed in Chapter 13, short-term notes payable are expected to be paid within a year or the operating cycle, whichever is longer. Long-term notes are similar in substance to a bond in that both have fixed maturity dates and carry either a stated or implicit interest rate. However, notes do not trade as readily as bonds in the organized public securities markets. Noncorporate and smaller corporate enterprises tend to issue notes as their long-term instruments, while larger-sized corporations issue both long-term notes and bonds.

Accounting for notes and bonds is quite similar. Like a bond, a note is valued at the present value of its future cash flows (interest and principal amount) with any discount or premium being amortized over the life of the note, using the effective interest or straight-line method. Determining the proper interest rate for valuation of a long-term note can be the most difficult aspect in accounting for notes.

Accounting for long-term notes will be examined under the following headings:

1. Notes issued solely for cash.
2. Notes issued for cash, but with some right or privilege also being exchanged.
3. Notes issued in a noncash exchange for property, goods, or services.

As you might expect, accounting for long-term notes payable parallels accounting for long-term notes receivable as presented in Chapter 7.

Notes Issued Solely for Cash

When the effective interest on a note is equal to its stated rate, the note sells at its face value. When the stated rate is different from the effective interest, the cash proceeds will be different from the face value of the note. As indicated earlier, the difference between the face value and the cash proceeds received is a discount or a premium that should be amortized over the life of a note.

When a note is issued solely for cash, the total interest expense is equal to the interest paid based on the stated rate times the face amount plus any discount or minus any premium. In such situations, the effective interest rate can be calculated by determining the interest rate which equates the amount of cash presently received with the present value of amounts (interest and principal) to be paid in the future.

An example of such a transaction is Beneficial Corporation's 1982 offering of $150 million of zero-coupon notes having a 1990 maturity date. With a face value of $1,000 each, these notes sold for $327—a deep discount of $673 each. Beneficial amortizes the discount over the eight-year life of the notes, using an effective interest rate of 15%. The present value of each note is the cash proceeds of $327, and the 15% effective interest rate is that rate which equates the $1,000 maturity value to be received in eight years to these proceeds.[17]

---

[17]Derived using the Present Value of an Amount of 1 Table at the end of Chapter 6:

$327 = \$1,000\, P_{\overline{8}|i}$

$P_{\overline{8}|i} = \$327/\$1,000 = .327$

$.327 = 15\%$ column interest rate at the 8-period row.

Notes Exchanged for Cash and Some Right or Privilege

Sometimes when a note is issued, additional rights or privileges are given to the recipient of the note. For example, a corporation may receive cash and issue a noninterest-bearing note payable that is to be repaid over five years with no stated interest, and in exchange agree to sell merchandise to the lender at less than the prevailing prices of its merchandise. As is typical of situations where no Canadian pronouncements exist, judgement must be applied. In this circumstance, the difference between the present value of the payable and the amount of cash received could be recorded by the issuer of the note (borrower/supplier) simultaneously as a discount (debit) on the note and as unearned revenue (credit) on the future sales. The discount would be amortized as a charge to interest expense over the life of the note. The unearned revenue, equal in amount to the discount, reflects a partial prepayment for sales transactions that will occur over the next five years. This unearned revenue would be recognized as revenue when sales are made to the lender over the next five years.

For example, assume that a company receives $100,000 cash in exchange for a five-year, noninterest-bearing note with a face or maturity value of $100,000. The appropriate rate at which to impute interest is determined to be 10% (i.e., the going market rate to the company for borrowing). Also, the conditions of the note provide that the recipient of the note (lender/customer) can purchase $500,000 of merchandise from the issuer of the note (borrower/supplier) at 88% of regular selling price over the next five years. To record the loan, the issuer of the note records a discount of $37,908, the difference between the $100,000 face amount of the loan and its present value of $62,092 ($100,000 × .62092 the present value factor for 5 years at 10% from Table 6-2). As the supplier of the merchandise, the issuer also records a credit to unearned revenue of $37,908. The issuer's journal entry is:

Cash	100,000	
Discount on Notes Payable	37,908	
Notes Payable		100,000
Unearned Revenue		37,908

The Discount on Notes Payable is subsequently amortized to interest expense using the effective interest or straight-line method. The Unearned Revenue is recognized as revenue from the sale of merchandise and is prorated on the same basis that each period's sales to the lender-customer bear to the total sales to that customer for the term of the note. In this situation the write-off of the discount and the recognition of the unearned revenue are at different rates.

Noncash Transactions

The third type of situation involves the issuance of a note for some noncash consideration, such as property, goods, or services. When the debt instrument is exchanged for property, goods, or services in a bargained transaction entered into at arm's length, the stated interest rate is presumed to be fair unless:

1. No interest rate is stated, or
2. The stated interest rate is unreasonable, or
3. The stated face amount of the debt instrument is materially different from the current cash sales price for the same or similar items or from the current market value of the debt instrument.

In these circumstances the present value of the debt instrument is measured by the fair value of the property, goods, or services or by an amount that reasonably approximates the market value of the note.[18] An implicit interest factor other than that reflected in the stated rate of interest, if such exists, is evidenced by any difference between the face amount of the note and the fair value of the property, goods, or services received.

For example, assume that Property Development Company sold land having a fair market value of $200,000 to Health Spa, Inc., in exchange for Health Spa's five-year, $293,860 noninterest-bearing note. The $200,000 represents the present value of the $293,860 note discounted at 8% for five years. If the transaction is recorded on the sale date at the face amount of the note by both parties, Health Spa's land account and Property's sales would be overstated by $93,860. This represents the interest for five years at an effective rate of 8%. Interest revenue to Property and interest expense to Health Spa for the five-year period correspondingly would be understated by $93,860.

The difference between the fair market value and the face amount of the note represents interest; therefore, the transaction is recorded at the exchange date as follows:

Entries for Noncash Note Transactions				
Health Spa, Inc. Books		Property Development Company Books		
Land	200,000	Notes Receivable	293,860	
Discount on Notes Payable	93,860	Discount on Notes Receivable		93,860
Notes Payable	293,860	Sales		200,000

During the five-year life of the note, Health Spa would amortize annually the discount as a charge to interest expense. Property Development would record interest revenue totalling $93,860 over the five-year period also by amortizing the discount. The effective interest method is appropriate, although the straight-line method may be used if the results obtained are not materially different.

Imputing an Interest Rate

In each of the previously illustrated situations, the effective or real interest rate was evident or determinable by other factors involved in the exchange, such as the fair market value of what was either given or received; but, if the fair value of the property, goods, or services is not determinable and if the debt instrument has no ready market, the problem of determining the present value of the debt instrument is more difficult. To estimate the present value of a debt instrument under such circumstances, an applicable interest rate is approximated that may differ from the stated interest rate. As previously discussed in regard to notes receivable, this process of interest rate approximation is called **imputation,** and the resulting interest rate is called an **imputed interest rate.** The imputed interest rate is used to establish the present value of the debt instrument by discounting, at that rate, all future payments on the debt instrument.

The choice of a rate requires the exercise of judgement, considering such factors

---

[18]"Interest on Receivables and Payables," *op. cit.,* par. 12.

as the credit standing of the issuer, restrictive covenants, the collateral, payments and other terms pertaining to the debt, and the existing prime interest rate. **Determination of the imputed interest rate is made at the time the debt instrument is issued; any subsequent changes in prevailing interest rates are ignored.**

The valuation of the note at the date of issuance using the imputed interest rate and the accounting entries at the date of issuance and for the interest and amortization of any discount or premium are illustrated in Chapter 7, pages 333–338. The balance sheet classification of a long-term note and any related discount or premium is similar to that for bonds.

MORTGAGE NOTES PAYABLE

The most common form of long-term note payable is a mortgage note payable. A **mortgage note payable** is a promissory note secured by a document called a mortgage that pledges title to property as security for the loan. Mortgage notes payable tend to be used more frequently by proprietorships and partnerships than by corporations, as corporations usually find that bond issues offer advantages in obtaining large loans.

On the balance sheet, the liability should be reported using a title such as ''Mortgage Notes Payable'' or ''Notes Payable—Secured,'' with a brief disclosure of the property pledged in notes to the financial statements.

Mortgages may be payable in full at maturity or in instalments over the life of the loan. If payable at maturity, the mortgage payable is shown as a long-term liability on the balance sheet until such time as the approaching maturity date warrants showing it as a current liability. If it is payable in instalments, the current instalments due are shown as current liabilities, with the remainder shown as a long-term liability.

SHORT-TERM OBLIGATIONS EXPECTED TO BE REFINANCED

Some short-term obligations are often expected to be refinanced on a long-term basis. While an enterprise may intend to refinance the obligations on a long-term basis, and can demonstrate an ability to consummate the refinancing, the *CICA Handbook* requires that a contractual arrangement must exist regarding the refinancing before such items can be reported as noncurrent liabilities.[19]

OFF-BALANCE SHEET FINANCING

OMIT FROM HERE

An issue of extreme importance to accountants is the question of off-balance sheet financing. **Off-balance sheet financing** is an attempt to borrow monies and to do it so that the obligations are not recorded. As was once noted, ''The basic drives of humans are few: to get enough food, to find shelter, and to keep debt off the balance sheet.''

Up to this point, we have discussed two off-balance sheet techniques:

Sales of receivables with recourse—Chapter 7 discussed transfers of receivables to third parties. It was noted that where the third party (buyer of the receivables) has full or partial recourse, the transaction may either be a sale or borrowing

---

[19]*CICA Handbook*, Section 1510, par. 6.

depending on the facts. When it is deemed to be a sale, no liability is reported on the balance sheet.

Product financing arrangements—In Chapter 8 it was noted that enterprises sometimes become involved in product financing arrangements in an attempt to generate income and to borrow monies without reporting the related borrowing on the financial statement. While this practice is no longer permitted in the U.S. (companies must report this type of arrangement as a liability), the Canadian practitioner must rely on professional judgement to assess the arguments regarding "substance over form" when determining how such arrangements will be reported. This challenge to the Canadian practitioner generally applies to many off-balance sheet activities.

Three additional off-balance sheet techniques are covered below:

1. Research and Development Arrangements
2. Project Financing Arrangements
3. Captive Finance Companies

In subsequent chapters, other off-balance sheet financing transactions (leasing and pensions) are examined.

Research and Development Arrangements

An interesting problem has recently developed in practice regarding the financing of R&D costs through innovative financing arrangements. To illustrate, assume that Helio Netics Corp. (HNC) needs $20 million to continue research on its photovoltaic (solar electric) cell. A limited partnership is established to raise the needed $20 million with the R&D being done by HNC. The limited partnership is granted the right to receive royalties on the future sale of the solar panels. The accounting question is: How should HNC account for this arrangement (in terms of the cash from the partnership and the expenditures incurred for R&D)? One view is that the limited partners simply lent money to HNC, which subsequently used it to finance its R&D activities. If such a view is adopted, R&D is reported as an expense on HNC's books along with a liability for the loan. Conversely, others argue that the R&D activities are those of the limited partnership (a separate enterprise). In this case, HNC reports neither the R&D expense nor the related liability, but instead provides note disclosure of the arrangement. From the perspective of HNC, the accounting treatment makes a substantial difference. Under one situation an expense and liability are reported; in the other, only a note is presented.

The accounting issue for HNC relates specifically to the question of whether or not the particular financing arrangement (the limited partnership) results in a separate accounting entity in substance. While the *CICA Handbook* does deal with accounting for research and development costs of a company (Section 3450 excludes R&D conducted for others under contract), it does not specify that R&D under such an arrangement is, in fact, that of HNC. Consequently, judgement is required to solve the problem.

In the U.S. the FASB, in *Statement No. 68*, "Research and Development Arrangements, " has taken the position that, to the extent that an enterprise is obligated to repay other parties for monies received, a liability and related charge to research and development expense should be estimated and recorded.[20] For

---

[20]"Research and Development Arrangements," *Statement of Financial Accounting Standards No. 68* (Stamford, Conn.: FASB, 1982), par. 5.

example, if HNC guarantees payments to the limited partnership, irrespective of the success of the project, the expense and related liability should be reported on the books of HNC.[21] Conversely, in the above situation if the risks associated with the R&D activities are with the limited partnership, then the debt and related expense need not be reported on HNC's books.

Project Financing Arrangements

In addition to product financing arrangements, companies also become involved in a variety of long-term commitments typically associated with project financing arrangements. **Project financing arrangements** arise when (1) two or more entities form another entity to construct an operating plant that will be used by both parties; (2) the new entity borrows funds to construct the project and repays the debt from the proceeds received from the project; (3) payment of the debt is guaranteed by the companies that formed the new entity. The advantage of such an arrangement is that the companies that formed the new entity do not have to report the liability on their books. To illustrate, assume that Dome Petroleum and Imperial Oil each put up $1 million and form a separate company to build a chemical plant to be used by both companies. The newly formed company borrows $48 million to construct the plant. In this way neither Dome nor Imperial reports the debt on their balance sheet—their only disclosure is the guarantee of the payment of the debt of the new company in case the proceeds from the project are insufficient to cover the debt service requirements.[22]

In some cases, these project financing arrangements become more formalized through the use of take-or-pay contracts, through-put contracts, or similar types of contracts. In a simple **take-or-pay contract,** a purchaser of goods signs an agreement with a seller to pay specified amounts periodically in return for products or services. The purchaser must make specified minimum payments even if delivery of the contracted products or services is not taken. Often these take-or-pay contracts are associated with project financing arrangements. For example, in the illustration above, Dome and Imperial could sign an agreement that they will purchase products from this new plant and that they will make certain minimum payments even if they do not take delivery of the goods.

Through-put agreements are similar in concept to take-or-pay contracts, except that a service instead of a product is provided by the asset under construction. For example, assume that Dome and Imperial become involved in a project financing arrangement to build a pipeline (instead of a plant) to transport their various products. An agreement is signed that requires each to pay specified amounts in return for the transportation of the product. In addition, these companies are obliged to provide specified minimum quantities to be transported in each period and are required to make cash payments even if they do not provide the minimum quantities to be transported.

---

[21]Some argued to the FASB that, as *Statement No. 68* was being implemented, many companies would no longer fund R&D in this manner. Thus, R&D expenditure would be reduced, which would hinder technological growth in the United States (an economic consequence argument). This example highlights both the complexity of accounting for R&D costs and the potential effect that the method of reporting these costs can have on the behaviour of corporate management.

[22]*CICA Handbook,* Section 3290. It should also be noted that, by the nature of particular agreements, such arrangements may, in fact, become joint ventures, in which case the recommendations of Section 3055 of the *Handbook* would apply.

Inconsistent methods have been used in practice to account for and disclose the unconditional obligation in a take-or-pay or through-put contract involved in a project financing arrangement. In general, most companies have attempted to develop these types of contracts to "get the debt off the balance sheet." Only in unusual situations would the acquisition of an asset and the incurrence of a liability have been reported on the balance sheet of the unconditionally obligated company. The only guidance provided in the *CICA Handbook*, Section 3280, is the recommendation that particulars of contractual obligations that are significant be disclosed. The method of such disclosures is left to judgement.

Captive Finance Companies

Companies often have created wholly owned subsidiaries to serve as vehicles for financing their operations. For example, General Motors Corp. has its General Motors Acceptance Corp. (GMAC), and Chrysler Corporation has its Chrysler Finance Corporation (CFC). These companies, often referred to as "captive" finance companies, usually assume a certain amount of receivables and debt at their inception. Subsequently, the captive finance company buys receivables from the major company and issues debt to fund the purchase. The question is whether these captive finance companies should be combined (consolidated) with the major company for financial reporting purposes.

Presently, these companies are usually not consolidated on the theory that combining such dissimilar entities as a manufacturing and financing operation will distort the financial statements and be misleading. Some would disagree with this, noting that the balance sheet of a company with a captive finance subsidiary that is not consolidated is not comparable to the balance sheet of a company that finances its own receivables. At this point, standard setters have not provided guidelines regarding solutions to such arrangements.

Rationale for Off-Balance Sheet Financing

The reasons for off-balance sheet financing are manifold. First, removing debt or otherwise keeping it from the balance sheet may enhance the quality of the balance sheet and permit credit to be obtained more readily or at less costly amounts. Second, loan covenants often impose a limitation on the amount of debt a company may have. As a result, off-balance sheet financing is used because these types of commitments might not be considered. Third, it is argued by some that the asset side of the balance sheet is severely understated. For example, companies that use LIFO inventories and depreciate assets on an accelerated basis will often have carrying amounts for inventories and property, plant, and equipment that are much lower than their current values. As an offset to these lower values, companies are tempted to use off-balance sheet financing to counteract the apparently high debt levels that would appear if such actions were not taken. In other words, if assets were reported at current values, then less pressure would exist for off-balance sheet financing arrangements.

Whether the above arguments have merit is debatable. The general idea "out of sight, out of mind" may not be true because many users of financial statements indicate that they factor off-balance sheet financing into their decisions when assessing debt-to-equity relationships. Similarly, many loan covenants do attempt to factor in these complex arrangements. Nevertheless, many managers believe that benefits will accrue to the company if these obligations are not reported on the balance sheet.

REPORTING LONG-TERM DEBT

Section 3210 of the *CICA Handbook* contains the following recommendations regarding presentations of long-term debt in the financial statements:

- For bonds, debentures, and similar securities, the title of the issue, the interest rate, maturity date, amount outstanding, and the existence of sinking fund, redemption, and conversion provisions should be disclosed. For mortgages and other long-term debt, similar particulars should be provided to the extent practical.
- The aggregate amount of payments estimated to be required in each of the next five years to meet sinking fund or retirement provisions should be disclosed.
- Any portion of long-term debt obligation payable within a year out of current funds should be included in current liabilities.
- Any of the company's own securities purchased and not yet cancelled should be shown separately as a deduction from the relative liability.
- Where long-term debt is payable in a currency other than that in which the balance sheet is stated, the currency in which the long-term debt is payable should be indicated. Where the carrying value differs from the liability translated at the rate of exchange prevailing at the date of the balance sheet, the amount of any significant difference should be disclosed.
- If any of the liabilities are secured, they should be stated separately and the fact that they are secured should be indicated.
- The details of any defaults of the company in principal, interest, sinking fund, or redemption provisions with respect to any outstanding obligation should be disclosed.
- The income statement should distinguish interest on indebtedness initially incurred for a term of more than one year (including the amortization of debt discount or premium and issue expenses).

Companies that have large amounts and numerous issues of long-term debt frequently report only one amount in the balance sheet and support this with comments and schedules in the accompanying notes. These note disclosures generally meet and often exceed the requirements of the *Handbook*. The illustrations on pages 666 and 667, drawn from financial statements of Canadian companies, provide examples of such reporting. Also, see Note 9 in the financial statements of Indal Limited in Appendix 5A.

The variety and complexity of long-term debt arrangements have grown considerably with the consequence that many accounting and reporting problems are emerging. Some believe the use of off-balance sheet financing to be one of the major financial reporting issues facing the accounting profession today. Likely many other problems associated with long-term debt will come forth. Resolving such issues will not be easy, as our understanding of long-term liabilities and the components of a conceptual framework to guide accounting are sufficiently imprecise that arguments can always be made for accounting or not accounting for an item in a particular manner. Therefore, sound judgement must continue to prevail in deciding upon such things as ''substance over form'' when reporting relevant and reliable information on particular situations to users of the financial statements.

Inglis Ltd.

Balance Sheet—current liabilities	(in thousands)	
	1982	1981
Current portion of long-term debt (Note 5)	1,700	850

Balance Sheet	1982	1981
Long-term debt less current portion (Note 5)	24,990	10,300

Note to financial statements

5.   Long-term debt

	(in thousands)	
	1982	1981
11% secured sinking fund debentures, Series "A" due $1,700,000 annually from 1983 to 1987 and $1,800,000 at maturity in 1988	$10,300	$11,150
12 1/4% convertible redeemable debenture, due 1987	7,000	
Mortgages, due 1984, with interest at 2% below prime	6,600	
Government of Canada noninterest-bearing capital assistance loans due 1985 to 1990	1,790	
Ontario Development Corporation debenture, interest free to 1984 and at 16 1/2% for 1985, due 1984 and 1985	1,000	
	26,690	11,150
Less current portion	1,700	850
	$24,990	$10,300

Security for long-term debt is set out below:
(a) First fixed charges on certain lands, buildings, machinery, and equipment to secure the 11% debentures, the 12 1/4% debenture, and the mortgages; and
(b) First and second floating charges on all property and assets to secure the 11% debentures and the Ontario Development Corporation debenture respectively.

In addition, the trust indenture for the 11% debenture includes provisions relating to the level of working capital and restrictions on payment of dividends. As at December 31, 1982, dividends of up to $11,500,00 could be distributed.

The 12 1/4% debenture carries an option, effective March 27, 1983, to convert the principal into common shares at a price of $29.41 per common share. The debenture may be redeemed by the Company at any time.

Repayments on long-term debt are as follows: 1984—$8,383,000; 1985—$2,885,000; 1986—$2,058,000; 1987—$9,058,000, and $2,606,000 thereafter.

KEY POINTS

1.   Long-term debt consists of probable future sacrifices of economic resources arising from present obligations that are not payable within the operating cycle, or within a year if there are several operating cycles within one year.

Dofasco Inc. (note regarding long-term debt)

(5) Long-term liabilities

	(in thousands)	
	1982	1981
Debt		
Sinking fund debentures—		
6 1/2% due May 15, 1987	$ 18,480	$ 19,670
9% due February 1, 1991	33,516	35,519
10% due June 1, 1994	36,331	38,556
10 7/8% due May 15, 1995	46,748	49,236
10 3/8% due March 15, 1996	48,748	51,877
9 3/8% due February 15, 1997	70,690	72,233
17% due May 1, 1997	60,000	—
13 1/2% due November 1, 2000	50,794	53,302
Eveleth Expansion Company first mortgage bonds		
(proportionate share)—		
9 1/2% due 1995		
(U.S. $22,880,000)	23,353	25,093
10% due 1995		
(U.S. $5,658,000)	5,577	6,006
Baycoat Limited first mortgage		
(proportionate share)—		
12% due July 1, 1983	94	187
Total long term debt at December 31	394,331	351,679
Less: Current requirements	2,269	2,262
	392,062	349,417
Accrued liability for relining blast furnace		
beyond one year	38,339	23,343
	$430,401	$372,760

Requirements for repayment of long-term debt within the next five years are as follows:

1983—$ 2,269,000; 1984—$ 2,180,000;
1985—$15,837,000; 1986—$20,231,000;
1987—$37,239,000.

The Corporation has revolving bank credit available until December 31, 1991, in the amount of $150,000,000 in Canadian funds plus an additional $50,000,000 in either Canadian or U.S. funds. Interest is at the rate of 3/8 of 1% above the prime commercial rate. During 1982 none of the revolving bank credit was used.

If the Eveleth Expansion Company first mortgage bonds were translated into Canadian dollars at the year-end rate of exchange, the long-term portion of this debt, outstanding at December 31, 1982, would increase by $5,614,000. This is not necessarily indicative of the amount which will be repaid when these obligations are retired.

2. A long-term debt usually has a specified maturity date, at which time the face value must be paid. Such debt normally bears an interest cost that must be paid periodically. A debt instrument confers no voting rights on the owner in most circumstances. These characteristics distinguish long-term debt financing from ownership equity financing, although the differences can become hazy in some situations.

3. Bonds payable can have a variety of characteristics. The particular characteristics of an issue are specified in a contract known as an indenture. Such

characteristics are concerned with security provided, term to maturity, conversion rights, transferability, interest rates and dates, and call privileges.

4. Considerable time, effort, and cost may be incurred in order to plan and prepare bonds for issuance. Accounting for and reporting of bonds begins at the time of issuance, flows through the life of the bonds in terms of interest payments and accruals, and ends when the bonds mature or are otherwise extinguished.

5. Issuance of bonds requires appropriate recognition of the liability, any discount or premium, and any accrual of interest since the last interest date.

6. Interest expense related to bonds is recorded on each interest date and at year end, if other than an interest date. Determination of the interest expense reflects an appropriate amortization of any premium or discount on the bonds. The effective interest method for amortizing a premium or discount is theoretically superior to the straight-line method because it results in interest expense being a constant rate multiplied by the carrying value of the debt at the beginning of the period. The straight-line method is simpler and can be used if its results do not differ materially from those of the effective interest method.

7. Extinguishment of debt results in the removal of the liability and any related accounts from the records in proportion to the amount of the debt extinguished. At this time, any discount, premium, or issue costs applicable to the debt should be amortized up to the extinguishment date. Removal of the liability and related accounts may result in a gain or loss which would likely be shown on the income statement as a component of income before extraordinary items.

8. Long-term notes payable are similar in substance to bonds in terms of having a fixed maturity date and an interest rate. As such, they are accounted for in a similar manner. This chapter illustrated particular situations involving the issuance of notes for cash, cash and some future right or privilege, and in noncash exchanges. Mortgages are a common form of long-term notes payable.

9. Off-balance sheet financing represents a significant challenge to accountants and management in terms of reporting information that is relevant to financial statement users. Essentially, such financing arrangements enable the borrowing of monies in such a way that one can argue that the obligation need not be reported as a liability in the body of the financial statements. Examples identified in this chapter were research and development arrangements, project financing arrangements, and captive finance companies.

10. Reporting of long-term debt in financial statements generally requires an indication of the nature of the liabilities, maturity dates, interest rates, call provisions, conversion privileges, restrictions imposed by the borrower, and assets pledged as security. Disclosure of such information is usually done in the notes. Long-term debt that matures within one year should be reported as a current liability, unless retirement is to be accomplished with other than current assets. If the debt is to be financed, converted into shares, or is to be retired from a bond retirement fund, it should continue to be reported as noncurrent and accompanied with a note explaining the method to be used in its liquidation.

APPENDIX

14A

ILLUSTRATION OF SERIAL BOND AMORTIZATION AND REDEMPTION BEFORE MATURITY

As mentioned in the chapter, a serial bond issue may be sold as though each series were a separate bond issue, or it may be sold as a package. Whether sold separately or as a package, one account for the total premium or discount is used in the general ledger for that serial issue. The total premium or discount to be amortized, whether computed for each series separately or for the entire issue, is entered as one amount in the Premium (or Discount) on Bonds Payable account. **The straight-line, bonds outstanding, or effective interest methods may be used to amortize the premium or discount.**

The following comprehensive illustration demonstrates (1) the amortization of a premium or discount on serial bonds using the straight-line, bonds outstanding, and effective interest methods; and (2) the accounting for redemption of serial bonds before maturity under all three methods of amortization.

AMORTIZATION OF A PREMIUM OR DISCOUNT ON SERIAL BONDS

A serial bond issue in the amount of $1,000,000, dated January 1, 1986, bearing 8% interest payable at December 31 each year, is sold by Yorkville School Products to yield 9% per annum; the bonds mature in the amount of $200,000 on January 1 of each year beginning in 1987. The bond price and discount are computed as follows:

		Selling Price	Discount
Bonds due 1/1/87 (one year away):			
Principal: $200,000 × 0.91743 (Table 6-2)	$183,486		
Interest: $16,000 × 0.91743 (Table 6-4)	14,679		
		$198,165	$ 1,835*
Bonds due 1/1/88 (two years away) Computations		196,482	3,518
Bonds due 1/1/89 (three years away) similar to		194,937	5,063
Bonds due 1/1/90 (four years away) those for		193,522	6,478
Bonds due 1/1/91 (five years away) 1/1/87 bonds.		192,220	7,780
Total price for all series		$975,326	
Total discount on all series			$24,674

*$1,835 = $200,000 − $198,165

Straight-line Amortization

The straight-line method of amortization may be used if the results are not materially different from those of the effective interest method. The total discount for the Yorkville School Products issue would be apportioned for each series over the five years as shown in the following schedule:

Amortization Schedule—Straight-line Method						
		Apportioned to				
Series Due Jan. 1	Total Discount	1986	1987	1988	1989	1990
1987	$ 1,835	$1,835				
1988	3,518	1,759	$1,759			
1989	5,063	1,688	1,688	$1,687		
1990	6,478	1,619	1,619	1,620	$1,620	
1991	7,780	1,556	1,556	1,556	1,556	$1,556
	$24,674	$8,457	$6,622	$4,863	$3,176	$1,556

Bonds Outstanding Method

If the entire issue of serial bonds is sold to underwriters at a stated price, the discount or premium is frequently amortized by the **bonds outstanding method,** since the discount or premium on each series is not definitely determinable. The bonds outstanding method applies the straight-line method to serial bonds and assumes that the discount applicable to each bond of the issue is the same dollar amount per bond per year.

The total discount for the Yorkville School Products issue would be apportioned over the five years as shown in the following schedule:

Amortization Schedule—Bonds Outstanding Method				
Year Ending Dec. 31	Bonds Outstanding During the Year	Bonds Outstanding During the Year ÷ Total of Bonds Outstanding Column	× Total Discount to be Amortized =	Discount to be Amortized During Each Year
1986	$1,000,000	10/30	$24,674	$ 8,224
1987	800,000	8/30	24,674	6,580
1988	600,000	6/30	24,674	4,935
1989	400,000	4/30	24,674	3,290
1990	200,000	2/30	24,674	1,645
	$3,000,000	30/30		$24,674

The effect of the column for "Bonds Outstanding During the Year" is to convert all the bonds into terms of bonds outstanding for one year, or a total of $3,000,000 for five years. Accordingly, during 1986 the premium to be amortized would be $1,000,000/$3,000,000 × $24,674, or $8,224. Similarly, during 1989 the premium to be amortized would be $400,000/$3,000,000 × $24,674, or $3,290.

An amortization schedule should be prepared for serial bonds in the same manner as the amortization schedule for single-maturity bonds, except that the maturity value of each serial must be deducted from the total carrying amount of the bonds when the serial is paid. The schedule shown below illustrates the amortization of the discount and the reduction in carrying amount for the serial bond issue described above using the bonds outstanding method.

Schedule of Bond Discount Amortization—Serial Bonds Bonds Outstanding Method					
Date	Credit Cash	Credit Bond Discount	Debit Interest Expense	Debit Bonds Payable	Carrying Value of Bonds
1/1/86					$975,326
12/31/86	$ 80,000[a]	$ 8,224[b]	$ 88,224[c]	—	$983,550[d]
1/1/87	200,000	—	—	$200,000	783,550
12/31/87	64,000	6,580	70,580	—	790,130
1/1/88	200,000	—	—	200,000	590,130
12/31/88	48,000	4,935	52,935	—	595,065
1/1/89	200,000	—	—	200,000	395,065
12/31/89	32,000	3,290	35,290	—	398,355
1/1/90	200,000	—	—	200,000	198,355
12/31/90	16,000	1,645	17,645	—	200,000
1/1/91	200,000	—	—	200,000	—
	$1,240,000	$24,674	$264,674	$1,000,000	

[a]$80,000 = $1,000,000 × 0.08
[b]$8,224 = $1,000,000/$3,000,000 × $24,674
[c]$88,224 = $80,000 + $8,224
[d]$983,550 = $975,326 + $8,224

A schedule with similar debit and credit columns could be prepared using the data from the straight-line amortization schedule. The credit to Bond Discount on December 31, 1986, would be $8,457 using the straight-line data.

Effective Interest Method

Application of the effective interest method to serial bonds is similar to that illustrated in the chapter regarding single-maturity bonds. Interest expense for the period is computed by multiplying the effective interest rate times the carrying amount of bonds outstanding during the period. The amount of amortization of bond discount or premium is the difference between the effective interest expense for the period and the actual interest payments. Under this method, the interest is at a constant rate relative to the carrying amount of the bonds outstanding. The following schedule illustrates the amortization of discount and the reduction in carrying amount for the Yorkville serial bond issue using the effective interest method.

Schedule of Bond Discount Amortization—Serial Bonds
Effective Interest Method
8% Bonds Sold to Yield 9%

Date	Credit Cash	Debit Interest Expense	Credit Bond Discount	Debit Bonds Payable	Carrying Value of Bonds
1/1/86					$975,326
12/31/86	$ 80,000[a]	$ 87,779[b]	$ 7,779[c]	—	983,105[d]
1/1/87	200,000	—	—	$ 200,000	783,105
12/31/87	64,000	70,479	6,479	—	789,584
1/1/88	200,000	—	—	200,000	589,584
12/31/88	48,000	53,063	5,063	—	594,647
1/1/89	200,000	—	—	200,000	394,647
12/31/89	32,000	35,518	3,518	—	398,165
1/1/90	200,000	—	—	200,000	198,165
12/31/90	16,000	17,835	1,835	—	200,000
1/1/91	200,000	—	—	200,000	—
	$1,240,000	$264,674	$24,674	$1,000,000	

[a]$80,000 = $1,000,000 × 0.08
[b]$87,779 = $975,326 × 0.09
[c]$7,779 = $87,779 − $80,000
[d]$983,105 = $975,326 + $7,779

The journal entries that would be recorded for the payment of the interest, amortization of the discount, and retirement of each series of bonds, can be determined from the column headings in the amortization schedule.

REDEMPTION OF SERIAL BONDS BEFORE MATURITY

If bonds of a certain series are redeemed before maturity date, it is necessary to compute the amount of unamortized discount (or premium) applicable to those bonds and to remove it from the Discount (or Premium) on Bonds Payable account.

Straight-line Method

Assume that on January 1, 1988, $200,000 of the Yorkville School Products serial bonds due January 1, 1991, are redeemed for $201,000. The unamortized discount on the $200,000 of bonds due on January 1, 1991, is $4,668 ($1,556 + $1,556 + $1,556; the discount apportioned to 1988, 1989, and 1990, respectively) as determined from the straight-line amortization schedule on page 670. The loss on early redemption of these bonds is computed as follows:

Purchase price of bonds redeemed	$201,000
Carrying value of 1/1/91 series bonds:	
($200,000 – $7,780 + $1,556 + $1,556) or	
($200,000 – $4,668)	195,332
Loss on bond redemption	$5,668

Bonds Outstanding Method

Using the same data, the computation of the applicable unamortized discount under the bonds outstanding method is as follows:

$$\frac{3 \text{ (number of years before maturity)} \times \$200,000 \text{ (par of bonds)} \times \$24,674 \text{ (total discount)}}{\$3,000,000 \text{ (total of bonds outstanding column)}} = \$4,935$$

Expressed a little differently, the discount to be amortized each year for each $200,000 of bonds is $200,000/$3,000,000 × $24,674, or $1,645. Therefore, if $200,000 of bonds are retired three years before maturity, the discount to be eliminated is 3 × $1,645, or $4,935.

Under the bonds outstanding method of amortization, the loss on early retirement of these bonds is computed as follows:

Purchase price of bonds redeemed	$201,000
Carrying value 1/1/91 series bonds:	
($200,000 – $4,935)	195,065
Loss on bond redemption	$5,935

Effective Interest Method

Under the effective interest method the carrying value of all the serial bonds outstanding at the time of an early retirement must be reduced by the present value of the bonds being retired. Reference to the effective interest amortization schedule shows that the carrying value of all the Yorkville bonds still outstanding at January 1, 1988, is $589,584. The carrying value of the bonds being retired is computed as the present value of the interest and principal obligations expected to be outstanding for the next three years (at 9%).

Present value of principal ($200,000 × .77218)	$154,436
Present value of interest payments ($16,000 × 2.53130)	40,501
Carrying value of bonds to be retired	$194,937

The entry to record the early redemption using the effective interest method would be as follows on January 1, 1988:

Bonds Payable	200,000	
Loss on Redemption of Bonds	6,063	
Discount on Bonds Payable ($200,000 − $194,937)		5,063
Cash		201,000

The gain or loss on redemption is the difference between the carrying value of the bonds ($194,937) and the cost to retire the bonds ($201,000); in this example, the loss is $6,063.

Note: All **asterisked** Questions, Cases, Exercises, or Problems relate to material contained in an Appendix.

QUESTIONS

1. (a) From what sources might a corporation obtain funds through long-term debt?
   (b) What is a bond indenture? What does it contain?
   (c) What is a mortgage?
2. Differentiate between a fixed-rate mortgage and a variable-rate mortgage.
3. Under what conditions may a short-term obligation be classified as a long-term debt?
4. (a) What is the typical denomination of corporate bonds?
   (b) How often is bond interest typically payable?
5. Differentiate between term bonds, mortgage bonds, collateral trust bonds, debenture bonds, income bonds, callable bonds, registered bonds, bearer bonds, convertible bonds, commodity-backed bonds, and deep discount bonds.
6. In what different ways may bonds be issued?
7. Distinguish between the following interest rates for bonds payable:
   (a) yield rate;   (b) nominal rate;
   (c) stated rate;   (d) market rate;
   (e) effective rate.
8. Distinguish between the following values relative to bonds payable:
   (a) par value;   (b) face value;
   (c) market value;   (d) maturity value.
9. Under what conditions of bond issuance does a discount on bonds payable arise? Under what conditions of bond issuance does a premium on bonds payable arise?
10. How should unamortized discount on bonds payable be reported on the financial statements? Unamortized premium on bonds payable?
11. What are the two methods of amortizing discount and premium on bonds payable? Explain each method.
12. Schwinn Company sells its bonds at a premium and applies the effective interest method in amortizing the premium. Will the annual interest expense increase or decrease over the life of the bonds? Explain.
13. How should the costs of issuing bonds be accounted for and classified in the financial statements?
14. Where should treasury bonds be shown on the balance sheet? Would treasury bonds be carried at par or at reacquisition cost?
15. What is the "call" feature of a bond issue? How does the call feature affect the amortization of bond premium or discount?
16. Why would a company wish to reduce its bond indebtedness before its bonds reach maturity? Indicate how this can be done and the accounting treatment for such a transaction.
17. How are gains and losses from extinguishment of debt classified in the income statement?

18. What must the accountant do to record a transaction involving the issuance of a noninterest-bearing long-term note in exchange for property?

19. How is the present value of a noninterest-bearing note computed?

20. When is the stated interest rate of a debt instrument presumed to be fair?

21. What are the considerations in computing an appropriate interest rate?

22. What are project financing arrangements?

23. What are take-or-pay contracts and through-put contracts?

24. What conditions must be met in order for a contractual obligation to be disclosed as an unconditional purchase obligation?

25. What disclosures are required relative to unconditional purchase obligations that have been recognized as balance sheet liabilities?

26. What disclosures are required relative to unconditional purchase obligations that have been disclosed only in the notes to the financial statements?

*27. (a) Describe the bonds-outstanding method of premium or discount amortization.

　　 (b) Describe the effective interest method of bond premium or discount amortization for serial bonds.

CASES

C14-1 On January 1, 1986, Cervaza Company issued for $1,075,230 its 20-year, 13% bonds that have a maturity value of $1,000,000 and pay interest semiannually on January 1 and July 1. Bond issue costs were not material in amount. Below are three presentations of the long-term liability section of the balance sheet that might be used for these bonds at the issue date:

1.	Bonds payable (maturing January 1, 2006)	$1,000,000
	Unamortized premium on bonds payable	75,230
	Total bond liability	$1,075,230
2.	Bonds payable—principal (face value $1,000,000, maturing January 1, 2006)	$ 97,220[a]
	Bonds payable—interest (semiannual payment $65,000)	978,010[b]
	Total bond liability	$1,075,230
3.	Bonds payable—principal (maturing, January, 2006)	$1,000,000
	Bonds payable—interest ($65,000 per period for 40 periods)	2,600,000
	Total bond liability	$3,600,000

[a]The present value of $1,000,000 due at the end of 40 (six-month) periods at the yield rate of 6% per period.
[b]The present value of $65,000 per period for 40 (six-month) periods at the yield rate of 6% per period.

Instructions

(a) Discuss the conceptual merit(s) of each of the date-of-issue balance sheet presentations shown above for these bonds.

(b) Explain why investors would pay $1,075,239 for bonds that have a maturity value of only $1,000,000.

(c) Assuming that a discount rate is needed to compute the carrying value of the obligations arising from a bond issue at any date during the life of the bonds, discuss the conceptual merit(s) of using for this purpose:
　　1. The coupon or nominal rate.
　　2. The effective rate or yield at date of issue.

(d) If the obligations arising from these bonds are to be carried at their present value computed by means of the current market rate of interest, how would the bond valuation at dates subsequent to the date of issue be affected by an increase or a decrease in the market rate of interest?

(AICPA adapted)

C14-2 The following article appeared in the June 19, 1979, issue of the *Wall Street Journal*:

Bond Markets
Giant Commonwealth Edison Issue Hits Resale Market With $70 Million Left Over
NEW YORK—Commonwealth Edison Co.'s slow-selling new 9 1/4% bonds were tossed onto the resale market at a reduced price with about $70 million still available from the $200 million offered Thursday, dealers said.

The Chicago utility's bonds, rated double-A by Moody's and double-A-minus by Standard & Poor's, originally had been priced at 99.803, to yield 9.3% in five years. They were marked down yesterday the equivalent of about $5.50 for each $1,000 face amount, to about 99.25, where their yield jumped to 9.45%.

Instructions

(a) How will the development above affect the accounting for Commonwealth Edison's bond issue?

(b) Provide several possible explanations for the markdown and the slow sale of Commonwealth Edison's bonds.

C14-3 **Part 1.** Theoretically, the appropriate method of amortizing a premium or discount on issuance of bonds is the effective interest method.

Instructions

(a) What is the effective interest method of amortization and how is it different from and similar to the straight-line method of amortization?

(b) How is amortization computed using the effective interest method, and why and how do amounts obtained using the effective interest method differ from amounts computed under the straight-line method?

Part 2. Gains or losses from the early extinguishment of debt that is refunded can theoretically be accounted for in three ways:

1. Amortized over remaining life of old debt.
2. Amortized over the life of the new debt issue.
3. Recognized in the period of extinguishment.

Instructions

(a) Develop supporting arguments for each of the three theoretical methods of accounting for gains and losses from the early extinguishment of debt.

(b) Which method do you prefer? Explain.

(AICPA adapted)

C14-4 As the accountant for Compost Perfume Company, you have prepared the balance sheet and have presented it to the president of the company. You are asked the following questions about it:

1. Why has depreciation been charged on equipment being purchased under a long-term instalment contract? Title has not passed to the company as yet and, therefore, they are not our assets. Why should the company not show on the asset side of the balance sheet only the amount paid to date instead of showing the full contract price, and the unpaid portion on the liability side?

2. What is bond discount? As a debit balance, why should it not be classified among the assets?

3. Bond interest payable is shown as a current liability. Did we not pay our trustee, Provincial Trust Company, the full amount of interest due this period?

4. Treasury bonds are shown as a deduction from bonds payable issued. Why should they not be shown as an asset, since they can be sold again? Are they the same as bonds of other companies that we hold as investments?

Instructions

Outline your answers to these questions by writing a brief paragraph that will justify your treatment.

EXERCISES

E14-1 Presented below are various accounts and related information for Christian Sisters Winery.

1. Unamortized premium of bonds payable, of which $2,800 will be amortized during the next year.
2. Bank loans payable due March 10, 1989. (The company's product requires aging for five years before sale.)
3. Serial bonds payable, $1,000,000, of which $200,000 are due each July 31.
4. Dividends payable in common shares on January 20, 1987.
5. Amounts withheld from employees' wages for income taxes.
6. Notes payable due January 15, 1988.
7. Credit balances in customers' accounts arising from returns and allowances after collection in full of account.
8. Bonds payable of $1,000,000 maturing June 30, 1987.
9. Overdraft of $500 in a bank account. (Debit balances are carried in two other accounts.)
10. Deposits made by customers who have ordered goods.

Instructions

Indicate whether each of the items above should be classified on December 31, 1986, as a current liability, a long-term liability, or under some other classification. Consider each one independently from all others. If the classification of some of the items is doubtful, explain why in each case.

E14-2 King Company authorized the issuance of 10% coupon bonds in the amount of $1,000,000, with interest coupons payable semiannually, and the bonds to be dated January 1, 1986. The financial events are as follows:

1. The authorization of 1,000 bonds of $1,000 each.
2. Subscriptions received for 700 bonds, at par.
3. Cash received in full on January 1, 1986, from subscribers to 600 bonds; bonds are issued.
4. On April 1, 1986, cash is received from subscribers to 100 bonds in the amount of the par value of the bonds plus accrued interest. The bonds are issued.
5. On July 1, 1986, six months' interest is paid on the bonds outstanding.

Instructions

Prepare entries to record the events listed above.

E14-3 In each of the following cases indicate whether the bond is sold at a premium or a discount and explain.

1. The stated interest rate for the bond is 16% and the effective rate is 15%.
2. The bond carries a coupon rate of 12% and is sold to yield 14%.
3. The market rate is 13% and the nominal rate of the bond is 13%.

E14-4 On June 30, 1975, Rolling Stones Company issued 14% bonds with a par value of $700,000 due in 20 years. They were issued at 99 and were callable at 103 at any date after June 30, 1985. Because of lower interest rates and a significant change in the company's credit rating, it was decided to call the entire issue on June 30, 1986, and to issue new bonds. New 12% bonds were sold in the amount of $800,000 at 101; they mature in 20 years. Rolling Stones Company uses straight-line amortization. Interest payment dates are December 31 and June 30.

Instructions

(a) Prepare journal entries to record the retirement of the old issue and the sale of the new issue on June 30, 1986.
(b) Prepare the entry required on December 31, 1986, to record the payment of the first six months' interest and the amortization of premium on the bonds.

E14-5   Fleetwood Mac Company had bonds outstanding with a maturity value of $200,000. On April 30, 1986, when these bonds had an unamortized discount of $4,000, they were called in at 106. To pay for these bonds, Fleetwood had issued other bonds a month earlier bearing a lower interest rate. The newly issued bonds had a life of 10 years. The new bonds were issued at 102 (face value $200,000). Issue costs related to the new bonds were $3,000.

Instructions

Ignoring interest, compute the gain or loss and record this refunding transaction.

E14-6   On January 2, 1980, Supertramp Corporation issued $1,200,000 of 13% bonds at 98 due December 31, 1989. Legal and other costs of $30,000 were incurred in connection with the issue. Interest on the bonds is payable annually each December 31. The $30,000 issue costs are being deferred and amortized on a straight-line basis over the 10-year term of the bonds. The discount on the bonds is also being amortized on a straight-line basis over the 10 years (straight-line is not materially different in effect from the effective interest method). The bonds are callable at 101 (that is, at 101% of face amount), and on January 2, 1985, Supertramp called $600,000 face amount of the bonds and retired them.

Instructions

Ignoring income taxes, compute the amount of loss, if any, to be recognized by Supertramp as a result of retiring the $600,000 of bonds in 1985 and prepare the journal entry to record the retirement.

(AICPA adapted)

E14-7   Speedwagon, Inc. had $6,000,000 of 12% bonds (interest payable July 9 and January 9) due in 10 years outstanding. On July 1, it issued $9,600,000 of 10% 15-year bonds (interest payable July 1 and January 1) at 99. A portion of the proceeds were used to call the 12% bonds at 103 on July 10. Unamortized bond discount and issue cost applicable to the 12% bonds were $60,000 and $30,000, respectively.

Instructions

Prepare the journal entries necessary to record the refunding of the bonds.

E14-8   Under the terms of its 9% bonds (interest payable June 30 and December 31), Styx Furniture Company must pay $2,000,000 to a trustee each year. The funds are to be used to retire as many bonds as possible in the open market. (Hint: Establish a bond retirement fund.)

On July 1, 1983, the company paid $2,000,000 to the trustee, who purchased $2,200,000 par value of bonds. Unamortized bond discount applicable to the bonds purchased was $50,000.

Instructions

Record the payment and purchase of the bonds on the Styx Furniture Company books.

E14-9   On July 1, 1986, Springsteen Company makes the two following acquisitions:

1. Purchases land having a fair market value of $100,000 by issuing a 4-year noninterest-bearing promissory note in the face amount of $174,901.
2. Purchases equipment by issuing a 5%, 8-year promissory note having a maturity value of $80,000 (interest payable annually). Springsteen Company has to pay 15% interest for funds from its bank.

Instructions

(a)   Provide the two journal entries that should be recorded by Springsteen Company for the two purchases on July 1.

(b)   Record the interest at the end of the first year (July 1, 1987) on both notes using the effective interest method.

E14-10   To secure a long-term supply, Fellerdemer Company entered into a take-or-pay contract with an aluminum recycling plant on January 1, 1984. Fellerdemer is obliged to purchase 40% of the output of the plant each period while the debt incurred to finance the plant remains outstanding. The annual cost of the aluminum to Fellerdemer will be the sum of 40% of the raw material costs, operating expenses, depreciation, interest on the debt used to finance the plant, and return on the owner's investment. The minimum amount payable to the plant under the contract, whether or not Fellerdemer is able to take delivery, is $5 million annually through December 31, 2003. Fellerdemer's total purchases under the agreement were $6 million in 1984 and $6.5 million in 1985. Funds to construct the plant were borrowed at an effective interest rate of 10%. Fellerdemer's incremental borrowing rate was 12% at January 1, 1984, and is 15% at December 31, 1985. Fellerdemer intends to disclose the contract in the notes to its financial statements at December 31, 1985.

Instructions

Assuming that the contract is an "unconditional purchase obligation," prepare the note disclosure for the contract at December 31, 1985.

*E14-11 Genesis Pen Company sells 12% bonds of a serial bond issue in the amount of $3,000,000 to underwriters for $3,090,000. The bonds are dated January 1, 1984, and mature in the amount of $600,000 on January 1 of each year beginning January 1, 1986.

Instructions

Compute the premium to be amortized during each of the years in which any of the bonds are outstanding, using the bonds outstanding method.

PROBLEMS

P14-1 On January 1, 1985, The Who Company sold 16% bonds having a maturity value of $100,000 for $103,353, which provides the bondholders with a 15% yield. The bonds are dated January 1, 1985, and mature January 1, 1990 with interest payable December 31 of each year. The Who Company allocates interest and unamortized discount on premium on the effective interest basis.

Instructions

(a) Prepare the journal entry at the date of the bond issuance.

(b) Prepare the journal entry to record the interest payment and the amortization for 1985. Preparation of a partial schedule of interest expense and bond amortization will aid in the solution.

(c) Prepare the journal entry to record the interest payment and the amortization for 1987.

P14-2 The following amortization and interest schedule reflects the issuance of 10-year bonds by Pink Floyd Corporation on January 1, 1986, and the subsequent interest payments and charges. The company's year end is December 31, and financial statements are prepared once yearly.

AMORTIZATION SCHEDULE

Year	Cash	Interest	Amount Unamortized	Carrying Value
1/1/86			$5,651	$ 94,349
1986	$11,000	$11,322	5,329	94,671
1987	11,000	11,361	4,968	95,032
1988	11,000	11,404	4,564	95,436
1989	11,000	11,452	4,112	95,888
1990	11,000	11,507	3,605	96,395
1991	11,000	11,567	3,038	96,962
1992	11,000	11,635	2,403	97,597
1993	11,000	11,712	1,691	98,309
1994	11,000	11,797	894	99,106
1995	11,000	11,894		100,000

Instructions

    (a) Indicate whether the bonds were issued at a premium or a discount and how you can determine this fact from the schedule.

    (b) Indicate whether the amortization schedule is based on the straight-line method or the effective interest method and how you can determine which method is used.

    (c) On the basis of the schedule above, prepare the journal entry to record the issuance of the bonds on January 1, 1986.

    (d) On the basis of the schedule above, prepare the journal entries to reflect the bond transactions and accruals for 1986.

    (e) On the basis of the schedule above, prepare the journal entries to reflect the bond transactions and accruals for 1994.

P14-3 AC-DC Company sells 14% bonds having a maturity value of $100,000 for $96,648. The bonds are dated January 1, 1986, and mature January 1, 1991. Interest is payable annually on January 1. (Hint: The effective interest rate or yield must be computed.)

Instructions

    (a) Set up a schedule of interest expense and discount amortization under the straight-line method.

    (b) Set up a schedule of interest expense and discount amortization under the effective interest method.

P14-4 In 1985, Kelona Winery was considering the issuance of bonds as of January 1, 1986, as follows:

Plan 1: $2,000,000 par value 12%, 1st mortgage, 20-year bonds, due Dec. 31, 2006, at 96, with interest payable annually.

Plan 2: $2,000,000 par value 12%, 1st mortgage, 20-year bonds, due Dec. 31, 2006, at 100, with provision for payment of a 4% ($80,000) premium at maturity, interest payable annually.

    Costs of issue such as printing and lawyers' fees may be ignored for the purpose of answering this question. Discount and premium are to be allocated to accounting periods on a straight-line basis.

Instructions

Give two separate sets of journal entries with appropriate explanations showing the accounting treatment that the foregoing bond issues would necessitate, respectively:

    (a) At time of issue.

    (b) Yearly thereafter.

    (c) On payment at date of maturity.

P14-5 In each of the following independent cases the company closes its books on December 31.

    1. Heather Co. sells $200,000 of 14% bonds on February 1, 1985. The bonds pay interest on February 1 and August 1. The due date of the bonds is August 1, 1988. The bonds yield 16%. Give entries through December 31, 1986.

    2. Dawna Co. sells $200,000 of 13% bonds on June 1, 1985. The bonds pay interest on June 1 and December 1. The due date of the bonds is June 1, 1989. The bonds yield 12%. On September 1, 1986, Dawna buys back and cancels $40,000 worth of bonds for $42,000 (includes accrued interest). Give entries through December 1, 1987.

Instructions

For the two cases above, prepare all of the relevant journal entries from the time of sale until the date indicated. (Round to the nearest dollar.) Use the effective interest method for discount and premium amortization, constructing amortization tables where applicable. Amortize premium or discount on interest dates and at year end. (Assume that no reversing entries are made.)

P14-6 Presented below are selected transactions on the books of Asmuth Corporation.

July 1, 1985   Bonds payable with a par value of $900,000, which are dated January 1, 1985, are sold at 102 plus accrued interest. They are coupon bonds, bear interest at 12% (payable annually at January 1), and mature January 1, 1995. (Use interest expense account for accrued interest.)

Dec. 31   Adjusting entries are made to record the accrued interest on the bonds, and the amortization of the proper amount of premium. (Use straight-line amortization.)

Jan. 1, 1986   Interest on the bonds is paid.

April 1   Bonds of par value of $450,000 are purchased at 101 plus accrued interest, and retired. (Bond premium is to be amortized only at the end of each year.)

Dec. 31   Adjusting entries are made to record the accrued interest on the bonds, and the proper amount of premium amortized.

Instructions

Prepare journal entries for the transactions above.

P14-7 Asia Company issued its 11% 30-year mortgage bonds in the principal amount of $5,000,000 on January 2, 1971, at a discount of $150,000, which it proceeded to amortize by charges to expense over the life of the issue on a straight-line basis. The indenture securing the issue provided that the bonds could be called for redemption in total but not in part at any time before maturity at 104% of the principal amount, but it did not provide for any sinking fund.

On December 18, 1985, the company issued its 9% 25-year debenture bonds in the principal amount of $6,000,000 at par, and the proceeds were used to redeem the 11% 30-year mortgage bonds on January 2, 1986. The indenture securing the new issue did not provide for any sinking fund nor for retirement before maturity.

Instructions

(a) Prepare journal entries to record the issuance of the 9% bonds and the retirement of the 11% bonds.

(b) Indicate the income statement treatment of the gain or loss from retirement and any note disclosure required. Assume 1986 income before extraordinary items of $3,460,000, a weighted-average number of shares outstanding of 1,500,000, and an income tax rate of 40%.

P14-8 On February 1, 1985, Arch Company sold 10,000 of its 12%, 20-year, $1,000 face value bonds at 98. Interest payment dates are February 1 and August 1, and the company uses the straight-line method of bond discount amortization. On March 1, 1986, Arch took advantage of favourable prices of its shares to extinguish 1,000 of the bonds by issuing 80,000 of its no-par value common shares. The company's shares were selling for $10 each on February 1, 1985 and $13 each on March 1, 1986.

Instructions

Prepare the journal entries needed on the books of Arch Company to record the following:

(a) February 1, 1985: issuance of the bonds.

(b) August 1, 1985: payment of semiannual interest.

(c) December 31, 1985: accrual of interest expense.

(d) February 1, 1986: payment of semiannual interest. (No reversing entries made.)

(e) March 1, 1986: extinguishment of 1,000 bonds.

P14-9   On January 1, 1983, Cosmetics Products Company sold $150,000 (face value) of bonds. The bonds are dated January 1, 1983, and will mature on January 1, 1988. Interest is paid annually on December 31. The bonds are callable after December 31, 1985, at 102. Issue costs related to these bonds amounted to $1,500, and these costs are being amortized by the straight-line method. The following amortization schedule was prepared by the accountant for the first two years of the life of the bonds:

Date	Cash	Interest	Amortization	Carrying Value of Bonds
Jan. 1, 1983				$139,186
Dec. 31, 1983	$15,000	$16,702	$1,702	140,888
Dec. 31, 1984	15,000	16,907	1,907	142,795
Dec. 31, 1985	15,000	17,135	2,135	144,930
Dec. 31, 1986	15,000	17,392	2,392	147,322

Instructions

On the basis of the information above, answer the following questions (round your answers to the nearest dollar or percent):

(a)   What is the nominal or stated rate of interest for this bond issue?

(b)   What is the effective or market rate of interest for this bond issue?

(c)   Present the journal entry to record the sale of the bond issue, including the issue costs.

(d)   Present the appropriate entry(ies) at December 31, 1985.

(e)   Present the disclosure of this bond issue on the December 31, 1985, balance sheet. Proper balance sheet subheadings must be indicated.

(f)   On June 30, 1986, $75,000 of the bond issue was redeemed at the call price. Present the journal entry for this redemption. ~~Amortization of the discount is recorded only at the end of the year.~~

(g)   Present the effects of the bond redemption on the 1986 income statement and any note disclosure. Proper income statement subheadings must be indicated. The income tax rate is 20%; 1986 income before extraordinary items is $31,023 with a weighted-average number of common shares outstanding during the year of 18,000. Working capital funds were used to redeem the bonds.

P14-10   Greg Teets Company issued 10-year coupon bonds in the amount of $1,000,000 on July 1, 1984. They were issued at par and bear interest at 12%, payable semiannually on July 1 and January 1. The Royal Bank is to act as trustee to handle the payment of interest.

On December 10, 1984, Greg Teets Company sent the Royal Bank a cheque for the interest due January 1, 1985, none of which was paid to bondholders before January 1, 1985.

Instructions

(a)   What balances will be shown in the ledger of Greg Teets Company on December 31, 1984, relating to the bonds and the interest on the bonds? How will these balances be shown in the financial statements? Establish a fund account for trustee payment.

(b)   Assume that in 1985 Greg Teets Company sent the Royal Bank cheques for the interest due July 1, 1985, and January 1, 1986, and that the bank returned to the company cancelled interest coupons in the amount of $114,000. Greg Teets Company sent the bank a cheque for $940 to cover the trustee expenses.

What balances will be shown in the ledger of Greg Teets Company on December 31, 1985, relating to the bonds and the interest on the bonds? How will these balances be shown in financial statements?

P14-11   Here are transactions of Led Zeppelin Company:

Jan. 1, 1985   Bonds payable (coupon bonds) in the amount of $1,000,000, and bearing interest at the rate of 12% payable semiannually on January 1 and July 1, due January 1, 2005, are issued at 96.

June 15	The First Bank and Trust Co. has been engaged as trustee to handle the payment of interest to individual bondholders. A cheque for the interest due July 1, 1985, is sent to the trustee.
June 30	Record the interest expense for the first six months of 1985. Bond discount is to be amortized only at the end of each year and by the straight-line method.
July 20	The trustee returns to the company cancelled interest coupons paid in the amount of $56,800 and reports that trustee's expenses charged against the account amount to $520.
Dec. 15	A cheque for the interest due January 1, 1986, and for the reported expenses is sent to the trustee (see July 20).
Dec. 31	Record the interest expense for the six months ended December 31, and amortize the proper amount of discount for the year.
Jan. 21, 1986	The trustee returns to the company cancelled interest coupons paid in the amount of $59,900.
Mar. 1	Bonds of par value $20,000 are bought on the market at 95 plus accrued interest, and retired. All interest coupons dated before July 1, 1986, have been removed.

Instructions

(a) Prepare entries in journal form on the books of Led Zeppelin for the transactions given above.

(b) What will be the amount of the cheque to the trustee for the interest for the first six months of 1986?

(c) What will be the amount of the discount amortized on December 31, 1986?

P14-12 Danish Inc. has been producing quality children's apparel for more than 25 years. The company's fiscal year runs from April 1 to March 31. The following information relates to the obligations of Danish as of March 31, 1986.

Bonds Payable. Danish issued $4,000,000 of 9% bonds on July 1, 1980 at 98, which yielded proceeds of $3,920,000. The bonds will mature on July 1, 1990. Interest is paid semiannually on July 1 and January 1. Danish uses the straight-line method to amortize the bond discount.

Notes Payable. Danish has signed several long-term notes with financial institutions and insurance companies. The maturity dates of these notes are given in the schedule below. The total unpaid interest for all of these notes amounts to $170,000 on March 31, 1986.

Due Date	Amount Due
April 1, 1986	$ 150,000
July 1, 1986	200,000
October 1, 1986	100,000
January 1, 1987	200,000
April 1, 1987–March 31, 1988	600,000
April 1, 1988–March 31, 1989	400,000
April 1, 1989–March 31, 1990	400,000
April 1, 1990–March 31, 1991	500,000
April 1, 1991–March 31, 1992	700,000
	$3,250,000

Estimated Warranties. Danish has a one-year product warranty on some selected items in its product line. The estimated warranty liability on sales made during the 1984–85 fiscal year and still outstanding as of March 31, 1985, amounted to $55,000. The warranty costs on sales made from April 1, 1985, through March 31, 1986 are estimated at $165,000. The actual warranty costs incurred during the current 1985-86 fiscal year are as follows:

Warranty claims honoured on 1984–85 sales	$ 55,000
Warranty claims honoured on 1985–86 sales	75,000
Total warranty claims honoured	$130,000

Other Information:

1. **Trade payables.** Accounts payable for supplies, goods, and services purchased on open account amount to $340,000 as of March 31, 1986.

2. **Payroll-related items.** Outstanding obligations related to Danish's payroll as of March 31, 1986 are:

Accrued salaries and wages	$150,000
CPP and UI payable	18,000
Income taxes withheld from employees	30,000
Other payroll deductions	3,000

3. **Taxes.** The following are taxes incurred but not due until the next fiscal year:

Income taxes	$305,000
Property taxes	125,000
Sales taxes	192,000

4. **Miscellaneous accruals.** Other accruals not separately classified amount to $62,000 as of March 31, 1986.

5. **Dividends.** On March 15, 1986, Danish's Board of Directors declared a cash dividend of $.40 per common share and a 10% common stock dividend. Both dividends were to be distributed on April 12, 1986, to the common shareholders of record at the close of business on March 31, 1986. Data regarding Danish no-par common shares follow:

Number of shares issued and outstanding	3,000,000 shares
Market values of common shares:	
March 15, 1986	$22.00 per share
March 31, 1986	21.50 per share
April 12, 1986	22.50 per share

Instructions

Prepare the liability section of the balance sheet and appropriate notes to the statement for Danish Inc. as of March 31, 1986, as they should appear in its annual report to the shareholders.

(CMA adapted)

P14-13 On December 31, 1985, Elton Company acquired a computer from John Corporation by issuing a $350,000 noninterest-bearing note, payable in full on December 31, 1988. Elton Company's credit rating permits it to borrow funds from its several lines of credit at 12%. The computer is expected to have a six-year life and a $50,000 salvage value.

Instructions

(a) Prepare the journal entry for the purchase on December 31, 1985.

(b) Prepare any necessary adjusting entries related to depreciation (use straight-line) and amortization (use effective interest method) on December 31, 1986.

(c) Prepare any necessary adjusting entries related to depreciation and amortization on December 31, 1987.

P14-14 Stevie Wonder and Associates, Inc. purchased machinery on December 31, 1984, at a price of $80,000, paying $20,000 down and agreeing to pay the balance in four equal instalments of $15,000 payable each December 31. An assumed interest of 12% is implicit in the purchase price.

Instructions

Prepare the journal entries that would be recorded for the purchase and for the payments and interest on the following dates:

(a) December 31, 1984.

(b) December 31, 1985.

(c) December 31, 1986.

(d) December 31, 1987.

(e) December 31, 1988.

*P14-15 On May 1, 1985, D. Parton Company sold a new serial bond issue with $600,000 par value for $642,000. The nominal interest rate on these bonds is 12%, and the interest is payable annually on May 1. One-half of the bonds will be retired on May 1 each year for two years, beginning in 1986. D. Parton Company closes its books on December 31 each year.

Instructions

Prepare all of the journal entries required over the life of these bonds to record the issuance, amortization, interest accruals and payments, and retirements. Use the bonds outstanding method.

*P14-16 On December 31, 1981, Olivia Newton Company sold a 12% serial bond issue in the amount of $2,800,000 for $2,794,400. The bonds mature in the amount of $400,000 on December 31 of each year, beginning December 31, 1982, and interest is payable annually.

On December 31, 1984, the company retired the $400,000 of bonds due on that date and, in addition, purchased at 99 and retired bonds in the amount of $200,000 which were due on December 31, 1986.

Instructions

(a) Prepare entries to record the payment of interest for 1982, and to record the amortization of discount for the year using the bonds outstanding method.

(b) Prepare entries to record the redemption of the bonds of $600,000 which were retired on December 31, 1984.

(c) Discuss the disclosures that are required relative to the bond transactions in 1984.

(d) What amount of discount would be amortized for the year 1986?

*P14-17 On January 1, 1983, Clapton/McCartney Corporation issued $1,000,000 of 5-year, 10% serial bonds to be repaid in the amount of $200,000 on January 1, 1984, 1985, 1986, 1987, and 1988. Interest is payable at the end of each year. The bonds were sold to yield a rate of 12%.

Instructions

(a) Prepare a schedule showing the computation of the total amount received from the issuance of the serial bonds. Show supporting computations in good form.

(b) Assume the bonds were originally sold at a discount of $46,506. Prepare a schedule of amortization of the bond discount for the first three years after issuance, using the effective interest method. Show supporting computations in good form.

(AICPA adapted)

PART

4

SHAREHOLDERS' EQUITY, DILUTIVE
SECURITIES, AND INVESTMENTS

15

SHAREHOLDERS' EQUITY: ISSUANCE AND REACQUISITION OF SHARE CAPITAL

In your first exposure to financial accounting you were probably taught that the credit side of the balance sheet represents the sources of enterprise assets. Liabilities represent the amount of assets that were financed by lending sources, and shareholders' equity represents (1) the amount that was contributed by the shareholders and (2) the portion that was earned and retained by the enterprise. While this explanation is accurate and may seem simple enough, shareholders' equity is generally the least understood section of the financial statements because of its distinctive accounting terminology and its legalistic nature.

THE NATURE OF SHAREHOLDERS' EQUITY

The owners of an enterprise bear the ultimate risks and uncertainties and receive the benefits of enterprise operations. Their interest in the enterprise is measured by the difference between the assets and the liabilities of the enterprise. **Owners' or shareholders' interest in a business enterprise is a residual interest** in the sense that it ranks after liabilities as a claim to or interest in the assets of an enterprise. As an amount, shareholders' equity represents the cumulative net contributions by shareholders plus recorded earnings that have been retained. As a residual interest, shareholders' equity has no existence apart from the assets and liabilities of the enterprise—shareholders' equity equals net assets. Shareholders' equity is not a claim to specific assets but a claim against a portion of the total assets. Its amount is not specified or fixed; it depends on the enterprise's profitability. Shareholders' equity grows if the enterprise is profitable and shrinks or may disappear entirely if the enterprise is unprofitable.

Sources of Shareholders' Equity

Accounting for shareholders' equity is greatly influenced by tradition and by corporate law. Although the legal aspects of equity must be respected and disclosed, legal requirements need not be the only accounting basis for classifying and reporting the components of equity.[1] **The two primary sources from which owners' equity is derived are (1) contributions by shareholders and (2) earnings retained by a corporation,** and these two components should be accounted for and reported by every corporation. The diagram below depicts the two major sources of changes in shareholders' equity:[2]

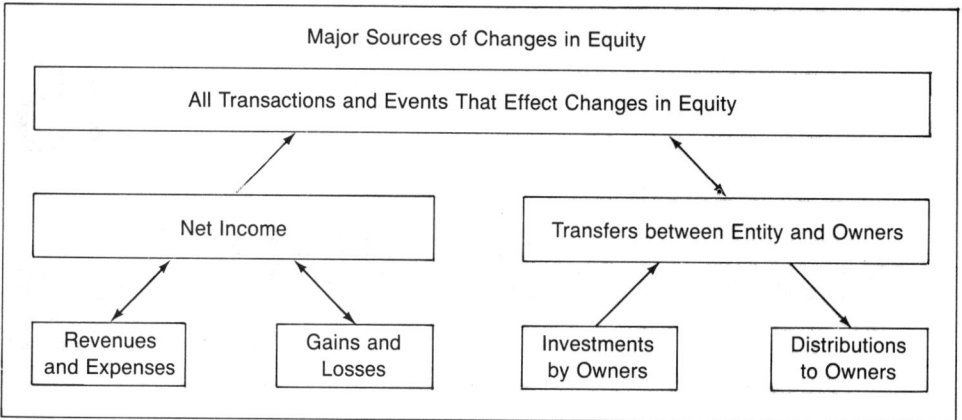

Changes in shareholders' equity may also occur by conversion of debt into equity and through capital donations to the corporations. In addition, changes within equity are brought about by stock dividends, stock conversions, and recapitalizations (quasi-reorganizations).

What Is Capital?

To this point, we have used the term shareholders' or owners' equity to denote the total of ownership capital of the enterprise. It is important to understand that many different meanings are attached to the word "capital" and, therefore, the word often is construed differently by various groups.

In **corporation finance,** for example, capital commonly represents the gross assets of the enterprise. In **law,** capital is considered that portion of shareholders'

---

[1]Beatrice Melcher, "Stockholders' Equity," *Accounting Research Study No. 15* (New York: AICPA, 1973), p. 2.

[2]Adapted from "Elements of Financial Statements of Business Enterprises," *Statement of Financial Accounting Concepts, No. 3* (Stamford, Conn.: FASB, 1980), p. 23.

equity that is required by statute to be retained in the business for the protection of creditors. Generally, **legal capital (stated capital)** is the full price received for shares issued as specified by the Canada Business Corporations Act (CBCA) and most provincial incorporation acts. In some jurisdictions ownership shares may have a par value, in which case that amount is considered to be the legal capital.

Accountants for the most part define capital more broadly than legal capital but more narrowly than total assets. When accountants refer to capital they usually mean shareholders' or owners' equity. They then subclassify shareholders' equity into various categories, the primary ones being **Share Capital, Contributed Surplus,** and **Retained Earnings.** Share Capital represents the legal or stated capital of a corporation as defined in the previous paragraph. Contributed Surplus would include such items as donations from owners and other sources, gains on forfeited shares, credits arising when shares are reacquired and cancelled at a cost less than their issue price, and amounts received in excess of par value when such shares are issued. Indeed, this subclassification of shareholders' equity may alternatively be titled Contributed Capital.[3] Retained Earnings consists of all undistributed income that remains invested in the enterprise. A comprehensive illustration of the shareholders' equity section of a balance sheet is given in Chapter 16 on page 751, which shows how these categories may be presented and provides examples of what they may include.

We have chosen to divide our coverage of shareholders' equity by discussing the accounting matters relating to share capital (issuance and reacquisition) in Chapter 15 and the other components (contributed surplus and retained earnings) in Chapter 16. Additional aspects that can have an impact on shareholders' equity (convertible debt, stock purchase warrants, and stock options) are covered in Chapter 17; but first, in order to account for shareholders' equity, one must understand the corporate form of entity.

THE CORPORATE FORM OF ENTITY

Of the **three primary forms of business organization—the proprietorship, the partnership, and the corporation,** the dominant form of business is the corporation in terms of the aggregate amount of resources controlled, goods and services produced, and people employed. Nearly all of the largest industrial firms are corporations. Although the corporate form has a number of advantages (as well as disadvantages) over the other two forms, the principal attribute that has helped it to reach its present dominant role is its facility for attracting and accumulating large amounts of capital.

Various types of corporations exist, distinguished by the nature of their ownership, their purpose, and the type of legislation under which they have been created. Such types as the following are common in Canada:

1. **Profit-seeking corporations** engaged in activities with the intent of making a financial return for owners. Ownership in such corporations may be widely traded and distributed (often called **publicly held corporations**) or held by a small number of shareholders with restrictions on the transferability of shares (often referred to as **privately held corporations**).

[3]While this subclassification of shareholders' equity will be referred to as Contributed Surplus, the accounts included in this subclassification will have, in their name, the words: "Contributed Capital—." This is done to assist in distinguishing between the subclassification heading and the separate accounts included therein. It is acceptable that these separate accounts have, in their name, the words: "Contributed Surplus—" rather than "Contributed Capital—."

2. **Not-for-profit corporations** that are created to provide educational, charitable, recreational, or similar services for its members or society in general.

3. **Crown corporations** that are created by special government statutes to provide services to the public, such as the Canadian Broadcasting Corporation and Canada Post.

The profit-seeking corporation is the type which will be examined in this book.

The owners' equity accounts of such corporations are considerably different from those of a proprietorship or partnership. It is not necessary to enter into a detailed discussion of the advantages or disadvantages of the corporate form of business enterprise at this point. However, certain characteristics of the corporation do have a direct effect on what may be termed proprietorship, owners' equity, or net worth accounting, and it is helpful if these are clearly understood.

Among the special characteristics of the corporate form that affect accounting are:

1. Influence of corporate law.
2. Use of the share capital or capital stock system.
3. Development of a variety of ownership interests.
4. Limited liability of shareholders.
5. Formality of profit distribution.

Corporate Law

In Canada, a corporation may be established provincially or federally by submitting the required documentation to the appropriate government office. If incorporated provincially, the company would be subject to the requirements and provisions of the respective province's business corporations act. Federally incorporated companies are created and operate under the provisions of the **Canada Business Corporations Act** (CBCA). While the provisions of most business corporation acts are reasonably similar, differences do exist. These differences create difficulties when trying to make generalizations in a discussion of shareholders' equity. Consequently, the CBCA will be the focal point when discussing legal aspects of accounting for shareholders' equity in this text.

Under the CBCA, one or more individuals over eighteen, of sound mind and not bankrupt, are entitled to incorporate. To do so, incorporators develop, sign and send **articles of incorporation**[4] to the Director, Department of Consumer and Corporate Affairs. The Director, who is responsible for the administration of the CBCA, will issue a **certificate of incorporation** after ensuring that the incorporating documents are appropriately completed. Incorporation is essentially a right under the CBCA because the Director has no discretion to refuse documents that are in order. When a certificate of incorporation is issued, the resulting business becomes a separate legal entity which may act in the capacity of a natural person when conducting its affairs. As with any person, it is bound by the laws of the country. In addition, the corporation (unless a particular exemption is explicitly granted) must act in accordance with all of the provisions of the CBCA. These provisions have significant implications regarding accounting for corporations in general and for shareholders' equity in particular, as will be discussed throughout this and the next chapter.

---

[4]The articles of incorporation must specify such things as the name of the company (which must use either the words "incorporated" or "limited" or their abbreviation or French equivalent as part of the name), place of registered office, classes and any maximum number of shares authorized, restrictions on rights to transfer shares, number of directors, and any restrictions on the corporation's business.

First, however, one important accounting aspect of the CBCA should be emphasized: the CBCA Regulations state that financial statements are to be prepared in accordance with the standards set out in the *CICA Handbook*. Consequently, this provision gives the *Handbook* a legal status. As its authors (members of the Accounting Standards Committee for the financial reporting sections of the *Handbook*) are primarily members of the accounting profession, the implication of this CBCA Regulation is that the Canadian accounting profession is self-regulating. This privilege and responsibility of the profession does not exist in many other countries in which government influences are significant to the determination of accounting practices and standards.[5]

Share Capital or Capital Stock System

The share capital of a corporation is generally made up of a large number of units or shares. For a given class of shares (stock) each share is exactly equal to every other share. Each owner's interest is determined by the number of shares possessed. If a company has but one class of stock divided into 1,000 shares, a person owning 500 shares controls one-half the ownership interest of the corporation; one holding 10 shares has a one-hundredth interest.

Each share has certain rights and privileges that can be restricted only by provisions in the articles of incorporation. In the absence of restrictive provisions, each share carries the following rights:

1. To share proportionately in profits.
2. To share proportionately in management (the right to vote at shareholder meetings).
3. To share proportionately in corporate assets upon liquidation.

In addition to these three rights, the CBCA allows a corporation to assign a **pre-emptive right** to any or all classes of shares through appropriate specification in the articles of incorporation. A pre-emptive right means that existing shareholders of a class of shares have a right to acquire additional issues of that class in proportion to their existing holdings before the newly issued shares can be offered to others.

A pre-emptive right may be used in a corporation to protect each shareholder's proportional interest in the enterprise. **The pre-emptive right protects an existing shareholder from involuntary dilution of ownership interest.** Without this right shareholders with a given percentage interest might find their interest reduced by the issuance of additional shares without their knowledge and at prices that were not favourable to them. Because assigning the pre-emptive right to shares makes it inconvenient for a corporation to make large issuances of additional stock, as is frequently done when acquiring other companies, it has not been used by many corporations.

The great advantage of the share system is the ease with which an interest in the business may be transferred from one individual to another. Generally, **individuals owning shares in a corporation may sell them to others at any time and at any price without obtaining the consent of the company or other shareholders.** Each share is the personal property of the owner and may be disposed of at will. All that is required of the corporation is that it maintain a list or subsidiary ledger of

---

[5]Chapter 1 examined the process by which Canadian accounting standards in the *Handbook* are developed and considered some of the implications to the profession resulting from the legal status conferred on the *Handbook*.

shareholders as a basis for dividend payments, issuance of share rights, voting proxies, and the like. It is necessary for the corporation to revise periodically the subsidiary ledger of shareholders, generally in advance of every dividend payment or shareholders' meeting, because shares are frequently transferred. As the number of shareholders grows, the need may develop for a more efficient system that can handle large numbers of share transactions. Also, the major stock exchanges require controls that the typical corporation finds uneconomic to provide. Thus **registrars and transfer agents** who specialize in providing services for recording and transferring shares are usually used.

Variety of Ownership Interests

Corporations may issue shares of various classes. Each class would have specified rights, privileges, restrictions, and conditions attached to it as stated in the company's articles of incorporation. The CBCA simply refers to the possible existence of classes of shares without specifying what they shall be called. Consequently, the name given to different classes of shares by corporations can be varied. Typical practice is to identify classes by a letter (i.e., Class A, Class B, etc.) followed by a brief identification of the nature of rights or restrictions that attach to the shares in the class. However, the rights and restrictions of Class A shares for one corporation are likely to be quite different from those of Class A shares of another corporation, so that the only means by which one can identify the rights and restrictions of a class of shares for a particular corporation is to examine the description that applies to that class. We will therefore be using the terms ''common shares'' and ''preferred shares'' in this book as a means to differentiate between basic ownership interest shares and shares that have specific privileges or restrictions regarding the rights identified in the previous section.

In every corporation, one class of shares must represent the basic ownership interest. This class will be referred to as common shares. **Common shares** are the residual corporate interest that bears the ultimate risk of loss and receives the benefits of success. They guarantee neither dividends nor assets upon dissolution, but common shareholders generally control the management of the corporation and tend to profit most if the company is successful. In the event that a corporation has only one authorized issue of shares, that issue is considered to be common shares, whether so designated or not.

To appeal to all types of investors, corporations may offer two or more share classes with different rights or privileges attached to each. The preceding section emphasized that each share of a given class has the same rights as other shares of the same class and that there are three rights inherent in every share. Through specification in the articles of incorporation, certain of these rights may be sacrificed, usually in return for other special rights or privileges. Thus special classes of shares are created, and because there are certain preferences and/or restrictions attached to these classes, they will be referred to as **preferred shares.**

Preferred shareholders typically have a prior claim on earnings. Therefore, they would receive a dividend, usually a stated amount, before any dividend may be distributed to the common shareholders. In return for this preference, the preferred shareholders may sacrifice the right to a voice in management or the right to share in profits beyond the stated amount.

A company may accomplish a variety of objectives by issuing more than one class of shares. For example, one company created two classes, A and B, when it decided to issue shares to the public several years ago. Both Class A and Class B participate equally (per share) in all dividend payments and have the same claim on assets on dissolution. The differences are that Class A is voting and Class B is not; Class B is traded publicly over the counter while Class A, which is "family owned," must be sold privately; and Class A shares are convertible, one for one, into Class B shares but not vice versa. By issuing two classes of shares, the Class A owners obtained a ready market for the company's shares and yet provided an effective shield against outside takeover.

In this example, using the interpretations specified above, the Class A shares would be thought of as common shares and the Class B as preferred shares (there is a restriction on the basic right to vote and no privileges given in return). While the labelling as common and preferred is beneficial for purposes of this text (because it saves some time and space otherwise necessary to continually describe the characteristics of a class of shares), it has the limitation of not accurately reflecting actual circumstances. (For example, the company referred to in the previous paragraph identified both Class A and B as common shares in their descriptions.)

An additional example of the variety of shares that may be issued is provided by NOVA, An Alberta Corporation which has ten types of preferred shares (which vary in terms of such factors as redemption prices and dates, dividend amounts, and sinking fund requirements) and two classes labelled as common shares (300,000,000 authorized Class A, with no voting rights except for the election of seven directors, and 2,004 authorized Class B).

Limited Liability of Shareholders

The shareholders of a corporation contribute either cash, other property, or services to the enterprise in return for ownership shares. The amount so invested in the enterprise is the extent of a shareholder's possible loss. That is, if the corporation sustains losses to such an extent that remaining assets are insufficient to pay creditors, no recourse can be held by the creditors against the personal assets of the individual shareholders. In a partnership or proprietorship, personal assets of the owners can be called upon to satisfy unpaid claims against the enterprise. Ownership interests in a corporation are legally protected against such a contingency; **the shareholders may lose their investment but they cannot lose more than their investment.**

While the corporate form of organization grants the protective feature of limited liability to the shareholders, it also requires that withdrawal of the amount of shareholders' investment represented by amounts in share capital accounts not occur unless all prior claims on corporate assets have been paid. The corporation must maintain this capital until dissolution; upon dissolution, it must satisfy all prior claims before distributing any amounts to the shareholders. In a proprietorship or partnership the owners can withdraw amounts at will, because all their personal assets may be called on to protect creditors from loss.

Shareholders invest in a corporation by purchasing its capital shares. While these may be continuously traded in the stock market, it is only the amount paid to the corporation when the shares were originally issued that appears on the company's financial statements as part of shareholders' equity.

Under the CBCA, all shares must be **without a nominal or par value.** This simply means that all proceeds from the corporation's issuance of shares must be credited to the appropriate share capital account.

Prior to the implementation of the CBCA, federally incorporated companies could have **par value shares** and some provincial acts continue to permit par value shares to be issued. Par value is simply an amount per share determined by the incorporators of the company and stated as such in the articles of incorporation. From an accounting point of view, par value is the amount credited to the appropriate share capital account when shares are issued. This par value amount represents legal capital, an amount that cannot be used as a basis for dividend distributions. As an arbitrary amount designated by incorporators, par value has little to do with the market value of shares issued. If shares are sold by a corporation at an amount in excess of par value, this excess is called a premium and is credited to a Contributed Capital account. In rare instances when shares are sold at less than par value, a discount on the shares would result. This discount would be shown as a contra account to the share capital account (set up at par value) in the shareholders' equity section of the balance sheet. Those who had bought the shares at a discount are liable for that amount should the corporation declare bankruptcy.

We will concentrate on the accounting for shares without par value in this book, because shares with par value are a rapidly diminishing phenomenon for companies incorporated in Canada. However, since par value shares continue to have limited applicability in Canada, issues related to them are covered in Appendix 15A at the end of this Chapter.

Formality of Profit Distribution

Generally, the directors of an enterprise (elected by shareholders) determine what is to be done with profits realized through operations. Profits may be left in the business to permit expansion or merely to provide a margin of safety, or they may be withdrawn and divided among the owners. In a proprietorship or partnership this decision is made by the owner or owners informally and requires no specific action. In a corporation, however, profit distribution is controlled by certain legal restrictions.

First, **no amounts may be distributed among the owners unless the corporate capital is maintained intact.** This reflects the presumption that sufficient security must be left in a corporation to satisfy the liability holders after any dividends have been distributed to shareholders. Various tests of corporate solvency have been used over the years. Under the CBCA, dividends may not be declared or paid if there are reasonable grounds for believing that (1) the corporation is, or would be after the dividend, unable to pay its liabilities as they become due, or (2) the realizable value of the corporation's assets would, as the result of the dividend, be less than the total of its liabilities and stated (legal) capital for all classes of shares.

Second, **distributions to shareholders must be formally approved by the board of directors** and recorded in the minutes of their meetings. As the top executive body in the corporation, the board of directors must make certain that no distributions are made to shareholders that are not justified by profits. Directors are generally held liable to creditors if liabilities cannot be paid because company assets have been illegally paid out to shareholders.

Third, **dividends must be in full agreement with the capital share provisions as to preferences, participation, and the like.** Once the corporation has created specific stipulations regarding the rights of various classes of shareholders, these stipulations must be observed.

CHARACTERISTICS OF PREFERRED SHARES

Preferred shares are a special class of shares because they possess certain preferences or restrictions not possessed by common shares. The following characteristics are those most frequently associated with preferred share issues:

1. Preference as to dividends (rights regarding priority, and whether or not they are cumulative and/or participating).
2. Preference as to assets in the event of liquidation.
3. Convertible into common shares.
4. Callable (redeemable) at the option of the corporation.
5. Retractable at the option of the shareholder.
6. Nonvoting.

A corporation may attach whatever preferences or restrictions in whatever combination it desires to a preferred share issue so long as it does not specifically violate its incorporation law, and it may issue more than one class of preferred shares. The features that distinguish preferred from common shares may be of a more restrictive and negative nature than preferences; for example, the preferred shares may be nonvoting, noncumulative, and nonparticipating. Unless specifically prohibited though, all of the basic rights of ownership apply to preferred shares.

A dividend for shares without par value is usually expressed as a **specific dollar amount per share.** A **priority preference as to dividends** is not an assurance that dividends will be paid; it is merely assurance that the stated dividend applicable to the preferred shares must be paid before dividends can be paid on the common shares.

In addition to a preference as to the priority of payment of dividends, various other features that may be attributed to a class of preferred shares are as follows:

1. **Cumulative.** Dividends not paid in any year must be made up in a later year before any profits can be distributed to common shareholders. If the directors fail to declare a dividend at the normal date for dividend action, the dividend is said to have been "passed." Any passed dividend on cumulative preferred shares constitutes a **dividend in arrears**. Because no liability exists until the board of directors declares a dividend, a dividend in arrears is not recorded as a liability but is disclosed in a note to the financial statements. (In common law, if the corporate articles are silent about the cumulative feature, preferred shares are considered to be cumulative.) Noncumulative preferred shares are seldom issued because a passed dividend is lost forever to the shareholder.

2. **Participating.** Holders of participating preferred shares share ratably with the common shareholders in any profit distributions beyond the prescribed amount. That is, $5 preferred shares, if fully participating, will receive not only their $5 return but also, after a proportional amount per share is paid to common shareholders, additional dividends at the same level as those paid to common shareholders. Moreover, participating preferred shares may not always be fully participating as described, but rather partially participating. For example, provisions may be made that $5 preferred shares will be participating up to a maximum total amount of $10 per share, after which they cease to participate in additional profit distributions. Participating preferred shares, popular in the early 1900s, have seldom been issued in the past few decades.

3. **Convertible.** The shareholders may, at their option, exchange their preferred shares for common shares at a predetermined ratio. The convertible preferred shareholder not only enjoys a prior claim on dividends but also has the option of converting into a common shareholder with unlimited participation in earnings. Convertible preferred shares have been widely used in the past two decades, especially in consummating

business combinations, and are favoured by investors who are attracted by the preferred dividend feature and the possibility of sharing in the long-term success of the company. The accounting problems related to convertible securities are discussed in Chapter 17.

4. **Callable.** The issuing corporation can call or redeem at its option the outstanding preferred shares at specified future dates and at stipulated prices. Many preferred issues are callable. The call or redemption price is ordinarily set slightly above the original issuance price. The callable feature permits the corporation to use the capital obtained through the issuance of such shares until the need has passed or it is no longer advantageous. The existence of a call price or prices tends to set a ceiling on the market value of the preferred shares unless they are convertible into common. When cumulative preferred shares are called for redemption, any dividends in arrears must be paid. For many decades some preferred share issues have contained provisions for redemption at some future date through sinking funds or other means. More recently, some preferred share issues have provided for mandatory redemption within five or ten years of issuance.

5. **Retractable.** The holder of a retractable preferred share may, at his or her option, have the issuing company buy it back, usually at a specified price and at a specified time.

The motivation for issuance of preferred shares instead of debt often lies in the existing debt-to-equity ratio of the issuer. As the ratio weakens because of increasing debt, an issuance of preferred shares may be used to improve upon the ratio. In other instances, issuances are made through private placements with other corporations at a lower than market dividend rate because the acquiring corporation receives some tax advantages.

Debt Characteristics of Preferred Shares

With the right combination of features (i.e., fixed return, no vote, redeemable), preferred shares may possess more of the characteristics of debt than of ownership equity. Preferred shares generally have no maturity date, but the preferred shareholder's relationship with the company may be terminated if the corporation exercises its call privileges. Despite these debt characteristics, preferred shares are usually accounted for as an equity security and reported in the shareholders' equity section of the balance sheet. This accounting emphasizes the legal form of such securities in that they do not have priority over claims of unsecured creditors, and payments to owners are likely to be governed by legal restrictions related to the solvency position of the corporation.

Preferred shares that have essentially the same characteristics as debt (set dividends; fixed term for redemption or are redeemable at the option of the holder) from the issuer's point of view have, however, created concerns over disclosures. In December, 1977, the Accounting Research Committee (renamed the Accounting Standards Committee in 1982) of the CICA issued an Accounting Guideline on **Term-Preferred Shares** (shares having the legal form of equity but many of the characteristics of debt) that stated:

> . . . to allow proper evaluation of the enterprise's financial position, the unique characteristics of term-preferred shares ought to be clearly disclosed in the financial statements. There are basic conceptual issues involved in accounting for term-preferred shares but the Steering Committee believes that until these issues are settled, term-preferred shares would normally be included in shareholders' equity, set out separately from other classes of share capital. In addition to the disclosure requirements of SHARE CAPITAL (in Section 3240 of the *CICA Handbook*), there ought

also to be disclosure of the terms of redemption, including the amounts required in each of the next five years to meet redemption provisions, and other special features.[6]

In the United States, the Securities and Exchange Commission (SEC) issued, in 1979, a rule that prohibited companies from combining preferred shares with common shares in financial statements. Amounts had to be separately presented for redeemable preferred shares,[7] nonredeemable preferred shares, and common shares. The amounts applicable to these three categories of equity items could not be totalled or combined for SEC reporting purposes.

Both the Canadian and U.S. statements have been triggered by concern about the increasing issuance of preferred shares having the attributes of debt and specifying redemption over such relatively short periods as five to ten years. Even though GAAP does not dictate (or prohibit) separate classification for such securities, application of the qualitative characteristic for information of representational faithfulness would suggest that economic substance rather than legal form or description should be a basic consideration regarding their classification in financial statements. To date, accounting standards have not answered the conceptual question of whether term or redeemable preferred shares are a liability or an owners' equity item.

ACCOUNTING FOR THE ISSUANCE OF SHARES

From the preceding discussion of the special features of the corporate system, it can be seen that a corporation obtains funds from its shareholders through a series of events and transactions. After the authorized classes of shares are established in the articles of incorporation, the shares would be offered for sale. Amounts received for shares would be collected and the shares issued. The accounting involved in the issuance of shares is discussed under the following topics:

1. Accounting for shares without par value.
2. Accounting for shares sold on a subscription basis.
3. Accounting for shares issued in combination with other securities.
4. Accounting for additional assessments.
5. Accounting for expenses related to issuance.

Shares Without Par Value

As previously indicated, the CBCA requires that almost all shares issued by com-

---

[6]*Term-Preferred Shares, Accounting Guideline* (Toronto: CICA, December, 1977). *Financial Reporting in Canada—1983* (Toronto: CICA, 1983) indicates that term-preferred shares were disclosed by 50 companies in 1982, 44 in 1981, 36 in 1980, and 32 in 1979. Such shares were generally disclosed as part of share capital in shareholders' equity but were set out separately from other classes of share capital.

[7]*Redeemable preferred shares* are subject to mandatory redemption requirements or have a redemption feature that is outside the control of the issuer. It includes preferred shares that (1) have a fixed or determinable redemption date, (2) are redeemable at the option of the holder, or (3) have conditions for redemption that are not solely within the control of the issuer. *Nonredeemable preferred shares* are not redeemable or are redeemable solely at the option of the issuer. *Securities and Exchange Commission Release No. 33-6097* (Washington, D. C.: SEC, July 27, 1979).

panies incorporated under it be without par or nominal value.[8] Assume that Video Electronics Ltd. is incorporated under the CBCA with 10,000 authorized common shares without par value. No entry, other than a memorandum entry, need be made for the authorization inasmuch as no dollar amount is involved. A memorandum entry or notation simply means that a Common Share account would be created and the number of shares authorized (10,000), and their nature (without par value) would be noted. Entries into this account would be made as share transactions between the company and investors take place. By having such a notation in the account, one can readily determine the number of shares authorized but not issued by deducting the number issued from the authorized number. There are more sophisticated systems for keeping track of the number of shares authorized and issued.

Authorized shares simply represent the classes and nature of shares that a company is entitled to issue. These would be specified in its articles of incorporation. The CBCA allows, but does not require, a corporation to specify a number of authorized shares for each class.

When shares without par value are issued, the full amount of the proceeds received is credited to the appropriate share capital account. If 500 common shares of Video Electronics Ltd. are sold for cash of $10 per share, the entry would be:

Cash	5,000	
Common Shares		5,000

If another 500 shares are sold at a later date for $11 per share, the entry would be:

Cash	5,500	
Common Shares		5,500

The price received for a share is governed by the market place. In determining market price, investors assess the share relative to other shares in terms of such things as rights, future earnings, and risk.

Entries for the sale of preferred shares without par value are of the same nature as illustrated above except that a Preferred Shares account would be credited.

The accounts titled Common Shares or Preferred Shares may alternately be titled Common Stock or Preferred Stock.

Shares Sold on a Subscription Basis

The preceding discussion assumed that the shares were sold for cash, but they may also be sold on a subscription basis. Texaco Canada, Placer Development, and Canada Development Corporation serve as examples of companies that have had subscription issues. When shares are sold on a subscription basis, the full price is not received initially. Normally only a partial payment is made initially, and the shares are not issued, nor rights associated with the shares given, until the full subscription price is received.

---

[8]The CBCA, in Section 26, subsection 1.2, states that, after November 8, 1977, shares issued in non-arm's length transactions (in the meaning of that term in the Income Tax Act) may have the whole or any part of the consideration received in exchange added to the stated capital amounts for the shares of the class. As such, assigning an amount less than that deemed to be received for shares is possible under this Act, but the circumstances under which such a treatment would be permitted pertain to tax issues and occur infrequently. When this does happen, the excess of amount received over the value assigned to the shares would be credited to a Contributed Capital account.

Accounting for Subscribed Shares   Two new accounts are used when shares are sold on a subscription basis. The first, **Common** (or **Preferred) Shares Subscribed**, indicates the corporation's obligation to issue shares upon payment of final subscription balances by those who have subscribed. This account thus signifies a commitment against the unissued capital shares. Once the subscription price is fully paid, the Common (or Preferred) Shares Subscribed account is debited and the Common (or Preferred) Shares account is credited. Shares Subscribed accounts are presented in the shareholders' equity section below the respective Common or Preferred Shares accounts.

The second account, **Subscriptions Receivable,** indicates the amount yet to be collected before subscribed shares will be issued. Controversy exists concerning the presentation of Subscriptions Receivable on the balance sheet. Some argue that Subscriptions Receivable should be reported in the current asset section (assuming that payment on the receivable will be received within the operating cycle or one year, whichever is longer). They note that it is a receivable similar to trade accounts receivable, but that it differs in conception. Trade accounts receivable grow out of sales transactions in the ordinary course of business; subscriptions receivable relate to the issuance of a concern's own shares and in a sense represent capital contributions not yet paid the corporation.

Others argue that Subscriptions Receivable should be reported as a deduction from Common (or Preferred) Shares Subscribed in the shareholders' equity section. Their reasoning is based on a concern that doing otherwise may result in users of financial statements misunderstanding the share capital accounts (i.e., not realizing that some shares are only partially paid for), and the fact that subscribers cannot be forced to pay the unpaid balance of a subscription receivable.

It should be emphasized that there is no ''right'' answer to this classification issue. Judgement must therefore be exercised. In the United States, practice generally follows the contra-equity approach, which is required in reports to the SEC.

The journal entries for handling shares sold on a subscription basis are illustrated by the following example. Lakehead Corp. offers 500 common shares of no-par value on a subscription basis at a price of $20 per share. Various individuals accept the company's offer and agree to pay 50% down in cash and the remaining 50% at the end of six months. At the date the subscriptions are received, the entries are:

Subscriptions Receivable	10,000	
Common Shares Subscribed		10,000
(To record receipt of subscriptions for 500 shares)		
Cash	5,000	
Subscriptions Receivable		5,000
(To record receipt of first instalment representing 50% of total due on subscribed shares)		

When the final payment is received and the shares are issued, the entries are:

Cash	5,000	
Subscriptions Receivable		5,000
(To record receipt of final instalment on subscribed shares)		
Common Shares Subscribed	10,000	
Common Shares		10,000
(To record issuance of 500 shares upon receipt of final instalment from subscribers)		

Assume that Lakehead Corp. had 10,000 common shares authorized, and had previously issued 5,000 shares for a total of $75,000. The receivable and subscribed accounts after the subscription was received could be shown as follows, using the contra-equity approach:

Lakehead Corp.
PARTIAL BALANCE SHEET

Shareholders' Equity
  Share Capital

Common shares, no-par value, 10,000 authorized, 5,000 issued.		$75,000
Common shares subscribed (500 shares)	$10,000	
Less: Subscriptions receivable	(5,000)	5,000
Total share capital		$80,000

Alternatively, the $5,000 subscription receivable could be shown as a current asset and the Common Shares Subscribed amount would be shown as the gross amount ($10,000) in Shareholders' Equity.

Defaulted Subscription Accounts   Sometimes a subscriber is unable to pay all instalments and defaults on the agreement. The question is then raised of what to do with the balance of the subscription account as well as the amount already paid in. The solution to this problem depends on the terms of the subscription contract, corporate policy, and any applicable law of the jurisdiction of incorporation. The possibilities include returning the amount already paid by the subscriber (possibly after deducting some expenses), treating the amount paid as forfeited and therefore transferred to a Contributed Capital account, or issuing shares to the subscriber equivalent to the number that previous subscription payments would have paid in full.

Shares Issued in Combination with Other Securities (Lump Sum Sales)

Generally, corporations sell classes of shares separately from one another so that the proceeds are known relative to each class, and ordinarily even relative to each lot. Occasionally, two or more classes of securities are issued for a single payment or lump sum. It is not uncommon for more than one type or class of security to be issued in the acquisition of another company. The accounting problem in a lump sum issuance is to determine the allocation of the proceeds between the several classes of securities. The two methods of allocation available for accountants are (1) the proportional method and (2) the incremental method.

Proportional Method   If the fair market value or another sound basis for determining relative value is available for each class of security, the **lump sum received is best allocated between the classes of securities on a proportional basis**—that is, in accordance with the ratio that each is to the total. For instance, if 1,000 common shares having a market value of $20 a share and 1,000 preferred shares having a market value of $12 a share are issued for a lump sum of $30,000, the allocation of the $30,000 to the two classes would be as shown on page 703:

Fair market value of common (1,000 × $20) = $20,000
Fair market value of preferred (1,000 × $12) =   12,000

Aggregate fair market value $32,000

Allocated to common: $\dfrac{\$20,000}{\$32,000}$ × $30,000 = $18,750

Allocated to preferred: $\dfrac{\$12,000}{\$32,000}$ × $30,000 = $11,250

Total allocation $30,000

Incremental Method   In instances **where the fair market value of all classes of securities is not determinable, the incremental method may be used.** The market value of the securities is used as a basis for those classes that are known, and the remainder of the lump sum is allocated to the class for which the market value is not known. For instance, if 1,000 common shares having a market value of $20 and 1,000 preferred shares having no established market value are issued for a lump sum of $30,000, the allocation of the $30,000 to the two classes would be as follows:

Lump sum receipt $30,000
Allocated to common (1,000 shares × $20 fair market value)   20,000

Balance allocated to preferred $10,000

If no fair market value is determinable for any of the classes of shares involved **in a lump sum exchange, the allocation may have to be arbitrary.** If it is known that one or more of the classes of securities issued will have a determinable market value in the near future, the arbitrary basis may be used with the intent to make an adjustment when the future market value is established.

Shares Issued in Noncash Transactions

It is not uncommon for a corporation to issue shares in exchange for property, services, or any form of asset other than cash. Accounting for the issuance of shares for property or services may involve a problem of valuation. **The general rule to be applied when shares are issued for services or property other than cash is that the property or services be recorded at either its fair market value or the fair market value of the shares issued, whichever is more clearly determinable.**

If the fair market value of the property or services is readily determinable, it is used as a basis for recording the exchange. If it is not readily determinable but the fair market value of the shares issued is, the transaction is recorded at the fair market value of the shares. If both are readily determinable and the transaction is the result of an arm's-length exchange, there will probably be little difference in their fair market values. In such cases it should not matter which value is regarded as the basis for valuing the exchange. If the fair market value of the shares being issued and the property or services being received are not readily determinable, the value to be assigned is generally established by the board of directors, usually through independent appraisals. The use of the book values as a basis of valuation for these transactions should be avoided.

When shares are issued for personal services by employees or outsiders, the fair value of the services as of the date of the contract for such services, rather than the date of issuance of the shares, should be the basis for valuation because the contract is viewed in an accounting sense as a subscription. In these exchanges, however, the fair market value of the shares issued is usually more readily determinable.

The following series of transactions illustrates recording the issuance of 10,000 common shares for a patent under various circumstances:

1. The fair market value of the patent is not readily determinable but the fair market value of the shares is known to be $140,000.

Patent	140,000	
Common Shares		140,000

2. The fair market value of the shares is not readily determinable, but the fair market value of the patent is determined to be $150,000.

Patent	150,000	
Common Shares		150,000

3. Neither the fair market value of the share nor the patent is readily determinable. An independent consultant values the patent at $125,000, and the board of directors agrees with that valuation.

Patent	125,000	
Common Shares		125,000

In corporate law, the board of directors is granted the power to set the value of noncash transactions. In some instances, this power has been abused. The issuance of shares for property or services has resulted in cases of overstated corporate capital through intentional overvaluation of the property or services received. The overvaluation of the shareholders' equity resulting from inflated asset values creates what is referred to as **watered stock.** The "water" can be eliminated from the corporate structure by writing down the overvalued assets.

If, as a result of the issuance of shares for property or services, the recorded assets are undervalued, **secret reserves** are created. A secret reserve may also be achieved by excessive depreciation or amortization charges, by expensing capital expenditures, by excessive write-downs of inventories or receivables, or by any other understatement of assets or overstatement of liabilities. An example of a liability overstatement is an excessive provision for estimated product warranties that correspondingly results in an understatement of owners' equity, thereby creating a secret reserve.

Assessments on Capital Shares

The laws of some jurisdictions provide that a corporation may assess shareholders an additional amount above their original contributions. Although this situation occurs rather infrequently, when shareholders are assessed they must either pay or possibly forfeit their existing shares. Upon receiving the assessments from the shareholders, the corporation would credit an account such as Contributed Capital Arising from Assessments. Shares issued by companies incorporated under the CBCA cannot be assessed.

Costs of Issuing Shares

The costs associated with the acquisition of corporate capital resulting from the issuance of securities include attorneys' fees, public accountants' fees, underwriters' fees and commissions, expenses of printing and mailing certificates and registration statements, clerical and administrative expenses of preparing, and costs of advertising the issue.

In practice there are two primary methods of accounting for initial issue costs. **The first method treats issue costs as a reduction of the amounts paid in.** In effect, such a treatment has the result of simply reducing the amount received for issued shares. This treatment is based on the premise that issue costs are unrelated to corporate operations and thus are not properly chargeable against earnings from operations; issue costs are viewed as a reduction of proceeds of the financing activity.

The second method treats issue costs as an organization cost that is charged neither to current earnings nor to corporate capital; such costs are capitalized and classified as a deferred charge and written off over an arbitrary time period. This treatment is based on the premise that amounts paid in as invested capital should not be violated, and that issue costs benefit the corporation over a long period of time or so long as the invested capital is used.

In addition to the costs of issuing shares, corporations annually incur costs of maintaining the shareholders' records and handling ownership transfers. These recurring costs, primarily registrar and transfer agents' fees, should be charged as expense to the period in which incurred.

REACQUISITION OF SHARES

Corporations may wish to purchase or redeem (in the case of redeemable preferred shares) their outstanding shares for a variety of reasons. These reasons include:

1. To have enough shares on hand to meet employee stock option contracts.
2. To reduce the shares outstanding in hopes of increasing earnings per share.
3. To buy out a particular ownership interest.
4. To attempt to make a market in the company's shares.
5. To contract the operations of the business.
6. To meet the share needs of a potential merger.
7. To change the debt ratio.
8. To settle a debt.
9. To eliminate fractional shares.
10. To fulfill terms of a contract.
11. To satisfy a claim of a dissenting shareholder.
12. To change from public to private corporation status.

Whether or not a corporation may purchase its own shares and what it may do with them depends on the terms and conditions of its articles of incorporation and the legal constraints imposed by the Act under which it is incorporated.

Assuming that a corporation may purchase or otherwise reacquire its own shares, they may either be (1) retired (cancelled) or (2) held in treasury for reissue. Issues related to each of these treatments are discussed under the separate headings that follow.

Reacquisition and Retirement

The CBCA and acts of various provinces permit a corporation to purchase or redeem its shares by special resolution of its board of directors as long as such an action would not result in the corporation's becoming insolvent. Insolvency (under the CBCA) would result if, after reacquisition, the corporation were unable to pay its liabilities or if the realizable value of its assets were less than its liabilities and stated capital. The reacquired shares would be cancelled or, if the articles have an authorized limit on the number of shares, restored to the status of authorized but unissued shares.

When shares are purchased or redeemed by the issuing corporation it is likely that the price paid will differ from the amount received for the shares when they were issued. It would be incorrect to treat any differences as a gain or loss shown in the income statement, owing to the capital nature of the transaction. Consequently, when shares are purchased or redeemed and cancelled, shareholders' equity accounts are adjusted. The accounts adjusted and the nature of the adjustment is specified in the *CICA Handbook*:

> Where a company redeems its own shares, or cancels its own shares that it has acquired, and the cost of such shares is equal to or greater than their par, stated, or assigned value, the cost should be allocated as follows:
>
> (a)   To share capital, in an amount equal to the par, stated, or assigned value of the shares;
>
> (b)   Any excess, to contributed surplus to the extent that contributed surplus was created by a net excess of proceeds over cost on cancellation or resale of shares of the same class;
>
> (c)   Any excess, to contributed surplus in an amount equal to the pro rata share of the portion of contributed surplus that arose from transactions, other than those in (b) above, in the same class of shares;
>
> (d)   Any excess, to retained earnings.[9]

In the case where the cost to purchase shares is less than the par, stated, or assigned value, the cost would be allocated as follows:

> (a)   To share capital in an amount equal to the par, stated or assigned value of the shares;
>
> (b)   The difference, to contributed surplus.[10]

These specifications are written to apply to both par and no-par value shares. For no-par value shares, the amount of the cost of reacquisition to be charged against the Share Capital account is an assigned value equal to the average per share amount in the account for that class of share at the date of the reacquisition of the shares.[11] This would, therefore, be the average of the amounts of the proceeds received for all of the no-par value shares that had been issued. For no-par value shares, reacquisition and cancellation at a cost in excess of assigned value would, following the steps in the *Handbook*, normally result in simply debiting the Share Capital (step a) and Retained Earnings (step d). An exception to this procedure would occur if a prior cancellation of some shares of this class had resulted in the creation of Contributed Surplus; that is, if the cost of the shares purchased was less than their assigned value at that time. In such a case, purchase for cancellation at a cost in excess of assigned value would result in a reduction of the Share Capital

---

[9]*CICA Handbook*, Section 3240, par. 15.

[10]*Ibid.*, par. 17.

[11]*Ibid.*, par. 18.

account for the assigned value (step a), the Contributed Surplus account created by the prior transaction (step b), and the Retained Earnings account if necessary (step d).

To illustrate the application of the accounting procedures for the purchase and cancellation of no-par shares, assume the following composition of shareholders' equity for Waterloo Corp. as a starting point.

Waterloo Corp.	
SHAREHOLDERS' EQUITY	
December 31, 1985	
Share Capital:	
Class A, 10,500 shares issued	
and outstanding, no-par value	$ 63,000
Class B, 50,000 shares issued	
and outstanding, no-par value	100,000
Total Share Capital	$163,000
Retained Earnings	300,000
Total Shareholders' Equity	$463,000

On January 30, 1986, Waterloo Corp. purchased and cancelled 500 Class A shares. The purchase cost was $4 per share. The required entry would be:

Class A Shares [500 ($63,000 ÷ 10,500)]	3,000	
Cash		2,000
Contributed Capital—Excess of Assigned Value		
over Reacquisition Cost		1,000

This entry is derived by following the allocation procedure when the cost to purchase is less than the assigned value of shares cancelled.

On September 10, 1986, the company purchased and cancelled an additional 1,000 Class A shares. The purchase cost was $8 per share. This transaction would be recorded as:

Class A Shares [1,000 ($60,000 ÷ 10,000)]	6,000	
Contributed Capital—Excess of Assigned Value		
over Reacquisition Cost	1,000	
Retained Earnings	1,000	
Cash		8,000

This entry is derived by following the steps for the situation where the cost of the shares purchased is greater than their assigned value. Specifically, the procedure would be as follows:

Step (a): Remove from share capital the assigned value of the Class A shares cancelled. The assigned value is the amount in the Class A Shares account ($60,000, which is the $63,000 on December 31 less the $3,000 debit for the reacquisition on January 30) divided by the number of shares issued and outstanding (10,000, which is the 10,500 on December 31 less the 500 reacquired on January 30) at the date of the reacquisition.

Step (b): If there is any contributed capital arising from previous cancellations of the same share class (i.e., when the cost of purchased shares was less than its assigned value), it would be removed by a debit to that account. The amount would be the lesser of the account's total balance or the amount by which the purchase cost exceeds the assigned value of the cancelled shares. From the cancellation of Class A shares on January 30, 1986, such a Contributed Capital account resulted in a $1,000 balance. Since the purchase cost of the present cancellation was $2,000 greater than the assigned value, the full $1,000 balance in this Contributed Capital account is debited.

Step (c):   If, after steps (a) and (b), there is still an excess of cost to be accounted for, this excess is to be charged against any Contributed Capital account—other than that in (b)—that arose from transactions in the same class of shares. The maximum that can be charged to such accounts is based on a pro rata share allocation of the account balance. A pro rata share allocation is determined by dividing the number of shares reacquired by the number of shares issued prior to the reacquisition and multiplying the result by the balance in the Contributed Capital account. There are no such Contributed Capital accounts in this example, and they would be rare in the case of no-par value shares (Contributed Capital on Forfeited Shares would be an example). Such accounts exist for par value shares in which the proceeds received in excess of par value are credited to a Contributed Capital account.

Step (d):   Since there is still an excess of $1,000 of the cost over allocations made in the previous steps, this amount is charged against Retained Earnings.

While this example has illustrated calculations associated with all steps in the process, it would not be necessary to continue through steps beyond those required to allocate the total purchase cost of the shares cancelled. For example, if the cost had been only $6,700, the full amount would be accounted for by debiting the Class A Shares for $6,000 and the Contributed Capital—Excess of Assigned Value over Reacquisition Cost account for $700. If there are no accounts in Contributed Surplus arising from transactions in the class of shares involved, steps (b) and (c) would be omitted.

TREASURY SHARES

Treasury shares or treasury stock are the terms used to describe a company's own shares that have been repurchased but have not been cancelled; they are being held for reissue.

While Canadian corporate law has allowed companies to issue redeemable preferred shares for some time, it was not until 1971 that corporations were permitted to purchase other types of their own shares. At that time, Ontario's incorporation act allowed for such transactions for the first time in a Canadian jurisdiction. Since then, the CBCA and provincial acts have allowed corporations to reacquire their own shares. Legislation varies, however, in terms of what companies may do with such shares. As previously stated, the CBCA requires that repurchased shares be cancelled and, if the articles limit the number of authorized shares, be restored to the status of authorized but unissued shares. Two exceptions allowed by the CBCA are (1) when acting in the capacity of a legal representative not receiving any beneficial interest from the shares and (2) when such shares are held as security for purposes of ordinary business transactions that involve the lending of money.

Consequently, with rare exception, there can be no such thing as treasury shares for companies incorporated under the CBCA. Alternatively, some provincial jurisdictions do permit such treasury shares to exist.[12] When a corporation holds treasury shares, voting rights and dividend declarations do not usually apply to these shares.

Two basic approaches of accounting for treasury shares have developed.[13] These are called the **two-transaction method** and the **single-transaction method.** The differences between the two are based upon the presumption of the underlying nature of treasury shares transactions.

---

[12]*"Financial Reporting in Canada—1983* reported that, of the 325 companies surveyed, 10 in 1982, 9 in 1981, 13 in 1980, and 10 in 1979 disclosed the acquisition of their own common shares. Also, it was reported that 24 companies in 1982, 14 in 1981, 11 in 1980, and 13 in 1979 disclosed cancellations of common shares purchased.

[13]*CICA Handbook,* Section 3240.

Two-Transaction Method   The presumption associated with this method is that the purchase by a company of its own shares terminates the relationship between the company and the shareholder. Such an acquisition therefore represents a completed, independent transaction in terms of the company's capital. A subsequent resale of the acquired shares is also viewed as a separate, independent transaction. Therefore, these two transactions (purchase and sale of shares) would be recorded independently of each other.

The purchase transaction under this method is recorded as if the shares were retired. Therefore, the journal entry would result in the reduction of shareholders' equity accounts in the same manner as was illustrated in the previous section dealing with reacquisition and retirement of shares. The reissuance transaction is treated in a manner similar to a transaction involving the original issuance of shares.

To illustrate the accounting entries under the two-transaction approach, assume as a starting point the information regarding the shareholders' equity of Waterloo Corp. as at December 31, 1985 (page 707). On January 15, 1986, the company reacquired as treasury stock 1,000 Class A shares by paying $7 per share. This repurchase would be recorded, under the repurchase steps, as follows:

Class A Shares	6,000	
Retained Earnings	1,000	
Cash		7,000

A variation on this entry would be to debit an account called Treasury Shares instead of the Class A Shares account. When such an account is used under this method it would be set up as a contra account to the Class A Shares balance in terms of balance sheet disclosure.

The treasury shares were sold on February 15 for $8 per share. When treasury shares with no-par value are sold, the full amount received is credited to the Share Capital account (i.e., as if the shares were being issued for the first time). Therefore, the entry to record the sale of these shares would be:

Cash	8,000	
Class A Shares		8,000

Had a Treasury Shares account been used in the January 15 entry, that account would be credited for its balance ($6,000) and the difference between this amount and the cash proceeds received would go to the Class A Shares account as follows:

Cash	8,000	
Treasury Shares		6,000
Class A Shares		2,000

Single-Transaction Method   The presumption underlying this method (also called the cost method) is that the purchase and sale of treasury shares are essentially two parts of a single procedure being used by a corporation. In essence, the acquisition of treasury shares is the initiation of a transaction that is consummated when the shares are resold. Consequently, the holding by a company of its own shares is viewed as a transition phase between the beginning and end of a single activity.

When shares are purchased under the single-transaction method, the total cost is debited to a Treasury Shares account. There are no direct reductions of any Shareholders' Equity accounts. The balance in the Treasury Shares account would be shown as a deduction from the total of the components of Shareholders' Equity in the balance sheet.[14] An example of such disclosure is as follows:

Shareholders' equity:	
Common shares, no-par value; authorized	
24,000,000 shares; issued 19,045,870 shares	$ 27,686,000
Retained earnings	253,265,000
Total	$280,951,000
Less: Cost of treasury shares (209,970 shares)	(7,527,000)
Total shareholders' equity	$273,424,000

When the shares are sold, the Treasury Shares account is credited for their cost. If they are sold for more than their cost, the excess is credited to a Contributed Capital account. If they are sold at less than their cost, the difference is debited to any balance in a Contributed Capital account resulting from previous sales or cancellations of treasury shares and any remaining difference is charged against Retained Earnings.

The entries associated with the single-transaction method are illustrated below, using the same information as was used for the two-transaction method. January 15, 1986—1,000 Class A shares were purchased as treasury stock at $7 per share:

Treasury Shares	7,000	
Cash		7,000

February 15, 1986—all treasury shares were sold for $8 per share:

Cash	8,000	
Treasury Shares		7,000
Contributed Capital—Excess of sale price		
of treasury shares over cost		1,000

If treasury shares recorded under the single-transaction method are subsequently retired (cancelled), then the procedure for cancelling shares is applied, with the balance in the Treasury Shares account being eliminated. For example, if instead of selling the treasury shares bought on February 15, Waterloo Corp. decided to cancel them, the entry at the time of that decision would be:

Class A Shares	6,000	
Retained Earnings	1,000	
Treasury Shares		7,000

The *CICA Handbook* states that the single-transaction method should be the method of accounting for the acquisition of treasury shares by a company.[15] Both methods may be used in the United States.

BASIC RECORDS RELATED TO SHARES

A share or stock certificate book and a share or stock transfer book are included among the special corporate records involved in accounting for shares. A share certificate book is similar to a cheque book in that printed share certificates are enclosed. A share transfer book simply tells who owns the shares at a given point

[14]*Ibid.*, par. 11.

[15]*Ibid.*, par 10.

in time. Obviously the corporation must be able to obtain at any time a list of the current shareholders so that dividend payments, notices of annual shareholder meetings, and voting proxies may be sent to the proper persons.

Many corporations avoid the problems concerned with handling share capital sales and transfers by engaging some organization that specializes in this type of work to serve as a **registrar and transfer agent.** Trust companies frequently serve in this capacity, keeping all the necessary records. The corporation is provided upon request with a list of registered shareholders for such purposes as mailing dividend cheques or voting proxies.

As might be expected, certain accounts act as controlling accounts in the general ledger, with subsidiary ledgers to supply necessary detail. These are:

General Ledger Account	Subsidiary Ledger
Common or Preferred Shares	Shareholders' Ledger
Subscriptions Receivable	Subscriptions Receivable Ledger
Common or Preferred Shares Subscribed	Subscribed Shares Ledger

KEY POINTS

1. The shareholders' equity section is generally the least understood part of the financial statements because of its legalistic nature and the use of distinctive accounting terminology.

2. Shareholders' equity represents the ownership interest in a corporation. It is the difference between total assets and liabilities (i.e., the net assets). Shareholders have a residual interest in an enterprise in the sense that they rank after liability holders in claim to the assets.

3. Direct contributions by shareholders and earnings retained by a corporation are the primary sources from which ownership equity is derived. The contributions by shareholders are generally subclassified on the balance sheet as share capital and contributed surplus. Share capital is that portion of equity that is required by statute to be retained in the business for the protection of creditors. Contributed surplus represents additional amounts received from shareholders, such as donations. Retained earnings is the undistributed income that remains invested in the enterprise.

4. Canadian companies may be incorporated under the Canada Business Corporations Act (CBCA) or a provincial incorporation act. For purposes of this book, we have concentrated on the CBCA, although it should be realized that acts of different jurisdictions may vary. A major aspect of the CBCA is that it confers legal status on the *CICA Handbook;* that is, regulations under this Act require that financial statements be prepared in accordance with the recommendations in the *Handbook.*

5. Ownership interests are represented by share certificates. Basic ownership rights are to share in profits, to share in management (vote at shareholder meetings), and to share in corporate assets upon liquidation. Shares possessing these basic rights have been called "common shares." Common shareholders bear the ultimate risk of failure and benefit of success. Other types of shares (called "preferred shares") may exist. Various rights, privileges, restrictions, and conditions would attach to preferred shares that differentiate them from the basic common shares. The particulars regarding preferred shares would be specified in an enterprise's articles of incorporation. While

the CBCA simply states that shares may be of different "classes" (i.e., A, B, C, etc.), we have used the terms "common" and "preferred" to represent the existence of these differences.

6. Preferred shares may have various rights, privileges, or restrictions assigned in terms of dividends or distribution of assets on liquidation, may be convertible, callable, or retractable, and usually are non-voting. In some cases (term preferred shares), the economic nature of a preferred share is that it has the characteristics of debt even though it may have the legal form of being equity. Such circumstances create a dilemma for accountants in terms of classification questions.

7. Accounting for share capital was examined with regard to issuance of shares without par value for cash and non-cash items, in combination with issuing different equity securities, and on a subscription basis. Accounting issues and procedures related to costs incurred for issuing shares were also identified. Although the notion of par value remains an aspect of accounting for share capital, its importance is rapidly diminishing in Canadian financial reporting. Consequently, coverage of par value shares has been relegated to Appendix 15A.

8. A corporation may purchase its own shares for various reasons. Such reacquired shares are not an asset of the enterprise because a corporation may not own part of itself.

9. While permitting reacquisition of shares, the CBCA requires that such shares be retired (cancelled) or restored to the status of authorized but unissued shares. Reacquisition and retirement of shares without par value is accounted for by removing the average amount received for the shares (assigned value) from the Share Capital account and charging any excess amount paid to a Contributed Capital account if such exists from previous similar transactions and then to Retained Earnings, if necessary. If the cost of reacquisition is less than the assigned value, the difference would be credited to a Contributed Capital account.

10. In some cases, the jurisdiction of incorporation may permit reacquisition without requiring cancellation. In such cases, the shares held are called treasury shares. The two-transaction method and the single-transaction method of accounting for treasury shares were illustrated. The *CICA Handbook* recommends that the single-transaction method should be used.

15A

ACCOUNTING FOR PAR VALUE SHARES

As indicated in the chapter, par value is an arbitrary amount per share determined by the incorporators of a company and stated as such in the articles of incorporation. When a par value exists, it is usually very low ($1, $5, $10 per share), which contrasts dramatically with the situation in the early 1900s when practically all shares had a par value of $100. The reason for having low par values is to permit the original sale of shares at low amounts per share and at the same time avoid the contingent liability of shareholders associated with shares sold below par. Shares with a low par value are rarely, if ever, sold by the issuing company below par value. A par value has nothing to do with the market value of the share. The accounting significance of par value is that it is the amount per share issued that is credited to the share capital account. Amounts received above or below par value are charged to other accounts, as will be illustrated shortly.

Par value shares were common in Canada until recent years. In 1975, the Canada Business Corporations Act (CBCA) decreed that par value shares were no longer permitted for companies incorporated under it. Such enterprises had five years from January 1, 1976, to file for continuance under the CBCA; that is, to switch from the requirements of the predecessor Canada Corporations Act to those of the CBCA. Most provincial incorporation acts followed the example of the CBCA in requiring that share capital would be of no-par value. The development of consistent regulations across all Canadian jurisdictions and the necessary conversion by companies from old to new requirements has taken considerable time. Indeed, at the time of writing this edition, it was evident that companies were still reporting par value. *Financial Reporting in Canada—1983* indicated that in 1982, of the 325 companies surveyed, 148 had all share classes without par value whereas 105 had disclosed a par value (or a stated value) for at least one class of shares (72 made no reference to either par or no-par value). Consequently, it would appear safe to conclude that Canadian practice is currently in a state of transition regarding the elimination of the use of par value shares. Although we have chosen basically to follow the CBCA requirements regarding the use of shares without par value throughout this book, we recognize that some may wish to consider the accounting aspects related to par value to a greater extent than is possible from the limited references to it in the chapter. Moreover, a more comprehensive examination of such accounting may be beneficial to understanding financial statements that incorporate par value shares (i.e., those of companies that are, as yet, continuing under old acts until it is no longer permitted, are operating in jurisdictions permitting par value, or are incorporated in such countries as the United States, which permits par value shares). For these reasons, the material in this Appendix is presented. The accounting for par value shares will be examined under the following headings:

- Issuance of par value shares for cash.
- Par value shares sold on a subscription basis.
- Reacquisition and retirement of par value shares.
- Treasury shares.

Issuance of Par Value Shares for Cash

To show the required information for issuance of par value shares, accounts must be kept for each class as follows:

1. **Preferred Shares or Common Shares.** Reflects the par value of the corporation's issued shares. These accounts are credited for the par value when the shares are originally issued. No additional entries are made in these accounts unless additional shares are issued or shares are retired.

2. **Contributed Capital in Excess of Par or Premium on Common (or Preferred) Shares.** Indicates any excess over par value paid in by shareholders in return for the shares issued to them. Once paid in, the excess over par becomes a part of the corporation's contributed surplus and the individual shareholder has no greater claim on the excess paid in than all other holders of the same class of shares.

3. **Discount on Shares.** Indicates that the shares have been issued at less than par. The holder of shares issued below par may be called on to pay in the amount of the discount if necessary to prevent creditors from sustaining a loss upon liquidation of the corporation. Sale of shares at a discount is generally not permitted in Canada.

To illustrate how these accounts are used, assume that Hamilton Corporation sold 100 common shares with a par value of $5 per share for $1,100. The entry to record the issuance is:

Cash	1,100	
Common Shares		500
Contributed Capital in Excess of Par		600
(Premium on Common Shares)		

If the shares had been sold for $300, the entry would have been recorded as follows:

Cash	300	
Discount on Common Shares (a contra account to		
common shares)	200	
Common Shares		500

While these entries reflect the receipt of cash for the shares, such shares could be issued in combination with other securities (lump sum sales) or for noncash items. In such situations, the basic issue is to determine the amount (fair value) received for the shares. Solutions to these issues are the same as those stated in Chapter 15 regarding shares without par value. Once the amount received for par value shares has been determined, the par value is credited to the appropriate Share Capital account, and any excess or deficiency goes to a Contributed Capital or Discount account respectively.

Par Value Shares Sold on a Subscription Basis

The journal entries for handling par value shares sold on a subscription basis are illustrated by the following example. Mercury Ltd. offers 500 common shares of $5 par value on a subscription basis at a price of $20 per share. Various individuals accept the company's offer and agree to pay 50% down and to pay the remaining 50% at the end of six months.

At date of issuance:

Subscriptions Receivable	10,000	
Common Shares Subscribed		2,500
Contributed Capital in Excess of Par		7,500
(To record receipt of subscriptions for 500 shares)		
Cash	5,000	
Subscriptions Receivable		5,000
(To record receipt of first instalment repre-		
senting 50% of total due on subscribed shares)		

When the final payment is received and the shares are issued, the entries are:

Six months later:

Cash	5,000	
Subscriptions Receivable		5,000
(To record receipt of final instalment on		
subscribed shares)		
Common Shares Subscribed	2,500	
Common Shares		2,500
(To record issuance of 500 shares upon receipt of		
final instalment from subscribers)		

Reacquisition and Retirement of Par Value Shares

To illustrate the accounting procedures for the purchase and cancellation of par value shares, the Waterloo Corp. example referred to in Chapter 15 regarding reacquisition and retirement of no-par value shares will be drawn upon. This will allow for comparison between par value and no-par value shares. Two modifications to the original shareholders' equity section are made: the Class A shares issued for $63,000 had a $5 par value resulting in a Premium on Class A Shares which is a Contributed Surplus account. Therefore, the starting point for this illustration is as shown on page 716.

Waterloo Corp.
SHAREHOLDERS' EQUITY
December 31, 1985

Share Capital	
Class A, 10,500 shares issued	
and outstanding, $5 par value	$52,500
Class B, 50,000 shares issued	
and outstanding, no-par value	100,000
Total Share Capital	$152,500
Contributed Surplus:	
Premium on Class A Shares	10,500
Retained Earnings	300,000
Total Shareholders' Equity	$463,000

On January 30, 1986, Waterloo Corp. purchased and cancelled 500 Class A shares. The purchase cost was $4 per share. The required entry would be:

Class A Shares	2,500	
Cash		2,000
Contributed Capital—Excess of Par Value over		
Reacquisition Cost (Class A)		500

This entry is derived by following the *CICA Handbook* allocation procedure as identified in Chapter 15 when the cost to purchase is less than the par value of shares cancelled.

On September 10, 1986, the company purchased and cancelled an additional 1,000 Class A shares. The purchase cost was $8 per share. This transaction would be recorded as:

Class A Shares	5,000	
Contributed Capital—Excess of Par Value over		
Reacquisition Cost	500	
Contributed Capital—Premium on Class A Shares	1,050	
Retained Earnings	1,450	
Cash		8,000

This entry is derived by following the steps in the *CICA Handbook* for the situations where the cost of the shares purchased is greater than their par or assigned value. Specifically, the procedure would be as follows:

Step (a): Remove from share capital the par value of the Class A shares cancelled. This is equal to the par value ($5) multiplied by the shares purchased (1,000).

Step (b): If there is any contributed capital arising from previous cancellations of the same share class (i.e., when cost of purchased shares was less than its par value), it would be removed by a debit to that account. The amount would be the lesser of the account's total balance or the amount by which the purchase cost exceeds the par value of the cancelled shares. From the cancellation of Class A shares January 30, 1986, such a Contributed Capital account resulted in a $500 balance. Since the purchase cost of the present cancellation was $3,000 greater than the par value, the full $500 balance in this Contributed Capital account is debited.

Step (c): If, after steps (a) and (b), there is still an excess of cost to be accounted for, this excess is to be charged against any Contributed Surplus account—other than that in (b)—that arose from transactions in the same class of shares. In this example, Premium on Class A Shares is such an account. The maximum that can be charged to such accounts is based on a pro rata share allocation of the account balance. A pro rata share allocation is determined by dividing the number of shares purchased (1,000) by the number of shares issued prior to the purchase (10,500 from December 31 less 500 retired on January 30 equals 10,000) and multiplying the result (0.1) by the account balance ($10,500). The maximum pro rata share allocation of $1,050 is debited to the Premium on Class A Shares account, because there is an excess of cost over allocations made in steps (a) and (b) of $2,500.

Step (d):   Since there is still an excess of $1,450 of the cost over allocations made in steps (a), (b), and (c), this amount is charged against Retained Earnings.

If the cost to reacquire the shares had been only $5,300, the full amount would be accounted for by debiting the Class A Shares for $5,000 and the Contributed Capital—Excess of Par Value over Reacquisition Cost account for $300.

Treasury Shares

The basic concepts of accounting for treasury shares under the two-transaction and the single-transaction methods were specified in Chapter 15 and continue to apply to par value shares. Again, for purposes of comparison between par value and no-par value shares accounting, we will use the example of the shareholders' equity section of Waterloo Corp. as at December 31, 1985, as a starting point. The events related to treasury shares transactions are:

January 15, 1986—the company acquired treasury shares of 1,000 Class A
$5 par value shares by paying $7 per share.
February 15, 1986—the treasury shares were sold for $8 per share.

Using the two-transaction method, the journal entries would be:

	January 15	
Class A Shares	5,000	
Premium on Class A Shares	1,000	
Retained Earnings	1,000	
Cash		7,000

$$*\text{Pro rata share allocation} = \frac{1,000 \text{ shares}}{10,500 \text{ shares}} \times \$10,500$$
$$= \$1,000$$

	February 15	
Cash	8,000	
Contributed Capital—Excess of sales price of treasury shares over par value		3,000
Class A Shares		5,000

If a Treasury Shares account had been used in the repurchase entry, that account rather than Class A Shares would have been credited for $5,000 when the shares were sold. However, if the treasury shares had been sold for less than par, the Class A Shares (Treasury Shares) account would still be credited for the par value and the excess would be debited first to any credit balance in a Contributed Capital account arising from previous sales or cancellations of treasury shares, and second to Retained Earnings.

Using the single-transaction method, the following entries would be made:

	January 15	
Treasury Shares	7,000	
Cash		7,000

	February 15	
Cash	8,000	
Treasury Shares		7,000
Contributed Capital—Excess of sale price of treasury shares over cost		1,000

If, instead of selling the treasury shares bought on February 15, Waterloo Corp. used the single-transaction method and decided to cancel them, the entry at the time of that decision would be:

Class A Shares	5,000	
Premium on Class A Shares	~~952~~ 1,000	
Retained Earnings	~~1,048~~ 1,000	
Treasury Shares		7,000

Note: All **asterisked** Questions, Cases, Exercises, or Problems relate to material contained in an Appendix.

QUESTIONS

1. Differentiate between capital in a legal sense, capital in a corporate finance sense, and capital in an accounting sense.

2. Distinguish between the following types of corporations: profit-seeking corporations, publicly held corporations, privately held corporations, not-for-profit corporations, and Crown corporations.

3. Discuss the special characteristics of the corporate form of business that have a direct effect on proprietorship or owners' equity accounting.

4. In the absence of restrictive provisions, what are the basic rights of the shareholders of a corporation?

5. Distinguish between common and preferred shares.

6. What features or rights may alter the character of preferred shares?

7. What is the difference between nonparticipating, partially participating, and fully participating shares?

8. (a) In what ways may preferred shares be more like a debt security than an equity security?
   (b) How should preferred shares be classified in the financial statements?

9. What are the legal restrictions that control the distribution of the profits of a corporation?

10. Explain each of the following terms: authorized share capital, unissued shares, issued shares, outstanding shares, subscribed shares, and treasury shares.

11. Why is it important to know the legal jurisdiction under which a company is incorporated?

12. When might the Subscriptions Receivable account be classified as a current asset? As a noncurrent asset? As a deduction in the shareholders' equity section?

13. Explain the difference between the proportional method and the incremental method of allocating the proceeds of lump sum sales of shares.

14. What are the different bases for share valuation when assets other than cash are received for shares?

15. Discuss the two methods of accounting for initial issue costs. Which do you support and why?

16. For what reasons might a corporation purchase its own shares?

17. When shares are purchased and cancelled, how is the cost of the shares assigned to the various shareholders' equity accounts under *CICA Handbook* recommendations?

18. Distinguish between the two-transaction method and the single-transaction (cost) method of accounting for treasury shares.

19. How is shareholders' equity affected differently by using the single-transaction (cost) method instead of the two-transaction method for treasury shares purchases?

*20. What is meant by par value, and what is its significance to shareholders?

*21. Describe the accounting for the subscription of common shares at a price in excess of their par value.

CASES

C15-1 Graham Pencil Company is a small, closely held corporation. Eighty percent of the issued shares are held by Joan Graham, President; of the remainder, 10% are held by members of her family and 10% by Lynn Chase, a former officer who is now retired. The balance sheet of the company at June 30, 1986, is substantially as shown below:

Assets		Liabilities and Capital	
Cash	$ 22,000	Current liabilities	$150,000
Other	570,000	Share capital	300,000
		Retained earnings	142,000
	$592,000		$592,000

Additional authorized share capital of 15,000 no-par value shares had never been issued. To strengthen the cash position of the company, Ms. Graham issued 5,000 shares to herself and paid $100,000 cash. At the next shareholders' meeting, Ms. Chase objected and claimed that her interests had been injured. All shares were issued for the same price of $20 per share.

Instructions

(a) Which shareholders' right may have been ignored in the issue of shares to Ms. Graham?

(b) How may the damage to Ms. Chase's interests be repaired most simply?

(c) If Ms. Graham offered Ms. Chase a personal cash settlement, and they agreed to employ you as an impartial arbitrator to determine the amount, what settlement would you propose? Present your calculations with sufficient explanation to satisfy both parties.

C15-2 Medical Equipment Corporation purchased $160,000 worth of equipment in 1986 for $100,000 cash and a promise to deliver an indeterminate number of shares with a market value of $20,000 on January 1 of each year for the next four years. Hence, $80,000 in "market value" of shares will be required to discharge the $60,000 balance due on the equipment.

Instructions

(a) Discuss the propriety of recording the equipment at:
1. $100,000 (the cash payment).
2. $160,000 (the cash price of the equipment).
3. $180,000 (the $100,000 cash payment + the $80,000 market value of the shares that must be transferred to the vendor in order to settle the obligation according to the terms of the agreement).

(b) Discuss the arguments for treating the balance due as:
1. A liability.
2. Common shares subscribed.

C15-3 It has been said that (1) the use of the LIFO inventory method during an extended period of rising prices and (2) the expensing of all human-resource costs are among the accounting practices that help create "secret reserves."

Instructions

(a) What is a "secret reserve"? How can "secret reserves" be created or enlarged?

(b) What is the basis for saying that the two specific practices cited above tend to create "secret reserves"?

(c) Is it possible to create a "secret reserve" in connection with accounting for a liability? If so, explain or give an example.

(d) What are the objections to the creation of "secret reserves"?

(e) It has also been said that "watered stock" is the opposite of a "secret reserve." What is "watered stock"?

(f) Describe the general circumstances in which "watered stock" can arise.

(g) What steps can be taken to eliminate "water" from a capital structure?

(AICPA adapted)

C15-4 In connection with your first audit of Happy Jack Mining Company, you note the following facts concerning its share capital transactions:

1. Authorized capital consists of 8,000,000 common shares of no-par value.
2. All 8,000,000 shares were issued initially in exchange for certain mineral properties, which were recorded at an amount of $16,000,000.
3. Soon thereafter, owing to the need for additional working capital, 3,000,000 of the shares were donated to the company and immediately sold for $4,500,000 cash, which resulted in a credit to contributed capital for this amount.

Instructions

(a) Describe, in order of preference, alternative methods of accounting for the receipt and immediate disposition of donated shares.
(b) 1. What values should be assigned to the mineral properties and the shareholders' equity? Discuss.
     2. What adjustment, if any, would you recommend?
*(c) Assume the shares had a $1 par value each. Give the journal entries to record the initial issuance, the receipt and sale of the donated shares, and any adjustments regarding the original value assigned to the mineral properties and the shareholders' equity accounts given the information in point 3.

EXERCISES

E15-1 Sportique Corp. is authorized to issue 500,000 common shares of no-par value. On November 30, 1986, 60,000 shares were subscribed to at $14 per share. A 40% down payment was made on the subscribed shares. On January 30, 1987, the balance due on the subscribed shares was collected except for a subscriber of 8,000 shares who defaulted on his subscription. The 8,000 shares were sold on February 10, 1987, at $15 per share, and the defaulting subscriber's down payment was returned.

Instructions

Prepare the required journal entries for the transactions above.

E15-2 On January 1, 1986, Elbert, Inc. received authorization to issue an additional 200,000 common shares of no-par value. Subscribers have contracted to purchase the shares at the subscription price of $50 per share with terms of 30% down in cash and the remaining 70% at the end of six months.

Instructions

(a) Give Elbert's journal entry for the situation above on the date of subscription.
(b) Assume that Will Galliart has subscribed to 600 of the shares but defaults after paying his 30% down payment. Assume also that the subscription contract affords the subscriber shares on a pro rata basis in the event of default. Give Elbert's journal entry for the disposition of the balances in the accounts related to Mr. Galliart.

E15-3 Saskquach, Inc. issues 500 common shares of no-par value and 100 preferred shares of no-par value for a lump sum of $100,000.

Instructions

(a) Prepare the journal entry for the issuance when the market value of the common shares is $185 each and the market value of the preferred shares is $250 each.
(b) Prepare the journal entry of the issuance when only the market value of the common shares is known and it is $150 per share.

E15-4　Comfort Wear Company was organized with 50,000 preferred shares of no-par value, $8 dividend, and 100,000 no-par value common shares. During the first year, 1,000 shares of preferred and 1,000 shares of common were issued for a lump sum price of $170,000.

Instructions

What entry should be made to record this transaction under each of the following independent conditions:

(a)　Shortly after the transaction described above, 500 preferred shares were sold at $109.

(b)　The market value per share of common shares was $80.

(c)　At the date of issuance, the preferred shares had a market price of $129 per share and the common shares had a market price of $43 per share.

E15-5　Sumptuous Furniture Ltd. has outstanding 50,000 common shares of no-par value, all of which had been issued at $30 per share. On July 5, 1986, Sumptuous repurchased 1,000 of these shares at $48 per share.

Instructions

(a)　Assuming the company is incorporated under the Canada Business Corporations Act, what entry would be made on July 5 to record the reacquisition?

(b)　Assuming the reacquired shares were to be held as treasury shares, what entry would be made on July 5 under (1) the two-transaction method and (2) the single-transaction method?

E15-6　Sumptuous Furniture Ltd., after having repurchased its shares on July 5, 1986, as indicated in E15-5, resold these shares on July 30, 1986. What entries would be made under (1) the two-transaction method and (2) the single transaction method if these treasury shares had been sold for:

(a)　$50 per share?

(b)　$40 per share?

E15-7　M. M. Yanker Corporation's articles authorizes 100,000 common shares of no-par value, and 25,000, $8, cumulative and nonparticipating preferred shares of no-par value. Yanker engages in the following share transactions through December 31, 1986: 30,000 common shares are issued for $350,000 and 5,000 preferred shares for machinery valued at $600,000. Subscriptions for 3,000 shares of common have been taken, and 40% of the subscription price of $18 per share has been collected. The shares will be issued upon collection of the subscription price in full. Treasury shares consisting of 500 common shares have been purchased for $14 and accounted for under the single-transaction (cost) method. The Retained Earnings balance is $85,000.

Instructions

Prepare the shareholders' equity section of the balance sheet as at December 31, 1986, in good form.

***E15-8**　The management of Topitout Contractors, Inc. has decided to sell common shares to raise additional capital to allow for expansion in the rapidly growing construction industry. The corporation decides to sell these shares through a subscription basis and publicly notifies the investment world. The shares have a $5 par value, and 18,000 shares are offered at $25 a share. The terms of the subscription are 40% down and the balance at the end of six months. All shares are subscribed to during the offering period.

Instructions

Give the journal entry for the original subscription, the collection of the down payments, the collection of the balance of the subscription price, and the issuance of the common shares.

*E15-9   On November 15, 1986, Country Publishing Corp. acquires 2,000 of its own $10 par value common shares in the market at a cost of $38 per share. These shares had originally sold for $32 each.

Instructions

(a)   Prepare Country's journal entries to record this acquisition as treasury shares under (1) the two-transaction method and (2) the single-transaction method.

(b)   Assume that Country resells the shares on December 20, 1986, for the market price of $48 per share. Prepare the journal entries to reflect this resale under (1) the two-transaction method and (2) the single-transaction method.

PROBLEMS

P15-1   Galloping Enterprises, Inc. (GEI) is a closely held toy manufacturer in the west. You have been engaged as the independent public accountant to perform the first audit of GEI. It is agreed that only current-year (1986) financial statements will be prepared.

The following shareholders' equity information has been developed from GEI records on December 31, 1985:

Common shares, no par value:

authorized 10,000 shares; issued 2,000 shares	$70,000
Retained earnings	38,000

The following transactions took place during 1986:

1.   On March 15, GEI issued 1,200 common shares to Kathy Norton for $54 per share.

2.   On March 31, GEI reacquired 800 shares from Floyd Beams (GEI's founder) for $60 per share. These shares were cancelled and retired upon receipt.

For the year 1986, GEI reported net income of $28,000.

Instructions

(a)   How should the shareholders' equity information be reported in the GEI financial statements for the year ended December 31, 1986?

(b)   How would your answer to (a) have been altered if GEI had treated the reacquired shares as treasury shares under the single-transaction method?

P15-2   Share transactions of Technicolour Coat Company are as follows:

April 1   Subscriptions to 700 common shares of no-par value are received, together with cheques from the various subscribers to cover a 25% down payment. The shares were subscribed to at a price of $108 each. The remainder of the subscription price is to be paid in three equal monthly instalments.

May   1   First instalments are collected from all subscribers.

June   1   Second instalments are received from all subscribers except Lyle McGinnis, who subscribed to 60 shares.

June   5   In reply to correspondence, Mr. McGinnis states that he is unable to complete his instalment payments and authorizes the company to dispose of the shares subscribed to by him.

June 17   The shares subscribed to by Mr. McGinnis are sold for cash at $101 each. Expenses of $90 are incurred in disposing of these shares.

June 25   A cheque is mailed to Mr. McGinnis equal to the refund due him.

July   1   The final instalments are collected on all open subscription accounts, and the shares are issued.

Instructions

Prepare entries in general journal form for the transactions above. Assume that defaulting subscribers are to receive a refund for amounts they have paid less deficiencies between the subscription price and amounts received when the subscribed shares are sold and any expenses incurred.

P15-3 On January 5, 1986, Fun & Humour Corporation began operations with authorized capital of 5,000 preferred shares of no-par value, $10 cumulative and nonparticipating, and 50,000 common shares of no-par value. It then completed these transactions:

Jan. 11 Accepted subscriptions to 20,000 common shares at $12 per share; 20% down payments accompanied the subscriptions.

Feb. 1 Issued Thomas J. Nessinger Corp. 2,700 preferred shares for the following assets: machinery with a fair market value of $35,000; a factory building with a fair market value of $85,000; and land with an appraised value of $175,000.

Mar. 16 Other machinery, with a fair market value of $85,000, was donated to the company.

Apr. 15 Collected the balance of the subscription price on the common shares and issued them.

July 29 Reacquired 1,200 of its own common shares at $9 per share. (Treat as treasury shares and use the single-transaction method.)

Aug. 10 Sold 1,100 of the treasury shares at $7 per share.

Aug. 26 Declared a 10% stock dividend on the common shares. The shares were selling at $7 each on the day of the declaration.

Sept. 15 Distributed the stock dividend.

Dec. 31 Declared a $0.10 per share cash dividend on common and declared the required preferred dividend.

Dec. 31 Closed the Income Summary account. There was a $61,000 net income.

Instructions

(a) Record the journal entries for the transactions listed above.

(b) Prepare the shareholders' equity section of Fun & Humour's balance sheet as of December 31, 1986.

P15-4 The shareholders' equity section of the CanPost Corporation balance sheet at December 31, 1985, was as follows:

Common shares—no-par value; 50,000 authorized; 12,000 issued and outstanding	$1,200,000
Contributed Surplus—Donated Land	240,000
Retained Earnings	120,000
	$1,560,000

On January 2, 1986, having idle cash, the company repurchased 480 of its outstanding shares for $60,000. These shares were handled in the manner specified in the Canada Business Corporations Act, the legislation under which the company was incorporated. During the year, CanPost sold some of these shares, as they had been restored to the status of authorized but unissued shares as permitted by the CBCA. The first such sale was on April 15, at which time the company received $135 per share for 120 shares. The second sale was made on August 13, when another 120 shares were sold for $122.50 per share.

Instructions

(a) Prepare the journal entries for the transactions identified for 1986.

(b) Assuming net income for 1986 was $23,000, prepare the shareholders' equity section of CanPost's balance sheet as at December 31, 1986.

P15-5 Entertainment Company Limited has the following shareholders' equity accounts at December 31, 1985:

Common Shares—no-par value, authorized 4,000, issued 3,200	$320,000
Retained Earnings	200,000

Instructions

(a) Prepare entries in journal form to record the following transactions, which took place during 1986. (Hint: Debit Retained Earnings in transaction 6.)

1. 160 of the issued shares were purchased for $96 per share. (These are to be accounted for using the single-transaction method.)
2. A $10 per share cash dividend was declared.
3. The dividend declared in (2) above was paid.
4. The treasury shares purchased in (1) above were resold for $102 per share.
5. 400 of the now-outstanding shares were purchased for a total of $40,800.
6. 80 additional outstanding shares were purchased at $105 per share and retired.
7. 240 of the shares purchased in (5) above were resold for $97 per share.

(b) Prepare the shareholders' equity section of Entertainment Company's balance sheet after giving effect to these transactions, assuming that the net income for 1986 was $46,000.

P15-6 During May, 1985, Gilroy, Inc. was organized with 3,000,000 authorized common shares of no-par value, and 300,000 shares were then issued for $3,300,000. Net income through December 31, 1985, was $125,000.

On July 13, 1986, Gilroy issued 500,000 common shares for $6,250,000. A 5% stock dividend was declared on October 2, 1986, and issued on November 6, 1986, to shareholders of record on October 23, 1986. The market value of the common shares was $11 per share on the declaration date. Gilroy's net income for the year ended December 31, 1986, was $350,000. (Hint: Retained Earnings should be reduced by the fair market value of the stock dividend.)

During 1987 Gilroy had the following transactions:

1. In February, Gilroy reacquired 30,000 common shares for $9 per share. Gilroy uses the single-transaction method to account for treasury shares.
2. In June, Gilroy sold 15,000 of its treasury shares for $12 per share.
3. On December 15, 1987, Gilroy declared its first cash dividend to shareholders of $0.10 per share, payable on January 10, 1988, to shareholders of record on December 31, 1987.
4. On December 21, 1987, Gilroy formally retired 10,000 of its treasury shares and had them revert to an unissued basis. The market value of the common shares was $16 per share on this date.
5. Net income for 1987 was $750,000.

Instructions

Prepare a schedule of all transactions affecting the share capital (shares and dollar amounts), contributed capital, retained earnings, treasury shares (shares and dollar amounts), and the amounts that would be included in Gilroy's balance sheet at December 31, 1985, 1986, and 1987, as a result of the above facts. Show supporting computations in good form.

(AICPA adapted)

P15-7 Turnaround Corporation's charter authorized issuance of 10,000 common shares of no-par value and 10,000 preferred shares of no-par value. The following transactions involving the issuance of shares were completed. Each transaction is independent of the others.

1. Issued a $10,000, 9% bond payable at par and gave as a bonus one preferred share, which was selling for $75 a share at that time.
2. Issued 40 common shares for machinery. The machinery had been appraised at $5,100; the seller's book value was $6,000. The most recent market price of the common shares was $122 each.
3. Voted an assessment of $5 for the 1,000 common shares outstanding and of $3 on the 500 preferred shares outstanding. The assessment was paid in full.
4. Issued 60 shares of common and 40 shares of preferred for a lump sum amounting to $12,625. The common had been selling at $125 and the preferred at $65.
5. Issued 20 shares of common and 10 shares of preferred for furniture and fixtures. The common had a fair market value of $150 per share, and the furniture and fixtures were appraised at $3,750.

Instructions

Record the transactions listed above in journal entry form.

P15-8 Galactica Corporation is a publicly owned company. At December 31, 1985, Galactica had 25,000,000 common shares of no-par value authorized, of which 15,000,000 shares were issued and 14,000,000 shares were outstanding.

The shareholders' equity accounts at December 31, 1985, had the following balances:

Common shares	$230,000,000
Retained earnings	50,000,000
Treasury shares	18,000,000

During 1986, Galactica had the following transactions:

On February 1, a secondary distribution of 2,000,000 common shares was completed. The shares were sold to the public at $18 per share, net of offering costs.

On February 15, Galactica issued at $110 per share, 100,000 preferred shares of no-par value, $8 cumulative dividend.

On March 1, Galactica reacquired 20,000 common shares for $18.50 per share. Galactica uses the single-transaction method to account for treasury shares.

On March 15, when the common shares were trading for $21 per share, a major shareholder donated 10,000 shares which were retired.

On March 31, Galactica declared a semiannual cash dividend on the common shares of $0.10 per share, payable on April 30, to shareholders of record on April 10. The cash dividends do not apply to treasury shares.

On April 30, employees exercised 100,000 options that were granted in 1984 under a noncompensatory stock option plan. When the options were granted, each option entitled the employee to purchase one common share for $20. On April 30, the market price of the common shares was $20 per share. Galactica issued new shares to settle the transaction.

On May 31, when the market price of the common shares was $20 per share, Galactica declared a 5% stock dividend distributable on July 1 to shareholders of record on June 1. The stock dividend is recorded using the market price. It does not apply to treasury shares.

On June 30, Galactica sold the 20,000 treasury shares reacquired on March 1 and an additional 280,000 treasury shares costing $5,600,000 that were on hand at the beginning of the year. The selling price was $25 per share.

On September 30, Galactica declared a semiannual cash dividend on the common shares of $0.10 per share and the yearly dividend on preferred shares, both payable on October 30, to shareholders of record on October 10. The cash dividends do not apply to treasury shares.

Net income for 1986 was $25,000,000.

Instructions

Prepare a work sheet to be used to summarize, for each transaction, the changes in Galactica's shareholders' equity accounts for 1986. The columns on this work sheet should have the following headings:

Date of transactions (or beginning date)
Common shares—number of shares
Common shares—amount
Preferred shares—number of shares
Preferred shares—amount
Contributed Surplus*
Retained earnings
Treasury shares—number of shares
Treasury shares—amount

Show supporting computations in good form.

*While there may be several individual accounts that would be recognized in Contributed Surplus, use this column to record the effects of transactions on the total amount of Contributed Surplus.

(AICPA adapted)

*P15-9 Transactions of Sandy Dawn Company Ltd. are as follows:

1. The company is incorporated with authorized capital of 12,000 preferred shares of $100 par value and 12,000 common shares without par value.
2. 9,600 common shares are issued to founders of the corporation for land valued by the board of directors at $506,000.
3. 6,000 preferred shares are sold for cash at $110 per share.
4. 600 common shares are sold to an officer of the corporation for $60 a share.
5. 300 of the preferred shares outstanding are purchased for cash at par and immediately cancelled.
6. 450 of the preferred shares outstanding are purchased for cash at $98 each and held as treasury shares.
7. 600 of the common shares outstanding are purchased at $62 a share and held as treasury shares.
8. 150 of the repurchased preferred shares are reissued at $102 per share.
9. 2,400 preferred shares are issued at $99 per share.
10. 300 of the reacquired common shares are reissued for $57 a share.
11. 120 common shares are repurchased for $53 a share and retired.

Instructions

(a) Prepare entries in journal form to record the transactions listed above. No other transactions affecting the Share Capital accounts have occurred. Treasury shares are to be entered in the Treasury Shares accounts using the single-transaction method. (Round to the nearest dollar.)

(b) Assuming that the company has retained earnings from operations of $95,000, prepare the shareholders' equity section of its balance sheet after considering all the transactions given.

*P15-10 Before Huskie Communications Corporation engages in the treasury shares transactions listed below, its general ledger reflects, among others, the following account balances (par value of each of its shares is $50).

Contributed Capital in Excess of Par	Common Shares	Retained Earnings
Balance $36,000	Balance $120,000	Balance $30,000

Instructions

Record the transactions listed below under the two generally accepted methods of handling treasury shares.

(a) Bought 300 common shares as treasury shares at $63 per share.
(b) Bought 150 common shares as treasury shares at $67 per share.
(c) Sold 225 of the treasury shares at $66 per share.
(d) Sold 120 of the treasury shares at $62 per share.
(e) Retired the remaining shares in the treasury.

*P15-11 The accounts shown below appear in the December 31 trial balance of the Alberta Company Limited:

Preferred shares authorized ($100 par value)	$500,000
Common shares authorized ($10 par value)	200,000
Unissued preferred shares	180,000
Unissued common shares	100,000
Subscriptions receivable, common	18,000
Subscriptions receivable, preferred	19,000
Preferred shares subscribed	30,000
Common shares subscribed	22,500
Treasury shares, preferred (700 shares at cost)	68,600
Contributed surplus (Excess of amount paid in over par value of common shares)	87,500

Instructions

Use the above accounts to determine the following:

(a) Total authorized share capital.

(b) Total unissued share capital.

(c) Total issued share capital.

(d) Share capital subscribed.

(e) Total share capital and contributed surplus.

16

SHAREHOLDERS' EQUITY: CONTRIBUTED SURPLUS AND RETAINED EARNINGS

The following three categories most frequently appear as part of shareholders' equity in a corporation's financial statements:

1. Share Capital or Capital Stock (legal or stated capital)
2. Contributed Surplus
3. Retained Earnings or Deficit

The first two categories, Share Capital and Contributed Surplus, constitute **contributed capital;** Retained Earnings represents the **earned capital** of the enterprise. The distinction between contributed capital and earned capital has a legal origin, but at present it serves the useful purpose of indicating the different sources from which the corporation has obtained its **equity capital.** The first source —share capital—was discussed in Chapter 15. The other sources are very diverse in nature and require careful analysis.

While these three categories represent the normal components of shareholders' equity, other categories may sometimes appear. Examples would be Treasury Shares accounted for using the single-transaction method (discussed in Chapter 15) and Appraisal Increase Credits (examined later in this Chapter).

TERMINOLOGY

The terminology used to report shareholders' equity varies from company to company: while Share Capital or Capital Stock, Contributed Surplus, and Retained Earnings are the names used to categorize the sources of shareholders' equity by many Canadian corporations, other names for these categories are sometimes used.[1]

A particular concern of the accounting profession has been the use of the term "surplus" in corporate reporting. The concern is derived from the belief that the word "surplus" connotes to many readers of financial statements a residue or "something not needed." Consequently, the word "surplus" has been eliminated in most cases (e.g., "Retained Earnings" has replaced the heading "Earned Surplus," which had been used formerly). Whenever the word "surplus" is used in contemporary reports, the CICA suggests that it be in conjunction with a descriptive adjective,[2] as in, for example, the heading "Contributed Surplus." A widely accepted term to replace "Contributed Surplus" has not yet been used in financial statements of Canadian corporations. In the United States, "Additional Paid-in Capital" is the frequently used heading for this category.

CONTRIBUTED SURPLUS

Contributed surplus may be derived from a considerable variety of transactions. The *CICA Handbook* states:

> "Contributed surplus" has frequently been taken to include only amounts paid in by shareholders, but it may include capital donations from other sources. Contributed surplus, in the form of surplus paid in by shareholders, includes premiums on shares issued, any portion of the proceeds of issue of shares without par value not allocated to share capital, gain on forfeited shares, proceeds arising from donated shares, credits resulting from redemption or conversion of shares at less than the amount set up as share capital, and any other contribution by shareholders in excess of amounts allocated to share capital.[3]

The basic transactions and events that may affect contributed surplus are expressed in account form on page 730.

An interesting aspect of the **Canada Business Corporations Act** (CBCA) is that, because of its requirements to have no-par value shares and to cancel reacquired shares, it eliminates most contributed surplus items. However, companies that had these items in their accounts before filing for continuance under the CBCA could carry the items forward.

No operating gains or losses or extraordinary gains and losses may be debited or credited to contributed surplus. The profession has long discouraged bypassing net income and retained earnings through the write-off of losses (e.g., write-offs of

---

[1]*Financial Reporting in Canada—1983* (Toronto: CICA, 1983) indicated that in 1982 (a) Share Capital was used by 82 of 325 companies surveyed and Capital Stock was used by 188 companies, while other headings used were Capital (11 companies), Stated Capital (12); (b) Contributed Surplus was used by 66 of 80 companies reporting such items, while the remaining companies used such headings as Premium on Shares Issued (4), Purchase or Redemption of Preferred Shares (3), Capital (3), Paid-in Capital (4); (c) Retained Earnings was used by 280 of the 325 companies, Deficit by 20, while other headings included Earnings Retained, Reinvested Earnings, Retained Income and Earnings Reinvested; (d) Shareholders' Equity was used by 299 companies as the title for the balance sheet section with 7 using Common Shareholders' Equity, 4 using Shareholders' Investment, and 15 using different titles.

[2]*CICA Handbook* (Toronto: CICA), Section 3250, par. 2.

[3]*Ibid.*, par. 5.

Contributed Surplus	
1. Discounts on capital shares issued.* 2. Sale of treasury shares below cost under the circumstances and to the extent described in Chapter 15. 3. Absorption of a deficit in a recapitalization (quasi-reorganization). 4. Distribution of a liquidating dividend. 5. Retirement of shares at a cost in excess of par* or assigned value.	1. Premiums on capital shares issued.* 2. Sale of treasury shares above cost. 3. Additional capital arising in recapitalizations or revisions in the capital structure (quasi-reorganizations). 4. Additional assessments on shareholders. 5. Conversion of convertible bonds or preferred shares.* 6. Capital donations from non-shareholders. 7. Retirement of shares acquired by purchase at a cost less than par* or assigned value or through donations.

*Items relate to shares having a par value. (See Appendix 15A for further explanation.)

bond discount, goodwill, or obsolete plant and equipment) to contributed surplus accounts or other capital accounts.

In balance sheet presentation, only one account (Contributed Surplus) and one amount (which is the net balance of all of these possible transactions) need appear. A subsidiary ledger or separate general ledger accounts may be kept of the different sources of contributed surplus. Furthermore, maintaining such separate records would greatly facilitate disclosure of changes in contributed surplus during a period as is required by the *CICA Handbook*, Section 3250, paragraph 13.

RETAINED EARNINGS

The basic source of retained earnings consists of income from operations. Shareholders assume the greatest risk in enterprise operations and stand any losses or share in any profits resulting from enterprise activities. Any income not distributed among the shareholders becomes additional shareholders' equity. The main operations of the enterprise, such as manufacturing and selling a given product, plus any ancillary activities, such as disposing of scrap or renting out unused space, plus the results of extraordinary and unusual items all give rise to net income that increases retained earnings. The more common items that either increase or decrease retained earnings are expressed in account form on page 731.

In Chapter 4 it was pointed out that, under the all-inclusive concept of income reporting, the results of unusual and extraordinary transactions should be placed in the income statement, not directly into the retained earnings statement. Prior period adjustments, error corrections, and retroactive adjustments resulting from changing accounting principles should be handled as adjustments to beginning retained earnings, bypassing completely the current income statement.

Retained Earnings	
1. Net loss. 2. Prior period adjustments, error corrections, and retroactive adjustments resulting from changes in accounting principles. 3. Cash dividends. 4. Stock dividends. 5. Property dividends. 6. Transactions involving share acquisitions.	1. Net income. 2. Prior period adjustments, error corrections, and retroactive adjustments resulting from changes in accounting principles.

DIVIDEND POLICY

As soon as retained earnings is recorded, two alternatives exist regarding its disposition: (1) the credit balance can be reduced by a distribution of assets (a dividend) to the shareholders, or (2) it can be left intact and the offsetting assets used in the operations of the business. Further decisions are required under each of these alternatives, but the original decision must be whether to distribute the increase in net assets generated by profitable operations in the form of dividends to the shareholders or to retain these resources in the enterprise and use them for business purposes.

Very few companies pay dividends in amounts equal to the retained earnings legally available for dividends. The reasons for this are varied and include at least the following:

1. Agreements (bond covenants) with specific creditors to retain all or a portion of the earnings (in the form of assets) to build up additional protection against possible loss for those creditors.
2. Desire to retain in the business the assets that would otherwise be paid out as dividends. This is sometimes called internal financing, reinvesting earnings, or "plowing" the profits back into the business.
3. Desire to smooth out dividend payments from year to year by accumulating earnings in good years and using such accumulated earnings as a basis for dividends in bad years.
4. Desire to build up a cushion or buffer against possible losses.
5. Legal restrictions included in the acts under which a company is incorporated. For example, a dividend may not be paid if it would render a corporation insolvent even if retained earnings existed. Also, in jurisdictions permitting treasury shares, the law may require that retained earnings equivalent to the cost of such shares be restricted against dividend declarations.

No particular explanation is required for any of these except the last. The laws of most jurisdictions require that the corporation's stated capital (legal capital) be restricted from distribution to shareholders so that it may serve as a protection against loss to creditors. If, for example, the corporation buys its own outstanding shares, it has reduced its stated capital and distributed assets to shareholders. Therefore, the corporation could, by purchasing shares at any price desired, return to the shareholders their investments and leave creditors with little or no protection against loss. Consequently, restricting dividends to the extent that retained earnings will not fall below the cost of the treasury shares is a way to overcome this problem.

If a company is considering declaring a dividend, two preliminary questions must be asked:

1. Is the condition of the corporation such that a dividend is legally permissible?
2. Is the condition of the corporation such that a dividend is economically sound?

Legality of a Dividend

The legality of a dividend can be determined only by reviewing the applicable incorporation law. Even then the law may not be clear, and eventually a decision may require recourse to courts of law. Frequently, the company's lawyer may provide an opinion on a dividend problem to reduce the possibility of misinterpretation of the law. For most general dividend declarations the following summary is adequate:

1. Retained earnings, unless legally encumbered in some manner, is usually the correct basis for dividend distributions.
2. Revaluation capital is seldom the correct basis for dividends (except possibly stock dividends).
3. In some jurisdictions, contributed surplus may be used for dividends.
4. Deficits must be eliminated before payment of any dividends.
5. In most jurisdictions that allow treasury shares, dividends may not reduce retained earnings below the cost of treasury shares held.

The CBCA prohibits the declaration or payment of dividends if there are reasonable grounds for believing that such an action would (1) result in the corporation being unable to pay its liabilities when they become due, or (2) result in the realizable value of the corporation's assets being less than the total of its liabilities and stated (legal) capital of all share classes. Adhering to the legal requirements associated with dividends is critical to a corporation's directors because, if such requirements are judged to have been violated, the directors can be held jointly and severally liable for the entire debts and obligations of the company.

Financial Condition and Dividend Distributions

Dividend distributions generally require that a corporation have a credit balance in retained earnings. From the standpoint of good management, attention must be given to other conditions as well. If we assume an extreme situation such as the following, these considerations become more apparent.

BALANCE SHEET			
Plant assets	$500,000	Share capital	$400,000
		Retained earnings	100,000
	$500,000		$500,000

This company has a retained earnings credit balance and, unless it is encumbered, legally can declare a dividend of $100,000. However, because all its assets are plant assets and used in operations, payment of a cash dividend of $100,000 requires the sale of plant assets or borrowing. Even if we assume a balance sheet showing current assets, there is still the further question of whether those assets are needed for other purposes.

BALANCE SHEET				
Cash	$100,000	Current liabilities		$ 40,000
Plant assets	440,000	Share capital	$400,000	
		Retained earnings	100,000	500,000
	$540,000			$540,000

The existence of current liabilities implies very strongly that some of the cash is needed to meet current debts as they mature. Furthermore, day-by-day cash requirements for payroll and other expenditures not included in current liabilities will also require cash.

Thus, before a dividend is declared, the question of **availability of funds to pay the dividend must be considered.** Availability of funds includes more than possession of a cash balance sufficiently large to pay the dividend. Other demands for cash such as those considered in preparing a cash forecast must be investigated, and a dividend should not be paid unless both the present and future financial position appear to warrant the distribution.

Directors must also consider the effect of inflation on reported income. During a period of significant inflation, some costs charged to expense under historical cost accounting are understated in the sense of comparative purchasing power. Income is thereby overstated because certain costs have not been adjusted for inflation. As an example, St. Regis Paper Company at one time reported historical cost net income of $179 million, but when it was adjusted for general inflation net income was $67.7 million. Yet St. Regis paid cash dividends of $72.3 million. Were cash dividends paid excessive? This subject is discussed in considerable depth in Chapter 25.

The conclusion to be reached regarding a decision to declare a dividend is clear. While the existence of available retained earnings is a necessity, many other factors are important. No corporate director should ever recommend a dividend based on the existence of retained earnings alone. The legal requirements as well as the present and expected future financial position must also be considered.

Types of Dividends

Dividend distributions are based either on accumulated profits—that is, retained earnings—or, in some cases, contributed surplus accounts. The natural expectation of any shareholder who receives a dividend is that the corporation has operated successfully and that the shareholder is receiving a share of its profits. Any dividend not based on retained earnings (a liquidating dividend) should be adequately described in the accompanying message to the shareholders so that there will be no misunderstanding of its source. Dividends are of the following types:

1. Cash dividends.
2. Property dividends.
3. Scrip dividends.
4. Liquidating dividends.
5. Stock dividends.

Dividends are commonly paid in cash but occasionally in stock, scrip, or some other asset. **Any dividend other than a stock dividend reduces the shareholders' equity in the corporation,** because a portion of the equity is reduced either through an immediate or promised future distribution of assets. When a stock dividend is declared, the corporation does not pay out assets or incur a liability. It merely issues additional shares to each shareholder. The individual shareholder receives nothing more than additional shares.

Cash Dividends   The board of directors votes on the declaration of dividends, and if the resolution is properly approved, the dividend is declared. It cannot be paid immediately, however, because transfers of shares from one holder to another require that a current list of shareholders be prepared. For this reason the dividend resolution generally allows a short period of time before payment. A dividend approved at the January 10 (date of declaration) meeting of the board of directors might be declared payable February 5 (date of payment) to all shareholders of record on January 25 (date of record).

The period from January 10 to January 25 gives time for any transfers in process to be completed and registered with the transfer agent. The time from January 25 to February 5 provides an opportunity for the transfer agent or accounting department, depending on who does this work, to prepare a list of shareholders as of January 25 and to prepare and mail dividend cheques.

A declared dividend, except a stock dividend, is a liability and, because payment is generally required very soon, it is usually a current liability. The following entries are required to record the declaration and payment of an ordinary dividend payable in cash. This example assumes that on June 10 a corporation declared a cash dividend of 50 cents a share on 1.8 million shares payable July 16 to all shareholders of record June 24.

At date of declaration (June 10):

Retained Earnings (Cash Dividends Declared)	900,000	
Dividends Payable		900,000

At date of record (June 24):
No entry

At date of payment (July 16):

Dividends Payable	900,000	
Cash		900,000

To keep track of the amount of dividends declared during the year, an account called Cash Dividends Declared might be debited instead of Retained Earnings at the time of declaration. This account is then closed to Retained Earnings at the end of the year.

Dividend declarations are made as a stated amount per share for no-par value shares issued and outstanding.[4] If a company holds treasury shares, dividends do not apply to these.[5]

Dividend policies vary among corporations. Some older, well-established firms take pride in a long, unbroken string of quarterly dividend payments and would lower or pass the dividend only if forced to do so by a sustained decline in earnings or a critical shortage of cash. The percentage of annual earnings distributed as cash dividends ("payout ratio") depends somewhat on the stability and trend of earnings, with 25% to 75% of earnings being paid out by many well-established corporations.

---

[4]For par value shares, dividends may be declared as a certain percentage of the par value.

[5]*CICA Handbook*, Section 3240, par. 22.

"Growth companies," on the other hand, pay little or no cash dividends because their policy is to expand as rapidly as internal and external financing permit.

Knowledge of a dividend policy for a particular corporation may be gained from an analysis of its successive financial statements. While no explicit recommendation regarding disclosure of dividend policy exists in Canada, in the U.S. the SEC encourages companies to disclose their dividend policy in their annual report. For example, companies that (1) have earnings but fail to pay dividends or (2) do not expect to pay dividends in the foreseeable future are encouraged to report this information. In addition, companies that have had a consistent pattern of paying dividends are encouraged to indicate whether they intend to continue this practice in the future.

Property Dividends   Dividends payable in assets of the corporation other than cash are called **property dividends** or **dividends in kind**. Property dividends may be in whatever form the board of directors designates; for example: merchandise, real estate, or investments; but because of the obvious difficulties of divisibility of units and delivery to the shareholders, the usual property dividend is in the form of securities of other companies that the distributing corporation has held as an investment.

A property dividend is a nonreciprocal transfer of nonmonetary assets between an enterprise and its owners.[6] Prior to the early 1970s, the accounting for such transfers was based on the carrying amount (book value) of the noncash assets transferred. This practice was based on the rationale that there is no sale or arm's-length transaction on which to base a gain or loss and that only this method is consistent with the historical cost basis of accounting. This practice changed, however, following the issuance of *APB Opinion No. 29* in the U.S. which provided direction to the accounting profession. It stated:

> A transfer of a nonmonetary asset to a stockholder or to another entity in a nonreciprocal transfer should be recorded at the fair value of the asset transferred, and a gain or loss should be recognized on the disposition of the asset.[7]

The **fair value** of the nonmonetary asset distributed is measured by the amount that would be realizable in an outright sale at or near the time of the declaration. Such amount should be determined by referring to estimated realizable values in cash transactions of the same or similar assets, quoted market prices, independent appraisals, and other available evidence.

The failure to recognize the fair value of nonmonetary assets transferred may both misstate the dividend and fail to recognize gains and losses on assets that have already been earned or incurred by the enterprise. Recording the dividend at fair value permits future comparisons of dividend rates and, if cash must be distributed to some shareholders in place of the nonmonetary asset, determination of the amount to be distributed is simplified. Recording fair value is especially appropriate when property dividends are given to a class of shares other than common. For example, preferred shareholders should not profit by property dividends, the market value of which exceeds the fixed dividend amount.

---

[6]A nonreciprocal transfer is a transfer of assets or services in one direction, either from an enterprise to its owners or another entity or from owners or another entity to the enterprise.

[7]"Accounting for Nonmonetary Transactions," *Opinions of the Accounting Principles Board No. 29* (New York: AICPA, 1973), par. 18. There is no Canadian-based recommendation on property dividends. Therefore, U.S. authoritative statements serve as a useful guide.

When a property dividend is declared, the corporation should restate at fair value the property to be distributed, recognizing any gain or loss as the difference between the fair value and carrying value of the property at date of declaration. The declared dividend may then be recorded as a debit to Retained Earnings (or Property Dividends Declared) and a credit to Property Dividends Payable at an amount equal to the fair value of the property to be distributed. Upon distribution of the dividend, Property Dividends Payable is debited, and the account containing the distributed asset (restated at fair value) is credited.

For example, Inuit, Inc. transferred some of its investments in marketable securities costing $1,250,000 to shareholders by declaring a property dividend on December 18, 1985, to be distributed on January 30, 1986, to shareholders of record on January 15, 1986. At the date of declaration the securities have a market value of $2,000,000. The entries are as below.

At date of declaration (December 18, 1985):

Investments in Securities	750,000	
Gain on Appreciation of Securities		750,000
Retained Earnings (Property Dividends Declared)	2,000,000	
Property Dividends Payable		2,000,000

At date of distribution (January 30, 1986):

Property Dividends Payable	2,000,000	
Investments in Securities		2,000,000

Scrip Dividend   A dividend payable in scrip means that the corporation, instead of paying the dividend now, has elected to pay it at some later date. **The scrip issued to shareholders as a dividend is merely a special form of note payable.** Scrip dividends may be declared when the corporation has a sufficient retained earnings balance but is short of cash. The recipient of the scrip dividend may hold it until the due date, if one is specified, and collect the dividend, or possibly, may sell (discount) it to obtain immediate cash. When a scrip dividend is declared, the corporation debits Retained Earnings (or Scrip Dividend Declared) and credits Scrip Dividend Payable, reporting the payable as a liability on the balance sheet. Upon payment, Scrip Dividend Payable is debited and Cash credited. If the scrip bears interest, the interest portion of the cash payment should be debited to Interest Expense and not treated as part of the dividend.

As an example, Berg Canning Company, when short of cash, avoided missing its 84th consecutive quarterly dividend by declaring on May 6, 1985, a scrip dividend in the form of two-month promissory notes amounting to 80 cents a share on 2,545,000 shares outstanding. The date of record was May 27, 1985, and the notes had an interest rate of 10% per annum with a maturity (payment) date of July 27. The entries related to this scrip dividend are as follows:

At date of declaration (May 6, 1985):

Retained Earnings (Scrip Dividend Declared)	2,036,000	
Notes Payable to Shareholders ($.80 × 2,545,000)		2,036,000

At date of payment (July 27, 1985):

Notes Payable to Shareholders	2,036,000	
Interest Expense ($2,036,000 × 2/12 × .10)[a]	33,933	
Cash		2,069,933

[a]The interest runs from the date of record to the date of payment.

Liquidating Dividend   Examples exist of corporations that have used contributed surplus as a basis for dividends. Without proper disclosure of this fact, shareholders may believe the corporation has been operating at a profit. A further result could be subsequent sale of additional shares at a higher price than is warranted. This type of deception, intentional or unintentional, can be avoided by requiring that a clear statement of the basis of every dividend accompany the dividend cheque.

Dividends based on other than retained earnings are sometimes described as liquidating dividends, thus implying that they are a return of the shareholder's investment rather than of profits. In fact, the distribution may be based on contributed capital that resulted from donations by outsiders or other shareholders and not be a return of the given shareholder's contribution. In a more general sense, however, **any dividend not based on earnings must be a reduction of corporation capital and, to that extent, it is a liquidating dividend.** We noted in Chapter 11 that companies in the extractive industries may pay dividends equal to the total of accumulated income and depletion. The portion of these dividends in excess of accumulated income represents a return of part of the shareholder's investment.

For example, McChesney Mines, Inc., in declaring a "dividend" to its common shareholders of $100,000, announced that $70,000 should be considered income and the remainder a return of capital. The entries are:

At date of declaration:

Retained Earnings	70,000	
Contributed Surplus	30,000	
Dividend Payable		100,000

At date of payment:

Dividend Payable	100,000	
Cash		100,000

Stock Dividends A stock dividend occurs when the board of directors of a company declares that a dividend will be paid to shareholders in the form of the company's own shares (of the same or different class).[8] This may occur because the board wishes to capitalize part of the earnings and thus retain earnings in the business on a permanent basis. Alternatively, a stock dividend may be declared because the board, unwilling or unable to pay a cash dividend, may still desire to provide the shareholders with something tangible for their interest in the company. Many would argue, however, that a stock dividend, while it may provide some psychological benefit in the mind of the shareholder, does not provide any real economic benefits. This is because, in a stock dividend, **no assets are distributed,** and each shareholder has exactly the same proportionate interest in the corporation and the same total book value after the stock dividend as before the dividend. Of course, the book value per share is lower because an increased number of shares is held.

Accounting for a stock dividend of no-par value shares results in transferring an amount from retained earnings to the appropriate share capital account. The question to be answered is: "What amount should be transferred?" The CICA has not made a recommendation regarding this. The CBCA states that, for stock dividends, the declared amount of the dividend shall be added to the stated capital account. The CBCA does not allow shares to be issued until they are fully paid for in an amount not less than the fair equivalent of money that the corporation would have

---

[8]*Financial Reporting in Canada—1983* indicated that, of the surveyed companies, there were 32 in 1982, 36 in 1981, 28 in 1980, and 13 in 1979 that disclosed the distribution of a stock dividend in their financial statements.

received if the shares had been issued for cash; therefore, the fair market value must be used for companies incorporated under it.

Ordinarily, fair value is taken to be the market price of the shares on the date of the dividend declaration. This is reasonable given the assumption that the market price will not change materially as the result of the stock dividend. When the market price is significantly affected (when a relatively large number of shares is being issued), it would be more appropriate to account for the event as a stock split (as described later), even though it may be called a stock dividend.

In the United States, the Committee on Accounting Procedure of the AICPA has stated that the **fair value** of the shares issued should be transferred from retained earnings.[9] This method of handling stock dividends is justified on the grounds "that many recipients of stock dividends look upon them as distributions of corporate earnings and usually in an amount equivalent to the fair value of the additional shares received."[10]

While the conclusion may be acceptable, this particular argument is not very convincing because it is generally agreed that stock dividends are not income to the recipients and, therefore, sound accounting should not recommend procedures simply because some recipients think they are income.[11] The stock dividend is not income to shareholders because it merely distributes the recipient's equity over a larger number of shares. Theoretically, while the number of shares held increases, the underlying worth of the total number of shares held has not changed because the net assets of the corporation have not changed. If, however, the market price per share does not decline in direct proportion to the increased number of shares now issued (i.e., the market does not respond perfectly), the recipients of the stock dividend could be better off; but, to realize their gain, they would have to sell their shares.

Given the direction in the CBCA and the guidance provided by U.S. accounting standards, we will illustrate the **accounting for stock dividends using the market value of the shares issued at the date of declaration as the appropriate amount involved.**[12]

Entries for Stock Dividends   Assume that a corporation has outstanding 1,000 common shares of no-par value issued for $100,000, and a retained earnings balance of $50,000. If it declares a 10% stock dividend, it issues 100 additional shares

---

[9]American Institute of Certified Public Accountants, *Accounting Research and Terminology Bulletins, No. 43* (New York: AICPA, 1961), Ch. 7, par. 10.

[10]*Ibid.*, par. 10.

[11]For Canadian income tax purposes, at the time of this writing, federal legislation was pending which would result in treating the receipt of a stock dividend in the same manner as a cash dividend with the amount being the fair value of the shares received. Prior to this, the receipt of a stock dividend was not considered as dividend income. However, as a result of a stock dividend, the average cost of shares held would be reduced and, therefore, the amount of capital gain (proceeds in excess of average cost) and the resulting tax would be increased when the shares were sold. The pending legislation would not call for a reduction in average share cost on receipt of a stock dividend but, because the tax consequences are likely to be higher for recipients, it is probable that stock dividends will occur less frequently than in the past.

[12]Arguments could be made that for stock dividends in no-par value shares no amount need be transferred (only the number of shares issued would be changed, as is the case for stock splits, resulting in the average "price" per share being reduced) or that amounts other than fair value could be transferred (i.e., if a fair market value were not determinable). In the case of stock dividends in par value shares, arguments have been made supporting the position that only the par value amount be transferred from retained earnings regardless of market value. Normally, however, the market value of par value shares is transferred from retained earnings with the par value going to share capital and the excess to a contributed capital account.

to present shareholders. Assuming that the fair market value per share was $130 at the time of the stock dividend declaration, the entry is:

Retained Earnings (Stock Dividend Declared)	13,000	
Common Stock Dividend Distributable		13,000

If a balance sheet is prepared between the dates of declaration and distribution, the Common Stock Dividend Distributable account should be shown in the shareholders' equity section as an addition to share capital (whereas cash or property dividends payable are shown as current liabilities).[13]

When the shares are issued the entry is:

Common Stock Dividend Distributable	13,000	
Common Shares		13,000

No matter what the fair value is at the time of the stock dividend, each shareholder retains the same proportionate interest in the corporation. The following illustration shows that the total net worth of each shareholder (A, B, and C) has not changed as a result of the stock dividend, and that each shareholder owns the same proportion of the total shares outstanding after as before the stock dividend.

Before dividend:	
Share capital, 1,000 common shares of no-par value	$100,000
Retained earnings	50,000
Total shareholders' equity	$150,000
Shareholders' interest:	
A—400 shares, 40% interest, book value	$ 60,000
B—500 shares, 50% interest, book value	75,000
C—100 shares, 10% interest, book value	15,000
	$150,000
After declaration but before payment of 10% stock dividend:	
If fair value ($130) is used as basis for entry	
Share capital, 1,000 shares	$100,000
Common stock dividend distributable, 100 shares	13,000
Retained earnings ($50,000 − $13,000)	37,000
Total shareholders' equity	$150,000
After declaration and payment of 10% stock dividend:	
If fair value ($130) is used as basis for entry	
Share capital, 1,100 shares	$113,000
Retained earnings ($50,000 − $13,000)	37,000
Total shareholders' equity	$150,000
Shareholders' interest:	
A—440 shares, 40% interest, book value	$ 60,000
B—550 shares, 50% interest, book value	75,000
C—110 shares, 10% interest, book value	15,000
	$150,000

[13]Some would argue that no entry need be made at date of declaration since court decisions have allowed for stock dividends to be revoked after declaration. Nevertheless, the declaration should be disclosed in financial statements. Journalizing at the time of declaration and disclosing in the statements as indicated is appropriate. A note could also be used.

Stock Splits

If a company has undistributed earnings each year over a long period of time so that a sizable balance in retained earnings has accumulated, the market value of its outstanding shares may increase to reflect the larger investment. Shares that were issued at prices less than $50 not infrequently attain a market value in excess of $100 a share. The higher the market price of a share, the less readily it can be purchased by most people. The managements of many corporations believe that for better public relations, broad ownership of a corporation's shares is desirable. They wish, therefore, to have a market price sufficiently low to be within range of the majority of potential investors. To reduce the market value of shares, the common device of a **stock split** is employed. For example when IBM's stock was selling at $304 a share, the company split its common shares four for one. The day after IBM's split (involving 583,268,480 shares) was effective, the stock sold for $76 a share, exactly one quarter of its price per share before the split. IBM's intent was to obtain a wider distribution of its shares by improving their marketability. From an accounting standpoint, **no entry is recorded for a stock split;** a memorandum note, however, may be made to indicate that the number of shares outstanding has increased.[14] The absence of any other changes in shareholders' equity information is indicated in the following illustration for a two-for-one stock split on 1,000 no-par value common shares.

Shareholders' Equity Before 2 for 1 Split		Shareholders' Equity After 2 for 1 Split	
Common, 1,000 shares,		Common, 2,000 shares,	
no-par value	$100,000	no-par value	$100,000
Retained earnings	50,000	Retained earnings	50,000
	$150,000		$150,000

Some companies use reverse stock splits. A **reverse stock split** reduces the number of shares outstanding and increases the per share price. This technique is used where the share price is unusually low or where management may wish to take control of the company. For example, two officers of Metropolitan Maintenance Co. took control of the company by forcing a 1 for 3,000 reverse stock split on their shareholders. For every 3,000 old shares, one new share was issued; but anyone who had fewer than 3,000 shares received only cash for their shares. Only the two officers owned more than 3,000 shares. A nice squeeze plan![15]

Stock Splits and Stock Dividends Differentiated

A stock split is distinguished from a stock dividend in that a stock split results in an increase (or decrease in a reverse stock split) in the number of shares outstanding with no change in share capital amount, whereas a stock dividend results in an increase in both the number of shares outstanding and the share capital amount.[16] Neither, however, results in any change to total shareholders' equity (the addition

---

[14]If shares have a par value, the memorandum note would indicate that the par value had changed as well as the number of shares outstanding.

[15]*Forbes* (November 19, 1984), p. 54.

[16]For par value shares, a split also requires the par value to be changed.

to share capital from a stock dividend comes from reducing retained earnings, leaving the total shareholders' equity unchanged).

The reasons for issuing a stock dividend are numerous and varied. Stock dividends can be more of a publicity gesture because they are considered by many as dividends and, consequently, the corporation is not criticized for retention of profits. In addition, the corporation may simply wish to retain profits in the business by capitalizing a part of retained earnings. In such a situation, a transfer is made on declaration of a stock dividend from earned capital to permanent capital.

A stock dividend, like a stock split, also may be used to increase the marketability of the shares, although marketability is often a secondary consideration. If the stock dividend is so large that the principal consideration appears to be a desire to reduce the price of the shares, the action results in a stock split, regardless of the form it may take. The AICPA Committee on Accounting Procedures stated that **whenever additional shares are issued for the purpose of reducing the unit market price, then the distribution more closely resembles a stock split than a stock dividend. This effect usually results only if the number of shares issued is more than 20% or 25% of the number of shares previously outstanding.**[17] The Committee recommended that such a distribution not be called a stock dividend, but it might properly be called "a split-up effected in the form of a dividend" or "a stock split." While no such guidelines have been specified for the Canadian practitioner, the U.S. standard is useful when one is required to exercise judgement regarding accounting for substance over form.

Dividend Preferences

It was previously indicated that various rights and privileges may be given to particular classes (preferred) of shares. In most cases, these rights and privileges pertain to dividends and reflect various combinations regarding cumulative and participating arrangements (defined in Chapter 15). The examples given below illustrate the effect of various provisions on dividend distributions to common and preferred shareholders. Assume that $50,000 is to be distributed as cash dividends, and that outstanding share capital consists of $400,000 received for 8,000 shares of no-par value common stock and $100,000 received for 1,000 shares of $6 preferred no-par value shares. Dividends would be distributed to each class according to the assumptions stated for each situation. It should be noted that the terms and bases for determining participating dividends can be different from those shown in these illustrations. The specific details related to participation would be described in the articles of incorporation.

1. Assumption—the preferred shares are noncumulative and nonparticipating:

	Preferred	Common	Total
$6 × 1,000 shares	$6,000		$ 6,000
The remainder to common		$44,000	44,000
Totals	$6,000	$44,000	$50,000

[17]*Accounting Research and Terminology Bulletins, No. 43,* par. 13. The U.S. SEC has added more precision to the 20–25% rule. Specifically, the SEC indicates that distributions of 25% or more should be considered a "split-up effected in the form of a dividend." Distributions of less than 25% should be accounted for as a stock dividend. Use these guidelines when doing homework problems on this subject.

2. Assumption—the preferred shares are cumulative and nonparticipating, and dividends have not been paid on them in the preceding two years:

	Preferred	Common	Total
Dividends in arrears, $6 × 1,000 shares for two years	$12,000		$12,000
Current year's dividend, $6 × 1,000 shares	6,000		6,000
The remainder to common		$32,000	32,000
Totals	$18,000	$32,000	$50,000

3. Assumption—the preferred shares are noncumulative and fully participating. Participation is in terms of the proportionate (percentage) relationship of the amounts paid for the shares (i.e., the amounts in the share capital accounts). Participation takes place after the stipulated preferred dividend is satisfied and common shareholders have been allocated an equal rate on their share capital:

	Preferred	Common	Total
Current year's dividend	$ 6,000	$24,000	$30,000
Participating dividend	4,000	16,000	20,000
Totals	$10,000	$40,000	$50,000

The amounts in this schedule were determined as follows:

Current year's dividend		
Preferred ($6 × 1,000 shares)	$ 6,000	
Common (Preferred rate × common share capital)		
[($6,000/$100,000) × $400,000]	24,000	$30,000
Amount available for participation	$ 20,000	
Total share capital ($100,000 + $400,000)	500,000	
Rate of participation		
$\dfrac{\text{Amount available}}{\text{Total share capital}} = \dfrac{\$ 20,000}{\$500,000}$	4%	
Participating dividend		
Preferred (4% × $100,000)		$ 4,000
Common (4% × $400,000)		16,000
		$20,000

An alternative to this calculation would be:

(a) determine the percentage of the total amount available for dividends to total share capital:

$$\frac{\$ 50,000}{\$500,000} = 10\%$$

(b) if this rate is greater than the rate committed to preferred for the year (6% = $6,000/$100,000), then it can be applied to the share capital for each class to determine their respective total dividend:

To preferred (10% × $100,000)	$10,000
To common (10% × $400,000)	40,000
Total	$50,000

(c) if the rate is less than the rate committed to preferred, the preferred are given their full amount ($6,000) if available, with the remainder, if any, going to the common shareholders.

4. Assumption—the preferred shares are cumulative and fully participating, and dividends have not been paid in the preceding two years. In this case, the dividends in arrears would be allocated to the preferred shareholders and the balance available would be allocated according to the procedures shown in illustration 3. Therefore, the distribution would be:

	Preferred	Common	Total
Preferred dividends in arrears			
(2 years × $6 × 1,000 shares)	$12,000		$12,000
Current year's dividend			
(6% of share capital)	6,000	$24,000	30,000
Participating dividend			
($8,000/$500,000) × share capital	1,600	6,400	8,000
Totals	$19,600	$30,400	$50,000

APPROPRIATIONS OF RETAINED EARNINGS

Appropriations (also called reserves) of retained earnings are nothing more than segregations of retained earnings, temporarily or perhaps even permanently established for a given purpose. When the appropriation is no longer necessary, the appropriated amount should be returned to unappropriated retained earnings. The consequence of an appropriation is to indicate to shareholders that a portion of retained earnings is not available for dividend distributions. An appropriation of retained earnings in no way results in the existence of any cash fund for reasons related to the appropriation. Should such a cash fund (e.g., sinking fund for bond retirement) be required or desired, actions apart from an appropriation of retained earnings must be taken. Under no circumstances may amounts be charged against appropriations that would otherwise be charged to income statement accounts.[18]

The act of appropriating retained earnings is a policy matter requiring approval by the board of directors. According to the *CICA Handbook*, the appropriation of retained earnings is acceptable practice, provided that it is shown within the shareholders' equity section of the balance sheet and is clearly identified as to the source from which it was created.[19]

Any improper use of such appropriations or failure to disclose properly their nature calls for comment by the independent auditor even though the retained earnings appropriation is basically a management problem.

Reasons for Retained Earnings Appropriations

Various reasons are advanced for establishing an appropriation of retained earnings. These include:

[18]*CICA Handbook*, Section 3260, par. 2–3.

[19]*Ibid.*, par. 4. As well, *Financial Reporting in Canada—1983* reported that nine of the surveyed companies indicated the existence of reserves (appropriations); all disclosed the source of shareholders' equity from which they were created.

1. **Legal restrictions**. As indicated earlier, some laws prohibit the purchase of treasury shares by the corporation unless earnings available for dividends are present. They then restrict the retained earnings in an amount equal to the cost of any treasury shares acquired. Such laws actually require that stated capital be maintained by requiring that earnings be retained to substitute for share capital temporarily acquired as treasury shares.

2. **Contractual restrictions**. Bond indentures frequently contain a requirement that retained earnings in specified amounts be appropriated each year during the life of bonds. The appropriation created under such a provision is commonly called Appropriation for Sinking Fund or Appropriation for Bond Indebtedness.

3. **Existence of possible or expected loss**. Some companies establish Appropriations for Anticipated Future Inventory Declines to reflect expected losses should a general decline in prices occur. Similar appropriations might be established for estimated losses due to lawsuits, unfavourable contractual obligations, and other contingencies.

4. **Protection of working capital position**. The board of directors may authorize the creation of an "Appropriation for Working Capital" out of retained earnings in order to indicate that the amount specified is not available for dividends because it is desirable to maintain a strong current position. Another example involves a decision made to finance a building program by internal financing. An "Appropriation for Plant Expansion" is created to indicate that retained earnings in the amount appropriated will not be considered by the directors as available for dividends.

Some corporations establish appropriations for general contingencies, or appropriate retained earnings for unspecified purposes. The real reason for the restriction may be any of those given above. The essence of the action is that the board of directors desires to reduce the amount of retained earnings **apparently** available for dividends without explaining to the shareholders exactly why. In some cases this is justified by statutory or contractual restrictions. In other cases no adequate explanation for such actions is possible. In general, however, the establishment of general or unspecified appropriations should not be encouraged.

Recording Appropriations of Retained Earnings

As soon as the board of directors has approved an appropriation of retained earnings, it becomes necessary to record the appropriation in the accounts. First, the unappropriated retained earnings must be reduced by the amount of the appropriation and, second, a new account must be established to receive the amount transferred. If the appropriation merely augments a previously established segregation, the account already in use should receive the credit. The appropriation is recorded as a debit to Retained Earnings and a credit to an appropriately named account that itself is really a subdivision of Retained Earnings. For example:

(a) An Appropriation for Plant Expansion is to be created by transfer from Retained Earnings of $40,000 a year for ten years. The entry for each year would be:

Retained Earnings	40,000	
Retained Earnings Appropriated for Plant Expansion		40,000

(b) At the end of ten years the appropriation would have a balance of $400,000. If we assume that the expansion plan has been completed, the appropriation is no longer required and can be returned to retained earnings by making the following entry:

Retained Earnings Appropriated for Plant Expansion	400,000	
Retained Earnings		400,000

Return of an appropriation to retained earnings has the effect of increasing unappropriated retained earnings without affecting the assets or current position. In effect, over the ten years the company has expanded by reinvesting earnings.

The term "reserve" may be used instead of "appropriation" in such account titles. The authors, however, have not condoned this practice because it results in confusion and misunderstanding owing to the public's general interpretation of the term and its diverse use by accountants in the past (i.e., Reserve for Depreciation, Reserve for Uncollectible Accounts, which were contra-asset items). Fortunately, some of this confusion has been eliminated by the *CICA Handbook*, which limits the use of the term "reserve" to appropriations of retained earnings or other surplus.[20]

Disclosure of Restrictions on Retained Earnings

In many corporations restrictions or conditions affecting the distribution of retained earnings exist, but no appropriation (reserve) account is established.[21] The *CICA Handbook* requires that disclosure of the details of such circumstances be made.[22]

Most restrictions for which journal entries are not made are of a contractual nature, resulting from agreements with creditors, and are best disclosed by note. Parenthetical notations are sometimes used, but restrictions imposed by bond indentures and loan agreements commonly require an extended explanation; notes provide a medium for more complete explanations and free the financial statements from abbreviated notations. The type of detail revealed by such notes could include identification of the source of the restriction, pertinent provisions, and the amount of retained earnings subject to restriction, or the amount not so restricted. The following examples from annual reports illustrate note disclosure relating to restrictions on retained earnings and dividends.

Domtar Inc.

9. Retained earnings

The Trust Deeds securing the sinking fund debentures contain restrictions on the payment of dividends, other than stock dividends, on common shares. Under the most restrictive provision, $129.1 million of retained earnings at December 31, 1982, is not available for payment as dividends on common shares other than through stock dividends.

Westcoast Transmission Co. Ltd.

8. Dividend Restriction:

The First Mortgage and the indentures relating to the Company's long-term debt and preferred shares contain restrictions as to the declaration or payment of dividends (other than stock dividends) on common shares. Under the most restrictive provision, the amount available for dividends at December 31, 1982, is $126,000,000 (December 31, 1981 − $108,000,000, December 31, 1980 − $89,000,000).

---

[20]*Ibid.*, par. 1.

[21]While the *CICA Handbook* states that reserves should be shown as part of shareholders' equity (Section 3260, par. 4), this applies only when the board has authorized the creation of such an account. The *Handbook* does not require the creation of appropriation accounts when restrictions exist.

[22]*CICA Handbook*, Section 3250, par. 10. *Financial Reporting in Canada—1983* stated that, in 1982, 79 of the surveyed companies made such disclosures (64 giving details). In 1981 there were 82, in 1980 there were 75, and in 1979 there were 77 companies disclosing such restrictions.

As noted previously, restrictions may be based on the retention of a certain amount of retained earnings, on the corporation's ability to observe certain working capital requirements, upon additional borrowing, and on other considerations. When there is more than one type of restriction relating to a particular contract, disclosure of the amount of retained earnings so restricted may be based on the most restrictive covenants. This is sufficient because restrictions seldom, if ever, pyramid in amount.

Appropriations or Disclosures for Contingencies and for Self-Insurance

A **contingency** is defined as an existing condition or situation involving uncertainty as to possible gain or loss to an enterprise that will ultimately be resolved when one or more future events occur or fail to occur.[23] Accounting for loss contingencies was examined in Chapter 5. It was pointed out that under certain conditions (loss is likely and can be reasonably estimated) such contingent losses may be accrued by a charge to income and the recording of a liability prior to their ultimate resolution. In most cases, however, these conditions are not met and the existence of the loss contingency is disclosed by a note. Shown below is an example of such a disclosure.

Southam Inc.

10. Legal proceedings
On May 1, 1981, the Attorney General of Canada charged the company and certain other companies with offenses under the Combines Investigation Act, including conspiring to lessen unduly competition of major English language daily newspapers published in certain areas and forming a merger or a monopoly in certain areas. The trial has been scheduled to commence during 1983 and the company will contest the charges. In the event of conviction, the court is empowered to order the dissolution of any merger or monopoly found to exist, to prohibit any act directed toward the continuation of an offense found to have been committed, and to impose fines. The outcome of these proceedings is not determinable at this time and the effect, if any, is expected to be accounted for in the consolidated statement of income in the year in which it is known.

In addition to such disclosures of contingencies, the board of directors of a corporation may, at its discretion, give further recognition to possible future losses by directing that a portion of retained earnings be restricted or that an appropriation of retained earnings (Appropriation for Contingencies) be made for a specific amount in the accounts. Disclosing the existence of restrictions of retained earnings for contingencies in the notes to the financial statements is more common than appropriating a specific portion of retained earnings.

A company may insure against many contingencies such as fire, flood, storm, and accident by taking out insurance policies and paying premiums to insurance companies. Some contingencies, however, are not insurable or the rates may be judged as being prohibitively high in the circumstances. In such situations, some companies may adopt a policy referred to as **self-insurance**. Self-insurance appears especially valid when a company's physical or operating characteristics permit application of the law of large numbers as used by insurance companies. Whenever the risk of loss can be spread over a large number of possible loss events that individually would be small in relation to the total potential loss, self-insurance is

---

[23]*Ibid.*, Section 3290, par. 2.

a temptation. It is based on the belief that the losses will be less over an extended period of time than the premiums that would be paid to insure against such losses; that is, the company avoids the insurance company's overhead costs including the insurance agent's commission. Examples of such situations are a car rental company with hundreds of cars in different locations, or a grocery chain with many stores scattered geographically.

Accounting for self-insurance could take one of at least three forms:

Record Losses as Incurred. Under this approach no accounting recognition is given to the fact that self-insurance is the mode of operation and that uninsured losses may have to be absorbed in some future period. Losses are charged against revenues of the period in which it is likely that an asset has been impaired or a liability has been incurred at the date of the financial statements and the amount of loss can be reasonably estimated.[24] **This approach is permitted under GAAP.**

Appropriate and Record Losses as Incurred. This approach treats uninsured losses in the same manner; that is, they are charged entirely to expense in the period in which they are sustained. Recognition is given to contingent losses in periods other than their incurrence, however, by appropriations of retained earnings. The annual appropriation is a debit to Retained Earnings and a credit to Appropriation for Self-Insurance. When the casualty loss occurs, a loss account is debited, the appropriate asset account is credited for the book value of the loss, and the entry creating the appropriation is reversed. The amount of the annual appropriation may approximate the premium cost of adequate insurance covering the risk, or it may be a prorated allocation of an estimated and anticipated future loss. The balance of the appropriation account normally does not exceed the maximum expected loss at any one time and is never charged with actual losses. The effect of this and the first method is a varying charge for actual losses instead of a stable charge to expense that would result from premium payments to an insurance company. **This approach is also permitted under GAAP.**

Accrue Expense. This approach avoids the irregular effects on net income resulting from irregularly occurring uninsured losses and makes the income statement of an uninsured company appear to be comparable to those of firms carrying insurance. This method accrues the estimated losses by charging operations each year with a hypothetical amount of insurance expense and crediting a similar amount to a liability account entitled Liability for Self-Insured Risks or Liability for Uninsured Losses. When the casualty losses occur, they are charged against the liability account. The liability account absorbs the impact of the loss; each year's income statement absorbs only a portion of the loss. **This approach is not permitted under GAAP.**

Self-insurance is no insurance, and any company that assumes its own risks puts itself in the position of incurring expenses or losses as the casualties occur. The improper application of the accrual method (third method) to self-insurance obscures a fundamental difference in circumstances between companies that transfer risks to others through insurance and those that do not. There is little theoretical justification for the establishment of a liability based on a hypothetical charge to insurance expense. This is "as if" accounting.[25] Can there be an expense in advance of the actual occurrence of a casualty, or a liability to incur a casualty loss in the future? The *CICA Handbook*'s answer to this question is:

[24]*Ibid.*, par. 12.

[25]A commentary in *Forbes* (June 15, 1974, p. 42) stated its position on this matter quite succinctly: "The simple and unquestionable fact of life is this: business is cyclical and full of unexpected surprises. Is it the role of accounting to disguise this unpleasant fact and create a fairyland of smoothly rising earnings? Or, should accounting reflect reality, warts and all—floods, expropriations, and all manner of rude shocks?"

Fires, explosions, and other similar perils are random in their occurrence and, since no impairment of an asset or incurrence of a liability can exist prior to the occurrence of such an event, accrual is inappropriate. Where, however, an enterprise lacks adequate insurance against a material risk that is normally insured, disclosure of this fact may be desirable.[26]

With respect to uninsured losses that may result from injury to others, damage to the property of others, or business interruptions that may occur after the balance sheet date, premature accrual is similarly objectionable.

Are Appropriations of Retained Earnings Necessary?

Creation of an appropriation of retained earnings can be caused by (1) requirements of a statute or contractual agreement (i.e., bond indenture) or (2) a discretionary decision of the board of directors. Regardless of the cause, the consequence is communication to financial statement users that a portion of retained earnings is not regarded as available for dividends.

While the first cause identified above represents a legal requirement that cannot be avoided, the necessity for making discretionary appropriations is debatable. While it may be a legitimate attempt to inform statement users that part of the retained earnings is restricted, a consequence may be that such users wonder why the balance of unappropriated retained earnings is not distributed as dividends. Therefore, disclosure of discretionary restrictions by notes to the statements may be much more informative and less confusing than simply using appropriations.

STATEMENTS PRESENTING CHANGES IN RETAINED EARNINGS AND CONTRIBUTED SURPLUS

The *CICA Handbook* recommends that changes in each of retained earnings and contributed surplus during the period should be disclosed.[27] Statements of changes in retained earnings and of contributed surplus are frequently presented to accomplish this. The basic format for presenting this information is:

1. Balance at the beginning of the period.
2. Additions.
3. Deductions.
4. Balance at the end of the period.

Although a large segment of the general public (investors and creditors) has gained an understanding of and appreciation for the balance sheet and income statement and, to some degree, the statement of retained earnings and statement of changes in financial position, only a small minority comprehend the items appearing in the statement of contributed surplus. Nevertheless, disclosure of changes in the separate accounts that make up contributed surplus (in addition to retained earnings) is helpful to making the financial statements sufficiently informative. Disclosure of such changes may take the form of separate statements or may be made in the basic financial statements or notes thereto. The following examples from financial statements indicate how such disclosure may be accomplished.

[26]*CICA Handbook*, Section 3290, par. 16.

[27]*Ibid.*, Section 3250, par. 13.

The New Brunswick Telephone Co. Ltd.

	(in thousands)	
Balance Sheet—in shareholders' equity	1982	1981
Contributed surplus	16,902	15,133
Retained earnings	63,494	55,602

CONSOLIDATED STATEMENT OF CONTRIBUTED SURPLUS

Year ended December 31	1982	1981
Balance at beginning of year	$15,133	$13,638
Discount on preferred shares purchased for cancellation	233	146
Premium on common shares issued	1,536	1,349
Balance at end of year	$16,902	$15,133

Steinberg Inc.

	(in thousands)	
Balance Sheet—in shareholders' equity	1982	1981
Contributed Surplus (Note 7)	1,257	757
Retained Earnings	244,750	224,766

Note to financial statements:

7. Contributed Surplus
The contributed surplus as at July 31, 1982, consisted of gains on redemption of 5 1/4% cumulative redeemable preferred shares, Series "A", and $1.95 cumulative redeemable second preferred shares, series one, amounting to $756,977 with respect to prior years and $500,537 with respect to the current year.

In order to disclose the changes in all shareholder equity items a **columnar format** report can be very useful. Such a format is used for the Statement of Shareholders' Equity in the financial statements of The Goodyear Tire & Rubber Company as shown below:

The Goodyear Tire & Rubber Company and Subsidiaries
CONSOLIDATED STATEMENT OF SHAREHOLDERS' EQUITY

(Dollars in millions except per share)

	Common Stock		Capital	Retained
	Shares	Amount	Surplus	Earnings
Balance at December 31, 1983 after deducting 1,219,698 treasury shares	105,425,079	91.5	589.4	2,678.8
Net income for 1984				411.0
Cash dividends paid in 1984 $1.50 per share				(158.7)
Common stock purchased for treasury	(250,001)	(.3)	(6.8)	
Common stock issued (including 46,220 treasury shares)	1,317,631	1.3	31.0	
Balance at December 31, 1984 after deducting 1,423,479 treasury shares	106,492,709	$92.5	$613.6	$2,931.1

APPRAISAL INCREASE CREDITS

Assets have normally been accounted for on a historical cost basis. The *CICA Handbook* recognizes, however, that some circumstances may warrant reflecting asset values that differ from cost.[28] When an asset's appraisal value is in excess of its book value and this fact is to be recognized in the accounts, the credit would be made to a shareholders' equity account such as Excess of Appraised Value of Fixed Assets Over Cost (or Depreciated Cost when appropriate)[29] or simply Appraisal Increase. Such appraisal increase credit accounts are to be shown as a separate item in shareholders' equity. An appraisal increase account balance may remain indefinitely or be amortized to retained earnings each period in amounts not greater than the realization of the appreciation through sale or depreciation provisions.[30]

ILLUSTRATION OF A COMPREHENSIVE SHAREHOLDERS' EQUITY SECTION

The illustration on page 751 is an example of a comprehensive shareholders' equity section of a balance sheet. It includes most of the equity items discussed in Chapters 15 and 16 although notes that would normally provide more details on the items have been omitted.

OMIT FROM HERE

QUASI-REORGANIZATION

A corporation that consistently suffers net losses accumulates negative retained earnings, or a deficit. Corporate laws often provide that no dividends may be declared and paid so long as a corporation's contributed capital (share capital and contributed surplus) has been impaired by a deficit. In these cases, a corporation with a debit balance of retained earnings must accumulate sufficient profits to offset the deficit before dividends may be paid.

This situation may be a real hardship on a corporation and its shareholders. For example, a company that has operated unsuccessfully for several years and accumulated a deficit may attain a position that gives promise of successful operation in the future. Development of new products and new markets, a new management group placed in control, or merely improved economic conditions may point to much improved operating results; but, if the law prohibits dividends until the deficit has been replaced by earnings, the shareholders must wait until such profits have been earned, which may take a considerable period of time. Furthermore, future success may depend on obtaining additional funds through the sale of shares. If no dividends can be paid for some time, however, the market price of any new share issue is likely to be low, if such shares can be marketed at all.

---

[28]*CICA Handbook*, Section 3060, par. 1. An example given is the case of appraisal values in a reorganization. Another may be recognition of a discovery value. Also, recent developments in accounting for changing prices have implications for accounting for assets at other than historical cost (see Chapter 25).

[29]*Ibid.*, Section 3270, par. 1.

[30]*Ibid.*, par. 2. Section 3060, par. 6 also states that when appraisal increases are recorded, depreciation of the asset should be based on the appraisal value. *Financial Reporting in Canada—1983* reported that, of the 325 companies surveyed, 13 had included appraisal increases in the shareholders' equity section in 1982 and 1981. In each year, 8 showed a current write-off and the remaining 5 did not.

Model Corporation
SHAREHOLDERS' EQUITY
December 31, 1986

Share Capital:
  Class A, preferred, $9 dividend,
  cumulative, no-par value,
  30,000 shares authorized, issued,
  and outstanding .... $ 3,150,000
  Class B, common, no-par value,
  400,000 shares issued and
  outstanding, no authorized
  limit 4,000,000
  Class B common stock dividend
  distributable, 20,000 shares 200,000
      Total share capital .... $ 7,350,000

Contributed Surplus:
  Excess of assigned value over cost
  of common shares purchased and
  cancelled .... $ 10,000
  Donated land 830,000
      Total contributed capital 840,000

Retained Earnings:
  Appropriated for plant expansion $2,100,000
  Unappropriated 2,160,000
      Total retained earnings 4,260,000
      Total capital and retained earnings $12,450,000

Excess of Appraised Value of
  Fixed Assets Over Depreciated Cost 100,000
      Total $12,550,000
Less cost of treasury stock (2,000
  shares, common) .... (80,000)
      Total shareholders' equity $12,470,000

Thus, a company with every prospect of a successful future may be prevented from accomplishing its plans because of a deficit, although present management may have had nothing whatever to do with the years over which the deficit was accumulated. To permit the corporation to proceed with its plans might well be to the advantage of all interests in the enterprise; to require it to make up the deficit out of profits might actually force it to liquidate to the possible injury of all parties at interest.

A procedure that eliminates an accumulated deficit and permits the company to proceed on much the same basis as if it had been legally reorganized, without the difficulty and expenses generally connected with a legal reorganization, is known as a "quasi-reorganization," and consists of the following steps:

1. All assets are revalued at appropriate current values so the company will not be burdened with excessive inventory or plant asset valuations in following years. Any loss on revaluation increases the deficit.

2. Contributed surplus must be available or must be created, at least equal in amount to the deficit. If no such surplus exists, it is created through donation of shares to the corporation by shareholders, by reduction of the value of shares outstanding, or by some similar means.
3. The deficit is then charged against the contributed surplus and thus eliminated.

The series of entries given below illustrate the steps taken in a quasi-reorganization. Assume that the concern shows a deficit of $20,000 before the quasi-reorganization is effected.

Retained Earnings	80,000	
Inventory		30,000
Plant Assets		50,000
(To revalue assets to recognize unrecorded losses)		
Common Shares	150,000	
Contributed Surplus		150,000
(To reduce the value of 3,000 common shares outstanding)		
Contributed Surplus	100,000	
Retained Earnings		100,000
(To charge deficit against contributed surplus)		

The contributed surplus created at the time of the quasi-reorganization may be called Reorganization Capital, Capital from Reduction in the Value of Share Capital, or other appropriate titles, depending on its source.

In connection with the foregoing steps, certain requirements must be fulfilled. (a) The proposed quasi-reorganization procedure should be submitted to and receive the approval of the corporation's shareholders before it is put into effect. (b) The new asset valuations should be fair and not deliberately understate or overstate assets and liabilities. (c) After the reorganization the corporation must have a zero balance of retained earnings, although it may have contributed surplus arising from the reorganization. (d) In subsequent reports the retained earnings must be "dated" for a period of at least three years to show the fact and the date of the quasi-reorganization, as illustrated in the following example of a 1986 balance sheet presentation.

Shareholders' equity		
Common shares of no-par value, authorized		
and issued, 30,000 shares	$150,000	
Capital arising from reduction in		
assigned value of common shares	50,000	
Earnings retained in the business		
(after quasi-reorganization on June 30, 1983)	33,500	$233,500

In times of general economic or specific industry recession (such as the early 1980s) or depression the use of the quasi-reorganization procedure becomes a more common occurrence as companies attempt to turn around, to get a fresh start, and make their financial statements more representative of the firm's changed economic status. For example, Lockheed Corporation, given its large losses on the L-1011 Tri-Star program, decided to use the quasi-reorganization approach to offset a large deficit balance in retained earnings; and Astrotech International

OMIT
TO
HERE

Corporation eliminated a $28 million deficit in Retained Earnings in 1984 as it changed from an investment company to an operating company through the quasi-reorganization approach.

KEY POINTS

1. The basic categories of shareholders' equity are Share Capital (Chapter 15), Contributed Surplus, and Retained Earnings. Such other categories as Appraisal Increase Credits or Treasury Shares may sometimes appear.

2. Contributed Surplus comes from a variety of sources that represent amounts contributed by shareholders and others to a corporation. Donations, assessments, sale of treasury shares above cost (single-transaction method), excess of assigned value of shares reacquired and cancelled over the cost, and forfeited shares are examples of sources of Contributed Surplus.

3. Retained Earnings is the sum total of all income earned by a corporation less the dividends declared.

4. Dividends are established by a resolution in the minutes of the board of directors on the date of declaration which, in addition to specifying amounts, specifies the date of record and the date of payment.

5. Dividend declaration decisions are governed by the corporation having sufficient retained earnings available and assets to distribute so that payment will not result in insolvency. Present and future financial positions are important aspects of such decisions.

6. Various types of dividends exist—cash, property, scrip, liquidating, and stock dividends.

7. Preferences as to dividends may exist between classes of shares in terms of priority for distribution, cumulative, and participation rights. Various combinations of such preferences may exist.

8. Restrictions may exist regarding the availability of retained earnings for dividends. These may be the result of statutory or contractual commitments, or a discretionary decision of the board of directors. Disclosure of such restrictions is necessary and may be accomplished through notes to the financial statements and/or establishment of an appropriation account.

9. Disclosure of changes in shareholders' equity accounts during a period is required in the financial statements. This may be accomplished in the basic financial statements, in separate statements designed to accomplish this objective, or through notes.

10. In some circumstances, appraisal increase credits (the excess of an appraisal value over the historical cost book value of an asset) may occur. These are to be shown as a separate item in shareholders' equity.

11. A quasi-reorganization is a procedure requiring formal approval by equity holders that essentially enables a company to get a fresh start. This procedure results in revaluing assets to current values and eliminating an accumulated deficit by a charge against existing or created contributed capital accounts.

QUESTIONS

1. Distinguish among: contributed capital, earned capital, and equity capital.
2. List the possible sources of "contributed surplus."
3. What equity accounts might conceivably have debit balances? Discuss.
4. Indicate the ways in which donated capital may originate.
5. What are some of the common items that increase or decrease retained earnings?
6. Very few companies pay dividends in amounts equal to their retained earnings legally available for dividends. Why?
7. What are the principal considerations of a board of directors in making decisions involving dividend declarations? Discuss briefly.
8. Distinguish among: cash dividends, property dividends, scrip dividends, liquidating dividends, and stock dividends.
9. What factors influence the dividend policy of a company?
10. Describe the accounting entry for a stock dividend. Describe the accounting entry for a stock split.
11. Stock splits and stock dividends may be used by a corporation to change the number of its shares outstanding.
    (a) What is meant by a stock split effected in the form of a dividend?
    (b) From an accounting viewpoint, explain how the stock split effected in the form of a dividend differs from an ordinary stock dividend.
    (c) How should a stock dividend which has been declared but not yet issued be classified in a statement of financial position (balance sheet)? Why?
12. For what reasons might a company appropriate a portion of its retained earnings?
13. How should appropriations of retained earnings be created and written off?
14. Indicate both the improper and the proper use of the term "reserve."
15. What are some of the ways that retained earnings may be restricted?
16. Is there a duplication of charges to current year's costs or expenses when an appropriation is created for fixed asset replacement, as well as there being accumulated depreciation with respect to the fixed assets? Explain your answer briefly.
17. What is self-insurance? What are two acceptable forms of accounting for self-insurance?
18. Dividends are sometimes said to have been paid "out of retained earnings." What is the error in this statement?
19. Under what circumstances would a corporation consider submitting itself to a quasi-reorganization?
20. Outline the accounting steps involved in accomplishing a quasi-reorganization.

CASES

C16-1 The directors of Aromatic Spray Corporation are considering the issuance of a stock dividend. They have asked you to discuss the proposed action by answering the following questions.

Instructions

(a) What is a stock dividend? How is a stock dividend distinguished from a stock split (1) from a legal standpoint? (2) from an accounting standpoint?
(b) For what reasons does a corporation usually declare a stock dividend? A stock split?
(c) Discuss the amount, if any, of retained earnings to be capitalized in connection with a stock dividend.

(AICPA adapted)

C16-2 Airfoil Boat Corporation, a client, is considering the authorization of an 8% common stock dividend to common shareholders. The financial vice-president of Airfoil wishes to discuss the accounting implications of such an authorization with you before the next meeting of the board of directors.

Instructions

(a) The first topic the vice-president wishes to discuss is the nature of the stock dividend to the recipient. Discuss the case **against** considering the stock dividend as income to the recipient.

(b) The other topic for discussion is the propriety of issuing the stock dividend to all "shareholders of record" or to "shareholders of record exclusive of shares held in the name of the corporation as treasury stock." Discuss the case **against** issuing stock dividends on treasury shares.

(AICPA adapted)

C16-3 Amy and Norton, a large retail chain store company, has outlets throughout Canada. Due to their many different locations, the president thinks that it would be advantageous to self-insure the outlets against the risk of any future loss or damage from fire or other natural causes. From past experience and by applying appropriate statistical and actuarial techniques, the president believes that the amount of future losses can be predicted with reasonable accuracy.

Instructions

The president has asked you how Amy and Norton should record this type of contingency and on what basis the current period should be allocated a portion of the estimated losses. What would you tell the president?

C16-4 The retained earnings section of Pacioli Publishing, Inc.'s balance sheet was presented as follows:

Retained Earnings	
Appropriation for plant expansion	$10,000,000
Appropriation for contingencies	2,000,000
Appropriation regarding bond indenture contract	1,000,000
Total appropriation	$13,000,000
Unappropriated (see Note 7)	15,000,000
Total retained earnings	$28,000,000

Note 7: The Board of Directors has restricted $7,000,000 of this amount, given that there are presently litigation proceedings against the company, claiming this as the maximum amount for damages.

Mike Jackson, a common shareholder in the company, was recently quoted as saying "I think appropriations mean that dividends can't be declared out of such amounts. Unfortunately, something must have gone wrong with the company's accounting because a special cash account for each of these appropriations was not shown in the asset section of the balance sheet. Also, I don't really understand why an appropriation was not set up for the $7,000,000 regarding litigation proceedings. The fact that this was disclosed by a note must mean that the restriction is of a second class nature to the listed appropriations. Furthermore, at the next shareholders' meeting, I think we should really get after management, as they don't appear to want to give us our fair amount of dividends. Even accepting the appropriations and restriction as being reasonable, that leaves $8,000,000 that should have been paid as dividends because management has given no reasons why it should be kept in the company.

Instructions

Discuss Mr. Jackson's points regarding his understanding of the reported information.

C16-5 Bista & Battaglia Co., a medium-sized manufacturer, has been experiencing losses for the 5 years that it has been doing business. Although the operations for the year just ended resulted in a loss, several important changes resulted in a profitable fourth quarter, and the future operations of the company are expected to be profitable.

The treasurer, Marty Larsen, suggests that there be a quasi-reorganization to (1) eliminate the accumulated deficit of $632,240, (2) write up the $702,300 cost of land and buildings to their fair value, and (3) set up an asset of $298,500 to represent the estimated future tax benefit of the losses accumulated to date, as they could be offset against future income, thereby reducing future taxes payable.

Instructions

(a) What are the characteristics of a quasi-reorganization? In other words, of what does it consist?

(b) List the conditions under which a quasi-reorganization generally is justified.

(c) Discuss the propriety of the treasurer's proposals to:

1. Eliminate the deficit of $632,240.
2. Write up the $702,300 cost of the land and buildings to their fair value.
3. Set up an asset of $298,500 to represent the estimated future tax benefit of the losses accumulated to date.

(AICPA adapted)

EXERCISES

E16-1 Shareholders' equity on the balance sheet is composed of three major sections. They are: A. Share Capital, B. Contributed Surplus, and C. Retained Earnings.

Instructions

Classify each of the following items as affecting one of the three sections above or as D, an item not to be included in shareholders' equity.

1. Net income.
2. Preferred shares subscribed.
3. Goodwill.
4. Donated land.
5. Cash dividends declared.
6. Preferred shares.
7. Retained earnings appropriated.
8. Allowance for doubtful accounts.
9. Sinking fund.
10. Common shares.
11. Contributed capital—forfeit of cash received on preferred shares subscribed but not paid for in full.

E16-2 The following information has been taken from the ledger accounts of PEI Potatoes Corporation:

Total income since incorporation	$125,000
Total cash dividends paid	50,000
Proceeds from sale of donated shares	25,000
Total value of stock dividends distributed	15,000
Gains on treasury shares transactions (single transaction method)	17,500
Unamortized discount on bonds payable	37,500
Appropriation for plant expansion	25,000

Instructions

Determine the current balance of unappropriated retained earnings.

E16-3 The shareholders' equity accounts of the Cameron Company, Inc. have the following balances on December 31, 1986:

Common shares, no-par value, 400,000 shares issued and outstanding	$6,000,000
Contributed surplus	1,600,000
Retained earnings	7,200,000

Shares of Cameron Company, Inc., are currently selling on the Prairie Stock Exchange at $42, each.

Instructions

Prepare the appropriate journal entries for each of the following unrelated items:

(a) A stock dividend of 10% is declared and issued.

(b) A stock dividend of 100% is declared and issued.

(c) A four-for-one stock split is declared and issued.

E16-4 The following data were taken from the balance sheet accounts of Kitty-Hawk Corporation on December 31, 1985:

Current Assets	$495,000
Investments	308,250
Common Shares no-par value, 45,000 authorized, 22,500 issued and outstanding	450,000
Contributed Surplus—Donations	72,000
Retained Earnings	780,000

Instructions

Prepare the required journal entries for the following unrelated items:

(a) A 10% stock dividend is declared and distributed at a time when the market value of a share is $30.

(b) A scrip dividend of $30,000 is declared.

(c) The shares are split five-for-one.

(d) A dividend is declared January 5, 1986, and paid January 25, 1986, in shares held as an investment; the shares have a book value of $37,000 and a fair market value of $67,500.

E16-5 The outstanding share capital of Comfortable Sleepwear Corporation consists of (1) 1,000 preferred shares with no-par value and with a stated dividend of $8 for which $100,000 was received when all were sold, and (2) 2,000 common shares of no-par value for which $200,000 was received.

Instructions

Assuming that the company has retained earnings of $52,000, all of which is to be paid out in dividends, and that preferred dividends were not paid during the two years preceding the current year, state how much each class of shares would receive under each of the following conditions:

(a) The preferred shares are noncumulative and nonparticipating.

(b) The preferred shares are cumulative and nonparticipating.

(c) The preferred shares are cumulative and participating.

E16-6 Alice Wonderland Company's ledger shows the following balances on December 31, 1986:

Preferred shares—no-par value, $1.05 dividend, outstanding 20,000 shares	$ 300,000
Common shares—no-par value, outstanding 30,000 shares	1,500,000
Retained earnings	540,000

Instructions

Assuming that the directors decide to declare total dividends in the amount of $195,000, determine how much each class of shares would receive under each of the conditions stated below. Dividends on the preferred have not been paid in the previous year.

(a) The preferred shares are cumulative and fully participating.

(b) The preferred shares are noncumulative and nonparticipating.

(c) The preferred shares are noncumulative and participating in distritions in excess of a 10% dividend rate on the common shares.

E16-7   Jerry Goodrich, as president of Ski Lift, Inc., has decided against purchasing casualty insurance to cover the company's 4 lifts. Recognizing the possibility of casualty losses, he has $15,000 a year appropriated as a reserve for such contingencies; the first appropriation was made in 1983. In 1986 a fire destroys one of his lifts. The lift had a 20-year life, no salvage value, and an original cost of $200,000 when it was built 12 years ago. After the fire in 1986, Goodrich changes his mind, buys insurance and pays an annual premium of $17,500 on January 2, 1987, and eliminates his casualty reserve.

Instructions

Prepare the entries to journalize the insurance and casualty transactions and the events of 1983, 1986, and 1987.

E16-8   The following account balances are available from the ledger of Turnaround Corporation on December 31, 1985:

Common Shares—no-par value, 15,000 shares	
authorized and outstanding	$1,050,000
Retained Earnings (deficit)	(315,000)

As of January 2, 1986, the corporation gave effect to a shareholder-approved quasi-reorganization by reducing the average (assigned) value of the shares to $42 a share, writing down plant assets by $52,500, and eliminating the deficit.

Instructions

Prepare the required journal entries for the quasi-reorganization of Turnaround.

E16-9   The condensed balance sheets of Snap Back Company immediately before and one year after it had completed a quasi-reorganization appear below:

	Before Quasi	One Year After		Before Quasi	One Year After
Current assets	$ 300,000	$ 420,000	Common shares	$2,250,000	$1,350,000
Plant assets (net)	1,500,000	1,050,000	Contributed Surplus	150,000	
			Retained Earnings	(600,000)	120,000
	$1,800,000	$1,470,000		$1,800,000	$1,470,000

For the year following the quasi-reorganization, the Snap Back Company reported net income of $150,000, depreciation expense of $75,000, and paid a cash dividend of $30,000. As part of the quasi-reorganization, the company wrote down inventories by $75,000. No purchases or sales of plant assets and no share transactions occurred in the year following the quasi-reorganization.

Instructions

Prepare all the journal entries made at the time of the quasi-reorganization.

E16-10 J-Cloth Co. Ltd. had its buildings appraised recently at $500,000. Orginally, they cost $750,000 and, to date, accumulated depreciation on them is $400,000.

Instructions

Assuming the company could legitimately recognize appraisals in its accounts, what journal entry would be made to reflect this information?

PROBLEMS

P16-1 As the newly appointed controller for Golf Cart Company, you are interested in analysing the "Additional Capital" account of the company in order to present an accurate balance sheet. Your assistant, Steve Kittleson, who has analysed the account from the inception of the company, submits the following summary:

	Debits	Credits
Cash dividends—preferred	$ 135,000	
Cash dividends—common	330,000	
Net income		$1,230,000
Appraisal increase credit for land		300,000
Additional assessments of prior years' income taxes	130,500	
Extraordinary gain		22,500
Donated building		195,000
Extraordinary loss	172,500	
Correction of a prior period error	67,500	
	$ 835,500	$1,747,500
Credit balance of additional capital account	912,000	
	$1,747,500	$1,747,500

Instructions

(a) Prepare a journal entry to close the single "Additional Capital" account now used and to establish appropriately classified accounts. Indicate how you derive the balance of each new account.

(b) If generally accepted accounting principles had been followed, what amount should have been shown as total net income?

P16-2 The balance sheet of Innovative, Inc. shows $300,000 share capital, consisting of 3,000 common shares, and retained earnings of $225,000. As controller of the company, you find that Earl Schultz, the assistant treasurer, is $60,000 short in his accounts and had concealed this shortage by adding the amount to the inventory. He owns 450 of the company's shares and, in settlement of the shortage, offers these shares at their book value. The offer is accepted; the company pays him the excess value and distributes the 450 shares thus acquired to the other shareholders. Assume that the addition to the inventory account took place after the income had been properly calculated and closed to the retained earnings.

Instructions

(a) What amount should Innovative, Inc. pay the assistant treasurer?

(b) By what journal entries should the foregoing transactions be recorded? (Treasury shares are recorded using the single transaction method.)

(c) What is the total shareholders' equity after the distribution noted above?

P16-3 The Board of Directors of Elm Corporation on December 1, 1986, declared a 2% stock dividend on the no-par value common shares of the corporation, payable on December 28, 1986, to the holders of record at the close of business December 15, 1986. They stipulated that cash dividends were to be paid in lieu of issuing any fractional shares. They also directed that the amount to be charged against retained earnings should be equal to the market value per share on the declaration date multiplied by the total of (a) the number of shares issued as a stock dividend, and (b) the number of shares on which cash is paid in place of the issuance of fractional shares. The following facts are given:

1. At the dividend date:

(a) Shares of Elm common issued	3,048,750
(b) Shares of Elm common held in treasury	1,100
(c) Shares of Elm common included in (a) above held by persons who will receive cash in lieu of fractional shares	222,750
(d) Shares of predecessor company that are exchangeable for Elm common at the rate of 1 1/4 shares of Elm common for each share of predecessor company (necessary number of shares of Elm common have been reserved but not issued). Provision was made for a cash dividend in lieu of fractional shares to holders of 180 of these 660 shares.	660

2. Values of Elm common were:

Market value at December 1st	$22
Book value at December 1st	$16

Instructions

Prepare entries and explanations to record the payment of the dividend.

(AICPA adapted)

P16-4   The books of Becca Corporation carried the following account balances as of December 31, 1985:

Cash	$271,500
Preferred shares, $0.60 cumulative dividend, nonparticipating, no-par value, 30,000 issued	300,000
Common shares, no-par value, 150,000 issued	750,000
Treasury shares (common 3,600 shares at cost)	21,600
Retained earnings	105,000

The preferred shares have dividends in arrears for the past year (1985).

The board of directors, at their annual meeting on December 21,1986, declared the following: "The current year dividends shall be $0.60 per share on the preferred and $0.50 per share on the common; the dividends in arrears shall be paid by issuing one share held as treasury stock for each 10 shares of preferred held."

The preferred is currently selling at $11 per share and the common at $6 per share. Net income for 1986 is estimated at $18,000.

Instructions

(a) Prepare the journal entries required for the dividend declaration and payment, assuming that they occur simultaneously. (Hint: Assume that all preferred dividends are paid before payment is made to holders of common shares.)

(b) Could Becca Corporation give the preferred shareholders two years' dividends and common shareholders a $0.50 per share dividend, all in cash?

P16-5   Kinniry TV, Inc. has outstanding 1,500 preferred shares of no-par, $14 dividend, that were issued for $300,000, and 500 common shares of no-par value for which $90,000 was received. The schedule on page 761 shows the amount of dividends paid out over the past four years.

Instructions

Allocate the dividends to each class of shares under assumptions (a) and (b). Express your answers in per-share amounts using the following format.

		Assumptions			
		(a) Preferred, Noncumulative, and Nonparticipating		(b) Preferred, Cumulative, and Fully Participating	
Year	Paid-out	Preferred	Common	Preferred	Common
1983	$12,000				
1984	$36,000				
1985	$58,500				
1986	$78,000				

P16-6 Peggy Nelson, Inc. began operations in January 1982, and had the following reported net income or loss for each of its five years of operations:

1982	$ 225,000 loss
1983	195,000 loss
1984	180,000 loss
1985	375,000 income
1986	1,500,000 income

At December 31, 1986, the company's share capital accounts were as follows:

Common, no-par value, authorized 100,000 shares, issued and outstanding 50,000 shares	$750,000
$4, nonparticipating noncumulative preferred, no-par value; authorized, issued and outstanding 1,500 shares	150,000
$12, fully participating cumulative preferred, no-par value, authorized, issued and outstanding 10,000 shares	1,500,000

Nelson has never paid a cash or stock dividend. There has been no change in the share capital accounts since Nelson began operations. The incorporation law permits dividends only from retained earnings given that their payment will not result in insolvency.

Instructions

Prepare a work sheet showing the maximum amount of retained earnings available for dividends on December 31, 1986, and how it would be distributable to the holders of the common shares and each of the preferred shares. Show supporting computations in good form.

(AICPA adapted)

P16-7 Some of the account balances of Kristan Corp. at December 31, 1985, are shown below:

$6 Preferred, no-par, 1,000 shares authorized and issued	$ 10,300
Common, no-par, 100,000 shares authorized, 50,000 issued	550,000
Unappropriated Retained Earnings	340,500
Treasury Shares—Preferred (50 shares at cost)	5,600
Treasury Shares—Common (1,000 shares at cost)	15,000
Retained Earnings Appropriated for Contingencies	75,000
Retained Earnings Appropriated for Fire Insurance	80,000

The price of the company's common shares has been increasing steadily on the market; it was $23 on January 1, 1986, advanced to $27 by July 1, and $30 at the end of the year 1986. The preferred shares are not openly traded but were appraised at $105 per share during 1986.

Instructions

Give the proper journal entries for each of the following which took place in 1986:

(a) The company incurred a fire loss of $57,000 to its warehouse.

(b) The company declared a property dividend on April 1. Each common shareholder was to receive one share of Akes & Panes for every 10 shares outstanding. Kristan Corp. owned 8,000 shares of Akes & Panes (2% of total outstanding shares) that were purchased as an investment in 1983 for $68,400. The market value of Akes & Panes shares was $16 each on April 1. Record appreciation only on the shares distributed.

(c) The company resold the 50 preferred shares held in the treasury for $116 per share.

(d) On July 1, the company declared a 4% stock dividend to the common shareholders.

(e) The city of Trenton, in an effort to persuade the company to expand into that city, donated to Kristan Corp. a plot of land with an appraised value of $26,000.

(f) At the annual board of directors' meeting, the board decided to "Set up an appropriation of retained earnings for the future construction of a new plant. Such appropriation to be for $60,000 per year." Also, it was decided to increase the appropriation for possible contingencies by $25,000, to eliminate the appropriation for fire insurance, and to begin purchasing such insurance from Danegeld Insurance Company.

P16-8 The controller of Scott Fraser Paint Company presents the owners' equity section of the company's December 31, 1986 balance sheet in the following form:

Net Worth

Common shares	$104,000
Preferred shares	220,000
Retained earnings	359,100
Appraisal capital	22,000
Total net worth	$705,100

A study of the company records revealed the following facts:

1. The company sold 8,000 common shares of no-par value for $13 per share at the time the firm was organized. The firm was incorporated in 1979.

2. In 1981, the company issued 2,000 no-par value, cumulative and nonparticipating, $6, preferred shares at a price of $110 per share.

3. In 1984, when the market value of the common shares was $21 each, a common stock dividend of 800 shares was issued but not recorded.

4. The company has bought and sold its own common shares on several occasions. It has received $7,000 in excess of cost from the resale of its own common shares, which were purchased in the market.

5. At the end of 1986, the company holds 100 common shares, which were acquired at a cost of $27 per share, in the treasury. The law does not permit stated capital to be impaired as a result of treasury shares purchases. (Treasury shares should be recorded using the single-transaction method.)

6. In 1985, certain shareholders donated 200 common shares to the company. These shares were immediately sold for $24 each.

7. The $22,000 that is shown as appraisal capital, represents the appraised value of land given to the firm by the local government.

8. From 1979 to the end of 1986, the company earned net income of $550,000, and distributed $200,000 of this net income in cash dividends to shareholders.

9. The total amount of the owners' equity was correctly computed by the company's accountants at the end of 1986.

Instructions

Prepare a revised shareholders' equity section of the balance sheet of Scott Fraser Paint Company as of December 31, 1986. (Accompany with a schedule indicating how the retained earnings balance of $359,100 was determined.)

P16-9 The following accounts and balances appear in Spangler Corporation's ledger after closing revenue and expense accounts to the Income Summary but before any entries resulting from the following resolutions:

Land Held for Investment	$ 76,000 dr.
Retained Earnings Appropriated for Possible Decline of Inventory Prices	129,000 cr.
Retained Earnings Appropriated for Contingencies	200,000 cr.
Retained Earnings	540,000 cr.
Income Summary	300,000 cr.

The following resolutions were passed by the board of directors of the Spangler Corporation at their last meeting for the year 1986:

1. A Retained Earnings Appropriated for Possible Additional Income Tax Assessments of Prior Years is to be created in the amount of $35,000.

2. An amount equal to 20% of the net income for the year is to be transferred to the Retained Earnings Appropriated for Contingencies.

3. The present Retained Earnings Appropriated for Possible Decline of Inventory Prices that was set up as a charge against Retained Earnings in 1985 is to be written off as no longer required.

4. A decline in the value of land purchased for investment is to be recorded. As measured by the sales value of other property in the area, the value of the Spangler's land has decreased 30% since date of purchase, and an equivalent write-down is to be made in the carrying value of the property.

5. A Retained Earnings Appropriated for Future Plant Expansion is to be established equal to 50% of the balance of the Retained Earnings account, after all transactions for the year noted above have been recorded and the Income Summary is closed to Retained Earnings.

6. A stock dividend of 8% on the common shares (5,000 no-par shares had been issued and are outstanding) is declared and issued. The market price of the shares on the date of declaration was $120 each.

Instructions

(a) Prepare entries in general journal form to record the board of directors' resolutions.

(b) What is the amount of retained earnings apparently available for dividends?

(c) What is the amount of retained earnings actually (legally) available for dividends?

P16-10 Bedard Company has the following shareholders' equity accounts:

	Issued Shares	Amount
Preferred shares, no-par value	2,400	$240,000
Treasury shares, preferred (at cost)	160	24,000
Common shares without par value (at issue price)	3,600	118,800
Retained earnings		494,640

In view of the large retained earnings, the board of directors resolves: (1) "to pay a 100% stock dividend on all shares outstanding, capitalizing amounts of retained earnings equal to the issue price of the preferred and common shares outstanding," respectively, and thereafter, (2) "to pay a cash dividend of $6 on preferred shares and a cash dividend of $3 a share on common."

Instructions

(a) Prepare entries in journal form to record declaration of these dividends.

(b) Prepare the shareholders' equity section of a balance sheet for Bedard Company after declaration but before distribution of these dividends.

P16-11 The following is a summary of all relevant transactions of Rob Russell Corporation since it was organized in 1984:

In 1984, 15,000 common shares were authorized and 7,500 (no-par value) were issued at a price of $55. In 1985, 1,500 shares were issued as a stock dividend when the shares were selling for $62 each. Three hundred common shares were bought in 1986 at a cost of $66 per share. These 300 shares are still in the company treasury. (Assume that the applicable incorporation law requires an appropriation of retained earnings equal to the cost of treasury shares.)

In 1985, 10,000 preferred shares were authorized and the company issued 3,000 of them (no-par value) at $104. In 1986, preferred shares were donated to the company and immediately resold for $18,900.

The corporation has earned a total of $600,000 in net income after income taxes, and paid out a total of $352,500 in cash dividends since incorporation. An appropriation of retained earnings was made in 1986 by the board of directors in the amount of $75,000 for Fixed Asset Replacements.

Instructions

Prepare the shareholders' equity section of the balance sheet in proper form for Rob Russell Corporation as of December 31, 1986. Account for treasury shares using the single-transaction method.

P16-12 Chewy Gum Corp. has outstanding 2,000,000 common shares of no-par value that were issued at $10 each. The balance in its retained earnings account at January 1, 1986 was $24,000,000. During 1986 the company's net income was $5,400,000. A cash dividend of $0.40 a share was paid June 30, 1986, and a 10% stock dividend was distributed to shareholders of record at the close of business on December 31, 1986 (declaration date was November 30). You have been asked to advise on the proper accounting treatment of the stock dividend.

The existing shares of the company are quoted on a national stock exchange. The market price per share has been as follows:

October 31, 1986	$22
November 30, 1986	24
December 31, 1986	29
Average price over the two-month period	26

Instructions

(a) Prepare a journal entry to record the cash dividend.

(b) Prepare a journal entry to record the stock dividend.

(c) Prepare the shareholders' equity section (including a schedule of retained earnings) of the balance sheet of the Chewy Gum Corp. for December 31, 1986 on the basis of the foregoing information. Draft a note to the financial statements setting forth the basis of the accounting for the stock dividend and add separately appropriate comments or explanations regarding the basis chosen.

P16-13 On December 15, 1985, the directors of Mike McEllen Corporation voted to appropriate $75,000 of retained earnings, and to retain in the business assets equal to the appropriation for use in expanding the corporation's factory building. This was the fourth of such appropriations; after it was recorded, the shareholders' equity section of McEllen's balance sheet appeared as follows:

Shareholders' equity:

Common shares, no-par value, 250,000 shares authorized, 200,000 shares issued and outstanding		$5,400,000
Retained earnings—		
Unappropriated	$1,300,000	
Appropriated for plant expansion	300,000	
Total retained earnings		1,600,000
Total shareholders' equity		$7,000,000

On January 9, 1986, the corporation entered into a contract for the construction of the factory addition for which the retained earnings were appropriated. On November 1, 1986, the addition was completed and the contractor paid the contract price of $287,500.

On December 14, 1986, the board of directors voted to return to the balance of the Retained Earnings Appropriated for Plant Expansion account to Unappropriated Retained Earnings. They also voted a 25,000 share stock dividend distributable on January 23, 1987 to the January 15, 1987 shareholders of record. The corporation's shares were selling at $34 in the market on December 14, 1986. McEllen reported net income for 1985 of $400,000 and for 1986 of $500,000.

Instructions

(a) Prepare the appropriate journal entries for McEllen Corporation for the information above (December 15, 1985 to January 23,1987, inclusive).

(b) Prepare the shareholders' equity section of the balance sheet for McEllen at December 31, 1986.

P16-14 The shareholders' equity section of McCartan Corp. balance sheet on January 1 of the current year is as follows:

Share Capital:		
Common shares, no-par, 20,000 shares authorized, 15,000 shares issued		$975,000
Retained Earnings:		
Unappropriated	$300,000	
Appropriated for plant expansion	150,000	
Appropriated for treasury shares	70,000	
Total retained earnings		520,000
		$1,495,000
Less: Cost of treasury shares (1,000 shares)		70,000
Total shareholders' equity		$1,425,000

The following selected transactions occurred during the year:

1. Paid cash dividends of $1.30 per share on the common shares. The dividend had been properly recorded when declared last year. The incorporation law prohibits cash or stock dividends on treasury shares.

2. Declared a 5% stock dividend on the common shares when the shares were selling at $87 each in the market.

3. Made a prior period adjustment to correct an error of $70,000 (net of tax) that overstated net income in the previous year. The error was the result of an overstatement of ending inventory. The applicable tax rate was 30%.

4. Sold all of the treasury shares for $92,000.

5. Issued the certificates for the stock dividend.

6. The board appropriated $65,000 of retained earnings for plant expansion, eliminated the appropriation for treasury shares, and declared a cash dividend of $1.65 per common share.

7. The company reported net income of $162,500 for the year.

Instructions

(a) Prepare journal entries for the selected transactions above.

(b) Prepare a retained earnings statement for the current year.

P16-15   The Shlee Company was formed on July 1, 1983. It was authorized to issue 200,000 common shares of no-par value and 50,000 preferred shares, $0.60 dividend, no-par value, cumulative and nonparticipating. Shlee Company has a July 1-June 30 fiscal year.

The following information relates to the shareholders' equity accounts of Shlee Company.

Common Shares

Prior to the 1985-86 fiscal year, Shlee Company had 105,000 common shares outstanding, issued as follows:

1. 95,000 shares were issued for cash on July 1, 1983, at $20 per share.

2. On July 24, 1983, 5,000 shares were exchanged for a plot of land that cost the seller $70,000 in 1977, and had an estimated market value of $130,000 on July 24, 1983.

3. 5,000 shares were issued on March 1, 1985; the shares had been subscribed for $32 per share on October 31, 1984.

During the 1985-86 fiscal year, the following transactions regarding common shares took place:

October 1, 1985	Subscriptions were received for 10,000 shares at $40 per share. Cash of $80,000 was received in full payment for 2,000 shares and share certificates were issued. The remaining subscription for 8,000 shares were to be paid in full by September 30, 1986, at which time the certificates were to be issued.
November 30, 1985	Shlee purchased 2,000 of its own shares on the open market at $38 per share. These shares were restored to the status of authorized but unissued shares.
December 15, 1985	Shlee declared a 2% stock dividend for shareholders of record on January 15, 1986, to be issued on January 31, 1986. Shlee was having a liquidity problem and could not afford a cash dividend at the time. Shlee's common shares were selling at $43 per share on December 15, 1985.
June 20, 1986	Shlee sold 500 common shares for $21,000.

Preferred Shares

Schlee issued 30,000 preferred shares for $15 each on July 1, 1985.

Cash Dividends

Shlee has followed a schedule of declaring cash dividends in December and June with payment being made to shareholders of record in the following month. Below are the cash dividends that have been declared since the inception of the company through June 30, 1986:

Declaration Date	Common Shares	Preferred Shares
December 14, 1984	$0.10 per share	$0.30 per share
June 15, 1985	$0.10 per share	$0.30 per share
December 15, 1985	—	$0.30 per share

No cash dividends were declared during June 1986 due to the company's liquidity problems.

Retained Earnings

As of June 30, 1985, Shlee's Retained Earnings account had a balance of $370,000. For the fiscal year ending June 30, 1986, Shlee reported net income of $20,000.

In March of 1985, Shlee received a term loan from the Commerce Bank. The bank requires Shlee to establish a sinking fund and restrict retained earnings for an amount equal to the sinking fund deposit. The annual sinking fund payment of $40,000 is due on April 30 each year; the first payment was made on schedule on April 30, 1986.

Instructions

Prepare the shareholders' equity section of the balance sheet, including appropriate notes, for Shlee Company as of June 30, 1986.

(CMA adapted)

P16-16 On June 30, 1986, the shareholders' equity section of the balance sheet of Carefree Clothes Company, Inc., appears as follows:

Shareholders' equity

$6 cumulative preferred shares			
Authorized and issued,			
2,000 shares, no-par			
value	$200,000		
Common shares			
Authorized 20,000 shares			
of no-par value, issued,			
10,400 shares	520,000	$720,000	
Retained earnings (deficit)		(140,000)	$580,000

A note to the balance sheet points out that preferred share dividends are in arrears in the amount of $48,000.

At a shareholders' meeting, a new group of officers was voted into power, and a quasi-reorganization plan proposed by the new officers was accepted by the shareholders. The terms of this plan are as follows:

1. Preferred shareholders are to cancel their claim against the corporation for dividends in arrears.
2. The assigned (average) value of the common shares is to be reduced from $50 a share to $20 in order to create contributed surplus.
3. Certain depreciable properties and inventories owned by the company are to be revalued downward $100,000 and $30,000, respectively.
4. The deficit is to be written off against the contributed surplus created by a reduction of the assigned value of the common shares.

Instructions

(a) Assuming that the various steps in the reorganization plan are carried out as of June 30, prepare journal entries to record the effect of the reorganization.
(b) Assuming that the company earns a net income of $50,000 for the year ended June 30, 1987, prepare the shareholders' equity section of the balance sheet as of that date.

17

DILUTIVE SECURITIES AND EARNINGS PER SHARE CALCULATIONS

The urge to merge that predominated the business scene in the 1960s has developed into merger mania in the 1980s. One consequence of heavy merger activity is an increase in the use of such dilutive securities as convertible bonds, convertible preferred shares, and share purchase warrants.

Dilutive securities are defined as securities that, although they are not common shares in form, enable their holders to obtain common shares upon exercise or conversion. A reduction in earnings per share often results when these securities become common shares. For example, during the sixties, corporate officers recognized that the issuance of these types of securities in a merger did not have the same immediate adverse effect on earnings per share as the issuance of common shares. In addition, many companies found that issuance of convertible securities did not seem to upset common shareholders, even though when these securities were later converted or exercised the common shareholders' interests were substantially diluted. For these reasons, such different terms as ''funny money'' were coined to indicate the peculiar nature of these types of securities and the unusual tricks that could be played on the uninformed investor.

The merger movement of the 1980s is somewhat different. Unlike the ''go-go'' years of the late 1960s, when mergers were often consummated as a means to increase earnings per share, the 1980 mergers appear to be based on a more substantive rationale. There are many reasons for merger mania in the 1980s. Among them the following are significant: (1) the federal government's attitude is not hostile to mergers, (2) financial institutions have developed sophisticated means of providing credit for acquisitions, (3) many owners of privately held companies wish to sell to acquire personal liquidity, and (4) it is believed that it is cheaper to buy rather than build, particularly when corporate equity securities are considered undervalued.

As a consequence of this step-up in merger activity, the use of dilutive securities is again increasing. Also on the rise is the use of such forms of compensation packages as stock option plans, which are dilutive in nature. These plans are used mainly to attract and retain executive talent and to provide tax relief for executives in high tax brackets.

The widespread use of different types of dilutive securities has led the accounting profession to examine the accounting in this area closely. Specifically, the profession has directed its attention to accounting for these securities at date of issuance and to the presentation of earnings per share figures that recognize the effect of these dilutive securities. The following discussion includes consideration of convertible securities, warrants, and stock options.

DILUTIVE SECURITIES AND COMPENSATION PLANS

Accounting for Convertible Debt

If bonds can be converted into other securities of the corporation during some specified period of time after issuance, they are called convertible bonds. A **convertible bond combines the benefits of a bond with the privilege of exchanging it for shares at the holder's option**. This security is purchased by investors who desire the security of a bond holding, but want the added option of conversion should the value of the shares appreciate significantly.

Corporations issue convertibles for two main reasons. One is the desire to raise equity capital that, assuming conversion, will arise when the original debt is converted. To illustrate, assume that a company wants to raise $1,000,000 at a time when its common shares are selling at $45 per share. Such an issue would require sale of approximately 22,222 shares (ignoring issue costs). By selling 1,000 bonds at $1,000 par, each convertible into 20 common shares, the enterprise may raise $1,000,000 by committing only 20,000 common shares. Most studies of convertible bonds indicate that the main purpose of issuing these securities has been to obtain common share financing at cheaper rates.

A second reason why companies issue convertible securities is that many enterprises could issue debt only at high interest rates unless a convertible covenant were attached. The conversion privilege entices the investors to accept a lower interest rate than would normally be the case on a straight debt issue. To illustrate, a company might have to pay 15% for a straight debt obligation, but it can issue a convertible at 9%. For this lower interest rate, the investor receives the right to buy the company's common shares at a fixed price until maturity, which is often 10 to 20 years.

Accounting for convertible debt involves reporting issues at the time of (1) issuance, (2) conversion, and (3) retirement.

At Time of Issuance   The method of recording convertible bonds at the date of issue follows that used in recording straight debt issues. Any discount or premium resulting from the issuance of convertible bonds is amortized on the basis of the maturity date, because it is difficult to predict when, if at all, conversion will occur. The accounting for convertible debt as a straight debt issue is controversial and is discussed more fully later in this chapter.

At Time of Conversion   If bonds are converted into other securities, the principal accounting problem is the determination of the amount at which to record the securities exchanged for the bond. For example, Hilton, Inc., issued at a premium of $60 a $1,000 bond convertible into 10 no-par common shares. At the time of conversion the unamortized premium is $50, the market value of the bond is $1,200, and the shares are quoted on the market at $120. Two possible methods of determining the issue price of the shares could be used.

1. The **market price** of the shares or bonds, $1,200.
2. The **book value** of the bonds, $1,050.

Market Value Approach

Recording the shares issued at the **market price** of the shares or bond offers a theoretically sound way to measure the price at which to record the transaction. If 10 common shares could be sold for $1,200, share capital of $1,200 should be recorded. Since at the time of sale bonds having a book value of $1,050 are converted, a loss on the conversion of the bonds of $150 occurs. The entry would be:

Bonds Payable	1,000	
Premium on Bonds Payable	50	
Loss on Redemption of Bonds Payable	150	
Common Shares		1,200

The use of the market price of the bonds can be supported on similar grounds. If the market price of the shares is not determinable, but the bonds can be purchased at $1,200, a good argument can be made that the shares have an issue price of $1,200.

The weakness in using the fair market value of the shares or bonds is the assumption that a gain or loss can be incurred by the corporation as a result of an equity transaction. Whereas the conversion may be favourable or unfavourable to the existing shareholder group because an increase or decrease in their equity occurs, the corporate entity, as a whole, is unaffected. Because the conversion described above is initiated by the holder of the debt instrument (rather than the issuer), it is not an "early extinguishment of debt." As a result, the gain or loss would not be classified as an extraordinary item.

Book Value Approach

From a practical point of view, if the market price of the shares or the market price of the bonds is not determinable, the **book value** of the bonds offers the best available measurement of the issue price. Furthermore, many accountants contend that even if market quotations are available, they should not be used, inasmuch as the common shares are merely substituted for the bonds and should be recorded at the carrying amount of the bonds that were converted.

In other words, supporters of this view argue that an agreement was established at the date of issuance to pay either a stated amount of cash at maturity or to issue a stated number of shares of equity securities. Therefore, when the debt is converted to equity in relation to preexisting contract terms, no gain or loss is recognized upon conversion. To illustrate the specifics of this approach, the entry for the foregoing transaction of Hilton, Inc. would be:

Bonds Payable	1,000	
Premium on Bonds Payable	50	
Common Shares		1,050

The book value method of recording convertible bonds is the method used in practice. As a result, for homework problems use the book value method unless the problem specifies otherwise.

Induced Conversions   Sometimes the issuer of a convertible security wishes to induce prompt conversion of its convertible debt to equity securities to reduce interest cost or improve its debt-to-equity ratio. As a result, the issuer may offer some form of additional consideration (cash, common shares) to the holder of the convertible securities to induce conversion. The additional consideration used to induce conversion should be reported as an expense of the current period. To illustrate, assume that Helloid, Inc. has outstanding $1,000,000 par value convertible debentures convertible into 100,000 shares of no-par value common stock. Helloid has decided it wishes to reduce its interest cost, and therefore agrees to pay the holders of the convertible debentures an additional $80,000 if they will convert. Assuming conversion occurs, the following entry is made:

Debt Conversion Expense	80,000	
Bonds Payable	1,000,000	
Common Shares		1,000,000
Cash		80,000

Note that the additional $80,000 is recorded as an expense of the current period and not as a reduction of equity. Some argue that an induced conversion is a capital-raising transaction and, similar to share issue costs, should be reported as a reduction of paid-in capital. However, some accounting authorities believe that, since the transaction involves both the issuance of equity and also the retirement of debt, it should be reported as an expense. Similarly, it should not be reported as an extraordinary loss because it is simply a payment to induce conversion and therefore is more in the nature of expense.[1]

Retirement of Convertible Debt

A special problem relates to the retirement of convertible debt for cash. The question is whether the retirement of convertible debt is a debt transaction or an equity transaction. If it is a debt transaction, the difference between the carrying amount of the retired convertible debt and the cash paid should result in a charge or credit to income; if it is an equity transaction, the difference should presumably go to contributed surplus.

The method for recording the **issuance** of convertible bonds follows that used in

---

[1] "Induced Conversions of Convertible Debt," *Statement of Financial Accounting Standards No. 84* (Stamford, Conn: FASB, 1985).

recording straight debt issues. Specifically this means that no portion of the proceeds should be attributable to the conversion feature and credited to Contributed Surplus. Although theoretical objections to this approach can be raised, to be consistent, a gain or loss on **retiring** convertible debt needs to be recognized in the same way as a gain or loss on **retiring** debt that is not convertible. For this reason, the differences between the cash acquisition price of debt and its carrying amount should be reported **currently in income as a gain or loss.**[2] As indicated in Chapter 14, material gains or losses on extinguishment of debt are considered extraordinary items.

Failure to recognize the equity feature of convertible debt when issued creates problems upon early extinguishment. To illustrate, assume that URL issues convertible debt at a time when the investment community attaches value to the conversion feature. Subsequently the price of URL shares decreases so sharply that the conversion feature has little or no value. If URL extinguishes their convertible debt early, a large gain develops because the book value of the debt will exceed the retirement price. Many accountants consider this treatment incorrect, because the reduction in value of the convertible debt relates to its equity features, not its debt features, and therefore an adjustment to Contributed Surplus should be made. As indicated earlier, however, present practice requires that an extraordinary gain or loss be recognized at the time of early extinguishment.

Convertible Preferred Shares

Convertible preferred shares are handled at the date of issue and at conversion in the same manner as convertible debt. The major difference in accounting for a convertible bond and a convertible preferred share is in the initial recording of the security investment. Convertible bonds are considered liabilities; convertible preferreds are considered a part of shareholders' equity.

In addition, when preferred share conversion privileges are exercised, there is no theoretical justification for recognition of a gain or loss. **The book value method is employed:** Preferred Share Capital is debited and Common Share Capital is credited.

To illustrate, Host Enterprises issued 1,000 no-par common shares upon conversion of 1,000 no-par preferred shares that were originally issued for $1,200. The entry would be:

Convertible Preferred Shares	1,200	
Common Shares		1,200

Stock Warrants

Warrants are certificates entitling the holder to acquire shares at a certain price within a stated period. This option is similar to the conversion privilege because warrants, if exercised, become common shares and have usually a dilutive effect (reduce earnings per share) similar to that of the conversion of convertible securities. A substantial difference between convertible securities and stock warrants is that upon exercise of the warrants, the holder has to pay a certain amount of money to obtain the shares.

---

[2]This method has been adopted as a standard in the U.S. by "Early Extinguishment of Debt," *Opinions of the Accounting Principles Board No. 26* (New York: AICPA, 1972).

The issuance of warrants or options to buy additional shares normally arises under three situations.

1. When issuing different types of securities, such as bonds or preferred shares, warrants are often included to make the **security more attractive,** to provide an "equity kicker."
2. Upon the issuance of additional common shares, existing shareholders may have a **preemptive right to purchase common shares** first. Warrants may be issued to evidence that right.
3. Warrants, often referred to as stock options, are given as **compensation to executives and employees.**

The problems in accounting for stock warrants are complex and present many difficulties. Many of the problems remain unresolved.

Stock Warrants Issued with Other Securities   Warrants issued with other securities are basically long-term options to buy common shares at a fixed price. Although some perpetual warrants are traded, generally their life is five years, with a few up to ten years.

Here is an illustration of the way a warrant works: Tenneco offered a unit composed of one share and one detachable warrant exercisable at $24.25 per share and good for five years. The unit sold for 22 3/4 ($22.75) and, since the price of the common the day before the sale was 19 7/8 ($19.87), it suggests a price of 2 7/8 ($2.87) for the warrants.

In this situation, the warrants had an apparent value of 2 7/8 ($2.87), even though it would not be profitable at present for the purchaser to exercise the warrant and buy the shares, because the price of the shares is much below the exercise price of $24.25.[3] The investor pays for the warrant to receive a possible future call on the shares at a fixed price when the price has risen significantly. For example, if the price of the shares rises to $30, the investor has gained $2.88 ($30 minus $24.25 minus $2.87) on an investment of $2.87—a 100% increase! Obviously, if the price does not rise, the investor loses the full $2.87.

The proceeds from the sale of debt with **detachable stock warrants** should be allocated between the two securities.[4] Two separable instruments are involved: that is, (1) a bond and (2) a warrant giving the holder the right to purchase common shares at a certain price. Warrants that are detachable can be traded separately from the debt and, therefore, a market value can be determined. The allocation of the sale's proceeds between the two securities would be made on the basis of their relative fair market values soon after the date of issuance.

To illustrate, AT & T's offering of detachable five-year warrants to buy one common share (no par value $5) at $25 (at a time when a share was selling for approximately $50) enabled it to price its offering of bonds at par with a competitive 8 3/4% yield. In this situation, to place a value on the two securities one would determine (1) the value of the bonds without the warrants and (2) the value of the warrants. For example, assume that AT & T's bonds (par $1,000) sold for 99 without the warrants soon after they were issued. The market value of the warrants at that time was $30. Prior to sale the warrants will not have a market value. The

---

[3]Later in this discussion it will be shown that the value of the warrant is normally determined on the basis of a relative market value approach because of the difficulty of imputing a warrant value in any other manner.

[4]A detachable warrant means that the warrant can sell separately from the bond. *APB Opinion No. 14* makes a distinction between detachable and nondetachable warrants because nondetachable warrants must be sold with the security as a complete package; thus, no allocation is permitted.

allocation is based on an estimate of market value, generally as established by an investment dealer or on the relative market value of the bonds and the warrants soon after they are issued and traded. The price paid for 10,000 $1,000 bonds with the warrants attached was par or $10,000,000. The allocation between the bonds and warrants would be made in this manner:

$$\frac{\text{Value of bonds without warrants}}{\text{Value of bonds without warrants} + \text{Value of warrants}} \times \text{Purchase price} = \text{Value assigned to bonds}$$

$$\frac{\$9,900,000}{\$9,900,000 + \$300,000} \times \$10,000,000 = \$9,705,883$$

$$\frac{\text{Value of warrants}}{\text{Value of bonds without warrants} + \text{Value of warrants}} \times \text{Purchase price} = \text{Value assigned to warrants}$$

$$\frac{\$300,000}{\$9,900,000 + \$300,000} \times \$10,000,000 = \$294,117$$

In this situation the entries are:

Cash	9,705,883	
Discount on Bonds Payable	294,117	
Bonds Payable		10,000,000
Cash	294,117	
Contributed Surplus—Stock Warrants		294,117

(The entries may be combined if desired; they are shown separately here to indicate that the purchaser of the bond is buying not only a bond, but also a possible claim on common shares in the future.)

Assuming that the warrants are exercised one warrant per one share of stock, the following entry would be made:

Cash	250,000	
Contributed Surplus—Stock Warrants	294,117	
Common Shares		544,117

If we assume, however, that the warrants are not exercised, Contributed Surplus—Stock Warrants is debited for $294,117 and Contributed Surplus from Expired Warrants is credited for a like amount. The contributed surplus reverts to the old shareholders.

The question arises whether the allocation of value to the warrants is consistent with the handling accorded convertible debt, in which case no value is allocated to the conversion privilege. The features of a convertible security are **inseparable** in the sense that choices are mutually exclusive; the holder either converts or redeems the bonds for cash, but cannot do both. No basis, therefore, exists for recognizing the conversion value in the accounts. However, the issuance of bonds with **detachable warrants** involves two securities, one a debt security, which will remain outstanding until maturity, and the other a warrant to purchase common shares. At the time of issuance, separable instruments exist, and therefore separate treatment is justified. **Nondetachable warrants**, however, do not require an allocation of the proceeds between the bonds and the warrants; that is, the entire proceeds are recorded as debt.

Many argue that the conversion feature is not significantly different in nature from the call represented by a warrant. The question is whether, although the legal forms are different, sufficient similarities of substance exist to support the same accounting treatment. Some contend that inseparability *per se* is not a valid basis for restricting allocation between identifiable components of a transaction. Examples of allocation between assets of value in a single transaction are not uncommon to the accountant's experience. To illustrate, such transactions as allocation of values in basket purchases, and separation of principal and interest in capitalizing long-term leases, indicate that the accountant has attempted to allocate values in a single transaction. To deny recognition of value to the conversion feature appears to be a recourse only to the form of the instrument and does not deal with the substance of the transaction. For example, debt with stock purchase warrants can have the essential attributes of a convertible bond—the warrants can be exercised and the debentures can be used as consideration for the exercise price.

In both situations (convertible debt and debt issued with warrants), the investor has made a payment to the firm for an equity feature; that is, the right to acquire an equity instrument in the future. The only real distinction between them is that the additional payment made when the equity instrument is formally acquired takes different forms. The warrant holder pays additional cash to the issuing firm; the convertible debt holder pays for shares by forgoing the receipt of interest from conversion date until maturity date and by forgoing the receipt of the maturity value itself. Thus, it is argued that the difference is one of method or form of payment only, rather than one of substance.

Rights to Subscribe to Additional Shares

If the directors of a corporation decide to issue new shares, the old shareholders generally have the right (preemptive privilege) to purchase newly issued shares in proportion to their holdings. The privilege, referred to as a **stock right,** saves existing shareholders from suffering a dilution of voting rights without their consent, and it may allow them to purchase shares somewhat below their market value. The warrants issued in these situations are of short duration, unlike the warrants issued with other securities.

The certificate representing the stock right states the number of shares that the holder of the right may purchase, as well as the price at which the new shares may be purchased. Each share owned ordinarily gives the owner one stock right. The price is normally less than the current market value of such shares, thereby giving the rights a value in themselves. From the time they are issued until they expire, they may be purchased and sold as any other security.

No entry is required when rights are issued to existing shareholders. Only a memorandum entry is needed to indicate the number of rights issued to existing shareholders and to insure that the company has additional unissued shares registered for issuance in case exercise of the rights occurs.

If the rights are exercised, usually a cash payment of some type is involved. Common Share Capital (no-par value) is credited with the amount of cash received.

Stock Compensations Plans

Another form of the warrant arises in stock compensation plans used to compensate employees. Stock compensation plans are usually defined as arrangements to

OMIT FROM HERE

issue shares to officers and employees as a group or individually. A common type of warrant is a **stock option plan** where **selected** employees are given the option to purchase common shares at a given price over an **extended period of time.** Other types of options exist also, such as the right to receive cash or shares if certain performance criteria are met in the future. In addition, a common type of warrant develops in a stock purchase plan, where **all** employees are given the option to purchase shares at a given price over a **short period of time.**

The *CICA Handbook* does not prescribe accounting procedures for stock option plans. Consequently, the following discussion refers to U.S. accounting standards which could be used in Canadian practice until the CICA issues a relevant addition to the *Handbook.*

For accounting purposes, stock option plans are usually considered compensatory —stock purchase plans are usually classified as noncompensatory.[5] **Compensatory** means that the plan was intended to compensate the employees; **noncompensatory** means that the primary purpose was not intended to compensate the employees, but rather to allow the employer to secure equity capital or to induce widespread ownership of an enterprise's common shares among employees. Specifically, the U.S. profession has concluded that noncompensatory plans have the following characteristics:

1. Participation by all employees who meet limited employment qualifications.
2. Equal offers of shares to all eligible employees.
3. Limitation of time permitted for exercise of an option or purchase right to a reasonable period.
4. Discount from the market price of the shares no greater than would be reasonable in an offer of shares to shareholders or others.[6]

For example, IBM has a stock purchase plan under which employees who meet minimal employment qualifications are entitled to purchase IBM shares at a 15% reduction from market price for a short period of time. Such a reduction from market price is not considered compensatory because the employer's objectives appear to be either to raise additional equity capital or to expand ownership of the enterprise's shares among the employees as a means of enhancing loyalty to the enterprise. This position is debatable because the employee is receiving a valuable fringe benefit. However, because it is difficult to determine the company's objectives, in practice, if the discount is in the amount of 10–15% of the market price, the foregoing type of stock purchase plan is considered noncompensatory. **Plans that do not possess all of the above mentioned four characteristics are classified as compensatory.**

Accounting for Stock Compensation Plans

Accounting for noncompensatory plans poses no practical difficulties for accoun-

---

[5]Plans in which employees pay cash, either directly or through payroll withholding, as all or a significant part of the consideration for stock they receive, are commonly referred to as stock option, stock purchase, or stock thrift or savings plans. Plans in which employees receive shares for current or future services without paying cash (or with a nominal payment) are commonly referred to as a stock bonus or stock award plans. Stock bonus and award plans are invariably compensatory. Stock thrift and savings plans are compensatory to the extent of contributions of an employer corporation. Stock option and purchase plans may be either compensatory or noncompensatory.

[6]"Accounting for Stock Issued to Employees," *Opinions of the Accounting Principles Board No. 25* (New York: AICPA, 1972), par. 7.

tants because compensation expense is not recorded by the employer corporations. The exercise of the option to purchase shares is simply accounted for as the normal share issue with shareholders' equity increased by the amount of the option price. Compensatory plans, however, present more difficulties. The following three questions must be resolved:

1. How should compensation expense be determined?
2. Over what periods should compensation expense be allocated?
3. What types of plans are used to compensate officers and key executives?

Determination of Compensation Expense   Total compensation expense is computed as the difference between the market price of the shares and the option price on the **measurement date.** The measurement date is the first date on which are known both (1) the number of shares that an individual employee is entitled to receive and (2) the option or purchase price, if any. The measurement date for many plans is the date an **option is granted** to an employee. The measurement date may be later than the date of grant in plans with variable terms (either number of shares or option price or both not known) that depend on events after date of grant. Usually the measurement date for plans with variable terms is the date of exercise.

If the number of shares or the option price or both are not known, compensation expense may have to be estimated on the basis of assumptions as to what will be the final number of shares and the option price.

Allocation of Compensation Expense   Compensation expense is recognized in the period(s) in which the **employee performs the services.** The total compensation expense is determined at the measurement date and allocated to the appropriate periods benefited by the employee's services. In practice, it is often difficult to specify the period of service, and considerable judgement is exercised in this determination. The general rule followed is that any method that is systematic and rational is appropriate, if the periods of service cannot be clearly defined. Assuming the measurement date is the date of grant, many enterprises recognize the compensation expense over an arbitrary period; others amortize it from the grant date to the date the option may be first exercised; and others record it as a current expense.

If the measurement date is later than the date of grant, the employer corporation should record the compensation expense each period from date of grant to the measurement date based on the market price of the shares at the end of each period.

Types of Plans   Many different types of plans are used to compensate key executives. Common to all these plans is that the amount of the reward depends upon future events. Consequently, continued employment is a necessary element in almost all types of plans. The popularity of a given plan usually depends on prospects in the stock market and tax considerations. For example, if it appears that appreciation will occur in a company's shares, a plan that offers the option to purchase shares is attractive to an executive. Conversely, if it appears that price appreciation is unlikely, then compensation might be tied to some performance measure such as an increase in book value or earnings per share. Three plans that illustrate different accounting issues are:

1. Stock option plans.
2. Stock appreciation rights plans.
3. Performance-type plans.

Accounting for Stock Option Plans

To illustrate the accounting for a stock option plan, assume that on November 1, 1985, the shareholders of Scott Company approve a plan that grants each of the company's five executives options to purchase 2,000 of the company's no-par value common shares. The options are granted on January 1, 1986, and may be exercised at any time within the next ten years. The option price per share is $60, and the market price of the shares at the date of grant is $70 per share. The total compensation expense is computed as follows. (Note that January 1, 1986, is the measurement date because the number of shares each executive can purchase and the option price are known on this date.)

Market value of 10,000 shares at date of grant ($70 per share)	$700,000
Option price of 10,000 shares at date of grant ($60 per share)	600,000
Total compensation expense	$100,000

To match revenue and expenses properly, the value of the options should be recognized as an expense in the period(s) in which the employee performs services. In the case of Scott Company, assume that documents associated with issuance of the options indicate that the expected period of benefit is two years, starting with the grant date. The entry to record the total compensation expense at the date of grant is as follows:

Deferred Compensation Expense	100,000	
Contributed Surplus—Stock Options		100,000

The deferred compensation expense (a contra shareholders' equity account) then is amortized to expense over the period of service involved (two years).[7] The credit balance in the Contributed Surplus—Stock Options account is treated as an element of shareholders' equity. An alternative to the entry above would be to record no formal entry at the date of grant, but accrue compensation expense at the end of each period as incurred. We will use the former approach for problem material because this method formalizes in the records the compensation element of these plans. On December 31, 1986, and on December 31, 1987, the following journal entry is recorded to recognize the compensation cost for the year attributable to the stock option plan.

Compensation Expense	50,000	
Deferred Compensation Expense		50,000

At December 31, 1986, the shareholders' equity section would be presented as follows, assuming that 1,000,000 no-par value shares were issued.

Shareholders' equity		
Common shares, no-par value, 1,000,000 shares issued and outstanding		$1,000,000
Contributed surplus—stock options	$100,000	
Less: Deferred compensation expense	50,000	50,000
Total shareholders' equity		$1,050,000

[7]The rationale for using a contra equity account is that deferred compensation expense represents an unearned compensation amount and is better reported as contra equity than as an asset.

If 20% or 2,000 of the 10,000 options were exercised on June 1, 1989 (three years and five months after date of grant), the following journal entry would be recorded:

Cash (2,000 × $60)	120,000	
Contributed Surplus—Stock Options (20% of $100,000)	20,000	
Common Shares		140,000

If the remaining stock options are not exercised before their expiry date, the balance in Contributed Surplus—Stock Options account should be transferred to a more properly titled contributed surplus account, such as Contributed Surplus from Expired Stock Options. The entry to record this transaction at the date of expiration would be as follows:

Contributed Surplus—Stock Options (80% of $100,000)	80,000	
Contributed Surplus from Expired Stock Options		80,000

The fact that a stock option is not exercised does not nullify the propriety of recording the costs of services received from the executives and attributable to the stock option plan. Compensation expense is, therefore, not adjusted upon expiry of the options. However, if a stock option is forfeited because **an employee fails to fulfill an obligation** (e.g., leaves employment) the estimate of compensation expense recorded in current period should be adjusted (as a change in estimate). This change in estimate would be recorded by debiting Contributed Surplus—Stock Options and crediting Compensation Expense, thereby decreasing compensation expense in the period of forfeiture.

Stock Appreciation Rights

In a stock appreciation rights (SAR) plan, the executive is given the right to receive **share appreciation,** which is defined as the excess of the market price of the stock at the date of exercise over a preestablished price. This share appreciation may be paid in cash, shares, or a combination of both. The major advantage of SARs is that the executive often does not have to make a cash outlay at the date of exercise, but receives a payment for the share appreciation which may be used to pay related income taxes. Unlike a stock option plan, the shares that constitute the basis for computing the appreciation in a SAR plan are not issued; only cash or shares having a market value equivalent to the appreciation is awarded the executive.

As indicated earlier, the usual date for measuring compensation related to stock compensation plans is the date of grant. However, with SARs, the final amount of cash or shares (or a combination of the two) to be distributed is not known until the date of exercise, and therefore total compensation cannot be measured until this date. Thus, the measurement date is the **date of exercise.**

How then should compensation expense be recorded during the interim periods from the date of grant to the date of exercise? Such a determination is not easy, because it is impossible to know what total compensation cost will be until the date of exercise, and the service period will probably not coincide with the exercise date. In order to allocate the compensation expense to interim periods, it is necessary to assume that the best estimate of total compensation cost for the plan at any interim period is the difference between the current market price of the shares and option price multiplied by the number of share appreciation rights outstanding. This total estimated compensation cost is then allocated over the service period to record an expense (or a decrease in expense if market price falls) in each period.[8] At the end of each interim period, total compensation expense reported to date should equal the percentage of the total service period that has elapsed multiplied by the estimated compensation cost. For example, if at an interim period the service period is 40% complete and total estimated compensation is $100,000, then total compensation expense reported to date should equal $40,000 ($100,000 times 40%).

When the exercise date is later than the service period, compensation expense should be adjusted each period in an amount sufficient to adjust total reported compensation expense to the estimated total compensation cost. In other words, after the service period elapses, compensation expense is adjusted whenever a change in the market price of the shares occurs in subsequent reporting periods until the rights expire or are exercised, whichever comes first.

Changes, either up or down, in the market value of these shares between the date of grant and the exercise date therefore result in a change in the measure of compensation. Some periods will have credits to compensation expense if the quoted market price of the shares falls from one period to the next; the credit to compensation expense, however, cannot exceed previously recognized compensation expense. In other words, total compensation expense cannot be negative.

To illustrate, assume that Bigger Hotels, Inc. establishes a SAR program on January 1, 1986, which entitles executives to receive cash at the date of exercise (anytime in the next five years) for the difference between the market price of the shares and the preestablished price of $10 on 10,000 SARs; the current market price of the shares is $13, and the service period runs for two years (1986-1987). The following schedule indicates the amount of compensation expense to be recorded each period, assuming that the executives hold the SARs for three years, at which time the rights are exercised.

STOCK APPRECIATION RIGHTS
Schedule of Compensation Expense

(1) Date	(2) Market Price	(3) Preestablished Price (10,000 SARs)	(4) Cumulative Compensation Recognizable[a]	(5) Percentage Accrued[b]	(6) Compensation Accrued to Date	Expense 1986	Expense 1987	Expense 1988
Dec. 31/86	$13	$10	$30,000	50%	$ 15,000	$15,000		
					55,000		$55,000	
Dec. 31/87	17	10	70,000	100%	70,000			
					(20,000)			$(20,000)
Dec. 31/88	15	10	50,000	100%	$ 50,000			

[a]Cumulative compensation for unexercised SARs to be allocated to periods of service.
[b]The percentage accrued is based upon a two-year service period (1986–1987).

In 1986, Bigger Hotels would record compensation expense of $15,000 because 50% of the $30,000 total compensation cost estimated at December 31, 1986, is allocable to 1986. In 1987, the market price increased to $17 per share; therefore, the additional compensation expense of $55,000 ($70,000 minus $15,000) was

---

[8]"Accounting for Stock Appreciation Rights and Other Variable Stock Option or Award Plans," *FASB Interpretation No. 28* (Stamford, Conn.: FASB, 1978), par. 2.

recorded. The SARs were held through 1988, during which time the share price decreased to $15. The decrease is recognized by recording a $20,000 credit to compensation expense and a debit to Liability Under Stock Appreciation Plan. Note that after the service period ends, since the rights are still outstanding, the rights are adjusted to market at December 31, 1988. Any such credit to compensation expense cannot exceed previous charges to expense attributable to that plan.

As the compensation expense is recorded each period, the corresponding credit should be to a liability account if the share appreciation is to be paid in cash. If shares are to be issued, then a more appropriate credit would be to Contributed Surplus. The entry to record compensation expense in the first year, assuming that the SAR ultimately will be paid in cash, is as follows:

Compensation Expense	15,000	
Liability Under Stock Appreciation Plan		15,000

The liability account would be credited again in 1987 for $55,000 and debited for $20,000 in 1988 when the negative compensation expense is recorded. The entry to record the negative compensation expense is as follows:

Liability Under Stock Appreciation Plan	20,000	
Compensation Expense		20,000

At December 31, 1988, executives receive $50,000; the entry removing the liability is as follows:

Liability Under Stock Appreciation Plan	50,000	
Cash		50,000

Because compensation expense is measured by the difference between market price of the shares from period to period, multiplied by the number of SARs, compensation expense can increase or decrease substantially from one period to the next.

Many accountants are disturbed about the accounting for SARs because the amount of compensation expense to be reported each period is subject to fluctuations in the stock market. As some accountants have questioned, "Shouldn't earnings determine share prices, rather than share prices determine earnings?" Even with this drawback, this type of plan is gaining in popularity because executives are required to make little, if any, cash outlay under these programs.

SARs are often issued in combination with compensatory stock options (referred to as **tandem** or **combination plans**) and the executives must then select which of the two sets of terms to exercise, thereby cancelling the other. The existence of alternative plans running concurrently poses additional problems from an accounting standpoint because the accountant must determine, on the basis of the facts available each period, which of the two plans has the higher probability of exercise and then account for this plan, and ignore the other.

Performance-Type Plans

Many executives have become disenchanted with stock compensation plans whose ultimate payment is a function of an increase in the market price of the common shares. This disenchantment arises because of the erratic behaviour of the stock market, coupled with the belief by some executives that their level of work and the market price of the shares are not well correlated. As a result, there has been a substantial increase in the use of plans where executives receive common shares (or cash) if specified performance criteria are attained during the performance period (generally three to five years).

The **performance criteria** employed usually are increases in return on assets or equity, growth in sales, growth in earnings per share (EPS), or a combination of these factors. A performance-type plan's **measurement date** is the date of exercise because the number of shares that will be issued or cash that will be paid out when performance is achieved is not known at the date of grant. The compensation cost is allocated to the periods involved in much the same manner as with stock apprecia-tion rights. Tandem or combination awards are popular with these plans; that is, the executive has the choice of selecting between a performance or stock option award. In these cases the executive has the best of both worlds because if either the share price increases, or the performance goal is achieved, the executive gains. In fact, in some plans the executive receives both types of plans, so that the monies received from the performance plan can finance the exercise price on the stock option plan.

Conceptual Issues Involving Stock Compensation Plans

Much debate surrounds the proper accounting and reporting for stock compensa-tion plans. Two primary conceptual questions that must be resolved before accept-able accounting standards may be adopted are discussed below.

Alternate Dates   What date should be used to measure total compensation cost? Many accountants favour the **date of grant** because the company forgoes an alterna-tive use of shares on that date. Others believe that some other date such as the date on which the **option becomes exercisable**, or on which the **option is exercised** is more appropriate. For example, the date the option becomes exercisable is favoured by some because at that date the employee has performed the option contract, and the company is obliged to issue shares at the option price.

Others state that the excess of the market price over the option price at the date the option becomes exercisable is still an incomplete valuation that understates the value of the option, particularly when this option may be held for several years before expiring. They believe that only at the date that the option is exercised is the final value of the employee's services recognizable. In short, the commitment to transfer cash or shares to employees under a plan is only a contingency until the date of exercise, when the amount of the transfer will be known.

Valuation   A second issue relates to how the option should be valued, assuming the measurement date is the date of grant.

One group believes that an attempt should be made to value the **option** itself.[9] They note that an option to buy shares at a price equal to or below the market price has value and cannot be considered worthless. In addition, because there is no risk of loss to the executive and a possibility, if not a probability, of great gain, the option may possess value that is greater than the spread between the option price

---

[9]For an interesting discussion of an attempt to value options, see Clifford W. Smith, Jr. and Jerold L. Zimmerman, "Valuing Employee Stock Option Plans Using Option Pricing Models," *Journal of Account-ing Research* (Autumn, 1976), pp. 357–364.

and the market price at the date of the grant. Similarly, others argue that although services are normally valued at the cost of the assets given in exchange for them, the **fair value of the services received** is also a proper and acceptable basis of valuation. Using this approach, an attempt is made to determine what type of cash trade-off the executives make in receiving an option for shares in lieu of a straight cash distribution. By imputing this cash trade-off, the total amount of compensation may be determined.

Others stress that the approaches described above are too subjective and argue for the approach adopted by the profession in the United States; namely, that compensation expense be measured by the difference between the market price and the option price at the **date of grant.** This argument is based on the premise that the only objective and verifiable amount that can be determined at the date of grant is the spread between the market and option price. Many are unhappy with this latter approach because little or no compensation is recorded for many stock option plans (for example, incentive stock option plans report zero compensation expense).

Finally, it is sometimes argued that **no compensation expense should be reported** at all because no cost to the entity results from the issuance of additional shares of stock; the cost to the shareholders is the possible dilution of their interest in the entity, and accountants should ignore this factor in their accounting. This does not appear to be a reasonable approach, because a cost to the existing shareholders is involved that should be considered a cost of operating the enterprise.

Disclosure of Compensation Plans   Disclosure of type and amount of compensation received by Canadian executives is not specifically required by the *CICA Handbook.* In a few provinces such information is required under securities legislation. Consequently, details about executive compensation are more difficult to obtain in Canada than in the United States. Users of financial statements could benefit from increased disclosure that would help them find answers to such questions as: Is the salary reasonable? Does the compensation package provide the proper types of incentives to executives? Will these plans lead to considerable dilution of existing shareholders' interest? Will these plans have an effect on corporate behaviour?

As indicated earlier, the answers to such questions are difficult because measurement of these plans is somewhat imprecise. Disclosure therefore plays an important role in helping users of the financial statements better understand these plans and their possible effects. Regardless of the basis used in valuing stock options, rights, and other types of awards, full disclosure should be made about the status of these plans at the end of the period, including the number of shares for which options or rights were exercised and are exercisable. The following example taken from Agra Industries Limited's 1984 annual report illustrates how these plans may be disclosed in the financial statements.

Note 8. Stock Option Plan
Under a Company stock option plan, dated November 6, 1979, options for 314,690 shares of the company have been accepted by employees of the Company as at July 31, 1984. The plan provides that employees shall pay to the Company 50 cents for each option, which shall be credited to the purchase price when validly exercised. The options are exercisable for a five-year period at a price not less than 90% of the market price at the time the options are granted. As at July 31, 1984, 156,600 shares have been issued to employees of the Company under the plan.

COMPUTING EARNINGS PER SHARE

Prior to the 1960s, the practice of reporting earnings per share (EPS) on outstanding common shares, while commonplace, was left to management's discretion. However, because of the importance of the earnings per share number, the profession in Section 3500 of the *CICA Handbook* required that earnings per share be disclosed either in the statement of income or in a note to the financial statements. In addition, this pronouncement required at least two presentations of earnings per share for companies with dilutive securities: (1) earnings per common share (basic earnings per share) and (2) fully diluted earnings per share.

Significantly, this is one area in which Canadian pronouncements do not follow those in the United States. Under Section 3500, Canadian firms are required to report "basic earnings per share," while in the U.S. *APB Opinion No. 15* requires reporting "primary earnings per share." In many cases basic earnings per share will not be equivalent to primary earnings per share. Thus, earnings per share of Canadian firms may not necessarily be compared with earnings per share of U.S. firms.

Simple Capital Structure

A corporation's capital structure is regarded as **simple** if it consists only of common shares or includes no potentially dilutive convertible securities, options, warrants, or other rights that upon conversion or exercise could in the aggregate dilute earnings per common share. A capital structure is regarded as **complex** if it includes securities that could have a dilutive effect on earnings per common share.

The appropriate presentation of earnings per share data for corporations having a simple capital structure is a **single presentation** expressed as "basic earnings per share" on the face of the income statement or in a note to the financial statements. The computation of earnings per common share is as follows:

$$\frac{\text{Net Income} - \text{Preferred Dividends}}{\text{Weighted Average of Shares Outstanding}} = \text{Earnings per Share}$$

Dividends on preferred stock (assuming it is a simple structure) should be subtracted from each of the components of income (income before extraordinary items and net income) to arrive at income available to common shareholders at these two levels. If the preferred is cumulative and the dividend is not declared in the current year, an amount equal to the dividend that should have been declared for the **current year** only should be subtracted from net income. If cumulative preference shares exist and a net loss occurs, the dividend requirement is added to the loss. Dividends in arrears for previous years should have been included in the previous years' computations.

Weighted Average Number of Shares

In all computations of earnings per share, the weighted average of shares outstanding during the period constitutes the basis for the per-share amounts reported. Shares issued or retired during a period are weighted by the fraction of the period in which they were outstanding. The weighted number of these shares is added to the number of shares outstanding for the entire period to obtain the weighted average number of shares outstanding during the period.

For example, assume that a corporation with 100,000 common shares outstanding on January 1 issued 6,000 additional common shares on March 1. The weighted average computed at different dates of the year would be as follows:

For quarters ended March 31	
100,000 + 1/3 (6,000)	= 102,000 shares
For six months ended June 30	
100,000 + 4/6 (6,000)	= 104,000 shares
For nine months ended September 30	
100,000 + 7/9 (6,000)	= 104,667 shares
For the year ended December 31	
100,000 + 10/12 (6,000)	= 105,000 shares

Reacquired shares are included in the weighted average only for the time they were outstanding. For example, assume that a corporation with 100,000 shares outstanding on January 1 reacquired 6,000 shares on March 1. The weighted average at different dates of the year could be computed as follows:

For quarter ended March 31	
94,000[a] + 2/3 (6,000)	= 98,000 shares
For six months ended June 30	
94,000 + 2/6 (6,000)	= 96,000 shares
For nine months ended September 30	
94,000 + 2/9 (6,000)	= 95,333 shares
For the year ended December 31	
94,000 + 2/12 (6,000)	= 95,000 shares

[a]100,000 − 6,000 = 94,000 shares outstanding for the full period

More complex methods of computing a weighted average may be used if the number of shares involved changes frequently. The sum of the shares outstanding

Computation of Weighted Average
Number of Shares

Date	Number of Shares Increase (Decrease)	Number of Shares Outstanding	Days Outstanding	Share-days
January 1		25,000	15[a]	375,000
January 16	1,000	26,000	78[b]	2,028,000
April 4	2,700	28,700	151	4,333,700
September 2	(1,500)	27,200	47	1,278,400
October 19	5,000	32,200	74	2,382,800
			365	10,397,900
			A	B

Weighted average number of shares outstanding (B ÷ A) = 28,487

[a]Days between 1/1 and 1/16 that 25,000 shares were outstanding.
[b]Days between 1/16 and 4/4 that 26,000 shares were outstanding.

each day divided by the number of days in the period would produce a precise average. The schedule on page 785 illustrates computation of a weighted average on a share-day basis. Ordinarily computations reflect outstanding shares to the nearest month.

When **stock dividends, stock splits, or reverse splits** occur, computation of the weighted average number of shares requires restatements of the shares outstanding before the stock dividend or split. Stock dividends or splits are treated as retroactive adjustments rather than transactions to be weighted by the number of days a stock dividend or split was outstanding. For example, assume that a corporation had 100,000 shares outstanding on January 1 and issued a 25% stock dividend on June 30. For purposes of computing a weighted average for the current year, the additional 25,000 shares outstanding as a result of the stock dividend are assumed to have been outstanding since the beginning of the year; thus the weighted average for the year would be 125,000 shares.

The weighted average number of shares outstanding includes a retroactive adjustment as a result of an issuance of a stock dividend or stock split, but the issuance or repurchase of stock for cash is included only from the transaction date. Why? The reason is that stock splits and stock dividends do not increase or decrease the net assets of the enterprise; only additional shares of stock are issued and, therefore, the weighted average shares for previous periods must be restated for comparison purposes. Conversely, the issuance or purchase of stock for cash changes the amount of net assets. As a result, the company either earns more or less in the future as a result of this change in net assets.

On a months-outstanding basis a restatement due to a stock dividend is illustrated in the schedule shown below.

In this schedule, the months-outstanding column indicates the period of time that shares are outstanding for the year 1986. For example, from January 1 to January 31, 25,000 shares were outstanding for one month; from January 31 to

---

Computation of Weighted Average Number of Shares
with Restatement for Stock Dividend
1986

| | | Number of Shares | | | Share Months | |
Date	Transaction	Increase (Decrease)	Outstanding	Months Outstanding	Original	Restated
January 1	—	—	25,000	1(1/1-1/31)	25,000	27,500[a]
January 31	Issued for cash	1,000	26,000	2(1/31-4/1)	52,000	57,200[a]
April 1	10% stock dividend	2,600	28,600	5(4/1-9/1)		143,000
September 1	Purchase stock	(1,500)	27,100	2(9/1-10/31)		54,200
October 31	Issued for cash	5,000	32,100	2(10/31-12/31)		64,200
				12		346,100
				A		B

Weighted average number of shares outstanding (B ÷ A) = 28,842 (rounded)

[a]Restatement of 25,000 and 52,000 amount by 10% stock dividend (April 1):
25,000 + .10(25,000) = 27,500; 27,500 × 1 month = 27,500 share months
26,000 + .10(26,000) = 28,600; 28,600 × 2 months = 57,200 share months

April 1, 26,000 shares were outstanding for two months; from April 1 to September 1, 28,600 shares were outstanding for five months, and so on. When a stock dividend or stock split occurs, transactions prior to the dividend or split must be adjusted. In this example, the shares outstanding from January 1 to April 1 are adjusted for the stock dividend, so that these shares are stated on the same basis as shares issued subsequent to the stock dividend.

If a stock dividend or stock split occurs after the end of the year, but before the financial statements are issued, the weighted average number of shares outstanding for the prior year (and any other years presented in comparative form) must be restated. The illustration on page 786, for example, indicates 28,842 shares outstanding on a weighted average basis for 1986; if a 2 for 1 stock split (100% stock dividend) occurred January 10, 1987 (the next year), the shares outstanding on a weighted average basis for 1986 would be 57,684 (2 $\times$ 28,842). Note that all problems in the text assume use of the months basis for computing weighted average rather than a weighted average on a share-day basis.

Complex Capital Structures and Dilutive Securities

One problem with a simple EPS computation is that it fails to recognize the dilutive impact on outstanding shares when a corporation has dilutive securities in its capital structure. **Dilutive securities** present a serious problem in determining the proper earnings per share because upon conversion or exercise an adverse effect on earnings per share occurs. This adverse effect can be significant and, more importantly, unexpected unless financial statements call attention, in some manner, to the potential dilutive effect. Because of the increasing use of dilutive securities in the 1960s, the profession could no longer ignore their significance and, therefore, now requires additional earnings per share disclosures for firms having complex capital structures. A **complex capital structure** exists when a corporation has convertible securities, options, warrants, or other rights that upon conversion or exercise could, in the aggregate, dilute earnings per share.

A complex capital structure requires a dual presentation of earnings per share, each with equal prominence either on the face of the income statement or in a note to the financial statements. In accounting parlance these two presentations are referred to as "basic earnings per share" and "fully diluted earnings per share." **Basic earnings per share** is based on the number of common shares outstanding. **Fully diluted earnings per share** is a pro forma presentation that reflects the dilution of earnings per share that would have occurred if **all** contingent issuances of common shares that would have reduced earnings per share had taken place. Because of disclosure rules, reported fully diluted earnings per share will always be less (less income per share or more loss per share) than or equal to basic EPS.

To provide relief from complex computations that have insignificant potential dilution, the profession exempts firms from the need to disclose immaterial potential dilution. The *CICA Handbook* does not specify a materiality threshold for earnings per share dilution. However, *APB Opinion No. 15* adopted 3% as the lower limit for material dilution. Any corporation whose capital structure has potential dilution of less than 3% of earnings per common share outstanding is considered to have a simple capital structure. To illustrate, Baxter Limited has earnings per share of $2.00, ignoring all dilutive securities in its capital structure. If the possible conversion or exercise of the dilutive securities in the aggregate would reduce earnings per share to $1.94 or below (97% $\times$ $2.00), a presentation stating the potential effect of dilutive securities would be required. Otherwise, the company reports earnings per share at $2.00 and no additional disclosure is required. It is to be assumed that the weighted average number of shares is the basis and that potential dilution, if any exists, is less than 3%. In computing the 3% dilution factor, the aggregate of all dilutive securities should be considered. The dilutive securities are not considered individually, but in total.

Whether the capital structure is simple or complex, where applicable, earnings per share data should be shown before and after extraordinary items. In addition, when the income statement includes a disposal of a subsidiary, Section 1600, par. 72, of the *CICA Handbook* recommends reporting results of continuing operations separately from the results of operations of the subsidiary that has been disposed of. Furthermore, earnings per share amounts must be shown for all periods presented; all prior period earnings per share amounts presented should be restated for stock dividends and stock splits. When results of operations of a prior period have been restated as a result of a prior period adjustment, the earnings per share data shown for the prior period should also be restated. The effect of the restatement, expressed in per share terms, should be disclosed in the year of restatement.

Basic Earnings per Share   Basic earnings per share must be computed and presented for all enterprises except business enterprises that do not have share capital; government-owned companies; wholly owned subsidiaries; and companies with only a few shareholders. If a corporation has more than one class of common stock (i.e., shares having equal participation rights after prescribed dividends), then it is necessary to compute and report separate basic earnings per share amounts for each class.

When common shares are issued on conversion of debt or senior shares, the shares issued are considered to have been outstanding from the date when interest or dividends ceased to be legally due on the securities converted. For example, if a firm had 100,000 shares outstanding on January 1 and on August 1 an additional 10,000 shares were issued as a result of bond conversions, the bond indenture specifies that interest on bonds converted will be paid to the regular interest payment date (June 30 and December 31) preceding the date of conversion. In this case the weighted average number of common shares for the year would be 105,000 (100,000 + 10,000/2).

Another case where the date of issue of common shares may not be the same as the date used in determining the term outstanding involves shares issued to effect a merger or an acquisition. If common shares are issued to effect a merger or an acquisition that is accounted for as a purchase, the shares so issued are considered to be outstanding from the date that earnings of the investee first accrue to the investor. If the merger is accounted for as a pooling-of-interests, the shares issued will be treated as outstanding retroactive to the beginning of the period.

Adjusted Basic Earnings per Share   In the computation of basic earnings per share, common shares issued during the year as a result of conversions of senior shares or debt are considered to be outstanding for only that portion of the year subsequent to the termination of the firm's obligation for interest or dividends. When such conversions take place during a fiscal period, firms are required to provide an additional earnings per share amount. This additional per share figure is known as "adjusted basic" earnings per share. Adjusted basic earnings per share is computed in the same way as basic earnings per share except that the shares issued in the conversion are treated as if they had been outstanding from the beginning of the year.

Income Available to Common Shares The numerator in the fraction used to compute earnings per share is the amount of net income (or loss) available to common shares. This amount is determined by deducting the dividends on senior shares from the reported income. If the senior shares are noncumulative, dividends declared is the appropriate deduction from reported income. When senior shares include cumulative preferred, it is necessary to deduct the amount of dividends prescribed, whether paid or not. For example, a firm reports $100,000 net income for a year during which it had 60,000 common shares outstanding, 10,000 $1.00 ordinary preferred, and 20,000 $1.00 cumulative preferred. Dividends of $0.50 per share were paid on both ordinary and cumulative preferred shares. The amount of income available to common shares would be $75,000 ($100,000 minus $5,000 paid on ordinary preferred and $20,000 prescribed on the cumulative preferred).

Fully Diluted Earnings per Share Firms having complex capital structures must present appropriate fully diluted earnings per share amounts if the potential dilution is material. Potential earnings per share dilution exists whenever a firm has convertible senior shares or debt outstanding or has issued stock rights, options, or warrants. The purpose of reporting fully diluted earnings per share is to disclose the maximum possible reduction in earnings per share that could take place if all qualifying issuable common shares were issued.

Computing fully diluted earnings per share involves a hypothetical calculation of the weighted average number of common shares and the amount of income available to those shares, assuming that holders of convertible securities, options, and warrants converted and/or exercised their options and warrants that would be dilutive at the beginning of the year or, if issued during the year, at the date of issue. The number of common shares outstanding must be increased by the number of issuable common shares. Issuable common shares include only those that are issuable under outstanding conversion privileges and/or options and warrants within a ten-year period from the balance sheet date. The term during which these issuable common shares are considered to be outstanding is the shorter of the full fiscal period or time during which the underlying security or option has been outstanding.

In addition to changing the weighted average number of common shares outstanding, it is necessary to recognize the "income effect" of the issuable common shares. If common shares are issuable as a result of outstanding convertible preferred, the income effect is equal to the dividends applicable to the convertible preferred. That is, if the holders of the convertible preferred shares converted their shares to common, the income available to common shareholders would now be increased by the amount of the dividends that would have otherwise been allocated to preferred shares. When the income effect involves an income statement item such as interest expense on convertible bonds, the amount of the adjustment is the amount by which the after-tax income would be increased. For example, if holders of convertible bonds exercised their conversion privilege, then income available to common shareholders would be increased by the amount of interest that would have been paid on the bonds less the amount by which income tax expense would be increased due to the reduction in interest expense.

Convertible Securities

Convertible securities that affect the calculation of fully diluted earnings per share include convertible senior shares and debt. Any outstanding rights to convert either senior shares or debt into common shares within a **ten-year term** that would result in dilution (reduction) of earnings per share should be included in the calculation of fully diluted earnings per share. As emphasized above, the number of issuable common shares outstanding as a result of the related convertible security are included in the computation of the weighted average number of common shares outstanding. Income is adjusted to reflect, on a pro forma basis, the changes that would occur if the conversion privileges had been exercised at the beginning of the year or date of issue, whichever is later. As an example, Marshy Field Limited has net income for the year of $310,000 and an average number of common shares outstanding during the period of 100,000. The company has two convertible debenture bond issues outstanding. One (outstanding at the beginning of the current year) is a 10% issue sold at 100 (total of $1,000,000) and convertible into 40,000 common shares. The other is a 15% issue sold at 100 (total of $1,000,000) on April 1 of the current year and convertible into 64,000 common shares. In addition, the firm has 50,000 noncumulative $1.00 convertible (one preferred for one common) preferred shares outstanding. Due to a cash shortage, dividends of only $0.75 per share were declared and paid during the current year. Assume that the tax rate at present is 40%. Fully diluted earnings per share would be $1.84.

Marshy Field Ltd. COMPUTATION OF EARNINGS PER SHARE		
	Number of Shares	Net Income
Net income		$310,000
Common shares	100,000	
Deduct:		
Preferred dividends declared		37,500
Income available to common shares	100,000	$272,500
Basic earnings per share ($272,500/100,000)		$2.73
From above	100,000	$272,500
Add assumed conversions:		
Convertible preferred		
Dividends (50,000 × $0.75)		37,500
Number of shares	50,000	
10% convertible debentures:		
Interest net of tax [$1,000,000 × (0.10 × 0.6)]		60,000
Number of shares	40,000	
15% convertible debentures:		
Interest net of tax [$1,000,000 × (0.15 × 0.6)] × 9/12		67,500
Number of shares (64,000 × 9/12)	48,000	
Totals	238,000	$437,500
Fully diluted earnings per share		$1.84

Options and Warrants

Stock options and warrants outstanding and their equivalents (if exercisable within the ten-year limit) are included in fully diluted earnings per share computations unless their effect on EPS is antidilutive (i.e., increase EPS). Stock purchase contracts, stock subscriptions not fully paid, deferred compensation packages providing for the issuance of common shares, and convertible securities that allow or require the payment of cash at issuance are treated as options and warrants. The number of common shares issuable upon exercise of outstanding options, warrants, and their equivalents is included in the weighted average number of common shares for the calculation of fully diluted earnings per share.

These calculations are based on the assumption that the options and/or warrants are exercised at the beginning of the year (or date of issue if later) and the proceeds from the exercise of the options and warrants are invested in operating assets of the firm. This amount is invested and, in turn, earns an assumed return that would increase the amount of income available to the common shares. The appropriate rate of return (net of tax) is left to the professional judgement of the accountant.

To illustrate the computation of fully diluted earnings per share when stock options and/or warrants are outstanding at the year end, assume that Kubitz Industries Limited has net income for the period of $220,000. The average number of common shares outstanding for the period was 50,000 shares. Options to purchase 5,000 common shares at a price of $10 per share were outstanding at the end of the year. Of the 5,000 options, 4,000 were outstanding at the beginning of the year and 1,000 were issued on October 1 of the current year. Kubitz's average rate of return on assets over the past three years has been 25% before income taxes of 40%.

In most cases, holders of convertible securities, options, rights, and warrants are protected against a dilution of the number of shares to which they are entitled in the event of either a stock split or a stock dividend. This protection is an antidilution clause that provides for a proportionate increase (decrease) in the conversion ratio or the number of shares that may be acquired with each option or warrant. For

---

Kubitz Industries Limited
COMPUTATION OF EARNINGS PER SHARE

		Number of Shares	Net Income
Net income			$220,000
Common shares		50,000	
Basic earnings per share			$4.40
From above		50,000	$220,000
Issuable common shares—stock options:			
Outstanding one year 4,000 × 1		4,000	
Outstanding three months 1,000 × 3/12		250	
Imputed earnings on option proceeds:			
Proceeds 4,000 × $10	$40,000		
Imputed earnings $40,000 × 0.25	10,000		
Less: Income taxes @ 40%	4,000		6,000
Proceeds 1,000 × $10	$10,000		
Imputed earnings $10,000 × 0.25	2,500		
Less: Income taxes @ 40%	1,000		
Net earnings for 12 months	1,500		
Imputed earnings for three months			
$1,500 × 3/12			375
Totals		54,250	$226,375
Fully diluted earnings per share			$4.17

example, a convertible bond with an original exchange ratio of 20 common shares for each $1,000 bond would, if so specified in an antidilution clause, have an exchange ratio of 40 to one after a two-for-one stock split.

Antidilution

When determining whether fully diluted earnings per share should be reported, all dilutive securities must be considered. In addition, any security that is antidilutive should be excluded and cannot be used to offset dilutive securities. Antidilutive securities are securities that would create an increase in earnings per share (or a reduction in net loss per share). For example, convertible debt is antidilutive whenever interest (net of tax) on the debt expensed per common share (based upon number of common shares issuable upon conversion) is greater than basic earnings per share. With options or warrants, whenever the imputed earnings (net of tax) expressed in per share terms (number of shares issuable under the associated options or warrants) is greater than basic earnings per share, they are considered antidilutive. A test for antidilution must be made before including any item in the fully diluted earnings per share calculation. This test involves simply comparing the per share effect of each potentially dilutive item with the basic earnings per share.[10] If the per share amount of the potentially dilutive item is greater than the basic earnings per share (less than net loss per share), then the item is antidilutive and must be omitted from the fully diluted earnings per share.

Pro Forma Earnings per Share

When transactions affecting common shares occur subsequent to the date of the balance sheet, earnings per share figures previously computed may not be relevant to users' needs. In these cases pro forma earnings per share amounts must be disclosed in a note to the financial statements. Pro forma basic earnings per share should be computed after any one of the following three kinds of transactions that occur subsequent to the date of the balance sheet.[11]

(a) Issuance of common shares when the proceeds are to be used to retire senior shares or debt outstanding at the date of the balance sheet.
(b) Common shares issued on the conversion of senior shares or debt outstanding at the balance sheet.
(c) When common shares are issued in a reorganization.

When computing pro forma earnings per share, common shares issued in any of the foregoing types of transactions are given retroactive recognition.

Type (b) transactions would have been anticipated in fully diluted earnings per share, and therefore are not used in computing pro forma fully diluted earnings per share. However, if type (a) or (c) transactions occur, then pro forma fully diluted earnings per share must be computed and disclosed in a note to the financial statements. Neither pro forma basic nor pro forma fully diluted earnings per share need to be reported for any prior periods. In addition, it is not necessary to report pro forma earnings figures that are not materially different from the basic and fully diluted earnings per share amounts.

---

[10]This test is an approximation of antidilution. Calculation of the exact amount includes the effects of other potentially dilutive securities as is illustrated in Exhibit 7 of Appendix 17A.

[11]*CICA Handbook*, Section 3500, par. 39.

Earnings per Share Presentations and Disclosures

If a corporation's capital structure is complex, the earnings per share presentations would be as follows:

Net Income per Common Share	
Basic	$3.30
Fully diluted	$2.70

When the income of a period includes special transactions, per share amounts (where applicable) should be shown for income before extraordinary items and net income. Reporting per share amount for gain or loss on extraordinary items is optional. A presentation reporting extraordinary items is illustrated below:

Net Income per Common Share	
Basic earnings per common share:	
Income before extraordinary item	$3.80
Extraordinary item	0.80
Net income	$3.00
Fully diluted earnings per common share:	
Income before extraordinary item	$3.35
Extraordinary item	0.65
Net income	$2.70

Earnings per share amounts must be shown for all periods presented; all prior period earnings per share amounts presented should be restated for stock dividends and stock splits. When results of operations of a prior period have been restated as a result of a prior period adjustment, the earnings per share data shown for the prior periods should be restated. The effect of the restatement should be disclosed in the year of restatement.

Some Canadian firms are required to report in jurisdictions outside of Canada. In these cases, the firms must disclose the earnings per share amounts required in Canada as well as those, if different, required in the foreign country.

SUMMARY

Computation of earnings per share has become a complex issue. Many accountants take a strong exception to some of the arbitrary rules contained in Section 3500 of the *CICA Handbook*. The situation facing accountants in this area is a difficult one, because many securities, although technically not common shares, have the basic characteristics of common shares. In addition, many companies have issued these types of securities rather than common shares in order to avoid an adverse effect on the earnings per share figure. Section 3500 was issued as an attempt to develop credibility in reporting earnings per share data.

KEY POINTS

1. Convertible bonds may be converted into other securities of the corporation.

2. The value of the conversion feature is not recognized in the issuer's books.

3. Conversions may be recorded at (1) book value, (2) market value of bonds, or (3) market value of the shares issued.

4. Convertible preference shares are recorded at issue price and conversions are recorded at book value.

5. Stock rights and warrants entitle holders to acquire shares at a certain price within a stipulated period.

6. When issued with other securities, rights and warrants are assigned values (usually using the relative market value method) and recorded separately.

7. Noncompensatory stock option plans offer share purchase options to employees to induce ownership interests. Shares issued under noncompensatory plans are recorded as ordinary share issues.

8. Compensatory stock option plans are intended as remuneration and convey value to employees at the date of the grant.

9. Compensation given under compensatory plans is measured by the excess of market value over option price on the measurement date.

10. Compensation expense is allocated to the periods during which the qualifying service is rendered. The value of the options is recorded as an element of contributed surplus.

11. Stock appreciation rights provide employees the opportunity to benefit from increases in share prices without having to purchase the shares. Precise measurement of the cost of the benefit is not possible until date of exercise. Compensation expense for interim periods is based on estimates of the number of shares and the difference between market price and option price at each year end. Changes in estimates of outstanding obligations are recorded in the period of the change.

12. Basic earnings per share is the amount of income attributed to each share of common stock outstanding. It is computed by dividing the income available to common shareholders (net income minus dividends paid on noncumulative preference shares and dividends prescribed on cumulative preference shares) by the weighted average number of common shares outstanding during the period.

13. Fully diluted earnings per share represents the lowest possible earnings per share amount (largest possible loss) that could have been reported **if** all potentially issuable common shares had been issued during the year.

14. Basic and fully diluted earnings per share should be reported for net income and income before extraordinary items.

15. When common shares have been issued during the year as a result of conversions of senior shares or debt, adjusted basic earnings per share should be reported. Adjusted basic earnings per share indicates the amount that basic earnings per share would have been if the conversions had taken place at the beginning of the year.

16. If common shares are issued after the end of the current year and before the financial statements have been issued and the proceeds used to retire senior shares or debt, pro forma basic and pro forma fully diluted earnings per share should be disclosed.

COMPREHENSIVE EARNINGS PER SHARE ILLUSTRATION

The following comprehensive illustration demonstrates how the methods for computing earnings per share would be handled in a complex situation. The following section of the balance sheet of Rhode Limited is presented for analysis; assumptions related to the capital structure follow.

```
                           Rhode Limited
                           BALANCE SHEET
              LIABILITIES AND SHAREHOLDERS' EQUITY
                        at December 31, 1986

Long-term debt:
  Notes payable, 7.2%                        $  500,000
  4% Convertible debentures                   1,500,000
  5% Convertible debentures                   2,500,000   $ 4,500,000
Shareholders' equity:
  $5 cumulative convertible preferred, no-par
    value, authorized 100,000 shares, issued
    25,000 shares                             2,500,000
  Common shares, no-par value, authorized
    5,000,000 shares, issued 500,000 shares     500,000
  Contributed surplus                         2,500,000
  Retained earnings (includes 1986 income of
    $1,000,000)                               9,000,000     14,500,000
                                                          $19,000,000
```

Notes and Assumptions
December 31, 1986

1. Options, exercisable at any time after July 1, 1989, were granted to purchase 50,000 common shares at $20 per share on July 2, 1986.
2. Warrants to purchase 100,000 common shares at $25 per share were issued in 1984. These warrants may be exercised at any time after January 1, 1991.
3. 4% and 5% convertible debentures are convertible into common shares at $25 per share (40 shares for each $1,000 bond).
4. $5 cumulative convertible preferred shares are convertible at the rate of four shares of common for each share of preferred ($25 conversion price).
5. All debt was issued at face value and all preferred was issued at $100 per share.
6. Except for the stock options in item 1 and the convertible debentures in item 11, all debt and securities were outstanding at the beginning and end of the year.
7. The average applicable income tax rate is 40%.
8. 25,000 shares of common were issued January 25, 1987, for $26 per share. The proceeds of this issue were used to retire 550 $1,000 5% convertible debentures.
9. On February 10, 1987, prior to issuance of the financial statements, directors of Rhode Limited voted to split the common shares two for one.
10. Net income for the year of $1,000,000 did not include any extraordinary items.
11. Holders of 1,000 4% convertible debentures exercised their conversion rights on September 30, 1986.
12. Rhode earns approximately 8% after taxes on net assets.

The computation of earnings per share amounts in accordance with Section 3500 of the *CICA Handbook* is as follows:

Computation of Earnings Per Share	Number of Shares	Income	Per Share Amount
Basic earnings per share (Exhibit 1)	940,000	$ 875,000	$0.93
Dilutive securities:			
4% convertible debentures (Exhibit 2)	180,000	54,000	0.30
5% convertible debentures (Exhibit 3)	200,000	75,000	0.375
Convertible preferred shares (Exhibit 4)	200,000	125,000	0.625
Stock options (Exhibit 5)	—	—	—
Stock warrants (Exhibit 6)	—	—	—
Fully diluted earnings per share	1,520,000	$1,129,000	$0.74
Adjusted basic earnings per share (Exhibit 10)	1,000,000	$ 893,000	$0.89

The following exhibits illustrate the computations for arriving at basic and fully diluted earnings per share. Exhibit 1 shows the calculation of basic earnings per share.

Exhibit 1	
Computation of Basic Earnings Per Share	
Net income as reported	$1,000,000
Deduct dividends prescribed on cumulative preferred shares (25,000 × $5.00)	125,000
Income attributed to common shares	$ 875,000

Common shares outstanding:	
For 12 months (500,000 − 40,000)	460,000
For three months (1,000 × $1,000)/$25 = 40,000	
40,000 × 3/12 =	10,000
Total	470,000
Adjustment for two-for-one stock split	× 2
Weighted average number of common shares outstanding	940,000
Basic earnings per share ($875,000/940,000)	$0.93

Exhibit 2 illustrates the calculation of the earnings per share effect of the 4% convertible debentures.

Exhibit 2
4% Convertible Debentures

Pro forma income effect of conversion:	
Interest expense reduction ($1,500,000 × 0.04) +	
($1,000,000 × 0.04) × 9/12	$ 90,000
Less: Income tax expense increase ($90,000 × 0.4)	36,000
Net increase in net income that would have	
occurred had conversion occurred Jan. 1, 1986	$ 54,000
Number of common shares issuable upon conversion	
($1,500,000/$25) + ($1,000,000/$25 × 9/12)	90,000
Adjustment for two-for-one stock split	× 2
Total issuable common shares	180,000
Earnings per share effect of possible conversion	
($54,000/180,000)	$0.30

Exhibit 3 presents the calculation of the pro forma earnings per share effect of the conversion of the 5% convertible debentures at January 1, 1986.

Exhibit 3
5% Convertible Debentures

Pro forma income effect of conversion:	
Interest expense reduction ($2,500,000 × 0.05)	$125,000
Less: Income tax expense increase ($125,000 × 0.4)	50,000
Net increase in net income that would have occurred	
had conversion taken place January 1, 1986	$ 75,000
Number of common shares issuable upon conversion	
($2,500,000/$25)	100,000
Adjustment for two-for-one stock split	× 2
Total issuable common shares	200,000
Pro forma earnings per share effect of conversion	
($75,000/200,000)	$0.375

Exhibit 4 illustrates the computation of the pro forma earnings per share effect of the conversion of the convertible preferred shares.

Exhibit 4
Convertible Preferred Shares

Income effect of conversion:	
Dividends prescribed (25,000 × $5.00)	$125,000
Number of common shares issuable upon conversion:	
(25,000 × 4)	100,000
Adjustment for two-for-one stock split	× 2
Issuable common shares	200,000
Earnings per share effect of conversion	
($125,000/200,000)	$0.625

Exhibit 5 shows the earnings per share effect of the exercise of the stock options from the date of issue (July 1, 1986).

Exhibit 5
Stock Options

Income that would have been earned on the proceeds from exercise of the options from date of issue to December 31, 1986 (50,000* × $20* × .08 × 6/12)	$40,000
Issuable common shares 50,000 × 6/12	25,000
Adjustable for two-for-one stock split	× 2
Issuable common shares	50,000
Earnings per share effect of exercise of stock options ($40,000/50,000)	$0.80

*At the time of the stock split the number of shares issuable under the options would be increased proportionately and the option price would be reduced to prevent dilution of the value of the options. (Options would be increased to 100,000 shares and the price would be reduced to $10 per share.)

Exhibit 6
Stock Warrants

Imputed income on proceeds from exercise of stock warrants ($12.50* × 200,000*) × 0.08	$200,000
Number of common shares issuable upon exercise of warrants	100,000
Adjustment for stock split	× 2
Total number of shares issuable	200,000
Earnings per share effect of exercise of stock warrants ($200,000/200,000)	$1.00

*Adjusted for stock split

Exhibit 6 on page 798 illustrates the calculation of the earnings per share effect of potential issuance of shares to holders of stock warrants. Notice that these are considered potentially dilutive securities since they may be exercised within the ten-year limit.

Exhibits 2 to 6 show the calculations of the per share effect of various potentially dilutive securities. Only those that cause reductions to basic earnings per share should be included in the calculation of fully diluted earnings per share. In order to determine which dilutive securities to include in the fully diluted earnings per share amount, it is necessary to rank the pro forma per share effects starting with the most dilutive. Fully diluted earnings per share is then computed by progressively including the dilutive securities until the lowest per share amount is determined. Any dilutive securities that cause this lowest possible amount to increase should be omitted from the calculations when determining the fully diluted earnings per share to be reported in the financial statements. This procedure is illustrated in Exhibit 7.

Exhibit 7
Fully Diluted Earnings Per Share

	Number of Shares	Income	Earnings Per Share
Basic earnings per share (Exhibit 1)	940,000	$ 875,000	$0.93
4% debentures (Exhibit 2)	180,000	54,000	
Subtotal	1,120,000	929,000	0.829
5% debentures (Exhibit 3)	200,000	75,000	
Subtotal	1,320,000	1,004,000	0.761
Convertible preferred (Exhibit 4)	200,000	125,000	
Subtotal	1,520,000	1,129,000	0.743
Stock options (Exhibit 5)	50,000	40,000	
Subtotal	1,570,000	1,169,000	0.745*
Stock warrants (Exhibit 6)	200,000	200,000	
Total	1,770,000	$1,369,000	0.773*

*Earnings per share increases; therefore, stock options and warrants are antidilutive and should be omitted from calculation of fully diluted earnings per share.

Exhibit 8
Pro Forma Basic Earnings Per Share

Net income attributed to common shares (Exhibit 1)		$875,000
Add: Interest expense reduction from debt		
retired January 25, 1987 ($550,000 × 0.05)	$27,500	
Less: Income tax expense increase ($27,500 × 0.4)	11,000	16,500
Pro forma income available to common shares		$891,500
Weighted average number of common shares		
outstanding (Exhibit 1)		940,000
Add: Common shares issued January 25, 1987		50,000
Pro forma weighted average number of common		
shares outstanding during 1986		990,000
Pro forma basic earnings per share ($891,500/990,000)		$0.90

The issuance of common shares subsequent to the end of the fiscal period and the proceeds used to retire debt necessitate computation and disclosure of pro forma basic and fully diluted earnings per share. These calculations are illustrated in Exhibits 8 and 9.

Exhibit 9
Pro Forma Diluted Earnings Per Share

Pro forma available to common shares (Exhibit 8)		$ 891,500
Add: Income attributed to assumed conversions		
4% convertible debentures (Exhibit 2)		54,000
5% convertible debentures (Exhibit 3)	$ 75,000	
Less: After-tax interest on debentures		
retired January 25, 1987 (Exhibit 8)	16,500	58,500
Convertible preferred shares (Exhibit 4)		125,000
Total		$1,129,000
Weighted average number of common shares		
Pro forma basic (Exhibit 8)		990,000
4% convertible debentures (Exhibit 2)		180,000
5% convertible debentures (Exhibit 3)	200,000	
Less: Debentures retired January 25, 1987		
($550,000/$25 adjusted for stock split)	44,000	156,000
Convertible preferred shares (Exhibit 4)		200,000
Total		1,526,000
Pro forma fully diluted earnings per share		
($1,129,000/1,526,000)		$0.74

When conversions of senior shares or debt occur during the fiscal period, adjusted basic earnings per share should be calculated as though the conversion had taken place at the beginning of the period. This calculation is presented in the following illustration, Exhibit 10.

Exhibit 10
Adjusted Basic Earnings Per Share

Income attributed to common shares (Exhibit 1)		$ 875,000
Add: Income effect of shares issued September 30		
on conversion of 4% debentures		
(1,000,000 × 0.4 × 9/12)		30,000
Deduct: Increases in income tax ($30,000 × 0.4)		(12,000)
Net income available to common shareholders		$ 893,000
Weighted average number of common shares outstanding		
(Exhibit 1)		940,000
Add: Shares issued September 30 on conversion		
restated to January 1 [(1,000,000/25) × 9/12]	30,000	
Adjustment for stock split	× 2	60,000
Weighted average number of common shares		
for adjusted basic earnings per share		1,000,000
Adjusted basic earnings per share ($893,000/1,000,000)		$0.89

Note: All **asterisked** Questions, Cases, Exercises, or Problems relate to material contained in an Appendix.

QUESTIONS

1. What are some of the major reasons for the increased merger activity in the early 1980s? Why might this increased activity lead to the issuance of dilutive securities?

2. Discuss the similarities and the differences between convertible debt and debt issued with stock purchase warrants.

3. What accounting treatment is required for convertible debt? What accounting treatment is required for debt issued with stock purchase warrants?

4. Explain how the conversion feature of convertible debt has a value (a) to the issuer, and (b) to the purchaser.

5. What are the arguments for giving separate accounting recognition to the conversion feature of debentures?

6. Assume that no value is assigned to the conversion feature upon issue of the debentures. Assume further that four years after issue, debentures with a face value of $100,000 and book value of $96,000 are tendered for conversion into 8,000 common shares immediately after an interest payment date when the market price of the debentures is 104 and the common shares are selling at $14 per share. The company records the conversion as follows:

Bonds Payable	100,000	
Discount on Bonds Payable		4,000
Common Shares (no-par value)		96,000

 Discuss the propriety of this accounting treatment.

7. On July 1, 1986, Harbecke Corporation issued $2,000,000 of 7% bonds payable in 10 years. The bonds include detachable warrants giving the bondholder the right to purchase for $30, one no-par value common share at any time during the next 10 years. The bonds were sold for $2,000,000. The value of the warrants at the time of issuance was $100,000. Prepare the journal entry to record this transaction.

8. What are stock rights? How does the issuing company account for them?

9. What are the advantages to an executive of receiving an incentive stock option? Why do some accountants believe that the present accounting for these options is inappropriate?

10. Erwin Corporation has an employee stock purchase plan which permits all full-time employees to purchase 10 common shares on the third anniversary of their employment and an additional 10 shares on each subsequent anniversary date. The purchase price is set at the market price on the date purchased, and no commission is charged. Discuss whether this plan would be considered compensatory.

11. What date or event does the AICPA believe should be used in determining the value of a stock option? What arguments support the AICPA position? What criticism may be brought against the date or event advocated by the AICPA?

12. What support can be offered for dates other than the date of grant on which to determine the value of a stock option?

13. What is the advantage to an executive of a stock appreciation right (SAR) plan? How is compensation expense measured in a SAR plan?

14. At December 31, 1986, the Wedgewood Company had 600,000 common shares issued and outstanding, 400,000 of which had been issued and outstanding throughout the year, and 200,000 of which were issued on October 1, 1986. Net income for 1986 was $2,144,000 and dividends declared on preferred were $394,000. Compute Wedgewood's earnings per common share. (Round to the nearest penny.)

15. Define the following terms:
    (a) 3% test for dilution.   (d) Potentially dilutive security.
    (b) Complex capital structure.   (e) Fully diluted earnings per share.
    (c) Basic earnings per share.

16. Earnings per share can affect market prices. Can market prices affect earnings per share? Explain.

17. What is meant by the term antidilution? Give an example.

CASES

C17-1 Incurring long-term debt with an arrangement whereby lenders receive an option to buy common shares during all or a portion of the time the debt is outstanding is a frequent corporate financing practice. In some situations the result is achieved through the issuance of convertible bonds; in others the debt instruments and the warrants to buy shares are separate.

Instructions

  (a) 1. Describe the differences that exist in current accounting for original proceeds of the issuance of convertible bonds and of debt instruments with separate warrants to purchase common shares.

        2. Discuss the underlying rationale for the differences described in (a) 1. above.

        3. Summarize the arguments that have been presented in favour of accounting for convertible bonds in the same manner as for debt with separate warrants.

  (b) At the start of the year, Bruce Budge Company issued $9,000,000 of 12% notes along with warrants to buy 600,000 shares of its no-par value common stock at $18 per share. The notes mature over the next 10 years starting one year from date of issuance, with annual maturities of $900,000. At the time, Budge had 4,800,000 common shares outstanding and the market price was $23 per share. The company received $10,020,000 for the notes and the warrants. For Bruce Budge Company, 12% was a relatively low borrowing rate. If offered alone, at this time, the notes would have been issued at a 22% discount. Prepare the journal entry (or entries) for the issuance of the notes and warrants for the cash consideration received.

(AICPA adapted)

C17-2 For various reasons, a corporation may issue warrants to purchase common shares at specified prices that, depending on the circumstances, may be less than, equal to, or greater than, the current market price. For example, warrants may be issued:

  1. To existing shareholders on a pro rata basis.

  2. To certain key employees under an incentive stock option plan.

  3. To purchasers of the corporation's bonds.

Instructions

For each of the three examples of how stock warrants are used:

  (a) Explain why they are used.

  (b) Discuss the significance of the price (or prices) at which the warrants are issued (or granted) in relation to (1) the current market price of the company's shares, and (2) the length of time over which they can be exercised.

  (c) Describe the information that should be disclosed in financial statements, or notes thereto, that are prepared when stock warrants are outstanding in the hands of the three groups listed above.

(AICPA adapted)

C17-3 On December 12, 1983, the board of directors of Michalmar Company authorized a grant of nonqualified options to company executives for the purchase of 20,000 common shares at 52 any time during 1986 if the executives still are employed by the company. The closing price of Michalmar common was 55 on December 12, 1983, 51 on January 2, 1986, and 49 1/8 on December 31, 1986. None of the options was exercised.

Instructions

  (a) Prepare a schedule presenting the computation of the compensation cost that should be attributed to the options of Michalmar Company.

  (b) Assume that the market price of Michalmar common rose to 58 (instead of declining to 51) on January 1, 1986, and that all options were exercised on that date. Would the company incur a cost for executive compensation? Why?

(c) Discuss the arguments for measuring compensation from executive stock options in terms of the spread between the:

1. Market price and option price when the grant is made.
2. Market price and option price when the options are first exercisable.
3. Market price and option price when the options are exercised.
4. Cash value of the executives' services estimated at date of grant and the amount of their salaries.

(AICPA adapted)

C17-4 In 1983 Smother Co. adopted a plan to give additional incentive compensation to its dealers to sell its principal product, fire extinguishers. Under the plan Smother transferred 9,000 of its no-par value common shares to a trust with the provision that Smother would have to forfeit interest in the trust and no part of the trust fund could ever revert to Smother. Shares were to be distributed to dealers on the basis of their shares of fire extinguisher purchases from Smother (above certain minimum levels) over the three-year period ending June 30, 1986.

In 1983 the shares were closely held. The book value of the shares was $6.90 per share as of June 30, 1983, and in 1983 additional shares were sold to existing shareholders for $7 per share. On the basis of this information, market value of the shares was determined to be $7 each.

In 1983 when the shares were transferred to the trust, Smother charged prepaid expenses for $63,000 ($7 per share market value) and credited capital stock for $63,000. The prepaid expense was charged to operations over a three-year period ended June 30, 1986. Smother sold a substantial number of its shares to the public in 1985 at $60 per share.

In June, 1986, all shares in the trust were distributed to the dealers. The market value of the shares at date of distribution from the trust had risen to $120 per share. Smother obtained a tax deduction equal to that market value for the tax year ended June 30, 1987.

Instructions

(a) How much should be reported as selling expense in each of the years noted above?
(b) Smother is also considering other types of option plans. One such plan is a stock appreciation right (SAR) plan. What is a SAR plan? What is a potential disadvantage of a SAR plan from the viewpoint of the company?

C17-5 Earnings per share (EPS) is the single most-featured financial statistic about modern corporations. Daily published quotations of stock prices have recently been expanded to include for many securities a "times earnings" figure which is based on EPS. Stock analysts often focus their discussions on the EPS of the corporations they study.

Instructions

Explain how dividends or dividend requirements on any class of preferred shares that may be outstanding affect the computation of EPS.

C17-6 Colleen Mackenzie Corporation, a new audit client of yours, has not reported earnings per share data in its annual reports to shareholders in the past. The treasurer requested that you furnish information about the reporting of earnings per share data in the current year's annual report in accordance with generally accepted accounting principles.

Instructions

(a) Define the term "earnings per share" as it applies to a corporation with a capitalization structure composed of only one class of common shares and explain how earnings per share should be computed and how the information should be disclosed in the corporation's financial statements.
(b) Discuss the treatment, if any, that should be given to each of the following items in computing earnings per common share for financial statement reporting.

1. The declaration of current dividends on cumulative preferred shares.
2. The acquisition of some of the corporation's outstanding common shares during the current fiscal year. The shares were classified as treasury shares.
3. A two-for-one stock split of common shares during the current fiscal year.
4. A provision created out of retained earnings for a contingent liability from a possible lawsuit.
5. Outstanding preferred shares issued at $46 with a $40 liquidation right.
6. The exercise at a price below market value but above book value of a common stock option issued during the current fiscal year to officers of the corporation.
7. The replacement of a machine immediately prior to the close of the current fiscal year at a cost 20% above the original cost of the replaced machine. The new machine will perform the same function as the old machine that was sold for its book value.

EXERCISES

E17-1 For each of the unrelated transactions described below, present the entry (entries) required and record each transaction.

1. Teddico Corp. issued $20,000,000 par value 11% convertible bonds at 99. If the bonds had not been convertible, the company's investment banker estimates they would have been sold at 95. Expenses of issuing the bonds were $80,000.
2. Anna Company issued $20,000,000 par value 10% bonds at 98. One detachable stock purchase warrant was issued with each $100 par value bond. At the time of issuance the warrants were selling for $4.
3. On July 1, 1986, Schmitt Company called its 11% convertible debentures for conversion. The $10,000,000 par value bonds were converted into 1,000,000 no-par value common shares which had been issued at $10,000,000. On July 1, there was $150,000 of unamortized discount applicable to the bonds, and the company incurred expenses of $75,000 in connection with the conversion of all the bonds. The company records the conversion using the book value method.

E17-2 Maxipump, Inc. issued $6,000,000 of 10%, 10-year convertible bonds on June 1, 1985, at 98 plus accrued interest. The bonds were dated April 1, 1985, with interest payable April 1 and October 1. Bond discount is amortized semiannually on a straight-line basis.

On April 1, 1986, $1,500,000 of these bonds were converted into 1,500 no-par value common shares. Accrued interest was paid in cash at the time of conversion.

Instructions

(a) Prepare the entry to record the interest expense at October 1, 1985. Assume that accrued interest payable was credited when the bonds were issued. (Round to nearest dollar.)

(b) Prepare the entry (entries) to record the conversion on April 1, 1986. (Book value method is used.) Assume that the entry to record amortization of the bond discount and interest payment has been made.

E17-3 Purdue Boiler Company has bonds payable outstanding in the amount of $500,000 and carries its account Premium on Bonds Payable in the amount of $7,500. Each $1,000 bond is convertible into 20 no-par preferred shares.

Instructions

(a) Assuming that the bonds are quoted on the market at 102 and that the preferred shares may be sold on the market at 50 7/8, make the entry to record the conversion of the bonds to preferred shares. (Use the market value approach.)

(b) Assuming that the book value method was used, what entry would be made?

E17-4 On September 1, 1986, T. Campbell Company sold at 104 (plus accrued interest) 4,000 of its 9%, 10-year, $1,000 face value, nonconvertible bonds with detachable stock warrants. Each bond carried two detachable warrants; each warrant was for one share of no-par common, at a specified option price of $15 per share. Shortly after issuance the warrants were quoted on the market for $3 each. No market value can be determined for the bonds above. Interest is payable on December 1 and June 1. Bond issue costs of $40,000 were incurred.

Instructions

Prepare, in general journal format the entry to record the issuance of the bonds.

(AICPA adapted)

E17-5 On January 1, 1984, when its common shares were selling for $80 per share, Linda Plumb Corp. issued $10,000,000 of 8% convertible debentures due in 10 years. The conversion option allowed the holder of each $1,000 bond to convert the bond into five shares of the corporation's no-par common. The debentures were issued for $10,900,000. The present value of the bond payments at the time of issuance was $8,500,000, and the corporation believes the difference between the present value and the amount paid is attributable to the conversion feature. On January 1, 1985, the corporation's common shares were split two-for-one. On January 1, 1986, when the corporation's common shares were selling for $135 per share, holders of 30% of the convertible debentures exercised their conversion options. The corporation uses the straight-line method for amortizing any bond discounts or premiums.

Instructions

(a) Prepare, in general journal form, the entry to record the original issuance of the convertible debentures.

(b) Prepare, in general journal form, the entry to record the exercise of the conversion option, using the book value method. Show supporting computations in good form.

E17-6 The December 31, 1985, balance sheet of Discorama Corp. is as follows:

8% callable, Convertible Bonds Payable [semiannual interest dates April 30 and October 31; convertible into 50 no-par value common (average issuance price of $25) per $1,000 of bond principal; maturity date April 30, 1991]	$400,000	
Discount on Bonds Payable	9,600	$390,400

On March 5, 1986, Discorama Corp. called all of the bonds as of April 30 for the principal plus interest through April 30. By April 30 all bondholders had exercised their conversion rights as of the interest payment date. Consequently, on April 30, Discorama Corp. paid the semiannual interest and issued common shares for the bonds. The discount is amortized on a straight-line basis. Discorama uses the book value method.

Instructions

Prepare the entry (entries) to record the interest expense and conversion on April 30, 1986. Reversing entries were made on January 1, 1986. (Round to the nearest dollar.)

E17-7 Atlantic Inc. has decided to raise additional capital by issuing $150,000 face value of bonds with a coupon rate of 10%. In discussions with their investment consultants, it was determined that to help the sale of the bonds, detachable stock warrants should be issued at the rate of one warrant for each $100 bond sold. The value of the bonds without the warrants is considered to be $132,000, and the value of the warrants in the market is $24,000. The bonds sold in the market at issuance for $147,000.

Instructions

(a) What entry should be made at the time of the issuance of the bonds and warrants?

(b) If the warrants were nondetachable, would the entries be different? Discuss.

E17-8 On January 1, 1985, Charmglo Corporation issued $4,000,000 of 10-year, 8% convertible debentures at 102. Interest is to be paid semiannually on June 30 and December 31. Each $1,000 debenture can be converted into eight shares of Charmglo Corporation no-par common after December 31, 1986.

On January 1, 1987, $400,000 of debentures are converted into common shares (average issuance price of $100), which are then selling at $112. An additional $400,000 of debentures is converted on March 31, 1987. The market price of the common shares is then $115.

Bond premium is amortized on a straight-line basis.

Instructions

Make the necessary journal entries for:

(a) December 31, 1986.   (c) March 31, 1987.
(b) January 1, 1987.   (d) June 30, 1987.

Record the conversions under both the fair market value method and the book value method.

E17-9 On November 1, 1983, Firewood Company adopted a stock option plan that granted options to key executives to purchase 45,000 shares of the company's no-par value common stock. The options were granted on January 1, 1984, and were exercisable two years after date of grant if the grantee was still an employee of the company; the options expired six years from date of grant. The option price was set at $35; market price at the date of the grant was $47 a share.

All of the options were exercised during the year 1986: 30,000 on January 3 when the market price was $67, and 15,000 on May 1 when the market price was $77 a share.

Instructions

(a) Compute the value of the stock option and the corresponding amount of executive compensation.

(b) Prepare journal entries relating to the stock option plan for the years 1984, 1985, and 1986. Assume that the employee performs services equally in 1984 and 1985.

E17-10 On November 2, 1982, the shareholders of Siska Company voted to adopt a stock option plan for Siska's key officers. According to terms of the option agreement, the officers of the company can purchase 30,000 shares of no-par common during 1985 and 54,000 shares during 1986. The shares that are purchasable during 1985 represent executive compensation for 1983, 1984, and 1985. If options for shares are not exercised during either year, they lapse as of the end of that year.

Options were granted to the officers of Siska on January 1, 1983, and at that time the option price was set for all shares at $30. During 1985, all options were exercised. During 1986, however, options for only 27,000 shares were exercised. The remaining options lapsed because the executives decided not to exercise them. Average issuance price of the shares was $10. The market prices of Siska common at various dates follows:

Dates	Market Price of Siska's Common
Option agreement accepted by shareholders	$32
Options granted	35
Options exercised in 1985	37
Options exercised in 1986	33

Instructions

Make any necessary journal entries related to this stock option for the following years: 1982, 1983, 1985, and 1986. (Siska closes its books on December 31.)

E17-11 On January 1, 1983, Bowie, Inc. granted stock options to officers and key employees for the purchase of 20,000 shares of the company's no-par common at $25 per share. The options were exercisable by grantees still in the employ of the company within a five-year period beginning January 1, 1985, and expiring December 31, 1989. The market price of Bowie's common was $33 per share at the date of grant. Bowie prepares a formal journal entry to record this award. The service period for this award is two years.

On April 1, 1984, 2,000 option shares were terminated when the employees resigned from the company. The market value of the common was $35 per share on this date.

On March 31, 1985, 12,000 option shares were exercised when the market value of the common was $40 per share.

Instructions

Prepare journal entries to record issuance of the stock options, termination of the stock options, exercise of the stock options, and charges to compensation expense, for the years ended December 31, 1983, 1984, and 1985.

(AICPA adapted)

E17-12 Mr. Max Rexroad has recently been elected president of CJO Company. As an incentive for Mr. Rexroad to become president, the company offered him the following pay package: (1) a salary of $85,000 per year, (2) an expense allowance of $16,000 per year, and (3) the right to purchase 5,000 no-par common shares at $10 per share; the current market price is $16 per share.

Instructions

(a) What entry is needed to record the granting of these stock options to Mr. Rexroad?

(b) Assume that the stock options had the following restriction attached: Mr. Rexroad must remain an employee of the company for three years before he is entitled to the shares. Consultation with investment bankers suggests that the value of these restricted shares is $14. What entry is needed to record the granting of these stock options to Mr. Rexroad?

E17-13 On December 31, 1984, Martin Bubley Soap Company issues 150,000 stock appreciation rights to its officers, entitling them to receive cash for the difference between the market price of its shares and a pre-established price of $10. The date of exercise is December 31, 1988. The market price fluctuates as follows: Dec. 31, 1985—$14; Dec. 31, 1986—$8; Dec. 31, 1987—$20; Dec. 31, 1988—$18. Rights are exercisable only if the officer is employed by the company at the date of exercise.

Instructions

(a) Prepare a schedule that shows the amount of compensation expense allocable to each year affected by the stock appreciation rights plan.

(b) Prepare the entry at Dec. 31, 1988, to record compensation expense, if any, in 1988.

(c) Prepare the entry on Dec. 31, 1988, assuming that all 150,000 SARs are exercised by all of the eligible officers.

E17-14 J. Brauer Company establishes a stock appreciation rights program that entitles its new president, Kay Roddick, to receive cash for the difference between the market price of the shares and a pre-established price of $30 (also market price) on December 31, 1985, on 30,000 SARs. The date of grant is December 31, 1985, and the required employment (service) period is 3 years. President Roddick exercises all of the SARs in 1991. The market value of the stock fluctuates as follows: Dec. 31, 1986—$36; Dec. 31, 1987—$39; Dec. 31, 1988—$45; Dec. 31, 1989—$36; Dec. 31, 1990—$48.

Instructions

(a) Prepare a five-year (1986-1990) schedule of compensation expense pertaining to the 30,000 SARs granted President Roddick.

(b) Prepare the journal entry for compensation expense in 1986, 1989, and 1990 relative to the 30,000 SARs.

E17-15 Hallmark Co. had 100,000 shares outstanding on January 1 and reacquired 24,000 shares on March 1.

Instructions

What is the weighted average number of shares outstanding:

(a) For the quarter ending March 31?

(b) For the six months ending June 30?

(c) For the year ending December 31?

E17-16 Subscription TV Company had 240,000 shares of common stock outstanding on December 31, 1986. During the year 1987 the company issued 12,000 shares on May 1 and retired 24,000 shares on October 31. For the year 1987, Subscription TV Company reported net income of $372,000 after a casualty loss of $62,000 (net of tax).

Instructions

What earnings per share data should be reported in the financial statements, assuming that the casualty loss is extraordinary?

E17-17 Barrel Winery, Inc. presented the following data:

Net income	$ 5,700,000
Preferred shares: 100,000 no-par shares outstanding, $7 cumulative, not convertible	10,000,000
Common shares: Outstanding Jan. 1	1,800,000
Issued for cash, May 1	900,000
Acquired treasury shares for cash, Aug. 1, two-for-one stock split, Oct. 1	240,000

Instructions

Compute earnings per share.

E17-18 A portion of the combined statement of income and retained earnings of Dave Murray, Inc. for the current year follows:

Income before extraordinary item		$ 17,000,000
Extraordinary loss, net of applicable income tax (Note 1)		1,700,000
Net income		15,300,000
Retained earnings at the beginning of the year		99,162,700
		114,462,700
Dividends declared:		
On preferred shares—$6.00 per share	$ 300,000	
On common shares—$1.75 per share	14,000,000	14,300,000
Retained earnings at the end of the year		$100,162,700

Note 1. During the year, Dave Murray, Inc. suffered a major casualty loss of $1,700,000 after applicable income tax reduction of $1,450,000.

At the end of the current year, Dave Murray, Inc. has outstanding 8,000,000 shares of no-par common and 50,000 shares of $6 preferred.

On April 1 of the current year, Dave Murray, Inc. issued 1,000,000 common shares for $32 per share to help finance the casualty.

Instructions

Compute the earnings per share on common for the current year as it should be reported to shareholders.

E17-19   On January 1, 1986, Pelzer Industries had shares outstanding as follows:

$5 Cumulative no-par preferred shares, issued and outstanding 8,000 shares.	$ 800,000
Common shares, no-par value, issued and outstanding 250,000 shares.	2,500,000

To acquire the net assets of three smaller companies, Pelzer authorized the issuance of an additional 160,000 common shares. The acquisitions took place as follows:

Date of Acquisition		Shares Issued
Company A	April 1, 1986	100,000
Company B	July 1, 1986	40,000
Company C	October 1, 1986	20,000

On May 14, 1986, Pelzer realized a $90,000 insurance gain on the expropriation of investments originally purchased in 1975.

On December 31, 1986, Pelzer recorded net income of $300,000 before tax and exclusive of the gain.

Instructions

Assuming a 50% tax rate, compute the earnings per share data that should appear on the financial statements of Pelzer Industries as of December 31, 1986. Assume that the expropriation is extraordinary.

E17-20   At January 1, 1986, H. R. Ford Company's outstanding shares included:

150,000 shares of no-par value, $6 cumulative preferred
1,000,000 shares of no-par value common

Net income for 1986 was $2,584,500. No cash dividends were declared or paid during 1986. On February 15, 1987, however, all preferred dividends in arrears were paid, together with a 5% stock dividend on common shares. There were no dividends in arrears prior to 1986.

On April 1, 1986, 400,000 shares of common were sold for $10 per share and on October 1, 1986, 120,000 shares of common stock were purchased for $20 per share and held as treasury stock.

Instructions

Compute earnings per share for 1986. Assume that financial statements for 1986 were issued in March, 1987.

E17-21   In 1985, C. Blough Enterprises issued, at par, 40 $500, 8% bonds, each convertible into 100 shares of no-par common. Blough had revenues of $12,400 and expenses other than interest and taxes of $7,600 for 1986. (Assume that the tax rate is 40%.) Throughout 1986, 2,000 shares of common were outstanding; none of the bonds was converted or redeemed.

Instructions

(a)   Compute earnings per share for 1986.

(b)   Assume the same facts as those assumed for (a), except that the 40 bonds were issued on October 1, 1986 (rather than in 1985), and none have been converted or redeemed.

(c)   Assume the same facts as assumed for (a), except that 20 of the 40 bonds were actually converted on July 1, 1986.

E17-22   On June 1, 1983, Pacioli Company and Wm. Paton Company merged to form PWP Inc. A total of 900,000 shares were issued to complete the merger. The new corporation reports on a calendar-year basis.

On April 1, 1985, the company issued an additional 200,000 common shares for cash. All 1,100,000 shares were outstanding on December 31, 1985.

PWP Inc. also issued $500,000 of 20-year, 8% convertible bonds at par on July 1, 1985. Each $1,000 bond converts to 40 shares of common at any interest date after January 1, 1998. None of the bonds has been converted to date.

PWP Inc. is preparing its annual report for the fiscal year ending December 31, 1985. The annual report will show earnings per share figures based upon a reported after-tax net income of $840,000. (The tax rate is 40%.)

Instructions

(a) Should PWP Inc. convertible bonds be treated in the calculation of earnings per share? Explain your answer.

(b) Without prejudice to your answer in (a), assume that the convertible bonds are not to be treated as dilutive securities. Determine for 1985:

    1. The number of shares to be used for calculating:
      a. Basic earnings per share.
      b. Fully diluted earnings per share.
    2. The earnings figures to be used for calculating:
      a. Basic earnings per share.
      b. Fully diluted earnings per share.

(CMA adapted)

E17-23 A. Lowes Dickinson's net income for 1986 is $40,000. The only potentially dilutive securities outstanding were 2,000 options issued during 1985, each exercisable for one share at $5. None has been exercised, and 10,000 shares of common were outstanding during 1986. Assume an aftertax rate of return of 10%.

Instructions

(a) Compute the relevant earnings per share amounts. (Round to nearest cent.)

(b) Assume the same facts as those assumed for (a), except that the 2,000 options were issued on November 1, 1986 (rather than in 1985).

E17-24 Zett Steel, Inc. indicates that its net income for 1986 is $20,100,000, which includes a gain on casualty (net of tax) of $1,800,000. Its capital structure includes some common shares reserved under employee stock options (114,000 shares). The common shares outstanding for the year remained at 6,600,000. The controller, Tony Zett, asks your advice concerning the earnings per share figure that they should present. The option price for the stock options is $32 per share.

Instructions

What would you tell the controller? (Assume that the gain is extraordinary.)

E17-25 Phil & Bailey Corporation earned $200,000 during a period when it had an average of 60,000 common shares outstanding. Also outstanding were 16,000 warrants that could be exercised to purchase one share of common for $15 for each warrant exercised. During the past five years, the company has earned a return of 10% before taxes of 40%.

Instructions

(a) Are the warrants dilutive?

(b) Compute basic earnings per share.

(c) Compute fully diluted earnings per share.

PROBLEMS

P17-1 The shareholders' equity section of R. H. Montgomery, Inc. at the beginning of the current year appears below:

Common shares, no-par value, authorized 500,000 shares, 100,000 shares issued and outstanding	$2,400,000
Retained earnings	380,000

During the current year the following transactions occurred:

1. The company issued to the shareholders 100,000 rights. Ten rights are needed to buy one share at $32. The rights were void after 30 days. The market price of the shares at this time was $34 per share.

2. The company sold to the public a $200,000, 10% bond issue at par. The company also issued with each $100 bond one detachable stock purchase warrant, which provided for the purchase of common at $28 per share. Shortly after issuance, the similar bonds without warrants were selling at 96 and the warrants at $8.

3. All but 10,000 of the rights issued in (1) were exercised in 30 days.

4. At the end of the year, 50% of the warrants in (2) had been exercised, and the remaining were outstanding and in good standing.

5. During the current year, the company granted stock options for 3,000 common shares to company executives. The market price of the shares on that date was $40 and the option price was $30. The options were to expire at year-end and were considered compensation for the current year.

6. All but 500 shares related to the stock option plan were exercised by year-end. The expiration resulted because one of the executives failed to fulfill an obligation related to the employment contract.

Instructions

    (a) Prepare general journal entries for the current year to record the transactions listed above.

    (b) Prepare the shareholders' equity section of the balance sheet at the end of the current year. Assume that retained earnings at the end of the current year is $680,000.

P17-2 A. C. Littleton Company issued $2,000,000 of convertible 10-year bonds on July 1, 1985. The bonds provide for 10% interest payable semiannually on January 1 and July 1. Expense and discount in connection with the issue was $39,000, which is being amortized monthly on a straight-line basis.

    The bonds are convertible after one year into eight shares of Littleton Company's no-par value common for each $1,000 of bonds.

    On August 1, 1986, $200,000 of bonds were turned in for conversion into common. Interest has been accrued monthly and paid as due. At the time of conversion any accrued interest on bonds being converted is paid in cash.

Instructions

Prepare the journal entries to record the conversion, amortization, and interest in connection with the bonds as of:

    (a) August 1, 1986.

    (b) August 31, 1986.

    (c) December 31, 1986, including closing entries for end of year.

                             (AICPA adapted)

P17-3 Steven Elbert Company adopted a stock option plan on November 30, 1984, that provided that 60,000 shares of no-par value common be designated as available for the granting of options to officers of the corporation at a price of $8 a share. The market value was $12 a share on November 30, 1984.

    On January 2, 1985, options to purchase 24,000 shares were granted to President Larry Mohrweis—12,000 for services to be rendered in 1985 and 12,000 for services to be rendered in 1986. Also on that date, options to purchase 12,000 shares were granted to Vice-President Karen Mortensen—4,000 for services to be rendered in 1985 and 8,000 for services to be rendered in 1986. The market value of the stock was $14 a share on January 1, 1985. The options were exercisable for a period of one year following the year in which the services were rendered.

    In 1986 neither the president nor the vice-president exercised their options because the market price of the stock was below the exercise price. The market value of the stock was $6 a share on December 31, 1986, when the options for 1985 services lapsed.

On December 31, 1987, both President Mohrweis and Vice-President Mortensen exercised their options for 12,000 and 8,000 shares, respectively, when the market price was $16 a share.

Instructions

(a) Prepare the necessary journal entries in 1984 when the stock option plan was adopted; in 1985 when options were granted; in 1986 when options lapsed; and in 1987 when options were exercised.

(b) What disclosure of the stock option plan should appear in the financial statements at December 31, 1984? At December 31, 1985? Assume that the stock options outstanding or exercised at any time are a significant financial item.

P17-4 As auditor for Search & Find, you have been assigned to check Cloudy Corporation's computation of earnings per share for the current year. The controller has supplied you with the following computations:

Net income	$3,413,928
Common shares issued and outstanding	
Beginning of year	1,204,761
End of year	1,004,901
Average	1,104,831
Earnings per share	

$$\frac{\$3,413,918}{1,104,831} = \$3.09 \text{ per share}$$

You have developed the following additional information:

1. There are no other equity securities in addition to the common shares.
2. There are no options or warrants outstanding to purchase common shares.
3. There are no convertible debt securities.
4. Activity in common shares during the year was as follows:

	1,204,761
Outstanding, Jan. 1	1,203,761
Treasury shares acquired, Oct. 1	(300,000)
	904,761
Shares reissued, Dec. 1	100,140
Outstanding, Dec. 31	1,004,901

Instructions

(a) On the basis of the information above, do you agree with the controller's computation of earnings per share for the year? If you disagree, prepare a revised computation of earnings per share.

(b) Assume the same facts as those in (a), except that options had been issued to purchase 150,000 shares of common at $10 per share. These options were outstanding at the beginning of the year and none had been exercised or cancelled during the year. The company earns a rate of return of 10% after taxes.

P17-5 Beams Nursery Company had the following account titles on its December 31, 1986, trial balance:

$14 cumulative convertible preferred shares
Common shares, no-par value
Retained earnings

The following additional information about the Beams Nursery Company was available for the year ended December 31, 1986:

1. 1,500,000 shares of preferred were authorized, of which 1,000,000 were outstanding. All 1,000,000 shares outstanding were issued on January 2, 1983, for $110 a share. Preferred shares are convertible into common shares on a one-for-one basis until

December 31, 1992; thereafter the preferred shares cease to be convertible and are callable at $100 per share by the company. No preferred shares have been converted into common, and there were no dividends in arrears at December 31, 1986.

2. Of the 5,500,000 common shares authorized, there were 3,900,000 outstanding at January 1, 1986. The market price of the outstanding common stock has increased slowly, but consistently, for the last five years.

3. The company has an employee stock option plan under which certain key employees and officers may purchase common shares at 100% of the market price at the date of the option grant. All options are exercisable in instalments of one-third each year, commencing one year after the date of the grant, and expire if not exercised within four years of the grant date. On January 1, 1986, options for 76,000 shares were outstanding at prices ranging from $47 to $83 a share. Options for 22,000 shares were exercised at $47 to $79 a share during 1986. No options expired during 1986, and additional options for 16,000 shares were granted at $86 a share during the year. The 70,000 options outstanding at December 31, 1986, were exercisable at $54 to $86 a share; of these, 32,500 were exercisable at that date at prices ranging from $54 to $79 a share.

4. The company also has an employee stock purchase plan under which the company pays one-half and the employee pays one-half of the market price of the stock at the date of the subscription. During 1986, employees subscribed to 65,000 shares at an average price of $87 a share. All 65,000 shares were paid for and issued late in September, 1986.

5. On December 31, 1986, a total of 400,000 shares of common were set aside for the granting of future stock options and for future purchases under the employee stock purchase plan. The only changes in the shareholders' equity for 1986 were those described above, 1986 net income, and cash dividends paid.

Instructions

(a) Prepare the shareholders' equity section of the balance sheet of Beams Nursery Company at December 31, 1986, substituting, where appropriate, Xs for unknown dollar amounts. Use good form and provide full disclosure. Write appropriate footnotes as they should appear in the published financial statements.

(b) Explain how the amount of the denominator should be determined to compute basic earnings per share for presentation in the financial statements. Be specific as to the handling of each item. If additional information is needed to determine whether an item should be included or excluded or the extent to which an item should be included, identify the information needed and how the item would be handled if the information were known. Assume Beams Nursery Company had substantial net income for the year ended December 31, 1986.

(AICPA adapted)

P17-6 The controller of Yukon Corporation has requested assistance in determining income, basic earnings per share, and fully diluted earnings per share for presentation in the company's income statement for the year ended September 30, 1987. As currently calculated, the company's net income is $700,000 for fiscal year 1986-1987. The controller has indicated that the income figure might be adjusted for the following transactions that were recorded by charges or credits directly to retained earnings. (The amounts are net of applicable income taxes.)

1. The sum of $280,000, applicable to a breached 1983 contract, was received as a result of a lawsuit. Prior to the award, legal counsel was uncertain about the outcome of the suit.

2. A gain of $300,000 was realized from an expropriation settlement (extraordinary).

3. A "gain" of $165,000 was realized on the sale of treasury shares.

4. A special inventory write-off of $190,000 was made, of which $120,000 applied to goods manufactured prior to October 1, 1986.

★ 5. The average <u>after-tax</u> return on assets is 10%. *for warrants.*

Your working papers disclose the following opening balances and transactions in the company's share capital accounts during the year:

1. Common shares (at October 1, 1986, no-par value, authorized 450,000 shares; effective December 1, 1986, no-par value, authorized 900,000 shares):
    Balance, October 1, 1986—issued and outstanding 90,000 shares.
    December 1, 1986—90,000 shares issued in a two-for-one stock split.
    December 1, 1986—420,000 shares issued at $39 per share.

2. Treasury shares—common:
    March 1, 1987—purchased 60,000 shares at $37.25 per share.
    April 1, 1987—sold 60,000 shares at $40 per share.

3. Stock purchase warrants, Series A (initially, each warrant was exchangeable with $60 for one common share; effective December 1, 1986, each warrant became exchangeable for two common shares at $30 per share):
    October 1, 1986—37,500 warrants issued at $6 each.

4. Stock purchase warrants, Series B (each warrant is exchangeable with $40 for one common share):
    April 1, 1987—30,000 warrants authorized and issued at $10 each.

5. First mortgage bonds, 9%, due 2000 (nonconvertible; priced to yield 8% when issued):
    Balance, October 1986—authorized, issued, and outstanding—the face value of $2,100,000.

6. Convertible debentures, 7%, due 2006 (initially, each $1,000 bond was convertible at any time until maturity into 12 1/2 common shares; effective December 1, 1986, the conversion rate became 25 shares for each bond):
    October 1, 1986—authorized and issued at their face value (no premium or discount) of $3,600,000.

Instructions

(a) Prepare a schedule computing net income as it should be presented in the company's income statement for the year ended September 30, 1987.

(b) Assuming that net income after income taxes for the year was $1,087,200 and that there were no extraordinary items, prepare a schedule computing (1) the basic earnings per share and (2) the fully diluted earnings per share that should be presented in the company's income statement for the year ended September 30, 1987. A supporting schedule computing the numbers of shares to be used in these computations should also be prepared. (Assume an income tax rate of 48% with no surcharge.)

(AICPA adapted)

P17-7 On February 1, 1986, when your audit and report are nearly complete, Joan Clay, the president of Clay Toy Corporation, asks you to prepare statistical schedules of comparative financial data for the past five years for inclusion in the company's annual report. Your working papers reveal the following information.

1. Income statements show net income amounts as follows:

    1981—$38,000
    1982— (40,000) (loss)
    1983— 50,000
    1984— 76,000
    1985— 98,000

2. On January 1, 1981, there were outstanding 2,000 no-par value common shares, and 1,000 shares of $3 cumulative preferred stock, no-par value.

3. A $5 dividend was paid in common stock to common shareholders on December 31, 1982. The fair market value was $145 per share at the time.

4. Eight hundred common shares were issued on March 31, 1983, to purchase another company. (The transaction was accounted for as a purchase, not a pooling of interests; use the weighted-average approach for purchase of a business.)

5. A dividend of cumulative preferred shares was distributed to common shareholders on July 1, 1983. One preferred share was distributed for every five common shares held. The fair market value of the preferred was $56 per share before the distribution and $54 per share immediately after the distribution.

6. Common shares were split two-for-one on December 31, 1984, and again on December 31, 1985.

7. Cash dividends are paid on preferred shares on June 30 and December 31. Preferred share dividends were paid in each year except 1982; the 1982 and 1983 dividends were paid in 1983.

8. Cash dividends on common shares are paid on June 30 and December 31. Dividends paid per outstanding share of common at the respective dates were:

1981	$ .50	$ .50
1982	None	None
1983	.75	.75
1984	1.00	.50[a]
1985	.75	.75[b]

[a]After two-for-one split.
[b]Before two-for-one split.

Instructions

(a) In connection with your preparation of the statistical schedule of comparative financial data for the past five years:

1. Prepare a schedule computing the number of common shares and preferred shares outstanding as of the respective year-end dates.

2. Prepare a schedule computing the current equivalent number of common shares outstanding as of the respective year-end dates. The current equivalent shares means the weighted average number of shares outstanding in the respective prior periods after restatement for stock splits and stock dividends.

3. Compute the total cash dividends paid to holders of preferred shares and to holders of common shares for each of the five years.

(b) Prepare a five-year summary of financial statistics to be included in the annual report. The summary should show by years "Net Income (or Loss)," "Basic Earnings Per Share," and "Cash Dividends Per Common Share."

(AICPA adapted)

P17-8 The shareholders' equity section of Seville Company's balance sheet as of December 31, 1986, contains the following:

$2.00 cumulative convertible preferred shares; authorized 1,600,000 shares, issued 1,400,000; converted to common 750,000, and outstanding 650,000 shares; involuntary liquidation value, $30 a share, aggregating $19,500,000	$16,250,000
Common shares, no-par value; authorized 15,000,000 shares, issued and outstanding 9,200,000 shares	2,300,000
Contributed surplus	30,500,000
Retained earnings	45,050,000
Total shareholders' equity	$94,100,000

On April 1, 1986, Seville Company acquired the business and assets and assumed the liabilities of Lockhart Corporation in a transaction accounted for as a pooling of interests. For each of Lockhart Corporation's 2,400,000 no-par value common shares outstanding, the owner received one share of Seville Company common. (**Hint:** In a pooling of interests, shares are considered outstanding for the entire year.)

Included in the liabilities of Seville Company are 10% convertible subordinated debentures issued at their face value of $20,000,000 in 1985. The debentures are due in 2000 and until then are convertible into the common shares of Seville Company at the rate of five shares of common for each $100 debenture. To date none of these has been converted.

On April 2, 1986, Seville Company issued 1,400,000 shares of convertible preferred shares at $40 per share. Quarterly dividends to December 31, 1986, have been paid on these shares. The preferred is convertible into common stock at the rate of two shares of common for each share of preferred. On October 1, 1986, 150,000 shares and on November 1, 1986, 600,000 shares of the preferred were converted into common shares.

During July, 1985, Seville Company granted options to its officers and key employees to purchase 600,000 shares of the company's common at a price of $20 a share. The options do not become exercisable until 1987.

During 1986, dividend payments and average market prices of the Seville common shares were:

	Dividend Per Share	Average Market Price Per Share
First quarter	$.11	$25
Second quarter	.13	30
Third quarter	.15	20
Fourth quarter	.12	25
Average for the year		25

The December 31, 1986, closing price of the common was $25 a share.

Seville Company's consolidated net income for the year ended December 31, 1986, was $11,400,000. The provision for income taxes was computed at a rate of 48% and the after-tax rate of return was 10%.

Instructions

(a) Prepare a schedule that shows for 1986 the computation of:

1. The weighted average number of shares for computing basic earnings per share.

2. The weighted average number of shares for computing fully diluted earnings per share.

(b) Prepare a schedule that shows for 1986 the computation to the nearest cent of:

1. Basic earnings per share.
2. Fully diluted earnings per share.

(AICPA adapted)

18

INVESTMENTS—TEMPORARY AND LONG-TERM

In order to engage in the production and sale of goods or services, a business enterprise must invest funds in many types of assets: monetary assets (cash and receivables); productive tangible assets (inventories, plant and equipment, and land); and intangible assets (patents, licences, trademarks, and goodwill). Sound financial management requires not only that cash and other assets be available when needed in the business, but also that cash and near cash assets not immediately needed in the conduct of regular operations be invested advantageously in a variety of securities and other assets. In many cases, transactions involving investments result in a considerable amount of revenue in addition to that derived from regular operations. The problems of accounting for investments involve the classification, measurement, and disclosure of the accounting methods used.

Investments are classified as either temporary (current) or long-term (noncurrent). This chapter covers both temporary and long-term investments and is divided into three sections. The first presents accounting for temporary investments (both debt and equity); the second covers accounting for long-term investments (both debt and equity); and the third discusses accounting for and reporting the cash surrender value of life insurance and special-purpose funds.

TEMPORARY INVESTMENTS

Temporary investments ordinarily consist of **short-term paper** (certificates of deposit, treasury bills, and commercial paper), **marketable debt securities** (government and corporate bonds), and **marketable equity securities** (preferred and common shares) acquired with cash not immediately needed in operations. The investments are held temporarily in place of cash and can be readily converted to cash when current financing needs make such conversion desirable. Temporary investments must be:

1. Readily marketable.
2. Intended to be converted into cash as needed within one year or the operating cycle, whichever is longer.

''Readily marketable'' means that the security can be sold quite easily. For example, if the shares are closely held (not publicly traded), there may be no market or a limited market at best for the security, and its classification as a long-term investment may be more appropriate. ''Intent to convert'' is an extremely difficult principle to apply in practice. Generally, intention to convert is substantiated when the invested cash is considered a contingency fund to be used whenever a need arises or when investment is made from cash temporarily idle because of the seasonality of the business. In classifying investments, management's expressed intent should be supported by rational argumentation and related evidence, such as the history of investment activities, events subsequent to the balance sheet date, and the nature and purpose of the investment.

In contrast, long-term investments are purchased as part of some long-range program or plan such as for long-term appreciation in the price of the security, ownership for control purposes, or maintaining or enhancing supplier or customer relationships.

Marketable Securities

Marketable securities consist of **marketable equity securities** and **marketable debt securities**. Accounting for these two kinds of investments differs as a result of the way that income is earned on each. Most equity securities generate dividend income, debt securities earn interest, and both types give rise to market gains or losses.

An **equity security** is ''any instrument representing ownership shares (for example, common and preferred) or the right to acquire (for example, warrants, rights, and call options) or dispose of (for example, put options) ownership shares in an enterprise at fixed or determinable prices.''[1] Treasury stock (shares of the company's own stock) and convertible bonds are excluded.

Acquisition of Marketable Equity Securities

Investments in marketable equity securities, like other assets, are recorded at cost when acquired. Cost includes the purchase price and such incidental acquisition costs as brokerage commissions and taxes.

---

[1]''Accounting for Certain Marketable Securities,'' *Statement of Financial Accounting Standards No. 12* (Stamford, Conn.: FASB, 1975), par. 7(a).

"Cost" is not specifically defined in the *CICA Handbook*. Some argue that it is "acquisition cost" as defined above. Others believe that it is acquisition cost less subsequent write-downs made on recognition of a permanent impairment in value or resulting from transfers between current and noncurrent classifications. A third opinion holds that cost is acquisition cost reduced by the sum of the periodic adjustments necessary to reduce the carrying value to the lower of cost and market. The following discussion follows the second of the above viewpoints.

Accounting for Changes in Market Value—Marketable Equity Securities

A single share or unit of a marketable equity security has a **market price**, which when multiplied by the number of shares or units of that specific security produces the aggregate market price referred to as the **market value**. The market price generally changes as transactions involving the security occur. The central issue for many years has been: To what extent should the financial statements reflect the changes in market value of marketable securities?

The CICA resolved this issue in relation to marketable securities by requiring that **when the market value of temporary investments has declined below the carrying value, they should be carried at market value.**[2] (Losses associated with write-downs to the lower of cost and market are not allowable for tax purposes.) Valuing securities at the lower of cost and market may be applied to the entire portfolio or to each security in the portfolio. When it is applied to the portfolio (the preferred method), then the amount by which aggregate cost exceeds market value (the net unrealized loss) of the short-term marketable equity securities portfolio should be accounted for as the "valuation allowance" and the unrealized loss reported in the determination of net income for the period. If, on the other hand, the lower of cost and market method of valuation is applied to each security, then the sum of individual security excesses of cost over market value is reported as a valuation allowance. Further, realized gains and losses and changes in the valuation allowance for a marketable equity securities portfolio should be used in the determination of net income of the period in which they occur. These valuation adjustments are recorded as part of the adjustment process whenever statements are to be prepared. In subsequent periods, recoveries of market value are recognized to the extent that the market valuation does not exceed the lesser of original cost and original cost adjusted for any impairment. In substance, this procedure involves adjusting carrying values down to market at each reporting date, and up only to the extent that previous write-downs to market have been recovered. Thus, unrealized losses and recoveries on short-term marketable equity securities flow through the income statement.[3]

The following discussion illustrates application of the lower of cost and market method to marketable equity securities classified as current assets.

National Service Corporation made the following purchases of marketable equity

---

[2]*CICA Handbook*, Section 3010, par. 6.

[3]Specialized industries (investment companies, brokers and dealers in securities, stock life insurance companies, and fire and casualty insurance companies) that carry marketable equity securities at market do not have to follow lower of cost and market. As indicated earlier, the accounting treatment for noncurrent marketable equity securities is different and is discussed in the section on long-term investments later in this chapter.

securities as temporary investments during the year 1985, which is the first year in which National invested in marketable equity securities:

> February 23, 1985—Purchased 10,000 shares of Northeast Industries, Ltd. common at a market price of $51.50 per share plus brokerage commissions[4] of $4,400 (total cost, $519,400).
>
> April 10, 1985—Purchased 10,000 shares of Bell Soup Co. common at a market price of $31.50 per share plus brokerage commissions of $2,500 (total cost, $317,500).
>
> August 3, 1985—Purchased 5,000 shares of Reggies Pulp Co. common at a market price of $28 per share plus brokerage commissions of $1,350 (total cost, $141,350).

Each of the purchases above is recorded at total acquisition cost (market price plus commissions) by a debit to "Marketable Equity Securities" and a credit to Cash.

During the year National made the following security sale:

> September 23, 1985—Sold 5,000 shares of Northeast Industries, Inc. common at a market price of $58 per share less brokerage commissions of $2,780 (proceeds, $287,220).

On December 31, 1985, National Service Corporation determined the carrying value of its portfolio in short-term marketable equity securities to be:

Short-term marketable equity securities	Cost	Market	Unrealized Gain (Loss)
		December 31, 1985	
Northeast Industries, Inc.	$259,700	$275,000	$ 15,300
Bell Soup Co.	317,500	304,000	(13,500)
Reggies Pulp Co.	141,350	104,000	(37,350)
Total of portfolio	$718,550	$683,000	$(35,550)
Balance required in the valuation allowance			$(35,550)

Applying the lower of cost and market method to National's securities portfolio results in a carrying value of $683,000. The net unrealized loss of $35,550 represents the aggregate excess of cost over the market value of National's portfolio of marketable equity securities classified as current assets. The unrealized loss of $35,550 is recorded as follows:

December 31, 1985

Unrealized Loss on Valuation of Marketable Equity Securities	35,550	
Allowance for Excess of Cost of Marketable Equity Securities over Market Value		35,550
(To recognize a loss equal to the excess of cost over market value of marketable equity securities)		

The loss account appears on the income statement in the "Other Expenses and Losses" section and therefore would be included in income before extraordinary items in National's 1985 financial statements. The allowance account appears on

[4]Brokerage commissions are incurred both when buying and selling securities; such commissions generally range between 1% and 3% of trade value on lots of 1,000 or less and $12.50 to $30.00 per hundred shares on lots between 1,000 and 100,000 shares.

the balance sheet among current assets as an asset valuation (contra account) deducted from the portfolio cost of $718,550 to produce a carrying amount of its portfolio of $683,000.

During 1986, National made the following sale and purchase of marketable equity securities:

> March 22, 1986—Sold 5,000 shares of Reggies Pulp Co. common at a market price of $17.50 per share less brokerage commissions of $1,590 (proceeds, $85,910).
>
> July 2, 1986—Purchased 10,000 shares of James Bay Gas & Electric common at a market price of $20.25 per share plus brokerage commissions of $2,300 (total cost, $204,800).

On December 31, 1986, National Service Corporation determined the carrying value of its portfolio in short-term marketable equity securities to be:

	December 31. 1986		
Short-term marketable equity securities	Cost	Market	Unrealized Gain (Loss)
Northeast Industries, Inc.	$259,700	$312,500	$52,800
Bell Soup Co.	317,500	327,500	10,000
James Bay Gas & Electric	204,800	202,500	(2,300)
Total of portfolio	$782,000	$842,500	$60,500
Balance required in the valuation allowance			$ –0–

Applying the lower of cost and market method to National's portfolio at December 31, 1986, results in a carrying value of $782,000 and elimination of the balance in the valuation allowance account of $35,550. The adjustment of the valuation allowance is recorded as follows:

December 31, 1986

Allowance for Excess of Cost of Marketable Equity Securities over Market Value	35,550	
Recovery of Unrealized Loss on Valuation of Marketable Equity Securities		35,550
(To record a reduction in the valuation allowance due to increase in market value of the marketable equity securities portfolio classified as current assets)		

The Recovery of Unrealized Loss on Valuation of Marketable Equity Securities $35,550 is reported in the "Other Revenues and Gains" section and therefore would be included in income before extraordinary items on National's 1986 income statement.

Note that **the recovery is recognized only to the extent that unrealized losses were previously recognized.** That is, the write-down of $35,550 in 1985, representing net unrealized losses, may be reversed but only to the extent that the resulting carrying value of the portfolio does not exceed original cost or, in other words, to the extent that a balance exists in the valuation allowance account at the date of write-up. Also, note that **the valuation is applied to the total portfolio and not to individual securities.**

Under this approach, the reversal of the write-down does not represent a recognition of an unrealized gain. The unrealized gain is the excess of market value over cost, or the $60,500 net difference between aggregate cost and aggregate market value of National's portfolio on December 31, 1986. The write-down is viewed as establishing a valuation allowance representing the estimated reduction in the realizable value of the portfolio, and subsequent market increases are viewed as having reduced or eliminated the requirements for such an allowance. In other words, the reversal of the write-down represents a change in an accounting estimate of an unrealized loss.[5]

If National's investment portfolio of short-term marketable equity securities had suffered an additional loss of market value during 1986 instead of the increase described above, a loss would have been charged to 1986 and the valuation allowance would have been increased (credited) by the amount of the additional write-down.

If a marketable equity security is **transferred from the current to the noncurrent portfolio**, or *vice versa*, the security should be transferred at the lower of its cost and market value at the date of transfer. If market value is less than cost, the market value becomes the new cost basis, and the difference is accounted for as if it were a realized loss and included in the determination of net income.[6] This procedure has the effect of accounting for an unrealized loss at the date of transfer in the same manner as if it had been realized, thus reducing the incentive to manipulate income by transferring securities between the current and noncurrent portfolios.

Disposition of Marketable Equity Securities

Marketable securities are sold when cash needs develop or when good investment management dictates a change in the securities held. The owner who sells the securities incurs such costs as brokerage commissions and receives only the net proceeds for the sale. The difference between the net proceeds from the sale of a marketable equity security and its cost represents the **realized gain or loss**. At the date of sale no regard is given to unrealized losses or recoveries or the amount accumulated in the valuation allowance account because the valuation allowance relates to the total portfolio and not to specific security holdings.

For example, in the previous illustration National Service Corporation sold 5,000 shares of Northeast Industries, Inc. common on September 23, 1985, for $58 per share, incurring $2,780 in brokerage commissions. The gain on the sale is computed as follows:

Gross selling price of 5,000 shares @ $58	$290,000
Less: Commissions	2,780
Net proceeds from sale	287,220
Cost of 5,000 shares ($519,400 ÷ 2)	259,700
Gain on sale	$ 27,520

[5]This method has been adopted in the United States by *FASB Statement No. 12*, par. 29(c).

[6]*Ibid.*, par. 10.

The sale is recorded as follows:

September 23, 1985

Cash	287,220	
Marketable Equity Securities		259,700
Realized Gain on Sale of Marketable Equity Securities		27,520
(To record sale of 5,000 shares of Northeast Industries common held as a temporary investment at a gain)		

National Service Corporation also sold 5,000 shares of Reggies Pulp Co. on March 22, 1986, for $17.50 per share, incurring $1,590 in brokerage commissions. The loss on the sale is computed as follows:

Cost of 5,000 shares		$141,350
Gross proceeds from sale	$87,500	
Less: Commissions	1,590	
Net proceeds from sale		85,910
Loss on sale		$ 55,440

As in the 1985 security sale, the amount of net proceeds from the 1986 sale of securities is compared with the original cost to determine the gain or loss and recorded as follows:

March 22, 1986

Cash	85,910	
Realized Loss on Sale of Marketable Equity Securities	55,440	
Marketable Equity Securities		141,350
(To record the sale of 5,000 shares of Reggies Pulp Co. common held as a temporary investment)		

The presence or absence of realized gains or losses recorded since the last portfolio valuation as a result of sales of marketable equity securities has no effect upon the method of computing the lower of cost and market for the remaining portfolio at the end of the period.

Valuation at Market

The use of the lower of cost and market and discontinuance of original cost as the carrying amount of a current asset portfolio of marketable equity securities is quite firmly established in Canadian practice. Using original cost as the basis when the market value of the portfolio is lower has the effect of deferring unrealized losses on the basis of the expectation of a future recovery in market value, which may or may not occur.

However, many accountants are unhappy with Section 3010 of the *CICA Handbook*. They argue that market value, whether higher or lower than cost, should be recognized in the accounts. It is considered inconsistent to reduce the carrying value of the securities to an amount below cost without increasing their carrying value when market value is above cost. **Market value proponents indicate that gains or losses develop when the value of the investments change and not when the investments are sold**. Recognition of losses only is conservative and does not reflect the underlying economics when prices increase.

A major objection to the use of market value is that fluctuations in earnings result as the market price of the equity securities changes. To illustrate, at one time Leaseway Transportation estimated that the use of market value in one year would have reduced earnings 28%, but that the use of market value a year later would have increased earnings approximately 21%. Most companies dislike these types of fluctuations in earnings because they have little control over these changes.

Recognition of impairment as opposed to improvement in the carrying amount of a securities portfolio is still the dominant attitude of accounting. As a result, it is not surprising that the profession adopted a compromise position between market valuation and historical cost (lower of cost and market). The following rationale was given for not using market value alone as the determinant of carrying value: "Consideration of that alternative would raise pervasive issues concerning the valuation of other types of assets, including the concept of historical cost versus current or realizable value."[7]

Marketable Debt (Nonequity) Securities

Most Canadian companies have adopted the **lower of cost and market** method for debt securities that are readily marketable and are classified as current assets. Marketable debt securities, such as bonds, may be carried at lower of cost and market, and any unrealized loss may be charged to expense and a valuation allowance used to carry the credit. The unrealized loss can be recovered and credited to revenue in the same manner as that accorded the marketable equity securities.

The acquisition of debt securities is recorded at cost. If the debt securities are bonds purchased between interest dates, the accrued interest at the date of purchase is segregated from the acquisition cost and classified appropriately. For example, Western Publishing Company invested some of its excess cash in the bond market by purchasing $100,000 10% bonds at 86 on April 1, 1985, interest payable semiannually on July 1 and January 1. The brokerage commission associated with this purchase was $1,720. The cash outlay is:

Purchase price of bonds	$86,000
Commission	1,720
Cost of bonds acquired	87,720
Accrued interest January 1 to April 1 ($100,000 × 10% × 3/12)	2,500
Cash payment	$90,220

The journal entry to record this transaction is:

April 1, 1985

Marketable Debt Securities	87,720	
Interest Revenue (or Accrued Interest Receivable)	2,500	
Cash		90,220

Generally, the discount or premium on temporary bond investments is not recorded in the accounts and not amortized because the investment is ordinarily held for only a short time.

[7]FASB Statement No. 12, par. 29(a)

The journal entry to record the receipt of interest as of July 1 is as follows, assuming that Interest Revenue was originally debited at the time of purchase:

July 1, 1985

Cash	5,000	
Interest Revenue		5,000

When marketable debt securities are sold, the difference between the cost (or carrying value) and the selling price is recorded as a gain or loss. For example, if Western Publishing Company sold the bonds on November 1, 1985, at 98 plus accrued interest (purchased above on April 1, 1985), the computation of the gain would be as follows, assuming that commissions associated with the sale are $1,870:

Selling price of bonds (100 × $980)	$98,000
Less: Commissions	(1,870)
Net proceeds	96,130
Carrying amount of bonds	87,720
Gain on sale of bonds	$ 8,410

The journal entry to record this transaction is:

November 1, 1985

Cash	99,463	
Interest Revenue (100,000 × .10 × 4/12)		3,333
Marketable Debt Securities		87,720
Gain on Sale of Temporary Investment		8,410

The gain on sale enters into the determination of income from operations before extraordinary items. In cases where there are numerous purchases of similar securities, some flow assumption must be applied to match the proper cost with the proceeds of sale. For financial reporting purposes, average cost is recommended.

Financial Statement Disclosure of Temporary Investments

Marketable equity securities usually rank next to cash in liquidity and should be listed in the current asset section of the balance sheet (assuming that they are held as temporary investments) immediately after cash. Marketable equity securities that are held for other than liquidity and temporary investment purposes should not be classified as current assets.

As of the date of each balance sheet presented, the aggregate cost (carrying value) and the aggregate market value of marketable equity securities should be disclosed either in the body of the financial statements or in the accompanying notes. When classified balance sheets are presented, the aggregate cost and the aggregate market value should be disclosed, segregated between current and non-current assets.

Further, **significant** reductions in market value arising **after** the date of the financial statements, but prior to their issuance, that are applicable to marketable securities in the portfolio should be disclosed.

To illustrate, we will use the data from National Service Corporation's December 31, 1985, and December 31, 1986, portfolio valuations presented on pages 820 and 821, respectively. National's marketable equity securities might be presented in the financial statements and the notes thereto as shown on page 826.

BALANCE SHEET

| | December 31 | |
	1986	1985
Current assets:		
Marketable equity securities, carried at lower of cost and market (Note 2)	$782,000	$683,000

INCOME STATEMENT

| | Year Ended December 31 | |
	1986	1985
Income from operations	$ XXX	$ XXX
Other revenues and gains		
Realized gain on sale of marketable equity securities		27,520
Recovery of unrealized loss on valuation of marketable equity securities	35,550	
Other expenses and losses		
Realized loss on sale of marketable equity securities	(55,440)	
Unrealized loss on valuation of marketable equity securities		(35,550)
Income before extraordinary items	$ XXXXX	$ XXXXX

Note 2—**Marketable Equity Securities.** Marketable equity securities are carried at the lower of cost and market at the balance sheet date; that determination is made by aggregating all current marketable equity securities. Marketable equity securities included in current assets had a market value at December 31, 1986, of $842,500 and a cost at December 31, 1985, of $718,550.

LONG-TERM INVESTMENTS

This section is devoted primarily to long-term investments in corporate securities: bonds of various types, preferred shares, and common shares. Numerous other items are commonly classified as long-term investments: funds for bond retirement, stock redemption, and other special purposes; investments in notes receivable, mortgages, and similar debt instruments; and such miscellaneous items as advances to affiliates, cash surrender value of life insurance policies, interests in estates and trusts, equity in joint ventures and partnerships, and real estate held for appreciation or future use. Some of these items are also discussed. Long-term investments are usually presented on the balance sheet just below current assets in a separate section called Long-term Investments, Investments and Funds, or just Investments.

Although many reasons prompt a corporation to invest in the securities of another corporation, **the primary motive is to enhance its own income**. A corporation may thus enhance its income (1) directly through the receipt of dividends or interest from the investment or through appreciation in the market value of the securities, or (2) indirectly by creating and insuring desirable operating relationships between companies to improve income performance. Frequently the most permanent of investments are those in the latter category: those for improving income performance. Benefits to the investors are derived from the influence or control that may be exercised over a major supplier, customer, or otherwise related company. As an illustration, at one time Sears, Roebuck held large stock interests in several of its leading suppliers: 22% of Kellwood, 31% of DeSoto, 40% of Roper, and 59% of Universal Rundle Co.

Investments in Bonds

Accounting for bonds as a long-term liability was presented in Chapter 14. In this chapter our attention is on accounting for these same securities from the investor's viewpoint. The types and characteristics of bonds that may be purchased are presented on pages 641–643; you should reread that discussion as background for this chapter. The variety in these features, along with the variability in interest rates, permits investors to shop for exactly the investment that satisfies their safety, yield, and marketability preferences.

Accounting for Bond Acquisitions

Investment in bonds should be recorded on the date of acquisition at cost, which includes brokerage fees and any other costs incidental to the purchase. **The cost or purchase price of a bond investment is its market value, which is the product of the market's appraisal of the risk involved and consideration of the stated interest rate in comparison with the prevailing market (yield) rate of interest for that type of security**. The cash amount of interest to be received periodically is fixed by the stated rate of interest on the face value (also called principal, par, or maturity value). If the rate of return desired by the investors is exactly equal to the stated rate, **the bond will sell at its face amount**. If investors demand a higher yield than the stated rate offers, **the bond will sell at a discount**. Purchasing the bond at an amount below the face amount, or at a discount, equates the yield on the bond with the market rate of interest. If the market rate of interest is below the stated rate, **investors will pay a premium**, more than maturity value, for the bond. The relationship between bond market values and interest rates is similar to that discussed under the heading of bonds payable, pages 643–645.

If bonds are **purchased between interest payment dates**, the investor must pay the owner the market price plus the interest accrued since the last interest payment date. The investor will collect this interest plus the additional interest earned by holding the bond to the next interest date. For example, assume the purchase on June 1 of bonds having a $100,000 face value, and paying 12% interest on April 1 and October 1, for 97. The entry to record purchase of the bonds and accrued interest is as follows:

Investments in Bonds	97,000	
Interest Revenue (or Accrued Interest		
Receivable $100,000 × .12 × 2/12)	2,000	
Cash		99,000

On October 1 the investor will receive interest of $6,000 consisting of $2,000 paid at date of acquisition and $4,000 earned for holding the bond for four months.

Investments acquired at par, at a discount, or at a premium are generally recorded in the accounts at cost, including brokerage and other fees but excluding the accrued interest; generally they are not recorded at maturity value. The use of a separate discount or premium account as a valuation account is acceptable procedure, but in practice it has not been widely used. If the discount of $3,000 were recorded separately and the bond recorded at maturity value, the entry to record the investment in bonds would be as follows:

Investments in Bonds	100,000	
Interest Revenue	2,000	
Discount on Investments in Bonds		3,000
Cash		99,000

When the investment is recorded net of the discount, at $97,000 as in the first example, the discount is amortized by debit entries recorded directly to the Investments in Bonds account. When the investment is recorded at maturity value, at $100,000 as in the second example, the discount is amortized by debiting the Discount on Investments in Bonds account. Both methods produce exactly the same net results on the financial statements. The following illustrations record the investment net of discount or premium.

Computing Prices of Bond Investments

Theoretically, the market price of a bond is the present value (PV) of its maturity amount plus the present value of its interest payments, both discounted at the market rate of interest. Using this as a basis, the price that should be paid for $10,000 of 8% bonds, interest payable semiannually, and maturing in six years with a 10% effective yield, is computed as follows:

$$
\begin{aligned}
\text{Purchase price} &= \text{PV of maturity amount plus PV of interest payments} \\
&= \$10,000 \times p_{6|10\%} + \$400 \times P_{12|5\%} \\
&= \$10,000 \times .56447 \text{ (Table 6-2)} + \$400 \times 8.86325 \text{ (Table 6-4)} \\
&= \$5,644.70 + \$3,545.30 \\
&= (\$9,190.00)
\end{aligned}
$$

Amortization of Bond Premium and Bond Discount

As discussed in Chapter 14, there are two widely used methods of amortizing bond premium and bond discount: (1) **the straight-line method**, and (2) **the effective interest method** (also called the present value or compound interest or effective yield method). Both methods are illustrated below. The write-off of discount on bond investments is sometimes referred to as discount "accumulation" instead of "amortization."

Straight-line Amortization of Premium   Assume that on March 1, 1987, bonds of a face value of $50,000, bearing 8% interest payable January 1 and July 1, are purchased for $53,008 plus accrued interest. The bonds mature January 1, 1995. The entry on March 1, 1987, is:

Investments in Bonds	53,008.00	
Interest Revenue	666.67	
Cash		53,674.67

The accrued interest of $666.67 represents interest at 8% for two months on $50,000, the par value of the bonds purchased.

When six months' interest is received on July 1, 1987, premium allocable to four months is written off under the straight-line method by a credit to the Investments account, and the revenue is reduced accordingly. The premium amortized would be 4/94 of $3,008, or $128, because the bonds have been held for four months and because there are 94 months from the date of purchase to maturity date. The entry on July 1, 1987, therefore, is:

Cash	2,000	
Investments in Bonds ($3,008 × 4/94)		128
Interest Revenue		1,872

The Interest Revenue account now has a balance of $1,872 less $666.67, or $1,205.33. This represents the revenue earned on the bonds during the four months from March 1 to July 1. This amount is analyzed as follows:

Interest received on July 1, 1987, 8% × $50,000 × 6/12	$2,000.00
Deduct: Interest accrued on Mar. 1, 1987, date of purchase of bonds, 8% × $50,000 × 2/12	666.67
Interest received that is applicable to the 4 months from Mar. 1 to July 1	1,333.33
Deduct: Premium amortized for 4 months, 4/94 × $3,008	128.00
Revenue earned during the 4 months	$1,205.33

On December 31, 1987, an adjusting entry would be made to accrue six months' interest and to amortize the premium applicable to six months.

Interest Receivable on Bonds	2,000	
Investments in Bonds ($3,008 × 6/94)		192
Interest Revenue		1,808

The $192 credit to the Investments account represents the premium amortization for the six months from July 1 to December 31, or 6/94 of $3,008. The credit to Interest Revenue, $1,808, represents the difference between the interest receivable of $2,000 and the premium amortized of $192, or the net amount taken up as revenue for the six months ended December 31, 1987.

During the next year and during each succeeding year, a premium of $384, representing 12/94 of the total premium paid, will be amortized. Thus, by the maturity date the entire amount of the premium will have been removed from the Investments account, and the bonds will be carried on the books at par at that time. The entry to be made at the maturity date of the bonds will therefore be:

Cash	50,000	
Investments in Bonds		50,000

In the entries shown above, the premium was amortized simultaneously with the interest received or accrued. They do not have to be combined in one entry, however, or entered at the same time. The entries for interest received or receivable are made at the proper times independently of the entries for premium amortization. The proper amount of premium may be amortized at the end of each fiscal year or any other acceptable time by debiting Interest Revenue and crediting Investments in Bonds. In the example above, the recognition of accrued interest and amortization of premium in separate entries would be as follows:

Interest Receivable on Bonds	2,000	
Interest Revenue		2,000
Interest Revenue	192	
Investments in Bonds		192

Separate entries are convenient when reversing entries are used because the entry for accrued interest would be reversed but no reversing entry is needed for premium amortization.

Straight-line Amortization (Accumulation) of Discount   If bonds are purchased below par, the straight-line method of amortization is similar to that illustrated above for amortization of premium. For discount, however, the amount of discount amortized is added to the interest revenue.

Assume that bonds with a par value of $50,000, bearing 8% interest payable January 1 and July 1, and maturing January 1, 1995, are purchased on March 1, 1987, for $46,992 plus accrued interest. In other words, assume that they are purchased at a discount of $3,008 instead of a premium of $3,008, as above. Because they have 94 months yet to run, the discount to be amortized for each month is 1/94 of $3,008, or $32. The entry to record the purchase is:

Investments in Bonds	46,992.00	
Interest Revenue	666.67	
Cash		47,658.67

When six months' interest is received on July 1, 1987, the entry is:

Cash	2,000	
Investments in Bonds	128	
Interest Revenue		2,128

The credit to Interest Revenue is the total of the interest received and the discount amortized. The discount amortized is debited to the asset account; by maturity date the book value of the bonds will be at par.

Thus, bonds purchased at a premium are written down to par through amortization of premium, and bonds purchased at a discount are written up to par through amortization of the discount.

Effective Interest Method   As discussed in Chapter 14, when a premium or discount is amortized under the straight-line method, the rate of return is not the same year after year. Although the interest received is constant from period to period, the carrying amount of the bond is either increasing or decreasing by the amount of the discount or premium amortization. The straight-line method produces a constant revenue, but also produces a variable rate of return on the book value of the investment. Although the effective interest method results in a varying amount being recorded as interest revenue from period to period, its virtue is that it produces a constant rate of return on the book value of the investment from period to period.

The straight-line method is the more popular method because (1) it is simple to apply; (2) it avoids the computations necessary under the effective interest rate method; and (3) it produces results not significantly different from the effective interest earned, unless the maturity date is many years distant or the premium or discount is exceptionally large. The effective interest method is preferable; however, the straight-line method may be used if the results obtained are not significantly different from those produced by the effective interest method.

Although the computations for the effective interest method are more complex, given the increased use of microcomputers by accountants, the effective interest method is now used extensively.

The effective interest method is applied to bond investments in a fashion similar to that described for bonds payable. The effective interest rate or yield is computed at the time of investment and is applied to the beginning carrying (book) value of the investment for each interest period. In each period the carrying value of the investment is increased by the amortized discount or decreased by the amortized premium.

To illustrate, assume that the Robinson Company is the purchaser of the Evermaster Corporation bonds discussed in Chapter 14, page 649. To restate the situation, Robinson Company purchased $100,000 of 8% bonds of Evermaster Corporation on January 1, 1986, paying $92,278. The bonds mature January 1, 1991; interest is payable each July 1 and January 1. The discount of $7,722 ($100,000 minus $92,278) provided an effective interest yield of 10%. The schedule below discloses the effect of the discount amortization on the interest revenue recorded each period using the effective interest method of amortization if the bonds are held to maturity. The investment is carried in the accounts net of the unamortized discount.

		Schedule of Interest Revenue and Bond Discount Amortization—Effective Interest Method 8% Bonds Purchased to Yield 10%		
Date	Debit Cash	Credit Interest Revenue	Debit Bond Investment*	Carrying Value of Bonds
Jan. 1,1986				$ 92,278
Jul. 1,1986	$ 4,000[a]	$ 4,614[b]	$ 614[c]	92,892[d]
Jan. 1,1987	4,000	4,645	645	93,537
Jul. 1,1987	4,000	4,677	677	94,214
Jan. 1,1988	4,000	4,711	711	94,925
Jul. 1,1988	4,000	4,746	746	95,671
Jan. 1,1989	4,000	4,783	783	96,454
Jul. 1,1989	4,000	4,823	823	97,277
Jan. 1,1990	4,000	4,864	864	98,141
Jul. 1,1990	4,000	4,907	907	99,048
Jan. 1,1991	4,000	4,952	952	100,000
	$40,000	$47,722	$7,722	

[a]$4,000 = $100,000 × .08 × 6/12
[b]$4,614 = $92,278 × .10 × 6/12
[c]$614 = $4,614 − $4,000
[d]$92,892 = $92,278 + $614
*Or, debit Discount on Investments in Bonds if the investment is carried at maturity value.

The journal entry to record the receipt of the first semiannual interest payment on July 1, 1986, (as shown on the schedule) is:

Cash	4,000	
Investments in Bonds	614	
Interest Revenue		4,614

Sale of Bond Investments Before Maturity Date

If bonds carried as long-term investments are sold before maturity date, entries must be made to amortize the discount or premium to the date of sale and to remove from the Investments account the book value of bonds sold.

For example, assume that the bonds described on page 830 are sold on April 1, 1993, at 99 1/2 plus accrued interest. Discount has been amortized at the rate of $32 per month from March 1, 1987, through the last closing date, December 31, 1992. An entry is made to amortize discount for the three months that have expired in 1993:

Investments in Bonds	96	
Interest Revenue		96

The entry to record the sale is:

Cash	50,750	
Interest Revenue		1,000
Investments in Bonds		49,328
Gain on Sale of Bond Investment		422

The credit to Interest Revenue represents accrued interest for three months, for which the purchaser pays cash. The debit to Cash represents the selling price of the bonds, $49,750, plus the accrued interest of $1,000. The credit to the Investments account represents the book value of the bonds on the date of the sale, and the credit to Gain on Sale of Bonds represents the excess of the selling price over the book value of the bonds. The computation of the latter two credits is shown below:

Selling price of bonds (exclusive of accrued interest)		$49,750
Deduct book value of bonds on April 1, 1993:		
Cost	$46,992	
Add discount amortized for the period from		
March 1, 1987, to April 1, 1993, 73/94 × $3,008	2,336	49,328
Gain on sale		$ 422

Long-term Investments in Shares

Shares may be acquired in the market from a firm's shareholders, from the issuing corporation, or from stockbrokers. Shares may also be acquired directly from an issuing company or from a private investor. When shares are purchased outright for cash, the full cost includes the purchase price of the security plus brokers' commissions and other fees incidental to the purchase. If shares are **acquired "on margin"** (part of the cost is borrowed from the broker), the share purchase should be recorded at its full cost, and a liability recognized for the unpaid balance. A share **subscription** or agreement to buy the stock of a corporation is recognized by a charge to an asset account for the security to be received and a credit to a liability account for the amount to be paid. Any interest on an obligation arising from a share purchase should be recognized as expense.

Shares acquired in **exchange for noncash consideration** (property or services) should be recorded at (1) the fair market value of the consideration given or (2) the fair market value of the shares received, whichever is more clearly determinable.

The absence of clearly determinable values for the property or services or a market price for the security acquired may force the use of appraisals or estimates to arrive at a cost.

The purchase of two or more classes of securities for a **lump sum price** calls for the allocation of the cost to the different classes in some equitable manner. If market prices are available for each class of security, the lump sum cost may be apportioned on the basis of the **relative market values**. If the market price is available for one security but not for the other, the market price may be assigned to the one and the cost excess to the other. If market prices are not available at the date of acquisition of several securities, it may be necessary to defer cost apportionment until evidence of at least one value becomes available. In some instances cost apportionment may have to wait until one of the securities is sold. In such cases, the proceeds from the sale of the one security may be subtracted from the lump sum cost, leaving the residual cost to be assigned as the cost of the other.

Accounting for numerous purchases of securities requires that information regarding the cost of individual purchases be preserved, as well as the dates of purchases and sales. Average cost should be used for multiple purchases of the same security.

Effect of Ownership Interest

The extent to which one corporation (**investor**) acquires an interest in the common shares in another corporation (**investee**)—that is, the degree of ownership interest —generally determines the accounting treatment for the investment. Long-term investments by one corporation in the common shares of another can be classified according to the percentage of the voting shares of the investee held by the investor:

1. Holdings of more than 50% (consolidated statements)—investor has controlling interest.
2. Holdings between 20% and 50% (equity method)—if investor has significant influence.
3. Holdings of less than 20% if investor does not have significant influence—investor has passive interest.

When one corporation acquires a voting interest of more than 50% (**controlling interest**) in another corporation, the investor corporation is referred to as the **parent** and the investee corporation as the **subsidiary**. The investment in the common shares of the subsidiary is presented as a long-term investment on the separate financial statements of the parent.

In addition to separate financial statements for both the parent and the subsidiary, **consolidated financial statements** are generally prepared. The parent treats the subsidiary as an investment in its separate financial statements, whereas in the consolidated financial statements the distinction between the separate legal entities is disregarded and the parent and subsidiary corporations are treated as a single economic entity. Whether or not consolidated financial statements are prepared, the investment in the subsidiary is generally accounted for on the parent's books using the **equity method** as explained in this chapter.

Although an investor corporation may hold an interest of less than 50% in an investee corporation and thus does not possess legal control, it "may be able to exercise significant influence over operating and financial decisions of an investee."[8] To provide a guide for accounting for investors when 50% or less of the voting

---

[8]*CICA Handbook*, Section 3050, par. 19.

interest is held and to develop an operational definition of "significant influence," the *CICA Handbook*, Section 3050, states:

> The ability to exercise significant influence may be indicated by, for example, representation on the board of directors, participation in policy making processes, material intercompany transactions, interchange of managerial personnel, or provision of technical information. If the investor holds less than 20% of the voting interest in the investee, it should be presumed that the investor does not have the ability to exercise significant influence, unless such influence is clearly demonstrated. On the other hand, the holding of 20% or more of the voting interest in the investee does not in itself confirm the ability to exercise significant influence. A substantial or majority ownership by another investor would not necessarily preclude an investor from exercising significant influence.[9]

In instances of "significant influence" (generally an investment of 20% or more) the investor is required to account for the investment using the **equity method**. When the investor lacks significant influence over the investee, presumably less than a 20% interest, or earnings of the investee are not likely to accrue to the investor, the investment is to be accounted for using **the cost method**. Circumstances in which investee earnings are not likely to accrue to the investor would include (1) the investee in receivership or bankruptcy, or (2) the investee located in a foreign country that has significant restrictions on transfers of funds.

Judgement is frequently required in determining whether an investment of 20% or more results in "significant influence" over the operating and financial decisions of an investee. In the later 1970s and early 1980s an increased number of "hostile" merger and takeover attempts created situations where "significant influence" over investees was difficult to determine.

In specialized industries, investments in certain securities of others are accounted for using the **market value method**. The following pages discuss and illustrate the four methods of accounting for long-term investments: namely, (1) the cost method, (2) the equity method, (3) the lower of cost and market method, and (4) the market value method, and their applicability.[10]

Cost Method

Under the **cost method** a long-term investment is originally recorded and reported at cost, and continues to be carried and reported at cost in the investment account until it is either partially or entirely disposed of, or until some fundamental change in conditions makes it clear that the value originally assigned can no longer be justified. Write-downs from cost are appropriate when the dividends received represent a distribution of earnings retained in the business prior to the acquisition of the shares by the investor (**liquidating dividend**). Ordinary cash dividends received from the investee are recorded as investment revenue.

To illustrate a liquidating dividend, assume that Queco, Inc. owns 5% of the common shares of Ontco Mining Company. Ontco Mining declares a dividend of

---

[9]*Ibid.*

[10]*Accounting Trends and Techniques—1984* reports that in 1983, of its 600 surveyed companies, 345 employed the equity method, 127 the cost method, 12 the cost less allowances for decline in value method, and 23 the lower of cost and market method as the basis for valuing investments in equity securities of other companies. The different methods resulted from differing circumstances and percentages of interest.

$200,000 and indicates that it should be considered a liquidating dividend. The entry made by Queco would be:

Dividend Receivable ($200,000 × .05)	10,000	
Investment in Shares		10,000

The cost method is applicable to passive investments in **nonmarketable** equity securities, such as shares in a closely held corporation. Such investments, having no market value, are not classified as current except when sale is imminent.

Equity Method

Under the **equity method** a substantive economic relationship is acknowledged between the investor and the investee. The investment is originally recorded at the cost of the shares acquired but is subsequently adjusted each period for changes in the net assets of the investee. That is, the **investment's carrying amount is periodically increased (decreased) by the investor's proportionate share of the earnings (losses) of the investee and decreased by all dividends received by the investor from the investee**. The equity method gives recognition to the fact that investee earnings increase investee net assets that underlie the investment, and that investee losses and dividends decrease these net assets.

To illustrate the cost and equity methods, assume that Maxi Company purchases a 20% interest in Mini Company. For purposes of applying the cost method in this illustration, assume that Maxi does not have the ability to exercise significant influence; where the equity method is applied, assume that the 20% interest permits Maxi to exercise significant influence. The entries are shown below.

Entries Under Cost and Equity Methods

Cost Method		Equity Method	

On January 2, 1986, Maxi Company acquired 48,000 shares (20% of Mini Company common stock) at a cost of $10 a share.

Cost Method			Equity Method		
Investment in			Investment in		
Mini Company	480,000		Mini Company	480,000	
Cash		480,000	Cash		480,000

For the year 1986, Mini Company reported net income of $200,000; Maxi Company's share is 20% or $40,000.

No entry		Investment in		
		Mini Company	40,000	
		Revenue from Investment		40,000

On January 28, 1987, Mini Company announced and paid a cash dividend of $100,000; Maxi Company received 20% or $20,000.

Cash	20,000		Cash	20,000	
Revenue from			Investment in		
Investment		20,000	Mini Company		20,000

For the year 1987, Mini reported a net loss of $50,000; Maxi Company's share is 20% or $10,000.

No entry		Loss on Investment	10,000	
		Investment in		
		Mini Company		10,000

Note that under the cost method only the cash dividends received from Mini Company are reported as revenue by Maxi Company. Under the equity method, Maxi Company reports as revenue its share of the net income reported by Mini Company; the cash dividends received from Mini Company are recorded as a decrease in the investment carrying value. The difference between the cost and equity methods can be significant. For example, at one time McCloth Steel Corporation reported that the use of the equity method had increased its income before taxes for the year by 55% or $3.5 million. Under either method, when the underlying value of the investment is permanently impaired—that is, there appears to be no chance of recovering a portion or all of the carrying value of the investment—the carrying amount of the asset should be written down, and the write-down recognized as a loss of the period.

Expanded Illustration of the Equity Method   Under the equity method, periodic investor revenue consists of the investor's proportionate share of investee earnings (adjusted to eliminate intercompany gains and losses) and **amortization of the difference between the investor's initial cost and the investor's proportionate share of the underlying book value of the investee at date of acquisition.** And, if the investee's net income includes extraordinary items, the investor treats a proportionate share of the extraordinary items as an extraordinary item rather than as ordinary investment revenue before extraordinary items.

To illustrate the equity method, assume that on January 1, 1986, Investor Company purchased 250,000 shares of Investee Company's 1,000,000 shares of outstanding common stock for $8,500,000. The book value of Investee Company's total net worth was $30,000,000 at the date of Investor Company's 25% investment. Investor Company thereby paid $1,000,000 in excess of book value [$8,500,000 − .25($30,000,000)]. It was determined that $600,000 of this is attributable to its share of **undervalued depreciable assets** of Investee Company and $400,000 to **unrecorded goodwill.** Investor Company estimated the average remaining life of the undervalued assets to be ten years and decided upon a 40-year amortization period for goodwill (the maximum length of time allowed). For the year 1986, Investee Company reported net income of $2,800,000 including an extraordinary loss of $400,000, and paid dividends at June 30, 1986, of $600,000 and at December 31, 1986, of $800,000. The following entries would be recorded on the books of Investor Company to report its long-term investment using the equity method:

January 1, 1986

Investment in Investee Company Shares	8,500,000	
Cash		8,500,000
(To record the acquisition of 250,000		
shares of Investee Company common shares)		

June 30, 1986

Cash	150,000	
Investment in Investee Company Shares		150,000
[To record dividend received		
($600,000 × .25) from Investee Company]		

December 31, 1986

Investment in Investee Company Shares	700,000	
Loss from Investment (extraordinary)	100,000	
Revenue from Investment (ordinary)		800,000
[To record share of Investee Company		
ordinary income ($3,200,000 × .25)		
and extraordinary loss ($400,000 × .25)]		

December 31, 1986

Cash	200,000	
Investment in Investee Company Shares		200,000
[To record dividend received ($800,000 × .25)		
from Investee Company]		

December 31, 1986

Revenue from Investment (ordinary)	70,000	
Investment in Investee Company Shares		70,000
(To record amortization of investment cost		
in excess of book value represented by:		
Undervalued depreciable assets—$600,000 ÷ 10 = $60,000		
Unrecorded goodwill—$400,000 ÷ 40 = 10,000		
Total $70,000)		

The investment in Investee Company is presented in the balance sheet of Investor Company at a carrying value of $8,780,000 computed as follows:

Investment in Investee Company		
Acquisition cost, Jan. 1, 1986	$8,500,000	
Plus: Share of 1986 income before extraordinary item	800,000	$9,300,000
Less: Share of extraordinary loss	100,000	
Dividends received Jun. 30 and Dec. 31	350,000	
Amortization of undervalued depreciable assets	60,000	
Amortization of unrecorded goodwill	10,000	520,000
Carrying value, Dec. 31, 1986 (250,000 shares)		$8,780,000

In the illustration above the investment cost exceeded the underlying book value. In some cases, an investor may acquire an investment at a **cost less than the underlying book value**. In such cases specific assets are assumed to be overvalued and, if depreciable, the excess of the investee's book value over the investor's acquisition cost is amortized into investment revenue over the remaining lives of the assets. Investment revenue is increased under the presumption that the investee's net income as reported is actually understated because the investee is charging depreciation on overstated asset values.

Investee Losses Exceed Carrying Amount   If an investor's share of the investee's losses exceeds the carrying amount of the investment, the question arises as to whether the investor should recognize additional losses. Ordinarily the investor should discontinue applying the equity method and not recognize additional losses. If the investor's potential loss is not limited to the amount of its original investment (by guarantee of the investee's obligations or other commitment to provide further financial support), it may be appropriate for the investor to recognize additional losses.

EASY ON
THIS

Change in Method *from* the Equity Method   If the investor level of influence or ownership falls below that necessary for continued use of the equity method, a change must be made to the cost method. The earnings or losses that relate to the stock retained by the investor and that were previously recognized by the investor should remain as part of the carrying amount of the investment with no retroactive restatement to the new method.

To the extent that dividends received by the investor in subsequent periods exceed its share of the investee's earnings for such periods (all periods following the change in method), they should be accounted for as a reduction of the investment carrying value, rather than as revenue. For example, using the data from the previous illustration, assume that on January 2, 1987, Investee Company issued 1,500,000 additional shares of its own common shares to the public, thereby reducing Investor Company's ownership from 25% to 10%, and that the net income (or loss) and dividends of Investee Company for the years 1987 through 1989 were as follows:

Year	Investor's Share of Investee Income (Loss)	Investee Dividends Received by Investor
1987	$600,000	$ 400,000
1988	350,000	400,000
1989	(200,000)	300,000
Totals	$750,000	$1,100,000

Assuming a change from the equity method to the cost method as of January 1, 1987, Investor Company's reported investment in Investee Company and its reported income would be as shown below.

Note from this illustration that when a change is made from the equity method to the cost method, the cost basis for accounting purposes is the carrying amount of the investment at the date of the change. Also, note the cessation of the amortization of the excess of acquisition price over the proportionate share of book value acquired attributable to undervalued depreciable assets and unrecorded goodwill when the change of method occurs. In other words, the new method is applied in its entirety once the equity method is no longer appropriate.

Year	Dividend Revenue Recognized	Cumulative Excess of Share of Earnings over Dividends Received	Investment at December 31
1987	$400,000	$200,000[a]	$8,780,000
1988	400,000	150,000[b]	8,780,000
1989	–0–	(350,000)[c]	8,780,000 – $350,000 = $8,430,000

[a]$600,000 – $400,000 = $200,000
[b]($350,000 – $400,000) + $200,000 = $150,000
[c]$150,000 – ($200,000 + $300,000) = ($350,000)

Change in Method *to* the Equity   An investment in common stock of an investee that has been accounted for by other than the equity method may become qualified for use of the equity method by an increase in the level of ownership. At the time that an investment qualifies for use of the equity method, the investor should adopt the equity method of accounting. Such a change is made **prospectively**. That is, the carrying amount of the investment account on the date that the equity method first becomes appropriate is used in determining subsequent entries required under equity accounting.

For example, on January 2, 1983, Amsted Corp. purchased for $500,000 cash 10% of the outstanding common shares of Cable Company. On that date, the net assets of Cable Company had a book value of $3,000,000. On January 1, 1985, Amsted Corp. purchased an additional 20% of Cable Company's common shares for $1,200,000 cash when the book value (and fair value) of Cable's net identifiable assets was $4,000,000. Now Amsted Corp. has a 30% interest (and assumed effective control) and must use the equity method. The net income reported by Cable Company and the Cable Company dividends received by Amsted during the period 1983 through 1985 were as follows:

Year	Cable Company Net Income	Cable Co. Dividends Paid to Amsted
1983	$ 500,000	$ 20,000
1984	1,000,000	30,000
1985	1,200,000	120,000

The journal entries recorded from January 2, 1983, through December 31, 1985, relative to Amsted Corp.'s investment in Cable Company reflecting the data above and a change from the cost method to the equity method are as follows:

January 2, 1983

Investment in Cable Company Common Shares	500,000	
Cash		500,000
(To record the purchase of a 10% interest in Cable Company)		

December 31, 1983

Cash	20,000	
Dividend Revenue		20,000
(To record the receipt of cash dividends from Cable Company)		

December 31, 1984

Cash	30,000	
Dividend Revenue		30,000
(To record the receipt of cash dividends from Cable Company)		

January 1, 1985

Investment in Cable Company Common Shares	1,200,000	
Cash		1,200,000
(To record the purchase of an additional interest in Cable Company)		

December 31, 1985

Investment in Cable Company Common Shares	347,500	
Revenue from Investment		347,500
[To record equity in earnings of Cable Company (30% of $1,200,000) less $12,500 amortization of goodwill[a]]		

[a]Goodwill is computed by deducting fair value owned at the date the equity method becomes mandatory (30% of $4,000,000) from the total cost of all shares held ($500,000 + $1,200,000). The amount thus determined is amortized over 40 years ($500,000 ÷ 40 = $12,400).

EASY UP
TO
HERE

Cash	120,000	
Investment in Cable Company Shares		120,000
(To record the receipt of cash		
dividends from Cable Company)		

In summary, changing to the equity method involves calculating the goodwill and fair value excess over book values of identifiable items at the date that the equity method first becomes appropriate and following the equity method from that date.

Disclosures Required under the Equity Method   The significance of an investment to the investor's financial position and operating results should be considered in evaluating the extent of disclosures about the investment and the investee company. According to the *CICA Handbook*, the following disclosures in the investor's financial statements are generally applicable to the equity method:

1.   The name of each investee and the investor's proportionate interest in each.
2.   The accounting policies of the investor with respect to investments.
3.   The difference, if any, between the amount of the cost of the investment at the date of acquisition and the amount of underlying equity in the net assets of the investee.
4.   When investments of 20% or more interest are in the aggregate material in relation to the financial position and operating results of an investor, it may be necessary to present summarized information concerning assets, liabilities, and results of operations of the investees, either individually or in groups, as appropriate.

Decline in Market Value Other Than Temporary   Occasionally a long-term investment in an individual marketable equity security suffers a decline in market value below cost that is other than temporary. If the decline is judged to be permanent, the cost basis of the individual security is written down to a new cost basis. The amount of a nontemporary write-down is accounted for as a **realized loss**. The new cost basis is not changed for subsequent recoveries in market value.

In judging whether a decline in market value below cost at the balance sheet date is other than temporary, a gain or loss realized on subsequent disposition or changes in market price occurring after the date of the financial statements but prior to their issuance should be taken into consideration along with other factors.[11]

Market Value Method

Although the profession has not yet sanctioned the market value method of accounting for long-term investments, this stand is being considered at the time of this writing. Under the market value method, the investor recognizes both dividends received and changes in market prices of the shares of the investee company as earnings or losses from the investment. Dividends received are accounted for as part of revenue from the investment. In addition, the investment account is adjusted for changes in the market value of the investee's shares. The change in market value since the preceding reporting date is included in the results of operations of the investor.

Reporting of investments in common shares at market value is considered by some accountants to meet most closely the objective of reporting the economic consequences of holding the investment. Although the market value method provides the best presentation of investments in some situations, the profession has

[11]"Changes in Market Value after the Balance Sheet Date," *FASB Interpretation No. 11* (Stamford, Conn.: FASB, 1976), par. 3.

concluded that further study will be necessary before the market value method is used as the sole basis.

Applicability of Methods

In summary, application of the cost and equity methods for long-term investments in shares is as follows:

Nature of Investment	Method
Investment in excess of 50% of voting equity and earnings likely to accrue to investor (Consolidated statements will be prepared)	Cost or Equity
Investment in excess of 50% of voting equity and earnings not likely to accrue to investor	Cost
Investment in excess of 20% of voting equity, except when evidence exists of an inability to exercise significant influence	Equity
Investment in excess of 20% of voting equity and earnings of investee not likely to accrue to investor	Cost
Investment is less than a 20% interest in voting equity and evidence exists of an ability to exercise significant influence; earnings likely to accrue to investor	Equity
Investment is less than a 20% interest in voting equity and no evidence of an ability to exercise significant influence exists	Cost
Investment in nonequity or nonmarketable securities	Cost

Even in cases of investments in excess of a 50% voting interest in common shares, certain conditions (for example, foreign subsidiaries operating under conditions of exchange restrictions, government controls, or other uncertainties) may militate against the use of the equity method. Two examples of such cases follow:

Borg-Warner Corporation

Principles in Consolidation—The consolidated financial statements include all subsidiaries except those in Mexico and South America, which are carried at cost owing to political and economic uncertainty, and the financial services companies. Investments in the financial services companies and in affiliated companies, at least 20% owned by Borg-Warner, are carried at equity in underlying net assets.

Insilco Corporation

Principles of Consolidation—The consolidated financial statements include the accounts of the Company and its significant majority-owned subsidiaries except its wholly-owned finance subsidiary and Times Fiber Communications, Inc., a joint venture in which the Company's 51% control is expected to be temporary. Investments in the finance subsidiary, joint ventures, and other associated companies are accounted for using the equity method.

The following schedule compares the various methods of accounting for long-term investments in terms of their effects upon the financial statements.

Comparison of the Effects of Methods of
Accounting for Long-term Investments in Shares[12]

	Balance Sheet	Income Statement
Cost Method	Investments are carried at acquisition cost.	Dividends are recognized as revenue.
Equity Method	Investments are carried at cost, are periodically adjusted by the investor's share of the investee's earnings or losses, and are decreased by all dividends received from the investee.	Revenue is recognized to the extent of the investor's share of the investee's earnings or losses reported subsequent to the date of investment (adjusted by amortization of the difference between cost and underlying book value).
Market Value Method	Investments are carried at market value.	Cash dividends received plus or minus the change in market price during the period are recognized as revenue.

Revenue from Investments in Shares

Revenue recognized from investments, whether under the cost, lower of cost and market, or the equity method, should be included in the income statement of the investor. Under the cost and the lower of cost and market methods, the dividends received (or receivable if declared but unpaid) are reported as investment revenue. Under the equity method, if the investee has extraordinary and prior period items reported during the period, the investor should report in a similar manner its proportionate share of the ordinary income, of the extraordinary items, and prior period adjustments unless separation into these components is considered immaterial.

The gains or losses on sales of investments also are factors in determining the net income for the period. The gain or loss resulting from the sale of long-term investments, unless it is the result of a major casualty, an expropriation, or the introduction of a new law prohibiting its ownership (which may be viewed as unusual and nonrecurring), is reported as part of current income from operations and is not an extraordinary item.

Dividends that are paid in some form of assets other than cash are called **property dividends**. In such instances, the fair market value of the property received becomes the basis for debiting an appropriate asset account and crediting Dividend Revenue (under the cost method).

Occasionally an investor receives a dividend that is in part, or entirely, a **liquidating dividend**. The investor should reduce the Investments account for the amount of the liquidating portion of the dividend and credit Dividend Revenue for the balance.

Stock Dividends

If the investee corporation declares a dividend payable in its own shares of the same class, instead of in cash, each shareholder owns a larger number of shares but

OMIT FROM HERE ↓

---

[12]Adapted and updated from Copeland, Strawser, and Binns, "Accounting for Investments in Common Stock," *Financial Executive* (February, 1972), p. 37.

retains the same proportionate interest in the firm as before. The issuing corporation has distributed no assets; it has merely transferred a specified amount of retained earnings to contributed surplus, thus indicating that this amount will not provide a basis in the future for cash dividends. Shares received as a result of a stock dividend or stock split-up do not constitute revenue to the recipients, because their interest in the issuing corporation is unchanged and because the issuing corporation has not distributed any of its assets.

The recipient of such additional shares would make no formal entry, but should make a memorandum entry and record a notation in the Investments account to show that additional shares have been received.

Although no dollar amount is entered at the time of the receipt of these shares, the fact that additional shares have been received must be considered in computing the carrying amount of any shares sold. The cost of the original shares purchased (plus the effect of any adjustments under the equity method) now constitutes the total carrying amount of both those shares plus the additional shares received, because no price was paid for the additional shares. The carrying amount per share is computed by dividing the total shares into the carrying amount of the original shares purchased.

To illustrate, assume that 100 shares of Flemal Company common stock are purchased for $9,600, and that two years later the company issues to shareholders one additional share for every two shares held; 150 shares of stock that cost a total of $9,600 are then held. Therefore, if 60 shares are sold for $4,300, the carrying amount of the 60 shares would be computed as shown below, assuming that the investment has been accounted for under the cost method.

Cost of 100 shares originally purchased	$9,600
Cost of 50 shares received as stock dividend	-0-
Carrying amount of 150 shares held	$9,600
Carrying amount per share is $9,600/150, or $64	
Carrying amount of 60 shares sold is 60 × $64, or $3,840	

The entry to record the sale is:

Cash	4,300	
Investments in Shares		3,840
Gain on Sales of Investments		460

A total of 90 shares is still retained, and they are carried in the Investments account at $9,600 minus $3,840, or $5,760. Thus the carrying amount for those shares remaining is also $64 per share, or a total of $5,760 for the 90 shares.

Stock Rights

When a corporation is about to offer for sale additional shares of an issue already outstanding, it may forward to present holders of that issue certificates permitting them to purchase additional shares in proportion to their present holdings. These certificates represent rights to purchase additional shares and are called **stock rights**. In rights offerings, rights generally are issued on the basis of one right per share, but it may take one or many rights to purchase one new share.

The certificate representing the stock rights, called a **warrant**, states the number of shares that the holder of the right may purchase and also the price at which they may be purchased. If this price is less than the current market value of such shares, the rights have a value in themselves, and from the time they are issued until they expire they may be purchased and sold like any other security.

Three dates are important to a proper understanding of stock rights: (1) the date the rights offering is announced, (2) the date as of which the certificates or rights are issued, and (3) the date the rights expire. From the date the right is announced until it is issued, the share of stock and the right are not separable, and the share is described as **rights-on**; after the certificate or right is received and up to the time it expires, the share and right can be sold separately. A share sold separately from an effective stock right is sold **ex-rights.**

When a right is received, the shareholders have actually received nothing that they did not have before, because the shares already owned brought them the right; they have received no distribution of the corporation assets. The carrying amount of the original shares held is now the carrying amount of those shares plus the rights and should be allocated between the two on the basis of their total market values at the time the rights are received.

Disposition of Rights   The investor who receives rights to purchase additional shares has three alternatives:

1. To exercise the rights by purchasing additional shares.
2. To sell the rights.
3. To permit them to expire without selling or using them.

If the investor buys additional shares, the carrying amount of the original shares allocated to the rights becomes a part of the carrying amount of the new shares purchased; if the investor sells the rights, the allocated carrying amount compared with the selling price determines the gain or loss on sale; and, if the investor permits the rights to expire, a loss is suffered, and the investment should be reduced accordingly. The following example illustrates the problem involved.

Note that the total cost of the shares and the rights is still $5,000 and, therefore, no entry is made in the Investments account in the general ledger at this time. The subsidiary records should reflect, however, the reduction in the carrying amount of the shares from $5,000 to $4,761.90 and the acquisition of the rights, with an

---

Shares owned before issuance of rights—100.

Cost of shares owned—$50 a share for a total cost of $5,000.

Rights received—one right for every share owned, or 100 rights; two
   rights are required to purchase one new share at $50.

Market values at date rights issued:

$$\text{Shares \$60 a share}$$
$$\text{Rights \$3 a right}$$

Total market value of shares (100 × $60)	$6,000
Total market value of rights (100 × $3)	300
Combined market value	$6,300

Cost allocated to stock: $\dfrac{\$6,000}{\$6,300} \times \$5,000 = \$4,761.90$

Cost allocated to rights: $\dfrac{\$300}{\$6,300} \times \$5,000 = \underline{\quad 238.10}$

$$\overline{\$5,000.00}$$

Cost allocated to each share of stock: $\dfrac{\$4,761.90}{100} = \$47.62$

Cost allocated to each right: $\dfrac{\$238.10}{100} = \$2.38$

allocated cost of $238.10. The general ledger account is not affected until the shares are sold, or the rights are sold or used or permitted to expire.

If some of the original shares are later sold, their cost for purposes of determining gain or loss on sale is $47.62 per share, as computed above. If 10 of the original shares are sold at $58 per share, the entry would be:

Cash	580.00	
Investments in Shares		476.20
Gain on Sale of Investments		103.80

Entries for Stock Rights   Rights may be sold, or used to purchase additional shares, or permitted to expire. The carrying amount allocated to the rights is part of the Long-term Investments account in the general ledger and, therefore, any entries made that are related to the rights are reflected in the Long-term Investments account. For example, assume that some of the rights are sold, some are used to purchase additional shares, and some are allowed to expire.

If 40 rights to purchase 20 shares are sold at $3.00 each, the entry is:

Cash	120.00	
Investments in Shares		95.20
Gain on Sale of Investments		24.80

The amount removed from the Long-term Investments account is the amount allocated to 40 rights, 40 × $2.38.

If rights to purchase 20 shares are exercised, and 20 additional shares are purchased at the offer price of $50, the entry is:

Investments in Shares	1,000.00	
Cash		1,000.00

If these shares are sold in the future, their cost should be considered to be $1,095.20, or $54.76 per share, the price paid of $50 per share plus the amount allocated to two rights of $4.76 which is already in the Long-term Investments account.

If the remaining 20 rights are permitted to expire, the amount allocated to these rights should be removed from the general ledger account by this entry:

Loss on Expiration of Stock Rights	47.60	
Investments in Shares		47.60

The balance of the general ledger account is now $5,381.00, as shown below.

Investments in Shares				
Purchase of original 100			Sale of 10 shares of	
shares @ $50 per share	5,000.00		original purchase	476.20
Purchase of 20 shares by			Sale of 40 rights	95.20
exercise of rights	1,000.00		Loss on expiration of	
			20 rights	47.60
			Balance	5,381.00
	6,000.00			6,000.00
Balance	5,381.00[a]			

[a]Analysis of Balance	
90 shares of original purchase, at allocated cost of $47.62 per share	$4,285.80
20 shares purchased through exercise of rights, carried at	
$54.76 per share (cash paid of $50.00, plus $4.76 for	
allocated cost of two rights)	1,095.20
Balance of account, as above	$5,381.00

The balance represents 110 shares, of which 90 are of the original purchase, and 20 are shares purchased through the exercise of stock rights.

CASH SURRENDER VALUE AND FUNDS

Cash Surrender Value of Life Insurance

There are many different kinds of insurance. The kinds usually carried by businesses include (a) casualty insurance, (b) liability insurance, and (c) life insurance. Accounting for casualty insurance is discussed in Appendix A of Chapter 10. Certain types of **life insurance** constitute an investment, whereas casualty insurance and liability insurance do not. The three common types of life insurance policies that companies often carry on the lives of their principal officers are (a) **ordinary life**, (b) **limited payment**, and (c) **term insurance**. During the period that ordinary life and limited payment policies are in force, there is a cash surrender value and a loan value. Term insurance ordinarily has no cash surrender value or loan value.

If the insured officers or their heirs are the beneficiaries of the policy, the premiums paid by the company represent expense to the company and, for income tax purposes, may represent income to the officer insured. In this case the cash surrender value of the policy does not represent an asset to the company.

If the company, however, is the beneficiary and has the right to cancel the policy at its own option, the cash surrender value of the policy or policies is an asset of the company. Accordingly, part of the premiums paid is not expense, because the cash surrender value increases each year. Only the difference between the premium paid and the increase in cash surrender value represents expense to the company.

For example, if Zima Corporation pays an insurance premium of $2,300 on a $100,000 policy covering its president and, as a result, the cash surrender value of the policy increases from $15,000 to $16,400 during the period, the entry to record the premium payment is:

Life Insurance Expense	900	
Cash Surrender Value of Life Insurance	1,400	
Cash		2,300

The cash surrender value of such life insurance policies should be reported in the balance sheet as a long-term investment, inasmuch as it is unlikely that the policies will be surrendered and cancelled in the immediate future. The premium is not deductible for tax purposes, however, and the proceeds of such policies are not taxable as income.

For example, Alico, Inc. recently reported information related to its cash surrender value as follows:

Other investments (Note 4)	
Cash surrender value of life insurance	448,000

Note 4. The company purchased, as owner and beneficiary, individual life insurance policies on the lives of such officers and employees as a means of funding substantially all of such additional benefits. The company's accounting policy with respect to such insurance coverage is to charge operations with the annual premium cost, net of increase in cash surrender value.

If the insured officer were to die half-way through the most recent period of coverage for which the $2,300 premium payment was made, the following entry would be made (assuming cash surrender value of $15,700 and refund of a pro rata share of the premium paid):

Cash [$100,000 + (1/2 of $2,300)]	101,150	
Cash Surrender Value of Life Insurance		16,400
Life Insurance Expense (1/2 × $900)		450
Gain on Life Insurance Coverage ($100,000 − $15,700)		84,300

The gain on life insurance coverage is generally reported as an extraordinary item because it is not considered to be a ''normal'' business transaction.

Funds

Assets may be held aside in special funds for specific purposes and, therefore, be unavailable for ordinary operations of the business. In this way the assets segregated in the special funds are available when needed for the intended purposes.

There are two general types of funds: (1) those in which cash is set aside to meet specific current obligations, and (2) those that are not directly related to current operations and therefore are in the nature of long-term investments.

Several funds of the first type, discussed in preceding chapters, include the following:

Fund	**Purpose**
Petty Cash	Payment of small expenditures, in currency
Payroll Cash Account	Payment of salaries and wages
Dividend Cash Account	Payment of dividends
Interest Fund	Payment of interest on long-term debt

In general, these funds are used to handle more conveniently and more expeditiously the payments of certain current obligations, to maintain better control over such expenditures, and to divide adequately the responsibility for cash disbursements. These funds are ordinarily shown as current assets (if immaterial, then as part of Cash) in the balance sheet, because the obligations to which they relate are ordinarily current liabilities.

As mentioned above, funds of the second type are similar to long-term investments, as they do not relate directly to current operations. The more common funds of this type and the purpose of each are listed below:

Fund	**Purpose**
Sinking Fund	Payment of long-term indebtedness
Plant Expansion Fund	Purchase or construction of additional plant
Stock Redemption Fund	Retirement of share capital (usually preferred shares)
Contingency Fund	Payment of unforeseen obligations

Because the cash set aside for such purposes as those listed above will not be needed until some time in the future, it is usually invested in securities so that revenue may be earned on the assets of the fund. The assets of a fund may or may not be placed in the hands of a trustee. If appointed, the trustee becomes the custodian of the assets, accounts to the company for them, and reports revenues and expenses of the fund. Funds of this second type are ordinarily shown in the long-term investments section of the balance sheet or in a separate section if relatively large in amount.

Entries for Funds

To account for the assets, revenues, and expenses of funds, it is desirable to keep separate accounts to accumulate such information. For example, if a fund is kept for the redemption of a preferred share issue that was issued with a redemption provision at par after a certain date, the following accounts might be kept:

> Stock Redemption Fund Cash
> Stock Redemption Fund Investments
> Stock Redemption Fund Revenue
> Stock Redemption Fund Expense
> Gain on Sale of Stock Redemption Fund Investments
> Loss on Sale of Stock Redemption Fund Investments

When cash is transferred from the regular cash account, perhaps periodically, the entry is:

Stock Redemption Fund Cash	30,000	
Cash		30,000

Securities purchased by the fund are recorded at cost:

Stock Redemption Fund Investments	27,000	
Stock Redemption Fund Cash		27,000

If securities purchased for the fund are to be held temporarily, they would be treated in the accounts in the same manner as temporary investments, described in the first section of this chapter. If they are to be held for a long period of time, they are treated in accordance with the entries described for long-term investments in the second section of this chapter. In both cases the securities purchased are recorded at cost when acquired, but in the case of bonds purchased as long-term investments for the fund, premium or discount should be amortized. If we assume that the entry above records the purchase at a premium of 10-year bonds of a par value of $25,000 on April 1, the issue date, and that the bonds bear interest at 8%, the entry for the receipt of semiannual interest on October 1 is:

Stock Redemption Fund Cash	1,000	
Stock Redemption Fund Revenue		1,000

At December 31, entries are made to record amortization of premium for nine months and to accrue interest on the bonds for three months:

Stock Redemption Fund Revenue	150	
Stock Redemption Fund Investments		150
(To record amortization of premium for 9 months, 9/12 of 1/10 of $2,000)		
Accrued Interest on Stock Redemption Fund Investments	500	
Stock Redemption Fund Revenue		500
(To record accrued interest for 3 months, 3/12 of 8% of $25,000)		

Expenses of the fund paid are recorded by debiting Stock Redemption Fund Expenses and crediting Stock Redemption Fund Cash.

When the investments held by the fund are disposed of, the entries to record the sale are in accord with the entries illustrated earlier in the chapter, using the accounts designated as relating to the redemption fund. Any revenue and expense accounts set up to record fund transactions should be closed to Income Summary at the end of the accounting period and reflected in earnings of the current period.

The entry for retirement of the preferred shares is:

Preferred Capital Stock	500,000	
Stock Redemption Fund Cash		500,000

Any balance remaining in the Stock Redemption Fund Cash account is transferred back to a general cash account.

Funds and Reserves Distinguished

Although funds and reserves (appropriations) are not similar, they are sometimes confused because they may be related and often have similar titles. **A simple distinction may be drawn: a fund is always an asset and always has a debit balance; a reserve (if used only in the limited sense recommended) is an appropriation of retained earnings, always has a credit balance, and is never an asset.**

The distinction is illustrated by reconsidering the entries made in connection with a stock redemption fund on the preceding pages.

The fund was originally established by the entry:

Stock Redemption Fund Cash	30,000	
Cash		30,000

Some of this cash was used to purchase investments; the assets of the fund were then cash and investments. Ultimately the investments were sold, and the stock redemption fund cash was used to retire the preferred shares.

If the company chose to do so, it could establish an appropriation for stock redemption at the same time to reduce the retained earnings apparently available for dividends. Appropriated retained earnings is established by periodic transfers from retained earnings, as follows:

Retained Earnings	30,000	
Appropriation for Stock Redemption		30,000

It will have a credit balance and will be shown in the shareholders' equity section of the balance sheet. When the shares are retired by payment of cash from the stock redemption fund, the appropriation is transferred back to retained earnings:

Appropriation for Stock Redemption	500,000	
Retained Earnings		500,000

The foregoing discussion indicates that the fund was an asset accumulated to retire shares and had a debit balance; the appropriation was a subdivision of Retained Earnings and had a credit balance. The fund was used to redeem the shares; the appropriation was transferred back to retained earnings.

KEY POINTS

1. Temporary investments usually include short-term paper, marketable debt securities, and marketable equity securities held temporarily.

2. Marketable securities are recorded at cost and the portfolio is adjusted to the lower of cost and market at the end of each period through the use of a valuation account.

3. Periodic income from marketable securities includes:
   (1) Unrealized gains (losses) (adjustments to the valuation account).
   (2) Realized gains (losses) resulting from dispositions or changes in classification (current to noncurrent or *vice versa*).
   (3) Dividend income on equity securities is recognized when the dividends are declared.
   (4) Interest income on debt securities is recognized as it accrues.

4. Long-term investments may be held in bonds or shares. Bonds are recorded at cost and carried at cost adjusted for amortization of discount or premium. Shares are recorded at cost and carried at either cost or equity.

5. Under the cost method of accounting, dividends received (except for liquidating dividends) are recorded as income.

6. A proportionate share of investee reported income adjusted for amortization of the purchase differential is recorded as income under the equity method of accounting. Dividends received are treated as recoveries of the investment and are credited to the investment account.

7. Under both cost and equity methods, material and apparent long-term impairments of the investment are recognized currently as losses and reductions to the carrying value of the investment.

8. Stock dividends received are not recognized as income since there is no change in either the investor's proportionate interest or the investee's net assets.

9. Stock rights and warrants are considered separate assets and are allocated a value usually based on relative market values.

10. Cash surrender value of life insurance to which the firm is beneficiary and holds rights to cancel is a noncurrent asset.

11. Funds are assets set aside for special purposes and may be classified as either current or noncurrent depending on the circumstances.

QUESTIONS

1. Distinguish between the nature of temporary and long-term investments. Give two examples of each type. Is it possible for securities of the same kind to be carried by one company as a long-term investment and by the other as a short-term investment? Explain.

2. Where on the balance sheet are long-term investments customarily presented? Identify six items customarily classified as long-term investments.

3. For what reasons would a company purchase bonds and shares of another company?

4. What purpose does the variety in bond features (types and characteristics) serve?

5. Distinguish between bond maturity value, bond market value, bond face value, bond par value, and bond principal value.

6. What factors cause a difference between the stated interest rate and the yield interest rate?

7. What are the problems of accounting for bond investments between interest dates?

8. Theoretically, what is the price of a bond?

9. Distinguish between the effective-interest method and the straight-line method relative to their effect on net income over the life of a bond investment. What are the merits of each method?

10. What is the cost of a long-term investment in bonds? What is the cost of a long-term investment in shares?

11. Contrast the accounting treatment of a premium or discount on long-term bond investments with the treatment of a premium or discount on a long-term bond debt. How is the premium or discount handled relative to a temporary investment?

12. On what basis should shares acquired in exchange for noncash consideration be recorded?

13. How should the purchase of two or more classes of securities for a lump sum price be accounted for if the market price of each class is known? If the market price of only one class is known? If no market prices are known?

14. Name three methods of accounting for long-term investments in shares subsequent to the date of acquisition. When is each method applicable?

15. What constitutes ''significant influence'' when an investor's financial interest is below the 50% level?

16. Distinguish between the cost and equity method of accounting for long-term investments in shares subsequent to the date of acquisition.

17. When the equity method is applied, what disclosures should be made in the investor's financial statements?

18. Distinguish between the accounting treatment for ''marketable securities—current'' and ''marketable securities—noncurrent.''

19. Magic, Inc. gradually acquired shares in Merlin Corp. (a nonsubsidiary) until its ownership exceeded 20%. How is this investment recorded and reported after the last purchase?

20. How is a stock dividend accounted for by the recipient? How is a stock split accounted for by the recipient?

21. What three dates are significant in relation to stock rights? What are the alternatives available to the recipient of stock rights?

22. In applying the equity method, what recognition, if any, does the investor give to the excess of its investment cost over its proportionate share of the investee book value at the date of acquisition? What recognition, if any, is given if the investment cost is less than the underlying book value?

23. Gigantic Corp. has an investment carrying value (equity method) on its books of $170,000 representing a 40% interest in Poquito Company, which suffered a $600,000 loss this year. How should Gigantic Corp. handle its proportionate share of Poquito's loss?

24. Distinguish between a fund and a reserve.

25. What are the two general types of funds? Give three examples of each type of fund.

CASES

C18-1 Presented below are four unrelated situations involving marketable equity securities:

1. A noncurrent portfolio with an aggregate market value in excess of cost includes 1 particular security whose market value has declined to less than one-half of the original cost. The decline in value is considered to be other than temporary.

2. The statement of financial position of a company does not classify assets and liabilities as current and noncurrent. The portfolio of marketable equity securities includes securities normally considered current that have a net cost in excess of market value of $13,000. The remainder of the portfolio has a net market value in excess of cost of $32,000.

3. A marketable security, whose market value is currently less than cost, is classified as noncurrent but is to be reclassified as current.

4. A company's noncurrent portfolio of marketable securities consists of the common stock of one company. At the end of the prior year the market value of the security was 50% of original cost, and this effect was properly reflected in a valuation allowance account. However, at the end of the current year the market value of the security has appreciated to twice the original cost. The security is still considered noncurrent at year end.

Instructions

What is the effect upon classification, carrying value, and earnings for each of the situations above? Complete your response to each situation before proceeding to the next.

C18-2 The *CICA Handbook* distinguishes between temporary investments (Section 3010) and long-term investments (Section 3050).

Instructions

(a) Why does a company maintain investment portfolios of current and noncurrent securities?

(b) What factors should be considered in determining whether investments in marketable securities should be classified as current or noncurrent, and how do these factors affect the accounting treatment for unrealized losses?

C18-3 For the past five years Flatt, Inc. has maintained an investment (properly accounted for and reported upon) in Trumbo Co. amounting to a 10% interest in the voting common shares of Trumbo Co. The purchase price was $1,050,000 and the underlying net equity in Trumbo at the date of purchase was $930,000. On January 2 of the current year, Flatt purchased an additional 15% of the voting common shares of Trumbo for $1,800,000; the underlying net equity of the additional investment at January 2 was $1,500,000. Trumbo has been profitable and has paid dividends annually since Flatt's initial acquisition.

Instructions

Discuss how this increase in ownership affects the accounting for and reporting upon the investment in Trumbo Co. Include in your discussion adjustments, if any, to the amount shown prior to the increase in investment to bring the amount into conformity with generally accepted accounting principles. Also include how current and subsequent periods would be reported.

(AICPA adapted)

C18-4 Beauty Cream, Inc. purchased marketable securities at a cost of $300,000 on February 1, 1985. When the securities were purchased, the company intended to hold the investment for more than one year. Therefore, the investment was classified as a noncurrent asset in the company's annual report for the year ended December 31, 1985, and stated at its then market value of $240,000.

On September 30, 1986, when the investment had a market value of $252,000, management reclassified it as a current asset because the company intended to sell the securities within the next 12 months. The market value of the investment was $270,000 on December 31, 1986.

The presentation of investments in marketable equity securities on a company's financial statement is affected by management's intentions regarding how long the investment is to be held and by the reporting requirements specified in the *CICA Handbook*.

Instructions

(a) Explain how the difference between cost and market value of the investment in the marketable securities would be reflected in the financial statements of Beauty Cream, Inc. prepared for the fiscal year ending December 31, 1985, when the investment was classified as a noncurrent asset.

(b) The consequence of management's decision to recognize the investment in marketable securities as short-term and reclassify it as a current asset was recorded in the accounts. At what amount would the investment be recorded on September 30, 1986, the date of this decision?

(c) How would the investment in the marketable equity securities be reported in the financial statements of Beauty Cream, Inc. as of December 31, 1986, so that the company's financial position and operations for the year 1986 would reflect and report properly the reclassification of the investment from a non-current asset to a current asset? Be sure to indicate the affected accounts, the related dollar amounts, and the note disclosures, if any.

C18-5 In the course of your examination of the financial statements of Macann Corporation as of December 31, 1985, the following entry came to your attention.

January 4, 1985

Receivable from Insurance Company	500,000	
Cash Surrender Value of Life Insurance Policies		68,000
Retained Earnings		79,500
Donated Capital from Life Insurance Proceeds		352,500
(Disposition of the proceeds of the life insurance policy on		
Mr. Macann's life. Mr. Macann died on January 1, 1985.)		

You are aware that Mr. Macann, an officer-shareholder in the small manufacturing firm, insisted that the corporation's board of directors authorize the purchase of an insurance policy to compensate for any loss of earning potential upon his death. The corporation paid $147,500 in premiums prior to Mr. Macann's death, and was the sole beneficiary of the policy. At the date of death, there had been no premium prepayment and no rebate was due. In prior years cash surrender value in the amount of $68,000 had been recorded in the accounts.

Instructions

(a) What is the "cash surrender value" of a life insurance policy?

(b) How should the cash surrender value of a life insurance policy be classified in the financial statements while the policy is in force? Why?

(c) Comment on the propriety of the entry recording the insurance receivable.

C18-6 **Part A.** To manufacture and sell its products a company must invest in inventories, plant and equipment, and other operating assets. In addition, a manufacturing company often finds it desirable or necessary to invest a portion of its available resources, either directly or through the operation of special funds, in shares, bonds, and other securities.

Instructions

(a) List the reasons why a manufacturing company might invest funds in shares, bonds, and other securities.

(b) What are the criteria for classifying investments as current or noncurrent assets?

Part B. Because of favourable market prices, the trustee of K & P Willrett Company's bond sinking fund invested the current year's contribution to the fund in the company's own bonds. The bonds are being held in the fund without cancellation. The fund also includes cash and securities of other companies.

Instructions

Describe three methods of classifying the bond sinking fund on the balance sheet of K & P Willrett Company. Include a discussion of the propriety of using each method.

C18-7 Terry McDowell Inc. administers the sinking fund applicable to its own outstanding long-term bonds. The following four proposals relate to the accounting treatment of sinking fund cash and securities.

1. To mingle sinking fund cash with general cash and sinking fund securities with other securities, and to show both as current assets on the balance sheet.

2. To keep sinking fund cash in a separate bank account and sinking fund securities separate from other securities, but on the balance sheet to treat cash as a part of the

general cash and the securities as part of general investments, both being shown as current assets.

3. To keep sinking fund cash in a separate bank account and sinking fund securities separate from other securities, but to combine the two accounts on the balance sheet under one caption, such as "Sinking Fund Cash and Investments," to be listed as a noncurrent asset.

4. To keep sinking fund cash in a separate bank account and sinking fund securities separate from other securities, and to identify each separately on the balance sheet among the current assets.

Instructions

Identify the proposal that is most appropriate. Give the reasons for your selection.

C18-8 Residue, Inc. a chemical processing company, has been operating profitably for many years. On March 1, 1985, Residue purchased 50,000 shares of Diversified Insurance Company stock for $2,000,000. The 50,000 shares represented 40% of Diversified's outstanding stock. Both Residue and Diversified operate on a fiscal year ending August 31.

For the fiscal year ended August 31, 1985, Diversified reported net income of $800,000 earned ratably throughout the year. During November, 1984, February, May, and August, 1985, Diversified paid its regular quarterly cash dividend of $100,000.

Instructions

(a) What criteria should Residue consider in determining whether its investment in Diversified should be classified as (1) a current asset (marketable security) or (2) a noncurrent asset (investment) in Residue's August 31, 1985, balance sheet? Confine your discussion to the decision criteria for determining the balance sheet classification of the investment.

(b) Assume that the investment should be classified as a long-term investment in the noncurrent asset section of Residue's balance sheet. The cost of Residue's investment equalled its equity in the recorded values of Diversified's net assets; recorded values were not materially different from fair values (individually or collectively). For the fiscal year ended August 31, 1985, how did the net income reported and dividends paid by Diversified affect the accounts of Residue? (Ignore income tax considerations.) Indicate each account affected, whether it increased or decreased, and explain the reason for the change in the account balance (such as Cash, Investment in Diversified, etc.). Organize your answer in the following format.

Account Name	Increase or Decrease	Reason for Change in Account Balance

EXERCISES

E18-1 The following data show the long-term investments of Tiptoe Shoe Company on June 30, 1985, the end of its fiscal year. These investments were purchased during the current year on the dates and at the costs shown.

February 1	Penwell Company $1,000, 11% bonds. Interest payable April 1 and Oct. 1. 50 bonds. Due March 1, 1987.	$ 52,000
March 30	Denson Company common stock, 4,000 shares (5% of the outstanding shares).	45,000
May 1	Rickety, Inc. $1,000, 10% bonds. Interest payable June 1 and Dec. 1. 25 bonds. Due September 1, 1988.	22,600
		$119,600

Instructions

(a) If amortization of premium or discount is recorded once a year on June 30, what entry would be necessary on June 30, 1985? (Apply the straight-line method.)

(b) What entry (if any) would be necessary if the market value of the investments were as follows on June 30:

Penwell Company	$ 51,200
Denson Company	40,800
Rickety, Inc.	25,400
	$117,400

E18-2 The transactions given below related to bonds purchased by Shoestring Company:

April 1, 1986	Bonds of Poe Company of a par value of $30,000 are purchased as a long-term investment at 95 plus accrued interest. The bonds bear interest at 9% payable annually on Dec. 1, and they mature Dec. 1, 1992.
Dec. 1	Interest of $2,700 is received on the Poe Company bonds. (Do not amortize discount at this time.)
Dec. 31	The proper amount of interest is accrued, and the entry is made to amortize the proper amount of discount for 1986.
June 1, 1987	Bonds of a par value of $7,500 are sold at 97 plus accrued interest. Assume that reversing entries are made January 1.

Instructions

Prepare journal entries required by Shoestring Company to record the transactions above, using straight-line amortization.

E18-3 On December 31, 1986, Fizzell Company owns long-term investments purchased on dates and at costs shown below:

Jan. 10, 1985	A Company common, 1,000 shares	$ 46,000
Mar. 20	B Company preferred, 300 shares	60,600
Apr. 1	C Company $1,000, 11% bonds due Apr. 1, 1995, interest payable Apr. 1 and Oct. 1, 25 bonds	27,400
June 1, 1986	D Company $1,000, 12% bonds due June 1, 1990, interest payable Dec. 1 and June 1, 22 bonds	20,800
		$154,800

Instructions

(a) Prepare the entry to record amortization of discount or premium on December 31, 1985. Assume that the company records amortization of discount and premium only at the end of each year, using the straight-line method, and records its debt securities at net cost.

(b) Prepare the entry to record amortization of discount or premium on December 31, 1986.

(c) The market value of the securities as of December 31, 1986, is as follows:

A Company common stock (representing a 2% interest)	$ 48,000
B Company preferred stock (representing a 5% interest)	52,600
C Company bonds	25,400
D Company bonds	23,000
	$149,000

What entry, if any, would you recommend be made with respect to this information, and what disclosures, if any, should be made in the financial statements?

E18-4 On January 1, 1986, Herbert Company purchases $200,000 of Bloyd Company 8% bonds for $154,119. The interest is payable semiannually on June 30 and December 31, and the bonds mature in 10 years. The purchase price provides a yield of 12% on the investment.

Instructions

(a) Prepare the journal entry on January 1, 1986, to record the purchase of the investment. (Record the investment at gross or maturity value.)

(b) Prepare the journal entry on June 30, 1986, to record the receipt of the first interest payment and any amortization, using the straight-line method.

(c) Prepare the journal entry on June 30, 1986, to record the receipt of the first interest payment and any amortization, using the effective interest method.

E18-5 On June 1, 1985, Warner, Inc. purchased as a long-term investment 800 of the $1,000 face value, 8% bonds of Universal Corporation for $738,300. The bonds were purchased to yield 10% interest. Interest is payable semiannually on December 1 and June 1. The bonds mature on June 1, 1990. Warner uses the effective interest method of amortization. On November 1, 1986, Warner sold the bonds for $785,000. This amount includes the appropriate accrued interest. (Round computations to the nearest dollar.)

Instructions

Prepare a schedule showing the income or loss, before income taxes, from the bond investment that Warner should record for the years ended December 31, 1985, and 1986.

(CMA adapted)

E18-6 Patrick Corp. was a 30% owner of Davis Company, holding 300,000 of Davis's common shares on December 31, 1984. The investment account had the following entries:

Investment in Davis

1/1/83	Cost	$3,240,000	12/6/83	Dividend received	$120,000
12/31/83	Share of income	480,000	12/31/83	Amortization of	
12/31/84	Share of income	600,000		undervalued assets	36,000
			12/5/84	Dividend received	240,000
			12/31/84	Amortization of	
				undervalued assets	36,000

On January 2, 1985, Patrick sold 150,000 shares of Davis for $3,000,000, thereby losing its significant influence. During the years 1985 and 1986, Davis experienced the following results of operations and paid the following dividends to Patrick.

	Davis Income (Loss)	Dividends Paid to Patrick
1985	$360,000	$48,000
1986	(240,000)	12,000

Instructions

(a) What effect does the January 2, 1985, transaction have upon Patrick's accounting treatment for its investment in Davis?

(b) Compute the carrying value of the investment in Davis as of December 31, 1986, assuming a market value of $1,800,000.

E18-7 Fantasy Clothes Company purchased 30,000 common shares (a 30% interest) of Cool-Jeans Company at $18 per share on January 2, 1985. During 1985, Cool-Jeans Company reported net income of $200,000 and paid dividends of $50,000. On January 2, 1986, Fantasy received 10,000 common shares as a result of a stock split by Cool-Jeans Company.

Instructions

(a) Prepare the entry to record the sale of 1,000 shares at $13.75 per share by Fantasy Clothes Company on January 3, 1986, applying the cost method in accounting for the investment (owing to lack of significant influence).

(b) Prepare the entry to record the sale of 1,000 shares at $13.75 per share on January 3, 1986, applying the equity method in accounting for the investment. Assume the acquisition cost approximated the book value acquired on January 2, 1985.

E18-8   On July 1, 1986, Keith Rissling Company purchased for cash 40% of the outstanding common shares of Ewert Company. Both Rissling Company and Ewert Company have a December 31 year end. Ewert Company, whose common shares are actively traded in the over-the-counter market, reported its total net income for the year to Rissling Company and also paid cash dividends on November 15, 1986, to Rissling Company and its other shareholders.

Instructions

How should Keith Rissling Company report the above facts in its December 31, 1986, balance sheet and its income statement for the year then ended? Discuss the rationale for your answer.

(AICPA adapted)

E18-9   At the end of its first year of operations, Jewel Kadlec Company had a current marketable securities portfolio with a cost of $500,000 and a market value of $550,000. At the end of its second year of operations, Jewel Kadlec Company had a current marketable securities portfolio with a cost of $525,000 and a market value of $475,000. No securities were sold during the first year. One security with a cost of $80,000 and a market value of $70,000 at the end of the first year was sold for $100,000 during the second year.

Instructions

How should Jewel Kadlec Company report the above facts in its balance sheets and income statements for both years? Discuss the rationale for your answer.

(AICPA adapted)

E18-10   Franzne Company pays the premiums on two insurance policies on the life of its president, Kim Franzne. Information concerning premiums paid in 1986 is given below.

					Cash Surrender Value	
Beneficiary	Face	Prem.	Dividends Cr. to Prem.	Net Prem.	Jan. 1, 1986	Dec. 31, 1986
1. Franzne Co.	$240,000	$7,800	$2,760	$5,040	$30,000	$32,400
2. President's husband	75,000	3,150		3,150	9,000	9,750

Instructions

(a) Prepare entries in journal form to record the payment of premiums in 1986.

(b) If the president were to die in January, 1987, and the beneficiaries were paid the face amounts of the policies, what entry would the Franzne Company make?

E18-11   Steve Robinson, Inc. has $100,000 in its bonds payable account at the beginning of 1985. Interest at 12% is payable April 1 and Oct. 1. On July 17, the sinking fund trustee for Steve Robinson, Inc. purchases at par $20,000 of the bonds.

Instructions

(a) Prepare the journal entries necessary on April 1 and October 1.

(b) What two methods may be used to disclose the holding on the balance sheet?

E18-12   The general ledger of Jacques Company shows an account for Bonds Payable with a balance of $1,000,000. Interest is payable on these bonds semiannually. Of the $1,000,000, bonds in the amount of $200,000 were recently purchased at par by the sinking fund trustee and are held in the sinking fund as an investment of the fund. The annual rate of interest is 11%.

Instructions

(a) What entry or entries should be made by Jacques Company to record payment of the semiannual interest? (The company makes interest payments directly to bondholders.)

(b) Illustrate how the bonds payable and the sinking fund accounts should be shown in the balance sheet. Assume that the sinking fund investments other than Jacques Company's bonds amount to $247,000, and that the sinking fund cash amounts to $9,100.

E18-13   The transactions given below relate to a fund being accumulated by the Martell Rug Company over a period of 20 years for the construction of additional buildings.

1. Cash is transferred from the general cash account to the fund.
2. Preferred shares of M. Frye Company are purchased as an investment of the fund.
3. Bonds of H. Castle Corporation are purchased between interest dates at a discount as an investment of the fund.
4. Expenses of the fund are paid from the fund cash.
5. Interest is collected on H. Castle Corporation bonds.
6. Bonds held in the fund are sold at a gain between interest dates.
7. Dividends are received on M. Frye Company preferred shares.
8. Common shares held in the fund are sold at a loss.
9. Cash is paid from the fund for building construction.
10. The cash balance remaining in the fund is transferred to general cash.

Instructions

Prepare journal entries to record the miscellaneous transactions listed above, with amounts omitted.

PROBLEMS

P18-1   On December 31, 1984, Dumbo Tool Company acquired 60,000 common shares of Lassie Corporation at a cost of $28 a share; the purchase represented 30% of Lassie Corporation's outstanding shares.

On May 1, 1985, Lassie Corporation paid a cash dividend of $1.50 a common share.

For the year 1985, Lassie Corporation reported net income of $400,000; the market value of the investment was $1,440,000 at December 31, 1985.

On May 1, 1986, Lassie Corporation paid a dividend of $0.50 a share. For the year 1986, Lassie Corporation reported a net income of $600,000; the market value of the investment was $1,620,000 at December 31, 1986.

Instructions

(a) Prepare the journal entries necessary to record the transactions listed above on Dumbo Tool Company's books, assuming that the investment in Lassie Corporation does not represent a significant influence and, therefore, is carried on the cost basis. December 31 is Dumbo Tool Company's year end.

(b) Prepare the journal entries necessary to record the transactions listed above on Dumbo Tool Company's books, assuming that the investment in Lassie Corporation is carried on the equity basis.

(c) What is the carrying value of the investment in Lassie Corporation shares on January 1, 1987, (1) under the cost basis, and (2) under the equity method?

P18-2   On January 1, 1983, Sherri Jenkins Company acquires $100,000 of Pontiff Products, Inc. 9% bonds at a price of $92,794. The interest is payable each December 31, and the bonds mature January 1, 1986. The investment will provide Sherri Jenkins Company with a 12% yield.

Instructions

(a)   Prepare a three-year schedule of interest revenue and bond discount amortization, applying the straight-line method.

(b)   Prepare a three-year schedule of interest revenue and bond discount amortization, applying the effective interest method.

(c)   Prepare the journal entry for the interest receipt of December 31, 1985, and the discount amortization under the straight-line method.

(d)   Prepare the journal entry for the interest receipt of December 31, 1985, and the discount amortization under the effective interest method.

P18-3   On January 1, 1984, Jeffries, Inc. paid $700,000 for 10,000 voting common shares of Wolf Company, which was a 10% interest in Wolf. At that date the net assets of Wolf totalled $6,000,000. The fair values of all of Wolf's identifiable assets and liabilities were equal to their book values. Jeffries does not have the ability to exercise significant influence over the operating and financial policies of Wolf. Jeffries received dividends of $0.90 per share from Wolf on October 1, 1984. Wolf reported net income of $400,000 for the year ended December 31, 1984.

On July 1, 1985, Jeffries paid $2,300,000 for 30,000 additional shares of Wolf Company's voting common shares, which represents a 30% investment in Wolf. The fair values of all of Wolf's identifiable assets net of liabilities were equal to their book value of $6,500,000. As a result of this transaction, Jeffries has the ability to exercise significant influence over the operating and financial policies of Wolf. Jeffries received dividends of $1.10 per share from Wolf on April 1, 1985, and $1.35 per share on October 1, 1985. Wolf reported net income of $500,000 for the year ended December 31, 1985, and $200,000 for the six months ended December 31, 1985. Jeffries amortizes goodwill over a 40-year period.

Instructions

(a)   Prepare a schedule showing the income or loss before income taxes for the year ended December 31, 1984, that Jeffries should report from its investment in Wolf in its income statement issued in March 1985.

(b)   During March, 1986, Jeffries issues comparative financial statements for 1984 and 1985. Prepare schedules showing the income or loss before income taxes for the years ended December 31, 1984, and 1985, that Jeffries should report from its investment in Wolf.

(AICPA adapted)

P18-4   On January 1, 1985, Mouse Corp. bought 3,500 shares of Cat Company common stock at $12 per share. At that time Cat Company's balance sheet showed total assets of $200,000, liabilities of $20,000, common stock (10,000 shares) of $100,000, and retained earnings of $80,000. The difference between book value acquired and the purchase price is attributable to assets having a remaining life of 10 years.

At the end of 1985, Cat Company reported net income of $25,000 and paid cash dividends of $7,500 on December 31, 1985. The market value of Cat Company was $13 per share at December 31, 1985.

On January 1, 1986, Mouse Corp. sold 875 shares of Cat Company stock at the market price of $14 per share.

Instructions

(a)   Prepare journal entries to record the events noted above and data on the books of Mouse Corp., assuming that it is unable to exercise significant influence over Cat Company during 1985 and, therefore, applies the cost method.

(b)   Prepare journal entries to record the events above and data on the books of Mouse Corp. applying the equity method. (Round to the nearest dollar.)

P18-5   On January 3, 1984, Varsity Company purchased for $500,000 cash a 10% interest in Summerset Corp. On that date the net assets of Summerset had a book value of $3,750,000. The excess of cost over the underlying equity in net assets is attributable to undervalued depreciable assets having a remaining life of 10 years from date of the Varsity purchase.

On January 2, 1986, Varsity purchased an additional 30% of Summerset's common shares for $1,900,000 cash when the book value of Summerset's net assets was $5,000,000. The excess was attributable to depreciable assets having a remaining life of eight years.

During 1984, 1985, and 1986 the following occurred:

	Summerset Net Income	Dividends Paid by Summerset to Varsity
1984	$375,000	$12,500
1985	450,000	18,750
1986	500,000	37,500

Instructions

On the books of Varsity Company prepare all journal entries in 1984, 1985, and 1986 that relate to its investment in Summerset Corp., reflecting the data above and a change from the cost method to the equity method.

P18-6   Tourigny Company has the following portfolio of long-term marketable securities at December 31, 1985.

Security	Quantity	Percent Interest	Per Share Cost	Per Share Market
Microtape, Inc.	2,000 shares	8%	$11	$16
Surley Corp.	6,000 shares	14%	23	17
Denson Company	4,000 shares	2%	31	26

Instructions

(a)   What descriptions and amounts should be reported on the face of Tourigny's December 31, 1985, balance sheet relative to long-term investments?

On December 31, 1986, Tourigny's portfolio of long-term marketable securities consisted of the following common stocks.

Security	Quantity	Percent Interest	Per Share Cost	Per Share Market
Surley Corp.	6,000 shares	14%	$23	$30
Denson Company	4,000 shares	2%	31	25
Denson Company	2,000 shares	1%	25	25

During the year 1986, Tourigny Company changed its intent relative to its investment in Microtape, Inc. and reclassified the shares to current asset status when they were selling for $8 per share.

(b)   What descriptions and amounts should be reported on the face of Tourigny's December 31, 1986, balance sheet relative to long-term investments? What descriptions and amounts should be reported to reflect the transactions above in Tourigny's 1986 income statement?

(c)   Assuming that comparative financial statements for 1985 and 1986 are presented, draft the footnote necessary for full disclosure of Tourigny's transactions and position in marketable securities.

P18-7 Calgary Wildcats Corp. makes the following long-term investments during 1985:

Security	Quantity	Percent Interest	Per Share Cost
Ottawa Forms Company	2,400 shares	2%	$80
Lavalle Grader Corp.	7,500 shares	16%	20
Regina Development Inc.	3,000 shares	4%	35

The following information concerning these investments relates to 1985 and 1986:

1. For the year 1985—Cash dividends received:
   Ottawa Forms $4.00 per share
   Lavalle Grader $0.60 per share
   Regina Development $1.50 per share
2. Market values per share, Dec. 31, 1985:
   Ottawa Forms $74
   Lavalle Grader $22
   Regina Development $28
3. For the year 1986—Cash dividends received:
   Ottawa Forms $4.00 per share
   Lavalle Grader $0.15 per share
   Regina Development $1.70 per share
4. On Sept. 30, 1986, the investment in Lavalle Grader was reclassified to current asset status when its market value per share was $15.
5. Market value per share, Dec. 31, 1986:
   Ottawa Forms $68
   Regina Development $46

Instructions

(a) Prepare all of the journal entries to reflect the transactions above and data in accordance with the *CICA Handbook*.

(b) Prepare the descriptions and amounts that should be reported on the face of Calgary Wildcats Corp.'s comparative financial statements for 1985 and 1986 relative to these long-term investments.

(c) Draft the footnote that should accompany the 1985–86 comparative statements relative to the noncurrent marketable securities.

P18-8 Taxi Corporation carries an account in its general ledger called "Investments," which contained the following debits for investment purchases, and no credits.

Feb. 1, 1985	RC Company common, 200 shares	$ 35,200
April 1	Government bonds, 11%, due April 1, 1995, interest payable April 1 and October 1, 100 bonds of $1,000 par each (current asset)	116,600
July 1	Noble Steel Company 12% bonds, par $50,000, dated March 1, 1985, purchased at 103 plus accrued interest, interest payable annually on March 1, due March 1, 2005 (noncurrent asset)	53,500

Instructions

(a) Prepare entries necessary to classify the amounts into proper accounts, assuming that, of the securities held, the government bonds are the only temporary investments.

(b) Prepare the entry to record the accrued interest and amortization of premium on December 31, 1985, using the straight-line method.

(c) The market values of the securities on December 31, 1985, were:

RC Company common shares	$ 33,000 (1% interest)
Government bonds	118,800
Noble Steel Company bonds	59,400

What entry or entries, if any, would you recommend be made?

(d) The government bonds were sold on July 1, 1986, for $117,700 plus accrued interest. Give the proper entry.

(e) Twenty additional shares of RC Company common were received on July 15, 1986, as a stock dividend and, on July 31, 1986, 30 shares of RC Company common were sold at $176 per share. What entries would be made for these two transactions?

P18-9 On January 10, 1985, Pontificate Company purchased 200 shares (a 3% interest) of Meteoric Corporation's common for $26,400 as a long-term investment. On July 12, 1985, Meteoric Corporation announced that one right would be issued for every two shares held.

July 30, 1985	Rights to purchase 100 shares at $100 per share are received. The market value of the shares is $150 per share and the market value of the rights is $20 per right.
Aug. 10	The rights to purchase 40 shares are sold at $20 per right.
Aug. 11	The additional 60 rights are exercised, and 60 shares are purchased at $100 per share.
Nov. 15	50 shares of Meteoric Corporation are sold at $130 per share.

Instructions

Prepare general journal entries on the books of Pontificate Company for the foregoing transactions.

P18-10 Discoteque Company purchases 200 common shares of Gary Nussbaumer, Inc. on February 17. The shares, costing $24,096, are to be a long-term investment for Discoteque Company.

1. On June 30, Gary Nussbaumer, Inc. announces that rights are to be issued. One right will be received for every two shares owned.
2. The rights mentioned in (1) are received on July 15. One hundred shares may be purchased with these rights at $100. The shares are currently selling for $118 per share. Market value of the stock rights is $15 per right.
3. On August 5, 70 rights are exercised, and 70 shares of stock are purchased at $100.
4. On August 12, the remaining stock rights are sold at $17 per right.
5. On September 28, Discoteque Company sells 50 shares at $130 a share.

Instructions

Prepare necessary journal entries for the five numbered items above.

P18-11 Mountainview Company holds 300 common shares of Joe Vidal Company that it purchased for $33,867 as a long-term investment. On January 15, 1986, it is announced that one right will be issued for every four shares of Joe Vidal Company stock held.

Instructions

(a) Prepare entries on Mountainview Company's books for the transactions below that occurred after the date of this announcement. Show all computations in good form.

  1. 100 shares are sold "rights-on" for $12,300.
  2. Rights to purchase 50 additional shares at $100 per share are received. The market value of the shares on this date is $105 per share and the market value of the rights is $6 per right.
  3. The rights are exercised, and 50 additional shares are purchased at $100 per share.
  4. 100 of the original shares are sold at $107 per share.

(b) If the rights had not been exercised but instead had been sold at $6 per right, what would have been the amount of the gain or loss on the sale of the rights?

(c) If the shares purchased through the exercise of the rights is later sold at $107 per share, what is the amount of the gain or loss on the sale?

(d) If the rights had not been exercised, but had been allowed to expire, what would be the proper entry?

P18-12 The transactions given below relate to a sinking fund for retirement of long-term bonds of Coed Corp.

1. In accordance with the terms of the bond indenture, cash in the amount of $125,000 is transferred at the end of the first year from the regular cash account to the sinking fund.
2. Alcan Company 10% bonds of a par value of $40,000, maturing in five years, are purchased for $37,000.
3. Four hundred of West Company's $4 preferred shares are purchased at $52 per share.
4. Annual interest of $4,000 is received on Alcan Company bonds. (Amortize the proper amount of discount, using straight-line amortization.)
5. Sinking fund expenses of $375 are paid from sinking fund cash.
6. Eastern Company 9% bonds with interest payable February 1 and August 1 are purchased on April 15 at par value of $40,000 plus accrued interest.
7. Dividends of $1,600 are received on West Company preferred shares.
8. All the Eastern Company bonds are sold on September 1 at $101 plus accrued interest. Assume interest collected August 1 was properly recorded.
9. Investments carried in the fund at $1,652,000 are sold for $1,601,000.
10. The fund contains cash of $1,611,000 after disposing of all investments and paying all expenses. $1,600,000 of this amount is used to retire the bonds payable at maturity date.
11. The remaining cash balance is returned to the general account.

Instructions

Prepare the journal entries required by Coed Corp. for the transactions above.

P18-13 Cheerleader Corporation has various long-term investments and maintains its books on the accrual basis. The books for the year ended December 31, 1986, have not been closed. Here is an analysis of the Investment account for the year.

Cheerleader Corporation
ANALYSIS OF INVESTMENT ACCOUNT
Year Ended December 31, 1986

1986	Transactions	Fol.	Debit	Credit
Jan. 1	5,000 shares Backand Oil Co.		$ 5,300	
	1,000 shares General Corp.		34,000	
	50 shares, $9 Pfd. Grey Steel		6,000	
	$10,000, 8% bonds Martin Co.		10,270	
Feb. 10	Purchased 5,000 shares, Wash Motors	CD	16,000	
Mar. 1	Cash dividend, Grey Steel	CR		$ 450
Apr. 1	Interest, Martin Co. bonds	CR		400
May 15	Sold 800 rights, General Corp.	CR		1,100
May 16	Exercised 200 rights, General Corp. to purchase 50 shares, General Corp.	CD	2,250	
Aug. 5	Sold 200 shares, Wash Motors	CR		2,500
Sept. 18	Sold 100 shares, General Corp.	CR		3,400
Oct. 1	Interest, Martin Co. bonds			400
			$73,820	$8,250

Your work sheets for the year ended December 31, 1985, show these securities in the Investment account as below.

Date of Acquisition	Number of Shares or Face Value of Bonds	Type of Security	Name of Issuer	Amount
Jan. 1, 1978	5,000	Common shares	Backand Oil Co.	$ 5,300
Apr. 1, 1979	1,000	Common shares	General Corp.	34,000
Nov. 15, 1979	50	$9 preferred shares	Grey Steel	6,000
Oct. 1, 1984	$10,000	8% bonds	Martin Co.	10,270
				$55,570

After inquiry, the following additional data was obtained:

1. The General Corporation on May 12 issued warrants representing the right to purchase, at $45 per share, one share for every four shares held. On May 12, the market value of the shares, rights on, was $50 and exrights was $49. Cheerleader Corporation sold 800 rights on May 15, when the market price of the shares was $51. On May 16, 200 rights were exercised.
2. On June 30, Wash Motors declared a reverse stock split of one-for-five.
3. Cheerleader Corporation acquired the Martin Company bonds, which are due September 30, 1989, for $10,360. Interest is payable April 1 and October 1.
4. The sale of 100 shares of General Corporation stock was part of the 1,000 shares purchased on April 1, 1979. The stock was sold for $65 per share.
5. The government of Backand in early 1986 confiscated the assets of the Backand Oil Company and nationalized the company. Despite the protest of the government, the Backand government has refused to recognize any claims of the shareholders or management of the Backand Oil Company.

Instructions

Prepare a work sheet showing the adjustments to arrive at the correct balance at December 31, 1986, in the Investment account. The work sheet should include the names of other accounts affected by the adjustments or reclassifications. (Formal journal entries are not required, but may be prepared to expedite and support the work sheet.)

(AICPA adapted)

P18-14 Pacemaker, Inc., a domestic corporation having a fiscal year ending June 30, has purchased common shares in several other domestic corporations. As of June 30, 1986, the balance in Pacemaker's Investments account was $1,741,200, the total cost of shares purchased less the cost of shares sold. Pacemaker wishes to restate the Investments account to reflect the provisions of the *CICA Handbook*.

Data concerning the investments follow:

	Ruby, Inc.	Howat, Inc.	Jewel, Inc.
Common shares outstanding	3,000	32,000	100,000
Shares purchased by Pacemaker	(a) 300 (b) 810	8,000	30,000
Date of purchase	(a) July 1, 1983 (b) July 1, 1985	June 30, 1984	June 30, 1985
Cost of shares purchased	(a) $ 98,800 (b) $ 284,000	$ 92,000	$1,340,000

Balance sheet at date indicated:

Assets	July 1, 1985	June 30, 1984	June 30, 1985
Current assets	$ 724,000	$ 79,200	$1,989,000
Fixed assets, net of depreciation	3,276,000	1,432,800	6,600,000
Patent, net of amortization			297,000
	$4,000,000	$1,512,000	$8,886,000

Liabilities and Capital			
Liabilities	$3,000,000	$1,144,000	$4,989,000
Common shares	520,000	160,000	2,800,000
Retained earnings	480,000	208,000	1,097,000
	$4,000,000	$1,512,000	$8,886,000

	July 1, 1985	June 30, 1984	June 30, 1985
Changes in common shares since July 1, 1983	None	None	None
Average remaining life of fixed assets at date of balance sheet (above)	12 years	9 years	22 years
Analysis of retained earnings:			
Balance, July 1, 1983	$ 468,000		
Net income, July 1, 1983, to June 30, 1984	106,800		
Dividend paid—April 1, 1984	(102,000)		
Balance, June 30, 1984	472,800	$ 208,000	
Net income (loss), July 1, 1984, to June 30, 1985	111,200	(4,000)	
Dividend paid—April 1, 1985	(104,000)		
Balance, June 30, 1985	480,000	204,000	$1,097,000
Net income, July 1, 1985, to June 30, 1986	50,000	36,000	660,000
Dividends paid:			
December 18, 1985			(300,000)
June 1, 1986		(11,200)	
Balance, June 30, 1986	$ 530,000	$ 228,800	$1,457,000

Pacemaker's first purchase of Ruby's shares was made because of the high rate of return expected on the investment. All later purchases of shares have been made to gain substantial influence over the operations of the various companies.

In December, 1985, changing market conditions caused Pacemaker to reevaluate its relation to Howat. On December 31, 1985, Pacemaker sold 6,400 shares of Howat for $108,800.

For Ruby and Howat, the fair values of the net assets did not differ materially from the book values as shown in the balance sheets above. For Jewel, fair values exceeded book values only with respect to the patent, which had a fair value of $600,000 and a remaining life of 15 years as of June 30, 1985.

Instructions

Prepare a work sheet to restate Pacemaker's Investments account as of June 30, 1986, and its investment income by year for the three years then ended. Transactions should be listed in chronological order, and supporting computations should be in good form. **Ignore income taxes.** Amortization of goodwill, if any, is to be over a 40-year period. Use the following columnar headings for your work sheet:

		Investments			Investment Income Year Ended June 30			Other Accounts	
		Ruby	Howat	Jewel	1984	1985	1986	Amount	Name
Date	Description	Dr.(Cr.)	Dr.(Cr.)	Dr.(Cr.)	Cr.(Dr.)	Cr.(Dr.)	Cr.(Dr.)	Dr.(Cr.)	

(AICPA Adapted)

PART

5

ISSUES RELATED TO
INCOME MEASUREMENT

19

REVENUE RECOGNITION

Revenue recognition is one of the most difficult and pressing problems facing the accounting profession. Although the profession has general guidelines to determine when revenue should be recognized, the many methods of marketing and selling products and services make it extremely difficult to develop guidelines that will apply to all situations. In the United States significant lawsuits involving revenue recognition problems, such as those involving U.S. Financial (related party transactions), National Student Marketing (revenue that did not materialize), and Equity Funding (sales that never were) illustrate the complexity of determining when and at what amount revenue should be recognized. Similar revenue recognition problems have emerged in Canada with the failure of the Canadian Commercial Bank (recognizing revenue before collection was reasonably assured) and Grandma Lee's (recognizing revenue before all significant acts were completed).

Revenue recognition is difficult in such cases as sales of personal property where right of unlimited returns exists, accounting for franchise fees, exchanges of nonmonetary assets, and service fee revenues from such businesses as health spas, mortuaries, advertising agencies, and travel agencies. In October, 1985, the CICA published an *Exposure Draft*, "Revenue," proposing accounting standards for revenue recognition. Until these proposed standards are adopted as a *Handbook* section, Canadian accountants will continue to refer to related authoritative literature in the United States.

One of the most complex and basic questions in measuring and timing revenue recognition is determining when a sale is a sale.

GUIDELINES FOR REVENUE RECOGNITION[1]

Revenue is defined as:

> ...the gross inflow of cash, receivables, or other consideration arising in the course of the ordinary activities of an enterprise from the sale of goods, from the rendering of services, and from the use by others of enterprise resources yielding interest, royalties, and dividends.[2]

As an element in the income measurement process, the revenue for a period is generally determined independently of expenses by applying the revenue recognition principle.[3]

To use the latest terminology contained in the *Exposure Draft*, "**revenue should be recognized when (1) all significant acts necessary to entitle the enterprise to the revenue have been performed; (2) reasonable assurance exists regarding the measurement of the consideration to be received; and (3) ultimate collection of the consideration is reasonably assured.**"[4] Revenues are **realized** when goods and services are exchanged for cash and claims to cash (receivables). Revenues are **realizable** when assets received in exchange are readily convertible to known amounts of cash or claims to cash. Finally, revenues are **earned** when the entity has substantially accomplished what it must do in order to be entitled to the benefits represented by the revenues; that is, when the earning process is complete or virtually complete.[5] In accordance with this principle: (a) revenue from selling products is usually recognized at the date of sale (when the vendor has transferred to the purchaser the "significant" risks and rewards attributed to ownership[6]), generally interpreted to mean the date of delivery to customers; (b) revenue from services rendered is recognized when the consideration due may be measured with reasonable assurance (implying that the service has been performed and is billable); (c) revenue from permitting others to use enterprise assets, such as interest, rent, and royalties, is recognized as time passes, as the assets are used, or according to the terms of the relevant agreement.

These statements describe the conceptual nature of revenue and are the basis of accounting for revenue transactions. Yet, in practice, there are departures from the revenue recognition principle; other points in the earning process are sometimes used in recognizing revenue, owing in great measure to the considerable variety of revenue transactions. For example, many revenue recognition problems develop because payment is not reasonably assured or because it is difficult to determine

---

[1]Most of the recent accounting pronouncements on revenue recognition, and much of present practice, are based on *Statement of Accounting Principles Board No. 4*, "Basic Concepts and Accounting Principles Underlying Financial Statements of Business Enterprises" (New York: AICPA, 1970).

[2]*CICA Exposure Draft*, "Revenue" (October, 1985).

[3]**Recognition** "is mainly concerned with when revenue is recognized in the financial statements of an enterprise." (*CICA Exposure Draft*, "Revenue," par. 5.) "Recognition includes depiction of an item in both words and numbers, with the amount included in the totals of the financial statements." *Statement of Financial Accounting Concepts No. 5* (Stamford, Conn.: FASB, 1980), par. 6.

[4]*Ibid.*

[5]**Gains** (as contrasted to revenues) commonly result from transactions and other events that involve no "earning process" and, for gain recognition, being earned is generally less significant than being realized or realizable. Gains are commonly recognized at the time of sale of an asset, disposition of a liability, or when prices of certain assets change.

[6]*CICA Exposure Draft*, "Revenue," par. 19.

when the earning process is complete. Real estate land sales provide a good example. To illustrate, in the United States at one time General Development recognized the entire sales price of real estate as revenue as soon as it received 5% of the purchase price or a minimum downpayment and two monthly payments. Cavenaugh Industries required that the percentage collected be only 3%. Dart Industries required a 10% down payment, as did Boise Cascade, yet McCulloch demanded 15%. Similar variations in revenue recognition practices might also be found in Canada.

The profession is continually developing criteria that should be met before a departure from the sale basis is acceptable. An FASB study found some common **reasons for departures from the sale basis.**[7] One reason is a desire to **recognize** the effect of earning activities (revenue) **earlier** in the earning process than the time of the sale if there is a high degree of certainty about the amount of revenue earned. A second reason is a desire to **delay recognition** of revenue beyond the time of sale if the degree of uncertainty concerning the amount of either revenue or costs is sufficiently high or if the sale does not represent substantial completion of the earning process.

The same FASB study concluded that there are significant inconsistencies in accounting pronouncements and, consequently, in practice for recognizing revenue. As a result similar transactions and other events are not treated similarly. Yet the study found some common threads underlying the rationale for particular methods. Recognition issues are frequently resolved by reference to such concepts as probability of collection, transfer of benefits and risks of ownership, measurability of revenues and costs, completion of the earning process, and substance over form. Unfortunately, these concepts are often applied differently.[8] Only time will determine whether or not the CICA's recently proposed criteria (transfer of risk and measurability of consideration) will be accepted and, if so, will provide sufficient guidance for standardizing future practice in revenue accounting.

This chapter is devoted exclusively to the discussion and illustration of two of the four general types of revenue transactions described earlier, namely, (1) selling products and (2) rendering services—both of which are **sales transactions.** Accounting for the other two types of revenue transactions, (3) revenue from permitting others to use enterprise assets, and (4) revenue from disposing of assets other than products, is discussed in several other sections of this text. Our discussion of product and certain service sales transactions is organized around the following topics:

1. Revenue recognition at point of sale (delivery).
2. Revenue recognition before delivery.
3. Revenue recognition after delivery.
4. Revenue recognition for special sales transactions—franchises and consignments.

Accounting for service sales transactions is presented in Appendix 19B of this chapter.

REVENUE RECOGNITION AT POINT OF SALE (DELIVERY)

Many business enterprises wish to market one or more products or services; retail stores purchase many different articles they wish to sell; manufacturers market the

[7]Henry R. Jaenicke, *Survey of Present Practices in Recognizing Revenues, Expenses, Gains, and Losses,* A Research Report (Stamford, Conn.: FASB, 1981), p. 11.

[8]*Ibid.*, p. 16.

products they have fabricated or processed; transportation companies offer to transport freight or persons; public accounting firms offer the services of their expert accountants; and so on. In return for the product or service sold, the enterprise usually receives cash or a promise of cash at some date in the future (credit sales). Thus sales transactions have two sides: on the one hand, a product or service is given; on the other, cash or a promise of cash in the future is received.

Inherent in any sales transaction is the element of gain or loss. Therefore, the enterprise does not merely record an increase in one asset and a decrease in another, but recognizes that the transaction involves both revenue and cost elements, each of which is recorded separately. Net income is measured when expenses are deducted from revenues.

Cash Sales versus Credit Sales

Many retail sales, such as those made by grocery stores and drug stores, are made for cash. Cash is collected when goods are transferred to the customer. Cash sales differ from credit sales in that once made they are complete in themselves; no additional steps are necessary to collect cash from the customer. In a credit sale (sales on account), the seller receives a promise by the purchaser to pay cash in the future. The consideration obtained by the seller is a receivable rather than cash in hand. (The accounting treatment accorded receivable transactions and related allowance for doubtful accounts was discussed in Chapter 7.)

Revenue Recognition When Right of Return Exists

Whether cash or credit sales are involved, a special problem arises with claims for returns and allowances. In Chapter 7, the accounting treatment for normal returns and allowances was presented. However, certain companies experience such a **high ratio of returned merchandise** to sales that they find it necessary to postpone reporting sales until the return privilege has substantially expired. For example, in the publishing industry the rate of return runs up to 25% for hardcover books and 65% for some magazines. Other types of companies that experience high return rates are perishable food dealers; rack jobbers or distributors who sell to retail outlets; record and tape companies; and some toy and sporting goods manufacturers. Returns in these industries frequently are made either through a right of contract or as a matter of practice involving "guaranteed sales" agreements or consignments.

Three alternative methods are available when the seller is exposed to continued risks of ownership through return of the product. These are: (1) not recording a sale until all return privileges have expired; (2) recording the sale, but reducing sales by an estimate of future returns; and (3) recording the sale and accounting for the returns as they occur in future periods. The FASB concluded that if a company sells its product but gives the buyer the right to return the product, revenue from the sales transaction shall be recognized at the time of sale only if **all** of the following six conditions have been met:[9]

1. The seller's price to the buyer is substantially fixed or determinable at the date of sale.

---

[9]"Revenue Recognition When Right of Return Exists," *Statement of Financial Accounting Standards No. 48* (Stamford, Conn.: FASB, 1981), par. 6.

2. The buyer has paid the seller, or the buyer is obligated to pay the seller and the obligation is not contingent on resale of the product.

3. The buyer's obligation to the seller would not be changed in the event of theft or physical destruction or damage to the product.

4. The buyer acquiring the product for resale has economic substance apart from that provided by the seller.

5. The seller does not have significant obligations for future performance to bring about resale of the product by the buyer directly.

6. The amount of future returns can be reasonably estimated.

These six conditions help to clarify whether the vendor has transferred the risks of ownership and to identify the factors influencing measurement of the consideration that is expected to be derived from the sales. Sales revenue and cost of sales that are not recognized at the time of sale because the six conditions above are not met should be recognized either when the return privilege has substantially expired or when those six conditions subsequently are met (whichever occurs first). Sales revenue and cost of sales reported in the income statement should be reduced to report estimated returns.[10]

REVENUE RECOGNITION BEFORE DELIVERY

Sometimes questions arise as to whether revenue should be recognized before the actual delivery of the product. For instance, revenue might be recognized:

1. At completion of production.
2. During production.

Revenue Recognition at Completion of Production

In certain cases revenue is recognized at the completion of production even though no sale has been made. Examples of such situations involve precious metals or agricultural products with assured prices. Revenue is recognized when these metals are mined or agricultural crops harvested because the sales price is reasonably assured, the units are interchangeable, and no significant costs are involved in distributing the product (see discussion in Chapter 9, page 422, "Valuation at Net Realizable Value").[11] When a sale or cash receipt precedes production and delivery, as in the case of magazine subscriptions, revenues may be recognized as earned by production and delivery.[12]

Revenue Recognition During Production

Such long-term contracts as construction contracts, contracts for development of military and commercial aircraft, weapons delivery systems, and space exploration hardware frequently provide that the seller (builder) may bill the purchaser at intervals as various points in the project are reached. When the project to be constructed consists of separable units (e.g., a group of buildings or many kilometres

---

[10]*Ibid.*, pars. 6 and 7.

[11]Such revenue satisfies the criteria of *Concepts Statement No. 5* since the assets are readily realizable and the earning process is virtually complete (see par. 84, item e).

[12]*Statement of Financial Accounting Concepts No. 5*, par. 84, item b.

of roadway), provision may be made for passage of title as well as billing at stated stages of completion, as with the completion of each building unit or every 10 km of road. Such contract provisions in effect provide for delivery in instalments, and the accounting records should report this by taking up sales as "delivered."[13]

Percentage-of-Completion versus Completed Contract   The accounting measurements associated with long-term projects are difficult because events and amounts must be estimated for a period of years. Construction companies, for example, often invest capital and labour over a considerable time. Production on one contract or job may extend over two or more accounting periods, and progress billings and collections for work performed at predetermined intervals are commonplace. Two distinctly different methods of accounting for long-term construction contracts are recognized by the accounting profession.[14]

1. **Percentage-of-completion method.** Revenues and gross profit are recognized each period based upon the progress of the construction; that is, the percentage of completion. Construction costs **plus gross profit earned to date** are accumulated in an inventory account (Construction in Process), and progress billings are accumulated in a contra inventory account (Billings on Construction in Process).
2. **Completed-contract method.** Revenues and gross profit are recognized only when the contract is completed. Construction costs are accumulated in an inventory account (Construction in Process), and progress billings are accumulated in a contra inventory account (Billings on Construction in Process).

When to use the Percentage-of-Completion Method   The rationale for using percentage-of-completion accounting is that under most of these contracts the buyer and seller have obtained enforceable rights. The buyer has the legal right to require specific performance on the contract; the seller has the right to require progress payments that provide evidence of the buyer's ownership interest. As a result, the economics of the situation suggest that a continuous sale occurs as the work progresses, and revenue should be recognized accordingly.

The accounting profession has for many years considered the percentage-of completion method preferable "**when estimates of costs to complete and extent of progress toward completion of long-term contracts are reasonably dependable.**"[15]

In the 1985 *Exposure Draft*, the CICA recommends that the completed-contract method and the percentage-of-completion method be used in specified circumstances, and that these two methods not be viewed as acceptable alternatives in the same circumstances. The method chosen should be the one that best relates "revenue to the work accomplished."[16] Further guidance in this regard may be found in a 1981 AICPA *Statement of Position* which recommends use of the percentage-of-completion method when estimates of progress toward completion, revenues, and costs are reasonably dependable and all the following conditions exist:[17]

---

[13]*Ibid.*, par. 84, item c.

[14]*Financial Reporting in Canada—1983* reports that in 1982, of the 35 of its 325 sample companies that referred to long-term construction contracts, 25 used the percentage-of-completion method, 7 used the completed-contract method, and 3 used both methods.

It is not uncommon for companies to use the completed-contract method for income tax purposes and the percentage-of-completion method for financial accounting purposes.

[15]Committee on Accounting Procedure, "Long-Term Construction-Type Contracts," *Accounting Research Bulletin No. 45* (New York: AICPA, 1955), p. 7.

[16]*CICA Exposure Draft*, "Revenue," par. 20.

[17]"Accounting for Performance of Construction-Type and Certain Production-Type Contracts," *Statement of Position 81-1* (New York: AICPA, 1981), par. 23.

1. The contract clearly specifies the enforceable rights regarding goods or services to be provided and received by the parties, the consideration to be exchanged, and the manner and terms of settlement.
2. The buyer can be expected to satisfy all obligations under the contract.
3. The contractor can be expected to perform the contractual obligation.

When to Use the Completed-Contract Method   The completed-contract method should be used only (1) when an entity has primarily short-term contracts, or (2) when the conditions for using the percentage-of-completion method cannot be met, or (3) when there are inherent hazards in the contract beyond the normal, recurring business risks. The presumption is that percentage-of-completion is the better method and that the completed-contract method should be used only when the percentage-of-completion method is inappropriate.

Percentage-of-Completion Method

The percentage-of-completion method recognizes revenues, costs, and gross profit as progress is made toward completion on a long-term contract. To defer recognition of these items until completion of the entire contract is to misrepresent the efforts (costs) and accomplishments (revenues); that is, the operations of the interim accounting periods. In order to apply the percentage-of-completion method, one must have some basis or standard for measuring the progress toward completion at particular interim dates.

Measuring the Progress Toward Completion   As one practising accountant recently wrote, "The big problem in applying the percentage-of-completion method that cannot be demonstrated in an example has to do with the ability to make reasonably accurate estimates of completion and the final gross profit."[18]

Various methods are used in practice to determine the **extent of progress toward completion;** the most common are "cost-to-cost method," "efforts-expended methods," and "units-of-work performed method." The objective of all the methods is to measure the extent of progress in terms of costs, units, or value added. The various measures (costs incurred, labour hours worked, tonnes produced, storeys completed, etc.) are identified and classified as input and output measures. **Input measures** (costs incurred, labour hours worked) are made in terms of efforts devoted to a contract. **Output measures** (tonnes produced, storeys of a building completed, kilometres of a highway completed) are made in terms of results. Neither is universally applicable to all long-term projects; their use requires careful tailoring to the circumstances and the exercise of judgement.

Both input and output measures have disadvantages in certain circumstances. The input measure is based on an established relationship between a unit of input and productivity. If inefficiencies cause the productivity relationship to change, inaccurate measurements result. Another potential problem of using an input method is known as "front-end loading," which produces higher estimates of completion by virtue of incurring significant costs up front. Some early-stage construction costs should be disregarded if they do not relate to contract performance; for example, costs of uninstalled materials or costs of subcontracts not yet performed.

---

[18]Richard S. Hickok, "New Guidance for Construction Contractors: 'A Credit Plus,' " *The Journal of Accountancy* (March, 1982), p. 46.

Output measures can result in inaccurate measurement if the units used as the basis are not comparable in time, effort, or cost to complete. For example, using storeys completed can be deceiving; to complete the first storey of an eight-storey building may require more than one-eighth the total cost, owing to the foundation and substructure.

One of the more popular input measures used to determine the progress toward completion is the **cost-to-cost method.** Under the cost-to-cost method, the percentage of completion is measured by comparing costs incurred to date with the most recent estimate of the total costs to complete the contract as shown in the following formula:

$$\frac{\text{Costs incurred to end of current period}}{\text{Most recent estimate of total costs}} = \text{Percentage complete}$$

The percentage that costs incurred bear to total estimated costs is applied to the total revenue and the estimated total gross profit on the contract. Thus, we arrive at the revenue and the gross profit amounts to be recognized to date. The amounts of revenue and gross profit recognized each year are computed using the following formula:

$$\frac{\text{Costs incurred to end of current period}}{\text{Most recent estimate of total costs}} \times \begin{matrix}\text{Estimated total}\\ \text{revenue}\\ \text{(or gross profit)}\\ \text{from the contract}\end{matrix} - \begin{matrix}\text{Total revenue}\\ \text{(or gross profit)}\\ \text{recognized}\\ \text{in prior periods}\end{matrix} = \begin{matrix}\text{Current period}\\ \text{revenue}\\ \text{(or}\\ \text{gross profit)}\end{matrix}$$

Because the cost-to-cost method is recommended in the United States (without excluding other bases for measuring progress toward completion), we have adopted it for use in our illustrations.[19]

Illustration of the Percentage-of-Completion Method (Cost-to-Cost Basis) Assume that the Pfeifer Construction has a contract starting July, 1986, to construct a $4,500,000 bridge that is expected to be completed in October, 1988, at total cost of $4,000,000. The following data pertain to the construction period. (Note that by the end of 1987 the estimated total cost has increased from $4,000,000 to $4,050,000.)

	1986	1987	1988
Costs to date	$1,000,000	$2,916,000	$4,050,000
Estimated costs to complete	3,000,000	1,134,000	—
Progress billings during the year	900,000	2,400,000	1,200,000
Cash collected during the year	750,000	1,750,000	2,000,000

The percentage completed would be computed as follows:

[19]See *ARB No. 45*, par. 4.

Pfeifer Construction Company
Percentage-of-Completion Method (Cost-to-Cost Basis)

	1986	1987	1988
Contract price	$4,500,000	$4,500,000	$4,500,000
Less: Estimated cost—			
Costs to date	1,000,000	2,916,000	4,050,000
Estimated costs to complete	3,000,000	1,134,000	–0–
Estimated total costs	4,000,000	4,050,000	4,050,000
Estimated total gross profit	$ 500,000	$ 450,000	$ 450,000
Percentage completed:	25%	72%	100%
	$\left(\dfrac{\$1,000,000}{\$4,000,000}\right)$	$\left(\dfrac{\$2,916,000}{\$4,050,000}\right)$	$\left(\dfrac{\$4,050,000}{\$4,050,000}\right)$

On the basis of the data above, the following entries would be prepared (1) to record the costs of construction, (2) to record progress billings, and (3) to record collections. (These entries appear as summaries of the many transactions that would be entered individually as they occur during the year.)

	1986		1987		1988	
To record cost of construction:						
Construction in Process	1,000,000		1,916,000		1,134,000	
Materials, cash,						
payables, etc.		1,000,000		1,916,000		1,134,000
To record progress billings:						
Accounts Receivable	900,000		2,400,000		1,200,000	
Billings on Construction						
in Process		900,000		2,400,000		1,200,000
To record collections:						
Cash	750,000		1,750,000		2,000,000	
Accounts Receivable		750,000		1,750,000		2,000,000

In this illustration, the costs incurred to date as a proportion of the estimated total costs to be incurred on the project is a measure of the extent of progress toward completion. The estimated revenue and gross profit to be recognized for each year is calculated as follows:

	1986	1987	1988
Revenue recognized in:			
1986 $4,500,000 × 25%	$1,125,000		
1987 $4,500,000 × 72%		$3,240,000	
Less: Revenue recognized in 1986		1,125,000	
Revenue in 1987		2,115,000	
1988 $4,500,000 × 100%			$4,500,000
Less: Revenue recognized in			
1986 and 1987			3,240,000
Revenue in 1988			$1,260,000

	1986	1987	1988
Gross profit recognized in:			
1986 $500,000 × 25%	$ 125,000		
1987 $450,000 × 72%		$ 324,000	
Less: Gross profit recognized in 1986		125,000	
Gross profit in 1987		$ 199,000	
1988 $450,000 × 100%			$ 450,000
Less: Gross profit recognized in 1986 and 1987			324,000
Gross profit in 1988			$ 126,000

The entries to recognize revenue and gross profit each year and to record completion and final approval of the contract are shown below. Note that Revenue from Long-Term Contracts is credited for the amounts as computed above, while gross profit as computed above is debited to Construction in Process. The difference between the amounts recognized each year for revenue and gross profit is debited to a nominal account, Construction Costs (similar to Cost of Goods Sold in a manufacturing enterprise), which is reported in the income statement.

	1986	1987	1988
To recognize revenue and gross profit:			
Construction in Process (gross profit)	125,000	199,000	126,000
Construction Costs	1,000,000	1,916,000	1,134,000
Revenue from Long-Term Contract	1,125,000	2,115,000	1,260,000
To record final approval of the contract:			
Billings on Construction in Process			4,500,000
Construction in Process			4,500,000

Note that the Construction in Process account is not affected by the entry to recognize construction expense. Costs must continue to be accumulated in the Construction in Process account to maintain a record of total costs incurred (plus recognized profit) to date. Although theoretically a series of "sales" takes place using the percentage-of-completion method, the inventory cost cannot be removed

Construction in Process				
1986 construction costs	$1,000,000	Dec. 31/88 to close		
1986 recognized gross profit	125,000	completed		
1987 construction costs	1,916,000	project	$4,500,000	
1987 recognized gross profit	199,000			
1988 construction costs	1,134,000			
1988 recognized gross profit	126,000			
Total	$4,500,000	Total	$4,500,000	

until the construction is completed and transferred to the new owner. The Construction in Process account would include the summarized entries over the term of the construction project shown on page 878.

The Pfeifer Construction Company illustration contained a change in estimate in the second year, 1987, where the estimated total costs increased from $4,000,000 to $4,050,000. By adjusting the percentage completed to the changed estimate of total costs and then deducting from revenues and gross profit computed for progress-to-date the amount of revenues and gross profit recognized in prior periods, the change in estimate was accounted for in a **cumulative catch-up manner.** That is, the change in estimate is accounted for in the period of change so that the balance sheet at the end of the period of change and the accounting in subsequent periods are as they would have been if the revised estimate had been the original estimate.

Financial Statement Presentation—Percentage of Completion   Generally when a receivable from a sale is recorded, the Inventory account is reduced by an accompanying entry; but in this case both the receivable and the inventory continue to be carried. By subtracting the balance in the Billings account from Construction in Process, double-counting the inventory is avoided.

During the life of the contract, the difference between the Construction in Process and the Billings on Construction in Process accounts is reported in the balance sheet as a current asset if a debit, and as a current liability if a credit. When the costs incurred plus the gross profit recognized to date (the balance in Construction in Process) exceed the billings, this excess is reported as a current asset entitled "Costs and Recognized Profit in Excess of Billings." The unbilled portion of revenue recognized to date can be calculated at any time by subtracting the billings to date from the revenue recognized to date as illustrated below for 1986 for Pfeifer Construction:

Calculation of Unbilled Contract Price at Dec. 31, 1986

Contract revenue recognized to date: $4,500,000 $\times \dfrac{\$1,000,000}{\$4,000,000}$ = $1,125,000

Billings to date	900,000
Unbilled	$ 225,000

When the billings exceed costs incurred and gross profit to date, this excess is reported as a current liability entitled "Billings in Excess of Costs and Recognized Profit." When a company has a number of projects, and costs exceed billings on some contracts, while billings exceed costs on others, the contracts should be segregated so that the asset side includes only those contracts on which costs and recognized profit exceed billings; the liability side includes only those on which billings exceed costs and recognized profit. Separate disclosures of the dollar volume of billings and costs are preferable to a presentation of the net difference only.

Using data from the previous illustration, the Pfeifer Construction Company would report the status and results of its long-term construction activities under the percentage-of-completion method as follows:

Pfeifer Construction Company
FINANCIAL STATEMENT PRESENTATION—PERCENTAGE-OF-COMPLETION METHOD

	1986	1987	1988
Income Statement			
Revenue from long-term contracts	$1,125,000	$2,115,000	$1,260,000
Costs of construction	1,000,000	1,916,000	1,134,000
Gross profit	$ 125,000	$ 199,000	$ 126,000

Balance Sheet (Dec. 31)

		1986	1987	
Current assets:				
Accounts receivable		$ 150,000	$ 800,000	
Inventories				
Construction in process	$ 1,125,000			
Less: Billings	900,000			
Costs and recognized profit				
in excess of billings		$ 225,000		
Current liabilities:				
Billings ($3,300,000) in excess of				
costs and recognized profit				
($3,240,000)			$ 60,000	

Note 1—Summary of significant accounting policies.
Long-Term Construction Contracts. The company recognizes revenues and reports profits from long-term construction contracts, its principal business, under the percentage-of-completion method of accounting. These contracts generally extend for periods in excess of one year. The amounts of revenues and profits recognized each year are based on the ratio of costs incurred to the total estimated costs. Costs included in construction in process include direct material, direct labour, and project-related overhead. Corporate general and administrative expenses are charged to the periods as incurred and are not allocated to construction contracts.

Completed-Contract Method

Under the completed-contract method, revenue and gross profit are recognized only at point of sale; that is, when the contract is completed. Costs of long-term contracts in process and current billings are accumulated, but there are no interim charges or credits to income statement accounts for revenues, costs, and gross profit.

The principal advantage of the completed-contract method is that reported revenue is based on final results rather than on estimates of unperformed work. Its major disadvantage is that a distortion of earnings may occur; it does not reflect current performance when the period of a contract extends into more than one accounting period. Although operations may be fairly uniform during the period of the contract, revenue is not reported until the year of completion.

The **annual entries** to record costs of construction, progress billings, and collections from customers would be identical to those illustrated under the percentage-of-completion method. An entry to recognize revenue and gross profit would not be made until the contract is completed. For the bridge project of Pfeifer Construction Company illustrated on the preceding pages, the following entries are made in

1988 under the completed-contract method to recognize revenue and costs and to close out the inventory and billing accounts:

Billings on Construction in Process	4,500,000	
Revenue from Long-Term Contracts		4,500,000
Costs of Construction	4,050,000	
Construction in Process		4,050,000

Comparing the two methods relative to the same bridge project, the Pfeifer Construction Company would have recognized gross profit as follows:

	Percentage-of-Completion	Completed-Contract
1986	$125,000	$ -0-
1987	199,000	-0-
1988	126,000	450,000
Total	$450,000	$450,000

Using the data from the illustration, the Pfeifer Construction Company would report the status and results of its long-term construction activities under the completed-contract method as follows:

Pfeifer Construction Company
FINANCIAL STATEMENT PRESENTATION—COMPLETED-CONTRACT METHOD

		1986	1987	1988
Income Statement				
Revenue from long-term contracts		—	—	$4,500,000
Costs of construction		—	—	4,050,000
Gross profit		—	—	$ 450,000
Balance Sheet (Dec. 31)				
Current assets:				
Accounts receivable		$ 150,000	$ 800,000	
Inventories				
Construction in process	$1,000,000			
Less: Billings	900,000			
Unbilled contract costs	$ 100,000			
Current liabilities:				
Billings ($3,300,000) in excess of				
contract costs ($2,916,000)			$ 384,000	

Note 1—Summary of significant accounting policies.
Long-term Construction Contracts. The company recognizes revenues and reports profits from long-term construction contracts, its principal business, under the completed-contract method. These contracts generally extend for periods in excess of one year. Contract costs and billings are accumulated during the periods of construction, but no revenues or profits are recognized until completion of the contract. Costs included in construction in process include direct material, direct labour, and project-related overhead. Corporate general and administrative expenses are charged to the periods as incurred and are not allocated to construction contracts.

Accounting for Long-term Contract Losses

Two types of losses may be recognized under long-term contracts:[20]

1. **Loss in current period on a profitable contract.** This condition arises when, during construction, there is a significant increase in the estimated total contract costs but the increase does not eliminate all profit on the contract. Under the percentage-of-completion method only, the estimated cost increase requires a current period adjustment of excess gross profit recognized on the project in prior periods. This adjustment is recorded as a loss in the current period because it is a **change in accounting estimate** (discussed in Chapter 23).

2. **Loss on an unprofitable contract.** Cost estimates at the end of the current period may indicate that a loss will result on completion of the entire contract. Under **both** the percentage-of-completion and the completed-contract methods, the entire expected contract loss must be recognized in the current period.

The treatment described for both types of losses are consistent with accounting's custom of anticipating foreseeable losses in order to avoid overstatement of current and future income (conservatism).

Losses in Current Period   To illustrate a loss in the current period on a contract originally expected to be profitable upon completion, assume that on December 31, 1987, Pfeifer Construction Company estimates the costs to complete the bridge contract at $1,468,962 instead of $1,134,000 (refer to page 877). Assuming all other data are the same as before, Pfeifer would compute the percentage completed and recognize the loss as follows:

Computation of Recognizable Loss—1987
Percentage-of-Completion Method

Costs to date (Dec. 31/87)	$2,916,000
Estimated costs to complete (revised)	1,468,962
Estimated total costs	$4,384,962
Percentage completed ($2,916,000 ÷ $4,384,962)	66 1/2%
Revenue recognized in 1987	
($4,500,000 × 66 1/2% − $1,125,000)	$1,867,500
Costs incurred in 1987	1,916,000
Loss recognized in 1987	$ 48,500

Compare these computations with those for 1987 on pages 877 and 878. Note the change in percentage completed from 72% to 66 1/2% owing to the estimated increase in future costs to complete.

The 1987 loss of $48,500 is a cumulative adjustment of the "excessive" gross profit recognized on the contract in 1986. Rather than restate the prior period, the prior period misstatement is absorbed entirely in the current period. In this illustration the adjustment was large enough to result in recognition of a loss.

Pfeifer Construction would record the loss in 1987 as follows:

Construction Expenses	1,916,000	
Construction in Process (Loss)		48,500
Revenue from Long-Term Contract		1,867,500

---

[20]Sak Bhamornsiri, "Losses from Construction Contracts," *The Journal of Accountancy* (April, 1982), p. 26.

The loss of $48,500 will be reported on the 1987 income statement as the difference between the reported revenues of $1,867,500 and the costs of $1,916,000.[21] **Under the completed-contract method, no loss is recognized in 1987 because the contract is still expected to result in a profit** that will be recognized in the year of completion.

EASY
ON
THIS
INFO

Loss on an Unprofitable Contract   To illustrate the accounting for an overall loss on a long-term contract, assume that at December 31, 1987, Pfeifer Construction Company estimates the costs to complete the bridge contract at $1,640,250 instead of $1,134,000. Revised estimates relative to the bridge contract appear as follows:

	1986 Original Estimates	1987 Revised Estimates
Contract price	$4,500,000	$4,500,000
Estimated total cost	4,000,000	4,556,250 *
Estimated gross profit (loss)	$ 500,000	$ (56,250)

*($2,916,000 + $1,640,250)

Under the **percentage-of-completion method**, $125,000 of gross profit was recognized in 1986 (see page 878). This $125,000 must be offset in 1987 because it is now not expected to be realized. In addition the cumulative loss of $56,520 must be recognized also in 1987 since losses must be recognized as soon as estimable. Therefore, a total loss of $181,250 ($125,000 + $56,250) must be recognized in 1987. The revenues and costs can be computed and recorded in the normal manner with a provision for the loss that would be recognized in 1988 added to the 1987 loss as computed under the percentage-of-completion method shown below:

Computation of Recognizable Loss—1987 Percentage-of-Completion Method	
Costs to date (Dec. 31/87)	$2,916,000
Estimated costs to complete	1,640,250
Estimated total costs	$4,556,250
Percentage completed ($2,916,000 ÷ $4,556,250)	64%
Revenue recognized in 1987 ($4,500,000 × 64% − $1,125,000)	$1,755,000
Costs incurred in 1987	1,916,000
Loss to date	161,000
Expected loss to complete project	20,250[a]
Loss recognized in 1987	$ 181,250
[a]1988 Revenue: ($4,500,000 − $1,125,000 − $1,755,000)	$1,620,000
1988 Estimated costs:	1,640,250
1988 Loss (percentage-of-completion basis)	$ 20,250

[21]In 1988 Pfeifer Construction will recognize the remaining 33 1/2% of the revenue, $1,507,500, with costs of $1,468,962 as estimated, and report a gross profit of $38,538. The total gross profit over the three years of the contract would be $115,038 [$125,000 (1986) − $48,500 (1987) + $38,538 (1988)], which is the difference between the total contract revenue of $4,500,000 and the total contract costs of $4,384,962.

Pfeifer Construction would record the loss in 1987 as follows. (Costs incurred in 1987 are increased by the anticipated 1988 loss recognized in 1987.)

Construction Expenses ($1,916,000 + $20,250)	1,936,250[22]	
Construction in Process		181,250
Revenue from Long-Term Contracts		1,755,000

At the end of 1987, Construction in Process has a balance of $2,859,750 as shown below:[23]

Construction in Process			
1986 Construction costs	$1,000,000		
1986 Recognized gross profit	125,000		
1987 Construction costs	1,916,000	1987 Recognized loss	$181,250
Balance, $2,859,750			

Under the **completed-contract method,** the contract loss $56,250 is also recognized in the year in which it first became evident through the following entry in 1987:

Loss from Long-Term Contracts	56,250	
Construction in Process (Loss)		56,250

In circumstances where the Construction in Process balance exceeds the billings, the recognized loss may be deducted on the balance sheet from such accumulated costs. That is, under both the percentage-of-completion and the completed-contract methods, the provision for the loss (the credit) may be combined with Construction in Process, thereby reducing the inventory balance. In those circumstances, however, such as in the above illustration (1987) where the billings exceed the accumulated costs, the amount of the estimated loss should be reported separately on the balance sheet as a current liability. That is, under both the percentage-of-completion and the completed-contract methods, the amount of the loss of $56,250, as estimated in 1987, would be taken from the Construction in Process account and reported separately as a current liability entitled Estimated Loss from Long-Term Contracts.[24]

---

[22]The total costs to be debited to Construction Expenses in 1987, the year in which the estimated loss became evident, may alternatively be computed as follows:

Estimated total cost to extent of total estimated revenue	$4,500,000
Percentage completed at Dec. 31/87	× 64%
Cost to Dec. 31/87 before inclusion of total loss	2,880,000
Add: Estimated total loss	56,250
Cost to date plus loss	2,936,250
Cost recognized in prior years (1986)	1,000,000
Cost recognizable in 1987	$1,936,250

[23]If the costs in 1988 are $1,640,250 as projected, at the end of 1988 the Construction in Process account will have a balance of $1,640,250 + $2,859,750, or $4,500,000, equal to the contract price. When the revenue remaining to be recognized in 1988 of $1,620,000 [$4,500,000 (total contract price) − $1,125,000 (1986) − $1,755,000 (1987)] is matched with the construction expense to be recognized in 1988 of $1,620,000 [total costs of $4,556,250 less the total costs recognized in prior years of $2,936,250 (1986, $1,000,000; 1987, $1,936,250)], a zero profit results. Thus the total loss has been recognized in 1987, the year in which it first became evident.

[24]*Construction Contractors, Audit and Accounting Guide* (New York: AICPA, 1981), pp. 148-149.

OMIT
FROM
HERE

Disclosures in Financial Statements

In addition to making the financial statement disclosures required of all businesses, construction contractors usually make some unique disclosures. Generally these additional disclosures are made in the notes to the financial statements. For example, a construction contractor should disclose the method of recognizing revenue,[25] the basis used to classify assets and liabilities as current (the nature and length of the operating cycle), the basis for recording inventory, the effects of any revision of estimates, the amount of backlog on uncompleted contracts, and the details about receivables (billed and unbilled, maturity, interest rates, and retainage provisions).

Other Revenue Recognition Bases in Advance of Delivery

Two additional revenue recognition bases that have been suggested as appropriate in certain circumstances are (1) the accretion basis and (2) the discovery basis. Both methods have conceptual merit, but because of practical problems and economic and tax consequences, neither the accounting profession nor the affected industries have pressed for their implementation.

Accretion Basis   Accretion is the increase in value resulting from natural growth or the aging processes. Farmers experience accretion by growing crops and breeding animals. Timberland and nursery stock increase in value as the trees and plants grow. Some wines improve with age. Is accretion revenue? Should it be recognized as revenue? Periodic recognition of accretion as revenue has not been adopted in practice.

Accounting theoreticians are somewhat divided on the nature of accretion. Some reject recognition of accretion as revenue. They contend that while there is no doubt that assets have increased, the technical process of production remains to be undertaken, followed by conversion into liquid assets.[26] Others conclude that, from an economic point of view, recognition of accretion may be justified but that the present discounted value (required to make the necessary comparative inventory valuations) is difficult to determine because it depends upon expectations of future market prices, future costs of providing growth, and future costs of harvesting and getting the product ready for market.[27]

The profession permits recognition of revenue at the completion of production for certain agricultural products that possess "immediate marketability at quoted prices that cannot be influenced by the producer."[28] The accounting profession's official pronouncements, however, are silent on the possible extension of that principle to agricultural products still in the growth or production stage even if they are readily marketable at quoted prices.

Discovery Basis   In the United States the SEC's recent proposal for reserve recognition accounting (RRA) for oil and gas producers has revived interest in the use of some form of discovery-basis accounting in the extractive industries. As with

---

[25]*Ibid.*, p. 30

[26]W. A. Paton and A. C. Littleton, *An Introduction to Corporate Accounting Standards* (Sarasota, Fla.: American Accounting Association, 1940), p. 52.

[27]E. S. Hendricksen, *Accounting Theory*, 3rd ed. (Homewood, Ill.: Richard D. Irwin, 1977), p. 186.

[28]"Basic Concepts and Accounting Principles Underlying Financial Statements of Business Enterprises," *APB Statement No. 4* (New York: AICPA, 1970), par. 184.

accretion, there is no doubt that an enterprise's assets may be greatly increased and enhanced by exploration and discovery. Many contend that the financial reporting of companies in the extractive industries would be vastly improved if discovered resources were recognized as assets and changes in oil and gas reserves were included in earnings. Their arguments for the discovery basis are based on the significance of discovery in the earning process and the view that the product's market price can be reasonably estimated. The arguments against revenue recognition at the time of discovery focus on the uncertainties surrounding the assumptions needed to determine discovery values, the cost of obtaining the necessary data, and the departure from historical cost-based accounting.[29]

Except for the SEC's requirement in the United States that RRA be used in supplemental data, the discovery basis of revenue recognition is sanctioned neither by current practice nor by official accounting pronouncements.

REVENUE RECOGNITION AFTER DELIVERY

In some cases, the collection of the sales price is not reasonably assured and revenue recognition is deferred. One of two methods is generally employed to defer revenue recognition until the cash is received: that is, **the cost recovery method** or **the instalment method.**[30]

Cost Recovery Method

Under the cost recovery method, equal amounts of revenue and expense are recognized as collections are made until all costs have been recovered. After all costs have been recovered, any additional cash receipts are included in revenue. This method is used where a high degree of uncertainty exists related to collection of receivables.

To illustrate the cost recovery method, assume that Fesmire Manufacturing sells machinery that had cost Fesmire $25,000 to Duckit Company with payments receivable of $18,000 in 1986, $12,000 in 1987, and $6,000 in 1988. If the cost recovery method is applicable to this sale transaction and the cash is collected on schedule, revenue, cost, and gross profit would be recognized as follows:

	1986	1987	1988
Cash collected	$18,000	$12,000	$6,000
Revenue recognized	$18,000	$12,000	$6,000
Cost	18,000	7,000	-0-
Gross profit	$ -0-	$ 5,000	$6,000

As shown above, under the cost recovery method equal amounts of revenue and expense are recognized and no profit is recognized until the cost of the merchandise sold is fully recovered through cash collections. After all costs have been recovered, the revenue that continues to be recognized represents income.

---

[29]*Survey of Present Practices in Recognizing Revenues, Expenses, Gains, and Losses,* op. cit., p. 80.

[30]Sometimes cash is received prior to delivery of the goods and is recorded as a deposit (customer advance) because the sale transaction is incomplete. In such cases, the seller has not performed under the contract and has no claim against the purchaser. Cash received represents advances and should be reported as a liability until the contract is performed by delivery of the product.

Instalment Sales Accounting Method

Under the instalment method, emphasis is placed on collection rather than on sale, and instalment sales lead to income recognition in the periods of collection rather than in the period of sale. The instalment basis of accounting is justified on the basis that, when there is no reasonable basis for estimating the degree of collectibility, revenue should not be recognized until cash is collected. The exercise of professional judgement is necessary in selecting between the instalment method and the cost recovery method. The resolution revolves around the degree of uncertainty in the collection of the receivable. The cost recovery method is adopted when there is a greater degree of uncertainty. Because the instalment method is used extensively in certain industries, this subject is discussed in more detail in the following sections.

The expression ''instalment sales'' is generally used to describe any type of sale for which payment is required in periodic instalments over an extended period of time. It is used in the retail field, where all types of farm and home equipment and furnishings are sold on an instalment basis. It is also used to a limited degree in the heavy equipment industry, where machine installations are sometimes paid for over a long period. A more recent application of the method is in the area of realty or land development sales. Because payment for the products or property sold is spread over a relatively long period, the risk of loss resulting from uncollectible accounts is greater in instalment sales transactions than in ordinary sales. Consequently, various devices are used to protect the seller. In the area of merchandise, the two most common are (1) the use of a conditional sales contract that provides that title to the item sold does not pass to the purchaser until all payments have been made, and (2) use of notes secured by a chattel (personal property) mortgage on the article sold. Either of these permits the seller to ''repossess'' the goods sold if the purchaser defaults on one or more payments. The repossessed merchandise is then resold at whatever price it will bring to compensate the seller for the uncollected instalments and the expense of repossession.

Under the instalment method of accounting, income recognition is deferred until the period of cash collection. Both revenues and cost of sales are recognized in the period of sale, but the related gross profit is deferred to those periods in which cash is collected. Thus, instead of the sale being deferred to the future periods of anticipated collection and then related costs and expenses being deferred, only the proportional gross profit is deferred, which is equivalent to deferring both sales and cost of sales. Other expenses (e.g., selling expense, administrative expense, and so on) are not deferred. **The cost of the goods sold is deferred proportionally to the deferred sales (by deferring gross profit),** but operating or financial expenses are considered as expenses in the period incurred.

Thus, the theory that cost and expenses should be matched against sales is applied in instalment sales transactions through the gross profit figure but no further. Concerns operating under the instalment sales method of accounting generally record operating expenses without regard to the fact that some portion of the year's gross profit is to be deferred. This practice is often justified on the basis that (1) these expenses do not follow sales as closely as does the cost of goods sold, and (2) accurate apportionment among periods would be so difficult that it could not be justified by the benefits gained.

Acceptability of Instalment Sales   The use of the instalment method as a method for revenue recognition has fluctuated widely. Until the early 1960s the instalment method of accounting was widely used and accepted for instalment sales transactions. As instalment sales transactions increased during the sixties, somewhat paradoxically, acceptance and application of the instalment method for financial accounting purposes decreased. In 1966 the profession in the United States concluded that, except in special circumstances, ''the instalment method of recognizing revenue is not acceptable.''[31]

The rationale for this position is that because the instalment method of accounting recognizes no revenue until cash is collected, it is not exactly in accordance with the concept of accrual accounting. The instalment method is frequently justified on the grounds that the risk of not collecting an accounts receivable may be so great that the sale itself is not sufficient evidence that recognition should occur. In some cases this reasoning may be valid, but not in a majority of cases. The general approach is that if a sale has been completed it should be recognized, and if bad debts are expected they should be recorded as separate estimates of uncollectibles. Current accounting practices indicate that although collection expenses, repossession expenses, and bad debts are an unavoidable part of instalment sales activities, the incurrence of these costs and the collectibility of the receivables are reasonably predictable.

The study of this topic is justified by its widespread use as a tax accounting method, the recent increased emphasis on cash flows, and the method's acceptability in cases where a reasonable basis of estimating the degree of collectibility is deemed not to exist. In addition, weaknesses in the sales method of revenue recognition became very apparent when the franchise and land development booms of the sixties and seventies produced many failures and disillusioned investors. Application of the sales method to **franchise and licence operations** resulted in the abuse described earlier as **''front-end loading''** (recognizing revenue prematurely; that is, when the franchise is granted or the licence issued rather than as it is earned or as the cash is received). Many **''land development''** ventures were susceptible to the same abuses. As a result, accounting for these transactions now leans toward revenue recognition on a cash basis.

Procedure for Deferring Revenue and Cost of Sales of Merchandise   One could easily work out a procedure that deferred both the uncollected portion of the sales price and the proportionate part of the cost of goods sold. Instead of apportioning both sales price and cost over the period of collection, however, **only the gross profit is deferred.** This procedure has exactly the same effect as deferring both sales and cost of sales but requires only one deferred account rather than two.

The steps to be used are described as follows:

For the sales in any one year—

1. During the year, record both sales and cost of sales in the regular way, using the special accounts described later, and compute the rate of gross profit on instalment sales transactions.
2. At the end of the year, apply the rate of gross profit to the cash collections of the current year's instalment sales to arrive at the realized gross profit.
3. The gross profit not realized should be deferred to future years.

---

[31]''Omnibus Opinion,'' *Opinions of the Accounting Principles Board No. 10* (New York: AICPA, 1966), par. 12.

For sales made in prior years—

> The gross profit rate of each year's sales must be applied against cash collections of accounts receivable resulting from that year's sales to arrive at the realized gross profit.

From the preceding discussion of the general practice followed in taking up income from instalment sales, it is apparent that special accounts must be used to provide certain information required to determine the realized and unrealized gross profit in each year of operations. The requirements are as follows:

1. Instalment sales transactions must be kept separate in the accounts from all other sales.
2. Gross profit on sales sold on instalment must be determinable.
3. The amount of cash collected on instalment sales accounts receivable must be known and, further, the total collected on the current year's and on each preceding year's sales must be determinable.
4. Provision must be made for carrying forward each year's deferred gross profit.

In each year, the ordinary operating expenses are charged to expense accounts as under customary accounting procedure and are closed to the Income Summary account. Thus, the one peculiarity in computing net income under the instalment sales method as generally applied is the deferment of gross profit until realized by collection of the accounts receivable.

To illustrate the instalment sales method in accounting for the sales of merchandise, assume the following data:

	1986	1987	1988
Sales (on instalment)	$200,000	$250,000	$240,000
Cost of sales	150,000	190,000	168,000
Gross profit	$ 50,000	$ 60,000	$ 72,000
Rate of gross profit on sales	25%[a]	24%[b]	30%[c]
Cash receipts			
1986 sales	$ 60,000	$100,000	$ 40,000
1987 sales		100,000	125,000
1988 sales			80,000

[a] $\dfrac{\$50,000}{\$200,000}$ [b] $\dfrac{\$60,000}{\$250,000}$ [c] $\dfrac{\$72,000}{\$240,000}$

To simplify the illustration, interest charges have been excluded. Summary entries in general journal form have been prepared for the transactions in the illustration. In reviewing these entries it must be remembered that as a practical matter they would not appear as summary entries, but the transactions would be entered individually as they occur. The following entries illustrate accounting for instalment sales transactions. All transactions not concerned with the instalment sales activity have been omitted.

1986

Instalment Accounts Receivable, 1986	200,000	
Instalment Sales		200,000
(To record sales made on instalment in 1986)		
Cash	60,000	
Instalment Accounts Receivable, 1986		60,000
(To record cash collected on instalment receivables)		

Cost of Instalment Sales	150,000	
Cost of Goods Sold		150,000
(To record cost of goods sold on instalment in 1986)		
Instalment Sales	200,000	
Cost of Instalment Sales		150,000
Deferred Gross Profit, 1986		50,000
(To close instalment sales and cost of instalment sales for the year)		
Deferred Gross Profit, 1986	15,000	
Realized Gross Profit on Instalment Sales		15,000
(To remove from deferred gross profit the profit realized through collections)		
Realized Gross Profit on Instalment Sales	15,000	
Income Summary		15,000
(To close profits realized by collections)		

The realized and deferred gross profit is computed for the year 1986 as follows:

1986	
Rate of gross profit current year	25%
Cash collected on current year's sales	$60,000
Realized gross profit (25% of $60,000)	15,000
Gross profit to be deferred ($50,000 − $15,000)	35,000

1987

Instalment Accounts Receivable, 1987	250,000	
Instalment Sales		250,000
(To record sales made on instalment in 1987)		
Cash	200,000	
Instalment Accounts Receivable, 1986		100,000
Instalment Accounts Receivable, 1987		100,000
(To record cash collected on instalment receivables)		
Cost of Instalment Sales	190,000	
Cost of Goods Sold		190,000
(To record cost of goods sold on instalment in 1987)		
Instalment Sales	250,000	
Cost of Instalment Sales		190,000
Deferred Gross profit, 1987		60,000
(To close instalment sales and cost of instalment sales for the year)		
Deferred Gross Profit, 1986	25,000	
Deferred Gross Profit, 1987	24,000	
Realized Gross Profit on Instalment Sales		49,000
(To remove from deferred gross profit the profit realized through collections)		
Realized Gross Profit on Instalment Sales	49,000	
Income Summary		49,000
(To close profits realized by collections)		

The realized and deferred gross profit is computed for the year 1987 as follows:

1987	
Current year's sales	
Rate of gross profit	24%
Cash collected on current year's sales	$100,000
Realized gross profit (24% of $100,000)	24,000
Gross profit to be deferred ($60,000 − $24,000)	36,000
Prior years' sales	
Rate of gross profit—1986	25%
Cash collected on 1986 sales	$100,000
Gross profit realized in 1987 on 1986 sales	
(25% of $100,000)	25,000
Total gross profit realized in 1987	
Realized on collections of 1986 sales	$ 25,000
Realized on collections of 1987 sales	24,000
Total	$ 49,000

The entries in 1988 would be similar to those of 1987, and the total gross profit taken up or realized would be $64,000, as shown by the computations below.

1988	
Current year's sales	
Rate of gross profit	30%
Cash collected on current year's sales	$ 80,000
Gross profit realized on 1988 sales (30% of $80,000)	24,000
Gross profit to be deferred ($72,000 − $24,000)	48,000
Prior years' sales	
1986 sales	
Rate of gross profit	25%
Cash collected	$ 40,000
Gross profit realized in 1988 on 1986 sales	
(25% of $40,000)	10,000
1987 sales	
Rate of gross profit	24%
Cash collected	$125,000
Gross profit realized in 1988 on 1987 sales	
(24% of $125,000)	30,000
Total gross profit realized in 1988	
Realized on collections of 1986 sales	$ 10,000
Realized on collections of 1987 sales	30,000
Realized on collections of 1988 sales	24,000
Total	$ 64,000

Additional Problems of Instalment Sales Accounting

In addition to computing realized and deferred gross profit currently, other problems are involved in accounting for instalment sales transactions. These problems are related to:

1. Interest on instalment contracts.
2. Uncollectible accounts.
3. Defaults and repossessions.

Interest on Instalment Contracts Because the collection of instalment receivables is spread over a long period, it is customary to charge the buyer interest on the unpaid balance. Interest charges are generally provided for in setting up the schedule of payments required by the sales contract; that is, each instalment payment consists of interest and principal. Generally, each payment is equal (level payment pattern) in amount to each successive payment. However, a smaller portion of each successive payment is attributable to interest and a correspondingly larger amount attributable to principal. For example, an item costing $5,000 is sold to a customer who pays $2,000 cash and signs a contract to pay the balance in three equal annual instalments with interest at 8%. The schedule below shows how each annual instalment is allocated between interest and a reduction of the principal amount.

	Instalment Payment Schedule			
Date	Cash (Debit)	Interest Earned (Credit)	Instalment Receivables (Credit)	Unpaid Balance
Jan. 2/86	—	—	—	$3,000.00
Jan. 2/87	$1,164.10[a]	$240.00[b]	$ 924.10	2,075.90
Jan. 2/88	1,164.10	166.07	998.03	1,077.87
Jan. 2/89	1,164.10	86.23	1,077.87	–0–

[a]Periodic payment = Original unpaid balance PV of an annuity of $1.00 for three periods at 8%; $1,164.10 = $3,000 ÷ 2.57710.
[b]$3,000 × .08 = $240.

When interest is involved in instalment sales, it should be accounted for separately as interest revenue distinct from the gross profit recognized on the instalment sales collections during the period. The interest is recognized as interest revenue at the time of the cash receipt. Also, interest accrued since the last collection date on the instalment receivables should be recorded as an adjusting entry at year end.

Uncollectible Accounts The problem of bad debts or uncollectible accounts receivable is somewhat different for concerns selling on an instalment basis because of a repossession feature commonly incorporated in the sales agreement. This feature gives the selling company an opportunity to recoup any uncollectible accounts through repossession and resale of repossessed merchandise. If the experience of the company indicates that repossessions do not, as a rule, compensate for uncollectible balances, it may be advisable to provide for such losses through charges to a special bad debts expense account just as is done for other credit sales. This matter was covered in detail in Chapter 7.

Defaults and Repossessions Depending on the terms of the sales contract and the policy of the credit department, the seller can repossess merchandise sold under an instalment arrangement if the purchaser fails to meet payment requirements. Repossessed merchandise may be reconditioned before it is offered for sale, and may be resold for cash or under a plan for instalment payments.

Repossession of merchandise sold is a recognition that the related instalment receivable account is not collectible and that it should be written off. Along with the account receivable, the applicable deferred gross profit must be removed from the ledger in an entry similar to the following:

Repossessed Merchandise (an inventory account)	XX	
Deferred Gross Profit	XX	
Instalment Accounts Receivable		XX

The entry above assumes that the repossessed merchandise is to be recorded on the books at exactly the amount of the uncollected account less the deferred gross profit applicable. This assumption may or may not be proper. The condition of the merchandise repossessed, the cost of reconditioning, and the market for second-hand merchandise of that particular type must all be considered. **The objective should be to put any asset acquired on the books at its fair value or, when fair value is not ascertainable, at the best possible approximation of fair value.** If the fair value of the merchandise repossessed is less than the uncollected balance less the deferred gross profit, a "loss on repossession" should be recorded at the date of repossession.

Some accountants contend that repossessed merchandise should be entered at a valuation that will permit the company to make its regular rate of gross profit on resale. If it is entered at its approximated cost to purchase, the regular rate of gross profit is provided for, but that is a secondary consideration. It is more important that the asset acquired by repossession be recorded at fair value in accordance with the general practice of carrying assets at acquisition price as represented by the fair market value at the date of acquisition.

To illustrate the required entry, assume that a refrigerator was sold to Susan Hunt for $500 on September 1, 1986. Terms require a down payment of $200 and $20 on the first of every month for 15 months thereafter. It is further assumed that the refrigerator cost $300, and is sold to provide a 40% rate of gross profit on selling price. At the year end, December 31, 1986, a total of $60 should have been collected in addition to the original down payment.

If Hunt makes her January and February payments in 1987 and then defaults, the account balances applicable to Hunt at time of default would be:

Instalment Account Receivable (Hunt)	200(dr.)
Deferred Gross Profit (40% × $240) Dec. 31, 1986	96(cr.)

The deferred gross profit applicable to the Hunt account still has the December 31, 1986, balance because no entry has been made to take up gross profit realized by cash collections in 1987. The regular entry at the end of 1987, however, will take up the gross profit realized by all cash collections including amounts received from Hunt. Hence, the balance of deferred gross profit applicable to Hunt's account may be computed by applying the gross profit rate for the year of sale to the balance of Hunt's account receivable, 40% of $200, or $80. The account balances should therefore be considered as:

Instalment Account Receivable (Hunt)	200 (dr.)
Deferred Gross Profit (applicable to Hunt after recognition of $16 of profit in January and February)	80 (cr.)

If the estimated fair value of the article repossessed is set at $70, the following entry would be required to record the repossession:

Deferred Gross Profit	80	
Repossessed Merchandise	70	
Loss on Repossession	50	
Instalment Account Receivable (Hunt)		200

The amount of the loss is determined by (1) subtracting the deferred gross profit from the amount of the account receivable to determine the unrecovered cost (or book value) of the merchandise repossessed, and (2) subtracting the estimated fair value of the merchandise repossessed from the unrecovered cost to get the amount of the loss on repossession.

Balance of account receivable (representing uncollected selling price)	$200
Less: Deferred gross profit	80
Unrecovered cost	120
Less: Estimated fair value of merchandise repossessed	70
Loss (Gain) on repossession	$ 50

As pointed out earlier, the loss on repossession may be charged to a special bad debts account or an Allowance for Doubtful Accounts if such an account is carried.

Financial Statement Presentation of Instalment Sales Transactions   If instalment sales transactions represent a significant part of total sales, full disclosure of instalment sales, the cost of instalment sales, and any expenses allocable to instalment sales is desirable. If, however, instalment sales transactions constitute an insignificant part of total sales, it may be satisfactory to include only the realized gross profit in the income statement as a special item following the gross profit on sales as shown below.

Health Machine Company
STATEMENT OF INCOME
For the Year Ended December 31, 1987

Sales	$620,000
Cost of goods sold	490,000
Gross profit on sales	130,000
Gross profit realized on instalment sales	51,000
Total gross profit on sales	$181,000

If more complete disclosure of instalment sales transactions is desired, a presentation similar to the following may be used:

Health Machine Company
STATEMENT OF INCOME
For the Year Ended December 31, 1987

	Instalment Sales	Other Sales	Total
Sales	$248,000	$620,000	$868,000
Cost of goods sold	182,000	490,000	672,000
Gross margin on sales	66,000	130,000	196,000
Less: Deferred gross profit on instalment sales of this year	47,000		47,000
Realized gross profit on this year's sales	19,000	130,000	149,000
Add: Gross profit realized on instalment sales of prior years	32,000		32,000
Gross profit realized this year	$ 51,000	$130,000	$181,000

The apparent awkwardness of this method of presentation is difficult to avoid if full disclosure of instalment sales transactions is to be provided in the income statement. One solution, of course, is to prepare a separate schedule showing instalment sales transactions with only the final figure carried into the income statement.

In the balance sheet it is generally considered desirable to classify instalment accounts receivable by year of collectibility. There is some question as to whether instalment accounts that are not collectible for two or more years should be included in current assets. If instalment sales are part of normal operations, they may be considered as current assets because they are collectible within the operating cycle of the business. Little confusion should result from this practice if maturity dates are fully disclosed as illustrated in the following example:

Current Assets		
Notes and accounts receivable		
Trade customers	$78,800	
Less: Allowance for doubtful accounts	3,700	
	75,100	
Instalment accounts collectible in 1988	22,600	
Instalment accounts collectible in 1989	47,200	$144,900

On the other hand, receivables from an instalment contract, resulting from a transaction **not** related to normal operations should be reported in the "other assets" section if due beyond the normal operating cycle.

Financial statement presentation of Repossessed Merchandise and of Gain or Loss on Repossessions is based on the nature of each of these items. Repossessed merchandise is a part of inventory and should be included as such in the current asset section of the balance sheet; any loss on repossessions should be included in the income statement in the Other Revenues and Gains or Other Expenses and Losses section.

Deferred gross profit on instalment sales is generally treated as consisting entirely of unearned revenue and classified as a current liability. Theoretically, deferred gross profit consists of three elements: (1) income tax liability to be paid when the sales are reported as realized revenue (current liability); (2) allowance for collection expense, bad debts, and repossession losses (deduction from instalment accounts receivable); and (3) a residual which will be reported as net income (retained earnings, restricted as to dividend availability) when realized. However, because of the difficulty in allocating deferred gross profit among these three elements, the whole amount is frequently reported as unearned revenue. *SFAC No. 3* presents the argument that "no matter how it is displayed in financial statements, deferred gross profit on instalment sales is conceptually an asset valuation; that is, a reduction of an asset."[32] While we support this position, we also recognize that until an official standard on this topic is issued, financial statements will probably continue to report such deferred gross profit as a current liability.

Summary of Product Revenue Recognition Bases

The revenue recognition bases or methods, the criteria for their use, and the reasons for departing from the sale basis are summarized in the following exhibit:

---

[32]See "Elements of Financial Statements of Business Enterprises," *Statement of Financial Accounting Concepts No. 3* (Stamford, Conn.: FASB, 1980) pars. 156-158.

**REVENUE RECOGNITION BASES
OTHER THAN THE SALE BASIS FOR PRODUCTS[33]**

Recognition Basis (or Method of Applying a Basis)	Criteria for Use of Basis	Reason(s) for Departing from Sale Basis
Completion-of-production basis	Immediate marketability at quoted prices; unit interchangeability; difficulty of determining costs.	Known or determinable revenues; inability to determine costs and thereby defer expense recognition until sale.
Percentage-of-completion method	Long-term construction of property; dependable estimates of extent of progress and cost to complete; reasonable assurance of collectibility of contract price; expectation that both contractor and buyer can meet obligations, and absence of inherent hazards that make estimates doubtful.	Availability of evidence of ultimate proceeds; better measure of periodic income; avoidance of fluctuations in revenues, expenses, and income; performance is a "continuous sale" and therefore not a departure from the sale basis.
Completed-contract method	Use on short-term contracts, and whenever percentage-of-completion cannot be used on long-term contracts.	Existence of inherent hazards in the contract beyond the normal, recurring business risks; conditions for using the percentage-of-completion method are absent.
Accretion basis	Criteria unspecified because accretion basis is not permitted by authoritative pronouncements.	Possible support for recognizing accretion as revenue includes product marketability at known prices and desirability of recognizing changes in assets.
Discovery basis	Criteria unspecified because discovery basis is not permitted by authoritative pronouncements.	Possible support for recognizing revenue at time natural resources are discovered includes the significance of discovery in the earning process and the view that sales prices can be estimated.
Instalment method and cost recovery method	Absence of a reasonable basis for estimating degree of collectibility.	Collectibility of the receivable is so uncertain that gross profit (or income) is not recognized until cash is actually received.

[33]Adapted from *Survey of Present Practices in Recognizing Revenues, Expenses, Gains, and Losses,* op, cit. pp. 12 and 13.

REVENUE FROM BARTERING

Owing to a variety of economic and tax circumstances, some companies engage in **barter transactions.** For example, radio and television stations often barter advertising time for merchandise or services. These transactions should be recorded at the estimated fair value of the merchandise or service received, with the barter revenue recognized when it is earned (in the period in which the commercial is broadcast). Barter revenue should be recorded for scripts, tapes, and programs obtained in exchange for commercials equivalent to the fair value of the programming received or the broadcast time given in exchange, whichever is more readily determinable.

Other companies also increasingly derive a portion of their revenues from barter transactions that result in inflows of nonfinancial assets or services instead of cash. For instance, a plumber may trade his services for those of an electrician, an attorney and a house painter may arrange for the house painter to paint the attorney's home in exchange for legal services, or an automobile dealer may sell a truck to a cleaning service company in exchange for a cleaning service contract. Barter clubs have even been established to accommodate the exchange of a great variety of services. Is revenue recognizable in these barter transactions? Is revenue realized or realizable in these situations? The accounting profession in Canada has not directly addressed barter transactions. (*APB Opinion No. 29* on nonmonetary exchanges addresses trade-in transactions that are similar to bartering.[34]) Accounting for barter transactions presents some real recognition and measurement problems for accountants. As these transactions grow in number and significance, the CICA may be prompted to issue accounting standards.

OMIT
TO
HERE

KEY POINTS

1. Revenue has been defined as an inflow or other enhancement of assets of an entity or settlement of its liabilities from delivering or producing goods, rendering services, or other earning activities of an enterprise during a period.

2. Revenue is said to be **earned** when the earning process is virtually complete, and revenues are **realized** when goods and services are exchanged for cash or claims to cash.

3. **Recognition** is formally recording or incorporating an item in the accounts and financial statements of an entity. Revenue is usually recognized when it is realized or realizable and it is earned.

4. Point of sale is most often used for recognition of revenue. However, departures in certain circumstances involve recognition before or after delivery. These departures are justified by the degree of measurability of the revenue.

5. Revenue may be recognized during production on certain long-term projects when the degree of completion is measurable and the realization of the resulting revenue is quite certain.

6. Under the completed-contract method of revenue recognition, revenue is not recognized until the related project is completed. Although this method is

---

[34]The Department of National Revenue claims that the fair market value of the goods or services received by each of the bartering parties is taxable. Even where no goods or services are received, a barter club member is taxable on the value of "credit or trading units" credited during the year.

more objective than the percentage-of-completion method, it sometimes results in erractic yearly revenue patterns.

7. Losses on long-term projects should be recognized in the year in which a loss is first estimated. This treatment is based on the principle of conservatism.

8. If a product is homogeneous in nature, produced by numerous suppliers and there is a ready market that is unaffected by the output from a single supplier (e.g., certain agricultural products and precious metals), revenue may be recognized upon completion of production rather than at point of sale.

9. When realization of the revenue is uncertain owing to such unpredictable factors as returns or collections, revenue recognition may be postponed until the uncertainties are resolved.

10. Under the instalment sales method, revenue is recognized proportionately as cash collections are made. In cases where ultimate realization is highly uncertain, the cost recovery method (in which costs are recovered before any profits are recognized) may be used.

REVENUE RECOGNITION FOR SPECIAL SALES TRANSACTIONS

To supplement and illustrate our presentation of revenue recognition, we have chosen to cover two common yet unique types of sales transactions—**franchise sales and consignment sales.**

FRANCHISES

Accounting for franchise sales was chosen because of its popularity, complexity, and applicability to many of the previously discussed revenue recognition bases. In accounting for franchise sales, the accountant must analyze the transaction and, considering all the circumstances, must use judgement in selecting and applying one or more of the revenue recognition bases and then, possibly, monitor the situation over a long period of time.

The Franchise Sales Phenomenon

As indicated earlier, the accountant determines when revenue is recognized, essentially on the basis of two criteria: (1) completion or virtual completion of the earning process, and (2) occurrence of an exchange. These criteria are appropriate for most business activities, but for some sales transactions they simply are not adequate in defining when revenue should be recognized. In some situations, the accountant is forced to look to the circumstances surrounding the contract to ascertain when to recognize revenue and income. Sales transactions in some industries (for example, land development, leasing, and franchising) require closer scrutiny. The fast-growing franchise industry has given accountants special concern and challenge.

Four types of franchising arrangements have evolved: (1) manufacturer-retailer, (2) manufacturer-wholesaler, (3) service sponsor-retailer, and (4) wholesaler-retailer. The fastest growing category of franchising, and the one that caused a reexamination of appropriate accounting, has been the third category, **service sponsor-retailer.** Included in this category are such industries and businesses as:

> Soft ice cream drive-ins (Tastee Freez, Dairy Queen)
> Food drive-ins (McDonald's, Kentucky Fried Chicken, Burger King)
> Restaurants (Perkins, Pizza Hut, Denny's)
> Motels (Holiday Inn, Howard Johnson, Best Western)
> Auto rentals (Avis, Hertz, Tilden)
> Part-time help (Manpower, Kelly Girl)
> Others (H & R Block, Arthur Murray Studios, Seven-Eleven Stores)

Franchise companies derive their revenue from one or both of two sources: (1) from the sale of initial franchises and related assets or services, and (2) from continuing fees based on the operations of franchises. The **franchisor** (the party who grants business rights under the franchise) normally provides the **franchisee** (the party who operates the franchised business) with the following services:

1. Assistance in site selection.
   (a) Analyzing location.
   (b) Negotiating leases.
2. Evaluation of potential income.
3. Supervision of construction activity.
   (a) Obtaining financing.
   (b) Designing building.
   (c) Supervising contractor while building.
4. Assistance in the acquisition of signs, fixtures, and equipment.
5. Provision of bookkeeping and advisory services.
   (a) Setting up franchisee's records.
   (b) Advising on income, real estate, and other taxes.
   (c) Advising on local regulations of the franchisee's business.
6. Provision of employee and management training.
7. Provision of quality control.
8. Provision of advertising and promotion.[35]

During the sixties and early seventies it was standard practice for franchisors to recognize the entire franchise fee at the date of sale whether the fee was received then or was collectible over a long period of time as represented by a long-term note. Frequently, franchisors recorded the entire amount as revenue in the year of sale even though many of the services were yet to be performed and uncertainty existed regarding the collection of the entire fee. In effect the franchisors were counting their fried chickens before they were hatched. For example, a **franchise agreement** may provide for refunds to the franchisee if certain conditions are not

---

[35]Archibald E. MacKay, "Accounting for Initial Franchise Fee Revenue," *The Journal of Accountancy* (January, 1970), pp. 66–67.

met, and the franchise fee profit can be reduced sharply by future costs of obligations and services to be rendered by the franchisor. The following discussion of accounting for franchise fees is based on procedures which, in the absence of *CICA Handbook* requirements, are acceptable for Canadian financial reporting.[36]

Initial Franchise Fees

The initial franchise fee is consideration for establishing the franchise relationship and providing some initial services. Initial franchise fees are to be recorded as revenue only when and as the franchisor makes "substantial performance" of the services it is obligated to perform and collection of the fee is reasonably assured. **Substantial performance** occurs when the franchisor has no remaining obligation to refund any cash received or excuse any nonpayment of a note and has performed all the initial services required under the contract. "The commencement of operations by the franchisee shall be presumed to be the earliest point at which substantial performance has occurred, unless it can be demonstrated that substantial performance of all obligations, including services rendered voluntarily, has occurred before that time."[37]

Illustration of Entries for Initial Franchise Fees

To illustrate, assume that Tum's Pizza, Inc. charges an initial franchise fee of $50,000 for the right to operate as a franchisee of Tum's Pizza. Of this amount, $10,000 is payable when the agreement is signed, and the balance is payable in five annual payments of $8,000 each. In return for the initial franchise fee the franchisor will help in locating the site, negotiate the lease or purchase of the site, supervise the construction activity, and provide the bookkeeping services. The credit rating of the franchisee indicates that money can be borrowed at 8%. The present value of an ordinary annuity of five annual receipts of $8,000 each discounted at 8% is $31,941.60. The discount of $8,058.40 represents the interest revenue to be accrued by the franchisor over the payment period. The above facts could, depending on the specific circumstances, give rise to any of the following entries.

1. If there is reasonable expectation that the downpayment may be refunded and if substantial future services remain to be performed by Tum's Pizza, Inc., the entry should be:

Cash	10,000.00	
Notes Receivable	40,000.00	
Discount on Notes Receivable		8,058.40
Unearned Franchise Fees		41,941.60

2. If the probability of refunding the initial franchise fee is extremely low, the amount of future services to be provided to the franchisee is minimal, collectibility of the note is reasonably assured, and substantial performance has occurred, the entry should be:

Cash	10,000.00	
Notes Receivable	40,000.00	
Discount on Notes Receivable		8,058.40
Revenue from Franchise Fees		41,941.60

---

[36]In the United States, accounting policy for franchise fee revenue is specified in "Accounting for Franchise Fee Revenue," *Statement of Financial Accounting Standards No. 45* (Stamford, Conn.: FASB, 1981).

[37]*Ibid.*, par. 5.

3. If the initial down payment is not refundable, represents a fair measure of the services already provided, with a significant amount of services still to be performed by the franchisor in future periods, and collectibility of the note is reasonably assured, the entry should be:

Cash	10,000.00	
Notes Receivable	40,000.00	
Discount on Notes Receivable		8,058.40
Revenue from Franchise Fees		10,000.00
Unearned Franchise Fees		31,941.60

4. If the initial down payment is not refundable and no future services are required by the franchisor, but collection of the note is so uncertain that recognition of the note as an asset is unwarranted, the entry should be:

Cash	10,000.00	
Revenue from Franchise Fees		10,000.00

5. Under the same conditions as those listed under 4 except that the down payment is refundable or substantial services are yet to be performed, the entry should be:

Cash	10,000.00	
Unearned Franchise Fees		10,000.00

In cases 4 and 5 above where collection of the note is extremely uncertain, cash collections may be recognized using the instalment method or the cost recovery method.

Continuing Franchise Fees

Continuing franchise fees are received in return for the continuing rights granted by the franchise agreement and for providing such services as management training, advertising and promotion, legal assistance, and other support. Continuing fees should be reported as revenue when they are earned and receivable from the franchisee, unless a portion of them has been designated for a particular purpose, such as providing a specified amount for building maintenance or local advertising. In that case, the portion deferred shall be an amount sufficient to cover the estimated cost in excess of continuing franchise fees and provide a reasonable profit on the continuing services.

Bargain Purchases

In addition to paying continuing franchise fees, franchisees frequently purchase some or all of their equipment and supplies from the franchisor. The franchisor would account for these sales as it would for any other product sales. Sometimes, however, the franchise agreement grants the franchisee the right to make **bargain purchases** of equipment or supplies after the initial franchise fee is paid. If the bargain price is lower than the normal selling price of the same product, or if it does not provide the franchisor a reasonable profit, then a portion of the initial franchise fee should be deferred. The deferred portion would be accounted for as an adjustment of the selling price when the franchisee subsequently purchases the equipment or supplies.

Options to Purchase

A franchise agreement may give the franchisor an **option to purchase** the franchisee's business. For example, as a matter of management policy, the franchisor may reserve the right to purchase a profitable franchised outlet, or to purchase one that is in financial difficulty. If it is probable at the time the option is given that the franchisor will ultimately purchase the outlet, then the initial franchise fee should not be recognized as revenue but should be recorded as a liability. When the option is exercised, the liability would reduce the franchisor's investment in the outlet.

Illustration of Entries for Continuing Fees, Bargain Purchases, and Options

To illustrate these concepts, assume the facts given on page 901 in the Tum's Pizza example. In addition, assume that Tum's Pizza, Inc. charges a continuing franchise fee of $4,200 annually for services rendered during the year.

1. If 20% of the continuing franchise fee is designated specifically for building maintenance to be provided by the franchisor, the entry to record the franchise fee should be:

Cash	4,200.00	
Revenue from Continuing Franchise Fees		3,360.00
Unearned Franchise Fees ($4,200 × .20)		840.00

When maintenance is provided, assuming that the franchisor will receive a 25% markup on selling price, the entries are:

Unearned Franchise Fees	840.00	
Revenue from Continuing Franchise Fees		840.00
Maintenance Expense [$840 − (840 × .25)]	630.00	
Cash (or Accounts Payable)		630.00

2. If during the year Tum's Pizza, Inc. sells supplies costing $3,000 to the franchisee at the normal $4,000 price, the entries are:

Cash (or Accounts Receivable)	4,000.00	
Franchise Product Sales		4,000.00
Cost of Franchise Product Sales	3,000.00	
Supplies Inventory		3,000.00

3. Collectibility of the note for the initial franchise fee is reasonably assured, and substantial performance by the franchisor has occurred. (See entry 2, page 901.) If after the initial franchise fee is paid, the franchisee has the right to purchase up to $20,000 of supplies at their cost of $15,000, the entry to record the initial franchise fee would be:

Cash	10,000.00	
Notes Receivable	40,000.00	
Discount on Notes Receivable		8,058.40
Revenue from Franchise Fees		36,941.60
Unearned Franchise Fees		5,000.00

When the franchisee subsequently purchases the supplies, the entries are:

Cash (or Accounts Receivable)	15,000.00	
Unearned Franchise Fees	5,000.00	
Franchise Product Sales		20,000.00
Cost of Franchise Product Sales	15,000.00	
Supplies Inventory		15,000.00

4. Collectibility of the note for the initial franchise fee is reasonably assured and substantial performance by the franchisor has occurred. (See entry 2, page 901.) The franchise agreement contains an option allowing Tum's Pizza, Inc. to purchase the outlet at any time during the next five years. If it is likely that this option will ultimately be exercised, the entry to record the initial franchise would be:

Cash	10,000.00	
Notes Receivable	40,000.00	
Discount on Notes Receivable		8,058.40
Deferred Franchise Purchase Option (liability)		41,941.60

Franchisor's Costs

Franchise accounting also involves proper accounting for the **franchisor's costs**. The objective is to match related costs and revenues by reporting them as components of income in the same accounting period. Franchisors should ordinarily defer **direct costs** (usually incremental costs) relating to specific franchise sales for which revenue has not yet been recognized. **Indirect costs** of a regular and recurring nature that are incurred irrespective of the level of franchise sales such as selling and administrative expenses (and other fixed costs) should be expensed as incurred. Costs should not be deferred, however, without reference to anticipated revenue and its realizability.[38]

Disclosures of Franchisors

Disclosure of all significant commitments and obligations resulting from franchise agreements, including a description of services that have not yet been substantially performed, is required. Any resolution of uncertainties regarding the collectibility of franchise fees should be disclosed. Initial franchise fees should be segregated from other franchise fee revenue if they are significant. Where possible, revenues and costs related to franchisor-owned outlets should be distinguished from those related to franchised outlets.

CONSIGNMENT SALES ACCOUNTING

In some sales arrangements the delivery of the goods by the manufacturer (or wholesaler) to the dealer (or retailer) is not considered to be full performance and a sale because the manufacturer retains title to the goods. This specialized method of marketing certain types of products makes use of a device known as a **consignment.** Under this arrangement, the **consignor** (manufacturer) ships merchandise to the **consignee** (dealer) who is to act as an agent for the consignor in selling the merchandise. Both consignor and consignee are interested in selling—the former to make a profit or develop a market, the latter to make a commission on the sales.

The consignee accepts the merchandise and agrees to exercise due diligence in caring for and selling the merchandise. Cash received from customers is remitted to the consignor by the consignee, after deducting a sales commission (and any chargeable expenses). A modified version of the sale basis of revenue recognition is used by the consignor. That is, revenue is recognized only after the consignor receives notification of sale and the cash remittance from the consignee. The

---

[38]"Accounting for Franchise Fee Revenue," *op. cit.*, p. 17.

merchandise is carried throughout the consignment as the inventory of the consignor, separately classified as Merchandise on Consignment. It is not recorded as an asset on the consignee's books. Upon sale of the merchandise, the consignee has a liability for the net amount due the consignor. The consignor periodically receives from the consignee an **account of sales** that shows the merchandise received, merchandise sold, expenses chargeable to the consignment, and the cash remitted. Revenue is then recognized by the consignor.

To illustrate consignment accounting entries, assume that Nelba Manufacturing Ltd. ships merchandise costing $36,000 on consignment to Best Value Stores. Nelba pays $3,750 of freight costs and Best Value pays $2,250 for local advertising costs that are reimbursable from Nelba. By the end of the period, two-thirds of the consigned merchandise is sold for $40,000 cash. Best Value notifies Nelba of the sales, retains a 10% commission, and remits the cash due Nelba. The following journal entries would be made by the consignor (Nelba) and the consignee (Best Value):

Transaction	Nelba Manufacturing Ltd. (Consignor)		Best Value Stores (Consignee)	

Shipment of consigned merchandise	Inventory on Consignment 36,000
	   Finished Goods Inventory
		36,000	No entry (record memo of
			  merchandise received)	

Payment of freight costs by consignor	Inventory on Consignment 3,750 Cash	3,750	No entry	
Payment of advertising by consignee	No entry until notified		Receivable from Consignor 2,250 Cash	2,250
Sales of consigned merchandise	No entry until notified		Cash 40,000 Payable to Consignor	40,000

Notification of sales and expenses and remittance of amount due	Cash 33,750
	Advertising Expense 2,250
	Commission Expense 4,000
	   Revenue from Consignment
	    Sales
		40,000	Payable to Consignor 40,000
			   Receivable from Consignor
			   Commission Revenue
			   Cash
				2,250
				4,000
				33,750

Adjustment of inventory on consignment for cost of sales	Cost of Goods Sold 26,500
	   Inventory on Consignment
	   [2/3 ($36,000 + $3,750)
	    = $26,500]
		26,500	No entry	

Under the consignment arrangement, the manufacturer (consignor) accepts the risk that the merchandise might not sell and relieves the dealer (consignee) of the need to commit part of its working capital to inventory. A variety of different systems and account titles are used to record consignments, but they all share the common goal of postponing the recognition of revenue until it is known that a sale to a third party has occurred.

ACCOUNTING FOR SERVICE SALES TRANSACTIONS

This appendix is more illustrative than authoritative, because the concepts presented are not officially GAAP. Service sales represent a significant portion of all sales made in our economy, and they are obviously being accounted for in some manner. Yet, no written official pronouncement provides specific standards of accounting for service sales transactions. Some of the methods presented on the following pages are being applied uniformly and properly in practice and, to that extent (and because they do not violate any existing accounting standard), they are GAAP. But because the profession has not issued specific guidelines, practice in accounting for revenue from service sales varies considerably, even between firms in the same industry.

This section is based on the recent combined effort of the FASB and the AICPA to establish standards of accounting for certain service transactions through their issuance in 1978 of an *Invitation to Comment*. Like many attempts to achieve uniformity in accounting practice, this effort is being resisted and criticized by special interest groups. We present this material (1) because of its instructional value and practical applicability, (2) because it fills an area long in need of standards, and (3) because it complements so well the subject matter of this chapter.

SERVICE INDUSTRIES AND SERVICE TRANSACTIONS

The number and variety of businesses that offer services to the public are increasing, and the range of services they offer is broadening. Examples include the industries listed below.

Accounting	Management consultants
Advertising agencies	Medical practitioners
Architects	Modeling agencies
Cemetery associations	Mortgage banking
Computer service organizations	Moving and storage firms
Correspondence schools	Perpetual care societies
Electronic security	Placement agencies
Employment agencies	Private and social clubs
Engineering firms	Public relations firms
Entertainers	Real estate brokerages
Garbage and waste removal firms	Retirement homes
Interior design or decoration firms	Research and development labs
Legal services	Transport firms
Health spas	Travel agencies

This list gives only a sampling of service industries; an all-inclusive list cannot be provided because the range of possible services is vast.

The major accounting questions facing these types of service organizations relate to when revenue should be recognized as being earned and when costs should be charged to expense. The following discussion represents newly developed concepts and methods that are still in the initial stages of reception and implementation.

> Service transactions are defined as transactions between a seller and a purchaser in which, for a mutually agreed price, the seller performs, agrees to perform at a later date, or agrees to maintain readiness to perform an act or acts, including permitting others to use enterprise resources that do not alone produce a tangible commodity or product as the principal intended result.[39]

Although this definition does not require that the act or acts to be performed be specified by a contract, in practice most service transactions performed over a period of time or requiring performance in the future are formalized by a contract. However, agreements to perform at a later date and agreements to maintain a readiness to perform an act are often only commitments or executory contracts, and these are not currently viewed as transactions to be recorded in accrual-based, transaction-oriented financial statements.

Some transactions may involve both services and products. **When the sale of a product is incidental to the rendering of a service, the transaction would be accounted for as a service transaction.** For example, a fixed-price equipment maintenance contract that includes parts would be considered a service transaction. Conversely, **if a service is incidental to the sale of a product, the transaction would be accounted for as a product transaction.** For example, the inclusion of a warranty or guarantee in the sale of a product is considered incidental.

Determining when a service or a product is incidental to a transaction can be difficult. An incidental nature may be indicated, however, in one of the following two ways:

1. The inclusion of a product or a service does not result in a variance in the total transaction price from what would be charged excluding the product or service.

[39]"Accounting for Certain Service Transactions," *FASB Invitation to Comment* (Stamford, Conn.: FASB, 1978), p. 1.

2. A product is not sold or a service is not rendered separately in the seller's normal business.[40]

If both the product and the service are stated separately and the total transaction price would vary because the product or the service is included, the transaction would be accounted for as both a product and a service transaction. For example, equipment maintenance contracts in which parts are charged separately would qualify for separable product and service transaction accounting.

REVENUE AND EXPENSE RECOGNITION FOR SERVICE TRANSACTIONS

Revenue from service transactions should be recognized on the basis of the seller's performance of the transaction. **Performance** is "the execution of a defined act or acts or occurs with the passage of time."[41]

Authoritative professional literature generally specifies that costs should be charged to expense in the period in which the revenue with which they are associated is recognized as earned. These costs should not be deferred unless they are expected to be recoverable from future revenue.[42]

For purposes of accounting for service transactions, related costs are identified as follows:[43]

1. **Initial direct costs** are costs that are directly associated with negotiating and consummating service agreements. They include, but are not necessarily limited to commissions, legal fees, costs of credit investigations, and instalment paper processing fees. No portion of supervisory and administration expenses or other indirect expenses, such as rent and facilities costs, is included in initial direct costs.
2. **Direct costs** are costs that have a clearly identifiable beneficial or causal relationship (i) to the services preformed or (ii) to the level of services performed for a group of customers; for example, service labour and repair parts included as part of a service agreement.
3. **Indirect costs** are all costs other than initial direct costs and direct costs. They include provisions for uncollectible accounts, general and administrative expenses, advertising expenses, and general selling expenses.

Indirect costs should be charged to expense as incurred regardless of the revenue recognition method applied to the transaction. The method of accounting for initial direct costs and direct costs is dependent upon the revenue recognition method applied to the transaction.

METHODS OF SERVICE REVENUE RECOGNITION

Four different methods of accounting for revenues on service transactions have been proposed. The major determinant of each method's applicability is the nature and extent of performance. The four recommended methods are:

1. Specific performance method.
2. Completed performance method.
3. Proportional performance method.
4. Collection method.

[40]*Ibid.*, pp. 10–11.

[41]*Ibid.*, p. 11.

[42]"Basic Concepts and Accounting Principles Underlying Financial Statements of Business Enterprises," *APB Statement No. 4* (New York: AICPA, 1970), par. 155.

[43]"Accounting for Certain Service Transactions," *op. cit.*, pp. 13 and 14.

Specific Performance Method   The specific performance method is appropriate when a service transaction consists of a **single act**. Revenue should be recognized at the time the act takes place. Initial direct costs and direct costs should be charged to expense at the time revenues are recognized. Thus initial direct costs and direct costs incurred before the service is performed should be deferred until the revenue is recognized.

This method can be used by a real estate broker who would record sales commissions as revenue when the real estate transaction is consummated at the "closing." This method might also apply to an employment agency whose fee is contingent upon the new employee's remaining at a job for a specified period of time. Because the agency has rendered its services in locating and placing an employee for its client, the fee would be recorded at the time the employee is placed. However, if experience shows that there is a reasonable possibility of having to refund the fee because of the employment period contingency, it is appropriate to record an allowance based on estimates of fees that will never be collected.

Completed Performance Method   The completed performance method is appropriate when services are performed in **more than one act** and the proportion of services to be performed is the last of a series of acts so significant in relation to the entire service transaction that **performance cannot be deemed to have occurred until the last act occurs.** For example, for a moving company that packs, loads, and delivers goods to various locations, the act of delivery is so significant to its completing the earning process that revenue should not be recognized until delivery occurs.

Under the completed performance method, initial direct costs and direct costs would be expensed when revenue is recognized. Costs incurred before the service is performed should be deferred until the revenue is recognized.

Proportional Performance Method   The proportional performance method is appropriate when services are performed in **more than one act** and revenue should be recognized as the various acts that make up the entire transactions occur; that is, in proportion to the performance of each act.[44] This method can be applied in a slightly different manner to three differing sets of circumstances:

1. **Specified number of identical or similar acts.** An equal amount of revenue would be recorded for each act expected to be performed. The processing of monthly mortgage payments by a mortgage banker is an appropriate application of this method.
2. **Specified number of defined but not identical acts.** Revenue is recognized in the ratio that the direct costs of performing each act have to the total estimated direct cost of the entire transaction. A correspondence school that provides progress evaluations, lessons, examinations, and grading might appropriately use this method. If the direct cost ratio is impractical or not objectively determinable as a measurement basis, a systematic and rational basis that reasonably relates revenue recognition to performance should be used. As a last resort, the straight-line method should be used.
3. **Unspecified number of identical or similar acts with a fixed period of performance**. Revenue is recognized on the straight-line method over the specified period unless there is evidence that another method more accurately represents the pattern of performance. A two-year club membership in which the club's facilities are available for the member's use throughout that period is an example of appropriate application of the straight-line method.

[44]Proportional measurement is necessary only if the acts are performed in more than one financial accounting period.

Under the proportional performance method, **initial direct costs** are recorded as expenses in the same manner as revenue is recorded. Because there is generally a close correlation between the incurrence of **direct costs** and the extent of performance achieved, direct costs are recorded as expenses as they are incurred.

Collection Method

If there is a significant degree of uncertainty surrounding the collectibility of service revenue, revenue should be recorded as cash is collected. Under this method, initial direct and direct costs should be recorded as expenses as incurred. The collection method is appropriate when a service is being provided to a customer whose ability to pay for those services is questionable.

Summary of Service Revenue Recognition Methods

The four service revenue recognition methods presented above are conceptually somewhat similar to several of the product sales revenue recognition methods presented earlier in the chapter, as shown below:

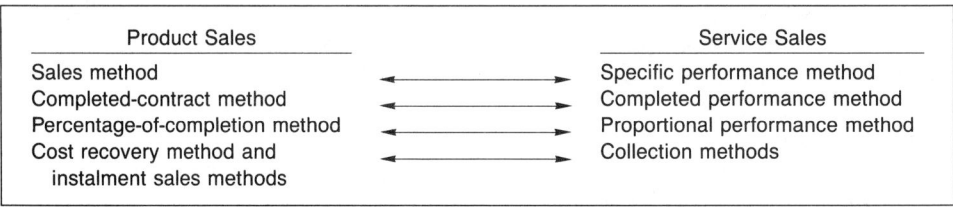

Product Sales	Service Sales
Sales method	Specific performance method
Completed-contract method	Completed performance method
Percentage-of-completion method	Proportional performance method
Cost recovery method and instalment sales methods	Collection methods

Note: All **asterisked** Questions, Cases, Exercises, or Problems relate to material contained in an Appendix.

QUESTIONS

1. What is revenue? When is revenue realized in a theoretical sense? According to the "realization principle," when is revenue realized?
2. When is revenue recognized in the following situations: (a) Revenue from selling products? (b) Revenue from services rendered? (c) Revenue from permitting others to use enterprise assets? (d) Revenue from disposing of assets other than products?
3. Identify several types of sales transactions and indicate the types of business for which that type of transaction is common.
4. When is revenue conventionally recognized? What conditions should exist for the recognition at date of sale of all or part of the revenue and income of any sale transaction?
5. What are the three alternative accounting methods available to a seller who is exposed to continued risks of ownership through return of the product?
6. Under what conditions may a seller, who is exposed to the continued risk of a high rate of return of the product sold, recognize sales transactions as current revenue?
7. How does the accounting for a "contract of sale" differ from the accounting for a "contract to sell"?

8. What are the two basic methods of accounting for long-term construction contracts? Indicate the circumstances that determine when one or the other of these methods should be used.

9. For what reasons should the percentage-of-completion method be used over the completed-contract method whenever possible?

10. What methods are used in practice to determine the extent of progress toward completion? Identify some "input measures" and some "output measures" that might be used to determine the extent of progress.

11. What are the two types of losses that can become evident in accounting for long-term contracts? What is the nature of each type of loss? How is each type accounted for?

12. What is accretion? Why is accretion generally not recognized as revenue?

13. What are the current arguments for and against using some form of discovery basis accounting in the extractive industries?

14. Identify and briefly describe the two methods generally employed to account for the cash received in situations where the collection of the sales price is not reasonably assured.

15. What is the nature of an instalment sale?

16. How do instalment sales differ from ordinary credit sales?

17. Describe the instalment sales method of accounting.

18. How are operating expenses (not included in cost of goods sold) handled under the instalment method of accounting? What is the justification for such treatment?

19. When interest is involved in instalment sales transactions, how should it be treated for accounting purposes?

20. How should the results of instalment sales be reported on the income statement?

21. What is the nature of a sale on consignment? When is revenue recognized from a consignment sale?

*22. Why in franchise arrangements may it not be proper to recognize the entire franchise fee as revenue at the date of sale?

*23. How does the concept of "substantial performance" apply to accounting for franchise sales?

*24. How should a franchisor account for continuing franchise fees and routine sales of equipment and supplies to franchisees?

*25. What changes are made in the franchisor's recording of the initial franchise fee when the franchise agreement:
    (a) Contains an option allowing the franchisor to purchase the franchised outlet, and it is likely that the option will be exercised?
    (b) Allows the franchisee to purchase equipment and supplies from the franchisor at bargain prices?

*26. At what time is it proper to recognize income in the following cases: (a) instalment sales with no reasonable basis for estimating the degree of collectibility; (b) sales for future delivery; (c) merchandise shipped on consignment; (d) profit on incomplete construction contracts; and (e) subscriptions to publications?

*27. When should revenue from service transactions be recognized?

*28. Identify and differentiate between the three types of service costs. What is the guideline for expensing costs in general? What are the general guidelines for recognizing the three types of service costs?

*29. What are the four methods of accounting for service transactions that have been recommended? Which product sales revenue recognition bases do each of these service methods most resemble in effect on revenue timing?

CASES

C19-1 Revenue is usually recognized at the point of sale. Under special circumstances, however, bases other than the point of sale are used for the timing of revenue recognition.

Instructions

(a) Why is the point of sale usually used as the basis for the timing of revenue recognition?

(b) Disregarding the special circumstances when bases other than the point of sale are used, discuss the merits of each of the following objections to the sales basis of revenue recognition:

1. It is too conservative because revenue is earned throughout the entire process of production.

2. It is not conservative enough because accounts receivable do not represent disposable funds, sales returns and allowances may be made, and collection and bad debt expenses may be incurred in a later period.

(c) Revenue may also be recognized (1) during production and (2) when cash is received. For each of these two bases of timing revenue recognition, give an example of the circumstances in which it is properly used and discuss the accounting merits of its use in lieu of the sales basis.

(AICPA adapted)

C19-2 The earning of revenue by a business enterprise is recognized for accounting purposes when the transaction is recorded. In some situations, however, accountants have developed guidelines for recognizing revenue by other criteria; for example, at the point of sale.

Instructions

(Ignore income taxes.)

(a) Explain and justify why revenue is often recognized as earned at time of sale.

(b) Explain in what situations it would be appropriate to recognize revenue as the productive activity takes place.

(c) At what times, other than those included in (a) and (b) above, may it be appropriate to recognize revenue? Explain.

C19-3 H & S Blue Stamps, Inc. was formed early this year to sell trading stamps throughout the west to retailers, who distribute the stamps free to their customers. Books for accumulating the stamps and catalogues illustrating the merchandise for which the stamps may be exchanged are given free to retailers for distribution to stamp recipients. Centres have been established with inventories of merchandise premiums for redemption of the stamps. Retailers may not return unused stamps to H & S.

The following schedule expresses H & S's expectations as to percentages that will be attained from a normal month's activity. For this purpose, a "normal month's activity" is defined as the level of operations expected when expansion of activities ceases or tapers off to a stable rate. The company expects that this level will be attained in the third year and that sales of stamps will average $4,000,000 per month throughout the third year.

Month	Actual Stamp Sales Percent	Merchandise Premium Purchases Percent	Stamp Redemptions Percent
6th	30%	40%	10%
12th	60	60	45
18th	80	80	70
24th	90	90	80
30th	100	100	95

H & S plans to adopt an annual closing date at the end of each 12 months of operation.

Instructions

(a) Discuss the factors to be considered in determining when revenue should be recognized as measuring the income of a business enterprise.

(b) Discuss the accounting alternatives that should be considered by H & S Blue Stamps, Inc. for the recognition of its revenues and related expenses.

(c) For each accounting alternative discussed in (b), give balance sheet accounts that should be used and indicate how each should be classified.

(AICPA adapted)

*C19-4   Planetary Products Inc. is a large conglomerate consisting of 44 subsidiary companies with plants and offices throughout Canada and the world. Dunlop & Co. is the international public accounting firm engaged to design and install a computerized total information, accounting, and cost control system in each of Planetary's subsidiaries. The CA firm is given three years to complete the engagement; it intends to work continuously on the project, but will assign the largest number of its staff to it during its least busy period each year (May to October). Dunlop & Co. obtained this consulting engagement after much study, planning, an elaborate presentation, and a bid of $5,200,000.

Instructions

(a) Name and describe four different methods of accounting for the revenues from service-type engagements, indicating when revenue is recognized.

(b) For each of the four methods, describe how initial direct costs and direct costs should be expensed.

(c) Discuss the method of revenue recognition and expensing of initial indirect costs and direct costs that you believe is appropriate for the CA firm in its performance of the engagement described above.

(d) How does the receipt of cash for payment of services affect revenue recognition in this and other service transactions?

*C19-5   Pizza Heaven Inc. sells franchises to independent operators throughout the eastern part of Canada. The contract with the franchisee includes the following provisions.

1.   The franchisee is charged an initial fee of $50,000. Of this amount $10,000 is payable when the agreement is signed and an $8,000 noninterest-bearing note is payable at the end of each of the five subsequent years.

2.   All of the initial franchise fee collected by Pizza Heaven Inc. is to be refunded and the remaining obligation cancelled if, for any reason, the franchisee fails to open his or her franchise.

3.   In return for the initial franchise fee, Pizza Heaven Inc. agrees to (a) assist the franchisee in selecting the location for their business, (b) negotiate the lease for the land, (c) obtain financing and assist with building design, (d) supervise construction, (e) establish accounting and tax records, and (f) provide expert advice over a five-year period relating to such matters as employee and management training, quality control, and promotion.

4.   In addition to the initial franchise fee, the franchisee is required to pay to Pizza Heaven Inc. a monthly fee of 2% of sales for menu planning, recipe innovations, and the privilege of purchasing ingredients from Pizza Heaven Inc. at or below prevailing market prices. Management of Pizza Heaven Inc. estimates that the value of the services rendered to the franchisee at the time the contract is signed amounts to at least $10,000. All franchisees to date have opened their locations at the scheduled time, and none has defaulted on any of the notes receivable.

The credit ratings of all franchisees would entitle them to borrow at the current interest rate of 10%. The present value of an ordinary annuity of five annual receipts of $8,000 and discounted at 10% is $30,326.

Instructions

(a) Discuss the alternatives that Pizza Heaven Inc. might use to account for the initial franchise fee. Evaluate each by applying generally accepted accounting principles to this situation, and give illustrative entries for each alternative.

(b) Given the nature of Pizza Heaven Inc.'s agreement with its franchisees, when should revenue be recognized? Discuss the question of revenue recognition for both the initial franchise fee and the additional monthly fee of 2% of sales, giving illustrative entries for both types of revenue.

(c) Assuming that Pizza Heaven Inc. sells some franchises for $70,000, which includes a charge of $20,000 for the rental of equipment for its useful life of 10 years, that $30,000 of the fee is payable immediately and the balance on noninterest-bearing notes at $8,000 per year, that no portion of the $20,000 rental payment is refundable in case the franchisee goes out of business, and that title to the equipment remains with the franchisor, what would be the preferable method of accounting for the rental portion of the initial franchise fee? Explain.

(AICPA adapted)

EXERCISES

E19-1 On June 3, Huskie Company sold to Gail Wark merchandise having a sales price of $4,500 with terms of 2/10, n/60, f.o.b. shipping point. An invoice totalling $135, terms n/30, was received by Gail Wark on June 8 from the Messenger Transport Service for the freight cost. Upon receipt of the goods on June 5, Gail Wark notified Huskie Company that merchandise costing $300 contained flaws that rendered it worthless; the same day Huskie Company issued a credit memo covering the worthless merchandise and asked that it be returned at company expense. The freight on the returned merchandise was $24, paid by Huskie Company on June 7. On June 12, the company received a cheque for the balance due from Gail Wark.

Instructions

(a) Prepare journal entries on Huskie Company books to record all the events noted above under each of the following bases:
   1. Sales and receivables are entered at gross selling price.
   2. Sales and receivables are entered net of cash discounts.

(b) Prepare the journal entry under basis 2, assuming that Gail Wark did not remit payment until July 29.

E19-2 In 1986, Mountain Tunnel Corp. began construction work under a three-year contract. The contract price was $1,000,000. Mountain uses the percentage-of-completion method for financial accounting purposes. The income to be recognized each year is based on the proportion of cost incurred to total estimated costs for completing the contract. The financial statement presentations relating to this contract at December 31, 1986, follow:

Balance Sheet		
Accounts receivable—construction contract billings		$18,750
Construction in progress	$62,500	
Less contract billings	58,750	
Cost of uncompleted contract in excess of billings		3,750

Income Statement	
Income (before tax) on the contract recognized in 1986	$12,500

Instructions

(a) How much cash was collected in 1986 on this contract?

(b) What was the initial estimated total income before tax on this contract?

(AICPA adapted)

E19-3 On April 1, 1986, Faivre, Inc. entered into a cost-plus-fixed-fee contract to construct an electric generator for Dalton Corporation. At the contract date, Faivre estimated that it would take two years to complete the project at a cost of $2,000,000. The fixed fee stipulated in the contract was $300,000. Faivre appropriately accounts for this contract under the percentage-of-completion method. During 1986 Faivre incurred costs of $700,000 related to the project; the estimated cost at December 31, 1986, to complete the contract is $1,400,000. Dalton was billed $500,000 under the contract.

Instructions

Prepare a schedule to compute the amount of gross profit to be recognized by Faivre under the contract for the year ended December 31, 1986. Show supporting computations in good form.

(AICPA adapted)

E19-4 Haid Construction Company uses the percentage-of-completion method of accounting. In 1986, Haid began work under contract #E2-D2, which provided for a contract price of $2,100,000. Other details follow:

	1986	1987
Costs incurred during the year	$ 300,000	$1,375,000
Estimated costs to complete, as of December 31	1,200,000	–0–
Billings during the year	360,000	1,740,000
Collections during the year	250,000	1,600,000

Instructions

(a) What portion of the total contract price would be recognized as revenue in 1986? 1987?

(b) Assuming the same facts as those above except that Haid uses the completed-contract method of accounting, what portion of the total contract price would be recognized as revenue in 1987?

(c) Prepare a complete set of journal entries for 1986.

E19-5 In 1986, Nagy Construction Company agreed to construct an apartment building at a price of $1,050,000. The information relating to the costs and billings for this contract is as follows:

	1986	1987	1988
Costs incurred to date	$240,000	$440,000	$ 840,000
Estimated costs yet to be incurred	560,000	360,000	–0–
Customer billings to date	100,000	360,000	1,050,000
Collection of billings to date	80,000	300,000	940,000

Instructions

(a) Assuming that the percentage-of-completion method is used, compute the amount of gross profit to be recognized in 1986 and 1987. Prepare journal entries for 1987.

(b) For 1987, show how the details related to this construction contract would be disclosed on the balance sheet and on the income statement.

E19-6 Barrington Construction Company began operations in 1985. Construction activity for the first year is shown below. All contracts are with different customers, and any work remaining at December 31, 1985, is expected to be completed in 1986.

Project	Contract Price	Total Billings Through 12/31/85	Cash Collections Through 12/31/85	Contract Costs Incurred Through 12/31/85	Estimated Additional Costs to Complete
1	$ 520,000	$ 350,000	$310,000	$424,000	$106,000
2	670,000	210,000	210,000	126,000	504,000
3	475,000	475,000	395,000	315,000	–0–
	$1,665,000	$1,035,000	$915,000	$865,000	$610,000

Instructions

Prepare a partial income statement and balance sheet to indicate how the above information would be reported for financial statement purposes. Barrington uses the completed-contract method.

E19-7 Delicate Construction Company began operations January 1, 1986. During the year, Delicate entered into a contract with Silo & Shed Corporation to construct a manufacturing facility. At that time, Delicate estimated that it would take five years to complete the facility at a total cost of $4,800,000. The total contract price for construction of the facility is $6,200,000. During the year, Delicate incurred $1,250,000 in construction costs related to the construction project. The estimated cost to complete the contract is $3,750,000. Silo & Shed was billed and paid 30% of the contract price.

Instructions

Prepare schedules to compute the amount of gross profit to be recognized for the year ended December 31, 1986, and the amount to be shown as ''cost of uncompleted contract in excess of related billings'' or ''billings on uncompleted contract in excess of related costs'' at December 31, 1986, under each of the following methods:

(a) Completed-contract method.

(b) Percentage-of-completion method.

Show supporting computations in good form.

(AICPA adapted)

*E19-8 On May 3, 1986, Don Ford Company consigned 60 freezers, costing $500 each, to Diana Company. The cost of shipping the freezers amounted to $600, and was paid by Don Ford Company. On December 30, 1986, an account of sales was received from the consignee, reporting that 40 freezers had been sold for $600 each. Remittance was made by the consignee for the amount due, after deducting a commission of 10%, advertising of $100, and total installation costs of $200 on the freezers sold.

Instructions

(a) Compute the inventory value of the units unsold in the hands of the consignee.

(b) Compute the profit for the consignor for the units sold.

(c) Compute the amount of cash that will be remitted by the consignee.

E19-9 Linda Plumb Co. appropriately uses the instalment sales method of accounting. On December 31, 1987, the books show balances as follows:

Instalment Receivables		Deferred Gross Profit		Gross Profit on Sales	
1985	$10,000	1985	$ 7,000	1985	35%
1986	40,000	1986	26,000	1986	34%
1987	90,000	1987	105,000	1987	32%

Instructions

(a) Prepare the adjusting entry or entries required on December 31, 1987, to recognize 1987 realized gross profit. (Cash receipts entries have already been made.)

(b) Compute the amount of cash collected in 1987 on accounts receivable of each year.

E19-10 Frank Lovell Corporation, which began business on January 1, 1985, appropriately uses the instalment sales method of accounting. The following data were obtained for the years 1985 and 1986:

	1985	1986
Instalment sales	$700,000	$840,000
Cost of instalment sales	560,000	630,000
General and administrative expenses	70,000	84,000
Cash collections on sales of 1985	300,000	250,000
Cash collections on sales of 1986	–0–	400,000

Instructions

(a) Compute the balance in the deferred gross profit accounts on December 31, 1985, and on December 31, 1986.

(b) A 1985 sale resulted in default in 1987. At the date of default, the balance on the instalment receivable was $12,000, and the repossessed merchandise had a fair value of $8,200. Prepare the entry to record the repossession.

(AICPA adapted)

E19-11 Sherri Schulzke Corporation sells farm machinery on the instalment plan. On July 1, 1985, Schulzke entered into an instalment sale contract with Agriculture, Inc. for an eight-year period. Equal annual payments under the instalment sale are $100,000 and are due on July 1. The first payment was made on July 1, 1985. Additional information follows:

1. The amount that would be realized on an outright sale of similar farm machinery is $556,000.

2. The cost of the farm machinery sold to Agriculture is $417,000.

3. The finance charges relating to the instalment period are $244,000 based on a stated interest rate of 12%, which is appropriate.

4. Circumstances are such that the collection of the instalments due under the contract is reasonably assured.

Instructions

What income or loss before income taxes should Schulzke record for the year ended December 31, 1985, as a result of the above transactions?

(AICPA adapted)

E19-12 Lowprice Outlet, Inc. was involved in two default and repossession cases during the year.

1. A refrigerator was sold to Ms. Alice Congdon for $1,800, including a 40% markup on selling price. Ms. Congdon made a down payment of 20%, four of the remaining 24 equal payments, and then defaulted on further payments. The refrigerator was repossessed, at which time the fair value was determined to be $800.

2. An oven that cost $1,200 was sold to Mr. Chuck Ehrlich for $1,600 on the instalment basis. Mr. Ehrlich made a down payment of $240 and paid $80 a month for six months, after which he defaulted. The oven was repossessed, and the estimated value at time of repossession was determined to be $720.

Instructions

Prepare the journal entries to record the repossessions.

E19-13 Semi-Trailer Company uses the instalment sales method in accounting for its instalment sales. On January 1, 1986, Semi-Trailer Company had an instalment account receivable from Elaine Wunderlich with a balance of $1,250. During 1986, $200 was collected from Wunderlich. When no further collection could be made, the merchandise sold to Wunderlich was repossessed. The merchandise, when repossessed, had a fair market value of $400. The company spent $50 for reconditioning of the merchandise. The merchandise was originally sold with a gross profit rate of 40%.

Instructions

Prepare the entries on the books of Semi-Trailer Company to record all transactions related to Wunderlich during 1986.

*E19-14 Herb Huskie Hamburgers, Inc. charges an initial franchise fee of $60,000. Upon the signing of the agreement, a payment of $30,000 is due; thereafter, three annual payments of $10,000 are required. The credit rating of the franchisee is such that it would have to pay interest at 10% to borrow money.

Instructions

Prepare the entries to record the initial franchise fee on the books of the franchisor under the following assumptions:

(a) The down payment is not refundable; no future services are required by the franchisor; and collection of the note is reasonably assured.

(b) The franchisor has substantial services to perform, and the collection of the note is very uncertain.

(c) The down payment is not refundable; collection of the note is reasonably certain; the franchisor has yet to perform a substantial amount of services; and the down payment represents a fair measure of the services already performed.

*E19-15   On January 1, 1985, Andrew Franklin signed an agreement to operate as a franchisee of Sickbay Hospital Supplies, Inc. for an initial franchise fee of $40,000. The amount of $15,000 was paid when the agreement was signed, and the balance is payable in five annual payments of $5,000, each beginning January 1, 1986. The agreement provides that the down payment is not refundable and that no future services are required of the franchisor. Franklin's credit rating indicates that he can borrow money at 12% for a loan of this type.

Instructions

(a) How much should Sickbay record as revenue from franchise fees on January 1, 1985? At what amount should Franklin record the acquisition cost of the franchise on January 1, 1985?

(b) What entry would be made by Sickbay on January 1, 1985, if the down payment were refundable and substantial future services remain to be performed by Sickbay?

(c) How much revenue from franchise fees would be recorded by Sickbay on January 1, 1985, if:

1. The initial down payment was not refundable; it represented a fair measure of the services already provided, with a significant amount of services still to be performed by Sickbay in future periods; and collectibility of the note is reasonably assured?

2. The initial down payment is not refundable and no future services are required by the franchisor, but collection of the note is so uncertain that recognition of the note as an asset is unwarranted?

3. The initial down payment has not been earned and collection of the note is so uncertain that recognition of the note as an asset is unwarranted?

PROBLEMS

P19-1   Highrise Construction Company has entered into a contract beginning January 1, 1985, to build a parking complex. It has been estimated that the complex will cost $700,000 and will take three years to construct. The complex will be billed to the purchasing company at $1,000,000. The following data pertain to the construction period.

	1985	1986	1987
Costs to date	$350,000	$490,000	$ 700,000
Estimated costs to complete	350,000	210,000	–0–
Progress billings to date	300,000	650,000	1,000,000
Cash collected to date	250,000	600,000	1,000,000

Instructions

(a) Using the percentage-of-completion method, compute the estimated gross profit that would be recognized during each year of the construction period.

(b) Using the completed-contract method, compute the estimated gross profit that would be recognized during each year of the construction period.

P19-2 Hardhat Construction Company has contracted to build an office building. The construction is scheduled to begin on January 1, 1985, and the estimated time of completion is July 1, 1988. The building cost is estimated to be $50,000,000 and will be billed at $56,000,000. The following data relate to the construction period.

	1985	1986	1987	1988
Costs to date	$15,000,000	$25,000,000	$35,000,000	$50,000,000
Estimated cost to complete	35,000,000	25,000,000	15,000,000	–0–
Progress billings to date	7,000,000	20,000,000	35,000,000	56,000,000
Cash collected to date	7,000,000	18,000,000	30,000,000	56,000,000

Instructions

(a) Compute the estimated gross profit for 1985, 1986, 1987, and 1988, assuming that the percentage-of-completion method is used. (Ignore income taxes.)

(b) Prepare the necessary journal entries for Hardhat Construction Company for the years 1987 and 1988.

P19-3 On February 1, 1985, Dainty Construction Company obtained a contract to build an athletic stadium. The stadium was to be built at a total cost of $4,500,000 and was scheduled for completion by September 1, 1987. One clause of the contract stated that Dainty was to deduct $10,000 from the $6,200,000 billing price for each week that completion was delayed. Completion was delayed five weeks, which resulted in a $50,000 penalty. Below are the data pertaining to the construction period.

	1985	1986	1987
Costs to date	$1,500,000	$3,220,000	$4,600,000
Estimated costs to complete	3,000,000	1,380,000	–0–
Progress billings to date	1,000,000	2,500,000	6,150,000
Cash collected to date	800,000	2,300,000	6,150,000

Instructions

(a) Using the percentage-of-completion method, complete the estimated gross profit recognized in the years 1985–1987.

(b) Prepare a partial balance sheet for December 31, 1986, showing the balances in the receivable and inventory accounts.

P19-4 On March 1, 1985, Concordia Construction Company contracted to construct a factory building for Montgomery Manufacturing, Inc., for a total contract price of $5,000,000. The building was completed by October 31, 1987. The annual contract costs incurred, estimated costs to complete the contract, and accumulated billings to Montgomery for 1985, 1986, and 1987 are given below:

	At Dec. 31, 1985	At Dec. 31, 1986	At Dec. 31, 1987
Contract costs incurred	$1,000,000	$2,840,000	$ 960,000
Estimated costs to complete the contract	3,000,000	960,000	–0–
Billings to Montgomery	800,000	3,000,000	1,200,000

Instructions

(a) Using the percentage-of-completion method, prepare schedules to complete the profit or loss to be recognized as a result of this contract for the years ended December 31, 1985, 1986, and 1987. (Ignore income taxes.)

(b) Using the completed-contract method, prepare schedules to compute the profit or loss to be recognized as a result of this contract for the years ended December 1985, 1986, and 1987. (Ignore income taxes.)

P19-5 Hartwick Construction Company commenced doing business on January 1, 1985. Construction activities for the first year of operations are shown in the table below. All contract costs are with different customers, and any work remaining at December 31, 1985, is expected to be completed in 1986.

Project	Total Contract Price	Cash Billings Through Dec. 31/85	Collections Through Dec. 31/85	Contract Costs Incurred Through Dec. 31/85	Estimated Additional Costs to Complete
A	$ 260,000	$175,000	$155,000	$212,000	$ 53,000
B	335,000	105,000	105,000	63,000	252,000
C	237,500	237,500	197,500	157,500	–0–
D	100,000	35,000	25,000	56,375	46,125
E	230,000	200,000	200,000	185,000	15,000
	$1,162,500	$752,500	$682,500	$673,875	$366,125

Instructions

(a) Prepare a schedule to compute income to be reported, unbilled contract costs and recognized profit, and billings in excess of costs and recognized profit using the percentage-of-completion method.

(b) Prepare a partial income statement and balance sheet to indicate how the information would be reported for financial statement purposes.

P19-6 On July 1, 1985, Compton Construction Company, Inc. contracted to build an office building for Judy Kehler for a total contract price of $4,000,000. On July 1, Compton estimated that it would take between two and three years to complete the building. On December 31, 1987, the building was deemed substantially completed. Following are accumulated contract costs incurred, estimated costs to complete the contract, and accumulated billings for 1985, 1986, and 1987.

	At Dec. 31, 1985	At Dec. 31, 1986	At Dec. 31, 1987
Contract costs incured	$ 350,000	$2,500,000	$4,250,000
Estimated costs to complete the contract	3,150,000	1,700,000	–0–
Billings to Kehler	720,000	1,160,000	3,600,000

Instructions

(a) Using the percentage-of-completion method, prepare schedules to compute the profit or loss to be recognized as a result of this contract for the years ended December 31, 1985, 1986, and 1987. (Ignore income taxes.)

(b) Using the completed-contract method, prepare schedules to compute the profit or loss to be recognized as a result of this contract for the years ended December 1985, 1986, and 1987. (Ignore income taxes.)

P19-7 Presented below is summarized information for Hazard Appliance Co., which sells merchandise on the instalment basis:

	1985	1986	1987
Sales (on instalment plan)	$200,000	$240,000	$200,000
Cost of sales	120,000	151,200	130,000
Gross profit	$ 80,000	$ 88,800	$ 70,000
Collections from customers on:			
1985 instalment sales	$ 60,000	$110,000	$ 20,000
1986 instalment sales		80,000	120,000
1987 instalment sales			70,000

Instructions

(a) Compute the realized gross profit for each of the years 1985, 1986, and 1987.

(b) Prepare in journal form all entries required in 1987, applying the instalment method of accounting.

P19-8 Regal Flatware sells merchandise on open account as well as on instalment terms.

	1985	1986	1987
Sales on account	$417,000	$389,000	$510,000
Instalment sales	240,000	320,000	380,000
Collections on instalment sales			
Made in 1985	80,000	120,000	40,000
Made in 1986		110,000	160,000
Made in 1987			125,000
Cost of sales			
Sold on account	291,900	268,410	351,900
Sold on instalment	151,200	192,000	224,200
Selling expenses	87,000	84,500	110,000
Administrative expenses	42,000	48,000	54,000

Instructions

From the data above, which cover the three years since Regal Flatware commenced operations, determine the net income for each year, applying the instalment method of accounting.

P19-9 Cutrate Company sells appliances for cash and also on the instalment plan. Entries to record cost of sales are made monthly.

Cutrate Company
TRIAL BALANCE
December 31, 1987

Cash	$ 145,200	
Instalment Accounts Receivable, 1986	48,000	
Instalment Accounts Receivable, 1987	152,000	
Inventory—New Merchandise	124,000	
Inventory—Repossessed Merchandise	24,000	
Accounts Payable		$ 96,600
Deferred Gross Profit, 1986		45,600
Capital Stock		200,000
Retained Earnings		84,800
Sales		424,000
Instalment Sales		300,000
Cost of Sales	330,000	
Cost of Instalment Sales	195,000	
Gain or Loss on Repossessions	800	
Selling and Administrative Expenses	132,000	
	$1,151,000	$1,151,000

The accounting department has prepared the following analysis of cash receipts for the year:

Cash sales (including repossessed merchandise)	$424,000
Instalment accounts receivable, 1986	104,000
Instalment accounts receivable, 1987	148,000
Other	38,000
Total	$714,000

Repossessions recorded during the year are summarized as follows:

	1986
Uncollected balance	$8,000
Loss on repossession	800
Repossessed merchandise	4,800

Instructions

From the trial balance and accompanying information:

(a) Compute the rate of gross profit for 1986 and 1987.

(b) Prepare closing entries as of December 31, 1987, under the instalment method of accounting.

(c) Prepare a statement of income for the year ended December 31, 1987. Include only the realized gross profit in the income statement.

P19-10 Selected transactions of Threedee TV Sales Company are presented below:

1. A television set costing $560 is sold to John Engstrom on November 1, 1986, for $800. Engstrom makes a down payment of $200 and agrees to pay $25 on the first of each month for 24 months thereafter.

2. Engstrom pays the $25 instalment due December 1, 1986.

3. On December 31, 1986, the appropriate entries are made to record profit realized on the instalment sales.

4. The first seven instalments for 1987 of $25 each are paid by Engstrom. (Make one entry.)

5. In August 1987 the set is repossessed after Engstrom fails to pay the August 1 instalment and indicates that he will be unable to continue the payments. The estimated fair value of the repossessed set is $130.

Instructions

Prepare journal entries to record on the books of Threedee TV Sales Company the transactions above.

P19-11 The following summarized information relates to the instalment sales activity of Allabuy Stores, Inc. for the year 1985:

Instalment sales during 1985	$600,000
Cost of goods sold on instalment basis	348,000
Collections from customers	170,000
Unpaid balance on merchandise repossessed	20,000
Estimated value of merchandise repossessed	6,600

Instructions

(a) Prepare journal entries at the end of 1985 to record on the books of Allabuy Stores, Inc. the summarized data above.

(b) Prepare the entry to record the gross profit realized during 1985.

P19-12 Cottonco Inc. sells merchandise for cash and also on the instalment plan. Entries to record cost of goods sold are made at the end of each year. Repossessions of merchandise (sold in 1986) were made in 1987 and were recorded correctly as follows:

Deferred Gross Profit, 1986	4,200	
Repossessed Merchandise	6,000	
Loss on Repossessions	1,800	
Instalment Accounts Receivable, 1986		12,000

Part of this repossessed merchandise was sold for cash during 1987, and the sale was recorded by a debit to Cash and a credit to Sales.

The inventory of repossessed merchandise on hand December 31, 1987, is $4,000; of new merchandise, $100,000. There was no repossessed merchandise on hand January 1, 1987.

Collections on accounts receivable during 1987 were:

Instalment Accounts Receivable, 1986	$80,000
Instalment Accounts Receivable, 1987	50,000

The cost of the merchandise sold under the instalment plan during 1987 was $108,800.

The rate of gross profit on 1986 and on 1987 instalment sales can be computed from the information given on page 922.

Cottonco Inc.
TRIAL BALANCE
December 31, 1987

	Dr.	Cr.
Cash	$101,400	
Instalment Accounts Receivable, 1986	72,000	
Instalment Accounts Receivable, 1987	110,000	
Inventory, Jan. 1, 1987	120,000	
Repossessed Merchandise	6,000	
Accounts Payable		$ 24,000
Deferred Gross Profit, 1986		53,200
Capital Stock, Common		200,000
Retained Earnings		40,000
Sales		400,000
Instalment Sales		160,000
Purchases	360,000	
Loss on Repossessions	1,800	
Operating Expenses	106,000	
	$877,200	$877,200

Instructions

(a) From the trial balance and other information given above, prepare adjusting and closing entries as of December 31, 1987.

(b) Prepare an income statement for the year ended December 31, 1987. Include only the realized gross profit in the income statement.

*P19-13 On January 1, 1985, Limbo's Restaurants, Inc. entered into a franchise agreement granting the franchisee the right to do business under Limbo's name. According to the terms of the franchise agreement, Limbo's has an option to purchase the restaurant at any time within the next five years. It is probable that this option will be exercised. The initial franchise fee is $75,000. The franchisee paid $45,000 down and gave a $30,000 four-year note payable on which interest should be imputed at 10%. Straight-line interest amortization is used. Collectibility of the note is reasonably assured, and Limbo's had substantially performed all services by January 1, 1985. Their terms of the franchise agreement provide that the franchisee must pay a continuing annual fee of $20,000. Half of this is for the purchase of food and supplies from Limbo's at the normal sales price. During 1985, Limbo's provided services costing $4,000 to the franchisee and provided food and supplies costing $7,000. At December 31, 1985, Limbo's purchased the restaurant from the franchisee, paying $100,000 and cancelling the franchisee's note.

Instructions

Prepare the journal entries needed on the books of Limbo's Restaurants, Inc. to record each of the following:

(a) January 1, 1985: receipt of the initial franchise fee.

(b) During 1985: receipt of the continuing franchise fee and provision of food, supplies, and services to the franchisee.

(c) December 31, 1985: amortization of discount on the note and the purchase of the restaurant. The straight-line method of discount amortization is used.

*P19-14   On January 1, 1985, Vacation QuikFoto, Inc. entered into a franchise agreement with a local business, allowing the business (franchisee) to open an outlet under Vacation's name. The franchisee paid 40% of the initial $15,000 franchise fee, and gave a $9,000, two-year, 12% note payable for the difference. Interest on the note is due annually on December 31. In return for the initial franchise fee, Vacation located a site in a shopping mall, negotiated the lease, and installed photo-processing equipment. According to the franchise agreement, the franchisee is to pay a $7,000 continuing annual franchise fee, of which 5% must be spent by Vacation on local advertising. When the initial franchise fee is paid, the franchisee has an option to purchase the photo-processing equipment at 50% of its fair market value. It is estimated that the equipment will be worth $10,000 on January 1, 1985. At January 1, 1985, collectibility of the franchisee's note was reasonably assured, and Vacation had substantially performed all contracted services. During 1985 and 1986, Vacation fulfilled its obligations to provide local advertising services, and incurred other annual costs of $2,500. On January 1, 1987, the franchisee paid the note and exercised its bargain purchase option on the equipment.

Instructions

Prepare the journal entries needed on the books of Vacation QuikFoto, Inc. to record each of the following:

(a) January 1, 1985: receipt of the initial franchise fee.

(b) During 1985: receipt of the continuing franchise fee and incurrence of advertising and other costs.

(c) December 31, 1985: receipt of annual interest on the note.

(d) During 1986: receipt of the continuing franchise fee and incurrence of advertising and other costs.

(e) December 31, 1986: receipt of annual interest on the note.

(f) January 1, 1987: collection of the note and sale of the photo-processing equipment.

P19-15   Curtiss Construction Company, Inc. entered into a firm fixed-price contract with Mellissa Packard Associates on July 1, 1985, to construct a four-storey office building. At that time, Curtiss estimated that it would take between two and three years to complete the project. The total contract price for construction of the building is $4,000,000. Curtiss appropriately accounts for this contract under the completed-contract method in its financial statements and for income tax reporting. The building was deemed substantially completed on December 31, 1987. Estimated percentage of completion, accumulated contract costs incurred, estimated costs to complete the contract, and accumulated billings to Packard under the contract were as follows:

	At December 31, 1985	At December 31, 1986	At December 31, 1987
Percentage of completion	10%	60%	100%
Contract costs incurred	$ 350,000	$2,500,000	$4,250,000
Estimated costs to complete the contract	$3,150,000	$1,700,000	–0–
Billings to Packard	$ 720,000	$2,160,000	$3,600,000

Instructions

(a) Prepare schedules to compute the amount to be shown as "cost of uncompleted contract in excess of related billings" or "billings on uncompleted contract in excess of related costs" at December 31, 1985, 1986, and 1987. Ignore income taxes. Show supporting computations in good form.

(b) Prepare schedules to compute the profit or loss to be recognized as a result of this contract for the years ended December 31, 1985, 1986, and 1987. Ignore income taxes. Show supporting computations in good form.

(AICPA adapted)

P19-16 On January 2, 1985, Frigidtemp Company entered into a contract with a manufacturing company to purchase room-size air conditioners and to sell the units on an instalment plan with collections over approximately 30 months with no carrying charge.

Frigidtemp elected to report income from its sales of air conditioners according to the instalment method.

Purchases and sales of new units were as follows:

	Units Purchased		Units Sold	
Year	Quantity	Price Each	Quantity	Price Each
1985	1,200	$120	1,000	$180
1986	1,800	108	2,000	168
1987	800	126	700	171.60

Collections on instalment sales were as follows:

	Collections Received		
	1985	1986	1987
1985 sales	$36,000	$72,000	$ 72,000
1986 sales		84,000	138,000
1987 sales			25,200

In 1987, 40 units from the 1986 sales were repossessed and sold for $87 each on the instalment plan. At the time of repossession $1,440 had been collected from the original purchasers and the units had a fair value of $3,024.

General and administrative expenses for 1987 were $60,000. No charge has been made against current income for the applicable insurance expense from a three-year policy expiring June 30, 1988, costing $3,600, and for an advance payment of $12,000 on a new contract to purchase air conditioners beginning January 1, 1988.

Instructions

Assuming that the weighted-average method is used for determining the inventory cost including repossessed merchandise, prepare schedules computing for 1985, 1986, and 1987:

(a) 1. The cost of goods sold on instalments.
    2. The average unit cost of goods sold on instalment for each year.

(b) The gross profit percentages for 1985, 1986, and 1987.

(c) The gain or loss on repossessions in 1987.

(d) The net income from instalment sales for 1987. (Ignore income taxes.)

(AICPA adapted)

P19-17 After a two-year search for a buyer, Hobson, Inc. sold its idle plant facility to Jackson Company for $700,000 on January 1, 1982. On this date the plant had a depreciated cost on Hobson's books of $500,000. Under the agreement Jackson paid $100,000 cash on January 1, 1982, and signed a $600,000 note bearing interest at 10%. The note was payable on instalments of $100,000, $200,000, and $300,000 on January 1, 1983, 1984, and 1985 respectively. The note was secured by a mortgage on the property sold. Hobson appropriately accounted for the sale under the cost recovery method since there was no reasonable basis for estimating the degree of collectibility of the note receivable. Jackson repaid the note with three late instalment payments, which were accepted by Hobson, as follows:

Date of Payment	Principal	Interest
July 1, 1983	$100,000	$90,000
December 31, 1984	200,000	75,000
February 1, 1986	300,000	32,500

On April 1, 1986, Hobson exchanged a tract of land, which it had acquired for $105,000 as a potential future building site, for a used printing press of Tyler Company, and paid a cash difference of $30,000. The fair value of the land was $190,000 on the exchange date based on a recent appraisal. The fair value of the printing press was not reasonably determinable, but it had a depreciated cost of $210,000 on Tyler's books at April 1, 1986.

Instructions

(a) Prepare a schedule (using the format shown below) to record the initial transaction for the sale of the idle plant facility, the application of cash collections on the note, and the necessary journal entry on the date the transaction is complete.

Date	Cash Received Debit	Note Receivable Dr. (Cr.)	Idle Plant (Net) (Credit)	Deferred Income Dr. (Cr.)	Income Recognized (Credit)
January 1, 1982	$100,000				
July 1, 1983	190,000				
December 31, 1984	275,000				
February 1, 1986	332,500				
February 1, 1986					

(b) Prepare the journal entry on Hobson's books to record the exchange transactions with Tyler. Show supporting computations in good form.

(AICPA adapted)

20

ACCOUNTING FOR CORPORATE INCOME TAXES

Income of an incorporated business is generally subject to federal and provincial income taxes (proprietorships and partnerships are not subject to income taxes as separate entities). In computing income taxes payable to government units, corporations must complete tax returns, including a statement showing the amount of income subject to tax. In general, the form and content of the tax return income statement are similar to the form and content of the accounting income statement. **Taxable income** in the tax return, however, is computed in accordance with prescribed tax regulations and rules, while **pretax accounting income** in the income statement is measured in accordance with generally accepted accounting principles. Differences between taxable income and accounting income exist because the basic objectives of measuring taxable income are different from those for measuring accounting income. The result is that tax rules frequently differ from accounting principles.

The differences between taxable income and pretax accounting income give rise to **tax differences**. The tax effects of these differences must be recognized in the accounting records and in the resultant financial statements. Our interest in analyzing these tax differences is to determine their effect on the measurement of income tax expense and related liability and asset accounts for corporations. This chapter deals primarily with the accounting for tax differences between periods (**interperiod**

tax allocation). The accounting requirements for tax allocation within a period (**intraperiod tax allocation**) were discussed in Chapter 4.

INCOME AND TAXABLE INCOME

A major cause of problems in accounting for income taxes is that the objectives of reporting income on financial statements to shareholders and others are not the same as the objectives for determining taxable income reported to the government.

Determination of income for financial statement purposes is based on the belief that costs incurred in the process of earning income should be charged to the period in which related revenues are reported in the accounts.[1] Thus, the generally accepted accounting principles of realization of revenue and matching apply. In this framework, income taxes are considered as a cost incurred in the process of earning income. The underlying objective of such an income determination is to provide relevant information to assist owners and others in making decisions.

From a company's point of view, determination of taxable income should rest on the objective of minimizing the present value of income taxes paid over the life of the company. This is accomplished by excluding all revenues and including all expenses permitted within the law when determining taxable income (avoidance but not evasion of tax). Furthermore, to be consistent with this objective, a company should calculate taxable income in a manner that would defer payment of taxes into the future rather than pay them in the present period. Therefore, for purposes of taxable income determination, this would mean deferring the inclusion of revenues or gains to future years and including all possible expenses and losses in the present year when such options exist under tax laws. This calculation principle is different from generally accepted accounting principles, and results in a difference between taxable income (on which the amount of taxes paid is based) and pretax accounting income (on which the amount of tax expense is based).

Differences between Taxable Income and Pretax Accounting Income

Numerous items create differences between taxable income and pretax accounting income. For purposes of accounting recognition these differences are of two types: (1) permanent differences and (2) timing differences.

Permanent Differences   Permanent differences refer to (1) items that enter into accounting income but **never** into taxable income, or (2) items that enter into taxable income but **never** into accounting income. Such differences arise from tax laws which (a) exclude certain accounting revenues from taxation (for example, dividends received from another Canadian corporation, life insurance proceeds received on the death of an insured company officer), (b) exclude certain accounting expenses as a tax deduction (for example, premiums paid on company officers' life insurance, cost allocations related to fair-value adjustments), and (c) allow certain deductions that are not taken into accounting income (for example, 3% inventory allowance, investment tax credits, manufacturing and processing allowance, resource allowances).

Since permanent differences affect only the period in which they occur, they will not be offset by corresponding differences or "reversals" in subsequent periods.

---

[1]*CICA Handbook*, Section 3470, par. 4.

When such items appear on the accounting income statement, they are simply treated as non-taxable or non-deductible items in the determination of the amount of tax expense to be reported. If a permanent difference item is on the tax return, it would be used to calculate tax expense to be reported even though the item itself was not in the accounting income statement.

For example, assume that taxable income was $100,000 and pretax accounting income was $98,000, the difference being due to a permanent difference expense item appearing in the latter. If the statutory tax rate was 45%, both the tax payable and the tax expense would be $45,000 as shown below:

```
Tax payable = tax rate × taxable income
            = 0.45 × $100,000
            = $45,000
Tax expense = tax rate × ⎡  pretax accounting income
                         ⎢ + permanent difference
                         ⎢   expenses in income statement
                         ⎢ + permanent difference revenues
                         ⎢   in taxable income
                         ⎢ − permanent difference revenues
                         ⎢   in the income statement
                         ⎢ − permanent difference expenses
                         ⎣   in taxable income
            = 0.45 ($98,000 + $2,000 + 0 − 0 − 0)
            = $45,000
```

If taxable income was $100,000 and pretax accounting income was $110,000, with the difference caused by a permanent difference expense item in the tax return, then the tax payable and tax expense would be $45,000. The tax expense determination in the above formula would be:

$$0.45 \ (\$110,000 + 0 + 0 - 0 - \$10,000).$$

These examples show that when only permanent differences exist, both the tax payable and tax expense equal the tax rate multiplied by the taxable income. It should be recognized, however, that when permanent differences exist, the apparent reported (effective) tax rate of 46% and 41% respectively in the previous examples (tax expense divided by pretax accounting income) would not correspond to the 45% statutory tax rate. Disclosure of such discrepancies is required in the financial statements of enterprises that trade securities in a public market or file annually with a securities commission and is deemed desirable for other enterprises.[2] The excerpt from a financial statement of Canadian General Electric Co. Ltd. shown on page 942 illustrates how this type of disclosure can be made.

Timing Differences   Timing differences arise when (1) the time period of including items of revenue and expense in the computation of pretax accounting income and (2) the time period of including them in the computation of taxable income do not coincide. Timing differences originate in one period and ''reverse'' or ''turn around'' in one or more subsequent periods. Some timing differences reduce income taxes that would otherwise be payable currently if taxes were based on pretax accounting income; others increase current income taxes payable that would otherwise not have been payable until the future if pretax accounting income were used

[2]*Ibid.*, Section 3470, par. 33.

as the basis for their calculation. The *CICA Handbook* identifies five situations from which timing differences arise:

(a) where expenses are claimed for tax purposes in one period but are not charged against income for accounting purposes until some later period, such as capital cost allowances in excess of depreciation charged, and certain other costs which are sometimes deferred in the accounts but claimed immediately for taxes, such as exploration and development costs, start-up costs, past service pension contributions, and accounting and legal expenses in connection with bond financing;

(b) where expenses are charged against income for accounting purposes in one period but are not deducted for tax purposes until some later period, such as provisions for warranties, provisions for deferred compensation payments, and depreciation of fixed assets or write-downs of inventories in excess of amounts allowed for tax purposes;

(c) where revenues are included in accounting income in one period but are not taxable until some later period, such as profit on instalment sales;

(d) where revenues are deferred in the accounts to a later period but are taxable in the current period, such as unearned profits on certain types of construction contracts and intercompany profits in inventories that are eliminated on consolidation;

(e) where capital gains and losses are recorded for accounting purposes in periods different from those in which they are recognized for tax purposes.[3]

To illustrate timing differences further, assume that Baker Ltd. bought a Class 10 (Capital Cost Allowance rate of 30%) asset on January 10, 1986, at a cost of $100,000.[4] While the company deducted the maximum allowed CCA for tax purposes, the asset was depreciated over a period of 10 years for financial reporting purposes using the straight-line method. The appropriate depreciation and CCA expense charges year by year would be as follows:

	Amount of Expense	
Year	CCA for Tax Purposes	Depreciation for Accounting Purposes
1986	$15,000*	$ 10,000
1987	25,500	10,000
1988	17,850	10,000
1989	12,495	10,000
1990	8,746	10,000
1991	6,123	10,000
1992	4,286	10,000
1993	3,000	10,000
1994	2,100	10,000
1995	1,470	10,000
Total	$96,570**	$100,000

*For the first year of ownership, CCA equals one-half of the CCA rate times the Undepreciated Capital Cost. Thereafter, CCA equals the CCA rate times the Undepreciated Capital Cost.
**Assume the asset class continues even though this asset may be disposed of after 10 years.

As a result of using CCA for determining taxable income rather than straight-line depreciation amounts, the company would pay less tax in the early years of the asset's life (1986–1989) but, if other things remained constant, more tax in later

[3]*Ibid.*, Section 3470, par. 6.
[4]See Chapter 11 for the capital cost allowance technique.

years (1990–1995). If we carry the preceding illustration a step further, the results of this practice become clearer. Assume that Baker Ltd. has gross revenue of $300,000, that it has expenses other than depreciation of $250,000, and that it is subject to an income tax rate of 45% on its taxable income. The following schedule presents partial income statements for tax and for accounting purposes for 1986, 1989, 1990, and 1995, assuming tax expense reported equals the tax payable as determined by the tax return (i.e., that there is no interperiod tax allocation).

Baker Ltd.
PARTIAL INCOME STATEMENT
(Without Interperiod Tax Allocation)

	For Tax Purposes	For Accounting Purposes
1986:		
Income before CCA or depreciation and taxes	$50,000	$50,000
CCA or depreciation	15,000	10,000
Income before taxes	$35,000	$40,000
Income tax payable and expense	$15,750	$15,750
Net income reported		$24,250
Effective tax rate		39.4%
1989:		
Income before CCA or depreciation and taxes	$50,000	$50,000
CCA or depreciation	12,495	10,000
Income before taxes	$37,505	$40,000
Income tax payable and expense	$16,877	$16,877
Net income reported		$23,123
Effective tax rate		42.2%
1990:		
Income before CCA or depreciation and taxes	$50,000	$50,000
CCA or depreciation	8,746	10,000
Income before taxes	$41,254	$40,000
Income tax payable and expense	$18,564	$18,564
Net income reported		$21,436
Effective tax rate		46.4%
1995:		
Income before CCA or depreciation and taxes	$50,000	$50,000
CCA or depreciation	1,470	10,000
Income before taxes	$48,530	$40,000
Income tax payable and expense	$21,838	$21,838
Net income reported		$18,162
Effective tax rate		54.6%

Owners and prospective investors acquainted only with the information found in the "accounting" income statement might get an erroneous impression of the company's profitability. Although the underlying economic activity of the company was the same each year, the reported income after taxes is shown to be declining each year. Futhermore, the apparent effective tax rate on accounting income (income taxes divided by pretax accounting income) is increasing each year. In order to overcome such anomalies and for sound conceptual reasons, interperiod income tax allocation has become a requirement of financial statement reporting by Canadian corporations with rare exceptions.[5]

INTERPERIOD TAX ALLOCATION

Given the existence of timing differences, the determination of the provision for income taxes (i.e., income tax expense) to be reported in the income statement could follow one of at least two basic approaches: (1) the tax payable (or taxes payable) approach and (2) the tax allocation approach.

The **tax payable approach** would report as tax expense the amount payable based on taxable income determined in the tax return. The previous example (without interperiod tax allocation) illustrates this approach. Reasons supporting such an approach are:

(a) since it is taxable income and not accounting income that attracts taxation, the taxes actually payable for the period represent the appropriate cost to be allocated to that period;

(b) it is unnecessary to provide for income taxes for which there is no legal liability at the end of the financial period;

(c) while timing differences in one period may give rise to the reverse situation in some future period, the date of the reversal may be indefinitely postponed, and accordingly there is no necessity to provide for an amount which may never become payable;

(d) even where the taxes may become payable in some future period, it is usually difficult to estimate the future tax effects with any degree of accuracy.[6]

As indicated by the previous example, application of the tax payable approach can lead to erroneous impressions regarding an enterprise's profitability—although the underlying economic activity remained unchanged, net income after taxes declined and the effective tax rate increased each year. The fundamental reason for this consequence is that the income tax expense reported was not totally related (matched) to the revenues and expenses reported in pretax accounting income because of the timing differences. Therefore, assuming that income taxes can be considered a cost incurred to earn net income, this approach would violate the basic concept that costs incurred to earn income should be charged to the period in which the related revenues are reported.

The **tax allocation approach** is designed to overcome this limitation through associating the income tax expense with related accounting income. In essence, this is a method of interperiod tax allocation that applies the notion of "let the tax follow the income" (a notion equally applicable to intraperiod tax allocation). **Under the tax allocation approach, tax expense is related to pretax accounting income when such tax expense differs from actual taxes paid because of the differences in the timing of revenue or expense recognition.**

While recognizing the arguments for the tax payable approach, the Accounting

---

[5]*CICA Handbook*, Section 3470, pars. 59–61, permits exception to tax allocation for regulated or similar enterprises when such allocation would be inappropriate to achieve a proper matching of costs and revenues.

[6]*Ibid.*, Section 3470, par. 9.

Standards Committee of the CICA concluded that interperiod tax allocation is the appropriate basis to account for timing differences.[7] The basic reasons given to support this recommendation were:

(a) the incidence of income taxes on specific transactions should be recorded in the period in which the transactions are recognized for accounting purposes;

(b) income fluctuations which may arise on the taxes payable basis because of wide variations from period to period in the relationship between accounting income and the provision for income taxes are avoided.[8]

While the *CICA Handbook* recommends the use of interperiod tax allocation, two concepts exist regarding the extent to which such an approach may be applied: (1) comprehensive allocation and (2) partial allocation.

Comprehensive Allocation versus Partial Allocation

Under **comprehensive allocation,** interperiod tax allocation is applied to **all timing differences.** Supporters of this view believe that reported income tax expense should reflect the tax effects of all timing differences included in pretax accounting income, regardless of the period in which the related income taxes are actually paid. This view recognizes that the amount of income tax currently payable is not necessarily the income tax reported in the financial statements relating to the current period. Consequently, deferred taxes (differences between the tax expense and tax payable) should be recognized when timing differences originate, even if it is virtually certain that their reversal in future periods will be offset by new originating differences at that time. As a practical matter, therefore, recurring differences between taxable income and pretax accounting income could give rise to an indefinite postponement of tax. As an example, a recurring timing difference occurs when the Capital Cost Allowance approach is used for income tax determination by a company that uses straight-line depreciation for accounting purposes. This results in the accumulation of deferred tax credits that will not be paid as long as the company is acquiring depreciable assets faster than it is retiring them. Although the deferred taxes associated with specific assets do indeed reverse, the aggregate balance in deferred taxes remains stable or continues to grow because of the recurring purchases of additional assets.

Supporters of **partial allocation** contend that, unless deferred tax amounts are expected to be paid or recovered within a relevant period of time, they should not affect reported income. Consequently, interperiod tax allocation is not appropriate for recurring timing differences that result in an indefinite postponement of tax. Under this view, the presumption is that reported tax expense for a period would be the same as the tax payable for the period even if recurring timing differences existed. Accordingly, only **nonrecurring** material differences between taxes payable and accounting tax expense should be recognized. These should be recognized and allocated between periods only if they are reasonably expected to be paid or recovered within a relatively short period of time. An example of a situation resulting in a nonrecurring difference would be an **isolated** instalment sale in which the gross profit is reported for accounting purposes at the date of sale and for tax purposes when collected.

---

[7]*Ibid.*, Section 3470, par. 13. *Financial Reporting in Canada—1983* (Toronto: CICA, 1983) indicated that, in 1982, 322 of the 325 surveyed companies had to deal with timing differences. Of these, 302 used the tax allocation basis.

[8]*Ibid.*, Section 3470, par. 8.

The supporters of comprehensive allocation contend that partial allocation is a departure from accrual accounting because it emphasizes cash outlays, whereas comprehensive allocation results in a thorough and consistent matching of revenues and expenses.

While the *CICA Handbook* recommends interperiod tax allocation, there is no explicit recommendation regarding partial versus comprehensive allocation. However, comprehensive allocation appears to be suggested. This is because the *Handbook* states that tax allocation should be used when there are timing differences between accounting income and taxable income. Accounting income is defined, for purposes of Section 3470, as income in the financial statements before provision for income taxes (including any income taxes applicable to extraordinary items) but after excluding permanent differences.[9] Under such a definition, accounting income reflects a comprehensive concept, because all timing differences are included.

Deferred Income Taxes

As indicated earlier, if interperiod allocation procedures are not employed, the amounts of income tax expense and income taxes payable are the same. With interperiod tax allocation, the amounts reported for income tax expense and income taxes payable are different. As a result, accounting tax expense is debited to Income Tax Expense, the taxes due and payable are credited to Income Tax Payable, and the difference between these two amounts is debited (or credited) to an account titled Deferred Income Taxes. In the period in which a timing difference reverses, the amount accumulated in Deferred Income Taxes is reduced, as it absorbs the difference between reported tax expense and the tax actually payable for those later years.

Example 1: Interperiod Tax Allocation When Tax Expense Is Initially Greater Than Tax Payable   To illustrate comprehensive interperiod tax allocation accounting, the information presented previously for Baker Ltd. will be used. The income tax expense reported in the income statement each year would be $18,000. This is determined by multiplying the tax rate (45%) by the pretax accounting income

	Baker Ltd.	Tax Expense versus Tax Payable	
Year	Tax Expense	Tax Payable	Difference Expense – Payable
1986	$18,000	$15,750	$ 2,250
1987	18,000	11,025	6,975
1988	18,000	14,468	3,532
1989	18,000	16,877	1,123
1990	18,000	18,564	(564)
1991	18,000	19,745	(1,745)
1992	18,000	20,571	(2,571)
1993	18,000	21,150	(3,150)
1994	18,000	21,555	(3,555)
1995	18,000	21,838	(3,838)

[9]*Ibid.*, Section 3470, footnote 1.

($40,000; the $50,000 income before taxes and depreciation less the depreciation expense of $10,000). The tax payable continues to be equal to the tax rate multiplied by the taxable income. The difference between the tax expense and the tax payable from 1986 through 1995 is shown on page 934.

During the first four years the tax expense is greater than the tax payable and the difference would be credited to the Deferred Income Taxes account as indicated in the following entries:

	1986	1987	1988	1989
Income Tax Expense	18,000	18,000	18,000	18,000
Income Tax Payable	15,750	11,025	14,468	16,877
Deferred Income Taxes	2,250	6,975	3,532	1,123

At the end of four years, the Deferred Income Taxes account would have four credit entries as follows:

Deferred Income Taxes	
1986	2,250
1987	6,975
1988	3,532
1989	1,123

The credit balance in Deferred Income Taxes would be presented in the balance sheet under a liability classification.

During the next six years, the income statement will continue to show income of $40,000 before taxes and a tax expense of $18,000. Tax payable, however, will be greater than this tax expense. Therefore, for each of these years, the Deferred Income Taxes account would be debited for the difference between the expense and payable amount, as illustrated below:

	1990	1991	1995
Income Tax Expense	18,000	18,000	18,000
Deferred Income Taxes	564	1,745	3,838
Income Tax Payable	18,564	19,745	21,838

At the end of 1995, the Deferred Income Taxes account would appear as follows:

Deferred Income Taxes			
1990	564	1986	2,250
1991	1,745	1987	6,975
1992	2,571	1988	3,532
1993	3,150	1989	1,123
1994	3,555		
1995	3,838		

The $1,543 debit balance at the end of 1995 resulted from the fact that application of the CCA method left some undepreciated capital cost for tax purposes. The disposition of the Deferred Income Taxes balance would depend on the nature of disposition of the undepreciated capital cost.

Thus, by this allocation of income taxes, the income tax expense during each period in which the asset is used is unaffected by the decision to use CCA for income tax purposes. The temporary tax advantage, although of real significance for financial reasons, has no influence on reported net income, as it would be $22,000 per year. The calculation of tax payable is unaffected by the allocation of tax expense to periods based on accounting pretax income.

Partial income statements for tax and accounting purposes for 1986, 1989, 1990, and 1995 based on interperiod tax allocation notions are presented below. These should be compared to the statements without allocation as presented on page 931.

	For Tax Purposes	For Accounting Purposes
Baker Ltd.		
PARTIAL INCOME STATEMENT		
(With Interperiod Tax Allocation—Accounting Income		
Initially Exceeds Taxable Income)		
1986:		
Income before CCA or depreciation and taxes	$50,000	$50,000
CCA or depreciation	15,000	10,000
Income before taxes	$35,000	$40,000
Income tax payable	$15,750	
Income tax expense		$18,000
Net income reported		$22,000
Effective tax rate		45%
1989:		
Income before CCA or depreciation and taxes	$50,000	$50,000
CCA or depreciation	12,495	10,000
Income before taxes	$37,505	$40,000
Income tax payable	$16,877	
Income tax expense		18,000
Net income reported		$22,000
Effective tax rate		45%
1990:		
Income before CCA or depreciation and taxes	$50,000	$50,000
CCA or depreciation	8,746	10,000
Income before taxes	$41,254	$40,000
Income tax payable	$18,564	
Income tax expense		18,000
Net income reported		$22,000
Effective tax rate		45%
1995:		
Income before CCA or depreciation and taxes	$50,000	$50,000
CCA or depreciation	1,470	10,000
Income before taxes	$48,530	$40,000
Income tax payable	$21,838	
Income tax expense		18,000
Net income reported		$22,000
Effective tax rate		45%

Note that the **tax effect of a timing difference** in any year is found by computing income taxes both with and without the timing difference. The difference in the computations is the amount charged or credited to the Deferred Income Taxes account.

This example has illustrated the accounting for interperiod tax allocation in the situation where the tax expense is initially greater than the tax payable. The cause of the difference was that an expense (depreciation) included in the determination of pretax accounting income was initially less than the amount of CCA deducted for taxable income determination. Similar results in terms of originating deferred tax credits and their reversals would occur for other timing differences that result in pretax accounting income being greater than taxable income (i.e., when accounting revenues are greater than or accounting expenses are less than those in taxable income).

Example 2: Interperiod Tax Allocation When Tax Expense Is Initially Less Than Tax Payable   Initial or originating timing differences can result in the tax expense being less than the tax payable. Such would occur when the originating timing difference results in taxable income being greater than pretax accounting income (i.e., when accounting revenues are less than or accounting expenses are greater than those in taxable income). Accounting for product warranties can serve as an example. In order to match expenses against revenues, accounting income may include warranty expense reflecting the estimated costs to be incurred under warranty contracts related to sales of the current period. Warranty costs can, however, only be deducted as they are incurred for purposes of determining taxable income. Consequently, when the expense recognized in pretax accounting income is greater than the actual costs incurred for the period, the amount of tax payable will exceed the amount of tax expense with the difference being debited to Deferred Income Taxes. The Deferred Income Taxes account would be credited in periods where the

	Baker Ltd. Interperiod Tax Allocation—Accounting Income Initially Less Than Taxable Income				
	1986	1987	1988	1989	1990
Income Tax Expense Calculations:					
Gross Revenue	$300,000	$300,000	$300,000	$300,000	$300,000
Expenses, including $20,000 for warranties	250,000	250,000	250,000	250,000	250,000
Depreciation (equals CCA)	15,000	25,500	17,850	12,495	8,746
Accounting Income Before Tax	$ 35,000	$ 24,500	$ 32,150	$ 37,505	$ 41,254
Income Tax Expense (45%)	15,750	11,025	14,468	16,877	18,564
Income Tax Payable Calculation:					
Accounting Income Before Tax	$ 35,000	$ 24,500	$ 32,150	$ 37,505	$ 41,254
Adjustment for Timing Differences					
Add: Warranty Expense	20,000	20,000	20,000	20,000	20,000
Deduct: Actual Warranty Costs	(10,000)	(15,000)	(25,000)	(28,000)	(21,000)
Taxable Income	$ 45,000	$ 29,500	$ 27,150	$ 29,505	$ 40,254
Income Tax Payable (45%)	20,250	13,275	12,218	13,277	18,114
Deferred Income Taxes:					
Tax Expense − Tax Payable	($4,500)	($2,250)	$ 2,250	$ 3,600	$ 450

actual warranty costs were greater than the expense recognized in the determination of accounting income.

To illustrate the accounting for deferred taxes in such situations, we will return to the Baker Ltd. example. To avoid the complication of having two sources of timing differences to account for, we will initially assume that depreciation expense in pretax accounting income equals the capital cost allowance each year. Also, assume that the company has included a $20,000 product warranty expense in its annual total expenses of $250,000. The actual warranty costs allowed for purposes of determining taxable income from 1986 through 1990 are $10,000, $15,000, $25,000, $28,000, and $21,000 respectively. The schedule on page 937 shows the determination of tax expense, tax payable, and deferred tax amounts for 1986 through 1990.

The entries to record the tax expense for the first two years are:

	1986	1987
Income Tax Expense	15,750	11,025
Deferred Income Taxes	4,500	2,250
Income Tax Payable	20,250	13,275

For the next three years the entries would be:

	1988	1989	1990
Income Tax Expense	14,468	16,877	18,564
Income Tax Payable	12,218	13,277	18,114
Deferred Income Taxes	2,250	3,600	450

The Deferred Income Taxes account would be:

Deferred Income Taxes			
1986	4,500	1988	2,250
1987	2,250	1989	3,600
		1990	450

As this account has a debit balance each year, it would be shown in the balance sheet under an asset classification.

Originating and Reversing Differences—Additional Clarification

As implied earlier, an **originating difference** is the initial timing difference between pretax accounting income and taxable income, whether the pretax accounting income exceeds, or is exceeded by, taxable income. Depending on whether taxable income exceeds pretax accounting income or *vice versa* in the year of origination, an originating difference may result in either a debit or credit to Deferred Income Taxes. A **reversing difference,** on the other hand, occurs when timing differences that originated in prior periods are eliminated and the tax effect is removed from the Deferred Income Taxes account. As a result, a reversing difference may result in a debit or credit, depending on the originating difference.

In Example 1 for Baker Ltd., the originating differences occur in the years 1986 through 1989 when credits flow into the Deferred Income Taxes account because tax expense is initially greater than tax payable in each year. Reversing differences occur from 1990 through 1995 when the Deferred Income Taxes account is debited and the built up credit balance is reduced.

Originating differences can result in debits to a Deferred Income Taxes account. This happens when the initial timing difference results in tax expense being less than tax payable, as was the case in Example 2 in 1986 and 1987. In this example, the reversing differences occurred from 1988 through 1990, when the Deferred Income Taxes account was credited.

From these examples, it can be seen that an originating difference can start either as a credit or debit to deferred income taxes and continues as an originating difference as long as the original balance established in the first period increases. Reversing differences occur when the balance in deferred income taxes is reduced for a given transaction.

Example 3: Interperiod Tax Allocation When More Than One Timing Difference Exists The previous examples illustrated interperiod tax allocation when only one timing difference existed. In many situations, many timing differences of various types occur causing tax expense to differ from tax payable. While the basic calculations illustrated apply to such situations, it is desirable to keep track of the nature of each timing difference (by source and whether it is an originating or reversing difference) in order to be able to meet financial statement presentation requirements and to apply accounting procedures when tax rates change from year to year. These aspects will be examined shortly. To conclude this set of examples, however, the following illustration indicates a basic approach to compiling information when two or more timing differences exist.

Baker Ltd.
Interperiod Tax Allocation—Two Timing Differences Exist

	1986	1987	1988	1989	1990
Income Tax Expense Calculation:					
Accounting Income Before Tax*	$40,000	$40,000	$40,000	$40,000	$40,000
Income Tax Expense (45%)	18,000	18,000	18,000	18,000	18,000

*Revenue of $300,000 less expenses of $250,000 (including warranty expense of $20,000) less depreciation of $10,000.

	1986	1987	1988	1989	1990
Income Tax Payable Calculation:					
Accounting Income Before Tax	$40,000	$40,000	$40,000	$40,000	$40,000
Adjustments for Timing Differences					
Warranties:					
Add: Warranty Expense	$20,000	$20,000	$20,000	$20,000	$20,000
Deduct: Actual Costs	(10,000)	(15,000)	(25,000)	(28,000)	(21,000)
Net Adjustment for Warranties	$10,000	$ 5,000	($5,000)	($8,000)	($1,000)
Depreciation:					
Add: Depreciation Expense	$10,000	$10,000	$10,000	$10,000	$10,000
Deduct: CCA	(15,000)	(25,500)	(17,850)	(12,495)	(8,746)
Net Adjustment for Depreciation	($5,000)	($15,000)	($7,850)	($2,495)	$ 1,254
Taxable Income	$45,000	$29,500	$27,150	$29,506	$40,254
Income Tax Payable (45%)	20,250	13,275	12,218	13,277	18,114
Deferred Income Taxes:					
Due to Timing Differences on:					
Warranties	($4,500)	($2,250)	$ 2,250	$ 3,600	$ 450
Depreciation	2,250	6,975	3,532	1,123	(564)
Total	($2,250)	$ 4,725	$ 5,782	$ 4,723	($ 114)

This example combines the previous two illustrations regarding Baker Ltd. Here we will assume that depreciation expense is $10,000 per year for accounting purposes while capital cost amounts are used for calculating taxable income. Additionally, the differences regarding the warranty expense in accounting income and the warranty costs deducted to determine taxable income are as identified in the previous example. Accordingly, the tax expense, tax payable, and deferred tax amounts for 1986 through 1990 are determined as shown on page 939.

The information presented in this schedule would be used to make the entries related to income taxes. These entries, however, may include a Deferred Income Taxes account for each of the items causing the timing differences. If only one account were used, the effect of the two timing differences would be combined, and the different nature of each would be lost. This could create problems regarding requirements for financial statement presentation as discussed in the following section.

Financial Statement Presentation—Balance Sheet

Example 1 in the previous section illustrated a situation in which the Deferred Income Taxes account had a credit balance because the originating timing difference resulted in income tax expense exceeding income tax payable. It was stated that such credit balances would be presented in the balance sheet under a liability classification. Example 2 resulted in the Deferred Income Taxes account having a debit balance due to the nature of the originating timing difference. It was stated that such debit balances would be shown under an asset classification in the balance sheet. The questions remain as to which classification (current or noncurrent) would apply and whether the debit and credit balance consequences of various types of timing differences can be netted into a single account.

To answer these questions, the *CICA Handbook* makes the following recommendations for balance sheet treatment:

1. Accumulated tax allocation credits and/or debits should be segregated in the balance sheet as either current or noncurrent, according to the classification of the assets and liabilities to which they relate.
2. Current accumulated tax allocation debits or credits should be shown in current assets or current liabilities.
3. Noncurrent accumulated tax allocation debits or credits should be shown as a deferred charge or as a deferred credit outside shareholders' equity.[10]

The critical distinction in these recommendations is that of classifying amounts between current and noncurrent portions of the balance sheet. Where both debit and credit tax allocation amounts are appropriately classified as current, it is acceptable to show the net amount as either a current asset or liability. Similarly, the net amount for noncurrent amounts is all that needs to be shown.[11]

In Example 1, the credit balance in Deferred Income Taxes would be shown in the balance sheet as a noncurrent liability (i.e. outside shareholders' equity) because it relates to timing differences regarding a noncurrent asset's cost allocation. Assuming the warranty contracts are for a year or less, the Deferred Income Taxes account debit balance in Example 2 would be classified as a current asset on the balance sheet because it relates to a current liability (liability under product warranties).

---

[10]*Ibid.*, Section 3470, pars. 24, 26, 27.
[11]*Ibid.*, Section 3470, pars. 23, 25.

Using these conclusions regarding Example 3, the annual balance sheets would have to present two accounts for Deferred Income Taxes; one shown as a noncurrent liability for the credit balance resulting from differences between depreciation expense and CCA, and one shown as a current asset for the debit balance resulting from the timing differences on the warranties. Because of this need for separate classification, separate Deferred Income Taxes accounts may be used. If this were done by Baker Ltd. in Example 3, the journal entries for 1986 through 1990 would be:

	1986	1987	1988	1989	1990
Income Tax Expense	18,000	18,000	18,000	18,000	18,000
Deferred Income Taxes—Warranties	4,500	2,250		2,250	3,600	450
Deferred Income Taxes—Depreciation		2,250	6,975	3,532	1,123	564
Income Tax Payable		20,250	13,275	12,218	13,277	18,114

Alternatively, assume that the warranty liability was noncurrent. In this case, the resulting debit balance for the related deferred taxes account could be netted against the deferred tax credit balance related to depreciation. Thus, a noncurrent asset for deferred taxes in the amount of $2,250 ($4,500 related to warranties less $2,250 related to depreciation) could be shown in the 1986 balance sheet.

Financial Statement Presentation—Income Statement

The *CICA Handbook* recommends that the amount by which the current income tax provision (expense) is increased or decreased as a result of tax deferrals should be disclosed.[12] This may be done through stating the amount in the statement of changes in financial position, by showing the current and deferred portions of the tax expense in the income statement, or by means of a note.

Using the data for Baker Ltd. in Example 3, this may be accomplished through the 1986 income statement as shown below:

Baker Ltd. PARTIAL INCOME STATEMENT		
		1986
Income Before Income Taxes		$40,000
Income Tax Expense		
Currently Payable	$20,250	
Deferred	(2,250)	18,000
Net Income		$22,000

The use of a note to fulfill this requirement is illustrated by the following excerpt from a financial statement. This also serves as an example of how differences between the statutory tax rate and a company's effective tax rate may be disclosed and reconciled, a requirement noted earlier in the discussion of permanent differences.

---

[12]*Ibid.*, Section 3470, par. 29.

Canadian General Electric Co. Ltd.

Income Statement	1982	1981
Earnings before income taxes and minority interest	$64,028	$81,052
Provision for income taxes (Note 5)	17,322	28,490

Note to financial statements:
5. Provision for income taxes ($000's)

For the years ended December 31	1982	1981
Currently payable	$20,086	$17,149
Deferred	(2,764)	11,341
	$17,322	$28,490

The Company's effective income tax rate is made up as follows:

	1982	1981
Combined basic federal and provincial income tax rate	50.9%	50.9%
Manufacturing and processing profits allowance	(4.7)	(4.7)
Inventory allowance	(7.5)	(6.5)
Scientific research allowance	(2.1)	(3.6)
Nontaxable capital gains	(5.0)	(1.4)
Other	(4.5)	0.5
	27.1%	35.2%

There are several reasons for these disclosures; some of the main reasons are:

1. **Assessment of quality of earnings** Many investors are interested in the reconciliation of the book income (pretax accounting income) to taxable income in order to assess the quality of a company's earnings. Earnings that are enhanced by a favourable tax effect should be examined carefully, particularly if the tax effect is nonrecurring. For example, one year Wang Laboratories reported net income of $3.3 million, or 82 cents a share, versus $3.1 million, or 77 cents per share in the preceding period. All of the increase in net income resulted from an effective tax rate that was lower in the current year than in the preceding year (32.6% versus 39%). The difference in the rates was due primarily to the investment tax credit.

2. **Better predictions of future cash flows** Examination of the deferred portion of income tax expense provides information as to whether taxes payable will be higher or lower in the future. For example, a close examination may disclose the company's policy in regard to capitalization of costs, recognition of revenue, and so on. As a result, it may be possible to predict substantial future reductions in deferred income tax credits that may lead to a loss of liquidity since actual tax payments will be higher than the tax expense reported on the income statement.

3. **Helpful in setting government policy** An understanding of the amount currently paid by a corporation as well as its effective tax rate is helpful to government policymakers. For example, when the oil companies were considered to have earned excess profits in the early seventies, many politicians and other interested parties attempted to determine the effective tax rates of these companies. Unfortunately, at that time this information was not available in published annual reports.

INTERPERIOD TAX ALLOCATION—PRACTICAL PROBLEMS

The preceding examples of deferred income taxes were fairly straightforward in that there were few timing differences between taxable income and pretax accounting income. It was relatively easy to determine the exact tax effect, the build-up of the deferral, and the reversal or turnaround for each timing difference. This method is called the **individual item basis.** In practice, however, it is typical for a corporation to have a multitude of items handled differently for tax purposes and accounting purposes. Because of the volume of records which must be kept, it becomes impractical to identify, follow, and account for each individual transaction. To simplify computation of the tax effects of numerous timing differences, one of two alternatives to the individual item basis may be employed. These two methods are called (1) the "group-of-similar-items, gross change basis," and (2) the "group-of-similar-items, net change basis," or simply the "gross change method" and the "net change method."

In addition, it was assumed in the preceding illustrations that the tax rate remained constant over several periods, and that the same tax rate was applicable to all components of income. In practice, however, these assumptions would not be valid. The tax rates experienced by a particular company vary because of legislative changes in the tax law, and because of changes in the company's amount of taxable income. Further, special tax rates may apply to the various components of income reported in a particular year. The **gross change method** and the **net change method** are alternative computational approaches that deal with the accounting problems arising from changes in tax rates. The **with and without technique** is a computational approach that deals with the accounting problems arising from such tax provisions as graduated rate schedules, special capital gains tax rates, investment tax credits, foreign tax credits, and carryovers of certain losses and expenses. This procedure is discussed in Appendix 20A at the end of this chapter.

Gross Change Method

Under the gross change method, the tax effects of timing differences originating in the current period are computed at current tax rates. Reversals of timing differences that originated in prior periods are removed from the Deferred Income Taxes account at the applicable prior tax rates. To facilitate the computations, the following steps are used:

1. Separate all timing differences, whether originating or reversing, into groups of similar items. For example, group all instalment sales transactions, or all depreciation items.
2. Classify the items within each group as either originating or reversing.
3. Determine the tax effect of the aggregate originating differences within a particular group by using the current tax rates.
4. Determine the tax effect of the aggregate reversing differences in the group by using the applicable prior tax rates (i.e., the rates in effect when the differences originated).
5. For each group, the difference between (3) and (4) constitutes the amount of change in the Deferred Income Taxes account for the period.

Under this method, when a group of similar timing differences reverses, the balance in deferred taxes is written down (amortized) at the same tax rates that were in effect when the timing differences originated. Since it is unlikely that all of the reversing timing differences within a particular group originated at the same tax rates, it is necessary to select an appropriate tax rate to be applied to these timing differences in the periods they reverse. In practice, either a FIFO flow assumption or an average rate assumption may be used to determine the tax effect of the reversing differences within a particular group. If the **FIFO basis** is employed, a record must be maintained of all the originating differences and the rates at which they originated. As these timing differences reverse, the first-in differences are the amounts first reversed. If an **average rate basis** is used, the amount of the reduction in deferred taxes is determined by multiplying the aggregate reversing differences within a particular group by the weighted-average tax rate in effect during prior periods. For each group, a different weighted-average tax rate may be appropriate. This weighted-average tax rate is equal to the total deferred taxes divided by the total timing differences as they existed at the beginning of the period for a specific group.

The gross change basis is similar to the individual item basis in that the tax effects of timing differences are reversed (drawn down) at the tax rate at which they originated. The two bases are different in that **the gross change method groups similar timing differences and the individual item basis does not.** The gross change method is a practical extension of the individual item basis.

Net Change Method

Under the net change method, the tax effect associated with a particular group of net timing differences is determined by using the current tax rates. The net change method is similar to the gross change method in that all timing differences are separated into groups of similar items. It is different in that tax effects are not computed separately for the originating items and the reversing items within a particular group. Reversing differences within a group are first offset against originating differences. The tax effect of the entire group of timing differences is then computed by applying **current** tax rates to the **net change in the aggregate timing differences** within the group.

Illustration of Gross Change and Net Change Methods

To illustrate these methods and the differences between them in terms of deferred taxes, assume that Magic Corp. determined its 1986 accounting income before taxes to be $118,000. The company was subject to a 46% tax rate and identified the following differences between its income before taxes and taxable income for 1986:

1. Dividend revenue received from Canadian corporations was $12,000. This is not subject to tax and, therefore, is a permanent difference.
2. Capital cost allowance taken was $10,000 greater than depreciation expense. This is an originating difference that results in tax expense exceeding tax payable.
3. There was $7,000 gross profit from instalment sales for tax purposes that had been recognized in prior years for accounting purposes. This, therefore, is a reversing difference which has the effect of reducing tax expense relative to tax payable.

Magic Corp. RECONCILIATION AND COMPUTATION OF INCOME TAX PAYABLE—1986	
Income before taxes	$118,000
Permanent difference	
Dividend from Canadian corporations (tax exempt)	(12,000)
Timing differences:	
Originating—CCA in excess of depreciation	(10,000)
Reversing—taxable gross profit on instalment sales	
in excess of accounting gross profit on instalment sales	7,000
Taxable income	$103,000
Tax rate	46%
Income tax payable	$ 47,380

The reconciliation of Magic Corp.'s income before taxes to taxable income and the computation of tax payable is as shown on page 944.

Magic Corp. has maintained the following record of timing differences and deferred taxes for prior years:

Magic Corp.
SUMMARY OF PRIOR TIMING DIFFERENCES

Year	Timing Difference	Tax Rate	Deferred Taxes
1983	$ 6,000	50%	$3,000
1984	5,000	44%	2,200
1985	3,000	47%	1,410
	$14,000		$6,610

The weighted-average tax rate in prior years was 47.2% ($6,610 divided by $14,000).

Computations of deferred taxes and tax expense for 1986 under the gross change (FIFO and average basis) and the net change method are shown as follows:

Magic Corp.
COMPUTATION OF DEFERRED TAXES AND TAX EXPENSE—1986

	Gross Change Method		Net Change Method
	FIFO	Average	
Income tax payable	$47,380 cr.	$47,380 cr.	$47,380 cr.
Tax effect of timing differences:			
Originating:			
$10,000 × 46%	$ 4,600 cr.	$ 4,600 cr.	
Reversing:			
$6,000 × 50% (from 1983)	3,000 dr.		
1,000 × 44% (from 1984)	440 dr.		
7,000 × 47.2% (average)		3,304 dr.	
Net difference:			
($10,000 − $7,000) × 46%			$ 1,380 cr.
Deferred income taxes	$ 1,160 cr.	$ 1,296 cr.	$ 1,380 cr.
Income tax expense (to balance)	$48,540 dr.	$48,676 dr.	$48,760 dr.

The **income tax payable** is unaffected whether the gross change or the net change method is employed. If the tax rate were the same in all periods, the tax expense and the deferred income tax amounts would also be unaffected by the choice of methods; but because of tax rate changes, the methods produce different results. Under both the gross change method and the net change method, the tax effects of originating differences are computed at current tax rates. **The tax effects of reversing differences, however, are computed at applicable prior tax rates under the gross change method, and at current tax rates under the net change method.** When tax rates change, this difference in approach yields different results.

Criteria for Choosing Between Methods

As long as cumulative timing differences are not expected to reverse, both the net change method and the gross change method represent a consistent approach to the computation of income tax expense. Since the net change method is the easier to apply, it appears more desirable in these circumstances.

On the other hand, when cumulative timing differences are expected to reverse, the net change method may not be appropriate. The entire Deferred Income Taxes account must be amortized in the periods of reversal, regardless of the amount that would have been determined currently. This can result in the reporting of tax expense that is considerably more (or less) than the current effective tax rate. This is not consistent with the approach used under the net change method during the periods when cumulative timing differences are increasing. Therefore, reported tax expense in the period of reversal would not be comparable to amounts computed in previous years. In these cases, the gross change method (or individual item basis) appears more appropriate.

When the gross change method is used where individual groupings of originating differences can be identified by year, the FIFO basis is usually considered more appropriate than the average rate basis. An example would be the establishment of a liability for warranties with actual costs being recognized in subsequent periods for tax purposes. When it is difficult to identify individual items or groupings, as it is with a great number of depreciable assets, the average basis is generally selected.

The *CICA Handbook* does not specifically recommend either method. However, in a discussion paragraph which pertains to reversing differences, the *Handbook* states:

> Where the difference between accounting and taxable income in a period gives rise to a transfer to income from the tax allocation balance accumulated in prior periods, such transfer will be computed at the rate of accumulation. Where there are practical difficulties in identifying the specific components, the transfer may be calculated at the effective average rate of accumulation; that is, the proportion that the accumulated deferred credit or charge bears to the accumulated difference between taxable and accounting income.[13]

Therefore, while the gross change method appears preferable, the actual choice of method rests on judgement regarding the practical difficulties associated with its use.

INTERPERIOD TAX ALLOCATION—CONCEPTUAL APPROACHES TO DEFERRED INCOME TAXES

The preceding discussion identified no allocation, partial allocation, and comprehensive allocation as different approaches to solving the problem of which transactions, if any, should be identified with interperiod tax allocation. **The three views differed as to whether, and for which transactions, accounting recognition should be given to the tax effects of timing differences**. The conclusion was that comprehensive allocation was generally accepted accounting practice. Because tax rates change over time, additional questions relate to what method of tax allocation should be used in accounting for tax effects, and how those effects should be presented in the financial statements. The examples of the comprehensive approach set up originating differences in the Deferred Income Taxes account based on the income tax rate that existed in the year of the difference. Changes to the income tax rate actually occurring or anticipated in years subsequent to that in which the originating difference was recorded were not incorporated into the

---

[13]*Ibid.*, Section 3470, par. 18.

deferred taxes amounts. This approach reflects what is called the **deferral method** of interperiod tax allocation and is the method currently recommended in the *CICA Handbook*.[14] Alternatively, it has been argued that such changes in the tax rates should be reflected in the deferred tax amounts. This approach is known as the **accrual** or **liability method** of income tax allocation. A third method—the **net of tax method**—has also been considered in terms of a possible approach to tax allocation and how the effects should be presented in the financial statements. While **comprehensive allocation using the deferral method represents current practice**, the Accounting Standards Committee of the CICA was reviewing the whole area of accounting for corporate income taxes at the time of writing this text. As these three methods will likely be considered in this review, their nature is briefly discussed below.

Deferral Method   **Under the deferral method the amount of deferred income tax is based on tax rates in effect when timing differences originate**. The balance in deferred taxes is not adjusted to reflect subsequent changes in tax rates or the imposition of new taxes. Consequently the balance in deferred taxes may not represent the actual amount of additional taxes payable or receivable in the periods that timing differences reverse. Under this method, deferred charges and credits relating to timing differences "represent the cumulative recognition given to their tax effects and as such do not represent receivables or payables" in the usual economic sense.[15] This method is an income statement oriented approach that emphasizes proper matching of expenses with revenue in the periods that timing differences originate. The gross change and net change methods previously discussed are practical applications of the deferral method.

Accrual (Liability) Method   **Under the accrual (liability) method the amount of deferred income tax is based on the tax rates expected to be in effect during the periods in which the timing differences reverse**. Advocates of this method believe that the initial computation of deferred taxes is a tentative estimate that is subject to future adjustment if the tax rate changes or new taxes are imposed. Ordinarily, the most reasonable assumption about future tax rates is that the current tax rate will continue. However, if a rate change is known or reasonably certain at the time of the initial computation, the anticipated rate would be used under the liability method. Moreover, because the initial computation is an estimate, it is subject to future adjustment if tax rates change or new taxes are imposed. When adjustments are made to accumulated tax allocation balances, the adjustment would be treated as an extraordinary item.[16] Under this method, deferred taxes are viewed as economic liabilities for taxes payable or assets for prepaid tax. Therefore it would be appropriate to discount them to the present value of the amounts ultimately expected to be paid or received. This method is considered a balance sheet oriented approach that emphasizes the usefulness of financial statements in evaluating financial position and predicting future cash flows.

Net-of-Tax Method   Under the net-of-tax method no Deferred Income Taxes account is reported on the balance sheet. Further, the amount of income tax expense reported

---

[14]Ibid., Section 3470, par. 20.

[15]"Accounting for Income Taxes," *Opinions of the Accounting Principles Board No. 11* (New York: AICPA, 1967), par. 56.

[16]*CICA Handbook*, Section 3470, par. 15.

on the income statement is the same as the taxes currently payable. The tax effects of timing differences (determined by either the deferral or accrual methods) are not reported separately. Instead, they are reported as **adjustments to the carrying amounts of specific assets or liabilities and the related revenues or expenses.** This view recognizes that future taxability and tax deductibility are important factors in the valuation of individual assets and liabilities. For example, depreciation is said to reduce the value of an asset both because of a decline in economic usefulness and because of the loss of a portion of future tax deductibility; capital cost allowance uses up this portion of the asset value more rapidly than does straight-line depreciation. Under this view, depreciation expense reported on the income statement would include, in addition to an amount for straight-line depreciation, an amount equal to the current tax effect of the excess of CCA over accounting depreciation. On the balance sheet the related cumulative tax effect would be reported as a reduction of the specific asset rather than as a credit balance in a Deferred Income Taxes account. Under this method the asset, liability, revenue, or expense accounts would be presented ''net-of-tax.''

An Illustration of the Different Methods

To illustrate the difference in these three methods to interperiod tax allocation, assume that on January 1, 1986, Orange Inc. acquires for $100,000 an asset which has an estimated 10-year useful life. There is no salvage value expected and the asset will be depreciated using the straight-line method for financial reporting purposes. The CCA rate is 30% for assets of this type. The tax rate for 1986 is 40%, but the anticipated tax rate for future years is 48%. Tax payable for 1986, assuming that income before depreciation and taxes is $200,000, is computed below:

Orange, Inc. COMPUTATION OF TAX PAYABLE—1986	
Income before depreciation and taxes	$200,000
Capital cost allowance [.5 ($100,000 × .30)]	15,000
Taxable income	$185,000
Tax rate	40%
Tax payable	$ 74,000

Orange, Inc., PARTIAL INCOME STATEMENT—1986	Deferral	Accrual	Net-of-Tax
Income before depreciation and income taxes	$200,000	$200,000	$200,000
Depreciation	10,000	10,000	12,000
Income before taxes	$190,000	$190,000	$188,000
Current taxes	$ 74,000	$ 74,000	$ 74,000
Deferred taxes	2,000	2,400	—
Income taxes	$ 76,000	$ 76,400	$ 74,000
Net income	$114,000	$113,600	$114,000

An abbreviated income statement for 1986 under the three interperiod tax allocation methods is as shown at the bottom of page 948.

Under the deferral method, the deferred portion of income taxes is determined as follows:

Capital cost allowance	$15,000
Depreciation per books	10,000
Difference	$ 5,000
Tax rate	40%
Deferred income taxes	$ 2,000

Under the accrual (liability) method, the computation of deferred income taxes is essentially the same except that the anticipated future tax rate is used instead of the current rate.

Capital cost allowance	$15,000
Depreciation per books	10,000
Difference	$ 5,000
Tax rate	48%
Deferred income taxes	$ 2,400

The computation for the net-of-tax method is more complicated. As indicated earlier, depreciation expense reported on the income statement would include, in addition to an amount for straight-line depreciation, an amount equal to the tax effect of the excess of CCA over book depreciation. This computation is as follows:

Depreciation per books	$10,000
Tax effect of excess of CCA over depreciation	
($5,000 × 40%*)	2,000
Depreciation expense	$12,000

*Using 40% reflects application of the deferral method concept. If 48% were used, it would reflect application of the accrual method concept.

Therefore, under the net-of-tax method, depreciation expense and accumulated depreciation are higher by $2,000 than under either of the other methods.

Both the deferral method and the net-of-tax method (using the 40% tax rate) report the same net income. In this example, the difference between these two methods relates to the classification of the expense and whether a deferred income tax account is created. The accrual method may use a different tax rate than the deferral method. In this case, net income is lower because the anticipated future tax rate applied is higher than the current rate.

Future Prospects

While the accounting profession has adopted the deferral method of comprehensive tax allocation, significant developments have taken place which have led to an increasing concern over the propriety of such practice. The following paragraphs identify some of the major aspects contributing to these concerns.

Continued Growth in the Amount of Deferred Taxes   Examination of corporate balance sheets will immediately confirm a trend for accelerated growth in the amount of deferred income tax credits being reported. In 1975, for example, NOVA, An Alberta Corporation's Deferred Income Taxes account had a credit balance of $20.2 million. In 1984 the balance was $496.8 million. Of the company's $150.2 million income tax expense in 1984, $3.7 million was currently payable and $146.5 was credited to deferred taxes. Growth in deferred tax balances is a phenomenon that many companies are experiencing, and such growth suggests that fairly long time periods will have to elapse before the timing differences reverse. Consequently, the size of such accounts and the question of their disposition create problems, particularly in terms of understanding. For example, a recent study showed that over 10% of the largest 250 companies in the United States have deferred income tax credit balances in excess of 20% of shareholders' equity.[17] As another writer has noted, "For many companies, deferred income tax credits have increased considerably more than retained earnings in the last decade."[18]

Cost/Benefit Considerations   The computations required can become very complex and give rise to varying interpretations when numerous timing differences are involved. Considerable analysis is required to determine that the allocations are made properly. For these reasons, some accountants believe that the information benefits provided by the present method of interperiod tax allocation are more than outweighed by the costs involved. In addition, many users of financial statements complain that it is difficult to understand the concept of deferred income taxes and its significance for financial reporting purposes.

Decreased Importance of Matching   The profession justified comprehensive allocation on the basis of the matching principle. However, matching is coming under increasing attack. One writer noted that matching is "too often an attractive but empty slogan rather than a meaningful concept one can look to for guidance" and that "what constitutes proper matching...is very much in the eyes of the beholders." Thus some believe that comprehensive allocation results in (1) amounts carried as assets that have no demonstrable value and that are never expected to be realized, (2) amounts carried as liabilities that are more in the nature of contingencies, and (3) corresponding charges or credits to income for contingent amounts. Apparently the FASB agrees. In *Concepts Statement No. 3*, the FASB indicates that the deferral method of tax allocation does not fit the definition of an asset or liability.

No doubt these and other concerns have had an impact on the Accounting Standards Committee's decision to review its recommendations regarding corporate income taxes. Additionally, before reaching any conclusions, the Committee has decided to wait and see what the FASB will do in the United States. There, the deferral-comprehensive approach is also accepted practice, but the concerns expressed above are even more evident than in Canada. Consequently, the decisions of the FASB are likely to have a very significant impact on Canadian recommendations.

To date the FASB has issued a discussion memorandum on the subject and

[17]"Rollover," *Forbes* (January 18, 1982).

[18]J. T. Ball, "Accounting for Income Taxes," *Accountants Handbook*, Lee J. Seidler and D. R. Carmichael, eds. (New York: John Wiley & Sons, 1981), Chapter 13.

intends to issue a new standard in the near future. In its preliminary views the FASB has indicated its continued support for the comprehensive method of tax allocation. However, it believes that the accrual (liability) method rather than the deferral method should be employed for interperiod tax allocation.

If the accrual (liability) method is adopted, the major changes would relate to the use of a future tax rate (if known) instead of a current tax rate to compute deferred income taxes. Furthermore, if tax rates drop (increase), it would be necessary to adjust the present balances in deferred income taxes to lower (higher) amounts. In addition, the classification guidelines for deferred income taxes would change because deferred income taxes would be considered receivables and payables instead of deferred charges and credits. Under the accrual (liability) approach, deferred income taxes would be classified on the basis of whether they will reverse in the next year or not. The present rule of "related to" would no longer be employed. Although some would then favour discounting these "assets and liabilities," it appears unlikely that such discounting will be adopted.[19]

ACCOUNTING FOR NET OPERATING LOSSES

A **net operating loss** occurs for tax purposes in a year when tax-deductible expenses exceed taxable revenues. An inequitable tax burden would result if companies were taxed during profitable periods without receiving any tax relief during periods of net operating losses. Therefore, the tax laws permit taxpayers to use the losses of one year to offset the profits of other years. This tax-averaging provision is accomplished through the **carryback and carryforward of net operating losses**. Under this provision, a company pays no income taxes for a year in which it incurs a net operating loss. In addition, it may utilize the loss for tax purposes in either or both of the following ways:

Loss Carryback   A corporation may elect to carry the loss back against taxable income of any or all of the immediately preceding three years, receiving refunds for income taxes paid in those years.[20]

Loss Carryforward   A corporation may elect to carry the loss forward to any or all of the immediate seven years following the loss, using it to offset taxable income and thereby reducing or eliminating taxes that would otherwise be payable in those years.

The decision as to how to use a loss for tax purposes will depend upon such factors as its size, results of the previous years' operations, past and anticipated future tax rates, and other factors in which management sees the greatest tax advantage.

Operating losses can be substantial.[21] For example, Chrysler Corporation's total losses exceeded three billion dollars for the years 1978 through 1981. Companies

---

[19]*CICA Handbook*, Section 3470, par. 22, recommends that tax allocation amounts (albeit on the deferral basis) should not be discounted.

[20]The number of years for which losses may be carried back or forward is stipulated by tax laws. These provisions change from time to time. Provisions existing in 1985 were the basis of years used in this text.

[21]*Financial Reporting in Canada—1983* indicated that, of the 325 companies surveyed, 100 in 1982, 29 in 1981, and 15 in 1980 disclosed tax recoveries from loss carrybacks. As well, 93 companies in 1982, 68 in 1981, and 57 in 1980 disclosed potential tax recoveries due to loss carryforwards.

that have suffered substantial losses are often attractive merger candidates, because in certain cases the acquirer may use these losses to reduce its income taxes. In a sense, companies that have suffered substantial losses may find themselves worth more "dead" than "alive" because of the economic value related to the tax benefit that may be derived from their losses by other companies.

The following discussion will indicate the accounting aspects of loss carrybacks and carryforwards, initially assuming the absence of consequences regarding deferred income tax amounts. After these procedures are examined, implications of loss carrybacks and carryforwards on interperiod tax allocation will be examined.

Loss Carryback

If a corporation suffers a loss in a period following periods of taxable income, a refund of the prior years' taxes may be claimed. In such cases, the accounting treatment as stated in the *CICA Handbook* is quite clear:

> Where a loss for tax purposes gives rise to a recovery of income taxes of the previous period, such recovery should be reflected in the income statement for the period of the loss either before "income (loss) before extraordinary items" or, if it relates to an extraordinary item, as a deduction therefrom.[22]

To illustrate, Can Corp. had a net operating loss in 1986 of $50,000. The company had a net operating income in 1985 of $80,000. The tax rates have been 50% in 1986 and 48% in 1985. Assume that accounting and taxable income or loss coincide for both years. Under the carryback provision, the loss in 1986 may be used to claim a refund of taxes paid in 1985. Since the 1985 income exceeded the loss in 1986, the entire loss can be carried back to that year. Consequently a refund of $24,000 ($50,000 × 48% tax rate paid in 1985) can be claimed. The journal entry to record the claim in 1986 would be:

Income Tax Refund Receivable	24,000	
Refund of Income Taxes Due to Loss Carryback		24,000

The refund is reported on the income statement in the year of the loss as follows:

Operating loss before income tax effect	$(50,000)
Less: Refund of prior year's income taxes due to loss carryback	24,000
Net loss	$(26,000)

The refund receivable should be reflected in the balance sheet as a current asset. If the loss in the current year exceeds the total income from the preceding year, the difference may be carried back against taxable income for 1984 and/or 1983. Alternatively, the remainder of the loss may be carried forward.

Loss Carryforward

If it is not possible or it is decided not to carry an operating loss back, or if the operating loss is not fully absorbed through a carryback, it can be carried forward

---

[22]*CICA Handbook*, Section 3470, par. 40.

for seven succeeding years. Because the value of the loss carryforward depends on future earnings to provide the income tax offset, the realization of a future tax savings is not assured, and the proper accounting treatment in the loss year is not obvious. Therefore, the *CICA Handbook* has identified the accounting and reporting treatment for loss carryforwards under two conditions. These conditions reflect the degree of uncertainty associated with the earning of income in the future from which the tax effects of the carryforwards can be realized.

The first treatment applies when there is **virtual certainty** of realizing tax benefits from the loss. Virtual certainty exists when all three of the following conditions exist:

1. the loss results from an identifiable and nonrecurring cause;
2. a record of profitability has been established over a long period by the corporation, or a predecessor business, with any occasional losses being more than offset by income in subsequent years; and
3. there is assurance beyond any reasonable doubt that future taxable income will be sufficient to offset the loss carryforward and will be earned during the carryforward period prescribed by the tax laws. In assessing its ability to earn sufficient future taxable income to offset the loss, a corporation may recognize that it can maximize its taxable income during the loss carryforward period by not claiming certain deductions allowable for tax purposes (e.g., capital cost allowances). This will result either in a reduction of accumulated deferred income tax credits or in the recording of deferred income tax debits during the carryforward period.[23]

When these conditions are met, the tax saving on the loss carryforward would be recognized in the year of the loss. An asset (Estimated Future Tax Benefits from Loss Carryforward) would be debited and an income statement item (Reduction of Loss Due to Tax Carryforward Benefits) would be credited. The income statement account would be shown in the calculation of ''income (loss) before extraordinary items'' or, if it relates to an extraordinary item, as a deduction therefrom.[24]

The second treatment applies when the conditions for virtual certainty of realizing the tax benefit of a loss carryforward are not present, which is more frequently the case. Under these circumstances, tax benefits that may be realized in the future from a loss carryforward are not recorded in the period of the loss.[25] Instead, the tax savings from a loss carryforward would be recorded and reported as an extraordinary item in the period in which they were actually realized.[26]

To illustrate the two possible accounting treatments, assume that Norton Corporation suffered a $200,000 net operating loss in 1986 when the tax rate was (and was expected to continue at) 40%. Furthermore, assume there were no timing differences between taxable income and accounting income. The tax savings value of the 1986 loss depends on future taxable income.

If realization of the future tax savings is ''virtually certain,'' Norton Corporation may recognize the tax carryforward as an **asset** (future tax benefit) and reduce the current operating loss by the amount of the tax benefit of the loss carryforward. The tax benefit of $80,000 ($200,000 × 40%) is recorded in 1986 through this journal entry:

---

[23]*Ibid.*, Section 3470, par. 43. In the discussion of virtual certainty situations (par. 45) the *Handbook* states that the tax benefit should be calculated on the basis of the known enacted tax rates of relevant future periods (i.e., the accrual approach).

[24]*Ibid.*, Section 3470, par. 46.

[25]Disclosure by note of the amount of the loss carryforwards for tax purposes and their expiration dates would be made (*CICA Handbook*, Section 3470, par. 54).

[26]*Ibid.*, Section 3470, par. 56.

Estimated Future Tax Benefits—Loss Carryforward	80,000	
Reduction of Loss Due to Tax Carryforward Benefit		80,000

The lower portion of the income statement in 1986 would appear as follows:

Operating loss before income tax effect	$(200,000)
Less: Reduction of loss due to tax carryforward benefit	80,000
Net loss	$(120,000)

If, in 1987, the Norton Corporation earns $600,000 income before taxes, the following entry is recorded in 1987 assuming a 40% tax rate:

Income Tax Expense	240,000	
Estimated Future Tax Benefits—Loss Carryforward		80,000
Income Tax Payable		160,000

The 1987 income statement would appear as follows:

Income before taxes	$600,000
Less: Income tax expense	240,000
Net income	$360,000

In situations where a company discovers that virtual certainty no longer exists, any tax benefit of a loss carryforward previously recorded should be written off and shown as an extraordinary item in the income statement.[27]

If the Norton Corporation is not virtually certain of future earnings against which to offset its 1986 loss, the tax benefit of the loss carryforward should not be recognized in the loss year. Instead, it should be recognized as an **extraordinary item** in the future periods when the tax savings are realized. Therefore, in 1986 Norton Corporation would make no entry for income tax, and would report a net operating loss of $200,000 on its income statement.

If, in this situation, the Norton Corporation experiences a $600,000 pretax accounting income in 1987, the following entry would be recorded:

Income Tax Expense	240,000	
Tax Reduction Due to Loss Carryforward—Extraordinary Item		80,000
Income Tax Payable		160,000

The lower portion of the income statement in 1987 would appear as follows:

Income before income taxes	$600,000
Less: Income tax expense	240,000
Income before extraordinary item	$360,000
Extraordinary item:	
Tax reduction due to loss carryforward	80,000
Net income	$440,000

[27]*Ibid.*, Section 3470, par. 50.

Accounting treatments similar to those illustrated above would occur beyond 1987 if the 1987 income had not been sufficient to absorb the entire amount of the loss carryforward.

Disclosure Requirements

The amounts of any operating loss carryforwards for tax purposes not recognized in the loss period along with the expiration period of these loss carryforwards should be disclosed through a note to the financial statements.[28] From this disclosure the reader of the financial statements can determine the amount of income that may be recognized in the future on which no income tax will be paid. For example, as mentioned earlier, Chrysler had over $3 billion in tax losses in the period 1978—1981; it is now using these losses to offset income. Its executive vice president of finance recently remarked that "it still has approximately $650 million loss carryforwards going into 1985."

LOSS CARRYBACKS AND CARRYFORWARDS INTEGRATED WITH INTERPERIOD INCOME TAX ALLOCATION

Interperiod tax allocation for timing differences should continue to be employed by a corporation through loss and loss carryback or carryforward periods.[29] Accounting for these situations can be very complex. The following examples are therefore designed to introduce the basic concepts, but they are limited as to the variety of possible circumstances.

Example 1   Assume that Brooke Corp. began operations in 1985. For that year, the following schedule reflects pertinent information regarding its operations given a 40% tax rate.

Brooke Corp. DATA FOR 1985		
Accounting income (including $12,000 depreciation expense)		$50,000
Timing difference:		
CCA in excess of depreciation		10,000
Taxable income		$40,000
Tax payable (40%)		16,000
Journal entry:		
Income Tax Expense	20,000	
Income Tax Payable		16,000
Deferred Income Taxes		4,000

In 1986, the company incurred an accounting loss of $62,000 including depreciation of $12,000. Although $20,000 CCA could be taken in 1986, management chose not to take any CCA during that year. Because of this decision, the tax loss for 1986 was $50,000 and a timing difference of depreciation expense exceeding CCA by $12,000 resulted. (Note that not taking CCA this year would mean it could still be taken in future years.)

[28]*Ibid.*, Section 3470, par. 54.
[29]*Ibid.*, Section 3470, par. 36.

Assuming that Brooke Corp. wishes to carry back the 1986 loss, it could recover the $16,000 taxes paid in 1985. The entry to record this would be:

Income Tax Refund Receivable	16,000	
Refund of Income Taxes Due to Loss Carryback		16,000

An additional element entering into this situation is that the company may refile prior years' tax returns amending the amount taken for CCA. This would occur if such an action were advantageous to the company. While a refiling associated with a loss carryback cannot result in the company claiming a refund in excess of the taxes paid in a prior year, it may be advantageous in terms of reinstating CCA taken previously to undepreciated capital cost, which could then be taken in future years to reduce taxable income. Reducing the CCA taken in previous tax returns would, however, necessitate adjusting the Deferred Income Taxes credit built up based on the excess CCA over depreciation in the prior year.

To illustrate, assume that Brooke Corp. does refile its 1985 tax return on which it reduces the CCA taken by $10,000 (the full timing difference in 1985). The amended return would then show taxable income of $50,000. However, the full $50,000 tax loss in 1986 would totally offset this taxable income, and no additional tax would be payable for 1985. Therefore, the $16,000 tax paid would still be refunded and the full loss would be carried back. After refiling, the $10,000 CCA could be taken in future years. This, however, means that the Deferred Income Tax credit recorded in 1985 is no longer applicable (the depreciation expense and CCA for 1985 would be the same after refiling). Consequently, the deferred taxes would have to be adjusted. In this regard, the *CICA Handbook* states:

> Where the recomputation of taxable income for the previous period results in an adjustment to accumulated deferred income taxes, such adjustment should be reflected in the income statement for the period of the loss.[30]

Therefore, the following entry would be made:

Deferred Income Taxes	4,000	
Income Tax Recoverable in the Future		4,000

The credited account would be shown in the income statement as a deferred tax recoverable item as illustrated on page 957. The Deferred Income Taxes account would now be reduced to a zero balance.

The fact that depreciation expense of $12,000 is included in the 1986 income determination, but no CCA was taken in calculating the tax loss for the year, means there is a timing difference in the loss year. The accounting loss is greater than the tax loss, as the former includes an expense not in the latter. Accounting for this difference depends on expectations as to whether the timing difference will reverse —that the company will eventually have taxable income. (Note that the period for reversal of a timing difference is not limited as is the case for a loss carryforward.) When there is "reasonable assurance" that the timing difference will reverse, then the tax effect of the difference is recorded in the year of the loss (even if there is an absence of virtual certainty of realizing the tax benefit of a loss carryforward).[31] Such an entry for Brooke Corp. in 1986 would be:

Deferred Income Taxes	4,800	
Income Tax Recoverable in the Future		4,800
(Timing difference of $12,000 × tax rate of 40%)		

---

[30]*Ibid.*, Section 3470, par. 42.

[31]*Ibid.*, Section 3470, pars. 46 and 52.

When there is doubt that there will be income in the future sufficient enough to absorb the reversal, deferred income tax debits would not be recognized.[32]

Assuming at least reasonable assurance regarding a reversal, the partial 1986 income statement for Brooke Corp. would be:

Brooke Corp.
PARTIAL INCOME STATEMENT
For the Year Ended December 31, 1986

Net loss before depreciation		$50,000
Depreciation expense		12,000
Net loss before income taxes		$62,000
Deduct:		
Current refund due to loss carryback	$16,000	
Deferred income taxes recoverable		
in the future ($4,000 + $4,800)	8,800	24,800
Net loss		$37,200

Example 2   For various reasons, a corporation may not be able to, or may choose not to, carry back a loss or portion thereof. In such circumstances, the previously discussed recommended accounting practice concerning loss carryforwards would apply. Additionally, timing differences in the loss year may have to be accounted for.

Assume, for example, that Brooke Corp. decided not to carryback its 1986 loss or to refile its tax return of 1985 as was the case in Example 1. Therefore, the question becomes how will the company account for the loss carryforward and the timing difference in 1986.

Assuming virtual certainty of the tax benefits from the carryforward and reasonable assurance that the timing difference will reverse, the following entries would be made:

Estimated Future Tax Benefits—Loss Carryforward	20,000	
Reduction of Loss Due to Tax Carryforward Benefit		20,000
($50,000 tax loss × 40% tax rate)		
Deferred Income Taxes	4,800	
Income Tax Recoverable in the Future		4,800
($12,000 excess depreciation over CCA × 40% tax rate)		

If virtual certainty did not exist but reasonable assurance that timing differences would reverse was present, then only the second entry would be made. If both virtual certainty and reasonable assurance did not exist, then deferred income tax debits should not be recognized. Since the Deferred Income Taxes account has a credit balance of only $4,000 resulting from 1985, this is the maximum amount by which it can be debited under such circumstances.

INTRAPERIOD TAX ALLOCATION

Tax allocation is the process of matching reported tax expense with reported income. **Interperiod** tax allocation involves determination of the **amount** of tax expense to be reported in a particular accounting period; this is done by matching tax expense to accounting income. **Intraperiod** tax allocation involves determination of the

---

[32]*Ibid.*, Section 3470, par. 52.

format to be used in disclosing tax expense within a particular period; this is done by apportioning reported taxes to the related components of reported items in financial statements. Thus, intraperiod tax allocation means assigning tax expense between "income before extraordinary items" and "extraordinary items" in the income statement. Additionally, it requires that prior period adjustments, corrections of errors made in previous periods, and retroactive adjustments for changes in accounting policies be reported net of their income tax consequences in the statement of retained earnings.

Intraperiod tax allocation was examined in Chapter 4, and the reader may wish to refer to that material in order to refresh the memory. The topic has been reintroduced at this point in order to provide a complete identification in this chapter of the accounting disclosures related to reporting income taxes in financial statements.

CONCLUDING COMMENT

Interperiod tax allocation is one of the most challenging and complex areas in accounting practice. Many complications encountered in actual practice have not been discussed in this chapter. For example, in the discussion of the tax effects of a loss carryforward, it was assumed that the current year's tax rate was the same as the tax rates expected to exist when the benefits of the loss are realized. The examples regarding the integration of loss carryforwards or carrybacks and interperiod allocation for timing differences, while reasonably complex, only scratched the surface of possible situations. Additionally, accounting for the tax effects of capital losses relative to taxable capital gains has not been covered in this chapter. Therefore, while many basic aspects have been examined, much remains if one is to acquire a complete understanding of interperiod tax allocation accounting.

KEY POINTS

1. Because the objectives and principles for determining pretax accounting income and taxable income differ, the amounts are likely to differ. The nature of the item causing the difference can be one of two types: permanent difference or timing difference.

2. Permanent differences are items that enter into the calculation of either pretax accounting income or taxable income, but never into both. When such differences occur in accounting income, they are simply treated as nontaxable or nondeductible when determining tax expense reported on the income statement. If they are part of the taxable income calculation, they are used to calculate the tax expense reported even though the items are not shown on the income statement.

3. Timing differences result when revenue or expense items are included in either pretax accounting income or taxable income of a period and in the taxable income or accounting income respectively of a subsequent period. That is, they originate in one period and reverse in a future period.

4. The tax effects of timing differences are to be accounted for using interperiod tax allocation. (Tax expense is based on pretax accounting income whereas tax payable is based on taxable income.) An alternative approach (tax payable approach) would result in reporting a tax expense equal to tax payable but this is not recommended in the *CICA Handbook*. Furthermore, the *Handbook*

implies that tax allocation is to be applied on a comprehensive basis rather than a partial basis.

5. Application of the tax allocation approach gives rise to deferred income taxes being reported in the balance sheet. The amount reflects the cumulative tax effects (originating and reversing) of the timing differences associated with the balance sheet classification (current or noncurrent) of the item (asset or liability) which caused the deferred taxes.

6. Disclosure in the financial statements of the portion of income tax expense related to current taxes payable and to deferred amounts is necessary. This may be accomplished by showing the current and deferred portions of tax expense in the body of the income statement, through a note, or by stating the increase or decrease in deferred taxes in the statement of changes in financial position.

7. The existence of a large number of timing differences and/or tax rate changes over the years complicates the accounting for deferred taxes. While the gross change method is preferred by the *CICA Handbook* as a means of dealing with such complexities, the net change method may be used when practical difficulties create problems in using it.

8. Tax rates may be expected to change over the years. Present recommendations in the *CICA Handbook* state that deferred tax amounts are to be determined using the tax rate existing in the year of origination, and are not to be adjusted for future years' expected or actual tax rate changes (the deferral method). Recognizing expected and actual tax rate changes when recording originating amounts or adjusting deferred tax balances (the accrual or liability method) is an alternative approach not currently recommended. A current review by the Accounting Standards Committee of accounting for corporate taxes may lead to a change regarding the acceptance of this latter approach in the future.

9. Tax laws permit operating losses to be carried back or forward for purposes of determining taxes due for previous or future years.

10. Carryback of a loss results in a tax refund and reporting the refund due to the loss carryback in the income statement.

11. Accounting for a loss carryforward depends on whether or not there is "virtual certainty" of realizing tax savings during the loss carryforward period. If virtual certainty exists, the future tax benefit is recorded and reported in the income statement of the year of the loss. Otherwise, the benefit (except for implications regarding deferred tax amounts) is not recorded and reported in the loss year but is recognized as an extraordinary item in the year the tax saving is realized. Amounts and expiration dates of loss carryforwards not recognized in the accounts should be disclosed through a note to the financial statements.

12. Loss carrybacks and carryforwards and implications for determining amounts in tax returns (e.g., CCA taken) often affect deferred income tax amounts. The circumstances of such situations are varied and often complex. Examples integrating the consequences of loss carrybacks and carryforwards with deferred income tax accounts served to illustrate basic accounting procedures associated with such situations.

13. Intraperiod tax allocation refers to the recommended practice of reporting separately the income tax related to income before extraordinary items, extraordinary items, prior period adjustments, correction of errors, and adjustments for changes in accounting policies.

APPENDIX

20A

THE WITH AND WITHOUT TECHNIQUE

The presentation in the chapter illustrated the deferred tax computation as simply the current tax rate multiplied by the timing differential. This is referred to as the **"short-cut method."** In practice, however, owing to the interplay of such items as graduated tax rates, special tax rates, investment tax credits, foreign tax credits, and operating losses, the deferred tax is frequently computed using the **"with and without timing differences technique."** The with and without technique is not an alternative to the gross change or the net change methods, but is used in conjunction with one of these methods. When the net change method is used, the following steps are involved in applying this technique:

1. Compute the **income tax payable** on taxable income. Taxable income is equal to pretax accounting income adjusted for any permanent differences and for **all timing differences.** All special tax rates and credits are applied in the determination of income tax payable. This represents the "with" portion of the computation (that is, **with** adjustment for timing differences).

2. Compute the income tax that would have been paid on "adjusted pretax income." Adjusted pretax income is equal to pretax accounting income adjusted for any permanent differences but without adjustment for timing differences. All special tax rates and credits are applied to adjusted pretax income **as if it were taxable income** on which

tax would be paid. This represents the "without" portion of the computation (that is, **without** adjustment for timing differences).

3. The difference between (1) the income tax payable **with** adjustment for timing differences and (2) the pro forma tax **without** adjustment for timing differences represents the current tax effect of net timing differences. It is debited (or credited) to the deferred tax account.

To illustrate, the following schedule presents data and the computation of tax payable for a hypothetical corporation that has the first $25,000 of income taxed at a rate of 22% and additional amounts subject to a 48% rate.

	Computation of Tax Payable	
	1986	1987
Pretax accounting income	$50,000	$35,000
Timing difference—		
Excess of CCA over book depreciation	(20,000)	(15,000)
Taxable income	$30,000	$20,000
Taxes currently payable (computed on taxable income)—	$ 5,500[a]	$ 4,400[b]
	2,400[c]	
Tax payable	$ 7,900	$ 4,400

[a]$25,000 × 22%
[b]$20,000 × 22%
[c]$ 5,000 × 48%

Based on this data, the deferred tax provisions for 1986 and 1987 are computed as follows using the with and without technique.

(1) Tax computed on pretax accounting income **with** timing difference:

Tax Bracket	1986 Income (With)	1986 Tax Payable	1987 Income (With)	1987 Tax Payable
$0–$25,000	$25,000 × 22% =	$5,500	$20,000 × 22% =	$4,400
Over $25,000	5,000 × 48% =	2,400	–0– × 48% =	–0–
	$30,000	$7,900	$20,000	$4,400

(2) Tax computed on pretax accounting income **without** timing difference:

Tax Bracket	1986 Income (Without)	1986 Tax Expense	1987 Income (Without)	1987 Tax Expense
$0–$25,000	$25,000 × 22% =	$ 5,500	$25,000 × 22% =	$ 5,500
Over $25,000	25,000 × 48% =	12,000	10,000 × 48% =	4,800
	$50,000	$17,500	$35,000	$10,300

(3)   Deferred tax provision:

	1986	1987
$17,500 − $7,900 (tax expense minus tax payable)	$ 9,600	
$10,300 − $4,400 (tax expense minus tax payable)		$ 5,900

Under the short-cut method the deferred tax would have been computed in 1986 as $9,600 ($20,000 × 48%) and in 1987 as $7,200 ($15,000 × 48%); 1986 would be correct but not 1987. The amount deferred in 1987 is not 48% of the timing difference, as happened to be the case in 1986. Owing to the interplay of the different tax rates applied to different portions of income, the deferral is at an effective rate somewhere between 22% and 48%. This illustrates that the "short-cut method" of applying the current tax rate to the amount of timing differences should be used only when there is no possibility that special tax rates or credits will apply.

Note: All **asterisked** Questions, Cases, Exercises, or Problems relate to material contained in an Appendix.

QUESTIONS

1. In what basic ways do the objectives of determining taxable income differ from the objectives of measuring accounting income?
2. It is sometimes contended that federal and provincial income tax is not an expense but a sharing of profits with the government. Do you agree? Why or why not?
3. As controller for Maksymetz Products Co. Ltd., you are asked to meet with the board of directors to discuss the company's income tax situation. Several members of the board express concern over the fact that the company is reporting a larger amount of income tax expense on its published income statements than is to be paid to the government with the company's income tax return for that same year.
    (a) Explain to the board members the accounting rationale for this discrepancy.
    (b) How might this difference between tax paid and tax expense have arisen?
4. Explain what a permanent difference is in the interperiod allocation of income taxes. Give three examples.
5. Explain what a timing difference is in the interperiod allocation of income taxes. Give three examples.
6. Describe two items that account for taxable income being higher than accounting income.
7. Describe two items that account for accounting income being higher than taxable income.
8. What is the theoretical rationale for allocating income taxes between periods?
9. Comprehensive allocation and partial allocation are two concepts that exist regarding the extent to which interperiod tax allocation could be applied. Explain what is meant by each. What is the *CICA Handbook* position regarding which should be used?
10. How are deferred charges and deferred credits, arising from income tax allocation, treated on the balance sheet?
11. Explain the "individual item basis" of interperiod tax allocation.

12. What are the steps that are involved in applying the "gross change method"?

13. Explain the "net change method" of applying interperiod income tax allocation.

14. What is the basic difference between the "gross change method" and the "net change method"?

15. In what circumstances is application of the "gross change method" more desirable than application of the "net change method"? In what circumstances is it less desirable?

16. The deferral method and the accrual (liability) method represent alternative approaches to interperiod tax allocation. Explain what is meant by each and identify the one recommended in the *CICA Handbook*.

17. What is the tax effect of a sustained large operating loss to a corporation after it has operated profitably for several consecutive years?

18. Differentiate between "carrybacks" and "carryforwards." Which can be accounted for with the greater certainty when they arise? Why?

19. What are the alternatives in accounting for a loss carryforward? What are the circumstances that determine the alternative to be applied?

*20. Explain what is meant by the "short-cut method" and the "with and without timing differences technique" for determining deferred tax amounts. Under what circumstances would the latter method be preferable to the former?

CASES

C20-1 Listed below are 18 items that are treated differently for accounting and tax purposes.

1. Excess of capital cost allowance over book (financial statement) depreciation.
2. Tax-exempt interest income.
3. Excess of percentage depletion for tax purposes over cost depletion for accounting income determination.
4. Excess of charge to tax return over charge to accounting records for estimated uncollectibles.
5. Excess of accrued pension expense over amount paid.
6. Excess of fair market value of a charitable contribution (deductible for taxes) over cost (charged to expense).
7. Instalment sales income for accounting purposes in excess of taxable income from the instalment sales.
8. Expenses incurred in obtaining tax-exempt income.
9. A trademark acquired directly from the government amortized more rapidly for tax purposes than it is expensed for accounting purposes in this period.
10. Prepaid advertising expense deferred on the accounting records and deducted as an expense for tax purposes.
11. Premiums paid on life insurance of officers (corporation beneficiary).
12. Receipt of tax-free dividends from a Canadian corporation.
13. Proceeds of life insurance policies on lives of officers.
14. Estimated future warranty costs that are not deductible for tax purposes until they are incurred.
15. Excess of research and development cost per tax return over financial statement amount.
16. Charitable contributions—excess of accounting expense over tax limitation.
17. Fine for polluting.
18. Income discovered after closing but included in the tax return.

Instructions

Indicate whether the items are **permanent** differences or **timing** differences and whether any **originating** difference will result in a debit to deferred taxes or a credit to deferred taxes.

C20-2 In its financial statements for 1986 the Clear Glass Company reports an item —Deferred Income Tax, $425,000. The president in his letter to shareholders states that this is in connection with a capital cost allowance allowed by the federal government.

Instructions

(a) Explain the nature of this item and the accounting theory related to reporting such an item on the financial statements.

(b) Assuming straight-line depreciation with no salvage value is used for financial statement purposes, give the journal entries that were probably made to record this item, and the entries that will affect this account in future years. Amounts for the journal entries need not be given. Assume that the direction of the difference between CCA and book depreciation reverses in the sixth year and that the life of the assets involved is 15 years.

C20-3 Income tax allocation is an integral part of generally accepted accounting principles. The applications of intraperiod tax allocation (within a period) and interperiod tax allocation (among periods) are both required.

Instructions

(a) Explain the need for **intraperiod** tax allocation (covered in Chapter 4).

(b) Accountants who favour **interperiod** tax allocation argue that income taxes are an expense rather than a distribution of earnings. Explain the significance of this argument. **Do not explain the definitions of expense or distribution of earnings.**

(c) Indicate and explain whether each of the following **independent** situations should be treated as a timing difference or a permanent difference.

1. Estimated warranty costs (covering a three-year warranty) are expensed for accounting purposes at the time of sale but deducted for income tax purposes when incurred.
2. Depreciation for accounting and capital cost allowance for tax purposes differ.
3. A company properly uses the equity method to account for its 30% investment in a non-Canadian company. The investee pays dividends that are about 10% of its annual earnings. Only dividends received are taxable.

(d) Discuss the nature of the deferred income tax accounts and possible classifications in a company's statement of financial position.

C20-4 **Part A.** This year Lorac Company has the following items in its income statement:

1. Gross profits on instalment sales.
2. Revenues on long-term construction contracts.
3. Estimated cost of product warranty contracts.
4. Premiums on officers' life insurance with Lorac as beneficiary.

Instructions

(a) Under what conditions would deferred income taxes need to be reported in the financial statements?

(b) Specify whether or not deferred income taxes would need to be recognized for each of the items above, and indicate the rationale for such recognition.

Part B. Eneri Company's president has heard that deferred income taxes can be variously classified in the balance sheet.

Instructions

Identify the conditions under which deferred income taxes would be classified as a noncurrent item in the balance sheet. What justification exists for such classification?

(AICPA adapted)

C20-5 During 1986, the Burke Corp. incurred interest cost of $600,000 during construction of a new office building, which was completed on December 31. For tax purposes, the interest cost is deductible in 1986. For accounting purposes, the interest is capitalized and depreciated over the 15-year life of the building. Based on a 1986 tax rate of 40%, Burke's accountant estimates that the company will enjoy an immediate tax saving of $240,000. He contends that recognition of an immediate deferred tax liability for the full $240,000 will distort the company's debt ratios, since payment of any additional future taxes depends on such uncertain factors as the company's future earnings and tax rates. He believes that use of the deferral method of interperiod tax allocation would be misleading to financial statement users, since the $600,000 timing difference is a "semipermanent difference" that will take 15 years to reverse fully. He believes that the accrual (liability) method is more appropriate for "semipermanent" differences such as this, and that the tax effect should be discounted to its present value.

Instructions

    (a) Describe the difference between the deferral method and the accrual (liability) method of interperiod tax allocation.

    (b) Assuming pretax accounting income of $2,000,000, prepare the journal entry needed to record income taxes for 1986 under the deferral method.

    (c) Assuming annual pretax accounting income of $2,000,000 and a 40% tax rate, prepare the journal entry needed annually to record income taxes during the 15 years subsequent to 1986 under the deferral method.

    (d) Assuming that the accrual (liability) method of interperiod tax allocation was appropriate, what journal entry might be prepared in 1986 to record income taxes? Assume that a 10% discount factor is used, a 40% tax rate is appropriate, and pretax accounting income is $2,000,000.

EXERCISES

E20-1 Cascada, Inc. reported the following tax and accounting income:

	1984	1985	1986
Taxable income	$ 90,000	$135,000	$225,000
Pretax accounting income	150,000	120,000	180,000

The company's income is taxed at a 46% rate.

Instructions

Prepare the year-end journal entries to accrue its income tax liability and to reflect tax allocation at the end of each of the three years. All differences between taxable income and pretax accounting income are the result of timing differences.

E20-2 The pretax accounting income of Costumes Company Ltd. has differed from that of its taxable income throughout each of the last four years as follows:

Year	Pretax Accounting Income	Taxable Income	Tax Rate
1983	$270,000	$180,000	50%
1984	300,000	225,000	40%
1985	330,000	270,000	40%
1986	360,000	480,000	40%

Pretax accounting income for each year includes an expense of $10,000 which is not deductible for tax purposes (it is a permanent difference).

Instructions

Prepare journal entries to reflect income tax allocation in all four years using the deferral method. Assume that the reversing differences in 1986 are accounted for using the gross change, FIFO basis method.

E20-3 The income statements of Airport Limo, Inc. for a three-year period provide the following data:

	1984	1985	1986
Income before depreciation	150,000	170,000	190,000
Depreciation (asset with three-year life, no salvage value)	30,000	30,000	30,000
Pretax income after depreciation	120,000	140,000	160,000

A 45% tax rate is applicable to all three years. The capital cost allowance method is used for tax purposes with a CCA rate of 50%. The asset class will continue after three years.

Instructions

Prepare the journal entry for each year to record the income tax expense and the income tax payable.

E20-4 The following information about Wiggley Gum Co. Ltd. is provided:

	1984	1985	1986
Pretax accounting income	$70,000	$90,000	$55,000
Taxable income	60,000	65,000	75,000

Instructions

(a) Assuming a tax rate of 40% and that the differences in income are entirely the result of timing differences, prepare the journal entries at the end of each year to reflect income tax allocation.

(b) Assume the same facts as in (a) except that, in 1985, $10,000 of the income reflected in pretax accounting income is from dividends from Canadian corporations (tax exempt). Prepare any journal entries that would change from what they were in (a).

E20-5 Darling Manufacturing Company has recently completed a $2,100,000 plant that is a Class 2 (CCA rate of 5%) asset for tax purposes. The company plans to depreciate the plant over a 30-year life with no salvage value. The plant became operational on November 1, 1986, and the fiscal and tax year ends are December 31.

Instructions

(a) Prepare entries in journal form to record depreciation (straight-line depreciation with no salvage value) of plant and to record income taxes for the year ended December 31, 1986. Assume that taxable income before CCA was $580,000 and that the applicable tax rate is 52%.

(b) Reproduce the deferred income taxes account as it should appear in the general ledger of Darling Manufacturing Company after closing December 31, 1994.

E20-6 At December 31, 1986, Bedding Corp.'s Deferred Income Taxes account had a $469,000 credit balance consisting of the following items:

Timing Difference	Resulting Balance in Deferred Taxes
1. Excess of capital cost allowance over accounting depreciation.	$490,000 cr.
2. Accrual, for accounting purposes, of estimated warranty costs which are expected to be incurred in 1987. For tax purposes such costs are deductible in the year incurred.	95,000 dr.
3. Capitalization, for accounting purposes, of interest and property taxes incurred during construction of a building in 1986. The expenditures were deducted on the 1986 tax return.	74,000 cr.
Total	$469,000 cr.

Instructions

Indicate the manner in which deferred taxes should be presented on Bedding Corp.'s December 31, 1986, balance sheet.

E20-7 African Imports Co., an instalment seller of furniture, records sales on the accrual basis for financial reporting purposes but on the instalment method for tax purposes. As a result, $75,000 of deferred income taxes have been accrued at December 31, 1986. In accordance with trade practice, instalment accounts receivable from customers are shown as current assets, although the average collection period is approximately three years.

At December 31, 1986, African Imports Co. has recorded a $30,000 deferred income tax debit arising from a book accrual of noncurrent deferred compensation expense which is **not** currently tax deductible.

Also at December 31, 1986, African Imports has accrued $22,500 of deferred income taxes resulting from the use of capital cost allowance for tax purposes and straight-line depreciation for financial reporting purposes.

Instructions

How should the deferred income taxes be classified on African Imports' December 31, 1986, balance sheet?

(AICPA adapted)

E20-8 Executone Corporation has an item costing $45,000 that was expensed for tax purposes but is amortized over three years for accounting purposes. The tax rate is 40% in the year of origination, 1985, and 30% in the years of "turn around," 1986 and 1987. The accounting and tax data for the three years is shown below.

	Financial Accounting	Tax Return
1985 (40% tax rate)		
Income before timing difference	$50,000	$50,000
Timing difference	15,000	45,000
Income after timing difference	$35,000	$ 5,000
1986 (30% tax rate)		
Income before timing difference	$50,000	$50,000
Timing difference	15,000	–0–
Income after timing difference	$35,000	$50,000
1987 (30% tax rate)		
Income before timing difference	$50,000	$50,000
Timing difference	15,000	–0–
Income after timing difference	$35,000	$50,000

Instructions

Prepare the journal entries to record the income tax expense and the income tax payable at the end of each year, applying the individual item basis and the deferral method.

E20-9 Bouquet Perfume Company Limited uses capital cost allowance for tax purposes and straight-line depreciation for accounting purposes. In the current year, 1986, the tax rate increased to 45%. The rate in all prior years was 35%. Pretax accounting income is $750,000 in 1986, while originating timing differences are $110,000 and reversing timing differences are $84,000.   Taxable Income $124,000

Instructions

(a) Compute the change in deferred taxes under (1) the gross change method and (2) the net change method.

(b) Prepare the journal entry to record the tax payable, the tax expense, and the deferred taxes for 1986 under (1) the gross change method and (2) the net change method.

E20-10 During your audit of Merry-Go-Round Company Ltd., the following information was disclosed:

1.

Year	Amount Due per Tax Return
1985	$80,000
1986	$65,000

2. On January 1, 1985, equipment costing $100,000 was purchased. The equipment has a life of five years and a salvage value of $10,000. Capital cost allowance is taken for income tax purposes and the straight-line depreciation method is used for accounting purposes. The appropriate CCA rate is 30%.

3. In January, 1986, $75,000 was collected in advance rental of a building for a three-year period. The entire $75,000 was reported as taxable income in 1986, but $50,000 was reported as unearned revenue in 1986 for accounting purposes.

4. The tax rate is 40% in both years.

5. The client company used the deferral method of income tax allocation, and uses a single Deferred Income Taxes account.

Instructions

(a) Determine the balance in the Deferred Income Taxes account at the end of 1985 and whether it is a debit or a credit balance.

(b) Determine the balance in the Deferred Income Taxes account at the end of 1986 and whether it is a debit or a credit balance.

E20-11 Istanbul Rug Company Ltd. purchased fixed assets that cost $1,500,000 on January 1, 1981. Assume that for tax purposes the company is permitted to depreciate the assets completely over three years at an equal amount per year. For accounting purposes the company will depreciate the assets over six years. The tax rates for the years involved are 1981, 40%; 1982, 40%; 1983, 50%; 1984, 50%; 1985, 50%; 1986, 50%. The straight-line method of depreciation is applied for accounting purposes with zero salvage value estimated.

Instructions

Determine the amount entered in the Deferred Tax account for each year and whether the amount is a debit or a credit to the Deferred Tax account. Assume that depreciation is the only timing difference involved and that the deferral method on the gross change basis is applied.

(a) Use the FIFO method to determine the tax rate applicable to reversing differences.

(b) Use the average rate method to determine the tax rate applicable to reversing differences.

E20-12 City Tax Corp. leases equipment under five-year leases, which require each year's rent to be paid in advance.

At the beginning of the year, there was $300,000 of deferred rental income which, for accounting purposes, was earned during the year. During the year, $500,000 of taxable rent was collected, of which $250,000 was earned, leaving a balance of $250,000 in the Deferred Rental Income account.

The tax rate in the current year was 40%; in prior years it had been 50%.

Instructions

Compute the income tax expense for the current year and the ending balance in deferred taxes using (a) the gross change method, and (b) the net change method. Accounting income before taxes was $1,000,000.

E20-13 Taxable income and pretax accounting income would be identical for Lindsay Corp. except for its treatments of gross profits on instalment sales and estimated costs of warranties. The following income computations have been prepared:

Taxable Income	1984	1985	1986
Excess of Revenues over Expenses	$100,000	$140,000	$50,000
Instalment Gross Profit Collected	16,000	16,000	16,000
Cost of Warranties	(5,000)	(5,000)	(5,000)
Taxable Income	$111,000	$151,000	$61,000

Pretax Accounting Income	1984	1985	1986
Excess of Revenues over Expenses	$100,000	$140,000	$50,000
Instalment Gross Profit—Earned	48,000	–0–	–0–
Estimated Cost of Warranties	(15,000)	–0–	–0–
Income Before Taxes	$133,000	$140,000	$50,000

The tax rates in effect were: 1984, 40%; 1985 and 1986, 50%.

Instructions

Prepare the journal entries to reflect income tax expense and payable for each of the years under:

(a) The net change method.

(b) The gross change method (FIFO basis).

E20-14 The pretax income (or loss) figures for the Cola Pepsi Company are as follows:

1981	$100,000 $\}$ 50%
1982	120,000
1983	60,000
1984	(100,000) N0 V.C. $\}$ 40%
1985	(200,000)
1986	80,000
1987	80,000

Pretax accounting income and taxable income were the same for all years involved. Assume a 50% tax rate for 1981 and 1982, and a 40% rate for the remaining years. In 1984 and 1985, the company is not virtually certain of future earnings against which to offset the loss.

Instructions

Prepare the journal entries for the years 1983 to 1987 to reflect income tax expense and the effects of the loss carrybacks and carryforwards, assuming Cola Pepsi Company chooses to carry back losses for the maximum allowable period of three years until all income available for such carrybacks is fully offset.

E20-15 Pretzel-Chip Corporation experienced pretax accounting income and taxable income from 1978 through 1986 as follows:

Year	Income (Loss)	Tax Rate
1978	$10,000	20%
1979	20,000	40%
1980	8,000	40%
1981	32,000	50%
1982	(80,000)	30%
1983	40,000	30%
1984	20,000	40%
1985	70,000	50%
1986	(40,000)	46%

The company follows a policy of carrying back a loss against taxable income for the maximum allowable three years.

Instructions

(a) What entry for income taxes should have been recorded in 1982 if there was not virtual certainty that taxable income would be reported in the next seven years?

(b)   What entry for income taxes should have been recorded in 1982 if taxable income was assured with virtual certainty in the next seven years?

(c)   Indicate what the bottom portion of the income statement in 1983 would look like, assuming that the situation as stated in (b) above existed in 1982.

E20-16   Taco Company Ltd. began operations in 1983 and earned the following pretax income (loss) for both accounting purposes and tax purposes:

Year	Pretax Income (Loss)	Tax Rate
1983	$40,000	50%
1984	20,000	50%
1985	(80,000)	40%
1986	60,000	40%

The company uses the loss carryback provision of tax laws for the maximum period allowable before considering loss carryforwards.

Instructions

(a)   Prepare the journal entries for the years 1983 to 1986 to reflect tax expense and the allocation of loss carrybacks and carryforwards, assuming that in 1985 Taco Company is not virtually certain of future earnings against which to offset the loss.

(b)   Prepare the journal entries for 1985 and 1986, assuming that Taco Company is virtually assured of future earnings against which to offset the loss.

E20-17   Baxter Corp. began operations in 1985. For that year (ended December 31) a credit balance of $12,000 resulted in the Deferred Income Taxes account as determined below:

Pretax accounting income	$200,000
Excess CCA over depreciation	25,000
Taxable income	$175,000
Tax payable (48%)	$ 84,000

Journal entry:

Income Tax Expense	96,000	
Income Tax Payable		84,000
Deferred Income Taxes		12,000

For 1986, the company incurred a tax loss of $180,000 excluding $30,000 CCA which management decided would not be claimed in that year. Depreciation expense of $10,000 was reported in the income statement, resulting in a pretax accounting loss of $190,000. Management, in order to recover $5,000 of CCA taken in 1985, refiled the tax return for that year and claimed the full available refund of $84,000.

Instructions

(a)   Give the 1986 journal entries to account for the loss and management's actions. Assume reasonable assurance exists regarding timing difference reversals.

(b)   Beginning with the pretax accounting loss, show the partial income statement for 1986.

E20-18   Assume the circumstances presented in E20-17 except that management decides not to amend the 1985 CCA amount taken but to carry forward the $5,000 remaining from the $180,000 tax loss after claiming a refund.

Instructions

Give the 1986 journal entries related to the loss and management's actions as well as a partial income statement beginning with the pretax accounting loss, assuming that for any tax benefit of a loss carryforward there is:

(a) Virtual certainty.

(b) No virtual certainty.

*E20-19 Assume the following for Family Films Company Limited:

Pretax accounting income	$200,000
Taxable income	90,000

Tax rates:	
$0–$100,000	22%
Over $100,000	46%

Pretax accounting income includes $30,000 of interest on tax-exempt municipal bonds. Depreciation expense computed using capital cost allowance for tax purposes exceeds the amount computed under the straight-line method (used for financial accounting purposes) by $80,000.

Instructions

Compute the amount of income tax expense that will be reported on the income statement, differentiating between the portion that is current and that which is deferred. Compute the tax, using the "with and without" technique.

*E20-20 The income of the Motts Juice Company for the year is as follows:

Pretax accounting income	$120,000
Taxable income	147,000

The income figures above include a $25,000 gain on the sale of land; this gain is taxed at a special capital gain rate of 30%. The difference between pretax accounting income and taxable income is a result of accruing warranty expense for accounting purposes, but recording the expense when paid for tax purposes.
The following tax rates are in effect for the noncapital gain income:

$0–$100,000	22%
Over $100,000	46%

Instructions

(a) Prepare the journal entry to record the tax payable, tax expense, and deferred tax for the year using the "with and without technique."

(b) What is the amount of the deferred tax that would have been arrived at by applying the short-cut method?

PROBLEMS

P20-1 The Band-Aid Company Ltd. acquired fixed assets that cost $500,000 on January 5, 1984, which are subject to a capital cost allowance rate of 20% for tax purposes. The company is taxed at a rate of 48%. No salvage value is expected and the asset class will continue indefinitely.

Instructions

What should be the balance of the Deferred Income Taxes account in the ledger of the Band-Aid Company after closing on December 31, 1984, 1988, and 1994, assuming for accounting purposes that the straight-line method is used and that (a) the fixed assets are to be depreciated over a 10-year life, (b) over a 5-year life?

P20-2 The following facts apply to the Compact Car Company Ltd. for the calendar year 1986.

1. Assets are purchased at the beginning of 1986 at a cost of $60,000 and having a 10-year life, with no salvage value. The capital cost allowance rate for tax purposes is 25%, whereas the company uses the straight-line method for financial reporting purposes.
2. Warranty liability of $8,400 provided for accounting purposes is not deductible for tax purposes until warranty costs are incurred.
3. Accounting income before taxes includes $12,000 related to construction-type contracts still in process which are accounted for on the percentage-of-completion method for accounting purposes and on the completed-contract method for tax purposes.
4. Amortization of goodwill in the amount of $800 is not deductible for tax purposes.
5. Included in accounting income is $4,500 of tax exempt dividends received from Canadian corporations.
6. Pretax accounting income is $73,200.

Instructions

Calculate the income tax payable and the income tax expense for the year 1986. Assume that the income tax rate is 48%.

P20-3   The following information is obtained from the records of Pine Oaks Company Ltd.:

Year	Pretax Accounting Income	CCA Over (Under) Book Depreciation	Taxable Income	Tax Paid at 48%
1981	$ 20,000	$ 20,000	–0–	–0–
1982	60,000	20,000	$ 40,000	$ 19,200
1983	120,000	100,000	20,000	9,600
1984	180,000	120,000	60,000	28,800
1985	80,000	(60,000)	140,000	67,200
1986	20,000	(200,000)	220,000	105,600
	$480,000	$ –0–	$480,000	$230,400

Instructions

Prepare a schedule that provides for each of the years above the amount for each of the following column heads:

Income Tax Expense	Income Tax Payable	Increase (Decrease) in Deferred Tax	Balance in Deferred Tax

P20-4   Crop-Keep Corp. manufactures, constructs, and sells huge silos. The company was organized and began operations on January 1, 1984. A silo sells for a gross profit of $75,000. One-third of the total sale is collected in the first year and one-third in each of the following two years. Twelve silos were sold in 1984, 18 in 1985, and 20 in 1986. There have been no bad debts, and none are expected. Gross profit is recognized in the year of sale for accounting purposes but is recognized in the year cash is received for tax purposes. Instalment accounts receivable are considered a current asset.

The company's plant and equipment, acquired on January 1, 1984, cost $1,800,000 and is depreciated over a nine-year life with no salvage value. A capital cost allowance rate of 25% is used for tax purposes, and straight-line is used for accounting purposes. The company owns $100,000 of 10% municipal bonds, the interest on which is nontaxable.

Pretax accounting income for 1986 is $512,000.

Instructions

(a) Prepare the necessary journal entry to record income taxes for 1986 under the deferral method. The tax rate has been 40% since the company was organized.

(b) Assume that there was a $567,500 credit balance in the Deferred Income Taxes account at December 31, 1985. Of this amount, $480,000 relates to the instalment sales and the remainder to the depreciation. Compute the balance in Deferred Income Taxes at December 31, 1986. Indicate the section(s) of the balance sheet where it would be shown.

(c) Prepare the necessary journal entry to record income taxes for 1986 under the deferral method, assuming that the tax rate changed to 30% for 1986. The gross change method should be used.

P20-5 The following data represent the differences between accounting and tax income for Oriental Import, Inc., whose pretax accounting income is $860,000 for the current year.

1. Capital cost allowance exceeded accounting depreciation expense by $102,500 in the current year.

2. Officer life insurance expense was $5,200 for the year, and you have determined that this expense is not deductible for tax purposes. The expense amount represents the difference between the premium paid ($7,400) and the increase in the cash value of the policy ($2,200).

3. Rents of $5,000, applicable to next year, had been collected in December and deferred for financial statement purposes but are taxable in the year received.

4. In a previous year, the company established an allowance for product warranty expense. A summary of the current year's transactions appears below:

Balance at January 1	$ 96,300
Provision for the year	35,600
	$131,900
Payments made on product warranties	26,000
Balance at December 31	$105,900

Instructions

(a) Compute the current and deferred, if any, income tax provision. (Assume a 40% tax rate and apply the individual item basis.)

(b) Draft the income statement for the current year, beginning with "income before income taxes" and identifying "taxes currently payable" and "deferred" (net tax effect of timing differences).

P20-6 Luxury Cars, Inc. recognizes gross margin in instalment sales for accounting purposes at the time of sale and defers such gross margin for tax purposes until subsequent periods when the receivables arising from the instalment sales are collected. For accounting purposes, the company uses the straight-line method for depreciation, and the capital cost allowance method for tax purposes.
    Additional information:

Property	
1986 CCA in excess of accounting depreciation	$105,000
All depreciable property acquired in 1984; estimated useful life	10 years
Instalment sales	
Gross margin on 1986 instalment sales uncollected at year end	$180,000
Gross margin on prior-years' instalment sales collected during 1986	$150,000
Taxes	
Pretax accounting income for 1986	$300,000
Tax rate for 1986	50%
Average rate for all prior deferred income taxes	48%

NT axable until collected.

Instructions

Compute taxable income and the tax payable in 1986, and summarize the 1986 changes in the Deferred Income Taxes account balance:

(a) Using the gross change method.

(b) Using the net change method.

P20-7 The Jaspule Company began operations on January 3, 1986. Taxable income and pretax accounting income would be identical except for the following items:

Item	Revenue (Expense) Reported on 1986 Income Statement	Revenue (Expense) Reported on 1986 Tax Return
1. Depreciation: Difference due to using CCA for tax purposes and straight-line method for accounting purposes.	$(60,000)	$(120,000)
2. Rental fees collected in advance: Recognized in entirety on 1986 tax return. $90,000 will be earned in 1987.	160,000	250,000
3. Prepaid advertising expenditures for 1987 ad campaign: Deferred for accounting purposes and deducted as an expense in 1986 for tax purposes.	–0–	(15,000)

The income tax rate was 40% during 1986.

Instructions

(a) Compute the balance in Jaspule Company's Deferred Income Taxes account at December 31, 1986.

(b) Indicate the manner in which the deferred taxes should be presented on Jaspule's December 31, 1986, balance sheet.

P20-8 The following information about Nature Products Company Ltd. is provided to you:

1. In 1985, $60,000 was collected in rent; for accounting purposes the entire amount was reported as revenue in 1986. In 1986, $75,000 was collected in rent; of this amount, $30,000 was reported as unearned revenue in 1986. For tax purposes, the rent is reported as revenue in the year of collection.

2. On January 1, 1982, the company purchased a machine costing $120,000. The machine has a salvage value of $7,500, and has a useful life of five years. The straight-line method of depreciation is used for accounting purposes, and the capital cost allowance method is used for income tax purposes. The capital cost allowance on this machine was $15,000 for 1986.

3. On January 1, 1986, equipment was purchased that had a cost of $180,000. The equipment has no salvage value, and has a useful life of six years. The straight-line method of depreciation is used for accounting purposes, and the capital cost allowance (rate 50%) method for tax purposes.

4. The tax rate for years prior to 1986 is 40%; for 1986, the tax rate is 50%.

5. Pretax accounting income of $322,500 for 1986 includes tax-exempt dividend revenue of $22,500.

6. On the 1986 tax return, the company reported $45,000 of gross profit from instalment sales. This profit was reported in 1985 for accounting purposes.

7. The balance (credit) in the Deferred Tax account as of December 31, 1985 was $90,000.

Instructions

(a) Using the gross change method, compute the tax expense for 1986, and the balance in the Deferred Tax account at December 31, 1986.

(b) Using the net change method, compute the tax expense for 1986, and the balance in the Deferred Tax account at December 31, 1986.

P20-9 You have been assigned to make a computation of Pickaberry Company's provision for income taxes for 1985 and 1986. On the basis of your review of the working papers, you have developed the following information.

Reconciliation of Accounting Income to Taxable Income	1985	1986
	(dollars in thousands)	
Pretax accounting income	$ 130	$ 910
Permanent accounting/tax differences:		
Amortization of goodwill in excess of allowed amount	70	80
Pretax accounting income after adjustment for permanent tax differences	200	990
Accounting/tax timing differences:		
Excess of CCA over depreciation expense	(400)	(200)
Provision for loss on sale of plant—booked in 1985 but sold in 1986	200	(200)
Provision for warranties:		
Provided during year	500	
Paid during year		(300)
Taxable income	$ 500	$ 290
Income tax rates	38%	50%

Instructions

Compute the provision for income taxes and net income for both years by drafting the lower portion of the comparative income statement beginning with "income before taxes" and presenting the portion of the tax "currently payable" and the amount due to increase or decrease in the deferral (net tax effect of timing differences). Apply the gross change method.

P20-10 Suntan Lotion, Inc. sustained a $110,000 net operating loss during the current year of operations when the applicable tax rate was 42%.

Instructions

(a) Assuming that the corporation is not virtually certain it will have future earnings against which it can offset the loss carryforward, prepare the entries for income taxes in the year of loss and in the succeeding year. (Assume a $140,000 pretax income and a 42% rate in the succeeding year.)

(b) Assuming that the corporation is virtually certain of earnings in the succeeding periods to cover the loss, prepare the entries for income taxes in the year of the loss and in the succeeding year. (Assume a $140,000 pretax income and a 42% tax rate in the succeeding year.)

(c) For both the loss year and the succeeding year, present the lower portion of the income statement (pretax accounting income or loss and below) for both assumptions (a) and (b).

P20-11 On January 2, 1985, Don & Diana Cafés Inc. commenced operations. The company had an accounting loss of $580,000 for that year. There were no timing differences during 1985. The loss carryforward cannot be assured with virtual certainty, because 1985 was the company's first year of operations. During 1986, the company had taxable income (equal to its accounting income) of $800,000. (Assume the tax rate for 1985 and 1986 was 46%.)

Instructions

(a) Prepare the comparative partial statement of income (loss) for Don & Diana Cafés Inc. for the year ended December 31, 1986, with comparative figures for 1985. The statement will start with "Income (loss) before income taxes and extraordinary items."

(b) Assume that Don & Diana Cafés Inc. has been in existence since January 1, 1980, and had taxable income (loss) as follows:

Year ended December 31	Taxable income (loss)
1980	$(60,000)
1981	70,000

1982	(10,000)
1983	70,000
1984	200,000

Assuming that the company uses loss carryback provisions for the maximum period (three years), prepare the partial statement of income (loss) for the years ended December 31, 1985 and 1986. Explain how the tax refund, if any, should be treated. (Assume the tax rate for all previous periods is 46%.)

P20-12   Your firm has been appointed to examine the financial statements of Chyron Energy, Inc. (CEI) for the two years ended December 31, 1986, in conjunction with an application for a bank loan. CEI was formed on January 2, 1975.

Early in the engagement you learned that the controller was unfamiliar with income tax accounting and that no tax allocations had been recorded.

During the examination, considerable information was gathered from the accounting records and client employees regarding interperiod tax allocation. This information, which has been audited, is as follows (with dollar amounts rounded to the nearest $100):

1. CEI uses a bad debt write-off method for tax purposes and a full accrual method for accounting purposes. The balance of the Allowance for Doubtful Receivables account at December 31, 1984, was $124,000. Following is a schedule of accounts written off and the corresponding year(s) in which the related sales were made.

Year(s) in Which Sales Were Made	Year(s) in Which Accounts Written Off	
	1986	1985
1984 and prior	$39,600	$58,000
1985	14,400	
1986		
	$54,000	$58,000

The following is a schedule of changes in the Allowance for Doubtful Receivables account for the two years ended December 31, 1986:

	Year Ended December 31	
	1986	1985
Balance at beginning of year	$132,000	$124,000
Accounting written off during the year	(54,000)	(58,000)
Bad debt expense for the year	76,000	66,000
Balance at end of year	$154,000	$132,000

2. Following is a reconciliation between net income per books and taxable income:

		Year Ended December 31	
		1986	1985
(1)	Net income per books	$ 666,100	$ 525,600
(2)	Income tax payable during year	364,600	473,600
(3)	Taxable income not recorded on the books this year:		
	Deferred sales commissions	20,000	
(4)	Expenses recorded on the books this year not deducted on the tax return:		
	(a) Allowance for doubtful receivables	22,000	8,000
	(b) Amortization of goodwill	16,000	16,000
(5)	Total of lines 1 through 4	$1,088,800	$1,023,200

(6)	Income recorded on the books this year not included on the tax return:		
	Tax exempt dividends from Canadian corporations	10,000	
(7)	Deductions on the tax return not charged against accounting income this year:		
	CCA in excess of depreciation	167,400	76,000
(8)	Total of lines 6 and 7	177,400	76,000
(9)	Taxable income (line 5 less line 8)	$ 911,400	$ 947,200

3. Assume that the effective tax rates are as follows: 1984 and prior years—60%; 1985—50%; 1986—40%.

4. In December, 1986, CEI entered into a contract to serve as distributor for Brown Manufacturer, Inc.'s engineering products. The contract became effective December 31, 1986, and $20,000 of advance commissions on the contract were received and deposited on December 31, 1986. Because the commissions had not been earned, they were accounted for as a deferred credit to income on the balance sheet at December 31, 1986.

5. Goodwill represents the excess of cost over fair value of the net tangible assets of a retiring competitor that were acquired for cash on January 2, 1981. The original balance was $160,000.

Instructions

(a) Prepare a schedule calculating (1) the balance of deferred income taxes at December 31, 1985 and 1986, and (2) the amount of the timing differences between actual income tax payable and financial income tax expense for 1985 and 1986. Round all calculations to the nearest $100. Use the gross change method.

(b) Independently of your solution to (a) and assuming the data shown below, prepare the section of the income statement beginning with pretax accounting income to disclose properly income tax expense for the years ended December 31, 1986 and 1985.

	1986	1985
Pretax accounting income	$960,800	$931,200
Income Tax payable currently	364,600	473,600
Deferred tax account change—Dr. (Cr.)	(56,200)	49,000
Balance of deferred tax at end of year—Dr. (Cr.)	(88,400)	(32,200)

P20-13 Data Computers Corp. began operations in 1984. The following summarizes differences between pretax accounting income and taxable income for 1984 and 1985 and the resulting deferred income tax entries:

	1984	1985
Pretax accounting income	$100,000	$120,000
Excess CCA over depreciation	20,000	30,000
Taxable income	$ 80,000	$ 90,000
Income Tax payable (40% rate)	$ 32,000	$ 36,000

Journal entries:				
Income Tax Expense	40,000		48,000	
Income Tax Payable		32,000		36,000
Deferred Income Taxes		8,000		12,000

The tax rate of 40% is expected to continue.

Part A. Assume that the company incurred a tax loss of $200,000 in 1986 without including any of the maximum allowable CCA of $25,000 in its determination. (Because of the loss, management decided that no CCA would be taken in

1986.) The pretax accounting loss was $230,000 because it included $30,000 depreciation expense. Furthermore, the company decided to refile for 1984 and 1985 in order to amend the amount of CCA taken in those years, so that the full amount of the loss could be carried back to those years, and the reduction in the CCA taken for those years would be available in the future. There was reasonable assurance that any timing difference involved would reverse in the future.

Instructions

(a) Give the journal entries for 1986 to account for the loss and the related management actions.

(b) Beginning with the pretax accounting loss, present the remaining portion of the 1986 income statement.

Part B. Assume the same circumstances as Part A except that the company, while claiming the full possible refund of 1984 and 1985 taxes, decided it would not refile to change the CCA claimed in previous years.

Instructions

Give (a) the journal entries for 1986 to account for the loss and related management actions and (b) the partial income statement beginning with the pretax accounting loss, assuming that the portion of the loss not carried back will be carried forward and that:

1. There is virtual certainty of realizing its tax benefits.

2. There is not virtual certainty.

Part C. Assume that the tax loss in 1986 was $300,000 (excluding CCA as stated in Part A). Management decides to obtain a refund of taxes paid in 1984 and 1985 as well as refile in order to amend the CCA taken in those years, so that the full amount of the excess CCA over depreciation is recovered. Any remaining portion of the loss will be carried forward.

Instructions

Give (a) the 1986 journal entries to account for the loss and (b) the partial income statement beginning with the pretax accounting loss, assuming that for any loss carryforward amount there is:

1. Virtual certainty.

2. Not virtual certainty.

21

ACCOUNTING FOR PENSION COSTS

Many business organizations have been concerned with providing for the retirement of employees since the late 1800s. During recent decades a marked increase in this concern has resulted in the establishment of private pension plans in most large companies and in some medium- and small-sized ones.

The substantial growth of these plans, both in numbers of employees covered and in amounts of retirement benefits, has increased the significance of pension cost in relation to the financial position and the results of operations of many companies. Widely divergent practices in accounting for the cost of pension plans have persisted until recent years. The complex array of social concepts, legal considerations, actuarial techniques, income tax regulations, and varying business philosophies that characterize the environment in which pension plans have developed were partly responsible for the accounting profession's tendency to standardize practice in this area.

Generally accepted accounting principles for accounting for pension plans by employers are provided in Section 3460 of the *CICA Handbook*. This section was issued in 1968 following the publication in 1963 of a research study, "Accounting for Costs of Pension Plans" by W. B. Coutts and R. B. Dale-Harris. A second research study, "Accounting for Pension Costs and Liabilities" by T. Ross Archibald, was published by the CICA in 1980. This latter study has emphasized concerns related to accounting practices in this area. These concerns were addressed in an *Exposure Draft*, "Pension Costs and Obligations," issued in January, 1985. As a result, the profession is in the process of evaluating public response to the proposed revisions to *CICA Handbook*, Section 3460, and may either adopt the changes recommended in the *Exposure Draft* or issue a re-exposure draft. The material presented in this chapter deals with the basic issues of pension cost determination and allocation and presents methods of accounting that may or may not be generally accepted if and when Section 3460 is amended.

The Nature of Pension Plans

A **private pension plan** is an arrangement under which a company undertakes to provide its retired employees with benefits (ordinarily, monthly payments) that can be determined or estimated in advance from the provisions of a document or from the company's practices (commonly called a **defined-benefit plan**). Some pension plans are **funded**; that is, the company sets funds aside for future pension benefits by making payments to a funding agency that is responsible for accumulating the assets of the pension fund and for making payments to the recipients as the benefits become due. In an insured plan, the funding agency is an insurance company; in a trust-fund plan, the funding agency is a trustee. The process of making the cash payments to a funding agency is called **funding.** Some plans are **unfunded**; that is, the fund is under the control of the company instead of an independent funding agency. Pension payments to retired employees are made directly by the company as they become due.

Some plans are **contributory**; the employees bear part of the cost of the stated benefits or voluntarily make payments to increase their benefits. Other plans are **noncontributory**, because the employer bears the entire cost. Companies generally design registered pension plans in accordance with federal income tax requirements that permit deductibility of the employees' contributions to the pension fund (within certain limits).

The above-mentioned differences, together with differences in eligibility requirements, specified retirement ages, level of benefits, and disability options, result in an almost infinite variety of plans. In all pension plans, however, the three primary accounting problems are (1) **measuring the amount** of pension obligation resulting from the plan, (2) **allocating the cost** of the plans to the proper accounting periods, and (3) **disclosing the status and effects** of the plan in the financial statements and the accompanying notes. Because the first problem involves complicated actuarial considerations, **actuaries** are engaged to measure the amount of the pension obligation. Actuaries also play a leading role in allocating pension costs to accounting periods.

Employer versus Plan (Fund) Accounting

The subject of pension accounting may be divided and separately treated as **accounting for the employer** and **accounting for the pension fund.** The company or employer is the organization sponsoring the pension plan; the employer incurs the cost and makes contributions to the pension fund. The fund or plan is the entity that receives the contributions from the employer, administers the pension assets, and makes the benefit payments to the pension recipients (retired employees). The diagram below shows the three distinct entities involved in a pension plan and indicates the flow of cash between them.

The need for proper administration of and sound accounting for pension funds becomes apparent when one appreciates the absolute as well as the relative size of these funds. For example, total pension funds in Canada on December 31, 1979, were estimated in excess of $85 billion.[1] On December 31, 1978, Imperial Oil Limited estimated the market value of their pension fund assets at $431 million.

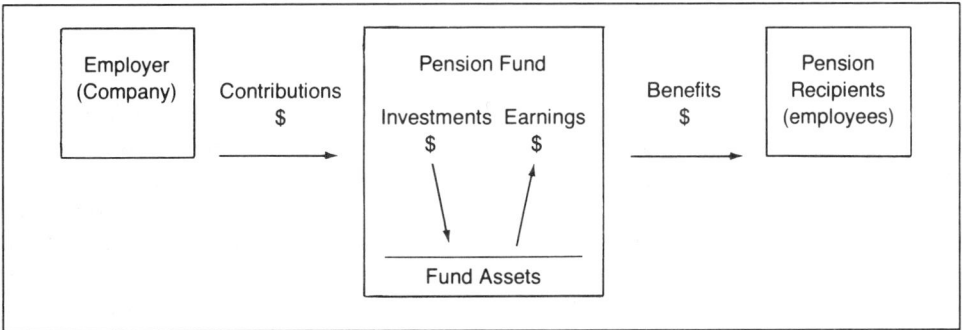

An unfunded pension plan is administered by the employer, while a funded plan is administered by a trustee. In either case, however, the fund should have separate legal and accounting identity for which a set of books is maintained and financial statements are prepared. Maintaining books and records and preparing financial statements for the fund, known as "accounting for employee benefit plans," is not the subject of this chapter. This chapter (with the exception of the last section) is devoted to the pension accounting and reporting problems of the employer as the sponsor of a pension plan.

The company as the employer records pension cost on its books in accordance with management policy within the standards prescribed by Section 3460 of the *CICA Handbook*. Contributions in the form of cash payments are made by the company to the pension fund in accordance with policies established jointly by the company and the trustees of the pension plan as well as the applicable federal or provincial statutes. Measurement of the pension cost and determination of the amount to be funded are separate, independent functions. If the recorded pension expense exceeds the cash contributions to the pension fund, the excess is reported as a pension liability on the company's balance sheet. Correspondingly, if the payments exceed the expense, the excess is reported as a deferred charge.

The pension fund administrator invests the contribution received from the employer, reinvests earnings therefrom, and pays pension benefits to retired employees. At any time the present value of expected future pension payments (the pension liability) may be actuarially computed. This liability represents the amount that the pension fund must equal now (assuming no further contributions by the employer) in order for earnings from the fund and the gradual reductions in the fund itself to exactly cover all expected future payments to present and expected future retirees over their expected lifetimes for employment services rendered to

---

[1]T. Ross Archibald, *Accounting for Pension Costs and Liabilities* (Toronto: CICA, 1980), p. 6.

date. If the pension fund assets equal or exceed the expected pension liability, the plan is **fully funded.**[2]

Pension liability has one meaning in reference to the pension fund and another in reference to the employer company. The expected pension liability of the pension fund is an actuarial concept representing an economic liability under the pension plan for future cash payments to retirees. The pension liability that may appear on company balance sheets represents an accounting credit that results from excess of amounts expensed over amounts contributed to the pension fund; it does not represent the amounts legally owed to the pension fund.

Cash Basis versus Accrual Basis

Until the mid-1960s, with few exceptions, companies applied the **cash basis** of accounting to pension plans by recognizing the amount paid in a particular accounting period for pension benefits as the pension expense for the period. The amount paid or funded in a fiscal period, as emphasized in the preceding example, depends upon financial management and may be discretionary; funding may be based on the availability of cash, the level of earnings, or other factors unrelated to accounting considerations. Application of the cash basis permits the manipulation of the amount of pension cost appearing in the income statement simply by varying the cash paid to the pension fund. Two once-common funding methods, **pay-as-you-go** (recognize pension costs only when benefits are paid directly to the retired employee) and **terminal funding** (recognize pension costs when annuity is purchased or contribution is made to the trust for retired employees), are no longer considered acceptable because they are cash basis oriented and do not recognize pension costs prior to the retirement of employees.

There is now broad agreement that pension cost should be accounted for on the **accrual basis**. Most accountants and an increasing number of business managers recognize that **accounting for pension plans requires measurement of the cost and its identification with the appropriate time periods**, which involves application of accrual, deferral, and estimation concepts in the same manner that they are applied in the measurement and time-period identification of other costs and expenses. The going-concern, matching, and consistency assumptions are all applicable and relevant to pension plan accounting.

Past Service Cost and Current Service Pension Cost

In determining future retirement benefits, many pension plans give employees credit for their years of service prior to adoption of the plan. For example, if on January 1, 1986, a company adopted a pension plan that granted benefits to employees on the basis of their total years of service to the company, an employee who had been employed since January 1, 1976, would already have 10 years of service toward pension credit. Some of the actuarial methods frequently used to determine pension cost compute separately the cost associated with the years prior to the date of adoption (this is called **past service cost)** and the cost associated with

---

[2]As used in this context, the term "funding" refers to the relationship between pension fund assets and the present value of expected future pension benefit payments. This usage contrasts with the use of "funding" to mean the contributions made by the employer to the pension fund. Thus, it is possible, and generally accurate, to say that a company is "fully funding" its accrued pension expense as recorded on the books, and yet state that the pension fund is "underfunded" in an actuarial sense.

the years after the date of adoption or amendment (this is called **current service cost).** The diagram below identifies past service cost and current service cost as they relate to the adoption date of a pension plan.

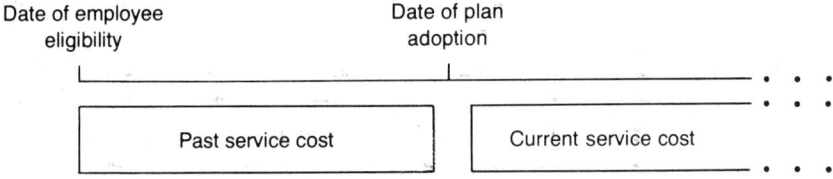

Past service cost arises from the granting of service credits to employees for years of service prior to adoption of a pension plan. The amount of past service cost is an actuarial estimate derived from a complicated actuarial method that takes into consideration such factors as life expectancy of employees, retirement age, employee turnover, future salary levels, interest rates, gains and losses of the fund, administrative costs, and pension benefits.

Current service pension cost is the cost assigned annually for the service credits earned by the employees during a given year. Current service cost also involves a complicated determination based on service credits for the current year with a separate determination made annually because of changes in the number of employees, salaries, and terms of the plan.

If a pension plan is initiated when a company is organized, no past service cost is recognized; only current service pension cost is incurred. Similarly, if no credits are given for service prior to inception of a pension plan, no past service cost arises.

Accountants generally agree that, although past service cost results from consideration given to years of service prior to adoption of the pension plan, this cost is related to periods subsequent to the adoption. Therefore, it should be treated as an expense of the years following adoption of the plan and should not be charged against retained earnings as something applicable to the past.

To illustrate these points, assume that the actuarial firm of Rowe and Satter Co. is hired by Ottawa Ltd. to prepare a report on a proposed pension plan that Ottawa Ltd. is considering. Ottawa Ltd. wishes to determine the past service cost and the current service cost that would be incurred for the typical employee. The following basic assumptions have been made by the actuary:

1. The plan is noncontributory, and plan assets will earn 6% interest.
2. The typical employee will receive at retirement $200 per year for each year employed by Ottawa Ltd.
3. Mortality table—1978 is used.
4. The typical employee is 50 years old, will retire at age 65, and has worked for the company for 10 years.

Ottawa Ltd. indicates that it will give credit for past service prior to adoption of the plan. **To compute the past service cost** the actuary first determines the expected life of the employee subsequent to retirement; the mortality table indicates that it is 13 years. Because the employee has already worked 10 years, the company has a future obligation of $2,000 ($200 X 10) for 13 years. The computation to determine the amount of monies the pension fund must have on hand at the date of this employee's retirement to meet the pension cost attributable to the period of past service is as follows:

(Attributable to 10 Years of Past Service)	
Amount to be paid each period	$ 2,000
Present value of ordinary annuity	
for 13 periods at 6% (Table 6-4)	× _____8.85268_
Amount needed at retirement	$17,705

Because the employee still has 15 years to go until retirement, the amount needed at retirement is discounted as follows:

Amount needed at retirement	$17,705
Present value of $17,705 for	
15 periods at 6% interest (Table 6-2)	× _____.41727_
Past service cost	$ 7,388

The present value of the past service cost pension obligation of $2,000 per year beginning in 15 years and continuing for 13 years is $7,388. The past service cost of $7,388 may be funded immediately or over some period of years that may or may not coincide with the amortization period.

To compute the current service cost, the actuary must determine the cost of the pension plan at the date of the employee's retirement for the service credits earned by the employee subsequent to adoption of the plan. This employee will work for 15 more years before retirement and will be entitled to receive $3,000 ($200 × 15) for each year of expected life subsequent to the age of 65, which in this case is 13 years. The following computation is made to determine the amount that the pension fund must have on hand at the date of the employee's retirement:

(Attributable to 15 Years of Future Service)	
Amount to be paid each period	$ 3,000
Present value of ordinary annuity	
for 13 periods at 6% (Table 6-4)	× _____8.85268_
Amount needed at retirement	$26,558

Assuming that Ottawa Ltd. desires a constant current service cost from year to year, the amount needed at retirement is divided by the amount of an ordinary annuity of 1 for 15 years at 6% to arrive at the current service cost per year, as follows: $1,141 = $26,558 ÷ 23.27597.[3] On the basis of the facts and assumptions given, current service cost each period is $1,141 for Ottawa Ltd. As illustrated later, other patterns for allocating the current service cost to each year may have been employed. This decision usually depends on the preferences of the company as to the earnings and funding patterns it wishes to follow. Moreover, to keep the illustration simple, we used data for one typical employee, whereas in practice pension costs are computed for groups of employees.

---

[3]An alternative computation is to find the amount needed at the date of the adoption of the plan to fund the current service cost. This value then should be divided by the present value of an ordinary annuity to arrive at the current service cost, as indicated below:

$$\$26,558 \times .41727 = \$11,082$$
$$\$11,082 \div 9.71225 = \$1,141$$

Amendments to Pension Plans and Prior Service Cost

Pension plans are frequently amended to increase retirement benefits. A change in benefits requires an actuarial valuation of the plan. Ordinarily, these amendments recognize service prior to the date of the amendment and the years thereafter. The period of service prior to the date of the amendment, or any actuarial valuation of the plan, is labelled the prior service period. Similarly, **prior service cost** refers to the portion of the total pension cost that, under the actuarial cost method in use, is identified with all periods prior to the date of an actuarial valuation of the plan (date of amendment). Therefore, as of the date of its computation, prior service cost includes (1) the past service cost, (2) the current service cost for years prior to that date, and (3) the increased pension cost arising from any amendment and attributable to years prior to that date. **Essentially, prior service cost is computed at any time in the same way that past service cost would be computed if the plan were being put into effect for the first time.** The diagram below identifies the prior service period.

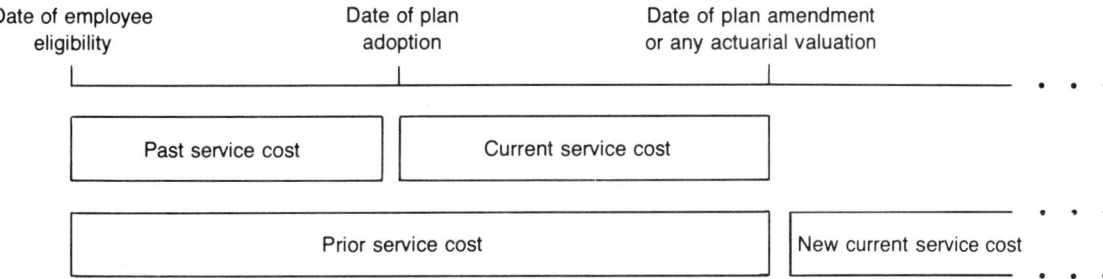

CICA Handbook, Section 3460, makes reference to a **specific part** of prior service cost; that is, any increases or decreases in prior service cost arising as a result of an amendment to the plan. Because this cost is accounted for in a manner similar to that used for past service cost, the term past service cost is used to refer to both types of cost.

One question that arises is whether a liability and a related expense should be reported at the time a plan is initiated or is amended to increase benefits. The profession takes the position that **no liability or expense** should be reported for these benefits at this point, because the employer would not increase benefits retroactively unless it expected to receive benefits in the future. This highly debatable point is one of the major issues confronting the CICA in its deliberations on accounting for pensions.

Actuarial Cost Methods

The major difficulties in estimating pension cost are in selecting the pertinent data relating to the employee group (employee age, years of service, compensation, etc.), designing the actuarial computations, and formulating the assumptions regarding future events (employee turnover and mortality, and pension fund earnings). Having made the necessary assumptions, the actuary would make a valuation using one of several actuarial cost methods to determine the periodic contributions the employer is to make to the pension fund. Recall that in our previous illustration with Ottawa Ltd., we arrived at a current service cost of $1,141 per year. In other words, if $1,141 were invested in the pension fund each year and earned 6%, the amount needed at retirement, $26,558, would be achieved.

Other approaches could be employed to fund this amount. For example, Ottawa Ltd. may wish to fund as a constant percentage of salaries each year. Such a procedure would lead to lower funding earlier and higher funding later as the salaries increased. Conversely, Ottawa Ltd. may wish to develop a funding procedure that maximizes the funding earlier. Although the actuarial methods are used primarily to determine the amounts to be funded, they may also be used to measure periodic pension expense. Two commonly used actuarial methods are:

1. Accrued benefit method.
2. Level contribution method.

Just as different depreciation methods result in different amounts of periodic depreciation expense, so the actuarial valuation methods above produce different amounts of pension expense. The accrued benefit method and its variants involve associating a distinct unit of retirement benefit with each year of credited service. The actuarially determined present value of the retirement benefit accruing as a result of employment service in a specific year is the presumed cost of pension benefits for that year. Variations in the amount of the estimated pension cost may be obtained using (1) actual employee salary and other actuarial factors for each year of service; (2) projected retirement benefits prorated over the employee's service life on a basis of salaries earned and projected; or (3) projected retirement benefits prorated over the years of service.

The level contribution methods assign the same dollar amount or an equal percentage of compensation to pension cost for each year of service. An employer's total pension cost will depend on (1) whether the calculation is made by summing the respective amounts determined for each employee (individual level cost method) or by computing the cost using aggregate data for the group of employees (aggregate level cost method); and (2) whether past service costs are included or excluded in making the calculation.

All of these actuarial cost methods are considered acceptable to provide pension costs consistent with the objectives of accrual accounting. The actuarial cost method chosen for accounting purposes does not have to be the same as the method used to fund the pension plan. The selection of the funding pattern is based on a number of considerations. For example, some companies employ shorter periods to fund in order to maximize tax deductions and build funds for increased future benefits. Others choose a longer period to fund in order to retain working capital. Where funding and pension expense are the same, companies that fund over a shorter period of time sometimes receive criticism from labour because lower pension expense is reported later in the plan. Acceptable accounting merely requires that the method be rational and systematic, be applied consistently, and result in a reasonable measure of pension cost from year to year.

Although the technical aspects of pension cost determination require the skill, experience, and judgement of an actuary, accountants must be familiar enough with actuarial methods and concepts to reach their own conclusions about the reasonableness of the estimated provision.

Accumulated Plan Benefits and Vesting

Accumulated plan benefits are those future benefit payments that are attributable under the plan's provision to employees' service to date. These **benefits** are expected to be paid to (1) retired or terminated employees or their beneficiaries, (2) beneficiaries of deceased employees, and (3) present employees or their beneficiaries. Accumulated plan benefits may be divided in terms of vested and unvested benefits. **Vested benefits** are earned pension benefits that are not contingent upon the employee's continuing in the service of the employer. Thus, to the extent that benefits vest, a present employee is entitled at some specified future date (normally retirement age) to benefits earned, even if the employee leaves the company before retirement. If payments for benefits already earned are contingent on staying with the same employer until retirement, the plan is "nonvesting." As long as prior service costs are being funded, vested benefits need not be accrued and recorded.

Interest Equivalents

A pension fund is established and maintained for the purpose of accumulating the amounts necessary to pay retirement benefits as they come due. The primary source of pension funds is, of course, the periodic contributions of the employer. Another source of funds assumed in actuarially determining the amount of the employer's contributions and expense is the **earnings** on pension fund assets. If the employer does not fund or underfunds the pension plan, earnings do not materialize in the amount actuarially assumed or necessary to meet the expected benefit payments. Therefore, when the amounts of the actuarially determined pension expense vary from the amounts funded, the annual accounting pension provision should be adjusted by "an amount equivalent to interest" on the accumulated difference. The annual pension expense is **increased** by an amount equivalent to interest on prior years' expense provisions not funded, or it is **decreased** by an amount equivalent to interest on prior years' funding in excess of expense provisions.

ACCOUNTING FOR PENSION COSTS

The amount of pension expense recognized during a particular accounting period depends on the factors listed below.

1. **The amount of past or prior service cost**. The amount of past or prior service cost is determined by an actuary and represents the present value of the future obligations resulting from the cost of credits for employee services rendered prior to the adoption or amendment of the pension plan.
2. **The funding or nonfunding of past or prior service cost**. The funding or nonfunding of the past or prior service cost is a financial decision of the employer. An amount equivalent to interest on the amount of any unfunded cost may be considered a part of the annual pension expense.
3. **The periods over which past or prior service cost is amortized**. The amortization of past or prior service cost is also the decision of the employer. Acceptable amortization periods vary from no amortization to the expected remaining service life of the employee group covered by the plan.
4. **The amount of current service cost.** This is determined by an actuary on the basis of employee service credits for the current year.
5. **The interest rate appropriate to the pension fund**. The interest rate determined by the actuary to be appropriate to the pension fund operation affects all computations of pension cost. Interest is an integral part of pension cost because time and annuity factors are inherent in pension concepts.

6. **The amounts funded annually**. These frequently reflect a financial decision of the employer and need not parallel the amounts expensed annually. Interest equivalents on the difference between the amounts expensed and the amounts funded can increase or decrease the periodic pension expense.

7. **The amount of vested benefits**. Pension expenses must include a provision for vested benefits only if the present value of vested past service benefits exceeds the cumulative amount of past service costs amortized.

Each of the foregoing factors must be considered and resolved before an accounting entry may be recorded to recognize annual pension cost.

To illustrate the accounting entries that result from different circumstances, assume that on January 1, 1986, the Odom Corporation, in business since 1970, adopts a funded pension plan for the benefit of its employees. The plan is noncontributory and provides for vesting after 15 years of service by each eligible employee. An insurance company is engaged as the trustee for the pension fund. An actuarial consulting firm recommends a 5% interest rate as appropriate and, applying an acceptable actuarial method, determines that the past service cost at the date of adoption (January 1, 1986) is $240,000 and that the current service cost for the year 1986 is $50,000, which is to be funded fully each year.

The management of Odom Corporation must now formulate an **amortization** policy and a **funding** policy for past service cost.

Case A—Amortization and Funding Periods the Same   Management decides to amortize and fund the past service cost of $240,000 over 15 years; equal payments are to be made to the pension fund trustee at the end of each year. The annual amortization of past service cost and the annual payment to the pension fund trustee are identical and are computed as follows:

$$\$240,000 \div \frac{\text{PV of an ordinary annuity}}{\text{of 1 for 15 periods at 5\%}} = \frac{\text{Periodic amortization}}{\text{and funding payment}}$$

$$\$240,000 \div 10.37966 \text{ (Table 6-4)} = \$23,122$$

Notice that in this illustration the sum of the past service pension cost for the 15-year amortization period will be $346,830 ($23,122 × 15). This amount exceeds the present value of the past service cost at January 1, 1987, by $106,830 ($346,830 − $240,000). The $106,830 amount represents an "interest equivalent" on the amount unfunded throughout the 15-year amortization period. Thus, the annual past service pension cost is made up of two components: (1) amortization of the present value of past service costs and (2) an interest equivalent on the unfunded balance. The method used to allocate past service cost in this example results in an equal amount ($23,122) being assigned to each fiscal year. Other methods of allocation would produce a different annual amount of past service expense for each of the fiscal periods in the amortization period. For example, amortizing the $240,000 on a straight-line basis over 15 years and adding an interest equivalent based on the annual outstanding balance of the unfunded portion would result in a past service pension expense of $28,000 for 1987 [($240,000 ÷ 15) + ($240,000 × .05)]. Since the interest equivalent would be based on the unfunded balance which declines annually, the total annual past service pension expense would gradually decrease in amount over the 15-year amortization term.

Alternatively, by using compound interest methods of amortizing past service pension cost, the annual pension expense may be determined as a constant, or very nearly constant, amount over the amortization period. This method is preferred by some accountants and will be used in the remaining illustrations in this chapter.

The entry on December 31, 1986, to recognize the annual pension expense and to record the Odom Corporation contributions to the pension fund trustee would appear as follows:

Pension Expense (current service cost)	50,000	
Pension Expense (past service cost)	23,122	
Cash		73,122

(Current service and past service costs are recorded separately merely for illustration purposes. These two amounts are generally combined and recorded in one pension expense account.)

The following schedule (first three years only) shows the relationship of the past service cost amortization and funding policies to the amount charged annually to pension expense.

Odom Corporation—Case A
SCHEDULE OF AMORTIZATION AND FUNDING OF PAST SERVICE COST

	Amortization—15 years			Funding 15 Years	Balance Sheet Deferred Expense/Liability	
Year	15-Year Annual Amount	Interest Reduction/ Addition	Pension Expense Debit	Cash Credit	Debit/ (Credit)	Dec. 31 Balance
	(a)	(b)	(c)	(d)	(e)	(f)
1986	$23,122	–0–	$23,122	$23,122	–0–	–0–
1987	23,122	–0–	23,122	23,122	–0–	–0–
1988	23,122	–0–	23,122	23,122	–0–	–0–

(a) $240,000 ÷ 10.37966.
(b) 5% of the preceding balance of (f).
(c) (a) plus (or minus) (b).
(d) $240,000 ÷ 10.37966.
(e) (d) minus (c).
(f) Preceding balance plus (or minus) (e).

Because the current provisions for pension expense, current service cost, and past service cost are fully funded each year, the balance sheet would contain neither a debit for deferred pension cost nor a credit for pension liability. At the end of 15 years when the past service cost is fully amortized and funded, only the current service pension cost would be expensed and funded each year.

It should be noted that it is difficult to understand what is being amortized because the principal amount to be amortized is **unrecorded.** Generally, amortization involves the write-off of an amount that has been recorded on the books as a debit or credit. The past or prior service cost that is amortized may be likened to an unrecorded deferred charge. In fact, if all past service costs were funded at the initiation of the pension plan, they might be recorded as a deferred charge, and the amortization could then be related to the write-off of the unamortized amount which would appear on the balance sheet.

Case B—Amortization Period Longer Than Funding Period Management decides to amortize past service cost of $240,000 over 15 years and to fund this cost by making equal payments at the end of each of the first ten years. The annual amortization and funding payments are computed as follows:

Amortization:

$$\$240,000 \div \frac{\text{PV of an ordinary annuity}}{\text{of 1 for 15 periods at 5\%}} = \text{Periodic amortization}$$

$$\$240,000 \div 10.37966 \text{ (Table 6-4)} = \$23,122$$

Funding:

$$\$240,000 \div \frac{\text{PV of an ordinary annuity}}{\text{of 1 of 10 periods at 5\%}} = \text{Periodic funding payment}$$

$$\$240,000 \div 7.72173 \text{ (Table 6-4)} = \$31,081$$

The following schedule shows the results from funding past service cost over a shorter period than the period of amortizing that cost. A deferred charge accumulates during the first 10 years and is depleted during the next 5 years. Also, the periodic amortization is reduced by the interest on the cumulative amount funded in excess of the amounts amortized.

Odom Corporation—Case B
SCHEDULE OF AMORTIZATION AND FUNDING OF PAST SERVICE COST

Year	Amortization—15 Years			Funding 10 Years	Balance Sheet Deferred Charge	
	15-Year Annual Amount	Interest Reduction	Pension Expense Debit	Cash Credit	Debit/ (Credit)	Dec. 31 Balance
	(a)	(b)	(c)	(d)	(e)	(f)
1986	$23,122	–0–	$ 23,122	$ 31,081	$ 7,959	$ 7,959
1987	23,122	$ 398	22,724	31,081	8,357	16,316
1988	23,122	816	22,306	31,081	8,775	25,091
1989	23,122	1,255	21,867	31,081	9,214	34,305
1990	23,122	1,715	21,407	31,081	9,674	43,979
1991	23,122	2,199	20,923	31,081	10,158	54,137
1992	23,122	2,707	20,415	31,081	10,666	64,803
1993	23,122	3,240	19,882	31,081	11,199	76,002
1994	23,122	3,800	19,322	31,081	11,759	87,761
1995	23,122	4,388	18,734	31,081	12,347	100,108
1996	23,122	5,005	18,117	–0–	(18,117)	81,991
1997	23,122	4,100	19,022	–0–	(19,022)	62,969
1998	23,122	3,148	19,974	–0–	(19,974)	42,995
1999	23,122	2,150	29,972	–0–	(20,972)	22,023
2000	23,122	1,099*	22,023	–0–	(22,023)	–0–
2001	–0–	–0–	–0–	–0–	–0–	–0–
			$310,810	$310,810		

*Adjusted for $2 discrepancy owing to rounding of computations.
(a) $240,000 ÷ 10.37966.
(b) 5% of the preceding balance of (f).
(c) (a) minus (b).
(d) $240,000 ÷ 7.72173.
(e) (d) minus (c).
(f) Preceding balance plus (e).

Using data from the schedule on page 990, the entries to recognize the annual pension expense (current service cost assumed to be $50,000 for all years, although it generally changes from year to year in actual practice) and to record Odom Corporation's annual contribution to the pension fund trustee would appear as follows for 1986, 1997, and 2001:

December 31, 1986

Pension Expense (current service cost)	50,000	
Pension Expense (past service cost)	23,122	
Deferred Pension Expense	7,959	
Cash ($50,000 + $31,081)		81,081

December 31, 1997

Pension Expense (current service cost)	50,000	
Pension Expense (past service cost)	19,022	
Deferred Pension Expense		19,022
Cash		50,000

December 31, 2001

Pension Expense (current service cost)	50,000	
Cash		50,000

Case C—Amortization Period Shorter Than Funding Period   Management decides to amortize past service cost of $240,000 over 15 years and to fund past service cost by making equal payments at the end of each of the first 20 years. The annual amortization and funding payments are computed as follows:

Amortization = $240,000 ÷ 10.37966 = $23,122
Funding   = $240,000 ÷ 12.46221 = $19,258

The schedule on page 992 shows the results from funding past service cost over a longer period than the period of amortizing that cost. A liability for the excess of the annual pension cost over the amount funded accumulates during the first 15 years and is eliminated during the next five years. Moreover, the periodic amortization is increased by the interest on the cumulative amount amortized in excess of the amounts funded.

Using data from the same schedule, the entries to recognize the annual pension expense (current service cost assumed to be $50,000 for all years) and to record Odom Corporation's annual contribution to the pension fund trustee would appear as follows for 1986, 2000, and 2006:

December 31, 1986

Pension Expense (current service cost)	50,000	
Pension Expense (past service cost)	23,122	
Liability for Pension Expense Not Funded		3,864
Cash		69,258

December 31, 2000

Pension Expense (current service cost)	50,000	
Pension Expense (past service cost)	26,907	
Liability for Pension Expense Not Funded		7,649
Cash		69,258

Odom Corporation—Case C
SCHEDULE OF AMORTIZATION AND FUNDING OF PAST SERVICE COST

	Amortization—15 Years			Funding 20 Years	Dec. 31 Balance Sheet Pension Liability	
Year	15-Year Annual Amount	Addition Due to Interest	Pension Expense Debit	Cash Credit	(Debit)/ Credit	Credit Balance
	(a)	(b)	(c)	(d)	(e)	(f)
1986	$23,122	–0–	$ 23,122	$ 19,258	$ 3,864	$ 3,864
1987	23,122	$ 193	23,315	19,258	4,057	7,921
1988	23,122	396	23,518	19,258	4,260	12,181
2000	23,122	3,785	26,907	19,258	7,649	83,346
2001	–0–	4,167	4,167	19,258	(15,091)	68,255
2005	–0–	915	915	19,258	(18,343)	–0–
2006	–0–	–0–	–0–	–0–	–0–	–0–
			$385,160	$385,160		

(a) $240,000 ÷ 10.37966.
(b) 5% of the preceding balance of (f).
(c) (a) plus (b).

(d) $240,000 ÷ 12.46221.
(e) (c) minus (d).
(f) Preceding balance plus (e).

December 31, 2001

Pension Expense (current service cost)	50,000	
Pension Expense (past service cost)	4,167	
Liability for Pension Expense Not Funded	15,091	
Cash		69,258

December 31, 2006

Pension Expense (current service cost)	50,000	
Cash		50,000

As indicated in the foregoing illustrations, the typical elements of periodic pension expense are (1) current service cost, (2) an amortized amount of past service cost, and (3) an amount equivalent to interest on the difference between amounts recorded for accounting purposes and the amounts funded.

The amortization and funding schedules above were presented to illustrate the effect on the annual expense provisions of differences in the amounts funded and the amounts amortized for past service cost. These differences occur in practice and are justifiable because the amortization or write-off of the past or prior service cost depends on the funding of that same amount, just as the depreciation of an asset is separate from the retirement of the liability incurred when the asset was acquired.

The preceding schedules are unrealistic in that the "real world" pension situation seldom remains so constant and unaltered for such long periods of time. It is not uncommon for pension plans to be amended as frequently as every three years. Therefore, computations for pension expense are made on a year-to-year basis and depend upon the amounts funded and accrued in the previous year.

Two Views of Pension Cost

Adoption of the accrual basis of accounting does not resolve a major controversy that exists relating to pension plan accounting. The question that still must be resolved is: What cost must be accounted for? And that question begs the question: What is the nature of pension cost? Two opposing views of the nature of pension cost exist among accountants.

Some accountants argue that pension cost is related to **the plan or the continuing employee group as a whole.** They believe that it is necessary to make specific expense charges for prior service cost if all future benefits payments can be met by annual provisions representing current service cost plus an amount equivalent to interest[4] on the unfunded prior service cost. The justification given for this treatment is that actuarial assumptions are a function of the mass of employees moving through the pension plan over the years and are not based on particular people at a particular time. In addition, they claim that an employer obtains diverse advantages of indefinite duration as a result of granting past service credits under a pension plan. The past service cost is, therefore, an intangible that does not diminish in value and thus does not need to be amortized.[5]

Other accountants believe that the annual expense of a pension plan is related to **the cost of specific pension benefits payable in the future to specific persons.** Proponents of this view advocate recognition of the past service cost over a period related to the remaining years of service of the employee group that is to receive credit for working years before adoption of the plan. Their argument is supported by the fact that past service cost is part of the cost of providing pensions for the employees initially covered. And although it may be true that the future periods benefited by the past service element of the plan are indefinite in length, by far the greatest part of the benefit is related to the service lives of the employees who will receive pensions measured in part by past service. Therefore, past service cost should be charged to expense over the remaining service lives of such employees.[6]

Experience (Actuarial) Gains or Losses

As discussed earlier, actuaries deal with several uncertainties in estimating the cost of a pension plan. In tentatively resolving these uncertainties, actuaries make assumptions. For example, assumptions usually have to be made about such items as the interest rate, mortality rate, retirement rate, turnover rate, disability rate, and salary amounts. Seldom does actual experience coincide with estimated results. Consequently, **adjustments may need to be made to reflect (1) deviations between estimated conditions and actual experience, and (2) revisions in the underlying assumptions.** These adjustments are referred to as ''actuarial revaluations'' in Section 3460 of the *CICA Handbook*. If the experience is favourable (actual earnings rate exceeds assumed earnings rate) or if the new assumptions are more optimistic, the adjustments that result are gains; if experience has been unfavourable (actual salary rates of employees higher than assumed salary rates) or if the new

---

[4]Such interest is necessary to keep the unfunded cost from growing; that is, to maintain the original size of unfunded past service cost stated at present value relative to the future benefits applicable to that past period.

[5]Ernest L. Hicks, ''Accounting for the Cost of Pension Plans,'' *Accounting Research Study No. 8* (New York: AICPA, 1965), pp. 345.

[6]*Ibid.*

assumptions are less optimistic, the adjustments are losses. The net effect of the gains and losses determined in a particular valuation is ordinarily dealt with as a single amount.

Once the gains and losses have been identified and measured, the problem becomes one of timing their recognition in providing for pension expense: the familiar problem of allocating gains and losses to accounting periods.

These items may be either charged to expense as part of current service cost of the current period or amortized over an appropriate period. The term representing an appropriate period varies from the period expected to elapse before the next revaluation and the remaining service life of the present employee group.

Plan Cancellation or Termination

On rare occasions firms may cancel a pension plan and replace it with an entirely new one. In these cases the gains or losses that arise are considered similar to those that result from deviations of actual earnings from actuarial estimates. Therefore, gains or losses arising from plan cancellation should be treated the same as experienced gains or losses and amortized over an appropriate period.

A plan termination occurs when the pension plan and the employee group are both terminated. That is, all employees previously covered by a plan are no longer employees of the firm, and the plan is terminated. The problem of accounting for gains or losses arising from the termination of a plan has not been resolved by the profession, and considerable judgement would have to be exercised in assessing the proper accounting methods.

Disclosure of Pensions in Financial Statements

Within the Financial Statements   The existence of a pension plan may result in recording not only an annual provision for pension expense, which is charged against revenue appearing on the income statement, but also accrued or deferred pension costs that are reported in the body of the balance sheet. As already indicated, if the amount paid (credit to Cash) by the employer to the pension trust is less than the annual provision (debit to Pension Expense), a credit balance accrual in the amount of the difference arises. This accrued pension cost usually appears in the long-term liability section and might be described as Liability for Pension Expense Not Funded, Provisions for Pension Cost in Excess of Payments, or Pension Costs Charged to Expense But Not Funded, or Due to Pension Fund. Classification as a current liability occurs when the liability requires the disbursement of cash within the next year.

If the cash paid (amount funded) to the pension trust during the period is greater than the amount charged to expense, a deferred charge equal to the difference arises. This deferral should be reported as Prepaid Pension Expense in the current asset section **if it is current in nature,** and as Deferred Pension Expense in the other asset section **if it is long-term in nature.**

Vested unfunded past service benefits present a special problem to employers. The present value of vested unfunded past service benefits, to the extent not previously charged to operations, should be recognized as a deferred charge offset by a liability. The liability account will be reduced by future funding payments, and the deferred charge is to be amortized to pension expense.

Note Disclosure Because company pension plans are frequently important to an understanding of financial position and the results of operations, the following information, if not disclosed in the body of the financial statements, should be disclosed in notes.[7]

1. The amount of past service costs remaining to be charged to operations and the rate at which such costs are being amortized.
2. Any change made in the method of accounting for pension costs.
3. The effect of any new plan or significant changes in an existing plan.

In addition to the above items, a recent research study recommends the following items be disclosed.[8]

1. The amount of unfunded past service costs.
2. When a firm administers its own pension fund, the balance sheet of the fund indicating the actuarial methods used and the valuation bases used for valuation of the fund assets.
3. Such key actuarial assumptions as mortality, turnover, retirement age, salary growth, and interest.

Past and Prior Service—Financial Statement Presentation

One question that arises is whether a liability should be reported on the balance sheet for unfunded past service cost. The CICA took the position that unfunded past service cost is not a liability that should be reported on the balance sheet, because the liability will be created in the future as the employee performs service.

  Others contend that an obligation to pay these costs arises immediately and, therefore, the balance sheet should report a liability with a related debit to a deferred charge account. This argument has gained support recently because, in most Canadian jurisdictions, firms are required to fund past service cost over a period not to exceed 15 years.

KEY POINTS

1. Private pension plans are arrangements in which companies undertake to provide retired employees with monthly benefits.
2. In funded pension plans the company sets funds aside for future pension benefits by making deposits with a funding agency that assumes responsibility for making pension benefit payments.
3. A company may choose to administer its own pension fund, in which case the plan is called an "unfunded" plan.
4. Accounting for the employer's pension costs involves (1) computing the amount, and (2) allocating it to the proper accounting periods.
5. The amount of pension cost is the present value of the estimated future benefits computed by using various actuarial assumptions and methods.
6. Under the accrued benefit method, a unit of retirement benefit is considered to be earned with each year of credited service. The cost of this unit of benefit is attributed to the service year in which it is earned.

---

[7]*CICA Handbook*, Section 3460, pars. 27 to 29.
[8]Archibald, *op. cit.*, p. 205.

7. The level contribution method uses an average of the estimated annual pension cost for each year. This results in a uniform annual pension cost over the service life of each employee or the employee group.

8. If the cost of pension benefits is not fully funded, an "interest equivalent" is added to the periodic pension cost to compensate for the earnings forgone on the unfunded amount.

9. Past service pension cost is the cost attributed to credited service rendered prior to the employer's adoption of the plan. Benefits for past service are granted to employees in the anticipation of future benefit to the employer; consequently, past service costs are amortized over a reasonable period subsequent to the adoption of the plan.

10. Prior service cost is the cost associated with deviations between the actuary's estimate of fund performance and actual fund earnings (experience) and amounts attributed to revisions in actuarial estimates.

11. Current service cost is the cost attributed to employee benefits earned during the current fiscal year.

12. The total annual pension cost is the sum of (1) amortization of past service cost, (2) amortization of prior service cost, (3) current service cost, and (4) an interest equivalent on unfunded or overfunded amounts.

13. Some accountants believe that pension costs should be derived from calculations using the employee group as a whole, while others argue that the annual pension cost is best determined by summing the pension cost determined for each employee in the group.

14. When a pension plan is cancelled and another plan is substituted for the original, any resulting cost adjustments should be amortized over a reasonable period.

QUESTIONS

1. Define a private pension plan. Differentiate between a funded and an unfunded pension plan. How does a contributory pension plan differ from a noncontributory plan?

2. Differentiate between "accounting for the employer" and "accounting for the pension fund."

3. Explain the term "funded" as it relates to (a) the pension fund and (b) the employer. Explain the meaning of "pension liability" as it relates to (c) the pension fund and (d) the employer.

4. Explain how cash basis accounting for pension plans differs from accrual basis accounting for pension plans.

5. Why is cash basis accounting generally considered unacceptable for pension plan accounting?

6. Why might a company select a shorter period to fund its pension plan?

7. Distinguish among (a) current service cost, (b) past service cost, and (c) prior service cost as they relate to pension plans.

8. A partial note to the financial statement of the Dryer Soap Company discloses the existence of the company's employee pension plan:

   Pension Plan. The company has a pension plan covering all employees. Total pension expense for the year was $528,400, which includes current service cost, and the amortization of past service cost, which originally totalled $1,400,000 (unamortized balance at year end being $1,033,826), over a 20-year period at 6%.

The company's policy is to fund the pension cost accrued with the trustee of the pension plan.

    (a)   What is meant by "past service cost"?

    (b)   Of the total annual pension expense, what amount is current service cost?

    (c)   What amount was paid to the pension fund trustee during the year?

    (d)   On the basis of the note above, what amounts appear in the body of the balance sheet relative to the pension plan?

  9.   What are accumulated plan benefits? What are "vested benefits" and under what circumstances must they be accrued?

10.   Upon what factors does the amount of pension expense recognized during a particular accounting period depend?

11.   What is the nature of "interest equivalents" and what is the justification for including them in the determination of pension cost?

12.   If accounting charges for past service costs exceed funding payments, what kind of account arises and how should it be reported in the financial statements? If the reverse occurs (payments exceed charges) what kind of account arises and how should it be reported?

13.   What are actuarial gains and losses as related to pension plans? What methods are applied in practice to account for actuarial gains or losses?

14.   In what situations should actuarial gains and losses be recognized immediately?

15.   What disclosures should be made in financial statements or their related notes for pension plans?

16.   (a)   What are the arguments in favour of accruing past service cost only to the extent funded?

       (b)   What are the arguments in favour of accruing past service cost regardless of the amount funded?

17.   What is a multiemployer plan and what accounting questions arise when a company is involved with one of these plans?

18.   One of the most controversial issues related to pension plan reporting is how to account for unfunded accumulated benefits arising from plan initiation and plan amendments that give retroactive benefit increases. What is accounting practice in this area? What other approach is advocated?

19.   What problems do interest rates and future salaries create in accounting for pension plans? Why are interest rates of such importance in accounting for pension plans?

CASES

C21-1   The following items frequently appear on financial statements.

  1.   Under the caption Deferred Charges:
Deferred Pension Cost (attributable to Funding of Past Service Liability).

  2.   Under the caption Retained Earnings Appropriation:
Reserve for Past Service Pension Cost (after deducting the related anticipated tax reduction).

  3.   On the Income Statement:
Current Service Cost.
Past Service Cost.
Trustee's Fees.

Instructions

With regard to "accounting for pension cost," explain the significance of each of the items above on corporate financial statements. Show how each is consistent with generally accepted accounting principles. (Note: All items set forth above are not necessarily to be found on the statements of a single company.)

(AICPA adapted)

C21-2 In examining the costs of pension plans, a CA encounters certain terms. The elements of pension costs that the terms represent must be dealt with appropriately if generally accepted accounting principles are to be reflected in the financial statements of entities with pension plans.

Instructions

(a) 1. Discuss the theoretical justification for accrual recognition of pension costs.

2. Discuss the relative objectivity of the measurement process of accrual versus cash (pay-as-you-go) accounting for annual pension costs.

(b) Explain the following terms as they apply to accounting for pension plans:

1. Actuarial valuations.
2. Actuarial cost methods.
3. Vested benefits.

(c) What information should be disclosed about a company's pension plans in its financial statements and its notes?

(AICPA adapted)

C21-3 Lahey Inc. has just acquired all of the capital stock of Golf Cart Corporation and has asked you to audit the balance sheet of the latter as of the date of acquisition. In the course of your examination you determine that the company has a noncontributory pension plan and has charged to income all payments made to the pension trust. There is no special provision in the pension plan that limits the company liability to an amount equal to assets in trust. The independent actuaries employed by the company have furnished you with the following summary of past service liability as of the audit date.

	Accrued Liability	Assets in Trust	Net Liability
For employees already retired	$1,307,900	$467,500	$ 840,400
For employees eligible to retire at their own option	524,700		524,700
For employees under retirement age	1,725,900		1,725,900
	$3,558,500	$467,500	$3,091,000

Instructions

Discuss the factors to be considered in making adjustments to set forth properly the financial position disclosed by the statements under audit. Lahey Inc. is in the 48% tax bracket.

(AICPA adapted)

C21-4 Sigma Oopsalon, Inc. was organized in 1966 and established a formal pension plan on January 1, 1982, to provide retirement benefits for all employees. The plan is noncontributory and is funded through a trustee, the Corner National Bank, which invests all funds and pays all benefits as they become due. Vesting occurs when the employee retires at age 65. Original past service cost of $220,000 is being amortized over 15 years and funded over 10 years. The company also funds an amount equal to current service cost net of actuarial gains and losses. There have been no amendments to the plan since its inception. Portions of the independent actuary's report follow:

Sigma Oopsalon, Inc.
BASIC NONCONTRIBUTORY PENSION PLAN
Actuarial Report as of June 30, 1986

I. Current Year's Funding and Pension Cost

Current service cost (before adjustment for actuarial gains) computed under the individual level cost method (with liability)		$ 68,300
Actuarial gains:		
Investment gains (losses):		
Excess of expected dividend revenue over actual dividend revenue		(700)
Gain on sale of investments		8,100
Gains in actuarial assumptions for:		
Mortality		6,800
Employee turnover		10,100
Reduction in pension cost from closing of plant		16,000
Net actuarial gains		40,300
Current service cost (funded currently)	$28,000	28,000
Past service costs:		
Funding	28,490	
Amortization		21,194
Total funded	$56,490	
Total pension cost for financial statement purposes		$ 49,194

II. Fund Assets (all available for benefits)

Cash		$ 8,400
Dividends receivable		3,050
Investment in common stocks, at cost (market value, $355,600)		325,500
		$ 336,950

III. Actuarial Liabilities (nonvested as of June 30, 1986)

Number of employees	92
Number of employees retired	–0–
Yearly earnings of employees	$1,196,000
Actuarial liability (present value of accumulated plan benefits)	$ 290,000

Instructions

(a) What interest rate is being used in the amortization and funding of the past service cost?

(b) On the basis of requirements for accounting for the cost of pension plans, evaluate the (1) treatment of actuarial gains and losses and (2) computation of pension cost for financial statement purposes. (Ignore income tax considerations.)

(c) Independent of your answer to (a), assume that the total amount to be funded is $65,326, the total pension cost for financial statement purposes is $58,030, and all amounts presented in the actuary's report are correct. In accordance with professional pronouncements, what type of information would be presented in the note to the financial statements of Sigma Oopsalon, Inc., for the year ended June 30, 1986?

(AICPA adapted)

EXERCISES

E21-1 On January 1, 1985, Taco Still Company adopts an employee pension plan. The following data relate to the operation of the plan for the year 1985:

1. Current service pension cost was actuarially computed to be $84,000 for 1985 and $89,000 for 1986 and is being funded annually.
2. The past service cost of $360,000 is to be amortized over 10 years.
3. It is estimated that investments of the pension fund will earn 10%.
4. The past service cost is being funded over 15 years with end-of-year payments.

Instructions

(Round to the nearest dollar.)

(a) Prepare the journal entry to record the payment to the pension trust and the provision for pension cost for 1985.

(b) Assuming that the same facts exist in 1986, prepare the journal entry to record the payment to the pension trust and the provision for pension cost for 1986.

E21-2 On January 2, 1986, Refrigfry Corp. adopted a pension plan covering all its employees. The plan's actuary estimated past service costs at $300,000. Refrigfry funds the entire amount of past service cost plus interest at the end of the first year of the plan, and each year funds current service costs in full at the end of the year. For accounting purposes, Refrigfry has chosen to record as annual pension expense 10% of past service cost, plus current service cost, plus (or minus) interest on any differences between amounts expensed and amounts funded. Current service cost is as follows: 1986, $60,000; 1987, $60,000; 1988, $70,000; and 1989, $80,000. The actuary recommends the use of a 9% rate for discounting.

Instructions

(Round to the nearest dollar.)

(a) Prepare the journal entry to record the pension expense and the amount funded in 1986.

(b) Prepare the journal entry to record the pension expense and the amount funded in 1989.

E21-3 On January 1, 1986, Mustafa Co. adopted a noncontributory pension plan. An actuary determined that the past service cost at the date of adoption was $650,000, and that the current service pension cost is $200,000. The actuary also indicated that the appropriate interest rate was 8%.

Management plans to fund the current service cost fully each year, and to fund the past service cost by making equal payments at the end of each of the first five years. The past service cost is to be amortized over 20 years.

Instructions

Prepare the journal entries to recognize the annual pension expense and to record the annual contribution to the pension fund for the years 1986, 1987, and 1988. (Round to the nearest dollar.)

E21-4 Gooie Bakeries, Inc. adopted a pension plan for its employees on January 1, 1985. The pertinent data relative to the cost of the plan are as follows:

1. Cost allocated to past service, $700,000.
2. Period of past service cost amortization, 20 years.
3. Current service cost, $75,000.
4. Amount funded annually, $100,000.
5. Rate of earnings on pension fund investments, 8%.

Instructions

(Round to the nearest dollar.)

(a) Prepare a five-year schedule that discloses for each year, beginning with the year of adoption, the amounts of (1) current service cost, (2) amortized past service cost, (3) interest equivalent on difference between prior years' provisions and amounts funded, (4) total annual charge to expense, (5) amount funded, and (6) cumulative difference between provisions and amounts funded.

(b) Using the data from (a), prepare the journal entry to record the amount funded in the fifth year and the provision for pension expense.

E21-5 As a result of labour negotiations, Camel Fur Co. adopts a pension plan for its employees. An actuarial firm estimates past service cost at $400,000 and current service cost for the first year of $50,000. Camel Fur Co. will amortize the past service cost at the rate of 10% per year and fund it over 20 years with end-of-the-year payments. Only half of each year's current service cost will be funded during the first three years.

Instructions

(Round to the nearest dollar.)

(a) Prepare the journal entry to record the pension provision and the amount funded during the first year.

(b) Prepare the journal entry to record the pension provision and the amount funded during the third year. Current service cost is $60,000 in the second year and $80,000 in the third year.

(c) What is reported on Camel Fur's balance sheet at the end of the third year?

E21-6 Cimple Energy Corp. adopts a pension plan on January 1, 1986. The following information relates to the operation of the plan for 1986 and 1987:

1. Current service pension cost was actuarially computed to be $44,000 for both years and is to be funded annually.

2. The past service cost of $270,000 is to be funded by making equal payments at the end of each of the first 20 years, and is to be amortized over 10 years.

3. It is estimated that investments of the pension fund will earn a 12% return.

Instructions

Compute the amount of pension expense recognized for the years 1986 and 1987. (Round to the nearest dollar.)

E21-7 Gunsmoke Chemicals, Inc. fully funds the current service portion of its pension expense. When the company started its pension plan early in 1986, it adopted a 16-year amortization period and a 20-year funding period for the past service cost of $350,000. The data below relate to the pension plan for 1986–88.

	1986	1987	1988
Current service cost	$100,000	$103,900	$110,100
Past service cost:			
Amortization on 16-year basis	30,037	30,037	30,037
Interest at 4% on accrued pension liability	–0–	171	349
Annual year-end payments to pension fund	25,754	25,754	25,754

Instructions

(Round to the nearest dollar.)

(a) Prepare the journal entries to recognize the annual pension expense and the annual contribution to the pension fund for 1986–88.

(b) Compute the accrued pension liability at the end of 1988.

E21-8 On January 1, 1986, Tonge Company adopted a noncontributory pension plan covering all of its employees. An actuary determined that the past service cost at the date of adoption was $800,000; the current service cost is $150,000 annually; and the appropriate interest rate is 8%. Tonge's accountant indicates that the past service cost is to be amortized over 15 years. Tonge has chosen Byrd National Bank as the trustee of the plan. According to the trust agreement, Tonge is to fund the current service cost fully at the end of each year, and to fund the past service cost by making equal payments at the end of each of the first 10 years. Reports issued by the trustee indicated the following:

	Dec. 31, 1986	Dec. 31, 1987
Fund Assets	$269,225	$ 561,790
Fund Liabilities	–0–	1,800
Actuarial Present Value of Accumulated Plan Benefits:		
Vested	100,000	150,000
Nonvested	900,000	1,000,000

Instructions

(a) Indicate the amounts that would be reflected on Tonge's income statement and balance sheet for 1986 and 1987.

(b) Prepare the note disclosure needed in Tonge's financial statements at December 31, 1987, relative to its pension plan.

E21-9   The notes to the financial statements of Gregory Company at December 31, 1986, include the following:

Pension Plan: On January 1, 1985, the Company adopted a pension plan covering all of its employees. The total pension expense for 1986 was $248,714, which includes current service cost, $150,000; amortization of past service cost over 15 years, $97,815; and an amount equivalent to interest (6%) on the excess of provisions over amounts funded. The company funds current service cost fully each year and is funding the past service cost in equal amounts over 20 years. A comparison of accumulated plan benefits and plan net assets for the company's pension plan is presented below:

	At Dec. 31, 1986
Actuarial Present Value of Accumulated Plan Benefits:	
Vested	$ 201,000
Nonvested	1,167,420
	$1,368,420
Net Assets	$ 479,620

The weighted-average assumed rate of return used in determining the actuarial present value of accumulated plan benefits was 6%.

Instructions

(a) Determine the amounts of the following:
   1. Past service cost at January 1, 1985. (Round to nearest dollar.)
   2. Amount of past service cost that is funded each year.

(b) Provide a brief explanation of each of the following amounts:
   1. $248,714.
   2. $97,815.
   3. $1,368,420.
   4. $479,620.
   5. What does the difference between $1,368,420 and $479,620 represent?

E21-10   DuPage Corporation, a calendar-year company, adopted a noncontributory defined benefit pension plan on January 1, 1986. DuPage's actuarial consulting firm recommended a 6% interest rate as appropriate and, applying an acceptable actuarial method, determined that the past service cost at the date of adoption of the plan is $300,000. Management decided to amortize the past service cost over 16 years and to fund the past service cost by making equal payments to the pension fund trustee at the end of each of the first 20 years. As of December 31, 1987, no benefits have vested. The current service pension cost is to be funded fully each year. Information relating to the pension plan provided by the actuarial consultant relating to the pension plan for the years 1986 and 1987 is as follows:

	1986	1987
Amortization of past service cost	$29,686	$29,686
Funding of past service cost	26,155	26,155
Current service pension cost	60,000	65,000

Instructions

(Round to the nearest dollar.)

Prepare schedules to compute the amounts relating to the pension plan that DuPage should report on its income statement and balance sheet for 1986 and 1987. Show supporting computations in good form.

(AICPA adapted)

E21-11 Rozanna Dana Inc. adopts a pension plan on January 1, 1986. According to actuarial computations, the past service cost is $1,350,000, which is to be amortized at 10% per year, and the current service cost for 1986 and 1987 is $400,000. The past service cost is completely funded on January 1, 1986; current service cost is funded each year. The pension fund is able to earn 6% on its investments.

Instructions

Prepare the journal entries for 1986 and 1987 to record pension expense and to record the payment to the pension fund. Support your entries with labelled computations. (Round to the nearest dollar.)

E21-12 Cathedral Filmstrips Co., a calendar-year corporation, adopted a company pension plan at the beginning of 1986. This plan is to be funded and noncontributory. Cathedral used an appropriate actuarial cost method to determine its current service annual pension cost for 1986 and 1987 as $15,000 and $16,000, respectively, which was paid in the appropriate year.

Cathedral's actuarially determined past service costs were funded on January 1, 1986, at an amount properly computed as $118,000. These past service costs are to be amortized at 10% per year. The interest factor assumed by the actuary is 9%.

Instructions

Prepare the journal entries to record the funding of past service cost and the pension expense for the years 1986 and 1987. Under each journal entry give the explanation or computation to support your entry. (Round to the nearest dollar.)

(AICPA adapted)

PROBLEMS

P21-1 Pine Oaks Company initiated a funded, noncontributory pension plan and gave employees credit for prior employment. The actuary estimated the past service cost at date of inception of the plan to be $120,000. Management decides to amortize past service cost over three years and to fund past service cost over four years using an 8% interest rate. Current service cost is actuarially determined to be $18,000 for year 1, $22,000 for year 2, $25,000 for year 3, and $27,000 for year 4, and is fully funded each year.

Instructions

(Round to the nearest dollar.)

(a) Prepare an amortization, funding, and expense schedule for the first four years.

(b) Prepare the entries for each of the first four years of the plan.

(c) Indicate the amounts that would be reflected on the income statement and the balance sheet for the first four years.

P21-2 Carefree Hospital Corp. initiated a funded, noncontributory pension plan and gave employees credit for prior employment (assume no vested benefits). The past service cost was actuarially estimated at the date of inception of the plan to be $840,000. Assume the past service cost is to be amortized over four years and funded over three years in equal amounts. Current service cost is actuarially determined to be $300,000 each year for the first two years and $380,000 for the next two years and is fully funded each year. The actuary recommends a 10% interest rate.

Instructions

(Round to the nearest dollar.)

(a) Prepare an amortization, funding, and expense schedule for the first four years.

(b) Prepare the entries for each of the first four years of the pension plan.

(c) Indicate the amounts that are reflected on the income statement and the balance sheet for the first four years.

P21-3 The notes to the financial statements of New Rose's Company, for the year ended December 31, 1986, include the following:

Retirement Plan: The charge to operations for pension expense of $2,373,858 includes current service cost of $2,000,000, past service cost amortization of $360,900, and interest (9%) equivalents of $12,958 on the excess of provisions over amounts funded. Current service cost is funded annually and, although the company's plan (adopted January 1, 1984) does not require funding of past service cost, this cost is currently being funded over 30 years. For accounting purposes the past service cost is being amortized over a 16-year period. As of the balance sheet date the unamortized past service cost allocable to future periods was $2,702,020.

Instructions

(Round to the nearest dollar.)

(a) Differentiate "current service cost" from "past service cost."

(b) What justification is there for allocating past service cost to future periods?

(c) What amounts relative to the company's pension plan appear in the body of the balance sheet at December 31, 1986?

(d) Prepare the journal entry, with explanation, to record the amount funded in 1986 and the pension provision for the year.

P21-4 Don Walker Piano Company is contemplating the adoption of a pension plan for its employees. President Walker wishes to know the effect such a plan might have on the company's earnings. An actuarial consulting firm has indicated that the cost of the proposed plan allocated to past service would be $800,000 and that current service cost would be $120,000. President Walker has indicated that the company will not fund the past service cost, but each year the company will pay to the pension trustee an amount equal to current service cost and interest at 8% on the unfunded past service cost. The past service cost is to be amortized over 20 years.

Instructions

(Round to the nearest dollar.)

(a) Compute for President Walker the amount of pension expense for the first year under the stipulations and data relative to the company's pension plan.

(b) Compute for President Walker the fifth year of the plan, assuming no change in actuarial method or the funding policies of the company.

P21-5 Several years after incorporation Wingtip Airlines Company initiated a funded, noncontributory pension plan. The past service cost at the date of inception of the plan was actuarially estimated to be $354,595. The past service cost is to be amortized over four years and funded over three years. Current service cost will be funded.

Instructions

(Round to the nearest dollar.)

(a) Prepare a schedule that reflects the amortization and funding of the past service cost, using a 12% interest rate.

(b) Assuming the actuary determined the current service cost to be $75,000 for year 1 and $80,000 for year 2, prepare the entries with respect to the pension plan for both years.

(c) Indicate the amounts that are reflected on the income statement and the balance sheet for each of the first two years.

P21-6 Vertigo Ladder Co. initiated a funded, noncontributory pension plan several years after incorporation. The actuary estimated the past service cost at the date of inception of the plan to be $188,609. The company decides to amortize the past service over three years and to fund past service cost over two years. Current service cost will be funded.

Instructions

(Round to the nearest dollar.)

(a) Prepare a schedule that reflects the amortization and funding of the past service cost, using a 10% interest rate.

(b) Assuming that the actuary determined the current service cost to be $70,000 for year 1 and $73,000 for year 2, prepare the entries with respect to the pension plan for both years.

(c) Indicate the amounts that are reflected on the income statement and the balance sheet for each of the first two years.

P21-7 Rittenberg Enterprises, which started operations in 1981, instituted a pension plan on January 1, 1986. The insurance company that is administering the pension plan has computed the present value of past service costs at $100,000 for the five years of operations through December 31, 1985. The pension plan provides for fully vested benefits when employees have completed 10 years of service. Therefore, there will be no vested benefits until December 31, 1990.

The insurance company proposed that Rittenberg Enterprises fund the past service cost in equal instalments over 25 years calculated by the present value method. Using an interest rate of 8%, the annual payment for past service cost would be $9,368. The company's treasurer agreed to this payment schedule. In addition, the controller concluded that a 25-year period was a reasonable period for amortizing the past service costs for book purposes. Consequently, the past service costs will also be amortized at the annual rate of $9,368 for 25 years.

The current service cost for the pension fund is estimated to be $30,000 each year for the next four years. The annual payment to the insurance company covering the current year's service cost and the annual instalment on the past service cost is payable on December 31 each year, the end of Rittenberg Enterprises' fiscal year. The insurance company was paid $39,368 ($30,000 + $9,368) on December 31, 1986, to cover the company's pension obligations for 1986.

Instructions

(Round to the nearest dollar.)

(a) Calculate and present the entries for the 1986 pension expense for Rittenberg Enterprises.

(b) Assume Rittenberg Enterprises will be unable to remit the full pension payment ($39,368) in 1987 and will submit only $30,000 to the insurance company. If Rittenberg Enterprises recognizes $39,368 as pension expense in 1987, show the entry required.

(CMA adapted)

P21-8 Aroma Winery Inc. adopts a pension plan on January 1, 1986. An actuarial firm advises that an 8% interest rate is appropriate, and determines that the past service cost as of January 1, 1986, is $525,000, and the current service cost for 1986 is $76,000. The plan provides for vesting after 30 years of service by employees.

Management decides to fund the current service cost fully each year and to fund the past service cost over 30 years. Past service cost is to be amortized over 25 years.

Instructions

Assuming that the current service cost remains the same for 1987 and 1988, prepare the following for the years 1986, 1987, and 1988. (Round to the nearest dollar.)

(a) A schedule that reflects the amortization and funding of past service cost, and the amounts to be reflected in the balance sheet.

(b) Journal entries at each year end to recognize the annual pension expense and to record the contribution to the pension fund.

P21-9 Kathy Crabtree Ad Agency initiated a pension plan several years after incorporation. The amount of the past service cost was computed at the date of adoption of the plan to be $730,000. Management decides to amortize the past service cost over four years and to fund it each year end over three years. The current service cost is computed to be $40,000 for the first four years of the plan; current service cost is completely funded each year. An interest rate of 9% is appropriate for the pension fund. Assume that there are no vested benefits.

Instructions

(Round to the nearest dollar.)

(a) Prepare a schedule that reflects the amortization and funding of past service cost and the amounts reflected on the balance sheet at the end of the first four years.

(b) Prepare the necessary journal entries for the first four years.

P21-10 On January 1, 1986, Gary Borling Publishing Co. adopts a funded, noncontributory pension plan. An actuarial firm computes the current service cost to be $54,000 for 1986 and 1987 and determines that the past service cost amounts to $440,000 at the date of the plan adoption. An interest rate of 9% is appropriate to the pension fund. Current service cost is fully funded each year. Past service cost is to be funded by equal payments at the end of each of the first 30 years.

Instructions

(Round to the nearest dollar.)

(a) Assuming that management decides to amortize past service costs over 30 years, prepare a schedule to reflect the amortization and funding of past service cost for 1986 and 1987.

(b) Prepare the journal entries to record the pension expense and the contribution to the pension fund for the years 1986 and 1987, using the funding information above and assuming that past service cost is amortized over (1) 30 years and (2) 20 years.

P21-11 Yogi Mattress Co., through labour negotiations, has been encouraged to amend as of January 1, 1986, its employee pension plan, which has been in operation for four years, having been adopted on January 1, 1982. At the time the plan was adopted, the past service cost was actuarially computed to be $800,000, with current service cost set at $100,000 annually. Since the inception of the plan, the company has been funding it in amounts equal to the annual provisions. The annual provisions for pension costs have included current service cost and amortization of past service cost over 25 years at a 6% interest rate.

As a result of the amendment, retirement benefits are to be increased. As well, because credit has been given for years of service prior to the date of amendment, prior service cost has increased $420,000, and current service cost has increased to $145,000. The increase in prior service cost is to be amortized over 21 years, but the company will continue to fund annually the same amount it funded during the first four years of the plan.

Annual provisions for pension cost from January 1, 1986, include current service cost, amortization of past service cost (until fully amortized), amortization of the increase in prior service cost, and interest equivalents at 6% on any difference between prior years' provisions and amounts funded.

Instructions

(Round to the nearest dollar.)

(a) Compute the amount of prior service cost as of the amendment date, January 1, 1986.

(b) What amounts relative to the pension plan appeared in the body of the December 31, 1985, balance sheet?

(c) Prepare the journal entry that was recorded in 1985 for the amount funded and the provision for pension cost. Show computations in your explanation.

(d) Prepare the journal entry, with explanation, to record the amount funded in 1986 and the provision for pension cost for that year.

(e) What amounts relative to the pension plan would appear in the body of the December 31, 1986, balance sheet?

(f) Prepare the journal entry, with explanation, to record the amount funded in 1987 (assuming no change in actuarial method or funding policy from 1986) and the provision for pension cost for 1987.

P21-12 Meditation Corporation, which has been in operation for the past 23 years, decided late in 1985 to adopt, beginning on January 1, 1986, a funded pension plan for its employees. The pension plan is to be noncontributory and will provide for vesting after five years of service by each eligible employee. A trust agreement has been entered into whereby a large national insurance company will receive the yearly pension fund contributions and administer the fund.

Management, through extended consultations with the fund trustee, internal accountants, and independent actuaries, arrived at the following conclusions:

1. The pension cost for current service in 1986 will be $30,000.

2. The present value of the past service cost at date of inception of the pension plan (January 1, 1986) is $200,000.

3. Because of the large sum of money involved, the past service costs will be funded at a rate of $17,765 per year for the next 30 years. The first payment will not be due until January 1, 1987.

4. Pension costs will be amortized over a 25-year period. The 25-year accrual factor is $18,736 per year.

5. Where applicable, an 8% interest rate was assumed.

Instructions

(a) Define current service pension costs and past service costs.

(b) Using xxx if the amount can't be calculated, determine what amounts will be reported in the company's:
   1. Income statement for 1986.
   2. Balance sheet as of December 31, 1986.
   3. Notes to the statements.
   Give account titles with the amounts.

(c) Using xxx if the amount can't be calculated, determine what amounts will be reported in the company's:
   1. Income statement for 1987.
   2. Balance sheet as of December 31, 1987.
   3. Notes to the statements.
   Give account titles with the amounts.

(CMA adapted)

P21-13 The following information has been obtained from the actuarial reports for the Fiedler Music Company. Assume that the market value of the securities in the pension fund is equal to book value, and that there is no past or prior service cost.

Year	Current Cost	Actuarial Gains (Losses)	Net Contribution
1976	$ 33,266	$ 998	$32,268
1977	39,113	6,609	32,504
1978	41,770	10,827	30,943
1979	51,548	(180)	51,728
1980	58,101	7,876	50,225
1981	50,940	50,940[a]	–0–
1982	64,063	28,701[b]	35,362
1983	69,948	27,552	42,396
1984	86,520	19,441	67,079
1985	96,900	25,624	71,276
1986	108,150	173,542[c]	–0–

[a]Includes $35,025 gain as a result of change in interest assumption from 6% to 6 1/2%.
[b]Includes $6,021 of gain carried over from 1978.
[c]Includes:
1. $27,000 gain due to withdrawal of two officers of the Company.
2. $65,600 gain as result of change in interest assumption from 6 1/2% to 7 1/2%.
3. $51,200 gain from withdrawals in connection with a plant closing 2/20/86.

Instructions

Fiedler Music Company amortizes its actuarial gains and losses over a period of 10 years. Compute the amount of pension expense for the years 1985 and 1986, giving proper consideration to the separately noted items a, b, and c.

P21-14 In December 1975 a noncontributory employee group-retirement plan was adopted by the Vitesse Cycle Company. Assume that the market value of the securities in the fund is equal to book value. The following information has been obtained from the actuary's reports.

Year	Current Cost	Actuarial Gains (Losses)	Net Contribution
1976	$133,064	$ 3,994	$129,070
1977	156,452	46,998	109,454
1978	167,978	43,306	123,772
1979	206,192	(720)	206,912
1980	232,404	22,614	209,790
1981	203,758	203,758[a]	–0–
1982	256,250	114,806[b]	141,444
1983	279,794	110,210	169,584
1984	346,078	77,764	268,314
1985	390,180	102,498	287,682
1986	394,501	272,878[c]	121,623

[a]Includes $170,112 gain from change in interest assumption from 5 to 5 1/2%.
[b]Includes $24,084 of gain carried over from 1981.
[c]Includes $85,000 gain due to withdrawal of two officers of the company.

Instructions

Vitesse Cycle Company company has adopted a 10-year period for allocation.
(a) Compute the pension expense for 1985 and 1986.
(b) What alternative methods could be used to allocate the actuarial gains and losses?

22

ACCOUNTING FOR LEASES

A **lease** is a contractual agreement between a **lessor** and a **lessee** that conveys to the lessee the right to use specific property (real or personal), owned by the lessor, for a specific period of time in return for stipulated, and generally periodic, cash payments (rents). An essential element of the lease agreement is that the lessor conveys less than the total interest in the property. Because of the financial, operating, and risk advantages that the lease arrangement provides, many businesses lease substantial amounts of property, both real and personal, as an alternative to ownership.

Prior to 1960, leasing chiefly affected retailing companies, which frequently lease their premises. Over the past two decades, leasing has grown tremendously in popularity; instead of borrowing money to buy an airplane, a computer, a nuclear core, or a satellite, a company leases it. Airlines and railroads lease huge amounts of equipment; many hotel and motel chains lease their facilities; and most retail chains lease the bulk of their retail premises and warehouses. Increasingly, utilities have turned to leasing, as it has become harder for them to borrow money. The increased significance and prevalence of lease arrangements in recent years have intensified the need for uniform accounting and complete informative reporting of these transactions.[1]

Advantages of Leasing

Although the lease arrangement is not without its disadvantages, the growth in its use suggests that leasing often has a genuine advantage over owning property. Some of the commonly discussed advantages to the lessee of leasing are:

1. **100% financing at fixed rates**—Leasing often requires no money down, which helps new and developing companies to conserve scarce cash. In addition, lease payments often remain fixed, protecting the lessee against inflation and increases in the cost of money. The following comment is typical: "Our local bank finally came up to 80% but wouldn't go any higher, and they wanted a floating rate. We just couldn't afford the down payment and we needed to lock in a final payment rate we knew we could live with."
2. **Protection against obsolescence**—Leasing permits rapid changes in equipment, reduces risk of obsolescence, and in many cases passes the risk in residual value to the lessor. For example, Syntex Corp. (pharmaceutical maker) leases Wang computers. Syntex is permitted under the lease agreement to turn in an old computer for a new model at any time, thus cancelling the old lease and writing a new one. The cost of the new lease is added to the balance due on the old lease, less the old computer's trade-in value. As the treasurer of Syntex recently remarked, "Our instinct is to purchase. But the first question, for us is, really, will a new one come along in a short time? If so, leasing is just a heck of a lot more convenient than purchasing."
3. **Flexibility**—Leasing is often more flexible because lease agreements may contain less restrictive provisions than other debt agreements. Innovative lessors can tailor a lease agreement to the special needs of a company. For instance, rentals can be structured to meet the timing of cash revenues so that payments are made when the equipment is productive. In addition, leased equipment may be exempt from floating liens held by major lenders on all newly acquired assets, thus eliminating the need for costly loan renegotiations.
4. **Less costly financing**—Some companies find leasing cheaper than other forms of financing. For example, start-up companies, depressed industries, or low tax companies lease as a way of claiming tax benefits that might otherwise be lost. Investment tax credits and depreciation deductions have no benefit to companies that have little if any taxable income. Through leasing, these tax benefits are used by the leasing companies or financial institutions which can pass on some of these tax benefits back to the user of the asset in the form of lower rental payments.
5. **Off-balance sheet financing**—Leasing in a certain manner leads to junior claims, does not add debt on a balance sheet, and does not affect financial ratios; hence, it may add to borrowing capacity.[2]

This point, commonly referred to as "off-balance sheet financing," is critical to some companies. For instance, the balance sheet of Chart House, Inc., a restaurateur operating over 500 restaurants in the United States, showed long-term debt of $127 million and total shareholders' equity of $88 million. Therefore, Chart House's debt-to-equity ratio was a high but manageable 1.4 to 1. But the company also was

---

[1]The popularity and general applicability of leasing are evidenced by the fact that 220 of 325 companies surveyed by the CICA in 1983 disclosed either capitalized or noncapitalized lease data: *Financial Reporting in Canada* (Toronto: CICA, 1983).

[2]As demonstrated later in this chapter, certain types of lease arrangements need not be capitalized on the balance sheet. The liability section is frequently relieved of large future lease commitments which if recorded would adversely affect the debt-to-equity ratio. The reluctance to record lease obligations as liabilities is one of the primary reasons capitalized lease accounting is resisted and circumvented by lessees.

obligated under leases, chiefly for restaurant land; the future rental payments related to those noncancelable operating leases was $125 million. Add the capitalized value of these payments to the long-term debt and Chart House's debt-to-equity ratio climbs well over 2 to 1. Safeway Stores was required to capitalize lease commitments with a present value of $748 million on a balance sheet showing only $131 million in long-term debt. Or, consider the situation of Glosser Bros., Inc., a retail department store chain, were it to capitalize its future minimum lease commitments on noncancelable leases of $70 million on its 1985 balance sheet, showing less than $4 million of long-term debt and $32 million of equity.

The existence or nonexistence of these advantages depends a great deal on the type and use required of the asset, the period of time involved, the financial condition of the company, and future tax and economic conditions. Therefore, the decision to lease or to purchase deserves thorough individual analysis.

Lease Provisions

Because a lease is a contract, the provisions agreed to by the lessor and lessee may vary widely and be limited only by their ingenuity and the peculiarities of the asset. The **duration** of the lease (lease term) may be from a few moments to the entire expected economic life of the asset. The **rental payments** may be level from year to year, increasing in amount, or decreasing; the rents may be predetermined or may vary with sales, the prime interest rate, the consumer price index, or some other factor; in most cases the rent is set to enable the lessor to recover the cost of the asset plus a fair return over the life of the lease. The **obligations for taxes, insurance, and maintenance** (executory costs) may be assumed by either the lessor or the lessee, or they may be divided between the lessor and the lessee. **Restrictions** somewhat comparable to those in bond indentures may limit the lessee's activities relative to dividend payments, or incurrence of further debt and lease obligation. The lease contract may be **noncancelable** or may grant the right to **early termination** on payment of a set scale of prices (prices often representing the unrecovered cost of the lessor) plus a penalty. In case of **default** the lessee may be liable for all future payments at once, receiving title to the property in exchange; or the lessor may enjoy the prerogative to sell and to collect from the lessee all or a portion of the difference between the sale price and the lessor's unrecovered cost. **Alternatives of the lessee at termination** of the lease may range from none, to the right to purchase the leased asset at the fair market value, or the right to renew or buy at a nominal price.[3]

In practice, any combination of provisions on these different points may be used, ranging from provisions that approach the purchase of a current service through the traditional short-term rental lease to those that seem to be purely financing devices for purchase/sale transactions. These different transactions call for different accounting methods to portray properly the substance of each situation.

CONCEPTUAL NATURE OF A LEASE

If Echo Bay Mines Ltd. borrows $15,000,000 on a 10-year note from the Royal Bank of Canada to purchase a Boeing 727 jet plane, it is clear that an asset and related

---

[3]John H. Myers, ''Reporting of Leases in Financial Statements,'' *Accounting Research Study No. 4* (New York: AICPA, 1964), pp. 10–11.

liability should be reported on Echo Bay's balance sheet in that amount. If Echo Bay purchases the 727 for $15,000,000 directly from Boeing through an instalment purchase over 10 years, it is equally clear that an asset and related liability should be reported. However, if Echo Bay leases the Boeing 727 for 10 years through a noncancelable lease transaction with payments of the same amount as the instalment purchase transaction, differences of opinion arise over how this and other types of lease transactions should be reported. The various views of accounting for leases are as follows:

Do Not Capitalize Any Leased Assets Because the lessee does not have ownership of the property, capitalization under this view is considered inappropriate. Furthermore, a lease is an executory contract requiring continuing performance by both parties. This view also contends that leases should not be capitalized because executory contracts (such as purchase commitments and employment contracts) are not capitalized at present.

Capitalize Those Leases Similar to Instalment Purchases Accountants should report transactions in accordance with their economic substance; therefore, if instalment purchases are capitalized, so also should leases that have the same characteristics as instalment purchases. For example, in the illustration above Echo Bay is committed to the same payments over a 10-year period for either a lease or instalment purchase; lessees simply make rental payments while owners make mortgage payments. Why shouldn't the financial statements report these transactions in the same manner?

Capitalize All Long-Term Leases Under this approach, the only requirement for capitalization is the long-term right to use the property. Often referred to as the property rights approach, it would lead to capitalization of all long-term leases.[4]

Capitalize Firm Leases Where the Penalty for Nonperformance is Substantial A final approach is to capitalize only firm (noncancelable) contractual rights and obligations. ''Firm'' means that it is unlikely that performance under the lease can be avoided without a severe penalty.[5]

To Capitalize or Not to Capitalize

In short, the various viewpoints range from no capitalization to capitalization of all leases. The CICA apparently agrees with the capitalization approach when it is similar to an instalment purchase situation, noting that a lease which transfers substantially all of the benefits and risks of ownership of property should be capitalized. This viewpoint leads to three basic conclusions. (1) The characteristics indicating that substantially all of the benefits and risks of ownership have been transferred must be identified. Such transactions include capital leases, which should be recorded as purchases and sales of assets. (2) For consistency, the same characteristics should apply to the lessee and the lessor. (3) Those leases that do not transfer substantially all the benefits and risks of ownership are operating

---

[4]See, for example, *Accounting Research Study No. 4*, which advocated this position.

[5]Yuji Ijiri, *Recognition of Contractual Rights and Obligations*, Research Report (Stamford, Conn.: FASB, 1980).

leases, and should not be capitalized but rather accounted for simply as rental payments and receipts.

If Capitalization, What Amount?

In stipulating the number, timing, and amounts of the rental payments, the lease provides the basis for measuring the asset and the liability involved. By capitalizing the present value of the future rental payments, **the lessee** records an asset and a liability at an amount generally representative of the asset's market value or purchase price. **The lessor**, having transferred substantially all the benefits and risks of ownership, transfers the asset and records a receivable in the amount of the future rentals. The lease rental payments are accounted for by both the lessee and the lessor as periodic payments consisting of interest and principal.

The remainder of the chapter presents the different types of leases and the specific criteria, accounting rules, and disclosure requirements set forth by the CICA in accounting for leases.

ACCOUNTING FOR LEASES—A BRIEF BACKGROUND

As indicated above, the CICA adopted the instalment purchase approach as far as determining when lease transactions should be capitalized. Prior to 1979, leases, irrespective of their duration or other character, were not capitalized and little about them was disclosed by the lessee or the lessor in the notes to the financial statements. Accounting for all leases was simply a matter of debiting rent expense by the lessee and crediting rent income by the lessor as lease payments were made or accrued. In January, 1979, the CICA, in *Handbook* Section 3065, required that leases that were in substance instalment purchases be capitalized by the lessee as asset purchases with a related obligation.

ACCOUNTING BY LESSEES

In attempting to standardize accounting for leases, the CICA tried to determine when the risks and benefits of ownership were transferred. If conditions were similar to an instalment purchase, the lessee should capitalize the lease and the lessor should remove the asset from its balance sheet. If the transaction did not meet certain criteria, the lease should not be capitalized. Therefore, from the standpoint of the lessee all leases may be classified for accounting purposes as follows:

(a) Operating leases (noncapitalization method).

(b) Capital leases (capitalization method).

If at the date of the lease agreement (inception of the lease)[6] the lessee is party to a noncancelable lease "that transfers substantially all of the benefits and risks of ownership related to the leased property from the lessor to the lessee," the lessee shall classify and account for the arrangement as a **capital lease**.[7] A lease is consid-

---

[6]*CICA Handbook*, Section 3065, par. 3(k).

[7]*Ibid*, Section 3065, par. 9,

ered to transfer substantially all of the benefits and risks of ownership when **one or more** of the following conditions are met:

1. There is reasonable assurance that the lessee will obtain ownership of the leased property by the end of the lease term.
2. The lease term is such that the lessee will receive substantially all of the economic benefits expected to be derived from the use of the leased property over its life span. This is usually assumed to occur if the lease term is 75% or more of the economic life of the leased property.
3. The present value of the minimum lease payments (excluding executory costs) is equal to substantially all (usually 90% or more) of the fair value of the leased property.

Leases that do not meet any of these three criteria listed above are classified and accounted for by the lessee as **operating leases**.

The flow chart below shows that a lease meeting any one of the three criteria above results in the lessee having a capital lease.

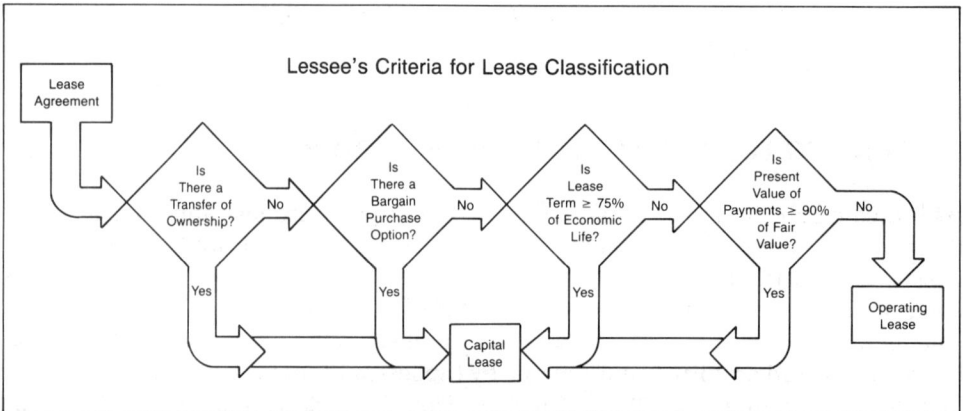

EXAMINATION OF CAPITALIZATION CRITERIA

The three capitalization criteria applicable to lessees are controversial and in some cases are difficult to apply in practice.

Transfer of Ownership Test

Logically, if the lease transfers ownership of the asset to the lessee, it is a capital lease and the asset should be capitalized. This criterion is not controversial and is easily implemented in practice.

The transfer of ownership may be facilitated at the end of the lease term without additional consideration or through a bargain purchase option. A bargain purchase option is a provision allowing the lessee to purchase the leased property for a price that is significantly lower than the expected fair value of the property at the date the option becomes exercisable; the difference between the purchase price and the expected fair market value must be large enough to make exercise of the option reasonably assured at the inception of the lease. For example, if you were to lease a Mercedes Benz 300SD for $750 per month for sixty months with an option to purchase it for $100 at the end of the sixty-month period, the $100 option to purchase is clearly a bargain and therefore capitalization is required. In other cases, the criterion may not be as easy to apply, and determining now that a certain future price is a bargain can be difficult.

Economic Life Test (75% Test)

If the lease period equals or exceeds 75% of the asset's economic life, it follows that most of the risks and rewards of ownership are transferred to the lessee and therefore capitalization is appropriate. However, determining the lease term and economic life of the asset may be troublesome. For example, **the lease term is generally considered the fixed noncancelable term of the lease.** However, this period is extended if a **bargain renewal option** is provided in the lease agreement. A bargain renewal option is a provision allowing the lessee to renew the lease for a rental that is lower than the expected fair rental at the date the option becomes exercisable. The difference between the renewal rental and the expected fair rental must be great enough to make the exercise of the option to renew reasonably assured at the inception of the lease. For example, if a personal computer is leased for three years at a rental of $100 per month, and then subsequently can be leased for $10 per month, it clearly is a bargain renewal option. However, as with bargain purchase options, it is sometimes difficult to determine what is a bargain.

The original lease term is also extended for: leases having substantial penalties for nonrenewal, periods for which the lessee has the option to renew or extend the lease, renewal periods preceding the date a bargain purchase option becomes exercisable, and renewal periods during which the lessee is expected to guarantee some of the lessor's debt. The lease term, however, can never extend beyond the time a bargain purchase option becomes exercisable.

Determining estimated economic life can also pose problems, especially if the leased item is a specialized item or has been used for a significant period of time. For example, determining the economic life of a nuclear core is extremely difficult because it is subject to much more than normal "wear and tear."

Recovery of Investment Test (90% Test)

This test indicates that if the present value of the minimum lease payments equals or exceeds 90% of the fair market value of the asset, then the leased asset should be capitalized. The rationale for this test is that if the present value of the minimum lease payments is reasonably close to the market price of the asset, the asset is being purchased.

In determining the present value of the minimum lease payments, four important concepts are involved: (1) minimum lease payments, (2) discount rate, (3) executory costs, and (4) residual value.

Minimum Lease Payments   These are payments the lessee is obligated to make or can be required to make in connection with the leased property. If the lease term contains a bargain purchase option, only the minimum rental payments over the lease term and the payment called for by the bargain purchase option should be included in the minimum lease payments. Otherwise, minimum lease payments include the following:

1. Minimum rental payments called for by the lease over the lease term.

2. The amount of any guarantee by the lessee of any residual value.
3. The amount payable for failure to renew or extend the lease.

Contingent rentals and executory costs (defined below) are not included in the lessee's computation of the present value of the minimum lease payments.

Discount Rate   The lessee computes the present value of the minimum lease payments using the **lessee's incremental borrowing rate**, which is defined as "the interest rate that, at the inception of the lease, the lessee would have incurred [in order] to borrow, over a similar term and with similar security for the borrowing, the funds necessary to purchase the leased asset."[8]

If, however, the lessee (1) knows the **implicit rate computed by the lessor** and (2) the implicit rate computed by the lessor is less than the lessee's incremental borrowing rate, then the lessee must use the implicit rate. The interest rate implicit in the lease is the discount rate that, when applied to the minimum lease payments and the unguaranteed residual value accruing to the lessor, causes the aggregate present value to be equal to the fair value of the leased property to the lessor.[9] In practice, the lessee frequently does not know the implicit rate. Because **the lessee's capitalized value of the leased property may not exceed its fair value**, the lessee is prevented from using an excessively low discount rate.

Executory Costs   Like most assets, leased tangible assets require the incurrence of insurance, maintenance, and property tax expenses (called **executory costs**) during their economic life. If the lessor retains responsibility for the payment of these "ownership-type costs," a portion of each lease payment that represents executory costs should be excluded in computing the present value of the minimum lease payments, because it does not represent payment on the reduction of the obligation. If the portion of the minimum lease payments representing executory costs is not determinable from the provisions of the lease, an estimate of such amount must be made. Many lease agreements, however, specify that these executory costs be assumed by the lessee; in these cases the rental payments can be used without adjustment in the present value computation.

Residual Value   The residual value is the estimated fair value of the leased property at the end of the lease term.[10] The lessor often transfers to the lessee or to a third party the risk of loss through a guaranteed residual value. The amount of a guaranteed residual value is (1) the certain or determinable amount at which the lessor has the right to require the lessee to purchase the asset, or (2) the amount the lessee or the third-party guarantor guarantees will be realized. According to Section 3065 of the *CICA Handbook*, the full amount of the guarantee rather than an estimate of the amount payable to make up the lessor's deficiency is to be included in the minimum lease payments. A lease provision requiring the lessee to make up a residual value deficiency that is attributable to damage, extraordinary wear and tear, or excessive usage is not usually included in the minimum lease payments. Such costs are similar to contingent rentals in that the amount is not determinable

[8]*Ibid.*, Section 3065, par. 3(p).
[9]*Ibid.*, Section 3065, par. 3(m).
[10]*Ibid.*, Section 3065, par. 3(r).

at the inception of the lease. Like **contingent rentals**, such costs are recognized as period costs when incurred.[11]

Asset and Liability Accounted for Differently

In a capital lease transaction the lessee is using the lease as a source of financing. The lessor finances the transaction (i.e., provides the investment capital) through the leased asset, and the lessee makes rent payments, which actually are instalment payments. Therefore, over the life of the property rented, the rental payments to the lessor constitute a payment of principal plus interest.

Under the capital lease method the lessee treats the lease transaction as if an asset were being purchased "by instalments"; that is, like a financing transaction in which an asset is acquired and an obligation is created. The lessee records a capital lease as an asset and a liability at the lower of (1) the present value of the minimum lease payments (excluding executory costs), or (2) the fair market value of the leased asset at the inception of the lease. The rationale for this approach is that the leased asset should not be recorded for more than its fair market value.

One troublesome aspect of accounting for the amortization of the capitalized leased asset relates to the period of amortization. For example, if the lease agreement satisfies criterion (1), on page 1014, that is, it transfers ownership of the asset to the lessee or contains a bargain purchase option, the leased asset is depreciated in a manner consistent with the lessee's normal depreciation policy for owned assets, using the economic life of the asset. In addition, if the asset has a residual value, it is subtracted from the leased asset to determine the depreciable amount.

On the other hand, if the lease does not transfer ownership at the end of the lease term or does not contain a bargain purchase option, the leased asset is depreciated over the term of the lease. In this case, either criterion (2) or (3) must have been met, and in both situations the leased asset reverts back to the lessor after a certain period of time. As a result, residual values are not subtracted from the carrying amount of the leased asset in determining the amount to depreciate, unless the residual amount is guaranteed.

Although the amount capitalized as an asset and the amount recorded as an obligation at the inception of the lease are computed at the same present value, the amortization of the asset and the discharge of the obligation are **independent accounting processes** during the term of the lease. The lessee should amortize the leased asset by applying the conventional depreciation methods: straight-line, sum-of-the-years'-digits, declining balance, units of production, and so on. The selection of a depreciation method should be in line with the objectives of income measurement and asset valuation.

The CICA uses the term "amortization" more frequently than the term "depreciation" in recognition of intangible leased property rights. The authors prefer the term "depreciation" as a description of the write-off of the costs of the expired services of a tangible asset.

Throughout the term of the lease, **the effective interest method** is used to allocate each lease payment between a reduction of the lease obligation and interest expense. This method produces a constant rate of interest in each period on the outstanding balance of the obligation.

---

[11]*Ibid.*, Section 3065, par. 19.

Whichever discount rate is used by the lessee in determining the present value of the minimum lease payments, that rate usually must be used by the lessee in applying the effective interest method to capital leases.

Capitalized Lease Method Illustrated (Lessee)

The preceding section discussed the theory and rules underlying the accounting treatment used by the lessee in recording capitalized lease transactions. The following presentation illustrates the accounting for the capitalized lease method.

Lessor Company and Lessee Company sign a lease agreement dated January 1, 1987, that calls for Lessor Company to lease equipment to Lessee Company beginning January 1, 1987. The lease agreement contains the following terms and provisions:

1. The term of the lease is five years, and the lease agreement is noncancelable, requiring equal rental payments of $25,981.62 at the beginning of each year (annuity due basis).
2. The equipment has a fair value at the inception of the lease of $100,000, an estimated economic life of five years, and no residual value.
3. Lessee Company pays all of the executory costs except for the property taxes of $2,000 per year, which are included in the annual payments.
4. The lease contains no renewal options and the equipment reverts to Lessor Company at the termination of the lease.
5. Lessee Company's incremental borrowing rate is 11% per year.
6. Lessee Company depreciates similar equipment that it owns on a straight-line basis.
7. Lessor Company set the annual rental to ensure a rate of return on its investment of 10% per year; this fact is known to Lessee Company. The lease meets the criteria for classification as a capital lease because (1) the lease term of five years, being equal to the equipment's estimated economic life of five years, satisfies the 75% test, and (2) the present value of the minimum lease payments ($100,000 as computed below) exceeds 90% of the fair value of the property ($100,000).

The minimum lease payments are $119,908.10 ($23,981.62 × 5) and the amount capitalized as leased assets is computed as the present value of the minimum lease payments (excluding executory costs—property taxes of $2,000) as follows:

```
Capitalized amount = ($25,981.62 – $2,000) × present value of an annuity due
                                              of 1 for 5 periods at 10%
                                              (Table 6-5)
                   = $23,981.62 × 4.16986
                   = $100,000
```

The lessor's implicit interest rate of 10% is used instead of the lessee's incremental borrowing rate of 11%, because (1) it is lower, and (2) the lessee has knowledge of it.

The entry to record the signing of the lease and the capitalization of the present value of the minimum lease payments net of executory costs (i.e., the recorded value of the asset and the liability) on Lessee Company's books on January 1, 1987, is:

Equipment Under Capital Leases   100,000
  Obligations Under Capital Leases   100,000

Note that the preceding entry records the obligation at the net amount of $100,000 (the present value of the future rental payments) rather than at the gross amount of $119,908.10 ($23,981.62 × 5).

The journal entry to record the **first lease payment on January 1, 1987**, is as follows:

Property Tax Expense	2,000.00	
Obligations Under Capital Leases	23,981.62	
Cash		25,981.62

Recording the annual lease payment in subsequent periods results in the recognition of additional expenses relative to the leased equipment, because in this case each lease payment of $25,981.62 consists of three elements: (1) a reduction in the lease obligation, (2) a financing cost (interest expense), and (3) executory costs (property taxes). The total financing cost (interest expense) over the term of the lease, is the difference between the present value ($100,000) of the lease payments and the actual cash disbursed, net of executory costs ($119,908.10), or $19,908.10. The annual interest should be computed by applying the effective interest method. Therefore, the annual interest expense is a function of the outstanding obligation, as illustrated in the following schedule:

Lessee Company
LEASE AMORTIZATION SCHEDULE
(Annuity due basis)

Date	Annual Lease Payment	Executory Costs	Interest (10%) on Unpaid Obligation	Reduction of Lease Obligation	Balance of Lease Obligation
	(a)	(b)	(c)	(d)	(e)
Jan. 1/87					$100,000.00
Jan. 1/87	$ 25,981.62	$ 2,000	–0–	$ 23,981.62	76,018.38
Jan. 1/88	25,981.62	2,000	$ 7,601.84	16,379.78	59,638.60
Jan. 1/89	25,981.62	2,000	5,963.86	18,017.76	41,620.84
Jan. 1/90	25,981.62	2,000	4,162.08	19,819.54	21,801.30
Jan. 1/91	25,981.62	2,000	2,180.32*	21,801.30	–0–
	$129,908.10	$10,000	$19,908.10	$100,000.00	

(a) Lease payment as required by lessor.
(b) Executory costs included in rental payment.
(c) Ten percent of the preceding balance of (e) except for Jan. 1/87; since this is an annuity due, no time has elapsed at the date of the first payment and no interest has accrued.
(d) (a) minus (b) and (c).
(e) Preceding balance minus (d).
 *Rounded by 19 cents.

At December 31, 1987, Lessee Company's fiscal year-end, **accrued interest** is recorded as follows. (If reversing entries are used, this entry would be reversed at January 1, 1988.)

Interest Expense	7,601.84	
Interest Payable		7,601.84

Depreciation of the leased equipment over its lease term of five years applying Lessee Company's normal depreciation policy (straight-line method) results in the following entry on December 31, 1987:

Depreciation Expense—Leased Equipment	20,000	
Accumulated Depreciation—Leased Equipment		20,000
($100,000 ÷ 5 years)		

At December 31, 1987, the assets recorded under capital leases are separately identified on the lessee's balance sheet. Similarly the related obligations are separately identified with the portion due within one year or the operating cycle, whichever is longer, classified with current liabilities and the balance with noncurrent liabilities. For example, the current portion of the December 31, 1987, total obligation of $76,018.38 in the lessee's amortization schedule is the amount of the reduction in the obligation in 1988, or $16,379.78. The liability section as it relates to lease transactions at December 31, 1987, would appear as follows:

Current Liabilities	
Interest Payable	$ 7,601.84
Obligation Under Capital Leases	16,379.78
Noncurrent Liabilities	
Obligations Under Capital Leases	$59,638.60

The journal entry to record the **lease payment of January 1, 1988**, is as follows:

Property Tax Expense	2,000.00	
Interest Expense (or Interest Payable)	7,601.84	
Obligations Under Capital Leases	16,379.78	
Cash		25,981.62

Entries through 1991 would follow the pattern above. Other executory costs (insurance and maintenance) assumed by Lessee Company would be recorded in a manner similar to that used to record any other operating costs incurred on assets owned by Lessee Company.

Upon expiration of the lease, the amount capitalized as leased equipment is fully amortized and the lease obligation is fully discharged. The equipment would be returned to the lessor, and the leased equipment and related accumulated depreciation accounts would be removed from the books. If the equipment is purchased at termination of the lease at a price of $5,000, and the estimated life of the equipment is changed from five to seven years, the following entry might be made:

Equipment ($100,000 + $5,000)	105,000	
Accumulated Depreciation—Capital Leases	100,000	
Leased Equipment Under Capital Leases		100,000
Accumulated Depreciation—Equipment		100,000
Cash		5,000

Operating Method (Lessee)

Under the **operating method,** rent expense (and a corresponding liability) accrues day by day to the lessee as the property is used. The lessee assigns rent to the periods benefiting from the use of the asset and ignores, in the accounting, any commitments to make future payments. Appropriate accruals are made if the accounting period ends between cash payment dates. For example, assume that the capital lease illustrated above had been accounted for as an operating lease.

The first-year charge to operations would have been $25,981.62, the amount of the rental payment. The journal entry to record this payment on January 1, 1987, would be as follows:

Rent Expense	25,981.62	
Cash		25,981.62

The rented asset and the liability for future rental payments, are not reported on the balance sheet. Rent expense would be reported on the income statement. In addition, note disclosure is required for operating leases that have initial lease terms in excess of one year. An illustration of the type of note disclosure required for an operating lease (as well as other types of leases) is provided later in this chapter.

Comparison of Capital Lease with Operating Lease

If the lease, as indicated above, had been accounted for as an operating lease, the first-year charge to operations would have been $25,981.62, the amount of the rental payment. Treating the transaction as a capital lease, however, resulted in a first-year charge of $29,601.84: depreciation of $20,000 (assuming straight-line), interest expense of $7,601.84 (per schedule on page 1019), and executory costs of $2,000. The following schedule shows that while the total charges to operations are the same over the lease term whether the lease is accounted for as a capital lease or as an operating lease, under the capital lease treatment the charges are higher in the earlier years and lower in the later years.[12]

Lessee Company
SCHEDULE OF CHARGES TO OPERATIONS
Capital Lease versus Operating Lease

	Capital Lease				Operating	
Year	Depreciation	Executory Costs	Interest	Total Charge	Lease Charge	Difference
1987	$ 20,000	$ 2,000	$ 7,601.84	$ 29,601.84	$ 25,981.62	$ 3,620.22
1988	20,000	2,000	5,963.86	27,963.86	25,981.62	1,982.24
1989	20,000	2,000	4,162.08	26,162.08	25,981.62	180.46
1990	20,000	2,000	2,180.32	24,180.32	25,981.62	(1,801.30)
1991	20,000	2,000	–0–	22,000.00	25,981.62	(3,981.62)
	$100,000	$10,000	$19,908.10	$129,908.10	$129,908.10	$ –0–

If an accelerated method of depreciation is used, the differences between the amount charged to operations under the two methods would be even larger in the earlier and later years.

In addition, using the capital lease approach would have resulted in an asset and related liability of $100,000 initially reported on the balance sheet; no such asset or liability would be reported under the operating method. Therefore, the following occurs if a capital lease, instead of an operating lease, is employed: (1) an increase

---

[12]The higher charges in the early years is one reason lessees are reluctant to adopt the capital lease accounting method. Lessees (especially those of real estate) claim that it is really no more costly to operate the leased asset in the early years than in the later years; thus, they advocate an even charge similar to that produced by the operating method.

in the amount of reported debt (both short-term and long-term), (2) an increase in the amount of total assets (specifically long-lived assets), and (3) a lower income early in the life of the lease and, therefore, lower retained earnings. Thus many companies believe that capital leases have a detrimental impact on their financial position as their debt-to-total-equity ratio increases and their rate of return on total assets decreases. As a result, the business community resists capitalizing leases.

Whether their resistance is well founded is a matter of conjecture. From the point of view of cash flow, the company is in the same position whether the lease is accounted for as an operating or a capital lease. The reason managers often argue against capitalization is that it can more easily lead to violation of loan covenants, can affect the amount of compensation received by owners (for example, a stock compensation plan tied to earnings), and finally can lower rates of return and increase debt-to-equity relationships, thus making the company less attractive to present and potential investors.[13]

ACCOUNTING BY LESSORS

Earlier in this chapter a number of advantages to the lessee of leasing were discussed. Three important benefits are available to the lessor:

1. **Interest Revenue**—Leasing is a form of financing; therefore, financial institutions and leasing companies find leasing attractive because it provides competitive interest margins.

2. **Tax Incentives**—Ownership of an asset provides substantial tax benefits if the company has high taxable income. In many cases, companies cannot use the tax benefit, but leasing provides them with an opportunity to transfer such tax benefits to another party in return for a lower rental rate on the leased asset. To illustrate, Boeing Aircraft recently sold one of its 767 jet planes to a wealthy investor who didn't need the plane but could use the tax benefit. The investor then leased the plane to a foreign airline which cannot use the tax benefits. Everyone gains. Boeing is able to sell its 767, the investor receives the tax benefits, and the foreign airline finds a cheaper way to acquire a 767.[14]

3. **High Residual Value**—Another advantage of leasing is the reversion of the property to the lessor at the end of the lease term. Residual values can produce very large profits. For example, Citicorp in the 1970s assumed that the commercial aircraft it was leasing to the airline industry would have a residual of 5% of its purchase price. In 1980 these planes were worth 150% of their cost—a handsome profit. However, by 1983 these same planes slumped to 80% of their cost.

Economics of Leasing

The lessor determines the amount of the rental, basing that amount on the rate of return needed to justify leasing the asset. The factors considered in establishing the rate of return are the credit standing of the lessee, the length of the lease, the status of the residual value (guaranteed versus unguaranteed), and so on. This rate

---

[13]A recent study indicates that management's behaviour did not change as a result of the profession's requirements to capitalize certain leases. For example, many companies restructure their leases to avoid capitalization; others increase their purchases of assets instead of leasing; and others, faced with capitalization, postpone their debt offerings or issue shares instead. However, it is interesting to note that the study found no significant effect on share or bond prices as a result of capitalization of leases. A. Rashad Abdel-khalik, "The Economic Effects on Leases of FASB Statement No. 13, Accounting for Leases," *Research Report* (Stamford, Conn.: FASB, 1981).

[14]Some would argue that there is a loser—the government. The tax benefits enable the profitable investor to reduce or eliminate taxable income.

is referred to as the **implicit rate of the lessor.** To illustrate, in the Lessor Company/ Lessee Company example on page 1018 the lessor's desired rate of return was 10%, the cost of the equipment to the lessor was $100,000, and the estimated residual value was zero. Lessor Company determined the amount of the rental payment in the following manner:

Cost of leased equipment	$100,000.00
Less: Present value of residual value	–0–
Amount to be recovered by lessor through lease payments	$100,000.00
Five beginning-of-the-year lease payments to yield a 10% return ($100,000 ÷ 4.16986)	$ 23,981.62

If a residual value were involved (whether guaranteed or not), the lessor would not have to recover as much from the rental payments. Therefore, the rental payments would be less. (This is illustrated later on page 1031.)

Classification of Leases by the Lessor

From the standpoint of the **lessor**, all leases may be classified for accounting purposes as follows:

(a) Operating leases.
(b) Direct financing leases.
(c) Sales-type leases.

If at the date of the lease agreement (inception) the lessor is party to a lease that meets **one or more** of the following Group I criteria (1,2, or 3) and **both** of the following Group II criteria (1 and 2), the lessor shall classify and account for the arrangement as a **direct financing lease** or a **sales-type lease**.[15] (Note that the Group I criteria are identical to the criteria that must be met for a lease to be classified as a capital lease by a lessee, per page 1014.)

Group I
1. There is reasonable assurance that the lessee will obtain ownership of the leased property by the end of the lease term.
2. The lease term is such that the lessee will receive substantially all of the economic benefits expected to be derived from the use of the leased property over its lifespan. This is usually assumed to occur if the lease term is 75% or more of the economic life of the leased property.
3. The present value of the minimum lease payments (excluding executory costs) is equal to substantially all (usually 90% or more) of the fair value of the leased property.

Group II
1. The credit risk associated with the lease is normal when compared to the risk of collection of similar receivables.
2. The amounts of any unreimbursable costs that are likely to be incurred by the lessor under the lease can be reasonably estimated.[16]

[15]*CICA Handbook*, Section 3065, par. 9.
[16]*Ibid.*, Section 3065, par. 7.

All leases that do not qualify as a direct financing lease or a sales-type lease are classified and accounted for by the lessor as operating leases.

Why the Group II requirements? The answer is that the profession wants to make sure that the lessor has really transferred the risks and benefits of ownership. If collectibility of payments is not predictable, or if performance by the lessor is incomplete, then it is inappropriate to remove this leased asset from the lessor's books. As an illustration, computer leasing companies at one time used to buy IBM equipment, lease it, and remove the leased assets from their balance sheets. In leasing the asset, the computer leasing companies stated that they would be willing to substitute new IBM equipment if obsolescence occurred. However, when IBM introduced a new computer line, they refused to sell it to the computer leasing companies. As a result, a number of computer leasing companies could not meet their contracts with their customers and were forced to take back the old equipment. What the computer leasing companies had taken off the books now had to be reinstated. Such a case demonstrates one reason for Group II requirements.

The distinction for the lessor between a direct financing lease and a sales-type lease is the presence or absence of a manufacturer's or dealer's profit (or loss). A sales-type lease involves a manufacturer's or dealer's profit, and a direct financing lease does not. The profit (or loss) to the lessor is evidenced by the difference between the fair value of the leased property at the inception of the lease and the lessor's cost or carrying amount (book value). Normally, sales-type leases arise when manufacturers or dealers use leasing as a means of marketing their products. For example, a computer manufacturer will lease its computer equipment to businesses and institutions. Direct financing leases generally result from arrangements with lessors that are primarily engaged in financing operations, such as lease-finance companies, banks, insurance companies, and pension trusts. However, a lessor need not be a manufacturer or dealer to realize a profit (or loss) at the inception of the lease that requires application of sales-type lease accounting.

All leases that do not qualify as direct financing or sales-type leases are classified and accounted for by the lessors as operating leases. The following flow chart shows the circumstances under which a lease is classified as operating, direct financing, or sales-type for the lessor.

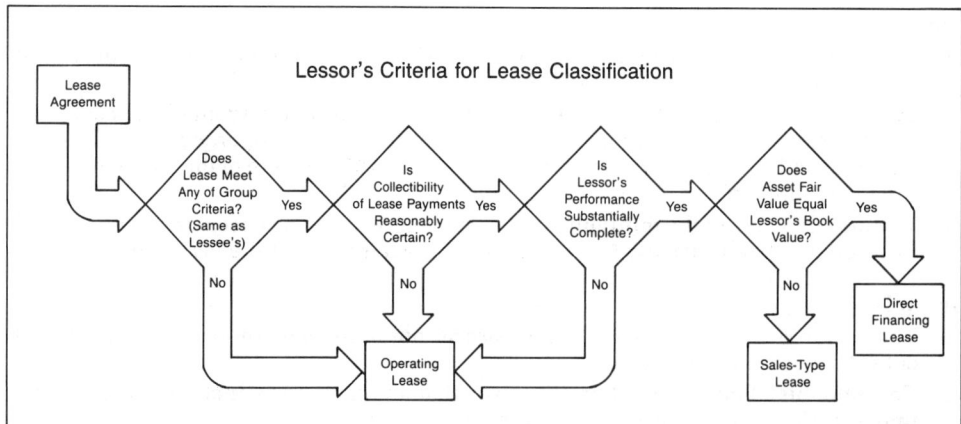

As a consequence of the additional Group II criteria for lessors, it is possible that a lessor not having met both criteria will classify a lease as an **operating** lease while the lessee will classify the same lease as a **capital** lease. In such an event, both the lessor and lessee will carry the asset on their books and both will depreciate the capitalized asset.

For purposes of comparison with the lessee's accounting, only the operating and direct financing leases will be illustrated in the following section. The more complex sales-type lease will be discussed later in the chapter.

Financing Method Applied to Direct Financing Leases   Leases that are in substance the financing of an asset purchase by a lessee require the lessor to substitute "net investment in lease" for the leased asset. The information necessary to record a direct financing lease is as follows:

1. **Gross investment** ("lease payments receivable"). The minimum lease payments plus any unguaranteed residual value accruing to the lessor at the end of the lease term.[17]
2. **Unearned finance (interest) revenue.** The difference between the gross investment (the receivable) and the fair market value of the property.
3. **Net investment.** The gross investment (the receivable) less the unearned interest (finance) revenue included therein.

The computation of the lease payments receivable is often confusing. This confusion arises because of the uncertainty as to how to account for residual values. Remember that the term "minimum lease payments" basically includes the following:

1. Rental payments (excluding executory costs).
2. Bargain purchase option (if any).
3. Guaranteed residual value (if any).

Thus the guaranteed residual value is included in the minimum lease payments definition. As a result, when lease payments receivable is defined as minimum lease payments plus unguaranteed residual value, it simply means that residual values, whether guaranteed or unguaranteed, are included as part of lease payments receivable.

In addition, note that if the lessor pays any executory costs, then the rental payment should be reduced by that amount for purposes of computing minimum lease payments. In other words, lease payments receivable includes:

1. Rental payments (less executory costs paid by the lessor).
2. Bargain purchase options (if any).
3. Guaranteed or unguaranteed residual values (if any).

The unearned interest revenue is amortized to revenue over the lease term by applying the effective interest method. Thus a constant rate of return is produced on the net investment in the lease. Any contingent rentals, including rentals based on variables such as machine hours or use or sales volume, are credited to revenue when they become receivable.

The following presentation, using the data from the preceding Lessor Company/ Lease Company illustration on page 1018, illustrates the accounting treatment accorded a direct financing lease. The information relevant to Lessor Company in accounting for the lease transaction is repeated below.

1. The term of the lease is five years beginning January 1, 1987, noncancelable, and requires equal rental payments of $25,981.62 at the beginning of each year; payments include $2,000 of executory costs (property taxes).

[17]Initially the unguaranteed residual value could be classified in a separate account. If the unguaranteed residual value is included in the Lease Payments Receivable account, it would be reclassified by the lessor at the end of the lease term if not purchased by the lessee.

2. The equipment has a cost of $100,000 to Lessor Company, a fair value at the inception of the lease of $100,000, an estimated economic life of five years, and no residual value.
3. No initial direct costs were incurred in negotiating and closing the lease transaction.
4. The lease contains no renewal options and the equipment reverts to Lessor Company at the termination of the lease.
5. Collectibility is reasonably assured and no additional costs (with the exception of the property taxes being collected from the lessee) are to be incurred by Lessor Company.
6. Lessor Company set the annual rentals to ensure a rate of return of 10% (implicit rate) on its investment as follows:

Cost of leased asset	$100,000
Less: Present value of residual value	–0–
Amount to be recovered by lessor through lease payments	$100,000
Five periodic lease payments: $100,000 ÷ 4.16986[a]	

[a]PV of an annuity due of 1 for 5 years at 10% (Table 6-5)

The lease meets the criteria for classification as a direct financing lease because (1) the lease term exceeds 75% of the equipment's estimated economic life, (2) the present value of the minimum lease payments exceeds 90% of the equipment's fair value, (3) collectibility of the payments is reasonably assured, and (4) there are no further costs to be incurred by Lessor Company. It is not a sales-type lease because there is no difference between the fair value ($100,000) of the equipment and the lessor's cost ($100,000).

The lease payments receivable (gross investment) is calculated as follows:

Lease payments receivable = Minimum lease payments minus executory costs paid by lessor plus unguaranteed residual value
= [($25,981.62 – $2,000) × 5] + $0
= $119,908.10

The unearned interest income is computed as the difference between the lease payment receivable and the lessor's cost or carrying amount of the leased asset:

Unearned interest income = Lease payments receivable minus asset fair market value
= $119,908.10 – $100,000
= $19,908.10

The net investment in this direct financing lease is $100,000; that is, the gross investment of $119,908.10 minus the unearned interest revenue of $19,908.10.

The lease of the asset, the resulting receivable, and the unearned interest income are recorded January 1, 1987, (the inception of the lease) as follows:

Lease Payments Receivable	119,908.10	
Equipment		100,000.00
Unearned Interest Revenue—Leases		19,908.10

The unearned interest income is classified on the balance sheet as a deduction from the lease payments receivable if the receivable is reported gross. Generally, the lease payments receivable, although **recorded** at the gross investment amount, is **reported** at the "net investment" amount (gross investment less unearned interest revenue) and entitled "Net investment in capital leases," classified between its current and noncurrent portions.

The leased equipment with a cost of $100,000, which represents Lessor Company's investment, is replaced with a lease receivable that includes the interest receivable. In a manner similar to the lessee's treatment of interest, Lessor Company applies the effective interest method and recognizes interest revenue as a function of the unrecovered net investment, as illustrated below:

Lessor Company
LEASE AMORTIZATION SCHEDULE
(Annuity due basis)

Date	Annual Lease Payment	Executory Costs	Interest (10%) on Net Investment	Net Investment Recovery	Net Investment
	(a)	(b)	(c)	(d)	(e)
Jan. 1/87					$100,000.00
Jan. 1/87	$ 25,981.62	$ 2,000.00	–0–	$ 23,981.62	76,018.38
Jan. 1/88	25,981.62	2,000.00	$ 7,601.84	16,379.78	59,638.60
Jan. 1/89	25,981.62	2,000.00	5,963.86	18,017.76	41,620.84
Jan. 1/90	25,981.62	2,000.00	4,162.08	19,819.54	21,801.30
Jan. 1/91	25,981.62	2,000.00	2,180.32*	21,801.30	–0–
	$129,908.10	$10,000.00	$19,908.10	$100,000.00	

(a) Annual rental that provides a 10% return on net investment.
(b) Executory costs included in rental payment.
(c) Ten percent of the preceding balance of (e) except for 1/1/87.
(d) (a) minus (b) and (c).
(e) Preceding balance minus (d).
   *Rounded by 19 cents

On January 1, 1987, the journal entry to record receipt of the first year's lease payment is as follows:

Cash	25,981.62	
Lease Payments Receivable		23,981.62
Property Tax Expense		2,000.00

On December 31, 1987, the interest revenue earned during the first year and included in the receipt above is recognized through the following entry:

Unearned Interest Revenue—Leases	7,601.84	
Interest Revenue—Leases		7,601.84

At December 31, 1987, the net investment under capital leases is reported in the lessor's balance sheet among current assets and/or noncurrent assets. The portion due within one year or the operating cycle, whichever is longer, is classified as a current asset and the balance with noncurrent assets. The total net investment at December 31, 1987, is equal to $83,620.22 (the balance at January 1, 1987, of $76,018.38 plus interest receivable for 1987 of $7,601.84). The current portion of the December 31, 1987, balance of $83,620.22 is the net investment to be received in 1988, $16,379.78, plus the interest of $7,601.84. The remainder, $59,638.60

[Lease Payments Receivable of $71,944.86 ($23,981.62 × 3) minus Unearned Interest Revenue of $12,306.26 ($5,963.86 + $4,162.08 + $2,180.32)] should be reported in the noncurrent asset section. The asset section as it relates to lease transactions at December 31, 1987, would appear as follows:

Current assets:	
Net investment in capital leases	$23,981.62
Noncurrent assets:	
Net investment in capital leases	$59,638.60

The following entries record receipt of the second year's lease payment and accrual of the interest earned:

January 1, 1988

Cash	25,981.62	
Lease Payments Receivable		23,981.62
Property Tax Expense		2,000.00

December 31,1988

Unearned Interest Revenue—Leases	5,963.86	
Interest Revenue—Leases		5,963.86

Journal entries through 1991 would follow the same pattern except that no entry would be recorded in 1991 (the last year) for accrued interest. Because the receivable is fully collected by January 1, 1991, no balance (investment) is outstanding during 1991 to which Lessor Company could attribute any interest. Upon expiration of the lease, the gross receivable and the unearned interest income would have zero balances. **Lessor Company recorded no depreciation** since no depreciable asset has been recognized. If the equipment is sold to Lessee Company for $5,000 upon expiration of the lease, Lessor Company would recognize disposition of the equipment as follows:

Cash	5,000	
Gain on Sale of Equipment Lease		5,000

Classification of Lease Obligation/Net Investment (Ordinary Annuity)

The classification of the lease obligation/net investment was presented in the previous section in an annuity due situation. As indicated on page 1020, the lessee's current liability is the payment ($23,981.62) to be made on January 1 of the next year. Similarly, as above, the lessor's current asset is the amount to be collected ($23,981.62) on January 1 of the next year. In both of these annuity due instances the balance sheet date is December 31 and the due date of the lease payment is January 1 (less than one year), so that the present value ($23,981.62) is the same as the rental payment ($23,981.62).

What happens if the situation is an ordinary annuity rather than an annuity due situation? For example, assume that the rent is to be paid at the end (December 31) of the next year rather than at the beginning (January 1) of the next year. *CICA Handbook*, Section 3065, does not indicate how to measure the current and noncurrent amounts; it requires that "any portion of lease obligations payable within a year out of current funds should be included in current liabilities."[18] Thus, two

---

[18]*CICA Handbook*, Section 3065, par. 23.

methods of measuring the current liability portion in ordinary annuity leases have evolved: (1) the change in the present value and (2) the present value of next year's payment.[19]

To illustrate the change in the present value method which is frequently used in practice, assume an ordinary annuity situation with the same facts as the Lessee Company/Lessor Company case excluding the $2,000 of executory costs. Because the rents are paid at the end of the period instead of at the beginning, the five rents are set at $26,379.73 to have an effective interest rate of 10%. The ordinary annuity amortization schedule appears as follows:

Date	Annual Lease Payment	Interest (10%)	Reduction of Principal	Balance of Lease Obligation/ Net Investment
	(a)	(b)	(c)	(d)
Jan. 1/87				$100,000.00
Dec. 31/87	$ 26,379.73	$10,000.00	$ 16,379.73	83,620.27
Dec. 31/88	26,379.73	8,362.03	18,017.70	65,602.57
Dec. 31/89	26,379.73	6,560.26	19,819.47	45,783.10
Dec. 31/90	26,379.73	4,578.31	21,801.42	23,981.68
Dec. 31/91	26,379.73	2,398.05	23,981.68	–0–
	$131,898.65	$31,898.65	$100,000.00	

Lessee Company/Lessor Company — LEASE AMORTIZATION SCHEDULE

The current portion of the lease obligation/net investment under the change in the present value method as of December 31, 1987, would be $18,017.70 ($83,620.27 − $65,602.57); and as of December 31, 1988, it would be $19,819.47 ($65,602.57 − $45,783.10). The portion of the lease obligation/net investment that is not current is classified as noncurrent; that is, $65,602.57 is the noncurrent portion at December 31, 1987.

Under the present value of next year's payment method, the current portion of the lease obligation/net investment would be reported at December 31, 1987, at the present value of $26,379.73 or $23,981.55 [$26,379.73 × .90909 $(p_{\overline{1}|10\%})$]. At December 31, 1988, the current portion would also be $23,981.55 ($26,379.73 × .90909). Under this method the current liability is the same amount each year for a given rent payment.

Because our discussion and homework assignments reflect the more typical annuity due lease arrangements that occur in practice, with the rents occurring in less than a year's time, the maturity value of the next rent (including principal and interest) is reported as the current portion.

Operating Method (Lessor)

Under the **operating method**, each rental receipt of the lessor is recorded as rental revenue on the use of an item carried as a plant asset. The plant asset is depreciated in the normal manner, with the depreciation expense of the period matched against the rental revenue. The amount of revenue recognized in each accounting period is a level amount (straight-line basis) regardless of the lease provisions, unless another

---

[19]For additional discussion on this approach and possible alternatives, see R. J. Swieringa, "When Current is Noncurrent and Vice Versa!" *The Accounting Review* (January, 1984), pp. 123–130.

systematic and rational basis better represents the time pattern in which the benefit is derived from the leased asset. In addition to the depreciation charge, maintenance costs and the cost of any other services rendered under the provisions of the lease that pertain to the current accounting period are charged against the recognized revenue. To illustrate the operating method, assume that the direct financing lease previously illustrated had been accounted for as an operating lease. The entry to record the cash rental payment, assuming the $2,000 was for property tax expense, would be as follows:

Cash	25,981.62	
Rental Revenue		23,981.62
Property Tax Expense		2,000.00

Depreciation is simply recorded by the lessor as follows (assuming the straight-line method, a cost basis of $100,000, and a five-year life):

Depreciation Expense—Leased Buildings	20,000	
Accumulated Depreciation—Leased Buildings		20,000

If real estate taxes, insurance, maintenance, and other operating costs during the year are the obligation of the lessor, they are recorded as expenses chargeable against the gross rental revenues.

If the lessor owned plant assets that it used in addition to those leased to others, the leased building would be separately classified with or near property, plant, and equipment in an appropriately titled account such as Building Leased to Others or Investment in Leased Property; Accumulated Depreciation is conventionally shown as a deduction from the investment. If significant in amount or in terms of activity, the rental revenues and accompanying expenses are separated in the income statement from sales revenue and cost of goods sold.

Rent is reported as revenue over the lease term as it becomes receivable according to the provisions of the lease. Generally, rentals under an operating lease are receivable on a straight-line basis; that is, in equal amounts at equal intervals. However, if the rentals depart from a straight-line basis, the revenue still should be recognized on a straight-line basis unless another basis more accurately reflects a decline in the service potential of the asset.

SPECIAL ACCOUNTING PROBLEMS

The features of lease arrangements that provide unique accounting problems are:

1. Residual values.
2. Sales-type leases.
3. Bargain purchase options.
4. Initial direct costs.
5. Sale leasebacks.

Residual Values

The residual value is the **estimated fair value** of the leased asset at the end of the lease term. Frequently, a significant residual value exists at the end of the lease term, especially when the economic life of the leased asset exceeds the lease term. If title does not pass automatically to the lessee or a bargain purchase option does not exist (criterion 1), the lessee returns physical custody of the asset to the lessor at the end of the lease term. The residual value may be unguaranteed or guaranteed by the lessee. If the lessee, for example, agrees to make up any deficiency below a stated amount that the lessor realizes in residual value at the end of the lease term, that stated amount is the **guaranteed residual value**.

The guaranteed residual value is employed in lease arrangements for two reasons. One is a business reason: it protects the lessor against any loss in estimated residual value, thereby ensuring the lessor of the desired rate of return on investment. The second is an accounting reason that has given added significance to the guaranteed residual value: as you will learn from the discussion at the end of this chapter, the guaranteed residual value is one of the devices frequently used to circumvent certain accounting rules.

The fact that the residual value is guaranteed or unguaranteed is of economic risk consequence to the lessor (i.e., a guaranteed residual value has more assurance of realization than does an unguaranteed residual value). As a result, some adjustment in rental rates may take place because the certainty of recovery has been increased for the lessor. After this rate is established, then it makes no difference from an accounting point of view whether the residual value is guaranteed or unguaranteed from the lessor's perspective. The net investment to be recorded by the lessor (once the rate is set) will be the same whether the residual value is guaranteed or unguaranteed. For example, assume the same data as in the Lessee Company/Lessor Company illustrations except that a residual value of $5,000 is estimated at the end of the five-year lease term. With an estimated residual value of $5,000 and an objective of earning a 10% return on investment (ROI),[20] whether the residual value is guaranteed or unguaranteed, Lessor Company would compute the amount of the lease payments as follows:

Lessor's Computation of Lease Payments (10% ROI)	
(Annuity due basis, including residual value)	
Guaranteed or Unguaranteed Residual Value	
Cost of leased asset to lessor	$100,000.00
Less: Present value of residual value	
($5,000 × .62092, Table 6-2)	3,104.60
Amount to be recovered by lessor through lease payments	$ 96,895.40
Five periodic lease payments (96,895.40 ÷ 4.16986, Table 6-5)	$ 23,237.09

The foregoing lease payment amount should be contrasted to the lease payments of $23,981.62 as computed on page 1023 where no residual value existed. The payments are less because the lessor's recoverable amount is less by the present value of the residual value.

Lessee Accounting for Residual Value   Whether the estimated residual value is guaranteed or unguaranteed is of both economic and accounting consequence to the lessee. The accounting difference is in the fact that the term "minimum lease payments," the basis for capitalization, includes the guaranteed residual value but

---

[20]Technically, the rate of return demanded by the lessor would be different depending upon whether the residual value was guaranteed or unguaranteed. We are ignoring this difference in subsequent sections to simplify the illustrations.

excludes the unguaranteed residual value, as illustrated in the next two sections.

Guaranteed residual value (lessee accounting). A guaranteed residual value affects the lessee's computation of the minimum lease payments and, therefore, the amounts capitalized as a leased asset and a lease obligation. In effect, the guaranteed residual value is an additional lease payment that will be paid in property or cash, or both, at the end of the lease term. Using the rental payments as computed by the lessor above, the minimum lease payments are $121,185.45 [($23,237.09 × 5) + $5,000]. The capitalized present value of the minimum lease payments (excluding executory costs) is computed as follows:

Lessee's Capitalized Amount (10% Rate) (Annuity due basis, including **guaranteed** residual value)	
Present value of five annual rental payments of $23,237.09 × 4.16986 (Table 6-5)	$ 96,895.40
Present value of guaranteed residual value of $5,000 due five years after date of inception: $5,000 × 0.62092	3,104.60
Lessee's capitalized amount	$100,000.00

A schedule of interest expense and amortization of the lease obligation of $100,000 that produces a guaranteed residual value of $5,000 at the end of five years is prepared by Lessee Company as follows:

		Lessee Company			
		LEASE AMORTIZATION SCHEDULE			
		(Annuity due basis, **guaranteed** residual value—GRV)			
Date	Annual Lease Payment Plus GRV	Executory Costs	Interest (10%) on Unpaid Obligation	Reduction of Lease Obligation	Lease Obligation
	(a)	(b)	(c)	(d)	(e)
Jan. 1/87					$100,000.00
Jan. 1/87	$ 25,237.09	$ 2,000.00	–0–	$ 23,237.09	76,762.91
Jan. 1/88	25,237.09	2,000.00	$ 7,676.29	15,560.80	61,202.11
Jan. 1/89	25,237.09	2,000.00	6,120.21	17,116.88	44,085.23
Jan. 1/90	25,237.09	2,000.00	4,408.52	18,828.57	25,256.66
Jan. 1/91	25,237.09	2,000.00	2,525.67	20,711.42	4,545.24
Dec. 31/91	5,000.00*		454.76**	4,545.24	–0–
	$131,185.45	$10,000.00	$21,185.45	$100,000.00	

(a) Annual lease payment as required by lease.
(b) Executory costs included in rental payment.
(c) Preceding balance of (e) × 10%, except January 1, 1987.
(d) (a) minus (b) and (c).
(e) Preceding balance minus (d).
*Represents the guaranteed residual value; this amount or any part of it will be paid if the residual value is less than $5,000 at December 31, 1991.
**Rounded by 24 cents.

If, at the end of the lease, the fair market value of the leased property is less than $5,000, Lessee Company may have to record a loss. For example, assume that

Lessee Company depreciated the leased asset down to its residual value of $5,000 but that the fair market value of the asset at December 31, 1991, was $3,000. In this case, the Lessee Company would have to report a loss of $2,000. The following journal entry would be made (assuming cash was paid to make up the residual value deficiency):

Loss on Capital Lease	2,000	
Obligations Under Capital Lease	5,000	
Accumulated Depreciation—Capital Lease	95,000	
Leased Equipment Under Capital Lease		100,000
Cash		2,000

If the fair market value exceeds $5,000, a gain may be recognized. Gains on guaranteed residual values may be apportioned to the lessor and lessee in whatever ratio the parties initially agree.

Unguaranteed residual value (lessee accounting). From the lessee's viewpoint, an unguaranteed residual value is the same as no residual value in terms of its effect upon the lessee's method of computing the minimum lease payments and the capitalization of the leased asset and the lease obligation. For example, assume the same facts as those above except that the $5,000 residual value is **unguaranteed instead of guaranteed.** The amount of the annual lease payments would be the same, $23,237.09, because whether the residual value is guaranteed or unguaranteed, Lessor Company's amount to be recovered through lease rentals is the same—that is, $96,895.40. The minimum lease payments are $116,185.45 ($23,237.09 × 5). Lessee Company would capitalize the following amount:

Lessee's Capitalized Amount (10% Rate) (Annuity due basis, including **unguaranteed** residual value)	
Present value of five annual rental payments of $23,237.09 × 4.16986 (Table 6-5)	$96,895.40
Unguaranteed residual value of $5,000 (Not capitalized by lessee)	–0–
Lessee's capitalized amount	$96,895.40

Assuming that the asset had a fair market value of $3,000 at the end of the lease term, no loss would be reported in this situation. Assuming that the leased asset has been fully depreciated and that the lease obligation has been fully amortized (as shown in the amortization schedule), no entry is required at the end of the lease term, except to remove the asset and its accumulated depreciation from the books.

If we continue the assumption that the fair value of the leased asset is $100,000, this lease still satisfies the 90% of fair value criterion because the present value of the minimum lease payments, $96,895.40, is approximately 97% of the fair value of $100,000. Note that if the unguaranteed residual value is sufficiently large, thereby reducing the minimum lease payments, the present value of the minimum lease payments can be less than 90% of the fair value of the leased asset, thereby disqualifying the transaction from capital lease status **for the lessee and the lessor** (assuming that the transaction did not qualify under any of the other two criteria). If, however, **the residual value is guaranteed by a third party** unrelated to either the lessee or lessor, it is treated by the lessee as an unguaranteed residual value but by the lessor as a guaranteed residual value. This anomaly in lease accounting has been used extensively in the business world to undermine the CICA's intent to maintain accounting symmetry between the lessee and the lessor. (See the last section of this chapter for a more extended discussion of these attempts at circumvention.)

Lessee entries involving residual values. The entries by Lessee Company for both a guaranteed and an unguaranteed residual value are shown below in comparative form.

Lessee Company Entries for Guaranteed and Unguaranteed Residual Values			
Guaranteed Residual Value		**Unguaranteed Residual Value**	
Capitalization of Lease January 1, 1987:			
Leased Equipment under		Leased Equipment under	
Capital Leases	100,000.00	Capital Leases	96,895.40
Obligations under		Obligations under	
Capital Leases	100,000.00	Capital Leases	96,895.40
First Payment January 1, 1987:			
Property Tax Expense	2,000.00	Property Tax Expense	2,000.00
Obligations under		Obligations under	
Capital Leases	23,237.09	Capital Leases	23,237.09
Cash	25,237.09	Cash	25,237.09
Adjusting Entry for Accrued Interest December 31, 1987:			
Interest Expense	7,676.29	Interest Expense	7,365.83
Interest Payable	7,676.29	Interest Payable	7,365.83
Entry to Record Depreciation December 31, 1987:			
Depreciation Expense—		Depreciation Expense—	
Capital Leases	19,000.00	Capital Leases	19,379.08
Accumulated Depreciation—		Accumulated Deprecia-	
Capital Leases	19,000.00	tion—Capital Leases	19,379.08
[($100,000 − $5,000) ÷ 5 years]		($96,895.40 ÷ 5 years)	
Second Payment January 1, 1988:			
Property Tax Expense	2,000.00	Property Tax Expense	2,000.00
Obligations under		Obligations under	
Capital Leases	15,560.80	Capital Leases	15,871.26
Interest Payable		Interest Payable	
(or Interest Expense)	7,676.29	(or Interest Expense)	7,365.83
Cash	25,237.09	Cash	25,237.09

Lessor Accounting for Residual Value As indicated earlier, the net investment to be recovered by the lessor is the same whether the residual value is guaranteed or unguaranteed. The lessor works on the assumption that the residual value will be realized at the end of the lease term whether guaranteed or unguaranteed. Therefore, as shown on page 1031, the lease payments required by the lessor to earn a certain return on investment are the same ($23,237.09) whether the residual value is guaranteed or unguaranteed. Lessor accounting for residual values varies only slightly for direct financing and sales-type leases, as discussed below and on pages 1036 and 1037.

Direct financing lease. Using the Lessee Company/Lessor Company data and assuming a residual value (either guaranteed or unguaranteed) of $5,000 and classification of the lease as a direct financing lease, the following necessary amounts are computed:

Gross investment = ($23,237.09 × 5) + $5,000 = $121,185.45
Unearned interest revenue = $121,185.45 − $100,000 = $21,185.45
Net investment = $121,185.45 − $21,185.45 = $100,000

The schedule for amortization of guaranteed and unguaranteed residual value is the same:

Lessor Company
LEASE AMORTIZATION SCHEDULE
(Annuity due basis, **guaranteed** or **unguaranteed** residual value)

Date	Annual Lease Payment Plus Residual Value	Executory Costs	Interest (10%) on Net Investment	Net Investment Recovery	Net Investment
	(a)	(b)	(c)	(d)	(e)
Jan. 1/87					$100,000.00
Jan. 1/87	$ 25,237.09	$ 2,000.00	–0–	$ 23,237.09	76,762.91
Jan. 1/88	25,237.09	2,000.00	$ 7,676.29	15,560.80	61,202.11
Jan. 1/89	25,237.09	2,000.00	6,120.21	17,116.88	44,085.23
Jan. 1/90	25,237.09	2,000.00	4,408.52	18,828.57	25,256.66
Jan. 1/91	25,237.09	2,000.00	2,525.67	20,711.42	4,545.24
Dec. 31/91	5,000.00		454.76*	4,545.24	–0–
	$131,185.45	$10,000.00	$21,185.45	$100,000.00	

(a) Annual lease payment as required by lease.
(b) Executory costs included in rental payment.
(c) Preceding balance of (e) × 10%, except for Jan. 1/87.
(d) (a) minus (b) and (c).
(e) Preceding balance minus (d).
*Rounded by 24 cents.

Using the amounts computed above, the following entries would be made by Lessor Company during the first year for this direct financing lease:

Lessor Entries for Either Guaranteed or Unguaranteed Residual Value

Inception of Lease Jan. 1/87:

Lease Payments Receivable	121,185.45	
Equipment		100,000.00
Unearned Interest Revenue—Leases		21,185.45

First Payment Received Jan. 1/87:

Cash	25,237.09	
Lease Payments Receivable		23,237.09
Property Tax Expense/Property Tax Payable		2,000.00

Adjusting Entry for Accrued Interest Dec. 31/87:

Unearned Interest Revenue—Leases	7,676.29	
Interest Revenue—Leases		7,676.29

The entries above may be compared to those of Lessee Company on page 1034.

Sales-Type Lease (Lessor)

As already indicated, the primary difference between a direct financing lease and a sales-type lease is the manufacturer's or dealer's profit (or loss). The information necessary to record the sales-type lease is as follows:

1. **Gross Investment** (also "lease payments receivable"). The minimum lease payments plus the unguaranteed residual value.
2. **Unearned Interest Revenue.** The gross investment less the fair market value of the asset.
3. **Sales Price of the Asset.** The present value of the minimum lease payments.
4. **Cost of Goods Sold.** The cost of the asset to the lessor, less the present value of any unguaranteed residual value.

From the above, note that the Gross Investment and the Unearned Interest Revenue account are the same whether a guaranteed or an unguaranteed residual value is involved. If the residual value is guaranteed, it is part of the minimum lease payment; if not guaranteed, it is still included as dictated by the definition. A difference does exist, however, in the accounting for guaranteed and unguaranteed residual values relative to the amount recorded for both sales and cost of goods sold. In the case of a guaranteed residual value, the residual value may be considered part of sales revenue because the lessor knows this amount will be received. In the case of an unguaranteed residual value, however, the residual value is not sold, so cost of goods sold is reduced. However, the gross profit on the sale of the asset is the same whether a guaranteed or unguaranteed residual value is involved. The difference in the two methods relates to the amounts recorded as sales and cost of goods sold.

To illustrate a sales-type lease with a guaranteed and unguaranteed residual value, assume the same facts as in the preceding direct financing lease situation (page 1031). The estimated residual value is $5,000 (the present value of which is $3,104.60) and the leased equipment has an $85,000 cost to the dealer, Lessor Company. At the end of the lease term assume that the fair market value of the residual value is $3,000.

Using this information, Lessor Company records the sales-type lease as follows:

	Sales-Type Lease	
	Guaranteed Residual Value	Unguaranteed Residual Value
Gross investment	$121,185.45	Same
	[($23,237.09 × 5) + $5,000]	
Unearned interest revenue	$21,185.45	Same
	($121,185.45 − $100,000)	
Sales price of the asset	$100,000.00	$96,895.40
	($96,895.40 + $3,104.60)	
Cost of goods sold	$85,000.00	$81,895.40
		($85,000.00 − $3,104.60)
Gross profit	$15,000.00	$15,000.00
	($100,000 − $85,000)	($96,895.40 − $81,895.40)

The entries to record this transaction on January 1, 1987, and the receipt of the residual value at the end of the lease term are as follows:

Lessor Company

Entries for Guaranteed and Unguaranteed Residual Values

Guaranteed Residual Values			Unguaranteed Residual Values		
To record sales-type lease at inception (January 1, 1987):					
Cost of Goods Sold	85,000.00		Cost of Goods Sold	81,895.40	
Lease Payments			Lease Payments		
Receivable	121,185.45		Receivable	121,185.45	
Sales Revenue		100,000.00	Sales Revenue		96,895.40
Unearned Interest Revenue		21,185.45	Unearned Interest Revenue		21,185.45
Inventory		85,000.00	Inventory		85,000.00
To record receipt of the first lease payment (January 1, 1987):					
Cash	25,237.09		Cash	25,237.09	
Lease Payments Receivable		23,237.09	Lease Payments Receivable		23,237.09
Property Tax Expense/			Property Tax Expense/		
Property Tax Payable		2,000.00	Property Tax Payable		2,000.00
To recognize interest revenue earned during the first year (December 31, 1987):					
Unearned Interest			Unearned Interest		
Revenue	7,676.29		Revenue	7,676.29	
Interest Revenue		7,676.29	Interest Revenue		7,676.29
(See lease amortization schedule, page 1035.)					
To record receipt of second lease payment (January 1, 1988):					
Cash	25,237.09		Cash	25,237.09	
Lease Payments Receivable		23,237.09	Lease Payments Receivable		23,237.09
Property Tax Expense/			Property Tax Expense/		
Property Tax Payable		2,000.00	Property Tax Payable		2,000.00
To recognize interest revenue earned during the second year (December 31, 1988):					
Unearned Interest			Unearned Interest		
Revenue	6,120.21		Revenue	6,120.21	
Interest Revenue		6,120.21	Interest Revenue		6,120.21
To record receipt of residual value at end of the leased term (December 31, 1991):					
Inventory	3,000.00		Inventory	3,000.00	
Cash	2,000.00		Loss on Capital Lease	2,000.00	
Lease Payments Receivable		5,000.00	Lease Payments Receivable		5,000.00

The profit recorded by Lessor Company at the point of sale is the same, $15,000, whether the residual value is guaranteed or unguaranteed, but the sales revenue and cost of goods sold amounts are different.

The **estimated unguaranteed residual value** in a sales-type lease (and a financing-type lease) must be reviewed periodically. If the estimate of the unguaranteed residual value declines, the accounting for the transaction must be revised using the changed estimate. The decline represents a reduction in the lessor's net investment and is recognized as a loss in the period in which the residual estimate is reduced. Upward adjustments in estimated residual values are not recognized.

Bargain Purchase Option (Lessee)

A bargain purchase option allows the lessee to purchase the leased property for a future price that is so much lower than the expected future fair value of the property that, at the inception of the lease, the future exercise of the option appears to be reasonably assured. If a bargain purchase option exists, **the lessee must increase the present value of the minimum lease payments by the present value of the option price.**

For example, assume that Lessee Company in the illustration on page 1018 had an option to buy the leased equipment for $5,000 at the end of the five-year lease term when the fair value is expected to be $18,000. The significant difference between the option price and the fair value creates a bargain purchase option, the exercise of which is reasonably assured. The computations of (1) the amount of the five lease payments necessary for the lessor to earn a 10% return on net investment, (2) the amount of the minimum lease payments, (3) the amount capitalized as leased assets and lease obligation, and (4) the amortization of the lease obligation are affected by a bargain purchase option in the same manner that they are by a guaranteed residual value. Therefore, the computations and amortization schedule that would be prepared for this $5,000 bargain purchase option are identical to those shown on pages 1032 and 1035 for the $5,000 guaranteed residual value.

The only difference between the accounting treatment given a bargain purchase option and a guaranteed residual value of identical amounts and circumstances is in the computation of the annual depreciation. In the case of a guaranteed residual value the lessee depreciates the asset over the lease life, while in the case of a bargain purchase option the lessee uses the economic life of the asset.

Initial Direct Costs (Lessor)

The incremental costs incurred by the lessor that are directly associated with negotiating and consummating a leasing transaction are called **initial direct costs**. Examples of initial direct costs are commissions, legal fees, costs of preparing and processing documents, and that portion of salespersons' and other employees' compensation that is applicable to the time spent on **completed** lease transactions.[21]

For **operating leases**, the lessor should defer initial direct costs and allocate them over the lease term in proportion to the recognition of rental income. In a **sales-type lease** transaction, the lessor expenses the initial direct costs in the year of incurrence; that is, the period in which the profit on the sale is recognized. In a **direct financing lease**, however, initial direct costs should be allocated over the term of the lease by charging any initial direct costs against income as incurred and recognizing as revenue in the same period a portion of the unearned income equal to the initial direct costs. To illustrate, if Lessor Company incurred $4,900 of initial direct costs in consummating the lease with Lessee Company, Lessor would make the following two entries:

Various natural expenses; i.e., Sales Commissions, Legal Expense,		
Travel Expense, etc.	4,900	
Cash and Accounts Payable		4,900
Unearned Interest Revenue	4,900	
Interest Revenue		4,900

The remaining unearned revenue is amortized over the lease term applying the effective interest method. Because the unearned income is reduced by the amount of the initial direct costs, a new implicit interest rate must be computed to amortize

---

[21]*CICA Handbook*, Section 3065, par. 3 (1).

the remaining unearned revenue. This dual entry method of allocating initial direct costs over the lease term is recommended by the CICA because this method has been used for some years throughout the leasing industry.

Sale-Leaseback

The term "sale-leaseback" describes a transaction in which the owner of property (seller-lessee) sells the property to another and simultaneously leases it back from the new owner. The use of the property is continued without interruption. For example, a company buys land, constructs a building to its specifications, sells the property to an investor, and then immediately leases it.

Generally, in such a transaction the property is sold at a price equal to or greater than current market value and is leased back for a term approximating the property's useful life and for lease payments sufficient to repay the buyer for the cash invested plus a reasonable return on investment. In addition, the lessee pays all executory costs (maintenance, insurance, and taxes), just as if title had passed. The sale price and the amount of the rents are related. The tax advantage for the seller-lessee is the deductibility of the entire lease payment, which may include interest and amortization of the cost of land and other, already partially depreciated, real property. Thus, the tax deduction under the lease arrangement may exceed allowable depreciation had title been retained. The sale-leaseback mechanism is used frequently where financing is a problem.

Lessee If the lease meets one of the three criteria for treatment as a capital lease (see page 1014), the **seller-lessee accounts for the lease as a capital lease.** If none of the criteria is satisfied, the seller-lessee accounts for the lease as an operating lease. Any profit or loss experienced by the seller-lessee from the sale of the assets that are leased back under a capital lease should be deferred and amortized over the lease term (or the economic life if criterion (1) is satisfied) in proportion to the amortization of the leased assets.[22] For example, if Lessee Company sells equipment having a book value of $580,000 and a fair value of $623,110 to Lessor Company for $623,110 and leases the equipment back for $50,000 a year for 20 years, the profit of $43,110 should be amortized over the 20-year period at the same rate that the $623,110 is depreciated. Under an operating lease such profit or loss should be deferred and amortized in proportion to the rental payments over the period of time the assets are expected to be used by the lessee. If the leased asset is land only, the amortization shall be on a straight-line basis over the lease term.

The profession requires, however, that when the fair value of the asset is less than the book value (carrying amount), a loss must be recognized immediately that is equal to the amount of the difference between the book value and fair value. For example, if Lessee Company sells equipment having a book value of $650,000 and a fair value of $623,110, the difference of $26,890 should be charged against current income.

Lessor If the lease meets one of the criteria in Group I and both the criteria in Group II (see page 1023), the **purchaser-lessor** records the transaction as a purchase and a direct financing lease. If the lease does not meet the criteria, the purchaser-lessor records the transaction as a purchase and an operating lease.

[22]*Ibid*, Section 3065, par. 68.

Sale-Leaseback Illustration

To illustrate the accounting treatment accorded a sale-leaseback transaction, assume that Lessee Company on January 1, 1987, sells an aircraft having a carrying amount on its books of $75,500,000 to Lessor Company for $80,000,000, and immediately leases the aircraft back under the following conditions:

1. The term of the lease is 15 years, noncancelable, requiring equal rental payments of $10,487,443 at the beginning of each year.
2. The aircraft has a fair value of $80,000,000 on January 1, 1987, and an estimated economic life of 15 years.
3. Lessee Company has the option to renew the lease, one year at a time, at the same rental payments upon expiration of the original lease.
4. Lessee Company pays all executory costs.
5. Lessee Company depreciates similar aircraft that it owns on a straight-line basis over 15 years.
6. The annual payments assure the lessor a 12% return.
7. The incremental borrowing rate of Lessee Company is 12%.

This lease is a capital lease to Lessee Company because the lease term exceeds 75% of the estimated life of the aircraft and because the present value of the lease payments exceeds 90% of the fair value of the aircraft to the lessor. Assuming that collectibility of the lease payments is reasonably predictable, and that no important uncertainties exist in relation to unreimbursable costs yet to be incurred by the lessor, Lessor Company should classify this lease as a direct financing lease.

The typical journal entries to record the transactions relating to this lease for both Lessee Company and Lessor Company for the first year are presented on page 1041.

LEASE ACCOUNTING—THE UNSOLVED PROBLEM

As indicated at the beginning of this chapter, lease accounting is a much abused area in which strenuous efforts are being made to circumvent *CICA Handbook*, Section 3065. In practice, the accounting rules for capitalizing leases have been rendered partially ineffective by the strong desires of lessees to resist capitalization. Leasing generally involves large dollar amounts which, when capitalized, materially increase reported liabilities and adversely affect the debt-to-equity ratio. Lease capitalization is also resisted because charges to expense made in the early years of the lease term are higher under the capital lease method than under the operating method, frequently without tax benefit. As a consequence, a great deal of effort has been devoted to beating the profession's lease capitalization rules.[23]

To avoid leased asset capitalization, lease agreements are designed, written, and interpreted so that none of the three capitalized lease criteria is satisfied from the lessee's viewpoint. Devising lease agreements in such a way has not been too difficult when the following specifications are met:

1. Make certain that the lease does not specify the transfer of title to the property to the lessee.
2. Do not write in a bargain purchase option.

---

[23]Richard Dieter, "Is Lessee Accounting Working?" *The CPA Journal* (August, 1979), pp. 13–19. This article provides interesting examples of abuses of lease accounting standards, discusses the circumstances that led to the current situation, and proposes a solution to the confusion.

Entries for Sale-Leaseback

Lessee Company		Lessor Company	

Sale of Aircraft by Lessee Company to Lessor Company, January 1, 1987:

Cash	80,000,000		Aircraft	80,000,000	
Aircraft		75,500,000	Cash		80,000,000

Unearned Profit on
  Sale-Leaseback   4,500,000   Lease Payments
                                               Receivable   157,311,645

Leased Aircraft Under   Aircraft   80,000,000
   Capital Leases   80,000,000   Unearned Interest
Obligations Under   Revenue—Leases   77,311,645
   Capital Leases   80,000,000   ($10,487,443 × 15 = $157,311,645)

First Lease Payment, January 1, 1987

Obligations Under   Cash   10,487,443
   Capital Leases   10,487,443   Lease Payments
   Cash   10,487,443   Receivable   10,487,443

Incurrence and Payment of Executory Costs by Lessee Company throughout 1987:

Insurance, Maintenance,   (No entry)
   Taxes, etc.   XXX
Cash or Accounts
   Payable   XXX

Depreciation Expense on the Aircraft, December 31, 1987:

Depreciation Expense   5,333,333   (No entry)
Accumulated Depreciation—
   Capital Leases   5,333,333
   ($80,000,000 ÷ 15)

Amortization of Profit on Sale-Leaseback by Lessee Company, December 31, 1987:

Unearned Profit on   (No entry)
   Sale-Leaseback   300,000
   Depreciation Expense   300,000
   ($4,500,000 ÷ 15)

Note: A case might be made for crediting Revenue
instead of Depreciation Expense.

Interest for 1987, December 31, 1987:

Interest Expense—   Unearned Interest
   Capital Leases   8,341,507[a]   Revenue   8,341,507
   Interest Payable   8,341,507   Interest Revenue—
                                     Lease   8,341,507[a]

[a]Partial Lease Amortization Schedule:

Date	Annual Rental Payment	Interest 12%	Reduction of Balance	Balance
Jan. 1/87				$80,000,000
Jan. 1/87	$10,487,443	–0–	$10,487,443	69,512,557
Jan. 1/88	10,487,443	$8,341,507	2,145,936	67,366,621

3. Set the lease term at something less than 75% of the estimated economic life of the leased property.
4. Arrange for the present value of the minimum lease payments to be less than 90% of the fair value of the leased property.

But the real challenge lies in disqualifying the lease as a capital lease to the lessee while having the same lease qualify as a capital (sales or financing) lease to the lessor. Unlike lessees, lessors try to avoid having lease arrangements classified as operating leases.

Avoiding the first two criteria is relatively simple, but it takes a little ingenuity to avoid the "90% recovery test" for the lessee while satisfying it for the lessor. Two of the factors involved in this effort are: (1) the use of the incremental borrowing rate by the lessee when it is higher than the implicit interest rate of the lessor, by making information about the implicit rate unavailable to the lessee; and (2) residual value guarantees.

The lessee's use of the higher interest rate is probably the more popular subterfuge. While lessees are knowledgeable about the fair value of the leased property and, of course, the rental payments, they generally are not aware of the estimated residual value used by the lessor. Thus the lessee does not know exactly the lessor's implicit rate and is free to use the incremental borrowing rate.

The residual value guarantee is the other unique, yet popular, device used by the lessees and lessors. In fact, a whole new industry has emerged to circumvent symmetry between the lessee and the lessor in accounting for leases. The residual value guarantee has spawned numerous companies whose principal, or even sole, function is to guarantee the residual value of leased assets. These "third-party guarantors" (insurers), for a fee, assume the risk of deficiencies in leased asset residual value.[24]

Because the guaranteed residual value is included in the minimum lease payments for the lessor, the 90% recovery of fair market value test is satisfied and the lease is a nonoperating lease to the lessor. Because the residual value is guaranteed by a third party, the minimum lease payments of the lessee do not include the guarantee. Thus by merely transferring some of the risk to a third party, lessees can alter substantially the accounting treatment by converting what would otherwise be capital leases to operating leases.

Much of this circumvention is encouraged by the nature of the criteria which stem from weaknesses in the basic objective of *CICA Handbook*, Section 3065. Accounting standard-setting bodies continue to have poor experience with arbitrary break points or other size and percentage criteria (i.e., rules like "90% of," "75% of," etc.). As indicated earlier, some accountants believe that a more workable solution would be to require capitalization of all leases that extend for some defined period (such as one year) on the basis that the lessee has acquired an asset (a property right) and a corresponding liability, rather than on the basis that the lease transfers substantially all the risks and rewards of ownership. Others take a less stringent stand, but nonetheless call for capitalization of more lease transactions.

---

[24]Third-party guarantors have experienced some difficulty. Lloyd's of London, for example, insured the fast-growing U.S. computer-leasing industry in the amount of $2 billion against revenue losses and losses in residual value if leases were cancelled. Because of "overnight" technological improvements and the successive introductions of more efficient and less expensive computers by IBM, lessees in abundance cancelled their leases. As the market for second-hand computers became flooded and residual values plummeted, third-party guarantor Lloyd's of London projected a loss of $400 million. Much of the third-party guarantee business was stimulated by the lessees' and lessors' desire to circumvent the profession's capitalization rules.

REPORTING LEASE DATA IN FINANCIAL STATEMENTS

Disclosures Required of the Lessee

The CICA requires that the following information on leases be disclosed in the lessee's financial statements or in the notes:

1. For **capital leases**:
   a. The gross amount of assets recorded under capital leases and related accumulated amortization as of the date of each balance sheet presented, in aggregate and, preferably, by major category.
   b. Future minimum lease payments as of the date of the latest balance sheet presented, in the aggregate and for each of the five succeeding fiscal years, with a separate deduction for amounts included in the minimum lease payments representing executory costs and imputed interest.
   c. The portion, if any, of the lease obligations that is payable within one year out of current funds should be reported as a current liability.
   d. Periodic interest expense related to lease obligations may be disclosed either separately or included in interest on long-term indebtedness.
   e. It may be desirable to disclose separately total contingent rentals (rentals based on a factor other than the passage of time) as well as the amount of future minimum rentals receivable from noncancelable sub-leases.
2. For **operating leases**:
   a. The future minimum lease payments both in aggregate and for each of the five succeeding years.
   b. A description of any other commitments under operating leases.[25]

Disclosures Required of the Lessor

The CICA requires that **lessors** disclose in the financial statements or in the notes the following information:

1. For **operating leases**:
   a. The cost of property held for leasing and the amount of accumulated depreciation.
   b. Rental income from operating leases.
   c. Minimum future rentals both in aggregate and for each of the five succeeding years are not explicitly required but are desirable.
2. For **sales-type and direct financing leases**:
   a. The lessor's net investment in sales-type and direct financing leases; it may also be desirable to present the components of the net investment—namely:
      i. Future minimum lease payments receivable.
      ii. Unguaranteed residual values.
      iii. Unearned finance income.
      iv. Executory costs included in the minimum lease payments receivable.
   b. Future minimum lease payments to be received for each of the five succeeding fiscal years as of the date of the balance sheet presented.
   c. Total contingent rentals included in income.

Illustrated Disclosures

The financial statement excerpts from the 1982 annual report of Loblaw Companies Ltd., which follow, present the statement and note disclosures typical of a lessee having capital leases.

---

[25]*CICA Handbook*, Section 3065, par. 32.

Loblaw Companies Ltd.

	1982	1981
Fixed Assets, at cost	(in thousands of dollars)	
Land	$ 48,942	$ 31,184
Buildings	114,422	88,347
Equipment and fixtures	347,253	335,627
Leasehold improvements	114,887	124,101
	625,504	579,259
Accumulated depreciation	249,499	239,345
	376,005	339,914
Property under capital leases, less accumulated depreciation (Note 6)	80,754	85,880
	$456,759	$425,794
Current Liabilities:		
Current portion of obligations under capital leases	6,152	5,389
Noncurrent Liabilities:		
Obligations under capital leases (Note 6)	86,798	89,498
Income Statement		
Operating expenses:		
Depreciation of property under capital leases	8,938	8,480
Interest on obligations under capital leases	10,789	11,431

Notes to Financial Statements

1. Summary of Significant Accounting Policies (in part)
    (h) Leases
    Leases entered into after December 30, 1978, which transfer substantially all of the benefits and risks incident to ownership of property are recorded as the acquisition of an asset and the incurrence of an obligation. Under this method of accounting for leases, the asset is amortized on a straight-line basis and the obligation, including interest thereon, is liquidated over the life of the lease. Rents on noncapital leases and on all leases entered into before December 31, 1978, are expensed as incurred.

6. Leases and Commitments
    The Company and its subsidiaries have obligations under long-term leases for retail outlets, warehousing facilities, equipment, and store fixtures. Assets under capital leases entered into after December 30, 1978, and recorded as assets are:

	1982	1981
	(in thousands of dollars)	
Buildings	$ 50,742	$ 48,137
Equipment and fixtures	55,368	54,159
	106,110	102,296
Accumulated depreciation	25,356	16,416
	$ 80,754	$ 85,880

Retroactive application of capitalization of leases entered into before December 31, 1978, would have increased net earnings in 1982 by $268,000 (1981—reduced by $619,000), and assets and obligations would have increased by $107,727,000 (1981—$125,803,000) and $131,917,000 (1981—$169,158,000) respectively.

The following table represents minimum lease commitments together with the present value of the obligations under capital leases entered into after December 31, 1978.

| | Capital Leases Entered into after December 30, 1978 | Other Leases | | |
		Gross	Expected Sub-lease Income	Expected Net Liability
	(in thousands of dollars)			
For the year				
1983	$ 17,232	$ 68,755	$ 23,348	$ 45,407
1984	17,432	65,135	21,382	43,753
1985	17,351	58,621	17,998	40,623
1986	17,427	54,043	14,618	39,425
1987	16,192	50,306	12,090	38,216
Thereafter to 2054	109,523	378,591	68,083	310,508
Total minimum lease payments	$195,157	$675,451	$157,519	$517,932
Less: Amounts representing executory costs and interest at 11.5%	102,207			
Balance of obligation	92,950			
Less: Current portion	6,152			
	$ 86,798			

In addition, subsidiaries of the Company are contingently liable under assigned leases, the gross rentals of which amount to approximately $36 million.

OPERATING LEASE DISCLOSURES **Glosser Bros., Inc.** (Lessee)

NOTE D—LEASING ARRANGEMENTS

The Company conducts its retail store operations primarily from leased facilities. Substantially all leases contain provisions for multiple renewal options. Leases are primarily net leases which require the payment of executory costs such as real estate taxes, incurrence, common area maintenance, and other operating costs in addition to minimum rentals. The remaining leases are gross leases which provide for minimum rentals that include executory costs. Certain leases require additional rentals based on percentages of sales exceeding specified amounts.

Following is a schedule by fiscal year of future minimum rental payments required under operating leases that have initial or remaining noncancelable lease terms in excess of one year as of January 26, 1985:

1985	$ 5,540,000
1986	5,528,000
1987	5,286,000
1988	4,759,000
1989	4,168,000
Later years	45,098,000
Total minimum rental payments required	$70,379,000

Rental expense is as follows:

	1984	1983	1982
Minimum rents	$4,690,000	$4,266,000	$4,122,000
Additional rents	633,000	458,000	357,000
Total	$5,323,000	$4,724,000	$4,479,000

Included in rental expenses are leases from affiliated lessors which approximated $520,000, $578,000, and $534,000 in 1984, 1983, and 1982 respectively.

For another illustration of lease disclosure by a lessee, see Indal Limited's Note 6 under "Leases" on page 229.

The note from the 1985 annual report of Glosser Bros. Inc. on page 1045 illustrates the disclosures of a lessee having only operating leases:

Illustration of Different Lease Arrangements

To illustrate a number of concepts discussed in this chapter, assume that Morgan Bakeries is involved in four different lease situations as described below. Each of these leases is noncancelable, and in no case does Morgan receive title to the properties leased during or at the end of the lease term. All leases start on January 1, 1987, with the first rental due at the beginning of the year. The additional information is as follows:

Lessor	Harmon Ltd.	Arden's Oven Co.	Mendota Truck Co.	Appleland Computer
Type of property	Cabinets	Oven	Truck	Computer
Yearly rental	$6,000.00	$15,000.00	$5,582.62	$3,557.25
Lease term	20 years	10 years	3 years	3 years
Estimated economic life	30 years	25 years	7 years	5 years
Purchase option	None	$35,000 at end of 10 years $4,000 at end of 15 years	None	$3,000 at end of 5 years, which approximates fair market value.
Renewal option	None	5-year renewal option at $12,000 per year	None	1-year at $1,500; no penalty for nonrenewal.
Fair market value at inception of lease	$60,000.00	$120,000.00	$20,000.00	$10,000.00
Cost of asset to lessor	$60,000.00	$120,000.00	$15,000.00	$10,000.00
Residual value				
Guaranteed	–0–	–0–	$7,000.00	–0–
Unguaranteed	$5,000.00	–0–	–0–	$3,000.00
Incremental borrowing rate of lessee	12%	12%	12%	12%
Executory costs paid by	Lessee $300 per year	Lessee $1,000 per year	Lessee $500 per year	Lessor Estimated to be $500 per year, including profit thereon.
Present value of minimum lease payments Using incremental borrowing rate of lessee	$50,194.68	$111,253.59	$20,000.00	$8,224.16
Using implicit rate of lessor	Not known	Not known	Not known	Known by lessee $8,027.45
Fair market value at end of lease	$5,000.00	$38,000 at end of 10 years $20,000 at end of 15 years	Not available	$3,000.00

Harmon Ltd. The following is an analysis of the Harmon Ltd. lease:

1. Transfer of title? No.
2. Bargain purchase option? No.
3. Economic life test (75% test): The lease term is 20 years and the estimated economic life is 30 years. Thus it does **not** meet the 75% test.
4. Recovery of investment test (90% test):

Fair market value	$60,000	Rental payments	$ 6,000.00
Rate	90%	PV of annuity due for	
	$54,000	20 years at 12%	8.36578
			$50,194.68

The present value of the minimum lease payments is less than 90% of the fair market value, and therefore this test is not met. Both Morgan and Harmon should account for this lease as an operating lease, as indicated by the entries shown below on January 1, 1987.

Morgan Bakeries (Lessee)			Harmon Ltd. (Lessor)		
Rental Expense	6,000		Cash	6,000	
Cash		6,000	Rental Revenue		6,000

Arden's Oven Co.   The following is an analysis of Arden's Oven Co.'s lease:

1. Transfer of title? No.
2. Bargain purchase option? The $35,000 option at the end of 10 years does not appear to be sufficiently lower than the expected fair value of $38,000 to be reasonably assured that it will be exercised. However, the $4,000 at the end of 15 years, when the fair value is $20,000, does appear to be a bargain. From the information given, test 1 is therefore met.
3. Economic life test (75% test): Given that a bargain purchase option exists, the lease term is the initial lease period of 10 years plus the five-year renewal option since it precedes a bargain purchase option. Even though the lease term is now 15 years, this test is still **not** met because 75% of the economic life of 25 years is 18.75 years.
4. Recovery of investment test (90%) test:

Fair market value	$120,000	Rental payments (1–10)	$ 15,000.00
Rate	90%	PV of annuity due for	
90% of the fair market value	$108,000	10 years at 12%	6.32825
		PV of rental payments 1 through 10	$ 94,923.75
		Rental payments (11-15)	$ 12,000.00
		PV of annuity due for 5 years beginning after 10 (7.62817 – 6.32825)	1.29992
		PV of rental payments 11 through 15	$ 15,599.04
		PV of rental payments	$110,522.79
		Bargain purchase option	$ 4,000.00
		PV of $1 due in 15 years at 12%	.18270
		PV of bargain purchase option	$ 730.80
		PV of minimum lease payments	$111,253.59

The present value of the minimum lease payments is greater than 90% of the fair market value; therefore, the 90% test is met. Morgan Bakeries should account for this as a capital lease as both criteria (a) and (c) are met. Assuming that Arden's Oven Co.'s implicit rate is the same as Morgan's incremental borrowing rate, the following entries are made on January 1, 1987:

Morgan Bakeries (Lessee)		Arden's Oven Co. (Lessor)		
Leased Asset—Oven	111,253.59	Lease Payments		
Obligation Under		Receivable	214,000*	
Capital Lease	111,253.59	Asset—Oven		120,000
		Unearned Interest		
		Revenue		94,000
		*[($15,000 × 10) + ($12,000 × 5) + $4,000]		

Morgan Bakeries would depreciate the lease asset over its economic life of 25 years, given the bargain purchase option. Arden does not use sales-type lease accounting because the fair market value and the cost of the asset are the same at the inception of the lease.

Mendota Truck Co.   The following is an analysis of the Mendota Truck Co. lease:

1. Transfer of title? No.
2. Bargain purchase option? No.
3. Estimated economic life test (75% test): The lease term is three years and the estimated economic life is seven years. Thus it does **not** meet the 75% test.
4. Recovery of investment test (90% test):

Fair market value	$20,000	Rental payments	$ 5,582.62
Rate	90%	PV on annuity due for	
90% of the fair market value	$18,000	3 years at 12%	2.69005
		PV of rental payments	$15,017.54*
		(*adjusted for .01 due to rounding)	
		Guaranteed residual value	$ 7,000.00
		PV of 1 for 3 years at 12%	.71178
		PV of guaranteed residual value	$ 4,982.46
		PV of rental payments	$15,017.54
		PV of guaranteed residual value	4,982.46
		PV of minimum lease payments	$20,000.00

The present value of the minimum lease payments is greater than 90% of the fair market value; therefore, the 90% test **is** met. Assuming that Mendota Truck Co.'s implicit rate is the same as Morgan's incremental borrowing rate, the following entries are made on January 1, 1987:

Morgan Bakeries (Lessee)		Mendota Truck Co. (Lessor)		
Leased Asset	20,000.00	Lease Payments		
Lease Obligation	20,000.00	Receivable	23,747.86*	
		Cost of Goods Sold	15,000.00	
		Asset—Truck		15,000.00
		Sales		20,000.00
		Unearned Interest		
		Revenue		3,747.86
		*[($5,582.62 × 3) + $7,000]		

The leased asset is depreciated over three years to its guaranteed residual value.

Appleland Computer The following is an analysis of the Appleland Computer lease:

1. Transfer of title? No.
2. Bargain purchase option? No. The option to purchase at the end of three years at approximate fair market value is clearly not a bargain.
3. Economic life test (75% test): The lease term is three years and no bargain renewal period exists. Therefore the 75% test is **not** met.
4. Recovery of investment test (90% test):

Fair market value	$10,000	Rental payments	$3,557.25
Rate	90%	Less: Executory costs	
90% of the fair market value	$ 9,000	and profit thereon	500.00
			$3,057.25
		PV of annuity due for	
		3 years at 12%	2.69005
		PV of minimum lease	
		payments using incre-	
		mental borrowing rate	$8,224.16

The present value of the minimum lease payments using the incremental borrowing rate is $8,224.16; using the implicit rate it is $8,027.48. The lessee uses the lower $8,027.45 when comparing to 90% of the fair market value. However, the present value of the minimum lease payments is lower than the adjusted fair market value, and therefore the recovery of investment test is **not** met.

The following entries are therefore made on January 1, 1987, indicating an operating lease.

Morgan Bakeries (Lessee)			Appleland Computer (Lessor)		
Rental Expense	3,557.25		Cash	3,557.25	
Cash		3,557.25	Rental Revenue		3,557.25

If the executory costs had not been deducted in this case, capital lease treatment would have been required, since the 90% test would have been met.

KEY POINTS

1. A lease is a contractual agreement between a lessor and a lessee that conveys the right to use a specific property owned by the lessor for a specific period of time.
2. For accounting purposes, leases are classified as either operating or capital.
3. When substantially all of the risks and rewards of ownership are transferred to the lessee through a lease, the lease is accounted for as a capital lease. Otherwise, leases are treated as operating leases.
4. Operating leases are recorded as expenses (revenues) over the lease term as the asset services are used (based on time or other contractually defined measurement).

5. Lessees record capital leases as a purchase of asset services, Assets Under Capital Leases, and an offsetting liability, Lease Payments Receivable. Each of these accounts at the inception of the lease is equal to the present value of the minimum lease payments as defined by the *CICA Handbook*.

6. Periodic expense associated with a capital lease is composed of: (1) amortization of the asset (lease rights), (2) interest on the unpaid balance of the capitalized lease payments, and (3) any executory costs paid by the lessee.

7. Lessors report capital leases as either financing or sales-type leases. When the asset leased has a fair value that differs from its carrying value on the lessor's books, the lease is recorded as a sales-type lease; otherwise the lessor records capital leases as financing leases.

8. Periodic revenue reported by a lessor in a capital lease consists of financing income (interest) on the unpaid balance of the capitalized lease payments. In addition, a trading margin on sales-type leases is reported in the originating year of the lease.

9. Residual value is the estimated fair value of the leased asset at the termination of the lease. If the lessee guarantees that the asset will have a certain residual value at the end of the lease term, this amount is included in the calculation of the lessee's capitalized value of the lease. The lessor will always include residual values, whether guaranteed or not, in calcuations of capitalized values.

10. A bargain purchase option is a clause in the lease agreement permitting the lessee to acquire the leased property at the end of the lease for a price substantially lower than its estimated residual value. Both lessor and lessee include the amount of a bargain purchase option in their calculations of capitalized values.

11. If the owner of property sells the property to another and simultaneously leases it back from the new owner, the transaction is known as a sale-leaseback. Any profit realized on the sale of property in these transactions should be deferred and recognized over the term of the lease.

12. Lessees (lessors) record expense (revenue) as it accrues under the lease agreement. Assets and/or liabilities arise only if related expenses (revenues) are recognized in different fiscal periods than those in which the related cash payments (receipts) occur.

13. The CICA requires extensive disclosure of details pertaining to capitalized leases. These include, among other items, assets held or leased under capital leases and future minimum lease payments (receivable) both in aggregate for the lease term and detailed for each of the five years following the date of the financial statements.

REAL ESTATE LEASES

Special problems can arise when leases involve land, or land and buildings, or equipment as well as real estate.

Land

If land is the sole item of property leased, the **lessee** should account for the lease as a capital lease only if criterion (1) is met; that is, if the lease transfers ownership of the property or contains a bargain purchase option; otherwise it is accounted for as an operating lease. The **lessor** accounts for a land lease either as a sales-type or direct financing lease, whichever is appropriate, if the lease transfers ownership or contains a bargain purchase option and meets both the collectibility and uncertainties tests; otherwise the operating method is used.

Land and Buildings

If both land and buildings are involved and the lease transfers ownership or contains a bargain purchase option, the land and the building(s) should be separately classified by the **lessee**. The present value of the minimum lease payments is allocated between land and buildings in proportion to their fair values at the inception of the lease. The **lessor** accounts for the lease as a single unit either as a sales-type, direct financing, or operating lease, as appropriate.

When both land and buildings are involved and the lease does not transfer ownership or contain a bargain purchase option, the accounting treatment depends upon the proportion of land to buildings. If the fair value of the land is "minor" in relation to the total fair value of the leased property, both lessee and lessor consider the land and the building as a single unit. However, if the fair value of the land at the inception of the lease is "significant" in relation to the total fair value of the leased property, the land and the building are considered separately by both lessee and lessor. The lessee accounts for the building as a capital lease and the land as an operating lease if one of the two remaining criteria (2) and (3) is met. If none of the criteria is met, the lessee uses the operating method on the land and the building. The lessor accounts for the building as a sales-type or direct financing lease as appropriate and the land element separately as an operating lease.

Real Estate and Equipment

If a lease involves both real estate and equipment, the portion of the lease payments applicable to the equipment should be estimated by whatever means are appropriate and reasonable. The equipment then should be treated separately for purposes of applying the criteria and accounted for separately according to its classification by both lessee and lessor.

QUESTIONS

1. VanBuer Fertilizer, Inc. is expanding its operations and is in the process of selecting the method of financing this program. After some investigation, the company determines that it may (a) issue bonds and with the proceeds purchase the needed assets, or (b) lease the assets on a long-term basis.

   Without knowing the comparative costs involved, answer these questions:
   1. What might be the advantages of leasing the assets instead of owning them?
   2. What might be the disadvantages of leasing the assets instead of owning them?
   3. In what way will the balance sheet be differently affected by leasing the assets as opposed to issuing bonds and purchasing the assets?

2. Gourmet Foods Corp. is considering leasing a significant number of assets. The president, Peggy Graham, is attending an informal meeting in the afternoon with a potential lessor. Because her legal advisor cannot be reached, she has called on you, the controller, to brief her on the general provisions of lease agreements to which she should give consideration in such preliminary discussions with a possible lessor.

   Identify the general provisions of the lease agreement that the president should be told to include in her discussion with the potential lessor.

3. Identify the lease classifications for lessees and the criteria that must be met for each classification.

4. Identify the two recognized lease accounting methods for lessees and distinguish between them.

5. The Lawn Mower Company rents a warehouse on a month-to-month basis for the storage of its excess inventory. The company periodically must rent space whenever its production greatly exceeds actual sales. For several years the company officials have discussed building their own storage facility, but this enthusiasm wavers when sales increase sufficiently to absorb the excess inventory.

   What is the nature of this type of lease arrangement, and what accounting treatment should be accorded it?

6. What disclosures should be made by a lessee if the leased assets and the related obligation are not capitalized?

7. Differentiate between the "lessee's incremental borrowing rate" and the "lessor's implicit rate" in accounting for leases, indicating when one or the other should be used.

8. Outline the accounting procedures involved in applying the operating method by a lessee.

9. Outline the accounting procedures involved in applying the capital lease method by a lessee.

10. Identify the lease classifications for lessors and the criteria that must be met for each classification.

11. Outline the accounting procedures involved in applying the operating method by a lessor.

12. Outline the accounting procedures involved in applying the direct financing method.

13. Microdot Company is a manufacturer and lessor of computer equipment. What should be the nature of its lease arrangements with lessees if the company wishes to account for its lease transactions as sales-type leases?

14. Vacuum Sweeper Corporation's lease arrangements qualify as sales-type leases at the time of entering into the transactions. How should the corporation recognize revenues and costs in these situations?

15. Why are present-value concepts appropriate and applicable in accounting for financing-type lease arrangements?

16. Jerry Moluf, M.D. (lessee) has a noncancelable 20-year lease with E.T. Elsner Realty, Inc. (lessor) for the use of a medical building. Taxes, insurance, and maintenance are paid by the lessee in addition to the fixed annual payments, of which the present value is equal to the fair market value of the leased property. At the end of the lease period, title to the property becomes the lessee's upon payment of a nominal price.

   Considering the terms of the lease described above, comment on the nature of the lease transaction and the accounting treatment that should be accorded it by the lessee.

17. The residual value is the estimated fair value of the leased property at the end of the lease term.
    (a) Of what significance is (1) an unguaranteed and (2) a guaranteed residual value in the lessee's accounting for a capitalized lease transaction?
    (b) Of what significance is (1) an unguaranteed and (2) a guaranteed residual value in the lessor's accounting for a direct financing lease transaction?

18. How should changes in the estimated residual value be handled by the lessor?

19. Describe the effect of a "bargain purchase option" on accounting for a capital lease transaction by a lessee.

20. What are "initial direct costs" and how are they accounted for?

21. What is the nature of a "sale-leaseback" transaction?

CASES

C22-1 Milton Corporation entered into a lease arrangement with Foxy Leasing Corporation for a certain machine. Milton will lease the machine for a period of three years, which is 50% of the machine's economic life. Foxy will take possession of the machine at the end of the initial three-year lease and lease it to another smaller company that does not need the most current version of the machine. Milton does not guarantee any residual value for the machine and will not purchase the machine at the end of the lease term.

   Milton's incremental borrowing rate is 10%, and the implicit rate in the lease is 8.5%. Milton has no way of knowing the implicit rate used by Foxy. Using either rate, the present value of the minimum lease payments is between 90% and 100% of the fair value of the machinery at the date of the lease agreement.

Milton has agreed to pay all executory costs directly, and no allowance for these costs is included in the lease payments.

Foxy is reasonably certain that Milton will pay all lease payments and, because Milton has agreed to pay all executory costs, there are no important uncertainties regarding costs to be incurred by Foxy. Assume that no indirect costs are involved.

Instructions

(a) With respect to Milton (the lessee), answer the following:

1. What type of lease has been entered into? Explain the reason for your answer.
2. How should Milton compute the appropriate amount to be recorded for the lease or asset acquired?
3. What accounts will be created or affected by this transaction, and how will the lease or asset and other costs related to the transaction be matched with earnings?
4. What disclosures must Milton make regarding this lease or asset?

(b) With respect to Foxy (the lessor), answer the following:

1. What type of leasing arrangement has been entered into? Explain the reason for your answer.
2. How should this lease be recorded by Foxy, and how are the appropriate amounts determined?
3. How should Foxy determine the appropriate amount of earnings to be recognized from each lease payment?
4. What disclosures must Foxy make regarding this lease?

(AICPA adapted)

EXERCISES

E22-1 Nancy Beasley Leasing Company leases a new machine that cost $36,000 to Patty Hart Corporation on a three-year noncancelable contract. Patty Hart Corporation agrees to assume all risks of normal ownership including such costs as insurance, taxes, and maintenance. The machine has a three-year useful life and no residual value. The lease was signed on January 1, 1986. Beasley Leasing Company expects to earn a 10% return on its investment. The annual rentals are payable on each December 31.

Instructions

(a) Discuss the nature of the lease arrangement and the accounting method that each party to the lease should apply.

(b) Prepare an amortization schedule that would be suitable for both the lessor and the lessee and which covers all the years involved.

E22-2 Stillwater Company enters into a lease agreement on July 1, 1985, for the purpose of leasing a machine to be used in its manufacturing operations. The following data pertain to this agreement:

1. The term of the noncancelable lease is three years, with no renewal option, and no residual value at the end of the lease term. Payments of $92,935.08 are due on July 1 of each year, beginning July 1, 1985.
2. The fair value of the machine on July 1, 1985 is $265,000. The machine has a remaining economic life of five years, with no salvage value. The machine reverts to the lessor on the termination of the lease.
3. Stillwater Company elects to depreciate the machine on the straight-line method.
4. Stillwater Company's incremental borrowing rate is 12% per year. Stillwater does not have knowledge of the implicit rate computed by the lessor.

Instructions

Prepare the journal entries on the books of the lessee that relate to the lease agreement through July 1, 1987. The accounting period of Stillwater Company ends on December 31. (Assume that reversing entries are made.)

E22-3 On January 1, 1986, Judy Nolan Paper Co. signs a 10-year, noncancelable lease agreement to lease a storage building from Temporary Storage Company. The following information pertains to this lease agreement:

1. The agreement requires equal annual rental payments of $135,000 beginning January 1, 1986.
2. The fair value of the building on January 1, 1986 is $800,000.
3. The building has an estimated economic life of 12 years with an unguaranteed residual value of $10,000. Nolan Paper Co. depreciates similar buildings on the straight-line method.
4. The lease is nonrenewable. At the termination of the lease, the building reverts to the lessor.
5. Nolan Paper's incremental borrowing rate is 12% per year. The lessor's implicit rate is not known by Nolan Paper Co.
6. The yearly rental payment includes $8,582.74 of executory costs related to taxes on the property.

Instructions

Prepare the journal entries on the lessee's books to reflect the signing of the lease agreement and to record the payments and expenses related to this lease for the years 1986 and 1987.

E22-4 Jones Housing Company leases an automobile with a fair value of ~~$6,000~~ $7,000 from Amazing Motors, Inc. on the following terms:

1. Noncancelable term of 50 months.
2. Rental of $150 per month (at end of each month; present value at 1% per month is $5,877).
3. Estimated residual value after 50 months is $910 (the present value at 1% per month is $552). Jones Housing Company guarantees the residual value of $910.
4. Estimated economic life of the automobile is 60 months.
5. Jones Housing Company's incremental borrowing rate is 12% a year (1% a month). Amazing's implicit rate is unknown.

Instructions

(a) What is the nature of this lease to Jones Housing Company?
(b) What is the present value of the minimum lease payments?
(c) Record the lease on Jones Housing Company's books at the date of inception.
(d) Record the first month's depreciation on Jones Housing Company's books (assume straight-line).
(e) Record the first month's lease payment.

E22-5 Electric Car Company leases a car at fair value to a salesman on January 1, 1986. The term on the noncancelable lease is four years. The following information about the lease is provided:

1. Title to the car passes to the lessee upon the termination of the lease when residual value is estimated at $1,000. insignificant
2. The fair value of the car is $10,000. The cost of the car to Electric Car Company is $6,000. The car has an economic life of five years.
3. Electric Car Company desires a rate of return of 15% on its investment.
4. Collectibility of the lease payments is reasonably predictable. There are no important uncertainties surrounding the amount of costs yet to be incurred by the lessor.
5. Equal annual lease payments are due at the beginning of each lease year.

Instructions

(a) Prepare a lease amortization schedule for Electric Car Company for the four-year lease term.
(b) What type of lease is this? Discuss.

    (c) Prepare the journal entries in 1986, 1987, and 1988 to record the lease agreement, the receipt of lease payments, and the recognition of income.

E22-6 Joe Williams Leasing Company signs a lease agreement on January 1, 1986 to lease electronic equipment to Hamsmith Company at cost. The term of the noncancelable lease is two years, and payments are required at the end of each year. The following information relates to this agreement:

1. Hamsmith Company has the option to purchase the equipment for $10,000 upon the termination of the lease.
2. The equipment has a cost of $60,000 to Joe Williams Company; the useful economic life is two years, with a salvage value of $10,000.
3. Hamsmith Company is required to pay $5,000 each year to the lessor for executory costs.
4. Joe Williams Company desires to earn a return of ~~8%~~ 12% on its investment.
5. Collectibility of the payments is reasonably predictable, and there are no important uncertainties surrounding the costs yet to be incurred by the lessor.

Instructions

    (a) Prepare the journal entries on the books of Joe Williams Company to reflect the payments received under the lease, and to recognize income, for the years 1986 and 1987.

    (b) Assuming that Hamsmith Company exercises its option to purchase the equipment on December 31, 1987, prepare the journal entry to reflect the sale.

E22-7 On January 1, 1986, Briarpatch Corporation sells land to Ski-Daddle Corporation for $1,100,000, and immediately leases the land back. The relevant information follows:

1. The land was carried on Briarpatch's books at a value of $800,000.
2. The term of the noncancelable lease is 20 years; title will pass to Briarpatch at the end of the lease term.
3. The lease agreement requires equal rental payments of $112,037.40 at the end of each year.
4. The incremental borrowing rate of Briarpatch Corporation is 10%. Briarpatch is aware that Ski-Daddle Corporation set the annual rental to ensure a rate of return of 8%.
5. The land has a fair value of $1,100,000 on January 1, 1986.
6. Briarpatch pays all executory costs. These costs consist of insurance and taxes amounting to $5,000 per year.

Instructions

    Prepare the journal entries for both the lessee and the lessor for 1986 to reflect the sale and leaseback agreement.

PROBLEMS

P22-1 Lease-What-You-Like, Inc. agrees to rent Bob Rode Winery Corporation the equipment that it requires to expand its production capacity to meet customers' demands for its products. The lease agreement calls for five annual lease payments of $200,000 at the end of each year. On the date the capital lease begins, the lessee recognizes the existence of leased assets and the related lease obligation at the present value of the five annual payments discounted at a rate of 15%, $670,432. The lessee uses the effective interest method of reducing lease obligations. The leased equipment has an estimated useful life of five years and no residual value; Rode Winery uses the sum-of-the-years'-digits method on similar equipment that it owns.

Instructions

(a) What would be the total amount of the reduction in the lease obligation of the lessee during the first year? The second year?

(b) Prepare the journal entry made by Rode Winery Corporation (lessee) on the date the lease begins.

(c) Prepare the journal entries to record the lease payment and interest expense for the first year; the second year.

(d) Prepare the journal entry at the end of the first full year to recognize depreciation of the leased equipment.

P22-2 Rob Isham Company leased a new crane to Hefty Products Company under a five-year noncancelable contract starting January 1, 1986. Terms of the lease require payments of $11,000 each January 1 starting January 1, 1986. Isham will pay insurance, taxes, and maintenance charges on the crane, that has an estimated life of 12 years, a fair value of $80,000, and a cost to Isham Company of $80,000. The estimated fair value of the crane is expected to be $10,000 at the end of the lease term. No bargain purchase or renewal options are included in the contract. Both Isham and Hefty adjust and close books annually at December 31. Collectibility is reasonably certain, and no uncertainties exist relative to unreimbursable lessor costs. Hefty's incremental borrowing rate is 7%, and Isham's implicit interest rate of 6% is unknown to Hefty.

Instructions

(a) Identify the type of lease involved and give reasons for your classification. Discuss the accounting treatment that should be applied by both the lessee and lessor.

(b) Prepare all the entries related to the lease contract and leased asset for the year 1986 for the lessee and lessor, assuming:
1. Insurance $160.
2. Taxes $80.
3. Maintenance $490.
4. Straight-line depreciation and salvage value of $2,000.

(c) Discuss what should be presented in the balance sheet and income statement and related notes of both the lessee and the lessor at December 31, 1986.

P22-3 Prairie Railroad and Loco-Motive Corporation enter into an agreement that requires Loco-Motive to build three diesel-electric engines to Prairie's specifications. Upon completion of the engines, Prairie has agreed to lease them for a period of 12 years and to assume all costs and risks of ownership. The lease is noncancelable, becomes effective on January 1, 1986, and requires annual rental payments of $280,000 due each January 1 beginning in 1986.

Prairie's incremental borrowing rate is 13%, and the implicit interest rate used by Loco-Motive and known to Prairie is 12%. The total cost of building the three engines is $1,550,000. The economic life of the engines is estimated to be 12 years with residual value set at zero. The railroad depreciates similar equipment on a straight-line basis. At the end of the lease, the railroad assumes title to the engines. Collectibility is reasonably certain, and no uncertainties exist relative to unreimbursable lessor costs.

Instructions

(Round all numbers to the nearest dollar.)

(a) Discuss the nature of this lease transaction from the viewpoint of both lessee and lessor.

(b) Prepare the journal entry or entries to record the transaction on January 1, 1986 on the books of Prairie Railroad.

(c) Prepare the journal entry or entries to record the transaction on January 1, 1986 on the books of Loco-Motive Corporation.

(d) Prepare the journal entries for both the lessee and the lessor to record the first rental payment on January 1, 1986.

(e) Prepare the journal entries to record interest expense (revenue) for both the lessee and lessor at December 31, 1986. (Prepare a two-year lease amortization schedule.)

(f) Show the items and amounts that would be reported on the balance sheet (not notes) at December 31, 1986 for both the lessee and the lessor.

P22-4 On January 1, 1986, Rainbow Company contracts to lease equipment for five years, agreeing to make a payment of $70,000 (including the executory costs of $10,000) at the beginning of each year commencing in 1986. The taxes, the insurance, and the maintenance, estimated at $10,000 a year, are the obligations of the lessee. The leased equipment is to be capitalized at $267,906. The asset is to be amortized on a straight-line basis, while the obligation is to be reduced on an effective-interest basis. Rainbow Company's incremental borrowing rate is 8%, and the implicit rate in the lease is 6%, which is known by Rainbow. Title to the equipment transfers to Rainbow when the lease expires. The asset has an estimated useful life of five years and no residual value.

Instructions

(Round all numbers to the nearest dollar.)

(a) Explain the probable relationship of the $267,906 amount to the lease arrangement.

(b) Prepare the journal entry or entries that should be recorded on January 1, 1986 by Rainbow Company.

(c) Prepare the journal entry to record depreciation of the leased asset for the year 1986.

(d) Prepare the journal entry to record the interest expense for the year 1986.

(e) Prepare the journal entry to record the lease payment of January 1, 1987.

(f) What amounts will appear on the lessee's December 31, 1986 balance sheet relative to the lease contract?

P22-5 Armaloy Company as lessee signed a lease agreement for equipment for five years, beginning December 31, 1986. Annual rental payments of $30,000 are to be made at the beginning of each lease year (December 31). The taxes, insurance, and the maintenance costs are the obligation of the lessee. The interest rate used by the lessor in setting the payment schedule is 11%; Armaloy's incremental borrowing rate is 12%. Armaloy is unaware of the rate being used by the lessor. At the end of the lease, Armaloy has the option to buy the equipment for $1, considerably below its then-estimated fair value. The equipment has an estimated useful life of eight years. Armaloy uses the straight-line method of depreciation on similar owned equipment.

Instructions

(Round all numbers to the nearest dollar.)

(a) Prepare the journal entry or entries, with explanations, that should be recorded on December 31, 1986 by Armaloy. (Assume no residual value.)

(b) Prepare the journal entry or entries, with explanations, that should be recorded on December 31, 1987 by Armaloy. (Prepare the lease amortization schedule for all five payments.)

(c) Prepare the journal entry or entries, with explanations, that should be recorded on December 31, 1988 by Armaloy.

(d) What amounts would appear on the December 31, 1988 balance sheet of Armaloy relative to the lease arrangement?

P22-6 Seeum, Inc. was incorporated in 1983 to operate as a computer software service firm with an accounting fiscal year ending August 31. Seeum's primary product is a sophisticated on-line inventory-control system; its customers pay a fixed fee plus a usage charge for using the system.

Seeum has leased a large, BIG-I computer system from the manufacturer. The lease calls for a monthly rental of $31,000 for the 144 months (12 years) of the lease term. The estimated useful life of the computer is 15 years.

Each scheduled monthly rental payment includes $5,000 for full-service maintenance on the computer to be performed by the manufacturer. All rentals are payable on the first day of the month beginning with August 1, 1985, the date the computer was installed and the lease agreement was signed.

The lease is noncancelable for its 12-year term, and it is secured only by the manufacturer's chattel lien on the BIG-I system. On any anniversary date of the lease after August, 1990, Seeum can purchase the BIG-I system from the manufacturer at 75% of the then-current fair value of the computer.

This lease is to be accounted for as a capital lease by Seeum, and it will be depreciated by the straight-line method with no expected salvage value. Borrowed funds for this type of transaction would cost Seeum 12% per year (1% per month). Following is a schedule of the present value of $1 for selected periods, discounted at 1% per period when payments are made at the beginning of each period.

Periods (Months)	Present Value of $1 per Period Discounted at 1% per Period
1	1.000
2	1.990
3	2.970
143	76.658
144	76.899

Instructions

Prepare, in general journal form, all entries Seeum should have made in its accounting records during August, 1985, relating to this lease. Give full explanations and show supporting computations for each entry. Remember, August 31 is the end of Seeum's fiscal accounting period, and it will be preparing financial statements on that date. **Do not prepare closing entries.**

(AICPA adapted)

P22-7 Sammie Jones Dairy leases its milking equipment from Zeff Finance Company under the following lease terms:

1. The lease term is five years, noncancelable, and requires equal rental payments of $46,500.00 due at the beginning of each year starting January 1, 1986.
2. The equipment has a fair value at the inception of the lease (January 1, 1986) of $200,100, an estimated economic life of five years, and a residual value (which is guaranteed by Jones Dairy) of $10,000.
3. The lease contains no renewable options, and the equipment reverts to Zeff Finance Company upon termination of the lease.
4. Jones Dairy's incremental borrowing rate is 10% per year; the implicit rate is also 10%.
5. Jones Dairy depreciates similar equipment that it owns on a straight-line basis.
6. Collectibility of the lease payments is reasonably predictable, and there are no important uncertainties surrounding the costs yet to be incurred by the lessor.

Instructions

(a) Describe the nature of the lease and in general discuss how the lessee and lessor should account for the lease transaction.

(b) Prepare the journal entries at January 1, 1986 for both parties.

(c) Prepare the journal entries at December 31, 1986 (both the lessee's and lessor's year end).

(d) Prepare the journal entries at January 1, 1987 for both the lessor and lessee. (Assume no reversing entries are needed.)

(e) On December 31, 1991, the residual value of the equipment is $4,000. Jones Dairy returns to Zeff Finance the equipment and makes good on its residual value guarantee. Prepare the journal entry to record this final transaction of the lease.

P22-8   Bear Company manufactures a desk-type computer with an estimated economic life of 12 years and leases it to Cougar Company for a period of 10 years. The normal selling price of the equipment is $259,569, and its unguaranteed residual value at the end of the lease term is estimated to be $20,000. Cougar will pay annual payments of $40,000 at the beginning of each year and all maintenance, insurance, and taxes.

Bear incurred costs of $200,000 in manufacturing the equipment and $7,000 in negotiating and closing the lease. Bear has determined that the collectibility of the lease payments is reasonably predictable, that there will be no additional costs incurred, and that the implicit interest rate is 12%.

Instructions

(Round all numbers to the nearest dollar.)

(a) Discuss the nature of this lease in relation to the lessor and compute the amount of each of the following items:
1. Gross investment.
2. Unearned income.
3. Sales price.
4. Cost of sales.

(b) Prepare a 10-year lease amortization schedule.

(c) Prepare all of the lessor's journal entries for the first year.

P22-9   On February 1, 1982, Duran Company buys land costing $300,000 and on that site has a large shopping centre constructed to its specifications at a cost of $2,700,000. The centre is completed on December 27, 1985. On January 1, 1986 Duran Company sells the shopping centre property to Fraseval Development Corporation for $3,000,000 cash and immediately signs an agreement to lease the entire property for 40 years, making annual payments of $278,870 on January 1 beginning in 1986. These payments are sufficient to repay the Fraseval Development Corporation its cash outlay and to provide a 10% return on the investment. Title to the property will revert to Duran Company at the termination of the lease. All maintenance and other services, and the cost of insurance, taxes, and utilities, are the responsibility of the lessee. The Duran Company has decided to amortize the property on a straight-line basis.

Instructions

(Round all numbers to the nearest dollar.)

(a) From the information above, prepare journal entries (on an annual basis), with explanations for Duran Company relative to the leased property for the year 1986.

(b) What accounts and amounts will appear in the December 31, 1986 financial statements of Duran Company relative to the leased property?

(c) From the information above, prepare for Fraseval Development Corporation's books journal entries relative to the leased property for the year 1986.

P22-10 Cribkeep Company owns land having a cost of $56,000 on which it constructs a warehouse that is completed on January 1, 1986, at a cost of $404,799. On that date Cribkeep sells the warehouse and the land to Knott Realty Inc. for $504,799 and simultaneously signs a lease under the following conditions:

1. 10 years and noncancelable.
2. Fair values at Jan. 1/86—land $100,000; warehouse $404,799.
3. Estimated life of the warehouse is 20 years with no residual value.
4. Lease payments are $82,154 payable each December 31.
5. Cribkeep Company's incremental borrowing rate is 10%; the lessor uses it to compute the annual payments.
6. Lessee has the option to buy the warehouse for $1 at the end of the lease term.
7. Lessee depreciates similar assets using the straight-line method.
8. Lessee assumes responsibility for executory costs.

9. Collectibility of the payments is reasonably certain, and no uncertainties exist relative to unreimbursable lessor costs.

Instructions

(Round all numbers to the nearest dollar.)

(a) Prepare a lease amortization schedule usable by both lessee and lessor through 1988 to record interest and reduction of principal.

(b) Prepare entries for the books of both the lessee and the lessor on January 1, 1986.

(c) Prepare entries for the books of both the lessee and the lessor for 1986 amortization and the first rental payment on December 31, 1986.

(d) Indicate the amounts and accounts that should appear on the December 31, 1986 balance sheet of both the lessee and the lessor.

(e) Prepare the notes that should accompany the December 31, 1986 financial statements of the lessee and the lessor.

P22-11 In 1985 the Intermountain Express Company negotiated and closed a long-term lease contract for newly constructed truck terminals and freight storage facilities. The buildings were erected to the company's specifications on land owned by the company. On January 1, 1986, Intermountain Express Company took possession of the leased properties.

On January 1, 1986 and 1987, the company made cash payments of $1,440,000 that were recorded as rental expenses.

Although the terminals have a composite useful life of 40 years, the noncancelable lease runs for 20 years from January 1, 1986, with a bargain purchase option available upon expiration of the lease.

The 20-year lease is effective for the period January 1, 1986, through December 31, 2005. Advance rental payments of $1,200,000 are payable to the lessor on January 1 of each of the first 10 years of the lease term. Advance rental payments of $360,000 are due on January 1 for each of the last 10 years of the lease. The company has an option to purchase all of these leased facilities for $1 on December 31, 2005. It also must make annual payments to the lessor of $90,000 for property taxes and $150,000 for insurance. The lease was negotiated to assure the lessor a 6% rate of return.

Instructions

(Round all numbers to the nearest dollar.)

(a) Prepare a schedule to compute for Intermountain Express Company the discounted present value of the terminal facilities and related obligation at January 1, 1986.

(b) Assuming that the discounted present value of terminal facilities and related obligation at January 1, 1986, was $12,000,000, prepare journal entries for Intermountain Express Company to record:

1. Cash payment to the lessor on January 1, 1988.

2. Amortization of the cost of the leased properties for 1988 using the straight-line method and assuming a zero salvage value.

3. Accrual of interest expense at December 31, 1988.

Selected present value factors are as follows:

Periods	For an Ordinary Annuity of $1 at 6%	For $1 at 6%
1	0.943396	0.943396
2	1.833393	0.889996
8	6.209794	0.627412
9	6.801692	0.591898
10	7.360087	0.558395
19	11.158117	0.330513
20	11.469921	0.311805

(AICPA adapted)

P22-12 During 1986, Sharko Leasing Co. began leasing equipment to small manufacturers. Below is information regarding leasing arrangements.

1. Sharko Leasing Co. leases equipment with terms from three to five years, depending on the useful life of the equipment. At the expiration of the lease, the equipment will be sold to the lessee at 10% of the lessor's cost, the expected salvage value of the equipment.

2. The amount of the lessee's monthly payment is computed by multiplying the lessor's cost of the equipment by the payment factor applicable to the term of lease.

Term of lease	Payment factor
3 years	3.32%
4 years	2.63%
5 years	2.22%

3. The excess of the gross contract receivable for equipment rentals over the cost (reduced by the estimated salvage value at the termination of the lease) is recognized as revenue over the term of the lease under the sum-of-the-years'-digits method computed on a monthly basis.

4. The following leases were entered into during 1986:

Machine	Dates of Lease	Period of Lease	Machine Cost
Die	July 1/86–June 30/90	4 years	$45,000
Press	Sept. 1/86–Aug. 31/89	3 years	$30,000

Instructions

(a) Prepare a schedule of gross contracts receivable for equipment rentals at the dates of the lease for the die and press machines.

(b) Prepare a schedule of unearned lease income at December 31, 1986 for each machine lease.

(c) Prepare a schedule computing the present dollar value of lease payments receivable (gross investment) for equipment rentals at December 31, 1986. (The present dollar value of the "lease receivables for equipment rentals" is the outstanding amount of the gross lease receivables less the unearned lease income included therein.) Without prejudice to your solution to (b), assume that the unearned lease income at December 31, 1986, was $29,000.

(AICPA adapted)

23

ACCOUNTING CHANGES AND ERROR ANALYSIS

Such headlines as the following often appear in the financial press:

"Accounting change aids White Farm."

"Aeronautical company revises estimates of service lives of Boeing 747s."

"Deficit would have been $20 million more if firm hadn't altered accounting."

"AT&T changes in accounting result in $7.3 billion charge to 1983 income."

Why do these changes in accounting occur? The reasons are numerous; to illustrate, we discuss three. First, the accounting profession may mandate the use of a new accounting method or principle. For example, in 1978 the CICA for the first time required expensing of research costs. Second, changing economic conditions may cause a company to change its methods of accounting. Third, changes in technology and in operations may require a company to revise the service lives, depreciation method, or the expected salvage value of depreciable assets. For example, the AT&T changed its estimates and depreciation methods as a result of changes in its competitive environment and in telecommunications technology. Whatever the cause, changes in accounting should result in more useful information for decision making. Accountants must determine whether such changes are appropriate and, if made, how they should be reported to facilitate analysis and understanding of financial statements.

While the qualitative characteristics of **usefulness** may be enhanced by changes in accounting, the characteristics of **comparability** and **consistency** may be adversely affected. Trends in comparative financial statements and historical 5- and 10-year summaries can be particularly affected by changes in accounting policies. Proper treatment and full disclosure should allow the readers of financial statements to comprehend and assess the effects of changes in accounting upon the financial information reported.

When accounting errors are discovered, the accountant faces similar problems. How should accounting errors be corrected and disclosed so that the usefulness of the financial information is enhanced? In this chapter we discuss the different types of accounting changes and error corrections and the varied procedures in accounting for them.

ACCOUNTING CHANGES

Before the issuance of *CICA Handbook*, Section 1506, ''Accounting Changes,'' in 1980, companies had considerable flexibility in reporting changes affecting comparability in accounting reports. This flexibility was evidenced by alternative accounting treatments that were developed and used in essentially equivalent situations. For example, when the steel companies changed their method of depreciating plant assets from that of accelerated depreciation to straight-line depreciation, the effect of the change was presented in different ways by different companies. The cumulative difference between the depreciation charges that had been recorded and what would have been recorded could have been reflected in the income statement of the period of change. The change could have been ignored, and the undepreciated asset balance simply depreciated on a straight-line basis in the future. Or, companies could simply have restated the prior periods as though the straight-line approach had always been used. Such alternatives diminish comparability of the statements between periods and between companies, and obscure historical-trend data.

An essential step in this area is to categorize the different types of changes that occur in practice.[1]

Types of Accounting Changes

1. **Change in accounting policy**. A change from one generally accepted accounting principle to another generally accepted accounting principle: for example, a change in the method of depreciation from declining balance to straight-line depreciation of plant assets.
2. **Change in accounting estimate.** A change that occurs as a result of the acquisition of additional information or as more experience is acquired. An example is a change in the service lives of depreciable assets.
3. **Change in reporting entity.** A change from reporting as one specific entity to another: for example, acquisition or disposal of a subsidiary company.

Correction of an Error in Previously Issued Financial Statements (not an accounting change)

Errors in financial statements that occur as a result of mathematical mistakes, mistakes in the application of accounting principles, or oversight or misuse of

---

[1]*CICA Handbook*, Section 1506.

facts that existed at the time financial statements were prepared: for example, the incorrect application of the retail inventory method for determining final inventory value.

Changes were classified into these categories because the individual characteristics of each category necessitate different methods of recognizing these changes in the financial statements. Each of these items is discussed separately to investigate its unusual characteristics and to determine how each item should be reflected in the accounts and how the information should be disclosed in comparative statements.

Changes in Accounting Policy

A change in accounting policy involves a change from one generally accepted accounting principle to another. The term "accounting principle" is defined to include changes in the method of application of an accounting principle. Below are examples of changes in accounting principles.

1. Changing the basis of inventory pricing from average cost to LIFO.
2. Changing the method of depreciation on plant assets from accelerated to straight-line.
3. Changing the accounting for construction contracts from the completed-contract to the percentage-of-completion method.

A careful examination must be made in each circumstance to ensure that a change in principle has occurred. **A change in accounting principle is not considered to result from the adoption of a new principle in recognition of events that have occurred for the first time or that were previously immaterial.** For example, adoption of a new and different depreciation method for newly acquired plant assets is not considered a change in accounting principle. Certain marketing expenditures that were previously deemed immaterial and expensed in the period incurred may now be material and acceptably deferred and amortized without being considered a change in accounting principle. Finally, **if the accounting principle previously followed was not acceptable, or if the principle was applied incorrectly, a change to a generally accepted accounting principle is considered a correction of an error.** For example, a switch from the cash basis of accounting to the accrual basis is considered a correction of an error. If the company deducted salvage value when computing declining-balance depreciation on plant assets and later recomputed depreciation without deduction of estimated salvage, a correction of an error occurs.

Three approaches have been suggested for reporting changes in accounting policies in the accounts:

Retroactively   The cumulative effect of the use of the new method on the financial statements at the beginning of the period is computed. A retroactive adjustment of the financial statement is then made, recasting the financial statements of prior years on a basis consistent with the newly adopted principle. Advocates of this position argue that only by restatement of prior periods can changes in accounting principles lead to comparable financial statements. If this approach is not used, the year previous to the change will reflect the old method; the year of the change will reflect the entire cumulative adjustment either in opening retained earnings or in income; and the following year will present financial statements on the new basis without the cumulative effect of the change. The question is how can public confidence in financial statements be maintained when the periods are not comparable? Consistency is considered essential for meaningful earnings-trend data and other financial relationships necessary to evaluate the business.

Currently   The cumulative effect of the use of the new method on the financial statements at the beginning of the period is computed. This adjustment is then reported in the current year's income statement as a special item between the captions "extraordinary items" and "net income." Advocates of this position argue that restating financial statements for prior years results in a loss of confidence in financial reports by investors. How will a present or prospective investor react when told that the earnings computed five years ago are now entirely different? Restatement, if permitted, also might upset many contractual and other arrangements that were based on the old figures. For example, profit-sharing arrangements computed on the old basis might have to be recomputed and completely new distributions made, possibly creating legal problems. Many practical difficulties also exist: the cost of restatement may be excessive, or restatement may be impossible on the basis of data available. Finally, some individuals argue that restatement permits possible manipulation of earnings, because changes affecting income favourably might be handled currently or in the future, while changes having an unfavourable effect might be handled retroactively.

Prospectively   No change is made in previously reported results. Opening balances are not adjusted, and no attempt is made to allocate charges or credits for prior events. Advocates of this position argue that once management presents to investors financial statements based on acceptable accounting principles, the statements are final, because management cannot change prior periods by adopting a new principle. According to this line of reasoning, the cumulative adjustment in the current year is not appropriate, because this approach would reflect in net income an amount that has little or no relationship to the current year's income or economic events.

Three Types of Accounting Changes

Before the adoption of *CICA Handbook*, Section 1506, all three of the approaches above were used. Section 1506, however, settled this issue by establishing guidelines that are to be used, depending on circumstances. We have classified these changes in accounting policy into three categories:

1. Retroactive-with-Restatement
2. Retroactive-without-Restatement
3. Prospective

Retroactive-with-Restatement   The retroactive method with restatement of prior periods should be used to account for changes in accounting policy. The basic requirements are as follows:

1. The newly adopted accounting policy should be applied retroactively.
2. Financial statements for prior periods included for comparative purposes should be restated to give effect to the new accounting policy.
3. The effect of the change on such significant items as net income, earnings per share, and working capital for the current year as well as for prior periods should be disclosed along with a brief description of the change.

To illustrate, assume that Lang Ltd. decided at the beginning of 1987 to change from the declining-balance method of depreciation to the straight-line method for financial reporting on its plant assets. For tax purposes, the company has claimed capital cost allowance that coincidentally is equal to the amount of the declining-balance depreciation, and this relationship will continue. The assets originally cost $100,000 in 1985 and have an estimated useful life of four years. The data assumed for this illustration are:

Year	Declining-Balance Depreciation	Straight-Line Depreciation	Difference	Tax Effect 40%	Effect on Income (net of tax)
1985	$40,000	$18,500	$21,500	$8,600	$12,900
1986	24,000	18,500	5,500	2,200	3,300
			$27,000	$10,800	$16,200

The entry made to record this change in accounting policy in 1987 should be:

Accumulated Depreciation	27,000	
Deferred Income Taxes		10,800
Retained Earnings—Cumulative Effect of		
Change in Accounting Policy—Depreciation		16,200

The debit of $27,000 to Accumulated Depreciation is the excess of the declining-balance depreciation over the straight-line depreciation. The Deferred Income Taxes of $10,800 are recorded to reflect interperiod tax allocation procedures. Prior to the change in accounting principle, depreciation and capital cost allowance were the same. However, if the straight-line method had been employed for book purposes in previous years, the excess of capital cost allowance over book depreciation would have created credits to Deferred Income Taxes totalling $10,800. The cumulative effect on Retained Earnings at the beginning of the year in which the change was made results from the difference between declining-balance and straight-line depreciation, reduced by the tax on that difference.

The information presented in the original income statements prior to the change for 1985 and 1986 is summarized below:

	1986	1985
Lang Ltd. SUMMARIZED COMPARATIVE INCOME STATEMENTS for the Years 1986 and 1985		
Income before extraordinary item (assumed)	$120,000	$111,000
Extraordinary item (assumed)	(30,000)	10,000
Net income	$ 90,000	$121,000
Earnings per share		
Basic earnings per share (100,000 shares)		
Income before extraordinary item	$1.20	$1.11
Extraordinary item	(0.30)	0.10
Net income	$0.90	$1.21

Lang's two-year comparative income statements for 1987 following the change in depreciation method would appear as follows:

Lang Ltd.
SUMMARIZED COMPARATIVE INCOME STATEMENTS
for the Years 1987 and 1986

	1987	1986
Income before extraordinary item (assumed)	$135,000	$123,300*
Extraordinary item (assumed)	18,000	(30,000)
Net income	$153,000	$ 93,300
Earnings per share		
Basic earnings per share (100,000 shares)		
Income before extraordinary item	$1.35	$1.23
Extraordinary item	0.18	(0.30)
Net income	$1.53	$0.93

*Restated

The 1987 comparative statement of retained earnings would reflect the portion of the cumulative effect of the accounting change not included in the 1986 comparative income statement (the portion attributed to 1985).

Lang Ltd.
COMPARATIVE STATEMENT OF RETAINED EARNINGS
for the Years 1987 and 1986

	1987	1986
Balance at beginning of year		
As previously reported (assumed)	$483,800	$450,000
Retroactive change in accounting policy (Note 2)	16,200	12,900
As restated	$500,000	$462,900
Net income	153,000	93,300
	$653,000	$556,200
Dividends	63,000	56,200
Balance at end of year	$590,000	$500,000

Note 2—Change in Depreciation Method for Plant Assets. In 1987 depreciation of plant equipment is computed by use of the straight-line method. In prior years, beginning in 1985, depreciation of plant and equipment was computed by the declining-balance method. The straight-line method has been applied retroactively to equipment acquisitions of prior years. The effect of the change in 1987 was to decrease net income by approximately $2,460 (or two cents per share). The 1986 comparative income statement has been retroactively restated to reflect the effect of the change on 1986 net income (an increase of $3,300, or approximately three cents per share). Income for 1985 and prior periods would have been increased by $12,900, or 13 cents per share.

Only the financial statements presented for comparison purposes are restated to show the effect of the change, and any change attributable to those periods prior to the earliest comparative period presented is shown as an adjustment to beginning Retained Earnings. Other balance sheet accounts affected by the change should also be restated.

Retroactive-without-Restatement   Retroactive restatement requires the use of information that may, in some cases, be unreasonably difficult to obtain. For example, if a construction firm wishes to change from the completed-contract method of accounting for long-term projects to the percentage-of-completion method, it would be necessary to obtain the estimated completion costs for each uncompleted project at various preceding year ends. In such cases where the total cumulative effect of a change in accounting policy may be determined but the effect on individual prior periods cannot be reasonably determined, the *CICA Handbook* permits retroactive adjustment without restatement of prior period financial statements.

To illustrate, assume that Denson Construction Limited has accounted for its income from long-term construction contracts using the completed-contract method. In 1987, the company changed to the percentage-of-completion method because the management believes that this approach provides a more appropriate measure of the income earned. For tax purposes (assume a 40% rate), the company has employed the completed-contract method and plans to continue using this method in the future.

The following information is available for analysis:

Construction in progress December 31, 1986:	
Percentage-of-completion method	$780,000
Completed-contract method	560,000
Difference	$220,000
Less: Tax effect (40%)	88,000
Income effect	$132,000

The entry to record the change in 1987 would be:

Construction in Progress	220,000	
Deferred Income Taxes		88,000
Retained Earnings		132,000

The Construction in Progress account is increased by $220,000, representing the increase in the inventory under the new method. The Deferred Taxes account is used to recognize interperiod tax allocation. If, in previous years, the percentage-of-completion method had been employed for accounting purposes while the completed-contract method was used for tax purposes, a difference of $220,000

STATEMENT OF RETAINED EARNINGS	
December 31, 1987	
Balance at beginning of year, as previously reported	$1,696,000
Add: Adjustment for the cumulative effect on prior years of applying retroactively the new method of accounting for long-term contracts (Note A)	132,000
Balance at beginning of year, as restated	$1,828,000
Net income (assumed)	120,000
Balance at end of year	$1,948,000

Note A—Change in Method of Accounting for Long-Term Contracts. The company has accounted for revenue and costs for long-term contracts by the percentage-of-completion method in 1987, whereas in all prior years revenue and costs were determined by the completed-contract method. The effect on financial statements of prior periods is not determinable, consequently these statements have not been restated. For income tax purposes, the completed-contract method has been continued. The effect of the accounting change on income of 1987 was an increase of $6,000 net of related taxes, and on income of prior periods an increase of $132,000 net of related taxes.

between book income and taxable income would have developed, on which $88,000 of tax would have been deferred.

The adjustment for the cumulative effect of the accounting change would be reported in the statement of retained earnings as shown on page 1069.

The foregoing example is similar to the case involving restatement of prior periods financial statements. The journal entries to record the accounting change are similar since the cumulative effect of the change on Retained Earnings is recorded as an adjustment to beginning Retained Earnings. The only difference between retroactive adjustment with restatement and without restatement is in the printed financial statements. Restatement provides financial statement readers with amounts that would have been reported had the new policy been adopted at an earlier date. On the other hand, retroactive adjustment without restatement leaves the comparative financial statements as originally reported and presents the cumulative effect of the change as an adjustment to beginning Retained Earnings of the current year. In both examples, as required by Section 1506 of the *CICA Handbook*, the effect of the change on the current year's income is disclosed in the note.

Prospective   Retroactive application of a change in an accounting policy may not be possible in some cases because it would be extremely difficult to obtain the necessary financial data. This situation could arise, for example, on the adoption of a new *Handbook* recommendation or legislative requirement such that the cumulative effect of the necessary accounting change could not be determined without incurring unreasonable cost or using imprecise data. In these rare circumstances, it is permissible to make the required or desired accounting change in the current year without restating the beginning Retained Earnings.

As an example, suppose that a new *Handbook* section requires capitalization of interest on certain long-term construction projects. Those firms having assets that have been constructed in the past and now qualifying for interest capitalization would find it extremely difficult to determine the adjusted cost and accumulated depreciation necessary to apply the method retroactively. In these cases, the *Handbook* permits prospective application of the accounting change. That is, the new accounting policy would be applied in the current and future years.

Change in Accounting Estimate

The preparation of financial statements requires estimating the effects of future conditions and events. Future conditions and events and their effects cannot be perceived with certainty; therefore, estimating requires the exercise of judgement. Accounting estimates will change as new events occur, as more experience is acquired, or as additional information is obtained. The following are examples of items that require estimates.

1. Uncollectible receivables.
2. Inventory obsolescence.
3. Useful lives and salvage values of assets.
4. Periods benefited by deferred costs.
5. Liabilities for warranty costs and income taxes.
6. Recoverable mineral reserves.

Changes in estimates must be handled prospectively; that is, no changes should be made in previously reported results. Opening balances are not adjusted, and no attempt is made to "catch up" for prior periods. Financial statements of prior periods are not restated, and pro forma amounts for prior periods are not reported. Instead, the effects of all changes in estimates are accounted for in (1) the period of change if the change affects that period only or (2) the period of change and future periods if the change affects both. As a result, changes in estimates are viewed as normal recurring corrections and adjustments, the natural result of the accounting process, and retroactive treatment is prohibited.

The circumstances related to a change in estimate appear to be very different from those surrounding a change in accounting policy. If changes in estimates were handled on a retroactive or catch-up basis, continual adjustments of prior years' income would occur. It seems proper to accept the view that because new conditions or circumstances exist, the revision fits the new situation and should be handled in the current and future periods.

To illustrate, Salamon Ltd. purchased for $300,000 a building that was originally estimated to have a life of 15 years and no salvage value. Depreciation has been recorded for five years on a straight-line basis. On January 1, 1987, the estimate of the useful life of the asset is revised, so that the asset is considered to have a total life of 25 years. The accounts at the beginning of the sixth year are as follows:

Building	$300,000
Less: Accumulated Depreciation—Building	100,000
Book Value of Building	200,000

The entry to record depreciation for the year 1987 is:

Depreciation Expense	10,000	
Accumulated Depreciation—Building		10,000

The $10,000 depreciation charge is computed as follows:

$$\text{Depreciation Charge} = \frac{\text{Book Value of Asset}}{\text{Remaining Service Life}} = \frac{\$200,000}{25 \text{ years} - 5 \text{ years}}$$

Differentiating between a change in an estimate and a change in an accounting principle is sometimes difficult. When, for example, a company changes from deferring and amortizing certain marketing costs to recording them as an expense as incurred because future benefits of the cost have become doubtful, is it a change in principle or a change in estimate? In such a case, **whenever it is impossible to determine whether a change in principle or a change in estimate has occurred, the change should be considered a change in estimate.**

A similar problem occurs in differentiating between a change in estimate and a correction of an error, although the answer is more clear cut. How do we determine whether the information was overlooked in earlier periods (an error) or whether the information is now available for the first time (change in estimate)? Proper classification is important because corrections of errors have a different accounting treatment from that given changes in estimates. The general rule is that **careful estimates that later prove to be incorrect should be considered changes in esti-**

mate. Only when the estimate was obviously computed incorrectly because of lack of expertise or in bad faith should the adjustment be considered an error. There is no clear demarcation line here, and the accountant must use good judgement in light of all the circumstances.

Reporting a Change in Entity

A change in the reporting entity is not defined as an accounting change in Section 1506 of the *CICA Handbook*. However, specific disclosure requirements for circumstances in which there has been a change in the reporting entity are mandated in Section 1580.

An accounting change that results in financial statements that are actually the statements of a different entity should be reported by (1) restating the financial statements of all prior periods presented to show the financial information for the new reporting entity for all periods or (2) by reporting the activities of the new entity prospectively from the date of acquisition (disposal) and presenting supplementary pro forma information in a note.

When a business combination transaction is accounted for as a pooling of interests, ''the results of operations for the period in which the combination occurs and for all prior periods should be reflected on a combined basis.''[2] Thus, a change in the reporting entity caused by a pooling of interests must be disclosed by retroactive application with restatement of all prior periods.

When an acquisition of another firm has been accounted for as a purchase transaction and the financial statements are consolidated following the acquisition, the resulting change in the reporting entity is disclosed on a prospective basis. That is, the statements of the current and future periods reflect the effect of the change. In addition, if the acquisition takes place on a date other than the beginning of the fiscal period, the acquiring firm should present supplementary information showing on a pro forma basis the amount of income that would have been earned had the acquisition taken place at the beginning of the fiscal period.

If a firm disposes of an investment in a firm previously included in the consolidated financial statements, then income from the remaining or continuing operations should be presented separately from the results of discontinued operations. The reason for this requirement is that projections of future income are facilitated by data about the earnings of that portion of the accounting entity which is expected to continue operations in the future.

In summary, a change in a reporting entity attributed to a pooling of interests requires retroactive restatement of the financial statements, while a change in a reporting entity resulting from either acquisitions or disposals of subsidiaries is disclosed on a prospective basis with supplementary pro forma information containing the full year's earnings of the continuing entity.

Correction of an Error

CICA Handbook, Section 1506, also discusses how a correction of an error should be handled in the financial statements. No business, large or small, is immune from errors. The risk of material errors, however, may be reduced through the installation of good internal controls and the application of sound accounting procedures.

---

[2]*CICA Handbook*, Section 1580, par. 69.

The following are examples of accounting errors:

1. A change from an accounting principle that is **not** generally accepted to an accounting principle that is acceptable. The rationale adopted is that the prior periods were incorrectly presented because of the application of an improper accounting principle: for example, a change from the cash basis of accounting to the accrual basis.

2. Mathematical mistakes that result from adding, subtracting, and so on. An illustration is the totalling of the inventory count sheets incorrectly in computing the inventory value.

3. Changes in estimate that occur because the estimates are not prepared in good faith: for example, the adoption of a clearly unrealistic depreciation rate.

4. An oversight, such as the failure to accrue or defer certain assets and liabilities at the end of the period.

5. A misuse of facts, such as the failure to use salvage value in computing the depreciation base for the straight-line approach.

6. The incorrect classification of a cost as an expense instead of an asset and vice versa.

As soon as they are discovered, errors must be corrected by proper entries in the accounts and reflected in the financial statements. **The profession requires that corrections of errors be accounted for retroactively**, be recorded in the year in which the error was discovered, and be reported in the financial statements as an adjustment to the beginning balance of retained earnings. If comparative statements are presented, the prior statements affected should be restated to correct for the error. The disclosures need not be repeated in the financial statements of subsequent periods.

To illustrate, in 1987, the bookkeeper for Sure Sale Company discovered that in 1986 the company failed to record in the accounts $20,000 of depreciation expense on a newly constructed building. The capital cost allowance is correctly included in the tax return. Because of numerous timing differences, reported net income for 1986 was $150,000, and taxable income was $110,000. The following entry was made for income taxes (assuming a 40% effective tax rate in 1986):

Income Tax Expense	60,000	
Income Tax Payable		44,000
Deferred Income Taxes		16,000

As a result of the $20,000 omission error in 1986:

Depreciation expense (1986) was understated	$20,000
Accumulated depreciation is understated	20,000
Income tax expense (1986) was overstated ($20,000 × 40%)	8,000
Net income (1986) was overstated	12,000
Deferred income taxes is overstated ($20,000 × 40%)	8,000

The entry made in 1987 to correct the omission of $20,000 of depreciation in 1986 would be:

1987 Correcting Entry

Retained Earnings	12,000	
Deferred Income Taxes	8,000	
Accumulated Depreciation—Buildings		20,000

The journal entry to record the correction of the error is the same whether single-period or comparative financial statements are prepared; however, presentation on the financial statements will differ. If single-period (noncomparative) statements are presented, the error should be reported as an adjustment to the opening balance of retained earnings of the period in which the error is discovered, as shown on page 1074

Retained earnings, January 1, 1987:		
As previously reported		$350,000
Correction of an error (depreciation)	$20,000	
Less: Applicable income tax reduction	8,000	(12,000)
Adjusted balance of retained earnings, January 1, 1987		338,000
Add: Net income 1987		400,000
Retained earnings, December 31, 1987		$738,000

If comparative financial statements are prepared, adjustments should be made to correct the amounts for all affected accounts reported in the statements for all periods reported. The data for each year being presented should be restated to the correct basis, and any catch-up adjustment should be shown as an adjustment to retained earnings for the earliest period reported. For example, in the case of Sure Sale Company, the error of omitting the depreciation of $20,000 in 1986, which was discovered in 1987, results in the restatement of the 1986 financial statements when presented in comparison with those of 1987. The following accounts in the 1986 financial statements (presented in comparison with those of 1987) would have been restated.

In the balance sheet:

Accumulated depreciation—buildings	$20,000 increase
Deferred income taxes	$ 8,000 decrease
Retained earnings, ending balance	$12,000 decrease

In the income statement:

Depreciation expense—buildings	$20,000 increase
Tax expense	$ 8,000 decrease
Net income	$12,000 decrease

In the statement of retained earnings:

Retained earnings, ending balance	$12,000 decrease
(owing to lower net income for the period)	

The 1987 financial statements comparing the year's figures with those of 1986 are prepared as if the error had not occurred. As a minimum, such comparative statements in 1987 would include a note calling attention to restatement of the 1986 statements and disclosing the effect of the correction on income before extraordinary items, net income, and the related per share amounts.

Summary of Accounting Changes and Corrections of Errors

The issuance of *CICA Handbook*, Section 1506, provided long-awaited guidelines for the orderly resolution of several significant and long-standing accounting problems. Yet, because of the diversity in situations in practice, professional judgement is of paramount importance. In applying these guidelines, the primary objective is to serve the user of the financial statements; achieving such service requires accuracy, full disclosure, and an absence of misleading implications. The principal distinctions and treatments presented in the foregoing discussion are summarized below.

1. **Changes in accounting policy** (General Rule).
    Employ the retroactive-with-restatement approach by:
    (a) Reporting current results on the new basis.
    (b) Restating all prior period financial statements presented for comparison.
2. **Changes in accounting policy** (Exceptions).
    Employ the retroactive-without-restatement approach by:
    (a) Reporting the current results on the new basis.
    (b) Reporting the cumulative effect of the adjustment in the statement of retained earnings as an adjustment to the beginning balance.
    (c) Disclosing the effect of the change on the current year's financial statements.
    Employ the prospective approach by:
    (a) Reporting the current results on the new basis.
    (b) Disclosing the effect of the change on the current year's financial statements.
3. **Changes in estimate.**
    Employ the prospective approach by:
    (a) Reporting current and future financial statements on the new basis.
    (b) Presenting prior period financial statements as previously reported.
    (c) Making no adjustment to current period opening balances for purposes of catch-up, and making no pro forma presentations.
4. **Changes in entity.**
    Employ the retroactive-with-restatement approach (pooling of interests) by:
    (a) Restating the financial statements of all prior periods presented.
    (b) Disclosing in the year of change the effect on net income for all prior periods presented.
    Employ the prospective approach with pro forma information (purchases or disposals of subsidiaries) by:
    (a) Reporting current financial statements on the new basis.
    (b) Providing pro forma supplementary information of the new income for the full year from the continuing entity.
5. **Changes due to errors.**
    Employ the retroactive-with-restatement approach by:
    (a) Correcting all prior period financial statements presented.
    (b) Restating the beginning balance of retained earnings for the first period presented when the effects of the error extend to a period prior to that one.

Changes in accounting principles are considered appropriate when the enterprise demonstrates that the alternative generally accepted accounting principle that is adopted **is preferable** to the existing one. Preferability among accounting principles should be determined on the basis of whether the new principle constitutes an improvement in financial reporting, not on the basis of the income tax effect alone; but it is not always easy to determine what is an improvement in financial reporting. **How does one measure preferability or improvement?** One enterprise might argue that a change in accounting principle from FIFO to LIFO inventory valuation better matches current costs and current revenues. Conversely, another enterprise might change from LIFO to FIFO because it wishes to report a more realistic balance sheet amount for inventory. How does an accountant determine which is the better of these two arguments? It appears that one must have some "standard" or "objective" as a basis for determining the method that is preferable. Because no universal standard or objective is generally accepted, the problem of determining preferability continues to be a difficult one.

ERROR ANALYSIS

As indicated earlier, material errors are unusual in large corporations because internal control procedures coupled with the diligence of the accounting staff are ordinarily sufficient to find any major errors in the system. Smaller businesses may face a different problem. These enterprises may not be able to afford an internal audit staff, or implement the necessary control procedures to ensure that accounting data are always recorded accurately. The following discussion, therefore, applies primarily to smaller firms whose internal control systems are inappropriate or inefficient for processing the accounting data.

In practice, firms do not correct for errors discovered that do not have a significant effect on the presentation of the financial statements. For example, the failure to record accrued wages of $5,000 when the total payroll for the year is $1,750,000 and net income is $940,000 is not considered significant, and no correction is made. Obviously, defining materiality is difficult, and accountants must rely on their experience and judgement to determine whether adjustment is necessary for a given error. **All errors discussed in this section are assumed to be material and to require adjustment.** Also, all of the tax effects are ignored in this section.

The accountant must answer three questions in error analysis:

1. What type of error is involved?
2. What entries are needed to correct for the error?
3. How are financial statements to be restated once the error is discovered?

Type of Error Involved

As indicated earlier, the profession requires that errors be treated as retroactive adjustments and corrections be reported in the current year as adjustments to the beginning balance of Retained Earnings. If comparative statements are presented, the prior statements affected should be restated to correct for the error.

Three types of error can occur; because each error has its own peculiarities, differentiation among the types is important.

Balance Sheet Errors

These errors affect only the presentation of the real accounts, that is, they result from the improper classification of an asset, liability, or shareholders' equity account. Examples are the classification of a short-term receivable as part of the investment section; the classification of a note payable as an account payable; and the classification of plant assets as inventory. Reclassification of the item to its proper position is needed when the error is discovered. If comparative statements that include the error year are prepared, the balance sheet for the error year is restated correctly.

Income Statement Errors

These errors affect only the presentation of the nominal accounts presented in the income statement. Errors involve the improper classification of revenues or expenses, such as recording interest revenue as part of sales; purchases as bad debt expense; and depreciation expense as interest expense. An income statement error has no effect on the balance sheet and no effect on net income; a reclassification entry is needed when the error is discovered, if it is discovered in the year it is made. If the error occurred in prior periods, no entry is needed at the date of discovery because the accounts for the current year are correctly stated. If comparative statements that include the error year are prepared, the income statement for the error year is restated correctly.

Balance Sheet and Income Statement Errors

The third type of error involves both the balance sheet and income statement. For example, assume that accrued wages payable were overlooked by the bookkeeper at the end of the accounting period. The effect of this error is to understate expenses, understate liabilities, and overstate net income for that period of time. This type of error affects both the balance sheet and the income statement and is classified in one of the following two ways—counterbalancing and noncounterbalancing.

Counterbalancing errors will be offset or corrected over two periods. In the previous illustration, the failure to record accrued wages is considered a counterbalancing error because over a two-year period the error will no longer be present. In other words the failure to record accrued wages in the previous period means: (1) net income for the first period is overstated; (2) accrued wages payable (a liability) is understated; and (3) wages expense is understated. In the next period, net income is understated; accrued wages payable (a liability) is correctly stated; and wages expense is overstated. For the **two years combined:** (1) net income is correct; (2) wages expense is correct; and (3) accrued wages payable at the end of the second year is correct. Most errors in accounting that affect both the balance sheet and income statement are counterbalancing errors.

Noncounterbalancing errors are errors that are not offset in the next accounting period; for example, the failure to capitalize equipment that has a useful life of five years. If we expense this asset immediately, expenses will be overstated in the first period but understated in the next four periods. At the end of the second period, the effect of the error is not fully offset. Net income is correct in the aggregate only at the end of five years, because the asset is fully depreciated at this point. Only in rare instances is an error never reversed; for example, when land is initially expensed. Because land is not depreciable, the effect of the error on the land account will not be offset until the land is sold.

Accountants define counterbalancing errors as errors that correct themselves over two periods, whereas noncounterbalancing errors are those that take longer than two periods to correct themselves. How these errors are handled in the accounting records is illustrated in the following sections.

Counterbalancing Errors

The usual types of counterbalancing errors are illustrated on the following pages. In studying these illustrations, a number of points should be remembered. First, determine whether or not the books have been closed for the period in which the error is found:

1. **The books have been closed.**
    (a) If the error is already counterbalanced, no entry is necessary.

    (b) If the error is not yet counterbalanced, an entry is necessary to adjust the present balance of Retained Earnings.

  2. **The books have not been closed.**

    (a) If the error is already counterbalanced and we are in the second year, an entry is necessary to correct the current period and to adjust the beginning balance of Retained Earnings.

    (b) If the error is not yet counterbalanced, an entry is necessary to adjust the beginning balance of Retained Earnings.

Second, if comparative statements are presented, restatement of the amounts for comparative purposes is necessary. This situation occurs even if a correcting journal entry is not required. To illustrate, assume that Sanford's Cement Co. failed to accrue income in 1984 when earned, but recorded the income in 1985 when received. The error was discovered in 1987. No entry is necessary to correct for this error because the effects have been counterbalanced by the time the error is discovered in 1987. However, if comparative financial statements for 1984 through 1987 are presented, the accounts and related amounts for the years 1984 and 1985 should be restated correctly for financial reporting purposes.

Failure to Record Accrued Wages   On December 31, 1986, accrued wages in the amount of $1,500 were not recognized. The entry in 1987 to correct this error, assuming that the books have not been closed for 1987, is:

Retained Earnings	1,500	
Wages Expense		1,500

    The rationale for this entry is as follows: (1) When the accrued wages of 1986 are paid in 1987, an additional debit of $1,500 is made to the 1987 Wages Expense. (2) Wages Expense—1987 is overstated by $1,500. (3) Because 1986 accrued wages were not recorded as Wages Expense—1986, net income for 1986 was overstated by $1,500. (4) Because 1986 net income is overstated by $1,500, the Retained Earnings account is overstated by $1,500 because net income is closed to Retained Earnings.

    If the books have been closed for 1987, no entry is made because the error is counterbalanced.

Failure to Record Prepaid Expenses   In January, 1986, Hurley Enterprises purchased a two-year insurance policy costing $1,000; Insurance Expense was debited and Cash was credited. No adjusting entries were made at the end of 1986.

    The entry on December 31, 1987, to correct this error, assuming that the books have not been closed for 1987, is:

Insurance Expense	500	
Retained Earnings		500

If the books have been closed for 1987, no entry is made because the error is counterbalanced.

Overstatement of Prepaid Revenue   On December 31, 1986, Hurley Enterprises received $50,000 as a prepayment for renting certain office space for the following year. The entry made at the time of receipt of the rent payment was a debit to Cash and a credit to Rent Revenue. No adjusting entry was made as of December 31, 1986. The entry on December 31, 1987, to correct for this error, assuming that the books have not been closed for 1987, is:

Retained Earnings	50,000	
Rent Revenue		50,000

If the books have been closed for 1987, no entry is made because the error is counterbalanced.

Overstatement of Accrued Revenue   On December 31, 1986, Hurley Enterprises accrued as interest revenue $8,000 that applied to 1987. The entry made on December 31, 1986, was to debit Accrued Interest Receivable and credit Interest Revenue. The entry on December 31, 1987, to correct for this error, assuming that the books have not been closed for 1987, is:

Retained Earnings	8,000	
Interest Revenue		8,000

If the books have been closed for 1987, no entry is made because the error is counterbalanced.

Understatement of Ending Inventory   On December 31, 1986, the physical count of the inventory was understated by $25,000 because the inventory crew failed to count one warehouse of merchandise. The entry on December 31, 1987, to correct for this error, assuming that the books have not been closed for 1987, is:

Inventory (beginning)	25,000	
Retained Earnings		25,000

If the books have been closed for 1987, no entry is made because the error is counterbalanced.

Overstatement of Purchases   Hurley Enterprise's accountant recorded a purchase of merchandise for $9,000 in 1986 that applied to 1987. The physical inventory for 1986 was correctly stated. The entry on December 31, 1987, to correct for this error, assuming that the books have not been closed for 1987, is:

Purchases	9,000	
Retained Earnings		9,000

If the books have been closed for 1987, no entry is made because the error is counterbalanced.

Overstatement of Purchases and Inventories   Sometimes both the physical inventory and the purchases are incorrectly stated. Assume, as in the previous illustration, that purchases for 1986 are overstated by $9,000 and that inventory is overstated by the same amount. The entry on December 31, 1987, to correct for this error, assuming that the books have not been closed for 1987, is:

Purchases	9,000	
Inventory		9,000[a]

[a]The net income for 1986 is correctly computed because the overstatement of purchases was offset by the overstatement of ending inventory in the cost of goods sold computation.

If the books have been closed for 1987, no entry is made because the error is counterbalanced.

Noncounterbalancing Errors

Because such errors do not counterbalance over a two-year period, the entries are more complex and correcting entries are needed, even if the books have been closed.

Failure to Record Depreciation   Assume that Hurley Enterprises purchased a machine for $10,000 on January 1, 1986, that had an estimated useful life of five years. The accountant incorrectly expensed this machine in 1986. The error was discovered in 1987. If we assume that the company desires to use straight-line depreciation on this asset, the entry in 1987, to correct for this error, given that the books have not been closed, is:

Machinery	10,000	
Depreciation Expense	2,000	
Retained Earnings		8,000[a]
Accumulated Depreciation		4,000[a]

[a]Computations:

Retained Earnings

Overstatement of expense in 1986	$10,000
Proper depreciation for 1986 (20% × $10,000)	(2,000)
Retained earnings understated as of Dec. 31, 1986	$8,000

Accumulated Depreciation

Accumulated depreciation (20% × $10,000 × 2)	$4,000

If the books have been closed for 1987, the entry is:

Machinery	10,000	
Retained Earnings		6,000[a]
Accumulated Depreciation		4,000

[a]Computations:

Retained Earnings

Retained earnings understated as of Dec. 31, 1986	$ 8,000
Proper depreciation for 1987 (20% × $10,000)	(2,000)
Retained earnings understated as of Dec. 31, 1987	$ 6,000

Failure to Adjust for Bad Debts   Companies sometimes use a specific charge-off method in accounting for bad debt expense when a percentage of sales is more appropriate. Adjustments are often made to change from the specific write-off to some type of allowance method. Assume that Hurley Enterprises has recognized bad debt expense because the debts have actually become uncollectible as follows:

	1986	1987
From 1986 sales	$550	$690
From 1987 sales		700

Hurley estimates that an additional $1,400 will be charged off in 1988; $300 applicable to 1986 Sales and $1,100 to 1987 Sales. The entry on December 31, 1987, assuming that the books have not been closed for 1987, is:

Bad Debt Expense	410[a]	
Retained Earnings	990[a]	
Allowance for Doubtful Account		1,400

[a]Computations:

Allowance for doubtful accounts—additional $300 for 1986 sales and $1,100 for 1987 sales.
Bad debts and retained earnings balance:

	1986	1987
Bad debts charged for	$1,240[a]	$ 700
Additional bad debts anticipated	300	1,100
Proper bad debt expense	1,540	1,800
Charges currently made to each period	(550)	(1,390)
Bad debt adjustment	$ 990	$ 410

[a]$550 + $690 = $1,240

If the books have been closed for 1987, the entry is:

Retained Earnings	1,400	
Allowance for Doubtful Accounts		1,400

Comprehensive Illustration: Numerous Errors

In some circumstances not one but a combination of errors occurs. A work sheet is therefore prepared to facilitate the analysis. To demonstrate the use of a work sheet, the following problem is presented for solution. The mechanics of the work sheet preparation should be obvious from the solution format.

The income statements of the Hudson Company for the years ended December 31, 1985, 1986, and 1987 indicate the following net incomes:

1985	$17,400
1986	20,200
1987	11,300

An examination of the accounting records of the Hudson Company for these years indicates that several errors were made in arriving at the net income amounts reported. The following errors were discovered:

(a) Wages earned by workers but not paid at December 31 were consistently omitted from the records. The amounts omitted were:

December 31, 1985	$1,000
December 31, 1986	1,400
December 31, 1987	1,600

These amounts were recorded as expenses when paid in the year following that in which they were earned.

(b) The merchandise inventory on December 31, 1985, was overstated by $1,900 as the result of errors made in the footings and extensions on the inventory sheets.

(c) Unexpired insurance of $1,200, applicable to 1987, was expensed on December 31, 1986.

(d) Interest receivable in the amount of $240 was not recorded on December 31, 1986.

(e) On January 2, 1986, a piece of equipment costing $3,900 was sold for $1,800. At the date of sale the equipment had accumulated depreciation pertaining to it of $2,400. The cash received was recorded as Miscellaneous Revenue in 1986. In addition, depreciation was recorded for this equipment in both 1986 and 1987 at the rate of 10% of cost.

Instructions   Prepare a schedule showing the corrected net income amounts for the years ended December 31, 1985, 1986, and 1987. Each correction of the amount originally reported should be clearly labelled. In addition, indicate the balance sheet accounts affected as of December 31, 1987.

Correcting entries **if the books have not been closed** on December 31, 1987, are:

(a) Retained Earnings	1,400	
Wages Expense		1,400
(To correct improper charge to wages expense for 1987)		
Wages Expense	1,600	
Wages Payable		1,600
(To record proper wages expense for 1987)		
(b) No entry		
(c) Insurance Expense	1,200	
Retained Earnings		1,200
(To record proper insurance expense for 1987)		
(d) Interest Revenue	240	
Retained Earnings		240
(To correct improper credit to interest revenue in 1987)		
(e) Retained Earnings	1,500	
Accumulated Depreciation	2,400	
Machinery		3,900
(To record write-off of machinery in 1986 and adjustment of retained earnings)		
Accumulated Depreciation	780	
Depreciation Expense		390
Retained Earnings		390
(To correct improper charge for depreciation expense in 1986 and 1987)		

Solution.

	Work Sheet Analysis of Changes in Net Income				Balance Sheet Correction at December 31, 1987		
	1885	1986	1987	Totals	Debit	Credit	Account
Net income as reported	$17,400	$20,200	$11,300	$48,900			
Wages unpaid, Dec. 31/85	(1,000)	1,000		-0-			
Wages unpaid, Dec. 31/86		(1,400)	1,400	-0-			
Wages unpaid, Dec. 31/87			(1,600)	(1,600)		1,600	Wages Payable
Inventory overstatement, Dec. 31/85	(1,900)	1,900		-0-			
Unexpired insurance, Dec. 31/86		1,200	(1,200)	-0-			
Interest receivable, Dec. 31/86		240	(240)	-0-			
Correction for entry made upon sale of equipment, Jan. 2/86[a]		(1,500)		(1,500)	2,400	3,900	Accumulated Depreciation Machinery
Overcharge of depreciation, 1986		390		390	390		Accumulated Depreciation
Overcharge of depreciation, 1987			390	390			Accumulated Depreciation
Corrected net income	$14,500	$22,030	$10,050	$46,580			

[a]Cost	$ 3,900
Accumulated depreciation	2,400
Book value	1,500
Proceeds from sale	1,800
Gain on sale	300
Income reported	(1,800)
Adjustment	$(1,500)

Correcting entries **if the books have been closed** on December 31, 1987, are:

(a)	Retained Earnings	1,600	
	Wages Payable		1,600
	(To record proper wages expense for 1987)		

(b), (c), (d) No entry

(e)	Retained Earnings	1,500	
	Accumulated Depreciation	2,400	
	Machinery		3,900
	(To record write-off of machinery in 1986 and adjustment of retained earnings)		
	Accumulated Depreciation	780	
	Retained Earnings		780
	(To correct improper charge for depreciation expense in 1986 and 1987)		

Preparation of Comparative Statements

Discussion of error analysis up to now has been concerned with the identification of the type of error involved and the accounting for its correction in the accounting records. The correction of the error should be presented on comparative financial statements. In addition, five- or ten-year summaries are given. The work sheet in Table 23-1 illustrates how a typical year's financial statements are restated, given many different errors. The resulting balance sheet, income statement, and the correcting entries are not presented because they should be self-explanatory.

To illustrate, Reynolds and Sons operate a small retail outlet in the town of Prescott. Lacking expertise in accounting, they did not keep adequate records; as a result, many errors occurred in recording the accounting information. Presented in Table 23-1 is a work sheet that begins with the unadjusted trial balance of Reynolds and Sons; the correcting entries and their effect on the financial statements can be determined by examining the work sheet. Supplementary information related to the correction of errors appears below and in the work sheet on page 1084.

1. The bookkeeper inadvertently failed to record a cash receipt of $1,000 on the sale of merchandise in 1987.
2. Accrued wages expense at the end of 1986 was $2,500; at the end of 1987, $3,200. The company did not accrue for wages; all wages are charged to administrative expense.
3. The beginning inventory was understated by $5,400 because goods in transit at the end of last year were not counted. The proper purchase entry had been made.
4. No allowance had been set up for estimated uncollectible receivables. It is decided to set up such an allowance for the estimated probable losses as of December 31, 1987, for 1986 accounts of $700, and for 1987 accounts of $1,500. It is also decided to correct the charge against each year so that it shows the losses (actual and estimated) relating to that year's sales.
   Accounts have been written off to bad debt expense (selling expense) as follows:

	In 1986	In 1987
1987 Accounts		$1,600
1986 Accounts	$400	2,000

5. Unexpired insurance not recorded at the end of 1986, $600; at the end of 1987, $400. All insurance expense is charged to Administrative Expense.
6. An account payable of $6,000 should have been a note payable.
7. During 1986, an asset that cost $10,000 and had a book value of $4,000 was sold for $7,000. At the time of sale Cash was debited and Miscellaneous Revenue was credited for $7,000.

8. As a result of the last transaction, the company overstated depreciation expense (an administrative expense) in 1986 by $800 and in 1987 by $1,200.

9. In a physical count, the company determined the final inventory to be $40,000.

Table 23-1
Work Sheet Analysis to Adjust Financial Statements for the Year 1987

	Trial Balance Unadjusted		Adjustments		Income Statement Adjusted		Balance Sheet Adjusted	
	Debit	Credit	Debit	Credit	Debit	Credit	Debit	Credit
Cash	3,100		(1) 1,000				4,100	
Accounts Receivable	17,600						17,600	
Notes Receivable	8,500						8,500	
Inventories, Jan. 1, 1987	34,000		(3) 5,400		39,400			
Property, Plant, & Equipment	112,000			(7) 10,000ª			102,000	
Accumulated Depreciation		83,500	(7) 6,000ª					
			(8) 2,000					75,500
Investments	24,300						24,300	
Accounts Payable		14,500	(6) 6,000					8,500
Notes Payable		10,000		(6) 6,000				16,000
Capital Stock		43,500						43,500
			(4) 2,700ᵇ	(3) 5,400				
Retained Earnings		20,000	(7) 4,000ª	(5) 600				17,600
			(2) 2,500	(8) 800				
Sales		94,000		(1) 1,000		95,000		
Purchases	21,000				21,000			
Selling Expenses	22,000			(4) 500ᵇ	21,500			
Administrative Expenses	23,000		(2) 700	(5) 400	22,700			
			(5) 600	(8) 1,200				
Totals	265,500	265,500						
Wages Payable				(2) 3,200				3,200
Allowance for Doubtful Accounts				(4) 2,200ᵇ				2,200
Unexpired Insurance			(5) 400				400	
Inventory, Dec. 31, 1987						(9) 40,000	(9) 40,000	
Net Income					30,400			30,400
Totals			31,300	31,300	135,000	135,000	196,900	196,900

Computations:

ªMachinery		ᵇBad Debts		1986	1987
Proceeds from sale	$7,000	Bad debts charged for		$2,400	$1,600
Book value of machinery	4,000	Additional bad debts anticipated		700	1,500
Gain on sale	3,000			3,100	3,100
Revenue credited	7,000	Charges currently made to each year		(400)	(3,600)
Retained earnings adjustment	$4,000	Bad debt adjustment		$2,700	$ (500)

KEY POINTS

1. Accounting changes occur when either an accounting policy, an accounting estimate, or the accounting entity is changed.

2. Accounting changes affect account balances for the current and/or future fiscal periods, and often those of a prior period or periods.

3. Three approaches to report changes in accounting policies are: (1) retroactively, (2) currently, and (3) prospectively. Retroactive recognition involves restatements of the prior periods affected, while current recognition requires adjustment of the opening balances of the current period's account balances. Prospective recognition, on the other hand, requires only current and future period financial statements.

4. If possible, changes in accounting policies are treated retroactively. However, if it is not practical due to excessive cost or unavailability of data, such changes may be recognized in the current period.

5. A change in the accounting entity is accounted for retroactively if it is attributed to a pooling-of-interests transaction. Otherwise, it is recognized currently.

6. Changes in accounting estimates occur frequently and, consequently, are given prospective recognition.

7. Errors result from mathematical mistakes, oversight or misuse of facts, or incorrect application of accounting principles.

QUESTIONS

1. What are the advantages of employing the retroactive-with-restatement approach for handling changes in accounting principle?

2. In recent years, *The Globe and Mail* has indicated that many companies have changed their accounting principles. What are the major reasons why companies change accounting methods?

3. Define a change in estimate and provide an illustration. When is a change in accounting estimate affected by a change in accounting principle?

4. Discuss and illustrate how a correction of an error in previously issued financial statements should be handled.

5. Indicate how the following items are recorded in the accounting records in the current year.
    (a) Change from the cash basis to accrual basis of accounting.
    (b) Change from LIFO to FIFO method for inventory valuation purposes.
    (c) Change in the estimate of service lives for plant assets.
    (d) Large write-off of goodwill.
    (e) A change in depreciating plant assets from accelerated to the straight-line method.
    (f) Large write-off of inventories because of obsolescence.

6. State how each of the following items is reflected in the financial statements:
    (a) Charge for failure to record depreciation in a previous period.
    (b) Change from straight-line method of depreciation to sum-of-the-years'-digits.
    (c) Change from FIFO to LIFO method for inventory valuation purposes.
    (d) Litigation won in current year, related to prior period.
    (e) Change in the realizability of certain receivables.
    (f) Write-off of receivables.
    (g) Change from the percentage-of-completion to the completed-contract method for reporting net income.

7. Bold, Inc. has followed the practice of capitalizing certain marketing costs and amortizing these costs over their expected life. In the current year, the company determined that the future benefits from these costs were doubtful. Consequently, the company adopted the policy of expensing these costs as incurred. How should this accounting change be reported in the comparative financial statements?

8. The Madsen Construction Co. had followed the practice of expensing all materials assigned to a construction job without recognizing any salvage inventory. On Decem-

ber 31, 1986, it was determined that salvage inventory should be valued at $41,500. Of this amount, $20,000 arose during the current year. How should this change in accounting principle be reflected in the financial statements?

9. Bolman, Inc. wishes to change from the sum-of-the-years'-digits to the straight-line depreciation method for financial reporting purposes. The auditor indicates that a change would be permitted only if it is to a preferable method. What difficulties develop in assessing preferability?

10. Porter Enterprises controlled four subsidiaries. One subsidiary was sold during the current year. How should this change in accounting principle be reflected in the financial statements?

11. Senn, Inc., a closely held corporation, is in the process of preparing financial statements to accompany an offering of its common shares. The company at this time has decided to switch from the accelerated depreciation to the straight-line method of depreciation to better represent its financial operations. How should this change in accounting principle be reported in the financial statements?

12. Prior to 1986, Ivery, Inc. excluded manufacturing overhead costs from work in process and finished goods inventory. These costs have been expensed as incurred. In 1986, the company decided to change its accounting methods for manufacturing inventories to full costing by including these costs as product costs. Assuming that these costs are material how should this change be reflected in the financial statements for 1985 and 1986?

13. Largo Company failed to record accrued salaries for 1983, $1,800; 1984, $2,100; and 1985, $4,200. What is the amount of the overstatement or understatement of Retained Earnings at December 31, 1986?

14. In January, 1985, installation costs of $7,000 on new machinery were charged to Repair Expense. Other costs of this machinery of $30,000 were correctly recorded and have been depreciated using the straight-line method with an estimated life of 10 years and no salvage value. At December 31, 1986, it is decided that the machinery has a useful life of 20 years, starting with January 1, 1986. What entry(entries) should be made in 1986 to record correctly transactions related to machinery, assuming the machinery has no salvage value? The books have not been closed for 1986.

15. An account payable of $9,000 for merchandise purchased on December 23, 1985 was recorded in January, 1986. This merchandise was not included in inventory at December 31, 1985. What effect does this error have on reported net income for 1985? What entry should be made to correct this error, assuming that the books are not closed for 1985?

16. On January 1, 1986, $100,000 of 10%, 20-year bonds were issued for $98,000. The $2,000 discount was charged to Interest Expense. The bookkeeper records interest only on the interest payment dates of January 1 and July 1. What is the effect of this error on reported net income for 1986, assuming straight-line amortization of the discount? What entry is necessary to correct this error, assuming that the books are not closed for 1986?

17. Equipment was purchased on January 2, 1986 for $14,000, but no portion of the cost has been charged to depreciation. The corporation wishes to use the straight-line method for these assets, which have been estimated to have a life of 10 years and no salvage value. What effect does this error have on net income in 1986? What entry is necessary to correct this error, assuming that the books are not closed for 1986?

CASES

C23-1 Various types of accounting changes can affect the financial statements of a business enterprise differently. Assume that the following list describes changes that have a material effect on the financial statements for the current year of your business enterprise.

1. Correction of a mathematical error in inventory pricing made in a prior period.
2. A change from prime costing to full absorption costing for inventory valuation.

3. A change from presentation of statements of individual companies to presentation of consolidated statements.

4. A change in the method of accounting for leases for tax purposes to conform with the financial accounting method. As a result, both deferred and current taxes payable changed substantially.

5. A change from the FIFO method of inventory pricing to the LIFO method of inventory pricing.

6. A change from the completed-contract method to the percentage-of-completion method of accounting for long-term construction-type contracts.

7. A change in the estimated useful life of previously recorded fixed assets based on newly acquired information.

8. A change from deferring and amortizing preproduction costs to recording such costs as an expense when incurred because future benefits of the costs have become doubtful. The new accounting method was adopted in recognition of the change in estimated future benefits.

9. A change from including the employer's share of CPP premiums with Payroll Expenses to including it with "Retirement Benefits" on the income statement.

Instructions

Identify the type of change that is described in each item above and indicate whether the prior year's financial statements should be restated when presented in comparative form with the current year's statements. Ignore possible pro forma effects.

C23-2 Composition Inc. has recently hired a new independent auditor who says she wants "to get everything straightened out." Consequently, she has proposed the following accounting changes in connection with Composition's 1986 financial statements:

1. In the past, the client has spread preproduction costs in its furniture division over five years. Because its latest furniture is of the "fad" type, it appears that the largest volume of sales will occur during the first two years after introduction. Consequently, the client proposes to amortize preproduction costs on a per-unit basis, which will result in expensing most of such costs during the first two years after the furniture's introduction. If the new accounting method had been used prior to 1986, retained earnings at December 31, 1985, would have been $300,000 less.

2. For the nursery division, the client proposes to switch from FIFO to LIFO inventories as it is believed that LIFO will provide a better matching of current costs with revenues. The effect of making this change on 1986 earnings will be an increase of $270,000. The client says that the effect of the change on retained earnings at December 31, 1986 cannot be determined.

3. To achieve a better matching of revenues and expenses in its building construction division, the client proposes to switch from the completed-contract method of accounting to the percentage-of-completion method. Had the percentage-of-completion method been employed in all prior years, retained earnings at December 31, 1985, would have been $1,237,500 greater.

4. At December 31, 1985, the client had a receivable of $787,500 from Scarlatti, Inc. on its balance sheet. Scarlatti, Inc. has gone bankrupt, and no recovery is expected. The client proposes to write off the receivable as a prior period item.

5. The client proposes the following changes in depreciation policies:

   (a) For office furniture and fixtures it proposes a change from a ten-year useful life to an eight-year life. If this change had been made in prior years, retained earnings at December 31, 1985 would have been $150,000 less. The effect of the change on 1986 income alone is a reduction of $15,000.

   (b) For its manufacturing assets the client proposes to change from double-declining balance depreciation to straight-line. If straight-line depreciation had been used for all prior periods, retained earnings would have been $285,000 greater at December 31, 1985. The effect of the change on 1986 income alone is a reduction of $18,000.

(c) For its equipment in the leasing division the client proposes to adopt the sum-of-the-years'-digits depreciation method. The client had never used SYD before. The first year the client operated a leasing division was 1986. If straight-line depreciation were used, 1986 income would be $60,000 greater.

6. In preparing its 1985 statements, one of the client's bookkeepers overstated ending inventory by $172,500 because of a mathematical error. The client proposes to treat this item as a prior period adjustment.

Instructions

(a) For each of the changes described above decide whether:
1. The change involves an accounting principle, accounting estimate, or correction of an error.
2. Restatement of opening retained earnings is required.
(b) Do any of the changes require presentation of pro forma amounts?
(c) What would be the proper adjustment to the December 31, 1985, retained earnings? What would be the "cumulative effect" shown separately in the 1986 Statement of Retained Earnings?

C23-3   Listed below are three independent, unrelated situations relating to accounting changes.

1. A company decides in January, 1987, to adopt the straight-line method of depreciation for plant equipment. The straight-line method will be used for new acquisitions as well as for previously acquired plant equipment for which depreciation had been provided on an accelerated basis.

2. A company determined that the depreciable lives of its fixed assets are too long at present to match fairly the cost of the fixed assets with the revenue produced. The company decided at the beginning of the current year to reduce the depreciable lives of all of its existing fixed assets by five years.

3. Cavanaugh Company is in the process of having its first audit. The company's policy with regard to recognition of revenue is to use the instalment method. However, the instalment method of revenue recognition is not a generally accepted accounting principle except in certain circumstances, which are not present here. Ms. Laura Cavanaugh, the president, is willing to change to an acceptable method.

Instructions

For each of the situations described, provide the information indicated below:
(a) Type of accounting change.
(b) Manner of reporting the change under current generally accepted accounting principles including a discussion, where applicable, of how amounts are computed.
(c) Effect of the change on the balance sheet and income statement.

C23-4   Denise L. Rode, controller of Handel Corp., is aware that there is a *CICA Handbook* section pertaining to accounting changes. After reading the section, she is confused and is not sure what action should be taken on the following items related to Handel Corp. for the year 1986:

1. All equipment sold by Handel is subject to a three-year warranty. It has been estimated that the expense ultimately to be incurred on these machines is 1% of sales. In 1986, because of a production breakthrough, it is now estimated that 0.5% of sales is sufficient. In 1984 and 1985, warranty expense was computed as $40,000 and $50,000, respectively. The company now believes that these warranty costs should be reduced by 50%.

2. In 1986, the company decided to change its method of inventory pricing from average cost to the FIFO method. The effect of this change on prior years is to increase 1984 income by $60,000 and decrease 1985 income by $20,000.

3. In 1986, Rode decided to change the company's policy on accounting for certain marketing costs. Previously, the company had chosen to defer and amortize all marketing costs over at least five years because Handel believed that a return on these expenditures did not occur immediately. Recently, however, the time differential has considerably shortened, and Handel is now expensing the marketing costs as incurred.

4. In 1986, the company examined its entire policy relating to the depreciation of plant equipment. Plant equipment had normally been depreciated over a 15-year period, but recent experience has indicated that the company was incorrect in its estimates and that the assets should be depreciated over a 20-year period.

5. One division of Handel Corp., Hayden Co., has consistently shown an increasing net income from period to period. On closer examination of their operating statement, it is noted that bad debt expense and inventory obsolescence charges are much lower than in other divisions. In discussing this with the controller of this division, it has been learned that the controller has increased his net income each period by knowingly making low estimates related to the write-off of receivables and inventory.

6. In 1986, the company purchased new machinery that should increase production dramatically. The company has decided to depreciate this machinery on an accelerated basis, even though other machinery is depreciated on a straight-line basis.

Instructions

Denise L. Rode has come to you, as her CA, for advice about the situations above. Indicate the appropriate accounting treatment that should be given each of these situations.

C23-5 Maher Manufacturing is preparing its year-end financial statements. The controller is confronted with several decisions about statement presentation with regard to the following items:

1. Upon making the year-end physical inventory adjustment for the current year, the prior year's physical inventory sheets for an entire warehouse were discovered to have been mislaid and excluded from last year's count.

2. The method of accounting used for financial reporting purposes for certain receivables has been approved for tax purposes during the current tax year by Revenue Canada. This change for tax purposes will cause both deferred and current taxes payable to change substantially.

3. Management has decided to switch from the FIFO inventory valuation method to the LIFO inventory valuation method for all inventories.

4. Maher's Custom Division manufactures large-scale custom designed machinery on a contract basis. Management decided to switch from the completed-contract method to the percentage-of-completion method of accounting for long-term contracts.

5. The Vice-President of Sales had indicated that one product line has lost its customer appeal and will be phased out over the next three years. Therefore, a decision has been made to lower the estimated lives on related production equipment from the remaining five years to three years.

6. Estimating the lives of new products in the Leisure Products Division has become very difficult owing to the highly competitive conditions in this market. Therefore, the practice of deferring and amortizing preproduction costs has been abandoned in favour of expensing such costs as they are incurred.

7. The Franck Building was converted from a sales office to offices for the Accounting Department at the beginning of this year. Therefore, the expense related to this building will now appear as an administrative expense rather than a selling expense on the current year's income statement.

Instructions

(a) *CICA Handbook*, Section 1506, identifies four types of accounting changes —changes in accounting principle, changes in estimates, changes in entity, and changes due to error. For each of these four types of accounting changes:

1. Define the type of change.
2. Explain the general accounting treatment required according to Section 1506 with respect to the current year and prior years' financial statements.

3. Discuss the impact of the changes on the external auditor's report.

(b) For each of the seven changes Mahler Manufacturing has made in the current year, identify and explain whether the change is a change in accounting principle, in estimate, in entity, or due to error. If any of the changes is not one of these four types, explain why.

(CMA adapted)

EXERCISES

E23-1   Giuseppe Vardi, Inc. acquired the following assets in January of 1984:

Equipment, estimated service life, 5 years; salvage value, $25,000	$625,000
Building, estimated service life, 30 years; no salvage value	$840,000

The equipment has been depreciated using the sum-of-the years'-digits method for the first three years, for financial reporting purposes. In 1987, the company decided to change the method of computing depreciation to the straight-line method for the equipment, but no change was made in the estimated service life or salvage value. It was also decided to change the total estimated service life of the building from 30 years to 45 years, with no change in the estimated salvage value. The building is depreciated on the straight-line method.

The company has 100,000 common shares outstanding. Results of operations for 1987 and 1986 are shown below:

	1987	1986
Income: (depreciation for 1987 has been computed on the straight-line basis for both the equipment and building[a])	$406,000	$400,000
Income per share	$4.06	$4.00

[a]It should be noted that the computation for depreciation expense for 1987 and 1986 for the building was based on the original estimate of service life of 30 years.

Instructions

(a) Compute the effect of the change in accounting principle to be reported in the income statement and the restatement of retained earnings for 1987, and prepare the journal entry to record the change. (Ignore tax effects.)

(b) Present comparative data for the years 1986 and 1987, starting with the income amounts calculated above for 1986 and 1987. Prepare pro forma data. Do not prepare the note. (Ignore tax effects.)

E23-2   Beethoven Organ Co. purchased equipment on January 1, 1984, for $660,000. At that time it was estimated that the machine would have a 10-year life and no salvage value. On December 31, 1987, the firm's accountant found that the entry for depreciation expense had been omitted in 1985. In addition, management has informed the accountant that they plan to switch to straight-line depreciation, starting with the year 1987. At present, the company uses the sum-of-the-years'-digits method for depreciating equipment.

Instructions

Prepare the general journal entries the accountant should make at December 31, 1987. (Ignore tax effects.)

E23-3 Bach Tool Co. purchased equipment for $348,000 which was estimated to have a useful life of ten years with a salvage value of $8,000 at the end of that time. Depreciation has been entered for seven years on a straight-line basis. In 1987, it is determined that the total estimated life should be 15 years with a salvage value of $6,000 at the end of that time.

Instructions

(a) Prepare the entry (if any) to correct the prior years' depreciation.

(b) Prepare the entry to record depreciation for 1987.

E23-4 Mozart Corporation owns equipment that originally cost $500,000 and had an estimated useful life of 20 years. The equipment had no expected salvage value.
   The two requirements below are independent and must be considered as entirely separate from each other.

Instructions

(a) After using the double-declining balance method for two years, the company decided to switch to the straight-line method of depreciation. Prepare the general journal entry(entries) necessary in the third year to account properly for (1) the change in accounting principle and (2) depreciation expense. (Ignore income tax effects).

(b) After using the straight-line method for two years, the company determined that the useful life of the equipment is 27 years (seven more than the original estimate). Prepare the general journal entry(entries) necessary to account properly for the depreciation expense in the third year.

E23-5 Chopin Industries changed from the double-declining balance to the straight-line method in 1987 on all its plant assets. The appropriate information related to this change follows. For tax purposes, assume that the amount of CCA claimed is higher than the double-declining balance depreciation for each of the three years.

Year	Double-declining Balance Depreciation	Straight-line Depreciation	Difference
1985	$300,000	$120,000	$180,000
1986	240,000	120,000	120,000
1987	192,000	120,000	72,000

Net income for 1986 was reported at $270,000 and for 1987 was reported at $285,000, excluding any adjustment for the cumulative effect of a change in depreciation methods. The straight-line method of depreciation was employed in computing net income for 1987.

Instructions

(a) Assuming a tax rate of 45%, what is the amount of the cumulative effect adjustment in 1987?

(b) Prepare the journal entry(entries) to record the cumulative effect adjustment in the accounting records.

E23-6 Liszt Construction Company changed from the completed-contract to the percentage-of-completion method of accounting for long-term construction contracts during 1987. For tax purposes, the company employs the completed-contract method and will continue this approach in the future. The appropriate information related to this change is as follows:

	Pretax Income From:		
	Percentage-of-completion	Completed-contract	Difference
1986	$870,000	$650,000	$220,000
1987	820,000	580,000	240,000

Instructions

    (a) Assuming that the tax rate is 40%, what is the amount of net income that would be reported in 1987?

    (b) What entry(entries) are necessary to adjust the accounting records for the change in accounting principle?

E23-7 Below is the net income of R. Wagner Instrument Co., a private corporation, computed under the three inventory methods using a periodic system.

	FIFO	Average Cost	LIFO
1984	$21,000	$20,000	$18,000
1985	27,000	22,000	19,000
1986	24,000	24,000	22,000
1987	30,000	27,000	24,000

Instructions

    (a) Assume that in 1987 Wagner decided to change from the FIFO method to the average cost method of pricing inventories. Prepare the journal entry necessary for the change that took place during 1987, and show all the appropriate information needed for reporting on a comparative basis.

    (b) Assume that in 1987 Wagner, which had been using the LIFO method since incorporation in 1981, changed to the FIFO method of pricing inventories. Prepare the journal entry necessary for the change, and show all the appropriate information needed for reporting on a comparative basis.

    (c) Assume that in 1987 Wagner, which had been using the FIFO method, changed to the LIFO method of pricing inventories. Prepare the journal entry necessary for the change, and show all appropriate information needed for reporting on a comparative basis.

E23-8 Mendelssohn Industries uses periodic procedures and on December 31, 1987 decides to change from FIFO to LIFO. The following information is available in the company records:

	Units	Unit Cost
1986: Beginning Inventory	3,000	$20
Purchases: #1	5,000	24
#2	4,000	28
#3	6,000	32
#4	5,000	33
#5	5,000	35
Ending Inventory	8,000	
1987: Beginning Inventory	8,000	
Purchases: #1	2,000	44
#2	5,000	47
#3	5,000	50
#4	7,000	56
#5	3,000	58
Ending Inventory	11,000	

Instructions

    (a) State the value at which Mendelssohn Industries reports the ending inventory for 1987.

    (b) Indicate what additional disclosures are necessary for this change (both within the body of the financial statements and in notes). Assume a 40% tax rate.

E23-9 The first audit of the books of Schumann Horn Company was made for the year ended December 31, 1987. In examining the books, the auditor found that certain items had been overlooked or incorrectly handled in the last three years. These items are:

1. Schumann Horn Company purchased another company early in 1985 and recorded goodwill of $380,000. Schumann had not amortized goodwill since its value had not diminished.
2. In 1987, the company changed its basis of inventory pricing from FIFO to LIFO. The cumulative effect of this change amounted to $72,000. The company debited this cumulative effect to Retained Earnings. LIFO was used in computing income in 1987.
3. In 1987, the company wrote off $95,500 of inventory considered to be obsolete; this loss was charged directly to Retained Earnings.
4. At the beginning of 1985, the company purchased a machine for $450,000 (salvage value of $30,000) that had a useful life of six years. The bookkeeper used straight-line depreciation, but failed to deduct the salvage value in computing the depreciation base for the three years.
5. At the end of 1986, the company failed to accrue sales salaries of $34,000.
6. A tax lawsuit that involved the year 1985 was settled late in 1987. It was determined that the company owned an additional $75,000 in taxes related to 1985. The company did not record a liability in 1985 or 1986 because the possibility of loss was considered remote, and charged the $75,000 to a loss account in 1987.

Instructions

Prepare the journal entries necessary in 1987 to correct the books, assuming that the books have not been closed. The proper amortization period for goodwill is 40 years. Disregard effects of corrections on income tax.

E23-10 Presented below are the comparative statements for Tchaikovsky, Inc.

	1987	1986
Sales	$300,000	$250,000
Cost of sales	180,000	142,000
Gross profit	120,000	108,000
Expenses	77,000	43,000
Net income	$ 43,000	$ 65,000
Retained earnings (Jan. 1)	125,000	80,000
Net income	43,000	65,000
Dividends	(25,000)	(20,000)
Retained earnings (Dec. 31)	$143,000	$125,000

The following additional information is provided:

1. In 1987, Tchaikovsky, Inc. decides to switch its depreciation method from sum-of-the-years'-digits to the straight-line method. The differences in the two depreciation methods for the assets involved are:

	1986	1987
Sum-of-the-years'-digits	$50,000	$40,000[a]
Straight-line	25,000	25,000

[a]The 1987 income statement contains depreciation expense of $40,000.

2. In 1987, the company discovers that the ending inventory for 1986 was overstated by $35,000. Ending inventory for 1987 is correctly stated.

Instructions

(a) Prepare the revised income and retained earnings statements for 1986 and 1987, assuming comparative statements (ignore income tax effects). Do not prepare notes or pro forma amounts.
(b) Prepare the revised income and retained earnings statement for 1987, assuming a noncomparative presentation (ignore income tax effects). Do not prepare notes or pro forma amounts.

E23-11 The reported net incomes for the first two years of Brahms Laboratory, Inc. were as follows: 1986—$147,000; 1987—$185,000. Early in 1988, the following errors were discovered:

1. Depreciation of equipment for 1986 was overstated by $12,000.
2. Depreciation of equipment for 1987 was understated by $41,200.
3. December 31, 1986 inventory was understated by $60,000.
4. December 31, 1987 inventory was overstated by $17,500.

Instructions

Prepare the correcting entry necessary when these errors are discovered. Assume that the books are closed.

E23-12 Bizet Camera Company's December 31 year-end financial statements contained the following errors:

	December 31, 1986	December 31, 1987
Ending inventory	$8,500 understated	$7,250 overstated
Depreciation expense	$1,200 understated	—

An insurance premium of $45,000 was prepaid in 1986 covering the years 1986, 1987, and 1988. In addition, on December 31, 1987, fully depreciated machinery was sold for $13,000 cash, but the entry was not recorded until 1988. There were no other errors during 1986 or 1987, and no corrections have been made for any of the errors.

Instructions

(a) Compute the total effect of the errors on 1987 net income.
(b) Compute the total effect of the errors on the amount of Bizet's working capital at December 31, 1987.
(c) Compute the total effect of the errors on the balance of Bizet's retained earnings at December 31, 1987.

E23-13 A partial trial balance of Grieg Lock Corporation is as follows on December 31, 1987:

	Dr.	Cr.
Supplies on hand	$ 2,000	
Accrued salaries and wages		$ 1,000
Accrued interest on investments	4,000	
Prepaid insurance	100,000	
Unearned rental income		-0-
Accrued interest payable		12,000

Additional adjusting data:

1. A physical count of supplies on hand on December 31, 1987, totalled $800.
2. Through oversight, the accrued salaries and wages account was not changed during 1987. Accrued salaries and wages on December 31, 1987, amounted to $3,300.
3. The accrued interest on investments account was also left unchanged during 1987. Accrued interest on investments amounted to $3,200 on December 31, 1987.
4. The unexpired portions of the insurance policies totalled $87,200 as of December 31, 1987.
5. $26,000 was received on January 1, 1987, for the rent of a building for both 1987 and 1988. The entire amount was credited to rental income.
6. Depreciation for the year was erroneously recorded as $3,000 rather than the correct figure of $30,000.
7. A further review of depreciation calculations of prior years revealed that depreciation of $5,400 was not recorded. It was decided that this oversight should be corrected by a prior period adjustment.

Instructions

      (a) Assuming that the books have not been closed, what are the adjusting entries necessary at December 31, 1987?

      (b) Assuming that the books have been closed, what are the adjusting entries necessary at December 31, 1987?

E23-14 The reported net income for Debussy Tape Co. for 1986 was $92,000 and $81,700 for 1987. However, the accountant noted that the following errors had been made:

    1. Sales for 1986 included amounts of $40,500 which had been received in cash during 1986, but for which the related products were delivered in 1987. Title did not pass to the purchaser until 1987.

    2. The inventory on December 31, 1986, was understated by $7,150.

    3. The bookkeeper in recording interest expense for both 1986 and 1987 on bonds payable made the following entry on an annual basis:

Interest Expense	13,200	
Cash		13,200

    The bonds have a face value of $220,000 and pay a stated interest rate of 6%. They were issued at a discount of $11,000 on January 1, 1986, to yield an effective interest rate of 7%. (Assume that the effective yield method should be used.)

    4. Ordinary repairs to equipment had been erroneously charged to the Equipment account during 1986 and 1987. Repairs in the amount of $8,500 in 1986 and $9,400 in 1987 were so charged. The company applies a rate of 10% to the balance in the Equipment account at the end of the year in its determination of depreciation charges.

Instructions

    Prepare a schedule showing the determination of corrected net income for 1986 and 1987.

E23-15 When the records of Dvorak Paper Corporation were reviewed at the close of 1987, the errors listed below were discovered. For each item indicate by a check mark in the appropriate column whether the error resulted in an overstatement, an understatement, or had no effect on net income for the years 1986 and 1987.

	1986			1987		
Item	Over-statement	Under-statement	No Effect	Over-statement	Under-statement	No Effect
1. Failure to record the correct amount of ending 1986 inventory. The amount was understated because of an error in calculation.						
2. Failure to record merchandise purchased in 1986. Merchandise was also omitted from ending inventory in 1986 but was not yet sold.						
3. Failure to record amortization of patent in 1987.						
4. Failure to record accrued interest on notes payable in 1986; amount was recorded when paid in 1987.						
5. Failure to reflect supplies on hand on balance sheet at end of 1986.						

E23-16   Presented below is the net income related to Copland Piano, Inc.:

1987	1986	1985
$225,000	$117,000	$210,000

Assume that depreciation entries for 1987 have not been recorded. The following information is also available.

 1. Copland purchased a truck on January 1, 1984, for $32,000 with a $2,000 salvage value and a five-year life. The company debited an expense account and credited cash on the purchase date.

 2. During 1987, Copland changed from the straight-line method of depreciation for its building to the double-declining method. The following computations present depreciation on both bases:

	1987	1986	1985
Straight-line	$25,000	$25,000	$25,000
Double-declining	40,500	45,000	50,000

 3. Early in 1987, Copland determined that a piece of equipment purchased in January, 1984, at a cost of $21,000 with an estimated life of five years and salvage value of $1,000, is now estimated to continue in use until December 31, 1991, and will have a $750 salvage value. Copland has been using straight-line depreciation.

4. Copland won a court case in 1987 related to a patent infringement in 1984. Copland will collect its $8,720 settlement of the suit in 1988. The company had not recorded any entries related to this suit in previous periods.

5. Copland, in reviewing its provision for uncollectibles during 1987, has determined that 1% of sales is the appropriate amount of bad debt expense to be charged to operations. The company had used 0.5% as its rate in 1986 and 1985 when the expense had been $9,000 and $6,000, respectively. The company would have recorded $8,000 of bad debt expense on December 31, 1987, under the old rate. An entry for bad debt expense in 1987 has not been recorded.

Instructions

For each of the foregoing accounting changes, errors, or prior period adjustments, present the journal entry(entries) Copland would have made to record them during 1987, assuming that the books have not been closed. If no entry is required, write ''none.''

E23-17   Rachmaninoff, Inc. purchases a computer for $150,000 on January 1, 1985. For financial reporting purposes, it is estimated that the computer will have a useful life of four years with no salvage value. For tax purposes, the computer is depreciated as Class 10 property at the rate of 30%. For book purposes, the company has used the sum-of-the-years'-digits depreciation method for 1985 and 1986, but decides to change to the straight-line method in 1987. The tax rate for all periods involved is 45%.

Instructions

(a) Prepare the journal entry to record the change in accounting method in 1987.

(b) Compute the amount of deferred income taxes that would be reported on the December 31, 1987, balance sheet and whether it would have a debit or credit balance.

E23-18   Sibelius Enterprises purchases on January 1, 1985, a number of light-duty trucks costing $350,000. For book purposes, the company depreciates these assets on a straight-line basis over five years. For tax purposes, the company uses the Class 10 rate of 30%. At the beginning of the second year, the company decides to change to the double-declining balance method of depreciation for book purposes. The tax rate for all periods involved is 40%.

Instructions

(a) Prepare the journal entry to record the change in accounting method in 1986.

(b) Compute the balance in deferred income taxes at the end of 1986.

PROBLEMS

P23-1 On December 31, 1987, before the books were closed, the management and accountants of Bernstein Brass, Inc. made the following determinations about three depreciable assets:

1. Depreciable asset A was purchased January 1, 1984. It originally cost $440,000 and, for depreciation purposes, the straight-line method was originally chosen. The asset was originally expected to be useful for 10 years and have a zero salvage value. In 1987, the decision was made to change the depreciation method from straight-line to sum-of-the-years'-digits, and the estimates relating to useful life and salvage value remained unchanged.

2. Depreciable asset B was purchased January 3, 1983. It originally cost $90,000 and, for depreciation purposes, the straight-line method was chosen. The asset was originally expected to be useful for ten years and have a zero salvage value. In 1987, the decision was made to shorten the total life of this asset to nine years and to estimate the salvage value at $3,000.

3. Depreciable asset C was purchased January 5, 1982. The asset's original cost was $85,000, and this amount was entirely expensed in 1982. This particular asset has a 10-year useful life and no salvage value. The straight-line method was chosen for depreciation purposes.

Additional data:

1. Income in 1987 before depreciation expense amounted to $370,000.
2. Depreciation expense on assets other than A, B, and C totalled $40,000 in 1987.
3. Income in 1986 was reported at $400,000.
4. Ignore all income tax effects.
5. 100,000 common shares were outstanding in 1986 and 1987.

Instructions

(a) Prepare all necessary entries in 1987 to record these determinations.

(b) Prepare comparative income statements for Bernstein Brass, Inc. for 1986 and 1987, starting with income before the cumulative effects of any change in accounting principle.

(c) Prepare comparative retained earnings statements for Bernstein Brass, Inc. for 1986 and 1987. The company had retained earnings of $200,000 at December 31, 1985.

P23-2 Ravel Company reported net income of $750,000 for 1985. Its preliminary calculations of net income for 1986 show $810,000. The books are still open for 1986.

Additional information follows:

1. On January 1, 1985, Ravel purchased equipment for $770,000. Ravel estimated its useful life to be ten years with a zero salvage value. Ravel uses sum-of-the-years'-digits depreciation. Based on new information available at the end of 1986, Ravel now estimates the asset's useful life should total eight years. Depreciation expense based on a 10-year useful life has already been recorded in 1986. *[handwritten: 7 years left at that time.]*

2. In reviewing the December 31, 1986, inventory, Ravel discovers errors in its inventory-taking procedures which caused inventories for the last three years to be incorrect. Inventory at the end of 1984 was overstated $7,000; at the end of 1985, it was overstated $17,000; and at the end of 1986, it was understated $21,000. Ravel uses a periodic inventory system and does not have a Cost of Goods Sold account. All information used to compute cost of goods sold is compiled in the Income Summary account. At the end of 1986, entries are made to remove the beginning inventory amount from the Inventory account (with a corresponding debit to Income Summary) and to establish the ending inventory amount in the Inventory account (with a corresponding credit to Income Summary). The Income Summary account is still open.

3. Ravel has failed to accrue wages payable at the end of each of the last three years, as follows:

December 31, 1984	$1,200
December 31, 1985	2,500
December 31, 1986	2,000

4. Ravel has two large blast furnaces that it uses in its manufacturing process. These furnaces must be periodically relined. Furnace A was relined in January, 1980, at a cost of $300,000 and again in January, 1985, at a cost of $400,000. Furnace B was relined for the first time in January, 1986, at a cost of $450,000. All these costs were charged to Maintenance Expense as incurred.

Since a relining will last for five years, a better matching of revenues and expenses would have resulted if the cost of the relining was capitalized and depreciated over five years. Ravel has decided to make a change in accounting principle from expensing relining costs as incurred to capitalizing them and depreciating them over five years on a straight-line basis. A full year's depreciation will be taken in the year of relining. This change meets the requirements for a change in accounting principle.

Instructions

(a) Prepare the journal entries necessary at December 31, 1986, to record the above corrections and changes. The books are still open for 1986. Income tax effects may be ignored.

(b) Ravel plans to issue comparative (1986 and 1985) financial statements. Starting with $810,000 for 1986 and $750,000 for 1985, prepare a schedule to derive the correct net incomes for 1986 and 1985 to be shown in these statements. Income tax effects may be ignored.

P23-3 Puccini Leggs Inc. was organized in late 1983 to manufacture and sell hosiery. At the end of its fourth year of operation, the company has been fairly successful, as indicated by the following reported net incomes.

1984	$175,000[a]	1986	230,000
1985	195,000[b]	1987	320,000

[a]Includes a $10,000 increase because of change in bad debt experience rate.
[b]Includes extraordinary gain of $30,000.

The company has decided to expand operations and has applied for a sizable bank loan. The bank officer has indicated that the records should be audited and presented in comparative statements to facilitate analysis by the bank. Puccini, therefore, hires the auditing firm of Rimsky and Korsakov Co. and has provided the following additional information.

1. In early 1985, Puccini changed their estimate from 2 to 1% on the amount of bad debt expense to be charged to operations. Bad debt expense for 1984, if a 1% rate had been used, would have been $10,000. The company, therefore, restated its net income of 1984.

2. In 1987, the auditor discovers that the company has changed its method of inventory pricing from LIFO to FIFO. The effect on the income statements for the previous years is as follows:

	1984	1985	1986	1987
Net income unadjusted—LIFO basis	$175,000	$195,000	$230,000	$320,000
Net income unadjusted—FIFO basis	190,000	200,000	240,000	295,000
	$ 15,000	$ 5,000	$ 10,000	($25,000)

3. In 1985, the company changed its method of depreciation from the accelerated method to the straight-line approach. The company used the straight-line method in 1985. The effect on the income statement for the previous year is as follows:

	1984
Net income unadjusted (accelerated method)	$150,000
Net income unadjusted (straight-line method)	156,000
	$ 6,000

4. In 1987, the auditor discovers that:
    (a) The company incorrectly overstated the ending inventory by $8,000 in 1986.
    (b) A dispute developed in 1985 with Revenue Canada over the deductibility of entertainment expenses. In 1984, the company was not permitted these deductions, but a tax settlement reached in 1987 allows for these expenses. As a result of the court's finding, tax expenses in 1987 are reduced by $50,000.

Instructions

(a) Indicate how each of these changes or corrections should be handled in the accounting records.

(b) Present comparative income statements for the years 1984 to 1987, starting with income before extraordinary items. Do not prepare pro forma amounts.

P23-4 Strauss Corporation has decided that in the preparation of its 1987 financial statements two changes will be made from the methods used in prior years:

1. **Depreciation.** Strauss has always used an accelerated method for tax and financial reporting purposes but has decided to change during 1987 to the straight-line method for financial reporting only. Assume that the accelerated method for tax and reporting purposes has been the same in the past. The effect of this change is as follows:

	Excess of Accelerated Depreciation Over Straight-line Depreciation
Prior to 1986	$1,365,000
1986	141,640
1987	132,360
	$1,639,000

Depreciation is charged to cost of sales and to selling, general, and administrative expenses on the basis of 75% and 25%, respectively.

2. **Bad debt expense.** In the past Strauss recognized that bad debt expense was equal to 1.5% of net sales. After careful review it has been decided that a rate of 1.75% is more appropriate for 1987. Bad debt expense is charged to selling, general, and administrative expenses.

The following information is taken from preliminary financial statements, prepared before giving effect to the two changes:

Strauss Corporation
CONDENSED BALANCE SHEET
December 31, 1987
With Comparative Figures for 1986

	1987	1986
Assets		
Current assets	$43,561,000	$43,900,000
Plant assets, at cost	45,792,000	43,974,000
Less accumulated depreciation	14,543,000	13,262,000
	$74,810,000	$74,612,000
Liabilities and Shareholders' Equity		
Current liabilities	$21,124,000	$26,650,000
Long-term debt	15,154,000	17,097,000
Capital stock	11,620,000	11,620,000
Retained earnings	26,912,000	19,245,000
	$74,810,000	$74,612,000

Strauss Corporation
INCOME STATEMENT
For the Year Ended December 31, 1987
With Comparative Figures for 1986

	1987	1986
Net sales	$92,340,000	$89,760,000
Cost of goods sold	54,847,000	53,074,000
	37,493,000	36,686,000
Selling, general, and administrative expenses	19,540,000	18,411,000
	17,953,000	18,275,000
Other income (expense), net	(1,198,000)	(1,079,000)
Income before income taxes	16,755,000	17,196,000
Income taxes	6,702,000	6,878,400
Net income	$10,053,000	$10,317,600

There have been no timing differences between any book and tax items prior to the changes above. The tax rate is 40%.

Instructions

For the items listed below compute the amounts that would appear on the comparative (1987 and 1986) financial statements of Strauss Corporation after adjustment for the two accounting changes. Show amounts for both 1987 and 1986 and prepare supporting schedules as necessary.

(a) Accumulated depreciation.
(b) Deferred income taxes (cumulative).
(c) Selling, general, and administrative expenses.
(d) Current portion of income tax expense.
(e) Deferred portion of income tax expense.
(f) Retained earnings.
(g) Pro forma net income.

(AICPA adapted)

P23-5   The management of Bartok Instrument Company has concluded, with the concurrence of its independent auditors, that results of operations would be more fairly presented if Bartok changed its method of pricing inventory from last-in, first-out (LIFO) to average cost in 1986. Given below is the five-year summary of income and a schedule of what the inventories might have been if stated on the average cost method.

Bartok Instrument Company
STATEMENT OF INCOME AND RETAINED EARNINGS
For the Years Ended May 31

	1982	1983	1984	1985	1986
Sales—net	$15,322	$18,143	$17,212	$19,687	$20,547
Cost of goods sold					
Beginning inventory	1,000	1,100	1,000	1,115	1,237
Purchases	13,000	13,900	15,000	15,900	17,100
Ending inventory	(1,100)	(1,000)	(1,115)	(1,237)	(1,369)
Total	12,900	14,000	14,885	15,778	16,968
Gross profit	2,422	4,143	2,327	3,909	3,579
Administrative expenses	700	763	832	907	989
Income before taxes	1,722	3,380	1,495	3,002	2,590
Income taxes (50%)	861	1,690	747	1,501	1,295

Net income	861	1,690	748	1,501	1,295
Retained earnings—beginning	1,206	2,067	3,757	4,504	6,005
Retained earnings—ending	$ 2,067	$ 3,757	$ 4,504	$ 6,005	$ 7,300
Earnings per share	$ 8.61	$ 16.90	$ 7.47	$ 15.01	$ 12.95

Schedule of Inventory Balances Using Average Cost Method

Years Ended May 31

1981	1982	1983	1984	1985	1986
$950	$1,124	$1,101	$1,270	$1,490	$1,699

Instructions

Prepare comparative statements for the five years, assuming that Bartok changed its method of inventory pricing to average cost. Indicate the effects on net income and earnings per share for the years involved. (All amounts except EPS are rounded to the nearest dollar.)

P23-6 Sousa Company is in the process of adjusting and correcting its books at the end of 1987. In reviewing its records, the following information is compiled.

1. On January 1, 1986, Sousa implemented a stock appreciation rights (SAR) plan for its top executives. The plan was to run from January 1, 1985, to December 31, 1987. This period was the intended service period and the date of exercise was December 31, 1987 (the measurement date). At December 31, 1987 (the measurement date), the executives were to receive in cash the appreciation in the market value of the shares over the three-year period. Using the market prices of the shares at the end of 1985 and 1986, respectively, Sousa estimated compensation expense of $30,800 for 1985 and $49,700 for 1986. At December 31, however, the market price of the stock was below its price at January 1, 1985.

2. Sousa has failed to accrue sales commissions payable at the end of each of the last two years, as follows:

December 31, 1986	$8,100
December 31, 1987	$4,600

3. In reviewing the December 31, 1987, inventory, Sousa discovers errors in its inventory-taking procedures which have caused inventories for the last three years to be incorrect, as follows:

December 31, 1985	Understated	$13,000—Physical
December 31, 1986	Understated	$17,000—Physical
December 31, 1987	Overstated	$ 3,000

    Sousa has already made an entry to establish the incorrect December 31, 1987, inventory amount.

4. At December 31, 1987, Sousa decides to change its depreciation method on its office equipment from double-declining balance to straight-line. Assume that CCA is higher than the double-declining depreciation taken for each period. The income tax rate is 30%. The following information is available:

	Double-Declining Balance	Straight-Line	Pretax Difference	Tax Effect	Difference, Net of Tax
Prior to 1987	$70,000	$40,000	$30,000	$9,000	$21,000
1987	12,000	10,000	2,000	600	1,400

    Sousa has already recorded the 1987 depreciation expense using the double-declining balance method.

5. Before 1987, Sousa accounted for its income from long-term construction contracts on the percentage-of-completion basis (while using the completed-contract method for tax purposes). Early in 1987, Sousa changes to the completed-contract basis on its books so it would be using the same method for its books as it uses for tax purposes. Income for 1987 has been recorded using the completed-contract method. The income tax rate is 30%. The following information is available:

	Pretax Income	
	Percentage-of-completion	Completed-contract
Prior to 1987	$175,000	$50,000
1987	60,000	20,000

Instructions

Prepare the journal entries necessary at December 31, 1987, to record the above corrections and changes. The books are still open for 1987. Sousa has not yet recorded its 1987 income tax expense and payable amounts so current-year tax effects may be ignored. Prior-year tax effects must be considered in items 4 and 5.

P23-7   On March 5, 1987, you were hired by a closely held company as a staff member of its newly created internal auditing department. While reviewing the company's records for 1985 and 1986, you discover that no adjustments have yet been made for the items listed below.

1. Interest income of $14,200 was not accrued at the end of 1985. It was recorded when received in February, 1986.

2. A word processor costing $8,000 was expensed when purchased on July 1, 1985. It is expected to have a four-year life with no salvage value. The company typically uses straight-line depreciation for all fixed assets.

3. Research costs of $30,000 were incurred early in 1985. They were capitalized and were to be amortized over a three-year period. Amortization of $10,000 was recorded for 1985 and $10,000 for 1986.

4. On January 2, 1985, the company leased a building for five years at a monthly rental of $7,000. On that date, the company paid the following amounts:

Security deposit	$25,000
First month's rent	7,000
Last month's rent	7,000
	$39,000

The entire amount of $39,000 was charged to rent expense in 1985.

5. The company received $33,000 from a customer at the beginning of 1985 for services to be performed evenly over a three-year period beginning in 1985. None of the amount received was reported as unearned revenue at the end of 1985.

6. Merchandise inventory costing $15,300 was in the warehouse at December 31, 1985, but was incorrectly omitted from the physical count at that date.

Instructions

Indicate the effect of any errors on the net income figure reported on the income statement for the year ending December 31, 1985, and the retained earnings figure reported on the balance sheet at December 31, 1986. Assume all amounts are material and ignore income tax effects. Using the following format enter the appropriate dollar amounts in the appropriate columns. Consider each item independent of the other items. It is unnecessary to total the columns on the grid.

	Net Income for 1985		Retained Earnings at December 31, 1986	
Item	Understated	Overstated	Understated	Overstated

P23-8 Brittan Hitech Industries has used the accrual basis of accounting for several years. A review of the records, however, indicates that some expenses and revenues have been handled on a cash basis because of errors made by an inexperienced bookkeeper. Income statements prepared by the bookkeeper reported $26,000 net income for 1986 and $34,000 net income for 1987. Further examination of the records reveals that the following items were handled improperly.

1. Rent was received from a tenant in December, 1986; the amount, $900, was recorded as income at that time, even though the rental pertained to 1987.

2. Wages payable on December 31 have been consistently omitted from the records of that date and have been entered as expenses when paid in the following year. The amounts of the accruals recorded in this manner were:

December 31, 1985	$ 850
December 31, 1986	1,340
December 31, 1987	780

3. Invoices for office supplies purchased have been charged to expense accounts when received. Inventories of supplies on hand at the end of each year have been ignored, and no entry has been made for them.

December 31, 1985	$1,000
December 31, 1986	460
December 31, 1987	1,070

Instructions

Prepare a schedule that will show the corrected net income for the years 1986 and 1987. All items listed should be labelled clearly.

P23-9 Berlin Shoe Corporation is in the process of negotiating a loan for expansion purposes. The books and records have never been audited and the bank has requested that an audit be performed. Berlin has prepared the following comparative financial statements for the years ended December 31, 1987 and 1986:

BALANCE SHEET
As of December 31, 1987 and 1986

	1987	1986
Assets		
Current assets		
Cash	$163,000	$ 82,000
Accounts receivable	392,000	296,000
Allowance for doubtful accounts	(37,000)	(18,000)
Marketable securities, at cost	78,000	78,000
Merchandise inventory	207,000	202,000
Total current assets	$803,000	$640,000
Plant assets		
Property, plant, and equipment	167,000	169,500
Accumulated depreciation	(121,600)	(106,400)
Total fixed assets	45,400	63,100
Total assets	$848,400	$703,100
Liabilities and Shareholders' Equity		
Liabilities		
Accounts payable	$121,400	$196,100
Shareholders' equity		
Common shares, no-par value authorized 50,000 shares, issued and outstanding 20,000 shares	260,000	260,000
Retained earnings	467,000	247,000
Total shareholders' equity	747,000	507,000
Total liabilities and shareholders' equity	$848,400	$703,100

STATEMENT OF INCOME
For the Years Ended December 31, 1987 and 1986

	1987	1986
Sales	$1,000,000	$900,000
Cost of sales	430,000	395,000
Gross profit	570,000	505,000
Operating expenses	210,000	205,000
Administrative expenses	140,000	105,000
	350,000	310,000
Net income	$ 220,000	$195,000

During the course of the audit, the following additional facts were determined.

1. An analysis of collections and losses on accounts receivable during the past two years indicates a drop in anticipated losses due to bad debts. After consultation with management it was agreed that the loss experience rate on sales should be reduced from the recorded 2% to 1%, beginning with the year ended December 31, 1987.

2. An analysis of marketable securities revealed that this investment portfolio consisted entirely of short-term investments in marketable equity securities that were acquired in 1986. The total market valuation for these investments as of the end of each year was as follows:

     December 31, 1986 $81,000
     December 31, 1987 $71,300

3. The merchandise inventory at December 31, 1986, was overstated by $15,100, and the merchandise inventory at December 31, 1987, was overstated by $19,800.

4. On January 2, 1986, equipment costing $30,000 (estimated useful life of 10 years and residual value of $5,000) was incorrectly charged to operating expenses. Berlin records depreciation on the straight-line method. In 1987 fully depreciated equipment (with no residual value) that originally cost $17,500 was sold as scrap for $2,800. Berlin credited the proceeds of $2,800 to property and equipment.

5. An analysis of 1986 operating expenses revealed that Berlin charged to expense a four-year insurance premium of $4,960 on January 15, 1986.

Instructions

(a) Prepare the journal entries to correct the books at December 31, 1987. The books for 1987 have not been closed. Ignore income taxes.

(b) Prepare a schedule showing the computations of corrected net income for the years ended December 31, 1987 and 1986, assuming that any adjustments are to be reported on comparative statements for the two years. The first items on your schedule should be the net income for each year. Ignore income taxes. (Do not prepare financial statements.)

P23-10 You have been asked by a client to review the records of Gershwin Company, a small manufacturer of precision tools and machines. Your client is interested in buying the business, and arrangements have been made for you to review the accounting records.

1. Gershwin Company commenced business on April 1, 1984, and has been reporting on a fiscal year ending March 31. The company has never been audited, but the annual statements prepared by the bookkeeper reflect the following income before closing and before deducting income taxes:

Year Ended March 31	Income Before Taxes
1985	$124,220
1986	160,450
1987	149,740

2. A relatively small number of machines have been shipped on consignment. These transactions have been recorded as ordinary sales and billed as such. On March 31 of each year, machines billed and in the hands of consignees amounted to:

1985	$9,360
1986	none
1987	9,100

   Sales price was determined by adding 30% to cost. Assume that the consigned machines are sold the following year.

3. On March 30, 1986, two machines were shipped to a customer on a C.O.D. basis. The sale was not entered until April 5, 1986, when cash was received for $6,100. The machines were not included in the inventory at March 31, 1986. (Title passed on March 30, 1986.)

4. All machines are sold subject to a five-year warranty. It is estimated that the expense ultimately to be incurred in connection with the warranty will amount to 0.5% of sales. The company has charged an expense account for warranty costs incurred.
   Sales per books and warranty costs were:

Year Ended March 31	Sales	Warranty Expense for Sales Made in 1985	1986	1987	Total
1985	$1,040,000	$760			$ 760
1986	1,120,000	360	$1,310		1,670
1987	1,980,000	320	1,620	$1,910	3,850

5. A review of the corporate minutes reveals the manager is entitled to a bonus of 0.5% of the income before deducting income taxes and the bonus. The bonuses have never been recorded or paid.

6. Bad debts have been recorded on a direct write-off basis. Experience of similar enterprises indicates that losses will approximate 0.25% of sales. Bad debts written off were:

	Bad Debts Incurred on Sales Made in 1985	1986	1987	Total
1985	$750			$ 750
1986	800	$ 520		1,320
1987	350	1,800	$1,700	3,850

7. The bank deducts 6% on all contracts financed. Of this amount 0.5% is placed in a reserve to the credit of Gershwin Company that is refunded to Gershwin as finance contracts are paid in full. The reserve established by the bank has not been reflected in the books of Gershwin. The excess of credits over debits (net increase) to the reserve account with Gershwin on the books of the bank for each fiscal year was as follows:

1985	$ 4,200
1986	4,700
1987	$ 5,600
	$14,500

8. Commissions on sales have been entered when paid. Commissions payable on March 31 of each year were:

1985	$ 1,400
1986	800
1987	1,120

Instructions

    (a) Present a schedule showing the revised income before taxes for each of the years ended March 31, 1985, 1986, and 1987. Make computations to the nearest whole dollar.

    (b) Prepare the journal entry or entries you would give the bookkeeper to correct the books. Assume the books have not yet been closed for the fiscal year ended March 31, 1987. Disregard correction of income taxes.

(AICPA adapted)

PART

6

PREPARATION AND ANALYSIS OF FINANCIAL STATEMENTS

24

STATEMENT OF CHANGES IN FINANCIAL POSITION

How did Petro-Canada Ltd. finance the large investment it made to acquire Petrofina Canada? How will De Havilland finance the new STOL aircraft that it is building for the airline industry? How was Sears Industries Inc. able to purchase long-term assets recently in the same year that it sustained a net loss? How much of the proposed expansion by Marriott Hotels will be financed through the reinvestment of net income? These types of questions are often asked by investors, creditors, and internal management who are interested in the financial operations of a business enterprise. However, an examination of the balance sheet, income statement, and statement of retained earnings often fails to provide ready answers to questions of this type.

The balance sheet presents the status of the assets and equities as of a specific date; the income statement presents a summary of the nature and results of transactions affecting net income. The statement of retained earnings provides an analysis of changes in retained earnings. These statements present to a limited extent and in a fragmented manner information about the financial activities of an enterprise during the period. Comparative balance sheets help to show what new assets have been acquired or disposed of and what liabilities have been incurred or liquidated. The income statement provides information as to resources provided by operations. The statement of retained earnings provides information as to the resources used to pay dividends. None of these statements, however, presents a detailed summary of all the resources provided during the period and the uses to which they are put.

EVOLUTION OF A NEW STATEMENT

A statement specifically designed to furnish this information is now issued by all major business enterprises as one of the primary financial statements. This statement, the **Statement of Changes in Financial Position**, is designed to present information on the financing and investing activities of a business enterprise. The evolution of this statement provides an interesting example of how the needs of financial statement users are met.

The statement originated in a simple analysis called the "Where-Got and Where-Gone Statement" that consisted of nothing more than a listing of the increases or decreases in the company's balance sheet items. After some years, the title of this statement was changed to "the funds statement." In 1961, the AICPA, recognizing the significance of this statement, sponsored research in this area that resulted in the publication of *Accounting Research Study No. 2* entitled "Cash Flow Analysis and the Funds Statement."[1] This study recommended that the funds statement be included in all annual reports to the shareholders and that it be covered by the auditor's opinion.

Prior to 1974 this statement was known as the "Statement of Source and Application of Funds." In 1974 the CICA revised and expanded Section 1540 of the *Handbook* that deals with this statement. In the revision, the statement was given the title "Statement of Changes in Financial Position." The objective of this statement was to provide information as to how the activities of the enterprise have been financed and how its **financial resources** have been used during the period covered by the statement. In September, 1985, an important revision to Section 1540 was released. In this revision the objective was changed to "provide information about the operating, financing, and investing activities of an enterprise and the effects of those activities on **cash resources**."[2] The change in emphasis from providing information about changes in financial resources to providing information about changes in cash resources has important implications for accountants. Under the previous *Handbook* requirements various alternatives such as working capital, quick assets, or cash were permitted. The revision requires information about cash or cash and its equivalents, restricting the number of alternatives previously available under Section 1540. Although the *Handbook* does not explicitly require all firms to present a statement of changes in financial position with their financial statements, most Canadian firms voluntarily include it in their annual reports.[3]

WHAT IS MEANT BY CHANGES IN FINANCIAL POSITION?

The changes that occur in financial position from one period to another can be measured in several different ways. The more common bases are discussed on page 1111.

---

[1]Perry Mason, " 'Cash Flow' Analysis and the Funds Statement," *Accounting Research Study No. 2* (New York: AICPA, 1961).

[2]*CICA Handbook*, Section 1540, par. 3.

[3]*Financial Reporting in Canada—1983* (Toronto: CICA, 1984), for example, indicates that all of the 325 companies surveyed presented a statement of changes in financial position in 1982.

Cash Basis

Under this concept the changes in the cash balance that occur over a period of time are summarized. Any transaction that either increases or decreases cash is considered in preparing the final statement. For example, the purchase of land for cash is considered a change in financial position because it decreases cash. A transaction that has no effect on cash, such as the purchase of land on credit, is not reported. Using cash only to measure changes in financial position has limitations, because many important transactions resulting in changes in financial position are of a noncash variety and are excluded from this statement.

An approach that is similar to cash which would also be permitted under the current *Handbook* provision is "cash and cash equivalents." Many believe that the distinction between cash and surplus cash temporarily invested is not substantive enough to warrant separation. Concepts similar to cash—such as (1) cash and temporary investments, (2) cash, temporary investments, and receivables (monetary assets), (3) cash, temporary investments, and receivables minus current liabilities (net monetary assets), and (4) cash less short-term bank loans—are sometimes suggested as means of measuring changes in financial position, but these concepts are not extensively employed in practice.[4]

Working Capital Basis

Changes in financial position used to be most commonly measured in terms of working capital (current assets minus current liabilities). Any transaction that increases or decreases working capital is shown in the statement. For example, the purchase of land for cash or short-term credit is reported in the changes statement because a change in working capital occurs. The use of working capital as the basis permits the exclusion of many routine transactions, such as cash collections on accounts receivable and the purchase of inventory on credit. All of these transactions are summarized in the amount reported as "resources (working capital) provided by operations."

All Financial Resources

If cash or working capital alone is used in measuring changes in financial position, some major financial transactions may be omitted. For example, issuing common shares for buildings or machinery has no effect on cash or working capital, but it is a significant financial transaction that should be disclosed. For this reason the definition of changes in financial position was expanded to include **all transactions that affect the firm's capital and asset structure.** This approach, known as the **all financial resources concept,** expands the definition of resources beyond cash or working capital to cover all significant financial occurrences. *CICA Handbook*, Section 1540, recommends the use of the all financial resources concept, indicating that a company may explain its changes in resources using such a concept as cash, or cash and cash equivalents, but that whichever concept is

---

[4]*Ibid.* In 1982 only 15 out of 325 companies surveyed used the cash and cash equivalent approach in measuring changes in financial position, while 280 of the companies surveyed analyzed the change in terms of working capital.

followed, it must be adjusted to disclose significant financial transactions that would otherwise be omitted under this concept.

The statement of changes in financial position should be based upon the all financial resources concept; at the same time, statements that employ a cash or cash equivalent approach disclose the change in cash or cash equivalents. To accomplish these two objectives, the statement (using cash as an illustration) must identify and analyze two categories of items: (1) sources of cash (inflows) and applications of cash (outflows), and (2) sources and applications of resources that did not affect (flow through) cash.

APPEAL OF THE CASH BASIS

Just a couple of years ago the working capital format was the most often used in preparing a statement of changes in financial position. The financial reporting environment, however, has changed dramatically in this area. For example, in a recently amended *Handbook* section, the CICA indicated that meaningful components of cash flow are generally more useful than reporting changes in working capital. This has been supported by the Financial Executives Institute which recommended that companies use the cash (or cash and cash equivalent) basis instead of the working capital basis in preparing this statement.[5] Also, many practitioners and academics have argued for a greater cash basis orientation to the statement of changes in financial position.[6] Furthermore, in its most recent *Concepts Statement No. 5*, the FASB strongly supports the inclusion in the primary financial statements of a **statement of cash flows** that reflects an entity's cash receipts classified by major sources and its cash payments classified by major uses.[7]

Why the sudden change in the financial reporting environment? One major reason is that investors and analysts are concerned that **accrual accounting has become too far removed from the underlying cash flows of the enterprise.** They contend that accountants are using too many arbitrary allocation devices (deferred taxes, depreciation, amortization of intangibles, accrual of revenues, etc.) and are therefore computing a net income figure that no longer provides an acceptable indicator of the earning power of the enterprise. Similarly, **because financial statements take no cognizance of the inflation besetting the economy today, many look for a more concrete standard like cash flow to evaluate operating success or failure.** In addition, others contend that the **working capital concept does not provide as useful information about liquidity and financial flexibility as does the cash approach.** For example, information on receivable and inventory financing is important; frequently receivable and inventory mismanagement leads to a lack of liquidity and other financial problems.

---

[5]Allen H. Seed, III, *The Funds Statement—Structure and Use* (Morristown, N. J.: Financial Executives Research Foundation, 1984), p. 3.

[6]For example, one writer has recommended that the statement of changes in financial position as currently prepared should be discontinued and replaced with three required statements: a statement of cash receipts and payments, a statement of financing activities, and a statement of investing activities. See Loyd C. Heath, *Accounting Research Monograph No. 3: Financial Reporting and the Evaluation of Solvency* (New York: AICPA, 1978); and Loyd C. Heath, "Let's Scrap the Funds Statement," *The Journal of Accountancy* (October, 1978), pp. 94–103. Also see Edward Swanson and Richard Vangermeersch, "Statement of Financing and Investing Activities," *The CPA Journal* (November, 1981), pp. 32–40.

[7]"Recognition and Measurement in Financial Statements of Business Enterprises," *Statement of Financial Accounting Concepts No. 5* (Stamford, Conn.: FASB, 1984), pars. 52–54.

ILLUSTRATIONS OF THE CASH APPROACH

The following illustrations disclose the change (increase or decrease) in cash, yet they are based upon the all financial resources concept. Therefore, in order to accommodate and identify the sources and uses of noncash resources as well as the sources and uses of cash, we will use the terms "resources provided" and "resources applied" as headings in the statements of changes.

Illustration 1—Butterfield Services Ltd.   To illustrate the preparation of a statement of changes in financial position, we will first assume a simple situation. The comparative account balances and differences between them for Butterfield Services Ltd. are shown below.

	Butterfield Services Ltd.			
	Balances		Changes	
	Dec. 31, 1986	Dec. 31, 1985	Dr.	Cr.
Cash	$ 17,000	$ 10,000	$ 7,000	
Accounts receivable	85,000	80,000	5,000	
Office furniture	24,000	24,000		
	$126,000	$114,000		
Accumulated depreciation	$ 12,000	$ 8,000		$ 4,000
Accounts payable	22,000	20,000		2,000
Share capital	50,000	50,000		
Retained earnings	42,000	36,000		6,000
	$126,000	$114,000	$12,000	$12,000

Assume that cash dividends of $3,000 were paid during the year 1986 and that the net income for 1986 was $9,000.

Because net income of $9,000 per the income statement is on an accrual basis, we must adjust it to a cash basis to report cash provided by operations. **The charge for depreciation expense that reduced net income did not require any cash expenditure during the current period.** Therefore, depreciation expense of $4,000 (as represented by the increase in accumulated depreciation from $8,000 to $12,000) must be added to net income in order to disclose the total cash provided by operations. Other charges to expense for the period that do not require the use of cash may be treated in the same manner as depreciation. Bond discount amortized, amortization of patents or goodwill, and changes in deferred income taxes are examples of such charges that are illustrated later in this chapter.

Other changes noted in the above schedule are an increase of $5,000 in Accounts Receivable and an increase of $2,000 in Accounts Payable. The operations of the period led to increased revenues but not all of these revenues resulted in an increase in cash. Some of the increase in revenues resulted in an increase in Accounts Receivable. In order to derive the amount of cash from operations we must deduct that portion of revenues not producing cash (that is, the $5,000 excess of revenues on account over cash collections from customers). The increase in Accounts Payable represents charges to expenses that did not yet require cash expenditures. The creditors are effectively, though temporarily, supplying cash. In order to derive the amount of cash from operations we must add that portion of expenses that did not require cash outflows (as represented by the increase in accounts payable).

The statement below, prepared on a cash basis, reports the changes identified and discussed on page 1113.

Butterfield Services Ltd.
STATEMENT OF CHANGES IN FINANCIAL POSITION
For the Year Ended December 31, 1986

Resources (cash) provided by
  Operations:
    Net income $ 9,000
    Add: Items not requiring cash outflows
      Depreciation expense $ 4,000
      Increase in accounts payable   2,000
    Less: Items not providing cash inflows
      Increase in accounts receivable   (5,000)   1,000
    Cash provided by operations   10,000

Resources (cash) applied to
  Payment of dividends   3,000
Increase in cash $ 7,000

This method of adjusting net income from operations on an accrual basis (as reported on the income statement) to cash from operations by adding back to net income the noncash expenses and losses and subtracting the noncash revenues and gains is referred to as the **indirect approach** (also called the reconciliation approach). An acceptable alternative approach that produces the same amount for cash provided from operations is the **direct approach** which starts with those revenues that provided cash and deducts operating costs and expenses that required the outlay of cash during the period. Both approaches are discussed in greater detail on pages 1132–1134.

Illustration 2—Doral Products Ltd. The preceding illustration was made simple to illustrate specific points. A more comprehensive example follows:

Doral Products Ltd.

Accounts	Dec. 31, 1986	Dec. 31, 1985	Differences Dr.	Differences Cr.
Cash	$ 4,600	$ 3,000	$ 1,600	
Accounts receivable (net)	11,300	15,000		$ 3,700
Inventories	11,500	25,000		13,500
Prepaid expenses	1,200	1,000	200	
Land	34,000	40,000		6,000
Equipment	95,000	60,000	35,000	
	$157,600	$144,000		
Accumulated depreciation—equipment	$ 23,000	$ 20,000		$ 3,000
Accounts payable	9,500	15,000	$ 5,500	
Bonds payable (long-term)	13,500	6,000		7,500
Share capital	80,000	80,000		
Retained earnings	31,600	23,000		8,600
	$157,600	$144,000	$42,300	$42,300

Additional information concerning some of the differences:

1. Land carried at $6,000 was sold for $7,000 during the year; the gain of $1,000 was not considered an extraordinary item.
2. Equipment costing $40,000 was purchased during the year; equipment with a cost of $5,000 was sold at its book value of $1,500. Depreciation expense for the year was $6,500.
3. Bonds payable in the amount of $7,500 were issued for cash.
4. Net income for the year was $19,600; cash dividends of $11,000 were declared and paid.

In preparing a statement of changes in financial position, a work sheet, described later, could be used, although it is possible to prepare the statement without using one. To prepare the statement, it is necessary to analyze the differences that occur in the accounts from one period to the next.

An analysis of the Retained Earnings account is a good starting point because the net income is the first item reported on a statement of changes in financial position. Then the changes in assets, liabilities, and other shareholders' equity accounts should be analyzed.

Increase in Retained Earnings. Retained earnings increased $8,600 for Doral Products Ltd. as a result of net income of $19,600 less cash dividends of $11,000. The net income amount would be reported as follows:

Resources (cash) provided by	
Operations:	
Net income	$19,600

The cash dividends are reported as a use of resources as follows:

Resources (cash) applied to	
Cash dividends	$11,000

Decrease in Accounts Receivable. A decrease in Accounts Receivable represents cash collections from customers in excess of credit sales made to customers during the current period. The $3,700 decrease is therefore added to income as a source of operating cash inflows and is reported as follows:

Resources (cash) provided by	
Operations:	
Add: Items not affecting cash	
Decrease in accounts receivable	$3,700

Decrease in Inventories. A decrease in the inventory balance from the beginning to the end of the current year represents a source of current period revenue and cash from a cash outlay made in a previous period. The $13,500 decrease is reported as a source of operating cash inflows as follows:

Resources (cash) provided by
  Operations:
    Net income
    Add: Items not affecting cash
      Decrease in inventories $13,500

Increase in Prepaid Expenses. An increase in Prepaid Expenses represents a current period cash outflow for an expense to be charged against a future income statement. The $200 increase in Prepaid Expenses would be reported as follows:

Resources (cash) applied to
  Operations:
    Net income
    Less: Items not affecting cash
      Increase in prepaid expenses $(200)

Decrease in Land. The decrease in the balance of Land account from the beginning to the end of the year is $6,000. The resources provided by the cash sale of the land are $7,000; the gain of $1,000 is included in net income for the year. On the statement of changes in financial position, the following information is reported:

Resources (cash) provided by
  Sale of land $7,000

The total proceeds from the sale of the land is reported as resources provided by sale of land. Note that the $1,000 gain on the sale of the land is included in net income. This gain of $1,000 must be deducted from net income when computing cash provided by operations to avoid double counting.

Resources provided by
  Operations:
    Net income
    Add (or deduct) items not affecting cash
      Gain on sale of land $(1,000)

Equipment and Related Depreciation. Equipment costing $40,000 was purchased for cash during the year; this purchase would be reported as follows:

Resources (cash) applied to
  Purchase of equipment $40,000

In addition, equipment costing $5,000 was sold for cash at its book value of $1,500. This transaction would be reported as follows:

Resources (cash) provided by
  Sale of equipment $1,500

Depreciation expense for the year is $6,500 and would be reported as an item added back to net income to show cash provided by operations. The difference of $3,000 in the Accumulated Depreciation—Equipment account is the net result of the increase of $6,500 from 1986 depreciation expense and the decrease of $3,500 from the sale of equipment. The depreciation expense for 1986 would be reported as follows:

```
Resources provided by
   Operations:
      Net income
      Add (or deduct) items not affecting cash
         Depreciation                                              $6,500
```

Decrease in Accounts Payable. A decrease in Accounts Payable represents cash payments to suppliers in excess of either charges to expense or inventory. In order to convert net income from an accrual basis to a cash basis, the $5,500 decrease in Accounts Payable is reported as follows:

```
Resources (cash) provided by
   Operations:
      Net income
      Less: Items not requiring cash outflows
         Decrease in accounts payable                              $(5,500)
```

Issuance of Bonds Payable. Bonds in the amount of $7,500 were issued for cash during the year. This transaction would be reported as follows:

```
Resources (cash) provided by
   Issuance of bonds payable                                       $7,500
```

Completed Statement—Illustration 2. Combining the foregoing items that were illustrated separately, a complete statement of changes in financial position would be presented as shown on page 1118.

Sources of Information for Statement of Changes

Listed below are important points to remember in the preparation of the statement of changes in financial position.

1. Comparative balance sheets provide the basic information from which the report is prepared. Additional information obtained from analyses of specific accounts is also included.
2. Both increases and decreases in plant assets, investments, long-term debt, and contributed capital stock are shown in the statement. This requires supplementary information obtained by analysis of related accounts.
3. An analysis of the Retained Earnings account is necessary to derive data relative to resources provided and applied. The net increase or decrease in retained earnings without any explanation is a meaningless amount in the statement, for it might repre-

---

Doral Products Ltd.
STATEMENT OF CHANGES IN FINANCIAL POSITION
For the Year Ended December 31, 1986

Resources (cash) provided by		
Operations:		
Net income		$19,600
Add: Items not requiring cash outflows		
Depreciation expense	$ 6,500	
Decrease in accounts receivable	3,700	
Decrease in inventories	13,500	
Less: Items not providing cash inflows		
Gain on sale of land	(1,000)	
Increase in prepaid expenses	(200)	
Decrease in accounts payable	(5,500)	17,000
Cash provided by operations		$36,600
Other sources of cash		
Sale of land	$ 7,000	
Sale of equipment	1,500	
Issuance of bonds payable	7,500	16,000
Total cash provided		$52,600
Resources (cash) applied to		
Payment of cash dividends	$(11,000)	
Purchase of equipment	(40,000)	
Total cash applied		51,000
Increase in cash		$ 1,600

---

sent the effect of net income, dividends declared, appropriations of retained earnings, and "prior period" adjustments.

4. The statement includes all changes that have passed through cash or have resulted in an increase or decrease in cash and, in addition, some significant financial transactions discussed later.

5. Write-downs, amortization charges, and similar "book" entries, such as depreciation of plant assets, are neither sources nor applications of resources, because they have no effect on cash. To the extent that they have entered into the determination of net income, however, they must be added back to or subtracted from net income to arrive at cash provided by operations.

Special Problems in Statement Analysis

Some of the special problems related to preparing the statement of changes in financial position were discussed in connection with the preceding illustrations. Other problems that arise with some frequency in the preparation of this statement may be categorized as follows:

1. Adjustments similar to depreciation.
2. Noncash (all financial resources) transactions.
3. Extraordinary items.
4. Net losses.

Adjustments Similar to Depreciation

Depreciation expense is the adjustment to net income that is made most commonly to arrive at cash provided by operations, but there are numerous other expense and revenue items that do not affect cash. Examples of expense items that must be added back to net income are the **amortization of intangible assets** such as goodwill and patents, and the **amortization of deferred charges** such as bond issue costs. These charges against income involve expenditures made in prior periods that are being amortized currently and reduce net income without affecting cash in the current period. Also, **amortization of bond discount or premium** on long-term bonds payable affects the amount of interest expense, but neither affects cash. As a result, amortization of these items should be added back to or subtracted from net income to arrive at cash provided from operations.

In a similar manner, **changes in deferred income taxes and deferred investment credit** accounts affect net income but have no effect on cash. For example, Walt Disney Productions recently experienced an increase in its liability for deferred taxes of approximately $12 million. Tax expense was increased and net income was decreased by this amount, but the flow of cash was not affected; therefore, $12 million was added back to net income. Conversely, Grand Union Company recently had a decrease in its liability for deferred taxes of $814,000 and subtracted this amount from net income to arrive at cash provided from operations.

A change related to an investment in common shares when the income or loss is accrued under the equity method is another common adjustment to net income. For example, Johns-Manville Corporation's equity in earnings of foreign subsidiaries recently increased by approximately $127 million. Such an increase, however, is not represented by a cash flow, so it was deducted from net income to arrive at cash provided by operations. Similarly, Dictaphone Corporation's equity in the net losses of its foreign subsidiaries was $132,000, and this amount was added back to net income. If the company receives a dividend from its equity investee, resources provided from a cash dividend should be reported. (Generally, these dividends are included in net income from operations.)

Noncash Transactions

Up to now, we have concentrated on those items that flow through, or effect a change in, cash. Under the all financial resources concept, the statement of changes in financial position must also include noncash transactions that are considered significant financing and investing activities of an enterprise.

Noncash Transactions Reported   The types of noncash transactions that are commonly reported in the statement of changes in financial position are: (1) the issuance of long-term debt or equity securities to purchase noncurrent assets; (2) the conversion of long-term debt or preferred shares to common shares; (3) the acquisition of long-term assets through gift or donation or the forgiveness of a long-term obligation; and (4) the retirement of debt through a sinking fund classified as long-term. To illustrate, assume that Posture Furniture Company acquired a $200,000 warehouse in exchange for a long-term $200,000 mortgage note on the property. This transaction does not affect cash but it has a significant impact on resources and would be reported in the statement of changes in financial position as follows:

Resources provided by		
Issuance of mortgage note for building	$200,000	
Resources applied to		
Purchase of buildings in exchange for long-term note		$200,000

For another illustration, assume that Calgary, Inc. converted bonds having a par of $50,000 for 50,000 no-par common shares. This transaction resulted in the issuance of additional common shares and the retirement of long-term debt with no effect upon cash. In a statement of changes in financial position, this information would be reported in the following manner:

Resources provided by		
Issuance of common shares for retirement of debt	$50,000	
Resources applied to		
Retirement of debt through issuance of common shares		$50,000

Noncash Transactions Not Reported   Certain financial transactions that affect only noncash accounts do not require reporting in the statement of changes in financial position because they do not provide or use resources. Examples of these types of transactions are **stock dividends, stock splits, and appropriations of retained earnings.** To illustrate, when a corporation declares a dividend distributable in **shares** instead of in **cash**, a transfer from Retained Earnings to Share Capital is usually made. *CICA Handbook*, Section 1540, recommends that this type of dividend not be disclosed in the statement of changes in financial position, because no change has occurred either in the amount or in the composition of shareholders' equity that has an effect on the resources of the enterprise. Similarly, stock splits and appropriations of retained earnings do not represent either resources provided or resources applied; therefore, they should not be reported in a statement of changes in financial position.

Extraordinary Items

The statement of changes in financial position begins with net income. Whenever extraordinary gains or losses are involved, the statement starts with income before extraordinary items. To this amount are added back or deducted items recognized in determining income or loss that did not use or provide cash. These items should be subtotalled and appropriately labelled "cash provided by operations, exclusive of extraordinary item." This subtotal should be followed by the extraordinary item.

Tandem Bike Company PARTIAL STATEMENT OF CHANGES IN FINANCIAL POSITION	
Resources (cash) provided by	
Operations:	
Income before extraordinary items	$30,000
Add (or deduct): Items not requiring cash outflows	
Depreciation expense	4,000
Cash provided by operations, exclusive	
of extraordinary item	$34,000
Extraordinary item—sale of investment including	
extraordinary gain of $9,000 (net of $3,000 tax)	25,000
	$59,000

To illustrate, assume that Tandem Bike Company reported net income of $39,000, which included an extraordinary gain of $9,000 (net of $3,000 tax) resulting from the sale of their only investment in equity securities (book value $16,000). Depreciation expense was $4,000 for the period. In the statement of changes in financial position the information on page 1120 would be reported.

In this illustration, the entire transaction is reported in one section of the statement. Because of its simplicity and ease of understanding, **this format should be used for problem material unless another approach is requested**. This format is also widely used in practice.

Net Losses

If an enterprise reports a net loss instead of a net income, the net loss must be adjusted for those items that do not result in a cash inflow or outflow. The presentation in the statement of changes in financial position differs depending on whether the net loss after adjusting for the charges or credits not affecting cash results in a negative or positive cash flow from operations. For example, if the net loss was $50,000 and the total amount of charges to be added back was $60,000, then resources are provided by operations in the amount of $10,000, as shown in the following computation.

Computation of Cash **Provided** by Operations		
Net loss		$(50,000)
Add (or deduct): Items not affecting cash		
Depreciation of plant assets	$55,000	
Amortization of patents	5,000	60,000
Cash provided by operations		$ 10,000

A presentation similar to the one above would appear in the statement of changes in financial position. If the company experienced a net loss of $80,000 and the total amount of the charges to be added back is $25,000, the presentation would appear as a negative amount in the resources **provided** section as illustrated below:

Computation of Cash **Provided** by Operations	
Net loss	$(80,000)
Add (or deduct): Items not affecting cash	
Depreciation of plant assets	25,000
Cash provided by operations	$(55,000)

COMPREHENSIVE ILLUSTRATION—USE OF A WORK SHEET

If numerous adjustments are necessary or if other complicating factors are present, many accountants prefer to use a work sheet to assemble and classify the data that will appear on the statement of changes in financial position. The work sheet is merely a device to aid in the preparation of the statement; its use is not required. The skeleton format of the work sheet for preparation of the statement of changes in financial position is shown below:

	End of Last Year Balances	Reconciling Items		End of Current Year Balances
		Debits	Credits	
Form of Work Sheet for Preparation of the Statement of Changes in Financial Position				
Debits:				
Totals				
Credits:				
Totals				
Resources provided by: Operations				
Other				
Resources applied to:				
Totals				

The use of T accounts or even the use of supplementary computations will often serve as suitable substitutes for the work sheet, and may prove less time-consuming to anyone experienced in preparing such statements. The T-account approach is illustrated in Appendix 24A.

A work sheet for Hanes Corporation is presented on pages 1129 and 1130. **The important items to note as you study the illustration are:**

1. The account balances listed on the work sheet are separated into those with debit balances and those with credit balances. The first column (far left) contains the beginning of the year balances, and the last column (far right) contains the end of the year balances. The transactions that affected the changes in these accounts during the period are the reconciling items that appear between these two columns.
2. The transactions for the current year are examined to determine whether they affected resources provided or applied. After the transactions are analyzed and entered in the work sheet, all the differences between the beginning and ending balances should be reconciled.
3. The adjustments shown on the work sheet are not entered in any journal or posted to any account. They are not adjustments to correct accounts; they are merely adjustments for this work sheet to facilitate the preparation of a statement of changes in financial position. The totals of the reconciling transaction debit and credit columns should balance.
4. The bottom portion of the work sheet provides the information necessary to prepare the formal statement of changes in financial position.

To illustrate procedures for preparation of the work sheet, the financial statements and other data related to the Hanes Corporation are presented with the balance sheet and the statement of income and retained earnings on pages 1123 and 1124. Additional explanations related to preparation of the work sheet are provided throughout the discussion presented on pages 1125–1128.

Hanes Corporation
COMPARATIVE BALANCE SHEET
December 31, 1986 and 1985

Assets	1986	1985	Difference Incr. or Decr.
Cash	$ 59,000	$ 66,000	$ 7,000 Decr.
Accounts receivable (net)	104,000	51,000	53,000 Incr.
Inventories	493,000	341,000	152,000 Incr.
Prepaid expenses	16,500	17,000	500 Decr.
Investments in shares of Porter Co.			
(equity method)	18,500	15,000	3,500 Incr.
Land	131,500	82,000	49,500 Incr.
Equipment	187,000	142,000	45,000 Incr.
Accumulated depreciation—equipment	(29,000)	(31,000)	2,000 Decr.
Buildings	262,000	262,000	—
Accumulated depreciation—buildings	(74,100)	(71,000)	3,100 Incr.
Goodwill	7,600	10,000	2,400 Decr.
Total Assets	$1,176,000	$884,000	

Liabilities			
Accounts payable	$ 132,000	$131,000	$ 1,000 Incr.
Accrued liabilities	43,000	39,000	4,000 Incr.
Income taxes payable	3,000	16,000	13,000 Decr.
Notes payable (long-term)	60,000	—	60,000 Incr.
Bonds payable	100,000	100,000	
Premium on bonds payable	7,000	8,000	1,000 Decr.
Deferred income taxes (long-term)	9,000	6,000	3,000 Incr.
Total Liabilities	$ 354,000	$300,000	

Shareholders' Equity			
Common shares	$ 247,000	$ 88,000	$159,000 Incr.
Retained earnings	592,000	496,000	96,000 Incr.
Treasury shares	(17,000)	—	17,000 Incr.
Total shareholders' equity	$ 822,000	$584,000	
Total Liabilities and Shareholders' Equity	$1,176,000	$884,000	

Hanes Corporation
COMBINED STATEMENT OF INCOME AND RETAINED EARNINGS
For the Year Ended 1986

Net sales	$524,500
Other revenue	3,500
Total revenues	$528,000
Expense	
Cost of goods sold	$310,000
Selling and administrative expense	47,000
Other expense and losses	12,000
Total expenses	$369,000

Income before income tax and extraordinary item	$159,000
Income Tax	
Current	47,000
Deferred	3,000
Income before extraordinary item	$109,000
Gain on expropriation of land (net of tax)	8,000
Net income	$117,000
Retained earnings, January 1	496,000
Less:	
Cash dividends	6,000
Stock dividend	15,000
Retained earnings, December 31	$592,000
Per Share:	
Income before extraordinary items	$1.98
Extraordinary item	0.15
Net income	$2.13

Additional information

(a) Other income of $3,500 represents Hanes Corporation's equity share in the net income of Porter Company, an equity investee. Hanes Corporation owns 22% of Porter Company.

(b) Land in the amount of $60,000 was purchased through the issuance of a long-term note; in addition, certain parcels of land (book value $10,500) were expropriated, resulting in an $8,000 gain, net of $2,500 tax.

(c) An analysis of the equipment account and related accumulated depreciation indicates the following:

	Equipment Dr./(Cr.)	Accum. Dep. Dr./(Cr.)	Gain or Loss
Balance at end of 1985	$142,000	$(31,000)	
Purchase of equipment	53,000		
Sale of equipment	(8,000)	2,500	$1,500L
Depreciation for the period		(11,500)	
Major repair charged to accumulated depreciation		11,000	
Balance at end of 1986	$187,000	$(29,000)	

(d) The change in the accumulated depreciation—building, goodwill, premium on bonds payable, and deferred income tax accounts resulted from depreciation and amortization entries.

(e) An analysis of the contributed capital accounts in shareholders' equity discloses the following:

	Common Shares
Balance at end of 1985	$ 88,000
Issuance of 2% stock dividend	15,000
Sale of shares for cash	144,000
Balance at end of 1986	$247,000

Analysis of Work Sheet Transactions

The following discussion (pages 1125–1128) provides an explanation of the individual adjustments that appear on the work sheet on page 1129.

Because cash is the basis for analysis, the cash account will be reconciled last. Income is the first item that appears on the statement of changes and will be analyzed first.

Change in Retained Earnings   Net income for the period comprises "income before extraordinary item" and an "extraordinary gain." Income before the extraordinary item is $109,000. The entry on the work sheet for certain items affecting retained earnings would be as follows:

(1)

Resources Provided by Income before Extraordinary Item	109,000	
Retained Earnings		109,000

The resources provided by income before extraordinary item is reported at the bottom of the work sheet and is the starting point for preparation of the statement of changes in financial position.

Retained earnings was also affected by a stock dividend and a cash dividend. The retained earnings statement reports a stock dividend of $15,000. The work sheet entry for this transaction is as follows:

(2)

Retained Earnings	15,000	
Common Shares		15,000

The issuance of stock dividends is not considered to be either resources provided or resources applied; therefore, although this transaction is entered on the work sheet for reconciling purposes, it is not reported in the statement of changes.

The cash dividend of $6,000 represents cash resources applied. The following work sheet entry is made:

(3)

Retained Earnings	6,000	
Resources Applied to Cash Dividends		6,000

The beginning and ending balances of retained earnings are reconciled by the entry of the three items above.

Accounts Receivable   The increase in Accounts Receivable of $53,000 represents revenues that did not result in cash inflows during 1986. The following work sheet entry is made:

(4)

Accounts Receivable	53,000	
Income before Extraordinary Item—		
Increase in Accounts Receivable		53,000

Inventories   The increase in Inventories of $152,000 represents an operating use of cash. The incremental investment in inventories during the year reduces cash without increasing the cost of goods sold. The work sheet entry is made as follows:

(5)

Inventories	152,000	
Income before Extraordinary Item—		
Increase in Inventories		152,000

Prepaid Expenses   The decrease in Prepaid Expenses of $500 represents a charge in the income statement for which there was no cash outflow in the current period. It should be added back to net income through the following entry:

(6)

Income before Extraordinary Item—Decrease in Prepaid Expenses	500	
Prepaid Expenses		500

Investment in Shares of Porter Co.   The investment in the shares of Porter Co. increased $3,500, which reflects Hanes Corporation's share of the income earned by its equity investee during the current year. Although revenue, and therefore income per the income statement, was increased $3,500 by the accounting entry that recorded Hanes' share of Porter Co.'s net income, no cash was provided. The following work sheet entry is made:

(7)

Investment in Shares of Porter Co.	3,500	
Income before Extraordinary Item—		
Equity in Earnings of Porter Co.		3,500

Land   Land in the amount of $60,000 was purchased through the issuance of a long-term note payable. Although this transaction did not affect cash, it is considered a significant resource transaction that should be reported because both resources provided and resources applied are affected. Two entries are necessary to record this transaction on the work sheet.

(8)

Land	60,000	
Resources Applied to Purchase of Land—		
Issuance of Long-term Note		60,000
Resources Provided by Issuance of Long-term Note—		
Purchase of Land	60,000	
Note Payable		60,000

In addition to the financial resources transactions involving the issuance of a note to purchase land, the Land account was decreased by the expropriation proceedings. The work sheet entry to record the book value portion of this transaction is as follows:

(9)

Resources Provided by Expropriation of Land	18,500	
Land		10,500
Retained Earnings		8,000

The $10,500 of resources provided by expropriation plus the $8,000 gain constitute the total resources of $18,500 related to the expropriation. The Land account balances are now reconciled.

Equipment and Accumulated Depreciation   An analysis of the Equipment account and its related Accumulated Depreciation account shows that a number of financial transactions have affected these accounts. Equipment in the amount of $53,000 was purchased during the year. The entry to record this transaction on the work sheet is as follows:

(10)

Equipment	53,000	
Resources Applied to the Purchase of Equipment		53,000

In addition, equipment with a book value of $5,500 was sold at a loss of $1,500. The entry to record this transaction on the work sheet is as follows:

(11)

Resources Provided by Sale of Equipment	4,000	
Income before Extraordinary Item—Loss on		
Sale of Equipment	1,500	
Accumulated Depreciation—Equipment	2,500	
Equipment		8,000

The proceeds from the sale of the equipment provided cash of $4,000. In addition, the loss on the sale of the equipment has reduced the income before extraordinary item, but has not affected cash; therefore, it must be added back to income before extraordinary item to report accurately cash provided by operations.

Depreciation on the equipment was reported at $11,500 and should be presented on the work sheet in the following manner:

(12)

Income before Extraordinary Item—		
Depreciation Expense—Equipment	11,500	
Accumulated Depreciation—Equipment		11,500

The depreciation expense is added back to the income before extraordinary item because it reduced income but did not affect cash.

Finally, a major repair to the equipment in the amount of $11,000 was charged to Accumulated Depreciation—Equipment. Because this expenditure required cash, the following work sheet entry is made:

(13)

Accumulated Depreciation—Equipment	11,000	
Resources Applied to Major Repairs of Equipment		11,000

The balances in the equipment and related accumulated depreciation accounts are reconciled after adjustment for the foregoing items.

Accumulated Depreciation and Amortization of Goodwill Depreciation expense on the buildings of $3,100 and amortization of goodwill of $2,400 are both expenses in the income statement that reduce net income but did not require a cash outflow in the current period. The following work sheet entry is made:

(14)

Income before Extraordinary Item—		
Depreciation Expense—Buildings	3,100	
Income before Extraordinary Item—		
Amortization of Goodwill	2,400	
Accumulated Depreciation—Buildings		3,100
Goodwill		2,400

Other Noncash Charges or Credits An analysis of the remaining accounts indicates that changes in the Accounts Payable, Accrued Liabilities, Income Taxes Payable, Premium on Bonds Payable, and Deferred Income Taxes balances resulted from charges or credits not affecting cash. The following compound entry to the work sheet could be made for these noncash, income-related items:

(15)

Income Taxes Payable	13,000	
Premium on Bonds Payable	1,000	
Income before Extraordinary Item—		
Increase in Accounts Payable	1,000	
Income before Extraordinary Item—		
Increase in Accrued Liabilities	4,000	
Income before Extraordinary Item—		
Increase in Deferred Income Taxes	3,000	
Income before Extraordinary Item—		
Decrease in Income Taxes Payable		13,000
Income before Extraordinary Item—		
Amortization of Bond Premium		1,000
Accounts Payable		1,000
Accrued Liabilities		4,000
Deferred Income Taxes		3,000

Common Shares and Related Accounts   A comparison of the common share balances and the contributed surplus balances shows that transactions during the year affected these accounts. First, a stock dividend of 2% was issued to shareholders. As indicated in the discussion of work sheet entry (2), no resources were provided or applied by the stock dividend transaction. In addition to the shares issued via the stock dividend, the Hanes Corporation issued common shares for $144,000. The work sheet entry to record this transaction is as follows:

(16)

Resources Provided by Sale of Common Shares	144,000	
Common Shares		144,000

Also, the company purchased its own common shares in the amount of $17,000. The work sheet entry to record this transaction is as follows:

(17)

Treasury Shares	17,000	
Resources Applied to Purchase of Treasury Shares		17,000

Final Summary Entry   The final entry to reconcile the change in cash and to balance the work sheet is as follows:

(18)

Decrease in Cash	7,000	
Cash		7,000

The amount is the difference between the beginning of the year and the end of the year cash balance.

Once it has been determined that the differences between the beginning and ending balances per the work sheet columns have been accounted for, the reconciling transactions columns can be totalled, and they should balance. The statement of changes in financial position can be prepared entirely from the items and amounts that appear at the bottom of the work sheet in the form of "resources provided by" and "resources applied to." The difference between the resources provided and the resources applied should equal the change in cash. This reconciliation provides evidence that the posting of the transactions during the period was performed accurately. However, the statement may still be incorrect if certain transactions were improperly analyzed.

Hanes Corporation
WORK SHEET FOR PREPARATION OF STATEMENT OF CHANGES IN FINANCIAL POSITION
For the Year Ended 1986

	Account Balance at End of 1985	Reconciling Transactions During 1986 Debit		Reconciling Transactions During 1986 Credit		Account Balance at End of 1986
Debits						
Cash	$ 66,000			(18)	$ 7,000	$ 59,000
Accounts receivable (net)	51,000	(4)	$ 53,000			104,000
Inventories	341,000	(5)	152,000			493,000
Prepaid expenses	17,000			(6)	500	16,500
Investment (equity method)	15,000	(7)	3,500			18,500
Land	82,000	(8)	60,000	(9)	10,500	131,500
Equipment	142,000	(10)	53,000	(11)	8,000	187,000
Buildings	262,000					262,000
Goodwill	10,000			(14)	2,400	7,600
Treasury shares	-0-	(17)	17,000			17,000
Total debits	$986,000					$1,296,100
Credits						
Accumulated depreciation— equipment	$ 31,000	(11) (13)	2,500 11,000	(12)	11,500	$ 29,000
Accumulated depreciation— buildings	71,000			(14)	3,100	74,100
Accounts payable	131,000			(15)	1,000	132,000
Accrued liabilities	39,000			(15)	4,000	43,000
Income taxes payable	16,000	(15)	13,000			3,000
Notes payable (long-term)	-0-			(8)	60,000	60,000
Bonds payable	100,000					100,000
Premium on bonds payable	8,000	(15)	1,000			7,000
Deferred income taxes	6,000			(15)	3,000	9,000
Common shares	88,000			(2) (16)	15,000 144,000	247,000
Retained earnings	496,000	(2) (3)	15,000 6,000	(9) (1)	8,000 109,000	592,000
Total credits	$986,000		$387,000		$387,000	$1,296,100

Resources provided by Operations:					
Income before extraordinary item	(1)	$109,000			
Increase in Accounts Receivable			(4)	$ 53,000	
Increase in Inventories			(5)	152,000	
Decrease in Prepaid Expense	(6)	500			
Equity in earnings of Porter Co.			(7)	3,500	
Loss on sale of equipment	(11)	1,500			
Depreciation expense—equipment	(12)	11,500			
Depreciation expense—buildings	(14)	3,100			
Amortization of Goodwill	(14)	2,400			
Increase in Accounts Payable	(15)	1,000			
Increase in Accrued Liabilities	(15)	4,000			
Deferred Income Taxes	(15)	3,000			
Decrease in Income Tax Payable			(15)	13,000	
Amortization of bond premium			(15)	1,000	
Expropriation of land	(9)	18,500			
Issuance of note payable to purchase land	(8)	60,000			

Sale of equipment	(11)	4,000
Sale of common shares	(16)	144,000
Decrease in cash	(18)	7,000

Resources applied to		
Payment of cash dividend	(3)	6,000
Purchase of land through issuance of note payable	(8)	60,000
Purchase of equipment	(10)	53,000
Major repairs of equipment	(13)	11,000
Purchase of treasury shares	(17)	17,000
	$369,500	$369,500

Preparation of Statement   Presented below is a formal statement of changes in financial position prepared from the data compiled in the lower portion of the work sheet. This is a cash basis statement presented in two primary sections, resources provided and resources applied.

Hanes Corporation
STATEMENT OF CHANGES IN FINANCIAL POSITION
For the Year Ended December 31, 1986

Resources provided by		
Operations:		
Income before extraordinary item		$109,000
Add (deduct): Items not providing or requiring cash		
Loss on sale of equipment	$ 1,500	
Depreciation expense	14,600	
Amortization of goodwill	2,400	
Deferred income taxes	3,000	
Decrease in prepaid expenses	500	
Increase in accounts payable	1,000	
Increase in accrued liabilities	4,000	27,000
Less: Items not requiring or providing cash		
Equity in earnings of Porter Co.	(3,500)	
Amortization of bond premium	(1,000)	
Increase in accounts receivable (net)	(53,000)	
Increase in inventories	(152,000)	
Decrease in income taxes payable	(13,000)	(222,500)
Cash provided by operations, exclusive of extraordinary item		(86,500)
Extraordinary item—Expropriation of land, including extraordinary gain of $8,000 (net of $2,500 tax)		18,500
Issuance of note payable to purchase land		60,000
Sale of equipment		4,000
Sale of common shares		144,000
Total resources provided		$140,000
Resources applied to		
Cash dividends	(6,000)	
Purchase of land through issuance of note payable	(60,000)	
Purchase of equipment	(53,000)	
Major repairs of equipment	(11,000)	
Purchase of treasury shares	(17,000)	
Total resources applied		147,000
Decrease in cash		$ 7,000

FORMS OF PRESENTATION

Owing to the issuance of the current Section 1540 of the *CICA Handbook*, the statement of changes in financial position is in a state of transition. Canadian firms will be adopting the cash basis for their fiscal years beginning after September, 1985. The traditional format for the content of the statement of changes in financial position is a **two-section form** referred to as the **provided and applied (or sources and uses) format,** which is the one we have used in our illustrations thus far in the chapter. The basic two-section outline is as follows:

1. Resources (cash) provided by—
2. Resources (cash) applied to—

The provided and applied (sources and uses) format has been the most popular. However, the **three-section form** referred to as the **activity format** is recommended in Section 1540. Consequently, it is anticipated that this format will be used extensively in the future. The activity format divides the statement into three major sections:

1. Operating activities—
2. Investment activities—
3. Financing activities—
   = Increase or decrease in cash

The content of the **operating activities section** is the same as that under the provided and applied format which shows cash flows from operations. The **investing activities section** discloses all acquisitions of long-term investments (including plant and equipment, investments in controlled companies, and deferred charges of various types) regardless of whether they were acquired for cash, for debt or equity securities, or in exchange for other noncash assets. All dispositions, retirements, and other decreases of long-term investments, plant, and equipment

---

Hanes Corporation
STATEMENT OF CHANGES IN FINANCIAL POSITION
For the Year Ended December 31, 1986
(Cash Basis—Activity Format)

Operating activities		
Cash provided by operations		$ (86,500)
(Same as operations section on page 1130)		
Extraordinary item—Expropriation of land,		
including gain of $8,000 (net of $2,500 tax)		18,500
Cash dividends paid		(6,000)
Investing activities		
Purchase of land through issuance of note	$ (60,000)	
Purchase of equipment	(53,000)	
Major repairs of equipment	(11,000)	
Sale of equipment	4,000	(120,000)
Financing activities		
Issuance of note for land	60,000	
Issuance of common shares	144,000	
Purchase of treasury shares	(17,000)	187,000
Decrease in cash		$ (7,000)

also appear in the investing activities section. The **financing activities section** discloses the acquisition of debt, the repayment of debt, and the issuance or retirement of shares. Cash dividends under the activity format may be classified as a separate category—neither operating or financing—between the operating and investing activities sections. Some, however, prefer to include dividends as a part of operating activities. The Hanes Corporation cash basis statement of changes in financial position in activity format is shown on page 1131 and should be compared to that same statement prepared in provided and applied format on page 1130.

CASH PROVIDED BY OPERATIONS— INDIRECT VERSUS DIRECT APPROACH

In all three previous illustrations, income from operations had to be adjusted for those revenues and gains and those expenses and losses that had no effect on cash. The two different approaches available to adjust income from operations on an accrual basis to cash provided from operations are the indirect (reconciliation) approach and the direct income statement approach.

Indirect Approach

For consistency and comparability, we used the indirect approach in all of the cash basis illustrations just presented. We determined cash from operations by adding back to or deducting from net income those revenues and expenses that had no effect on cash. The following diagram illustrates the common types of adjustments that are made to net income to arrive at cash provided by operations.

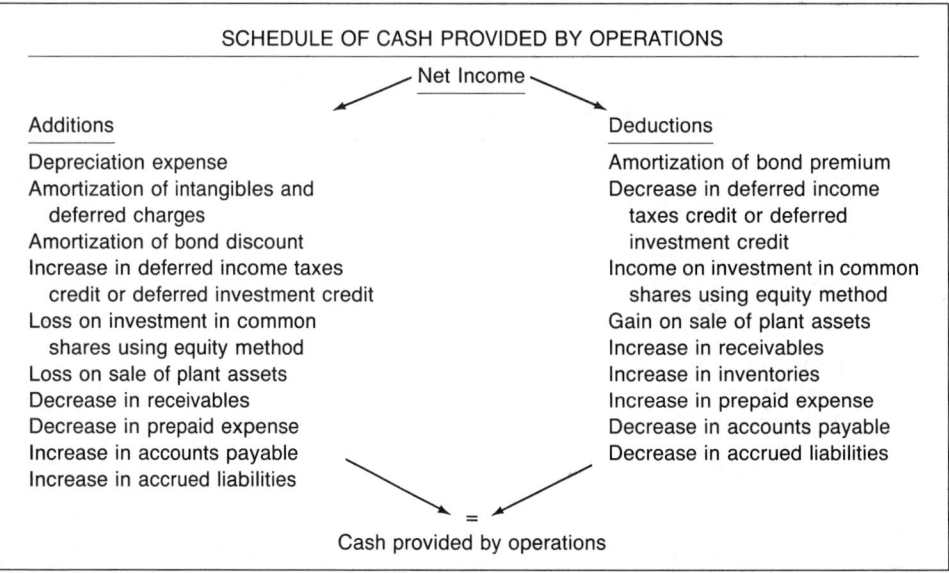

SCHEDULE OF CASH PROVIDED BY OPERATIONS

Net Income

Additions	Deductions
Depreciation expense	Amortization of bond premium
Amortization of intangibles and deferred charges	Decrease in deferred income taxes credit or deferred investment credit
Amortization of bond discount	Income on investment in common shares using equity method
Increase in deferred income taxes credit or deferred investment credit	Gain on sale of plant assets
Loss on investment in common shares using equity method	Increase in receivables
Loss on sale of plant assets	Increase in inventories
Decrease in receivables	Increase in prepaid expense
Decrease in prepaid expense	Decrease in accounts payable
Increase in accounts payable	Decrease in accrued liabilities
Increase in accrued liabilities	

= Cash provided by operations

The additions and deductions listed in the preceding diagram reconcile net income to cash provided by operations, thus the reason for referring to the indirect approach as the reconciliation approach. Application of the indirect approach to the Hanes Corporation illustration results in the following schedule of adjustments.

Hanes Corporation
SCHEDULE OF CHANGE FROM ACCRUAL TO CASH BASIS
(Indirect Approach)

Operations	Cash Provided
Income before extraordinary item	$109,000
Add: Items providing or not requiring cash	
Loss on sale of equipment	1,500
Depreciation expense	14,600
Amortization of goodwill	2,400
Deferred income taxes	3,000
Decrease in prepaid taxes	500
Increase in accounts payable	1,000
Increase in accrued liabilities	4,000
Deduct: Items requiring or not providing cash	
Equity in earnings of Porter Co.	(3,500)
Amortization of bond premium	(1,000)
Increase in accounts receivable (net)	(53,000)
Increase in inventories	(152,000)
Decrease in income taxes payable	(13,000)
Cash provided from operations exclusive, of extraordinary item	$ (86,500)

The items added or deducted in the indirect approach schedule above reconcile income from operations to cash provided by operations.

Hanes Corporation
SCHEDULE OF CHANGE FROM ACCRUAL TO CASH
BASIS INCOME STATEMENT (Partial)
(Direct Approach)

	Accrual Basis	Adjustment	Add (Subtract)	Cash Basis
Net sales	$524,500	– Increase in accounts receivable	$(53,000)	$471,500
Other income	3,500	– Equity in earnings of Porter Ltd.	(3,500)	-0-
Total revenues	528,000			471,500
Expenses				
Cost of goods sold	310,000	– Increase in accounts payable	(1,000)	
		+ Increase in inventories	152,000	461,000
Selling and administrative				
expense	47,000	– Depreciation expense	(14,600)	
		– Decrease in prepaid expenses	(500)	27,900
		– Increase in accrued liabilities	(4,000)	
Other expenses				
and losses	12,000	– Loss on sale of equipment	(1,500)	
		– Amortization of goodwill	(2,400)	
		+ Amortization of bond premium	1,000	9,100
Total expenses	369,000			498,000
Income (loss) before				
income tax	159,000			(26,500)
Income tax				
Current	47,000	+ Decrease in Income Taxes Payable	13,000	60,000
Deferred	3,000	– Increase in Deferred Income Taxes	(3,000)	-0-
Net income (loss)	$109,000			$(86,500)*

*Note that the cash provided (applied) by operations computed here, a negative $88,000, equals the amount computed earlier using the reconciliation format.

Direct Approach

Another approach is the direct method, which computes cash revenues and cash expenses directly. To illustrate this method, a portion of Hanes Limited's accrual basis income statement is adjusted to a cash basis. For purposes of this illustration, the increase in accounts payable is related to cost of goods sold; depreciation expense, prepaid expense, and accrued liabilities are related to selling and administrative expenses; and amortization of goodwill and bond premium are related to other expenses and losses. Other relationships should be apparent. This illustration is presented below.

Presentation of the direct approach for reporting cash provided by operations takes the form of a condensed cash basis income statement. For example, the cash from operations section of Hanes Corporation's statement of changes in financial position would appear as follows using the direct approach:

Hanes Corporation
STATEMENT OF CHANGES IN FINANCIAL POSITION (Partial)
(Cash Basis—Direct Approach)

Resources (Cash) provided by		
Cash from operations:		
Receipts from customers		$ 471,500
Payments to suppliers		(461,000)
		10,500
Selling and administrative expenses paid	$27,900	
Other expenses paid	9,100	
Income taxes paid	60,000	(97,000)
Cash provided by operations		$ (86,500)

Comparative Advantages of the Two Approaches

According to a recent study sponsored by the Financial Executives Research Foundation, "practically all companies use the reconciliation (indirect) approach for external reporting purposes, and most use it internally as well."[8] The study also found that the indirect approach to reporting is preferred by financial executives, financial analysts, rating agencies, and commercial banks, and that individual investors prefer the direct approach. These findings were the primary reasons for our use of the indirect method in our illustrations.

If a cash basis statement of changes in financial position is employed, should the indirect (reconciliation approach) or direct method be employed? Those who favour the indirect approach argue that by providing a reconciliation between net income and cash provided from operations, the differences are highlighted; such is not the case with the direct approach. Furthermore, some contend that the direct approach is nothing more than a cash basis income statement, which will confuse and create uncertainty for financial statement users who are familiar with accrual-based income statements. Finally, some question whether the direct approach is cost-justified. They maintain that additional preparation costs would probably be required because the financial records are not maintained on a cash basis.

[8]Seed, *op. cit.*, p. 6.

Conversely, others argue that by reporting sources and uses of cash, the direct method will be more helpful to users in understanding past trends and in estimating future cash flows. Futhermore, it is argued that a better understanding of the relationship between net income and cash flows is achieved through the use of the direct method. Only by reporting the cash revenues and cash expenses can one understand how the cash is generated. Use of the indirect approach implies that net income and certain expenses (for example, depreciation, amortization of intangibles) are sources of cash, which is misleading.

WORKING CAPITAL BASIS

Working capital is the difference between current assets and current liabilities. As a fund, working capital is viewed as containing all current assets (increases in working capital) and all current liabilities (decreases in working capital). **Any transaction that results in a net increase in working capital is a "source" of working capital**; that is, it provides working capital. **Any transaction that results in a net decrease in working capital is a "use" of working capital**; that is, it applies working capital. Some transactions merely rearrange the internal content of working capital; that is, they neither increase nor decrease working capital. For example, the collection of cash from an account receivable, the write-off of an account receivable (under the allowance method), the payment of an account payable, and the purchase of inventory for cash or on short-term credit, are neither sources nor applications of working capital, because the net balance does not change. Thus, in an analysis of working capital we must separate the transactions that cause changes (increases or decreases) in working capital from those that merely change the composition but not the total of working capital. It is the change in the working capital balance, along with other significant (nonworking capital) changes in resources, that the statement of changes in financial position on a working capital basis reports.

The diagram below illustrates the type of events and transactions that result in working capital being provided and applied.

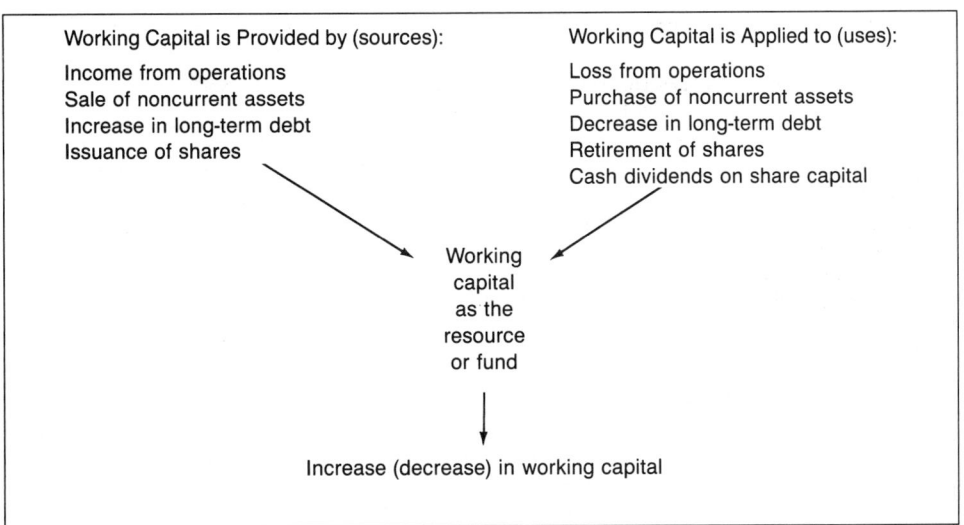

Working Capital is Provided by (sources):	Working Capital is Applied to (uses):
Income from operations	Loss from operations
Sale of noncurrent assets	Purchase of noncurrent assets
Increase in long-term debt	Decrease in long-term debt
Issuance of shares	Retirement of shares
	Cash dividends on share capital

Working capital as the resource or fund

Increase (decrease) in working capital

WORKING CAPITAL ILLUSTRATION

To illustrate the preparation of a statement of changes in financial position on a working capital basis and to permit ready comparisons with the cash basis, we will use the Doral Products Ltd. financial information. For convenience the illustration is repeated below:

Accounts	Dec. 31, 1986	Dec. 31, 1985	Differences Dr.	Differences Cr.
Cash	$ 4,600	$ 3,000	$ 1,600	
Accounts receivable (net)	11,300	15,000		$ 3,700
Inventories	11,500	25,000		13,500
Prepaid expenses	1,200	1,000	200	
Land	34,000	40,000		6,000
Equipment	95,000	60,000	35,000	
	$157,600	$144,000		
Accumulated depreciation—equipment	$ 23,000	$ 20,000		$ 3,000
Accounts payable	9,500	15,000	$ 5,500	
Bonds payable (long-term)	13,500	6,000		7,500
Share capital	80,000	80,000		
Retained earnings	31,600	23,000		8,600
	$157,600	$144,000	$42,300	$42,300

Doral Products Ltd.

Additional information concerning some of the differences:

1. Land carried at $6,000 was sold for $7,000 during the year; the gain of $1,000 was not considered an extraordinary item.
2. Equipment costing $40,000 was purchased during the year; equipment with a cost of $5,000 was sold at its book value of $1,500. Depreciation expense for the year was $6,500.
3. Bonds payable in the amount of $7,500 were issued for cash.

Doral Products Ltd.
SCHEDULE OF WORKING CAPITAL CHANGES
For the Year Ended December 31, 1986

	Working Capital Change Increase	Working Capital Change Decrease
Current Assets		
Increase in cash	$ 1,600	
Decrease in accounts receivable (net)		$ 3,700
Decrease in inventories		13,500
Increase in prepaid expenses	200	
Current Liabilities		
Decrease in accounts payable	5,500	
	$ 7,300	$17,200
Decrease in working capital	9,900	
	$17,200	$17,200

4. Net income for the year was $19,600; cash dividends of $11,000 were declared and paid.

The starting point in the development of the statement of changes in financial position on a working capital basis is computation of the working capital change. The working capital change is computed as shown on page 1136.

After the change in working capital is computed, an analysis of the nonworking capital accounts is performed. **An analysis of the Retained Earnings account is a good starting point** because the net income is the first item reported on a statement of changes in financial position. Then the noncurrent assets, liabilities, and shareholders' equity accounts should be analyzed. Note that **under the working capital basis all of the changes in the current assets and current liabilities have been aggregated or netted into one amount—the change in working capital.** Therefore, we need not separately analyze and report each current asset and current liability item as to its effect on the resources provided and applied. These changes in working capital items are reported, however, in a separate schedule below, yet as part of the statement of changes in financial position.

Increase in Retained Earnings   Retained earnings increased $8,600 for Doral Products Ltd. as a result of net income of $19,600 less cash dividends of $11,000. The net income amount would be reported as follows:

Resources provided by
  Operations:
    Net income
	$19,600

The cash dividends are reported as a use of resources as follows:

Resources applied to Cash dividends	$11,000

Working Capital Provided by or Applied to Operations   The working capital basis is similar to the cash basis in that net income must be adjusted for items that did not increase or decrease working capital in order to determine the actual effect of operations on working capital.

Depreciation expense is the adjustment to net income that is made most commonly to arrive at working capital provided by operations, but there are numerous other expense or revenue items that do not affect working capital. Examples of expense items that must be added back to net income are the **amortization of intangible assets** such as goodwill and patents, and the **amortization of deferred charges** such as bond issue costs. These charges to expense involve expenditures made in prior periods that are being amortized currently and reduce net income without affecting working capital in the current period. Also, **amortization of bond discount or premium** on long-term bonds payable affects the amount of interest expense, but neither affects working capital. As a result, amortization of these items should be added back to or subtracted from net income to arrive at working capital provided by operations. In a similar manner, **changes in deferred income taxes and deferred investment credit** accounts affect net income but have no effect on working capital.

The diagram shown below illustrates the common types of adjustments that are made to net income to arrive at working capital provided by operations.

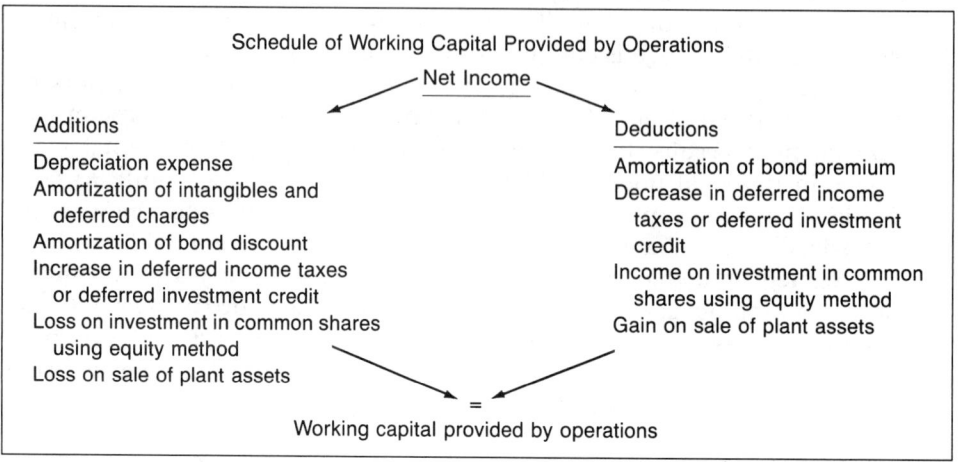

Some current asset adjustments such as the allocation of prepaid expenses are similar to depreciation in that they involve an allocation to expense during the current period but represent an expenditure made in a prior period. They are treated differently in the statement, however, because prepaid expenses are part of working capital, and the net increase or decrease in working capital is reported in the statement in one amount, whereas changes in long-term assets are shown separately.

The same holds true for any other charge or credit that might occur in the current asset or current liability section. For example, an increase in the allowance for doubtful accounts is a part of the computation of an increase or decrease in working capital without adjustment or special treatment. Similarly, a decrease in a current liability such as unearned revenue would be shown in the schedule of working capital changes but not as a separate adjustment to net income to arrive at working capital provided by operations.

Decrease in Land   The decrease in the balance of the Land account from the beginning to the end of the year is $6,000. The resources provided by the sale of the land are $7,000; the gain of $1,000 is included in net income for the year. On the statement of changes in financial position, the following information is reported:

The total proceeds from the sale of the land is reported as resources provided by sale of land. Note that the $1,000 gain on the sale of the land is included in net income. To avoid double counting, this gain of $1,000 must be deducted from net income when computing working capital provided by operations.

Equipment and Related Depreciation   Equipment costing $40,000 was purchased during the year; this purchase would be reported as follows:

Resources applied to Purchase of equipment	$40,000

In addition, equipment costing $5,000 was sold at its book value of $1,500. This transaction would be reported as follows:

Resources provided by Sale of equipment	$1,500

Depreciation expense for the year is $6,500 and would be reported as an item added back to net income to show working capital provided by operations. The difference of $3,000 in the Accumulated Depreciation—Equipment account is the net result of the increase of $6,500 from 1984 depreciation expense and the decrease of $3,500 from the sale of equipment.

Issuance of Bonds Payable   Bonds in the amount of $7,500 were issued during the year. This transaction would be reported as follows:

Resources provided by Issuance of bonds payable	$7,500

Completed Statement—Doral Products Ltd.   Combining the foregoing items that were illustrated separately results in a complete statement of changes in financial position as shown below.

Doral Products Ltd.
STATEMENT OF CHANGES IN FINANCIAL POSITION
For the Year Ended December 31, 1986

Resources provided by		
Operations:		
Net income		$19,600
Add or (deduct): Items not affecting working capital		
Gain on sale of land	$ (1,000)	
Depreciation expense	6,500	5,500
Working capital provided by operations		$25,100
Sale of land		7,000
Sale of equipment		1,500
Issuance of bonds payable		7,500
Total resources provided		$41,100
Resources applied to		
Cash dividends	$11,000	
Purchase of equipment	40,000	
Total resources applied		51,000
Decrease in working capital		$ 9,900

SCHEDULE OF WORKING CAPITAL CHANGES

	Working Capital Change	
Current Assets	Increase	Decrease
Increase in cash	$ 1,600	
Decrease in accounts receivable (net)		$ 3,700
Decrease in inventories		13,500
Increase in prepaid expenses	200	
Current Liabilities		
Decrease in accounts payable	5,500	
	$ 7,300	$17,200
Decrease in working capital	9,900	
	$17,200	$17,200

As with the cash basis, either the indirect (reconciliation) or direct approach to computing working capital provided by operations can be used. Likewise, either the two-section provided and applied format or the three-section activity format (operations, investing, and financing) may be used in preparing a working capital based statement of changes in financial position. Of course, the work sheet may be used to facilitate preparation of the statement on a working capital basis in the same manner as the cash basis illustration on pages 1129–1130.

Working Capital Basis—Hanes Corporation   To allow you to compare the Hanes Corporation statement of changes in financial position prepared on a cash basis (page 1130) with one prepared on a working capital basis, the working capital basis statement is presented on page 1141.

DISCLOSURE

CICA Handbook, Section 1540, indicates that the statements may take the form, include content, and use terminology that is necessary to achieve the objective of providing information about a firm's investing and financing activities. Specifically, Section 1540 recommends the following:

1. The statement summarizing changes in financial position should portray all aspects of the financing and investing activities (all financial resources).
2. The recommended title to be used for summarizing changes in financial position is Statement of Changes in Financial Position.
3. The statement should show the extent to which cash or cash equivalents have been generated from operations. Separate disclosure is required for items classified on the income statement as extraordinary.
4. Effects of financing and investing activities should be disclosed individually when material. For example, both outlays for acquisitions and proceeds from retirements of property should be reported; both long-term borrowings and repayments of long-term debts should be reported; and outlays for purchases of consolidated subsidiaries should be summarized by major assets obtained and obligations assumed.

Hanes Corporation
STATEMENT OF CHANGES IN FINANCIAL POSITION
For the Year Ended December 31, 1986
(Working Capital Basis)

Resources provided by
Operations:

Income before extraordinary item		$109,000
Add (deduct): Items not affecting working capital		
Equity in earnings of Porter Co.	$ (3,500)	
Loss on sale of equipment	1,500	
Depreciation expense	14,600	
Amortization of goodwill	2,400	
Deferred income taxes	3,000	
Amortization of bond premium	(1,000)	17,000
Working capital provided by operations, exclusive of extraordinary item		$126,000
Extraordinary item—Expropriation of land, including extraordinary gain of $8,000 (net of $2,500 tax)		18,500
Issuance of note payable to purchase land		60,000
Sale of equipment		4,000
Sale of common shares		144,000
Total resources provided		$352,500
Resources applied to		
Cash dividends	$ 6,000	
Purchase of land through issuance of note payable	60,000	
Purchase of equipment	53,000	
Major repairs of equipment	11,000	
Purchase of treasury shares	17,000	
Total resources applied		147,000
Increase in working capital		$205,500

SCHEDULE OF WORKING CAPITAL CHANGES

	Working Capital Change	
	Increase	Decrease
Current Assets		
Decrease in cash		$ 7,000
Increase in accounts receivable (net)	$ 53,000	
Increase in inventories	152,000	
Decrease in prepaid expenses		500
Current Liabilities		
Increase in accounts payable		1,000
Increase in accrued liabilities		4,000
Decrease in income taxes payable	13,000	
Totals	$218,000	$ 12,500
Increase in working capital		205,500
	$218,000	$218,000

USEFULNESS OF STATEMENT OF CHANGES IN FINANCIAL POSITION

Some of the benefits of a statement of changes in financial position are as follows:

Assessing Future Cash Flows   *FASB Concepts Statement No. 1* indicates that the primary objective of financial reporting is to predict the amount, timing, and uncertainty of future cash flows. Income data, when augmented with data from a statement of changes in financial position provides a good basis for assessing future cash flows.

Assessing Quality of Income   Operating capability is the ability of an enterprise to maintain a given physical level of operations. Whether an enterprise is able to maintain its operating capability, provide future growth, and distribute dividends to the owners depends on whether adequate funds are being or will be generated.

Assessing Financial Flexibility and Liquidity   Financial flexibility is the ability of an enterprise to take effective actions to alter the amounts and timing of cash flows so it can respond to unexpected needs and opportunities. Information on cash flow data (particularly cash provided by operations) should be useful in determining whether a company will be able to survive adverse operating conditions. The term "liquidity" relates to the amount of time that is expected to elapse until an asset is realized or otherwise converted into cash or until a liability has to be paid. Information on the enterprise's ability to generate funds from operations is important because it indicates whether a company might have difficulty in meeting obligations as they fall due, paying dividends, and meeting other recurring costs.

Providing Information on Financing and Investing Activities   The statement of changes in financial position can provide answers to such questions as:

> How was it possible to distribute dividends in excess of current earnings or in the presence of a net loss for the period?
> How did cash increase even though there was a net loss for the period?
> Why was money borrowed during the period?
> How was the expansion in plant and equipment financed?
> What happened to the proceeds from the sale of plant and equipment?
> How was the retirement of debt accomplished?
> What became of the assets derived from the increase in outstanding share capital?
> What became of the proceeds of the bond issue?
> How was the increase in cash financed?

In addition, many meaningful relationships can be established (e.g., funds provided by operations to debt, to capital expenditures, to dividends, or a combination of these items). Moreover, the statement provides insight into changes occurring in the company that cannot be determined from examination of a balance sheet and income statement.

KEY POINTS

1. The statement of changes in financial position is designed to present information on the operating, financing, and investing activities of a business enterprise.
2. Currently, the *CICA Handbook* requires that the statement be presented using the cash or the cash and cash equivalents basis.
3. Under the cash basis, changes in the cash balances that have occurred during a period of time are summarized, usually grouped by major activities (e.g., operating, financing, and investing).

4. When financial position is defined as working capital, the statement summarizes transactions that caused a change in the firm's net working capital.

5. Under the all financial resources approach, transactions that did not either provide or use cash (or working capital) but affected the firm's capital and asset structure (such as exchanges of shares for assets or exchanges of debt securities for assets) are reported in the statement of changes in financial position. The all financial resources concept must be used with the cash basis for Canadian financial reporting.

6. If the indirect approach is used, items included in the determination of income that did not either provide or use resources in the current year are added to or deducted from net income from operations to arrive at resources provided by operations.

7. Under the direct approach, cash revenues and cash expenses are computed directly so that cash provided from revenue-earning activities and cash expended for operating purposes may be reported.

8. The two-section format of the statement of changes in financial position has been the most common in the past. One section is headed "resources provided" and the other "resources applied."

9. *CICA Handbook*, Section 1540, requires the three-section or activity format. The major sections of this format are: (1) operating activities, (2) investing activities, and (3) financing activities.

10. Working capital has been the most prevalent basis used in Canada until 1986 and is also the most popular in the United States.

24A

THE T-ACCOUNT APPROACH TO PREPARATION OF THE STATEMENT OF CHANGES IN FINANCIAL POSITION

Many accountants find the work sheet approach to preparing a statement of changes in financial position cumbersome. In some cases, the detail of a work sheet is not needed and time does not permit the preparation of a work sheet. Therefore, the **T-account approach** to preparing a statement of changes in financial position has been devised. This procedure provides a quick and systematic method of accumulating the appropriate information to be presented in the formal statement of changes in financial position. The T accounts used in this approach are not part of the general ledger or any other ledger; they are developed only for use in this process.

To illustrate the T-account approach, we will use the information of the Hanes Corporation presented on pages 1123–1124.

Illustration

When the T-account approach is employed, the net change in the working capital for the period is computed by comparing the beginning and ending balances of the working capital accounts. After the net change is computed, a T account for working capital is prepared and the net change in working capital is entered at the top of this account on the left if working capital increased, and on the right if it decreased (see illustration of T account on page 1147). The T account is then structured into four separate classifications: (1) Sources—Operations and (2) Sources—Other, both on the left; and (3) Applications—Operations and (4) Applications—Other, on the right. T accounts are then set up for nonworking capital items that have had activity during the period, with the net change entered at the top of each account. The objective of the T-account approach is to explain the net change in working capital through the various changes that have occurred in the nonworking capital accounts. The working capital T account acts as a summarizing account. Most of the changes in the nonworking capital items are explained through the working capital account. Significant financial transactions that did not affect working capital are assumed to provide and apply working capital and are entered in this summary account to ensure their inclusion in the final statement. To illustrate, a complete version of the T-account approach is presented on the following pages.

The following items caused the change in working capital. (You should trace each entry to the accounts that are presented beginning on page 1147.)

1. Net income for the period, comprising income before extraordinary item of $109,000 and an extraordinary gain of $8,000 (net of tax), increased retained earnings by $117,000. To avoid the detail of nonworking capital revenues and expenses, we employ a short-cut by starting with income before extraordinary item and then, in subsequent entries, adjusting it to reflect resources provided by operations, exclusive of extraordinary item. In general journal form, the entry to report this increase and the extraordinary item would be:

Working Capital—Operations	109,000	
Retained Earnings		109,000

2. The Retained Earnings account also discloses stock dividends of $15,000. Because this transaction is not considered investing or financing activity, the Working Capital account is not affected, and the following entry would be made:

Retained Earnings	15,000	
Common Shares		15,000

3. Further analysis of the Retained Earnings account indicates that a cash dividend of $6,000 was declared during the current period. The entry to record the transaction would be:

Retained Earnings	6,000	
Working Capital—Other		6,000

   Note that the net change in the retained earnings balance of $96,000 is now reconciled. This reconciliation procedure is basic to the T-account approach because it ensures that all appropriate transactions have been considered.

4. The equity in the earnings of Porter Co. must be subtracted from income before extraordinary item because this income item does not increase working capital. The journal entry to recognize this equity in the earnings of Porter Co. is as follows:

Investment in Shares of Porter Co.	3,500	
Working Capital—Operations		5,500

5. A note of $60,000 was issued to purchase land. Although this transaction did not affect working capital, it is a significant financial transaction that should be reported. The transaction is therefore assumed both to have increased working capital and to have decreased working capital in order to report this amount in the Working Capital account. The following entry would be made:

Land	60,000	
Working Capital—Other		60,000

Working capital—Other	60,000	
Note Payable		60,000

An alternative to this approach is simply to adjust the Land and Note Payable account, noting that in a formal preparation of a statement of changes in financial position this transaction must be reported.

6. In addition, land with a book value of $10,500 was expropriated. The entry to record this transaction is as follows:

Working Capital—Other	18,500	
Land		10,500
Retained Earnings		8,000

Note that adding the $10,500 book value of this expropriation to the $8,000 extraordinary gain net of $2,500 tax provides total resources of $18,500 related to the expropriation.

7. Equipment and the related Accumulated Depreciation account indicate that a number of financial transactions affected these accounts. The first transaction is the purchase of equipment, which is recorded as follows:

Equipment	53,000	
Working Capital—Other		53,000

8. In addition, equipment with a book value of $5,500 was sold at a loss of $1,500. The entry to record this transaction is as follows:

Working Capital—Other	4,000	
Working Capital—Operations	1,500	
Accumulated Depreciation—Equipment	2,500	
Equipment		8,000

Note that the loss on the sale of the equipment reduced the income before extraordinary item, but did not affect working capital. The loss must therefore be added back to income before extraordinary item to report accurately resources provided by operations.

9. Depreciation on the equipment of $11,500 must be recorded as follows:

Working Capital—Operations	11,500	
Accumulated Depreciation—Equipment		11,500

10. The major repair reduced working capital, so the necessary journal entry is as follows:

Accumulated Depreciation—Equipment	11,000	
Working Capital—Other		11,000

The Equipment account and related Accumulated Depreciation account are now reconciled.

11. Analysis of the remaining accounts indicates changes in Accumulated Depreciation —Building, Premium on Bonds Payable, and Deferred Income Taxes that must be accounted for in determining the resources provided by operations, exclusive of extraordinary item. The entry to record these transactions is as follows:

Working Capital—Operations	3,100	
Working Capital—Operations	2,400	
Working Capital—Operations	3,000	
Premium on Bonds Payable	1,000	
Accumulated Depreciation—Buildings		3,100
Goodwill		2,400
Deferred Income Taxes		3,000
Working Capital—Operations		1,000

12. Examination of the Common Shares account indicates that in addition to the stock dividend (transaction 2), common stock was issued at $16 per share. The entry to record this transaction is as follows:

Working Capital—Other	144,000	
Common Shares		144,000

13. The company also purchased treasury shares, which is recorded as follows:

Treasury Shares	17,000	
Working Capital—Other		17,000

After the entries above are posted to the appropriate accounts, the working account (shown below) is used as the basis for preparing the statement of changes in financial position. The debit side of the working capital account contains the resources provided and the credit side contains the resources applied. The difference between the two sides of the working capital account should reconcile to the increase or decrease in working capital. The completed statement of changes in financial position is presented on page 1130.

Working Capital

Increases		Decreases	
Net change	$205,000		
Sources—Operations:		**Applications—Operations:**	
1. Income before extraordinary item	109,000	4. Equity in earnings of Porter Co.	$ 3,500
8. Loss on sale of equipment	1,500	11. Bond premium amortization	1,000
9. Depreciation expense	11,500		4,500
11. Depreciation expense	3,100		
11. Goodwill amortization	2,400		
11. Deferred income taxes	3,000		
	130,500		
Sources—Other:		**Applications—Other:**	
2. Issuance of note	60,000	3. Cash dividends	6,000
6. Expropriation of land	18,500	5. Purchase of land	60,000
8. Sale of equipment	4,000	7. Purchase of equipment	53,000
12. Sale of common shares	144,000	10. Major repair of equipment	11,000
	$226,500	13. Purchase of treasury shares	17,000
			$147,000

Investment in Stock of Porter Co. (equity method)

Net change	$ 3,500		
4. Equity in earnings	3,500		

Land

Net change	$ 49,500		
5. Purchase of land	60,000	6. Expropriation	10,500

Equipment

Net change	$ 45,000		
7. Purchase	53,000	8. Sale of equipment	8,000

Accumulated Depreciation—Equipment

Net change	$ 2,000		
8. Sale of equipment	2,500	9. Depreciation expense	11,500
10. Major repair	11,000		

Accumulated Depreciation—Buildings

		Net change	$ 3,100
		11. Depreciation expense	3,100

Goodwill

		Net change	$ 2,400
		11. Amortization of goodwill	2,400

Notes Payable

		Net change	$ 60,000
		5. Issuance of note	60,000

Premium on Bonds Payable

Net change	$ 1,000		
11. Bond premium amortization	1,000		

Deferred Income Taxes

		Net change	$ 3,000
		11. Increase	3,000

Common Shares

		Net change	$ 10,000
		2. Stock dividend	15,000
		12. Sale of common shares	144,000

Retained Earnings

		Net change	$ 96,000
2. Stock dividend	15,000	1. Net income	109,000
3. Cash dividend	6,000	6. Gain on expropriation of land	8,000

Treasury Shares

Net change	$ 17,000		
13. Purchase of treasury shares	17,000		

SUMMARY OF T-ACCOUNT APPROACH

Short-cut approaches are often used with the T-account approach. For example, the journal entries may not be prepared because the transactions are obvious. Also, only the nonworking capital T accounts that have a number of changes, such as Equipment, Accumulated Depreciation—Equipment, and Retained Earnings, need be presented in T-account form. Other more obvious changes in nonworking capital items can be determined simply by examining the comparative balance sheet and other related data. The T-account approach provides certain advantages over the work sheet method in that (1) a statement usually can be prepared much faster using the T-account method and (2) the use of the T-account method helps in understanding the relationship between working capital and nonworking capital items. Conversely, the work sheet on highly complex problems provides a more orderly and systematic approach to preparing the statement of changes in financial position. In addition, in practice the work sheet is used extensively to ensure that all items are properly accounted for. The mechanics of the T-account approach are equally applicable to the cash basis.

The following steps are used in the T-account approach:

1. Determine the increase or decrease in working capital for the year.
2. Post the increase or decrease to the working capital T account and establish four classifications within this account: Sources—Operations, Sources—Other, Applications—Operations, and Applications—Other.
3. Determine the increase or decrease in each nonworking capital account. Accounts that have no change can be ignored unless two transactions have occurred in the same account of the same amount, which is highly unlikely. A short-cut approach is to prepare T accounts only for nonworking capital accounts that have a number of transactions. All other changes can be immediately posted to the working capital account after examining the additional information related to the changes in the balance sheet for a period.
4. Reconstruct entries in nonworking capital accounts and post them to the nonworking capital account affected and to the working capital T account.
5. Using the postings from the working capital T account, prepare the formal statement of changes in financial position.

One word of caution: the T-account approach will have to be modified if an all financial resources transactions occurs, such as the issuance of bonds to purchase a building. Although these transactions do not affect the working capital T accounts directly, an assumption may be made that they affect working capital indirectly and can be reported in the working capital account as sources and uses. An alternative is simply to adjust the two accounts affected, remembering that these transactions must be reported on a formal statement of changes in financial position.

QUESTIONS

1. What is the purpose of the statement of changes in financial position? How does it differ from a balance sheet or income statement?
2. What are the common funds or approaches that are used as the basis in preparing a statement of changes in financial position? Which approach is recommended by *CICA Handbook*, Section 1540? Why?
3. The following differences result from comparing the amounts in two successive balance sheets. Do the following items represent resources provided, resources applied, or neither?

	Differences		
	Debit	Credit	Explanation
(a) Equipment	$82,000		Equipment purchased
(b) Goodwill		$12,000	Amortization of goodwill
(c) Common shares distributable		40,000	Declaration of stock dividend
(d) Common shares	16,000		Purchase of treasury shares
(e) Retained earnings	7,000		Net income of $15,000 and dividends of $22,000

4. The net income for the year for Polytech, Inc. is $231,000, but the statement of changes in financial position indicates that the resources provided by operations is $296,000. What might account for the difference?

5. Give three examples of financial transactions that would be omitted if a working capital concept not including all financial resources were used as the basis for preparing a statement of changes in financial position.

6. On a statement of changes in financial position (working capital basis) why is the amortization of prepaid expenses treated differently than the depreciation taken on a plant asset?

7. Give four examples of changes in the capital structure that do not appear on the statement of changes in financial position.

8. Give four examples of items added back to income before extraordinary items to arrive at cash provided by operations.

9. The working capital provided by operations in Woodstock Ltd.'s statement of changes in financial position for 1986 was $8,000,000. For 1986, depreciation on plant assets was $3,800,000, amortization of goodwill was $100,000, and dividends on common shares were $2,000,000. Compute Woodstock's net income for 1986.

10. Each of the following items must be considered in preparing a statement of changes in financial position for Steel Plate, Inc. for the year ended December 31, 1986. For each item, state where it is to be shown in the statement, if at all.
    (a) Plant assets that had cost $20,000 six and one-half years before and were being depreciated on a straight-line basis over 10 years with no estimated scrap value were sold for $6,000.
    (b) During the year 1,000 no-par value shares were issued for $40 a share.
    (c) Uncollectible accounts receivable in the amount of $22,000 were written off against the allowance for doubtful accounts.
    (d) The company sustained a net loss for the year of $5,000. Depreciation amounted to $2,000 and patent amortization to $1,000.

11. Master Loan Inc. has a net income for the year of $650,000. Included in this net income are: a gain on casualty (extraordinary item), net of tax of $60,000; depreciation expense of $130,000; and amortization of bond premium of $10,000. What amount should Master Loan Inc. report on its statement of changes in financial position for cash provided by operations, exclusive of extraordinary item?

12. Chris Lahey, a student in intermediate accounting, decided that he would have no difficulty in preparing a statement of changes in financial position on the next exam if the problem were straightforward. He still, however, had difficulty understanding the following items. Explain how these items should be treated in a statement of changes in financial position.
    (a) The maturing portion of a long-term serial bond.
    (b) A long-term note given for the purchase of inventory.
    (c) Gain on the sale of marketable securities (current).
    (d) A common stock split.

13. Why are more business enterprises switching to a cash basis approach in preparing a statement of changes in financial position?

14. Harbecke, Inc. reported net income of $2 million in 1986. Depreciation for the year was $210,000, receivables increased $300,000, and accounts payable increased

$160,000. Compute cash provided from operations, assuming the receivable and payable increases related to operations.

15. Nair, Inc. reported sales on an accrual basis of $100,000. If gross receivables increased $80,000, and the allowance for bad debts increased $12,000 after a write-off of $6,000, compute cash sales.

16. Does a separate schedule of working capital have to be included if a cash approach is adopted? Discuss.

17. What are some of the arguments in favour of using the indirect (reconciliation approach) as opposed to the direct approach for reporting a cash basis statement of changes in financial position?

18. Of what use is the statement of changes in financial position?

CASES

C24-1 **Part A.** After considerable discussion and research in recent years concerning the reporting of changes in financial position (sources and applications of funds), The Accounting Standards Committee states in *CICA Handbook*, Section 1540:

. . . that the statement summarizing changes in financial position should be based on a broad concept embracing all changes in financial position and that the title of the statement should reflect this broad concept. The Board therefore recommends that the title be Statement of Changes in Financial Position.

Instructions

(a) What are the two common meanings of "funds" as used when preparing the statement of changes in financial position? Explain.

(b) What is meant by ". . . a broad concept embracing all changes in financial position . . ." as used by the AcSC in *CICA Handbook*, Section 1540? Explain.

Part B. Ace Company is a young and growing producer of electronic measuring instruments and technical equipment. You have been retained by Ace to advise it in the preparation of a statement of changes in financial position. For the fiscal year ended October 31, 1986, you have obtained the following information concerning certain events and transactions of Ace.

1. The board of directors declared a $400,000 cash dividend on October 20, 1986, payable on November 18, 1986, to shareholders of record on November 5, 1986.

2. The amount of reported earnings for the fiscal year was $800,000, which included a deduction for an extraordinary loss of $83,000 (see item 6 below).

3. Depreciation expense of $350,000 was included in the earnings statement.

4. Uncollectible accounts receivable of $38,000 was written off against the allowance for doubtful accounts. Also, $45,000 of bad debts expense was included in determining income for the fiscal year, and the same amount was added to the allowance for doubtful accounts.

5. A gain of $5,200 was realized on the sale of a machine; it originally cost $75,000, of which $30,000 was undepreciated on the date of sale.

6. On April 1, 1986, a freak flood caused an uninsured inventory loss of $83,000 ($170,000 loss, less reduction in income taxes of $87,000). This extraordinary loss was included in determining income as indicated in 2 above.

7. On July 3, 1986, a building and land were purchased for $600,000. Ace gave in payment $75,000 cash, $200,000 market value of its unissued common shares, and a $325,000 mortgage.

8. On August 3, 1986, $750,000 face value of Ace's 10% convertible debentures were converted into 7,500 no-par value of its common shares. The bonds were originally issued at face value.

Instructions

Explain whether each of the eight numbered items above is a source or use of cash and explain how it should be disclosed in Ace's statement of changes in financial position for the fiscal year ended October 31, 1986. If any item is neither a source nor a use of cash, explain why it is not and indicate the disclosure, if any, that should be made of the item in Ace's statement of changes in financial position for the fiscal year ended October 31, 1986.

C24-2 Presented below is the financial statement related to Shakespeare Book Co.:

Shakespeare Book Co.
STATEMENT SHOWING CAUSES
OF NET CHANGE IN WORKING CAPITAL

Funds were obtained from:		
Operations (net income transferred to retained earnings)		$185,220.40
Current assets used up in year's operations:		
Cash on hand and in banks	$ 35,627.25	
Postage stamps	20.00	35,647.25
Increase in common shares outstanding		31,000.00
		$251,867.65
Funds were applied to:		
Payments of cash dividends		$ 35,331.00
Declaration of stock dividends (not yet issued)		26,400.00
Investment in additions to		
Accounts receivable—trade	$ 12,504.83	
Notes receivable—trade	2,500.00	
Inventories	103,742.51	
Marketable securities	10,600.01	
Cash surrender value of life insurance	1,141.25	
Fixed assets (net increase)	15,450.52	
Patents	20,000.00	
Prepaid expense	2,502.04	168,441.16
Payments of serial bond maturities		10,000.00
Reduction in current liabilities		11,695.49
		$251,867.65

Instructions

You are to criticize the statement above, considering mainly its **function** and **content**. (There are differences of opinion concerning the general form of such a statement and the terminology used. You need not concern yourself with these matters in your criticism except where you believe them to be essential to the accomplishment of the statement's function.) Mention in your discussion specific items that the data supplied lead you to believe (a) may have been omitted incorrectly from the statement or (b) should have been excluded from the statement. For each item that you mention, give your reason for inclusion or deletion and state how you would treat the item. You need not prepare a revised statement.

C24-3 The following statement was prepared by Solar Corporation's accountant:

Solar Corporation
STATEMENT OF SOURCE AND APPLICATION OF FUNDS
For the Year Ended September 30, 1986

Source of funds	
Net income	$ 72,000
Depreciation and depletion	61,000
Increase in long-term debt	189,000
Common shares issued under employee option plans	16,000
Changes in current receivables and inventories, less current liabilities (excluding current maturities of long-term debt)	14,000
	$352,000
Application of funds	
Cash dividends	$ 44,000
Expenditures for property, plant, and equipment	224,000
Investments and other uses	20,000
Change in cash	64,000
	$352,000

The following additional information relating to Solar Corporation is available for the year ended September 30, 1986:

1. The corporation received $16,000 in cash from its employees on its employee stock option plans, and wage and salary expense attributable to the option plans was an additional $22,000.

2.

Expenditures for property, plant, and equipment	$242,000
Proceeds from retirements of property, plant, and equipment	18,000
Net expenditures	$224,000

3. A stock dividend of 10,000 shares of Solar Corporation's no-par common was distributed to common shareholders on April 1, 1986, when the per-share market price was $7.

4. On July 1, 1986, when its market price was $6 per share, 16,000 common of Solar Corporation were issued in exchange for 4,000 shares of preferred.

5. The balance sheet of Solar Corporation distinguishes between current and noncurrent assets and liabilities.

6.

Depreciation expense	$ 58,000
Depletion expense	3,000
	$ 61,000

7.

Increase in long-term debt	$610,000
Retirement of debt	421,000
Net increase	$189,000

Instructions

(a) In general, what are the objectives of a statement of the type shown above for the Solar Corporation? Explain.

(b) Identify the weaknesses in the form and format of the Solar Corporation's statement of changes in financial position without reference to the additional information.

(c) For each of the seven items of additional information for the statement of changes in financial position, indicate the preferable treatment and explain why the suggested treatment is preferable.

(AICPA adapted)

C24-4   The statement of changes in financial position is normally a required basic financial statement for each period for which an earnings statement is presented. The reporting entity has flexibility in form, content, and terminology with this statement to meet the objectives of differing circumstances. For example, the concept of "funds" may be interpreted to mean, among other things, cash or working capital. However, the statement should be prepared based on the "all financial resources" concept.

Instructions

(a)   What is the "all financial resources" concept?

(b)   What are two types of financial transactions that would be disclosed under the "all financial resources" concept and which would not be disclosed without the concept?

(c)   What effect, if any, would each of the following seven items have upon the preparation of a statement of changes in financial position prepared in accordance with generally accepted accounting principles using the cash concept of funds?
1.   Accounts receivable—trade.
2.   Inventory.
3.   Depreciation.
4.   Deferred income tax credit from interperiod allocation.
5.   Issuance of long-term debt in payment for a building.
6.   Payoff of current portion of debt.
7.   Sale of a fixed asset resulting in a loss.

(AICPA adapted)

C24-5   Each of the following items must be considered in preparing a statement of changes in financial position for Denson Originals, Inc. for the year ended December 31, 1986.

1.   Fixed assets that had cost $10,000 six and one-half years before and were being depreciated on a 10-year basis, with no estimated scrap value, were sold for $3,125.
2.   During the year, goodwill of $100,000 was completely written off to expense.
3.   During the year, 500 common shares were issued for $31 a share.
4.   The company sustained a net loss for the year of $2,100. Depreciation amounted to $900, and patent amortization was $400.
5.   An Appropriation for Contingencies in the amount of $80,000 was created by a charge against Retained Earnings.
6.   Uncollectible accounts receivable in the amount of $2,000 were written off against the Allowance for Doubtful Accounts.
7.   Investments that cost $12,000 when purchased 4 years earlier were sold for $11,000. The loss was considered ordinary.
8.   Bonds payable with a par value of $24,000 on which there was an unamortized bond premium of $1,800 were redeemed at 102. The gain was credited to income.

Instructions

For each item, state first where it is to be shown in the statement and then illustrate how you would present the necessary information, including the amount. Consider each item to be independent of the others. Assume that correct entries were made for all transactions as they took place.

EXERCISES

E24-1   Don and Diana are equal partners in the Five Flys Restaurant. Don withdraws from the partnership at the end of 1986, terminating the partnership. Below, you are given comparative financial data and other pertinent information.

	Dec. 31, 1985	Dec. 31, 1986	Increase or (Decrease)
Cash	$ 5,700	$ 7,400	$ 1,700
Receivables	7,800	10,300	2,500
Allowance for doubtful accounts	(900)	(1,000)	100
Marketable securities	5,000	5,000	—
Prepaid expenses	1,300	1,100	(200)
Land	10,000	10,000	—
Building and equipment	31,600	35,600	4,000
Accumulated depreciation	(3,700)	(5,300)	1,600
	$56,800	$63,100	
Accounts payable	$ 3,000	$ 2,600	(400)
Notes payable (short-term)	1,700	1,000	(700)
Accrued expenses	1,500	1,800	300
Mortgage payable	22,100	20,000	(2,100)
Don, capital	17,400	22,500	5,100
Diana, capital	11,100	15,200	4,100
	$56,800	$63,100	

1. Equipment for $4,000 was purchased in 1986.
2. At the time of the termination, Don makes withdrawals totalling, $1,700; Diana has withdrawn $4,000.

Instructions

Prepare a statement of changes in financial position (working capital approach) for the year 1986.

E24-2 Condensed financial data of Tennyson Company for the years ended December 31, 1985, and December 31, 1986, are presented below:

Tennyson Company
COMPARATIVE POSITION STATEMENT DATA
as of December 31, 1985 and 1986

	1985	1986
Cash	$ 38,400	$124,800
Receivables, net	49,000	83,200
Inventories	61,900	92,500
Investments	97,000	90,000
Plant assets	212,500	240,000
	$458,800	$630,500
Accounts payable	$ 67,300	$100,000
Mortgage payable	74,900	50,000
Accumulated depreciation	52,000	30,000
Common shares	131,100	175,000
Retained earnings	133,500	275,500
	$458,800	$630,500

Tennyson Company
INCOME STATEMENT
For the Year Ended December 31, 1985

Sales	$320,000	
Interest and other revenue	20,000	$340,000
Less:		
Cost of goods sold	130,000	
Selling and administrative expenses	10,000	
Depreciation	24,000	
Income taxes	5,000	
Interest charges	3,000	
Loss on sale of plant asset	6,000	178,000
Net income		162,000
Dividends		20,000
Income retained in business		$142,000

Additional information: New plant assets costing $80,000 were purchased during the year. Investments were sold at book value.

Instructions

From the foregoing information, prepare a statement of changes in financial position (working capital approach).

E24-3   Comparative adjusted trial balances for Lisa Herrington, Inc. are presented below:

Lisa Herrington, Inc.
ADJUSTED TRIAL BALANCE

	Dec. 31, 1985		Dec. 31, 1986	
	Dr.	Cr.	Dr.	Cr.
Cash	$ 5,400		$ 8,200	
Marketable securities	20,000		22,000	
Receivables (net)	60,000		66,800	
Inventories	64,000		72,000	
Delivery equipment	29,000		33,500	
Accumulated depreciation— delivery equipment		$ 17,000		$ 20,000
Machinery	14,500		17,500	
Accumulated depreciation— machinery		8,500		10,500
Building	55,000		55,000	
Accumulated depreciation— buildings		7,000		15,000
Land	15,000		15,000	
Accounts payable		47,500		43,000
Accrued expenses		8,000		9,500
Long-term notes payable		11,000		5,000
Bonds payable		50,000		50,000
Common shares		65,000		65,000
Retained earnings		38,000		48,900
Sales		294,900		335,100
Cost of goods sold	220,000		245,000	
Operating expenses	48,000		51,000	
Income taxes	16,000		16,000	
	$546,900	$546,900	$602,000	$602,000

Instructions

Using the information above, prepare a statement of changes in financial position (cash approach).

E24-4 Condensed financial data of Covaleski Company for 1985 and 1986 are presented below:

Covaleski Company
COMPARATIVE BALANCE SHEET DATA
As of December 31, 1985 and 1986

	1985	1986
Cash	$1,150	$1,200
Receivables, net	1,300	1,600
Inventory	1,700	1,600
Plant assets	1,700	1,900
Accumulated depreciation	(1,150)	(1,200)
Long-term investments	1,400	1,300
	$6,100	$6,400
Accounts payable	$ 900	$1,300
Taxes payable	600	550
Bonds payable	1,500	1,150
Share capital	1,700	1,800
Retained earnings	1,400	1,600
	$6,100	$6,400

Covaleski Company
INCOME STATEMENT
For the Year Ended 1986

Sales		$6,900
Cost of goods sold		5,200
Gross margin		$1,700
Operating expenses:		
Selling expenses	$600	
Administrative expense	650	
Depreciation expense	50	1,300
Net income		$ 400
Cash dividends		200
Income retained in business		$ 200

Additional information: There were no gains or losses in any noncurrent transactions during 1986.

Instructions

(a) Prepare a statement of changes in financial position (cash basis) using the indirect approach.

(b) Prepare a statement of changes in financial position (cash basis) using the direct approach.

E24-5 Presented below are data taken from the records of S. Kopp Company.

	December 31, 1985	December 31, 1986
Cash	$ 12,000	$ 16,500
Other current assets	35,000	63,500
Long-term investments	58,000	10,000
Plant assets	237,000	396,000
	$342,000	$486,000
Accumulated depreciation	$ 40,000	$ 30,000
Current liabilities	32,000	35,000
Bonds payable	-0-	105,000
Share capital	250,000	250,000
Donated capital	-0-	31,000
Retained earnings	20,000	35,000
	$342,000	$486,000

1. Securities carried at a cost of $48,000 on December 31, 1985, were sold during 1986 for $39,000. The loss (not extraordinary) was incorrectly charged directly to Retained Earnings.
2. Plant assets that cost $50,000 and were 70% depreciated were sold during the year for $8,000. The loss (not extraordinary) was incorrectly charged directly to Retained Earnings.
3. Net income as reported on the income statement for the year was $29,000.
4. Dividends paid amounted to $14,000.
5. Depreciation charged for the year was $25,000.
6. Land was donated to S. Kopp Company by the city. The land was worth $31,000. (Assume credit to Donated Capital is correct.)

Instructions

Prepare a statement of changes in financial position (cash basis). No schedule of working capital changes is required.

E24-6 Comparative balance sheets at December 31, 1985 and 1986, for Melton Brick Company follow.

	1985	1986
Cash	$ 48,000	$ 54,000
Receivables	66,000	60,000
Inventory	112,000	110,000
Prepaid expenses	8,000	9,000
Plant assets	220,000	312,000
Accumulated depreciation	(61,000)	(86,000)
Patents	40,000	35,000
	$433,000	$494,000
Accounts payable	$ 87,000	$75,000
Taxes payable	66,000	68,000
Mortgage payable	95,000	—
Preferred shares	—	156,000
Common shares	150,000	150,000
Retained earnings	35,000	45,000
	$433,000	$494,000

1. The only entries in the Retained Earnings account are for dividends paid in the amount of $20,000 and for the net income for the year.

2. The income statement for 1986 is as follows:

Sales	$132,000
Cost of sales	94,000
Gross profit	38,000
Operating expenses	8,000
Net income	$ 30,000

3. The only entry in the Accumulated Depreciation account is the depreciation expense for the period.

Instructions

(a) From the information above, prepare a statement of changes in financial position (working capital approach).

(b) From the information above, prepare a statement of changes in financial position (cash approach). Use the indirect approach.

E24-7 Candice Urbanak, Inc. had the following condensed balance sheet at the end of operations for 1985.

Candice Urbanak, Inc.
BALANCE SHEET
December 31, 1985

Current assets	$ 37,500	Current liabilities	$ 15,000
Investments	20,000	Long-term notes payable	25,500
Plant assets (net)	67,500	Bonds payable	25,000
Land	40,000	Share capital	75,000
		Retained earnings	24,500
	$165,000		$165,000

During 1986 the following occurred:

1. A tract of land was purchased for $7,750.
2. Bonds payable in the amount of $6,000 were retired at par.
3. An additional $12,500 in share capital was issued.
4. Dividends totalling $9,375 were paid to shareholders.
5. Net income for 1986 was $26,250 after allowing depreciation of $11,250.
6. Land was purchased through the issuance of $22,500 in bonds.
7. Candice Urbanak, Inc. sold part of its investment portfolio for $12,875. This transaction resulted in a gain of $375 for the firm. The company often sells and buys securities of this nature.

Instructions

(a) Prepare a statement of changes in financial position for 1986. A supporting schedule of working capital changes need not be prepared.

(b) Prepare the condensed balance sheet for Candice Urbanak, Inc. as it would appear at December 31, 1986. Assume that current liabilities remained at $15,000.

E24-8 The accounts below appear in the ledger of Chaucer Company.

Retained Earnings		Dr.	Cr.	Bal.
Jan. 1, 1986	Credit Balance			$ 42,000
Aug. 15	Dividends (Cash)	$19,600		22,400
Dec. 31	Net Income for 1986		$12,000	34,400

	Machinery	Dr.	Cr.	Bal.
Jan. 1, 1986	Debit Balance			$140,000
Aug. 3	Purchases of Machinery	$42,000		182,000
Sept. 10	Cost of Machinery Constructed	28,000		210,000
Nov. 15	Machinery sold		$56,000	154,000

	Accumulated Depreciation— Machinery	Dr.	Cr.	Bal.
Jan. 1, 1986	Credit Balance			$ 84,000
Apr. 8	Extraordinary Repairs	$21,000		63,000
Nov. 15	Accum. Depreciation of Machinery Sold	25,200		37,800
Dec. 31	Depreciation for 1986		$11,200	49,000

Instructions

From the information given, prepare all adjustments that should be made on a work sheet for a statement of changes in financial position (working capital concept). The loss on sale of equipment (Nov. 15) was $12,600.

E24-9   Presented below is some information related to Browning International:

1. Convertible bonds payable with a par value of $400,000 were exchanged for unissued common shares. The market price of both types of securities was par.
2. The net income for the year was $60,000.
3. Depreciation charged on the building was $16,000.
4. Organization costs in the amount of $10,000 were written off during the year as a charge to expense.
5. Some old office equipment was traded in on the purchase of some dissimilar office equipment and the following entry was made:

Office Equipment	5,000	
Accum. Depreciation—Office Equipment	3,000	
Office Equipment		4,000
Cash		3,400
Gain on Disposal of Plant Assets		600

The Gain on Disposal of Plant Assets was credited to current operations as ordinary income.

6. Dividends in the amount of $24,000, payable in cash, were declared near the end of the year, and an entry was made to record them. They are payable in January of next year.
7. The Appropriations for Bonded Indebtedness in the amount of $240,000 was returned to Retained Earnings during the year, because the bonds were retired during the year.

Instructions

Show by journal entries the adjustments that would be made on a work sheet for a statement of changes (cash basis) in financial position.

E24-10   Below is the comparative balance sheet for Yeats Printing Corporation.

	Dec. 31, 1985	Dec. 31, 1986
Cash	$ 20,000	$ 15,500
Short-term investments	20,000	25,000
Accounts receivable	45,000	43,000
Allowance for doubtful accounts	(2,000)	(1,800)
Prepaid expenses	2,500	3,200

Inventories	65,000	73,000
Land	50,000	50,000
Buildings	73,500	100,000
Accumulated depreciation—buildings	(21,000)	(30,000)
Equipment	47,000	53,000
Accumulated depreciation—equipment	(16,500)	(19,000)
Delivery equipment	39,000	39,000
Accumulated depreciation—delivery equipment	(20,500)	(24,000)
Patents	-0-	10,000
	$302,000	$336,900
Accounts payable	$ 18,000	$ 26,000
Short-term notes payable	6,000	4,000
Accrued payables	5,000	3,000
Mortgage payable	53,000	65,000
Bonds payable	62,500	50,000
Share capital	106,000	115,500
Retained earnings	51,500	73,400
	$302,000	$336,900

Dividends in the amount of $5,000 were declared and paid in 1986.

Instructions

From this information, prepare a work sheet for a statement of changes in financial position (cash). Make reasonable assumptions as appropriate.

E24-11 Presented below is information related to G. Ohlendorf, Inc. for the years 1985 and 1986 to aid in preparing a statement of changes in financial position (cash concept).

G. Ohlendorf, Inc.
BALANCE SHEETS

	December 31,	
Assets	1986	1985
Current assets:		
Cash	$ 128,000	$100,000
Marketable securities	62,000	
Accounts receivable—net	415,000	290,000
Merchandise inventory	345,000	210,000
Prepaid expenses	50,000	25,000
	1,000,000	625,000
Property, plant, and equipment	565,000	300,000
Less: Accumulated depreciation	55,000	25,000
	510,000	275,000
	$1,510,000	$900,000
Equities		
Current liabilities:		
Accounts payable	$ 272,000	$220,000
Accrued expenses	70,000	65,000
Dividends payable	40,000	-0-
	382,000	285,000
Note payable—due 1989	245,000	-0-

Shareholders' equity:		
Common shares	600,000	450,000
Retained earnings	283,000	165,000
	883,000	615,000
	$1,510,000	$900,000

G. Ohlendorf, Inc.
INCOME STATEMENTS

	Year Ended December 31,	
	1986	1985
Net sales—including service charges	$3,275,000	$2,000,000
Cost of goods sold	2,525,000	1,600,000
Gross profit	750,000	400,000
Expenses (including income taxes)	500,000	260,000
Net income	$ 250,000	$ 140,000

Additional information available included the following:

1. Although Ohlendorf will report all changes in financial position, management has adopted a format emphasizing the flow of cash.
2. All accounts receivable and accounts payable relate to trade merchandise. Cash discounts are not allowed to customers, but a service charge is added to an account for late payment. Accounts payable are recorded net and are always paid in time to take all of the discount allowed. The Allowance for Doubtful Accounts at the end of 1986 was the same as at the end of 1985; no receivables were charged against the Allowance during 1986.
3. The proceeds from the note payable were used to finance a new store building. Common shares were sold to provide additional working capital.

Instructions

Compute the following for the year 1986:

(a) Cash collected from accounts receivable, assuming that all sales are on account.
(b) Cash payments made on accounts payable to suppliers, assuming that all purchases of inventory are on account.
(c) Cash dividend payment.
(d) Cash receipts that were not provided by operations.
(e) Cash payments for assets that were not reflected in operations.

E24-12 Fresno Canning Co. has recently decided to go public and has hired you as the independent CA. One statement that the enterprise is anxious to have prepared is a statement of changes in financial position. Financial statements of Fresno Canning Co. for 1985 and 1986 are provided below.

		Dec. 31/85		Dec. 31/86
Cash		$ 13,000		$ 21,000
Accounts receivable		14,000		33,000
Merchandise inventory		35,000		22,000
Property, plant, and equipment	$78,000		$60,000	
Less: Accumulated depreciation	(24,000)	54,000	(22,000)	38,000
		$116,000		$114,000

Accounts payable	23,000	30,000
Income taxes payable	30,000	25,000
Bonds payable	33,000	35,000
Common shares	14,000	6,000
Retained earnings	16,000	18,000
	$116,000	$114,000

INCOME STATEMENT
For the Year Ended December 31, 1986

Sales		$220,000
Cost of sales		180,000
Gross profit		40,000
Selling expenses	$18,000	
Administrative expenses	6,000	24,000
Income from operations		16,000
Interest expense		5,000
Income before taxes		11,000
Income taxes		2,000
Net income		$ 9,000

The following additional data were provided:

1. Dividends for the year 1986 were $5,000.
2. During the year equipment was sold for $10,000. This equipment cost $18,000 originally and had a book value of $12,000 at the time of sale. The loss on sale was incorrectly charged to retained earnings.
3. All depreciation expense is in the selling expense category.

Instructions

(a) Prepare a statement of changes in financial position, using a working capital approach.

(b) Prepare a statement of changes in financial position that emphasizes a cash approach, using the indirect approach. All sales and purchases are on account.

E24-13 Clarence Hankes Co. reported $210,000 of net income for 1986. The accountant, in preparing the statement of changes in financial position on a working capital basis, noted several items that might offset working capital provided by operations. These items are listed below:

1. During 1986, Hankes purchased 100 treasury shares at a cost of $20 per share. These shares were then reissued at $25 per share.
2. During 1986, Hankes sold 100 shares of IBM common at $250 per share. Acquisition cost of these shares was $150 per share. This investment was shown on Hankes' December 31, 1985, balance sheet as a current asset.
3. During 1986, Hankes changed from the straight-line method to the double-declining balance method of depreciation for its machinery. The debit to the Cumulative Effect (Retained Earnings) account was for $19,000 net of tax.
4. During 1986, Hankes revised its estimate for bad debts. Before 1986, Hankes' bad debts expense was 1% of its net sales. In 1986, this percentage was increased to 1.5%. Net sales for 1984 were $500,000.
5. During 1986, Hankes issued 500 shares of its no-par common for a patent. The market value of the shares on the date of the transaction was $23 per share.
6. Depreciation expense for 1986 was $23,000.

7. Hankes Co. holds 40% of the Seabrook Company's common shares as a long-term investment. Seabrook Company reported $14,000 of net income for 1986.

8. Seabrook Company paid a total of $2,000 of cash dividends in 1986.

9. A comparison of Hankes' December 31, 1985, and December 31, 1986, balance sheets indicates that the credit balance in Deferred Income Taxes (classified as a long-term liability) decreased $4,000.

10. During 1986, Hankes declared a 10% stock dividend. One thousand shares of no-par common were distributed. The market price at date of issuance was $20 per share.

Instructions

Prepare a schedule that shows working capital provided by operations.

E24-14 Odon Company has not yet prepared a formal Statement of Changes in Financial Position for the 1986 fiscal year. Comparative Statements of Financial Position as of December 31, 1985 and 1986, and a Statement of Income and Retained Earnings for the year ended December 31, 1986, are presented below.

Odon Company
STATEMENT OF INCOME AND RETAINED EARNINGS
Year Ended December 31, 1986
(000 omitted)

Sales		$2,408
Expenses		
Cost of goods sold	$1,100	
Salaries and benefits	850	
Heat, light, and power	75	
Depreciation	60	
Property taxes	18	
Patent amortization	25	
Miscellaneous expense	10	
Interest	55	2,193
Income before income taxes		215
Income taxes		105
Net income		110
Retained earnings—Jan. 1, 1986		310
		420
Stock dividend declared and issued		130
Retained earnings—Dec. 31, 1986		$ 290

Odon Company
STATEMENT OF INCOME AND RETAINED EARNINGS
Year Ended December 31, 1986
(000 omitted)

Assets	1985	1986
Current assets		
Cash	$ 100	$ 60
Treasury notes	50	-0-
Accounts receivable	500	610
Inventory	600	720
Total current assets	1,250	1,390

Long-term assets		
Land	70	80
Buildings and equipment	600	710
Accumulated depreciation	(120)	(180)
Patents (less amortization)	130	105
Total long-term assets	680	715
Total assets	$1,930	$2,105

Liabilities and Shareholders' Equity		
Current liabilities		
Accounts payable	$ 300	$ 360
Taxes payable	20	25
Notes payable	400	400
Total current liabilities	720	785
Term notes payable—due 1999	200	200
Total liabilities	920	985
Shareholders' equity		
Common shares outstanding	700	830
Retained earnings	310	290
Total shareholders' equity	1,010	1,120
Total liabilities and shareholders' equity	$1,930	$2,105

Instructions

Prepare a Statement of Changes in Financial Position that reconciles the change in cash balance. Use the direct approach. Changes in accounts receivable and accounts payable relate to sales and cost of sales. Taxes payable relates only to income taxes.

(CMA adapted)

E24-15 Presented below are comparative balance sheets for El Matador, Incorporated.

	December 31	
	1986	1985
Cash	$ 450,000	$ 500,000
Accounts receivable, net	1,150,000	900,000
Inventory	3,100,000	2,175,000
Prepaid expenses	50,000	75,000
Land	500,000	200,000
Plant and equipment	5,500,000	4,890,000
Accumulated depreciation	(1,900,000)	(1,500,000)
Investments in other companies	350,000	160,000
Total assets	$9,200,000	$7,400,000
Accounts payable	$1,775,000	$1,210,000
Income taxes payable	200,000	250,000
Notes payable—current portion	500,000	—
Long-term notes	1,250,000	1,750,000
Deferred taxes	400,000	250,000
Share capital	3,500,000	2,800,000
Retained earnings	1,575,000	1,140,000
Total liabilities and equities	$9,200,000	$7,400,000

The 1986 income statement follows:

Sales	$8,000,000
Cost of goods sold	3,820,000
Gross margin	4,180,000
Operating expenses	2,900,000
Gain on sale of equipment	120,000
Income before taxes	1,400,000
Income tax expense	500,000
Net income	$ 900,000

The following additional information is available.

1. The company issued $190,000 of its own shares in exchange for 10% of the shares of another company.
2. Fully depreciated equipment costing $100,000 new was retired and removed from the books.
3. A stock dividend of $200,000 was declared and issued during the year; a cash dividend was also declared and paid.
4. A $300,000 fabricating plant was acquired during 1986 by giving $200,000 in common shares and $100,000 in cash.
5. Depreciation expense totalled $650,000, of which $550,000 was included in cost of goods sold and $100,000 in operating expenses.
6. Unneeded equipment with an original cost of $350,000 and a book value of $200,000 was sold for $320,000.
7. Five thousand common shares were issued at $22 per share.
8. Five hundred thousand dollars in long-term notes were reclassified to current status.

Instructions

(a) Prepare a statement of changes in financial position (cash basis), using the indirect approach.
(b) Prepare a statement of changes in financial position (cash basis), using the direct approach. Assume that the accounts receivable and accounts payable relate solely to sales and cost of sales. Amortization of prepaid expenses relates to operating expenses.

PROBLEMS

P24-1 The comparative balance sheets for Railway Car Corporation show the following information:

	December 31	
	1986	1985
Cash	$ 38,500	$ 7,000
Accounts receivable	12,000	10,000
Inventory	12,000	6,000
Investments	—	2,000
Building	—	29,750
Equipment	50,000	35,000
Patent	5,000	6,250
Totals	$117,500	$96,000

Allowance for doubtful accounts	$ 3,000	$ 4,500
Accumulated depreciation on equipment	2,000	4,500
Accumulated depreciation on building	—	11,000
Accounts payable	5,000	3,000
Dividends payable	—	6,000
Notes payable, short-term (nontrade)	3,000	4,000
Long-term notes payable	36,000	25,000
Common shares	38,000	33,000
Retained earnings	30,500	5,000
	$117,500	$96,000

Additional data related to 1986 are as follows:

1. Equipment that had cost $7,000 and was 50% depreciated at time of disposal was sold for $2,500 (net of tax).
2. Five thousand dollars of the long-term note payable was paid by issuing common shares.
3. The only cash dividends paid were $6,000.
4. On January 1, 1986, the building was completely destroyed by a flood. Insurance proceeds on the building were $29,750 (net of tax).
5. Investments (long-term) were sold at $3,700 (net of tax) above their cost. The company has made similar sales and investments in the past.
6. Cash of $6,000 was paid for the acquisition of equipment.
7. A long-term note for $16,000 was issued for the acquisition of equipment.

Instructions

Prepare a statement of changes in financial position (cash basis). Flood damages are unusual and infrequent in that part of the country.

P24-2 The following schedule showing net changes in balance sheet accounts at December 31, 1986, compared to December 31, 1985, was prepared from the records of The Oshawa Company. The statement of changes in financial position for the year ended December 31, 1986, has not yet been prepared.

Assets	Net Change Increase (Decrease)
Cash	$ 70,000
Accounts receivable, net	66,000
Inventories	37,000
Prepaid expenses	1,000
Property, plant, and equipment, net	54,000
Total assets	$228,000
Liabilities	
Accounts payable	$ (50,500)
Notes payable—current	(15,000)
Accrued expenses	28,000
Bonds payable	(29,000)
Less: Decrease in unamortized bond discount	2,200
Total liabilities	(64,300)

Shareholders' Equity

Common shares	700,000
Retained earnings	(437,700)
Appropriation of retained earnings for possible future inventory price decline	30,000
Total shareholders' equity	292,300
Total liabilities and shareholders' equity	$228,000

Additional information:

1. The net income for the year ended December 31, 1986, was $198,800. There were no extraordinary items.

2. During the year ended December 31, 1986, uncollectible accounts receivable of $26,400 were written off by a charge to allowance for doubtful accounts.

3. A comparison of property, plant, and equipment as of the end of each year follows:

	December 31, 1986	December 31, 1985	Net Increase (Decrease)
Property, plant, and equipment	$565,500	$510,000	$55,500
Less: Accumulated depreciation	229,500	228,000	(1,500)
Property, plant, and equipment, net	$336,000	$282,000	$54,000

During 1986, machinery was purchased at a cost of $47,000. In addition, machinery that was acquired in 1979 at a cost of $48,000 was sold for $5,400. At the date of sale, the machinery had an undepreciated cost of $8,400. The remaining increase in property, plant, and equipment resulted from the acquisition of a tract of land for a new plant site.

4. The bonds payable mature at the rate of $29,000 every year.

5. In January, 1986, the company issued an additional 18,000 common shares at $14 per share upon the exercise of outstanding stock options held by key employees. In May, 1986, the company declared and issued a 4% stock dividend on its outstanding shares (market price $14). During the year, a cash dividend was paid on common. On December 31, 1986, there were 832,000 common shares outstanding.

6. The appropriation of retained earnings for possible future inventory price decline was provided by a charge against retained earnings, in anticipation of an expected future drop in the market related to goods in inventory.

Instructions

Prepare a statement of changes in financial position for the year ended December 31, 1986, based upon the information presented above. The statement should be prepared using a cash format.

(AICPA adapted)

P24-3 You have completed the field work in connection with your audit of Garfield Corporation for the year ended December 31, 1986. The following schedule shows the balance sheet accounts at the beginning and end of the year.

	Dec. 31, 1986	Dec. 31, 1985	Increase or (Decrease)
Cash	$ 287,900	$ 320,000	$ (32,100)
Accounts receivable	487,800	410,000	77,800
Inventory	691,700	660,000	31,700
Prepaid expenses	12,000	8,000	4,000
Investment in subsidiary	106,800	—	106,800

Cash surrender value of life insurance	2,304	1,800	504
Machinery	187,000	190,000	(3,000)
Buildings	566,500	407,900	158,600
Land	52,500	52,500	—
Patents	69,000	60,000	9,000
Goodwill	40,000	50,000	(10,000)
Bond discount and expense	3,276	—	3,276
	$2,506,780	$2,160,200	$346,580

	Dec. 31, 1986	Dec. 31, 1985	Increase or (Decrease)
Accrued taxes payable	$ 94,000	$ 79,600	$ 14,400
Accounts payable	299,280	280,000	19,280
Dividends payable	70,000	—	70,000
Bonds payable—8%	125,000	—	125,000
Bonds payable—12%	—	100,000	(100,000)
Allowance for doubtful accounts	35,300	40,000	(4,700)
Accumulated depreciation—building	407,000	400,000	7,000
Accumulated depreciation—machinery	141,000	130,000	11,000
Premium on bonds payable	—	2,400	(2,400)
Share capital—no par	1,315,200	1,453,200	(138,000)
Appropriation for plant expansion	10,000	—	10,000
Retained earnings—unappropriated	10,000	(325,000)	335,000
	$2,506,780	$2,160,200	$346,580

STATEMENT OF RETAINED EARNINGS

January	1, 1986	Balance (deficit)	$(325,000)
March	31, 1986	Net income for first quarter of 1984	25,000
April	1, 1986	Transfer from paid-in capital	300,000
		Balance	-0-
December 31, 1986		Net income for last three quarters of 1986	90,000
		Dividend declared—payable January 20, 1987	(70,000)
		Appropriation for plant expansion	(10,000)
		Balance	$ 10,000

Your working papers contain the following information:

1. On April 1, 1986, the existing deficit was written off against share capital created by reducing the stated value of the no-par stock.
2. On November 1, 1986, 29,600 no-par shares were sold for $162,000.
3. A patent was purchased for $15,000.
4. Machinery was purchased for $5,000 and installed in December, 1986. A cheque for this amount was sent to the vendor in January, 1987.
5. During the year, machinery that had a cost basis of $8,000 and on which there was accumulated depreciation of $5,200 was sold for $1,000. No other plant assets were sold during the year.
6. The 12%, 20-year bonds were dated and issued on January 2, 1974. Interest was payable on June 30 and December 31. They were sold originally at 106. These bonds were retired at 101 (net of tax) plus accrued interest on March 31, 1986.
7. The 8%, 40-year bonds were dated January 1, 1986, and were sold on March 31 at 98 plus accrued interest. Interest is payable semiannually on June 30 and December 31. Expense of issuance was $839.

8. Garfield Corporation acquired 80% control in the Subsidiary Company on January 2, 1986, for $100,000. The income statement of the Subsidiary Company for 1986 shows a net income of $8,500.

9. Extraordinary repairs to buildings of $7,200 were charged to Accumulated Depreciation—Building.

Instructions

From the information above, prepare a statement of changes in financial position (cash basis). A work sheet is not necessary, but the principal computations should be supported by schedules or skeleton ledger accounts.

P24-4   The manager of Yummy Cookie Company has reviewed the annual financial statements for the year 1986 and is unable to determine from a reading of the balance sheet the reasons for the changes in working capital during the year. You are given the following balance sheets of Yummy Cookie Company.

	Dec. 31/86	Dec. 31/85	Increase (Decrease)
Land	$ 138,000	$ 150,000	$ (12,000)
Machinery	335,000	200,000	135,000
Tools	40,000	70,000	(30,000)
Bond investment	17,000	15,000	2,000
Inventories	210,000	218,000	(8,000)
Goodwill	-0-	210,000	(210,000)
Buildings	810,000	550,000	260,000
Accounts receivable	178,000	92,000	86,000
Notes receivable—trade	21,000	27,000	(6,000)
Cash in bank	27,000	8,000	19,000
Cash on hand	2,600	1,000	1,600
Unexpired insurance—machinery	700	1,400	(700)
Unamortized bond discount	2,000	2,500	(500)
	$1,781,300	$1,544,900	$ 236,400
Share capital	$ 700,000	$ 400,000	$ 300,000
Bonds payable	160,000	100,000	60,000
Accounts payable	56,000	52,000	4,000
Notes payable—trade	7,000	10,000	(3,000)
Bank loans—short term	4,500	6,800	(2,300)
Accrued interest	9,000	6,000	3,000
Accrued taxes	4,000	3,000	1,000
Allowance for doubtful accounts	4,700	2,300	2,400
Accumulated depreciation	269,000	181,000	88,000
Retained earnings	567,100	783,800	(216,700)
	$1,781,300	$1,544,900	$ 236,400

You are advised that the following transactions took place during the year:

1. The income statement for the year 1986 was:

Sales (net)		$1,271,300
Operating charges:		
Material and supplies	$250,000	
Direct labour	210,000	
Manufacturing overhead	181,500	
Depreciation	120,900	
Selling expenses	245,000	
General expenses	230,000	
Interest expense (net)	15,000	
Unusual items:		
Write-off of goodwill	210,000	
Write-off of land	12,000	
Loss on machinery	1,600	1,476,000
Net loss		$ 204,700

2. A 3% cash dividend was declared and paid on the outstanding shares at January 1, 1986.

3. There were no purchases or sales of tools. The cost of tools used is in depreciation.

4. Old machinery that cost $4,500 was scrapped and written off the books. Accumulated depreciation on such equipment was $2,900.

Instructions

(a) Prepare a statement of changes in financial position using a cash basis approach. Use the indirect approach. Assume that the bank loan—short-term and bank overdraft were related to transactions involving the purchase of materials and supplies. All sales and purchases of inventory are made on account.

(b) Prepare a statement of changes in financial position, using a working capital approach.

P24-5 The balance sheet of Vacuum Pack Company at December 31, 1985, is as follows:

Vacuum Pack Company
BALANCE SHEET
December 31, 1985

Cash			$ 42,000
Receivables			108,000
Inventories			214,000
Prepaid expenses			28,000
Total current assets			392,000
Investments (long-term)			84,000
Land		$ 45,000	
Buildings	$570,000		
Less: Accumulated depreciation	110,000	460,000	
Equipment	385,000		
Less: Accumulated depreciation	180,000	205,000	710,000
Patents			122,000
			$1,308,000
Accounts payable			$ 85,000
Notes payable			120,000
Taxes payable			188,000
Total current liabilities			393,000
Bonds payable			500,000
Preferred shares		$200,000	
Common shares		200,000	
Retained earnings		15,000	415,000
			$1,308,000

Vacuum Pack Company's management predicts the following transactions for the coming year:

Sales (accrual basis)	$4,840,000
Payments for salaries, purchases, interest, taxes, etc. (cash basis)	4,486,000
Decrease in prepaid expenses	5,500
Increase in receivables	110,000
Increase in inventories	35,000
Depreciation:	
Buildings	33,000
Equipment	55,000
Patent amortization	11,000
Increase in accounts payable	22,000
Increase in taxes payable	99,000

Reduction in bonds payable	500,000
Sales of investments (all those held December 31, 1985)	110,000
Issuance of common shares	220,000

Instructions

(a) Prepare a balance sheet as it will appear December 31, 1986, if all the anticipated transactions work out as expected.

(b) Prepare a statement of changes in financial position (cash approach) for 1986, assuming that the expected 1986 transactions are all completed. Use the indirect approach.

(c) Prepare a statement of changes in financial position (working capital approach) for 1986, assuming that the expected 1986 transactions are all completed. Assume that the sale of investments is not an extraordinary item.

(d) Compute cash provided by operations, using the direct approach.

P24-6 The following financial data were furnished to you by Cunico Corporation:

1. A six-month note payable for $55,000 was issued toward the purchase of new equipment.
2. The long-term note payable requires the payment of $16,000 per year plus interest until paid.
3. Treasury shares were sold for $1,000 more than its cost.
4. All dividends were paid by cash.
5. All purchases and sales were on account.
6. The sinking fund will be used to retire the long-term bonds.
7. Equipment with an original cost of $15,000 was sold for $6,000.
8. Selling and General Expenses includes the following expenses:

Expired Insurance	$ 2,000
Building depreciation	7,500
Equipment depreciation	15,500
Bad debts expense	7,000
Interest expense	18,000

Cunico Corporation
COMPARATIVE TRIAL BALANCES
At Beginning and End of Fiscal Year Ended October 31, 1986

	October 31, 1986	Increase	Decrease	November 1, 1985
Cash	$ 228,000	$178,000		$ 50,000
Accounts receivable	146,000	46,000		100,000
Inventories	291,000		$ 9,000	300,000
Unexpired insurance	2,500	500		2,000
Long-term investments at cost	10,000		30,000	40,000
Sinking fund	90,000	10,000		80,000
Land and building	195,000			195,000
Equipment	215,000	125,000		90,000
Discount on bonds payable	8,400		600	9,000
Treasury stock at cost	5,100		4,900	10,000
Cost of goods sold	530,000			
Selling and general expense	296,000			
Income tax	31,000			
Loss on sale of equipment	2,000			
Capital gains tax	3,000			
Total debits	$2,053,000			$876,000

Allowance for doubtful accounts	$ 8,000	$ 3,000		$ 5,000
Accumulated depreciation—building	30,000	7,500		22,500
Accumulated depreciation—equipment	36,000	8,500		27,500
Accounts payable	50,000		10,000	60,000
Notes payable—current	75,000	55,000		20,000
Accrued expenses payable	20,000	5,000		15,000
Taxes payable	33,000	23,000		10,000
Unearned revenue	3,000		6,000	9,000
Note payable—long-term	44,000		16,000	60,000
Bonds payable—long-term	250,000			250,000
Share capital—common	401,000	196,000		205,000
Appropriation for sinking fund	90,000	10,000		80,000
Unappropriated retained earnings	90,000		22,000	112,000
Sales	912,000			
Gain on sale of investments (ordinary)	11,000			
Total credits	$2,053,000			$876,000

Instructions

(a) Prepare schedules computing:
   1. Collections of accounts receivable.
   2. Payments of accounts payable.

(b) Prepare a statement of changes in financial position—cash approach for Cunico Corporation. Use the indirect approach.

(AICPA adapted)

P24-7 Tampa Drilling Company has prepared its financial statements for the year ended December 31, 1985, and for the three months ended March 31, 1986. You have been asked to prepare a statement of changes in financial position on a working capital basis for the three months ended March 31, 1986. The company's balance sheet data at December 31, 1985, and March 31, 1986, as well as its income statement data for the three months ended March 31, 1986, follow. You have previously satisfied yourself as to the correctness of the amounts presented.

	Balance Sheet	
	December 31, 1985	March 31, 1986
Cash	$ 24,400	$ 87,400
Marketable investments	17,600	7,300
Accounts receivable, net	24,620	49,320
Inventory	29,590	48,590
Total current assets	96,210	192,610
Land	41,300	18,700
Building	250,000	250,000
Equipment	-0-	83,000
Accumulated depreciation	(15,000)	(17,750)
Investment in 30%-owned company	60,920	67,100
Other assets	15,100	15,100
Total	$448,530	$608,760
Accounts payable	$ 21,220	$ 16,000
Dividend payable	-0-	9,000
Income taxes payable	-0-	34,946
Total current liabilities	21,220	59,946
Other liabilities	186,000	186,000
Bonds payable	45,000	115,000
Discount on bonds payable	(2,400)	(2,150)
Deferred income taxes	5,610	846

Preferred shares	30,000	-0-
Common shares	80,000	110,000
Dividends declared	-0-	(9,000)
Retained earnings	83,100	148,118
Total	$448,530	$608,760

	Income Statement Data for the Three Months Ended March 31, 1986
Sales	$242,807
Gain on sale of marketable investments	3,400
Equity in earnings of 30%-owned company	6,180
Gain on expropriation of land (extraordinary)	10,400
	$262,787
Cost of sales	$138,407
General and administrative expenses	22,010
Depreciation	2,750
Interest expense	1,150
Income taxes	33,452
	197,769
Net income	$ 65,018

Your discussion with the company's controller and a review of the financial records have revealed the following information:

1. On January 8, 1986, the company sold marketable securities for cash.
2. The company's preferred shares are convertible into common at a rate of one share of preferred for two shares of common.
3. On January 17, 1986, three hectares of land were expropriated. An award of $33,000 in cash was received on March 22, 1986. Purchase of additional land as a replacement is not contemplated by the company. (Treat as a capital gain for tax purposes.)
4. On March 25, 1986, the company purchased equipment for cash.
5. On March 29, 1986, bonds payable were issued by the company at par for cash.
6. The company's tax rate is 40% for regular income and 20% for capital gains.

Instructions

Prepare in good form a statement of changes in financial position, including any supporting schedules needed, on a cash basis for Tampa Drilling Company for the three months ended March 31, 1986.

(AICPA adapted)

25

FINANCIAL REPORTING AND CHANGING PRICES

It has often been said that only two things in life are certain—death and taxes. However, a third could probably now be added—inflation. That is, the value of every currency in the world steadily decreases. For example, during the decade of the 1970s the compound annual inflation rate (the average) was 7.5% in Canada, 6.7% in the United States, 9% in France, 13.2% in Great Britain, 15% in Mexico, 28.3% in Brazil, 117.2% in Argentina, and 163.6% in Chile. Each of these increases in prices has been accompanied by a comparable decrease in the value of that country's currency. Inflation in the 1980s, although not as severe so far for Canada, continues to be substantial for many countries. For example, in 1984, Brazil experienced an inflation rate of over 400% and Argentina over 560%. As another example, Bolivia's inflation rate recently (1985) was estimated to be the highest in the world (116,000%). In this situation, prices go up by the hour. The 1,000 peso bill, the most commonly used, now costs more to print than what it can purchase.[1]

In Canada prior to 1970 it was easy to ignore inflation's impact because the changes from year to year were considered insignificant. With the general price level doubling between 1970 and 1980, and the continued inflation of the 1980s,

[1]*Wall Street Journal*, February 7, 1985, p. 1.

this is no longer the case. In fact, as the diagram on page 1177 illustrates, we have been experiencing a significant decline in the purchasing power of the Canadian dollar over the period 1949-1981 when the rate of inflation is compounded. The effects of this phenomenon are substantial. Many companies are experiencing liquidity problems, even though they are reporting record net income figures. The problem is that they lack the necessary funds to replace their inventories and productive capacity at increased prices.

A difficult, exciting, and extensive experimental and educational process is currently taking place. Already, substantial experimentation has occurred, and some consensus is developing on changing price information. Adjusting for price changes will likely continue to be much debated. Preparers of financial statements and users alike must grasp what the new information is intended to portray. Such is the purpose of this chapter.

ALTERNATIVE FINANCIAL REPORTING APPROACHES

As indicated in Chapter 2, a long-standing principle of accounting holds that transactions should be recorded at historical cost. However, many accountants are unhappy with the present reporting model, noting that historical cost financial statements have severe limitations. Criticism is especially strong when one perceives the effects of double-digit inflation in Canada in the late 1970s. At such times cost is no longer adequate because the cost figures of prior years are not comparable to current cost amounts. To meet these criticisms, a number of different solutions have been proposed. Three models that have been discussed extensively are:

1. **Constant Dollar Accounting**. Change the measuring unit but retain the historical cost reporting model.
2. **Current Cost Accounting**. Retain the measuring unit but depart from the historical cost reporting model.
3. **Current Cost/Constant Dollar Accounting**. Change the measuring unit and depart from the historical cost reporting model.

Constant Dollar Accounting (General Price-Level Model)   A dollar is valued in terms of its ability to purchase "a number of items in general," or more appropriately, its "purchasing power." If a dollar today cannot buy the same bundle of goods that a dollar bought a number of years ago, then inflation has occurred. This phenomenon has great relevance to accountants because we assume that our measuring unit (the dollar) is stable; unfortunately, the truth is that our measuring unit changes and, as it changes, distortions develop.

Those who advocate the adjustment of accounting data for changes in the purchasing power of the dollar, referred to as **constant dollar accounting** or **general price-level accounting,** ask the question: Is it possible to add 1963 dollars, 1975 dollars, and 1983 dollars and arrive at any meaningful sum because of the differences in their purchasing power? Adding 20,000 1963 dollars with 30,000 1975 dollars and 40,000 1983 dollars may total 90,000 dollars, but the sum may have no more economic significance than the addition of 20,000 Canadian dollars to 30,000 French francs and 40,000 German marks for a total of 90,000 monetary units. The monetary units are just not equivalent.

The **objective of constant dollar accounting**, therefore, is to maintain capital in terms of constant purchasing power as measured by a general index of the level of

INFLATION IN CANADA
(Based on Consumer Price Index)

Year	Consumer Price Index 1981 = 100[a]	Purchasing Power of Dollar 1984 = $1.00	Rate of Inflation[b]
1960	31.3	3.91	1.0
1961	31.6	3.87	1.0
1962	32.0	3.82	1.3
1963	32.6	3.75	1.9
1964	33.2	3.68	1.8
1965	34.0	3.60	2.4
1966	35.2	3.47	3.5
1967	36.5	3.35	3.7
1968	38.0	3.22	4.1
1969	39.7	3.08	4.5
1970	41.0	2.98	3.3
1971	42.2	2.90	2.9
1972	44.2	2.77	4.7
1973	47.6	2.57	7.7
1974	52.8	2.32	10.9
1975	58.5	2.09	10.8
1976	62.9	1.94	7.5
1977	67.9	1.80	7.9
1978	73.9	1.65	8.8
1979	80.7	1.52	9.2
1980	88.9	1.38	10.2
1981	100.0	1.22	12.5
1982	110.8	1.10	10.8
1983	117.2	1.04	5.8
1984	122.3	1.00	4.4

[a]Source: Statistics Canada

[b]Rate of Inflation $= \dfrac{CPI_t - CPI_{t-1}}{CPI_{t-1}}$

DECLINE IN THE PURCHASING POWER
OF THE DOLLAR
(Based on Consumer Price Index)

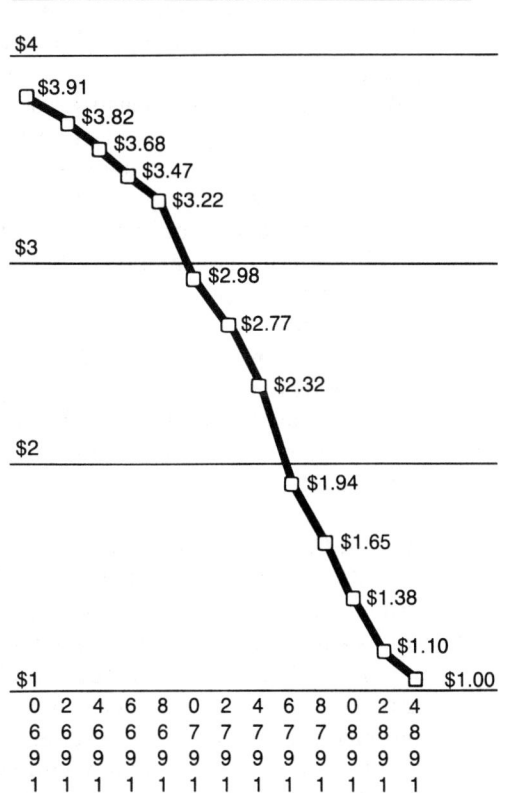

prices. This concept implies that business must maintain at a constant level its ability to purchase a wide variety of goods and services throughout the economy. In the operation of a business, a certain amount of purchasing power is given up through the process of acquiring, producing, and selling goods over a period of time. The investors in and the managers of the business need to know whether the purchasing power sacrificed is being restored and maintained.

The information provided by constant dollar accounting is of limited value since it does not reflect changes in prices due to such factors as changes in demand, technological innovations, and so on. The profession appears to be moving away from previous preferences for this method and towards various measures of current values. The discussion of constant dollar accounting in this chapter is presented to help readers understand the principle of indexing financial statement values, and to describe the source of certain gains and losses resulting from inflation.

Current Cost Accounting   A second approach, called current cost accounting, abandons historical cost as a basis for financial statements and shifts to some measure of current cost. Proponents of this approach argue that the problem is not with the unit of measure but rather with the historical cost model.

Their position is that users of financial statements are primarily interested in current values, rather than what costs were incurred at some point in the past. Their argument is based on the notion of economic asset value, which conceptually is the present value of the future net receipts from the particular asset in question.

A popular means to measure the change in the cost of specific assets is current cost. Current cost is the cost of replacing the identical asset owned; that is, one of the same age and of the same operating capacity. Current cost may be approximated in a variety of ways but often is computed by applying a specific price index to the historical cost or book value of assets. Unlike the constant dollar approach, which is simply a restatement of historical dollars into constant purchasing power, the current cost approach changes the basis of measurement from historical cost to current value.

The **objective of current cost accounting** is to maintain capital in terms of operating capacity or the ability to provide goods and services at the same level at the end of a period as the beginning. This approach assumes that all resources consumed or sold will be replaced with resources preforming a similar function at the same or better level of production.

Current Cost/Constant Dollar Accounting   A third group contends that both the unit of measurement and the historical cost model should be changed. As two writers noted in discussing constant dollar accounting: "We feel that the modification is a necessary one, but hope that the doctor, having cured the hangnail, does not fail to diagnose the pneumonia."[2] Advocates of this approach argue that the unit of measurement must be standardized (or else we are using "a rubber ruler" in measuring dollars), and that after standardization some form of current cost accounting should be employed. Only under this combined approach will the effects of real changes in enterprise wealth and earning power be determined.[3]

Simplified Example of the Various Methods   To illustrate the above concepts more fully, assume that Hardent Ltd. purchased land at the beginning of 1986 at a cost of $10,000. At the end of 1986, the value of the land increased to $18,000. In addition, during 1986, the general price level rose 10%. Using **historical cost**, the balance sheet and income statement effects of these events are reported for 1986 as follows:

Balance Sheet	Income Statement
Land $10,000	No effect

The land is reported at its original cost on the balance sheet. No changes are reported even though the value of the land and the general price level have increased. No income effect is recorded because the land was not sold.

[2]Edgar O. Edwards and Philip W. Bell, *The Theory and Measurement of Business Income* (Berkeley: University of California Press, 1961), p. 16.

[3]For discussion that supports this approach, see Robert R. Sterling, "Relevant Financial Reporting in a Period of Changing Prices," *Journal of Accountancy* (February, 1975).

Under **constant dollar accounting** the balance sheet and income statement effects of these events are reported for 1986 as follows:

Balance Sheet	Income Statement
Land $11,000	No effect

In the constant dollar situation the historical cost of the asset is simply restated to $11,000 ($10,000 × 1.10) because the purchasing power of the dollar has changed. Net income is not affected because constant dollar accounting is simply a restatement of historical cost numbers. Thus, because the land was not sold, no income is recognized.

Under **current cost** the balance sheet and income statement effects of these events are reported for 1986 as follows:

Balance Sheet	Income Statement
Land $18,000	Net income effect $8,000

In a current cost system the valuation model has changed. As a result, the land is now reported at its current cost, or $18,000. Given that the land has increased $8,000 while being owned, the company experiences a holding gain, which normally is reported as part of income.

Under a **combined current cost/constant dollar system** the balance sheet and income statement effects of these events are reported for 1986 as follows:

Balance Sheet	Income Statement
Land $18,000	Net income effect $7,000

In this case, the land is stated at current cost in end-of-year dollars on the balance sheet. Although a nominal holding gain of $8,000 ($18,000 − $10,000) has occurred, in real terms Hardent Inc. has experienced an increase of only $7,000 as computed below:

Current cost (end of period)	$18,000
Historical cost (adjusted to constant dollars) $10,000 × 1.10	11,000
Holding gain, net of inflation	$ 7,000

Thus, the income effect on a current cost/constant dollar basis is $7,000.[4]

Each of these concepts will be discussed in more detail in this chapter.

[4]As indicated later, many question whether this holding gain is reported as part of income or as an adjustment to capital. Given an emphasis upon comprehensive income, we believe that this amount would be reported as part of this income number, although still not as a part of net income as we define it today.

PROFESSIONAL PRONOUNCEMENTS

The profession has been reluctant to incorporate changing price information in financial statements because the effects of reporting on a basis other than historical cost are not considered significant enough to justify the additional expenditures. However, in the mid-to-late 1970s Canada experienced unprecedented increases in the inflation rate. As a result, the profession came under extreme pressure to disclose some type of changing price information. In 1982 the CICA issued *Handbook*, Section 4510, which required certain large, publicly held enterprises to disclose supplementary information on both a current cost and a current cost/ constant dollar basis. The AcSC noted that this requirement for disclosure of changing price information on two different bases was intended to encourage experimentation. When the results of using various methods in reporting the effects of changing prices are known, the Committee will make modifications to Section 4510.

ORGANIZATION OF THIS CHAPTER

To help you in understanding accounting for changing prices, this chapter is divided into three main sections as follows:

Constant Dollar Accounting—The preparation of comprehensive financial statements on a constant dollar basis.

Current Cost Accounting—The preparation of comprehensive financial statements on a current cost basis.

CICA Handbook, **Section 4510, Accounting**—Comprehensive financial statements, adjusted for changing prices, are not required; however, a partial restatement on a current cost basis containing information about the effects of changes in the general level of prices is mandated. These supplementary schedules and disclosures that satisfy this requirement are illustrated.

We believe it is important that the student master each of these three topics in order to understand accounting for changing prices. In addition, we have provided in the appendix to this chapter a detailed explanation and illustration of accounting for changing prices on a current cost/constant dollar basis.

CONSTANT DOLLAR ACCOUNTING

As indicated earlier, in addition to being a medium of exchange, the dollar has a "real" value that is determined by the amount of goods and services for which it can be exchanged. **This real value is commonly called purchasing power.** As the economy experiences periods of inflation (rising price levels) or deflation (declining price levels), the amount of goods and services for which a dollar can be exchanged changes; that is, the purchasing power of the dollar changes over time.

Fortunately, the need to measure purchasing power is neither new nor restricted to accounting. Statistics Canada, an agency of the Canadian government, like those of many foreign countries, publishes indices designed to measure changes in the general price level. When such indices provide acceptable measures of general price-level changes, they can be used in accounting to adjust historical costs for changes in general purchasing power.

Measuring General Price-Level Changes

A price index is a weighted-average relation between money and a given set of goods and services. Constructing a price index that measures the change in purchasing power of the dollar is a complex problem; it involves the exercise of judgement in accumulating and appraising data.

It is fair to say, however, that the general indices now available are reasonably useful to most persons and business managers as gauges of the change in the purchasing power of the dollar. The more widely used indices of price change that are computed regularly by Statistics Canada are:

1. The Gross National Expenditure Implicit Price Index.
2. The Consumer Price Index.
3. The Wholesale Price Index.

The Consumer Price Index (CPI) reflects the average change in the retail prices of a fairly broad but select "basket" of consumer goods. It has been the most popular index because it is reported monthly by Statistics Canada.

Restatement in Common Dollars

The procedure for restating the dollars of varying purchasing power reported in historical cost financial statements into dollars of current purchasing power is mathematically a simple, although sometimes time-consuming, process. The restatement (frequently called translation or conversion) is accomplished by multiplying the amount to be restated by a fraction, the numerator of which is the index for current prices and the denominator of which is the index for prices that prevailed at the date related to the amount being restated. For example, the cost of an asset acquired for $1,000 on June 30, 1976, is restated in terms of December 31, 1986, dollars as follows:

$$\frac{1986 \text{ index}}{1976 \text{ index}} \times \$1,000 = \text{cost of asset in terms of 1986 dollars}$$

Technically, the index at date of acquisition, June 30, 1976, should be used for the denominator. The average index for June, 1976, may be used because daily price-level indices are not available. The average annual index may be used with satisfactory results in the absence of rampant inflation or deflation and, particularly, in the initial restatement when price-level adjustments are being made for the first time, a large number of amounts are to be adjusted, and the amounts to be restated are several years removed.

To illustrate further the method of restating historical dollars to current dollars, assume the facts presented below relative to acquired assets and the preparation of financial statements in 1986:

Year	Acquisition Cost	Consumer Price Index
1959	$10,000	87
1967	$10,000	99
1974	$10,000	140
1986	$10,000	335 (Estimated)

To express all of these acquisition costs in terms of one year's prices, say 1986, the restatement process is:

1959	$10,000 × 335/87	$38,505.75
1967	10,000 × 335/99	33,838.38
1974	10,000 × 335/140	23,928.57
1986	10,000 × 335/335	10,000.00
Total in terms of 1986 dollars		$106,272.70

Thus, the total acquisition cost of the assets, $40,000, is modified on a constant dollar basis to $106,272.70 in terms of 1986 prices.

Monetary and Nonmonetary Classifications

In preparing constant dollar financial statements, it is essential to distinguish between (1) the amounts that are by their nature already stated in current dollars and, therefore, require no restatement, and (2) the amounts that require restatement in order to be stated in terms of current dollars. The former are classified as **monetary items,** the latter as **nonmonetary items.**

Monetary assets include cash, contractual claims to a fixed amount of cash in the future, such as accounts and notes receivable, and investments that pay a fixed amount of interest or dividends and will be repaid at a fixed amount in the future (the date of repayment, however, need not be specified—as for an investment in preferred shares). **Monetary liabilities** include accounts and notes payable, such accruals as wages and interest payable, and long-term obligations payable in a fixed sum (including preferred shareholders' equity).

All assets and liabilities not classified as monetary items are classified as "nonmonetary" for constant dollar accounting purposes. **Nonmonetary assets** are the items whose prices in terms of the monetary unit may change over time: for example, inventories, investments in common shares, property, plant, and equipment, and deferred charges that represent costs expended in the past. **Nonmonetary liabilities** are obligations to provide given amounts of goods and services or an equivalent amount of purchasing power (even though the payment may be in the form of cash): for example, advances received on sales contracts, liabilities for rent collected in advance, and certain deferred credits.

The importance of distinguishing between monetary and nonmonetary items in reporting the impact of changing price levels is demonstrated by Raymond J. Chambers:

> The importance of the distinction lies in the fact that monetary assets and nonmonetary assets are subject to quite different risks. Holdings of monetary assets are subject to the risk of changes in the purchasing power of money. If for whatever reasons the general level of prices rises, the purchasing power of a unit of money tends to fall; a greater number of units is required to buy a given good. Clearly, then, nonmonetary assets are subject to the same influences, but in the opposite direction. If the price level is expected to rise, it is clearly preferable to hold goods and to incur fixed obligations than it is to hold monetary assets.[5]

[5]Raymond J. Chambers, *Accounting, Evaluation and Economic Behavior* (Englewood Cliffs, N.J.: Prentice-Hall, 1966), p. 196.

A list of the more common monetary and nonmonetary items is presented below. Note that inventories, property, plant, and equipment, and intangibles are nonmonetary in nature. Conversely, most liabilities are monetary because they involve a fixed claim to pay cash, except for liabilities that are liquidated through the exchange of goods or services. Shareholders' equity accounts, such as common shares and contributed surplus, are nonmonetary in nature. Retained earnings is computed separately each period by adding constant dollar net income less any dividends to the restated beginning balance of retained earnings.

CLASSIFICATION OF MONETARY AND NONMONETARY ITEMS[a]

Monetary Items:

Assets

Cash on hand and demand bank deposits
Time deposits
Preferred shares (nonconvertible and nonparticipating)
Bonds (other than convertible)
Accounts and notes receivable
Allowance for doubtful accounts
Loans to employees
Long-term receivables
Refundable deposits
Advances to unconsolidated subsidiaries
Cash surrender value of life insurance
Advances to suppliers (not on a fixed price contract)

Liabilities

Accounts and notes payable
Accrued expenses payable
Cash dividends payable
Advances from customers (not on a fixed price contract)
Accrued losses in firm purchase commitments
Refundable deposits
Bonds payable and long-tern debt
Unamortized premium or discount on bonds or notes payable
Convertible bonds payable

Nonmonetary Items:

Assets

Inventory (other than inventories used on contracts)
Investment in common shares in most situations
Property, plant, and equipment
Accumulated depreciation of property, plant, and equipment
Purchase commitments (portion paid on fixed price contracts)
Patents, trademarks, licences, and formulas
Goodwill
Deferred property acquisition costs
Other intangible assets and deferred charges

Liabilities

Sales commitments (portion collected on fixed price contracts)
Obligations under warranties
Deferred investment tax credit

Items Requiring Individual Analysis:

Assets

Investment in preferred shares (convertible or participating) and convertible bonds:

If the market values the security primarily as a bond, it is monetary; if it values the security primarily as a stock, it is nonmonetary.

Inventories:

If the future cash receipts will not vary because of future changes in prices, they are monetary. Goods priced at market upon delivery are nonmonetary.

Prepaid insurance, advertising, rents, and other prepayments:

Claims to future services are nonmonetary. Prepayments that are deposits, advance payments, or receivables are monetary because the prepayment does not obtain a given quantity of future services but rather is a fixed money offset.

Pension, sinking, and other funds under enterprise control:

The specific assets in the fund should be classified as monetary or nonmonetary.

Liabilities
Accrued vacation pay:

If it is paid at the wage rates as of the vacation dates and if those rates may vary, it is nonmonetary. If they do not vary, then it is monetary.

Deferred revenue:

Nonmonetary if an obligation to furnish goods or services is involved.

Accrued pension obligations:

Fixed amounts payable to a fund are monetary; all other amounts are nonmonetary.

Special Items

Deferred income tax charges and credits:

Deferred income tax charges and credits are considered nonmonetary by the CICA.

Preferred shares (shareholders' equity):

If, as is commonly the case, the preferred shareholders' equity is fixed in terms of the number of dollars to be paid in liquidation, then the aggregate par or stated value of the preferred shares may be treated (from the viewpoint of common shareholders' equity) as a monetary item.

[a]Adapted from "Financial Reporting and Changing Prices," *Statement of Financial Accounting Standards No. 33* (Stamford, Conn.: FASB, 1979).

Effects of Holding Monetary and Nonmonetary Items

Holders of money lose general purchasing power during inflation because a given amount of money buys progressively fewer goods and services. This same loss in purchasing power occurs when any "monetary" asset is held during a period of inflation. For instance, in the case of accounts or notes receivable, or any claim to a fixed amount of money, the amount of money expected to be received represents a diminishing amount of general purchasing power simply as a result of inflation. Similarly, accounts, notes, and bonds payable, or any fixed amount of money payable in the future becomes less burdensome during inflation because they are payable in dollars of reduced general purchasing power.

The resulting gains and losses have been variously described as "inflation gains or losses," "monetary gains or losses," "purchasing power gains and losses," and "general price-level gains or losses." The CICA in *Handbook*, Section 4510, calls them "**general purchasing power gain or loss on net monetary items**."[6] Whatever their name, these explicit measurements of the gains and losses resulting from monetary assets and liabilities are the unique product of constant dollar adjustments of historical amounts.

To illustrate the effects of holding a monetary asset during a period of inflation, assume that you have the following balance sheet at the beginning of the period.

Balance Sheet (Beginning of Period)			
Cash	$100	Owners' equity	$100

[6]*CICA Handbook*, Section 4510, par. 45.

If the general price level doubles during the year, and no transactions take place, then to be in the same economic position you should have the balance sheet shown below at the end of the year.

Balance Sheet (End of Period)			
Cash	$200	Owners' equity	$200

However, the fact is that you have only $100 and have experienced a purchasing power loss of $100 in holding monetary items in a period of inflation. Your balance sheet would be presented as follows on a constant dollar basis.

Balance Sheet (End of Period)			
Cash	$100	Owners' equity	$200
		Retained earnings	(100)
			$100

In summary, you have lost $100 in end-of-year dollars.

Nonmonetary items, on the other hand, do not represent a fixed claim to receive or pay cash. If, for example, the price level doubles, and you hold inventory, the cost of the inventory should be adjusted because, like other nonmonetary items, it retains its purchasing power. To illustrate the effects of holding a nonmonetary asset during a period of inflation, assume that you have the following balance sheet at the beginning of the period.

Balance Sheet (Beginning of Period)			
Inventory	$100	Owners' equity	$100

If the price level doubles and the inventory was purchased at the beginning of the period, then your balance sheet in constant dollars is as follows.

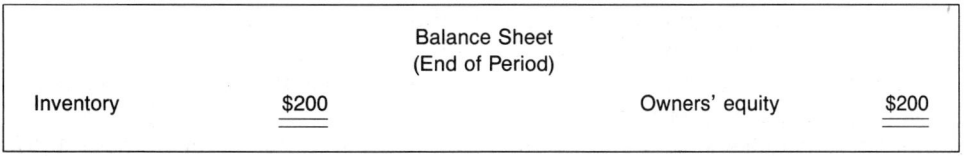

Balance Sheet (End of Period)			
Inventory	$200	Owners' equity	$200

In summary, monetary assets and liabilities are generally stated in dollars of current purchasing power in the historical dollar balance sheet. The fact that the end-of-the-year amounts are the same in historical dollars as in constant dollar statements does not obscure the fact, however, that purchasing power gains or losses result from holding them during a period of general price-level change. Nonmonetary items are reported at different amounts in the constant dollar statements than they are in the historical cost statements, assuming a change in the general price level.

Selection of a Constant Dollar Index

The discussion on constant dollar accounting to this point has implied the use of an index that presents information in end-of-year dollars. The use of the end-of-the-year index has the advantage that all elements of the financial statements are reported in terms of current end-of-year dollars. In addition, monetary assets and liabilities reported for the current year on the balance sheet do not need adjustment because they are already stated in end-of-the-year dollars.

Instead of using an index that reports in end-of-year dollars, many professionals advocate the use of an average index. An average index restates the historical cost numbers to average-for-the-year prices instead of end-of-the-year prices. One advantage of this approach is that many items on the income statement do not need adjustment because they are earned or incurred evenly throughout the year. For example, sales revenue and most expenses often can be considered to be earned or incurred evenly throughout the period. As a result these elements need not be adjusted when converting from a historical cost to a constant dollar system. Ease of computation is therefore a real advantage of using an average-for-the-year index instead of an end-of-year index.

A disadvantage of the average-for-the-year approach is that monetary items that are stated in end-of-year dollars must be converted back to average-for-the-year dollars. To many, this conversion causes confusion because a monetary item, such as cash, is restated to average-for-the-year dollars, and therefore is not reported at the same amount as the historical cost balance at the year end.

The CICA has sanctioned the use of either the average or year-end index in preparing the supplementary information required under Section 4510. In order to simplify the discussion, we will illustrate the use of the end-of-the-year index in making computations.

Constant Dollar Accounting—Lia Corporation

When financial statements are being adjusted to constant dollars for the first time, it is necessary to analyze completely the amounts in each account to determine their year of origin. The initial adjustment process involves considerably more work than subsequent adjustments. When comparative financial statements are being adjusted, the previous period's amounts must be restated in terms of the price level at the latest statement date. If adjusted statements have been prepared for the previous year, the restatement of that year can be accomplished by multiplying each amount in the previous year's adjusted statements by the ratio of the current index to the index of the immediately preceding year.

To illustrate the procedures peculiar to constant dollar accounting, the accounts of Lia Corporation are presented on a historical cost basis in the form of abbreviated comparative balance sheets and an intervening income statement on page 1187 (Exhibit 1). Price-level changes are magnified to illustrate their effects. Only the first six items of additional information have relevance in computing a constant dollar set of financial statements. Assume that Lia Corporation started business on January 1, 1986.

Adjustment of Balance Sheet Items

Monetary Items   The amounts of the monetary items at the end of the year December 31, 1986, do not need to be restated because they are reported in end-of-year

Exhibit 1
Lia Corporation
COMPARATIVE BALANCE SHEETS
As of January 1, 1986, and December 31, 1986
(Historical Cost Basis)

	January 1, 1986	December 31, 1986
Cash, receivables, and other monetary assets	$ 200,000	$ 325,000
Inventories	250,000	300,000
Equipment (net)	150,000	140,000
Land	450,000	450,000
Total assets	$1,050,000	$1,215,000
Current liabilities (all monetary)	$ 100,000	$ 200,000
Long-term liabilities (all monetary)	650,000	650,000
Total liabilities	750,000	850,000
Share capital	300,000	300,000
Retained earnings	-0-	65,000
Total shareholders' equity	300,000	365,000
Total liabilities and shareholders' equity	$1,050,000	$1,215,000

Lia Corporation
STATEMENT OF INCOME AND RETAINED EARNINGS
For the Year Ended December 31, 1986
(Historical Cost Basis)

Sales		$800,000
Cost of goods sold:		
Inventory, January 1, 1986	$250,000	
Purchases	520,000	
Goods available for sale	770,000	
Inventory, December 31, 1986	300,000	470,000
Gross profit		330,000
Selling and administrative expenses		170,000
Depreciation expense		10,000
Income before income taxes		150,000
Income taxes		75,000
Net income		75,000
Retained earnings, January 1, 1986		-0-
		75,000
Cash dividends		(10,000)
Retained earnings, December 31, 1986		$ 65,000

Additional related information:

Constant Dollar Information

1. The following CPI-U index numbers are assumed for use in the illustration:

Jan. 1/86	Opening of the business	100
1986	Average	160
Dec. 31/86	Year end	200

2. The inventory is priced on a first-in, first-out (FIFO) basis. The beginning inventory was purchased at the opening of the business. The ending inventory was acquired in November and December at a price level of 180.
3. Acquisition of the equipment and land took place at the opening of the business.

4. The equipment has a useful life of 15 years and is depreciated on a straight-line basis with no salvage value.
5. All revenue and expenses, except for that portion of the cost of goods sold represented by the beginning inventory, are earned or incurred evenly throughout the year.
6. Dividends are declared and paid at the end of the year.

Current Cost Information

7. Cost of goods sold on a current cost basis at different dates during the year is $760,000 (assume incurred evenly). Current cost of the inventory at the end of 1986 is $500,000.
8. Current cost of the equipment at the end of 1986 excluding accumulated depreciation is $180,000. Net current cost is $168,000.
9. Current cost of the land at the end of 1986 is $900,000.
10. Historical cost and current cost are identical for the inventory, equipment, and land at the beginning of the year Jan. 1, 1986.
11. Selling and administrative expenses and income taxes are the same on both a historical and current cost basis.

dollars. The amounts at the beginning of the period, however, must be restated in order to express them in terms of purchasing power at the end of the year. These computations are shown below.

Cash, receivables, and other monetary assets	
Dec. 31, 1986 $325,000 × 200/200	$ 325,000
Jan. 1, 1986 $200,000 × 200/100	$ 400,000
Current liabilities (all monetary)	
Dec. 31, 1986 $200,000 × 200/200	$ 200,000
Jan. 1, 1986 $100,000 × 200/100	$ 200,000
Long-term liabilities (all monetary)	
Dec. 31, 1986 $650,000 × 200/200	$ 650,000
Jan. 1, 1986 $650,000 × 200/100	$1,300,000

The balances of the monetary items at December 31, 1986, are stated in terms of the price level on December 31, 1986, and remain the same. The cash, receivables, and other monetary items have greater purchasing power on January 1, 1986, than they have on December 31, 1986. Therefore, the January 1, 1986, balances must be increased to December 31, 1986, dollars to restate the beginning balances in end-of-year dollars. The current and long-term liabilities at January 1, 1986, must also be converted to December 31, 1986, dollars.

Inventories Inventories can present a special problem because restatement in terms of the current price level requires knowledge of the dates of acquisition and their historical cost. If the specific identification method is used, the identified number of historical dollars is multiplied by a fraction, the numerator of which is the current index and the denominator of which is the index for the date of acquisition. Typically, however, a FIFO, LIFO, or average cost assumption is used. The price-level restatement should be consistent with that assumption. In this case it is assumed that the FIFO method is applied and that the year-end inventory consists of goods acquired during the last two months at an average index of 180 for those months:

Dec. 31, 1986	Inventories—ending $300,000 × 200/180	$333,333
Jan. 1, 1986	Inventories—beginning $250,000 × 200/100	$500,000

Equipment   The equipment would be restated in end-of-year dollars as follows:

Dec. 31, 1986	Equipment (net)—$140,000 × 200/100	$280,000
Jan. 1, 1986	Equipment (net)—$150,000 × 200/100	$300,000

Land   The restatement of the land in end-of-year dollars is the same on both balance sheets:

Dec. 31, 1986	Land—$450,000 × 200/100	$900,000
Jan. 1, 1986	Land—$450,000 × 200/100	$900,000

The computations above illustrate that, while price-level restatements for equipment and land are straightforward, the initial restatement process can be tedious when a large number of items and acquisition dates is involved.

Common Shares and Retained Earnings   The common shares account balances at December 31, 1986, and at January 1, 1986, are converted to end-of-year dollars as follows:

Dec. 31, 1986	Common shares—$300,000 × 200/100	$600,000
Jan. 1, 1986	Common shares—$300,000 × 200/100	$600,000

Retained earnings is computed as the amount needed to balance the balance sheet. The following balances are reported:

Dec. 31, 1986	Retained earnings	$388,333
Jan. 1, 1986	Retained earnings	-0-

Note that the amount of retained earnings at December 31, 1986, should be reconcilable to the amount of restated income for the year 1986 taking into consideration dividends paid during the year (see Exhibit 2, page 1193).

In preparing constant dollar financial statements, common shares, contributed surplus, and retained earnings may all be viewed as shareholders' equity and treated as one residual, inseparable sum. Price-level adjusted common shareholders' equity may then be measured as the difference between (1) total **restated** assets and (2) total **restated** liabilities plus preferred shareholders' equity (if any):

Dec. 31, 1986	Common shareholders' equity—$1,838,333 (assets) – $850,000 (liabilities) =	$988,333
Jan. 1, 1986	Common shareholders' equity—$2,100,000 (assets) – $1,500,000 (liabilities) =	$600,000

The abbreviated comparative balance sheet of Lia Corporation prepared on a comprehensive constant dollar basis is presented on page 1193 (Exhibit 2).

Adjustment of Combined Income and Retained Earnings Statement Items

Sales   Because sales were spread evenly over the year, the average index for 1986 may be used to restate sales to end-of-year dollars:

$$\$800,000 \times 200/160 = \$1,000,000$$

If sales (or other operating items) are seasonal or if the price-level changes are not reasonably constant during the year, quarterly sales (or other operating items) are restated using quarterly indices.

Cost of Goods Sold   The cost of goods sold can be restated in December 31, 1986, dollars as follows (purchases are assumed to be made evenly over the year and therefore the average index for 1986 is used):

Beginning inventory	$250,000 × 200/100 =	$ 500,000
Purchases	520,000 × 200/160 =	650,000
Goods available for sale	770,000	1,150,000
Ending inventory	300,000 × 200/180 =	333,333
Cost of goods sold	$470,000	$ 816,667

Selling and Administrative Expenses   Assuming that these expenses were incurred evenly throughout the period, they would be restated as follows:

$$\$170,000 \times 200/160 = \$212,500$$

Depreciation Expense   Since the equipment was purchased at the beginning of the year, depreciation expense would be restated to end-of-year dollars as follows:

$$\$10,000 \times 200/100 = \$20,000$$

Income Taxes   Assuming that these expenses were incurred evenly throughout the period, they would be restated as follows:

$$\$75,000 \times 200/160 = \$93,750$$

Cash Dividends   Cash dividends were paid to common shareholders at the end of the year when the index was 200. No adjustment is necessary, as the following computation illustrates:

$$\$10,000 \times 200/200 = \$10,000$$

Purchasing Power Gain or Loss

Analyzing the effects of price-level changes on monetary items reveals management's effectiveness in coping with such changes. The computation of the purchasing power gain or loss on net monetary items involves preparing a detailed **statement of sources and uses of monetary items** for the period under consideration, restated item by item. The statement of sources and uses of net monetary items reports the beginning balance of net monetary items, the additions to net monetary items during the period, the deductions to net monetary items during the period, and the ending balance of net monetary items.

As indicated in the schedule below, at the beginning of the period monetary liabilities exceeded monetary assets by $550,000. The only source of monetary assets during the period was sales of $800,000, whereas there were numerous uses of monetary assets totalling $775,000 during the period. As a result, monetary liabilities exceeded monetary assets at the end of the period by $525,000.

Lia Corporation
COMPUTATION OF PURCHASING POWER GAIN OR LOSS—1986
(End-of-Year Dollars)

		1986 Historical	Restatement Ratio	Restated to Dec. 31/86 Dollars
Net monetary items, historical —Jan. 1/86:				
Cash, receivables, and other monetary assets	$ 200,000			
Current liabilities (all monetary)	(100,000)			
Long-term liabilities (all monetary)	(650,000)	$(550,000)	× 200/100	$(1,100,000)
Add (sources of monetary items):				
Sales		800,000	× 200/160	1,000,000
Sub-total		250,000		(100,000)
Deduct (uses of monetary items):				
Purchases		520,000	× 200/160	650,000
Selling and administrative expenses		170,000	× 200/160	212,500
Income taxes		75,000	× 200/160	93,750
Cash dividends		10,000	× 200/200	10,000
Total uses		775,000		966,250
Net monetary items, historical—Dec. 31/86:				
Cash, receivables, and other monetary assets	$ 325,000			
Current liabilities (all monetary)	(200,000)			
Long-term liabilities (all monetary)	(650,000)	$(525,000)		
Net monetary items restated				(1,066,250)
Net monetary income, historical		$(525,000)	× 200/200	(525,000)
Purchasing power gain on net monetary items				$ 541,250

After the statement of sources and uses of monetary items is prepared on a historical cost basis, each of the components of this statement (beginning balance, additions, and subtractions) is restated in year-end dollars. The restated beginning balance plus additions and less deductions is then the ending balance of net monetary items in year-end dollars. In Lia Corporation's case, this number is $1,066,250. This $1,066,250 balance is then compared to the actual historical cost ending balance of net monetary items in year-end dollars. The historical cost balance in year-end dollars shows an excess of monetary liabilities over monetary assets of $525,000. As a result, Lia Corporation reports a purchasing power gain on net monetary items of $541,250. This should be expected because whenever the price level increases and a company is holding an excess of monetary liabilities over monetary assets, it should experience a gain in purchasing power. The statement of income and retained earnings (along with comparative balance sheets) on a constant dollar basis is illustrated on page 1193 (Exhibit 2).

Advantages and Disadvantages of Constant Dollar Accounting

Constant dollar financial statements have been lauded widely by many as a means of overcoming reporting problems during perids of inflation or deflation. The following arguments have been submitted in support of preparing such statements:

1. Constant dollar accounting provides management with an **objectively** determined quantification of the impact of inflation on its business operations.
2. Constant dollar accounting eliminates the effects of inflation from financial information by requiring each enterprise to follow the same objective procedure and use the same price-level index, thereby **preserving comparability of financial statements between firms.**
3. Constant dollar accounting **enhances comparability between the financial statements of a single firm** by eliminating differences due to price-level changes and thereby improves trend analysis.
4. Constant dollar accounting eliminates the effects of price-level changes without having to develop a new structure of accounting; in other words, it **preserves the historical cost-based accounting system** that is currently used and understood.
5. Constant dollar accounting **eliminates the necessity of and attraction to the "piecemeal" approaches** used in combatting the effects of inflation on financial statements; namely, LIFO inventory costing and accelerated depreciation of property, plant, and equipment.

In spite of widespread publicity, discussion, and authoritative support both inside and outside the accounting profession, the preparation and public issuance of constant dollar financial statements up to this point have been negligible, probably because of the following disadvantages said to be associated with constant dollar financial statements.

1. The additional **cost** of preparing constant dollar statements is not offset by the benefit of receiving sufficient relevant information.
2. Constant dollar financial statements will cause **confusion** and be misunderstood by users.
3. Restating the "value" of nonmonetary items at historical cost adjusted for general price-level changes **is no more meaningful than historical cost alone;** that is, it suffers all the shortcomings of the historical cost method.
4. The reported purchasing power gain from monetary items is **misleading** because it does not necessarily represent successful management or provide funds for dividends, plant expansion, or other purposes.

Exhibit 2
Lia Corporation
COMPARATIVE BALANCE SHEETS
As of January 1, 1986, and December 31, 1986
(Constant Dollar Basis)

	January 1, 1986	December 31, 1986
Cash, receivables, and other monetary assets	$ 400,000	$ 325,000
Inventories	500,000	333,333
Equipment (net)	300,000	280,000
Land	900,000	900,000
Total assets	$2,100,000	$1,838,333
Current liabilities (all monetary)	$ 200,000	$ 200,000
Long-term liabilities (all monetary)	1,300,000	650,000
Total liabilities	1,500,000	850,000
Share capital	600,000	600,000
Retained earnings	-0-	388,333
Total shareholders' equity	600,000	988,333
Total liabilities and shareholders' equity	$2,100,000	$1,838,333

Lia Corporation
STATEMENT OF INCOME AND RETAINED EARNINGS
For the Year Ended December 31, 1986
(Constant Dollar Basis)

Sales		$1,000,000
Cost of goods sold		
Inventory, January 1, 1986	$ 500,000	
Purchases	650,000	
Goods available for sale	1,150,000	
Inventory, December 31, 1986	333,333	816,667
Gross profit		183,333
Selling and administrative expenses		212,500
Depreciation expense		20,000
Loss before income taxes		(49,167)
Income taxes		93,750
Loss before purchasing power gain on net monetary items		(142,917)
Purchasing power gain on net monetary items		541,250
Constant dollar net income		398,333
Retained earnings, January 1, 1986		-0-
Cash dividends		(10,000)
Retained earnings, December 31, 1986		$ 388,333

5. Constant dollar accounting **assumes that the impact of inflation falls equally** on all businesses and on all classes of assets and costs, which is not true.

Probably the greatest deterrent to widespread and mandatory adoption of constant dollar accounting in the past has been **what it is not;** constant dollar accounting is not present value, net realizable value, or current cost accounting, and therein lies much of the opposition to its use.

CURRENT COST ACCOUNTING

As indicated earlier, current cost[7] is the cost of replacing the identical asset owned; that is, with another of the same age and of the same operating capacity.[8] An alternative method of measuring current cost is to use the cost of replacing the "service potential" of the asset owned. This method has been adopted by the CICA in *Handbook*, Section 4510. To illustrate the current cost accounting model, assume that Andrea Limited purchased inventory at the beginning of Period 1 for $100,000; the current cost of the inventory at the end of Period 1 is $125,000; at the end of Period 2 the current cost is $155,000; and the inventory is sold in Period 3 for $170,000 when the inventory has a current cost of $160,000. Net income under the current cost and historical cost models for the three periods would be reported as shown below.

Andrea Limited COMPARISON OF CURRENT COST AND HISTORICAL COST			
Current Cost Model			
	Period 1	Period 2	Period 3
Revenues	$ –0–	$ –0–	$170,000
Cost of goods sold	–0–	–0–	160,000
Current cost income from continuing operations	–0–	–0–	10,000
Holding gain	$25,000	$30,000	5,000
Current cost net income	$25,000	$30,000	$ 15,000
Historical Cost Model			
Revenue	$ –0–	$ –0–	$170,000
Cost of goods sold	–0–	–0–	100,000
Historical cost net income	$ –0–	$ –0–	$ 70,000

The total net income is the same over the three years using either the current cost or the historical cost approach. The current cost approach recognizes the income as the inventory increases in value, whereas the historical cost approach delays recognition until the inventory is sold. In this illustration, the term **holding gain is employed to measure the increase in current cost that arises from holding the inventory from period to period.**

[7]Although the terms are used interchangeably, a subtle but important distinction exists between current cost and replacement cost. Current cost is the current purchase price of an asset owned, whereas replacement cost is the current purchase price of assets that will replace existing assets. In many cases, such as inventories, current cost and replacement cost are the same, because replacement will be with similar assets. However, with long-term assets, significant differences can develop. For example, assume that a Boeing 727 aircraft is going to be replaced with a new Boeing 767. In computing the current cost of the Boeing 727, we would take the cost of the Boeing 767 and adjust that cost for the value of the differences in service potential due to the differences in life, output capacity, and nature of service, including any operating cost savings associated with the new aircraft. However, under replacement cost only the difference in output capacity is considered, and no allowances are made for differences in useful life or operating costs.

[8]For a complete discussion of current cost, see Lawrence Revsine, *Replacement Cost Accounting* (Englewood Cliffs, N. J.: Prentice-Hall, 1973); Edgar O. Edwards and Phillip W. Bell, *The Theory and Measurement of Business Income* (Berkeley: University of California Press, 1961); and James A. Largay, III, and John Leslie Livingstone, *Accounting for Changing Prices* (Santa Barbara, Calif.: Wiley/Hamilton, 1976).

Current Cost—Complex Illustration

In a comprehensive current cost model, holding gains and losses are usually segregated between those that are realized and those that are unrealized. **Realized holding gains and losses** are the difference between the current cost and the historical cost of the asset sold or consumed during the period. **Unrealized holding gains and losses** relate to assets on hand at the end of the year. These gains and losses are the total increase in the current cost of the assets from the date they were acquired to the end of the current year. **The total holding gain recognized for any period will then be:**

1. **The holding gains and losses realized during the year.**
2. **The change in the unrealized holding gain or loss between the beginning and the end of the year.**

To illustrate, assume the same information as in the preceding illustration. A current cost accounting system would report the following:

	Period 1	Period 2	Period 3
Andrea Limited COMPREHENSIVE APPROACH Current Cost Model			
Revenues	$ –0–	$ –0–	$170,000
Cost of goods sold	–0–	–0–	160,000
Current cost income from operations	–0–	–0–	10,000
Realized holding gain	–0–	–0–	60,000
Realized income	–0–	–0–	70,000
Unrealized holding gain (loss)	25,000	30,000	(55,000)
Current cost net income	$ 25,000	$ 30,000	$ 15,000

The realized holding gain in Period 3 is $60,000, the difference between the current cost of inventory ($160,000) and the historical cost of inventory ($100,000); it is reported when the asset is sold. The unrealized holding gain or loss reported in each period is the change in the total unrealized holding gain from one period to the next. For example, in Period 2 the total unrealized holding gain at the beginning of the period is $25,000 and at the end of the period is $55,000. The unrealized holding gain reported in Period 2 is therefore $30,000 ($55,000 – $25,000). In Period 3 the total unrealized holding gain at the beginning of the period is $55,000 and at the end of the period is zero because the inventory is sold. As a result, an unrealized holding loss of $55,000 ($55,000 – $0) is reported in the third period.[9]

In the current cost model, three different income numbers are reported. **Current cost income from operations** reflects current cost margins—sales revenues less the current cost of inputs. **Realized income** measures the total income realized during the year. Realized income and historical cost income are always the same. Classifi-

---

[9]This system is basically the approach adopted by Edwards and Bell (see footnote 8). Note that only the change in the unrealized holding gain is considered in computing current cost net income. If current cost net income included realized holding gains and total unrealized holding gains, double counting could occur because the realized holding gain would recognize unrealized holding gains of prior periods.

cation within the income statement is different, however, because the current cost model subdivides historical cost income into two components—current cost income from operations and realized holding gains. **Current cost net income** measures the total income of the enterprise for one period and takes into account both realized and unrealized holding gains. Many consider this income number to provide the most appropriate measure of whether an enterprise is successful from one period to the next.

Current Cost Accounting—Lia Corporation

To illustrate the procedures peculiar to current cost accounting, accounts of Lia Corporation are presented on a historical cost basis in the form of abbreviated comparative balance sheets and an intervening income statement on page 1187 (Exhibit 1).

Adjustment of Balance Sheet Items

Preparation of the balance sheet on a current cost basis is relatively straightforward. The current cost of each item is reported at its current cost. The abbreviated comparative balance sheets for Lia Corporation would be presented as indicated on page 1199 (Exhibit 3).

All the monetary items are stated at face value, which is also current value. The inventory, equipment, and land in both balance sheets are reported at their current cost. Share capital is not adjusted because changes in the purchasing power of the dollar are not considered. The retained earnings is simply the difference between the assets and liabilities less the share capital. Retained earnings also can be computed by adding the beginning balance to the current cost net income less dividends for 1986. Dividends are not adjusted in a current cost system.

Adjustment of Income Statement Items

As indicated earlier, the current cost income statement usually reports three types of income: current cost income (loss) from operations, realized income (loss), and current cost net income (loss). If the data from Lia Corporation are used, the following would be reported on the income statement.

Sales   Because revenues are stated at their current price when sold, their amount is the same in either a historical cost or a current cost system.

Sales	$800,000

Cost of Goods Sold   Current cost of goods sold as given in the additional information in Exhibit 1 is the result of adjusting the historical cost of goods sold to the current cost of these items at the date of sale.

Cost of goods sold	$760,000

Selling and Administrative Expenses   These expenses are reported at their current cost, which in this case is the same as their historical cost.

Selling and administrative expenses	$170,000

Depreciation Expense   In a current cost accounting system, it is appropriate to assume that depreciation expense is incurred evenly through the year. As a result, average current cost balances should be used as the basis for computing depreciation.[10] In this case, depreciation expense on the equipment is computed and reported as follows:

$$\text{Average current cost balance} = \frac{\$150,000 + \$180,000}{2} = \$165,000$$

$$\text{Depreciation expense} = \$165,000 \div 15 = \$11,000$$

Income Taxes   These expenses are reported at their current cost, which is the same as their historical cost:

Income taxes	$75,000

Realized and Unrealized Holding Gains   The computation of the unrealized, realized, and total holding gain is shown on page 1198.

An explanation of the unrealized and realized holding gains follows:

Inventory, cost of goods sold, and purchases. Since the historical cost of goods sold was $470,000, but their replacement cost had risen to $760,000 by the date of sale, a holding gain of $290,000 would be recognized. Similarly, the ending inventory which cost $300,000 would cost $500,000 to replace at year end. The company, therefore, has an unrealized holding gain of $200,000 on these goods. Note that a holding gain on the purchases does not take place because at the date of purchase the historical cost and current cost are the same.

Equipment and depreciation expense. The computation for the holding gains involving the equipment and related depreciation expense is complex. As indicated earlier, the current cost depreciation for the period is $11,000 computed on the average current cost balance for the year. The difference of $1,000 ($11,000 – $10,000) between the current cost depreciation and the historical cost depreciation is reported as a realized holding gain. A portion of the equipment that has appreciated in value is now consumed (depreciated), and a holding gain should be realized.

An additional complication, however, arises in relation to depreciation because the December 31, 1986, balance sheet reports the equipment at a total current cost of $180,000 (per current cost information at top of page 1188), not $165,000 (average balance of current cost). In order to report the proper accumulated deprecia-

---

[10]Note that some theorists would argue for depreciation expense to be reported on the basis of the ending balance. Our presentation is in accordance with *CICA Handbook*, Section 4510.

Exhibit 2A
Lia Corporation
UNREALIZED AND REALIZED HOLDING GAINS

	Historical Cost	Current Cost	Unrealized Holding Gain (Loss)	Realized Holding Gain (Loss)
Inventory Dec. 31/86[a]	$300,000	$500,000	$200,000	$ -0-
Cost of goods sold	470,000	760,000	-0-	290,000
Purchases	520,000	520,000	-0-	-0-
Equipment (net) Dec. 31/86	140,000	168,000	28,000	-0-
Depreciation expense	10,000	11,000	-0-	1,000
Land Dec. 31/86	450,000	900,000	450,000	-0-
Total unrealized holding gain			$678,000	
Total realized holding gain				$291,000
Increase (decrease) in current cost of assets held during the year (total holding gain) ($678,000 + $291,000)				$969,000

[a]Note that beginning inventory, equipment (net), and land are ignored here because historical cost and current cost are the same.

tion balance of $12,000 ($180,000 ÷ 15 years), a **catch-up deprecation charge** (often referred to as **backlog depreciation**) must be made. In other words, depreciation expense based on the average balances in equipment ($165,000) was $11,000, not $12,000. As a result, the ending current cost balance for equipment adjusted for accumulated depreciation is incorrect unless it is adjusted for catch-up depreciation. For example, the computation for Lia Corporation would be as follows:

Current cost of equipment (gross)	$180,000
Current cost of equipment (net) unadjusted	168,000
Accumulated depreciation to date	12,000
Depreciation expense to date	(11,000)
Catch-up depreciation	1,000
Current cost of equipment (net)	$168,000

As a result of restating the equipment balance from $169,000 to $168,000, the unrealized holding gain is reduced by $1,000.

As shown in Exhibit 2A, an realized holding gain of $28,000, after deducting catch-up depreciation, must be recognized. This unrealized holding gain is the difference between the current cost of the equipment at the end of the year minus the current cost of the equipment at the beginning of the year adjusted for depreciation. No unrealized holding gains exist from previous periods.

Note that in Exhibit 2A above we assume that the catch-up depreciation entry is recorded and is incorporated into the reported financial information. As a result, the equipment (net) on a current cost basis was stated at $168,000 ($180,000 − $12,000) on December 31, 1986. Another way to compute the unrealized holding gain is to assume that the catch-up depreciation entry has not been recognized. In this case, the unrealized holding gain is computed at $29,000 ($169,000 − $140,000). Therefore, it would be necessary to reduce the unrealized holding gain by the catch-up depreciation adjustment in a separate computation. In either approach, the unrealized holding gain should be the same.

Land   The current cost of the land has increased $450,000 ($900,000 − $450,000), and an unrealized holding gain in this amount should be recognized.

The current cost financial statements for Lia Corporation are presented below.

Exhibit 3
Lia Corporation
COMPARATIVE BALANCE SHEETS
As of January 1 and December 31, 1986
(Current Cost Basis)

	January 1, 1986	December 31, 1986
Cash, receivables, and other monetary assets	$ 200,000	$ 325,000
Inventories	250,000	500,000
Equipment (net)	150,000	168,000
Land	450,000	900,000
Total assets	$1,050,000	$1,893,000
Current liabilities (all monetary)	$ 100,000	$ 200,000
Long-term liabilities (all monetary)	650,000	650,000
Total liabilities	750,000	850,000
Share capital	300,000	300,000
Retained earnings	–0–	743,000
Total shareholders' equity	300,000	1,043,000
Total liabilities and shareholders' equity	$1,050,000	$1,893,000

Lia Corporation
STATEMENT OF INCOME AND RETAINED EARNINGS
For the Year Ended December 31, 1986
(Current Cost Basis)

Sales	$ 800,000
Cost of goods sold	760,000
Gross profit	40,000
Selling and administrative expense	170,000
Depreciation expense	11,000
Loss before income taxes	(141,000)
Income taxes	75,000
Current cost loss from continuing operations	(216,000)
Realized holding gain	291,000
Realized income	75,000
Unrealized holding gain	678,000
Current cost net income	753,000
Retained earnings, January 1, 1986	–0–
	753,000
Cash dividends	(10,000)
Retained earnings, December 31, 1986	$ 743,000

The current cost loss from continuing operations and the realized holding gain when added together equal historical cost net income. An advantage of the current cost over the historical cost income statement is the segregation of income into these two components.

Advantages and Disadvantages of Current Cost

A distinct advantage that current cost has over both historical cost and constant dollar accounting is that the specific changes (up and down) in individual items are considered. While the general level of prices may be increasing, specific items may be decreasing. Such items as calculators, tennis balls, watches, microwave ovens, and television sets, for example, have decreased in price, whereas the general level of prices has increased. Constant dollar accounting using a general price index does not make an allowance for these changes in prices as effectively as a current cost system does.

The major arguments for the use of a current cost approach are:

1. **Current cost provides a better measure of efficiency.** If, for example, depreciation is based on current costs, not historical costs, a better measure of operating efficiencies is obtained. For example, assume that you are a new manager in an operation that includes a number of assets purchased recently at current prices, and your performance is compared with that of someone in a similar job elsewhere who is using similar assets that were purchased five years ago when the price was substantially lower. You probably would contend that the five-year-old assets should be revalued because the other manager will show a lower depreciation charge and higher net income than you will.

2. **Current cost is an approximation of the service potential of the asset.** It is difficult, if not impossible, to determine the present discounted values of specific cash flows that will occur from the use of certain assets; but current cost frequently is a reasonable approximation of this value. As the current cost increases, the implication is that the enterprise has a holding gain (an increase from one period to another in the current cost of that item) because the aggregate value of the asset's service potential has increased.

3. **Current cost provides for the maintenance of physical capital.** Assume that an asset is purchased for one dollar, sold for two dollars, and replaced for two dollars. How much income should be reported and how much tax should be paid? Under traditional accounting procedures, one dollar of income would be earned (which is subject to tax and a claim for dividend distribution). If current cost is used, however, no income exists to be taxed and claims for dividend distributions would probably be fewer.

4. **Current cost provides an assessment of future cash flows.** Information on current cost margins may be useful for assessing future cash flows when the selling price of a product is closely related to its current cost. In addition, reporting holding gains (losses) may provide help in assessing future cash flows.

The major arguments against current cost adjustments are:

1. **The use of current cost is subjective because it is difficult to determine the exact current cost of all items at any point in time.** A good second-hand market for all types of assets does not exist. In most cases, the asset is not replaced with an identical asset; it is replaced with a better one, a faster one, an improved one, an altogether different one, or not replaced at all.

2. **The maintenance of physical capital is not the accountant's function.** It is generally conceded that it is management's function to ensure that capital is not impaired.

3. **Current cost is not always an approximation of the fair market value.** An asset's value is a function of the future cash flows generated by it. Current cost, however, does not necessarily measure an increase in the service potential of that asset.

CICA POSITION

Up to this point, two comprehensive sets of financial statements have been prepared, one on a constant dollar basis and the other on a current cost basis. An understanding of these two bases of computation is necessary to understand the price-level adjusted information required to be reported by *CICA Handbook*, Section 4510.

As indicated earlier, *CICA Handbook*, Section 4510, was issued in 1982. The AcSC indicated that no major changes were to be made to the primary financial statements but that something must be done to augment them with information about the effects of price changes. One of the purposes of Section 4510 is to encourage experimentation rather than to establish rigid rules. Consequently, two alternative capital maintenance approaches may be used: financial capital or operating capability.

Certain enterprises are required to report the following as supplementary information:

1. **Current cost amounts of**
   (a) cost of goods sold;
   (b) depreciation, depletion, and amortization of property, plant, and equipment;
   (c) change during the reporting period in inventories, property, plant, and equipment; and
   (d) income before extraordinary items (after recognizing the above current cost amounts).
2. **Constant dollar amounts of**
   (a) the purchasing power gain or loss on net monetary items; and
   (b) the amount of change during the reporting period in inventories, and property, plant, and equipment attributed to general inflation.
3. **Other items**
   (a) the amount of the "financing" adjustment; and
   (b) current and deferred amounts of income tax expense.

In addition to the above items pertaining to the current period, comparative information for the corresponding preceding period should be restated for the change in general purchasing power. Because of the costs involved, all the information regarding the effects of changing prices is to be reported only by certain large public corporations. Furthermore, the information may be presented in supplementary statements, schedules, or supplementary notes in the financial reports attached to the primary financial statements.[11]

In summary, the CICA is requiring companies to report selected current cost and constant dollar information. What is proposed is a set of disclosures that falls short of requiring comprehensive financial statements of either of these approaches. While this may not be sufficient for those who would like to see complete financial statements restated, it does represent an effort to deal with some of the major financial statement distortions caused by general and specific price changes.

CICA Approach—Lia Corporation

CICA Handbook, Section 4510, does not require the preparation of comprehensive financial statements on a current cost/constant dollar basis. Rather, supplemental price-level information required by the CICA is simplified in a number of ways. First, **restatement is necessary only for inventory, property, plant, and equipment, cost of goods sold, and depreciation and depletion expense**; sales and other

---

[11]*CICA Handbook*, Section 4510, par. 12.

revenues, and other expenses do not have to be adjusted. In addition, investments in subsidiaries, intangibles, and deferred charges and credits do not have to be restated. The CICA took this approach because the differences between historical cost and current cost/constant dollar amounts are likely to be great for inventories and property, plant, and equipment, but not so great for the other items.

Second, the CICA permits presentation of this limited information in either **average-for-the-year dollars** or **year-end-dollars**. Using average-for-the-year dollars has significant computational advantages in that revenues and expenses assumed to occur evenly throughout the year will be the same in historical as well as constant dollars. Current cost/constant dollar measures of cost of goods sold and depreciation expense also approximate measures in average-for-the-year dollars without further adjustment.

Third, **no distinction is made between realized and unrealized holding gains and losses**. The total holding gain or loss, net of inflation, referred to as "the excess of the increase in specific prices over the increase in the general price level," must be presented.

To illustrate the current cost/constant dollar approach required, assume the information for Lia Corporation on page 1187 (Exhibit 1). When a partial income statement is prepared, either average-for-the-year dollars or year-end dollars may be used. It should be emphasized that even if revenues and other expenses are not incurred evenly throughout the year, the profession permits an assumption of an even incurrence to simplify the computations. However, this advantage is reduced somewhat when comprehensive financial statements are presented. Monetary items would need to be stated in average-for-the-year dollars rather than end-of-the-year dollars and would, therefore, not be at the same amount as the historical cost balances.

Adjustments to Income Statement Items

Cost of Goods Sold   The cost of goods sold adjustment is the amount necessary to restate the historical cost of goods sold to its current cost amount at the date of sale. The cost of goods sold adjustment of $290,000 is equal to the realized holding gain (Exhibit 2A).

Current cost of goods sold (Exhibit 1)	$760,000
Historical cost of goods sold (Exhibit 1)	470,000
Cost of goods sold adjustment	$290,000

Depreciation Expense   The depreciation, depletion, and amortization expense adjustment represents the difference between depreciation, depletion, and amortization of property, plant, and equipment based on average current costs and the amount as shown on the historical cost statement on top of page 1203.

The Financing Adjustment   When inventory and property, plant, and equipment are partially financed by net monetary liabilities, a benefit or cost may accrue to common shareholders as a result of changes in current costs. The amount of this benefit or cost is termed "the financing adjustment." Calculation of this adjustment involves three steps: (1) compute the average net monetary liabilities for the

Current Cost of Property, Plant, and Equipment:	
January 1, 1986	$150,000
December 31, 1986	180,000
Average current cost (150 + 180) ÷ 2	165,000
Depreciation on average current cost	
(1/15 of $165,000) (Exhibit 3)	$ 11,000
Depreciation on historic cost (Exhibit 1)	10,000
Depreciation adjustment	$ 1,000

period; (2) compute the average common shareholders' equity on a current cost basis for the period; and (3) multiply the aggregate current cost income adjustments (cost of goods sold, depreciation, etc.) by the debt financing ratio. The debt financing ratio is the amount determined in (1), above, divided by the sum of the amounts of (1) and (2). This calculation is illustrated for Lia Corporation as follows:

	January 1, 1986	December 31, 1986
Net Monetary Liabilities (historical):		
January 1, 1986		$ 550,000
December 31, 1986		525,000
Average net monetary liabilities (550 + 525) ÷ 2		$ 537,500
Average Common Shareholders' Equity on a Current Cost Basis:		
Net assets (common shareholders' equity) on a historical cost basis	$300,000	$ 365,000
Difference between current cost and historical cost of inventory and property, plant, and equipment:		
Inventory at current cost	250,000	500,000
Inventory at historic cost	250,000	300,000
	–0–	200,000
Property, plant, and equipment at current cost, net of depreciation	600,000	1,068,000
Property, plant, and equipment at historical cost, net of depreciation	600,000	590,000
	–0–	478,000
Net assets (common shareholders' equity) on a current cost basis	$300,000	$1,043,000
Average common shareholders' equity on a current cost basis (300,000 + 1,043,000) ÷ 2		$ 671,500
Calculation of the financing adjustment:[12]		
Current cost adjustments:		
Cost of goods sold	$290,000	
Depreciation	1,000	
	291,000	
Debt financing ratio: $\dfrac{537,500}{537,500 + 671,500} = .44$		
Financing adjustment (.44 × 291,000)		$ 128,040

[12]The financing adjustment may also be calculated by multiplying the increase in current cost amounts of inventory and property, plant, and equipment occurring during the year by the debt financing ratio.

Income Attributable to Common Shareholders on a Current Cost Basis—Operating Capability Under the operating capability concept of capital maintenance, income attributed to common shareholders on a current cost basis is determined as follows: The foregoing three adjustments (cost of goods sold, depreciation, and the financing adjustment) are deducted (added) to the historical cost income available to common shareholders (income before extraordinary items less dividends paid on nonparticipating preferred shares). The resulting income attributable to common shareholders on a current cost basis may be disclosed either as a restatement of the historical cost income statement or in a schedule as illustrated below:

Historical income attributed to common shareholders (Exhibit 1)		$ 75,000
Less: Current cost adjustments:		
Cost of goods sold	$290,000	
Depreciation	1,000	(291,000)
Income on a current cost basis		(216,000)
Financing adjustment		128,040
Income attributable to common shareholders on a current cost basis under an operating capability concept of capital		$ (87,960)

Income Attributable to Common Shareholders on a Current Cost Basis under a Financial Concept of Capital As an alternative to using an operating capability concept of capital, firms may report using a financial concept of capital. Under this concept, historical cost income is adjusted to include (1) current cost of goods sold, (2) depreciation on a current cost basis, (3) increase (decrease) in the current cost (net of general inflation) of inventories, property, plant, and equipment during the year, and (4) gain or loss in purchasing power attributed to holding net monetary items. Items 1, 2, and 4 have been calculated in previous sections of this chapter. The computation of item 3 involves combining current cost and constant dollar methods in order to determine the increase in current cost of inventories, property, plant, and equipment during the year, and the amount of the increase (decrease) that is attributed to general inflation. These amounts for Lia Corporation's inventories are computed on page 1205.

Inventory The amount defined as "the change in the current cost amounts of inventory" represents the total realized and unrealized holding gains (losses) that have occurred on inventory items during the period. This may be computed by deducting the current cost of inventory "inputs" (opening inventory and purchases) during the period from the current cost of inventory "outputs" (cost of goods sold and ending inventory) that have occurred during and at the end of the period. The excess (deficiency) of the current cost of outputs over the current cost of inputs is the amount of the increase (decrease) in current cost of inventory during the period. This amount is also known as the total holding gains (realized and unrealized).

When the current cost of inventory outputs and inputs in the above calculation is restated to average-for-the-year dollars, the amount of the increase (decrease) in the current cost of inventory during the year may be derived in constant dollars. The difference between the amount in nominal dollars and the amount in constant dollars is the amount of the increase or decrease that may be attributed to general inflation. These calculations are illustrated below:

	Current Costs	Conversion Factor	Average 1986 Dollars
Current Cost Outputs:			
Cost of goods sold (current cost at date of sale)	$ 760,000	160/160	$ 760,000
Inventory, December 31, 1986	500,000	160/200	400,000
Subtotal	1,260,000		1,160,000
Deduct Current Cost Inputs:			
Inventory, January 1, 1986	(250,000)	160/100	(400,000)
Purchases (assumed purchased evenly throughout the year)	(520,000)	160/160	(520,000)
Increase in current cost of inventory	$ 490,000		$ 240,000
Increase in current cost of inventory in nominal dollars			$ 490,000
Less: Increase in current cost of inventory in constant dollars			240,000
Increase in current cost of inventory due to general inflation			$ 250,000

Property, Plant, and Equipment   A similar procedure is necessary to compute the increase in current cost of property, plant, and equipment items during the year and the portion of the increase that results from general inflation. The change in the current cost amounts of property, plant, and equipment and the general inflation component may be determined by computing the **net increase in current costs during the year in both nominal and constant dollars.**

	Current Costs	Conversion Factor	Average 1986 Dollars
Outputs at Current Cost:			
Property, plant, and equipment at current cost at December 31, 1986	$1,068,000*	160/200	$ 854,400
Depreciation expense	11,000	160/160	11,000
Less: Inputs at Current Cost:			
Property, plant, and equipment at January 1, 1986	(600,000)		(960,000)
Net increase in the current cost of property, plant, and equipment	$ 479,000		$ (94,600)
Increase in current cost in nominal dollars			$ 479,000
Plus: Decrease in current cost in constant dollars			(94,600)
Amount of the increase in the current cost of property, plant, and equipment attributable to general inflation			$ 573,600

*The difference between gross current cost minus accumulated depreciation ($1,080,000 – $11,000) and net current cost ($1,068,000) is attributed to backlog depreciation. Since complete restatement of financial statements is not required, the amount ($1,000) is not separately disclosed.

An income statement prepared under the financial concept of capital maintenance would appear as follows:

Lia Corporation
SUPPLEMENTARY INFORMATION DISCLOSING AFFECT OF CHANGING PRICES
For the Year Ended December 31, 1986

Sales		$ 800,000
Cost of goods sold (current cost)		760,000
Selling, general and administrative expenses		170,000
Depreciation (current cost)		11,000
Total		941,000
Income (loss) before income taxes		(141,000)
Income taxes		75,000
Income (loss) on a current cost basis		(216,000)
Increase in current cost of		
Inventories	$490,000	
Property, plant, and equipment	479,000	969,000
Income attributable to common shareholders on		
a current cost basis in nominal dollars		753,000
Deduct: Increase in current cost attributable		
to general inflation:		
Inventories	250,000	
Property, plant, and equipment	573,600	823,600
		(70,600)
Add: Gain in general purchasing power from		
having net monetary liabilities		433,000
Income attributable to common shareholders on		
a current cost basis in constant dollars		$ 362,400

Adjustments of Balance Sheet Items

Although Section 4510 does not require a complete balance sheet, in order to compute the excess of the increase in specific prices over the increases in the general price level (total holding gain, net of inflation) a number of balance sheet items must be adjusted. The required information about changes in current costs (holding gains and losses) that have occurred during the period could be summarized and presented as follows:

	Change in Current Costs	General Inflation Component	Increase Net of General Inflation
Inventory	$490,000	$250,000	$240,000
Property, plant, and equipment	479,000	573,600	(94,600)
	$969,000	$823,600	$145,400

In addition to the above balance sheet items, Section 4510 requires firms to disclose the following items at the **lower of current cost and recoverable amount:**

  Inventory
  Property, plant, and equipment
  Resources used on partly completed contracts

General Purchasing Power Gain or Loss on Net Monetary Items   Monetary items are defined as **"money and claims to money, the value of which, in terms of the**

monetary unit, whether foreign or domestic, is fixed by contract or otherwise.'' As indicated in the preceding discussion, some items must be examined on an individual basis when being classified as either monetary or nonmonetary. For example, nonparticipating preferred shares are considered monetary, while participating preferred shares would be classified as nonmonetary. Deferred income taxes are specifically defined as nonmonetary. Computing the general purchasing power gain or loss on net monetary items is done in two steps. First, compute the net monetary items at the beginning and end of the current period.

Net Monetary Items	January 1, 1986	December 31, 1986
Cash, receivables, and other monetary assets	$ 200,000	$ 325,000
Current liabilities (all monetary)	(100,000)	(200,000)
Long-term liabilities (all monetary)	(650,000)	(650,000)
Net monetary items	$(550,000)	$(525,000)

The second step in computing the purchasing power gain or loss is to restate the beginning and ending balance of monetary items, and sources and uses of monetary items during the period, to either average-for-the-year dollars or end-of-the-year dollars. The computation of the purchasing power gain or loss on net monetary items using end-of-the-year dollars is illustrated on page 1191. The same calculation using average-for-the-year dollars is shown below.

	1986 Historical	Conversion Factor	Restated
Net monetary items Jan. 1, 1986	$(550,000)	160/100	$(880,000)
Add (sources):			
Sales	800,000	160/160	800,000
	250,000		(80,000)
Deduct (uses):			
Purchases	520,000	160/160	520,000
Selling and administrative expenses	170,000	160/160	170,000
Income taxes	75,000	160/160	75,000
Cash dividends	10,000		8,000
Total uses	775,000		773,000
Net monetary items restated			(853,000)
Net monetary items at Dec. 31, 1986 historical restated to average-for-the-year dollars	$(525,000)	160/200	(420,000)
Purchasing power gain on net monetary items			$ 433,000[a]

[a]This may also be computed by multiplying the amount of gain (loss) determined in year-end dollars by the conversion factor of 160/200.

In the computation above, those items that occurred continuously during the year (sales, purchases, selling, and administrative expenses and income taxes) are already stated in average-for-the-year dollars; the isolated lump-sum use (payment of dividend) was restated using the index applicable to the date of occurrence.

Comparative Information

Comparative information should be restated for the effects of changes in general purchasing power. Furthermore, the accounting principles used in computing the income attributable to common shareholders on a current cost basis should be consistent with those used in computing income on a historical cost basis.

Additional Highlights

Other matters of importance are as follows:

1. Use of recoverable amount.
2. Income taxes.
3. Determination of current costs.

Recoverable Amount   The term "recoverable amount" means net realizable value or the present value (value in use) expected to be recoverable from the sale or use of the asset. The *CICA Handbook* states that when the recoverable amount of an asset or group of assets is materially and permanently below current cost, the recoverable amount should be used as the measure of the assets and of the expense associated with the use or sale of the assets for that measure of income. This concept is similar to that used for historical cost statements (lower of cost and market for inventories is an illustration). To state assets at a cost figure that exceeds its recoverable amounts is inappropriate. A better approach is to recognize the loss immediately.

Income Taxes   The total income tax is to be based on historical cost and be charged as an expense in arriving at income from operations. The CICA wishes to highlight the impact of the income taxes on overstated profits and thereby inform users of the excessive taxation that often occurs in a period of inflation. Others disagree with this approach, and argue that a portion of the income taxes should be imputed to the realized holding gain. Still others contend that income taxes should be imputed on the unrealized holding gain as well. Those who consider that the purpose is to disclose the economic change from one period to another argue that the unrealized holding gain should have a tax effect associated with it.

Determination of Current Costs   The CICA has identified the following bases for determining the current cost of inventories and property, plant, and equipment.
    Direct pricing. Current invoice and vendor's prices and price lists or other quotations or estimates are acceptable methods of valuing both inventories and property, plant, and equipment.
    Indexation. Either external or specific internal indices might be used to value both inventories and property, plant, and equipment.
    Reference pricing. Reference to prices of other similar assets may be used with caution when determining current costs.
    Discounted cash flow. If the amounts and timing of future cash flows can be reasonably estimated, discounted cash flow may be used in estimating current costs. When discounted cash flow is used, accountants must take care in the selection of a discount rate that appropriately reflects the risk of the activities and the industry, as well as the nature of the asset being valued.

Exhibit 4
Lia Corporation
COMPARATIVE ANALYSIS OF DIFFERENT SYSTEMS
December 31, 1986

Balance Sheet	Historical Cost (Exhibit 1)	Constant Dollar (Exhibit 2)	Current Cost (Exhibit 3)	CICA Approach (Partial)
Cash, receivables, and other monetary assets	$ 325,000	$ 325,000	$ 325,000	NA
Inventories	300,000	333,333	500,000	$500,000*
Equipment (net)	140,000	280,000	168,000	168,000
Land	450,000	900,000	900,000	900,000
Total assets	$1,215,000	$1,838,333	$1,893,000	
Current liabilities (all monetary)	200,000	200,000	200,000	NA
Long-term liabilities (all monetary)	650,000	650,000	650,000	NA
Total liabilities	850,000	850,000	850,000	NA
Share capital	300,000	600,000	300,000	NA
Retained earnings	65,000	388,333	743,000	NA
Total shareholders' equity	365,000	988,333	1,043,000	NA
Total liabilities and shareholders' equity	$1,215,000	$1,838,333	$1,893,000	

*The current cost of inventories and property, plant, and equipment must be disclosed.

Balance Sheet	Historical Cost (Exhibit 1)	Constant Dollar (Exhibit 2)	Current Cost (Exhibit 3)	CICA Approach (Partial)
Sales	$ 800,000	$1,000,000	$ 800,000	$800,000
Cost of goods sold	470,000	816,667	760,000	760,000
Gross profit	330,000	183,333	40,000	40,000
Selling and administrative expenses	170,000	212,500	170,000	170,000
Depreciation expense	10,000	20,000	11,000	11,000
Income taxes—current	75,000	93,750	75,000	75,000
Income (loss) from operations	75,000	(142,917)	(216,000)	(216,000)
Financing adjustment				(128,040)
Income attributable to common shareholders on a current cost basis				$(87,960)
Realized holding gain (loss)	NA	NA	291,000	NA
Realized income (loss)	NA	NA	75,000	NA
Unrealized holding gain	NA	NA	678,000	NA
Specific increase (decrease) in inventories, equipment, land, net of inflation	NA	NA	NA	$145,400
Purchasing power gain (or loss) on net monetary items	NA	541,250	NA	$433,000
Net income	75,000	398,333	753,000	
Beginning retained earnings	–0–	–0–	–0–	
	75,000	398,333	753,000	
Cash dividends	10,000	10,000	10,000	
Ending retained earnings	$ 65,000	$ 388,333	$ 743,000	

Comparative Analysis

Presented as Exhibit 4 (page 1209) is a comparative set of financial statements prepared under the different valuation approaches illustrated in this chapter. Note that, for balance sheet purposes, the CICA requires only that inventories and property, plant, and equipment be reported at current values.

Examination of the income statement shows that Lia Corporation's profitability is the result of purchasing power gain on net monetary items due principally to holding a large amount of debt during a period of price inflation. During a period of inflation, companies with large real estate holdings and large loans outstanding report higher income under constant dollar and current cost/constant dollar statements. Note also that Lia Corporation would report a loss from operations on a constant dollar, current cost system, and the CICA approach, but would still be paying income taxes. This presentation illustrates why many have contended that the historical cost income numbers are an illusion, vanishing after phantom inventory profits are considered and depreciation expense is adjusted for the cost of replacing aging assets. The year 1974 in the United States provided a good illustration of this problem. As one article noted, "corporations were paying an effective tax rate of 63% on inflation-adjusted earnings." It was estimated that many manufacturing companies paid out more than 150% of their adjusted earnings.[13]

Finally, note that historical cost net income, $75,000, equals current cost realized income, $75,000. This occurrence in our illustration is not a coincidence; it demonstrates that the current cost approach segregates the historical cost income into two components: income (loss) from operations and realized holding gain (loss).

Concluding Observations

Now that certain enterprises have been requested to report price-level information, the CICA will be able to determine whether some type of consensus will emerge in support of the appropriate method or methods of valuation. It is quite conceivable that some users will find all or some of the information provided by the new *Handbook* section helpful, whereas others will find little if any usefulness in these supplementary disclosures. The eventual resolution of this issue depends upon continued experimentation and analysis.

KEY POINTS

1. The objective of constant dollar accounting is to maintain capital in terms of constant purchasing power as measured by a general index of the level of prices. The objective of current cost accounting is to maintain capital in terms of operating capacity to provide goods and services at the same level at the end of a period as at the beginning.
2. Current cost/constant dollar accounting measures elements in terms of current cost but adjusts for a standard unit of measurement.
3. The CICA permits information on changing prices to be based on the Consumer Price Index for adjusting for the effect of general inflation.

---

[13]"The Profit Illusion," *Business Week*, March 19, 1979.

4. Monetary assets and liabilities are assets and liabilities whose claims to or claims on cash do not change as the general price-level changes. Nonmonetary items are items whose price may change over time.

5. Holders of monetary assets in a period of inflation lose purchasing power and, in a period of deflation, gain purchasing power. Holders of monetary liabilities gain purchasing power in a period of inflation and lose it in a period of deflation. The term purchasing power gain or loss is used to describe this gain or loss that occurs in holding monetary items during a period of changing prices.

6. The CICA permits the use of either average-for-the-year or end-of-the-year index to compute constant dollar restatements.

7. In a current cost model, three different income numbers are reported. Current cost income from operations reflects current cost margins—sales revenue less the current cost of inputs. Realized income measures the total income realized through sale or consumption during the period. Current cost net income measures the total income of the enterprise for one period and takes into consideration both realized and unrealized holding gains.

8. Enterprises of a certain size are required to report the following as supplemental information: (1) income attributed to common shareholders on a current cost basis; (2) purchasing power gains and losses on net monetary items; (3) increases or decreases in current cost amounts of inventory and property, plant, and equipment both gross and net of inflation (same as total holding gain, net of inflation); (4) current cost amounts of inventory and property, plant, and equipment at the end of the year.

9. When the recoverable amount of an asset is permanently lower than current cost, it should be reported at the lower amount.

10. Income taxes are reported at historical cost amounts.

11. Current cost amounts are determined through direct pricing, indexation, or appraisals.

25A

CURRENT COST/CONSTANT DOLLAR ACCOUNTING

As indicated in Chapter 25, the CICA has adopted an approach using some current cost/constant dollar information. The purpose of this appendix is to present a comprehensive set of financial statements on a current cost/constant dollar basis. These statements may then be compared with the constant dollar, current cost, and the CICA approaches presented in the chapter. In addition, the CICA has encouraged experimentation which could lead to use of current cost/constant dollar financial statements.

Balance Sheet Adjustments

In developing a current cost/constant dollar balance sheet, it is necessary to find the current cost for all of the balance sheet items in average-for-the-year dollars. Exhibit 3 on page 1199 reports the current cost of the balance sheet items in end-of-the-year dollars; therefore, restatement to average-for-the-year dollars is needed. This restatement of the December 31, 1986, balance sheet is as follows:

End-of-year Current Cost (Exhibit 3)		×	Index	=	Current Cost/Constant Dollar (Average-for-the-year dollars)
Cash, receivables, and					
other monetary assets	$ 325,000	×	160/200	=	$ 260,000
Inventories	500,000	×	160/200	=	400,000
Equipment	168,000	×	160/200	=	134,400
Land	900,000	×	160/200	=	720,000
Total assets	$1,893,000				$1,514,400
Current liabilities	$ 200,000	×	160/200	=	$ 160,000
Long-term liabilities	650,000	×	160/200	=	520,000
Total liabilities	$ 850,000				$ 660,000

Shareholders' equity accounts are computed somewhat differently. The common share account was stated at $300,000. To restate the common shares in average-for-the-year dollars, it must be adjusted from the beginning of the period as follows:

Common shares:	$300,000 × 160/100 = $480,000

The retained earnings amount may be a plug figure ($354,400), or it may be computed by adding the beginning retained earnings to current cost/constant dollar net income and subtracting any dividends declared during the year.

Note that the balance sheet at the beginning of the year 1986 is stated in current cost; it too must be adjusted to average-for-the-year dollars. This is accomplished by multiplying each item by 160/100.

Income Statement Adjustments

No adjustment is required for the following items, as the current cost income statement numbers are already stated in average-for-the-year dollars.

	Current Cost/Constant Dollars (Average-for-the-year dollars)
Sales	$800,000
Cost of goods sold	760,000
Selling and administrative expenses	170,000
Depreciation expense	11,000
Income taxes	75,000

As part of the current cost/constant dollar presentations, two other items must be reported. First, the purchasing power gain or loss must be computed. As indicated on page 1207, the purchasing power gain in average-for-the-year dollars is $433,000. Secondly, the realized and unrealized holding gains, net of inflation, should be reported. These are computed in average-for-the-year dollars as shown on page 1214.

Note that the amount of the total holding gain net of inflation computed in the schedule above ($145,400) is the same as the amount determined in the computation of information required under *CICA Handbook*, Section 4510. The calculation

Lia Corporation
UNREALIZED AND REALIZED HOLDING GAINS

	Constant Dollar	Current Cost	Unrealized Holding Gain (Loss)	Realized Holding Gain (Loss)
Inventory 12/31/86	$266,667[1]	$400,000	$133,333	$ -0-
Cost of goods sold	653,333[2]	760,000	-0-	106,667
Purchases	520,000[3]	520,000	-0-	-0-
Equipment (net)	224,000[4]	134,400	(89,600)	-0-
Depreciation expense	16,000[5]	11,000	-0-	(5,000)
Land 12/31/86	720,000[6]	720,000	-0-	-0-
Total unrealized holding gain			$ 43,733	
Total realized holding gain				$101,667
Increase (decrease) in current cost of assets held during the year, net of inflation (total holding gain net of inflation)		($43,733 + $101,667)		$145,400

*Note that beginning inventory, equipment (net), and land are ignored here because historical cost and current cost are the same.
[1]Ending inventory at historical cost restated to average $'s ($300,000 × 160/180)
[2]Cost of goods sold at historical cost restated to average $'s
[3]Purchases at historical cost is the same as average $'s
[4]Equipment (net) at 12/31/86 in restated historical cost ($140,000 × 160/100)
[5]Depreciation at historical restated to average $'s ($10,000 × 160/100)
[6]Land at year-end historical cost restated to average $'s ($450,000 × 160/100)

above, however, identifies the realized and unrealized portions of the total holding gain.

Current Cost/Constant Dollar Financial Statements

A comprehensive set of financial statements on a current cost/constant dollar basis in average-for-the-year dollars is presented in Exhibit A.

Advantages and Disadvantages of Current Cost/Constant Dollar Accounting

Many of the arguments indicated earlier for and against current cost and constant dollar accounting apply here. Some arguments that have particular relevance are presented below:

Arguments for current cost/constant dollar accounting:

1   Current cost/constant dollar accounting both **stabilizes that measuring unit and provides current, comparable data.**
2.   A current cost/constant dollar system provides **more information** than either system alone. Holding gains and losses adjusted for inflation and deflation are reported, as well as the purchasing power gain or loss on net monetary items.
3.   Because it is not certain what is the most useful income figure, by providing these additional disclosures, users through **experimentation** will identify the most useful data.

Arguments against current cost/constant dollar accounting:

1.   The **cost** to prepare this information is significant and is perhaps not justified by the benefits received.

Exhibit A
Lia Corporation
COMPARATIVE BALANCE SHEET
As of December 31, 1986
(Current Cost/Constant Dollar Basis)
Average-for-the-year Dollars

	January 1, 1986	December 31, 1986
Cash, receivables, and other monetary assets	$ 320,000	$ 260,000
Inventories	400,000	400,000
Equipment (net)	240,000	134,400
Land	720,000	720,000
Total assets	$1,680,000	$1,514,400
Current liabilities (all monetary)	$ 160,000	$ 160,000
Long-term liabilities (all monetary)	1,040,000	520,000
Total liabilities	1,200,000	680,000
Share capital	480,000	480,000
Retained earnings	–0–	354,400
Total shareholders' equity	480,000	834,400
Total liabilities and shareholders' equity	$1,680,000	$1,514,400

Lia Corporation
STATEMENT OF INCOME AND RETAINED EARNINGS
For the Year Ended December 31, 1986
(Current Cost/Constant Dollar Basis)
Average-for-the-year Dollars

Sales	$ 800,000
Cost of goods sold	760,000
Gross profit	40,000
Selling and administrative expenses	170,000
Depreciation expense	11,000
Loss before income taxes	(141,000)
Income taxes	75,000
Loss from operations	(216,000)
Realized holding gain, net of inflation	101,667
Realized loss	(114,333)
Unrealized holding gain, net of inflation	43,733
	70,600
Purchasing power gain on net monetary items	433,000
Current cost/constant dollar net income	362,400
Retained earnings, January 1, 1986	–0–
	362,400
Cash dividends	8,000
Retained earnings, December 31, 1986	354,400

2. Very few people will understand the new data. Providing this additional information may be more harmful than helpful. More information is not always better information, because it **may confuse readers or lead to information overload.**

3. The conceptual superiority of the current cost/constant dollar accounting system is **untested and unproven.** For example, there is no body of literature that indicates that the information might lead to better predictions of cash flow.

Note: All **asterisked** Questions, Cases, Exercises, or Problems relate to material contained in an Appendix.

QUESTIONS

1. What is a price index? How does a general price index differ from a specific price index?

2. What is constant dollar accounting? How does constant dollar accounting differ from current cost accounting?

3. Assume that the Consumer Price Index has increased to 155 from 100 six years ago. How many end-of-year dollars are needed today to purchase what $30,000 purchased three years ago?

4. Distinguish between monetary and nonmonetary items. What is a purchasing power gain or loss on net monetary items?

5. If the general price level is rising steadily, which of the following would be most realistically valued for balance sheet purposes: (a) equipment, (b) cash, or (c) real estate?

6. Jenny Van Alstyne purchased a 10-year, 16% bond at par for $1,000, collected interest annually during the life of the bond, and realized the principal amount of the bond at maturity. If the price level were half as high at maturity date as it was at the date of purchase, how would Jenny fare?

7. Mark DeFlippo purchased a 20-year, 10% bond at par for $1,000, collected interest annually during the life of the bond, and realized the principal amount of the bond at maturity. If the price level were twice as high at maturity date as it was at the date of purchase, how would Mark fare?

8. Assume a decade of rising prices. Would the following items give rise to (a) purchasing power gains, (b) purchasing power losses, or (c) neither purchasing power gains nor losses?
   (a) Owning land during the period.
   (b) Holding a long-term note payable.
   (c) Holding cash in a pension fund.
   (d) Having preferred shares outstanding during the period.
   (e) Holding a note receivable.
   (f) Having patents during the period.
   (g) Having an investment in common shares.

9. Classify each of the following as monetary or nonmonetary items:
   (a) Equipment
   (b) Premium on bonds payable
   (c) Common shares
   (d) Bonds
   (e) Preferred shares (par value to be paid in liquidation)
   (f) Investment in common shares
   (g) Refundable deposits
   (h) Accumulated depreciation—equipment
   (i) Accounts receivable
   (j) Deferred income taxes

10. Indicate whether a company gains or loses under each of the following conditions:
   (a) A company maintains equal amounts of monetary assets and monetary liabilities during a period of price-level increases.
   (b) A company maintains an excess of liabilities over monetary assets during a period of price-level increases.
   (c) A company maintains an excess of monetary assets over monetary liabilities during a period of price-level increases.
   (d) A company maintains an excess of monetary assets over monetary liabilities during a period of price-level decreases.

11. What are the major arguments in opposition to modifying financial statements for general price-level changes?

12. Explain three commonly advocated concepts of current value.

13. Some theorists have argued that the present value of future discounted cash flows should be used as the basis for measuring assets and liabilities. What are the major disadvantages to this approach?

14. Many noted that the major difference between constant dollar and current cost accounting is related to the view of capital maintenance. What is the theory of capital maintenance and how does the constant dollar approach differ from the current cost approach in this regard?

15. A comprehensive current cost model emphasizes three different income numbers. Explain the rationale for these three income numbers.

16. At the beginning of 1986, a company purchased inventory for $60,000. During the year, the company sold half this inventory for $70,000 at a time when the current cost of the inventory sold was $45,000. At the end of the year, the remaining inventory had a current cost of $65,000. Compute the current cost income from operations, the realized holding gain, the unrealized holding gain, and the current cost net income.

17. MacDonald and Robertson has decided that it wishes to report current cost information related to its inventories. What approaches might be used to find the current cost for inventories?

18. Tam Bridges Inc. purchased equipment at the beginning of the year for $100,000 that had an estimated life of 10 years and no salvage value. The current cost of the equipment at the end of the year was $120,000. Assuming straight-line depreciation on a current cost basis, how much depreciation would be reported as a charge to current cost income from continuing operations? How much should be charged to the unrealized holding gain?

19. Many believe that if a partial or complete current cost income statement is prepared, income taxes should be allocated to the realized or unrealized holding gain. Explain the rationale for this approach. Indicate the CICA position on this matter.

20. What are the major advantages of current cost accounting? Expain the differences between current cost accounting and replacement cost accounting.

21. Why might the use of the specific price-level adjustments (current cost) produce a better indicator of disposable wealth than constant dollar accounting?

22. Some argue that a current cost approach is not acceptable, unless the historical cost numbers are adjusted to a constant dollar basis. Explain the rationale for this approach.

23. On January 1, 1986, Pritchett, Ltd. had cash of $20,000 and inventories whose historical cost and current cost were $28,000. During the year, the general price level increased 10% on an even basis throughout the period, and the current cost of the inventories at the end of the year was $36,000. Assuming that the company held these assets for the entire year, compute the unrealized holding gain if a current cost/constant dollar approach were employed and reported in (1) end-of-year dollars and (2) average-for-the-year dollars.

*24. What are the major differences between the current cost/constant dollar approach and the current cost approach?

25. *CICA Handbook*, Section 4510, ''Financial Reporting and Changing Prices,'' was issued in 1982. Indicate the major reporting requirements of this section.

*26. What are the major advantages of the current cost/constant dollar approach?

CASES

C25-1 A business entity's financial statements could be prepared by using historical cost or current value as a basis. In addition, the basis could be stated in terms of unadjusted dollars or dollars restated for changes in purchasing power. The various permutations of these two separate and distinct areas are shown in the following matrix:

	Unadjusted Dollars	Dollars Restated for Changes in Purchasing Power
Historical cost	1	2
Current value	3	4

Block number 1 of the matrix represents the traditional method of accounting for transactions in accounting today, wherein the absolute (unadjusted) amount of dollars given up or received is recorded for the asset or liability obtained (**relationship between resources**). Amounts recorded in the method described in block number 1 reflect the original cost of the asset or liability and do not give effect to any change in value of the unit of measure (**standard of comparison**). This method assumes the validity of the accounting concepts of going concern and stable monetary unit. Any gain or loss (including holding and purchasing power gains or losses) resulting from the sale or satisfaction of amounts recorded under this method is deferred in its entirety until sale or satisfaction.

Instructions

For each of the remaining matrix blocks (2, 3, and 4), respond to the following questions. **Limit your discussion to nonmonetary assets only**.

(a)   How will this method of recording assets affect the relationship between resources and the standard of comparison?

(b)   What is the theoretical justification for using each method?

(c)   How will each method of asset valuation affect the recognition of gain or loss during the life of the asset and ultimately from the sale or abandonment of the asset? Your response should include a discussion of the timing and magnitude of the gain or loss and conceptual reasons for any difference from the gain or loss computed using the traditional method.

(AICPA adapted)

C25-2   Shipman Corp., a wholesaler with large investments in plant and equipment, began operations in 1944. The company's history has been one of expansion in sales, production, and physical facilities. Recently, some concern has been expressed that the conventional financial statements do not provide sufficient information for decisions by investors. After consideration of proposals for various types of supplementary financial statements to be included in the 1986 annual report, management has decided to present a balance sheet as of December 31, 1986, and a statement of income and retained earnings for 1986, both restated for changes in the general price level.

Instructions

(a)   On what basis can it be contended that Shipman's conventional statements should be restated for changes in the general price level?

(b)   Distinguish between financial statements restated for general price-level changes and current value financial statements.

(c)   Distinguish between monetary and nonmonetary assets and liabilities as the terms are used in constant dollar accounting. Give examples of each.

(d)   Outline the procedures Shipman should follow in preparing the proposed supplementary statements. (Assume statements are computed in year-end dollars.)

(e)   Indicate the major similarities and differences between the proposed supplementary statements and the corresponding conventional statements.

(f)   Assuming that in the future Shipman will want to present comparative supplementary statements, can the 1986 supplementary statements be presented in 1987 without adjustment? Explain.

(AICPA adapted)

C25-3   The general purchasing power of the dollar has declined considerably because of inflation in recent years. To account for this changing value of the dollar, many accountants suggest that financial statements be adjusted for general price-level changes. Three independent, unrelated statements regarding general price-level adjusted financial statements follow. Each statement contains some fallacious reasoning.

1. When adjusting financial data for general price-level changes, a distinction must be made between monetary and nonmonetary assets and liabilities, which, under the historical cost basis of accounting, have been indentified as "current" and "noncurrent." When using the historical cost basis of accounting, no purchasing power gain or loss is recognized in the accounting process, but when financial statements are adjusted for general price-level changes, a purchasing power gain or loss will be recognized on monetary and nonmonetary items.

2. The accounting profession has not seriously considered price-level adjusted financial statements before because the rate of inflation usually has been so small from year to year that the adjustments would have been immaterial in amount. Price-level adjusted financial statements represent a departure from the historical cost basis of accounting. Financial statements should be prepared on the basis of facts, not estimates.

3. If financial statements were adjusted for general price-level changes, depreciation charges in the income statement would permit the recovery of dollars of current purchasing power and, thereby, equal the cost of new assets to replace the old ones. General price-level adjusted data would yield statement-of-financial-position amounts closely approximating current values. Furthermore, management can make better decisions if constant dollar financial statements are published.

Instructions

Evaluate each of the independent statements and identify the areas of fallacious reasoning in each and explain why the reasoning is incorrect. Complete your discussion of each statement before proceeding to the next statement.

(AICPA adapted)

C25-4   The controller for Trophy, Inc. has recently hired you as assistant controller. Recognizing that you should be quite familiar with the recent pronouncement on accounting for changing prices, the controller shows you supplementary data for the year. Part of the information follows:

Trophy, Inc.
STATEMENT OF INCOME FROM OPERATIONS
ADJUSTED FOR CHANGING PRICES
For the Year Ended December 31, 1986
(Financial concept of capital)

(In 000s of Average 1986 Dollars)

Income from operations, as reported in the income statement		$ 27,000
Adjustments to restate historical costs to current costs:		
Costs of goods sold	(25,224)	
Depreciation and amortization expense	(28,500)	(53,724)
Loss from operations on a current cost basis		(26,724)
Increase in current cost amounts of:		
Inventories, property, plant, and equipment held during the year[a]		73,824
General purchasing power adjustments:		
Increase in current cost amounts of inventory and property, plant, and equipment attributal to the effects of general inflation		(56,877)
Purchasing power gain on net monetary items		23,187
Income attributal to common shareholders on a current cost basis in constant dollars		$ 13,410

---

[a]At December 31, 1986, current cost of inventory was $197,100 and current cost of property, plant, and equipment, net of accumulated depreciation, was $255,300.

Instructions

The controller is interested in the answer to the following questions:

(a) Why is the statement presented in average 1986 dollars?

(b) What is meant by general inflation?

(c) What is the difference in the two losses from operations?

(d) Why are the other expenses such as officers' salaries not reported on this statement?

(e) What is the purchasing power gain on net monetary items? (Explain.)

(f) Why are taxes not allocated to the increase in specific prices of inventories and property, plant, and equipment?

(g) Must Trophy, Inc. report this information in this manner, or are other alternatives available? (Assume that the company is required to present supplementary price-level data.)

C25-5   In 1982, *CICA Handbook*, Section 4510, "Financial Reporting and Changing Prices," was released. This section applies to public enterprises that have either (1) inventories and property, plant, and equipment (before deducting accumulated depreciation) of more than $125 million or (2) total assets amounting to more than $1 billion (after deducting accumulated depreciation). No changes are required in the basic financial statements, but information required by Section 4510 is to be presented in supplementary statements, schedules, or notes in the financial reports.

Instructions

(a) A number of terms are defined and used in *CICA Handbook*, Section 4510.

1. Differentiate between the terms constant dollar and current cost.

2. Explain what is meant by current cost/constant dollar accounting and how it differs from historical cost accounting.

(b) Identify the accounts for which an enterprise must measure the effects of changing prices in order to present the supplementary information required by Section 4510.

(c) *FASB Concepts Statement No. 1*, "Objectives of Financial Reporting by Business Enterprises," concludes that financial reporting should provide information to help investors, creditors, and other financial statement users assess the amounts, timing, and uncertainty of prospective net cash inflows to the enterprise.

1. Explain how *CICA Handbook*, Section 4510, may help in attaining this objective.

2. Identify and discuss two ways in which the information required by Section 4510 may be useful for internal management decisions.

(CMA adapted)

EXERCISES

E25-1   Excerpts from the balance of Power Equipment Company as of December 31, 1986, when the price index was 150, include the following accounts.

Bonds payable (due 1993)	$300,000
Depreciation expense—building	11,000
Inventory (LIFO basis)	60,000
Sales (made evenly throughout the year)	400,000
Cash	40,000
Notes receivable	60,000
Land	100,000
Building	440,000
Accounts payable	30,000

During 1986, the average price index was 135. The land was purchased in 1978 when the price index was 105, and the building was constructed in 1982 when the index was 120. The bonds were issued November, 1981, when the index was 115. The LIFO inventory was built up during 1983 when the average index was 125.

Instructions

At what amounts would these accounts be presented in constant dollar financial statements in (a) end-of-year dollars and (b) average-for-the-year dollars?

E25-2　You have been asked to prepare constant dollar financial statements for Kitchen Products Company. At the end of the period for which statements are being prepared, the price index being used stands at 180. The index values prevailing when each item (amount) was first recorded on the books are shown below.

Item	Index	Item	Index
1. Equipment	160	5. Bonds payable (long-term)	175
2. Accounts payable	135	6. Insurance expense	140
3. Land	180	7. Notes receivable (short-term)	130 and 150
4. Depreciation on equipment	160	8. Rent income	178

Instructions

Indicate which of the items above would be increased, decreased, or remain unchanged on constant dollar statements as compared to the historical cost statements.

E25-3　Presented below are selected price indices for specific dates or periods:

Dec. 31, 1958—100	June 30, 1985—204
Feb. 15, 1959—106	Dec. 31, 1985—215
Mar. 21, 1959—108	Average 1985—206
May 1, 1974—169	June 19, 1986—220
Sept. 23, 1978—190	Dec. 31, 1986—233
Dec. 31, 1981—197	Average 1986—222

1. Cash (on hand December 31, 1986).
2. Equipment (purchased March 21, 1959).
3. Common stock, no par, issued December 31, 1958.
4. Land (acquired February 15, 1959).
5. Preferred stock, $6 (issued September 23, 1978).
6. Accounts receivable (balance December 31, 1986).
7. Inventory (LIFO accumulated throughout 1985).
8. Depreciation expense for 1986 (on equipment purchased March 21, 1959).
9. Sales made during 1986.
10. Investments in common shares (purchased May 1, 1974).
11. Accounts payable (balance December 31, 1986).
12. Bonds payable (issued December 31, 1981, maturing December 31, 1998).
13. Purchases made during 1986.
14. Interest expense (incurred evenly through 1986).
15. Allowance for doubtful accounts (balance December 31, 1986).

Instructions

Given the dates and respective price indices above, indicate what the numerator and the denominator would be to adjust the items for price-level changes for presentation in December 31, 1986, constant dollar balance sheet, in end-of-year dollars.

E25-4   Express Transport Co. purchased equipment for $60,000 on January 1, 1985, when the price index was 120. The equipment has an estimated life of 10 years with no scrap value. At December 31, 1985, the price index was 140 and at December 31, 1986, it was 150.

Instructions

(a)   At what amounts is the equipment carried on constant dollar balance sheets at December 31, 1985, and December 31, 1986? (Assume amounts reported in end-of-year dollars.) Round answers to nearest dollar.

(b)   What is the amount of depreciation expense (use the straight-line method) on the constant dollar income statements for the years ended December 31, 1985, and December 31, 1986? (Assume amounts reported in end-of-year dollars.)

(c)   Assuming that the average price level in 1985 was 130 and in 1986 was 144, indicate the amount at which equipment and the related depreciation would be reported on the related financial statements for each of these years. (Assume average-for-the-year dollars is employed.)

E25-5   Earlville Grain Company began operations on January 1, 1986. At that time merchandise was purchased for $40,000. Additional merchandise was purchased uniformly throughout the year for $210,000. The inventory at December 31, 1986, consists of goods purchased throughout December, at a cost of $29,000. Earlville used a FIFO cost assumption. Assume the following price-level indices:

January 1, 1986	126
1986 Year Average	144
December, 1986, Average	150
December 31, 1986	153

Instructions

Compute the cost of goods sold as it would appear in a constant dollar income statement for 1986 in (a) end-of-year dollars and (b) average-for-the-year dollars.

E25-6   At the beginning of 1986, Cortland Carmel Co. had net monetary assets of $80,000. During the period, the following items increased or decreased this balance:

1.   Equipment was purchased in the first quarter for $11,000 and dividends were paid on December 31 of $6,000.
2.   Sales of $230,000 were made evenly throughout the period.
3.   Purchases of $150,000 were made evenly throughout the period.
4.   Selling expenses (excluding depreciation) of $40,000 were incurred in the first quarter.

The Consumer Price Index was as follows:

January 1, 1986	100
First quarter, 1986	105
Average 1986	110
December 31, 1986	120

Instructions

(a)   Compute the purchasing power gain or loss on net monetary items for 1986 in end-of-year dollars.

(b)   Compute the purchasing power gain or loss on net monetary items for 1986 in average-for-the-year dollars as is recommended in Section 4510.

E25-7   The books of New Glarus Company carried the following selected items on December 31.

	1986	1985
Plant and equipment	$125,500	$225,500
Accumulated depreciation—plant and equipment	30,000	85,000
Share capital (no par value, 25,000 shares)	100,000	100,000
Net monetary items	42,700	30,500

Other relevant information:

1. The Consumer Price Index was as follows:

December 31, 1985	115
April 15, 1986	110
June 15, 1986	115
December 15, 1986	130
December 31, 1986	130
Average for 1986	120

2. Equipment costing $100,000 and having $60,000 of accumulated depreciation was sold on April 15, 1986, for its book value.
3. The company paid a $0.10/share cash dividend on June 15, 1986, and December 15, 1986.
4. Assume that all other transactions that affect such net monetary items as sales occur evenly through 1986.

Instructions

(a) Compute the purchasing power gain or loss on net monetary items for 1986 in end-of-year dollars.

(b) Compute the purchasing power gain or loss on net monetary items for 1986 in average-for-the-year dollars.

E25-8 Ohara Foundry Co. owns a patent for a milling device. The device has a remaining life of four years. Ohara estimates the future cash flows from the patent to be as follows:

Year	Cash Receipts Received at the End of Each Year	Cash Disbursements Made at the End of Each Year	Net Cash Inflows
1	$50,000	$22,000	$28,000
2	40,000	18,000	22,000
3	25,000	14,000	11,000
4	21,000	14,000	7,000

Instructions

(a) Assuming a 10% discount factor, determine the present value of the patent. (Round to nearest dollar.)

(b) Many contend that the present value of future cash flows is the proper method for valuation purposes. Speculate as to why this approach was not adopted in *CICA Handbook*, Section 4510.

E25-9 Regina Poultry, Inc. adopted a current cost system in its first year of operation. At the start of the first year, 1986, the company purchased $24,000 of inventory, and at the end of the year had an inventory of $14,000 on a historical cost basis and $22,800 on a current cost basis. At the time the inventory was sold, the current cost of the inventory was $13,200. Sales for the year were $18,000. Ignore all tax effects and assume that the Consumers Price Index did not change over this period. Other expenses were $1,200 on both historical cost and current cost bases.

Instructions

(a) Prepare a current cost income statement.

(b) Prepare the current cost income statement's supplementary information in accordance with *CICA Handbook*, Section 4510.

E25-10 Assume the same information as Exercise 25-9, and that the Consumer Price Index was as follows:

Beginning of 1986	100
Average for 1986	130
End of 1986	160

Instructions

Compute the increase (decrease) in the current cost of inventory, less the effect of the increase in the general price level. Assume that the goods were sold at the time when the general price level was at the average for the year. The beginning inventory was acquired at the beginning price level. The company is presenting only a partial income statement as recommended in *CICA Handbook*, Section 4510.

E25-11 Silo Mfg. Co. is considering the adoption of a current cost system. Presented below is the enterprise's balance sheet at the end of the year based on historical cost.

Silo Mfg. Co.
BALANCE SHEET
as of December 31, 1986

Cash	$25,000	Accounts Payable	$ 9,000
Inventory	42,000	Share Capital	50,000
Land	16,000	Retained Earnings	24,000
	$83,000		$83,000

The following additional information is presented:

1. Cost of goods sold on a historical cost basis is $60,000; on a current cost basis, $68,000.
2. No dividends were paid in the first year of operation.
3. Ending inventory on a current cost basis is $47,000; land on a current basis is $24,000 at the end of the year.
4. Operating expenses for the first year were $20,000.

Instructions

(a) Prepare an income statement for the current year on a (1) historical cost basis and (2) current cost basis. No unrealized holding gains exist at the beginning of the year.

(b) Prepare a balance sheet for the current year on a current cost basis.

E25-12 Presented below is the historical cost income statement of Cindy Ubl, Inc.

Cindy Ubl, Inc.
INCOME STATEMENT
For the Year Ended December 31, 1986

		Historical
Sales		$1,000,000
Cost of goods sold:		
Inventory Jan. 1, 1986	$ 40,000	
Purchases	500,000	
	540,000	
Inventory Dec. 31, 1986	100,000	
Cost of goods sold		440,000
Gross profit		560,000

Depreciation	400,000	
Operating expenses	190,000	
Total expenses		590,000
Net loss		$ (30,000)

Additional information:

1. Revenues were earned and operating expenses were incurred evenly throughout the year.
2. Inventory was acquired during the last week of the year (FIFO basis).
3. Depreciable assets have a five-year life and were acquired as follows:

    January 1, 1983—$1,500,000
    January 1, 1985—   500,000

4. The Consumer Price Index was as follows:

    | January 1, 1983 | 175 |
    | Average, 1983 | 160 |
    | January 1, 1985 | 140 |
    | Average, 1985 | 130 |
    | January 1, 1986 | 115 |
    | Average, 1986 | 105 |
    | December 31, 1986 | 80 |

5. The purchasing power loss on net monetary items was $29,000.

Instructions

(a) Using the data provided above, prepare a comprehensive constant dollar income statement in year-end dollars.

(b) What are the major differences between a comprehensive income statement on a constant dollar basis and the supplementary income statement information prepared in accordance with the provisions of *CICA Handbook*, Section 4510?

E25-13 Presented below is the historical cost income statement of Cutlass, Ltd.

Sales	$37,000
Cost of goods sold	15,000
Gross profit	22,000
Depreciation expense	2,500
Other expenses	7,500
Income before taxes	12,000
Income taxes (50%)	6,250
Net income	$ 5,750

Assume that the current cost of goods sold was $18,750 and that depreciation on a current cost basis was $6,250. Current cost and historical cost are the same on all other items. The general price level has not changed.

Instructions

(a) Prepare the current cost partial income statement per *CICA Handbook*, Section 4510. Assume that no unrealized holding gains exist.

(b) If a portion of the income tax were allocated to the realized holding gain, how would the income statement differ?

(c) What might be the rationale of the CICA for not allocating the income tax?

E25-14 Hydrants & Plugs Co. purchased 100 bolts of cloth for $520 each on July 1, 1985. On December 15, 50 bolts were sold for $650 each; the current cost to replace the sold bolts was $585 each. On March 31, 1986, the remaining bolts were sold for $715 each; their current cost had risen to $663.

Instructions

Compute the current cost net income in 1985 and 1986. Indicate the realized and unrealized holding gains (losses) reported in each year. Ignore income taxes.

E25-15   Presented below is information related to equipment purchased by Chocolate Company.

Historical cost (acquired July 1, 1984)	$18,000
Current cost January 1, 1986 (gross)	21,600
Current cost December 31, 1986 (25% increase in specific price index)	27,000
Accumulated depreciation January 1, 1986:	
Historical cost	5,400
Current cost	6,480
Life of asset	5 years
Depreciation method	Straight-line

Instructions

(a) Compute the amount of depreciation expense that would be reported in arriving at income from operations on a current cost basis per *CICA Handbook*, Section 4510. (One-half year's depreciation was taken in the year of acquisition.)

(b) Compute the increase in current cost of equipment (holding gain) that will be reported per *CICA Handbook*, Section 4510.

PROBLEMS

P25-1   Retail Showcase Mart was organized on December 15, 1985. The company's initial Statement of Financial Position is presented below.

Retail Showcase Mart
STATEMENT OF FINANCIAL POSITION
December 31, 1985

Assets

Cash	$200,000
Inventory (at historical cost which equals market value; FIFO; periodic)	400,000
Furniture and fixtures	200,000
Land (held for future store site)	100,000
Total assets	$900,000

Liabilities and Shareholders' Equity

Accounts payable	$300,000
Share capital (no par, 200,000 shares authorized; 120,000 issued and outstanding)	600,000
Total liabilities and shareholders' equity	$900,000

The Statement of Income and the Statement of Financial Position prepared at the close of business on December 31, 1986, are presented below.

Retail Showcase Mart
STATEMENT OF INCOME
For the Year Ended December 31, 1986

Sales			$1,100,000
Cost of goods sold:			
Inventory January 1, 1986		$ 400,000	
Purchases		1,000,000	
Goods available		$1,400,000	
Inventory December 31, 1986		600,000	800,000
Gross profit			$ 300,000
Operating expenses			
Rent		$ 36,000	
Depreciation		20,000	
Other (all required cash expenditures)		44,000	100,000
Income before taxes			$ 200,000
Income tax expense			80,000
Net income			$ 120,000
Earnings per share			$1.00

Retail Showcase Mart
STATEMENT OF FINANCIAL POSITION
December 31, 1986

Assets

Cash	$ 240,000
Accounts receivable	400,000
Inventory (at historical cost; FIFO; periodic)	600,000
Furniture and fixtures (net)	180,000
Land (held for future store site)	100,000
Total assets	$1,520,000

Liabilities and Shareholders' Equity

Accounts payable	$ 800,000
Share capital (no par, 200,000 shares authorized; 120,000 issued and outstanding)	600,000
Retained earnings	120,000
Total liabilities and shareholders' equity	$1,520,000

Retail Showcase Mart rents its showroom facilities on an operating lease basis at a cost of $3,000 per month. The rent would be $5,000 per month if it were based on the current cost of the facility. All sales and cash outlays for costs and expenses occur uniformly throughout the year.

The following information indicates changing prices since Retail Showcase Mart began its operations.

1. The Consumer Price Index is as follows:

December 31, 1985	200
October 1, 1986	216
December 31, 1986	220
Average for 1986	212

2. The ending inventory is acquired on October 1, 1986.
3. Inventory at current cost on December 31, 1986, is $700,000.
4. Cost of good sold at current cost as of date of sale is $875,000.
5. Current cost of the land on December 31, 1986, is $150,000.
6. The sales and purchases occur uniformly throughout 1986.
7. The "net recoverable amounts" for inventories and fixed assets have been determined by management to be in excess of the net current costs.

The accounting manager of Retail Showcase Mart has decided to comply voluntarily with the reporting requirements presented in Section 4510 of the *CICA Handbook*.

Instructions

(a) Compute Retail Showcase Mart's purchasing power gain or loss for 1986 in terms of December 31, 1986, dollars. Round all computations to the nearest $100.

(b) Prepare a constant dollar income statement for 1986 for Retail Showcase Mart in terms of December 31, 1986, dollars. Round all computations to the nearest $100.

(c) Identify and explain the advantages and disadvantages of constant dollar financial statements.

(CMA adapted)

P25-2 The following information is taken from the historical cost income statement of Batavia Electronics:

Sales revenue	$1,000,000
Cost of goods sold	600,000
Selling and administrative expenses	29,000
Depreciation expense	91,000
Interest expense	64,000
Income taxes	16,000

The historical cost balance sheet for Batavia Electronics is as follows:

Assets	December 31, 1985	December 31, 1986
Cash and accounts receivable	$ 80,000	$ 190,000
Inventory	500,000	520,000
Equipment	130,000	250,000
Accumulated depreciation—equipment	(11,500)	(30,500)
Building	800,000	800,000
Accumulated depreciation—building	(80,000)	(152,000)
	$1,418,500	$1,577,500

Liabilities and Owners' Equity		
Accounts payable	$ 40,000	$ 50,000
8% bonds payable	600,000	650,000
Preferred shares	100,000	100,000
Common shares	300,000	300,000
Retained earnings	378,500	477,500
	$1,418,500	$1,577,500

The following additional information is provided:

1. The general price-level index at December 31, 1985, was 160; the average index for the year 1986 was 170; the index at December 31, 1986, was 180.
2. Sales revenues and material purchases occurred uniformly throughout the year. The expenses, other than depreciation, were paid uniformly throughout the year.

3. The inventories are based on a FIFO cost assumption. The December 31, 1985, inventory consists of goods acquired during the last three months of the year; the average index during those three months was 150. The December 31, 1986, inventory consists of goods acquired during the last month of 1986; the average index for that month was 176.

4. The equipment account consists of the following:

Acquisitions date	Amount	Index
June 5, 1985	$ 50,000	120
October 27, 1985	80,000	148
October 9, 1986	120,000	174
	$250,000	

Depreciation is calculated using the straight-line method, a useful life of 10 years, and no expected salvage value. Company policy is to take one-half year's depreciation in the year of acquisition or retirement.

5. The building was acquired in 1985, when the index was 135. The building has a 20-year life, with an estimated salvage value of $50,000. Depreciation is calculated using the double-declining balance method. Company policy with respect to buildings is to take a full year's depreciation in the year of acquisition.

6. Bonds with a face value of $600,000 were issued in 1968, when the company was organized. Bonds with a face value of $50,000 were issued in 1986, when the index was 171.

7. The preferred shares have no par value, and a fixed liquidation value of $110.

8. Dividends of $101,000 were paid uniformly throughout the year.

9. The common shares were issued when the company was organized in 1968, when the index was 95.

Instructions

(a) Prepare a schedule computing the purchasing power gain or loss on net monetary items in end-of-year dollars.

(b) Prepare a constant dollar income statement in end-of-year dollars.

(c) Prepare a constant dollar balance sheet for 1986 in end-of-year dollars, and restate the 1985 balance sheet to the current end-of-year price level.

(d) Prepare a schedule computing the purchasing power gain or loss on net monetary items in average-for-the-year dollars as permitted in Section 4510 of the *CICA Handbook*.

P25-3 Flack Records, Inc. is discussing the possibility of reporting its cost of goods sold and ending inventory on a historical cost, constant dollar, current cost, and current cost/constant dollar basis. Assume that you are given the following information with respect to Flack Records, Inc.

	Historical Cost	Current Cost	Consumer Price Index
Beginning inventory	$ 40,000	$40,000	100
Purchases	160,000	a	125 (average)
Ending inventory	50,000	65,000	150

aNote: the current cost of goods sold is $192,000 (incurred evenly through the year).

Assume that the beginning and ending inventory were purchased when the general price-level indices were 100 and 150, respectively. Purchases were made evenly throughout the year.

Instructions

(a) Compute the cost of goods sold and ending inventory under a historical cost, constant dollar, and current cost approach in year-end dollars.

(b) At what amount would cost of goods sold and inventory be reported in accordance with *CICA Handbook*, Section 4510, assuming that comprehensive financial statements are not prepared. (Hint: The conversion factor for 125/150 to be used is .833.)

(c) Compute the realized and unrealized holding gain, net of inflation effects. Indicate the realized and unrealized holding gain, net of inflation. Compute the average-for-the-year dollars.

P25-4 Presented below is information related to Osco Stores, Inc., at the beginning of the year 1986:

Osco Stores, Inc.
BALANCE SHEET
January 1, 1986

Assets		Equities	
Cash	$ 10,000	Long-term debt	$ 40,000
Inventory	20,000		
Land	15,000	Share capital	35,000
Building	55,000	Retained earnings	25,000
Total assets	$100,000	Total equities	$100,000

Additional information related to transactions occurring in 1986 follows:

Sales	$100,000
Purchases of inventory in 1986	60,000
Ending inventory, Dec. 31, 1986, historical cost	22,000
Ending inventory, Dec. 31, 1986, current cost	26,000
Cost of goods sold on current cost basis at different dates during the year (average current cost of goods sold the same)	65,000

1. Land's current cost increased to $19,000 during the year.
2. Building's current cost is $70,000 excluding accumulated depreciation.
3. Operating expenses on both a historical cost and current cost basis were $20,000.
4. All applicable transactions were on a cash basis.
5. The company uses a perpetual system for recording inventories.
6. The building has an estimated useful life of 25 years and is being depreciated on the straight-line basis.
7. Current cost and historical cost for inventory, and buildings, are identical at the beginning of the period.

Instructions

(a) Prepare an income statement and balance sheet on a historical cost basis for 1986.

(b) Prepare an income statement and balance sheet on a current cost basis for 1986.

P25-5 Assume the same information as in Problem 25-4 and that the following changes occurred in the Consumers Price Index:

Beginning of 1986	100
Average	130
End of 1986	180

Instructions

(a) Prepare an income statement and balance sheet on a constant dollar basis in end-of-year dollars. Assume that sales, purchases, and operating expenses were incurred evenly throughout the year. Land, building, and beginning inventory were acquired when the general price-level index was at 100. Ending inventory comprised goods purchased when the general price level was 130. (Hint: Use the conversion factor of 1.3846 for the 180/130; do not use the fraction approach.) Round to nearest dollar.

(b) Assume the same information as (a) and prepare the partial income statement that is required to be presented under *CICA Handbook*, Section 4510, using the financial concept of capital. (Hint: Use the conversion factor of .7222 for 130/180; do not use the fraction approach.)

*P25-6 Assume the same information as in Problems 25-4 and 25-5.

Instructions

Prepare an income statement and a balance sheet on a current cost/constant dollar basis in end-of-the-year dollars. (Hint: Make certain the data from instruction (a) of Problem 25-5 are used.)

P25-7 Presented below is information related to Moyer Development Corp.

1984 Purchased land for $80,000 cash on December 31.
Current cost at year end was $80,000.
1985 Held this land all year.
Current cost at year end was $104,000.
1986 October 31—sold this land for $136,000. Current cost of land at date of sale is $130,000.

General price-level index:

December 31, 1984	100
December 31, 1985	110
October 31, 1986	120

Instructions

(a) Determine the amount that the land would be stated on a balance sheet at December 31, 1984 and 1985, under the following assumptions (end-of-year dollars):
1. Constant dollar accounting.
2. Current cost accounting.

(b) Determine the following items:
1. Constant dollar income for 1984, 1985, and 1986 (end-of-year dollars).
2. Unrealized holding gain (loss) on current cost basis for 1985, unadjusted for inflation.
3. Income from operations on a current cost basis for 1986.
4. Realized holding gain (loss) on a current cost basis in 1986, unadjusted for inflation.

(c) Indicate the amount of income from operations that would be reported under *CICA Handbook*, Section 4510, for 1984, 1985, and 1986. Assume that the general indices presented above also reflect the average index for the year; that is, 1984 average index equals 100; 1985 average index equals 110; 1986 average index equals 120.

*P25-8 Assume the same information as in Problem 25-7.

Instructions

(a) Determine the amount at which the land would be stated on a balance sheet at December 31, 1984 and 1985, assuming current cost/constant dollar accounting in end-of-year dollars.

(b) Determine the realized holding gain (loss) on a current cost/constant dollar basis for 1986.

(c) Determine the unrealized holding gain (loss) on a current cost/constant dollar basis for 1986.

P25-9 Pockets & Cuffs Inc. started operations on January 1, 1986, with the following balance sheet:

Pockets & Cuffs Inc.
BALANCE SHEET
As of January 1, 1986

Cash	$15,000	Share capital	$90,000
Inventories	45,000		
Equipment	30,000		
Total assets	$90,000		$90,000

Transaction data for 1986 were as follows:

Current cost of ending inventory at year end	$ 75,000
Current cost of equipment at year end	
(five-year life—straight-line depreciation)	37,500
Income taxes (50% rate)	
Sales (cash)	157,500
Purchases (cash)	90,000
Ending inventory, historical cost	67,500
Cash operating expenses (excludes depreciation)	30,000
Current cost of goods sold (incurred evenly through year)	82,500

Instructions

(a) Prepare a historical cost income statement and balance sheet for Pockets & Cuffs Inc. for 1986.

(b) Prepare a comprehensive current cost income statement and balance sheet for Pockets & Cuffs Inc. for 1986. Assume that the historical cost of the inventory and equipment is the same as its current cost at the beginning of 1986. Depreciation expense is computed on the average current cost asset balances. Charge catch-up depreciation to the unrealized holding gain. Operating expenses on a historical and current cost basis are the same.

P25-10 Assume the same data as in Problem 25-9, and that the Consumer Price Index was as follows:

Beginning of 1986	100
Average	120
End of 1986	150

Assume that all revenues, purchases, and expenses (excluding depreciation) and the ending inventory were incurred at the average price level.

Instructions

(a) Prepare a constant dollar income statement and balance sheet for Pockets & Cuffs Inc. for 1986 in end-of-year dollars.

(b) Prepare a constant dollar income statement and balance sheet for Pockets & Cuffs Inc. in average-for-the-year dollars.

(c) Prepare a partial income statement as required by *CICA Handbook*, Section 4510. (Use the operating capability concept of capital. Ignore the computation for the increase in specific prices, net of inflation, that appears on this statement.)

*P25-11 Assume the same data as in Problems 25-9 and 25-10.

Instructions

(a) Prepare a current cost/constant dollar income statement and balance sheet for Pockets & Cuffs Inc. for 1986 in end-of-year dollars.

(b) Prepare a current cost/constant dollar income statement and balance sheet for Pockets & Cuffs Inc. for 1986 in average-for-the-year dollars.

P25-12 Calgary Drilling Inc. is experimenting with the use of current cost in its accounting. At the beginning of 1986, the company purchased inventory that had a cost of $60,000, of which $36,000 was sold evenly during the year at a sales price of $54,000. The general price level was 100 at the beginning of 1986 and 150 at the end of the period. The average price level for the period was 120. It is estimated that the current cost of the inventory at the date of sale was $39,600 and the current cost of the ending inventory at December 31, 1986, is $26,400. Assume that the company has no other beginning inventory or purchases and uses a perpetual system. (Ignore income taxes.)

Instructions

(a) Prepare an income statement on a historical cost basis for the year 1986.

(b) Prepare an income statement on a constant dollar basis for the year 1986 in end-of-year dollars.

(c) Prepare a comprehensive income statement on a current cost basis for the year 1986.

(d) Prepare, in an income statement format, income from operations in accordance with *CICA Handbook*, Section 4510 (financial concept of capital), and other related disclosures, where possible, for the year 1986.

*P25-13 Assume the same data as in Problem 25-12.

Instructions

Prepare a comprehensive income statement on a current cost/constant dollar basis for the year 1986 in end-of-year dollars.

P25-14 The balance sheet of Red Rock, Inc. appeared as follows on December 31, 1986:

Red Rock, Inc.
BALANCE SHEET
December 31, 1986
(in millions)

Assets		Equities	
Cash	$ 100	Liabilities	
		Long-term note payable	$ 600
Inventory, at FIFO cost	200	Shareholders' equity	
		Common shares (100	
Equipment	700	shares)	400
Total assets	$1,000	Total equities	$1,000

At December 31, 1986, the historical cost and current cost of the inventory were the same. The equipment was purchased new on December 31, 1986. Red Rock uses straight-line depreciation and estimates the equipment will have a useful life of five years with no salvage value.

Financial and economic events experienced by Red Rock, Inc. during 1987, the first year of operations, included:

Sales, all on account	$1,100
Cash purchases of inventory	500
Accounts receivable, December 31, 1987	300
Inventory at historical cost, December 31, 1987	100
Inventory at current cost, December 31, 1987	130
Cost of goods sold at current cost as of date of sale	675
Equipment at current cost, December 31, 1987	850

The general price level index was 100 at the end of 1986, 200 at the end of 1987, with an average of 160 for 1987. The price shifts occurred uniformly throughout 1987. The index at the time ending inventory was acquired was 175. The "net recoverable amounts'' for inventory and equipment have been determined by management to be in excess of net current costs. All sales and purchases occurred evenly throughout the year.

Instructions

(a) Prepare an income statement for the year ended 1987 and comparative balance sheets as of December 31, 1986 and 1987, using each of the following measurements:

1. Historical cost.
2. Constant dollar, in 1987 year-end dollars.
3. Current cost (disclose realized and unrealized holding gains separately).

(b) Prepare an income statement for the year ended 1987 in accordance with the disclosure requirements of *CICA Handbook*, Section 4510, using the financial concept of capital. Include the purchasing power gain or loss and the increases or decreases for the current year in the current cost amounts of inventory and equipment, net of inflation. Also, prepare the five-year summary information for 1986 and 1987.

(All computations should be to the nearest dollar.)

26

BASIC FINANCIAL STATEMENT ANALYSIS

The interpretation and evaluation of financial statement data require familiarity with the basic tools of financial statement analysis. Naturally, the type of financial analysis that takes place depends on the particular interest that the analyst (whether creditor, shareholder, potential investor, manager, government agency, or labour leader) has in the enterprise. For example, such **short-term creditors** as banks and suppliers are primarily interested in the ability of the firm to pay its currently maturing obligations. The composition of the current assets and their relation to short-term liabilities are examined closely to evaluate the short-run solvency of the firm. **Bondholders**, on the other hand, look to more long-term indicators, such as the enterprise's capital structure, past and projected earnings, and changes in financial position. **Shareholders**, present or prospective, also are interested in many of the features considered by a long-term debtor. Their examination focuses on the earnings picture, because changes in it can greatly affect the market price of their investment. Shareholders are concerned also with the financial position of the firm, because it affects indirectly the stability of the earnings.

The **management** of a company is necessarily concerned about the composition of its capital structure and about the changes and trends in earnings. This financial information has a direct influence on the type, amount, and cost of external financing that the company may obtain. As the financial statements are a primary means by which management communicates information to other groups regarding the results of their decisions in terms of financial position, results of operations, and changes in financial position, management certainly has considerable interest in the information contained therein. A company's management may often be prone to consider the consequences of major decisions in terms of their impact on financial statements. In addition, management may find financial information useful on a day-to-day operating basis in such areas as capital budgeting, breakeven analysis, variance analysis, gross margin analysis, and for internal control purposes, although accounting information applicable to such areas is more likely to be related to internal reports prepared using concepts examined in management accounting books.

The accountant's function is twofold: (1) to identify and measure economic events and transactions and (2) to communicate economic information about them to interested parties. Thus far in this book we have discussed accounting in terms of measurement and report preparation, but communication in accounting means more than just preparing the reports; accountants, as well as others, must be able to analyze and interpret financial statements.

A GENERAL PERSPECTIVE ON FINANCIAL STATEMENT ANALYSIS

Expertise in financial statement analysis reflects a skill that one acquires primarily by experience. Nevertheless, in order to develop this skill, one must have an idea of the techniques used in financial statement analysis and how to interpret the results. These aspects can be examined in books and courses, and serve as a basis for building the skill required to conduct a useful analysis.

Information from financial statements can be gleaned by examining relationships between items on the statements (ratios, percentages) and identifying trends in these relationships (comparative analysis). A problem with learning how to analyze statements is that the means may become an end in themselves. There are thousands of possible relationships that could be calculated and trends identified. If one knows only how to calculate ratios and trends without realizing how such information can be used, little is accomplished. Therefore, a logical approach to financial statement analysis is necessary. Such an approach may consist of the following steps:

1. **Know the questions for which you want to find answers.** As indicated at the beginning of this chapter, there are various groups with different types of interests in a company. Depending on the perspective of the user, particular questions of interest to them can be identified.
2. **Know the questions that particular ratios and comparisons are able to help answer.** These will be discussed in the remainder of this chapter.
3. **Match 1 and 2 above.** By such a matching, the statement analysis will have a logical direction and purpose.

While having such an approach is useful, several caveats must be attached to basic financial statement analysis. **Financial statements report on the past**. Thus, analysis of this data examines the past. Whenever such information is incorporated into a decision-making (future-oriented) process, a critical assumption is that the past is a reasonable basis for predicting the future. This is usually a reasonable approach, but the limitations associated with it should be recognized. Also, ratio and trend analyses will help identify present strengths and weaknesses of a company. In many cases, however, such analyses will not reveal why things are as they are. Thus, ratios and trends may serve as "red flags" regarding problem areas. Finding answers about "why" problems exist usually requires an in-depth analysis and an awareness of many factors about a company that are not reported in the financial statements—for instance, the impact of inflation, actions of competitors, technological developments, a strike at a major supplier's or buyer's operations.

Another point is that **a single ratio by itself is not likely to be very useful**. For example, a current ratio of 2:1 (current assets are twice current liabilities) may be viewed as satisfactory. If, however, the industry average is 3:1, such a conclusion may be questioned. Even given this industry average, one may conclude that the particular company is doing well if the ratio last year was 1.5:1. Consequently, to derive meaning from ratios, some standard against which to compare them is needed. Such a standard may come from industry averages, past years' amounts, a particular competitor, or planned levels.

Finally, **awareness of the limitations of accounting numbers used in an analysis** is important. Some of these limitations and their consequences will be discussed throughout this chapter. Understanding the many accounting issues and alternatives presented throughout this book provides a background against which the limitations of accounting numbers can be more fully appreciated.

Basic Approaches of Financial Analysis

Various approaches are used in the analysis of financial statement data to bring out the comparative and relative significance of the financial information presented. These approaches include ratio analysis, comparative analysis, and percentage analysis. Such approaches, and the information they generate, should be assessed in combination with additional data available in notes and other sources of information about a company. It is difficult to say that one approach is more useful than another because every situation facing the analyst is different, and the answers needed are often obtained only upon close examination of the interrelationships among all the data provided. Consequently, combining all approaches when performing an analysis is likely to result in more informed conclusions.

RATIO ANALYSIS

Ratio analysis is the usual starting point in deriving information desired by the analyst of financial statements. A ratio is simply an expression of the relationship between two numbers drawn or derived from the financial statements. As such, ratios serve as summary indicators that can distill some key information about a business enterprise.

Ratios can be classified as follows:

> **Liquidity ratios.** Measures of the short-run ability of the enterprise to pay its maturing obligations.
> **Activity ratios.** Measures of how effectively the enterprise is using the assets employed.
> **Profitability ratios.** Measures of the degree of success or failure of a given enterprise for a given period of time.
> **Coverage ratios.** Measures of the degree of protection for long-term creditors and investors.

The use of these ratios will be illustrated through a case example adapted from the annual report of a large chemical concern that we have disguised under the name of Anetek Chemical Corporation.

Anetek Chemical Corporation is a worldwide enterprise offering more than 1,400 products and services in the following major classifications: chemicals, plasters, pharmaceuticals, metals, agricultural chemicals, packaging, and industrial chemical cleaning. Anetek products are manufactured through the recovery and upgrading of chemicals found in underground brines, salt deposits, petroleum, and seawater. Production is accomplished through the intensive application of technology developed, in large part, by the company's own research organization. Anetek employees number some 50,000 in 48 countries. The comparative consolidated income statement and balance sheet (as shown) are the basis for the illustrations of ratio calculations. **The numbers used in the ratios, like the numbers used in the financial statements, have the last three digits (000) omitted**.

Anetek Chemical Corporation
CONSOLIDATED INCOME STATEMENT
For the Year Ended December 31
(in thousands of dollars)

	1986	1985
Sales and other revenue:		
Net sales	$1,600,000	$1,350,000
Interest revenue	25,000	20,000
Other revenue	50,000	30,000
Total revenue	$1,675,000	$1,400,000
Cost and other charges:		
Cost of goods sold	$1,000,000	$ 850,000
Depreciation and amortization	150,000	150,000
Selling and administrative expenses	225,000	150,000
Interest expense	50,000	25,000
Total	$1,425,000	$1,175,000
Income before taxes	$ 250,000	$ 225,000
Income taxes	100,000	75,000
Net income	$ 150,000	$ 150,000
Earnings per share[a]	$5.00	$4.50

[a]Additional information:
Number of shares outstanding in 1986 is 30 million.
Market price of Anetek's shares at end of 1986 is $60 each.
Cash dividend per share in 1986 is $2.25.

Liquidity Ratios

The ability of a firm to meet its current debts is important in evaluating its financial position. For example, Anetek Chemical has current liabilities of $575,000 on December 31, 1986. Can these current obligations be met when due? Certain basic ratios can be computed that provide some guides for determining the enterprise's short-term debt-paying ability.

Anetek Chemical Corporation
CONSOLIDATED BALANCE SHEET[a]
December 31
(in thousands of dollars)

	1986	1985
Assets		
Current assets:		
Cash	$ 40,000	$ 25,000
Marketable securities (at cost)	100,000	75,000
Accounts receivable	350,000	300,000
Inventories (at lower of cost and market)	310,000	250,000
Total current assets	$ 800,000	$ 650,000
Investments (at cost)	$ 300,000	$ 325,000
Fixed assets:		
Property, plant, and equipment (at cost)	$2,000,000	$1,900,000
Less: Accumulated depreciation	(900,000)	(800,000)
	$1,100,000	$1,100,000
Goodwill	$ 50,000	$ 25,000
Total assets	$2,250,000	$2,100,000
Debt and Equity		
Current liabilities:		
Accounts payable	$ 125,000	$ 100,000
Notes payable	250,000	200,000
Accrued and other liabilities	200,000	150,000
Total current liabilities	$ 575,000	$ 450,000
Long-term debt:		
Bonds and notes payable	725,000	550,000
Total liabilities	$1,300,000	$1,000,000
Shareholders' equity:		
Common shares	$ 150,000	$ 150,000
Contributed surplus	550,000	650,000
Retained earnings	250,000	300,000
Total equity	$ 950,000	$1,100,000
Total debt and equity	$2,250,000	$2,100,000

[a]The notes and some detail that accompanied this statement are excluded for purposes of simplicity and brevity.

1. Current Ratio   The current ratio expresses the relationship of total current assets to total current liabilities. Although the quotient is the dollars of current assets available to cover each dollar of current debt, it is most frequently expressed as a coverage of so many times. Sometimes it is called the working capital ratio, because working capital is the excess of current assets over current liabilities. The computation of the current ratio for Anetek is:

$$\text{Current Ratio} = \frac{\text{Current Assets}}{\text{Current Liabilities}} = \frac{\$800,000}{\$575,000} = 1.39 \text{ times}$$

$$\text{Industry Average}^1 = 2.30 \text{ times}$$

The current ratio of 1.39 to 1 compared with the industry average of 2.3 to 1 indicates that Anetek's safety factor to meet maturing short-term obligations is noticeably low. Does the relatively low current ratio signal a liquidity problem? Or, considering that the ratio is greater than 1 to 1, is the situation well in hand? The current ratio is only one measure of determining liquidity, and it does not answer all of the liquidity questions. How liquid are the receivables and inventory? What effect would the omission of the inventory have on the analysis of liquidity? To answer these and other questions, additional analysis of other related data is required.

2. Acid-Test Ratio   A satisfactory current ratio does not disclose the fact that a portion of the current assets may be tied up in slow-moving inventories. With inventories, especially raw material and work in process, there is a question of how long it will take to transform them into the finished product and what ultimately will be realized on the sale of the merchandise. It must also be remembered that different companies may be using different inventory valuation methods. Elimination of the inventories, along with any prepaid expenses, from the current assets might provide better information for the short-term creditor. Many analysts favour a "quick" or "acid-test" ratio that relates total current liabilities to cash, marketable securities, and receivables. The acid-test ratio is computed for Anetek as follows:

$$\text{Acid-test Ratio} = \frac{\text{Cash} + \text{Marketable Securities} + \text{Net Receivables}}{\text{Current Liabilities}} = \frac{\$490,000}{\$575,000} = 0.85$$

$$\text{Industry Average}^1 = 1.20 \text{ times}$$

The acid-test ratio for Anetek as compared with the industry average is low. This means that Anetek may have difficulty in meeting its short-term needs unless the firm is able to obtain additional current assets through conversion of some of its long-term assets, through additional financing, or through profitable operating results.

3. Defensive-Interval Ratio   Neither the current-ratio nor the acid-test ratio gives a complete explanation of the current debt-paying ability of the company. The matching of current assets with current liabilities assumes that the current assets will be employed to pay off the current liabilities. Some analysts argue that a better measure of liquidity is provided by the defensive-interval ratio. The defensive-interval ratio is computed by dividing defensive assets (cash, marketable securities, and net receivables) by projected daily expenditures from operations. This ratio

---

[1] The industry average ratios are taken from Dun and Bradstreet, *Key Business Ratios in 25 Lines*, and Leo Troy's *The Almanac of Business and Industrial Financial Ratios*. The industry average ratios provide some basis for comparison with other companies in the same industry.

measures the time span in which a firm can operate on present liquid assets without resorting to funds that would be generated by future operations. Projected daily expenditures are computed by dividing cost of goods sold plus selling and administrative expenses and other ordinary cash expenses by 365 days.[2]

The defensive-interval measure for Anetek is:

$$\text{Defensive-Interval Ratio} = \frac{\text{Defensive Assets}}{\substack{\text{Projected Daily Operational Expenses (based} \\ \text{on past expenses)} - \text{Noncash Charges}}}$$

$$= \$490,000 \div \left(\frac{\$1,525,000 - \$150,000}{365} \right)$$

$$= 130 \text{ days}$$

$$\text{Industry Average} = 80 \text{ days}$$

Whether this ratio provides a better measure of liquidity than the current ratio or acid-test ratio is difficult to evaluate, but it does provide another useful tool for analyzing the liquidity position of the enterprise.[3] This ratio establishes a safety factor or margin for the investor in determining the capability of the company to meet its basic operational costs.[4] It would appear that 130 days provides the company with a relatively high degree of protection, and tends to offset the weakness indicated by the low current and acid-test ratios.

Activity Ratios

Another way of evaluating liquidity is to determine how quickly certain assets can be turned into cash. How liquid, for example, are the receivables and inventory? In addition, this type of calculation (an activity ratio) provides information related to how efficiently the enterprise uses its assets. Activity ratios are computed for Anetek Chemical on the basis of receivables, inventories, and total assets.

4. Receivables Turnover   The receivables turnover ratio is computed by dividing net sales by average receivables outstanding during the year. Theoretically, the numerator should include only net credit sales. This information is frequently not available, however, and if the relative amounts of charge and cash sales remain fairly constant, the trend indicated by the ratio will still be valid. Unless seasonal factors are significant, average receivables outstanding can be computed from the beginning and ending balance of the trade receivables. Net trade receivables instead of gross trade receivables are used for this computation.

[2]The only necessary adjustments to the total expense figure are deductions of any noncash charges such as depreciation and provisions for any known changes in planned operations from previous periods. Income tax expense has been included in the illustration to determine total expenses for the year.

[3]For other approaches to measuring short-term liquidity, see Harold Bierman, "Measuring Financial Liquidity," The Accounting Review (October, 1960), pp. 628–632, where he argues for the ratio of net working capital to resources provided by operations; and James Walter, "Determination of Technical Solvency," Journal of Business (January, 1957), pp. 30–43, where he uses the ratio of resources provided by operations to current debt.

[4]See George H. Sorter and George Benston, "Appraising the Defensive Position of the Firm: The Interval Measure," Accounting Review (October, 1960), pp. 633–640; and Sidney Davidson, George H. Sorter, and Hemu Kalle, "Measuring the Defensive Position of a Firm," Financial Analyst's Journal (January-February, 1964), pp. 23–29.

Accounts Receivable Turnover = $\dfrac{\text{Net Sales}}{\text{Average Trade Receivables (net)}}$

$$= \$1,600,000 \div \left(\frac{\$350,000 + \$300,000}{2}\right)$$

= 4.92 times or every 74 days (365 days ÷ 4.92)

Industry Average[5] = 7.15 times or every 51 days

This information provides some indication of the quality of the receivables, and also an idea of how successful the firm is in collecting its outstanding receivables. If possible, an aging schedule should also be prepared to determine how long the receivables have been outstanding. It is possible that the receivables turnover is quite satisfactory, but this situation may have resulted because certain receivables have been collected quickly whereas others have been outstanding for a relatively long period. In Anetek's case, the receivables turnover appears low. The general rule is that the time allowed for payment by the selling terms should not be exceeded by more than 10 or 15 days. Dividing 365 days by the turnover provides a measure (74 days for Anetek) of the average number of days to collect accounts receivable. Therefore, the higher the turnover, the shorter this period of time.

5. Inventory Turnover   Inventory turnover is computed by dividing the average inventory into the cost of goods sold. The inventory turnover ratio for Anetek Chemical is:

Inventory Turnover = $\dfrac{\text{Cost of Goods Sold}}{\text{Average Inventory}} = \dfrac{\$1,000,000}{\dfrac{\$310,000 + \$250,000}{2}}$

= 3.57 times or every 102 days (365 days ÷ 3.57)

Industry Average = 4.62 times or every 79 days

The inventory turnover measures how quickly inventory is sold. Dividing 365 days by the inventory turnover indicates the average number of days it takes to sell inventory (or average number of days' sales for which inventory is on hand).

Generally, the higher the inventory turnover, the better the enterprise is performing. It is possible, however, that a high inventory turnover enterprise is incurring high "stockout costs" because not enough inventory is available. The ratio is useful because it provides a basis for determining whether obsolete inventory is present or pricing problems exist. In Anetek's case, the turnover ratio is lower than the industry average, indicating that some slow-moving inventory may exist. Remember that this ratio is an average, which means that many goods may be turning over quite rapidly, whereas others may have failed to sell at all. In addition, it was assumed that an average of the beginning and ending inventory represented the average for the year. If this situation is not correct, additional computations must be made, assuming that the required information is available.

Inventory must be divided into cost of sales (a cost figure) instead of into sales,

[5]Often the receivables turnover is transformed to an average collection period. In this case, 4.92 is divided into 365 days to obtain 74 days. Several figures other than 365 could be used here; a common alternative is 360 days. Because our industry average was based on 365 days, we used this figure in our computations.

which includes some margin of profit, because it is stated at cost. Occasionally analysts use sales instead of cost of goods sold as a substitute, but this practice has no theoretical support unless inventories are valued at retail prices.

The method of inventory valuation can affect the computed turnover and the current ratio. The analyst should be aware of the different valuations that can be used in costing inventory (e.g., FIFO, Average Cost, LIFO) and the effect that these different valuation procedures might have on the ratios.

From the accounts receivable and inventory turnover information, a **total conversion period** can be determined. The total conversion period is the average number of days it takes from acquiring inventory to collecting cash from its sale. It is calculated by adding the average number of days it takes to sell inventory to the average number of days to collect accounts receivable. For Anetek, the total conversion period is 176 days (102 + 74). Examining the conversion period and its two components can be useful in identifying differences between companies or between years for the same company when evaluating the effectiveness of marketing, credit granting, and collection policies.

The conversion period is often referred to as the **operating cycle**, which is the time between the spending of cash on inventory and the collection of cash from sales of that inventory. However, the operating cycle could be shorter than the conversion period if inventory is bought on credit.

6. Asset Turnover The asset turnover ratio is determined by dividing average total assets into net sales for the period. The asset turnover for Anetek is:

$$\text{Asset Turnover} = \frac{\text{Net Sales}}{\text{Average Total Assets}} = \frac{\$1{,}600{,}000}{\dfrac{\$2{,}250{,}000 + \$2{,}100.000}{2}} = 0.74 \text{ times}$$

$$\text{Industry Average} = 0.94 \text{ times}$$

This ratio supposedly indicates how efficiently the company utilizes its assets. If the turnover ratio is high, the company is presumed to be using its assets effectively to generate sales. (A turnover of 0.74 indicates that for each $1 of assets, $0.74 of sales revenue was earned.) The problem with this turnover calculation is that it places a premium on using old assets because their book value is low. In addition, this ratio is affected by the depreciation method employed by the company. For example, a company that employs an accelerated method of depreciation will have a higher turnover than a company using straight-line, all other factors being equal. For these reasons, this ratio should not be the only one considered in evaluating the efficiency of the company in terms of activity.

Profitability Ratios

Profitability ratios indicate how well the enterprise has operated during the year. These ratios help to answer such questions as: Was the net income adequate? What rate of return does it represent? What is the rate of net income by activities? What rate of income was paid in dividends? What amount was earned by different equity claimants? Generally, the ratios are computed either on the basis of sales or on an investment base such as total assets. Profitability is frequently used as the ultimate test of management effectiveness.

7. Profit Margin on Sales   The profit margin on sales is computed by dividing net income by net sales for the period. Anetek's ratio is:

$$\text{Profit Margin on Sales} = \frac{\text{Net Income}}{\text{Net Sales}} = \frac{\$150,000}{\$1,600,000} = 9.4\%$$

$$\text{Industry Average} = 6\%$$

This ratio indicates that Anetek is achieving an above-average rate of profit on each sales dollar received. It provides some indication of the buffer available in case of higher costs or lower sales in the future.

8. Rate of Return on Assets   While the profit margin discloses useful information regarding the average net income made per dollar of net sales, it does not answer the important question of how profitable the enterprise was for the given time period. This can be examined only by relating profit margin on each dollar of sales to the volume of sales per dollar invested in the company (asset turnover). The resulting relationship is called the rate of return on assets and can be determined as follows:

$$\text{Rate of Return on Assets} = \text{Profit Margin on Sales} \times \text{Asset Turnover}$$

$$\text{Rate of Return on Assets} = \frac{\text{Net Income}}{\text{Net Sales}} \times \frac{\text{Net Sales}}{\text{Average Total Assets}}$$

$$= \frac{\$150,000}{\$1,600,000} \times \frac{\$1,600,000}{\dfrac{\$2,250,000 + \$2,100,000}{2}}$$

$$= 6.9\%$$

$$\text{Industry Average} = 5.6\%$$

Rather than multiply the profit margin by the asset turnover, the rate of return on assets can be computed simply by dividing net income by average total assets as shown below:

$$\text{Rate of Return on Assets} = \frac{\text{Net Income}}{\text{Average Total Assets}}$$

$$= \$150,000 \div \left(\frac{\$2,250,000 + \$2,100,000}{2}\right)$$

$$= 6.9\%$$

$$\text{Industry Average} = 5.6\%$$

Examining the profit margin and asset turnover components of the rate of return on assets is likely to reveal important information that is not evident from the simpler calculation (net income divided by average total assets). For example, Anetek's relatively high profit margin (compared to the industry) has more than offset its lower-than-average asset turnover, resulting in a rate of return on assets (6.9% under either calculation) that is somewhat above the average for the industry. In terms of corporate strategy, Anetek's management appears to have established a policy of setting higher prices for its products (assuming costs are fairly similar across the industry) and accepting a lower volume of sales relative to assets invested.

Analysis of profit margin and asset turnover is helpful in determining the particular strategies of companies within an industry when attempting to understand and evaluate rate of return on assets. Many enterprises have a small profit margin on sales and a high turnover (grocery and discount stores), whereas other enterprises have a relatively high profit margin but a low inventory turnover (jewellery and furniture stores). Even companies in the same type of business may follow different strategies that turn out to be equally profitable. For example, in the restaurant business McDonald's follows a strategy of charging relatively low prices compared to a high-class restaurant. While McDonald's margin would be lower, the volume of sales (turnover) would be higher. Consequently, both types of strategies may prove to be successful for overall profitability.

One of the most interesting applications of the fact that overall profitability results from many factors is called the du Pont system of financial control.[6] The basic components in the du Pont system are presented in the following diagram.

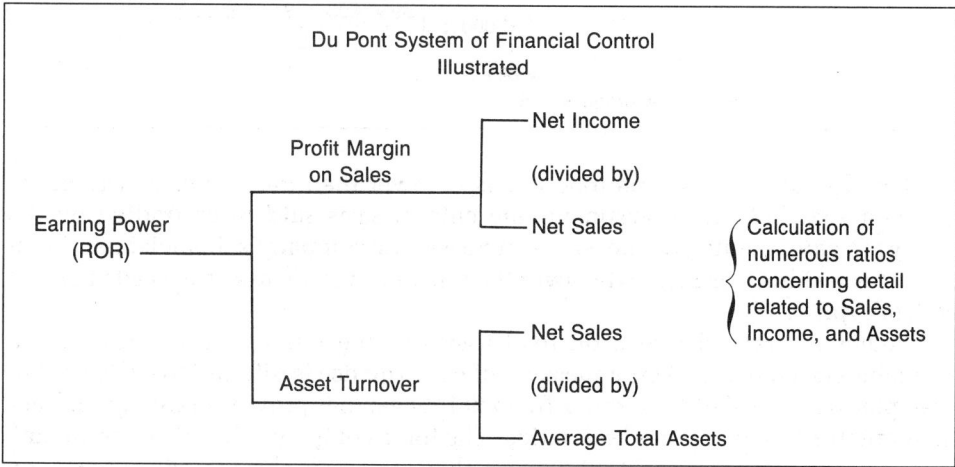

In this system, ratios can be defined in enough detail to give the analyst the information desired. The significant point is that all ratios can help explain the different effects leading to the rate of return on invested capital.

Because of a belief that operating activities should be separated from financing activities when analyzing a company, some contend that a better measure of the rate earned on the assets results from the use of net income before subtraction of the interest charge.[7] This ratio is computed by dividing net income plus after-tax interest expense by average total assets. Interest expense (net of tax effect), including discount amortization, is added back to income because the interest represents a cost of securing additional assets and therefore should not be considered as a deduction in arriving at the amount of return on assets. The ratio for Anetek is:

---

[6]Descriptions of this system are available in T. C. Davis, *How the du Pont Organization Appraises Its Performance*, Financial Management Series, No. 94 (New York: American Management Assocation Treasurer's Dept., 1950); and C. A. Kline, Jr. and H. L. Hissler, "The du Pont Chart System for Appraising Operating Performance," *N.A.C.A. Bulletin* (August, 1953), pp. 1595–1619.

[7]Public utility companies often compute their rate of return on the basis of this approach.

$$\text{Rate of Return on Assets} = \frac{\text{Net Income} + \text{Interest Expense} - \text{Tax Savings}[8]}{\text{Average Total Assets}}$$

(after eliminating interest expense and related tax savings)

$$= \frac{\$150,000 + \$50,000 - 0.40\,(\$50,000)}{\dfrac{\$2,250,000 + \$2,100,000}{2}}$$

$$= 8.3\%$$

9. Rate of Return on Common Shareholders' Equity This ratio is defined as net income after interest, taxes, and preferred dividends divided by average common shareholders' equity. Anetek's ratio is computed in this manner:

$$\text{Rate of Return on Common Shareholders' Equity} = \frac{\text{Net Income} - \text{Preferred Dividends}}{\text{Average Common Shareholders' Equity}}$$

$$= \$150,000 \div \left(\frac{\$950,000 + \$1,100,000}{2}\right)$$

$$= 14.6\%$$
$$\text{Industry Average} = 9.5\%$$

When the rate of return on total assets is lower than the rate of return on the common shareholders' investment, the enterprise is said to be trading on the equity at a gain. Trading on the equity increases the company's financial risk, but it enhances residual earnings whenever the rate of return on assets exceeds the cost of debt capital.

Whether the rate of return on total assets or the rate of return on common shareholders' equity is a better measure of performance is difficult to evaluate. For example, when *Forbes* (a popular financial magazine) provides basic guidelines for profitability, it computes both ratios. The three companies listed below all rank fairly close in return on equity; however, they are not as close in rate of return on total assets.

Comparisons of Different Types of Profitability Indices

Company	5-Year Return on Common Shareholders' Equity Rank[a]	Percentage	5-Year Return on Total Assets Rank	Percentage
Teledyne	24	35.4	34	34.2
Superior Oil	26	34.8	418	12.2
Pioneer	33	32.9	152	17.4

[a]Rank amongst 500 publicly owned U.S. companies.

[8]The tax savings is computed by multiplying the interest expense by the effective tax rate. The effective rate, if not reported, may be determined by dividing the income tax expense by income before taxes.

When these three companies are evaluated, Superior Oil stands out as a company that is highly leveraged; that is, a great deal of debt is in its capital structure. Leveraging per se is not wrong, but in an economic downturn chances are that Superior Oil would turn less profitable more quickly than the other two companies.

On the other hand, many companies are leveraged very little; can they be considered less profitable? For example, Avon Products has a rate of return on assets of 30.5% (Rank 11) and rate of return on common shareholders' equity of 30.8% (Rank 42). Is Avon more or less profitable than Superior Oil? It is a difficult question to evaluate, and both ratios should be considered in the analysis.

Trading on the Equity   The expression "trading on the equity" describes the practice of using borrowed money at fixed interest rates or issuing preferred shares with constant dividend amounts in hopes of obtaining a higher rate of return from the use of the money acquired than the interest or preferred dividends paid. Because debtors or preferred shareholders are usually given a prior claim on some or all of the corporate assets, the advantage to common shareholders must come from borrowing at a lower rate than the rate of return obtained by the corporation on the assets borrowed. If this can be done, the capital obtained from bondholders or preferred shareholders earns enough to pay the interest or preferred dividends, and to leave a margin for the common shareholders. When this condition exists, trading on the equity is profitable. A comparison of the rate of return on total assets with the rate applicable to common shareholders indicates the profitability of trading on the equity in any given case. To illustrate, Anetek's rate of return on total assets is 6.9%, whereas the rate of return on the common shareholders' equity is 14.6%. Anetek traded on the equity at a gain. In essence, the liability claimants were paid a lower rate than 6.9%. Anetek is a very highly leveraged company that has achieved an excellent rate of return on common shareholders' equity by using its debt effectively. A similar conclusion applies to Indal Limited (see Appendix 5A of Chapter 5 for the company's ten-year summary, which shows rates of return on total assets and on common shareholders' equity) for 1984 and 1983 when the rate of return on common shareholders' equity was more than twice that on total assets. A word of caution—trading on the equity is a two-way street: just as a company's ownership gains can be magnified, so also can losses. In 1982, Indal Limited reported its lowest net income given in the ten-year summary and showed a rate of return on common shareholders' equity of only one-half that of the rate of return on total assets.

10. Earnings Per Share   The earnings per share figure is probably the ratio most used by investment analysts, yet it is one of the most deceptive. If no dilutive securities are present in the capital structure, then earnings per share is simply computed by dividing net income minus preferred dividends by the weighted average number of common shares outstanding. If, however, convertible securities, stock options, warrants, or other dilutive securities are included in the capital structure, (1) basic earnings per common share and (2) fully diluted earnings per share figures would have to be examined.[9] The 1986 computation for Anetek is shown at the top of page 1248.

Because no dilutive securities that are common share equivalents or potentially dilutive securities are present in Anetek's capital structure, fully diluted earnings per share amounts are not calculated.

---

[9]See Chapter 17 for a discussion of how dilutive securities should be handled to compute fully diluted earnings per share.

$$\text{Basic Earnings Per Share} = \frac{\text{Net Income} - \text{Preferred Dividends}}{\text{Weighted Average Number of Shares Outstanding}} = \frac{\$150,000}{30,000} = \$5.00$$

Certain dangers exist when the earnings per share ratio is computed. For example, earnings per share can be increased simply by reducing the number of shares outstanding through the purchase and cancellation of a company's own stock. In addition, the earnings per share figure fails to recognize the probable increasing base of the shareholders' investment. That is, earnings per share, all other factors being equal, will probably increase year after year if the corporation reinvests earnings in the business, because a larger earnings figure should be generated without a corresponding increase in the denominator (the number of shares outstanding). Because even the well-informed public attaches such importance to earnings per share, caution is warranted, and the figure should not be given more emphasis than it deserves. The common problem is that the per-share figure draws the investor's attention from the enterprise as a whole—with its differing magnitudes of sales, costs, volumes, and invested capital—and concentrates too much attention on the single share.

11. Price Earnings Ratio   The price earnings (P/E) ratio is an oft-quoted statistic used by analysts in discussing the investment possibility of a given enterprise. It is computed by dividing the market price of a share by its earnings per share. For Anetek, the ratio is:

$$\text{Price Earnings Ratio} = \frac{\text{Market Price Per Share}}{\text{Earnings Per Share}} = \frac{\$60}{\$5} = 12.0$$

A steady drop in a company's price earnings ratio indicates that investors are wary of the firm's growth potential. Some companies have high P/E multiples, while others have low multiples. The reason for differences is linked to several factors: relative risk, stability of earnings, trends in earnings, and the market's perception of the growth potential of the shares. The inverse of the price earnings ratio (earnings per share divided by market price per share) provides a measure of the **rate of return on the market value of the share**. For Anetek, this would be 8.33%. Other things being equal, an investor would prefer a lower price earnings ratio.

12. Payout Ratio   The payout ratio is the ratio of cash dividends to net income. If preferred shares are outstanding, this ratio is computed for common shareholders by dividing cash dividends paid to common shareholders by income available to common shareholders. Given that the 1986 cash dividends are $67,500, the payout ratio for Anetek is:

$$\text{Payout Ratio} = \frac{\text{Cash Dividends}}{\text{Net Income less Preferred Dividends}} = \frac{\$67,500}{\$150,000} = 45\%$$

It is important to many investors that a fairly substantial payout ratio exist; however, speculators view appreciation in the value of shares as more important. Generally, growth companies are characterized by low payout ratios because they reinvest most of their earnings. For example, Anetek has a rather high payout ratio when compared with IPSCO Inc., which paid out approximately 34% of earnings in 1984, but a relatively low ratio when compared with EMCO Limited's payout of approximately 80% of net earnings to common shareholders in 1984.

While the payout ratio helps in assessing dividend policy, care must be exercised when comparing the ratio of different companies over time periods. For example, when a company is going through difficult times (incurring low earnings or losses), it may continue to pay dividends, thereby showing a very high payout ratio. Such was the case from 1981 through 1984 for INCO Limited, which paid dividends to common shareholders despite losses each year. Also, the existence of extraordinary gains or losses in the net income figure would distort the meaningfulness of a trend in payout ratios. For this reason, calculation of a payout ratio based on net income before such items may be more useful when examining trend relationships.

Another closely related ratio that is often used is the **dividend yield**; it is simply the cash dividend per share divided by the market price per share. The cash dividend per share for Anetek is $2.25, so the dividend yield is 3.75% ($2.25/$60). This ratio affords investors some idea of the rate of return that will be received in cash dividends in the short run from their investment.

Coverage Ratios

The coverage ratios are computed to help in predicting the long-run solvency of a company. These ratios are of interest primarily to bondholders and other long-term debtors who need some indication of the measure of protection available to them. In addition, such ratios reflect part of the risk involved in investing in common shares because the more debt that is added to the capital structure, the more uncertain is the return to common shareholders.

13. Debt to Total Assets This ratio provides the creditors with some idea of the corporation's ability to withstand losses without impairing the interests of creditors. The lower this ratio the more "buffer" there is available to creditors before the corporation becomes insolvent. From the creditor's point of view a low ratio of debt (total liabilities) to total assets is desirable.

The ratio for Anetek is:

$$\text{Debt to Total Assets} = \frac{\text{Debt}}{\text{Total Assets}} = \frac{\$1,300,000}{\$2,250,000} = 58\%$$

$$\text{Industry Average} = 38\%$$

There are other ways of expressing this ratio, such as the ratio of debt to shareholders' equity, the ratio of shareholders' equity to the sum of debt and shareholders' equity, or the ratio of long-term debt to total assets less current liabilities. Essentially, these ratios all provide similar answers to the question: How well protected are the creditors in the case of possible insolvency of the enterprise?[10] This ratio has a very definite effect on the company's ability to obtain additional financing in terms of interest rates and security provisions required. Anetek is highly leveraged compared to the industry average; further growth through debt financing could prove to be difficult.

14. Times Interest Earned   The times interest earned ratio is computed by dividing income before interest charges and taxes by the interest charge. This ratio stresses the importance of a company's covering all interest charges. Note that the times interest earned ratio uses income before interest and income taxes, because this amount represents the amount of income available to cover interest. Income taxes are paid only after interest charges have been met. The ratio for Anetek is:

$$\text{Times Interest Earned} = \frac{\text{Income Before Taxes and Interest Charges}}{\text{Interest Charges}} = \frac{\$300,000}{\$50,000} = 6 \text{ times}$$

In this case Anetek's interest coverage appears to be adequate.

If a company pays preferred dividends, the number of times the preferred dividends are earned is computed by dividing the net income for the year by the annual preferred dividend requirements.

15. Book Value Per Share   A much-used basis for evaluating the net worth and any changes in it from year to year is found in the book value or equity value per share. Book value per share is the amount each share would receive if the company were liquidated **on the basis of amounts reported on the balance sheet.** The figure loses much of its relevance if the valuations on the balance sheet do not approximate fair market value of the assets. It is computed by allocating the shareholders' equity items among the various classes of shares and then dividing the total so allocated to each class by the number of shares outstanding.

The book value per common share for Anetek is:

$$\text{Book Value Per Share} = \frac{\text{Common Shareholders' Equity}}{\text{Outstanding Shares}} = \frac{\$950,000}{30,000} = \$31.67$$

Preferred shares are not a part of the capital structure of Anetek. When this type of security is present, an analysis of the covenants involving the preferred shares should be studied. If preferred dividends are in arrears, the preferred shares are participating, or if preferred shares have a redemption or liquidating value higher than their carrying amount, retained earnings must be allocated between the preferred and common shareholders.

To illustrate, assume that the situation as shown at the top of page 1251 exists.

In the computation it is assumed that no preferred dividends are in arrears and that the preferred is not participating. Now assume that the same facts exist except that the $5 preferred is cumulative, participating up to $8 per share, and that dividends for three years before the current year are in arrears. The book value

---

[10]Additional protection, of course, is afforded through specified liens and collateral and through contractual restrictive covenants.

Shareholders' equity	Preferred	Common
Preferred shares, $5 dividend per share	$300,000.00	
Common shares		$400,000.00
Contributed surplus		37,500.00
Retained earnings		162,582.00
Totals	$300,000.00	$600,082.00
Shares outstanding	3,000	4,000
Book value per share	$ 100.00	$ 150.02

of each class of shares is then computed as follows, assuming that no action has yet been taken concerning dividends for the current year:

Shareholders' equity	Preferred	Common
Preferred shares,[11] $5	$300,000.00	
Common shares		$400,000.00
Contributed surplus		37,500.00
Retained earnings:		
Dividends in arrears (three years at $15,000 a year)	45,000.00	
Current year dividends ($5 per share)	15,000.00	20,000.00
Participating—additional $3 per share	9,000.00	12,000.00
Remainder to common		61,582.00
Totals	$369,000.00	$531,082.00
Shares outstanding	3,000	4,000
Book value per share	$ 123.00	$ 132.77

In connection with the book value computation, the analyst must know how to handle such items as the number of authorized and unissued shares, any commitments with respect to the issuance of unissued shares, and the relative rights and privileges of the various types of shares authorized. Although the book value per share figure is useful in some cases, in many instances it is not meaningful for decision-making purposes.

16. Cash Flow Per Share   One of the most popular yet least understood ratios used today is cash flow per share. It is computed by dividing net income plus noncash charges (such as depreciation and amortization) by the number of common shares outstanding. The cash flow per share for Anetek is:

$$\text{Cash Flow Per Share} = \frac{\text{Net Income} + \text{Noncash Adjustments}}{\text{Outstanding Shares}}$$

$$= \frac{\$150,000 + \$150,000}{30,000} = \$10.00$$

[11]If the preferred shares have a liquidating preference as to assets, this is considered in determining book value. For example, if the preferred shareholders receive $360,000 at liquidation instead of $300,000, an additional $60,000 is allocated to the preferred.

This amount represents neither the flow of cash through the enterprise nor the residual of the cash received minus the cash disbursed divided by the outstanding shares. It is frequently used to determine approximately the amount of resources generated internally. For most purposes, however, "cash flow per share" is extremely misleading and too frequently used as a measure of "real" profitability.

Until recently, the position taken in the *CICA Handbook* regarding cash or funds flow data per share was:

> The presentation of cash flow per share and price/cash flow ratios reflects a tendency on the part of some users of financial statements to place more emphasis on cash flow than on net income as a measure of results of operations. The amount of cash or other funds provided from operations is not a substitute for or an improvement upon properly determined net income as a measure of results of operations. Figures relating to such measures, therefore, should not be presented in a manner that would seem to give them greater authority and prominence than conventionally computed earnings.[12]

The revison to Section 1540 made in 1985 resulted in deletion of this paragraph, likely due, in part, to the belief that such summary figures as per share information require further study.

In the United States, the profession strongly recommends that isolated statistics of working capital or cash provided from operations, especially per-share amounts, not be presented in annual reports to shareholders.[13] The concern has been that cash flow per share can be misleading and may be used as a measure of profitability.

LIMITATIONS OF RATIO ANALYSIS

A summary of the financial ratios examined in this chapter, their formulas, and an example using data for Anetek Chemical Corporation is presented on page 1253. While ratio analysis is a useful technique for drawing information from financial statements, several of its limitations must be recognized.

Because a ratio can be computed precisely, it is easy to attach a high degree of reliability or significance to it. Financial analysis involves many alternative approaches, and ratio analysis is only one of several means of gaining an understanding about a business enterprise from the financial data. Such different and supplementary approaches as careful investigation of notes, examination of the company's accounting policies, analysis of product-line breakdowns, and inspection of interim data are discussed in the next chapter.

The reader of financial statements must understand the basic limitations associated with ratio analysis when evaluating an enterprise. As analytical tools, ratios are attractive because they are simple and convenient. Frequently, decisions are based on only these simple computations involving relationships between financial data. The ratios are only as good as the data upon which they are based.

One important limitation of ratios is that they are **based on historical cost which can lead to distortions in measuring performance.** By failing to incorporate changing price information, many believe that inaccurate assessments of the enterprise's financial condition and performance result. To illustrate, Imasco Limited, a major Canadian corporation dealing in consumer products and services, in its 1985 statements carried its investment in the common shares of Canada Northwest

[12]*CICA Handbook*, Section 1540, par. 43, as per August, 1974 (prior to revision, September, 1985). Note that the cash flow discussed above is highly simplified because it does not adjust for changes in receivables, payables, and other current assets and liabilities affecting operations. See Chapter 24 for an in-depth discussion regarding determination of cash flow information.

[13]"Reporting Changes in Financial Position," *APB Opinion No. 19* (New York: AICPA, 1971), par. 15.

Energy Limited at the cost of approximately $8,632,000 although the approximate fair market value of the investment was $50,032,000. Such significant information tends to be obscured by the enthusiasm for computing precise ratios.

Anetek Chemical Corporation
SUMMARY OF FINANCIAL RATIOS

Ratio	Formula for Computation	Computation
I. Liquidity		
1. Current ratio	$\dfrac{\text{Current assets}}{\text{Current liabilities}}$	$\dfrac{\$800,000}{\$575,000} = 1.39 \text{ times}$
2. Quick, or acid-test	$\dfrac{\text{Cash, marketable securities, and receivables}}{\text{Current liabilities}}$	$\dfrac{\$490,000}{\$575,000} = 0.85 \text{ times}$
3. Defensive-interval measure	$\dfrac{\text{Defensive assets}}{\frac{\text{Projected daily expenditures minus noncash expenditure}}{365}}$	$\dfrac{\$490,000}{\frac{\$1,525,000 - \$150,000}{365}} = 130 \text{ days}$
II. Activity		
4. Receivable turnover	$\dfrac{\text{Net sales}}{\text{Average trade receivables (net)}}$	$\dfrac{\$1,600,000}{\frac{\$350,000 + \$300,000}{2}} = 4.92 \text{ times, every 74 days}$
5. Inventory turnover	$\dfrac{\text{Cost of goods sold}}{\text{Average inventory}}$	$\dfrac{\$1,000,000}{\frac{\$310,000 + \$250,000}{2}} = 3.57 \text{ times, every 102 days}$
6. Asset turnover	$\dfrac{\text{Net sales}}{\text{Average total assets}}$	$\dfrac{\$1,600,000}{\frac{\$2,250,000 + \$2,100,000}{2}} = 0.74 \text{ times}$
III. Profitability		
7. Profit margin on sales	$\dfrac{\text{Net income}}{\text{Net Sales}}$	$\dfrac{\$150,000}{\$1,600,000} = 9.4\%$
8. Rate of return on assets	$\dfrac{\text{Net income}}{\text{Average total assets}}$	$\dfrac{\$150,000}{\frac{\$2,250,000 + \$2,100,000}{2}} = 6.9\%$
9. Rate of return on common shareholders' equity	$\dfrac{\text{Net income minus preferred dividends}}{\text{Average common shareholders' equity}}$	$\dfrac{\$150,000}{\frac{\$950,000 + \$1,100,000}{2}} = 14.6\%$
10. Earnings per share	$\dfrac{\text{Net income minus preferred dividends}}{\text{Weighted average number of shares outstanding}}$	$\dfrac{\$150,000}{30,000} = \$5.00$
11. Price earnings ratio	$\dfrac{\text{Market price per share}}{\text{Earnings per share}}$	$\dfrac{\$60}{\$5} = 12 \text{ times}$
12. Payout ratio	$\dfrac{\text{Cash dividends}}{\text{Net income}}$	$\dfrac{\$67,500}{\$150,000} = 45\%$
IV. Coverage		
13. Debt to total assets	$\dfrac{\text{Debt}}{\text{Total assets or equities}}$	$\dfrac{\$1,300,000}{\$2,250,000} = 58\%$
14. Times interest earned	$\dfrac{\text{Income before interest charges and taxes}}{\text{Interest charges}}$	$\dfrac{\$300,000}{\$50,000} = 6 \text{ times}$
15. Book value per share	$\dfrac{\text{Common shareholders' equity}}{\text{Outstanding shares}}$	$\dfrac{\$950,000}{30,000} = \$31.67$
16. Cash flow per share	$\dfrac{\text{Income plus noncash adjustments}}{\text{Outstanding shares}}$	$\dfrac{\$150,000 + \$150,000}{30,000} = \$10.00$

Also, investors must remember that **where estimated items (such as depreciation and amortization) are significant, income ratios lose some of their credibility.** Income recognized before the termination of the life of the business is an approximation. In analyzing the income statement, the user should be cognizant of the uncertainty surrounding the computation of net income. "The physicist has long since conceded that the location of an electron is best expressed by a probability curve. Surely an abstraction like earnings per share is even more subject to the rules of probability and risk."[14]

Probably the greatest criticism of ratio analysis is the **difficult problem of achieving comparability among firms in a given industry.** Achieving comparability among firms that apply different accounting procedures is difficult and requires that the analyst (1) identify basic differences existing in their accounting and (2) adjust the balances to achieve comparability.

Basic differences in accounting usually involve one of the following areas:

1. Inventory valuation (FIFO, LIFO, average cost).
2. Depreciation methods, particularly the use of straight-line versus accelerated deprecation.
3. Capitalization versus expense of certain costs, particularly costs involved in developing natural resources.
4. Pooling versus purchase in accounting for business combinations.
5. Capitalization of leases versus noncapitalization.
6. Investments in common shares carried at cost, equity, and sometimes market.
7. Differing treatments of pension costs.

The use of these different alternatives can make quite a significant difference in the ratios computed. For example, in the brewing industry, at one time Anheuser-Busch noted that if it had used average cost for inventory valuation instead of LIFO, inventories would have increased approximately $33,000,000; such an increase would have a substantive impact on the current ratio. Several studies have already analyzed the impact of different accounting methods on financial statement analysis. The differences in income that can develop are staggering in some cases, depending on the company's accounting policies.[15] The average investor may find it difficult to grasp all these differences, but investors must be aware of the potential pitfalls if they are to be able to make the proper adjustments.

Finally, it must be recognized that a **substantial amount of important information about a company is not in its financial statements**. Events involving such things as industry changes, management changes, competitors' actions, technological developments, government actions, and union activities are often critical to the successful operation of a company. These events occur continuously, and information regarding them must come from careful analysis of financial reports in the media and other sources. Indeed many would argue, under what is known as the **efficient market hypothesis**, that financial statements should contain "no surprises" to those engaged in market activities because the effect of these events should be known before the issuance of such reports. Appendix 26A elaborates on some of these events.

---

[14]Richard E. Cheney, "How Dependable Is the Bottom Line?" *The Financial Executive* (January, 1971), p. 12.

[15]Examples of such descriptive studies are: Curtis L. Norton and Ralph E. Smith, "A Comparison of General Price Level and Historical Cost Financial Statements in the Prediction of Bankruptcy," *The Accounting Review* (January, 1979), pp. 72–87; Robert Alan Cerf, "Price Level Changes and Financial Ratios," *Journal of Business* (July, 1957), pp. 180–192; and Thomas A. Nelson, "Capitalizing Leases —The Effect on Financial Ratios," *Journal of Accountancy* (July, 1963), pp. 49–58.

PRICE-LEVEL DATA AND RATIOS

The analyst must recognize that traditional financial statements are based on historical cost. Depending upon the type and age of the assets involved, inflation or deflation can greatly affect financial data. As a result, some users restate historical cost based statements to determine whether there has been any real increase from year to year in the elements included therein. As one individual stated in a recent research study on the use of price-level data: "The use of constant dollars helps management unclutter its thinking. . . . The effect of inflation at even 7 to 8 percent per year boggles the mind."[16]

Alternatively, many believe that current cost data provide a better measure for determining the overall performance of the enterprise. To illustrate how current cost information might be used in ratio analysis, certain selected ratios have been developed from a recent annual report of Borg-Warner Corporation.[17] The ratios and their significance are provided below.

Selected Rates on Current Cost Basis
(millions of dollars)

Formula	Computation	Significance
$\dfrac{\text{Current Cost Income}}{\text{Historical Cost Income}}$	$= \dfrac{\$76}{\$126} = 60.3\%$	The lower the ratio, the higher the impact of inflation.
$\dfrac{\text{Income Taxes}}{\substack{\text{Income before Income Taxes}\\ \text{(current cost)}}}$	$= \dfrac{\$47}{\$52} = 90.4\%$	Shows the tax rate on current cost income is higher than that on historical cost income.
$\dfrac{\text{Holding Gains}}{\text{Physical Assets}}$	$\dfrac{\$57}{\$1,381} = 4.1\%$	Indicates whether the company has assets that are appreciating in value.

These ratios are simply examples of the type of information that can be developed from current cost data. As the investment community becomes familiar with this data, and more companies incorporate it in their reporting process, these ratios and variants thereof will take on added significance to many users of financial statements.

REPORTING RATIOS—SOME ISSUES

Computation of ratios requires that appropriate information regarding the components of the ratios be provided in the financial statements. For example, because rate of return on assets or equity is commonly computed, it follows that sufficient data should be provided in the financial statements to enable its calculation. In fact, it could be argued that the profession should require the reporting of the more common ratios in the financial statements rather than leave the computation to the analyst.

[16]Allen H. Seed, "Measuring Financial Performance in an Inflationary Environment," *Financial Executive* (January, 1982), pp. 41–46.

[17]*Ibid.*

Whether the Accounting Standards Committee should establish standards for reporting of ratios is debatable. Some would argue that the *CICA Handbook* is already involved in establishing standards in the area of ratios, given its requirement that EPS information be disclosed on the face of the income statement or in a note cross-referenced to this statement. Because EPS is the only required ratio, many believe that undue emphasis is given to it. To discourage this emphasis and to enhance financial reporting, it could be argued that additional ratio information should be presented, such as rate of return on assets or equity.

Others, however, are of the opinion that the profession should not be involved in developing standards related to the determination and presentation of ratios. A basic argument favouring this position relates to the issue of how far the profession should go if such a responsibility were assumed. That is, where does financial reporting end and financial analysis begin? Furthermore, we know so little concerning which ratios are used and in what combinations that attempting to require disclosure of certain ratios may not be very helpful.[18] One reason for the profession's reluctance to mandate disclosures is that research regarding the use and usefulness of summary indicators is still limited and inconclusive. Some of the major findings to date are as follows:

Predictability Studies   One interesting approach using ratios has been the use of prediction models to determine whether a company is headed for bankruptcy or increased profitability. Several studies have been partially successful in using a combination of ratios to predict a possible bankruptcy situation, whereas attempts to determine profitability have met with dismal failure. For example, one study found that the ratio of cash flow to total debt was the best predictor of bankruptcy. This study showed how financial ratios can be used to predict failure five years prior to its actual occurrence.[19] Ratios have also been used to predict other types of events, such as bank lending decisions, credit ratings, mergers and acquisitions, and so on, although success has been limited in these areas.

Survey and Interview Studies   These studies generally attempt to determine what financial statement users believe are the most appropriate ratios for analysis purposes. One of the most significant studies suggests that information on return on investment, cash flows, changes in financial position, effects of inflation, and components of earnings are considered more important than earnings per share.[20]

Behavioural Research   Experiments that examine the decision-making process given the use of certain information (often referred to as behavioural research) are few and limited in scope. In short, we do not know how information is used, except in a very controlled environment. Some limited evidence on credit-granting activities by bank loan officers suggests that reasonable predictions of business failure can be made using only certain key ratios.[21]

[18]For an expanded discussion of these points, see Paul Frishkoff, "Reporting of Summary Indicators: An Investigation of Research and Practice," *Research Report* (Stamford, Conn.: FASB, 1981).

[19]William H. Beaver, "Financial Ratios as Predictors of Failure," Empirical Research in Accounting, Selected Studies, 1966, *Journal of Accounting Research*, pp. 71–127; and William H. Beaver, "Alternative Accounting Measures as Predictors of Failures," *The Accounting Review* (January, 1968), pp. 113–122. See also E. B. Deakin, "Discriminate Analysis of Predictors of Business Failure," *Journal of Accounting Research* (Spring, 1972), pp. 167–179.

[20]Louis Harris and Associates, Inc., "A Study of the Attitudes Toward an Assessment of the Financial Accounting Standards Board" (Stamford, Conn.: Financial Accounting Foundation, 1980).

[21]See, for example, Robert Libby, "Accounting Ratios and the Prediction of Failure: Some Behavioral Evidence," *Journal of Accounting Research* (Spring, 1975), pp. 150–161.

Such studies indicate the potential that ratio analysis holds. Although this type of analysis has many limitations, the merits of ratio analysis as a method for analyzing a business situation should be appreciated.

COMPARATIVE ANALYSIS

In comparative analysis the same reports or data are presented for two or more different dates or periods so that like items may be compared. Ratio analysis provides only a single snapshot, the analysis being for one given point or period in time. In a comparative analysis, an investment analyst can concentrate on a given item and determine whether it appears to be growing or diminishing year by year and the proportion of such change to related items.

The *CICA Handbook* states that, "when it is meaningful, financial statements should be prepared on a comparative basis showing the figures for the corresponding preceding period" (Section 1500, paragraph 9). Generally, companies present comparative financial statements.[22] Indeed, many companies include in their annual reports five- or ten-year summaries of pertinent data that permit the reader to examine and analyze trends. An illustration of a five-year condensed statement with additional supporting data as presented by Anetek Chemical Corporation is shown below.

Anetek Chemical Corporation
CONDENSED COMPARATIVE STATEMENTS
(in millions of dollars, except where noted)

Income	1986	1985	1984	1983	1982	10 Years Ago 1976	20 Years Ago 1966
Sales and other revenue:							
Net sales	$1,600.0	$1,350.0	$1,309.7	$1,176.2	$1,077.5	$636.2	$170.7
Other revenue	75.0	50.0	39.4	34.1	24.6	9.0	3.7
Total	1,675.0	1,400.0	1,349.1	1,210.3	1,102.1	645.2	174.4
Costs and other charges:							
Cost of sales	1,000.0	850.0	827.4	737.6	684.2	386.8	111.0
Depreciation and depletion	150.0	150.0	122.6	115.6	98.7	82.4	14.2
Selling and admin- istrative expenses	225.0	150.0	144.2	133.7	126.7	66.7	10.7
Interest expense	50.0	25.0	28.5	20.7	9.4	8.9	1.8
Taxes on income	100.0	75.0	79.5	73.5	68.3	42.4	12.4
Total	1,525.0	1,250.0	1,202.2	1,081.1	987.3	587.2	150.1
Net income for the year	150.0	150.0	146.9	129.2	114.8	58.0	24.3

[22]*Financial Reporting in Canada—1983* (Toronto: CICA, 1984) reported that all 325 of the surveyed companies provided comparative figures for the immediate preceding fiscal period in their annual reports.

Other Statistics							
Earnings per share on common shares (in dollars)[a]	$ 5.00	$ 4.50	$ 4.09	$ 3.58	$ 3.11	$ 1.68	$ 1.06
Cash dividends per share paid to shareholders on common shares (in dollars)[a]	2.25	2.15	1.95	1.79	1.71	1.11	.25
Cash dividends declared on common shares	67.5	66.1	59.9	54.1	53.3	30.8	5.0
Stock dividend at approximate market value				46.8		27.3	
Taxes (major)	144.5	125.9	116.5	105.6	97.8	59.8	17.0
Wages paid	389.3	325.6	302.1	279.6	263.2	183.2	48.6
Cost of employee benefits	50.8	36.2	32.9	28.7	27.2	18.4	4.4
Number of employees at year end (thousands)	47.4	36.4	35.0	33.8	33.2	26.6	14.6
Additions to property	306.3	192.3	241.5	248.3	166.1	185.0	49.0

[a]Adjusted for stock splits and stock dividends.

PERCENTAGE ANALYSIS

Analysts also use percentage analysis to help them evaluate an enterprise. Percentage analysis consists of reducing a series of related amounts to a series of percentages of a given base. All items in an income statement are frequently expressed as a percentage of sales or sometimes as a percentage of cost of goods sold; a balance sheet may be analyzed on the basis of total assets. This analysis facilitates comparison and is helpful in evaluating the relative size of items or the relative change in items. A conversion of absolute dollar amounts to percentages may also facilitate comparison between companies of different size.

To illustrate, here is a comparative analysis of the expense section on the income statement of Anetek for the last two years.

Anetek Chemical Corporation				
	1986	1985	Difference	% Change Increase (Decrease)
Cost of sales	$1,000.0	$850.0	$150.0	17.6%
Depreciation and depletion	150.0	150.0	–0–	–0–
Selling and administrative expenses	225.0	150.0	75.0	50.0
Interest expense	50.0	25.0	25.0	100.0
Taxes	100.0	75.0	25.0	33.3

This approach, normally called a **horizontal analysis,** indicates the proportionate change over a period of time. It is especially useful in evaluating a trend, because absolute changes are often deceiving.

Another approach, called **vertical analysis**, is the expression of each item on a financial statement in a given period to a base figure. For example, Anetek Chemical's income statement using this approach appears below.

	1986 Amount	Percentage of Total Revenue
Anetek Chemical Corporation		
INCOME STATEMENT		
(in millions of dollars)		
Net sales	$1,600.0	96%
Other revenue	75.0	4
Total revenue	$1,675.0	100%
Less:		
Cost of goods sold	$1,000.0	60%
Depreciation and depletion	150.0	9
Selling and administrative expenses	225.0	13
Interest expense	50.0	3
Income tax	100.0	6
Total expenses	$1,525.0	91%
Net income	$ 150.0	9%

A variation of vertical analysis, referred to as **common-size analysis**, is the presentation of percentages without the dollar amounts given.

KEY POINTS

1. Once financial statements have been prepared and distributed, analysis and interpretation of the information contained therein is necessary.

2. Fundamental financial statement analysis employs basic approaches (ratio analysis, comparative analysis, percentage analysis) which generate numerical information. This information in combination with additional data (notes to statements and other information about the company and the industry) is used to interpret and evaluate a company's financial position, changes therein, and results of operations for purposes of helping the analyst reach conclusions.

3. The purposes for analyzing financial statements vary and depend on the objectives of the interested party. Because of their different interests, short-term creditors, bondholders, shareholders, management, and other groups would employ financial statement analysis to help answer questions of particular concern to them. Therefore, the choice of ratios and their comparisons should be directly related to the questions being addressed. Without such a perspective, the calculation of ratios and the making of comparisons could become an end in itself rather than a means to an end.

4. A ratio is an expression of the relationship between two numbers that can serve as a summary indicator regarding the financial data of a business enterprise.

5. Liquidity ratios are designed to help assess the short-run ability of an enterprise to pay its maturing obligations. Liquidity ratios include the current ratio, acid-test ratio, and defensive-interval ratio.

6. Activity ratios help assess how effectively an enterprise is using its assets. Such ratios include the receivables turnover, inventory turnover, and asset turnover.

7. Profitability ratios help assess the degree of success or failure of an enterprise's operations during a period of time. Rate of return on assets and on common shareholders' equity is particularly relevant in this regard. Assessing rate of return in terms of profit margin and asset turnover reveals significant insight into an enterprise's strategy regarding profitability. Earnings per share, price earnings ratio, and payout ratio are other measures used to assess profitability.

8. Coverage ratios are designed to help assess the degree of protection for, and risk attached to, long-term creditors and investors. Coverage ratios include debt to total assets, times interest earned, book value per share, and cash flow per share.

9. While ratio analysis is useful, its limitations must be recognized. These include the facts that ratios are traditionally based on historical cost numbers, and that many ratios use estimates in their calculation. A significant criticism is that comparison of ratios between different enterprises is very difficult because each may be using different accounting policies and procedures.

10. With the exception of earnings per share, accounting standards do not require that any ratios need to be reported in the financial statements.

11. Comparative analysis means that the analyst compares like items for two or more accounting periods. From such analysis, trend relationships are identified.

12. Percentage analysis consists of reducing a series of amounts to a series of percentages of a given base. Horizontal analysis provides the percentage change in an item over time, and vertical analysis expresses each item on a financial statement as a percentage of a base amount.

26A

FUNDAMENTAL ANALYSIS VERSUS CAPITAL MARKET ANALYSIS

The approach presented in this chapter assumes that a present or potential shareholder analyzes financial information to determine whether a common share is under- or overvalued. This approach, often referred to as **fundamental analysis,** attempts to find the **intrinsic value** of the security, which is defined as "that value which is justified by the facts (e.g., assets, earnings, dividends, definite prospects including the factor of management)."[23] An investor who, therefore, finds a common share that has an intrinsic value higher than the current market price will buy or continue to hold the security. Conversely, if the intrinsic value of the common shares is lower than the current market price, the investor will sell or not purchase them. The assumption of fundamental analysis is that by careful investigation, under- and overvalued common shares may be detected and appropriate investment decisions made.

To illustrate, at one time Del Monte Corporation's shares dropped from $29 to $23 per share. This drop was attributed to the fact that its most recent earnings per share had dropped from $2.16 to $1.65. However, certain analysts concluded after careful investigation that Del Monte's income would have increased 48 cents

---

[23]Benjamin Graham, David L. Dodd, and Sidney Cottle, *Security Analysis: Principles and Techniques,* 4th ed. (New York: McGraw-Hill Book Co., 1962), p. 28.

instead of declining 51 cents if not for some nonrecurring charges that had little to do with the operations of the business. Apparently many other investors arrived at the same conclusion, because the share price increased 87% to $44 a share a short time later. This example demonstrates that many believe that fundamental analysis is a most useful technique for analyzing financial statements.

Proponents of **capital market analysis** (efficient market hypothesis) believe that the current market price of common shares at any given point in time reflects all available public information and, therefore, analysis of financial statements will not enable an investor to find an under- or overvalued security. The implication of this approach is that attempts to ''beat the market'' through fundamental analysis are fruitless because the market is efficient with respect to incorporating publicly available information into the common share price. It should be emphasized that capital market analysis states only that the current price reflects such publicly available information as that found in financial statements; if you happen to have inside information, you may be able to use it advantageously.

What then does an investor do when he or she believes that the capital market is efficient with respect to publicly available information? To answer this question, we have to recognize that **an investor in common shares is interested in determining the return that would be received and the risk level that would be assumed if the common shares were purchased.** The return on each common share is measured by the change in the market price plus the dividend payment received; the risk level is computed by assessing the probability of achieving a desired return. It follows that the higher the return, the greater the risk, and vice versa. A rational investor will attempt to achieve the highest return possible, given the risk level assumed.

In fundamental analysis, it is extremely difficult to determine the risk level that an investor is assuming. Although an analysis of the financial condition of the business enterprise provides indications as to the possible variability in the returns from the common shares, no theory of risk measurement has been well formulated. This is not the case in capital market analysis. A capital market advocate notes that the risk (variability) associated with the return on common shares comprises two components, a **systematic risk** and an **unsystematic risk.** The systematic risk, often referred to as **beta**, measures the average change in a common share's return for each change in the return on the market as a whole. For example, if a common share has a beta of one, a 10% increase in the market would mean that a 10% increase in the return on those common shares should be expected. Conversely, if a common share has a beta of minus one, the return on the security moves directly opposite to changes in the overall market. The nonsystematic risk, however, cannot be correlated with any factor and is considered random. By acquiring a portfolio of shares, the investor can avoid this unsystematic risk entirely, because over a number of shares this risk component cancels and is eliminated from consideration.

The implication of capital market analysis is that an investor should be concerned with the acquisition of a portfolio of common shares and not with the purchase of an individual security. Purchase of a number of shares provides two important advantages. First, the investor can eliminate the unsystematic risk because this component cancels out for a number of shares. Second, the investor can determine the risk level desired and hopefully can attain this level.

To illustrate the difference between fundamental analysis and capital market analysis, assume that you are interested in purchasing some shares of Seagram Co. Ltd. Adherents of fundamental analysis would suggest that you analyze the financial statements of Seagram to determine its intrinsic value or what you think the shares are "worth." Comparison of the present price to the intrinsic value will then provide the answer as to whether the shares should be purchased. Proponents of capital market analysis, however, would argue that you should determine the beta of Seagram shares and how this beta interacts with the other shares held in your portfolio. If the purchase of Seagram increases the beta in your portfolio, and if you desire this additional risk, then the appropriate investment decision is evident.

It should be emphasized that capital market analysis is highly controversial in the investment community. Only after continual experimentation will the financial community be able to determine its conceptual and operational validity.

Note: All **asterisked** Questions, Cases, Exercises, or Problems relate to material contained in an Appendix.

QUESTIONS

1. "The significance of financial statement data is not in the amount alone." Discuss the meaning of this statement.
2. Distinguish between ratio analysis and percentage analysis relative to the interpretation of financial statements. What is the value of these two types of analysis?
3. A close friend of yours, who is a Psychology major and who has not had any college courses or any experience in business, is receiving the financial statements from companies in which he has minor investments (acquired for him by his now-deceased father). He asks you what he needs to know to interpret and to evaluate the financial statement data that he is receiving. What would you tell him?
4. The controller of a large chemical company has requested you to include in your report certain balance sheet and income statement ratios so that comparisons may be made. Indicate the types or categories of ratios that might be provided and explain their significance.
5. Of what significance is the current ratio? If this ratio is too low, what may it signify? Can this ratio be too high? Explain.
6. How does the acid-test ratio differ from the current ratio? How are they similar? Of what benefit is the defensive-interval ratio?
7. Answer each of the questions in the following unrelated situations:
   (d) A company has current assets of $90,000 (of which $40,000 is inventory and prepaid items) and current liabilities of $30,000. What is the current ratio? What is the acid-test ratio? If the company borrows $15,000 cash from a bank on a 120-day loan, what will its current ratio be? What will the acid-test ratio be?
   (b) A company has current assets of $600,000 and current liabilities of $240,000. The board of directors declares a cash dividend of $160,000. What is the current ratio after the declaration, but before payment? What is the current ratio after the payment of the dividend?
   (c) The current ratio of a company is 5:1 and its acid-test ratio is 1:1. If the inventories and prepaid items amount to $500,000, what is the amount of current liabilities?
   (d) A company had an average inventory last year of $190,000, and its inventory turnover was 4.2 times. If sales volume and unit cost remain the same this year as last and inventory turnover is 7.0 times this year, what will average inventory have to be during the current year?
8. In calculating inventory turnover, why is cost of goods sold used as the numerator? As the inventory turnover increases, what increasing risk does the business assume?
9. What is the relationship of the asset turnover ratio to the rate of return on assets?
10. One member of the board of directors suggests that the corporation maximize trading on equity, that is, using shareholders' equity as a basis for borrowing

additional funds at a lower rate of interest than the expected earnings from the use of the borrowed funds.
(a) Explain how a change in income tax rates affects trading on equity.
(b) Explain how trading on equity affects earnings per common share.
(c) Under what circumstances should a corporation seek to trade on equity to a substantial degree?

11. Explain the meaning of the following terms:
(a) Dividend yield.
(b) Price-earnings ratio.
(c) Payout ratio.
(d) Earnings per share.

12. What is meant by book value? Of what significance are preferred shares in the computation of book value?

13. Of what importance are the following ratios in financial analysis?
(a) Shareholders' equity to total assets or equities.
(b) Debt to total assets or equities.
(c) Times interest earned.
(d) Ratio of plant assets to long-term liabilities.

14. Discuss the inherent limitations of single-year statements for purposes of analysis and interpretation. Include in your discussion the extent to which these limitations are overcome by the use of comparative statements.

15. Comparative balance sheets and comparative income statements that show a firm's financial history of each of the last 10 years may be misleading. Discuss the factors or conditions that might contribute to misinterpretations. Include a discussion of the additional information and supplementary data that might be included in or provided with the statements to prevent misinterpretations.

16. Explain the meaning of the following terms: (a) common-size analysis, (b) vertical analysis, (c) horizontal analysis, (d) percentage analysis.

17. Presently, the profession requires that earnings per share be disclosed on the face of the income statement or in a note cross-referenced to this statement. What are some disadvantages of reporting ratios on the financial statements?

*18. A student who just completed his first finance course commented, ''We didn't use ratio analysis; our instructor indicated that ratio analysis was no longer fashionable.'' Discuss.

*19. Some believe that the stock market is efficient with respect to incorporating publicly available information into share prices. What implication does this statement have for financial statement analysis?

CASES

C26-1 The transactions listed below relate to Demco, Inc. You are to assume that on the date on which each of the transactions occurred the corporation's accounts showed only common shares outstanding, a current ratio of 2.7:1, and a substantial net income for the year to date (before giving effect to the transaction concerned). On that date the book value per share was $151.53.

Each numbered transaction is to be considered completely independent of the others, and its related answer should be based on the effect(s) of that transaction alone. Assume that all numbered transactions occurred during 1986 and that the amount involved in each case is sufficiently material to distort reported net income if improperly included in the determination of net income. Assume further that each transaction was recorded in accordance with generally accepted accounting principles.

For each of the numbered transactions you are to decide whether it:

(a) Increased the corporation's 1986 net income.
(b) Decreased the corporation's 1986 net income.
(c) Increased the corporation's total retained earnings directly (i.e., not via net income).

(d) Decreased the corporation's total retained earnings directly.

(e) Increased the corporation's current ratio.

(f) Decreased the corporation's current ratio.

(g) Increased each shareholder's proportionate share of total shareholders' equity.

(h) Decreased each shareholder's proportionate share of total shareholders' equity.

(i) Increased each shareholder's equity per share (book value).

(j) Decreased each shareholder's equity per share (book value).

(k) Had none of the foregoing effects.

Instructions

List the numbers 1 through 8. Beside them, place as many letters as you deem appropriate to reflect the effect(s) of each of the following transactions as of the date of the transaction.

1. In January the board directed the write-off of certain patent rights that had suddenly and unexpectedly become worthless.

2. The corporation wrote off all of the unamortized discount and issue expense applicable to bonds that it refinanced in 1986.

3. The corporation sold at a profit land and a building that had been idle for some time. Under the terms of the sale, the corporation received a portion of the sales price in cash immediately, the balance maturing at six-month intervals.

4. The board of directors authorized the write-up of certain fixed assets to values established in a competent appraisal.

5. The corporation called in all its outstanding shares and exchanged them for new shares on a 2-for-1 basis.

6. The corporation paid a cash dividend which had been recorded in the accounts at time of declaration.

7. Litigation involving Demco, Inc. as defendant was settled in the corporation's favour, with the plaintiff paying all court costs and legal fees. The corporation had appropriated retained earnings in 1980 as a special contingency appropriation for this court action, and the board directs abolition of the appropriation. (Indicate the effect of reversing the appropriation only.)

8. The corporation received a cheque from its insurance company to cover the theft of a truck. No entries concerning the theft had been made previously, and the proceeds reduce but do not cover completely the loss.

(AICPA adapted)

C26-2 As the accountant for Badger Meters Inc., you have been requested to develop some key ratios from the comparative financial statements. This information is to be used to convince creditors that Badger Meters Inc. is solvent and to support the use of going-concern valuation procedures in the financial statements.

The data requested and the computations developed from the financial statements follow:

	1986	1985
Current ratio	2.6 times	2.1 times
Acid-test ratio	.8 times	1.3 times
Property, plant, and equipment to shareholders' equity	2.5 times	2.2 times
Sales to shareholders' equity	2.4 times	2.7 times
Net income	Up 32%	Down 9%
Earnings per share	$3.30	$2.50
Book value per share	Up 6%	Up 9%

Instructions

(a) Badger Meters' management asks you to prepare a list of brief comments stating how each of these items supports the solvency and going-concern potential of the business. The company wishes to use these comments to support its presentation of data to its creditors. You are to prepare the comments as requested, giving the implications and the limitations of each item separately, and then the collective inference that may be drawn from them about Badger's solvency and going-concern potential.

(b) Having completed the requirement requested in (a), prepare a brief listing of additional ratio-analysis data for Badger which you think its creditors are going to ask for to supplement the data provided in (a). Explain why you think the additional data will be helpful to these creditors in evaluating Badger's solvency.

(c) What warnings should you offer these creditors about the limitations of ratio analysis for the purposes stated here?

C26-3 Antique Furniture, Inc. went public three years ago (1984). The board of directors will be meeting shortly after the end of the year to decide on a dividend policy. In the past, growth has been financed primarily through the retention of earnings. A stock or a cash dividend has never been declared. Presented below is a brief financial summary of Antique Furniture, Inc. operations.

| | ($000 omitted) | | | | |
	1986	1985	1984	1983	1982
Sales	$20,000	$16,000	$14,000	$6,000	$4,000
Net income	$ 3,000	$ 1,600	$ 800	$1,000	$ 200
Average total assets	$22,000	$19,000	$11,500	$4,200	$3,000
Current assets	$ 8,000	$ 6,000	$ 3,000	$1,200	$1,000
Working capital	$ 3,600	$ 3,200	$ 1,200	$ 500	$ 400
Common shares:					
Number of shares outstanding (000)	2,000	2,000	2,000	20	20
Average market price	$9	$6	$4	—	—

Instructions

(a) Suggest factors to be considered by the board of directors in establishing a dividend policy.

(b) Compute the rate of return on assets, profit margin on sales, asset turnover, earnings per share, and price-earnings ratio for each of the five years for Antique Furniture, Inc.

(c) Comment on the appropriateness of declaring a cash dividend at this time, using the ratios computed in (b) as a major factor in your analysis.

C26-4 The owners of Fermi Labs, Inc., a closely held corporation, have offered to sell their 100% interest in the company's common shares at an amount equal to their book value. They will retain their interest in the company's preferred shares.

The president of Trendler Corporation, your client, would like to combine the operations of Fermi Labs with the Metal Products Division, and she is seriously considering having Trendler Corporation buy the common shares of Fermi Labs. She questions the use of "book value" as a basis for the sale, however, and has come to you for advice.

Instructions

Draft a report to your client, covering the following points:

(a) Define book value. Explain its significance in establishing a value for a business that is expected to continue in operation indefinitely.

(b) Describe the procedure for computing book values of ownership equities.

(c) Why should your client consider the accounting policies and methods of Fermi Labs, Inc. in her evaluation of the company's reported book value? List the areas of accounting policy and methods relevant to this evaluation.

(d) What factors, other than book value, should your client recognize in determining a basis for the sale?

(AICPA adapted)

C26-5 The Finance Committee of the Farnsworth Corporation was established to appraise and screen departmental requests for plant expansions and improvements at a time when these requests totalled $11,200,000. The committee then sought your professional advice and help in establishing the minimum performance standards that it should demand of these projects in the way of anticipated rates of return before interest and taxes.

Farnsworth Corporation is a closely held family corporation in which the shareholders exert an active and unified influence on the management. At this date, the company has no long-term debt and has 1,000,000 common shares outstanding which were sold at $20 per share. It is currently earning $5 million (income before interest and taxes) per year. The applicable tax rate is 40%.

If the projects under consideration are approved, management is confident that the $11,200,000 of required funds can be obtained either:

1. By borrowing: via the medium of an issue of $11,200,000, 11%, 20-year bonds.

2. By equity financing: via the medium of an issue of 560,000 common shares to the general public. It is expected that the ownership of these 560,000 shares will be widely dispersed and scattered.

The company has been earning a 15% return after taxes. The management and the dominant shareholders consider this rate of earnings to be a fair price-earnings ratio (6.67 times earnings) as long as the company remains free of long-term debt. A lowering of the price-earnings ratio to five times earnings constitutes an adequate adjustment to compensate for the risk of carrying $11,200,000 of long-term debt. They believe that this reflects, and is consistent with, current market appraisals.

Instructions

(a) Prepare columnar schedules comparing minimum returns, considering interest, taxes, and earnings ratio, which should be produced by each alternative to maintain the present capitalized value per share (of $20).

(b) What minimum rate of return on new investment is necessary for each alternative to maintain the present capitalized value per share (of $20)?

(AICPA adapted)

*C26-6 Two students are discussing the merits of ratio analysis as a basis for financial analysis. In discussing the valuation of common shares, one student notes that many securities sell too high in normal markets. These shares, often referred to as "blue chip"—the prosperous leaders of the industry—have a popularity that is not supported by their assets and earnings. It seems that certain companies and certain industries attract a bullishness that overvalues the shares. Through fundamental analysis, therefore, we can determine whether these shares are overvalued in relation to their intrinsic value.

The second student argues that this type of analysis is no longer used in the investment community for evaluating common shares. The student notes that a new theory of investment selection based on capital market analysis is now used extensively. Unfortunately, the student cannot explain this concept beyond suggesting that it has something to do with "beta" and a "portfolio of shares."

Instructions

(a) Define the term "intrinsic value" and explain why an investment analyst would be interested in finding this value.

(b) Explain the term "beta" and its importance to the theory of capital market analysis.

(c) Why is a portfolio of shares necessary in the capital market analysis approach to selection of common shares?

EXERCISE

E26-1   Presented below is information related to Media Network Inc.:

Media Network Inc.
BALANCE SHEET
December 31, 1986

Cash		$ 40,000	Notes payable (short-term)	$ 60,000
Receivables	$110,000		Accounts payable	26,000
less allowance	10,000	100,000	Accrued liabilities	5,000
Inventories		150,000	Share capital	
Prepaid insurance		3,000	(50,000 common shares)	250,000
Land		20,000	Retained earnings	132,000
Equipment (net)		160,000		
		$473,000		$473,000

Media Network Inc.
STATEMENT OF INCOME
Year Ended December 31, 1986

Sales		$1,100,000
Cost of sales		
Inventory, Jan. 1, 1986	$100,000	
Purchases	790,000	
Cost of goods available for sale	$890,000	
Inventory, Dec. 31, 1986	150,000	
Cost of goods sold		740,000
Gross profit on sales		$ 360,000
Operating expenses		170,000
Net income		$ 190,000

Instructions

(a)   Compute the following ratios or relationships of Media Network Inc. Assume that the ending account balances are representative unless the information provided indicates differently.

1.   Current ratio.
2.   Inventory turnover.
3.   Receivables turnover.
4.   Earnings per share.
5.   Profit margin on sales.
6.   Rate of return on common shareholders' equity on December 31, 1986.

(b)   Indicate for each of the following transactions whether the transaction would improve, weaken, or have no effect on the current ratio of Media Network Inc. at December 31, 1986.

1.   Write off an uncollectible account receivable, $2,200.
2.   Sell additional capital shares for cash.
3.   Pay $24,000 on notes payable (short-term).
4.   Collect $23,000 on accounts receivable.
5.   Buy equipment on account.
6.   Give an existing creditor a short-term note in settlement of his account.

E26-2   Expandabelt Company has been operating for several years, and on December 31, 1986, presented the following balance sheet:

Expandabelt Company
BALANCE SHEET
December 31, 1986

Cash	$ 20,000	Accounts payable	$ 70,000
Receivables (net)	70,000	Mortgage payable	130,000
Inventories	80,000	Common shares	120,000
Plant assets (net)	180,000	Retained earnings	30,000
	$350,000		$350,000

The net income for 1986 was $20,000. Projected annual operating expenditures (based on past data) exclusive of depreciation are $45,000. Assume that total assets are the same in 1985 and 1986.

Instructions

Compute each of the following ratios, indicating the manner in which each is computed and its significance as a tool in the analysis of the financial soundness of the company.

(a) Current ratio
(b) Acid-test ratio.
(c) Defensive interval measure.
(d) Debt to total assets.
(e) Rate of return on assets.

E26-3 Financial information for Airtrain Company is presented below.

Assets	Dec. 31, 1986	Dec. 31, 1985
Cash	$ 140,000	$ 142,000
Receivables (net)	270,000	198,000
Inventories	1,200,000	1,050,000
Short-term investments	200,000	400,000
Prepaid items	60,000	80,000
Land	300,000	300,000
Building and equipment (net)	2,000,000	1,760,000
	$4,170,000	$3,930,000

Equities		
Accounts payable	$ 630,000	$ 430,000
Notes payable	200,000	200,000
Accrued liabilities	100,000	100,000
Bonds payable due 1991	700,000	800,000
Common shares	2,000,000	2,000,000
Retained earnings	540,000	400,000
	$4,170,000	$3,930,000

Airtrain Company
COMPARATIVE INCOME STATEMENT
Years Ended December 31, 1986 and 1985

	1986	1985
Sales	$4,200,000	$3,900,000
Cost of goods sold	3,400,000	3,100,000
Gross profit	$ 800,000	$ 800,000
Operating expenses	480,000	400,000
Net income	$ 320,000	$ 400,000

Instructions

From these data compute as many ratios presented in the chapter, for both years, as possible. Assume that the ending account balances for 1985 are representative unless the information provided indicates differently. The beginning inventory for 1985 was 800,000.

E26-4 Shown below is the equity section of the balance sheet for Sampson Company and Delilah Company. Each has assets totalling $4,200,000.

	Sampson Co.		Delilah Co.
Current liabilities	$ 300,000	Current liabilities	$ 500,000
Long-term debt, 10%	1,500,000	Common shares ($20 per share)	3,000,000
Common shares ($20 per share)	1,800,000	Retained earnings	700,000
Retained earnings	600,000		
	$4,200,000		$4,200,000

For the last two years each company has earned the same income before interest and taxes.

	Sampson Co.	Delilah Co.
Income before interest and taxes	$820,000	$820,000
Interest expense	150,000	-0-
	$670,000	$820,000
Income taxes (40%)	268,000	328,000
Net income	$402,000	$492,000

Instructions

(a)   Which company is more profitable in terms of return on total assets?

(b)   Which company is more profitable in terms of return on shareholders' equity?

(c)   Which company has the greater net income per share? Why?

(d)   From the point of view of income, is it advantageous to the shareholders of Sampson Co. to have the long-term debt outstanding? Why?

E26-5 The controller of Winnipeg Merchandise Company Ltd. finds that, although the company continues to earn about the same net income year after year, the rate of return on shareholders' equity is decreasing. Most of the profits remain in the business so that total assets are increasing year by year, but there is very little increase in net income. As the recently hired chief accountant, you are requested to assist the controller in locating the difficulty and to suggest remedial measures. Among the matters of interest that you find is the following:

	Inventory Dec. 31	Cost Goods Sold
1983	$257,000	$2,850,000
1984	292,000	2,650,000
1985	365,000	2,800,000
1986	407,000	2,980,000

Instructions

(a)   What conclusions can be reached on the basis of this information only?

(b)   What further investigation does it suggest? State exactly how you would proceed.

(c)   If your conclusions are confirmed in the additional investigation, what recommendations would you make concerning remedial measures?

E26-6   Presented below is information related to Serveyou Inc.

Operating income	$ 498,750
Bond interest expense	180,000
	$ 318,750
Income taxes	165,750
Net income	$ 153,000
Bonds payable	$1,500,000
Common shares	525,000
Appropriation for contingencies	75,000
Retained earnings, unappropriated	300,000

Instructions

Is Serveyou Inc. trading on the equity successfully? Explain.

E26-7   Hardy Luggage Company's condensed financial statements provide the following information:

BALANCE SHEET		
	Dec. 31, 1986	Dec. 31, 1985
Cash	$ 40,000	$ 60,000
Accounts receivable (net)	130,000	80,000
Marketable securities (short-term)	80,000	40,000
Inventories	460,000	360,000
Prepaid expenses	3,000	7,000
Total current assets	$ 713,000	$ 547,000
Property, plant, and equipment (net)	637,000	653,000
Total assets	$1,350,000	$1,200,000
Current liabilities	$ 200,000	$ 160,000
Bonds payable	400,000	400,000
Common shareholders' equity	750,000	640,000
Total liabilities and shareholders' equity	$1,350,000	$1,200,000

INCOME STATEMENT For the Year Ended 1986	
Sales	$1,100,000
Cost of goods sold	(700,000)
Gross profit	$ 400,000
Selling and administrative expense	(106,000)
Interest expense	(40,000)
Net income	$ 254,000

Instructions

(a)   Determine the following:
    1.   Current ratio at December 31, 1986.
    2.   Acid-test ratio at December 31, 1986.

3. Accounts receivable turnover for 1986.
4. Inventory turnover for 1986.
5. Rate of return on assets for 1986.
6. Rate of return on common shareholders' equity for 1986.

(b) Prepare a brief evaluation of the financial condition of Hardy Luggage Company and of the adequacy of its profits.

E26-8 As loan analyst for Commerce Bank, you have been presented the following information:

Assets

	James Co. Ltd.	Salamon Co. Ltd.
Cash	$ 80,000	$ 255,000
Receivables	152,000	222,000
Inventories	455,000	460,000
Total current assets	$ 687,000	$ 937,000
Other assets	500,000	612,000
Total assets	$1,187,000	$1,549,000

Liabilities and Capital

	James Co. Ltd.	Salamon Co. Ltd.
Current liabilities	$ 280,000	$ 320,000
Long-term liabilities	400,000	500,000
Share capital and retained earnings	507,000	729,000
Total liabilities and capital	$1,187,000	$1,549,000
Annual sales	$1,050,000	$1,500,000
Rate of gross profit on sales	30%	41%

Each of these companies has requested a loan of $50,000 for six months with no collateral offered. Inasmuch as your bank has reached its quota for loans of this type, only one of these requests is to be granted.

Instructions

Which of the two companies, as judged by the information given above, would you recommend as the better risk and why? Assume that the ending account balances are representative of the entire year.

E26-9 Presented below is information related to Fishery Company for 1986:

Sales	$720,000
Net income	60,000
Average total assets	360,000
Average shareholders' equity	200,000
Market price of shares at year end	$70 per share
Cash dividend per share	$1.60
Earnings per share	$2.40

Instructions

(a) Compute the following ratios for 1986:
1. Profit margin on sales.
2. Rate of return on shareholders' equity.
3. Rate of return on total assets.
4. Dividend yield.
5. Price-earnings ratio.

(b) Compute the following for 1987, assuming that all other factors remain constant:

1. Total sales if the profit margin on sales is 10%.
2. Average total assets if the asset turnover is two times.
3. Net income if the earnings per share is $3.50.
4. Rate of return on shareholders' equity, assuming shareholders' equity increases 10%.
5. Asset turnover, assuming that average total assets increase $40,000.

E26-10 Wingtip Company is a wholesale distributor of professional equipment and supplies. The company's sales have averaged about $900,000 annually for the three-year period 1984–1986. The firm's total assets at the end of 1986 amounted to $850,000.

The president of Wingtip Company has asked the controller to prepare a report that summarizes the financial aspects of the company's operations for the past three years. This report will be presented to the board of directors at their next meeting.

In addition to comparative financial statements, the controller has decided to present a number of relevant financial ratios which can assist in the identification and interpretation of trends. At the request of the controller, the accounting staff has calculated the following ratios for the three-year period:

	1984	1985	1986
Current ratio	1.80	1.92	1.96
Acid-test (quick) ratio	1.08	0.99	0.87
Accounts receivable turnover	8.75	7.71	6.42
Inventory turnover	4.73	4.32	3.42
Percentage of total debt to total assets	48	45	42
Percentage of long-term debt to total assets	28	24	21
Sales to fixed assets (fixed asset turnover)	1.58	1.69	1.79
Sales as a percentage of 1984 sales	1.00	1.03	1.05
Gross profit percentage	36.0	34.7	34.6
Net income to sales	7.0%	7.0%	7.2%
Return on total assets	7.7%	7.7%	7.8%
Return on shareholders' equity	13.6%	13.1%	12.7%

In the preparation of his report, the controller has decided first to examine the financial ratios independently of any other data to determine if the ratios themselves reveal any significant trends over the three-year period.

Instructions

(a) The current ratio is increasing while the acid-test (quick) ratio is decreasing. Using the ratios provided, identify and explain the contributing factor(s) for this apparently divergent trend.

(b) In terms of the ratios provided, what conclusion(s) can be drawn regarding the company's use of financial leverage during the 1984-1985 period?

(c) Using the ratios provided, what conclusion(s) can be drawn regarding the company's net investment in plant and equipment?

(CMA adapted)

E26-11 Gerhardt Gears, Inc. began operations in January, 1984, and reported the following results for each of its three years of operations.

1984	$ 320,000 net loss
1985	$ 40,000 net loss
1986	$1,200,000 net income

At December 31, 1986, Gerhardt Gears, Inc. capital accounts were as follows:

$12 cumulative preferred shares, authorized,
  issued, and outstanding 10,000 shares $1,000,000
Common shares, authorized, 2,000,000 shares;
  issued and outstanding 1,000,000 shares $1,000,000

Gerhardt Gears, Inc. has never paid a cash or stock dividend. There has been no change in the capital accounts since Gerhardt began operations.

Instructions

(a) Compute the book value per common share and preferred share at December 31, 1986.

(b) Compute the book value per common share and preferred share at December 31, 1986, assuming that the preferred shares have a liquidating value of $106 per share.

PROBLEMS

P26-1   Smith Bros. Corporation's management is concerned over the corporation's current financial position and return on investment. They request your assistance in analyzing their financial statements, and furnish the following statements:

Smith Bros. Corporation
STATEMENT OF WORKING CAPITAL DEFICIT
December 31, 1986

Current liabilities		$224,500
Less: Current assets		
Cash	$ 10,000	
Accounts receivable (net)	75,600	
Inventory	109,098	194,698
Working capital deficit		$ 29,802

Smith Bros. Corporation
INCOME STATEMENT
For the Year Ended December 31, 1986

Sales (90,500 units)	$778,300
Cost of goods sold	452,500
Gross profit	$325,800
Selling and administrative expenses, including $24,860 depreciation	155,660
Income before income taxes	$170,140
Income taxes	74,000
Net income	$ 96,140

Additional information: Assets other than current assets consist of land, building, and equipment with a book value of $377,000 on December 31, 1986. Assume that ending account balances represent amounts existing throughout the year.

Instructions

Assuming that Smith Bros. Corporation operates 300 days per year, compute the following (using 300 days in all computations):

(a) Accounts receivable turnover.

(b) Inventory turnover.

(c) Number of days' operations (working capital provided by operations) to cover the working capital deficit.

(d) Return on total assets as a product of asset turnover and the profit margin on sales (profit margin ratio).

P26-2 Mistue Corp. is listed on the Toronto Stock Exchange. The market value of its common shares was quoted at $19 per share at December 31, 1986, and 1985. Mistue's balance sheet at December 31, 1986, and 1985, and statement of income and retained earnings for the years then ended, are presented below:

Mistue Corp.
BALANCE SHEET

	December 31	
Assets	1986	1985
Current assets:		
Cash	$ 3,500,000	$ 3,600,000
Marketable securities, at cost which approximates market	13,000,000	11,000,000
Accounts receivable, net of allowance for doubtful accounts	120,000,000	95,000,000
Inventories, lower of cost and market	134,000,000	154,000,000
Prepaid expenses	2,500,000	2,400,000
Total current assets	$273,000,000	$266,000,000
Property, plant, and equipment, net of accumulated depreciation	311,000,000	308,000,000
Investments, at equity	2,000,000	3,000,000
Long-term receivables	14,000,000	16,000,000
Goodwill and patents, net of accumulated amortization	6,000,000	6,500,000
Other assets	7,000,000	8,500,000
Total assets	$613,000,000	$608,000,000

Liabilities and Shareholders' Equity		
Current liabilities:		
Notes payable	$ 5,000,000	$ 15,000,000
Accounts payable	38,000,000	48,000,000
Accrued expenses	24,500,000	27,000,000
Income taxes payable	1,000,000	1,000,000
Payments due within one year on long-term debt	6,500,000	7,000,000
Total current liabilities	$ 75,000,000	$ 98,000,000
Long-term debt	$169,000,000	$180,000,000
Deferred income taxes	$ 74,000,000	$ 67,000,000
Other liabilities	$ 9,000,000	$ 8,000,000
Shareholders' equity:		
Common shares, authorized 20,000,000 shares; issued and outstanding 12,000,000 shares	$ 12,000,000	$ 10,000,000
$10 cumulative preferred shares, $100.00 liquidating value; authorized 50,000 shares; issued and outstanding 40,000 shares	4,000,000	4,000,000
Contributed surplus	107,000,000	107,000,000
Retained earnings	163,000,000	134,000,000
Total shareholders' equity	$286,000,000	$255,000,000
Total liabilities and shareholders' equity	$613,000,000	$608,000,000

Mistue Corp.
STATEMENT OF INCOME AND RETAINED EARNINGS

	Year ended December 31	
	1986	1985
Net sales	$700,000,000	$500,000,000
Cost and expenses:		
Cost of goods sold	$540,000,000	$400,000,000
Selling, general, and administrative expenses	66,000,000	60,000,000
Other, net	7,000,000	6,000,000
Total costs and expenses	$613,000,000	$466,000,000
Income before income taxes	$ 87,000,000	$ 34,000,000
Income taxes	35,000,000	15,600,000
Net income	$ 52,000,000	$ 18,400,000
Retained earnings at beginning of period	134,000,000	126,000,000
Dividends on common shares	22,600,000	10,000,000
Dividends on preferred shares	400,000	400,000
Retained earnings at end of period	$163,000,000	$134,000,000

Instructions

On the basis of the information above, compute the following for 1986 only:

(a) Current (working capital) ratio.

(b) Quick (acid-test) ratio.

(c) Number of days' sales in average receivables, assuming a business year consisting of 300 days and all sales on account.

(d) Inventory turnover.

(e) Book value per common share, assuming that there is no dividend arrearage on the preferred shares.

(f) Earnings per common share.

(g) Price-earnings ratio on common shares.

(h) Dividend-payout ratio on common shares.

P26-3   Warford Corporation was formed five years ago through a public subscription of common shares. Lucinda Street, who owns 15% of the common shares, was one of the organizers of Warford and is its current president. The company has been successful, but currently is experiencing a shortage of funds. On June 10, Street approached the Toronto-Dominion Bank, asking for a 24-month extension on two $30,000 notes, which are due on June 30, 1986, and September 30, 1986. Another note of $7,000 is due on December 31, 1986, but she expects no difficulty in paying this note on its due date. Street explained that Warford's cash-flow problems are due primarily to the company's desire to finance a $300,000 plant expansion over the next two fiscal years through internally generated funds.

The commercial loans officer of the bank requested financial reports for the last two fiscal years. These reports are reproduced below:

Warford Corporation
STATEMENT OF FINANCIAL POSITION
March 31

Assets	1985	1986
Cash	$ 12,500	$ 16,400
Notes receivable	104,000	112,000
Accounts receivable (net)	68,500	81,600
Inventories (at cost)	50,000	80,000
Plant and equipment (net of depreciation)	646,000	680,000
Total assets	$881,000	$970,000

Liabilities and Shareholders' Equity

Accounts payable	$ 72,000	$ 69,000
Notes payable	54,500	67,000
Accrued liabilities	6,000	9,000
Common shares (60,000 shares, issued and outstanding)	600,000	600,000
Retained earnings[a]	148,500	225,000
Total liabilities and shareholders' equity	$881,000	$970,000

[a]Cash dividends were paid at the rate of $1.00 per share in fiscal year 1985 and $1.25 per share in fiscal year 1986.

Warford Corporation
INCOME STATEMENT
For the Fiscal Years Ended March 31

	1985	1986
Sales	$2,700,000	$3,000,000
Cost of goods sold[a]	1,720,000	1,902,500
Gross margin	$ 980,000	$1,097,500
Operating expenses	780,000	845,000
Income before income taxes	$ 200,000	$ 252,500
Income taxes (40%)	80,000	101,000
Net income	$ 120,000	$ 151,500

[a]Depreciation charges on the plant and equipment of $100,000 and $102,500 for fiscal years ended March 31, 1985 and 1986, respectively, are included in cost of goods sold.

Instructions

(a) Compute the following items for Warford Corporation:
   1. Current ratio for fiscal years 1985 and 1986.
   2. Acid-test (quick) ratio for fiscal years 1985 and 1986.
   3. Inventory turnover for fiscal year 1986.
   4. Return on assets for fiscal years 1985 and 1986.
   5. Percentage change in sales, cost of goods sold, gross margin, and net income after taxes from fiscal year 1985 to 1986.

(b) Identify and explain what other financial reports and/or financial analyses might be helpful to the commercial loan officer in evaluating Street's request for a time extension on Warford's notes.

(c) Assume that the percentage changes experienced in fiscal year 1986 as compared with fiscal year 1985 for sales, cost of goods sold, gross margin, and net income after taxes will be repeated in each of the next two years. Is Warford's desire to finance the plant expansion from internally generated funds realistic? Discuss.

(d) Should the Toronto-Dominion Bank grant the extension on Warford's notes considering Street's statement about financing the plant expansion through internally generated funds? Discuss.

(CIA adapted)

P26-4 Optima Corporation has, in recent years, maintained the following relationships among the data on its financial statements:

1.	Gross profit rate on net sales	40%
2.	Net profit margin on net sales	10%
3.	Rate of selling expenses to net sales	20%
4.	Accounts receivable turnover	8 per year
5.	Inventory turnover	6 per year

6.	Acid-test ratio	2 to 1
7.	Current ratio	3 to 1
8.	Quick asset composition: 8% cash, 32% marketable securities, 60% accounts receivable	
9.	Asset turnover	2 per year
10.	Ratio of total assets to intangible assets	20 to 1
11.	Ratio of accumulated depreciation to cost of fixed assets	1 to 3
12.	Ratio of accounts receivable to accounts payable	1.5 to 1
13.	Ratio of working capital to shareholders' equity	1 to 1.6
14.	Ratio of total debt to shareholders' equity	1 to 2

The corporation had a net income of $240,000 for 1986, which resulted in earnings of $9.38 per common share. Additional information includes the following:

1. Share capital authorized, issued (all in 1978), and outstanding:
   Common, no-par value, issued at $11 per share.
   Preferred, $11 nonparticipating, no-par value, issued at $110 per share.
2. Market value per share of common at December 31, 1986: $112.56.
3. Preferred dividends paid in 1986: $5,500.
4. Times interest earned in 1986: 17.
5. The amounts of the following were the same at December 31, 1986, as at January 1, 1986: inventory, accounts receivable, 10% bonds payable—due 1988, and total shareholders' equity.
6. All purchases and sales were "on account."

Instructions

(a) Prepare in good form the condensed (1) balance sheet and (2) income statement for the year ending December 31, 1986, presenting the amounts you would expect to appear on Optima's financial statements (ignoring income taxes). Major captions appearing on Optima's balance sheet are: Current Assets; Property, Plant, and Equipment; Intangible Assets; Current Liabilities; Long-term Liabilities; and Shareholders' Equity. In addition to the accounts divulged in the problem, you should include accounts for Prepaid Expenses, Accrued Expenses, and Administrative Expenses.

(b) Compute the following for 1986 (showing your computations):
   1. Rate of return on common shareholders' equity.
   2. Price-earnings ratio for common shares.
   3. Dividends paid per common share.
   4. Dividends paid per preferred share.
   5. Dividend yield on common shares.

(AICPA adapted)

P26-5 The Heartland Corporation has been operating successfully for a number of years. The balance sheet of the company as of December 31 is presented here.

The Heartland Corporation
BALANCE SHEET
December 31, 1986

Current assets		Current liabilities	
Cash	$ 50,000	Notes payable	$ 80,000
Accounts receivable (net)	140,000	Accounts payable	77,000
Notes receivable	80,000	Taxes payable	61,000
Inventories	270,000	Total current liabilities	$ 218,000
Prepaid items	20,000		
Total current assets	$ 560,000		

			Long-term bank loan, due in		
Fixed assets			2001, 9% interest		140,000
Land	$ 30,000		Shareholders' equity		
Building (net)	165,000		Common shares		
Equipment (net)	330,000		(35,000 issued)	$350,000	
Total fixed assets		525,000	Retained earnings	377,000	727,000
		$1,085,000			$1,085,000

The balance sheet indicates that the bulk of the company's growth has been financed by the common shareholders, because $377,000 of past net income of the company has been retained and is now invested in various operating assets. For the last three years the company has earned an average net income of $110,000 after interest ($15,000) and taxes ($61,000).

The board of directors has been considering an expansion of operations. Estimations indicate that the company can double its volume of operations with an additional investment of about $800,000. Of this amount $600,000 would be used to add to the present building, to purchase new equipment, and to reorganize certain operations. The remaining amount would be needed for working capital —inventories and higher receivables. Competitive conditions are such that the added volume can probably be sold at the existing prices and that income before taxes and interest will total $350,000. The tax rate of about 36% on income after interest will continue.

Three alternative plans for financing the expansion are under consideration:

1. Sell enough additional shares to raise $800,000. For this purpose it is estimated the shares would sell at $32 each.
2. Sell 20-year bonds at 12% interest, totalling $620,000. In addition, sell 10,000 shares at a price of $32 per share. Use part of the proceeds to pay off the present long-term bank loan.
3. Sell 20-year bonds at 12% interest, totalling $730,000. Use part of the proceeds to pay off present long-term bank loans. The remaining funds are to be provided by short-term creditors. The cost of these funds (in interest and discounts not taken) is estimated at $27,000 a year.

Assume that the financing alternative selected will take place immediately.

Instructions

(a) 1. Compute the current ratio under each plan and compare it with the present current ratio.
2. Compute earnings per share under each plan and compare with the present earnings per share.
3. Compute the rate of return on common shareholders' equity under each plan and compare with the present return.
4. Compute the ratio of debt to total equity under each plan and compare it with the present ratio.

(b) Which alternative financing plan do you recommend? Why?

P26-6 The shareholders' equity in Ranchero Manufacturing, Inc. is as follows:

Preferred shares—$12 cumulative, nonparticipating, no-par value; authorized 10,000 shares, of which 4,500 are issued and out-standing	$ 450,000	
Common shares—no-par value; authorized 1,000,000 shares, issued 900,000 shares	1,110,000	$1,560,000

Contributed capital arising from the acquisition and cancellation of preferred shares		3,000
Retained earnings		
Appropriation for contingencies	$ 46,000	
Appropriation for sinking fund	280,000	
Appropriation for possible inventory decline	75,000	
Unrestricted	516,000	917,000
		$2,480,000

Instructions

Compute the book value per share of the common and the preferred shares under each of the following conditions:

(a)   Assume that there are no preferred share dividends in arrears.

(b)   Assume the same situation as stated above except that preferred share dividends are $108,000 in arrears including the current year.

(c)   Assume the same situation as in (a) except that the preferred shares are fully participating, based on the ratio of the total capitalized value of the respective shares outstanding.

(d)   Assume the same situation as in (a) except that, instead of retained earnings, the company has a deficit of $300,000.

P26-7   Presented below are comparative balance sheets for the Eversonic Company.

Eversonic Company
COMPARATIVE BALANCE SHEET
December 31, 1986 and 1985

Assets	1986	1985
Cash	$ 150,000	$ 230,000
Accounts receivable (net)	220,000	160,000
Investments	160,000	150,000
Inventories	860,000	930,000
Prepaid expenses	25,000	20,000
Fixed assets	2,400,000	1,800,000
Accumulated depreciation	(1,000,000)	(700,000)
	$ 2,815,000	$2,590,000

Liabilities and Shareholders' Equity	1986	1985
Accounts payable	$ 50,000	$ 30,000
Accrued expenses	150,000	200,000
Bonds payable	300,000	200,000
Share capital	2,000,000	1,770,000
Retained earnings	315,000	390,000
	$ 2,815,000	$2,590,000

Instructions

(a)   Prepare a comparative balance sheet of Eversonic Company, showing the percentage each item is of the total assets that each item constitutes.

(b)   Prepare a comparative balance sheet of Eversonic Company, showing the dollar change and the percentage change for each item.

(c)   Of what value is the information in (a)?

(d)   Of what value is the information in (b)?

P26-8 Compustatic Company is planning to invest $10,000,000 in an expansion program that is expected to increase income by $2,300,000 before interest and taxes. The company currently is earning $4 per share on 1,000,000 common shares outstanding. The capital structure prior to the investment is:

Debt	$10,000,000
Equity	30,000,000
	$40,000,000

The expansion can be financed by sale of 250,000 shares at $40 net each, or by issuing long-term debt at a 10% interest cost. The firm's recent income statement was as follows:

Sales	$100,000,000
Variable cost	$ 60,000,000
Fixed cost	31,000,000
	$ 91,000,000
Income before interest and taxes	$ 9,000,000
Interest	1,000,000
Income before income taxes	$ 8,000,000
Income taxes (50%)	4,000,000
Net income	$ 4,000,000

Instructions
(a) Assuming that the firm maintains its current income and achieves the anticipated income from the expansion, what will be the earnings per share (1) if the expansion is financed by debt? (2) if the expansion is financed by equity?
(b) At what level of income before interest and taxes will the earnings per share be the same amount under either alternative?
(c) The choice of financing alternatives influences the earnings per share. The choice might also influence the earnings multiple (price to earnings ratio) used by the "market." Discuss the factors inherent in the choice between the debt and equity alternatives that might influence the earnings multiple. Be sure to indicate the direction in which these factors might influence the earnings multiple.

(CMA adapted)

P26-9 Near the close of your audit, the treasurer of Clausing Corporation, your client, informs you that the company is planning to acquire the Nelson Corporation and requests that you prepare certain financial statistics for 1986 and 1985 from the following statements of Nelson Corporation.

Nelson Corporation
BALANCE SHEET
December 31, 1986 and 1985

Assets

	1986	1985
Current assets		
Cash	$ 1,610,000	$ 387,000
Marketable securities, at cost (market value $550,000)	510,000	
Accounts receivable, less allowance for doubtful accounts: 1986, $125,000; 1985, $110,000	4,075,000	3,669,000
Inventories, at lower of cost and market	7,250,000	7,050,000
Prepaid expenses	125,000	218,000
Total current assets	$13,570,000	$11,324,000

Plant and equipment, at cost		
Land and buildings	$13,500,000	$13,500,000
Machinery and equipment	9,250,000	8,520,000
Total plant and equipment	$22,750,000	$22,020,000
Less: Accumulated depreciation	13,470,000	12,549,000
Total plant and equipment—net	$ 9,280,000	$ 9,471,000
Long-term receivables	$ 250,000	$ 250,000
Other assets	$ 25,000	$ 75,000
Total assets	$23,125,000	$22,120,000

Liabilities and Shareholders' Equity

Current liabilities		
Accounts payable	$ 2,950,000	$ 3,426,000
Accrued expenses	1,575,000	1,644,000
Income taxes payable	875,000	750,000
Current maturities on long-term debt	500,000	500,000
Total current liabilities	$ 5,900,000	$ 6,320,000
Other liabilities		
5% sinking-fund debentures, due January 1, 1997 ($500,000 redeemable annually)	$ 5,000,000	$ 5,500,000
Deferred taxes on income, related to depreciation	350,000	210,000
Total other liabilities	$ 5,350,000	$ 5,710,000
Shareholders' equity		
Preferred shares, $1.00 cumulative, preference on liquidation $25 per share (authorized: 100,000 shares; issued and outstanding: 50,000 shares)	$ 1,000,000	$ 1,000,000
Common shares (authorized 900,000 shares; issued and outstanding; 1986, 550,000 shares; 1985, 500,000 shares)	550,000	500,000
Contributed surplus	3,075,000	625,000
Retained earnings	7,250,000	7,965,000
Total shareholders' equity	$11,875,000	$10,090,000
Total liabilities and shareholders' equity	$23,125,000	$22,120,000

Nelson Corporation
STATEMENT OF INCOME AND RETAINED EARNINGS
For the Years Ended December 31, 1986 and 1985

	1986	1985
Revenues		
Net sales	$48,425,000	$41,700,000
Royalties	70,000	25,000
Interest	30,000	
Total	$48,525,000	$41,725,000
Costs and expenses		
Cost of goods sold	$31,460,000	$29,190,000
Selling, general, and administrative	12,090,000	8,785,000
Interest on 5% sinking-fund debenture	275,000	300,000
Income taxes	2,315,000	1,695,000
Total	$46,140,000	$39,970,000

Net income	$ 2,385,000	$ 1,755,000
Retained earnings, beginning of year	7,965,000	6,760,000
Total	$10,350,000	$ 8,515,000
Dividends paid		
Preferred, $1.00 per share in cash	$ 50,000	$ 50,000
Common		
Cash—$1.00 per share	550,000	500,000
Stock (10%)—50,000 shares at market value		
of $50 per share	2,500,000	
Total	$ 3,075,000	$ 550,000
Retained earnings, end of year	$ 7,250,000	$ 7,965,000

Additional information:

1. The inventory at January 1, 1985, was $6,850,000.
2. The market prices of the common shares at December 31, 1986 and 1985, were $73.50 and $47.75 per share, respectively.
3. The cash dividends for both preferred and common shares were declared and paid in December of each year. The stock dividend on common was declared and distributed in August, 1986.
4. Plant and equipment sales and retirements during 1986 and 1985 were $375,000 and $425,000, respectively. The related depreciation allowances were $215,000 in 1986 and $335,000 in 1985. At December 31, 1984, the plant and equipment asset balance was $21,470,000, and the related depreciation allowances were $11,650,000.

Instructions

Prepare a schedule computing the following selected statistics for 1986 and 1985. The current equivalent number of shares outstanding as of the respective year-end dates should be used in computing per-share statistics. (The current equivalent shares means the number of shares outstanding in the prior period, adjusted retroactively for the stock dividend.)

(a) At December 31:
  1. Current ratio.
  2. Acid-test (quick) ratio.
  3. Book value per common shares.

(b) Year ended December 31:
  1. Gross margin rate.
  2. Inventory turnover rate.
  3. Times interest earned.
  4. Earnings per common share.
  5. Common share price-earnings ratio (end of year value).
  6. Gross capital expenditures.

(AICPA adapted)

27

FULL DISCLOSURE IN FINANCIAL REPORTING

Accountants have long recognized that attempting to present all essential information about an enterprise in a balance sheet, income statement, and statement of changes in financial position is an extremely difficult if not impossible task.

For example, *FASB Concepts Statement No. 1* notes that although financial reporting and financial statements have essentially the same objectives, some useful information is better provided in the financial statements and some is better provided by means of financial reporting other than financial statements. A good illustration of the types of financial information used in investment, credit, and other decisions is provided in Figure 27-1 on page 1285.

Financial statements, notes to the financial statements, and supplementary information are areas directly affected by CICA standards. In addition, financial reporting includes such other types of information found in the annual report as management's discussion and analysis.

FULL DISCLOSURE PRINCIPLE

As indicated in Chapter 2, the profession has adopted a **full disclosure principle** that calls for financial reporting of any financial facts significant enough to influence the judgement of an informed reader. In some situations, the benefits from

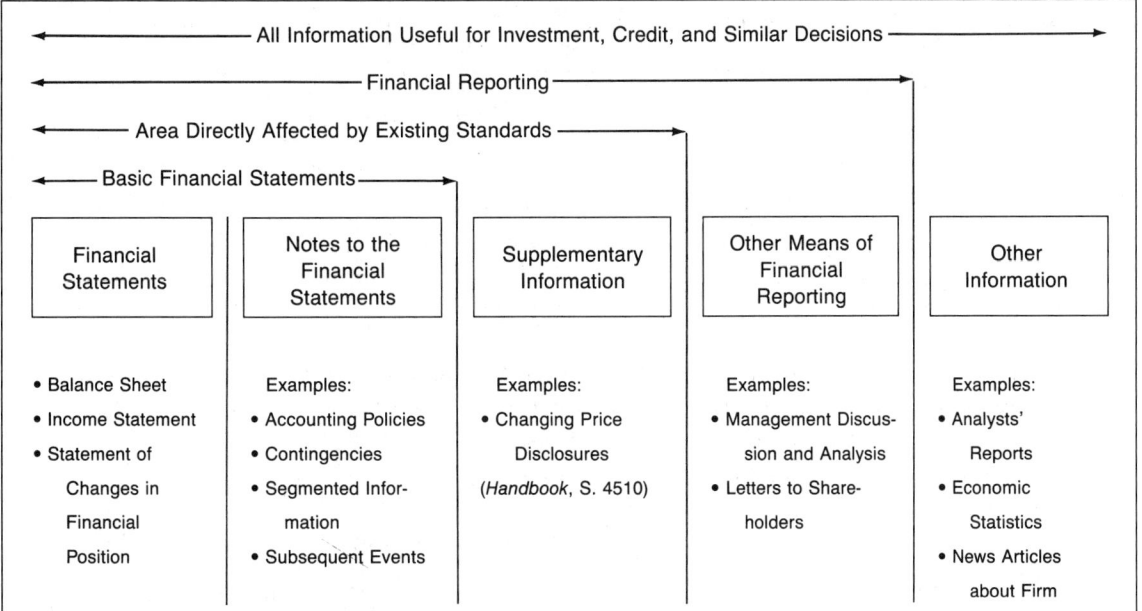

FIGURE 27-1   Types of Financial Information[1]

disclosure may be apparent but the costs uncertain; whereas in other instances the costs may be certain but the benefits of disclosure not as apparent.

The costs of disclosure cannot be dismissed. For example, *The Wall Street Journal* indicated that, if U.S. government reporting rules on segmented reporting were adopted, a company like Fruehauf would have to increase its accounting staff 50%, from 300 to 450 people. Many accountants and managers believe that the present reporting requirements are so substantial that users have a difficult time absorbing the information; they charge the profession with engaging in **information overload.** Conversely, others contend that even more information is needed to assess an enterprise's financial position and earnings potential.

The complexity of this situation is highlighted by such financial disasters as White Farm, W. T. Grant, or Canadian Commercial Bank. Was the information presented about these companies not comprehensible? Was it buried? Was it too technical? Or was it simply not there? No easy answers are forthcoming. One problem is that the profession is still in the process of developing the guidelines that tell whether a given transaction should be disclosed and what format this disclosure should take. Different users want different information, and it becomes exceedingly difficult to develop disclosure policies that meet their varied objectives.[2]

INCREASE IN REPORTING REQUIREMENTS

Disclosure requirements have increased substantially in recent years. Each new *Handbook* section issued by the CICA, has additional disclosure requirements for

[1]Adapted from "Recognition and Measurement in Financial Statements of Business Enterprises," *Statement of Financial Accounting Concepts No. 5* (Stamford, Conn.: FASB, 1984), p. 5.

[2]See, for example, Stephen Buzby, "The Nature of Adequate Disclosure," *The Journal of Accountancy* (April, 1974) for an interesting discussion of issues related to disclosure.

both financial and nonfinancial information. The reasons for this increase in disclosure requirements are varied; some of them are listed below.

Complexity of the Business Environment   The difficulty of distilling economic events into summarized reports has been magnified by the increasing complexity of business operations in such areas as leasing, business combinations, pensions, financing arrangements, revenue recognition, and deferred taxes. As a result, notes are used extensively to explain these transactions and their future effects.

Necessity for Timely Information   Today, more than ever before, information that is current and predictive is being demanded. For example, more complete interim data are required; and published financial forecasts, long avoided and even feared by some accountants, have been recommended in a recent research study.[3]

Accounting as a Control and Monitoring Device   Federal and provincial governments, through such statutes as the Canada Business Corporations Act and acts regulating securities, require public disclosure of certain specific information in addition to that mandated in the *CICA Handbook*. This leads in part toward differential disclosure of information to government agencies and to the public.

The purpose of this chapter is to acquaint the student with (1) the general types of disclosure currently required, (2) some recent trends in financial reporting, and (3) the breadth of responsibility that has been placed on the accounting profession.

NOTES TO THE FINANCIAL STATEMENTS

Notes are an integral part of the financial statements of a business enterprise, but they are often overlooked because they are highly technical and often appear in small print. Notes to the financial statements are the accountant's means of amplifying or explaining the items presented in the main body of the statements. Information pertinent to specific financial statement items can be explained in qualitative terms, and supplementary data of a quantitative nature can be provided to expand the information in the financial statements. Restrictions imposed by financial arrangements or basic contractual agreements also can be explained in notes. It is generally conceded that, although notes may be technical and difficult to understand, they provide meaningful information for the user of the financial statements.

Accounting Policies

Accounting policies of a given entity are the specific principles and methods currently employed and considered most appropriate to present fairly the financial statements of the enterprise. The profession, in *CICA Handbook*, Section 1505, concluded that information about the accounting policies adopted and followed by a reporting entity is essential for financial statement users in making economic decisions. It recommended that when financial statements are issued, a statement identifying the accounting policies adopted and followed by the reporting entity should also be presented as an integral part of the financial statements. The disclo-

---

[3]Robert H. Kidd, *Earnings Forecasts* (Toronto: CICA, 1976).

sure should be given in either a separate summary or as the first note to the financial statements. This information should answer such questions as: What method of depreciation is used on plant assets? What valuation method is employed on inventories? What amortization policy is followed in regard to intangible assets? How is the investment tax credit handled for plant assets?

Refer to Appendix 5A following Chapter 5 for an illustration of note disclosure of accounting methods and other notes accompanying the audited financial statements of Indal Limited.

Some of the excerpts from the notes to Inco Limited's 1984 financial statements and other Canadian firms are used for illustrative purposes. Following the quoted note is an analysis of the information provided by part of the note disclosing significant accounting policies.

Basis of Consolidation

The consolidated financial statements include the accounts of the Company and its subsidiaries and are prepared in conformity with generally accepted accounting principles as established in Canada which, in the Company's case, generally conform with those established in the United States, except as explained in Note 2.

Analysis This note discloses the fact that the company has acquired other businesses during prior years. These acquisitions and subsequent operations have been reported in accordance with the relevant sections of the *CICA Handbook*. Since the Company's shares are listed on stock exchanges in the United States, financial statements must be filed with the SEC. For this purpose accounting principles generally accepted in the U.S.A. must be used. Note 2 (not reproduced here) explains the sources and amount of differences between account balances computed under Canadian generally accepted accounting principles and those properly determined for U.S. reporting purposes.

Pension Plans The Company has pension plans covering essentially all employees. Pension costs are calculated and funded based on actuarial estimates, except that funding is subject to limitations under applicable tax regulations. Prior service costs, which will be charged to operations within the next 13 years, approximated $100 million at December 31, 1984.

Analysis This note informs users of the statements that Inco is amortizing prior service pension costs over an extended period. As of December 31, 1984, $100 million remains unamortized.

Disclosure of Gain or Loss Contingencies

In some cases, enterprises have either gain or loss contingencies that are not disclosed in the body of the financial statements. As indicated in earlier chapters, these contingencies may take a variety of forms such as pending lawsuits, either favourable or unfavourable, a contingent liability on an accommodation endorsement, and possible renegotiation refunds on contracts. A note from Inco's financial statements is presented on page 1288.

Note 3. Discontinued Business Segments

The Consolidated balance sheet reflects the investment in discontinued business segments at an estimated net realizable value of $140 million at December 31, 1982. The Company completed the withdrawal from these businesses in 1983.

Under agreements with the purchasers of these businesses, the Company made certain representations concerning the condition of the businesses and assumed, or agreed to assume, certain liabilities. The Company may therefore be required in future years to provide indemnification to the purchasers under these agreements or make payments in connection with assumed liabilities. Any indemnification would be made primarily through the reduction of notes received by the Company in connection with such sales and, to a lesser degree, in cash. The Company cannot presently estimate the amount of possible note reductions or payments which might be required, but believes that the total amount of such indemnification or payments would not be material in relation to the Company's financial position.

Analysis   The nature of the contingency in relation to the notes receivable is explained to the investor. The opinion of the company regarding possible losses is also considered. The investor should read this section of the notes carefully, even reading between the lines, to measure the potential impact of these contingencies.

Examination of Credit Claims

An investor normally finds it extremely useful to determine the nature and cost of creditorship claims. The liability section in the balance sheet can provide the major types of liabilities outstanding only in aggregate. Note schedules regarding such obligations provide additional information about how the company is financing its operations, the costs that will have to be borne in future periods, and the timing of future cash outflows as shown in the following note:

Note 8. Long-Term Debt

The Company's long-term debt consists of the following (the applicable weighted-average interest rates and repayment periods as at December 31, 1984, are shown in parentheses):

December 31	1984	1983	1982
	(in thousands)		
Inco Limited			
6.85% U.S. $ Debentures (1988–1993)	$ 87,765	$ 97,293	$ 103,850
8.625% Cdn. $ Debentures (1987–1991)	40,278	47,660	49,986
9.25% Cdn. $ Debentures (1988-1990)	38,599	46,019	48,076
9.0% Eurodollar Debentures (1988–1992)	69,672	80,936	89,316
8.25% Eurodollar Notes	-0-	48,334	50,000
12.375% U.S. $ Debentures (1991-2010)	100,000	100,000	100,000
15.75% Sterling Unsecured Loan Stock (2006)	49,500	49,500	49,500
U.S. $ Term loans (10.1%) (1985–1989)*	85,100	100,000	50,000
U.S. $ Revolving loans (9.8%) (1986-1993)*	393,500	287,000	216,300
Cdn. $ Revolving loans (11.3%) (1986–1991)**	3,785	34,796	40,401

P.T. International Nickel Indonesia

Eurodollar bank loans (11.4%) (1985–1989)*	75,000	75,000	103,848
Export and supplier credits (9.0%) (1985-1989)	94,516	100,010	146,340
8.0625% U.S. $ Production sharing loan (1985–1986)	5,400	6,750	12,600
Exmibal			
Export and supplier credits (8.3%) (1985–1988)	19,403	26,246	32,794
9.5% U.S. $ International agency loans (1985–1988)	3,600	5,700	7,800
Other Indebtedness			
(8.5%)(1985–2002)	24,527	49,623	96,453
	1,090,645	1,154,867	1,197,264
Long-term debt due within one year	40,295	99,162	67,971
Long-term debt	$1,050,350	$1,055,705	1,129,293

*Interest is based on Eurocurrency rates.

**Interest is based on Canadian money market and bank's prime commercial lending rates.

The average interest rate on long-term debt at December 31, 1984, was 9.8%. Approximately 52% of such debt carries interest rates that are subject to periodic adjustments based on market interest rates. Interest expense on long-term debt for the years 1984, 1983, and 1982 was $119,302,000, $108,508,000, and $129,091,000 respectively. After reflecting forward exchange hedging contracts, 99% of the long-term debt is payable in U.S. dollars.

The Company has not extended a financial guarantee of the debt of P.T. Inco. However, under the terms of an amended Completion Guarantee Agreement, the Company has agreed, subject to *force majeure*, to provide sufficient funds in the form of equity and/or loans to enable P.T. Inco to meet its financial obligations as they become due, including scheduled debt service payments, until all existing senior funded debt of P.T. Inco, $174,916,000 at December 31, 1984, has been repaid.

At the end of 1984, the Company had unutilized committed credit facilities of $335 million. Substantially all of these facilities contain a covenant which requires that the ratio of the Company's consolidated debt to its net worth not exceed 50:50; at December 31, 1984, this ratio was 46:54. Under these facilities, net worth is essentially defined as the sum of preferred shares and common shareholders' equity, and consolidated debt is defined to include borrowings, guarantees, and certain other minimal obligations. Under this covenant, the maximum that the Company could have borrowed under its unutilized credit facilities was $180 million at December 31, 1984. In the near term, the Company expects that these unutilized credit facilities should provide sufficient liquidity. Additional liquidity will also be provided by a restructuring of the Company's pension plan in the United States which, upon receipt of the required governmental approvals, is expected to generate about $100 million, and possibly by exercises of warrants to purchase Common Shares (see Note 9). During 1984 the Company incurred fees of $1,120,000 to compensate banks for undrawn credit facilities.

Long-term debt maturities and sinking fund requirements for each of the five years through 1989 are: 1985—$40,295,000; 1986—$86,546,000; 1987—$114,710,000; 1988—$122,240,000; 1989—$175,175,000.

Analysis   The note discloses the composition and details of the outstanding long-term debt. For example, the company has debentures ranging in cost from 6.85% to over 15%. In addition, the amount of debt to be retired in each of the next five years is disclosed. The interest rates represent a fixed annual cost. The maturity dates indicate when large cash outlays will have to be made or refinancing will have to take place. Although not currently a liability, the company's line of credit indicates the amount available to meet future cash needs.

Claims of Equity Holders

Many companies present in the body of the balance sheet the number of shares issued and outstanding for each type of equity security. Such data may also be presented in a note. Beyond that, the most common type of equity note disclosure relates to contracts and senior securities outstanding that might affect the various claims of the residual equity holders—for example, the existence of outstanding stock options, outstanding convertible debt, and convertible preferred shares. In addition, it is necessary to disclose to equity claimants certain types of restrictions currently in force. Generally, these types of restrictions involve the amount of earnings available for dividend distribution. The note below illustrates the type of data often presented for shareholders' equity.

Note 9. Preferred and Common Shares

At December 31, 1984, the authorized share capital of the Company consisted of 30,000,000 preferred shares and an unlimited number of common shares.

The Series A Preferred Shares, which do not have general voting rights, have a cumulative floating rate dividend equal to half of the Canadian bank prime rate plus 1 1/4 per cent. The shares are redeemable at the option of the Company and are retractable at the option of the holders in 1987 at $25 (Cdn.) per share. The purchase price of the Canadian dollars required to redeem these shares is hedged by forward exchange contracts at an effective average rate of $1.00 (Cdn.) to $.81 (U.S.). The dividends of $13,576,000 paid in 1984 on these preferred shares reflected an average annual dividend rate of approximately 7.0% (1983—7.4%; 1982—10.3%).

The 7.85% cumulative Series B Preferred Shares have general voting rights and were redeemable at $25.60 (Cdn.) commencing December 1, 1984, such price decreasing annually to $25.00 (Cdn.) by December 1, 1987. The Company is required to purchase 150,000 Series B Preferred Shares annually if such shares are available at a price not greater than $25.00 (Cdn.) per share.

In August, 1984, the Company sold 3,600,000 10% Cumulative Redeemable Commodity-Indexed Series C Preferred Shares at $25 (Cdn.) per share. These shares, which have general voting rights, are retractable at $25 (Cdn.) per share at the option of the holders in 1991. The commodity-indexed exchange feature gives each holder the right to receive the cash equivalent of specified amounts of either nickel or copper, provided that, if exchanges are made prior to August 1, 1987, the Company may make payments in cash or common shares, at its option. The exchange privilege may not be exercised prior to August 1, 1987, unless the average London Metal Exchange cash price exceeds U.S. $2.90 per pound for nickel or U.S. $.80 per pound for copper.

Series B Preferred shareholders have the right to elect to receive Series B Preferred Shares or Common Shares in lieu of cash dividends. Under the Inco Optional Stock Dividend Program, common shareholders may elect to receive Common Shares, valued at a five per cent discount from the market price of the shares, in lieu of cash dividends.

At December 31, 1984, 3,449,070 warrants were outstanding, each of which entitles the holder to purchase one Common Share at $16 (Cdn.). The warrants expire August 20, 1985.

Changes in the Series B Preferred Shares and Common Shares for the years 1982–1984 are shown below. There were no changes in the 10,000,000 Series A Preferred Shares issued in 1977 or the 3,600,000 Series C Preferred Shares issued in 1984.

	Series B Preferred Shares		Common Shares	
	Number of shares	$ in thousands	Number of shares	$ in thousands
December 31, 1981	4,499,256	$102,548	76,850,493	$141,794
Shares purchased	(150,000)	(3,420)	—	—
Shares issued in lieu of cash dividends	10,585	216	532,742	5,144
Shares sold under Share Purchase Plan	—	—	59,412	601
Shares sold under public offerings	—	—	12,900,000	124,514
December 31, 1982	4,359,841	99,344	90,342,647	272,053
Shares purchased	(149,000)	(3,397)	—	—
Options exercised	—	—	43,877	442
Shares sold under Share Purchase Plan	—	—	50,435	749
Shares sold under public offering	—	—	6,600,000	80,435
Warrants exercised	—	—	925	12
December 31, 1983	4,217,708	96,086	97,462,791	359,695
Shares purchased	(151,600)	(3,457)	—	—
Options exercised	—	—	7,170	65
Shares issued in lieu of cash dividends	7,297	141	550,833	6,048
Shares sold under Share Purchase Plan	—	—	41,480	484
December 31, 1984	4,073,405	$ 92,770	98,062,274	$366,292

Analysis   This note provides information about (1) the capital changes during the years and (2) the dividend, redemption, and other provisions related to the various classes of shares. This note indicates the magnitude of the changes that occurred in the equity section during the three-year period and also the potential changes that may develop from existing contractual arrangements. For example, the number of shares outstanding during 1984 changed very little, even though some shares were issued in lieu of cash dividends.

Executory Commitments

An enterprise often becomes involved in several executory contracts. When two parties contract to some undertaking on the basis that neither party has yet performed, the contract is executory. Examples in accounting are pension agreements, lease arrangements, and purchase commitments. Most companies do not recognize these items in the accounts, although many accountants believe that these items should be recorded, notwithstanding the difficult valuation problems. Accountants agree that some type of disclosure is necessary because these commitments will affect the cash flow of the enterprise in the future. An example of Inco's pension commitments is as follows:

Note 12. Retirement Benefits

Pension expense totalled $34,503,000 in 1984, $45,382,000 in 1983, and $34,335,000 in 1982. A comparison of accumulated plan benefits and plan net assets for the Company's Canadian, United States, and United Kingdom pension plans is shown below. The actuarial present value of accumulated plan benefits and the net assets available for benefits have not been calculated for other pension plans; such benefits and related net assets are not material. At December 31, 1984, vested and nonvested benefits exceeded the related net assets of one of the Company's major Canadian pension trust funds by approximately $60 million.

December 31	1984	1983	1982
	(in thousands)		
Actuarial present value of accumulated plan benefits, using an assumed discount rate of 7.4% (1983 and 1982—7.3%):			
Vested benefits	$670,000	$674,800	$607,400
Nonvested benefits	127,400	132,400	149,400
	$797,400	$807,200	$756,800
Net assets, at market value, available for benefits	$962,500	$989,200	$876,200

On January 21, 1985, the Company filed applications with certain U.S. governmental agencies for approval to implement a plan to restructure its U.S. Retirement System. Under the plan, the Company purchases annuities for participants and, having discharged those responsibilities, would be entitled to any surplus in the pension fund. The surplus is expected to approximate $100 million. Approval is expected in 1985. Proceeds would be used to reduce debt.

The Company provides certain health care and life insurance benefits for retired employees. Substantially all employees in Canada, the United States, and the United Kingdom may become eligible for these benefits upon retirement from the Company. The cost of these benefits, which are generally provided through insurance companies, approximated $9 million for 1984.

Analysis   Examination indicates that the company has provided funds in excess of the amounts estimated necessary to provide future pension benefits. As a consequence, the excess funds, subject to anticipated government approval, will be available for current operations. In addition to pensions, retired employees may also be eligible for health care benefits. The cost of these benefits is recorded on a pay-as-you-go basis. Consequently, no liability for estimated future costs has been recorded.

Disclosure of Special Transactions or Events

Related party transactions, errors and irregularities, and subsequent events pose especially sensitive and difficult problems for the accountant. The accountant/auditor who has responsibility for reporting on these types of transactions has to be extremely careful that the rights of the reporting company and the needs of users of the financial statements are properly balanced.

Related party transactions arise when a business engages in transactions in which one of the transacting parties has the ability to exercise, directly or indirectly, control or significant influence over the operating and financing decisions of the other.[4]

[4]*CICA Handbook*, Section 3840.

Transactions involving related parties cannot be presumed to be carried out on an arm's-length basis because the requisite conditions of competitive, free-market dealings may not exist. Such transactions as borrowing or lending money at abnormally low or high interest rates, real estate sales at amounts that differ significantly from appraisal value, exchanges of nonmonetary assets, and transactions involving enterprises that have no economic substance (''shell corporations'') suggest that related parties may be involved. The accountant is expected to report the economic substance rather than the legal form of these transactions and to make adequate disclosures. Section 3840 of the *CICA Handbook* requires the following disclosures of material related party transactions:

1. A description of the nature and extent of transactions:
2. A description of the relationship;
3. Amounts due to or from related parties as of the date of each balance sheet presented.[5]

An example of the disclosure of related party transactions is taken from the 1984 Annual Report of Numac Oil & Gas Ltd.

Note 11 - Related Party Information

Numac Oil & Gas Ltd. (Numac) participates in oil and gas exploration and development ventures in Alberta with Union Enterprises Ltd. (Union). Union at March 1, 1985, beneficially owns 18.32% of the outstanding shares of Numac's common stock. From January 1 to December 31, 1984, Numac invoiced Union for $182,817 ($829,224 in 1983) for exploration and development expenditures. William S. McGregor is the President and a director of Numac and is a director of Union and owns 1,000 shares of Union. W. Darcy McKeough is Chairman, President, Chief Executive Officer, and a director of Union and owns 600 shares of Numac.

Numac's wholly-owned subsidiary, Numac Oil & Gas Inc., participates in oil and gas exploration and development joint ventures in the United States with Shield Resources, Inc., a wholly-owned subsidiary of Precambrian Shield Resources Limited (Precambrian). Numac at March 1, 1985, held 1.8% of the outstanding shares of Precambrian's common stock. Union Enterprises Ltd. beneficially owns 65.4% of Precambrian. W. Darcy McKeough (a director of Numac) is a director of Precambrian and owns 34,300 shares of Precambrian. Paul F. Little (a director of Numac) is a director of Precambrian and owns 100 shares of Precambrian.

For legal services rendered during 1984, the Company paid the law firm of Jackson, Arlette, MacIver and Skitsko of Edmonton, Alberta, the sum of $23,828. Alex N. MacIver is a partner of the said law firm and is a director of the Company.

Errors are defined as unintentional mistakes, whereas **irregularities** (frauds) are intentional distortions of financial statements. As indicated in earlier chapters of this book, when errors are discovered, the financial statements should be corrected. The same treatment should be given irregularities. The discovery of irregularities, however, gives rise to a whole different set of suspicions, procedures, and responsibilities on the part of the accountant/auditor.

Subsequent events are events occurring after the financial statement date which either provide further evidence of conditions that existed at the financial statement date or indicate conditions that arose subsequent to the financial statement date.[6] In these situations, the accountant/auditor must evaluate the adequacy of disclosure in the financial statements. For example, the allowance for doubtful accounts

[5]*Ibid.*, par. 13.
[6]*Ibid.*, par. 1.

may have appeared adequate at year end. However, after the year end but before the preparation of the financial statements, bankruptcy proceedings against an important debtor have been initiated. In this case, if the effect on the financial statements is material, the financial statements should be adjusted. Subsequent events that provide additional evidence about conditions at the date of the financial statements should be disclosed, if material, by making adjustments to the financial statements.

If the subsequent event relates to conditions that arose subsequent to the date of the financial statements and has a material effect on the assets and liabilities or future operations of the firm, then a descriptive note is required. Examples of these kinds of subsequent events include fire or flood losses, declines in market values of investments, or the commencement of litigation when the cause of litigation arose subsequent to the date of the financial statements.

The following excerpt from the notes to the 1984 financial statements of Echo Bay Mines Limited is an example of disclosure of subsequent events:

---

15. Subsequent events

Pursuant to an underwriting agreement dated January 24, 1985, entered into between the Company and Burns Fry Limited and Wood Gundy Inc., and an underwriting agreement dated January 24, 1985, and to be entered into between the Company and a number of United States underwriters managed by Solomon Brothers Inc., Goldman, Sachs & Co., Burns Fry and Timmins Inc. and Wood Gundy Corp., the Company proposes to sell an aggregate of 3,600,000 Common Shares of the Company for a total consideration of $38,719,950. The net proceeds will be applied to reduce bank indebtedness incurred to finance the acquisition of Copper Range Company.

On January 11, 1985, the Company acquired from The Louisiana Land and Exploration Company (LL&E) of New Orleans all of the issued shares of Copper Range Company (Copper Range). Copper Range owns a 50% undivided interest in the Round Mountain gold mining project located in Nye County, Nevada, other exploration prospects in the United States, and the inactive White Pine copper mining complex in the upper peninsula of Michigan. The acquisition will be accounted for by the purchase method, with the results of operations being included in the Company's results from January 1, 1985.

Assets acquired and values assigned thereto are as follows:

(stated in thousands of U.S.$)	White Pine	Round Mountain	Other
Net working capital	$ 5,600	$ 3,400	$ –
Copper assets held for sale[1]	23,000	–	–
50% of Round Mountain property, plant, and equipment[1]	–	10,000	–
Resource properties[1]	–	3,000	3,000
Round Mountain ore reserves[2]	–	18,000	–
	$28,600	$34,400	$3,000

[1]at estimated net realizable value.
[2]represents the difference between the purchase price
of Copper Range and the costs allocated to identifiable assets.
The assigned fair value of the assets acquired are estimates, and may be adjusted based on further study.

The purchase price was U.S. $55 million cash and assumption of certain reclamation and holding costs. The discounted value of these reclamation and holding costs as of the acquisition date is approximately U.S. $11.0 million. Included in these costs is a lease obligation for a refinery, presently available to the copper mining project, with a three year lease term commencing January 1, 1985, and terminating January 4, 1988, at an annual rental of U.S. $2.0 million. The Company has the exclusive irrevocable option to purchase the refinery as of January 1, 1988, for the sum of U.S. $13.5 million. Prior to the acquisition, Copper Range granted to LL&E a 3% gross royalty interest commencing January 1, 1989, based on revenues generated from Copper Range's interest in production from the Nevada precious metal properties, with the royalty percentage reducing to 11/2% after an aggregate of U.S. $75 million has been paid by Copper Range.

If the acquisition and related financing had been consummated on January 1, 1983, the pro forma consolidated revenue and net income from continuing operations of the Company would have been $118 million and $27 million for the year ended December 31, 1984, and $90 million and $14 million for the year ended December 31, 1983. The pro forma earnings per share from continuing operations would have been $0.67 in 1984 and $0.28 in 1983. The Company expects some ongoing costs related to the discontinued operations of the White Pine copper mining project.

On January 10, 1985, Echo Bay Inc., a wholly-owned subsidiary of the Company, arranged a term credit facility with a Canadian chartered bank for up to U.S. $60.0 million as interim financing for the acquisition of Copper Range. This credit is nonrevolving, bears interest at U.S. prime, is repayable in full by June 15, 1985, and is secured by shares of the subsidiary and guaranteed by the Company. On January 11, 1985, U.S. $55.5 million of this facility was utilized and U.S. $30.0 million was repaid the same day from the proceeds of a gold loan. This credit facility includes certain covenants including restrictions on other indebtedness and guarantees and pledges.

On January 10, 1985, a subsidiary of the Company borrowed 100,000 ounces of gold from a Canadian chartered bank. This gold was delivered against previously contracted forward sales and realized U.S. $30.6 million, of which U.S. $30.0 million was utilized on January 11, 1985, to partially repay the interim financing for the Copper Range acquisition. This gold loan is nonrevolving, is repayable in 60 equal monthly instalments and is secured by the shares of Copper Range and guaranteed by the Company. The interest rate on the loan varies with the bank's cost of funds and with the pricing option selected by the Company, and at present is approximately I.5%. This term credit includes certain covenants including restrictions on other indebtedness and guarantees and pledges. There is an option to convert the gold loan to borrowings in U.S. dollars at an interest rate of New York prime or LIBOR prime plus 1/2%.

REPORTING FOR DIVERSIFIED (CONGLOMERATE) COMPANIES

In the last two decades business enterprises have evidenced an increasing tendency to diversify their operations. As a result, investors and investment analysts have sought more information concerning the details behind conglomerate financial statements. Particularly, they are requesting revenue and income information on the **individual segments** that constitute the **total** business income figure. In addition, some attention has also been given to the segmentation of the balance

Office Equipment and Auto Parts Company INCOME STATEMENT DATA (in millions)			
	Consolidated	Office Equipment	Auto Parts
Net sales	$78.8	$18.0	$60.8
Manufacturing costs:			
Inventories, beginning	12.3	4.0	8.3
Materials and services	38.9	10.8	28.1
Wages	12.9	3.8	9.1
Inventories, ending	(13.3)	(3.9)	(9.4)
	50.8	14.7	36.1
Selling and administrative expense	12.1	1.6	10.5
Total operating expenses	62.9	16.3	46.6
Operating income	15.9	1.7	14.2
Income taxes	(9.3)	(1.0)	(8.3)
Net income	$ 6.6	$ 0.7	$ 5.9

sheet and statement of changes in financial position for the various divisions or subsidiaries comprised of the consolidated group.

An illustration of segmentation is presented in the example of a hypothetical office equipment and auto parts company on page 1295.

If only the consolidated figures are available to the analyst, much information regarding the composition of these figures is hidden in aggregated figures. There is no way to tell from the consolidated data the extent to which the differing product lines **contribute to the company's profitability, risk, and growth potential.**[7] For example, in the illustration above, if the office equipment segment is deemed a risky venture, the segmentation provides useful information for purposes of making an informed investment decision.

Companies have been somewhat hesitant to disclose segmented data for the reasons listed below.

1. Without a thorough knowledge of the business and an understanding of such important factors as the competitive environment and capital investment requirements, the investor may find the segmented information meaningless or even draw improper conclusions about the reported earnings of the segments.
2. Additional disclosure may harm reporting firms because it may be helpful to competitors, labour unions, suppliers, and certain government regulatory agencies.
3. Additional disclosure may discourage management from taking intelligent business risks because segments reporting losses or unsatisfactory earnings may cause shareholder dissatisfaction with management.
4. The wide variation among firms in the choice of segments, cost allocation, and other accounting problems limits the usefulness of segmented information.
5. The investor is investing in the company as a whole and not in the particular segments, and it should not matter how any single segment is performing if the overall performance is satisfactory.
6. Certain technical problems, such as classification of segments and allocation of segment revenues and cost (especially "common costs"), are formidable.

On the other hand, the advocates of segmented disclosures offer these reasons:

1. Segmented information is needed by the investor to make an intelligent investment decision regarding a diversified company.
   (a) Sales and earnings of individual segments are needed to forecast consolidated profits because of the differences between segments in growth rate, risk, and profitability.
   (b) Segmented reports disclose the nature of a company's businesses and the relative size of the components as an aid in evaluating the company's investment worth.
2. The absence of segmented reporting by a diversified company may put its unsegmented, single product-line competitors at a competitive disadvantage because the conglomerate may obscure information that its competitors must disclose.

The advocates of segmented disclosure appear to have a much stronger case. For example, many users indicate that segmented data are the most informative financial information provided, aside from the basic financial statements. As a result the CICA has issued extensive reporting guidelines in this area.

---

[7]One writer has shown that data provided on a segmented basis allows an analyst to predict future total sales and earnings better than data presented on a nonsegmented basis. See D. W. Collins, "Predicting Earnings with Sub-Entity Data: Some Further Evidence," *Journal of Accounting Research* (Spring, 1976).

Professional Pronouncements

Recognizing the need for guidelines in the area of segmented reporting, the profession issued *CICA Handbook*, Section 1700, in 1979. This standard, however, only applies to enterprises whose securities are traded in a public market or that are required to file financial statements annually with a securities commission. The basic requirements of this pronouncement are discussed below.

Accounting Principle Selection   Segment information required to be reported must be prepared on the same accounting basis as that used in the enterprise's consolidated financial statements. The exception is intersegment sales which are eliminated for consolidated purposes but are shown when individual segments are presented. **Intersegment sales** are transfers of products or services between segments of the enterprise. An example of segment disclosures required by the profession is shown for Inco Limited on page 1298.

Note that Inco Limited reports three segments: primary metals, alloy products, and other. Each segment follows the same accounting principles that are used to prepare the consolidated financial statements. The profession also requires that the **segment's revenues**, **operating profit (loss)**, and **identifiable assets** be reconciled to the consolidated financial statements. In addition, depreciation expense and the amount of capital expenditures must be reported.

Selecting Reportable Segments   A number of methods might have been used by Inco Limited to identify its industry segments, such as the Statistics Canada Standard Industrial Classification Code, currently existing profit centres, or relating common risk factors to products or product groups. The CICA concluded that none of these methods by itself is universally applicable and that management should exercise its judgement in determining industry segments. The CICA, however, did indicate that there are three factors that should be seriously considered.[8]

1. The nature of the product or service.
2. The nature of the production process. Such factors as sharing of common facilities and the type or types of raw materials used should be considered.
3. The nature of markets or marketing methods. This includes types of markets and the sensitivity of the respective markets to risk of changes in demand.

After the company decides on the segments it wishes to disclose, a quantitative test is made to determine whether the segment is significant enough to disclose. An industry segment is regarded as significant and therefore identified as a reportable segment, if it satisfies one or more of the following tests.

1. Its revenue is 10% or more of the total revenue of all industry segments (including intersegment sales).
2. Its operating profit or loss is 10% or more of the greater, in absolute amount, of either:
    (a) the total operating profit of all industry segments that earned an operating profit; and
    (b) the total operating loss of all industry segments that incurred an operating loss.
3. Its identifiable assets are 10% or more of the total identifiable assets of all industry segments.[9]

[8]*CICA Handbook*, Section 1700, par. 17.
[9]*Ibid.*, par. 23.

Data by Business Segment	1984				
	Primary metals	Alloy products	Other	Elimin- ations	Total
Net sales to customers	$1,052	$393	$ 23	$ –	$1,468
Intersegment sales	89	4	–	(93)	–
Total net sales	$1,141	$397	$ 23	$ (93)	$1,468
Operating earnings (loss)	$ 100	$ (5)	$ (6)	$ (14)	$ 75
Non-operating expenses*					(130)
Loss before income and mining taxes					$ (55)
Capital expenditures	$ 74	$ 27	$ 3	$ –	$ 104
Depreciation and depletion	$ 109	$ 22	$ 9	$ –	$ 140
Identifiable assets at December 31	$2,346	$542	$100	$ (39)	$2,949
Other assets					161
Total assets at December 31					$3,110

Data by Geographic Area	Canada	United States	Europe	Other	Total after elimin- ations
Net sales to customers	$ 265	$526	$460	$217	$1,468
Sales between geographic areas	711	21	9	9	–
Total net sales	$ 976	$547	$469	$226	$1,468
Operating earnings (loss)	$ 101	$ 7	$ (10)	$ (1)	$ 75
Identifiable assets at December 31	$1,463	$462	$277	$878**	$2,949

*Includes interest expense, general corporate income and expenses, equity in earnings of affiliates, and currency translation adjustments.

**Includes assets of $768 million relating to the Company's nickel operations in Indonesia.

The Company's business is organized around two principal product groups: primary metals and alloy products. The Company's principal primary metals are nickel and copper. Wrought nickel, high-nickel alloys in rolling mill forms, and forgings are the Company's major alloy products. Other business includes the Company's venture capital program, metals reprocessing operations, and oil and gas interests.

Other assets include investments in discontinued business segments of $140 in 1982; and corporate assets, principally cash, securities, and certain receivables and fixed assets of $161 in 1984 (1983—$200; 1982—$137).

The Company's intersegment sales are generally made at approximate prices used for sales to unaffiliated customers. Sales between geographic areas are generally made at prevailing market prices, except that sales of primary metals from Canada to other primary metals affiliates are net of discounts. In 1984, sales to customers include $57 (1983—$49; 1982—$35) exported from Canada and $12 (1983—$11; 1982—$29) exported from the United States. In 1984, total sales by Canadian companies include $322 (1983—$231; 1982—$243) exported to Europe. Geographic Area—Other includes sales to affiliated companies in Japan as follows: Shimura Kako Company, Ltd.—$103 in 1984 (1983—$118; 1982—$88) and Tokyo Nickel Company, Ltd.—$54 in 1984 (1983—$1).

In applying these rules, two additional factors must be considered. First, segment data must explain a significant portion of the company's business. Therefore, if data are segmented, the segmented results must equal or exceed 75% of the combined sales to unaffiliated customers for the entire enterprise. The reason for this rule is that it prevents a company from providing limited information on only a few segments and lumping all the rest into one category. Secondly, the profession recognized that reporting too many segments may overwhelm users with detailed information that may not be useful. Although the CICA did not issue any specific guidelines regarding how many segments are too many, this point is generally reached when a company has ten or more reportable segments.

To illustrate these requirements, assume that a company has identified six possible reporting segments (000's omitted):

Segments	Total Revenue (Unaffiliated)	Operating Profit (Loss)	Identifiable Assets
A	$ 100	$10	$ 60
B	50	2	30
C	700	40	390
D	300	20	160
E	900	18	280
F	100	(5)	50
	$2,150	$85	$970

The respective tests may now be applied as follows:

Revenue test: 10% × $2,150 = $215; C, D, and E meet this test.

Operating profit (loss) test: 10% × $90 = $9; A, C, D, and E meet this test—the $5 loss is ignored.

Identifiable assets test: 10% × $970 = $97; C, D, and E meet this test.

The reportable segments are therefore A, C, D, and E, assuming that these four segments have enough sales to meet the 75% of combined sales test. The 75% test is computed as follows:

75% of combined sales test: 75% × $2,150 = $1,612.50; the sales of A, C, D, and E total $2,000 ($100 + $700 + $300 + $900); therefore the 75% test is met.

Information to be Reported   As indicated above, the primary basis for segmenting the results of Inco Limited was by product line. The profession requires segmented information on other bases when appropriate. The three general areas are:

1. Service or product line
2. Foreign geographic segments
3. Export sales

Geographic segment operating profit, revenues, and identifiable assets are reported when revenues of this type are 10% or more of total revenue or total identifiable assets are more than 10% of the total assets of the firm. Export sales must be reported when a company derives 10% or more of its revenue from sales from this source. For example, Inco provides information about sales to customers, intercompany transfers between segments, operating earnings, and identifiable assets for each geographic segment. This information is extremely useful to investors who are concerned about the political and economic stability of a given geographic area.

Inco also discloses its level of export sales. **Export sales** are sales to customers in foreign countries by Inco's domestic operation. Since Inco's shares are listed on

U.S. stock exchanges, the company must report to the SEC. Consequently, export sales from the United States is also disclosed. Information of this type enables an investor to determine the level of sales made to foreign countries and thereby provides insight into the level of stability, risk, and growth potential of this revenue source.

Continuing Controversy

The area of segment reporting is controversial from a number of perspectives. For example, one frequent complaint is that this information is costly to develop. As a result, the Accounting Standards Committee of the CICA decided that nonpublic companies are not required to disclose segmented data. Conversely, others argue that segmented reporting should be extended to interim reports. The following issues also are still hotly debated.

Definition of a Segment   A general view that seems to prevail among accountants is that the enterprise should be free to select the breakdown that best represents the underlying activities of the business. An organizational unit approach probably reflects this point of view, because enterprises normally devise some way of relating responsibilities to various segments of the business. The problem with using this procedure is that the organizational unit is continually changing as operations are expanded or contracted. A problem of comparability between periods can develop.

In addition to the problem of determining the basis for identifying the segments, there is the question of what percentage to use. As indicated earlier, a 10% factor is applied to one of the following items: revenue, income or loss, or identifiable assets; but these criteria are still subject to interpretation. In general, however, the disclosure requirements associated with *CICA Handbook*, Section 1700, appear quite reasonable, and the flexibility afforded management seems desirable. Management is in the best position to judge which is the most meaningful breakdown of its divisional data, and with experimentation useful information should be forthcoming.

Allocation of Common Costs   One of the critical problems in providing segmented income statements for conglomerate companies is the allocation of common costs. Common costs are those incurred for the benefit of more than one segment and whose interrelated nature prevents a completely objective division of costs among segments. For example, the president's salary is very difficult to allocate to various segments. The significance of common costs is indicated by a Financial Executive Research Foundation survey that shows that the average ratio of common costs to net sales is greater than that of net income to net sales.

Many different bases for allocation have been suggested, such as sales, gross profit, assets employed, investment, and marginal income. The choice of basis is difficult because it can materially influence the relative profitability of the segments.

Transfer Pricing Problems   Transfer pricing is the practice of charging a price for goods ''sold'' between divisions or subsidiaries of a company, commonly called intracompany transfers. A transfer price system is used for several reasons, but the primary objective is to measure the performance and profitability of a given segment of the business in relation to other segments. In addition, a pricing system is needed to ensure control over the flow of goods through the enterprise.

Transfer pricing is not a problem of the same magnitude as common costs, but it still is very significant in many business enterprises. At present, different approaches to transfer pricing are used. Some firms transfer the goods at market prices; others use cost plus a fixed fee; and some use variable cost. In some situations, the company lets the division bargain for the price of the item in question.

In evaluating a specific division, we must consider the transfer pricing problem. If, for example, Division A sells certain goods to Division B using a market price instead of cost, the operating results of both divisions are affected. Transfer pricing in many situations does not occur on an arm's-length basis and, therefore, the final results of a given division must be suspect. The basis of accounting for intersegment sales and transfers should be disclosed.

INTERIM REPORTS

One further source of information for the investor is interim reports, which are reports that cover periods of less than one year. At one time, interim reports were referred to as the forgotten reports; such is no longer the case. The stock exchanges and the accounting profession have taken an active role in developing guidelines for the presentation of interim information. The CICA issued Section 1750 of the *Handbook* in 1971, which attempted to narrow the reporting alternatives related to interim reports. A recent quarterly report of Drummond Petroleum Ltd. on page 1302, illustrates the disclosure of selected quarterly data.

Because of the short-term nature of these reports, however, there is considerable controversy as to the general approach that should be employed. One group **(discrete view)** believes that each interim period should be treated as a separate accounting for annual reports. Accounting transactions should be reported as they occur and timing of expense recognition should not change with the period of time covered by the interim report. Conversely, another group **(integral view)** believes that the interim report is an integral part of the annual report and that deferrals and accruals should take into consideration what will happen for the entire year. In this approach, estimated expenses are assigned to parts of a year on the basis of sales volume or some other activity base. Under Section 1750, companies are required to follow the discrete approach.

INTERIM REPORTING REQUIREMENTS

CICA Handbook, Section 1750,indicates that the same accounting principles used for annual reports should be employed for interim reports. Revenues should be recognized in interim periods on the same basis as they are for annual periods. For example, if the instalment sales method is used as the basis for recognizing revenue on an annual basis, then the instalment basis should also be applied to interim reports as well. Furthermore, costs directly associated with revenues (product costs), such as material, labour and related fringe benefits, and manufacturing overhead should be treated in the same manner for interim reports as for annual reports.

Companies generally should use the same inventory pricing methods (FIFO, weighted-average, etc.) for interim reports that they use for annual reports. Determination of the interim inventory valuation should include consideration of such factors as current market or replacement value; losses due to obsolescence, shrinkage, and theft; and temporary encroachments of LIFO or base stock inventories. In

CONSOLIDATED STATEMENT OF LOSS AND DEFICIT
For the Three Months Ended March 31, 1985
(Unaudited)

	1985	1984
	$	$
INCOME		
Oil and gas sales	6,126,000	5,839,000
EXPENSES		
Operating	785,000	828,000
Administrative	387,000	483,000
Interest	2,790,000	2,585,000
	3,962,000	3,986,000
Income from operations		
before the following	2,164,000	1,943,000
Depletion, depreciation, and amortization	3,703,000	3,233,000
Net Loss for the Period	1,539,000	1,290,000
Deficit—Beginning of Period	108,318,000	101,797,000
Deficit—End of Period	109,857,000	103,087,000
Cash Flow per Share	$0.05	$0.05
Net Loss per Share	$0.03	$0.03
Common Shares Outstanding		
(weighted average)	51,659,095	46,029,783

CONSOLIDATED STATEMENT OF CHANGES IN FINANCIAL POSITION
For the Three Months Ended March 31, 1985
(Unaudited)

	1985	1984
	$	$
Source of Funds		
Cash flow from operations	2,822,000	2,341,000
Proceeds from sale of property,		
plant, and equipment	11,000	55,000
Petroleum Incentives Program Grants	705,000	716,000
Long-term debt	698,000	3,047,000
Common shares issued for cash	–0–	72,000
	4,236,000	6,231,000
Use of Funds		
Property, plant, and equipment	5,995,000	5,937,000
Other assets	49,000	145,000
Repayment of long-term debt	–0–	2,561,000
	6,044,000	8,643,000
Decrease in Working Capital	1,808,000	2,412,000
Working Capital—Beginning of Period	2,286,000	2,633,000
Working Capital—End of Period	478,000	221,000

addition, companies may use the retail inventory or gross profit methods of estimating interim inventory pricing.

Costs and expenses other than product costs, often referred to as period costs, should be allocated among interim periods on the basis of an estimate of time expired, benefit received, or activity associated with the periods.

Regarding disclosure, the following interim data should be reported as a minimum:

1. Sales or gross revenue, investment income, amount charged for depreciation and amortization, interest expense, income taxes, income before extraordinary items, extraordinary items (net of income taxes), and net income.
2. Basic and fully diluted earnings per share.
3. Details of any significant changes in financial position such as in working capital, fixed assets, long-term liabilities, and shareholders' equity.
4. Changes in accounting principles.
5. Subsequent events.
6. Other material matters not previously reported.[10]

In addition, the profession requires companies to publish all financial summaries in a comparative form on a basis consistent from period to period. This, in the event of accounting changes, requires retroactive restatement of both the current year's interim reports and any prior period interim data presented for comparison.

Unique Problems of Interim Reporting

In *CICA Handbook*, Section 1750, the Committee indicated that it favoured the discrete approach. However, within this broad guideline, a number of unique reporting problems develop related to the following items.

Advertising and Similar Costs The general guidelines are that such costs as advertising should be deferred in an interim period if the benefits extend beyond that period; otherwise they should be expensed as incurred. But such a determination is difficult and, even if they are deferred, how should they be allocated between quarters? Because of the vague guidelines in this area, accounting for advertising varies widely. One method, for example, would involve charging advertising costs as a percentage of sales and adjusting to actual at year end, whereas under another acceptable method these costs would be charged to expense as incurred.

The same type of problem relates to such items as the employer's contributions to the Canada Pension Plan, research and development costs, major repairs, and tax loss carry-back or carry-forward. For example, should the company expense Canada Pension Plan contributions on the highly paid personnel early in the year or allocate and spread them to subsequent quarters? Should major repair that occurs later in the year be anticipated and allocated proportionately to earlier periods?

Expenses Subject to Year-End Adjustment Allowance for bad debts, executive bonuses, pension costs, and inventory shrinkage are often not known with a great deal of certainty until year end. **These costs should be estimated and allocated in the best possible way to interim periods.** It should be emphasized that companies use a variety of allocation techniques to accomplish this objective.

Income Taxes Not every dollar of corporate taxable income is assessed at the same tax rate if, for example, the company is eligible for the small business deduction. In these cases certain corporations would be taxed at 21% less on the first $200,000 of income. As a result, there is a progressive aspect of business income taxes which poses a problem in preparing interim financial statements. Should the income to date be annualized and the proportionate income tax accrued for the

---

[10]*Ibid.*, Section 1750, par. 6.

period to date? Or should the first amount of income earned be taxed at the lower rate of tax applicable to such income? Section 1750 permits either method with the stipulation that the method used be consistent from period to period.[11]

Extraordinary Items   Extraordinary items consist of unusual and nonrecurring material gains and losses. In the past, they were handled in interim reports in one of three ways: (1) absorbed entirely in the quarter in which they occurred; (2) prorated over the four quarters; or (3) disclosed only by note. **The required approach is to charge or credit the loss or gain in the quarter in which it occurs instead of attempting some arbitrary multiple-period allocation.** This approach is consistent with the way in which extraordinary items are currently handled on an annual basis; no attempt is made to prorate the extraordinary items over several years. Some accountants favour the omission of extraordinary items from the quarterly net income because they believe that the inclusion of extraordinary items that may be large in proportion to interim results naturally distorts the predictive value of interim reports. Many accountants, however, consider this approach inappropriate because it deviates from the actual situation.

Earnings Per Share (EPS)   Interim reporting of earnings per share has all the problems inherent in computing and presenting annual earnings per share, and then some. If shares are issued in the third period, EPS for the first two periods will not indicate year-end EPS. If an extraordinary item is present in one period and new equity shares are sold in another period, the EPS figure for the extraordinary item will change for the year. On an annual basis only one EPS figure is associated with an extraordinary item, and that figure does not change; the interim figure is subject to change. **For purposes of computing earnings per share and making the disclosure determinations required by Section 1750, each interim period should stand alone; that is, all applicable tests should be made for that single period.**

Seasonality   Seasonality occurs when sales are compressed into one short period of the year while certain costs are fairly evenly spread throughout the year. For example, the natural gas industry has its heavy sales in the winter months, as contrasted with the beverage industry, which has its heavy sales in the summer months.

The problem of seasonality is related to the matching concept in accounting. Expenses should be matched against the revenues they create. In a seasonal business, wide fluctuations in profits occur because off-season sales may not absorb the company's fixed costs (e.g., manufacturing, selling, and administrative costs that tend to remain fairly constant regardless of sales or production).

To illustrate why seasonality is a problem, assume the following information:

Selling price per unit	$1
Annual sales for the period (projected and actual)	
100,000 units @ $1.00	$100,000
Manufacturing costs:	
Variable	$0.10 per unit
Fixed	$0.20 per unit or $20,000 for the year
Nonmanufacturing costs:	
Variable	$0.10 per unit
Fixed	$0.30 per unit or $30,000 for the year

[11]*Ibid.*, par. 17.

Sales for four quarters and the year (projected and actual) were:

		Percentage of Sales
1st Quarter	$ 20,000	20%
2nd Quarter	5,000	5
3rd Quarter	10,000	10
4th Quarter	65,000	65
Total for the Year	$100,000	100%

Under the present accounting framework, the income statements for the quarters might be presented as follows:

	1st Qtr	2nd Qtr	3rd Qtr	4th Qtr	Year
Sales	$20,000	$ 5,000	$10,000	$65,000	$100,000
Manufacturing costs					
Variable	(2,000)	(500)	(1,000)	(6,500)	(10,000)
Fixed[a]	(4,000)	(1,000)	(2,000)	(13,000)	(20,000)
	14,000	3,500	7,000	45,500	70,000
Nonmanufacturing costs					
Variable	(2,000)	(500)	(1,000)	(6,500)	(10,000)
Fixed[b]	(7,500)	(7,500)	(7,500)	(7,500)	(30,000)
Net income	$ 4,500	($ 4,500)	($ 1,500)	$31,500	$ 30,000

[a]The fixed manufacturing costs are inventoried, so that equal amounts of fixed costs do not appear during each quarter.
[b]The fixed nonmanufacturing costs are not inventoried so that equal amounts of fixed costs appear during each quarter.

An investor who uses the first quarter's results can be misled. If the first quarter's earnings are $4,500, should this figure be multiplied by four to predict annual earnings of $18,000? Or, as the analysis suggests, inasmuch as $20,000 in sales is 20% of the predicted sales for the year, net income for the year should be $22,500 ($4,500 × 5). Either figure is obviously wrong, and after the second quarter's results occur, the investor may become even more confused.

The problem with the conventional approach is that the fixed nonmanufacturing costs are not charged in proportion to sales. Some enterprises have adopted a way of avoiding this problem by making all fixed nonmanufacturing costs follow the sales pattern, as shown below:

	1st Qtr	2nd Qtr	3rd Qtr	4th Qtr	Year
Sales	$20,000	$ 5,000	$10,000	$65,000	$100,000
Manufacturing costs					
Variable	(2,000)	(500)	(1,000)	(6,500)	(10,000)
Fixed	(4,000)	(1,000)	(2,000)	(13,000)	(20,000)
	14,000	3,500	7,000	45,500	70,000
Nonmanufacturing costs					
Variable	(2,000)	(500)	(1,000)	(6,500)	(10,000)
Fixed	(6,000)	(1,500)	(3,000)	(19,500)	(30,000)
Net income	$ 6,000	$ 1,500	$ 3,000	$19,500	$ 30,000

This approach solves some of the problems of interim reporting; sales in the first quarter are 20% of total sales for the year, and net income in the first quarter is 20% of total income. In this case, as in the previous example, the investor cannot rely on multiplying any given quarter by four, but can use comparative data or rely on some estimate of sales in relation to income for a given period.

The greater the degree of seasonality experienced by a company, the greater the possibility for distortion. Because no definitive guidelines are available for handling such items as the fixed nonmanufacturing costs, variability in income can be substantial. To alleviate this problem, the profession recommends that companies should present comparative financial information using consistent methods.

The two illustrations above highlight the difference between the discrete and integral viewpoints. The fixed nonmanufacturing expenses would be expensed as incurred under the discrete viewpoint, but under the integral method they would be charged to income on the basis of some measure of activity.

Continuing Controversy   The profession has developed some standards for interim reporting. However, within the constraint that interim reports should be comparable from period to period, much is left to professional judgement. The *CICA Handbook* tends to support the discrete approach but, as emphasized earlier, certain items must be estimated on an annual basis (integral approach) and prorated quarterly.

Discussion also persists concerning the independent auditor's involvement in interim reports. Many auditors are reluctant to express an opinion on interim financial information, arguing that the data are too tentative and subjective. Conversely, an increasing number of individuals advocate some type of examination of interim reports. Since there is no statutory responsibility for auditors to perform a review of such information, the auditor may, on request from the client, permit his or her name to be associated with the interim report if a limited review in accordance with *CICA Handbook*, Section 8200, has been made.

Analysts want financial information as soon as possible, before it becomes old news. We may not be far from a continuous database system where corporate financial records can be accessed by microcomputer as often as analysts desire and the information put in the format they need. Thus investors could learn about sales slippage, cost increases, or earnings changes as they happen, rather than wait until after the quarter has ended.

SUPPLEMENTARY INFORMATION

Supplementary information may include information that presents a different perspective from that adopted in the financial statements. This may be quantifiable information that is high in relevance but low in reliability, or information that is helpful, but not essential. The major supplementary information required is the data and schedules that must be provided by certain companies on the effects of changing prices (constant dollar and current cost information). In addition, certain disclosures related to the oil and gas industry may be required as supplementary information, although these may be part of the notes. Supplementary information related to many other matters may also be reported. Some of the more important are discussed and illustrated in the following sections.

MANAGEMENT'S RESPONSIBILITIES FOR FINANCIAL STATEMENTS

The public accounting profession has attempted for many years to educate the public to the fact that a company's management has the primary responsibility for the preparation, integrity, and objectivity of the company's financial statements. Only recently have management letters acknowledging such responsibility appeared in annual reports to shareholders. Presented below is the management statement that served as a prelude to the 1984 financial statement of Inco Limited.

Management's Statement on Financial Reporting

The information and representations in this Annual Report have been prepared by management. The consolidated financial statements have been prepared in conformity with generally accepted accounting principles in Canada and, where appropriate, reflect management's judgements. The financial information presented throughout this Report is consistent with the data presented in the financial statements.

Systems of internal accounting control are maintained in order to assure on a reasonable basis the reliability of this financial information. These systems include formal policies and procedures, the careful selection and training of qualified personnel, and an organization providing for appropriate delegation of authority and segregation of responsibilities. These systems are monitored by our internal auditors who perform extensive tests and related procedures at major locations worldwide. Our independent auditors, whose report on their examinations of the consolidated financial statements appears on page 30, also review our systems of internal accounting control in accordance with generally accepted auditing standards for the purpose of expressing their opinion on the consolidated financial statements.

Financial management personnel, our internal auditors, and our independent auditors meet with the Audit Committee of the Board of Directors at least three times a year to report on accounting, auditing, internal accounting control, and financial reporting matters. The Audit Committee also has other duties which are described on page 35.

This Annual Report has been reviewed and approved by the Board of Directors.

Chairman and
Chief Executive Officer

Executive Vice-President
(Chief Financial Officer)

REPORTING ON FORECASTS

In recent years, the investing public's demand for more and better information has focused on disclosure of corporate expectations for the future through publication of earnings forecasts. Financial forecasts have therefore become the subject of intensive discussion with journalists, corporate executives, the various provincial securities commissions, financial analysts, accountants, and others making their views known. Predictably, there are strong arguments on either side.

Arguments for requiring published forecasts:

1. Investment decisions are based on future expectations; therefore, information about the future facilitates better decisions.
2. Forecasts are already circulated informally, but are uncontrolled, frequently misleading, and not available equally to all investors. This confused situation should be brought under control.
3. Circumstances now change so rapidly that historical information is no longer adequate for prediction.

Arguments against requiring published forecasts:

1. No one can foretell the future. Therefore forecasts, while conveying an impression of precision about the future, will inevitably be wrong.
2. Organizations will strive only to meet their published forecasts, not to produce results that are in the shareholders' best interest.
3. When forecasts are not proved to be accurate, there will be recriminations and probably legal actions.
4 Disclosure of forecasts will be detrimental to organizations, because it will fully inform not only investors, but also competitors (foreign and domestic).[12]

In Canada the publication of financial forecasts has not been officially encouraged. **The *CICA Handbook* fails to prescribe either accounting or auditing procedures for the preparation and audit of forecasted information.** In addition, the Ontario Securities Act allows firms to publish estimates of future earnings in a prospectus only after securing consent of the Director of the Ontario Securities Commission. As a result, financial forecasts are not presented as part of the formal financial reports.

The subject of preparation and dissemination of financial forecasts is a topic of current interest to both provincial securities commissions and the accounting profession. A research study generally favouring the publication of forecasts was published by the CICA in 1976 and the auditing implications are currently being studied.

Experience in the United States and Great Britain   Great Britain has permitted financial forecasts for years, and the results have been fairly successful. A typical British forecast adapted from a construction company's report to support a public share offering is as follows:

> Profits have grown substantially over the past 10 years and directors are confident of being able to continue this expansion . . . While the rate of expansion will be dependent on the level of economic activity in Ireland and in England, the group is well structured to avail itself of opportunities as they arise, particularly in the field of property development, which is expected to play an increasingly important role in the group's future expansion.
>
> Profits before taxation for the half year ended 30th June, 1986, was 402,000 pounds. On the basis of trading experiences since that date and the present level of sales and completions, the directors expect that in the absence of unforeseen circumstances, the group's profits before taxation for the year to 31st December, 1986, will be not less than 960,000 pounds . . . .
>
> No dividends will be paid in respect of the year December 31, 1986. In a full financial year, on the basis of the above forecasts (not including full year profits) it would be the intention of the board, assuming current rates of tax, to recommend dividends totalling 40% (of after-tax profits), of which 15% payable would be as an interim dividend in November, 1987, and 25% as a final dividend in June, 1988.

In the United States the legal environment is not as favourable towards publication of financial forecasts. A general narrative-type forecast would be preferred over the more quantitative British forecast. The following illustrates a forecast that a U.S. company might issue:

[12]Joseph P. Cummings, *Financial Forecasts and the Certified Public Accountant* (New York: Peat, Marwick, Mitchell & Co., November 30, 1972).

On the basis of promotions planned by the company for the second half of fiscal 1987, net earnings for that period are expected to be approximately the same as those for the first half of fiscal 1987, with net earnings for the third quarter expected to make the predominant contribution to net earnings for the second half of 1987.

Many Unresolved Problems   What happens if a company does not meet its forecasts? Are the company and the auditor going to be sued? If a company, for example, projects an earnings increase of 15% and achieves only 5%, should the shareholder be permitted to have some judicial recourse against the company? One possible solution to this problem would require passage of "safe harbour" legislation which would protect companies that have used "good faith" and "reasonable assumptions" in their forecasting.

In addition to the question of liability, several other issues must be resolved before earnings projections should be made mandatory. The role and responsibility of the Chartered Accountant as an attestor of forecasts must be determined. Should forecasts consist of general expectations or detailed disclosures? Should a single value ($1.50) or a range of values ($1.50 ± $.20) be presented? What should be the length of the period to be forecasted?

Financial forecasts provide such highly relevant investment information that the demand for them will not subside. Although there are some disadvantages to requiring forecasts, they are outweighed by the advantages. We believe that the publication of forecasts is a natural and inevitable extension of corporate disclosure.

EXAMINATION OF THE AUDITOR'S REPORT

Another important source of information that is often overlooked by investors in their examination of the financial statements is the auditor's report. An **auditor** is a professional who conducts an independent examination of the accounting data presented by the business enterprise. If the auditor is satisfied that the financial statements represent the financial position and results of operations, an **opinion** is expressed on audited statements in the following manner:

We have examined the consolidated financial statements and explanatory financial section appearing on pages 20 through 29 of this report. Our examination was made in accordance with generally accepted auditing standards, and accordingly included such tests and other procedures as we considered necessary in the circumstances.

In our opinion, these consolidated financial statements present fairly the financial position of Inco Limited at December 31, 1984, 1983, and 1982 and the results of its operations and the changes in its financial position for the years then ended in accordance with generally accepted accounting principles as established in Canada applied on a consistent basis except for the change in 1983, with which we concur, in the method of currency translation described in Note 1 of the explanatory financial section.

In preparing this report, the auditor follows these reporting standards:

1. The report shall state whether the financial statements are presented in accordance with generally accepted accounting principles.
2. The report shall state whether such principles have been consistently observed in the current period in relation to the preceding period.

3. The report shall contain either an expression of opinion regarding the financial statements taken as a whole or an assertion to the effect that an opinion cannot be expressed. When an overall opinion cannot be expressed, the reasons therefore should be stated. In all cases where an auditor's name is associated with financial statements, the report should contain a clear-cut indication of the character of the auditor's examination, if any, and the degree of responsibility being taken.

4. Informative disclosures in the financial statements are to be regarded as reasonably adequate unless otherwise stated in the report.

In most cases, the auditor issues a standard unqualified, or "clean" opinion; that is, the auditor believes that the financial statements do present fairly the financial position on a basis consistent with that used in the preceding year. There are situations in which the auditor, however, is required to (1) express a qualified opinion, (2) express an adverse opinion, or (3) deny an opinion.

A qualified opinion contains an exception to the standard opinion. Ordinarily the exception is not of sufficient magnitude to invalidate the statements as a whole; if it were, an adverse opinion would be rendered. The unusual circumstances in which the auditor may deviate from the standard unqualified short-form report on financial statements are as follows:

1. The scope of the examination is limited or affected by conditions or restrictions.
2. The statements do not fairly present financial position or results of operations because of:
   (a) Failure to adhere to generally accepted accounting principles.
   (b) Failure to disclose essential information.
3. Generally accepted accounting principles are not consistently applied.
4. The auditors do not agree with the valuation of an item in the financial statements.
5. Any other matter that may have an effect on the fairness of the financial statements.[13]

If the auditor is confronted with one of the situations noted above, the opinion must be qualified. The qualification is made in the audit report by using the phrase "except for" followed by a brief description of the situation.

An adverse opinion is required in any report in which the exceptions to fair presentation are so material that in the independent auditor's judgement a qualified opinion is not justified. In such a case, the financial statements taken as a whole do not provide a fair presentation in accordance with generally accepted accounting principles. Adverse opinions are rare, because most enterprises change their accounting to conform with the auditor's desires. A disclaimer of an opinion is normally issued when the auditor has determined that the statements are misleading.

Our point should be clear: the sophisticated analyst should examine closely the auditor's report in conjunction with the examination of the other financial data. Although the information usually can be found in other parts of the financial statements, the auditor's report can be a convenient and useful source of highly pertinent information.

CRITERIA FOR MAKING ACCOUNTING AND REPORTING CHOICES

Throughout this text, and especially in this chapter, we have stressed the need to make judicial choices between alternative accounting concepts, methods, and means of disclosures. You probably are surprised and even discouraged at the large

---

[13]*CICA Handbook*, Section 5500, par. 29.

number of choices among acceptable alternatives that accountants are required to make. As "a help to those who have to choose from among such alternatives," the FASB has issued "Qualitative Characteristics: Criteria for Selecting and Evaluating Financial Accounting and Reporting Policies."[14] This recent pronouncement is an addition to its series of "concept statements." The qualitative criteria offered by the FASB for selecting and evaluating financial accounting and reporting policies and methods are: decision usefulness, relevance, reliability, timeliness, understandability, neutrality, verifiability, representational faithfulness, comparability, completeness, consistency, and materiality.

The FASB's concept statements on objectives of financial reporting, elements of financial statements, and qualitative criteria for selecting financial accounting policies are somewhat reminiscent of other false starts at developing a theoretical framework for accounting practice. Nevertheless, the profession must continue its vigilance to develop a sound foundation upon which accounting standards and practice can be built. As Aristotle said, "The correct beginning is more than half the whole."

KEY POINTS

1. Financial statements, notes to the financial statements, and supplementary information are areas directly affected by CICA standards. In addition, financial reporting includes other types of information found in the annual report. Finally, there is other financial information that may be helpful, but is not part of the formal reporting system.

2. An increase in disclosure has occurred because of (1) the complexity of the business environment, (2) the necessity for timely information, and (3) the use of accounting as a control and monitoring device.

3. If only the consolidated figures are available to the user, much information regarding the composition of these figures is hidden in aggregated amounts. There is no way to tell from the consolidated data the extent to which the differing product lines contribute to the company's profitability, risk, and growth potential. As a result, segmented information is required by the profession in certain situations.

4. The same accounting principles used for consolidated data should be used for segmented data. Segmented data may be prepared for a service or product line, foreign operations, or export sales.

5. Interim reports cover periods of one year or less. Two viewpoints exist regarding interim reports. One (the discrete view) believes that each interim period should be treated as a separate accounting period. Another (the integral view) is that the interim report is an integral part of the annual report, and that deferrals and accruals should take into consideration what will happen for the entire year.

6. Publication of financial forecasts has not been incorporated into the formal reporting requirements, although the matter is being discussed in the profession. One of the main problems deterring the presentation of forecasts is the

[14]"Qualitative Characteristics: Criteria for Selecting and Evaluating Financial Accounting and Reporting Policies," Exposure draft of *Proposed Statement of Financial Accounting Concepts* (Stamford, Conn.: FASB, August 9, 1979).

nature and extent of liability assumed by the company and its auditors for the accuracy of the forecast.

7. Management has responsibility for the financial statements, and this responsibility is often indicated in a letter to shareholders in the annual report.

8. Certain supplementary information is often presented with financial statements to help users understand such relationships as the effect of changing prices on the firm.

9. An important source of information is the auditor's report. In most cases, the auditor issues a standard unqualified, or "clean" opinion. There are situations, however, in which the auditor is required to (1) express a qualified opinion, (2) express an adverse opinion, or (3) disclaim an opinion.

QUESTIONS

1. A recent annual report of a major steel company states: "Income tax expense includes provision for deferred income taxes of $8.8 million in 1986 and $13.1 million in 1985. Tax expense was reduced by a flow-through of the allowable investment credit of $7.3 million in 1986 and $3.1 million in 1985." What does this note mean?

2. Some financial writers have described the 1970s as the age of disclosure. What is the full disclosure principle in accounting? Why has disclosure increased substantially in the last 10 years?

3. What are the major advantages of notes to financial statements? What types of items are usually reported in the notes?

4. The auditor for Sandab, Ltd. is debating whether the major categories of property, plant, and equipment and related accumulated depreciation should be reported in a note or in the summary of significant accounting policies. What would be your recommendation? Why?

5. Dublin Co. is liable for a 7% mortgage payable of $24,600, secured by land and buildings, which is payable in semiannual instalments (including principal and interest) of $4,500. Indicate the balance sheet presentation of long-term debt and current maturities and, in general terms, the necessary disclosure.

6. At the beginning of 1986, Pagliais' Ltd. entered into an eight-year, nonrenewable lease agreement that requires the client to make substantial reconditioning and restoration expenditures at the end of the lease. What type of disclosure do you believe is necessary for this type of situation?

7. A recent annual report of Cocina Industries states: "The company and its subsidiaries have long-term leases expiring on various dates after December 31, 1986. Amounts payable under such commitments, without reduction for related rental income, are expected to average approximately $5,711,000 annually for the next three years. Related rental income from certain subleases to others is estimated to average $3,094,000 annually for the next three years." What information is provided by this note?

8. An annual report of Ford Motor Corporation states: "Net income per share is computed based upon the average number of shares of capital stock of all classes outstanding. Additional shares of common stock may be issued or delivered in the future on conversion of outstanding convertible debentures, exercise of outstanding employee stock options, and for payment of defined supplemental compensation. Had such additional shares been outstanding, net income per share would have been reduced by $0.10 in the current year and $0.30 in the previous year."

"As a result of capital stock transactions by the company during the current year (primarily the purchase of Class A Stock from Ford Foundation), net income per share was increased by $0.06." What information is provided by this note?

9. What type of disclosure or accounting do you believe is necessary for the following items:

    (a) The client reports an extraordinary item (net of tax) correctly on the income statement. No other mention is made of this item in the annual report.

    (b) The client expects to recover a substantial amount in connection with a pending refund claim for a prior year's taxes. Although the claim is being contested, counsel for the company has confirmed the client's expectation of recovery.

    (c) Because of a general increase in the number of labour disputes and strikes, both within and outside the industry, there is an increased likelihood that the client will suffer a costly strike in the near future.

10. The following information was described in a note to the financial statements of Rochelle Packing Co. "During August, 1986, Halco Products Corporation purchased 311,003 common shares of the Company which constitute approximately 35% of the shares outstanding. Halco has since obtained representation on the Board of Directors.

    "An affiliate of Halco Products Corporation acts as a food broker for the Company in the greater Toronto marketing area. The commissions for such services after August, 1986, amounted to approximately $20,000." Why is this information disclosed?

11. What is the difference between a CA's unqualified opinion or "clean" opinion and a qualified one?

12. When does a CA render a "subject to" qualified opinion? When does a CA render an adverse opinion?

13. What are diversified companies? What accounting problems are related to diversified companies?

14. Explain the following terms:
    (a) Identifiable assets.
    (b) Defined profit.
    (c) Industry segment.
    (d) Common cost.

15. The controller for Unity, Inc. recently commented: "If I have to disclose our segments individually, the only people who will gain are our competitors and the only people who will lose are our present shareholders." Evaluate this comment.

16. One student of Intermediate Accounting was heard to remark after a class discussion on diversified reporting: "All this is very confusing to me. First we are told that there is merit in presenting the consolidated results, and now we are told that it is better to show segmented results. I wish they would make up their minds." Evaluate this comment.

17. A financial writer notes recently: "There are substantial arguments for including earnings projections in annual reports and the like. The most compelling is that it would give anyone interested something now available to only a relatively select few—like large shareholders, creditors, and attentive bartenders." Identify some arguments against providing earnings projections.

18. An article discussing the negative aspects of forecasts noted: "What if Ford had made official projections early last year of 1987 and 1988 earnings? Did it correctly foresee OPEC's running amok and estimate billion-dollar losses in each of these years for its North American automobile operations?" Identify some arguments for providing earnings forecasts.

19. What are interim reports? Why are balance sheets often not provided with interim data?

20. What are the accounting problems related to the presentation of interim data?

21. What approaches have been suggested to overcome the seasonal problem related to interim reporting?

CASES

C27-1   Presented below are three independent situations.

1. A company has adopted a policy of recording self-insurance for any possible losses resulting from injury to others by the company's vehicles. The premium for an insurance policy for the same risk from an independent insurance company would have an annual cost of $3,000. During the period covered by the financial statements, there were no accidents involving the company's vehicles that resulted in injury to others.

2. A company offers a one-year warranty for the product that it manufactures. A history of warranty claims has been compiled and the probable amount of claims related to sales for a given period can be determined.

3. Subsequent to the date of a set of financial statements, but prior to the issuance of the financial statements, a company enters into a contract that will probably result in a significant loss to the company. The amount of the loss can be reasonably estimated.

Instructions

Discuss the accrual or type of disclosure necessary (if any) and the reason(s) why such disclosure is appropriate for each of the three independent sets of facts above.

(AICPA adapted)

C27-2   Pacific Inc. produces electronic components for sale to manufacturers of radios, television sets, and phonographic systems. In connection with her examination of Pacific's financial statements for the year ended December 31, 1986, Melissa Melton, CA, completed field work two weeks ago. Ms. Melton is now evaluating the significance of the following items prior to preparing her auditor's report. Except as noted, none of these items has been disclosed in the financial statements or notes.

1. A major electronics firm has introduced a line of products that will compete directly with Pacific's primary line, now being produced in the specially designed new plant. Because of manufacturing innovations, the competitor's line will be of comparable quality but priced 50% below Pacific's line. The competitor announced its new line during the week following completion of field work. Ms. Melton read the announcement in the newspaper and discussed the situation by telephone with Pacific executives. Pacific will meet the lower prices that are high enough to cover variable manufacturing and selling expenses but will permit recovery of only a portion of fixed costs.

2. The company's new manufacturing plant building, which cost $1,200,000 and has an estimated life of 25 years, is leased from Eastern National Bank at an annual rental of $240,000. The company is obliged to pay property taxes, insurance, and maintenance. At the conclusion of its 10-year noncancellable lease, the company has the option of purchasing the property for $1.00. In Pacific's income statement the rental payment is reported on a separate line.

3. A 10-year loan agreement, which the company entered into three years ago, provides that dividend payments may not exceed net income earned after taxes subsequent to the date of the agreement. The balance of retained earnings at the date of the loan agreement was $317,000. From that date through December 31, 1986, net income after taxes has totalled $450,000 and cash dividends have totalled $220,000. On the basis of these data the staff auditor assigned to this review concluded that there was no retained earnings restriction at December 31, 1986.

   Recently Pacific interrupted its policy of paying cash dividends quarterly to its shareholders. Dividends were paid regularly through 1985, discontinued for all of 1986 to finance equipment for the company's new plant, and resumed in the first quarter of 1987. In the annual report dividend policy is to be discussed in the president's letter to stockholders.

Instructions

For each of the items above discuss any additional disclosures in the financial statements and notes that the auditor should recommend to her client. (The cumulative effect of the items should not be considered.)

C27-3 Spify Container Corporation is in the process of preparing its annual financial statements for the fiscal year ended April 30, 1986. The company manufactures plastic, glass, and paper containers for sale to food and drink manufacturers and distributors.

Spify Container Corporation maintains separate control accounts for its raw materials. Inventories are valued at the lower of cost and market.

The company's property, plant, and equipment are classified in the following major categories: land, office buildings, furniture and fixtures, manufacturing facilities, manufacturing equipment, leasehold improvements. All fixed assets are carried at cost. The depreciation methods employed depend upon the type of asset (its classification) and when it was acquired.

Spify Container Corporation plans to present the inventory and fixed asset amounts in its April 30, 1986, balance sheet as shown below.

Inventories	$2,956,906
Property, plant, and equipment (net of depreciation)	$4,875,574

Instructions

What information regarding inventories and property, plant, and equipment must be disclosed by Spify Container Corporation in the audited financial statements issued to shareholders, either in the body or the notes, for the 1985-1986 fiscal year?

(CMA adapted)

C27-4 You are completing an examination of the financial statements of Cabinet Manufacturing Corporation for the year ended February 28, 1986. Cabinet's financial statements have not been examined previously. The controller of Cabinet has given you the following draft of proposed notes to the financial statements:

Cabinet Manufacturing Corporation
NOTES TO FINANCIAL STATEMENTS
Year Ended February 28, 1986

Note 1. With the approval of the Minister of Finance, the company changed its method of accounting for inventories from the first-in, first-out method to the average cost method on March 1, 1985. In the opinion of the company the effects of this change on the pricing of inventories and cost of goods manufactured were not material in the current year but are expected to be material in future years.

Note 2. The investment property was recorded at cost until December, 1985, when it was written up to its appraisal value. The company plans to sell the property in 1986, and an independent real estate agent in the area has indicated that the appraisal price can be realized. Pending completion of the sale the amount of the expected gain on the sale has been recorded in an unearned income account.

Note 3. The stock dividend described in our May 24, 1985, letter to shareholders has been recorded as a 110-for-100 stock split-up. Accordingly, there were no changes in the shareholders' equity account balances from this transaction.

Instructions

For each of the notes above discuss the note's adequacy and needed revisions, if any, of the financial statements or the note.

C27-5 You have completed your audit of Van Buren Iron Ware Inc. and its consolidated subsidiaries for the year ended December 31, 1986, and were satisfied with the results of your examination. You have examined the financial statements of Van Buren for the past three years. The corporation is now preparing its annual report to shareholders. The report will include the consolidated financial statements of Van Buren and its subsidiaries and your short-form auditor's report. During your audit the following matters came to your attention:

1. In 1986 the corporation changed its method of accounting for the investment tax credit applicable to research. An investment tax credit of $161,000 deferred in prior years was credited to income and the full 1986 investment tax credit of $62,000 was recorded as a reduction of income tax expense. As a result, net income after taxes for 1986 was increased by $223,000. You approved of this change as an acceptable alternative accounting treatment.

2. Revenue Canada is currently examining the corporation's 1983 federal income tax return and is questioning the amount of a deduction claimed by the corporation's domestic subsidiary for a loss sustained in 1983. The examination is still in process, and any additional tax liability is indeterminable at this time. The corporation's tax counsel believes that there will be no substantial additional tax liability.

3. A vice-president who is also a shareholder resigned on December 31, 1986, after an argument with the president. The vice-president is soliciting proxies from shareholders and expects to obtain sufficient proxies to gain control of the board of directors so that a new president will be appointed. The president plans to have a note to the financial statement prepared that would include information of the pending proxy fight, management's accomplishments over the years, and an appeal by management for the support of stockholders.

Instructions

(a) Prepare the notes, if any, that you would suggest for the items listed above.

(b) State your reasons for not making disclosure by note for each of the listed items for which you did not prepare a note.

(AICPA adapted)

C27-6   Musketeer Enterprises acquired a large tract of land in a small town approximately 10 miles from Capital City. The company executed a firm contract on November 15, 1985, for the construction of a one-mile race track, together with related facilities. The track and facilities were completed December 15, 1986. On December 31, 1986, a 15% instalment note of $150,000 was issued along with other consideration in settlement of the construction contract. Instalments of $50,000 fall due on December 31 of each of the next three years. The company planned to pay the notes from cash received from operations and from sale of additional capital stock.

The company adopted the double-declining balance method of computing depreciation. No depreciation was taken in 1986 because all racing equipment was received in December after the completion of the track and facilities.

The land on which the racing circuit was constructed was acquired at various dates for a total of $61,000, and its approximate market value on December 31, 1986, is $78,000.

Through the sale of tickets to spectators, parking fees, concession income, and income from betting, the company officials anticipated that approximately $275,000 is taken in during a typical year's racing season. Cash expenses for a racing season were estimated at $173,000.

You have made an examination of the financial condition of Musketeer Enterprises as of December 31, 1986. The balance sheet and statement of operations as of that date follow.

Musketeer Enterprises
BALANCE SHEET
December 31, 1986

Assets

Cash	$ 14,500
Accounts receivable	1,000
Prepaid expenses	7,500

Property (at cost)		
Land	$ 61,000	
Grading and track improvements	80,200	
Grandstand	110,000	
Buildings	65,000	
Racing equipment	45,000	361,200
Organization costs		300
Total assets		$384,500

Liabilities and Shareholders' Equity

Accounts payable		$ 22,000
Instalment note payable—15%		150,000
Shareholders' equity		
Share capital, no par value, authorized		
200,000, issued and outstanding 47,800 shares		222,500
Retained earnings (deficit)		(10,000)
Total liabilities and shareholders' equity		$384,500

Musketeer Enterprises
STATEMENT OF INCOME
For the Period from Inception, December 1, 1983
to December 31, 1986

Income	
Profit on sales of land	$ 8,000
Other	200
	8,200
General and administrative expenses	24,300
Net loss for the period	$16,100

On January 15, 1987, legislation that declared betting to be illegal was enacted by the provincial government. A discussion with management on January 17 about the effect of the legislation revealed that revenue is now estimated to be reduced to approximately $80,000 and cash expenses will be reduced to one-third the original estimate.

Instructions

(Disregard income tax implications.)

(a) Prepare the explanatory notes to accompany the balance sheet.

(b) What opinion do you believe the auditor should render? Discuss.

(AICPA adapted)

C27-7 Boxit Corporation, a publicly traded company, is preparing the interim financial data which it will issue to its shareholders at the end of the first quarter of the 1986-1987 fiscal year. Boxit's financial accounting department has compiled the following summarized revenue and expense data for the first quarter of the year:

Sales	$15,000,000
Cost of goods sold	9,000,000
Variable selling expenses	450,000
Fixed selling expenses	750,000

Included in the fixed selling expenses was the single lump-sum payment of $600,000 for television advertisements for the entire year.

Instructions

    (a) Boxit Corporation must issue its quarterly financial statements in accordance with generally accepted accounting principles regarding interim financial reporting.

        1. Explain whether Boxit should report its operating results for the quarter as if the quarter were a separate reporting period in and of itself or if the quarter were an integral part of the annual reporting period.

        2. State how the sales, cost of goods sold, and fixed selling expenses would be reflected in Boxit Corporation's quarterly report prepared for the first quarter of the 1983-1984 fiscal year. Briefly justify your presentation.

    (b) What financial information, as a minimum, must Boxit Corporation disclose to its shareholders in its quarterly reports?

(CMA adapted)

C27-8 The following statements are summarized from *CICA Handbook*, Section 1750, ''Interim Financial Reporting to Shareholders'':

It is important for shareholders that more frequent and timely information be available than that provided by the annual financial statements. Interim financial reports should present information with respect to the results of operations of a company for a specified period rather than a proration of expected results for the annual period. Consistent with this position, the interim financial reports have to be prepared on the same basis as annual statements. In general, the results for each interim period should be based on the accounting principles and practices used by an enterprise in the preparation of its latest annual financial statements unless a change in an accounting practice or policy has been adopted in the current year. The Committee concluded, however, that certain accounting principles and practices followed for annual reporting purposes may require modification at interim reporting dates so that the reported results for the interim period may better relate to the results of operations for the annual period.

Instructions

Listed below are six independent cases on how accounting facts might be reported on an individual company's interim financial reports. For each of these cases, state whether the method proposed for interim reporting would be acceptable under generally accepted accounting principles applicable to interim financial data. Support each answer with a brief explanation.

1. Morris Company wrote inventory down to reflect lower of cost and market in the first quarter of 1986. At year end the market exceeds the original acquisition cost of this inventory. Consequently, management plans to write the inventory back up to its original cost as a year-end adjustment.

2. Marbella Company realizes a large gain on the sale of investments at the beginning of the second quarter. The company wants to report one-third of the gain in each of the remaining quarters.

3. Engstrom Company has estimated its annual audit fee. They plan to prorate this expense equally over all four quarters.

4. Baker Company was reasonably certain they would have an employee strike in the third quarter. As a result, they shipped heavily during the second quarter but plan to defer the recognition of the sales in excess of the normal sales volume. The deferred sales will be recognized as sales in the third quarter when the strike is in progress. Baker Company management thinks this is more nearly representative of normal second- and third-quarter operations.

5. Iliff Company takes a physical inventory at year end for annual financial statement purposes. Inventory and cost of sales reported in the interim quarterly statements are based on estimated gross profit rates, because a physical inventory would result in a cessation of operations. Iliff Company does have reliable perpetual inventory records.

6. Zima Company is planning to report one-fourth of its pension expense each quarter.

(CMA adapted)

C27-9 Magneto Manufacturing Company, a British Columbia corporation listed on the Pacific Coast Stock Exchange, budgets activities for 1987 as follows:

	Amount	Units
Net sales	$9,000,000	1,000,000
Cost of goods sold	5,400,000	1,000,000
Gross margin	$3,600,000	
Selling, general, and administrative expenses	2,100,000	
Operating income	$1,500,000	
Nonoperating revenues and expenses	–0–	
Income before income taxes	$1,500,000	
Estimated income taxes (current and deferred)	825,000	
Net income	$ 675,000	
Earnings per common share	$6.75	

Magneto has operated profitably for many years and has experienced a seasonal pattern of sales volume and production similar to those below forecasted for 1987. Sales volume is expected to follow a quarterly pattern of 10%, 20%, 35%, 35%, respectively, because of seasonality of the industry. Also, owing to production and storage capacity limitations, it is expected that production will follow a pattern of 20%, 25%, 30%, 25%, per quarter, respectively.

At the conclusion of the first quarter of 1987, the controller of Magneto has prepared and issued the following interim report for public release:

	Amount	Units
Net sales	$ 900,000	100,000
Cost of goods sold	540,000	100,000
Gross margin	$ 360,000	
Selling, general, and administrative expenses	412,500	
Operating loss	$ (52,500)	
Loss from warehouse fire	(262,500)	
Loss before income taxes	$(315,000)	
Estimated income taxes	–0–	
Net loss	$(315,000)	
Loss per common share	(3.15)	

The following additional information is available for the first quarter just completed, but was not included in the public information released:

1. Assume that the warehouse fire loss met the conditions of an extraordinary loss. The warehouse had an undepreciated cost of $480,000; $217,500 was recovered from insurance on the warehouse. No other gains or losses are anticipated this year from similar events or transactions, and Magneto had no similar losses in preceding years; thus, the full loss will be deductible as an ordinary loss for income tax purposes.

2. The company uses a standard cost system in which standards are set at currently attainable levels on an annual basis. At the end of the first quarter there was under-applied fixed factory overhead (volume variance) of $75,000 that was treated as an asset at the end of the quarter. Production during the quarter was 200,000 units, of which 100,000 were sold.

3. The selling, general, and administrative expenses were budgeted on a basis of $1,350,000 fixed expenses for the year plus $0.75 variable expenses per unit of sales.

4. The effective income tax rate is expected to average 55% of earnings before income taxes during 1987. There are no permanent differences between pretax accounting earnings and taxable income.

5. Earnings per share were computed on the basis of 100,000 common shares outstanding. Magneto has only one class of shares issued, no long-term debt outstanding, and no stock option plan.

Instructions

(a) Without reference to the specific situation described above, what are the standards of disclosure for interim financial data (published interim financial reports) for publicly traded companies? Explain.

(b) Identify the weaknesses in form and content of Magneto's interim report without reference to the additional information.

(c) For each of the five points of additional information, indicate the preferable treatment for each item for interim reporting purposes and explain why that treatment is preferable.

(AICPA adapted)

C27-10 An article in *Barron's* noted:

Okay. Last fall, someone with a long memory and an even longer arm reached into that bureau drawer and came out with a moldy cheese sandwich and the equally moldy notion of corporate forecasts. We tried to find out what happened to the cheese sandwich—but, rats!, even recourse to the Freedom of Information Act didn't help. However, the forecast proposal was dusted off, polished up and found quite serviceable. The SEC, indeed, lost no time in running it up the old flagpole —but no one was very eager to salute. Even after some of the more objectionable features —compulsory corrections and detailed explanations of why the estimates went awry—were peeled off the original proposal. Seemingly, despite the Commission's smiles and sweet talk, those craven corporations were still afraid that an honest mistake would lead down the primrose path to consent decrees and class-action suits. To lay to rest such qualms, the Commission last week approved a "Safe Harbor" rule that, providing the forecasts were made on a reasonable basis and in good faith, protected corporations from litigation should the projections prove wide of the mark (as only about 99% are apt to do).

Instructions

(a) What are the arguments for preparing profit forecasts?

(b) What is the purpose of the "safe harbour" rule?

(c) Why are corporations concerned about presenting profit forecasts?

C27-11 The following article appeared in *The Wall Street Journal*:

Washington—The Securities and Exchange Commission staff issued guidelines for companies grappling with the problem of dividing up their business into industry segments for their annual reports. An industry segment is defined by the Financial Accounting Standards Board as a part of an enterprise engaged in providing a product or service or a group of related products or services primarily to unaffiliated customers for a profit.

Although conceding that the process is a "subjective talk" that "to a considerable extent, depends on the judgement of management," the SEC staff said companies should consider the nature of the products, the nature of their production and their markets and marketing methods to determine whether products and services should be grouped together or in separate industry segments.

Instructions

(a) What does financial reporting for segments of a business enterprise involve?

(b) Identify the reasons for requiring financial data to be reported by segments.

(c) Identify the possible disadvantages of requiring financial data to be reported by segments.

(d) Identify the accounting difficulties inherent in segmented reporting.

C27-12 The most recently published statement of consolidated income of Scotia Industries, Inc. appears below:

Ginger Baumgartner, a representative of a firm of security analysts, visited the central headquarters of Scotia Industries to obtain more information about the company's operations.

In the annual report Scotia's president stated that Scotia was engaged in the pharmaceutical, food-processing, toy-manufacturing, and metal-working industries. Ms. Baumgartner's firm complained that the published income statement was of limited utility in her analysis of the firm's operations. She said that Scotia should have disclosed separately the profit earned in each of its component industries. Further, she maintained that several items appearing on the statement of consolidated retained earnings should have been included on the income statement; a gain of $950,000 on the sale of the furniture division in early March of the current year and an assessment for additional income taxes of $247,350 resulting from an examination of the returns covering the years ended March 31, 1983 and 1984 (normally recurring).

Scotia Industries, Inc.
STATEMENT OF CONSOLIDATED INCOME
For the Year Ended March 31, 1986

Net sales	$57,061,800
Other revenue	611,100
Total revenue	57,672,900
Cost of products sold	40,759,950
Selling and administrative expenses	13,031,250
Interest expense	445,350
Total cost and expenses	54,236,550
Income before income taxes	3,436,350
Income taxes	1,507,800
Net income	$ 1,928,550

Instructions

(a) Explain what is meant by a "conglomerate" company.

(b) 1. Discuss the accounting problems involved in measuring net profit by industry segments within a company.

   2. With reference to Scotia Industries' statement of consolidated income, identify the specific items where difficulty might be encountered in measuring profit by each of its industry segments, and explain the nature of the difficulty.

(c) 1. What criteria should be applied in determining whether a gain or loss should be excluded from the determination of net income?

   2. What criteria should be applied in determining whether a gain or loss that is properly includable in the determination of net income should be included in the results of ordinary operations or shown separately as an extraordinary item after all other items of revenue and expense?

   3. How should the gain on the sale of the furniture division and the assessment of additional taxes each be presented in Scotia's financial statements?

(AICPA adapted)

INDEX